KETTERING COLLEGE
MEDICAL ARTS LIBRARY

D0146040

A GUIDE TO ASSESSMENTS THAT WORK

Oxford Series in Clinical Psychology

Editorial Board

Bruce Bongar
Lillian Comas-Diaz
Gerald P. Koocher
Annette M. La Greca
John C. Norcross

Comprehensive Textbook of Psychotherapy: Theory and Practice
Edited by Bruce Bongar and Larry E. Beutler

Clinical Personality Assessment: Practical Approaches, Second Edition
Edited by James N. Butcher

Principles of Therapeutic Change That Work
Edited by Louis G. Castonguay and Larry E. Beutler

Oxford Textbook of Psychopathology
Edited by Theodore Millon, Paul H. Blaney, and Roger D. Davis

Child and Adolescent Psychological Disorders: A Comprehensive Textbook
Edited by Sandra D. Netherton, Deborah Holmes, and C. Eugene Walker

Handbook of Psychotherapy Integration, Second Edition
Edited by John C. Norcross and Marvin R. Goldfried

Family Psychology: The Art of the Science
Edited by William M. Pinsof and Jay L. Lebow

Handbook of Girls' and Women's Psychological Health
Edited by Judith Worell and Carol D. Goodheart

A Guide to Assessments That Work
Edited by John Hunsley and Eric J. Mash

A GUIDE TO ASSESSMENTS THAT WORK

EDITED BY

John Hunsley and Eric J. Mash

New York Oxford

OXFORD

UNIVERSITY PRESS

2008

11/08

OXFORD

UNIVERSITY PRESS

Oxford University Press, Inc., publishes works that further
Oxford University's objective of excellence
in research, scholarship, and education.

Oxford New York
Auckland Cape Town Dar-es-Salaam Hong Kong Karachi
Kuala Lumpur Madrid Melbourne Mexico City Nairobi
New Delhi Shanghai Taipei Toronto

With offices in
Argentina Austria Brazil Chile Czech Republic France Greece
Guatemala Hungary Italy Japan Poland Portugal Singapore
South Korea Switzerland Thailand Turkey Ukraine Vietnam

Copyright © 2008 by Oxford University Press, Inc.

Published by Oxford University Press, Inc.
198 Madison Avenue, New York, New York 10016

www.oup.com

Oxford is a registered trademark of Oxford University Press

All rights reserved. No part of this publication may be reproduced,
stored in a retrieval system, or transmitted, in any form or by any means,
electronic, mechanical, photocopying, recording, or otherwise,
without the prior permission of Oxford University Press.

Library of Congress Cataloging-in-Publication Data
A guide to assessments that work / edited by John Hunsley and Eric J. Mash.
p.   ;   cm.—(Oxford series in clinical psychology)
Includes bibliographical references.
ISBN: 978-0-19-531064-1
1. Psychodiagnostics.   2. Evidence-based psychiatry.   I. Hunsley,
John, 1909-   II. Mash, Eric J.   III. Series.
[DNLM: 1. Mental Disorders—diagnosis.   2. Evidence-Based Medicine.
WM 141 G9457 2008]
Rc469.G78   2008
616.89'075—dc22   2007027382

1 3 5 7 9 8 6 4 2

Printed in the United States of America
on acid-free paper

To Catherine—my best friend and partner—J.H.

To Heather—the light of my life—E.J.M

Table of Contents

Contributor List

Carolyn S. Abramowitz, MD: Centre for Addiction and Mental Health, University of Toronto, Toronto, Ontario, Canada

Jonathan S. Abramowitz, PhD: Department of Psychology, University of North Carolina at Chapel Hill, Chapel Hill, North Carolina

Martin M. Antony, PhD: Department of Psychology, Ryerson University, Toronto, Ontario, Canada and St. Joseph's Healthcare Anxiety Treatment and Research Centre, Hamilton, Ontario, Canada

Howard E. Barbaree, PhD: Centre for Addiction and Mental Health and Centre of Criminology, University of Toronto, Toronto, Ontario, Canada

Yitzchak M. Binik, PhD: Department of Psychology, McGill University, Montreal, Quebec, Canada

Michelle G. Craske, PhD: Department of Psychology, University of California at Los Angeles, Los Angeles California

Shawn R. Currie, PhD: Hillhurst Mental Health & Addictions Services Office, Calgary, Alberta, Canada

Tara L. Deliberto, BS: Department of Psychology, Harvard University, Cambridge, Massachusetts

Lea R. Dougherty, PhD: Department of Psychology, Stony Brook University, Stony Brook, New York

Michel J. Dugas, PhD: Department of Psychology, Concordia University and Hôpital du Sacré-Coeur de Montréal Clinique des Troubles Anxieux, Montreal, Quebec, Canada

Lori Eisner, MS: Department of Psychology, University of Miami, Miami, Florida

Amy Fiske, PhD: Department of Psychology, West Virginia University, Morgantown, West Virginia

David M. Fresco, PhD: Department of Psychology, Kent State University, Kent, Ohio

Paul J. Frick, PhD: Department of Psychology, University of New Orleans, New Orleans, Louisiana

Nicole J. Gervais, BS: Department of Psychology, Concordia University, Montreal, Quebec, Canada

Shirley M. Glynn, PhD: VA Greater Los Angeles Healthcare System and Department of Psychiatry and Biobehavioral Sciences, David Geffen School of Medicine University of California at Los Angeles, Los Angeles, California

Kelly Green, MS: Rutgers Center of Alcohol Studies The State University of New Jersey, Piscataway, New Jersey

Stephen N. Haynes, PhD: Department of Psychology, University of Hawaii at Manoa, Honolulu, Hawaii

Richard E. Heyman, PhD: Department of Psychology, Stony Brook University, Stony Brook, New York

David C. Hodgins, PhD: Department of Psychology, University of Calgary, Calgary, Alberta, Canada

John Hunsley, PhD: School of Psychology, University of Ottawa, Ottawa, Ontario, Canada

Irene Belle Janis, MA: Department of Psychology, Harvard University, Cambridge, Massachusetts

Charlotte Johnston, PhD: Department of Psychology, University of British Columbia, Vancouver, British Columbia, Canada

Sheri L. Johnson, PhD: Department of Psychology, University of Miami, Miami, Florida

Terence M. Keane, PhD: Boston University School of Medicine, VA Boston Healthcare System, Boston, Massachusetts

Melody L. Keller, MA: Department of Psychology, University of California at Los Angeles, Los Angeles, California

Daniel N. Klein, PhD: Department of Psychology, Stony Brook University, Stony Brook, New York

Rebecca S. Laptook, MA: Department of Psychology, Stony Brook University, Stony Brook, New York

Janet W. T. Mah, MA: Department of Psychology, University of British Columbia, Vancouver, British Columbia, Canada

Eric J. Mash, PhD: School of Psychology, University of Calgary, Calgary, Alberta, Canada

Randi E. McCabe, PhD: Department of Psychiatry and Behavioral Neurosciences, McMaster University, Anxiety Treatment and Research Centre, St. Joseph's Healthcare, Hamilton, Ontario, Canada

Barbara McCrady, PhD: Center on Alcoholism, Substance Abuse, and Addictions, The University of New Mexico, Albuquerque, New Mexico

Patrick J. McGrath, PhD: Dalhousie University and Centre for Pediatric Pain Research, IWK Health Centre, Halifax, Nova Scotia, Canada

Robert J. McMahon, PhD: Department of Psychology, University of Washington, Seattle, Washington

C. Meghan McMurtry, BA: Dalhousie University and Centre for Pediatric Pain Research, IWK Health Centre, Halifax, Nova Scotia, Canada

Marta Meana, PhD: Department of Psychology, University of Nevada Las Vegas, Las Vegas, Nevada

David Menges, MS: Rutgers, The State University of New Jersey, Center of Alcohol Studies, Piscataway, New Jersey

Christopher Miller, BA: Department of Psychology, University of Miami, Miami, Florida

Erin C. Moon, BA: Dalhousie University and Centre for Pediatric Pain Research, IWK Health Centre, Halifax, Nova Scotia, Canada

Kim T. Mueser, PhD: Department of Psychiatry and Department of Community and Family Medicine, Dartmouth Medical School, Hanover, New Hampshire

Matthew K. Nock, PhD: Department of Psychology, Harvard University, Cambridge, Massachusetts

Akiko Okifuji, PhD: Department of Anesthesiology, University of Utah, Salt Lake City, Utah

Thomas M. Olino, MA: Department of Psychology, Stony Brook University, Stony Brook, New York

Thomas H. Ollendick, PhD: Department of Psychology, Virginia Polytechnic Institute and State University, Blacksburg, Virginia

Alisa A. O'Riley, MA: Department of Psychology, West Virginia University, Morganstown, West Virginia

Jacqueline B. Persons, PhD: Department of Psychology, University of California, Berkeley and San Francisco Bay Area Center for Cognitive Therapy, San Francisco, California

Damaris J. Rohsenow, PhD: Center for Alcohol and Addiction Studies, Veterans Affairs Medical Center, Brown University, Providence, Rhode Island

Karen Rowa, PhD: Department of Psychiatry and Behavioral Neurosciences, McMaster University, Anxiety Treatment and Research Centre, St. Joseph's Healthcare, Hamilton, Ontario, Canada

Michael C. Seto, PhD: Centre for Addiction and Mental Health and Centre of Criminology, University of Toronto, Toronto, Ontario, Canada

Amy K. Silberbogen, PhD: Boston University School of Medicine, VA Boston Healthcare System, Boston, Massachusetts

Wendy K. Silverman, PhD: Department of Psychology, Florida International University, Miami, Florida

Michelle Skinner, MS: Department of Psychology, University of Utah, Salt Lake City, Utah

Douglas K. Snyder, PhD: Department of Psychology, Texas A&M University, College Station, Texas

Randy Stinchfield, PhD: Center for Adolescent Substance Abuse, University of Minnesota Medical School, Minneapolis, Minnesota

Robyn Sysko, MS: VA Connecticut Healthcare, West Haven, Connecticut

Lea Thaler, BA: Department of Psychology, University of Nevada Las Vegas, Las Vegas, Nevada

Dennis C. Turk, PhD: School of Medicine, University of Washington, Seattle, Washington

Michelle M. Wedig, MA: Department of Psychology, Harvard University, Cambridge, Massachusetts

Mariann R. Weierich, PhD: Boston University School of Medicine, VA Boston Healthcare System, Boston, Massachusetts

Thomas A. Widiger, PhD: Department of Psychology, University of Kentucky, Lexington, Kentucky

Blaise Worden, MS: Rutgers, The State University of New Jersey, Center of Alcohol Studies, Piscataway, New Jersey

Preface

BACKGROUND

Evidence-based practice principles in health care systems emphasize the importance of integrating information drawn from systematically collected data, clinical expertise, and patient preferences when considering health care service options for patients (Institute of Medicine, 2001; Sackett, Rosenberg, Gray, Haynes, & Richardson, 1996). These principles are now a driving force in most health care systems and have recently been endorsed as a necessary foundation for the provision of professional psychological services (American Psychological Association Presidential Task Force on Evidence-Based Practice, 2006). As psychologists, it is difficult for us to imagine how any type of health care service, including psychological services, can be provided to children, adolescents, adults, couples, or families without using some type of informal or formal assessment methods. Nevertheless, until recently, there has been an almost exclusive focus on issues related to developing, disseminating, and providing evidence-based interventions, with only cursory acknowledgment of the role that evidence-based assessment (EBA) activities play in the promotion of evidence-based services.

The idea for this book began several years ago when, over a series of conversations, we became increasingly aware of (and increasingly puzzled by) this disconnect between the centrality of assessment in both professional and scientific activities and the almost exclusive focus in the professional and scientific literatures on the issue of evidence-based psychological treatments. After repeatedly ending these conversations with a conclusion along the lines of "Somebody should do something about this," we were eventually forced to admit that simply waiting for some kind of *deus ex machina* solution to occur was a less than ideal coping strategy. After all, if we were repeatedly grumbling about the lack of attention to the need for EBA principles, maybe we had a responsibility to do more than mutter and complain. It was at this point that we decided that, as frequent contributors to the assessment literature, we would attempt to tackle the complex and thorny issues related to delineating the essential features of EBA.

Aided by some outstanding colleagues, our initial efforts to encourage greater attention to the need for EBA in the development of a scientifically supported clinical psychology resulted in special sections in the *Journal of Clinical Child and Adolescent Psychology* (Mash & Hunsley, 2005) and *Psychological Assessment* (Hunsley & Mash, 2005). The articles in these special sections outlined a host of issues related to the assessment of commonly encountered clinical conditions. As frequently mentioned in these articles, despite the voluminous literature on psychological instruments relevant to the assessment of clinical conditions, there have been few concerted attempts to draw on the empirical evidence to develop assessment guidelines.

The present volume is intended to help fill this void in the psychological literature. It was designed to complement the series of books published by Oxford University Press that focus on bringing the best of psychological science to bear on questions of clinical importance. These volumes, A *Guide To Treatments That Work* (Nathan & Gorman, 1998, 2002, 2007), *Psychotherapy Relationships That Work* (Norcross, 2002), and *Principles of Therapeutic Change That Work* (Castonguay & Beutler, 2006) address intervention issues; the present volume specifically addresses the role of assessment in providing evidence-based services. Our primary goal for the book was to have it address the needs of professionals providing psychological services and those training to provide such services. A secondary goal, however, was to provide guidance to researchers on scientifically supported assessment tools that could be used for both psychopathology research and treatment research purposes. Relatedly, we hope that the summary tables provided in each chapter will provide some inspiration for assessment researchers to try to (a) develop instruments for specific assessment purposes and disorders for which, currently, few good options exist and (b) expand our limited knowledge base on the clinical utility of our assessment instruments.

ORGANIZATION

Consistent with evidence-based psychology and evidence-based medicine, the chapters in this volume are organized around specific disorders or conditions. Although we recognize that some clients do not have clearly defined or diagnosable problems, the vast majority of people seeking psychological services do have identifiable diagnoses or conditions. Accurately assessing these disorders and conditions is a prerequisite to (a) understanding the patient's or client's needs and (b) accessing the scientific literature on evidence-based treatment options. We also recognize that many patients or clients will present with multiple problems; to that end, the reader will find frequent references within a chapter to the assessment of common co-occurring problems that are addressed in other chapters in the volume. To be optimally useful to potential readers, we have included chapters that deal with the assessment of the most commonly encountered disorders or conditions among children, adolescents, adults, older adults, and couples.

Ideally, we want readers to come away from each chapter with a sense of the best scientific assessment options that are clinically feasible and useful. To help accomplish this, we were extremely fortunate to be able to assemble a stellar group of contributors for this volume. The authors are all active contributors to the scientific literature on assessment and share a commitment to the provision of EBA and treatment services.

To enhance the accessibility of the material presented throughout the book, we asked the authors, as much as possible, to follow a common structure in writing their chapters. Without being a straitjacket, we expected the authors to use these guidelines in a flexible manner that allowed for the best possible presentation of assessment work relevant to each disorder or clinical condition. The chapter format generally used throughout the volume is as follows:

Introduction: A brief overview of the chapter content.

Nature of the Disorder/Condition: This section includes information on (a) general diagnostic considerations, such as prevalence, incidence, prognosis, and common comorbid conditions, (b) evidence on etiology, and (c) contextual information such as relational and social functioning and other associated features.

Purposes of Assessment: To make the book as clinically relevant as possible, authors were asked to focus their review of the assessment literature to three specific assessment purposes: (a) diagnosis, (b) case conceptualization and treatment planning, and (c) treatment monitoring and evaluation. We fully realize the clinical and research importance of other assessment purposes but, rather than attempting to provide a compendium of assessment measures and strategies, we wanted authors to target these three key clinical assessment purposes. We also asked authors to consider ways in which age, gender, ethnicity, and other relevant characteristics may influence both the assessment measures and the process of assessment for the disorder/condition.

For each of the three main sections devoted to specific assessment purposes, authors were asked to focus on assessment measures and strategies that either have demonstrated their utility in clinical settings or have a substantial likelihood of being clinically useful. Authors were encouraged to consider the full range of relevant assessment methods (e.g., interviews, self-report, observation, performance tasks, computer-based methods, physiological, etc.), but both scientific evidence and clinical feasibility was to be used to guide decisions about methods to include.

Assessment for Diagnosis: This section deals with assessment measures and strategies used specifically for formulating a diagnosis. Authors were asked to focus on best practices and were encouraged to comment on important conceptual and practical issues in diagnosis and differential diagnosis.

Assessment for Case Conceptualization and Treatment Planning: This section presents assessment measures and strategies used to augment diagnostic information to yield a full psychological case conceptualization that can be used to guide decisions on treatment planning. Specifically, this section addresses the domains that the research literature indicates should be covered in an EBA to develop (a) a clinically meaningful and useful case conceptualization and (b) a clinically sensitive and feasible service/treatment plan (which may or may not include the involvement of other professionals).

Assessment for Treatment Monitoring and Treatment Outcome: In this third section, assessment measures and strategies were reviewed that can be used to (a) track the progress of treatment and (b) evaluate the overall effect of treatment on symptoms, diagnosis, and general functioning. Consistent with the underlying thrust of the volume, the emphasis is on assessment options that have supporting empirical evidence.

Within each of these three sections, standard tables are used to provide summary information about the psychometric characteristics of relevant instruments. Rather than provide extensive psychometric details in the text, authors were asked to use these rating tables to convey information on the psychometric adequacy of instruments. To enhance the utility of these tables, rather than presenting lists of specific psychometric values for each assessment tool, authors were asked to make global ratings of the quality of the various psychometric indices (e.g., norms, internal reliability, construct validity) as indicated by extant research. Details on the rating system used by the authors are presented in the introductory chapter. Our goal is to have these tables serve as valuable summaries for readers. In addition, by using the tables to present psychometric information, the authors were able to focus their chapters on both conceptual and practical issues without having to make frequent detours to discuss psychometrics.

At the conclusion of each of these three main sections there is a subsection entitled *Overall Evaluation* that includes concise summary statements about the scientific adequacy and clinical relevance of currently available measures. This is where authors comment on the availability (if any) of demonstrated scientific value of following the assessment guidance they have provided.

Conclusions and Future Directions: This final section in each chapter provides an overall sense of the scope and adequacy of the assessment options available for the disorder/condition, the limitations associated with these options, and possible future steps that could be taken to remedy these limitations. Some authors also used this section to raise issues related to the challenges involved in trying to ensure that clinical decision-making processes underlying the assessment process (and not just the assessment measures themselves) are scientifically sound.

ACKNOWLEDGMENTS   To begin with, we would like to express our gratitude to the authors. They diligently reviewed and summarized often-voluminous assessment literatures, and then presented this information in a clinically informed and accessible manner. The authors also worked hard to implement the guidelines we provided for both chapter structure and the ratings of various psychometric characteristics. Their efforts in constructing their chapters are admirable and the resulting chapters consistently provide invaluable clinical guidance.

We would also like to thank Joan Bossert, Vice-President and Publisher at Oxford University Press, for her initial interest in the topic and her ongoing support for the book. We greatly appreciate her enthusiasm and her efficiency throughout the process of developing and producing this book. We are also indebted to Mallory Jensen, Assistant Editor, Academic Division at Oxford University Press, who helped us to get the process of assembling the book underway and to Abby Gross, Associate Editor, Brain and Behavioral Sciences at Oxford University Press, who continued to help us the rest of the way with the book. Abby's assistance with the myriad issues associated with the publication process and her rapid response to queries was invaluable. The final stage of the process was overseen by Angelique Rondeau, Production Editor at Oxford University Press, who closely monitored the production of this volume and provided important assistance to us in finalizing this volume.

Finally, we would like to thank all the colleagues and contributors to the psychological assessment and measurement literatures who, over the years, have shaped our thinking about assessment issues. We are especially appreciative of the input from those colleagues who have discussed with us the host of problems, concerns, challenges, and promises associated with our efforts to promote greater awareness of the need for EBA within professional psychology.

References

American Psychological Association Presidential Task Force on Evidence-Based Practice. (2006). Evidence-based practice in psychology. *American Psychologist, 61*, 271–285.

Castonguay, L. G., & Beutler, L. E. (2006). *Principles of therapeutic change that work*. New York: Oxford University Press.

Hunsley, J., & Mash, E. J. (Eds.). (2005). Developing guidelines for the evidence-based assessment (EBA) of adult disorders [Special section]. *Psychological Assessment, 17(3)*.

Institute of Medicine. (2001). *Crossing the quality chasm: A new health system for the 21st century*. Washington, DC: National Academy Press.

Mash, E. J., & Hunsley, J. (Eds.). (2005). Developing guidelines for the evidence-based assessment of child and adolescent disorders [Special section]. *Journal of Clinical Child and Adolescent Psychology, 34(3)*.

Nathan, P. E., & Gorman, J. M. (Eds.). (2007). *A guide to treatments that work* (3rd ed.). New York: Oxford University Press.

Norcross, J. C. (Ed.). (2002). *Psychotherapy relationships that work: Therapist contributions and responsiveness to patients*. New York: Oxford University Press.

Sackett, D. L., Rosenberg, W. M. C., Gray, J. A. M., Haynes, R. B., & Richardson, W. S. (1996). Evidence based medicine: What it is and what it is not. *British Medical Journal, 312*, 71–72.

Foreword

I believe *A Guide to Assessments that Work* is the right book at the right time by the right editors and authors.

The mental health professions have been intensively engaged for a decade and a half and more in establishing empirically supported treatments. This effort has led to the publication of evidence-based treatment guidelines by both the principal mental health professions, clinical psychology (Chambless & Ollendick, 2001; Division 12 Task Force, 1995), and psychiatry (American Psychiatric Association, 1993, 2006) A substantial number of books and articles on evidence-based treatments have also appeared. Notable among them is a series by Oxford University Press, the publishers of *A Guide to Assessments that Work*, which began with the first edition of *A Guide to Treatments that Work* (Nathan & Gorman, 1998), now in its third edition, and the series includes *Psychotherapy Relationships that Work* (Norcross, 2002) and *Principles of Therapeutic Change that Work* (Castonguay & Beutler, 2006).

Now we have an entire volume given over to evidence-based assessment. It doesn't appear *de novo*. Over the past several years, its editors and like-minded colleagues tested and evaluated an extensive series of guidelines for evidence-based assessments for both adults and children (e.g., Hunsley & Mash, 2005; Mash & Hunsley, 2005). Many of this book's chapter authors participated in these efforts. It might well be said, then, that John Hunsley, Eric Mash, and the chapter authors in *A Guide to Assessments that Work* are the right editors and authors for this, the first book to detail the assessment evidence base.

There is also much to admire within the pages of the volume. Each chapter follows a common format prescribed by the editors and designed, as they point out, "to enhance the accessibility of the material presented throughout the book." First, the chapters are syndrome-focused, making it easy for clinicians who want help in assessing their patients to refer to the appropriate chapter or chapters. When they do so, they will find reviews of the assessment literature for three distinct purposes: diagnosis, treatment planning, and treatment monitoring. Each of these reviews is subjected to a rigorous rating system that culminates in an overall evaluation of "the scientific adequacy and clinical relevance of currently available measures." The chapters conclude with an overall assessment of the limits of the assessments available for the syndrome in question, along with suggestions for future steps to confront them. I believe it can well be said, then, that this is the right book by the right editors and authors.

But is this the right time for this book? Evidence-based treatments have been a focus of intense professional attention for many years. Why wouldn't the right time for this book have been several years ago rather than now, to coincide with the development of empirically supported treatments? The answer, I think, reflects the surprisingly brief history of the evidence-based medical practice movement. Despite lengthy concern for the efficacy of treatments for mental disorders that dates back more than 50 years, (e.g., Eysenck, 1952; Lambert & Bergin, 1994; Luborsky, Singer, & Luborsky, 1976; Nathan, Stuart, & Dolan, 2000), it took the appearance of a *Journal of the American Mental Association* article in the early 1990s advocating evidence-based medical practice over medicine as an art to mobilize mental health professionals to achieve the same goals for treatments for mental disorders. The *JAMA* article "ignited a debate about power, ethics, and responsibility in medicine that is now threatening to radically change the experience of health care" (Patterson, 2002). This effort resonated widely within the mental health community, giving impetus to the efforts of psychologists and psychiatrists to base treatment decisions on valid empirical data.

Psychologists had long questioned the uncertain reliability and utility of certain psychological tests, even though psychological testing was what many psychologists spent much of their time doing. At the same time, the urgency of efforts to heighten the support base for valid assessments was limited by continuing concerns over the efficacy of psychotherapy, for which many assessments were done. Not surprisingly, then, when empirical support for psychological treatments began to emerge in the early and middle 1990s, professional and public support for psychological intervention grew. In turn, as psychotherapy's worth became more widely recognized, the value of psychological assessments to help in the planning and evaluation of psychotherapy became increasingly recognized. If my view of this history is on target, the intense efforts that have culminated in this book could not have begun until psychotherapy's evidence base had been established. That has happened only recently, after a lengthy process, and that is why I claim that the right time for this book is now.

Who will use this book? I hope it will become a favorite text for graduate courses in assessment so that new generations of graduate students and their teachers will come to know which of the assessment procedures they are learning and teaching have strong empirical support. I also hope the book will become a resource for practitioners, including those who may not be used to choosing assessment instruments on the basis of

evidence base. To the extent that this book becomes as influential in clinical psychology as I hope it does, it should help precipitate a change in assessment test use patterns, with an increase in the utilization of tests with strong empirical support and a corresponding decrease in the use of tests without it. Even now, there are clinicians who use assessment instruments because they learned them in graduate school, rather than because there is strong evidence that they work. Now, a different and better standard is available.

I am pleased the editors of this book foresee it providing an impetus for research on assessment instruments that currently lack empirical support. I agree. As with a number of psychotherapy approaches, there remain a number of understudied assessment instruments whose evidence base is currently too thin for them to be considered empirically supported. Like the editors, I believe we can anticipate enhanced efforts to establish the limits of usefulness of assessment instruments that haven't yet been thoroughly explored. I also anticipate a good deal of fruitful discussion in the professional literature—and likely additional research—on the positions this book's editors and authors have taken on the assessment instruments they have evaluated. I suspect their ratings for "psychometric adequacy and clinical relevance" will be extensively critiqued and scrutinized. While the resultant dialogue might be energetic—even indecorous on occasion—as has been the dialogue surrounding the evidence base for some psychotherapies, I am hopeful it will also lead to more helpful evaluations of test instruments.

Perhaps the most important empirical studies we might ultimately anticipate would be research indicating which assessment instruments lead both to valid diagnoses and useful treatment planning for specific syndromes. A distant goal of syndromal diagnosis for psychopathology has always been diagnoses that bespeak effective treatments. If the system proposed in this volume leads to that desirable outcome, we could all celebrate.

I congratulate John Hunsley and Eric Mash and their colleagues for letting us have this eagerly anticipated volume.

Peter E. Nathan

References

American Psychiatric Association. (1993). Practice Guidelines for the Treatment of Major Depressive Disorder in Adults. *American Journal of Psychiatry, 150* (4 Supplement), 1–26.

American Psychiatric Association (2006). *Practice guidelines for the treatment of psychiatric disorders: Compendium, 2006.* Washington, DC: Author.

Castonguay, L. G., & Beutler, L. E. (2006). *Principles of therapeutic change that work.* New York: Oxford University Press.

Chambless, D. L., & Ollendick, T. H. (2001). Empirically supported psychological interventions: Controversies and evidence. In S. T. Fiske, D. L. Schacter, & C. Zahn-Waxler (Eds.), *Annual review of psychology* (vol. 52) (pp. 685–716). Palo Alto, CA: Annual Review.

Division 12 Task Force. (1995). Training in and dissemination of empirically-validated psychological treatments: Report and recommendations. *The Clinical Psychologist, 48,* 3–23.

Eysenck, H. J. (1952). The effects of psychotherapy: An evaluation. *Journal of Consulting Psychology, 16,* 319–324.

Hunsley, J., & Mash, E. J. (Eds.). (2005). Developing guidelines for the evidence-based assessment (EBA) of adult disorders (special section). *Psychological Assessment,* 17(3).

Lambert, M. J., & Bergin, A. E. (1994). The effectiveness of psychotherapy. In S.L. Garfield & A.E. Bergin (Eds.), *Handbook of psychotherapy and behavior change,* 4th ed. (pp. 143–189). New York: Wiley.

Luborsky, L., Singer, B., & Luborsky, L. (1976). Comparative studies of psychotherapies: Is it true that "everybody has won and all must have prizes?" In R. L. Spitzer & D. F. Klein (Eds.), *Evaluation of psychological therapies* (pp. 3–22). Baltimore, MD: Johns Hopkins University Press.

Mash, E. J., & Hunsley, J. (Eds.). (2005). Developing guidelines for the evidence-based assessment of child and adolescent disorders (special section). *Journal of Clinical Child and Adolescent Psychology,* 34(3).

Nathan, P. E., & Gorman, J. M. (1998, 2002, 2007). *A guide to treatments that work.* New York: Oxford University Press.

Nathan, P. E., Stuart, S. P., & Dolan, S. L. (2000). Research on psychotherapy efficacy and effectiveness: Between Scylla and Charybdis? *Psychological Bulletin, 126,* 964–981.

Norcross, J. C. (Ed.) (2002). *Psychotherapy relationships that work: Therapist contributions and responsiveness to patients.* New York: Oxford University Press.

Patterson, K. (2002). What doctors don't know (almost everything). *New York Times Magazine,* May 5, 74–77.

Part I

Introduction

1

Developing Criteria for Evidence-Based Assessment: An Introduction to Assessments That Work

John Hunsley

Eric J. Mash

For many professional psychologists, assessment is viewed as a unique and defining feature of their expertise (Krishnamurthy et al., 2004). Historically, careful attention to both conceptual and pragmatic issues related to measurement has served as the cornerstone of psychological science. Within the realm of professional psychology, the ability to provide assessment and evaluation services is typically seen as a required core competency. Indeed, assessment services are such an integral component of psychological practice that their value is rarely questioned but, rather, is typically assumed. However, solid evidence to support the usefulness of psychological assessment is lacking and many commonly used clinical assessment methods and instruments are not supported by scientific evidence (e.g., Hunsley, Lee, & Wood, 2003; Hunsley & Mash, 2007; Neisworth & Bognato, 2000; Norcross, Koocher, & Garofalo, 2006). Indeed, as Peterson (2004) recently commented, "For many of the most important inferences professional psychologists have to make, practitioners appear to be forever dependent on incorrigibly fallible interviews and unavoidably selective, reactive observations as primary sources of data" (p. 202).

In this era of evidence-based health-care practices, the need for scientifically sound assessment methods and instruments is greater than ever (Barlow, 2005). Assessment is the key to the accurate identification of patients' problems and strengths. Whether construed as individual patient monitoring, ongoing quality assurance efforts, or program evaluation, assessment is central to efforts to gauge the impact of health-care services provided to ameliorate these problems (Hermann, Chan, Zazzali, & Lerner, 2006). Furthermore, the increasing availability of research-derived treatment benchmarks holds out great promise for providing clinicians with meaningful and attainable targets for their intervention services (Hunsley & Lee, 2007; Weersing, 2005). Unfortunately, even in psychology, statements about evidence-based practice and best-practice guidelines rarely pay more than nominal attention to how critical assessment is to the provision of evidence-based services (e.g., American Psychological Association Presidential Task Force on Evidence-Based Practice, 2006). Without drawing upon a scientifically supported assessment literature, the prominence accorded to evidence-based treatment has been likened to constructing a magnificent house without bothering to build a solid foundation (Achenbach, 2005). Indeed, as the identification of evidence-based treatments rests entirely on the data provided by assessment tools, ignoring the quality of these tools places the whole evidence-based enterprise in jeopardy.

DEFINING EVIDENCE-BASED ASSESSMENT (EBA)

As we have described previously, there are three critical aspects that should define EBA (Hunsley & Mash, 2005, 2007; Mash & Hunsley, 2005). First, research findings and scientifically supported theories on both psychopathology and normal human development should be used to guide the selection of constructs to be assessed and the assessment process. As Barlow (2005) suggested, EBA measures and strategies should also be designed to be integrated into interventions that have been shown to work with the disorders or conditions that are targeted in the assessment. Therefore, while recognizing that most disorders do not come in clearly delineated neat packages, and that comorbidity is often the rule rather than the exception, we see EBAs as being disorder- or problem-specific. A problem-specific approach is consistent with how most assessment and treatment research is conducted and would facilitate the integration of EBA into evidence-based treatments (cf. Kazdin & Weisz, 2003; Mash & Barkley, 2006, 2007; Mash & Hunsley, 2007). Although formal diagnostic systems provide a frequently used alternative for framing the range of disorders and problems to be considered, commonly experienced emotional and relational problems, such as excessive anger, loneliness, conflictual relationships, and other specific impairments that may occur in the absence of a diagnosable disorder, may also be the focus of EBAs. Even when diagnostic systems are used as the framework for the assessment, a narrow focus on assessing symptoms and symptom reduction is insufficient for both treatment planning and treatment evaluation purposes (cf. Kazdin, 2003). Many assessments are conducted to identify the precise nature of the person's problem(s). It is, therefore, necessary to conceptualize multiple, interdependent stages in the assessment process, with each iteration of the process becoming less general in nature and increasingly problem-specific with further assessment (Mash & Terdal, 1997). In addition, for some generic assessment strategies, there may be research to indicate that the strategy is evidence based without being problem-specific. Examples of this include functional analytic assessments (Haynes, Leisen, & Blaine, 1997) and some recently developed patient monitoring systems (e.g., Lambert, 2001).

A second requirement is that, whenever possible, psychometrically strong measures should be used to assess the constructs targeted in the assessment. The measures should have evidence of reliability, validity, and clinical utility. They should also possess appropriate norms for norm-referenced interpretation and/ or replicated supporting evidence for the accuracy (e.g., sensitivity, specificity, predictive power, etc.) of

cut-scores for criterion-referenced interpretation (cf. Achenbach, 2005). Furthermore, there should be supporting evidence to indicate that the EBAs are sensitive to key characteristics of the individual(s) being assessed, including characteristics such as age, gender, race, ethnicity, and culture (Bell, Foster, & Mash, 2005; Ramirez, Ford, Stewart, & Teresi, 2005; Sonderegger & Barrett, 2004). Given the range of purposes for which assessment instruments can be used (i.e., screening, diagnosis, prognosis, case conceptualization, treatment formulation, treatment monitoring, treatment evaluation) and the fact that psychometric evidence is always conditional (based on sample characteristics and assessment purpose), supporting psychometric evidence must be considered for each purpose for which an instrument or assessment strategy is used. Thus, general discussions concerning the relative merits of information obtained via different assessment methods have little meaning outside of the assessment purpose and context. For example, as suggested in many chapters in this volume, semistructured diagnostic interviews are usually the best option for obtaining diagnostic information; however, in some instances, such interviews may not have incremental validity or utility once data from brief symptom rating scales are considered (Pelham, Fabiano, & Massetti, 2005). Similarly, not all psychometric elements are relevant to all assessment purposes. The group of validity statistics that includes specificity, sensitivity, positive predictive power, and negative predictive power is particularly relevant for diagnostic and prognostic assessment purposes and contains essential information for any measure that is intended to be used for screening purposes (Hsu, 2002). Such validity statistics may have little relevance, however, for many methods intended to be used for treatment monitoring and/or evaluation purposes; for these purposes, sensitivity to change is a much more salient psychometric feature (e.g., Vermeersch, Lambert, & Burlingame, 2000).

Finally, even with data from psychometrically strong measures, the assessment process is inherently a decision-making task in which the clinician must iteratively formulate and test hypotheses by integrating data that are often incomplete or inconsistent. Thus, a truly evidence-based approach to assessment would involve an evaluation of the accuracy and usefulness of this complex decision-making task in light of potential errors in data synthesis and interpretation, the costs associated with the assessment process, and, ultimately, the impact the assessment had on clinical outcomes. There are an increasing number of illustrations of how assessments can be conducted in an evidence-based manner (e.g., Doss, 2005; Frazier & Youngstrom, 2006; Youngstrom & Duax, 2005). These provide invaluable guides for clinicians and provide a preliminary framework that could lead to the eventual empirical evaluation of EBA processes themselves.

FROM RESEARCH TO PRACTICE: USING A "GOOD-ENOUGH" PRINCIPLE

Perhaps the greatest single challenge facing efforts to develop and implement EBAs is determining how to start the process of operationalizing the criteria we just outlined. The assessment literature provides a veritable wealth of information that is potentially relevant to EBA; this very strength, though, is also a considerable liability, for the size of the literature is beyond voluminous. Not only is the literature vast in scope, but the scientific evaluation of assessment methods and instruments can also be without end because there is no finite set of studies that can establish, once and for all, the psychometric properties of an instrument (Kazdin, 2005; Sechrest, 2005). On the other hand, every single day, clinicians must make decisions about what assessment tools to use in their practices, how best to use and combine the various forms of information they obtain in their assessment, and how to integrate assessment activities into other necessary aspects of clinical service. Moreover, the limited time available for service provision in clinical settings places an onus on using assessment options that are maximally accurate, efficient, and cost-effective. Thus, above and beyond the scientific support that has been amassed for an instrument, clinicians require tools that are brief, clear, clinically feasible, and user-friendly. In other words, they need instruments that have clinical utility and that are good enough to get the job done (Barlow, 2005; Lambert & Hawkins, 2004).

As has been noted in the assessment literature, there are no clear, commonly accepted guidelines to aid clinicians or researchers in determining when an instrument has sufficient scientific evidence to warrant its use (Kazdin, 2005; Sechrest, 2005). The Standards for Educational and Psychological Testing (American Educational Research Association,

American Psychological Association, & National Council on Measurement in Education, 1999) set out generic standards to be followed in developing and using psychological instruments, but are silent on the question of specific psychometric values that an instrument should have. The basic reason for this is that psychometric characteristics are not properties of an instrument per se but, rather, are properties of an instrument when used for a specific purpose with a specific sample. Quite understandably, therefore, assessment scholars, psychometricians, and test developers have been reluctant to explicitly indicate the minimum psychometric values or evidence necessary to indicate that an instrument is scientifically sound (cf. Streiner & Norman, 2003). Unfortunately, this is of little aid to the clinicians and researchers who are constantly faced with the decision of whether an instrument is good enough, scientifically speaking, for the assessment task at hand.

There have been some isolated attempts to establish criteria for the selection and use of measures for research purposes. Robinson, Shaver, and Wrightsman (1991), for example, developed evaluative criteria for the adequacy of attitude and personality measures, covering the domains of theoretical development, item development, norms, inter-item correlations, internal consistency, test–retest reliability, factor analytic results, known groups validity, convergent validity, discriminant validity, and freedom from response sets. Robinson and colleagues also used specific psychometric criteria for many of these domains, such as describing a coefficient α of .80 as exemplary. More recently, there have been efforts to establish general psychometric criteria for determining the suitability of measures for clinical use in measuring disability in speech/language disorders (Agency for Healthcare Research and Quality, 2002). A different approach was taken by the Measurement and Treatment Research to Improve Cognition in Schizophrenia Group to develop a consensus battery of cognitive tests to be used in clinical trials in schizophrenia (MATRICS, 2006). Rather than setting precise psychometric criteria for use in rating potential instruments, expert panelists were asked to rate, on a nine-point scale, each proposed tool's characteristics, including test–retest reliability, utility as a repeated measure, relation to functional outcome, responsiveness to treatment change, and practicality/tolerability.

Clearly any attempt to develop a method for determining the scientific adequacy of assessment instruments is fraught with the potential for error. The application of criteria that are too stringent could result in a solid set of assessment options, but one that is so limited in number or scope as to render the whole effort clinically worthless. Alternatively, using excessively lenient criteria could undermine the whole notion of an instrument or process being evidence based. So, with a clear awareness of this assessment equivalent of Scylla and Charybdis, we sought to construct a framework for the chapters included in this volume that would employ good-enough criteria for rating psychological instruments. In other words, rather than focusing on standards that define ideal criteria for a measure, our intent was to provide criteria that would indicate the minimum evidence that would be sufficient to warrant the use of a measure for specific clinical purposes. We assume, from the outset, that although our framework is intended to be scientifically sound and defensible, it is a first step, rather than the definitive effort in designing a rating system for evaluating psychometric adequacy.

In brief, to operationalize the good-enough principle, we developed specific rating criteria to be used across categories of psychometric properties that have clear clinical relevance; each category has rating options of adequate, good, and excellent. In the following sections, we describe the assessment purposes covered by our rating system, the psychometric properties included in the system, and the rationales for the rating options. The actual rating system, used by authors in this volume to construct their summary tables of instruments, is presented in two tables later in the chapter.

ASSESSMENT PURPOSES

Although psychological assessments are conducted for many reasons, it is possible to identify a small set of interrelated purposes which form the basis for most assessments. These include (a) diagnosis (i.e., determining the nature and/or cause[s] of the presenting problems, which may or may not involve the use of a formal diagnostic or categorization system), (b) screening (i.e., identifying those who have or who are at risk for a particular problem and who might be helped by further assessment or intervention), (c) prognosis and other predictions (i.e., generating predictions about the course of the problems if left untreated, recommendations for possible courses of action to be considered, and their likely impact on the course of the problems), (d) case conceptualization/ formulation (i.e., developing a comprehensive and clinically relevant understanding of the patient, generating hypotheses regarding critical aspects of the patient's psychosocial functioning and context that are likely to influence the patient's adjustment), (e) treatment design/planning (i.e., selecting/developing and implementing interventions designed to address the patient's problems by focusing on elements identified in the diagnostic evaluation and the case conceptualization) (f) treatment monitoring (i.e., tracking changes in symptoms, functioning, psychological characteristics, intermediate treatment goals, and/or variables determined to cause or maintain the problems), and (g) treatment evaluation (i.e., determining the effectiveness, social validity, consumer satisfaction, and/or cost-effectiveness of the intervention).

Our intent in conceptualizing this volume is to provide a summary of the best assessment methods and instruments for commonly encountered clinical assessment purposes. Therefore, although recognizing the importance of other possible assessment purposes, chapters in this volume focus on (a) diagnosis, (b) case conceptualization and treatment planning, and (c) treatment monitoring and treatment evaluation. Although separable in principle, we combined the purposes of case conceptualization and treatment planning because they tend to rely on the same assessment data. Similarly, we combined the purposes of treatment monitoring and evaluation because they often, but not exclusively, use the same assessment methods and instruments. Clearly, there are some overlapping elements, even in this set of purposes; for example, it is relatively common for the question of diagnosis to be revisited as part of evaluating the outcome of treatment. In the instrument summary tables that accompany each chapter, the psychometric strength of instruments used for these three main purposes are presented and rated. Within a chapter, the same instrument may be rated for more than one assessment purpose and thus appear in more than one table. As an instrument may possess more empirical support for some purposes than for others, the ratings given for the instrument may not be the same in each of the tables.

The chapters in this volume present information on the best available instruments for diagnosis, case conceptualization and treatment planning, and treatment monitoring and evaluation. They also provide details on clinically appropriate options for the range of data to collect, suggestions on how to address some of the challenges commonly encountered in conducting assessment, and suggestions for the assessment process itself. Consistent with the problem-specific focus within EBA outlined above, each chapter in this volume focuses on one or more specific disorders or conditions. However, many patients present with multiple problems and, therefore, there are frequent references within a given chapter to the assessment of common co-occurring problems that are addressed in other chapters in the volume. To be optimally useful to potential readers, the chapters are focused on the most commonly encountered disorders or conditions among children, adolescents, adults, older adults, and couples. With the specific focus on the three critical assessment purposes of diagnosis, case conceptualization and treatment planning, and treatment monitoring and treatment, within each disorder or condition, the chapters in this volume provide readers with essential information for conducting the best EBAs currently possible.

PSYCHOMETRIC PROPERTIES AND RATING CRITERIA

Clinical assessment typically entails the use of both idiographic and nomothetic instruments. Idiographic measures are designed to assess unique aspects of a person's experience and, therefore, to be useful in evaluating changes in these individually defined and constructed variables. In contrast, nomothetic measures are designed to assess constructs assumed to be relevant to all individuals and to facilitate comparisons, on these constructs, across people. Most chapters include information on idiographic measures such as self-monitoring forms and individualized scales for measuring treatment goals (e.g., goal attainment scaling). For such idiographic measures, psychometric characteristics such as reliability and validity may, at times, not be easily evaluated or even relevant. It is crucial, however, that the same items and instructions are used across assessment occasions—without this level of standardization it is impossible to accurately determine changes that may be due to treatment (Kazdin, 1993).

Deciding on the psychometric categories to be rated for the nomothetic instruments was not a simple task, nor was developing concrete rating options for each of the categories. In the end, we focused on nine categories: norms, internal consistency, inter-rater reliability, test–retest reliability, content validity, construct validity, validity generalization, sensitivity to treatment change, and clinical utility. Each of these categories is applied in relation to a specific assessment purpose (e.g., case conceptualization and treatment planning) in the context of a specific disorder or clinical condition (e.g., eating disorders, self-injurious behavior, relationship conflict). Consistent with our previous comments, factors such as gender, ethnicity, and age must be considered in making ratings within these categories. For each category, a rating of less than adequate, adequate, good, excellent, unavailable, or not applicable was possible. The precise nature of what constituted adequate, good, and excellent varied, of course, from category to category. In general, though, a rating of adequate indicated that the instrument meets a minimal level of scientific rigor, good indicated that the instrument would generally be seen as possessing solid scientific support, and excellent indicated there was extensive, high quality supporting evidence. Accordingly, a rating of less than adequate indicated that the instrument did not meet the minimum level set out in the criteria. A rating of unavailable indicated that research on the psychometric property under consideration had not yet been conducted or published. A rating of not applicable indicated that the psychometric property under consideration was not relevant to the instrument (e.g., inter-rater reliability for a self-report symptom rating scale).

When considering the clinical use of a measure, it would be desirable to only use those measures that would meet, at a minimum, the criteria for good. However, as measure development is an ongoing process, we thought it was important to provide the option of the adequate rating in order to fairly evaluate (a) relatively newly developed measures and (b) measures for which comparable levels of research evidence are not available across all psychometric categories in the rating system. That being said, the only instruments included in chapter summary tables were those that had adequate or better ratings on the majority of the psychometric dimensions. Thus, the instruments presented in these tables represent only a subset of available assessment tools.

Despite the difficulty inherent in promulgating scientific criteria for psychometric properties, we believe that the potential benefits of fair and attainable criteria far outweigh the potential drawbacks (cf. Sechrest, 2005). Accordingly, we used both reasoned

TABLE 1.1 Criteria at a Glance: Norms and Reliability

Norms

Adequate = Measures of central tendency and distribution for the total score (and subscores if relevant) based on a large, relevant, clinical sample are available

Good = Measures of central tendency and distribution for the total score (and subscores if relevant) based on several large, relevant samples (must include data from both clinical and nonclinical samples) are available

Excellent = Measures of central tendency and distribution for the total score (and subscores if relevant) based on one or more large, *representative* samples (must include data from both clinical and nonclinical samples) are available

Internal consistency

Adequate = Preponderance of evidence indicates α values of .70–.79

Good = Preponderance of evidence indicates α values of .80–.89

Excellent = Preponderance of evidence indicates α values $\geq$ .90

Inter-rater reliability

Adequate = Preponderance of evidence indicates κ values of .60–.74; the preponderance of evidence indicates Pearson correlation or intraclass correlation values of .70–.79

Good = Preponderance of evidence indicates κ values of .75–.84; the preponderance of evidence indicates Pearson correlation or intraclass correlation values of .80–.89

Excellent = Preponderance of evidence indicates κ values $\geq$ .85; the preponderance of evidence indicates Pearson correlation or intraclass correlation values $\geq$ .90

Test–retest reliability

Adequate = Preponderance of evidence indicates test–retest correlations of at least .70 over a period of several days to several weeks

Good = Preponderance of evidence indicates test–retest correlations of at least .70 over a period of several months

Excellent = Preponderance of evidence indicates test–retest correlations of at least .70 over a period of a year or longer

arguments from respected psychometricians, assessment scholars, and, whenever possible, summaries of various assessment literatures to guide our selection of criteria for rating the psychometric properties associated with an instrument. Table 1.1 presents the criteria used in rating norms and reliability indices; Table 1.2 presents the criteria used in rating validity indices and clinical utility.

Norms

When using a standardized, nomothetically based instrument, it is essential that norms, specific criterion-related cutoff scores, or both are available to aid in the accurate interpretation of a client's test score (American Educational Research Association, American Psychological Association, & National Council on Measurement in Education, 1999). For example, norms can be used to determine the client's pre- and post-treatment levels of functioning and to evaluate whether any change in functioning is clinically meaningful (Achenbach, 2001; Kendall, Marrs-Garcia, Nath, & Sheldrick, 1999). Selecting the target population(s) for the norms and then ensuring that the

norms are adequate can be difficult tasks, and several sets of norms may be required for a measure. One set of norms may be needed to determine the meaning of the obtained score relative to the general population, whereas a different set of norms could be used to compare the score to specific subgroups within the population (Cicchetti, 1994). Regardless of the population to which comparisons are to be made, a normative sample must be truly representative of the population with respect to demographics and other important characteristics (Achenbach, 2001). Ideally, whether conducted at the national level or the local level, this would involve probability-sampling efforts in which data are obtained from the majority of contacted respondents. As those familiar with psychological instruments are aware, such a sampling strategy is rarely used for the development of test norms. The reliance on data collected from convenience samples with unknown response rates reduces the accuracy of the resultant norms. Therefore, at a minimum, clinicians need to be provided with an indication of the quality and likely accuracy of the norms for a measure. Accordingly, the ratings for norms required, at a minimum for a rating of adequate, data from a single, large clinical sample. For a rating of good,

TABLE 1.2 Criteria at a Glance: Validity and Utility

Content validity

Adequate = The test developers clearly defined the domain of the construct being assessed and ensured that selected items were representative of the entire set of facets included in the domain

Good = In addition to the criteria used for an *adequate* rating, all elements of the instrument (e.g., instructions, items) were evaluated by judges (e.g., by experts or by pilot research participants)

Excellent = In addition to the criteria used for a *good* rating, multiple groups of judges were employed and quantitative ratings were used by the judges

Construct validity

Adequate = Some independently replicated evidence of construct validity (e.g., predictive validity, concurrent validity, and convergent and discriminant validity)

Good = Preponderance of independently replicated evidence, across multiple types of validity (e.g., predictive validity, concurrent validity, and convergent and discriminant validity), is indicative of construct validity

Excellent = In addition to the criteria used for a *good* rating, evidence of incremental validity with respect to other clinical data

Validity generalization

Adequate = Some evidence supports the use of this instrument with either (a) more than one specific group (based on sociodemographic characteristics such as age, gender, and ethnicity) or (b) in multiple contexts (e.g., home, school, primary care setting, inpatient setting)

Good = Preponderance of evidence supports the use of this instrument with either (a) more than one specific group (based on sociodemographic characteristics such as age, gender, and ethnicity) or (b) in multiple settings (e.g., home, school, primary care setting, inpatient setting)

Excellent = Preponderance of evidence supports the use of this instrument with more than one specific group (based on sociodemographic characteristics such as age, gender, and ethnicity) *and* across multiple contexts (e.g., home, school, primary care setting, inpatient setting)

Treatment sensitivity

Adequate = Some evidence of sensitivity to change over the course of treatment

Good = Preponderance of independently replicated evidence indicates sensitivity to change over the course of treatment

Excellent = In addition to the criteria used for a *good* rating, evidence of sensitivity to change across different types of treatments

Clinical utility

Adequate = Taking into account practical considerations (e.g., costs, ease of administration, availability of administration and scoring instructions, duration of assessment, availability of relevant cutoff scores, acceptability to patients), the resulting assessment data are likely to be clinically useful

Good = In addition to the criteria used for an *adequate* rating, there is some published evidence that the use of the resulting assessment data confers a demonstrable clinical benefit (e.g., better treatment outcome, lower treatment attrition rates, greater patient satisfaction with services)

Excellent = In addition to the criteria used for an *adequate* rating, there is *independently replicated* published evidence that the use of the resulting assessment data confers a demonstrable clinical benefit

normative data from multiple samples, including non-clinical samples, were required; when normative data from large, representative samples were available, a rating of excellent was applied.

Reliability

Reliability is a key psychometric element to be considered in evaluating an instrument. It refers to the consistency of a person's score on a measure (Anastasi, 1988), including whether (a) all elements of a measure contribute in a consistent way to the data obtained (internal consistency), (b) similar results would be obtained if the measure was used or scored by another clinician (inter-rater reliability),[1] or (c) similar results would be obtained if the person completed the measure a second time (test–retest reliability or test stability). Not all reliability indices are relevant to all assessment methods and measures, and the size of the indices may vary on the basis of the samples used.

With respect to internal consistency, we focused on α, which is the most widely used index (Streiner, 2003). Recommendations in the literature for what constitutes adequate internal consistency vary, but most authorities seem to view .70 as the minimum acceptable value (e.g., Cicchetti, 1994), and Charter (2003) reported that the mean internal consistency value among commonly used clinical instruments was .81. Accordingly, a rating of adequate was given to values of .70–.79, a rating of good required values of .80–.89, and, finally, because of cogent arguments that an α value of at least .90 is highly desirable in clinical assessment contexts (Nunnally & Bernstein, 1994), we required values ≥ .90 for an instrument to be rated as having excellent internal consistency. It should be noted that it is possible for α to be too (artificially) high, as a value close to unity typically indicates substantial redundancy among items (cf. Streiner, 2003).

These value ranges were also used in rating evidence for inter-rater reliability when assessed with Pearson correlations or intraclass correlations. Appropriate adjustments were made to the value ranges when κ statistics were used, in line with the recommendations discussed by Cicchetti (1994; see also Charter, 2003). Importantly, evidence for inter-rater reliability could only come from data generated among clinicians or clinical raters—estimates of cross-informant agreement, such as between parent and teacher ratings, are not indicators of reliability.

In establishing ratings for test–retest reliability values, our requirement for a minimum correlation of .70 was influenced by summary data reported on typical test–retest reliability results found with clinical instruments (Charter, 2003) and trait-like psychological measures (Watson, 2004). Of course, not all constructs or measures are expected to show temporal stability (e.g., measures of state-like variables, life stress inventories), so test–retest reliability was only rated if it was relevant. A rating of adequate required evidence of correlation values of .70 or greater, when reliability was assessed over a period of several days to several weeks. We then faced a challenge in determining appropriate criteria for good and excellent ratings. In order to enhance its likely usefulness, we wanted a rating system that was relatively simple. However, test–retest reliability is a complex phenomenon that is influenced by (a) the nature of the construct being assessed (i.e., it can be state-like, trait-like, or influenced by situational variables), (b) the time frame covering the reporting period instructions (i.e., whether respondents are asked to report their current functioning, functioning over the past few days, or functioning over an extended period, such as general functioning in the past year), and (c) the duration of the retest period (i.e., whether the time between two administrations of the instrument involved days, weeks, months, or years). In the end, rather than emphasize the value of increasingly large test–retest correlations, we decided to maintain the requirement for .70 or greater correlation values, but require increasing retest period durations of (a) several months and (b) at least a year for ratings of good and excellent respectively.

Validity

Validity is another central aspect to be considered when evaluating psychometric properties. Foster and Cone (1995) drew an important distinction between representational validity (i.e., whether a measure really assesses what it purports to measure) and elaborative validity (i.e., whether the measure has any utility for measuring the construct). Attending to the content validity of a measure is a basic, but frequently overlooked, step in evaluating representational validity (Haynes, Richard, & Kubany, 1995). As discussed by Smith, Fischer, and Fister (2003), the overall reliability and validity of an instrument is directly affected by the extent to which items in the instrument adequately represent the various aspects or facets of the construct the instrument is designed to measure. Assuming that representational validity has been established, it is elaborative validity that is central to clinicians' use of a measure. Accordingly, replicated evidence for a measure's concurrent, predictive, discriminative, and, ideally, incremental validity (Hunsley & Meyer, 2003) should be available to qualify a measure for consideration as evidence based. We have indicated already that validation is a context-sensitive concept—inattention to this fact can lead to inappropriate generalizations being made about a measure's validity. There should be, therefore, replicated elaborative validity evidence for each purpose of the measure and for each population or group for which the measure is intended to be used. This latter point is especially relevant when considering an instrument for clinical use, and thus it is essential to consider evidence for validity generalization—that is, the extent to which there is evidence for validity across a range of samples and settings (cf. Messick, 1995; Schmidt & Hunter, 1977).

For ratings of content validity evidence, we followed Haynes et al.'s (1995) suggestions, requiring explicit consideration of the construct facets to be included in the measure and, as the ratings increased, involvement of content validity judges to assess the measure. Unlike the situation for reliability, there are no commonly accepted summary statistics to evaluate either construct validity or incremental validity (but see, respectively, Westen & Rosenthal [2000] and Hunsley & Meyer [2003]). As a result, our ratings were based on the requirement of increasing amounts of replicated evidence of predictive validity, concurrent validity, convergent validity, and discriminant validity; in addition, for a rating of excellent, evidence of incremental validity was also required. We were unable to find any clearly applicable standards in the literature to guide us in developing criteria for validity generalization or treatment sensitivity (a dimension rated only for instruments used for the purposes of treatment monitoring and treatment evaluation). Therefore, adequate ratings for these dimensions required some evidence of, respectively, the use of the instrument with either more than one specific group or in multiple contexts and evidence of sensitivity to change over the course of treatment. Consistent with ratings for other dimensions, good and excellent ratings required increasingly demanding levels of evidence in these areas.

Utility

It is also essential to know the utility of an instrument for a specific clinical purpose. The concept of clinical utility, applied to both diagnostic systems (e.g., Kendell & Jablensky, 2003) and assessment tools (e.g., Hunsley & Bailey, 1999; Yates & Taub, 2003), has received a great deal of attention in recent years. Although definitions vary, they have in common an emphasis on garnering evidence regarding actual improvements in both decisions made by clinicians and service outcomes experienced by patients. Unfortunately, despite thousands of studies on the reliability and validity of psychological instruments, there is only scant attention paid to matters of utility in most assessment research studies (McGrath, 2001). This has directly contributed to the present state of affairs in which there is very little replicated evidence that psychological assessment data have a direct impact on improved provision and outcome of clinical services. At present, therefore, for the majority of psychological instruments, a determination of clinical utility must often be made on the basis of likely clinical value, rather than on empirical evidence.

Compared to the criteria for the psychometric dimensions presented thus far, our standards for evidence of clinical utility were noticeably less demanding. This was necessary because of the paucity of information on the extent to which assessment instruments are acceptable to patients, enhance the quality and outcome of clinical services, and/or are worth the costs associated with their use. Therefore, we relied on authors' expert opinions to classify an instrument as having adequate clinical utility. The availability of any supporting evidence of utility was sufficient for a rating of good and replicated evidence of utility was necessary for a rating of excellent.

The instrument summary tables also contain one final column, used to indicate instruments that are the best measures currently available to clinicians for specific purposes and disorders and, thus, are highly recommended for clinical use. Given the considerable differences in the state of the assessment literature for different disorders/conditions, chapter authors had some flexibility in determining their own precise requirements for an instrument to be rated, or not rated, as highly recommended. However, to ensure a moderate level of consistency in these ratings, a highly recommended rating could only be considered for those instruments having achieved ratings of good or excellent in the majority of its rated psychometric categories.

SOME FINAL THOUGHTS

We are hopeful that the rating system described in this chapter, and applied in each of the chapters of this book, will serve to advance the state of evidence-based psychological assessment. We also hope that it will serve as a stimulus for others to refine and improve upon our efforts. Whatever the possible merits of the rating system, we wish to close this chapter by drawing attention to three critical issues related to its use.

First, although the rating system used for this volume is relatively simple, the task of rating psychometric properties is not. Results from many studies must be considered in making such ratings and precise quantitative standards were not set for how to weight the results from studies. Furthermore, in the spirit of evidence-based practice, it is also important to note that we do not know whether these ratings are, themselves, reliable. Reliance on individual expert judgment, no matter how extensive and current the knowledge of the experts, is not as desirable as basing evidence-based conclusions and guidance on systematic reviews of the literature conducted according to a consensually agreed upon rating system (cf. GRADE Working Group, 2004). However, for all the potential limitations and biases inherent in our approach, reliance on expert review of the scientific literature is the current standard in psychology and, thus, was the only feasible option for the volume at this time.

The second issue has to do with the responsible clinical use of the guidance provided by the rating system. Consistent with evaluation and grading strategies used through evidence-based medicine and evidence-based psychology initiatives, many of our rating criteria relied upon the consideration of the preponderance of data relevant to each dimension. Such a strategy recognizes both the importance of replication in science and the fact that variability across studies in research design elements (including sample composition and research setting) will influence estimates of these psychometric dimensions. However, we hasten to emphasize that reliance on the preponderance of evidence for these ratings does not imply or guarantee that an instrument is applicable for all patients or clinical settings. Our intention is to have these ratings provide indications about scientifically strong measures that warrant consideration for clinical and research use. As with all evidence-based efforts, the responsibility rests with the individual professional to determine the suitability of an instrument for the specific setting, purpose, and individuals to be assessed.

Third, as emphasized throughout this volume, focusing on the scientific evidence for specific assessment tools should not overshadow the fact that the process of clinical assessment involves much more than simply selecting and administering the best available instruments. Choosing the best, most relevant, instruments is unquestionably an important step. Subsequent steps must ensure that the instruments are administered in an appropriate manner, accurately scored, and then individually interpreted in accordance with the relevant body of scientific research. However, to ensure a truly evidence-based approach to assessment, the major challenge is to then integrate all of the data within a process that is, itself, evidence based. Much of our focus in this chapter has been on evidence-based methods and instruments, in large part because (a) methods and specific measures are more easily identified than are processes and (b) the main emphasis in the assessment literature has been on psychometric properties of methods and instruments. As we indicated early in the chapter, an evidence-based approach to assessment should be developed in light of evidence on the accuracy and usefulness of this complex, iterative decision-making task. Although the chapters in this volume provide considerable assistance for having the assessment process be informed by scientific evidence, the future challenge will be to ensure that the entire process of assessment is evidence based.

Note

1. Although we chose to use the term "inter-rater reliability," there is some discussion in the assessment literature about whether the term should be "inter-rater agreement." Heyman et al. (2001), for example, suggested that, as indices of inter-rater reliability do not contain information about individual differences among participants and only contain information about one source of error (i.e., differences among raters), they should be considered to be indices of agreement, not reliability.

References

Achenbach, T. M. (2001). What are norms and why do we need valid ones? *Clinical Psychology: Science and Practice, 8,* 446–450.

Achenbach, T. M. (2005). Advancing assessment of children and adolescents: Commentary on evidence-based assessment of child and adolescent disorders. *Journal of Clinical Child and Adolescent Psychology, 34,* 541–547.

Agency for Healthcare Research and Quality. (2002). *Criteria for determining disability in speech–language disorders.* AHRQ Publication No. 02-E009.

American Educational Research Association, American Psychological Association, National Council on Measurement in Education. (1999). *Standards for educational and psychological testing.* Washington, DC: Author.

American Psychological Association Presidential Task Force on Evidence-Based Practice. (2006). Evidence-based practice in psychology. *American Psychologist, 61,* 271–285.

Anastasi, A. (1988). *Psychological testing* (6th ed.). New York: Macmillan.

Barlow, D. H. (2005). What's new about evidence based assessment? *Psychological Assessment, 17*, 308–311.

Bell, D., Foster, S. L., & Mash, E. J. (Eds.). (2005). *Handbook of behavioral and emotional problems in girls.* New York: Kluwer/Academic.

Charter, R. A. (2003). A breakdown of reliability coefficients by test type and reliability method, and the clinical implications of low reliability. *Journal of General Psychology, 130,* 290–304.

Cicchetti, D. V. (1994). Guidelines, criteria, and rules of thumb for evaluating normed and standardized assessment instruments in psychology. *Psychological Assessment, 6,* 284–290.

Doss, A. J. (2005). Evidence-based diagnosis: Incorporating diagnostic instruments into clinical practice. *Journal of the American Academy of Child & Adolescent Psychiatry, 44,* 947–952.

Foster, S. L., & Cone, J. D. (1995). Validity issues in clinical assessment. *Psychological Assessment, 7,* 248–260.

Frazier, T. W., & Youngstrom, E. A. (2006). Evidence-based assessment of attention-deficit/hyperactivity disorder: Using multiple sources of information. *Journal of the American Academy of Child & Adolescent Psychiatry, 45,* 614–620.

GRADE Working Group. (2004). Grading quality of evidence and strength of recommendations. *British Medical Journal, 328,* 1490–1497.

Haynes, S. N., Leisen, M. B., & Blaine, D. D. (1997). Design of individualized behavioral treatment programs using functional analytic clinical case methods. *Psychological Assessment, 9,* 334–348.

Haynes, S. N., Richard, D. C. S., & Kubany, E. S. (1995). Content validity in psychological assessment: A functional approach to concepts and methods. *Psychological Assessment, 7,* 238–247.

Hermann, R. C., Chan, J. A., Zazzali, J. L., & Lerner, D. (2006). Aligning measure-based quality improvement with implementation of evidence-based practices. *Administration and Policy in Mental Health and Mental Health Services Research, 33,* 636–645.

Heyman, R. E., Chaudhry, B. R., Treboux, D., Crowell, J., Lord, C., Vivian, D., et al. (2001). How much observational data is enough? An empirical test using marital interaction coding. *Behavior Therapy, 32,* 107–123.

Hsu, L. M. (2002). Diagnostic validity statistics and the MCMI-III. *Psychological Assessment, 14,* 410–422.

Hunsley, J., & Bailey, J. M. (1999). The clinical utility of the Rorschach: Unfulfilled promises and an uncertain future. *Psychological Assessment, 11,* 266–277.

Hunsley, J., & Lee, C. M. (2007). Research-informed benchmarks for psychological treatments: Efficacy studies, effectiveness studies, and beyond. *Professional Psychology: Research and Practice, 38,* 21–33.

Hunsley, J., Lee, C. M., & Wood, J. M. (2003). Controversial and questionable assessment techniques. In S. O. Lilienfeld, S. J. Lynn, & J. M. Lohr (Eds.), *Science and pseudoscience in clinical psychology* (pp. 39–76). New York: Guilford.

Hunsley, J., & Mash, E. J. (2005). Introduction to the special section on developing guidelines for the evidence-based assessment (EBA) of adult disorders. *Psychological Assessment, 17,* 251–255.

Hunsley, J., & Mash, E. J. (2007). Evidence-based assessment. *Annual Review of Clinical Psychology, 3,* 57–79.

Hunsley, J., & Meyer, G. J. (2003). The incremental validity of psychological testing and assessment: Conceptual, methodological, and statistical issues. *Psychological Assessment, 15,* 446–455.

Kazdin, A. E. (1993). Evaluation in clinical practice: Clinically sensitive and systematic methods of treatment delivery. *Behavior Therapy, 24,* 11–45.

Kazdin, A. E. (2003). Psychotherapy for children and adolescents. *Annual Review of Psychology, 54,* 253–276.

Kazdin, A. E. (2005). Evidence-based assessment of child and adolescent disorders: Issues in measurement development and clinical application. *Journal of Clinical Child and Adolescent Psychology, 34,* 548–558.

Kazdin, A. E., & Weisz, J. R. (Eds.). (2003). *Evidence-based psychotherapies for children and adolescents.* New York: Guilford.

Kendall, P. C., Marrs-Garcia, A., Nath, S. R., & Sheldrick, R. C. (1999). Normative comparisons for the evaluation of clinical significance. *Journal of Consulting and Clinical Psychology, 67,* 285–299.

Kendell, R., & Jablensky, A. (2003). Distinguishing between the validity and utility of psychiatric diagnoses. *American Journal of Psychiatry, 160,* 4–12.

Krishnamurthy, R., VandeCreek, L., Kaslow, N. J., Tazeau, Y. N., Miville, M. L., Kerns, R., et al. (2004). Achieving competency in psychological assessment: Directions for education and training. *Journal of Clinical Psychology, 60,* 725–739.

Lambert, M. J. (Ed.). (2001). Patient-focused research [Special section]. *Journal of Consulting and Clinical Psychology, 69,* 147–204.

Lambert, M. J., & Hawkins, E. J. (2004). Measuring outcome in professional practice: Considerations in selecting and using brief outcome instruments. *Professional Psychology: Research and Practice, 35,* 492–499.

Mash, E. J., & Barkley, R. A. (Eds.). (2006). *Treatment of childhood disorders* (3rd ed.). New York: Guilford.

Mash, E. J., & Barkley, R. A. (Eds.). (2007). *Assessment of childhood disorders* (4th ed.). New York: Guilford.

Mash, E. J., & Hunsley, J. (2005). Evidence-based assessment of child and adolescent disorders: Issues and challenges. *Journal of Clinical Child and Adolescent Psychology, 34,* 362–379.

Mash, E. J., & Hunsley, J. (2007). Assessment of child and family disturbance: A developmental systems approach. In E. Mash & R. A. Barkley (Eds.), *Assessment of childhood disorders* (pp. 3–50). New York: Guilford.

Mash, E. J., & Terdal, L. G. (1997). Assessment of child and family disturbance: A behavioral-systems approach. In E. J. Mash & L. G. Terdal (Eds.), *Assessment of childhood disorders* (3rd ed., pp. 3–68). New York: Guilford.

MATRICS. (2006). *Results of the MATRICS RAND Panel Meeting: Average medians for the categories of each candidate test.* Retrieved August 23, 2007, from http://www.matrics.ucla.edu/matrics-psychometrics-frame.htm

McGrath, R. E. (2001). Toward more clinically relevant assessment research. *Journal of Personality Assessment, 77,* 307–332.

Messick, S. (1995). Validity of psychological assessment: Validation of inferences from persons' responses and performances as scientific inquiry into score meaning. *American Psychologist, 50,* 741–749.

Neisworth, J. T., & Bagnato, S. J. (2000). Recommended practices in assessment. In S. Sandall, M. E. McLean, & B. J. Smith (Eds.), *DEC recommended practices in early intervention/early child special education* (pp. 17–27). Longmont, CO: Sopris West.

Norcross, J. C., Koocher, G. P., & Garofalo, A. (2006). Discredited psychological treatments and tests: A Delphi poll. *Professional Psychology: Research and Practice, 37,* 515–522.

Nunnally, J. C., & Bernstein, I. H. (1994). *Psychometric theory* (3rd ed.). New York: McGraw-Hill.

Pelham, W. E., Fabiano, G. A., & Massetti, G. M. (2005). Evidence-based assessment of attention deficit hyperactivity disorder in children and adolescents. *Journal of Clinical Child and Adolescent Psychology, 34,* 449–476.

Peterson, D. R. (2004). Science, scientism, and professional responsibility. *Clinical Psychology: Science and Practice, 11,* 196–210.

Ramirez, M., Ford, M. E., Stewart, A. L., & Teresi, J. A. (2005). Measurement issues in health disparities research. *Health Services Research, 40,* 1640–1657.

Robinson, J. P., Shaver, P. R., & Wrightsman, L. S. (1991). Criteria for scale selection and evaluation. In J. P. Robinson, P. R. Shaver, & L. S. Wrightsman (Eds.), *Measures of personality and social psychological attitudes* (pp. 1–16). New York: Academic Press.

Schmidt, F. L., & Hunter, J. E. (1977). Development of a general solution to the problem of validity generalization. *Journal of Applied Psychology, 62,* 529–540.

Sechrest, L. (2005). Validity of measures is no simple matter. *Health Services Research, 40,* 1584–1604.

Smith, G. T., Fischer, S., & Fister, S. M. (2003). Incremental validity principles in test construction. *Psychological Assessment, 15,* 467–477.

Sonderegger, R., & Barrett, P. M. (2004). Assessment and treatment of ethnically diverse children and adolescents. In P. M. Barrett & T. H. Ollendick (Eds.), *Handbook of interventions that work with children and adolescents: Prevention and treatment* (pp. 89–111). New York: John Wiley.

Streiner, D. L. (2003). Starting at the beginning: An introduction to coefficient alpha and internal consistency. *Journal of Personality Assessment, 80,* 99–103.

Streiner, D. L., & Norman, G. R. (2003). *Health measurement scales: A practical guide to their development and use* (3rd ed.). New York: Oxford University Press.

Vermeersch, D. A., Lambert, M. J., & Burlingame, G. M. (2000). Outcome questionnaire: Item sensitivity to change. *Journal of Personality Assessment, 74,* 242–261.

Watson, D. (2004). Stability versus change, dependability versus error: Issues in the assessment of personality over time. *Journal of Research in Personality, 38,* 319–350.

Weersing, V. R. (2005). Benchmarking the effectiveness of psychotherapy: Program evaluation as a component of evidence-based practice. *Journal of the American Academy of Child & Adolescent Psychiatry, 44,* 1058–1062.

Westen, D., & Rosenthal, R. (2003). Quantifying construct validity: Two simple measures. *Journal of Personality and Social Psychology, 84,* 608–618.

Yates, B. T., & Taub, J. (2003). Assessing the costs, benefits, cost-effectiveness, and cost-benefit of psychological assessment: We should, we can, and here's how. *Psychological Assessment, 15,* 478–495.

Youngstrom, E. A., & Duax, J. (2005). Evidence-based assessment of pediatric bipolar disorder, Part I: Base rate and family history. *Journal of the American Academy of Child & Adolescent Psychiatry, 44,* 712–717.

Part II

Attention-Deficit and Disruptive Behavior Disorders

2

Child Attention-Deficit/
Hyperactivity Disorder

Charlotte Johnston
Janet W. T. Mah

This chapter focuses on the assessment of childhood Attention-Deficit/Hyperactivity Disorder (ADHD) in clinical settings and on measures appropriate for 6- to 12-year-old children, as this age group is most frequently referred for assessment and treatment of ADHD. We hasten to note that this limited age focus is, to some degree, inconsistent with the developmental psychopathology perspective, which we believe most useful in understanding ADHD (Johnston & Mash, 2001). Information regarding the assessment of ADHD during the preschool years, adolescence, and into adulthood has only recently begun to emerge (e.g., Barkley, 2006) and more is sorely needed. A significant challenge in understanding, assessing, and treating ADHD across the life span (both within and across individuals) will be the integration of assessment tools and information from each of these age groups.

The relatively high prevalence of ADHD, combined with the pernicious nature of the problems associated with it and the persistence of the disorder over time, make comprehensive and accurate clinical assessment an imperative for guiding clinical care in this population. In addition, perhaps more than most child diagnoses, the ADHD diagnosis has been the subject of considerable controversy. Much of this controversy is fuelled by frequent, and at times sensationalistic, media reports. Many parents, whose children undergo assessments for ADHD, express fear that this is an overused diagnostic label designed merely to control children's naturally rambunctious nature and to justify the use of psychotropic medications. Contrary to these concerns, the scientific community has provided ample evidence to support the validity of the disorder and its associated treatments (Barkley, 2002; National Institutes of Health, 2000). Further evidence suggests that although the diagnosis may sometimes be overused, it is just as frequently missed (e.g., Angold, Erkanli, Egger, & Costello, 2000; Sayal, Goodman, & Ford, 2006). However, for each individual child there is no substitute for careful, evidence-based assessment to provide the best possible clinical service and to assist parents and children in understanding the meaning of the diagnostic label, the link between assessment and treatment recommendations, and the need to monitor impairments and treatment effects over time.

We begin with an overview of ADHD, providing a sense of the core characteristics of the disorder that need to be assessed. We then review assessment measures that serve three purposes, along with the unique challenges that may accompany each purpose: (a) measures used for diagnostic purposes, (b) measures useful for case formulation and treatment planning, and (c) assessments for monitoring the course and outcome of interventions. For each purpose, we have constructed a table indicating measures that meet psychometric criteria set out by the editors of this volume. In the text, we offer brief descriptions of these measures and occasionally mention other promising assessment tools that do not, as yet, meet the criteria used for including measures in the tables. Finally, we conclude with an overview of the state-of-the-art assessment in childhood ADHD, with a focus on the challenges that remain for research and clinical practice.

THE NATURE OF ADHD

The study of ADHD is one of the largest empirical literatures in child psychopathology and encompasses emerging evidence regarding the genetic, biological, neurological, psychological, social, and cultural characteristics of the disorder. Significant advances are being made in our understanding of ADHD, including exciting theoretical and empirical works probing the core causes and nature of the disorder (e.g., Nigg, Willcutt, & Doyle, 2005; Waldman & Gizer, 2006). The vibrant nature of research on ADHD bodes well for advancing our ability to clinically assess, treat, and potentially even prevent this disorder. However, the rapidly expanding and dynamic nature of the research also means that evidence-based assessment of ADHD must continually change as it incorporates new evidence. Thus, one challenge to the assessment of ADHD is the need for clinicians to update their knowledge constantly about the disorder, and to update assessment tools and methods accordingly. The first and perhaps most critical recommendation we offer for the assessment of ADHD is that the information in this chapter has an expiry date, and only by keeping abreast of the science of ADHD can clinical practice in this area remain appropriate.

ADHD is defined in the most recent edition of the Diagnostic and Statistical Manual (DSM-IV-Text Revision; American Psychiatric Association [APA], 2000) as a disorder characterized by developmentally inappropriate and maladaptive levels of inattention, impulsivity, and hyperactivity. ADHD has a prevalence rate among school-aged children of 3% to 7%, with more boys than girls affected. ADHD symptoms are persistent over time, and as many as 66% to 80% of children who meet diagnostic criteria will continue either to meet diagnostic criteria or to suffer impairment due to symptoms into adolescence and adulthood (e.g., Barkley, Fischer, Smallish, & Fletcher, 2002). Beyond the core symptoms of the disorder, children with ADHD frequently experience difficulties in areas such as academic performance, classroom and home behavior (including oppositional defiant and conduct disorders), peer relations, and internalizing problems (anxiety and mood disorders).

Depending on the type of symptoms present in the child, ADHD subtype diagnoses are assigned as Predominantly Inattentive, Predominantly Hyperactive-Impulsive, or Combined. Children with the Predominantly Inattentive subtype have problems with inattention, such as difficulties in paying close attention to details or sustaining attention. The Predominantly Hyperactive-Impulsive subtype is characterized by behaviors such as motor over activity or restlessness, and difficulties inhibiting behavior. Children with the Combined subtype experience both types of problems. The two symptom dimensions, inattention and hyperactivity-impulsivity, are highly related (e.g., Pillow, Pelham, Hoza, Molina, & Stultz, 1998), and many children show elevations in both types of symptoms. The Predominantly Hyperactive-Impulsive subtype appears most common in younger children and the predominance of these symptoms may reflect a developmental stage of the disorder rather than a unique subtype (e.g., Hart et al., 1995). Children with the Predominantly Inattentive subtype present as quite different from children with the Combined subtype, not only in symptoms but also in associated problems (e.g., Milich, Balentine, & Lynam, 2001), and some have argued that the Inattentive subtype should be viewed as a distinct disorder (e.g., Barkley, 2006). Not only had subtype been associated with different stages of development and patterns of comorbidity, but also emerging evidence suggests that subtype may predict some elements of treatment response (e.g., Barkley, DuPaul, & McMurray, 1990; MTA Cooperative Group, 1999b).

The evidence on differential validity of the subtypes means that the determination of ADHD subtype is critical. However, the practical challenge in doing so is to operationalize the measurement of symptom predominance. Although DSM criteria specify only that fewer than six symptoms of hyperactivity-impulsivity be present for a child to be classed as Predominantly Inattentive, studies have found large differences between Inattentive children with few or no hyperactive-impulsive symptoms compared to those children who fall just below the six-symptom threshold on this dimension (e.g., Weiss, Worling, & Wasdell, 2003). Unfortunately, little research is available to guide the clinician in the task of how to best determine subtype cutoffs.

The assessment of ADHD in childhood shares the conundrum faced by many childhood disorders, where multiple sources of information must be considered. As defined by DSM, ADHD is characterized by symptoms and impairment that occur cross-situationally. In the practicalities of assessment, this means that information from both home and school contexts is considered essential to the assessment process. Given the limitations of child self-report, particular for externalizing behaviors (e.g., Loeber, Green, Lahey, & Stouthamer-Loeber, 1991), the assessment of childhood ADHD places a heavy reliance on parents' and teachers' reports of the child's behavior. Although information from multiple informants and contexts is seen as critical to the assessment of ADHD, there is abundant evidence that these sources frequently show only minimal convergence (e.g., Achenbach, McConaughy, & Howell, 1987). In addition, little evidence is available with respect to the best methods for combining this information (Gadow, Drabick et al., 2004; Piacentini, Cohen, & Cohen, 1992) or specifying which combinations of information offer the best incremental validity in the assessment process (Johnston & Murray, 2003). The influence of rater characteristics (e.g., depressed mood or ADHD symptoms in the parent) must also be considered in evaluating the information provided by the multiple sources (e.g., Chi & Hinshaw, 2002; Faraone, Monuteaux, Biederman, Cohan, & Mick, 2003).

In this section, we have highlighted three general issues that arise in the assessment of ADHD: the continually evolving nature of assessment methods and tools, the imprecision of current subtype classifications, and the puzzle of how to best combine multiple, often discrepant, pieces of information. In the following sections, we feature other assessment issues more specifically linked with the assessment goals of diagnoses or treatment planning and evaluation. In all cases, as yet, research has offered limited insight into how assessments might most effectively address these issues and there is a need for further empirical study.

PURPOSES OF ADHD ASSESSMENT

Clinical assessments of childhood ADHD serve a variety of purposes, ranging from confirming an ADHD diagnosis to ruling out differential diagnoses such as anxiety disorders or learning problems, to assessing the response of a child's ADHD symptoms and functioning to a change in medication regimen. Varied assessment approaches and tools may be needed for addressing each of these different purposes. In this chapter, we focus on assessments for the purpose of diagnosis, treatment planning, and treatment monitoring. In selecting and evaluating assessment tools

for each of these purposes, we employed the rating system used throughout the chapters of this volume.

At this point, we offer a caveat regarding our selection and evaluation of the assessment measures included in our tables. We searched broadly for measures and information supporting their use. However, we used practical criteria that limited this search. To meet the dual goals of accessibility and independent research validation of the measures, we include measures that are commercially or publicly available, but which also have evidence of reliability, validity, or both reported by independent investigators in published studies. Given the breadth of the assessment literature, we acknowledge that we may have missed a small number of measures or information that would allow measures to meet the psychometric criteria required for inclusion in the tables. Within the text of the chapter, we occasionally describe other measures that do not meet the psychometric criteria required for table entry, but which hold promise in the assessment of ADHD. For such measures, although we continue in an attempt to be comprehensive, the sheer number of measures with limited psychometrics requires a more selective approach to inclusion.

ASSESSMENT FOR DIAGNOSIS

Although most evidence supports a dimensional view of ADHD symptoms (e.g., Sonuga-Barke, 1998), assessment for diagnosis requires a categorical decision. In addition, as noted above, reports of whether or not the child shows particular symptoms will be influenced by variables such as the context in which the child is observed (e.g., home vs. school) or characteristics of the rater (e.g., expectations, mood). In making diagnostic decisions, the clinician must remain aware of the assumptions underlying the use of diagnostic categories and of the multiple explanations for discrepancies across informants, and the clinician is best advised to resist unwarranted adherence to the use of arbitrary cutoffs or algorithms for combining information.

According to DSM-IV-TR (APA, 2000), an ADHD diagnosis requires not only that at least six of the nine symptoms of either inattention or hyperactivity-impulsivity be present, but also that these symptoms must have been present for at least 6 months, at a level that is maladaptive and inconsistent with developmental level. The symptoms must have presented before the age of 7 years, and lead to clinically significant impairment in social or academic functioning evidenced in two or more settings. In addition, the symptoms should not be better explained by other conditions such as pervasive developmental disorders and anxiety disorders. Thus, the assessment of ADHD requires not only measuring symptoms but also assessing these symptoms, their onsets, and their associated impairments in multiple settings and gathering information regarding co-occurring problems. Each of these requirements presents an assessment challenge.

Defining symptoms as developmentally inappropriate requires that assessment tools permit comparisons to a same-aged normative group. In addition, consideration should be given to the gender and ethnic composition of the normative sample. DSM-IV criteria do not specify gender or ethnic differences in how the disorder is displayed and would suggest the use of norms combined across child gender and based on samples with representative numbers of ethnic-minority children. However, epidemiological studies have revealed differences in the rates of ADHD symptoms across genders (e.g., Lahey et al., 1994) and ethnic groups (e.g., Epstein et al., 2005). With particular regard to gender, many investigators have questioned whether the existing symptom descriptions are more appropriate for boys than girls (e.g., Ohan & Johnston, 2005; Waschbusch, King, & North Partners in Action for Children and Youth, 2006). Short of modifying diagnostic criteria to be gender-specific, this view would at least encourage the use of gender-specific norms. However, such use carries a strong caveat given that the DSM diagnostic criteria are specified without regard to such child characteristics. Clinicians would be wise to consider comparisons to both gender-specific and general norms in order to obtain the most informed picture of the relative level of ADHD symptoms presented by the child.

Assessing the diagnostic criteria related to the age of symptom onset and duration of symptoms can also be challenging. Few established measures tap this information, and clinicians typically rely on more informal parent interviews to provide this information. With respect to research on memory and assessment, such practices carry a psychometric liability. For example, Angold, Erkanli, Costello, and Rutter (1996) reported that the reliability and validity of parents' recall of symptom onsets is far below required psychometric standards.

Given that ADHD is defined by its presence in multiple situations, strategies are needed for combining assessment information from parent and teacher reports into a single diagnostic decision. Many rely on the criteria used in the DSM-IV field trials and employ an either/or rule, counting symptoms as present if they are reported by either the parent or the teacher (e.g., Lahey et al., 1994). Although some studies suggest that teacher ratings do not add information beyond that contained in parent reports (e.g., Biederman, Keenan, & Faraone, 1990), other research studies suggest that both parent and teacher reports add useful information (e.g., Power, Andrews, et al., 1998). Still other researchers find that rater or source variance is substantial and often accounts for more variance in rating scale scores than the inattentive and hyperactive-impulsive dimensions of behavior (e.g., Gadow, Drabick, et al., 2004; Gomez, Burns, Walsh, & De Moura, 2003). Until further empirical evidence is available, clinicians must rely on clinical judgment, grounded in a solid knowledge of the empirical literature, in combining information from multiple sources and methods to arrive at a final diagnostic decision in childhood ADHD.

Finally, in assessments intended to offer a diagnosis of ADHD, the clinician must have a working knowledge of other childhood disorders in order to make informed differential and comorbid diagnoses. The process of teasing apart whether inattentive or impulsive behaviors are best accounted for by ADHD or by problems such as fetal alcohol effects, learning disorders, and anxiety remains a challenge. Given the space limitations of this chapter, we cannot cover measures useful for assessing these other childhood disorders and instead refer the reader to other child assessment resources (e.g., Kamphaus & Frick, 2005; Mash & Barkley, 2007) and the relevant chapters in this volume. However, we note that the limitations of our current knowledge and diagnostic systems often contribute to the difficulties of discriminating among disorders and the clinician may need to assign an ADHD diagnosis as a "working hypothesis" rather than as a confirmed decision. To the extent that the core nature of ADHD remains under debate, best practices for discriminating this condition from other related conditions (e.g., learning problems) will remain elusive.

A related problem of discriminating among disorders arises in the use of assessment measures, especially older measures, in which conceptualizations of

TABLE 2.1 Ratings of Instruments Used for Diagnosis

Instrument	Norms	Internal Consistency	Inter-Rater Reliability[a]	Test–Retest Reliability	Content Validity	Construct Validity	Validity Generalization	Clinical Utility	Highly Recommended
Narrowband ADHD Rating Scales									
ADHD RS IV									
Parent	E	G	NA	A	A	G	G	A	
Teacher	E	G	NA	A	A	G	G	A	
CRS-R ADHD Index									
Parent	E	G	NA	G	A	G	E	A	✓
Teacher	E	E	NA	G	A	G	E	A	✓
ADDES-3									
Parent	G	E	NA	A	G	A	G	A	
Teacher	E	E	NA	A	G	A	G	A	
Structured Interviews									
DISC-IV									
Parent	NA	NA	U	A	G	G	A	A	

[a] This column reflects inter-rater agreement between clinical judges, and this information is not available for most measures where, instead, parent and teacher agreement is more commonly assessed.

Note: ADHD RS IV: ADHD Rating Scale IV; CRS-R: Conners Rating Scales-Revised; ADDES-3: Attention-Deficit Disorder Evaluation Scales; DISC-IV: Diagnostic Interview Schedule for Children-IV; A = Adequate; G = Good; E = Excellent; U = Unavailable; NA = Not Applicable.

ADHD are confounded with symptoms of other disorders. For example, the hyperactivity scales of earlier versions of the Conners Parent and Teacher Rating Scales (Goyette, Conners, & Ulrich, 1978) included items more characteristic of oppositional problems. Similarly, the hyperactivity subscale of the 1982 version of the Personality Inventory for Children-Revised (Lachar, 1982) assesses behaviors such as cheating and peer relations, which are not core ADHD symptoms. Clinicians are advised not to judge the appropriateness of measures on the basis of titles or scale names but, rather, to give careful consideration to actual item content and whether this content is congruent with current conceptualizations of ADHD.

Overview of Measures for Diagnosis

Narrowband ADHD Checklists

Among measures designed to assess ADHD symptoms, we include only those that map onto the most recent version of the DSM. A number of rating scales have been produced that are tied, more or less directly, to DSM-IV symptoms of ADHD. One of the most widely used of these is the ADHD Rating Scale IV (ADHD RS IV; DuPaul, Power, Anastopoulos, & Reid, 1998). This brief rating scale, which can be completed by parents or teachers, lists the 18 DSM-IV symptoms of ADHD. For both parent and teacher ratings, age- and gender-specific norms are available for large representative normative samples, and for relatively large groups of children diagnosed with ADHD. Norms combined across genders are not available. The reliability and validity of the measure are generally good (refer to Table 2.1). Scores on the ADHD RS IV correlate with other ADHD measures and discriminate children with ADHD from nonproblem controls and from clinical controls. Sensitivity and specificity information is available, with some evidence that teacher ratings on the ADHD RS IV provide greater specificity and parent ratings provide greater sensitivity in making ADHD diagnoses (e.g., DuPaul et al., 1998; Kadesjo, Kadesjo, Hagglof, & Gillberg, 2001; Pappas, 2006; Power, Andrews, et al., 1998; Power, Doherty, et al., 1998). The measure provides a total score and has inattentive and hyperactivity-impulsivity subscales, supported by factor analysis, that are useful in determining ADHD subtype. The ADHD Rating Scale IV manual outlines evidence of small, but potentially meaningful, differences in scores across ethnic groups and these demand attention when using the measure with minority group children.

In addition to the ADHD RS IV, a number of very similar questionnaires exist, all with items listing the current DSM symptoms of ADHD (e.g., the SNAP, Swanson, 1992). Although it might be assumed that the psychometric properties of these various measures are consistent with those of the ADHD RS IV, most have not been investigated thoroughly and do not have large normative samples. Other measures that are described for assessing ADHD offer content that is not entirely consistent with DSM criteria and are not recommended for diagnostic purposes. For example, the Brown Attention-Deficit Disorder Scales for Children and Adolescents (Brown, 2001) is a parent and teacher report measure of the deficits in executive functioning that are thought to be associated with ADHD.

The ADHD Index from the Conners Rating Scales-Revised (CRS-R; Conners, 1997) is a brief measure consisting of the 12 items from the longer parent and teacher forms of the Conners that best discriminate ADHD and nonclinical children. Although not all of these items are worded exactly as the DSM symptoms, they appear synonymous. As part of the CRS-R, the ADHD Index is well validated and it has reasonable sensitivity and specificity in identifying ADHD. The normative sample is large and generally representative, and information regarding the scores of a large clinical group of children with ADHD is available. Norms are available only for the genders separately. The ADHD Index has satisfactory psychometric properties (Conners, Parker et al., 1998; Conners, Sitarenios et al., 1998; refer to Table 2.1) and the long history of the Conners Rating Scales in the study of ADHD provides an extensive research background for this measure. In addition to the ADHD Index, the CRS-R also includes subscales directly related to the DSM criteria for ADHD, as well as empirically derived scores assessing inattention and hyperactivity.

The Attention-Deficit Disorder Evaluation Scales (ADDES-3; McCarney, 2004) are recently updated versions of parent (46 items) and teacher (60 items) forms that yield inattention and hyperactive-impulsive subscale scores reflecting DSM-IV symptoms of ADHD. There are multiple earlier versions of this scale and several indices that can be calculated from the measure. Unfortunately, these multiple versions can lead to confusion. Although the manual for the ADDES-3 links scale interpretation to a variety of treatment recommendations, empirical support for these approaches is not provided. The normative sample is quite large and generally representative. Information from a large sample of children with ADHD (although method of diagnosis is not clearly specified) is also available for the teacher version.

Separate age and gender scores are calculated. The reliability and validity information for the measure as reported in the manual is generally good (McCarney, 2004; refer to Table 2.1); however, a limited number of independent validation studies are available (e.g., Zelko, 1991), and these have sometimes suggested limited sensitivity and specificity (e.g., Bussing, Schulmann, Belin, Widawski, & Perwien, 1998).

Structured Interviews

We included one structured interview, The Diagnostic Interview Schedule for Children-IV (DISC-IV; Shaffer, Fisher, Lucas, Dulcan, & Schwab-Stone, 2000), in Table 2.1. It is recognized that structured interviews often have limited psychometric information. In particular, the categorical model underlying these measures means that normative information is considered unnecessary. However, given the heavy reliance on structured interviews in many research and medical settings, we opted to include at least one such measure. We caution the clinician to consider carefully the costs of such interviews (e.g., heavy investment of clinician and family time) in contrast to the relatively low incremental validity offered by these measures compared to parent and teacher ratings of ADHD symptoms (e.g., Power, Costigan, Leff, Eiraldi, & Landau, 2001; Wolraich et al., 2003).

The DISC-IV (Shaffer et al., 2000) maps directly onto DSM-IV diagnostic criteria for a range of child disorders, including ADHD. The interview is available in multiple languages and in parent and youth versions. The child version has limited psychometric properties, although some studies support the use of combined responses across parents and children (Shaffer et al., 2000). The highly structured nature of the DISC-IV diminishes the importance of estimating inter-rater reliability or inter-judge agreement for this measure. Psychometric information for the fourth version of the DISC is just emerging; however, combined with information on earlier versions, support is generally adequate for the reliability of the measure for making ADHD diagnoses (Shaffer et al., 2000). Similarly, emerging evidence supports the convergent validity of ADHD diagnoses on the DISC-IV (e.g., de Nijs et al., 2004; Derks, Hudziak, Dolan, Ferdinand, & Boomsma, 2006; McGrath, Handwerk, Armstrong, Lucas, & Friman, 2004). One potential advantage to the measure is the inclusion of impairment questions, although the psychometric properties of these have not been extensively documented. Given the heavy reliance on this measure in many large research studies, we anticipate that further psychometric evidence will emerge.

Other structured and semistructured interviews often used in the assessment of ADHD include the Diagnostic Interview for Children and Adolescents (DICA; Reich, 1998) and the Child and Adolescent Psychiatric Assessment (CAPA; Angold & Costello, 2000). As with the DISC-IV, these interviews typically have not been subjected to extensive psychometric study. Structured teacher interviews, designed to be administered by telephone, have also been developed (e.g., Holmes et al., 2004). Although further work is required on the psychometric properties of these tools, they offer a promising avenue for gathering teacher information in a practical and clinically efficient manner.

Measures of Impairment

As noted above, the assessment of impairment is required to make an ADHD diagnosis according to DSM criteria. Although it is most common in clinical practice for this information to be gathered informally during unstructured interviews, such assessments may fail to meet minimal standards for reliability and validity. To compound the assessment problems facing the clinician, existing measures of impairment fall into two camps, neither of which is ideal for diagnosing ADHD. Some measures are brief and focus on impairment specific to ADHD symptoms (e.g., Impairment Rating Scale, Fabiano et al., 2006), but these measures are relatively new and do not enjoy extensive psychometric support or validation. In contrast, established measures, such as the Vineland Adaptive Behavior Scales–II (Sparrow, Cichetti, & Balla, 2005), are psychometrically sound, but at the same time are lengthy and may lack sensitivity and specificity in detecting impairments related to ADHD symptoms. Given that the greatest value of measures of impairment may be in treatment planning, we reserve further discussion of these measures for the following section of the chapter.

Measures not Useful in the Assessment of ADHD Diagnoses

The current diagnostic criteria for ADHD remain relatively subjective, and the drive to access more objective indicators of the disorder has been strong. A number of cognitive performance measures have been proposed as useful in this regard, most common versions of continuous performance tests. Some of these measures have come considerable distances in providing normative information, evidence of stability over time, and sensitivity to the effects of medication treatments (e.g., the Gordon Diagnostic System, Gordon, 1983; the Conners CPT II, Conners & MHS Staff, 2000), yet they remain limited in their clinical utility (Nichols & Waschbusch, 2004; Rapport, Chung, Shore, Denney, & Isaacs, 2000). Although these measures offer the promise of an objective measurement of ADHD symptoms (in contrast to the subjectivity inherent in parent and teacher reports), their relations to other measures of ADHD symptoms are often modest and there is limited evidence to support their predictive or discriminate validity. In particular, scores on these measures produce high rates of false negative diagnoses such that normal range scores are often found in children who meet diagnostic criteria for ADHD according to other measures. Neuropsychological and executive functioning tests have also been proposed as markers of ADHD. For example, the Tests of Everyday Attention in Children (Manly, Robertson, Anderson, & Nimmo-Smith, 1999) is described as assessing selective attention, sustained attention, and attentional control in children aged between 6 and 16 years. Although this measure shows promising psychometric development (Manly et al., 2001), its ability to identify core ADHD symptoms and its sensitivity and specificity as a diagnostic tool have not been verified. Thus, none of these measures are, as yet, sufficiently developed to meet the psychometric criteria for this volume or to be useful in making diagnostic decisions for individual children. Similarly, although clinical lore promotes the use of patterns of subscale scores on intelligence tests as indicative of ADHD, these measures have not demonstrated validity for this purpose (Kaufman, 1994). Nor have medical tests such as blood work or various brain imaging tests and measures of physical activity levels (e.g., actimeters) been of use in the clinical assessment of ADHD.

Overall Evaluation

Based on ease of use and predictive power, combining information from teacher and parent versions of brief DSM-IV-based rating scales appears to offer the best available option in the diagnosis of ADHD. Some evidence suggests that shorter versions of these measures based on items with the strongest discriminating power may be useful (e.g., Owens & Hoza, 2003; Power et al., 2001); however, these measures as yet do not have adequate psychometric properties.

Although structured diagnostic interviews are a mainstay in research on ADHD, recommended in pediatric and psychiatric assessment guidelines (American Academy of Child and Adolescent Psychiatry, 1997; American Academy of Pediatrics, 2000) and may be required in some clinical contexts for administrative purposes, evidence would suggest that they do not add incrementally to the information gathered more efficiently with rating scales (e.g., DuPaul, Power, McGoey, Ikeda, & Anastopoulos, 1998; Pelham, Fabiano, & Massetti, 2005; Ostrander, Wernfrut, Yarnold, & August, 1998; Wolraich et al., 2003). One advantage to structured interviews is the inclusion of the assessment of impairment, a required aspect of the diagnosis. If the clinician relies on rating scales in making the diagnosis, care must be taken to supplement these measures with information regarding impairment and history of the symptoms.

ASSESSMENT FOR CASE CONCEPTUALIZATION AND TREATMENT PLANNING

Three treatments have received empirical support for childhood ADHD (Chronis, Jones, & Raggi, 2006; Pelham, Wheeler, & Chronis, 1998): pharmacotherapy, behavioral treatment, and their combination. In assessments for treatment planning, the clinician is seeking information such as that needed to assist with prioritizing treatment targets or goals (e.g., which ADHD symptoms are most impairing or most likely to respond quickly to treatment), matching difficulties to recommended treatments (e.g., do this child's primary difficulties match the ADHD problems that have been targeted with behavioral or medication treatments), or identifying environmental elements that may be used in treatment (e.g., does the teacher offer rewards for the work completed). Information regarding factors that may interfere with treatment success (e.g., does this child have a physical condition that may limit the utility of medication) or strengths (e.g., sports interests or skills) will also be useful.

In this section, we review measures that provide information relevant to conceptualizing the nature of the problems experienced by children with ADHD and the planning of treatments targeting ADHD symptoms or symptom-related impairment.

However, we caution the reader that this focus is narrow and that much case conceptualization and treatment planning for ADHD involves consideration of co-occurring difficulties in child, family, academic, or peer functioning. Pelham and colleagues (2005), in their excellent review of evidence-based assessments for ADHD, offer a cogent and convincing argument that adaptations and impairments in functioning, rather than ADHD symptoms per se, should form the basis for treatment planning in ADHD. Thus, adequate treatment planning for ADHD necessitates gathering and integrating information far beyond diagnostic status. Information from a variety of sources, regarding a wide range of child and family functioning, is necessary to inform treatments that match the needs and resources of each child and family. For example, the clinician must consider the child's family, social and cultural context, relevant medical and educational history and concerns, the child's and family's goals for treatment, and available treatment options. Although difficulties in domains such as academics and social relationships are often closely linked to ADHD (and may even be the result of ADHD symptoms), assessment methodologies in these areas are not specific to ADHD and are not considered here. The parent–child relationship or parenting style, the parent's psychological or marital functioning, and the child's classroom behavior and performance, peer relationships, and self-esteem are among the areas that might be considered in a broader definition of treatment planning for ADHD.

We recommend the reader to chapters within this volume and to other excellent child assessment resources (e.g., Kamphaus & Frick, 2005; Mash & Barkley, 2007; Special Issue of the *Journal of Clinical Child and Adolescent Psychology*, Vol. 34, No. 3, 2005) for detailed information regarding assessment of the problems and conditions that are frequently associated with ADHD and that often figure prominently in treatment planning for children with this disorder. We cannot state strongly enough how important these other domains of assessment are in planning treatments for children with ADHD that will be maximally sensitive to the child and family's needs and concerns, and that will hold the greatest potential for altering, not only the child's current functioning but also long-term outcomes.

Overview of Measures for Treatment Planning

Broadband Checklists

Parent and teacher reports on broadband measures of child psychopathology provide useful information in planning treatments for children with ADHD (see Table 2.2). These measures provide insight into a range of difficulties, in addition to ADHD, and may direct the clinician to more in-depth assessments of co-existing disorders or disorders that may account for ADHD-like symptoms. Scores on these broadband measures also allow the clinician to incorporate knowledge of potential comorbidities into treatment planning as appropriate. For example, some evidence suggest that behavioral treatments for ADHD may have better outcomes among children with comorbid anxiety disorders (MTA Cooperative Group, 1999b), and behavioral treatments are empirically supported for addressing the oppositional, conduct disorder problems, or both that are frequently comorbid with ADHD (e.g., Kazdin, 2003; McMahon & Frick, 2005).

We include only broadband rating scales with subscales specifically targeting ADHD symptoms or behaviors. These measures vary in the extent to which their subscales map directly onto DSM ADHD criteria or symptom dimensions. For example, the Attention Problems subscale of the Child Behavior Checklist comprises both inattention and impulsivity items, and the Hyperactivity subscale of the Behavioral Assessment System for Children has several items that are more related to oppositionality than to ADHD (e.g., bothers other children, throws temper tantrums). Thus, these subscale measures typically cannot be substituted for the narrowband checklists described above (the exception to this would be the Conners ADHD Index). However, the subscales relevant to attention or hyperactivity-impulsivity found on many broadband checklists will offer supplemental information that may be useful in arriving at diagnostic decisions, particularly in complex cases. As the role of these broadband measures in treatment planning is to provide a screening-level assessment of a range of behavior problems, we require satisfactory psychometric properties at the level of subscale scores (as well as total scores).

The parent (Children Behavior Checklist; CBCL) and teacher (Teacher Report Form; TRF) versions from the Achenbach System of Empirically Based Assessment (ASEBA; Achenbach & Rescorla, 2001) are well-known and widely used measures, available in several languages, that have lengthy clinical and research traditions. A Youth Self-Report form is available for children 11–18 but is not described here. The parent and teacher checklists are used for children 6 to 18 years of age (a version for younger children is also available), and norms are based on large representative normal samples, as well as samples of clinic-referred children (although norms specific to different clinical diagnoses are not generally available). There are 118 items, requiring 15 to 20 minutes to complete, as well as subscales assessing competence (although the psychometric properties of the competence subscales are generally not as strong as the behavior problem scales). The ASEBA provides empirically derived subscales that are similar across the multiple informant versions of the measure and assess a variety of emotional and behavior problems such as attention, rule breaking, and aggression. The measures also yield overall Internalizing and Externalizing scores, as well as rationally derived subscales that map onto DSM diagnostic categories. The similarity in item content across informants allows for the calculation of inter-rater agreements, and information is available to compare levels of agreement to those in the normative sample. Considerable validity evidence is presented in the ASEBA manual, and numerous reviews provide additional evidence of the convergent, discriminant, and content validity of the measures (e.g., Gladman & Lancaster, 2003; Kamphaus & Frick, 2005; McConaughy, 2001; Pelham et al., 2005). As indicated in Table 2.2, both parent and teacher versions have solid psychometric properties. However, as with many of the measures reviewed in this chapter, few studies have examined the incremental validity or clinical utility of ASEBA scores and some studies suggest the superiority of other measures for some assessment purposes (e.g., Goodman & Scott, 1999; Vaughn, Riccio, Hynd, & Hall, 1997).

The Behavior Assessment System for Children, 2nd Edition (BASC-2; Reynolds & Kamphaus, 2002) is a multidimensional measure of adaptive and problem behaviors that has teacher and parent versions for children aged 6–11 (as well as preschool and adolescent versions not considered here). The measure takes approximately 10 to 20 minutes to complete and has multiple language versions. The BASC-2 provides rationally derived clinical subscales including Hyperactivity and Attention Problems, as well as composite scores for Adaptive Behavior, Externalizing

TABLE 2.2 Ratings of Instruments Used for Case Conceptualization and Treatment Planning

Instrument	Norms	Internal Consistency	Inter-Rater Reliability[a]	Test–Retest Reliability	Content Validity	Construct Validity	Validity Generalization	Clinical Utility	Highly Recommended
Broadband Rating Scales									
ASEBA									
CBCL (parent)	E	G	NA	E	A	G	E	A	✓
TRF (teacher)	E	E	NA	G	A	G	E	A	✓
BASC-2 (parent)	E	A	NA	G	A	G	E	A	
BASC-2 (teacher)	E	G	NA	G	A	G	E	A	
CPRS-R (parent)	E	G	NA	G	A	G	E	A	✓
CTRS-R (teacher)	E	G	NA	G	A	G	E	A	✓
CSI-4 (parent)	E	A	NA	A	A	G	E	A	
CSI-4 (teacher)	E	A	NA	A	A	G	E	A	
DSMD (parent)	L	G	NA	A	A	G	E	A	
DSMD (teacher)	L	G	NA	A	A	G	E	A	
Vand. (parent)	L	E	NA	U	A	G	G	A	
Vand. (teacher)	E	U	NA	U	A	G	E	A	
Measures of Impairment									
VABS-II (parent)	E	E	NA	A	G	G	G	A	
VABS-II (teacher)	E	E	NA	U	G	G	G	A	
CAFAS	U	A	E	U	A	G	U	A	
IRS (parent)	L	U	NA	G	A	G	A	A	
IRS (teacher)	L	U	NA	G	A	G	A	A	

[a] This column reflects inter-rater agreement between clinical judges, and this information in not available for most measures where, instead, parent and teacher agreement is more commonly assessed.

Note: ASEBA: Achenbach System of Empirically Based Assessment; CBCL: Child Behavior Checklist; TRF: Teacher Report Form; BASC-2: Behavior Assessment System for Children -2; CPRS-R: Conners Parent Rating Scale-Revised; CTRS-R: Conners Teacher Rating Scale-Revised; CSI-4: Child Symptom Inventory-4; DSMD: Devereux Scales of Mental Disorders; Vand.: Vanderbilt ADHD Diagnostic Parent and Teacher Rating Scales; VABS-II: Vineland Adaptive Behavior Scales, 2nd Edition; CAFAS: Child and Adolescent Functional Assessment Scale; IRS: Impairment Rating Scale; L = Less than Adequate; A = Adequate; G = Good; E = Excellent; U = Unavailable; NA = Not Applicable.

and Internalizing Problems, and a total Behavioral Symptoms Index. The teacher version has also scales related to school problems. One unique advantage of the BASC-2 over other broadband measures is that it offers validity checks to assist the clinician in detecting careless or untruthful responding, misunderstanding, or other threats to validity. BASC-2 norms are based on large representative samples, and are available both in aggregate form and differentiated according to the age, gender, and clinical status of the child. As noted above, not only does this measure evaluate behavioral and emotional problems, it also identifies the child's positive attributes, an aspect with obvious use in planning treatment. For both parent and teacher versions, extensive psychometric information is available in the manual and is reviewed elsewhere (e.g., Kamphaus, Reynolds, Hatcher, & Kim, 2004; Pelham et al., 2005; Sandoval & Echandia, 1994). Studies have reported high correlations between the BASC and ASEBA (e.g., Vaughn et al., 1997), and Ostrander and colleagues (1998) found that the BASC was more parsimonious and afforded greater predictive ability for ADHD-Combined subtype than the CBCL, which was superior for predicting ADHD-Inattentive type.

The Conners Rating Scales-Revised (CRS-R; Conners, 1997) are the most recent revision to a set of scales that have been closely allied with research and clinical work in ADHD for many years. The Revised scales have multiple language versions and numerous clinically useful aspects such as computer scoring and feedback forms. There are parent and teacher versions (as well as an adolescent self-report not described here), each with both short (5 to 10 minutes) and long (15 to 20 minutes) forms available. The short forms focus on symptoms of ADHD, cognitive problems, and oppositionality, whereas the longer forms also include subscales assessing other comorbid disorders. A Conners Global Index, useful for monitoring change in overall psychopathology, as well as the ADHD Index (described in the section on measures for diagnosis), is provided. Norms are based on a large sample of children, including males and females ages 3–17. The normative sample is generally representative, although with some underrepresentation of minority groups. Norms are only available for the genders separately. Information regarding scores of children diagnosed with ADHD is also available. The CRS-R manual and empirical studies outline the strong psychometric properties of both parent and

teacher versions of the measure (e.g., Conners, 1997; Conners, Parker, et al., 1998; Conners, Sitarenios, et al., 1998) and numerous reviews support the validity of the measure (e.g., Angello et al., 2003; Collett, Ohan, & Myers, 2003; Gadow et al., 2001; Kollins, Epstein, & Conners, 2004; Pelham et al., 2005).

Another broadband measure that directly reflects DSM symptomatology is the Child Symptom Inventory-4 (CSI-4; Gadow & Sprafkin, 2002), a behavior rating scale for assessing children between 5 and 12 years. Ninety-seven-item parent and 77-item teacher versions are available, each assessing a variety of DSM-IV emotional and behavioral disorders, including ADHD, oppositional defiant disorder, and conduct disorder. The CSI-4 can be scored to derive Symptom Count scores (diagnostic model) or Symptom Severity scores (normative data model). Normative samples are somewhat limited, and are not as representative as one would like; however, data for both normal and clinic-referred reference groups are available (although norms are not available for specific child diagnoses). As described in the manual and supporting publications (e.g., Mattison, Gadow, Sprafkin, & Nolan, 2002; Sprafkin, Gadow, Salisbury, Schneider, & Loney, 2002), CSI-4 scores demonstrate adequate reliability, although this evidence is often derived solely from clinical samples. The authors of the scale have reported convergent, discriminant, and predictive validity for both parent and teacher versions (e.g., Gadow, Sprafkin, Salisbury, Schneider, & Loney, 2004; Mattison et al., 2002; Mattison, Gadow, Sprafkin, Nolan, & Schneider, 2003; Sprafkin et al., 2002), although independently replicated findings are not widely available. Derived from the CSI-4, the ADHD Symptom Checklist-4 (Gadow & Sprafkin, 1999) is a 50-item scale, completed by parents or teachers. It assesses ADHD symptoms, as well as oppositional defiant disorder, peer aggression, and side effects commonly associated with stimulant medication. The measure has the same limitations as the full CSI, and, unfortunately, the psychometric properties of the side effects and peer aggression subscales are less than adequate, diminishing the overall value of the measure.

Other broadband questionnaires have been developed that may prove useful in treatment planning for ADHD, although these measures do require further research. The Devereux Scales of Mental Disorders (DSMD; Naglieri, LeBuff, & Pfeiffer, 1994) is a multidimensional behavior rating scale completed by a parent or teacher that assesses a wide range of child psychopathology (ages 5–12). Item content was drawn directly from the DSM-IV, with six factor analytically derived subscales including Conduct, Attention/ Delinquency, Depression, and Anxiety. Although norms were generated from a large national standardization sample, no clinical norms are available. The DSMD demonstrates adequate reliability and concurrent and discriminant validity (Naglieri et al., 1994). Independent studies acknowledge the DSMD as comparable to the CBCL and BASC (Eiraldi, Power, Karustis, & Goldstein, 2000; Smith & Reddy, 2002). Some evidence suggest that the DSMD is better suited to detecting acute or serious pathology, whereas the CBCL and BASC are better for assessing externalizing symptoms (Smith & Reddy, 2002), and the DSMD appears better in ruling in subtypes, whereas the CBCL is better at ruling out subtypes (Eiraldi et al., 2000). Finally, the Vanderbilt ADHD Diagnostic Parent and Teacher Rating Scales (Wolraich et al., 1998; Wolraich et al., 2003) is another DSM-based symptom rating scale for ADHD, which also includes items assessing oppositional and conduct problems as well as anxiety and depression. Unfortunately, despite its relatively wide spread use, at this time, the measure lacks evidence of test–retest reliability and the normative sample for parent ratings is less than adequate.

Measures of Impairment

Global and multidimensional measures of impairment are valuable in a comprehensive assessment of the psychosocial functioning of children with ADHD. In particular, these measures are likely to be useful in decisions regarding the absolute need for treatment and in identifying appropriate treatment foci. We concur with arguments made by others (e.g., Pelham et al., 2005) that impairments in adaptive behavior must figure prominently in treatment planning and monitoring for children with ADHD, more so than absolute levels of ADHD symptoms. Unfortunately, the need for psychometrically sound measures of impairment that are sensitive to the difficulties commonly experienced by children with ADHD has far outstripped the development of such tools. At present, the clinician must choose between measures that appear promising, but do not yet have extensive psychometric support, or well-established measures of adaptive behavior that are broad, and may not be particularly appropriate to ADHD-related difficulties

(e.g., the Vineland Adaptive Behavior Scales, Sparrow et al., 2005).

The Vineland Adaptive Behavior Scales, Second Edition (VABS-II; Sparrow et al., 2005) has been a leading measure of the personal and social skills needed for everyday living. Although typically used to identify individuals with developmental problems, some evidence supports the use of earlier versions of the VABS in groups of children with ADHD (e.g., Stein, Szumowski, Blondis, & Roisen, 1995; Wilson & Marcotte, 1996). Consisting of a Survey Interview Form, Parent/Caregiver Rating Form, and Expanded Interview Form for ages 0 through 90 years, and a Teacher Rating Form for ages 3 through 21 years, as a semistructured interview the VABS-II requires 20 to 60 minutes to complete. It is organized around four behavior domains (communication, daily living skills, socialization, and motor skills) and has demonstrated strong psychometric properties. Norms for the parent and teacher rating scale forms are based on large representative groups, including a variety of clinical groups, and the reliability and validity of the measure range from adequate to excellent as reported in the manual (Sparrow et al., 2005; refer to Table 2.2). A similar measure of adaptive functioning is the Scales of Independent Behavior-Revised (SIB-R; Bruininks et al., 1996). In addition to adaptive behavior assessment, it contains a behavior problem scale and an overall independence score. This measure has demonstrated satisfactory psychometric properties as well.

The Child and Adolescent Functional Assessment Scale (CAFAS; Hodges & Wong, 1996) is an additional multidimensional measure of impairment that may serve as an aid in treatment planning for children with ADHD. The CAFAS uses interviewer ratings to assess a child's (ages 7–17 years) degree of impairment due to emotional, behavioral, or psychiatric problems. Consisting of 315 items, and measuring functioning in areas such as school, home, and community, and behaviors such as emotional regulation, self-harm, and substance use, it requires only 10 minutes to complete. Although normative data are not available, reliability and validity criteria for this measure are generally satisfactory, as indicated in Table 2.2.

Other broad measures of impairment, such as the Columbia Impairment Scale (CIS; Bird et al., 1996) and the Child Global Assessment Scale (CGAS; Weissman, Warner, & Fendrich, 1990), are brief, one-dimensional, interviewer-administered ratings.

Although items on these scales assess functioning in a range of domains (e.g., interpersonal relations, school), they ultimately yield single, global scores. This feature, although providing an overall index of impairment that may meet the needs of a diagnostic assessment, fails to yield information of sufficient detail to be useful for treatment planning purposes.

A relatively new measure, the Impairment Rating Scale (IRS; Fabiano et al., 2006), was developed to assess the areas of functioning that are frequently problematic for children with ADHD. Parent and teacher versions are available in the public domain (http://wings.buffalo.edu/adhd), with questions pertaining to areas such as academic progress, self-esteem, peer relations, problem behavior, impact on the family, and overall functioning. Test–retest reliability has been established over periods up to a year. Within samples of ADHD and control children, convergent and discriminant validity have been demonstrated, and evidence suggests that parent and teacher IRS ratings accounted for unique variance in predicting child outcomes beyond ADHD symptoms (Fabiano et al., 2006; refer to Table 2.2). This measure holds considerable promise and we hope that further efforts will be devoted to further establishing its psychometric properties, including evidence of the clinical benefits that may accrue from its use.

Observational Measures

Informal observations of children in clinical settings have little clinical utility in detecting ADHD or planning for its treatment (e.g., Edwards et al., 2005). However, more structured observational measures do have potential utility in treatment planning. Using such measures clearly identify the ADHD symptoms and the impairments that ensue from these symptoms, which should be targeted in treatment plans. Unfortunately, despite variability in the psychometric information available, all the measures located failed to demonstrate adequate levels of the criteria used for table inclusion. For example, these observational measures seldom have norms or report the temporal stability of scores. These limitations preclude the inclusion of these measures in the tables; however, we do offer suggestions for available observational measures designed for classroom use or for assessing parent–child interactions.

The Direct Observation Form (DOF), the observational component of the ASEBA (Achenbach & Rescorla, 2001), uses a 10-minutes observation of the child's behavior in a classroom context, recommended to be repeated on three to six occasions. Although the measure includes a narrative and ratings of the child's behavior, psychometric information is reported primarily for the time sampling of 96 behaviors (the behaviors overlap with items on the CBCL and TRF). For normative comparisons, the DOF recommends that two nonproblem children be observed simultaneously with the target child in order to provide individualized norms. Although the manual also presents norms based on moderate size samples of clinic-referred and nonproblem children, the value of these norms is likely to be limited by the variability across classroom contexts (e.g., variables such as classroom rules, physical structure, and ratio of problem to nonproblem children will undoubtedly influence the rates of problem behaviors displayed by children). The manual reports moderate to high levels of inter-rater reliability using the DOF, and DOF scores correlate in expected ways with other measures and with clinical status (Achenbach & Rescorla, 2001).

One of the earliest developed observational systems used in children with ADHD is the Classroom Observation Code (COC; Abikoff, Gittelman-Klein, & Klein, 1977; Abikoff, Gittelman, & Klein, 1980). This structured system for conducting observations in school settings uses a time-sampling procedure to record 14 categories of behavior designed to be sensitive to ADHD symptoms and related impairments, including interference, off-task, aggression, noncompliance, motor movement, and extended verbalization. The COC has adequate inter-observer reliability, discriminates between ADHD and non-ADHD children, and there is no evidence of reactivity effects (Abikoff et al., 1997; 1980). The application of this observation system has extended beyond mainstream classrooms, and its inter-observer reliability and concurrent and discriminant validity have also been supported in classroom settings within psychiatric hospitals (Horn, Conners, Wells, & Shaw, 1986). Among the limitations of these findings is that the reliability and validity estimates were based on an average of 12 days of observations for each child; whether similar psychometric properties would hold over more clinically feasible, shorter observational periods is not known.

The Individualized Target Behavior Evaluation (ITBE; Pelham et al., 2002) is a simple observational scheme that uses teacher- or parent-implemented frequency counts of problematic behavior that are selected as relevant for each particular child. Similar to the procedures of a daily report card, this measure not only affords ongoing assessment of ADHD-related treatment targets but also serves as an integral part of treatment implementation. The ITBE operationalizes the child's target behaviors and sets a criterion of improvement for each behavior evaluated. During each observational period (typically one class period or part of a day), the teacher or parent observes the child and decides whether the child has met each behavioral goal. An overall percentage of targets met can be calculated, and contingencies are delivered depending on the child's performance. The ITBE demonstrates good internal consistency and correlates moderately with teacher and parent rating scales and other observation measures (Pelham et al., 2001). It does not require a high degree of training, independent observers, or a special setting for implementation, making it an appealing tool for clinical use (Pelham et al., 2005). Because it is highly individualized according to unique problems within each child, normative data and content validity are judged not applicable, and research regarding inter-rater reliability and temporal stability is lacking. Given the potential clinical value of this measure, future research and independent validation are strongly encouraged.

To assess aspects of ADHD that are problematic within parent–child interactions, a number of observational systems developed in research contexts are available, although most are too complex to provide reliable estimates in clinical practice. Perhaps one exception to this is the Behavioral Coding System (BCS; McMahon & Forehand, 2003). Using the BCS, the clinician codes parent and child behaviors in two 5-minutes interactions: (1) The Child's Game, a free-play situation in which the parent is instructed to engage in any activity that the child chooses and to allow the child to determine the nature and rules of the interaction; and (2) The Parent's Game, in which the parent has command over the rules and nature of the interaction. The presence of six parent behaviors (rewards, commands, time out, etc.) and three child behaviors (compliance, noncompliance, etc.) are recorded every 30 seconds, and the sequence of behaviors specifying parental antecedents, child responses, and parental consequences can be analyzed. Such information is readily translated into treatment goals

for either behavioral or pharmacological treatments. Inter-observer agreement and test–retest reliability of the BCS are adequate and the system is sensitive to differences in compliance between clinic-referred and nonreferred children (evidence reviewed in McMahon & Forehand, 2003). Unfortunately, independent reports of the measure's psychometrics and use within ADHD samples are not available.

Overall Evaluation

Broadband parent and teacher checklists provide essential information regarding behavior problems that may accompany ADHD and which may inform treatment planning. These measures are typically well developed and possess solid psychometric properties, and the clinician can feel confident in the information they provide. However, even more relevant information for treatment planning is likely to be derived from assessment of the child's functioning and impairments in daily situations. Measures of impairment, particularly those designed to be sensitive to the aspects of functioning most closely linked to ADHD, have clear potential in identifying appropriate treatment targets and assisting the clinician in prioritizing these targets. Unfortunately, these measures suffer from a limited psychometric base that diminishes the confidence that can be placed in their results. In a similar fashion, the context-specific and objective nature of observational assessments of the child's behavior, both in school and at home, have great potential for treatment planning. These measures may also assess environmental antecedents and consequences of the child's behaviors, yielding information of immediate relevance to the planning of behavioral interventions. Unfortunately, the psychometric properties of these observational systems remain largely unknown. Much work is needed to translate these promising measures into solid assessment tools with adequate psychometric properties and which allow normative comparisons. Most importantly, the clinical utility of these measures must be demonstrated.

ASSESSMENT FOR TREATMENT MONITORING AND TREATMENT OUTCOME

In conducting assessments to monitor and evaluate treatment implementation or progress in children with ADHD, there is a need for measures that are reliable over time, sensitive to relatively small changes in behavior or symptoms, and practical to use on a frequent basis (e.g., brief, inexpensive). In monitoring medication treatments, measurement of side effects is also recommended, although standardized measures for this purpose are not available. One prominent issue in considering assessment measures to be used in treatment monitoring is the stability of scores over time, and the vulnerability of measures to the effects of repeated assessments. For example, does a decrease in symptom severity on a measure over time reflect the benefits of treatment, or could the change be predicted solely on the basis of regression of scores to the mean? If treatment effects are to be assessed over a longer period, the availability of age norms will also be important in order to place score changes within the appropriate context of developmental changes in the behavior. As with disagreements in diagnostic information gathered from multiple sources, discrepancies in reports of treatment-related changes in child behaviors are also expected across informants and settings. Again, clinicians must struggle with how to combine or prioritize the multiple bits of information in reaching an overall conclusion regarding the progress of treatment.

In this section, we consider measures that have demonstrated not only basic psychometric properties but also sensitivity to change due to medication, behavioral interventions, or both. Although several measures meet these criteria, almost all of the evidence of this sensitivity is derived from studies aggregating across groups of children and information regarding performance of the measures in individual cases awaits investigation. Recent studies evaluating treatments for ADHD provide information on the sensitivity of various measures to treatment, and have aggregated scores not only across children but also across measures. For example, the large-scale, multi-site Multimodal Treatment Study of Attention-Deficit/Hyperactivity Disorder (MTA) provides extensive data on treatment outcomes for medication, behavioral, and combined interventions for ADHD at multiple end points. However, to create the most reliable scores for use in the group comparisons reported in this trial, multiple measures are typically amalgamated into composite scores (e.g., Arnold et al., 2004; Conners et al., 2001; MTA Cooperative Group, 1999a; 2004). Although advantageous from a research perspective, this approach limits the ability

of such studies to inform us regarding the sensitivity to treatment of any of the measures individually or for individual children.

Overview of Measures for Treatment Monitoring and Treatment Evaluation

Narrowband ADHD Checklists

As indicated in Table 2.3, among the narrowband, ADHD-specific rating scales, the ADHD RS IV and the ADHD Index from the CRS-R, as completed by teachers, parents, or both, have demonstrated sensitivity to medication treatment, at a group level, in numerous studies (e.g., Daviss et al., 2001; Greenhill et al., 2006; Weiss et al., 2005). The ADHD Index has also demonstrated sensitivity to behavioral interventions (e.g., Anastopoulos, Shelton, DuPaul, & Guevremont, 1993). Other symptom-level measures, although lacking in some psychometric characteristics, may bear consideration for treatment monitoring depending on the specific clinical needs of each case. For example, the IOWA Conners (Loney & Milich, 1982) is a brief teacher measure that may be useful, although it is less than adequate in terms of normative information. This 10-item measure was derived from items on the Conners' Teacher Rating Scale that provided discrimination between inattentive-overactive and aggressive symptoms. Considerable evidence support the construct validity (Atkins, Pelham, & Licht, 1989; Johnston & Pelham, 1989), internal consistency (Pelham, Milich, Murphy, & Murphy, 1989), and short-term stability of the measure (Loney & Milich, 1982). At a group level, the measure has been proven useful in multiple studies assessing the effectiveness of medication treatments for ADHD (e.g., Gadow, Nolan, Sverd, Sprafkin, & Paolicelli, 1990; Wolraich et al., 2001).

The BASC Monitor (Kamphaus & Reynolds, 1998), created using items from the BASC that cover DSM-IV symptoms of ADHD, was designed to allow frequent assessment of the core symptoms of ADHD (as well as adaptive competencies and general internalizing problems), with a specific goal of assessing the effectiveness of treatments for the disorder. Teacher, parent, and observation forms are available, and software provides a graphical depiction of change in a child's scores over time. Normative performance on the Monitor can be estimated from the BASC

TABLE 2.3 Ratings of Instruments Used for Treatment Monitoring and Treatment Outcome Evaluation

Instrument	Norms	Internal Consistency	Inter-Rater Reliability[a]	Test–Retest Reliability	Content Validity	Construct Validity	Validity General-ization	Treatment Sensitivity	Clinical Utility	Highly Recommended
Narrowband ADHD Rating Scales										
ADHD RS IV										
Parent	E	G	NA	A	A	G	G	E	A	✓
Teacher	E	G	NA	A	A	G	G	E	A	✓
CRS-R ADHD										
Parent	E	G	NA	G	A	G	E	G	A	
Teacher	E	E	NA	G	A	G	E	G	A	
IOWA Conners	L	G	NA	A	A	G	A	G	A	
Broadband Rating Scales										
ASEBA										
CBCL (parent)	E	G	NA	E	A	G	E	G	A	
TRF (teacher)	E	E	NA	G	A	G	E	G	A	
CPRS-R (parent)	E	G	NA	G	A	G	E	E	A	
CTRS-R (teacher)	E	G	NA	G	A	G	E	E	A	
Measures of Impairment										
CAFAS	U	A	E	A	A	G	U	A	A	

[a] This column reflects inter-rater agreement between clinical judges, and this information in not available for most measures where, instead, parent and teacher agreement is more commonly assessed.

Note: ADHD RS IV: ADHD Rating Scale IV; CRS-R: Conners Rating Scales-Revised; ASEBA: Achenbach System of Empirically Based Assessment; CBCL: Child Behavior Checklist; TRF: Teacher Report Form; CPRS-R: Conners Parent Rating Scale-Revised; CTRS-R: Conners Teacher Rating Scale-Revised; CAFAS: Child and Adolescent Functional Assessment Scale; L = Less than Adequate; A = Adequate; G = Good; E = Excellent; U = Unavailable; NA = Not Applicable.

norms (although not all Monitor items are found on the BASC), and both the internal consistency and test–retest stability of the measure appear satisfactory. Unfortunately, despite being developed with the explicit purpose of treatment monitoring, there is little evidence of the validity of the scale for this purpose. A similar measure, the SKAMP (Swanson, 1992), is a brief 10-item scale assessing academic impairment related to inattention and disruptive behavior. Although the measure lacks norms and little psychometric information is available, it has demonstrated satisfactory single day stability (e.g., Wigal et al., 1998) and is sensitive to the effects of stimulant treatment on classroom behavior (e.g., Greenhill et al., 2001; Swanson et al., 1998). Although only examined in a research context, daily electronic diaries may also prove to have clinical utility in assessing ADHD symptom change, as reported by either parents or children (e.g., Whalen et al., 2006).

Broadband Checklists

As indicated in Table 2.3, the parent and teacher versions of the AESBA (including older versions of these measures) have demonstrated sensitivity to behavioral

interventions in children with disruptive disorders (e.g., Ialongo et al., 1993; Kazdin, 2003). The Conners Rating Scales-Revised (Conners, 1997), both parent and teacher versions, in both earlier and the most recent versions, have consistently demonstrated sensitivity to medication treatments for children with ADHD (e.g., Gadow et al., 1999; Weiss et al., 2005) and some evidence supports their sensitivity to behavioral interventions as well (e.g., Horn, Ialongo, Popovich, & Peradotto, 1987; Pisterman et al., 1989).

Measures of Impairment

Among the measures of impairment, the CAFAS has demonstrated sensitivity to behavioral or mental health interventions, with generally adequate psychometric properties as indicated in Table 2.3 (e.g., Timmon-Mitchell, Bender, Kishna, & Mitchell, 2006; Vernberg, Jacobs, Nyre, Puddy, & Roberts, 2004). However, this sensitivity has not been examined specifically within ADHD samples. Although it is hoped that newer impairment measures, such as the IRS (Fabiano et al., 2006), will soon have evidence of treatment sensitivity, none is yet available.

Observational Measures

As noted above, using observational measures in treatment planning often yields ongoing assessment of treatment progress and documentation of treatment outcome. For example, the ITBE (Pelham et al., 2002), based on frequency counts of problematic behavior that are individualized for each child, has an obvious utility in treatment monitoring and this measure has proven sensitive to the effects of both medication and classroom behavior management strategies (Pelham et al., 2001). Other individualized behavioral assessments, including curriculum-based measurement, have also been reported as useful in monitoring treatment responses among students with ADHD (e.g., Stoner, Carey, Ikeda, & Shinn, 1994). Similarly, the BCS, assessing parent and child behavior, has demonstrated sensitivity to the effects of behavioral parent training (evidence reviewed in McMahon & Forehand, 2003). Despite the clear relevance of these behavioral measures for assessing treatment-related change in child or parent behavior, the advantages of these measures are combined with a lack of information regarding expected normative changes in scores over time and a lack of traditional validity evidence (Kollins, 2004).

Overall Evaluation

As with measures useful for treatment planning, the measures with the strongest psychometric properties (i.e., ADHD symptom scales and broadband checklists), although potentially useful in monitoring treatment outcomes, may be limited by their failure to assess impairments or to be sensitive to the relatively rapid changes in child behavior that are common in medication and behavioral interventions. In addition, the length of the broadband checklists is often prohibitive for repeated assessments. Clinicians are advised to give careful consideration to supplementing these measures with others that may more directly assess the child's daily functioning (e.g., the IRS or observational measures), with appropriate caution in the use of these measures due to their psychometric limitations. Clinical research is urgently needed to address the missing normative comparisons for these measures, to expand the evidence of their reliability and validity, and most importantly, to provide empirical support for the clinical utility these measures are assumed to possess.

CONCLUSIONS AND FUTURE DIRECTIONS

A multitude of tools for assessing childhood ADHD are available, both commercially and in the public domain, and new additions emerge regularly. In contrast to this abundant quantity of measures, far fewer measures are available that possess substantial psychometric qualities or that have been validated for uses beyond diagnostic questions. In this final section of the chapter, we draw attention to prominent unanswered questions regarding assessments for ADHD diagnoses and for treatment planning and monitoring. We again note that our focus on assessment measures should not overshadow the fact that the process of assessing a child with ADHD involves much more than simple administration of a standard set of measures. Clinicians must make client-specific decisions regarding which measures are best suited for each individual child and family (e.g., is this child represented in the measure's normative group), at which point in the assessment process (e.g., is the measure needed primarily for assigning a diagnosis or for monitoring the child's response to a new medication), and how information from multiple sources and measures is best combined to answer the assessment question. In addition, information derived from the measures presented here must be supplemented with clinical judgments regarding each individual child's situation and context (e.g., cultural factors) and must be employed within the context of a caring and supportive therapeutic relationship between clinician and family.

In diagnosing ADHD, the use of unstructured interviews as a guide for identifying general areas of concern (both in terms of ADHD and comorbid disorders), developmental and treatment history, and information specific to the child and family's circumstances remains a common assessment recommendation (e.g., Barkley, 2006), despite the known limitations of this assessment method. Efforts to develop and evaluate more structured tools for gathering this information would be clinically valuable. In terms of more structured assessment methods used in diagnosis, consensus appears to be that information from both parents and teachers is necessary (e.g., Pelham et al., 2005), although methods for combining this information have seldom been compared or validated. There is less agreement among experts regarding the relative merits of symptom-specific rating scales versus structured interviews, or both, in assigning diagnoses. Arguments based on little evidence of incremental validity for structured interviews, combined with the impressive practicality of rating scale measures, suggest quite convincingly that rating scales should be the measures of choice (e.g., Pelham et al., 2005). However, this issue demands further studies comparing the alternatives.

Other unresolved questions in assigning ADHD diagnoses focus on the role of age, gender, and ethnicity in normative comparisons. Although most agree on the need for developmentally appropriate norms, whether gender-specific or even ethnicity-specific norms are needed is more controversial. Until further research indicates whether or not the ADHD diagnosis holds differential validity across gender and ethnic groups, clinicians are perhaps best advised to consider all possible comparisons, and to consider normative comparisons within the context of the possibility that the construct of ADHD may be represented differently across diverse client groups.

Beyond the need to refine the measures and process of assessing ADHD, we have been struck by the disconnect that exists between assessments of ADHD diagnoses and assessments relevant to the treatment of the disorder. Among children referred with ADHD, it is often the case that the most pressing clinical problems are those related to functional impairments (e.g., in parent–child interactions, peer relations, or academic functioning) or to comorbid conditions (e.g., oppositional defiant disorder or learning disorders). Symptom severity, the target of diagnostic assessment, is clearly related to these impairments, but not synonymous with them. Knowing the child's level of ADHD symptoms, or even the subtype, offers little treatment guidance and changes in these symptom levels may not mirror changes in the functional problems that instigated help-seeking.

Although a few standardized measures with adequate psychometric properties have proven their value in planning and monitoring treatment progress in children, the most promising measures in this area originate from a behavioral perspective, but lack standardization, norm development, and broad psychometric evaluation. We believe that these measures have the greatest potential for enhancing the selection of appropriate treatment targets for children with ADHD and for providing careful, continuous, and objective feedback regarding treatment progress. However, one cannot ignore the inadequacies of

these measures in terms of traditional psychometric properties. Research is urgently needed to address these limitations, and to develop and test clinically useful measures appropriate to assessing and monitoring change in the functional impairments that form the core of ADHD treatment planning.

In closing, we acknowledge a number of useful resources on the assessment of ADHD and refer clinicians to these resources for additional guidelines and information useful in this endeavor. Recent books by Barkley (2006) and Anastopoulos and Shelton (2001) provide excellent coverage of assessment issues in ADHD. Clinical guidelines for assessing ADHD have been provided by the American Academy of Pediatrics (2000) and the American Academy of Child and Adolescent Psychiatry (1997). Pelham and colleagues' (2005) contribution on evidence-based assessment for ADHD is an excellent resource. Review articles by Collett and colleagues (2003), Angello and colleagues (2003), and Tripp, Schaughency, and Clarke (2006) provide extremely useful summaries of available rating scales. Finally, Evans and Youngstrom (2006) and Frazier and Youngstrom (2006) provide interesting illustrations of how clinicians may approach the task of ADHD assessment in an evidence-based manner. We trust that this chapter, along with these additional resources, provides the clinician with an overview of the issues prominent in the assessment of ADHD, and with a guide to currently available and useful measures.

References

Abikoff, H., Gittelman, R., & Klein, D. F. (1980). Classroom observation code for hyperactive children: A replication of validity. *Journal of Consulting and Clinical Psychology, 48,* 555–565.

Abikoff, H., Gittelman-Klein, R., & Klein, D. F. (1977). Validation of a classroom observation code for hyperactive children. *Journal of Consulting and Clinical Psychology, 45,* 772–783.

Achenbach, T. M., McConaughy, S. H., & Howell, C. T. (1987). Child/adolescent behavioral and emotional problems: Implications of cross-informant correlations for situational specificity. *Psychological Bulletin, 101,* 213–232.

Achenbach, T. M., & Rescorla, L. A. (2001). *Manual for the ASEBA school-age forms & profiles.* Burlington, VT: University of Vermont, Research Center for Children, Youth, & Families.

American Academy of Child and Adolescent Psychiatry. (1997). Practice parameters for the assessment and treatment of children, adolescents, and adults with attention-deficit/hyperactivity disorder. *Journal of the American Academy of Child & Adolescent Psychiatry, 36*(Suppl.), 85–121.

American Academy of Pediatrics. (2000). Clinical practice guideline: Diagnosis and evaluation of the child with attention-deficit/hyperactivity disorder. *Pediatrics, 105,* 1158–1170.

American Psychiatric Association. (2000). *Diagnostic and statistical manual-IV (Text Revision).* Washington, DC: Author.

Anastopoulos, A. D., & Shelton, T. L. (2001). *Assessing attention-deficit/hyperactivity disorder.* Dordrecht, The Netherlands: Kluwer Academic Publishers.

Anastopoulos, A. D., Shelton, T. L., DuPaul, G. J., & Guevremont, D. C. (1993). Parent training for Attention-Deficit Hyperactivity Disorder: Its impact on parent functioning. *Journal of Abnormal Child Psychology, 21,* 581–596.

Angello, L. M., Volpe, R. J., DiPerna, J. C., Gureasko-Moore, S. P., Gureasko-Moore, D. P., Nebrig, M. R. et al. (2003). Assessment of attention-deficit/hyperactivity disorder: An evaluation of six published rating scales. *School Psychology Review, 32,* 241–262.

Angold, A., & Costello, J. (2000). The Child and Adolescent Psychiatric Assessment (CAPA). *Journal of the American Academy of Child & Adolescent Psychiatry, 39,* 49–58.

Angold, A., Erkanli, A., Costello, E. J., & Rutter, M. (1996). Precision, reliability and accuracy in the dating of symptom onset in child and adolescent psychopathology. *Journal of Child Psychology and Psychiatry, 37,* 657–664.

Angold, A., Erkanli, A., Egger, H. L., & Costello, E. J. (2000). Stimulant treatment for children: A community perspective. *Journal of the American Academy of Child & Adolescent Psychiatry, 39,* 975–984.

Arnold, L. E., Davies, M., Abikoff, H. B., Conners, C. K., Elliott, G. R., Greenhill, L. L., et al. (2004). Nine months of multicomponent behavioral treatment for ADHD and effectiveness of MTA fading procedures. *Journal of Abnormal Child Psychology, 32,* 39–51.

Atkins, M. S., Pelham, W. E., & Licht, M. H. (1989). The differential validity of teacher ratings of inattention/overactivity and aggression. *Journal of Abnormal Child Psychology, 17,* 423–435.

Barkley, R. A. (2006). *Attention-deficit/hyperactivity disorder: A handbook for diagnosis and treatment.* New York: Guilford.

Barkley, R A., and 84 other behavioral scientists. (2002). International consensus statement on ADHD, January 2002. *Clinical Child and Family Psychology Review, 5,* 89–111.

Barkley, R. A., DuPaul, G. J., & McMurray, M. B. (1990). A comprehensive evaluation of attention deficit disorder with and without hyperactivity. *Journal of Consulting and Clinical Psychology, 58,* 775–789.

Barkley, R. A., Fisher, M., Smallish, L., & Fletcher, K. (2002). The persistence of attention-deficit/hyperactivity disorder into young adulthood as a function of reporting source and definition of disorder *Journal of Abnormal Psychology, 111,* 279–289.

Biederman, J., Keenan, K., & Faraone, S. (1990). Parent-based diagnosis of attention deficit disorder predicts a diagnosis based on teacher report. *Journal of the American Academy of Child & Adolescent Psychiatry, 29,* 298–701.

Bird, H. R., Andrews, H., Schwab-Stone, M., Goodman, S., Dulcan, M., Richters, J., et al. (1996). Global measures of impairment for epidemiologic and clinical use with children and adolescents. *International Journal of Methods in Psychiatric Research, 6,* 295–307.

Brown, T. E. (2001). *Brown attention-deficit disorder scales for children and adolescents.* San Antonia, TX: Psychological Corporation.

Bruininks, R. H., Woodcock, R. W., Weatherman, R. F., & Hill, B. K. (1996). *Scales of independent behavior-revised.* Itasca, IL: Riverside Publishing.

Bussing, R., Schuhmann, E., Belin, T. R., Widawski, M., & Perwien, A. R. (1998). Diagnostic utility of two commonly used ADHD screening measures among special education students. *Journal of the American Academy of Child & Adolescent Psychiatry, 37,* 74–82.

Chi, T. C., & Hinshaw, S. P. (2002). Mother-child relationships of children with ADHD: The role of maternal depressive symptoms and depression-related distortions. *Journal of Abnormal Child Psychology, 30,* 387–400.

Chronis, A. M., Jones, H. A., & Raggi, V. L. (2006). Evidence-based psychosocial treatments for children and adolescents with attention-deficit/hyperactivity disorder. *Clinical Psychology Review, 26,* 486–502.

Collett, B. R., Ohan, J. L., & Myers, K. M. (2003). Ten-year review of rating scales. V: Scales assessing attention-deficit/hyperactivity disorder. *Journal of the American Academy of Child & Adolescent Psychiatry, 42,* 1015–1037.

Conners, C. K. (1997). *Conners' rating scales—revised.* Toronto, ON: Multi-Health Systems.

Connors, C. K., Epstein, J. N., March, J. S., Angold, A., Wells, K. C., & Klaric, J. (2001). Multimodal treatment of ADHD in the MTA: An alternative outcome analysis. *Journal of the American Academy of Child & Adolescent Psychiatry, 40,* 159–167.

Conners, C. K., & MHS Staff (2000). *Conners continuous performance test II.* Tonawanda, NY: Multi-Health Systems.

Conners, C. K., Parker, J. D. A., Sitarenios, G., & Epstein, J. N. (1998). The Revised Conners' Parent Rating Scale (CPRS-R): Factor structure, reliability, and criterion validity. *Journal of Abnormal Child Psychology, 26,* 257–268.

Conners, C. K., Sitarenios, G., Parker, J. D. A., & Epstein, J. N. (1998). Revision and restandardization of the Conners Teacher Rating Scale (CTRS-R): Factor structure, reliability, and criterion validity. *Journal of Abnormal Child Psychology, 26,* 279–291.

Daviss, W. B., Bentivoglio, P., Racusin, R., Brown, K. M., Bostic, J. Q., & Wiley, L. (2001). Bupropion sustained release in adolescents with comorbid attention-deficit/hyperactivity disorder and depression. *Journal of the American Academy of Child & Adolescent Psychiatry, 40,* 307–314.

de Nijs, P. F. A., Ferdinand, R. F., de Bruin, E. I., Dekker, M. C. J., van Duijn, C. M., & Verhulst, F. C. (2004). Attention-deficit/hyperactivity disorder (ADHD): Parents' judgment about school, teacher's judgment about home. *European Child and Adolescent Psychiatry, 13,* 315–320.

Derks, E. M., Hudziak, J. J., Dolan, C. V., Ferdinand, R. F., & Boomsma, D. I. (2006). The relations between DISC-IV DSM diagnoses of ADHD and multi-informant CBCL- AP syndrome scores. *Comprehensive Psychiatry, 47,* 116–122.

DuPaul, G. J., Power, T. J., Anastopoulos, A. D., & Reid, R. (1998). *ADHD-IV Rating Scale: Checklists, norms, and clinical interpretation.* New York: Guilford.

DuPaul, G. J., Power, T. J., McGoey, K. E., Ikeda, M. J., & Anastopoulos, A. D. (1998). Reliability and validity of the parent and teacher ratings of attention-deficit/hyperactivity disorder symptoms. *Journal of Psychoeducational Assessment, 16,* 55–68.

Edwards, M. C., Schulz, E. G., Chelonis, J., Gardner, E., Philyaw, A., & Young, J. (2005). Estimates of the validity and utility of unstructured clinical observations of children in the assessment of ADHD. *Clinical Pediatrics, 44,* 49–56.

Eiraldi, R. B., Power, T. J., Karustis, J. L., & Goldstein, S. G. (2000). Assessing ADHD and comorbid disorders in children: The Child Behavior Checklist and the Devereux Scales of Mental Disorders. *Journal of Clinical Child Psychology, 29,* 3–16.

Epstein, J. N., Willoughby, M., Valencia, E. Y., Tonev, S. T., Abikoff, H. B., Arnold, L. E., et al. (2005). The role of children's ethnicity in the relationship between teacher ratings of attention-deficit/hyperactivity disorder and observed classroom behavior. *Journal of Consulting and Clinical Psychology, 73,* 424–434.

Evans, S. W., & Youngstrom, E. (2006). Evidence-based assessment of attention-deficit/hyperactivity disorder: Measuring outcomes. *Journal of the American Academy of Child & Adolescent Psychiatry, 45,* 1132–1137.

Fabiano, G. A., Pelham, W. E., Waschbusch, D. A., Gnagy, E. M. Lahey, B. B., Chronis, A. M., et al. (2006). A practical measure of impairment: Psychometric properties of the impairment rating scale in samples of children with attention deficit hyperactivity disorder and two school-based samples. *Journal of Clinical Child and Adolescent Psychology, 35,* 369–385.

Faraone, S. V., Monuteaux, M. C., Biederman, J., Cohan, S. L., & Mick, E. (2003). Does parental ADHD bias maternal reports of ADHD symptoms in children? *Journal of Consulting and Clinical Psychology, 71,* 168–175.

Frazier, T. W., & Youngstrom, E. A. (2006). Evidence-based assessment of attention-deficit/hyperactivity disorder: Using multiple sources of information. *Journal of the American Academy of Child & Adolescent Psychiatry, 45,* 614–620.

Gadow, K. D., Drabick, D. A. G., Loney, J., Sprafkin, J., Salisbury, H., Azizian, A., et al. (2004). Comparison of ADHD symptom subtypes as source-specific syndromes. *Journal of Child Psychology and Psychiatry, 45,* 1135–1149.

Gadow, K. D., Nolan, E. E., Sverd, J., Sprafkin, J., & Paolicelli, L. (1990). Methylphenidate in aggressive-hyperactive boys, I: effects on peer aggression in public school settings. *Journal of the American Academy of Child & Adolescent Psychiatry, 29,* 710–718.

Gadow, K. D. & Sprafkin, J. (1999). *ADHD symptom checklist-4 manual.* Stony Brook, NY: Checkmate Plus.

Gadow, K. D., & Sprafkin, J. (2002). *Child symptom inventory-4 norms manual.* Stony Brook, NY: Checkmate Plus.

Gadow, K. D., Sprafkin, J., Salisbury, H., Schneider, J., & Loney, J. (2004). Further validity evidence for the teacher version of the child symptom inventory-4. *School Psychology Quarterly, 19,* 50–71.

Gadow, K. D., Sverd, J., Sprafkin, J., Nolan, E. E., Gianarris, W. J., Golden, C. J., et al. (2001). The Conners' parent rating scales: A critical review of the literature. *Clinical Psychology Review, 21,* 1061–1093.

Gadow, K. D., Sverd, J., Sprafkin, J., Nolan, E. E., & Grossman, S. (1999). Long term methylphenidate therapy in children with comorbid attention deficit hyperactivity disorder and chronic multiple tic disorder. *Archives of General Psychiatry, 56,* 334–336.

Gladman, M., & Lancaster, S. (2003). A review of the Behavior Assessment System for Children. *School Psychology International, 24,* 276–291.

Gomez, R., Burns, G. L., Walsh, J. A., & De Moura, M. A. (2003). Multitrait-multisource confirmatory factor analytic approach to the construct validity of ADHD rating scales. *Psychological Assessment, 15,* 3–16.

Gordon, M. (1983). *The Gordon diagnostic system.* DeWitt, NY: Gordon Systems.

Goodman, R., & Scott, S. (1999). Comparing the Strengths and Difficulties Questionnaire and the Child Behavior Checklist: Is small beautiful? *Journal of Abnormal Child Psychology, 27,* 17–24.

Goyette, C. H., Conners, C. K., & Ulrich, R. F. (1978). Normative data on revised Conners Parent and Teacher Rating Scales. *Journal of Abnormal Child Psychology, 6,* 221–236.

Greenhill, L. L., Swanson, J. M., Vitiello, B. Davis, M., Clevenger, W., Wu, M., et al. (2001). Impairment and deportment responses to different methylphenidate doses in children with ADHD: The MTA titration trial. *Journal of the American Academy of Child & Adolescent Psychiatry, 40,* 180–187.

Greenhill, L. L., Biederman, J., Boeliner, S. W., Rugino, T. A., Sangal, R. B., Earl, C. Q., et al. (2006). A randomized, double-blind, placebo-controlled study of modafinil film-coated tablets in children and adolescents with attention-deficit/hyperactivity disorder. *Journal of the American Academy of Child & Adolescent Psychiatry, 45,* 503–511.

Hart, E. L, Lahey, B. B., Loeber, R., Applegate, B., Green, S. M., & Frick, P. J. (1995). Developmental change in attention-deficit hyperactivity disorder in boys: A four-year longitudinal study. *Journal of Abnormal Child Psychology, 23,* 729–749.

Hodges, K., & Wong, M. M. (1996). Psychometric characteristics of a multidimensional measure to assess impairment: The Child and Adolescent Functional Assessment Scale. *Journal of Child and Family Studies, 5,* 445–467.

Holmes, J., Lawson, D., Langley, K., Fitzpatrick, H., Trumper, A., Pay, H., et al. (2004). The child attention-deficit hyperactivity disorder teacher telephone interview (CHATTI): Reliability and validity. *The British Journal of Psychiatry, 184,* 74–78.

Horn, W. F., Conners, C. K., Wells, K. C., & Shaw, D. (1986). Use of the Abikoff Classroom Observation Coding System on a children's inpatient psychiatric unit. *Journal of Psychopathology and Behavioral Assessment, 8,* 9–23.

Horn, W. F., Ialongo, N., Popovich, S., & Peradotto, D. (1987). Behavioral parent training and cognitive-behavioral self-control therapy with ADD-H children: Comparative and combined effects. *Journal of Clinical Child Psychology, 16,* 57–68.

Ialongo, N. S., Horn, W. F., Pascoe, J. M., Greenberg, G., Packard, T., Lopez, M., et al. (1993). The effects of a multimodal intervention with Attention-deficit Hyperactivity Disorder children: A 9-month follow-up. *Journal of the American Academy of Child & Adolescent Psychiatry, 32,* 182–189.

Johnston, C., & Mash, E. J. (2001). Families of children with Attention Deficit Hyperactivity Disorder: Review and recommendations for future research. *Clinical Child and Family Psychology Review, 4,* 183–207.

Johnston, C., & Murray, C. (2003). Incremental validity in the psychological assessment of children and adolescents. *Psychological Assessment, 15,* 496–507.

Johnston, C., & Pelham, W. E. (1986). Teacher ratings predict peer ratings of aggression at 3-year follow-up in boys with attention deficit disorder with hyperactivity. *Journal of Consulting and Clinical Psychology, 54,* 571–572.

Kadesjo, C., Kadesjo, B., Hagglof, B., & Gillberg, C. (2001). ADHD in Swedish 3- to 7-year old children. *Journal of the American Academy of Child & Adolescent Psychiatry, 40,* 1021–1028.

Kamphaus, R. W., & Frick, P. J. (2005). *Clinical assessment of child and adolescent personality and behavior* (2nd ed.). New York: Springer.

Kamphaus, R. W., & Reynolds, C. R. (1998). *Behavior Assessment System for Children (BASC) ADHD Monitor.* Circle Pines, MN: American Guidance Systems.

Kamphaus, R. W., Reynolds, C. R., Hatcher, N. M., & Kim, S. (2004). Treatment planning and evaluation with the Behavior Assessment System for Children (BASC). In M. E. Maruish (Ed.), *The use of psychological testing for treatment planning and outcomes assessment* (pp. 331–354). Mahwah, NJ: LEA.

Kaufman, A. S. (1994). *Intelligent testing with the WISC-III.* New York: Wiley.

Kazdin, A. E. (2003). Problem-solving skills training and parent management training for conduct disorder. In A. E. Kazdin & J. R. Weisz (Eds.), *Evidence-based psychotherapies for children and adolescents* (pp. 241–262). New York: Guilford.

Kollins, S. H. (2004). Methodological issues in the assessment of medication effects in children diagnosed with attention deficit hyperactivity disorder (ADHD). *Journal of Behavioral Education, 13,* 247–266.

Kollins, S. H., Epstein, J. N., & Conners, C. K. (2004). Conners rating scales—Revised. In M. E. Mariush (Ed.), *The use of psychological testing for treatment planning and outcomes assessment: Vol. 2. Instruments for children and adolescents* (pp. 215–233). Mahwah, NJ: LEA.

Lachar, D. (1982) *Personality Inventory for Children-Revised (PIC-R)*. Los Angeles, CA: Western Psychological Services.

Lahey, B. B., Applegate, B., McBurnett, K., Biederman, J., Greenhill, L., Hynd, G., et al. (1994). DMS-IV field trials for attention deficit hyperactivity disorder in children and adolescents. *American Journal of Psychiatry, 151,* 1673–1685.

Loeber, R., Green, S. M., Lahey, B. B., & Stouthamer-Loeber, M. (1991). Differences and similarities between children, mothers, and teachers as informants on disruptive child behavior. *Journal of Abnormal Child Psychology, 19,* 75–95.

Loney, J., & Milich, R. (1982). Hyperactivity, inattention, and aggression in clinical practice. In D. K. Routh (Ed.), *Advances in developmental and behavioral pediatrics* (pp. 113–147). New York: Plenum.

Manly, T., Anderson, V., Nimmo-Smith, I., Turner, A., Watson, P., & Robertson, I. H. (2001). The differential assessment of children's attention: The Test of Everyday Attention for Children (TEA-Ch): normative sample and ADHD performance. *Journal of Child Psychology and Psychiatry, 42,* 1065–1081.

Manly, T., Robertson, I. H., Anderson, V., & Nimmo-Smith, I. (1999). *The test of everyday attention for children: Manual.* Bury St. Edmunds, England: Thames Valley Test Company Limited.

Mash, E. J., & Barkley, R. A. (2007). *Assessment of childhood disorders* (4th ed.). New York: Guilford.

Mattison, R. E., Gadow, K. D., Sprafkin, J., & Nolan, E. E. (2002). Discriminant validity of a DSM-IV based teacher checklist: Comparison of regular and special education students. *Behavioral Disorders, 27,* 304–316.

Mattison, R. E., Gadow, K. D., Sprafkin, J., Nolan, E. E., & Schneider, J. (2003). A DSM-IV referenced teacher rating scale for use in clinical management. *Journal of the American Academy of Child & Adolescent Psychiatry, 42,* 443–449.

McConaughy, S. H. (2001). The Achenbach System of Evidence Based Assessment. In J. J. W. Andrews, D. H. Saklofsky, & H. L. Jensen (Eds.), *Handbook of psychoeducational assessment: Ability, achievement, and behavior in children* (pp. 289–324). San Diego: Academic Press.

McCarney, S. B. (2004). *The attention deficit disorders evaluation scale, home and school versions, Technical Manual.* Columbia, MO: Hawthorne Educational Services.

McGrath, A. M., Handwerk, M. L., Armstrong, K. J., Lucas, C. P., & Friman, P. C. (2004). The validity of the ADHD section of the diagnostic interview schedule for children. *Behavior Modification, 28,* 349–374.

McMahon, R. J., & Forehand, R. L. (2003). *Helping the noncompliant child, second edition: Family-based treatment for oppositional behavior.* New York: Guilford Press.

McMahon, R. J., & Frick, P. J. (2005). Evidence-based assessment of conduct problems in children and adolescents. *Journal of Clinical Child and Adolescent Psychology, 34,* 477–505.

Milich, R., Balentine, A. C., & Lynam, D. R. (2001). ADHD combined type and ADHD predominately inattentive type are distinct and unrelated disorders. *Clinical Psychology: Science and Practice, 8,* 463–488.

MTA Cooperative Group. (1999a). A 14-month randomized clinical trial of treatment strategies for attention-deficit/hyperactivity disorder. *Archives of General Psychiatry, 56,* 1073–1086.

MTA Cooperative Group. (1999b). Moderators and mediators of treatment response of children with attention-deficit/hyperactivity disorder: The multimodal treatment study of children with attention-deficit/hyperactivity disorder. *Archives of General Psychiatry, 56,* 1088–1096.

MTA Cooperative Group. (2004). National Institute of Mental Health multimodal treatment study of ADHD follow-up: 24-month outcomes of treatment strategies for attention-deficit/hyperactivity disorder. *Pediatrics, 113,* 754–761.

Naglieri, J. A., LeBuffe, P. A., & Pfeiffer, S. I. (1994). *The Devereux Scales of Mental Disorders.* San Antonio, TX: The Psychological Corporation.

National Institutes of Health (2000). Consensus Development Conference Statement: Diagnosis and treatment of attention deficit hyperactivity disorder (ADHD). *Journal of the American Academy of Child & Adolescent Psychiatry, 39,* 182–193.

Nichols, S. L., & Waschbusch, D. A. (2004). A review of the validity of laboratory cognitive tasks used to assess symptoms of ADHD. *Child Psychiatry and Human Development, 34,* 297–315.

Nigg, J. T., Willcutt, E. G., & Doyle, A. E. (2005). Causal heterogeneity in attention-deficit/hyperactivity disorder: Do we need neuropsychological impaired subtypes? *Biological Psychiatry, 57,* 1224–1230.

Ohan, J. L., & Johnston, C. (2005). Gender appropriateness of symptom criteria for attention-deficit/hyperactivity disorder, oppositional defiant disorder, and conduct disorder. *Child Psychiatry and Human Development, 35,* 359–381.

Ostrander, R., Weinfurt, K. P., Yarnold, P. R., & August, G. J. (1998). Diagnosing Attention Deficit Disorders with the Behavioral Assessment System for Children and the Child Behavior Checklist: Test and construct validity analyses using optimal discriminant classification trees. *Journal of Consulting and Clinical Psychology, 66,* 660–672.

Owens, J. S., & Hoza, B. (2003). Diagnostic utility of DSM-IV TR symptoms in the prediction of

DSM-IV TR ADHD subtypes and ODD. *Journal of Attention Disorders, 7,* 11–27.

Pappas, D. (2006). ADHD Rating Scale IV: Checklists, norms, and clinical interpretation. *Journal of Psychoeducational Assessment, 24,* 172–178.

Pelham, W. E., Fabiano, G. A., & Massetti, G. M. (2005). Evidence-based assessment of attention deficit hyperactivity disorder in children and adolescents. *Journal of Clinical Child and Adolescent Psychology, 34,* 449–476.

Pelham, W. E., Gnagy, E. M., Burrows-Maclean, L., William, A., Fabiano, G. A., et al. (2001). Once-a-day Concerta methylphenidate versus three times daily methylphenidate in laboratory and natural settings. *Pediatrics, 107,* E105.

Pelham, W. E., Hoza, B., Pillow, D. R., Gnagy, E. M., Kipp, H. L., Greiner, A. R., et al. (2002). Effects of methylphenidate and expectancy on children with ADHD: Behavior, academic performance and attributions in a summer treatment program and regular classroom settings. *Journal of Consulting and Clinical Psychology, 70,* 320–335.

Pelham, W. E., Milich, R., Murphy, D., & Murphy, H. (1989). Normative data on the IOWA Conners Teacher Rating Scale. *Journal of Clinical Child Psychology, 18,* 259–262.

Pelham, W. E., Wheeler, T., & Chronis, A. (1998). Empirically supported psychosocial treatments for attention deficit hyperactivity disorder. *Journal of Clinical Child Psychology, 27,* 190–205.

Piacentini, J. C., Cohen, P., & Cohen, J. (1992). Combining discrepant diagnostic information from multiple sources: Are complex algorithms better than simple ones? *Journal of Abnormal Child Psychology, 20,* 51–63.

Pillow, D. R., Pelham, W. E., Hoza, B., Molina, B. S. G., & Stultz, C. H. (1998). Confirmatory factor analyses examining attention deficit hyperactivity disorder symptoms and other childhood disruptive behaviors. *Journal of Abnormal Child Psychology, 26,* 293–309.

Pisterman, S., McGrath, P. J., Firestone, P., Goodman, J. T., Webster, I., & Mallory, R. (1989). Outcome of parent-mediated treatment of preschoolers with attention deficit disorder with hyperactivity. *Journal of Consulting and Clinical Psychology, 59,* 628–635.

Power, T. J., Andrews, T. J., Eiraldi, R. B., Doherty, B. J., Ikeda, M. J., DuPaul, G. J., et al. (1998). Evaluating attention deficit hyperactivity disorder using multiple informants: The incremental utility of combining teacher with parent reports. *Psychological Assessment, 10,* 250–260.

Power, T. J., Costigan, T. E., Leff, S. S., Eiraldi, R. B., & Landau, S. (2001). Assessing ADHD across settings: Contributions of behavioral assessment to categorical decision making. *Journal of Clinical Child Psychology, 30,* 399–412.

Power, T. J., Doherty, B. J., Panichelli-Mindel, S. M., Karustis, J. L., Eiraldi, R. B., Anastopoulos, A. D., et al. (1998). The predictive validity of parent and teacher reports of ADHD symptoms. *Journal of Psychopathology and Behavior, 20,* 57–81.

Rapport, M. D., Chung, K., Shore, G., Denney, C. B., & Isaacs, P. (2000). Upgrading the science and technology of assessment and diagnosis: Laboratory and clinic-based assessment of children with ADHD. *Journal of Clinical Child Psychology, 29,* 555–568.

Reich, W. (2000). Diagnostic Interview for Children and Adolescents (DICA). *Journal of the American Academy of Child & Adolescent Psychiatry, 39,* 59–66.

Reynolds, C. R., & Kamphaus, R. W. (2002). *The clinician's guide to the Behavior Assessment Scale for Children.* New York: Guilford.

Sandoval, J., & Echandia, A. (1994). Behavior Assessment System for Children. *Journal of School Psychology, 32,* 419–425.

Sayal, K., Goodman, R., & Ford, T. (2006). Barriers to the identification of children with attention deficit/hyperactivity disorder. *Journal of Child Psychology and Psychiatry, 47,* 744–750.

Shaffer, D., Fisher, P., Lucas, C. P., Dulcan, M. K., & Schwab-Stone, M. E. (2000). NIMH Diagnostic Interview Schedule for Children Version IV (NIMH DISC-IV): Description, differences from previous versions, and reliability of some common diagnoses. *Journal of the American Academy of Child & Adolescent Psychiatry, 39,* 28–38.

Smith, S. R., & Reddy, L. A. (2002). The concurrent validity of the Devereux Scales of Mental Disorders. *Journal of Psychoeducational Assessment, 20,* 112–127.

Sonuga-Barke, E. J. S. (1998). Categorical models of childhood disorder: A conceptual and empirical analysis. *Journal of Child Psychology and Psychiatry, 39,* 115–133.

Sparrow, S. S., Cicchetti, D. V., & Bala, D. A. (2005). *Vineland adaptive behavior scales* (2nd ed.). Circle Pines, MN: American Guidance Service.

Sprafkin, J., Gadow, K. D., Salisbury, H., Schneider, J., & Loney, J. (2002). Further evidence of reliability and validity of the Child Symptom Inventory-4: Parent checklist in clinically referred boys. *Journal of Clinical Child and Adolescent Psychology, 31,* 513–524.

Stein, M. A., Szumowski, E., Blondis, T. A., & Roizen, N. J. (1995). Adaptive skills dysfunction in ADD and ADHD children. *Journal of Child Psychology and Psychiatry, 36,* 663–670.

Stoner, G., Carey, S. P., Ikeda, M. J., & Shinn, M. R. (1994). The utility of curriculum-based measurement for evaluating the effects of methylphenidate of academic performance. *Journal of Applied Behavior Analysis, 27,* 101–113.

Swanson, J. M. (1992). *School based assessments and interventions for ADD students.* Irvine, CA: K.C.

Swanson, J. M., Wigal, S. B., Udrea, D., Lerner, M., Agler, D., Flynn, D., et al. (1998). Evaluation of individual subjects in the analog classroom setting: I. Examples of graphical and statistical procedures for within-subject rankings of responses to different delivery patterns of methylphenidate. *Psychopharmacology Bulletin, 34,* 825–832.

Timmons-Mitchell, J., Bender, M. B., Kishna, M. A., & Mitchell, C. C. (2006). An independent effectiveness trail of multisystemic therapy with juvenile justice youth. *Journal of Clinical Child and Adolescent Psychology, 35,* 227–236.

Tripp, G., Schaughency, E. A., & Clarke, B. (2006). Parent and teaching rating scales in the evaluation of attention-deficit hyperactivity disorder: Contribution to diagnosis and differential diagnosis in clinically referred children. *Developmental and Behavioral Pediatrics, 2,* 209–218.

Vaughn, M. L., Riccio, C. A., Hynd, G. W., & Hall, J. (1997). Diagnosis in ADHD (predominantly inattentive and combined type subtypes): Discriminant validity of the Behavior Assessment System for Children and the Achenbach Parent and Teacher Rating Scales. *Journal of Clinical Child Psychology, 26,* 349–357.

Vernberg, E. M., Jacobs, A. K., Nyre, J. E., Puddy, R. W., & Roberts, M. C. (2004). Innovative treatment for children with serious emotional disturbance: Preliminary outcomes for a school-based intensive mental health program. *Journal of Clinical Child and Adolescent Psychology, 33,* 359–365.

Waldman, I. D., & Gizer I. R. (2006). The genetics of attention deficit hyperactivity disorder. *Clinical Psychology Review, 26,* 396–432.

Waschbusch, D. A., King, S., & Northern Partners in Action for Children and Youth. (2006). Should sex-specific norms be used to assess attention-deficit/hyperactivity disorder or oppositional defiant disorder? *Journal of Consulting and Clinical Psychology, 74,* 179–185.

Weiss, M. D., Worling, D. E., & Wasdell, M. B. (2003). A chart review study of the inattentive and combined types of ADHD. *Journal of Attention Disorders, 7,* 1–9.

Weiss, M., Tannock, R., Kratochvil, C., Dunn, D., Velex-Borras, J., Thomason, C., et al. (2005). A randomized, placebo-controlled study of once-daily atomoxetine in the school setting in children with ADHD. *Journal of the American Academy of Child & Adolescent Psychiatry, 44,* 647–655.

Weissman, M. M., Warner, V., & Fendrich, M. (1990). Applying impairment criteria to children's psychiatric diagnoses. *Journal of the American Academy of Child & Adolescent Psychiatry, 29,* 789–795.

Whalen, C. K., Henker, B., Jamner, L. D., Ishikawa, S. S., Floro, J. N., Swindle, R., et al. (2006). Toward mapping daily challenges of living with ADH: Maternal and child perspectives using electronic diaries. *Journal of Abnormal Child Psychology, 34,* 115–130.

Wigal, S., Gupta, S., Guinta, D., & Swanson, J. (1998). Reliability and validity of the SKAMP Rating Scale in a laboratory school setting. *Pharmacological Bulletin, 34,* 47–53.

Wilson, J. M., & Marcotte, A. C. (1996). Psychosocial adjustment and educational outcome in adolescents with a childhood diagnosis of attention deficit disorder. *Journal of the American Academy of Child & Adolescent Psychiatry, 35,* 579–587.

Wolraich, M. L., Greenhill, L. L., Pelham, W. E. Swanson, J., Wilens, T., Palumbos, D., et al. (2001). Randomized, controlled trial of OROS methylphenidate once a day in children with attention-deficit/hyperactivity disorder. *Pediatrics, 108,* 883–892.

Wolraich, M. L., Lambert, E. W., Baumgaertal, A., Garcia-Torner, S., Feurer, I. D., Bickman, L., et al. (1998). Teachers' screening for attention deficit/hyperactivity disorder: Comparing multinational samples on teacher ratings of ADHD. *Journal of Abnormal Child Psychology, 31,* 445–455.

Wolraich, M. L., Lambert, W., Doffing, M. A., Bickman, L., Simmons, T., & Worley, K. (2003). Psychometric properties of the Vanderbilt ADHD diagnostic parent rating scale in a referred population. *Journal of Pediatric Psychology, 28,* 559–568.

Zelko, F. A. (1991). Comparison of parent-completed behavior rating scales: Differentiating boys with ADD from psychiatric and normal controls. *Journal of Developmental and Behavioral Pediatrics, 12,* 31–37.

3

Child and Adolescent Conduct Problems

Paul J. Frick

Robert J. McMahon

Conduct problems (CP) in youth is one of the most common reasons that children and adolescents are referred to mental health clinics (Frick & Silverthorn, 2001). This is not surprising given that CP often cause significant disruptions for the child at home (Frick, 1998) and school (Gottfredson & Gottfredson, 2001), and it is the form of psychopathology that has been most strongly associated with delinquency and violence (Moffitt, 1993). An extensive body of research has led to an increased understanding of the many processes that may be involved in the development of severe CP (Dodge & Pettit, 2003; Frick, 2006). This research has many important implications for designing more effective interventions to prevent or treat these problems (Conduct Problems Prevention Research Group, 2000; Frick, 2006) and for improving the methods for assessing children and adolescents with severe CP (McMahon & Frick, 2005). The focus of this chapter is on the implications for assessments.

In the next section, we provide a brief overview of several key findings from research on CP in children and adolescents and highlight several findings that we feel have the most direct relevance to the assessment process. Specifically, we focus on research illustrating the great heterogeneity in the types, severity, and course of CP in youth, as well as the frequent co-occurring problems in adjustment that often accompany CP. We also summarize research showing important dispositional and contextual risk factors that have been related to CP and that could play an important role in the development or maintenance of CP. We then review some recent causal models that have been proposed to explain how these many risk factors could affect the development of the child and lead to CP.

After the brief overview of these select but critical areas of research, we then focus on the implications of this research for three types of assessments that are often conducted for children with CP. First, we focus on methods for determining whether the level of CP is severe, impairing, and developmentally inappropriate enough to be considered "disordered." Second, we focus on assessments that can be used for developing case conceptualizations, which can guide comprehensive and individualized treatment plans for children with CP. Using interventions that rely on multiple types of interventions, which are tailored to the child's individual needs, have proven to be the most effective for treating children and adolescents with CP (Conduct Problems Prevention Research Group, 2000; Frick, 2006). Third, we focus on measures that can be used to monitor and evaluate treatment progress and outcomes. Unfortunately, the availability of measures for this crucial assessment purpose is quite limited.

After summarizing research on CP and its implications for assessment, we conclude this chapter with a section highlighting some overriding issues related to assessing children with CP, such as the need to assess children with multiple measures that provide information on their adjustment in multiple contexts. We also provide a summary of some of the major limitations in the existing assessment technology and make recommendations for future work to overcome these limitations.

THE NATURE OF CP

Types and Severity of CP and Common Co-Occurring Conditions

CP constitutes a broad spectrum of "acting-out" behaviors, ranging from relatively minor oppositional behaviors such as yelling and temper tantrums to more serious forms of antisocial behavior such as physical destructiveness, stealing, and physical violence. There have been numerous methods used to divide CP into more discrete and homogenous types of behaviors (see Frick & Marsee, 2006; Hinshaw & Lee, 2003 for comprehensive reviews). For example, the *Diagnostic and Statistical Manual of Mental Disorders* (4th Edition–Text Revision; DSM-IV-TR; American Psychiatric Association, 2000) makes a distinction between the categories of oppositional defiant disorder (ODD) and conduct disorder (CD). ODD is a pattern of negativistic (e.g., deliberately doing things that annoy other people and blaming others for own mistakes), disobedient (e.g., defying or not complying with grown-ups' rules or requests), and hostile behaviors (e.g., losing temper). CD consists of more severe antisocial and aggressive behavior that involves serious violations of others' rights or deviations from major age-appropriate norms. The behaviors are categorized into four groups: aggressiveness to people and animals (e.g., bullying and fighting), property destruction (e.g., firesetting and other destruction of property), deceptiveness or theft (e.g., breaking and entering, stealing without confronting victim), and serious rule violations (e.g., running away from home or being truant from school before age 13).

In addition to this division in the DSM-IV-TR, factor analyses have resulted in another method for differentiating among types of CP. In a meta-analysis of over 60 published factor analyses, Frick et al. (1993) found that CP could be described by two bipolar dimensions. The first dimension was an overt–covert dimension. The overt pole consisted of directly confrontational behaviors such as oppositional defiant behaviors and aggression. In contrast, the covert pole consisted of behaviors that were nonconfrontational in nature (e.g., stealing and lying; see also Tiet, Wasserman, Loeber, Larken, & Miller, 2001; Willoughby, Kupersmidt, & Bryant, 2001). The second dimension divided the overt behaviors into those that were overt-destructive (aggression) and those that were overt-nondestructive (oppositional), and it divided the covert behaviors into those that were covert-destructive (property violations) and those that were covert-nondestructive (status offenses; i.e., those behaviors that are illegal because of the child or adolescent's age). One way in which this clustering of CP is useful is that the four-symptom patterns are fairly consistent with the distinctions made in many legal systems for differentiating types of delinquent behaviors, which generally distinguish between violent offenses (overt-destructive), status offenses (covert-nondestructive), and property offenses (covert-destructive; e.g., Office of Juvenile Justice and Delinquency Prevention, 1995).

Two specific forms of CP—noncompliance and aggression—deserve additional attention. Noncompliance (i.e., excessive disobedience to adults) appears to be important as one of the earliest predictors of the development of CP and it seems to play an important role in many of the subsequent academic and social problems exhibited by children with CP (Chamberlain & Patterson, 1995; McMahon & Forehand, 2003). Most importantly, however, research has shown that when child noncompliance is improved as a result of intervention, there is often concomitant improvement in other CP behaviors as well and a subsequent reduction in later risk for CP (Russo, Cataldo, & Cushing, 1981; Wells, Forehand, & Griest, 1980).

There is also evidence that aggression is an important dimension of CP. By its very nature, aggression results in harm to another child (Crick & Dodge, 1996). Furthermore, research has consistently shown that aggressive behavior in children and adolescents is often quite stable after the preschool years (Broidy et al., 2003). Importantly, research has found that there appears to be several different forms of aggressive behavior (Crick & Dodge, 1996; Poulin & Boivin, 2000). The first type of aggression is often referred to as retaliatory aggression, hostile aggression, or reactive aggression, in which aggression is viewed as a defensive reaction to a perceived threat and is characterized by anger and hostility (Crick & Dodge, 1996). The second type of aggressive behavior is generally unprovoked and is used for personal gain (instrumental) or to influence and coerce others (bullying and dominance). This type of aggressive behavior is referred to as instrumental aggression, premeditated aggression, or proactive aggression (Poulin & Boivin, 2000).

Importantly, although these different types of aggression are often correlated (e.g., correlations ranging from $r = .40$ to .70 in school-aged samples; Frick & Marsee, 2006), studies have consistently documented different correlates to the two forms of aggression (see Dodge & Petit, 2003; Frick & Marsee, 2006 for reviews). For example, reactive but not proactive aggression has been consistently linked to a tendency to misinterpret ambiguous behaviors as hostile provocation (Crick & Dodge, 1996; Hubbard, Dodge, Cillessen, Coie, & Schwartz, 2001) and to poorly regulated responses to emotional stimuli (Vitaro, Brengden, & Tremblay, 2002). In contrast, proactive but not reactive aggression has been associated with the tendency to view aggression as an effective means to reach goals (Crick & Dodge, 1996) and with reduced levels of emotional reactivity (i.e., skin conductance and heart rate acceleration; Hubbard et al., 2002; Muñoz, Frick, Kimonis, & Aucoin, in press).

In addition to proactive and reactive forms of aggression, both of which are overt in nature, several researchers have identified a form of indirect aggression, called relational aggression, that involves strategies that attempt to harm another child through harming his or her social relationships (Crick & Grotpeter, 1995). These behaviors include excluding a child from groups, rumor spreading, and friendship manipulation. Several studies have shown that when girls behave aggressively, they are more likely to use relational aggression than overt aggression (e.g., Crick & Grotpeter, 1995; Underwood, 2003). Further, research has suggested that it may be possible to divide relational aggression into instrumental and reactive forms, similar to overt aggression (Little, Jones, Henrich, & Hawley, 2003). Importantly, children who show relational aggression show many of the same social (e.g., peer rejection) and dispositional (e.g., impulsivity and callousness) risk factors as physically aggressive youth (Crick, Grotpeter, & Bigbee, 2002; Marsee & Frick, in press).

Epidemiology of CP

Prevalence estimates for CP in community samples of youth generally range between 6% and 10% (Loeber, Burke, Lahey, Winters, & Zera, 2000). When broken down by type of CP diagnoses found in DSM-IV-TR, ODD seems to be present in 3% to 5% of youth and CD is found in about 1% to 4% of youth (Loeber et al., 2000). Differences in prevalence rates across ethnic groups have not been found consistently. For example, higher rates of CP in African American youth have been found in some samples (Fabrega, Ulrich, & Mezzich, 1993) but not in others (McCoy, Frick, Loney, & Ellis, 2000). More importantly, it is unclear whether any association with minority status and CP is independent of the fact that ethnic minorities are more likely to experience economic hardships and live in urban neighborhoods with higher concentrations of crime than nonminority individuals (Lahey, Miller, Gordon, & Riley, 1999).

There is, however, consistent evidence for differences in prevalence rates of CP for children of different ages. The level of CP tends to decrease from the preschool to school-age years (Keenan & Shaw, 1997) and increase again in adolescence (Loeber et al., 2000). For example, Loeber et al. (2000) reported prevalence rates for CD of 5.6, 5.4, and 8.3 for boys aged 7, 11, and 13, respectively, and prevalence rates for ODD of 2.2, 4.8, and 5.0 for boys of the same age in a sample of 1,517 youth in a large urban area. However, the increase in the prevalence of CP from childhood to adolescence may not be consistent for all types of CP. Specifically, there is evidence that mild forms of physical aggression (e.g., fighting) show a decrease in prevalence rates across development, whereas nonaggressive and covert forms of antisocial behavior (e.g., lying and stealing) and serious aggression (e.g., armed robbery and sexual assault) show an increase in prevalence rates from childhood to adolescence (Loeber & Hay, 1997).

There also appear to be sex differences in the prevalence of CP. Overall estimates of the sex ratio for boys and girls with CP range from 2:1 to 4:1 (Loeber et al., 2000). However, this overall ratio hides several important developmental differences. Specifically, there are few sex differences between boys and girls in the prevalence rate of most types of CP prior to age 5 (Keenan & Shaw, 1997). However, after age 4 the rate of girls' behavior problems decreases while the rate of behavioral problems for boys either increases or stays at the same rate, leading to a male predominance of CP throughout much of childhood (Loeber et al., 2000). Numerous studies have also noted that the sex ratio between girls and boys with CP narrows dramatically from about 4:1 in childhood to about 2:1 in adolescence due to an increase in the number of girls engaging in CP in adolescence (see Silverthorn & Frick, 1999 for a review).

CP and Co-Occurring Problems in Adjustment

A consistent finding in research with children who show CP is that they often have a number of problems in adjustment, in addition to their CP, and these problems are critical to address in interventions. Attention-Deficit Hyperactivity Disorder (ADHD) is one of the most common comorbid conditions associated with CP. In a meta-analytic study, Waschbusch (2002) reported that 36% of boys and 57% of girls with CP had comorbid ADHD. Importantly, this review also suggested that the presence of ADHD often signals the presence of a more severe and more chronic form of CP in children. Internalizing disorders, such as depression and anxiety, also co-occur with CP at rates higher than expected by chance (Zoccolillo, 1992). In most cases, CP precedes the onset of depressive and anxiety symptoms and these symptoms are often viewed as consequences of the many adjustment problems experienced by a child with CP (Frick, Lilienfeld, Ellis, Loney, & Silverthorn, 1999; Loeber & Keenan, 1994). CP is also related to substance use (e.g., Hawkins, Catalano, & Miller, 1992). The comorbidity between CP and substance abuse is important because, when youths with CP also abuse substances, they tend to show an early onset of substance use and they are more likely to abuse multiple substances (Lynskey & Fergusson, 1995). With preschool-aged children, language impairment may be associated with CP (Wakschlag & Danis, 2004) and, in older children, CP is often associated with academic achievement below a level predicted by their intellectual level (Hinshaw, 1992).

Multiple Risks Associated with CP

Most researchers agree that CP is the result of a complex interaction of multiple causal factors (Frick, 2006; Hinshaw & Lee, 2003; McMahon, Wells, & Kotler, 2006). These factors can be summarized in five categories: biological factors, cognitive correlates, family context, peer context, and the broader social ecology (e.g., neighborhood and community). Although a number of biological correlates (e.g., neurochemical and autonomic irregularities) to CP have been identified and are likely important for causal theories (see Dodge & Pettit, 2003; Raine, 2002), they are not reviewed here because the current state of knowledge is not sufficiently developed to have clear implications for assessment.

In contrast, there are several aspects of the youth's cognitive and learning styles that have been associated with CP that may be important to the assessment process (see Frick & Loney, 2000). First, compared to others, youths with CP tend to score lower on intelligence tests, especially in the area of verbal intelligence (Loney, Frick, Ellis, & McCoy, 1998; Moffitt, 1993). Furthermore, these scores are predictive of the persistence of CP and engagement in delinquent behaviors during adolescence (Frick & Loney, 1999). Second, many children and adolescents with CP tend to show a learning style that is more sensitive to rewards than punishments. This has been labeled as a reward-dominant response style, and could explain why many of these youths persist in their maladaptive behaviors, despite the threat of serious potential consequences (Frick et al., 2003; O'Brien & Frick, 1996). Third, many youths with CP show a variety of deficits in their social cognition—that is, the way they interpret social cues and use them to respond in social situations (Crick & Dodge, 1994; Webster-Stratton & Lindsay, 1999). For example, children and adolescents with CP have been shown to have deficits in encoding social cues (e.g., lack of attention to relevant social cues), to make more hostile attributional biases and errors in the interpretation of social cues, to have deficient quantity and quality of generated solutions to social conflict, and to evaluate aggressive solutions more positively (Dodge & Petit, 2003).

The critical role of parenting practices in the development and maintenance of CP has been well established (e.g., Chamberlain & Patterson, 1995; Loeber & Stouthamer-Loeber, 1986). Types of parenting practices that have been closely associated with the development of CP include inconsistent discipline, irritable explosive discipline, poor supervision, lack of parental involvement, and rigid discipline (Chamberlain, Reid, Ray, Capaldi, & Fisher, 1997). In addition to parenting practices, various other risk factors that may have an impact on the family and may serve to precipitate or maintain CP have been identified. These familial factors include parental social cognitions (e.g., perceptions of the child), parental personal and marital adjustment (e.g., depression, ADHD, antisocial behavior, and substance abuse), and parental stress (McMahon & Estes, 1997; McMahon & Frick, 2005).

Research suggests that the child's relationship with peers can also play a significant role in the development, maintenance, and escalation of CP. Research has documented a relationship between peer rejection in elementary school and the later development of CP (Roff & Wirt, 1984). In addition, peer rejection in elementary school is predictive of an association with a deviant peer group (i.e., one that shows a high rate of antisocial behavior and substance abuse) in early adolescence (e.g., Fergusson, Swain, & Horwood, 2002). This relationship is important because association with a deviant peer group leads to an increase in the frequency and severity of CP (Patterson & Dishion, 1985), and it has proven to be a strong predictor of later delinquency (Patterson, Capaldi, & Bank, 1991) and substance abuse (Dishion, Capaldi, Spracklen, & Li, 1995; Fergusson et al., 2002).

Finally, there are factors within the youth's larger social ecology that have been associated with CP. One of the most consistently documented of these correlates has been low socioeconomic status (SES; Frick, Lahey, Hartdagen, & Hynd, 1989). However, several other ecological factors, many of which are related to low SES, such as poor housing, poor schools, and disadvantaged neighborhoods, have also been linked to the development of CP (see Frick, 1998; Peeples & Loeber, 1994). In addition, the high rate of violence witnessed by youths who live in impoverished inner-city neighborhoods has also been associated with CP (Osofsky, Wewers, Hann, & Fick, 1993).

Causal Theories of CP

Although there is general agreement that CP in children and adolescents is associated with multiple risk factors, there is less agreement as to how these risk factors play a role in the development of CP. Also, in addition to accounting for the large number of risk factors, causal theories of CP need to consider research suggesting that there may be many different causal pathways through which youth may develop these behaviors, each involving a different constellation of risk factors and each involving somewhat different causal processes (Frick, 2006).

The most widely accepted model for delineating distinct pathways in the development of CP distinguishes between childhood-onset and adolescent-onset subtypes of CP. That is, the DSM-IV-TR (American Psychiatric Association, 2000) makes the distinction between youths who begin showing CP before age 10 (i.e., childhood-onset) and those who do not show CP before age 10 (i.e., adolescent-onset). This distinction is supported by a substantial amount of research

documenting important differences between these two groups of youths with CP (see Moffitt, 2003; Frick, 2006 for reviews). Specifically, youths in the childhood-onset group show more serious aggression in childhood and adolescence and are more likely to continue to show antisocial and criminal behavior into adulthood (Frick & Loney, 1999; Moffitt & Caspi, 2001). More relevant to causal theory, many of the dispositional (e.g., temperamental risk and low intelligence) and contextual (e.g., family dysfunction) correlates that have been associated with CP are more strongly associated with the childhood-onset subtype. In contrast, the youths in the adolescent-onset subtype do not consistently show these same risk factors. If they do differ from other youths, it seems primarily to be in showing greater affiliation with delinquent peers and scoring higher on measures of rebelliousness and authority conflict (Moffitt & Caspi, 2001; Moffitt, Caspi, Dickson, Silva, & Stanton, 1996).

The different characteristics of youths in the two subtypes of CP have led to theoretical models that propose very different causal mechanisms operating across the two groups. For example, Moffitt (1993, 2003) has proposed that youth in the childhood-onset group develop CP behavior through a transactional process involving a difficult and vulnerable child (e.g., impulsive, with verbal deficits, and with a difficult temperament) who experiences an inadequate rearing environment (e.g., poor parental supervision and poor quality schools). This dysfunctional transactional process disrupts the child's socialization, leading to poor social relations with persons both inside (i.e., parents and siblings) and outside (i.e., peers and teachers) the family, which further disrupts the child's socialization. These disruptions lead to enduring vulnerabilities that can negatively affect the child's psychosocial adjustment across multiple developmental stages. In contrast, Moffitt views youths in the adolescent-onset pathway as showing an exaggeration of the normative developmental process of identity formation that takes place in adolescence. Their engagement in antisocial and delinquent behaviors is conceptualized as a misguided attempt to obtain a subjective sense of maturity and adult status in a way that is maladaptive (e.g., breaking societal norms) but encouraged by an antisocial peer group. Given that their behavior is viewed as an exaggeration of a process specific to the adolescent developmental stage and not due to enduring vulnerabilities, their CP is less likely to persist beyond adolescence. However, they may still have impairments that persist into adulthood due to the consequences of their CP (e.g., a criminal record, dropping out of school, and substance abuse; Moffitt & Caspi, 2001).

This distinction between childhood-onset and adolescent-onset trajectories to severe CP has been very influential for delineating different pathways through which youths may develop CP, although it is important to note that clear differences between the pathways are not always found (Lahey et al., 2000) and the applicability of this model to girls requires further testing (Silverthorn & Frick, 1999). Researchers have also begun extending this conceptualization in a number of important ways. For example, research has identified a subgroup of youths within the childhood-onset pathways who show high rates of callous and unemotional (CU) traits (e.g., lacking empathy and guilt). Importantly, Frick and Dickens (2006) reviewed 22 published studies showing that CU traits either co-occurred with ($n = 10$) or predicted ($n = 12$) serious antisocial and aggressive behavior. They also reviewed five studies showing that CU traits were related to poorer treatment response among youths with CP.

There is also evidence that the subgroup of CP youth with CU traits exhibits a distinct temperamental style from other youth with CP that has been variously labeled as low fearfulness (Rothbart & Bates, 1998) or low behavioral inhibition (Kagan & Snidman, 1991). This temperament could place a young child at risk for missing some of the early precursors to empathetic concern that involve emotional arousal evoked by the misfortune and distress of others (Blair, 1995; Frick & Morris, 2004), make them less responsive to typical parental socialization practices than other youths (Oxford, Cavell, & Hughes, 2003; Wootton, Frick, Shelton, & Silverthorn, 1997), and lead to impairments in their moral reasoning and empathic concern toward others (Blair, 1999; Pardini, Lochman, & Frick, 2003).

The few studies that have distinguished between youths within the childhood-onset group who differ on the presence of CU traits also provide some clues as to the mechanisms that may be involved in the development of CP in children and adolescents without these traits. These youths with CP who are not elevated on CU traits are less likely to be aggressive than those who are high on CU traits and, when they do act aggressively, it is more likely to be reactive in nature (Frick, Cornell, Barry, Bodin, & Dane, 2003)

and in response to real or perceived provocation by others (Frick, Cornell, Bodin, et al., 2003). Also, antisocial youths who do not show CU traits have CP that is more strongly associated with dysfunctional parenting practices (Oxford et al., 2003; Wootton et al., 1997). Finally, youths with CP, who do not show CU exhibit high levels of emotional distress (Frick et al., 1999; Frick, Cornell, Bodin, et al., 2003), are more reactive to the distress of others in social situations (Pardini et al., 2003) and are highly reactive to negative emotional stimuli (Kimonis, Frick, Fazekas, & Loney, 2006; Loney, Frick, Clements, Ellis, & Kerlin, 2003).

Overall, these findings suggest that a large number of children and adolescents with CP but without CU traits have problems regulating their emotions (Frick & Morris, 2004). These problems in emotion regulation can lead to very impulsive and unplanned aggressive and antisocial acts for which the child or adolescent may be remorseful afterwards but still may have difficulty controlling in the future (Pardini et al., 2003). The problems in emotion regulation can also make a youth particularly susceptible to becoming angry due to perceived provocations from peers leading to violent and aggressive acts within the context of high emotional arousal (Hubbard et al., 2002; Loney et al., 2003).

ASSESSMENT FOR DIAGNOSIS

When a child or adolescent with CP is referred for assessment, there are four primary goals for the assessment. First, it is important to determine whether or not the youth is, in fact, demonstrating significant levels of CP to rule out the possibility of the occasional inappropriate referral due to unrealistic parental or teacher expectations. Second, it is important to identify the types and severity of the youth's CP and to determine the degree and types of impairment associated with them. Some level of CP is normative and, as noted previously, there can be quite a range of CP that vary greatly in terms of how severe and impairing the behaviors are for the child. Assessing the level and severity of CP displayed by the child is critical to determine whether treatment is indicated and how intensive it needs to be. Third, given the high degree of comorbidity associated with CP, it is critical to at least screen for a wide variety of emotional, behavioral, social, and academic problems that can further influence the child's adjustment. Fourth, given the large number of risk factors that can contribute to the development and maintenance of CP, and that could be important targets of intervention, it is critical to assess the many dispositional and contextual risk factors that research has linked to CP in children and adolescents.

There are three primary assessment methods that can be used to accomplish these goals: behavior rating scales, structured diagnostic interviews, and behavioral observations. Each of these methods has specific strengths and weaknesses that they bring to the assessment process and we summarize these in the following paragraphs. In Table 3.1, we list some of the most commonly used empirically supported instruments for each method of assessment and we provide summary evaluations of their adequacy in terms of normative data, reliability, validity, generalizability, and clinical utility.

Behavior Rating Scales

Behavior rating scales are a core part of an assessment battery for assessing children and adolescents with CP. As noted in Table 3.1, there are a number of rating scales that are commercially available and they have a number of useful characteristics for meeting the goals outlined above.

First, most scales have subscales assessing different types of CP and they can be completed by adults who observe the youth in important psychosocial contexts (i.e., parents and teachers) and by the youth himself or herself. By having multiple informants who see the child in different settings, this can provide important information on the pervasiveness of the child's behavior problems and can help to detect potential biases in the report of any single informant. Most of the scales listed in Table 3.1 provide analogous content across the different raters. One notable exception is the Behavior Assessment System for Children, 2nd Edition (BASC-2; Reynolds & Kamphaus, 2004). In this scale, the teacher and parent versions are fairly similar in content, with the main difference being that teachers also rate behaviors indicative of learning problems and study skills. The content of the self-report version, however, is quite different. For example, the child does not rate his or her own level of CP but, instead, the self-report version provides more extended coverage of the child's attitudes (e.g., attitudes toward parents and teachers), his or her self-concept (e.g., self-esteem and sense of inadequacy), and his or her social relationships.

Second, rating scales provide some of the best norm-referenced data on a child's behavior. The most widely used rating scales (see Table 3.1) have large standardization samples that allow the child's ratings to be compared to the ratings of other children of the same age. This provides critical information to aid in determining whether the child's behavior is abnormal, given the child's age. For example, the standardization sample for the Achenbach System of Empirically Based Assessment (ASEBA; Achenbach & Rescorla, 2000, 2001) is representative of the 48 contiguous United States for SES, gender, ethnicity, region, and urban–suburban–rural residence (Achenbach & Rescorla, 2000, 2001). Similarly, the BASC-2 standardization samples ranged from 3,400 to 4,800 children and adolescents spanning 375 testing sites across the United States and Canada (Reynolds & Kamphaus, 2004).

Third, most rating scales contain many subscales, in addition to those assessing CP. These typically include scales assessing anxiety, depression, social problems, and family relationships. Thus, these rating scales can be very helpful in providing a broad screening of many of the most common co-occurring problems that are often found in children with CP and many of the risk factors that can play a role in the development and maintenance of CP. However, rating scales can vary on how well they assess the various co-occurring conditions. For example, the ASEBA does not include separate depression and anxiety scales, nor does it include a hyperactivity scale. Further, with the exception of the Child Symptom Inventory-IV (CSI-IV; Gadow & Sprafkin, 1998), which was explicitly designed to assess content reflected in the DSM-IV-TR, some of the scales do not correspond well to this classification system. For example, the attention problems scales on the ASEBA include items related to attention deficits (e.g., "can't concentrate" and "can't pay attention for long"), as well as items such as "acts too young for his/her age" and "nervous or high strung" that are not specific to inattention. However, the ASEBA now also includes DSM-oriented scales, such as Oppositional Defiant Problems and CP on the CBCL/6-18 (Achenbach, Dumenci, & Rescorla, 2003), and parent ratings on a Dutch version of the CBCL have been shown to predict DSM-IV diagnoses (Krol, De Bruyn, Coolen, & van Aarle, 2006).

Although an advantage of these rating scales is the breadth of their coverage of multiple areas of child functioning, the cost is that they often have only

TABLE 3.1 Ratings of Instruments Used for Diagnosis

Instrument	Norms	Internal Consistency	Inter-Rater Reliability	Test–Retest Reliability	Content Validity	Construct Validity	Validity Generalization	Clinical Utility	Highly Recommended
Rating Scales									
ASEBA	E	E	A	E	G	E	E	A	✓
BASC-2	E	E	A	E	E	G	E	A	✓
CSI-IV	G	A	A	A	E	G	G	A	
ECBI/SESBI-R	G	E	A	G	E	E	G	A	✓
Structured Interviews									
DICA	NA	NA	G	G	E	E	G	A	
DISC	NA	NA	G	G	E	E	G	A	✓
Behavioral Observations									
BCS	U	NA	A	U	A	G	G	A	✓
DPICS	L	NA	A	L	A	G	E	A	✓
Compliance test	L	E	E	A	A	G	A	A	
BASC-SOS	NA	NA	A	G	E	E	A	A	
ASEBA-DOF	NA	NA	G	G	E	E	A	A	
Impairment Indices									
CAFAS	G	NA	G	G	E	E	G	G	✓
CGAS	A	NA	G	G	E	E	G	G	

Note: ASEBA = Achenbach System of Empirically Based Assessment; BASC-2 = Behavior Assessment System for Children, 2nd Edition; CSI-IV = Child Symptom Inventory for DSM-IV; ECBI = Eyberg Child Behavior Inventory; SESBI-R = Sutter–Eyberg Child Behavior Inventory-Revised; DICA = Diagnostic Interview for Children and Adolescents; DISC = Diagnostic Interview Schedule for Children; BCS = Behavioral Coding System; DPICS = Dyadic Parent–Child Interaction Coding System; BASC-SOS = The BASC-2-Student Observational System; ASEBA-DOF = ASEBA Direct Observation Form; CAFAS = Child and Adolescent Functional Assessment Scale; CGAS = Children's Global Assessment Scale; L = Less than Adequate; A = Adequate; G = Good; E = Excellent; U = Unavailable; NA = Not Applicable.

minimal coverage of CP. There are, however, several rating scales that focus solely on CP and provide a more comprehensive coverage of various types of CP. For example, the Eyberg Child Behavior Inventory and Sutter–Eyberg Student Behavior Inventory-Revised (ECBI & SESBI-R; Eyberg & Pincus, 1999) are completed by parents and teachers, respectively. Both scales include 36 items describing specific CP behaviors and are scored on both a frequency-of-occurrence (Intensity) scale and a yes–no problem identification (Problem) scale. The inclusion of both frequency and problem ratings is very helpful in the diagnostic process to determine the level of impairment associated with the child's or adolescent's CP.

Interviews

The second major method for assessing CP is interviews. Interviews can be divided into two general categories: unstructured clinical interviews and structured diagnostic interviews. The clinical interview with the parent is important in the assessment of CP for a number of reasons. Besides providing a method for assessing the type, severity, and impairment associated with CP, the clinical interview with the parent helps to assess typical parent–child interactions that may be contributing to the CP, the antecedent conditions that may make CP behaviors more likely to occur, and the consequences that accompany such behaviors and either increase or decrease the likelihood that CP will reoccur. A number of interview formats are available to aid the clinician in obtaining information from the parents about their child's behavior and parent–child interactions (e.g., McMahon & Forehand, 2003; Patterson, Reid, Jones, & Conger, 1975; Wahler & Cormier, 1970). An individual interview with the child or adolescent may also be useful in providing the therapist with an opportunity to assess the child's perception of why he or she has been brought to the clinic and the child's subjective evaluation of his or her cognitive, affective, and behavioral characteristics (e.g., Bierman, 1983).

One criticism of the unstructured interview has been the difficulty in obtaining reliable information in this format. Structured interviews were developed in attempt to improve the reliability of the information that is obtained. As listed in Table 3.1, two structured diagnostic interviews that are frequently used in the assessment of children with CP are the Diagnostic Interview Schedule for Children (DISC;

e.g., Shaffer, Fisher, Lucas, Dulcan, & Schwab-Stone, 2000) and the Diagnostic Interview for Children and Adolescents (DICA; e.g., Reich, 2000). These and other similar interviews (see Loney and Frick, 2003, for a review) provide a structured format for obtaining parent and youth reports on the symptoms that constitute the criteria for ODD and CD according to DSM-IV-TR.

Similar to behavior rating scales, these interviews provide very structured question and answer formats and, thus, often lead to very reliable scores. The questions are typically asked in a stem and follow-up format. That is, a stem question is asked (e.g., "Does your child get into fights?") and follow-up questions are only asked if the stem question is answered affirmatively (e.g., "Is this only with his or her brothers and sisters?" and "Does he or she usually start these fights?"). Also similar to behavior rating scales, most structured interviews assess many other types of problems in adjustment, in addition to CP. Thus, they can be very helpful for providing an assessment of possible comorbid conditions that are often present in youth with CP.

However, as noted in Table 3.1, unlike behavior rating scales, structured interviews often do not provide normative information on a child's or parent's responses. Instead, structured interviews typically focus on assessing how much CP and other problems in adjustment impair a child's or adolescent's social and academic functioning. Also, unlike behavior ratings scales, most interview schedules provide standard questions that assess the age at which a child's behavioral difficulties began to emerge and how long they have caused problems for the child. As noted previously, the age at which CP emerge can be very important for designating distinct groups of youth with CP who have different factors leading to their behavior problems. Also, the assessment of age of onset of CP and other problems in adjustment allows for some estimate of the temporal ordering of a child's problems, such as whether the child's CP predated his/her emotional difficulties. Such information could help in determining whether the emotional distress is best conceptualized as being a result of the impairments caused by the CP.

However, there are a number of limitations in the information provided by structured interviews (see Loney & Frick, 2003). If the child has a number of problems, and many stem questions are answered affirmatively requiring the administration of extensive follow-up questions, the interviews can be very lengthy. That is, their administration time can range from 45 minutes for youths with few problems to over 2 hours for youths with many problems in adjustment (Loney & Frick, 2003). Further, most structured interviews do not have formats for obtaining teacher information, and obtaining reliable information from young children (below age 9) has been difficult with most structured interviews (Kamphaus & Frick, 2005). Perhaps one of the major limitations in the use of structured interviews, however, is evidence that the number of symptoms reported declines within an interview schedule. That is, parents and youths tend to report more symptoms for diagnoses assessed early in the interview, regardless of which diagnoses are assessed first (Jensen, Watanabe, & Richters, 1999; Piacentini et al., 1999). This finding calls into question the validity of diagnoses assessed later in the interview. Unfortunately, CP is often assessed last in most of the available interview schedules and, as a result, could be most influenced by this limitation.

Behavioral Observation

Behavioral observations provide a third common way of assessing CP behaviors. Behavioral observations in a child's or adolescent's natural setting (e.g., home, school, and playground) can make an important contribution to the assessment process by providing an assessment of the youth's behavior that is not filtered through the perceptions of an informant and by providing an assessment of the immediate environmental context of the youth's behavior. For example, behavioral observations can indicate how others in the child's environment (e.g., parents, teachers, and peers) respond to the child's CP; this could be very important for identifying factors that may be maintaining these behaviors.

Two widely used, structured, microanalytic observation procedures available for assessing CP and parental responses to these behaviors in younger (3–8 years) children in the clinic and the home are the Behavioral Coding System (BCS; Forehand & McMahon, 1981) and the Dyadic Parent–Child Interaction Coding System (DPICS; Eyberg, Nelson, Duke, & Boggs, 2005). The BCS and the DPICS are modifications of the assessment procedure developed by Hanf (1970) for the observation of parent–child interactions in the clinic. As employed in clinic settings, both the BCS and DPICS place the parent–child dyad in standard

situations that vary in the degree to which parental control is required, ranging from a free-play situation (i.e., Child's Game and Child-Directed Interaction) to one in which the parent directs the child's activity, either in the context of parent-directed play (i.e., Parent's Game and Parent-Directed Interaction) or in cleaning up the toys (i.e., Clean Up). Each task typically lasts 5 to 10 minutes. In the home setting, observations usually occur in a less structured manner (e.g., the parent and child are instructed to "do whatever you would normally do together"). In each coding system, a variety of parent and child behaviors are scored, many of which emphasize parental antecedents (e.g., commands) or consequences (e.g., use of verbal hostility) to the child's behavior. One of the main limitations of these observational systems is the very intensive training (e.g., 20 to 25 hours for the BCS) required of observers so that they reliably code the parent and child behaviors. This characteristic often limits the usefulness of these systems in many clinical settings (Frick, 2000). However, simplified versions of both the DPICS and the BCS have been developed to reduce training demands and may ultimately prove to be more useful to clinicians (Eyberg, Bessmer, Newcomb, Edwards, & Robinson, 1994; McMahon & Estes, 1994).

As noted previously, an important type of CP, especially in young children, is noncompliance. A direct observational assessment of child noncompliance can also be obtained in the clinic with the Compliance Test (CT; Roberts & Powers, 1988). In the CT, the parent is instructed to give a series of 30 standard commands without helping or following up on the commands with other verbalizations or nonverbal cues. In one version of the CT, two-part commands are given (e.g., "[Child's name], put the [toy] in the [container]."). In another version, the commands are separated into two codeable units (e.g. "[Child's name], pick up the [toy]. Put it in the [container]."). The CT takes between 5 and 15 minutes to complete. The CT has proven useful in identifying noncompliant preschool children in research and clinical settings (Roberts & Powers, 1990).

Many common CP behaviors are by nature covert (e.g., lying, stealing, and firesetting), which makes them more difficult to capture through observational techniques. However, Hinshaw and colleagues have developed and evaluated an analogue observational procedure to assess stealing, property destruction, and cheating in children ages 6–12 (Hinshaw,

Heller, & McHale, 1992; Hinshaw, Simmel, & Heller, 1995; Hinshaw, Zupan, Simmel, Nigg, & Melnick, 1997). Samples of boys (ages 6–12) with ADHD (most of whom also had ODD or CD) and a comparison group were asked to complete an academic worksheet alone in a room that contained a completed answer sheet, money, and toys. Stealing was measured by conducting a count of objects in the room immediately following the work session, whereas property destruction and cheating were assessed by ratings derived from observing the child's behavior during the session. Each of these observational measures of covert CP was correlated with parental ratings of covert CP. Stealing and property destruction were also associated with staff ratings.

There are also several behavioral observational systems that have been developed for use in school settings (Nock & Kurtz, 2005). For example, the BCS (Forehand & McMahon, 1981) has been modified for use in the classroom to assess teacher–child interactions, both alone (e.g., Breiner & Forehand, 1981) and in combination with a measure of academic engaged time (AET; McNeil, Eyberg, Eisenstadt, Newcomb, & Funderburk, 1991). Academic engaged time is the amount of time that a child or adolescent is appropriately engaged in on-task behavior during class time and is assessed using a simple stopwatch recording procedure (Walker, Colvin, & Ramsey, 1995).

The BASC-2-Student Observational System (SOS; Reynolds & Kamphaus, 2004) provides a system for observing children's behavior in the classroom using a momentary time-sampling procedure. The SOS specifies 65 behaviors that are common in classrooms settings and includes both adaptive (e.g., "follows directions" and "returns material used in class") and maladaptive (e.g., "fidgets in seat" and "teases others") behaviors. The observation period in the classroom involves 15 minutes that are divided into 30 intervals of 30 seconds each. The child's behavior is observed for 3 seconds at the end of each interval and the observer codes all behaviors that were observed during this time window. Scores from this observation system have differentiated students with CP from other children (Lett & Kamphaus, 1997).

Another classroom observational system, the ASEBA-DOF (Achenbach & Rescorla, 2001) was designed to observe students, ages 5–14, for 10-minute periods in the classroom. Three types of information are recorded. First, at the end of each minute during the observational period, the child's behavior is coded as being on- or off-task for 5 seconds. Second, at the end of the observational period, the observer writes a narrative of the child's behavior throughout the 10-minute observational period, noting the occurrence, duration, and intensity of specific problems. Third, and also at the end of the observational period, the observer codes 96 behaviors on a 4-point scale (0 = "behavior was not observed," through 3 = "definite occurrence of behavior with severe intensity or for greater than 3 minutes duration"). These ratings can be summed into Total Problem, Internalizing, and Externalizing behavior composites. The ASEBA-DOF has been shown to discriminate between referred and nonreferred children in the classroom (e.g., Reed & Edelbrock, 1983), as well as between children with CP from children with other behavior problems (e.g., McConaughey, Achenbach, & Gent, 1988).

One limitation in observational systems is the potential for reactivity, whereby the child's behavior can change because the child knows that he or she is being observed (Aspland & Gardner, 2003). An alternative to observations by independent observers that can reduce reactivity is to train significant adults in the child's or adolescent's environment to observe and record certain types of behavior. The most widely used procedure of this type is the Parent Daily Report (PDR; Chamberlain & Reid, 1987), a parent observation measure that is typically administered during brief (5 to 10 minutes) telephone interviews. Parents are asked which of a number of overt and covert behaviors have occurred in the past 24 hours. The PDR has shown moderate convergent validity with other parent report measures of child CP (Chamberlain & Reid, 1987; Webster-Stratton & Spitzer, 1991).

Functional Impairment

Most of the measures described above focus on the type, frequency, and severity of the child's CP. However, it is being increasingly recognized that the child's or adolescent's level of functional impairment can vary greatly, even with similar levels of CP (Bird, 1999; Bloomquist & Schnell, 2002). Knowledge of impairment is important for a number of reasons. First, it can determine how intensive an intervention may need to be for a child and the most appropriate setting for this treatment (Frick, 2004), it can provide useful information to the clinician concerning possible intervention targets (Frick, 2006), and it may also serve as an important indicator of intervention outcome (Hodges, Xue, & Wotring, 2004). As noted above, structured interviews based on the DSM-IV-TR allow for the assessment of impairment. In Table 3.1, we list two measures designed specifically to assess the youth's level of impairment: the Children's Global Assessment Scale (CGAS; Shaffer et al., 1983; Bird et al., 1993) and the Child and Adolescent Functional Assessment Scale (CAFAS; Hodges, 2000). Also, several of the broad rating scales summarized in Table 3.1 include subscales that assess important areas of potential impairment of children with CP. For example, the BASC-2 (Reynolds & Kamphaus, 2004) contains scales assessing the child's academic adjustment (e.g., learning problems, attitude toward school and teacher, and study skills), social adjustment (e.g., social stress and interpersonal relations), and self-concept (e.g., self-concept and sense of inadequacy).

Overall Evaluation

In summary, assessing the types, severity, and age of onset of CP displayed by the child, as well assessing common co-occurring problems in adjustment, are all critical to the assessment of children and adolescents with CP. Behavior rating scales, unstructured and structured interviews, and behavioral observations all can help in this process and each have their unique strengths and weaknesses. Thus, typical assessments of children with CP would include multiple methods of assessment that utilize the strengths of these different approaches.

Behavior rating scales, similar to the BASC-2 and ASEBA, typically provide the best norm-referenced information that allows for the comparison of a child's level of CP to a normative comparison group. Rating scales also typically have formats for obtaining information from several different informants who see the child in different settings (e.g., parents and teachers) and they provide a time-efficient method for assessing a number of possible co-occurring problems that may be present in youths with CP. In contrast, structured interviews, similar to the DICA and DISC, tend to be more time-consuming and are often limited in the normative information that they provide. However, they typically provide more information on the level of impairment associated with the child's CP and the age at which the problem behavior began. Finally, behavioral observation systems, such as the BCS and DPICS, provide an assessment of the child's behavior that is not filtered through the perceptions of an informant, and they provide a method for assessing the environmental contingencies that can be involved in the development or maintenance of CP. However, many behavioral observation systems require extensive training to reliably code the child's behavior and they are often limited in the normative information they provide.

ASSESSMENT FOR CASE CONCEPTUALIZATION AND TREATMENT PLANNING

The research reviewed previously indicated that children with CP often have multiple comorbid conditions that are important to consider in treatment planning and there are often multiple risk factors that can be involved in the development or maintenance of CP. As a result, many of the rating scales and structured interviews described in the previous section on diagnosis are also included in Table 3.2 because they are also critical for case conceptualization and treatment planning purposes. These measures provide a broad assessment of the child's functioning and capture the many important co-occurring problems in adjustment and risk factors that can be used in treatment planning.

A key area of research for guiding the assessment process is the research documenting various potential developmental pathways to CP. As reviewed previously, children with CP can fall into childhood-onset or adolescent-onset pathways, depending on when in development their level of severe antisocial and aggressive behavior started. Also, within the childhood-onset group, there seems to be important differences between those who do and do not show high levels of CU traits. Knowledge of the characteristics of children in these different pathways, and the different causal mechanisms involved, can serve as a guide for structuring and conducting the assessment (McMahon & Frick, 2005). Further, interventions can be tailored to the unique needs of youth in these different pathways (Frick, 2006).

Specifically, knowledge of the developmental pathways can provide a set of working hypotheses concerning the nature of the CP behavior, the most likely comorbid conditions, and the most likely risk factors (McMahon & Frick, 2005). For example, for a youth whose CP appears to onset in adolescence, one would hypothesize based on the available literature

TABLE 3.2 Ratings of Instruments Used for Case Conceptualization and Treatment Planning

Instrument	Norms	Internal Consistency	Inter-Rater Reliability	Test–Retest Reliability	Content Validity	Construct Validity	Validity Generalization	Clinical Utility	Highly Recommended
Rating Scales									
APSD	A	A	A	G	E	G	A	A	✓
ASEBA	E	E	A	E	G	E	E	A	✓
BASC-2	E	E	A	E	E	G	E	A	✓
CSI-IV	G	NA	A	A	E	G	G	A	
ECBI/SESBI-R	G	E	A	G	E	E	G	A	
Structured Interviews									
DICA	NA	NA	G	G	E	E	G	A	
DISC	NA	NA	G	G	E	E	G	A	✓
Behavioral Observations									
BCS	U	NA	A	U	A	G	G	A	✓
DPICS	L	NA	A	L	A	G	E	A	✓
Compliance test	L	E	E	A	A	G	A	A	
PDR	L	U	E	A	A	G	E	A	✓
BASC-SOS	NA	NA	A	G	E	E	A	A	
ASEBA-DOF	NA	NA	G	G	E	E	A	A	

Note: APSD = Antisocial Process Screening Device; ASEBA = Achenbach System of Empirically Based Assessment; BASC-2 = Behavior Assessment System for Children, 2nd Edition; CSI-IV = Child Symptom Inventory for DSM-IV; ECBI = Eyberg Child Behavior Inventory; SESBI-R = Sutter–Eyberg Child Behavior Inventory-Revised ; DICA = Diagnostic Interview for Children and Adolescents; DISC = Diagnostic Interview Schedule for Children; BCS = Behavioral Coding System; DPICS = Dyadic Parent–Child Interaction Coding System; PDR = Parent Daily Report; BASC-SOS = The BASC-2-Student Observational System; ASEBA-DOF = ASEBA Direct Observation Form; L = Less than Adequate; A = Adequate; G = Good; E = Excellent; U = Unavailable; NA = Not Applicable.

that he or she is less likely to be aggressive, to have intellectual deficits, to have temperamental vulnerabilities, and to have comorbid ADHD. However, the youth's association with a deviant peer group and factors that may contribute to this deviant peer group affiliation (e.g., lack of parental monitoring and supervision) would be especially important to assess for youth in this pathway. In contrast, for a youth whose serious CP began prior to adolescence, one would expect more cognitive and temperamental vulnerabilities, comorbid ADHD, and more serious problems in family functioning. For those youths in this childhood-onset group who do not show CU traits, the cognitive deficits would more likely be verbal deficits and the temperamental vulnerabilities would more likely be problems regulating emotions, leading to higher levels of anxiety, depression, and aggression involving anger. In contrast, for a youth with childhood-onset CP who shows high levels of CU traits, the cognitive deficits are more likely to involve a lack of sensitivity to punishment and the temperamental vulnerabilities are more likely to involve a preference for dangerous and novel activities and a failure to experience many types of emotion (e.g., guilt and empathy). Further, assessing the level and severity of aggressive behavior, especially the presence of instrumental aggression, would be critical for youths in this group.

As most clinicians recognize, people do not often fall neatly into the prototypes that are suggested by research. Therefore, these descriptions are meant to serve as hypotheses around which to organize an evidence-based assessment. They also highlight several specific important pieces of information that are needed when assessing children and adolescents with CP. One of the most critical pieces of information in guiding assessment, and perhaps ultimately intervention, is determining the age at which various CP behaviors began. This information provides some indication as to whether or not the youth may be on the childhood-onset pathway. Unfortunately, there has been little consistency in the literature concerning the most appropriate operational definition of childhood- versus adolescent-onset or even whether this distinction should be based on chronological age or on the pubertal status of the child (Moffitt, 2003). For example, the DSM-IV-TR makes the distinction between children who begin showing severe CP behaviors before age 10 (i.e., childhood-onset) and those who do not show severe CP before age 10 (i.e., adolescent-onset) in its definition of CD. However, other research studies have used age 11

(Robins, 1966) or age 14 (Patterson & Yoerger, 1993; Tibbets & Piquero, 1999) to define the start of adolescent onset. Thus, onset of severe CP before age 10 seems to be clearly considered childhood-onset and onset after age 13 clearly adolescent-onset. However, how to classify children whose CP onset between the ages of 11 and 13 is less clear and probably dependent on the level of physical, cognitive, and social maturity of the child.

Based on this research, it is therefore important for treatment planning to assess the age at which the child began showing serious CP. As noted above, an important advantage that many structured interviews have over behavior rating scales and behavioral observations is that they provide a structured method for assessing when a youth first began showing serious CP, thereby providing an important source of information on the developmental trajectory of the CP behavior. For example, in the DISC-IV (Shaffer et al., 2000), any question related to the presence of a CD symptom that is answered affirmatively is followed by questions asking the parent or youth to estimate at what age the first occurrence of the behavior took place. Obviously, such questions can also be integrated into an unstructured interview format as well.

In either case, however, there is always some concern about how accurate the parent or youth is in reporting the timing of specific behaviors. There are three findings from research that can help in interpreting such reports. First, the longer the time frame involved in the retrospective report (e.g., a parent of a 17-year-old reporting on preschool behavior vs. a parent of a 6-year-old reporting on preschool behavior), the less accurate the report is likely to be (Green, Loeber, & Lahey, 1991). Second, although a parental report of the exact age of onset may not be very reliable over time, typical variations in years are usually small and the relative rankings within symptoms (e.g., which symptom began first) and within a sample (e.g., which children exhibited the earliest onset of behavior) seem to be fairly stable (Green et al., 1991). As a result, these reports should be viewed as rough estimates of the timing of onset and not as exact dating procedures. Third, there is evidence that combining informants (e.g., such as a parent or youth) or combining sources of information (e.g., self-report and record of police contact), and taking the earliest reported age of onset from any source, provide an estimate that shows somewhat greater validity than any single source of information alone (Lahey et al., 1999).

If the youth's history of CP is consistent with the childhood-onset pathway, then additional assessment to examine the extent to which CU traits may also be present is important. The Antisocial Process Screening Device (Frick & Hare, 2001), described in Table 3.2, is a behavior rating scale completed by parents and teachers to identify children with CP who also exhibit CU traits (Christian et al., 1997; Frick, Bodin, & Barry, 2000; Frick, O'Brien, Wootton, & McBurnett, 1994). A self-report version of this scale is also available for older children and adolescents and it has been validated in a number of studies (Muñoz & Frick, 2007). A more extended assessment of these traits is also in the early stages of development (Essau, Sasagawa, & Frick, 2006; Kimonis et al., in press). However, both these scales currently lack normative data from which to make interpretations and, as a result, are not included in Table 3.2.

The key implication from research on the developmental pathways to CP is that the most appropriate treatment for a child or adolescent with CP may differ depending on characteristics of the child and factors in his or her environment that are operating to maintain these behaviors. This approach is very consistent with functional behavioral assessment (FBA) methods that focus on conducting an individualized assessment of each child's needs and matching intervention strategies to those needs (LaRue & Handelman, 2006; Walker, Ramsey, & Gresham, 2004). The typical FBA involves a specification of problem behaviors in operational terms (e.g., what types of CP are being exhibited in the classroom), as well as identification of events that reliably predict and control behavior through an examination of antecedents and consequences. For example, an FBA at school would determine whether the child's CP is occurring only in certain classes or situations (e.g., during class change and at lunch) and if there are certain factors that reliably lead to the CP (e.g., teasing by peers and disciplinary confrontations with teachers). It would also determine the consequences that are associated with the CP that may contribute to their likelihood of occurring in the future (e.g., getting sent home from school and preventing further teasing). Information relevant to an FBA can be gathered through interviews with significant others in the child's environment or through direct observations of the child in his or natural environment. Thus, several of the behavioral observation systems described previously are also quite important for case conceptualization and treatment planning for the child with CP.

Overall Evaluation

In summary, this section highlighted several critical issues for using assessment information for planning treatment for children with CP. First, because children with CP often have many co-occurring problems in adjustment that are important to address in treatment, it is critical that methods for assessing potential comorbid problems, such as behavior rating scales and structured interviews, can be used in treatment planning. Second, because children who show different developmental trajectories of their CP may require different approaches to treatment, it is critical to assess key characteristics that distinguish among children in these trajectories. Specifically, assessing the age at which the child began to exhibit CP, either through structured or unstructured interviews, and assessing the presence of CU traits using a scale such as the APSD, are both critical to the treatment planning process. Third, because environmental contingencies have proven to be very important for understanding factors that can either lead to or maintain CP in children and adolescents, assessment of these contingencies through unstructured interviews or behavior observations is also critical for the treatment planning process.

ASSESSMENT FOR TREATMENT MONITORING AND TREATMENT OUTCOME

Most of the applications of research for guiding the assessment process have focused on making diagnostic decisions (e.g., determining whether CP should be the primary source of concern and whether it is severe and impairing enough to warrant treatment) and on treatment planning (e.g., determine what types of intervention may be needed by the child; McMahon & Frick, 2005). However, an important third goal of the assessment process is monitoring the progress of intervention and evaluating treatment outcome. That is, evidence-based assessments should provide a means for testing whether interventions have brought about meaningful changes in the child's or adolescent's adjustment, either for better or worse (i.e., an iatrogenic effect). This is particularly important in the area of CP, given a number of documented cases in which treatments have lead to increases, rather than decreases, in problem behavior for some youth with CP (Dishion, McCord, & Poulin, 1999; Dodge, Dishion, & Lansford, 2006).

A few of the behavior rating scales and observational measures described previously have demonstrated sensitivity to intervention outcomes. These are described in Table 3.3. For example, scores from the ASEBA have proven to be sensitive to changes brought about by the treatment of youth with CP (e.g., DeGarmo, Patterson, & Forgatch, 2004; Eisenstadt, Eyberg, McNeil, Newcomb, & Funderburk, 1993). Also, the ECBI/SESBI-R scales have proven to change after parent management training interventions with young children (e.g., Eisenstadt et al., 1993; McNeil et al., 1991; Nixon, Sweeney, Erickson, & Touyz, 2003; Webster-Stratton & Hammond, 1997). Importantly, because these rating scales often provide norm-referenced scores, these scales can be critical for determining not only whether or not the intervention has led to significant decreases in the child's level of CP but also whether the behavior has been brought within a level that is normative for the child's age.

However, behavior rating scales completed by parents who are involved in treatment could be influenced by expectancy effects on the part of the parents who anticipate positive responses to an intervention. Thus, it is important to include ratings of the child's behavior from others who may not have been involved in the treatment or to include behavioral observations of treatment effects whenever possible, especially if the observer is unaware if the child and his or her parents were involved in treatment or unaware if the observation is pre- or posttreatment. Two observational systems described previously, the BCS and the DPICS, have been used in this way as an outcome measure for parenting interventions for CP (e.g., Eisenstadt et al., 1993; Herschell, Calzado, Eyberg, & McNeil, 2002; McMahon, Forehand, & Griest, 1981; Peed, Roberts, & Forehand, 1977; Webster-Stratton & Hammond, 1997). The PDR, which uses the parent as an observer, has also been used as a treatment outcome indicator but, similar to behavior rating scales, the observations by parents who are involved in treatment could be biased (Bank, Marlowe, Reid, Patterson, & Weinrott, 1991; Chamberlain & Reid, 1991; Webster-Stratton & Hammond, 1997).

As noted previously in the discussion of measures used to diagnose severe levels of CP, children with the same level of CP can vary greatly on the level of impairment associated with their CP. Thus, assessing the child's level of functional impairment after treatment is also an important assessment goal. The two measures of functional impairment included in Table 3.3, the CAFAS and the CGAS, have both proven to be sensitive to treatment effects (Hodges et al., 2004; Shaffer et al., 1983). Also, a number of the rating scales noted in Table 3.3, such as the ASEBA and BASC-2, assess important areas of potential impairment for children with CP such as the child's academic and social adjustment.

Although many measures have been used to assess treatment outcome, there has been very little research on the use of assessment measures to monitor the effects of ongoing intervention for CP. Exceptions to this are the structured observational analogues employed in some parent management training programs for young oppositional children that are employed repeatedly throughout the course of treatment, not only to monitor progress, but also to determine whether the parent has met specific behavioral performance criteria necessary for progression to the next step of the parenting intervention (Herschell et al., 2002; McMahon & Forehand, 2003).

Another assessment domain related to treatment outcome that has had only minimal research focus is in the assessment of treatment satisfaction. This is a form of social validity that may be assessed in terms of satisfaction with the outcome of treatment, therapists, treatment procedures, and teaching format (McMahon & Forehand, 1983). Given the diversity of treatments that are needed for youth with CP, no single consumer satisfaction measure is appropriate for use with all types of interventions for youth with CP and their families. The Therapy Attitude Inventory (TAI; Brestan, Jacobs, Rayfield, & Eyberg, 1999; Eyberg, 1993) and the Parent's Consumer Satisfaction Questionnaire (PCSQ; McMahon & Forehand, 2003; McMahon, Tiedemann, Forehand, & Griest, 1984) are examples of measures designed to evaluate parental satisfaction with parent management training programs (e.g., Brinkmeyer & Eyberg, 2003; McMahon & Forehand, 2003). Importantly, these measures largely focus on the parents' satisfaction with treatment. Children and adolescents themselves have rarely been asked about their satisfaction with treatment, with the exception of some evaluations of Multisystemic Therapy with adolescents (e.g., Henggeler et al., 1999).

TABLE 3.3 Ratings of Instruments Used for Treatment Monitoring and Treatment Outcome Evaluation

Instrument	Norms	Internal Consistency	Inter-Rater Reliability	Test–Retest Reliability	Content Validity	Construct Validity	Validity Generalization	Treatment Sensitivity	Clinical Utility	Highly Recommended
Rating Scales										
ASEBA (DSM scales)	E	E	A	E	G	E	E	G	A	✓
ECBI/SESBI-R	G	E	A	G	E	E	G	G	A	✓
Behavioral Observations										
BCS	U	NA	A	U	A	G	G	G	A	✓
DPICS	L	NA	A	L	A	G	E	G	A	✓
Compliance test	L	E	E	A	A	G	A	G	A	
PDR	L	U	E	A	A	G	E	E	A	✓
Impairment Indices										
CAFAS	G	NA	G	G	E	E	G	G	G	
CGAS	A	NA	G	G	E	E	G	G	G	✓
Treatment Satisfaction surveys										
PCSQ	U	U	NA	U	A	A	U	NA	A	
TAI	U	E	NA	G	A	G	A	NA	A	✓

Note: ASEBA = Achenbach System of Empirically Based Assessment; ECBI = Eyberg Child Behavior Inventory; SESBI-R = Sutter–Eyberg Child Behavior Inventory-Revised; BCS = Behavioral Coding System; DPICS = Dyadic Parent–Child Interaction Coding System; PDR = Parent Daily Report; CAFAS = Child and Adolescent Functional Assessment Scale; CGAS = Children's Global Assessment Scale; PCSQ = Parent's Consumer Satisfaction Questionnaire; TAI = Therapy Attitude Inventory; L = Less than Adequate; A = Adequate; G = Good; E = Excellent; U = Unavailable; NA = Not Applicable.

There are several important issues involved in selecting measures suitable for treatment monitoring and outcome evaluation (McMahon & Frick, 2005; McMahon & Metzler, 1998). First, the way questions on a rating scale are framed could affect its sensitivity to change. For example, the response scale on a behavior rating scale may be too general (e.g., "never" vs. "sometimes" vs. "always") or the time interval for reporting the frequency of a behavior (e.g., the past 6 months) may not be discrete enough to detect changes brought about by treatment. Second, a consistent finding when using structured interviews is that parents and children often report fewer symptoms on the second administration (Jensen et al., 1999; Piacentini et al., 1999). Thus, structured interviews are typically not good measures of treatment outcome because it is unclear whether any reductions in CP between pre- and posttreatment measures are due to the treatment or due to this normal decrease in symptoms over repeated administrations. Third, assessment-by-intervention interactions may occur when evaluating treatment outcomes. For example, as a function of intervention, parents may learn to become more effective monitors of their child's behavior. As a consequence, they may become more aware of their children's CP. Comparison of parental reports of their child's behavior prior to and after the intervention may actually suggest that parents perceive deterioration in their children's behavior, when in reality the parents have simply become more accurate reporters of such behavior (Dishion & McMahon, 1998).

Overall Evaluation

Unfortunately, the development of measures to adequately monitor treatment progress and treatment outcome for children and adolescents with CP has not advanced as far as the development of measures for diagnosis and treatment planning. This is a particularly unfortunate state of affairs in the treatment of CP, given that several treatments have proven to have potentially harmful effects on youth by leading to increases in behavior problems after treatment. However, several behavior rating scales, most notably the ASEBA and ECBI, have proven to be sensitive to the effects of treatment and they both provide norm-referenced scores to determine whether the child's level of CP was brought within a level that is normative for his or her age. Several behavioral observations systems, such as the BCS and DPICS, have also been used to both monitor the progress of treatment, as well as to evaluate treatment outcome. There have been a few measures developed to assess child's or parent's satisfaction with treatment. However, development of better evidence-based measures for this purpose is a critical area for future research.

CONCLUSIONS AND FUTURE DIRECTIONS

In this chapter, we have summarized several areas of research that have important implications for guiding assessments for youth with CP and summarized some recommended methods for accomplishing three primary assessment goals: diagnosis of non-normative and impairing forms of CP; case conceptualization and treatment planning; and monitoring and evaluating treatment outcome. In this concluding section, we seek to highlight some overarching issues that influence methods for meeting all of these assessment goals and to highlight some important areas for future research.

The first overarching issue is the need for a comprehensive assessment in most cases when assessing youth with CP. That is, an adequate assessment of a youth with CP must assess multiple aspects of the child's or adolescent's adjustment (e.g., CP, anxiety, and learning problems) in multiple settings (e.g., home and school; Kamphaus & Frick, 2005; McMahon & Estes, 1997; McMahon & Frick, 2005). However, it is also important to note that all of the individual assessment techniques summarized in Tables 1 through 3 have limitations. Thus, it is critical to assess the child using multiple methods whenever possible (Kamphaus & Frick, 2005). Because of issues of time, expense, and practicality, how best to acquire and interpret this large array of information become important issues. One approach is to use a multistage method, which starts with more time-efficient measures (e.g., broadband behavior rating scales and unstructured clinical interviews) that are followed by more time-intensive measures (e.g., structured interviews and behavioral observations) when indicated (McMahon & Estes, 1997; McMahon & Frick, 2005; Nock & Kurtz, 2005).

Whether or not a multistage method is used, there are few guidelines available to guide clinicians as to how to integrate and synthesize the multiple pieces of information that are obtained in the assessment to make important clinical decisions. This endeavor is made more complicated by the fact that information from different informants (Achenbach, McConaughy, & Howell, 1987; De Los Reyes & Kazdin, 2005) and from different methods (Barkley, 1991) often shows only modest correlations with each other. As a result, after collecting multiple sources of information on a youth's adjustment, the assessor often must make sense out of an array of often conflicting information.

Several strategies for integrating and interpreting information from comprehensive assessments have been proposed (Kamphaus & Frick, 2005; McMahon & Forehand, 2003; Wakschlag & Danis, 2004). For example, Kamphaus and Frick (2005) outline a multistage strategy for integrating results from a comprehensive assessment into a clear case conceptualization to guide treatment planning. At the first step, the assessor documents all clinically significant findings regarding the youth's adjustment (e.g., elevations on ratings scales, diagnoses from structured interviews, and problem behaviors from observations). At the second step, the assessor looks for convergent findings across these methods. At the third step, the assessor attempts to explain, using available research as much as possible, any discrepancies in the assessment results. For example, a finding that a child and parent are reporting high rates of anxiety but not the teacher may be explained by research suggesting that teachers may not be aware of a student's level of anxiety in the classroom (Achenbach et al., 1987). At the fourth step, the assessor then develops a profile of the areas of most concern for the child and develops a coherent explanation for the child's CP, again using existing research as much as possible. This process was illustrated previously in using research on the developmental pathways to CP to guide a case conceptualization. Although this approach to interpreting results of a comprehensive assessment is promising, much more research is needed to guide this process of integrating data from comprehensive assessments.

Another issue that requires further attention is the great need to enhance the clinical utility of evidence-based assessment tools (Frick, 2000; Hodges, 2004). Many of the assessment measures that have been used in research have not been developed in such as way that make them useful in clinical practice. For example, Frick and Loney (2000) reviewed a number of performance-based measures that have been used in research with children with CP. They concluded that few of these measures have been used in the

same format across multiple samples that would allow for the development of meaningful cutoff scores that could be used in clinical assessments. Also, as noted previously, many of the observational systems used to assess parent–child interactions require such intensive training of observers that their potential utility in many clinical assessments is also limited. Although we did review a few attempts to develop brief and clinically useful assessment methods, there are still too few such methods available.

Perhaps the most important limitation to evidence-based assessments of CP is the remaining disconnect between assessment concerning case conceptualization and treatment planning, on the one hand, and the availability of evidence-based interventions that map onto those assessment findings on the other. For example, interventions for youth who are engaging primarily in covert forms of CP (e.g., stealing and firesetting) are much less developed than those for more overt types of CP such as noncompliance and aggression (McMahon et al., 2006). Similarly, subtype-specific interventions for reactive and proactive aggression, and for relational aggression (e.g., Leff, Angelucci, Grabowski, & Weil, 2004; Levene, Walsh, Augimeri, & Pepler, 2004) and for the treatment of youths with and without CU traits (e.g., Frick, 1998, 2001, 2006) are in relatively early stages of development. Of note, however, is the clear evidence suggesting that high levels of noncompliance in a preschool-age child are best treated using one of several well-validated parent management training interventions (McMahon et al., 2006).

A critical issue in advancing the link between evidence-based assessment and treatment planning involves emerging research on the different developmental pathways to CP. As noted previously, this area of research may be the most important for understanding youths with CP because it could explain many of the variations in severity, the multiple co-occurring conditions, and the many different risk factors that have been associated with CP. This research could also be very important for designing more individualized treatments for youths with CP, especially older children and adolescents with more severe antisocial behaviors (Frick, 2006). However, in order for research on developmental pathways to be translated into practice, it is critical that better assessment methods for reliably and validly designating youths in these pathways be developed. This is especially the case for girls and for ethnically diverse youth (McMahon & Frick, 2005). Further, the different causal processes and developmental mechanisms (e.g., lack of empathy and guilt and poor emotion regulation) that may be involved in the different pathways need to be assessed, and this typically involves translating measures that have been used in developmental research into forms that are appropriate for clinical practice (Frick & Morris, 2004; Lahey, 2004).

In conclusion, it is hard to make a summary evaluation of the state of evidence-based practice related to the assessment of CP. In some areas, there have been great improvements over the past several decades, such as in the development of behavior ratings scales with large and representative normative samples. In other areas, such as in the development of measures to assess satisfaction with treatment, there have been fewer advances. Also, as the research base for understanding CP grows and evolves, so too must the guidelines for using this research in practice. Thus, evidence-based assessment is a moving target. However, the hallmark of an evidence-based approach to assessment is the commitment to never quit attempting to hit this moving target. The goal of this chapter is to highlight what we feel are currently some critical ways in which research on CP can inform the assessment process and to provide a structure whereby future advances in this research can be used to further enhance the process.

References

Achenbach, T. M., Dumenci, L., & Rescorla, L. A. (2003). DSM-oriented and empirically based approaches to constructing scales from the same item pools. *Journal of Clinical Child and Adolescent Psychology, 32,* 328–340.

Achenbach, T. M., McConaughy, S. H., & Howell, C. T. (1987). Child-adolescent behavioral and emotional problems: Implications of cross-informant correlations for situational specificity. *Psychological Bulletin, 101,* 213–232.

Achenbach, T. M., & Rescorla, L. A. (2000). *Manual for the ASEBA preschool forms and profiles.* Burlington, VT: University of Vermont, Department of Psychiatry.

Achenbach, T. M., & Rescorla, L. A. (2001). *Manual for the ASEBA school-age forms and profiles.* Burlington, VT: University of Vermont, Research Center for Children, Youth, & Families.

American Psychiatric Association. (2000). *The diagnostic and statistical manual of mental disorders* (4th ed., text revision). Washington, DC: Author.

Aspland, H., & Gardner, F. (2003). Observational measures of parent–child interaction: An introductory review. *Child and Adolescent Mental Health, 8,* 136–143.

Bank, L., Marlowe, J. H., Reid, J. B., Patterson, G. R., & Weinrott, M. R. (1991). A comparative evaluation of parent training interventions for families of chronic delinquents. *Journal of Abnormal Child Psychology, 19,* 15–33.

Barkley, R. A. (1991). The ecological validity of laboratory and analogue assessment methods of ADHD. *Journal of Abnormal Child Psychology, 19,* 149–178.

Bierman, K. L. (1983). Cognitive development and clinical interviews with children. In B. B. Lahey & A. E. Kazdin (Eds.), *Advances in clinical child psychology* (Vol. 6, pp. 217–250). New York: Plenum Press.

Bird, H. R. (1999). The assessment of functional impairment. In D. Shaffer, C. P. Lucas, & J. E. Richters (Eds.), *Diagnostic assessment in child and adolescent psychopathology* (pp. 209–229). New York: Guilford Press.

Bird, H. R., Shaffer, D., Fisher, P., Gould, M. S., Staghezza, B., Chen, J., et al. (1993). The Columbia Impairment Scale (CIS): Pilot findings on a measure of global impairment for children and adolescents. *International Journal of Methods in Psychiatric Research, 3,* 167–176.

Blair, R. J. R. (1995). A cognitive developmental approach to morality: Investigating the psychopath. *Cognition, 57,* 1–29.

Blair, R. J. R. (1999). Responsiveness to distress cues in the child with psychopathic tendencies. *Personality and Individual Differences, 27,* 135–145.

Bloomquist, M. L., & Schnell, S. V. (2002). Helping children with aggression and conduct problems: Best practices for interventions. New York: Guilford Press.

Breiner, J. L., & Forehand, R. (1981). An assessment of the effects of parent training on clinic-referred children's school behavior. *Behavioral Assessment, 3,* 31–42.

Brestan, E. V., Jacobs, J. R., Rayfield, A. D., & Eyberg, S. M. (1999). A consumer satisfaction measure for parent–child treatments and its relation to measures of child behavior change. *Behavior Therapy, 30,* 17–30.

Brinkmeyer, M., & Eyberg, S. M. (2003). Parent–Child Interaction Therapy for oppositional children. In A. E. Kazdin & J. R. Weisz (Eds.), *Evidence-based psychotherapies for children and adolescents* (pp. 204–223). New York: Guilford Press.

Broidy, L. M., Nagin, D. S., Tremblay, R. E., Bates, J. E., Brame, B. U., Dodge, K. A., et al. (2003). Developmental trajectories of childhood disruptive behaviors and adolescent delinquency: A six-site, cross-national study. *Developmental Psychology, 39,* 222–245.

Chamberlain, P., & Patterson, G. R. (1995). Discipline and child compliance in parenting. In M. H. Bornstein (Ed.), *Handbook of parenting: Vol. 4. Applied and practical parenting* (pp. 205–225). Hillsdale, NJ: Erlbaum.

Chamberlain, P., & Reid, J. B. (1987). Parent observation and report of child symptoms. *Behavioral Assessment, 9,* 97–109.

Chamberlain, P., & Reid, J. B. (1991). Using a specialized foster care community treatment model for children and adolescents leaving the state mental health hospital. *Journal of Community Psychology, 19,* 266–276.

Chamberlain, P., Reid, J. B., Ray, J., Capaldi, D. M., & Fisher, P. (1997). Parent Inadequate Discipline (PID). In T. A. Widiger, A. J. Frances, H. A. Pincus, R. Ross, M. B. First, & W. Davis (Eds.), *DSM-IV sourcebook* (Vol. 3, pp. 569–629). Washington, DC: American Psychiatric Association.

Christian, R. E., Frick, P. J., Hill, N. L., Tyler, L., & Frazer, D. R. (1997). Psychopathy and conduct problems in children: II. Implications for subtyping children with conduct problems. *Journal of the American Academy of Child & Adolescent Psychiatry, 36,* 233–241.

Conduct Problems Prevention Research Group. (2000). Merging universal and indicated prevention programs: The Fast Track model. *Addictive Behaviors, 25,* 913–927.

Crick, N. R., & Dodge, K. A. (1994). A review and reformulation of social information-processing mechanisms in children's social adjustment. *Psychological Bulletin, 115,* 74–101.

Crick, N. R., & Dodge, K. A. (1996). Social information-processing mechanisms in reactive and proactive aggression. *Child Development, 67,* 993–1002.

Crick, N. R., & Grotpeter, J. K. (1995). Relational aggression, gender, and social-psychological adjustment. *Child Development, 66,* 710–722.

Crick, N. R., Grotpeter, J. K., & Bigbee, M. A. (2002). Relationally and physically aggressive children's intent attributions and feelings of distress for relational and instrumental peer provocations. *Child Development, 73,* 1134–1142.

DeGarmo, D. S., Patterson, G. R., & Forgatch, M. S. (2004). How do outcomes in a specified parent training intervention maintain or wane over time? *Prevention Science, 5,* 73–89.

De Los Reyes, A., & Kazdin, A. E. (2005). Informant discrepancies in the assessment of childhood psychology: A critical review, theoretical framework, and recommendations for further study. *Psychological Bulletin, 131,* 483–509.

Dishion, T. J., Capaldi, D., Spracklen, K. M., & Li, F. (1995). Peer ecology of male adolescent drug use. *Development and Psychopathology, 7,* 803–824.

Dishion, T. J., McCord, J., & Poulin, F. (1999). When interventions harm: Peer groups and problem behavior. *American Psychologist, 54,* 755–764.

Dishion, T. J., & McMahon, R. J. (1998). Parental monitoring and the prevention of child and adolescent problem behavior: A conceptual and empirical formulation. *Clinical Child and Family Psychology Review, 1,* 61–75.

Dodge, K. A., Dishion, T. J., & Lansford, J. E. (2006). *Deviant peer influences in programs for youth: Problems and solutions.* New York: Guilford Press.

Dodge, K. A., & Pettit, G. S. (2003). A biopsychosocial model of the development of chronic conduct problems in adolescence. *Developmental Psychology, 39,* 349–371.

Eisenstadt, T. H., Eyberg, S., McNeil, C. B., Newcomb, K., & Funderburk, B. (1993). Parent–Child Interaction Therapy with behavior problem children: Relative effectiveness of two stages and overall treatment outcome. *Journal of Clinical Child Psychology, 22,* 42–51.

Essau, C. A, Sasagawa, S., & Frick, P. J. (2006). Callous-unemotional traits in a community sample of adolescents. *Assessment, 13,* 454–469.

Eyberg, S. (1993). Consumer satisfaction measures for assessing parent training programs. In L. VandeCreek, S. Knapp, & T. L. Jackson (Eds.), *Innovations in clinical practice: A source book* (Vol. 12, pp. 377–382). Sarasota, FL: Professional Resource Press.

Eyberg, S., Bessmer, J., Newcomb, K., Edwards, D., & Robinson, E. (1994). *Dyadic Parent–Child Interaction Coding System II: A manual.* Unpublished manuscript, University of Florida, Gainesville.

Eyberg, S. M., Nelson, M. M., Duke, M., & Boggs, S. R. (2005). *Manual for the Dyadic parent–child interaction coding system* (3rd ed.). Available online at www.PCIT.org.

Eyberg, S. M., & Pincus, D. (1999). The Eyberg Child Behavior Inventory and Sutter–Eyberg Student Behavior Inventory: Professional manual. Lutz, FL: Psychological Assessment Resources (PAR).

Fabrega, J. H., Ulrich, R., & Mezzich, J. E. (1993). Do Caucasian and Black adolescents differ at psychiatric intake? *Journal of the American Academy of Child & Adolescent Psychiatry, 32,* 407–413.

Fergusson, D. M., Swain, N. R., & Horwood, L. J. (2002). Deviant peer affiliations, crime and substance use: A fixed effects regression analysis. *Journal of Abnormal Child Psychology, 30,* 419–430.

Forehand, R., & McMahon, R. J. (1981). *Helping the noncompliant child: A clinician's guide to parent training.* New York: Guilford Press.

Frick, P. J. (1998). *Conduct disorders and severe antisocial behavior.* New York: Plenum Press.

Frick, P. J. (2000). Laboratory and performance-based measures of childhood disorders. *Journal of Clinical Child Psychology, 29,* 475–478.

Frick, P. J. (2001). Effective interventions for children and adolescents with conduct disorder. *Canadian Journal of Psychiatry, 46,* 26–37.

Frick, P. J. (2004). Developmental pathways to conduct disorder: Implications for serving youth who show severe aggressive and antisocial behavior. *Psychology in the Schools, 41,* 823–834.

Frick, P. J. (2006). Developmental pathways to conduct disorder. *Child and Adolescent Psychiatric Clinics of North America, 15,* 311–331.

Frick, P. J., Bodin, S. D., & Barry, C. T. (2000). Psychopathic traits and conduct problems in community and clinic-referred samples of children: Further development of the Psychopathy Screening Device. *Psychological Assessment, 12,* 382–393.

Frick, P. J., Cornell, A. H., Barry, C. T., Bodin, S. D., & Dane, H. A. (2003). Callous-unemotional traits and conduct problems in the prediction of conduct problem severity, aggression, and self-report of delinquency. *Journal of Abnormal Child Psychology, 31,* 457–470.

Frick, P. J., Cornell, A. H., Bodin, S. D., Dane, H. A., Barry, C. T., & Loney, B. R. (2003). Callous-unemotional traits and developmental pathways to severe conduct problems. *Developmental Psychology, 39,* 246–260.

Frick, P. J., & Dickens, C. (2006). Current perspectives on conduct disorder. *Current Psychiatry Reports, 8,* 59–72.

Frick, P. J., & Hare, R. D. (2001). *The Antisocial Process Screening Device (APSD).* Toronto: Multi-Health Systems.

Frick, P. J., Lahey, B. B., Hartdagen, S. E., & Hynd, G. W. (1989). Conduct problems in boys: Relations to maternal personality, marital satisfaction, and socioeconomic status. *Journal of Clinical Child Psychology, 18,* 114–120.

Frick, P. J., Lahey, B. B., Loeber, R., Tannenbaum, L. E., Van Horn, Y., Christ, M. A. G., et al. (1993). Oppositional defiant disorder and conduct disorder: A meta-analytic review of factor analyses and cross-validation in a clinic sample. *Clinical Psychology Review, 13,* 319–340.

Frick, P. J., Lilienfeld, S. O., Ellis, M. L., Loney, B. R., & Silverthorn, P. (1999). The association between anxiety and psychopathy dimensions in children. *Journal of Abnormal Child Psychology, 27,* 381–390.

Frick, P. J., & Loney, B. R. (1999). Outcomes of children and adolescents with conduct disorder and oppositional defiant disorder. In H. C. Quay & A. Hogan (Eds.), *Handbook of disruptive behavior disorders* (pp. 507–524). New York: Plenum Press.

Frick, P. J., & Loney, B. R. (2000). The use of laboratory and performance-based measures in the assessment of children and adolescents with conduct disorders. *Journal of Clinical Child Psychology, 29,* 540–554.

Frick, P. J., & Marsee, M. A. (2006). Psychopathic traits and developmental pathways to antisocial behavior in youth. In C. J. Patrick (Ed.), *Handbook of psychopathic traits* (pp. 355–374). New York: Guilford Press.

Frick, P. J., & Morris, A. S. (2004). Temperament and developmental pathways to conduct problems. *Journal of Clinical Child and Adolescent Psychology, 33,* 54–68.

Frick, P. J., O'Brien, B. S., Wootton, J. M., & McBurnett, K. (1994). Psychopathy and conduct problems in children. *Journal of Abnormal Psychology, 103,* 700–707.

Frick, P. J., & Silverthorn, P. (2001). Psychopathology in children. In P. B. Sutker & H. E. Adams (Eds.), *Comprehensive handbook of psychopathology* (3rd ed., pp. 881–920). New York: Kluwer Academic/Plenum.

Gadow, K. D., & Sprafkin, J. (1998). *CSI-4 screening manual.* Stony Brook, NY: Checkmate Plus.

Gottfredson, G. D., & Gottfredson, D. C. (2001). What schools do to prevent problem behavior and promote safe environments. *Journal of Educational & Psychological Consultation, 12,* 313–344.

Green, S. M., Loeber, R., & Lahey, B. B. (1991). Stability of mothers' recall of the age of onset of their child's attention and hyperactivity problems. *Journal of the American Academy of Child & Adolescent Psychiatry, 30,* 135–137.

Hanf, C. (1970). *Shaping mothers to shape their children's behavior.* Unpublished manuscript, University of Oregon Medical School.

Hawkins, J. D., Catalano, R. F., & Miller, J. Y. (1992). Risk and protective factors for alcohol and other drug problems in adolescence and early adulthood: Implications for substance abuse prevention. *Psychological Bulletin, 112,* 64–105.

Henggeler, S. W., Rowland, M. D., Randall, J., Ward, D. M., Pickrel, S. G., Cunningham, P. B., et al. (1999). Home-based Multisystemic Therapy as an alternative to the hospitalization of youths in psychiatric crisis: Clinical outcomes. *Journal of the American Academy of Child & Adolescent Psychiatry, 38,* 1331–1339.

Herschell, A., Calzada, E., Eyberg, S. M., & McNeil, C. B. (2002). Clinical issues in Parent–Child Interaction Therapy: Clinical past and future. *Cognitive and Behavioral Practice, 9,* 16–27.

Hinshaw, S. P. (1992). Externalizing behavior problems and academic underachievement in childhood and adolescence: Causal relationships and underlying mechanisms. *Psychological Bulletin, 111*, 127–155.

Hinshaw, S. P., Heller, T., & McHale, J. P. (1992). Covert antisocial behavior in boys with Attention-deficit Hyperactivity Disorder: External validation and effects of methylphenidate. *Journal of Consulting and Clinical Psychology, 60*, 274–281.

Hinshaw, S. P., & Lee, S. S. (2003). Conduct and oppositional defiant disorders. In E. J. Mash & R. A. Barkley (Eds.), *Child psychopathology* (2nd ed., pp. 144–198). New York: Guilford Press.

Hinshaw, S. P., Simmel, C., & Heller, T. L. (1995). Multimethod assessment of covert antisocial behavior in children: Laboratory observation, adult ratings, and child self-report. *Psychological Assessment, 7*, 209–219.

Hinshaw, S. P., Zupan, B. A., Simmel, C., Nigg, J. T., & Melnick, S. (1997). Peer status in boys with and without attention-deficit hyperactivity disorder: Predictions from overt and covert antisocial behavior, social isolation, and authoritative parenting beliefs. *Child Development, 68*, 880–896.

Hodges, K. (2000). *Child and Adolescent Functional Assessment Scale* (2nd rev. ed.). Ypsilanti: Eastern Michigan University.

Hodges, K. (2004). Using assessment in everyday practice for the benefit of families and practitioners. *Professional Psychology: Research and Practice, 35*, 449–456.

Hodges, K., Xue, Y., & Wotring, J. (2004). Use of the CAFAS to evaluate outcomes for youths with severe emotional disturbance served by public mental health. *Journal of Child and Family Studies, 13*, 325–339.

Hubbard, J. A., Dodge, K. A., Cillessen, A. H. N., Coie, J. D., & Schwartz, D. (2001). The dyadic nature of social information processing in boys' reactive and proactive aggression. *Journal of Personality and Social Psychology, 80*, 268–280.

Hubbard, J. A., Smithmyer, C. M., Ramsden, S. R., Parker, E. H., Flanagan, K. D., Dearing, K. F., et al. (2002). Observational, physiological, and self-report measures of children's anger: Relations to reactive versus proactive aggression. *Child Development, 73*, 1101–1118.

Jensen, P. S., Watanabe, H. K., & Richters, J. E. (1999). Who's up first? Testing for order effects in structured interviews using a counterbalanced experimental design. *Journal of Abnormal Child Psychology, 27*, 439–445.

Kagan, J., & Snidman, N. (1991). Temperamental factors in human development. *American Psychologist, 46*, 856–862.

Kamphaus, R. W., & Frick, P. J. (2005). *Clinical assessment of child and adolescent personality and behavior* (2nd ed.). New York: Springer.

Keenan, K., & Shaw, D. S. (1997). Developmental and social influences on young girls' behavioral and emotional problems. *Psychological Bulletin, 121*, 95–113.

Kimonis, E. R., Frick, P. J., Fazekas, H., & Loney, B. R. (2006). Psychopathic traits, aggression, and the processing of emotional stimuli in non-referred children. *Behavioral Sciences and the Law, 24*, 21–37.

Kimonis, E. R., Frick, P. J., Skeem, J. L., Marsee, M. A., Cruise, K., Muñoz, L. C., et al. (in press). Assessing callous-unemotional traits in adolescent offenders: Validation of the inventory of callous-unemotional traits. *Journal of the International Association of Psychiatry and Law.*

Krol, N. P. C. M., De Bruyn, E. E. J., Coolen, J. C., & van Aarle, E. J. M. (2006). From CBCL to DSM: A comparison of two methods to screen for DSM-IV diagnoses using CBCL data. *Journal of Clinical Child and Adolescent Psychology, 35*, 127–135.

Lahey, B. B. (2004). Commentary: Role of temperament in developmental models of psychopathology. *Journal of Clinical Child and Adolescent Psychology, 33*, 88–93.

Lahey, B. B., Goodman, S. H., Waldman, I. D., Bird, H., Canino, G., Jensen, P., et al. (1999). Relation of age of onset to the type and severity of child and adolescent conduct problems. *Journal of Abnormal Child Psychology, 27*, 247–260.

Lahey, B. B., Miller, T. L., Gordon, R. A., & Riley, A. (1999). Developmental epidemiology of the disruptive behavior disorders. In H. Quay & A. Hogan (Eds.), *Handbook of the disruptive behavior disorders* (pp. 23–48). New York: Plenum.

Lahey, B. B., Schwab-Stone, M., Goodman, S. H., Waldman, I. D., Canino, G., Rathouz, P. J., et al. (2000). Age and gender differences in oppositional behavior and conduct problems: A cross-sectional household study of middle childhood and adolescence. *Journal of Abnormal Psychology, 109*, 488–503.

LaRue, R. H., & Handleman, J. (2006). A primer on school-based functional assessment. *The Behavior Therapist, 29*, 48–52.

Leff, S. S., Angelucci, J., Grabowski, L., & Weil, J. (2004). Using school and community partners to design, implement, and evaluate a group intervention for relationally aggressive girls. In S. S. Leff (Chair), *Using partnerships to design, implement, and evaluate aggression prevention programs.* Symposium conducted at the meeting of the American Psychological Association, Honolulu.

Lett, N. J., & Kamphaus, R. W. (1997). Differential validity of the BASC Student Observation System and the BASC Teacher Rating Scale. *Canadian Journal of School Psychology, 13,* 1–14.

Levene, K. S., Walsh, M. M., Augimeri, L. K., & Pepler, D. J. (2004). Linking identification and treatment of early risk factors for female delinquency. In M. M. Moretti, C. L. Odgers, & M. A. Jackson (Eds.), *Girls and aggression: Contributing factors and intervention principles* (pp. 147–163). New York: Kluwer Academic/Plenum Publishers.

Little, T. D., Jones, S. M., Henrich, C. C., & Hawley, P. H. (2003). Disentangling the "whys" from the "whats" of aggressive behavior. *International Journal of Behavioural Development, 27,* 122–133.

Loeber, R., Burke, J. D., Lahey, B. B., Winters, A., & Zera, M. (2000). Oppositional defiant and conduct disorder: A review of the past 10 years, part I. *Journal of the American Academy of Child & Adolescent Psychiatry, 39,* 1468–1482.

Loeber, R., & Hay, D. F. (1997). Key issues in the development of aggressive and violence from childhood to early adulthood. *Annual Review of Psychology, 48,* 371–410.

Loeber, R., & Keenan, K. (1994). Interaction between conduct disorder and its comorbid conditions: Effects of age and gender. *Clinical Psychology Review, 14,* 497–523.

Loeber, R., & Stouthamer-Loeber, M. (1986). Family factors as correlates and predictors of juvenile conduct problems and delinquency. In M. Tonry & N. Morris (Eds.), *Crime and justice* (Vol. 7, pp. 29–149). Chicago: University of Chicago Press.

Loney, B. R., & Frick, P. J. (2003). Structured diagnostic interviewing. In C. R. Reynolds & R. W. Kamphaus (Eds.), *Handbook of educational assessment of children* (2nd ed., pp. 235–247). New York: Guilford Press.

Loney, B. R., Frick, P. J., Clements, C. B., Ellis, M. L., & Kerlin, K. (2003). Callous-unemotional traits, impulsivity, and emotional processing in antisocial adolescents. *Journal of Clinical Child and Adolescent Psychology, 32,* 139–152.

Loney, B. R., Frick, P. J., Ellis, M., & McCoy, M. G. (1998). Intelligence, psychopathy, and antisocial behavior. *Journal of Psychopathology and Behavioral Assessment, 20,* 231–247.

Lynskey, M. T., & Fergusson, D. M. (1995). Childhood conduct problems, attention deficit behaviors, and adolescent alcohol, tobacco, and illicit drug use. *Journal of Abnormal Child Psychology, 23,* 281–302.

Marsee, M. A., & Frick, P. J. (in press). Exploring the cognitive and emotional correlates to proactive and reactive aggression in a sample of detained girls. *Journal of Abnormal Child Psychology.*

McConaughy, S. H., Achenbach, T. M., & Gent, C. L. (1988). Multiaxial empirically based assessment: Parent, teacher, observational, cognitive, and personality correlates of Child Behavior Profile types for 6- to 11-year-old boys. *Journal of Abnormal Child Psychology, 16,* 485–509.

McCoy, M. G., Frick, P. J., Loney, B. R., & Ellis, M. L. (2000). The potential mediating role of parenting practices in the development of conduct problems in a clinic-referred sample. *Journal of Child and Family Studies, 8,* 477–494.

McMahon, R. J., & Estes, A. (1994). *Fast Track parent-child interaction task: Observational data collection manuals.* Unpublished manuscript, University of Washington, Seattle.

McMahon, R. J., & Estes, A. M. (1997). Conduct problems. In E. J. Mash & L. G. Terdal (Eds.), *Assessment of childhood disorders* (3rd ed., pp. 130–193). New York: Guilford Press.

McMahon, R. J., & Forehand, R. (1983). Consumer satisfaction in behavioral treatment of children: Types issues, and recommendations. *Behavior Therapy, 14,* 209–225.

McMahon, R. J., & Forehand, R. L. (2003). *Helping the noncompliant child: Family based treatment or oppositional behavior* (2nd ed.). New York: Guilford Press.

McMahon, R. J., Forehand, R., & Griest, D. L. (1981). Effects of knowledge of social learning principles on enhancing treatment outcome and generalization in a parent training program. *Journal of Consulting and Clinical Psychology, 49,* 526–532.

McMahon, R. J., & Frick, P. J. (2005). Evidence-based assessment of conduct problems in children and adolescents. *Journal of Clinical Child and Adolescent Psychology, 34,* 477–505.

McMahon, R. J., & Metzler, C. W. (1998). Selecting parenting measures for assessing family-based preventive interventions. In R. S. Ashery, E. B. Robertson, & K. L. Kumpfer (Eds.), *Drug abuse prevention through family interventions.* (NIDA Research Monograph No. 177, pp. 294–323). Rockville, MD: National Institute on Drug Abuse.

McMahon, R. J., Tiedemann, G. L., Forehand, R., & Griest, D. L. (1984). Parental satisfaction with parent training to modify child noncompliance. *Behavior Therapy, 15,* 295–303.

McMahon, R. J., Wells, K. C., & Kotler, J. S. (2006). Conduct problems. In E. J. Mash & R. A. Barkley (Eds.), *Treatment of childhood disorders* (3rd ed., pp. 137–268). New York: Guilford Press.

McNeil, C. B., Eyberg, S., Eisenstadt, T. H., Newcomb, K., & Funderburk, B. (1991). Parent–child interaction therapy with behavior problem children: Generalization of treatment effects to the school setting. *Journal of Clinical Child Psychology, 20*, 140–151.

Moffitt, T. E. (1993). Adolescence-limited and life-course persistent antisocial behavior: A developmental taxonomy. *Psychological Review, 100*, 674–701.

Moffitt, T. E. (2003). Life-course persistent and adolescence-limited antisocial behavior: A 10-year research review and research agenda. In B. B. Lahey, T. E. Moffitt, & A. Caspi (Eds.), *Causes of conduct disorder and juvenile delinquency* (pp. 49–75). New York: Guilford Press.

Moffitt, T. E., & Caspi, A. (2001). Childhood predictors differentiate life-course persistent and adolescence-limited antisocial pathways in males and females. *Development and Psychopathology, 13*, 355–376.

Moffitt, T. E., Caspi, A., Dickson, N., Silva, P., & Stanton, W. (1996). Childhood-onset versus adolescent-onset antisocial conduct problems in males: Natural history from ages 3 to 18 years. *Development and Psychopathology, 8*, 399–424.

Muñoz, L. C. & Frick, P. J. (in press). The reliability, stability, and predictive utility of the self-report version of the Antisocial Process Screening Device. *Scandinavian Journal of Psychology, 48*, 299–312.

Muñoz, L. C., Frick, P. J., Kimonis, E. R., & Aucoin, K. J. (in press). Types of aggression, responsiveness to provocation, and callous-unemotional traits in detained adolescents. *Journal of Abnormal Child Psychology.*

Nixon, R. D. V., Sweeney, L., Erickson, D. B., & Touyz, S. W. (2003). Parent–Child Interaction Therapy: A comparison of standard and abbreviated treatments for oppositional defiant preschoolers. *Journal of Consulting and Clinical Psychology, 71*, 251–260.

Nock, M. K., & Kurtz, S. M. S. (2005). Direct behavioral observation in school settings: Bringing science to practice. *Cognitive and Behavioral Practice, 12*, 359–370.

O'Brien, B. S., & Frick, P. J. (1996). Reward dominance: Associations with anxiety, conduct problems, and psychopathy in children. *Journal of Abnormal Child Psychology, 24*, 223–240.

Office of Juvenile Justice and Delinquency Prevention. (1995). *Juvenile offenders and victims: A focus on violence.* Pittsburgh, PA: National Center for Juvenile Justice.

Osofsky, J. D., Wewers, S., Hann, D. M., & Fick, A. C. (1993). Chronic community violence: What is happening to our children? *Psychiatry, 56*, 36–45.

Oxford, M., Cavell, T. A., & Hughes, J. N. (2003). Callous-unemotional traits moderate the relation between ineffective parenting and child externalizing problems: A partial replication and extension. *Journal of Clinical Child and Adolescent Psychology, 32*, 577–585.

Pardini, D. A., Lochman, J. E., & Frick, P. J. (2003). Callous/unemotional traits and social cognitive processes in adjudicated youth. *Journal of the American Academy of Child & Adolescent Psychiatry, 42*, 364–371.

Patterson, G. R., Capaldi, D., & Bank, L. (1991). An early starter model for predicting delinquency. In D. J. Pepler & K. H. Rubin (Eds.), *The development and treatment of childhood aggression* (pp. 139–168). Hillsdale, NJ: Erlbaum.

Patterson, G. R., & Dishion, T. J. (1985). Contributions of family and peers to delinquency. *Criminology, 23*, 63–79.

Patterson, G. R., Reid, J. B., Jones, R. R., & Conger, R. E. (1975). *A social learning approach to family intervention: Vol. 1. Families with aggressive children.* Eugene, OR: Castalia.

Patterson, G. R., & Yoerger, K. (1993). Developmental models for delinquent behavior. In S. Hodgins (Ed.), *Mental disorder and crime* (pp. 140–172). Newbury Park: Sage.

Peed, S., Roberts, M., & Forehand, R. (1977). Evaluation of the effectiveness of a standardized parent training program in altering the interaction of mothers and their noncompliant children. *Behavior Modification, 1*, 323–350.

Peeples, F., & Loeber, R. (1994). Do individual factors and neighborhood context explain ethnic differences in juvenile delinquency? *Journal of Quantitative Criminology, 10*, 141–158.

Piacentini, J., Robper, M., Jensen, P., Lucas, C., Fisher, P., Bird, H., et al. (1999). Informant-based determinants of symptom attenuation in structured child psychiatric interviews. *Journal of Abnormal Child Psychology, 27*, 417–428.

Poulin, F., & Boivin, M. (2000). Reactive and proactive aggression: Evidence of a two-factor model. *Psychological Assessment, 12*, 115–122.

Raine, A. (2002). Biosocial studies of antisocial and violent behavior in children and adults: A review. *Journal of Abnormal Child Psychology, 30*, 311–326.

Reed, M. L., & Edelbrock, C. (1983). Reliability and validity of the Direct Observation Form of the Child Behavior Checklist. *Journal of Abnormal Child Psychology, 11*, 521–530.

Reich, W. (2000). Diagnostic interview for children and adolescents (DICA). *Journal of the American Academy of Child & Adolescent Psychiatry, 39*, 59–66.

Reynolds, C. R., & Kamphaus, R. W. (2004). *Behavior Assessment System for Children-2 (BASC-2).* Bloomington, MN: Pearson Assessments.

Roberts, M. W., & Powers, S. W. (1988). The Compliance Test. *Behavioral Assessment, 10,* 375–398.

Roberts, M. W., & Powers, S. W. (1990). Adjusting chair timeout enforcement procedures for oppositional children. *Behavior Therapy, 21,* 257–271.

Robins, L. N. (1966). *Deviant children grown up.* Baltimore, MD: Williams and Wilkins.

Roff, J. D, & Wirt, R. D. (1984). Childhood aggression and social adjustment as antecedents of delinquency. *Journal of Abnormal Child Psychology, 12,* 111–126.

Rothbart, M. K., & Bates, J. E. (1998). Temperament. In W. Damon (Ed.), *Handbook of child psychology: Vol. 3, Social, emotional, and personality development* (pp. 105–176). New York: Wiley.

Russo, D. C., Cataldo, M. F., & Cushing, P. J. (1981). Compliance training and behavioral covariation in the treatment of multiple behavior problems. *Journal of Applied Behavior Analysis, 14,* 209–222.

Shaffer, D., Fisher, P., Lucas, C. P., Dulcan, M. K., & Schwab-Stone, M. E. (2000). NIMH Diagnostic Interview Schedule for Children version IV (NIMH DISC-IV): Description, differences from previous versions, and reliability of some common diagnoses. *Journal of the American Academy of Child & Adolescent Psychiatry, 39,* 28–38.

Shaffer, D., Gould, M. S., Brasic, J., Ambrosini, P., Fisher, P., Bird, H., et al. (1983). A Children's Global Assessment Scale (CGAS). *Archives of General Psychiatry, 40,* 1228–1231.

Silverthorn, P., & Frick, P. J. (1999). Developmental pathways to antisocial behavior: The delayed-onset pathway in girls. *Development and Psychopathology, 11,* 101–126.

Tibbetts, S. G., & Piquero, A. R. (1999). The influence of gender, low birth weight, and disadvantaged environment in predicting early onset of offending: A test of Moffitt's interactional hypothesis. *Criminology, 37,* 843–877.

Tiet, Q. Q., Wasserman, G. A., Loeber, R., Larken, S. M., & Miller, L. S. (2001). Developmental and sex differences in types of conduct problems. *Journal of Child and Family Studies, 10,* 181–197.

Underwood, M. K. (2003). *Social aggression among girls.* New York: Guilford Press.

Vitaro, F., Brendgen, M., & Tremblay, R. E. (2002). Reactively and proactively aggressive children: Antecedent and subsequent characteristics. *Journal of Child Psychology and Psychiatry and Allied Disciplines, 43,* 495–506.

Wahler, R. G., & Cormier, W. H. (1970). The ecological interview: A first step in out-patient child behavior therapy. *Journal of Behavior Therapy and Experimental Psychiatry, 1,* 279–289.

Wakschlag, L. S., & Danis, B. (2004). Assessment of disruptive behaviors in young children: A clinical-developmental framework. In R. Del Carmen & A. Carter (Eds.), *Handbook of infant and toddler mental health assessment* (pp. 421–440). New York: Oxford University Press.

Walker, H. M., Colvin, G., & Ramsey, E. (1995). *Antisocial behavior in school: Strategies and best practices.* Pacific Grove, CA: Brooks/Cole.

Walker, H. M., Ramsey, E., & Gresham, F. M. (2004). *Antisocial behavior in school: Evidence-based practice.* Belmont, CA: Wadsworth/Thomas Learning.

Waschbusch, D. A. (2002). A meta-analytic examination of comorbid hyperactive-impulsive-attention problems and conduct problems. *Psychological Bulletin, 128,* 118–150.

Webster-Stratton, C., & Hammond, M. (1997). Treating children with early-onset conduct problems: A comparison of child and parent training programs. *Journal of Consulting and Clinical Psychology, 65,* 93–109.

Webster-Stratton, C., & Lindsay, D. W. (1999). Social competence and conduct problems in young children: Issues in assessment. *Journal of Clinical Child and Adolescent Psychology, 28,* 25–43.

Webster-Stratton, C., & Spitzer, A. (1991). Development, reliability, and validity of the Daily Telephone Discipline Interview. *Behavioral Assessment, 13,* 221–239.

Wells, K. C., Forehand, R., & Griest, D. L. (1980). Generality of treatment effects from treated to untreated behaviors resulting from a parent training program. *Journal of Clinical Child Psychology, 8,* 217–219.

Willoughby, M., Kupersmidt, J., & Bryant, D. (2001). Overt and covert dimensions of antisocial behavior in early childhood. *Journal of Abnormal Child Psychology, 29,* 177–187.

Wootton, J. M., Frick, P. J., Shelton, K. K., & Silverthorn, P. (1997). Ineffective parenting and childhood conduct problems: The moderating role of callous-unemotional traits. *Journal of Consulting and Clinical Psychology, 65,* 301–308.

Zoccolillo, M. (1992). Co-occurrence of conduct disorder and its adult outcomes with depressive and anxiety disorders: A review. *Journal of the American Academy of Child & Adolescent Psychiatry, 31,* 547–556.

Part III

Mood Disorders and Self-Injury

4

Depression in Children
and Adolescents

Lea R. Dougherty

Daniel N. Klein

Thomas M. Olino

Rebecca S. Laptook

This chapter provides a review on evidence-based assessments of depression in children and adolescents. We focus on three phases of assessment: diagnosis and prognosis, case conceptualization and treatment planning, and treatment monitoring/evaluation. Our goal is to outline the parameters of a general assessment strategy and evaluate the efficacy of various assessment tools. Nevertheless, we acknowledge that additional areas will have to be explored for particular cases or contexts.

Currently, there is disagreement over what is the most useful and valid approach to conceptualizing and defining depression in children and adolescents. For example, there are controversies regarding whether depression should be defined in categorical or dimensional terms, whether and how depressive disorders should be divided into more homogeneous subtypes, and where the boundaries should be drawn between depression and other conditions such as the anxiety disorders (Klein, Shankman, & McFarland, 2006). The definition and classification of depression is further complicated by questions of whether depression presents differently at different developmental levels, and indeed, whether depression in children, adolescents, and adults are all manifestations of the same disorder. In this chapter, we focus on major depressive disorder (MDD), and, to a lesser extent, dysthymic disorder (DD), as defined by the fourth edition of the *Diagnostic and Statistical Manual of Mental Disorders* (DSM-IV-TR; American

Psychiatric Association, 2000). We believe that the diagnoses of MDD and DD have a moderate degree of clinical utility and construct validity in children and adolescents. However, as understanding of the etiology and the development of depression increases, the classification of depression in young people will undoubtedly change in significant ways.

An assessment strategy should be driven by the available data on the clinical features, associated characteristics, course, and treatment of depression, as well as what is known about the processes involved in the maintenance and recurrence of episodes. Hence, we begin with a brief overview of the literature on the psychopathology and treatment of depressive disorders in children and adolescents. This is followed by a review and evaluation of the assessment tools used in each phase of assessment.

THE NATURE OF DEPRESSION

Psychopathology

In the DSM-IV-TR, MDD in children and adolescents is defined by a period of at least 2 weeks characterized by the presence of a depressed or irritable mood or loss of interest or pleasure, and at least five of nine symptoms (including depressed mood and loss of interest). DD is defined as a period of at least 1 year characterized by depressed or irritable mood and at least two of six symptoms. The two conditions are not mutually exclusive—many children with MDD have a preexisting DD, and most children with DD experience episodes of MDD at some point (Kovacs, 1996), a phenomenon that has been referred to as "double depression."

Prevalence

Knowledge of base rates is an important consideration in assessment, as they can have a significant impact on the utility of assessment instruments and the validity of clinical decisions. For example, it is difficult for assessment instruments to improve on chance prediction in situations with very high or very low base rates, and for instruments with a given sensitivity and specificity, the positive predictive power of tests is maximized in high base rate situations, whereas negative predictive power is maximized in low base rate situations (Meehl & Rosen, 1955).

Depressive disorders are relatively uncommon in children, but are more frequent in adolescents. Recent research into the prevalence of emotional and behavioral disorders in preschoolers shows rates of MDD ranging from 0% to 2% (Egger & Angold, 2006). In community samples, the 6-month prevalence of depressive disorders is 1% to 3% in school-age children and 5% to 6% in adolescents; the lifetime prevalence in adolescents is 15% to 20% (Garber & Horowitz, 2002; Lewinsohn & Essau, 2002). Not surprisingly, the prevalence of depression is much higher in clinical settings, with estimated rates of 8% to 15% in children and over 50% in adolescents (Garber & Horowitz, 2002). There is no consistent gender difference in the prevalence of depressive disorders in children; however, the rates diverge in early adolescence, and by age 15 the prevalence is approximately two times higher in females than in males (Hankin et al., 1998).

Associated Features

Two associated features that are important to consider in assessing depression are functional impairment and comorbidity, as both may influence course and treatment response, as well as constituting important treatment targets in their own right.

Functional Impairment

Depressive disorders in children and adolescents are associated with significant problems in psychosocial functioning. Depressed children and adolescents often exhibit significant impairment in family, school, and peer functioning, and some degree of impairment may persist even after recovery from the depressive episode (Garber & Horowitz, 2002; Lewinsohn & Essau, 2002). Depression is the leading risk factor for youth suicide and may be a risk factor for the development of other disorders such as substance abuse (Birmaher, Arbelaez, & Brent, 2002). The causal relationship between depression and functional impairment is complex: depression causes significant impairment, but poor functioning may also be a risk factor for depression.

Comorbidity

In a meta-analysis of studies using community samples, Angold, Costello, and Erkanli (1999) reported that the median odds ratios for the associations of depression with anxiety, conduct, and attention deficit disorder were 8.2, 6.6, and 5.5, respectively. Depression is also often comorbid with eating, reading, and developmental disorders, and general medical conditions. In depressed preschoolers, two preliminary studies reported rates of comorbidity much higher than that would be expected from studies of older children (Egger & Angold, 2006).

There are a number of possible reasons for high comorbidity rates in children and adolescents, and identifying the causes of comorbidity could have important implications for revising the classification system (Klein & Riso, 1993). However, even without understanding the nature of the causal processes, comorbidity is clinically important because it can obscure the existence of a depressive disorder, is associated with greater impairment and a poorer course and treatment response, and comorbid conditions may require attention in their own right.

Course

Almost all children and adolescents with an episode of MDD recover, although many continue to experience subsyndromal (or residual) symptomatology. The length of episodes varies. The mean duration of episodes of MDD is approximately 7 to 8 months in clinical samples, and episodes of DD last an average of 48 months (Birmaher et al., 2002; Kovacs, 1996). Rates of relapse and recurrence of MDD are high, with the majority of depressed juveniles experiencing another episode within several years (Birmaher et al., 2002; Kovacs, 1996). Long-term follow-up studies indicate that adolescents with MDD are at high risk for experiencing depressive episodes in adulthood; however, the evidence for children with MDD is less consistent (Birmaher et al., 2002).

The mechanisms and processes that serve to maintain depressive episodes and cause recurrences are poorly understood. However, longitudinal studies of the course of depression in children and adolescents have identified a number of factors that appear to predict the duration of MDD episodes and the probability of recurrence. Variables that are associated with a longer time to recovery include an early age of onset, greater severity of depression, suicidality, double depression, the presence of comorbid anxiety or disruptive behavior disorders, depressotypic cognitions, and an adverse family environment. Variables that have been associated with an increased risk of recurrence include greater severity, psychotic symptoms, suicidality, a prior history of recurrent MDD, double depression, the presence of subthreshold symptoms after recovery, a depressotypic cognitive style, recent stressful life events, an adverse family environment, and a family history of MDD (particularly if it is recurrent; Birmaher et al., 2002).

Children and adolescents with MDD and DD are also at risk for developing manic and hypomanic episodes. The probability of "switching" to bipolar disorder is higher in patients with psychotic symptoms, psychomotor retardation, a family history of bipolar disorder, and a high familial loading for mood disorders (Birmaher et al., 2002; Geller, Fox, & Clark, 1994).

Treatment

There is relatively strong support for the efficacy of cognitive-behavioral therapy (CBT) and interpersonal therapy (IPT) for depressed adolescents (Asarnow, Jaycox, & Thompson, 2001; Kaslow, McClure, & Connell, 2002). The few studies examining the effects of family therapy, either alone or in conjunction with treatment for the adolescent, have generally failed to support its efficacy (Asarnow et al., 2001). However, Diamond, Reis, Diamond, Siqueland, and Isaacs (2002) reported promising data on the efficacy of attachment-based family therapy for adolescent depression.

Even fewer data are available on the efficacy of psychosocial interventions in school-aged children.

Almost all of the clinical trials in this age group have used variants of CBT, generally administered in a group format to children with elevated levels of depressive symptoms, but not necessarily diagnoses (Weisz, McCarty, & Valeri, 2006). Although the findings have varied, the majority of studies have reported evidence supporting the efficacy of CBT (Kaslow et al., 2002; Weisz et al., 2006).

Little is known about the mechanisms underlying the effects of CBT and IPT on depression in children, adolescents, or adults (Kazdin, 2003). In addition, despite the efficacy of psychosocial interventions for depressed children and adolescents in clinical trials, there is evidence that the types of treatments routinely provided in community settings are less successful than these evidence-based treatments (Weersing & Weisz, 2002). Finally, there are no data on the efficacy of treatments for very young children with depression.

Controlled clinical trials of antidepressant medications in children and adolescents are also limited. The available evidence indicates that the cyclic antidepressants are not efficacious. The data on newer medications, such as the selective serotonin reuptake inhibitors and atypical antidepressants, are mixed. Several double-blind placebo-controlled trials have reported benefits in adolescents or mixed samples of children and adolescents, but other published and unpublished studies have failed to find differences (Vasa, Carlino, & Pine, 2006). Questions have also been raised about whether several of the newer antidepressants are associated with increased suicidal ideation and behavior in children and adolescents (Vasa et al., 2006). At present, the only SSRI that is *cautiously* recommended for use with children and adolescents is fluoxetine.

Similar to adult depression, it appears that there are high rates of relapse and recurrence when psychosocial and pharmacological treatments are terminated. Unfortunately, there are few studies of continuation or maintenance treatments for depressed children and adolescents. Extrapolating from the adult literature, it may be prudent to consider continuation and maintenance treatment for patients with residual symptoms or characteristics associated with an increased risk of recurrence (e.g., history of recurrent episodes, double depression, family history of MDD, ongoing family conflict, and other stressors).

Data on predictors of treatment response in depressed children and adolescents are limited. However, it appears that many of the same variables that predict a more protracted recovery in naturalistic studies also predict a poorer response to treatment (Emslie, Mayes, Laptook, & Batt, 2003; Kaslow et al., 2002). Unfortunately, there are even fewer data on predictors of differential treatment response; that is, which patients respond better to some treatments than others. An exception is one study that reported that the presence of a comorbid anxiety disorder predicted a better response to CBT than to systemic-behavioral family therapy or supportive therapy (Brent et al., 1998).

PURPOSES OF ASSESSMENT

Clinical assessment can be thought of as a sequence including at least three phases: (1) diagnosis and prognosis; (2) case conceptualization and treatment planning; and (3) treatment monitoring and evaluation. The major goal of the first phase is to develop a preliminary diagnosis and prognosis. For depression, this includes determining whether criteria are met for MDD or DD, and ruling out exclusionary diagnoses such as bipolar disorder and depression due to a general medical condition or substance. As part of the assessment of depression, the clinician must assess key symptoms (e.g., suicidal ideation and psychotic symptoms) that might influence treatment decisions. In addition, it is important to assess carefully the previous course of depression (e.g., prior episodes and chronicity) due to its prognostic value and possible implications for long-term treatment. It is also important to assess comorbid psychiatric, developmental, and general medical disorders, and areas of significant functional impairment (e.g., family, school, and peers) in order to determine whether depression is the principle diagnosis that should be the primary target of intervention, and because of their prognostic implications. Given the high comorbidity between the mood and anxiety disorders, we refer the reader to Chapter 9 in this volume on the assessment of child and adolescent anxiety disorders.

The second phase of assessment involves developing a case conceptualization and treatment planning. In addition to variables already described, a comprehensive assessment of personal, interpersonal, or systemic dynamics is crucial in order to provide clues to the development and maintenance of symptoms and dysfunctional life patterns and to provide the focus of

treatment. First, it is important to assess the child's family environment, school functioning, peer relationships, significant stressors and traumas, and family history of psychopathology, as these factors have considerable prognostic value and may be involved in the development and maintenance of the disorder.

Second, it is important to consider other social factors such as race, culture, ethnicity, and socioeconomic status. Poverty, race, social stressors, and ethnicity have all been linked to greater depression symptomatology in youth (Taylor & Turner, 2002; Wight, Aneshensel, Botticello, & Sepulveda, 2005). Furthermore, as current views of depression are primarily shaped by Western culture, depression may manifest itself differently across cultures and ethnicity. This is suggested by differences in the phenomenology and prevalence of depression across cultures and ethnic groups (e.g., Chen, Roberts, & Aday, 1998). Moreover, we need to examine the validity of assessment tools across cultures as evidence suggests that they may also vary across cultures (e.g., Weisz, Chaiyasit, Weiss, Eastman, & Jackson, 1995).

Third, data on the severity and prior course of depression, key symptoms such as suicidal ideation/behavior and psychotic symptoms, comorbidity, and functional impairment are important for determining the appropriate treatment setting (e.g., inpatient vs. outpatient), the intensity and duration of treatment, and perhaps the treatment modality. As noted above, however, few data are available to guide these decisions. Information on comorbidity is also necessary to determine whether other disorders should be monitored or targeted for treatment. Finally, it is critical to take a detailed history of previous treatment, and assess the goals, attitudes, and motivation of the child and parents with respect to the relevant treatment options. This information is critical both for treatment selection and for engaging the child and family in treatment. As children and parents often disagree on the selection of treatment targets (Hawley & Weisz, 2003), it may take considerable negotiation to develop a treatment plan that is acceptable to all parties.

The third phase of assessment involves treatment monitoring and evaluation. This entails systematically assessing the degree of change in target symptoms and impairments in order to determine whether treatment should be continued, intensified, augmented, changed, or terminated. As few guidelines are available to help clinicians determine when treatment should be modified, this is an important area for future research.

Information Source

It is important to obtain data from multiple informants, including the child, parents, and teachers. Child report is critical, as parents and teachers tend to report lower levels of depressive and other internalizing symptoms in children than youths report themselves (Jensen et al., 1999). However, it is useful to supplement youths' reports with information from collaterals to assess externalizing disorders. Parent reports are particularly important for preadolescent children. Owing to developmental limitations in cognitive processes and language abilities, children are less reliable reporters of psychopathology than adolescents (Edelbrock, Costello, Dulcan, Kalas, & Conover, 1985). In addition, younger children have difficulty reporting on information regarding temporal parameters; therefore, parents must be relied on for information on course such as age of onset, previous episodes, and duration of current episode (Kovacs, 1986). Finally, parents are more involved in the day-to-day lives of children than adolescents, and therefore are more knowledgeable about their behavior and activities.

Although obtaining data from multiple informants is optimal, agreement between informants is only fair-to-moderate (Achenbach, McConaughy, & Howell, 1987). In addition, depressed parents appear to have a lower threshold for detecting depression in their children; hence, their reports tend to yield higher rates of both true and false positives (i.e., increased sensitivity but decreased specificity; Richters, 1992; Youngstrom, Izard, & Ackerman, 1999). Despite the substantial disagreement between informants, there is evidence for the validity of both parent and child reports (Jensen et al., 1999). In addition, several studies have demonstrated that child, parent, teacher, and clinician ratings all account for significant unique variance in predicting subsequent outcomes (Ferdinand et al., 2003; Verhulst, Dekker, & van der Ende, 1997).

The low agreement between data sources presents a significant challenge for clinicians who must decide how to interpret and integrate conflicting information. A variety of approaches to integrating data from multiple informants has been discussed in the literature, including assuming that the feature or diagnosis is present if any informant reports it (the "or" rule), requiring several informants to confirm the feature or diagnosis (the "and" rule), or developing various statistical procedures for optimizing prediction (e.g., Kraemer et al., 2003). The approach that most closely mirrors clinical practice is the "best estimate" procedure, in which the clinician uses his/her best judgment to integrate and resolve conflicting reports. This raises the possibility of introducing the unreliability and idiosyncrasy that structured interviews and standardized ratings scales were developed to prevent (see below). However, there is evidence from the adult literature that, when applied following appropriate guidelines (e.g., self-report takes precedence for internalizing disorders; informant report is given priority for externalizing disorders), the reliability of best estimate diagnoses can be very high (Klein et al., 1994).

Attenuation Effect

Studies of interviews and rating scales for both juvenile and adult psychopathology have often found that rates of diagnoses and ratings of symptom severity tend to decrease with repeated administrations, a phenomenon referred to as the "attenuation effect" (Egger & Angold, 2004). As this has been observed in nonclinical samples, it cannot be attributed to treatment or regression to the mean. This has important implications for treatment monitoring and evaluation, as it is difficult to distinguish the attenuation effect from a positive response to treatment for the individual patient. Although there is no solution to this problem at present, it behooves the clinician to be aware of this phenomenon and to consider alternative explanations for what appears to be improvement on rating scales.

Psychometric Considerations

In reviewing available instruments for each of the assessment phases described earlier in this section, accompanying tables will be used to present general information on a measure's psychometric properties and clinical utility. Thus, the presentation of specific psychometric data is kept to a minimum in the text and tables. As a general rule, we chose to include more widely used assessment tools that have been independently examined by two research groups. We made exceptions to this rule when a new measure appeared exceptionally promising due to unique features of the instrument. However, these *newer* measures will not be included in the tables as there are insufficient data to evaluate their efficacy at this time.

Measures were evaluated according to the criteria presented in Hunsley and Mash's introductory chapter in this volume. Nevertheless, we would like to mention several factors that influenced our ratings. First, inter-rater reliability can be examined by raters independently rating a case vignette, a videotaped or audiotaped assessment, a live assessment (paired-rater design), or by two examiners administering the same instrument at two different time points usually spanning only a few days (test–retest design). The first three approaches hold information constant across raters; hence, reliability should be higher than test–retest designs, in which information presented to each examiner can vary substantially. In making the ratings, we tried to take the type of design into account. In addition, examining the test–retest reliability of depression in youth over several months or a year is relatively uncommon as depression in youth is often intermittent/episodic. Therefore, most ratings of test–retest reliability cannot receive more than an adequate rating due to the shorter time frames assessed.

Second, evaluating convergent and divergent validity of an instrument can be difficult as depression tends to co-occur with many other forms of psychopathology (e.g., anxiety and disruptive behavior disorder). Although depression measures should correlate more highly with other depression measures than with measures of other forms of psychopathology, there should be substantial correlates between measures of depression and measures of anxiety and behavior problems. Similarly, depressed youth are likely to differ from non-depressed youth not only on measures of depression, but also on other measures of psychological dysfunction. Thus, modest discriminant validity may not be a limitation of the instrument, but instead might reflect the comorbidity between depression and other disorders. Finally, very little work has examined the clinical utility of youth depression measures. We are aware of only one such study (Hughes et al., 2005) that used the K-SADS; therefore, all other measures did not receive above an adequate rating on this criterion. Obviously, this is an area of research that needs much attention.

ASSESSMENT FOR DIAGNOSIS OF DEPRESSION IN CHILDREN AND ADOLESCENTS

The two major approaches to diagnosing and assessing depression in children and adolescents involve interviews and rating scales. Unfortunately, there are no laboratory measures of psychosocial or biological variables that are useful for clinical assessment at this time (Garber & Kaminski, 2000). Several observational measures/coding systems have been used for assessing depression in children; however, there is insufficient evidence to recommend their use (Garber & Kaminski, 2000).

Interviews can be unstructured, semistructured, or fully structured. Unstructured clinical interviews vary from clinician to clinician with respect to format, duration, focus, and coverage, and, therefore, in the amount and type of information elicited. The literature indicates that clinicians using unstructured interviews often fail to inquire about key aspects of psychopathology, particularly if it is inconsistent with their initial diagnostic impressions (Angold & Fisher, 1999), and formulate fewer diagnoses than clinicians using structured interviews (Zimmerman, 2003). With semistructured interviews the interviewer is responsible for rating the criteria as accurately as possible, using all available information, and improvising additional questions or confronting the respondent with inconsistencies when necessary. In contrast, the interviewer's role in fully structured interviews is limited to reading the questions as written and recording the respondent's answers. Both approaches require judgments about the presence of symptoms and other clinical features. In semistructured interviews, these judgments are made by the interviewers, whereas in fully structured interviews they are made by the respondents. As a result, semistructured interviews were designed for use by mental health professionals or well-trained and supervised technicians, and seek to capitalize on their clinical training and experience, whereas fully structured interviews were developed for lay interviewers in large-scale epidemiological studies where the cost of interviewers with clinical training is prohibitive. There have been few direct comparisons with respect to the validity of semistructured versus fully structured interviews. In the absence of evidence to the contrary, we assume that the semistructured approach yields higher quality data than the structured approach because the interviewer presumably has a better sense of the constructs being assessed than does the respondent.

Rating scales include clinician-administered, self-report, and parent and teacher measures. Clinician-administered rating scales are actually semistructured interviews that focus on a circumscribed area of symptomatology (e.g., depression). Unlike diagnostic interviews, they do not collect sufficient information to make a diagnosis (e.g., duration and exclusion criteria are generally not assessed). Self-report and parent and teacher rating scales are typically questionnaires that are self-administered by the designated informant, although they can be read to younger children. Similar to clinician-administered rating scales, self, parent, and teacher rating scales typically focus on current symptoms and behavior, and therefore do not provide sufficient information to make diagnoses.

Owing to their economy, self, parent, and teacher rating scales can be especially valuable as screening instruments, with elevated scores leading to a more intensive evaluation. Self-rating scales are generally superior to parent and teacher rating scales in screening for internalizing disorders due to their greater sensitivity. However, even the best self-rating scales have only moderate sensitivity and specificity, producing a substantial number of false positives and false negatives (Kendall, Cantwell, & Kazdin, 1989). As the prevalence of child and adolescent depression tends to be fairly low in most screening contexts, the use of screeners often results in false positives greatly outnumbering the true positives (Matthey & Petrovski, 2002; Roberts, Lewinsohn, & Seeley, 1991). Thus, the potential economy and efficiency of screening must be weighed against the costs of unnecessary extended evaluations for false positive cases and the risks associated with missing false negative cases.

In the next section, we briefly describe several of the better-researched and more widely used semistructured diagnostic interviews, fully structured diagnostic interviews, and rating scales. We also chose to include a few promising assessment tools that are worth noting due to some unique features of the instrument. We have been highly selective, and there are a number of equally good, but less widely used, measures that we have not included. For more information on this broader range of instruments, readers are referred to some excellent recent reviews (Angold & Fisher, 1999; Brooks & Kutcher, 2001; Myers & Winters, 2002; Silverman & Rabian, 1999). There are also a number of measures of specific components of the depressive syndrome, such as self-esteem, hopelessness, depressive cognitions, and suicidality (see Winters, Myers, & Proud, 2002, for a review) that may be useful for particular cases, but are not reviewed here.

Semistructured Diagnostic Interviews

In this section, we briefly review the three most widely used semistructured diagnostic interviews for child and adolescent psychopathology: the Schedule for Affective Disorders and Schizophrenia in School-Age Children (K-SADS; Puig-Antich & Chambers, 1978), the Diagnostic Interview for Children and Adolescents (DICA; Herjanic & Reich, 1982), and the Child and Adolescent Psychiatric Assessment (CAPA; Angold et al., 1995). Information on these instruments is provided in Table 4.1. Each interview assesses the criteria for most of the major child and adolescent psychiatric disorders and provides parallel versions for children and parents. Although some of the instruments are used to interview 6- and 7-year-old children, it is questionable whether children younger than 8 or 9 can provide valid information in a diagnostic interview (Angold & Fisher, 1999).

Evaluating the validity of semistructured diagnostic interviews is complex, as they are usually used as the "gold standard" that other measures are compared against. Construct validity is probably the best standard, but given the current state of the literature it is impossible to distinguish the construct validity of semistructured interviews from the diagnoses that they are designed to assess. In order to try to disentangle the construct validity of interviews from diagnostic constructs, it is necessary to conduct head-to-head comparisons of several interviews using the same sample and the same criteria for construct validation (e.g., family history and course). Unfortunately, such studies have not been conducted. Although the distinction between MDD and DD has important prognostic implications (Kovacs, 1996), the majority of studies combine them in a higher order depressive disorder category or focus solely on MDD. Hence, for present purposes, we will focus on depressive disorders as broadly conceived.

The K-SADS (Puig-Antich & Chambers, 1978) is the most widely used semistructured interview for children and adolescents (6–18 years). It is also the least structured of the semistructured interviews, and therefore requires the greatest amount of clinical training and experience. The K-SADS was modeled after the adult Schedule for Affective Disorders and Schizophrenia (SADS). There are a number of versions of the K-SADS that assess DSM-IV criteria. These versions vary in format, whether they assess lifetime as well as current psychopathology, and whether they also provide dimensional measures of symptom severity. Ratings are based on all sources of information and clinical judgment. Administration

TABLE 4.1 Ratings of Instruments Used for Diagnosis and Prognosis

Instrument	Norms	Internal Consistency	Inter-Rater Reliability	Test–Retest Reliability	Content Validity	Construct Validity	Validity Generalization	Clinical Utility	Highly Recommended
Diagnostic Instruments									
K-SADS	NA	U	G	A	G	E	E	G	✓
DICA	NA	U	A	A	G	A	E	A	
CAPA	NA	U	G	A	G	G	A	A	✓
DISC	NA	U	A	A	G	A	E	A	
Prognostic Instruments									
CDRS-R	G	G	G	A	G	G	E	A	✓
CDI	E	G	NA	A	G	G	E	A	✓
MFQ	E	G	NA	A	A	G	E	A	✓
RCDS	E	E	NA	A	G	A	A	A	
RADS	E	E	NA	G	G	G	E	A	✓

Note: K-SADS = Schedule for Affective Disorders and Schizophrenia in School-Age Children; DICA = Diagnostic Interview for Children and Adolescents; CAPA = Child and Adolescent Psychiatric Assessment; DISC = Diagnostic Interview Schedule for Children; CDRS-R = Children's Depression Rating Scale-Revised; CDI = Children's Depression Inventory; MFQ = Mood and Feelings Questionnaire; RCDS = Reynolds Child Depression Scale; RADS = Reynolds Adolescent Depression Scale; A = Adequate; G = Good; E = Excellent; U = Unavailable; NA = Not Applicable.

time of the parent and child interviews range from 35 minutes to 2.5 hours each, depending on the severity of the child's psychopathology. Inter-rater reliability has been reported to be adequate to excellent for depressive disorders in several studies, and has been particularly impressive with the more recent versions of the K-SADS (Ambrosini, 2000; Kaufman et al., 1997). Evidence for convergent validity derives from numerous studies reporting correlations between the K-SADS and a variety of clinician, self, and parent rating measures of depression and internalizing behavior problems (Ambrosini, 2000; Kaufman et al., 1997). In addition, youths diagnosed with MDD using the K-SADS differed from controls on psychosocial impairment, familial aggregation of mood disorders, numerous neurobiological parameters, and K-SADS diagnoses of depression predicted continued risk for recurrence of affective disorders (Ambrosini, 2000). Nevertheless, it has been suggested that MDD K-SADS diagnoses may identify a more severe clinical group than other assessment tools (Hamilton & Gillham, 1999).

The DICA (Herjanic & Reich, 1982) was originally designed as a fully structured interview but recent versions have been semistructured in nature. The most recent version of the DICA (Reich, 2000) assesses both DSM-III-R and DSM-IV criteria, and includes separate interviews for children (6–12 years), adolescents (13–17 years), and parents. The interview adopts a lifetime time frame and takes approximately 1 to 2 hours to complete. Data on inter-rater reliability have varied across studies, ranging from poor to good (Boyle et al., 1993; Brooks & Kutcher, 2001; Reich, 2000). DICA diagnoses are moderately correlated with clinicians' diagnoses, and clinician and self-rated measures of depressive symptoms (Brooks & Kutcher, 2001; Reich, 2000), providing some evidence of convergent validity. DICA MDD specificity rates are generally high, but its sensitivity rates are low, which suggests that the DICA tends to underdiagnose MDD compared to other measures (Ezpeleta et al., 1997; Olsson & von Knorring, 1997).

The CAPA (Angold, Prendergast, et al., 1995) assesses the criteria for most major diagnoses in children aged 9–17 years. The time frame for symptom assessment is the preceding 3 months, and administration time takes from 1 to 2 hours (Angold & Costello, 2000). Although there are few data on the CAPA by investigators who were not involved in its development, the interview has several very attractive features.

First, it is unique in that it includes an extensive glossary defining specific symptoms and distress and frequency ratings. As a result, the CAPA can be used by interviewers with minimal clinical experience, as long as they adhere closely to the definitions and conventions in the glossary. Second, it includes a section for assessing impairment in a number of areas, including family, peers, school, and leisure activities, and also includes sections assessing the family environment and life events and traumas. Test–retest reliability of the CAPA has only been reported in one study. Angold and Costello (1995) reported that the kappas for MDD and DD were .90 and .85, respectively, and that the intraclass correlation for the MDD symptom scale was .88. In another study, the inter-rater reliability using audiotaped interviews of the child version of the CAPA ranged from .78 to 1.0 for all diagnoses (Wamboldt, Wamboldt, Gavin, & McTaggart, 2001). Data on the association between CAPA diagnoses of depression and other measures of depression have not been published. However, Angold and Costello (2000) report that depression as diagnosed by the CAPA is associated with significant levels of functional impairment and higher concordance among monozygotic than dizygotic twins, supporting the construct validity of the interview.

Fully Structured Diagnostic Interviews

In this section, we review the most widely used fully structured diagnostic interview for child and adolescent psychopathology, the Diagnostic Interview Schedule for Children (DISC; Costello et al., 1984) and a newer instrument, the Children's Interview for Psychiatric Syndromes (ChIPS; Weller, Weller, Fristad, Rooney, & Schecter, 2000), whose preliminary investigations seem promising.

The DISC (Costello et al., 1984) assesses a broad range of psychiatric disorders which, in the latest version (DISC-IV), reflect DSM-IV and ICD-10 criteria (Shaffer, Fisher, Lucas, Dulcan, & Schwab-Stone, 2000). The DISC includes separate interviews for youth (9–17 years) and parents of 6- to 17-year-olds. The time frame includes the past 12 months and the past 4 weeks, and takes between 1 and 2 hours. Inter-rater reliability of the DISC was adequate (Costello et al., 1984). Test–retest reliability for MDD for the earlier versions range from poor to good (Hodges, 1994; Shaffer et al., 2000). However, preliminary results obtained with the DISC-IV suggest that it has better test–retest reliability than its predecessors, especially in clinical samples (Shaffer et al., 2000). Concordance between DISC diagnoses and clinicians' diagnoses (Hodges, 1994; Lewczyk, Garland, Hurlbert, Gearity, & Hough, 2003; Schwab-Stone et al., 1996) and self-rated measures of depressive symptoms (Angold, Costello, Messer, & Pickles, 1995; Hodges, 1994) range from poor to good, providing only limited evidence of convergent validity. Moreover, the DISC evidenced very low concordance with the K-SADS for MDD and poor discriminant validity (Hodges, 1994). Finally, prevalence studies have suggested that the DISC (original version) has good sensitivity but poor specificity, leading to overdiagnosing (Hodges, 1994).

The ChIPS (Weller et al., 2000) is a promising interview based on DSM-IV criteria, however, only one research group has investigated its psychometric properties. The potential advantages of the ChIPS over the DISC are its brief duration (20 to 50 minutes depending on the severity of the sample), its simple language appropriate for children 6 to 18 years old and their parents, and its easy-to-interpret summary sheet. For each of the five validity studies on the ChIPS, inter-rater reliability was excellent. Moderate levels of agreement were found between the ChIPS and the DICA and between ChIPS and clinicians' diagnoses. Even though preliminary data on the ChIPS are encouraging, more research into its validity using larger samples and by other research groups is strongly recommended.

Rating Scales

In this section and in Table 4.1, we review some of the more widely used clinician, self-report, and multi-informant rating scales for depression. Information on rating scales designed for adults that are often used with older adolescents can be found in Persons and Fresco's (2007) chapter in this volume. The Hamilton Rating Scale for Depression (HAM-D), Beck Depression Inventory (BDI), and Center for Epidemiological Studies-Depression Scale (CES-D) have similar psychometric properties in adolescent and adult samples (Roberts et al., 1991), have comparable reliability and validity compared to measures that were specifically designed for juveniles, and have been sensitive to treatment effects (Weisz et al., 2006). Hence, these measures appear to be acceptable alternatives for older adolescents.

The most widely used clinician scale for rating depression in children is the Children's Depression Rating Scale (CDRS; Poznanski, Cook, & Carroll, 1979). Based on the HAM-D, the CDRS was developed to assess current severity of depression in children aged 6 to 12 years and is often used for adolescents as well. The revised version (CDRS-R; Poznanski & Mokros, 1999) contains 17 items assessing cognitive, somatic, affective, and psychomotor symptoms and draws both on the respondent's report and the interviewer's behavioral observations. It takes 15 to 20 minutes to administer. It is designed to be administered separately to the child and an informant, with the clinician subsequently integrating the data using clinical judgment. Cutoff scores are provided to aid in interpreting levels of depression severity. The CDRS has good internal consistency and good inter-rater reliability (Brooks & Kutcher, 2001; Myers & Winters, 2002). Its convergent validity has been supported by moderate-to-high correlations with the HAM-D and several self-rated depression scales (Brooks & Kutcher, 2001; Myers & Winters, 2002). However, although some degree of discriminant validity has been suggested by children diagnosed as depressed scoring higher than those with other diagnoses, the CDRS has difficulty distinguishing between depression and anxiety and overestimates depression severity in children with general medical conditions due to its emphasis on somatic symptoms (Brooks & Kutcher, 2001; Myers & Winters, 2002).

There are a number of widely used self-rating scales for child and adolescent depression. We will briefly review four: the Children's Depression Inventory (CDI; Kovacs, 1992), Mood and Feelings Questionnaire (MFQ; Angold, Costello, et al., 1995), Reynolds Child Depression Scale (RCDS; Reynolds, 1989), and Reynolds Adolescent Depression Scale (RADS; Reynolds, 1987). Some of these measures, such as the MFQ, are based on older versions of the DSM. However, their use is still warranted as there have been few changes in symptoms and criteria for depressive disorders among DSM-III, DSM-III-R, and DSM-IV/DSM-IV-TR.

The CDI (Kovacs, 1992) is the most widely used depression rating scale for children and adolescents. Developed as a modified version of the BDI, it assesses severity of depression during the previous 2 weeks in children aged 7 to 17 years. It includes 27 items covering a broad range of depressive symptoms and associated features, with a particular emphasis on cognitive symptoms, and takes 10 to 20 minutes to complete. A number of studies have reported that the CDI has good internal consistency and many, but not all, studies have also reported good short-term test–retest reliability (Brooks & Kutcher, 2001; Kovacs, 1992; Silverman & Rabian, 1999). Studies of the factor structure of the CDI have produced inconsistent findings, with some indication that the factor structure varies by age (Cole, Hoffman, Tram, & Maxwell, 2000; Weiss & Garber, 2003). The CDI is moderately/highly correlated with the CDRS, a number of other self-rated depression scales, and other measures of related constructs supporting its convergent validity (Brooks & Kutcher, 2001; Myers & Winters, 2002; Silverman & Rabian, 1999). However, the discriminant validity of the CDI is questionable, as it is almost as highly correlated with measures of anxiety as it is with other measures of depression, and studies examining its ability to distinguish depressed from nondepressed patients have yielded conflicting findings (Myers & Winters, 2002; Silverman & Rabian, 1999).

The Mood and Feelings Questionnaire (MFQ; Angold, Costello et al., 1995) was developed to assess depression over the past 2 weeks in youths ages 8 to 18 years. It consists of 32 items covering the DSM-III-R criteria for depression and additional symptoms, such as loneliness, and feeling unloved or ugly. Angold, Costello et al. (1995) also developed a shorter 13-item version (SMFQ) by selecting items that yielded optimal discriminating power and internal consistency. The MFQ takes approximately 10 minutes to complete. It has good internal consistency and adequate test–retest reliability (Angold, Costello, et al., 1995; Wood, Kroll, Moore, & Harrington, 1995). In addition, the MFQ has demonstrated good convergent validity with respect to the CDI, DISC, CAPA, and K-SADS (Angold, Costello, et al., 1995; Thapar & McGuffin, 1998; Wood et al., 1995). The MFQ was also relatively successful in discriminating youths with diagnoses of depression from those with non-mood disorders (Kent, Vostanis, & Feehan, 1997; Thapar & McGuffin, 1998).

The Reynolds Child Depression Scale (RCDS; Reynolds, 1989) and Reynolds Adolescent Depression Scale (RADS; Reynolds, 1987) are 30-item scales designed to assess depressive symptomatology (as represented in DSM-III) during the previous 2 weeks in youths ages 8–12 and 13–18 years, respectively. Each scale takes approximately 10 minutes to complete, although children may require some additional time.

The Reynolds scales have been used primarily with school, rather than clinical, samples. Both scales have excellent internal consistency and good test–retest reliability (Brooks & Kutcher, 2001; Myers & Winters, 2002). In addition, both are correlated with interview diagnoses and other depression rating scales such as the CDRS, HAM-D, CDI, BDI, and CES-D (Brooks & Kutcher, 2001; Myers & Winters, 2002). Discriminant validity has not been well studied, although similar to most depression rating scales, the RADS is moderately correlated with measures of anxiety (Myers & Winters, 2002). A revised version of the RADS (RADS-2), which is based on the symptoms of depression found in the DSM-IV, has been recently developed, and Reynolds (2004) reports similar reliability and validity data for the RADS-2.

As noted earlier, it is important to obtain information about child and adolescent depression from informants other than the youths themselves. Several of the self-rating scales, such as the CDI, have been reworded for use by parents, and in some cases, by teachers and peers. Some psychometric data have been reported on these adaptations. Kovacs (2003) reported data on the norms and factor structure of the parent and teacher versions of the CDI, as well as good internal consistency for these measures. In addition, Cole et al. (2000) compared child- and parent-report versions of the CDI. They reported that the two versions had similar internal consistencies and test–retest reliabilities, and that the factor structure of the CDI was relatively similar, although not identical, across informants.

There are also a number of multi-informant rating scales that were designed to assess a broad range of child and adolescent psychopathology using instruments that are comparable across informants (Hart & Lahey, 1999). The most widely used is the parent-report Child Behavior Checklist (CBCL; Achenbach & Rescorla, 2001) and its accompanying teacher report (Teacher Report Form [TRF]) and child report (Youth Self-Report [YSR]) versions. The CBCL and TRF are appropriate for youths ages 5 to 18, whereas the YSR is designed for youths ages 11 to 18. The CBCL and YSR assess the child's behavior over the past 6 months, whereas the TRF uses a 2-month time frame. All three measures take approximately 10 to 15 minutes to complete.

The CBCL includes 118 items assessing two broad-band and eight narrowband scales identified using factor analysis, as well as a social competence scale.

Extensive norms for the CBCL, TRF, and YSR are available for both clinical and community samples, and favorable psychometric properties of the instruments have been documented in hundreds of studies. Unfortunately, the CBCL's utility in assessing depression, at least as conceptualized in the DSM-IV-TR, is limited. The scale that is most relevant to depression is the narrowband Anxious/Depressed scale, which combines symptoms of anxiety and depression. In addition, some other depressive symptoms are included on other narrowband scales. Indeed, a latent class analysis of the Anxiety/Depression scale was unable to distinguish distinct classes for depression and anxiety (Wadsworth, Hudziak, Heath, & Achenbach, 2001). A series of diagnostic scales that are more closely geared to DSM diagnoses has recently been added to the CBCL; however, studies of their association with semistructured interview-derived diagnoses have not yet been reported.

Assessment of Younger Children

As noted above, the diagnosis and assessment of depression in infants and preschool aged children are still largely uncharted territory (Egger & Angold, 2006). Moreover, the administration of semistructured interviews and self-rating scales to children under the age of 8 or 9 years is questionable (Angold & Fisher, 1999), although there is some evidence for the validity of the CDI in children as young as 5 to 6 years old (Ialongo, Edelsohn, & Kellam, 2001).

The most widely used measures of psychopathology in preschoolers are the CBCL 1½–5, a parent rating scale, and the TRF 1½–5, a teacher rating scale (Achenbach & Rescorla, 2004). In addition, the Early Childhood Inventory-4 (ECI-4; Gadow & Sprafkin, 2000) is a rating scale that assesses symptoms of the most relevant DSM-IV-TR psychiatric disorders for preschool children. There are parent and teacher versions of the ECI-4, and both categorical and dimensional scoring procedures.

Diagnostic clinical interviews have also been developed for this age group. Egger and Angold (2004) developed a downward extension of the CAPA for 2- to 5-year-old children entitled the Preschool Age Psychiatric Assessment (PAPA). The PAPA's inter-rater and test–retest reliability are comparable to semistructured interviews with older children and adults (Egger et al., 2006). A downward extension of the DISC-IV for preschoolers has also been developed

(DISC-IV Young Child; Lucas, Fisher, & Luby, 1998). Limited psychometric data are available for the DISC-IV Young Child; however, Luby and colleagues have used this instrument and provided encouraging results for the diagnosis of depression, as well as data on the external validity of MDD DISC-IV diagnoses in this age group (Luby, Mrakotsky, Heffelfinger, Brown, & Spitznagel, 2004; Luby, Sullivan, Belden, Stalets, Blankenship, & Spitznagel, 2006).

Finally, a group of investigators sponsored by the McArthur Foundation have developed a battery of assessment instruments for children in the early school-age period (ages 4.5 to 7.5 years). It includes a parent and teacher rating scale, the McArthur Health and Behavior Questionnaire (HBQ; Essex et al., 2002), and a semistructured interview, the Berkeley Puppet Interview (BPI; Ablow et al., 1999) that uses puppets in order to provide a more developmentally sensitive assessment. Both measures include scales tapping various domains of symptomatology (including a subscale for depressive symptoms), physical health, and peer and school functioning. In the initial reports from this group, the depression scale from the HBQ parent and teacher forms had adequate internal consistency and good test–retest reliability, and discriminated clinic from community subjects (Ablow et al., 1999). Although a categorical measure of depression from the HBQ parent form was not correlated with diagnoses of MDD derived from the parent version of the DISC, it was associated with a number of teacher-rated indices of impairment (Luby et al., 2002). Finally, the BPI depression scale had adequate internal consistency in a clinic sample, but poor internal consistency in a community sample, moderate test–retest reliability in both samples, and discriminated the clinic from community subjects (Ablow et al., 1999).

Overall Evaluation

For the purpose of diagnosis, we recommend the use of semistructured interviews, as they provide greater flexibility and allow for the clarification of questions and responses, and the clinical judgment of the interviewer. In particular, we recommend the K-SADS because of its fairly strong psychometric properties. In addition, we feel that the CAPA is very promising, particularly because it includes assessments of functional impairment and life stress (see below) and has a companion instrument for preschoolers. Fully structured interviews, such as the DISC-IV and ChIPS, can also play an important role in large-scale epidemiological studies and in screening. However, as fully structured interviews tend to overdiagnose, it is important that, when used for screening, screen-positive cases receive more extensive assessments to confirm the diagnosis.

As with fully structured interviews, we advise that rating scales not be used alone when formulating diagnoses, as many of the scales appear to measure general distress rather than depression specifically. In addition, they do not provide the necessary information to make a diagnosis (e.g., onset, duration, frequency of symptoms), and when they are used to approximate diagnoses, they tend to overidentify youths as depressed. However, rating scales provide useful information on the level of symptom severity and can be used for screening. Our recommendations for rating scales differ depending on sample characteristics. The RCDS and the RADS have been widely used in community and school samples. They both exhibit generally good psychometric properties and function well as screening tools in such populations, despite their lack of discriminant validity. In clinical samples, we recommend the use of the clinician-rated CDRS-R along with the self-report CDI. Although both lack good discriminant validity, they have functioned well in numerous studies of depressed youth, and when used in conjunction, they tend to yield prevalence rates that are consistent with studies using diagnostic interviews (Myers & Winters, 2002).

ASSESSMENT FOR THE PURPOSE OF CASE CONCEPTUALIZATION AND TREATMENT PLANNING

In this section, we briefly discuss measures of psychosocial functioning, life stress, and family history of psychopathology due to the importance of these variables for prognosis, case conceptualization, and treatment planning. Information on these measures is presented in Table 4.2. Also included in Table 4.2 are depression rating scales (described above) that assess symptom severity, which is also important for treatment planning as the initial severity of depressive symptoms has been related to poorer course and poorer treatment response (Goodyer, Herbert, Tamplin, Secher, & Pearson, 1997; Huey et al., 2005). Moreover, greater depression severity provides

information about the appropriate treatment setting (e.g., inpatient vs. outpatient) and the use of psychotropic medications. Furthermore, rating scales provide information about symptomatology that can inform treatment plans that incorporate components targeting specific symptoms (e.g., decreased interest and activity, low self-esteem/worthlessness).

Psychosocial Functioning

Depression in children and adolescents is associated with significant impairment in family and peer relationships and academic performance. The families of depressed youths are often characterized by a lack of cohesion and high levels of disengagement and criticism (Sheeber, Hops, & Davis, 2001). The parents of depressed children and adolescents exhibit less warmth and support and greater control and rejection than parents of controls (Garber & Horowitz, 2002). Depressed youths have significant peer difficulties and social skills deficits (Rudolph, Hammen, & Burge, 1994) and often exhibit academic underachievement, school attendance problems, and school failure (Hammen, Rudolph, Weisz, Rao, & Burge, 1999).

There are a variety of approaches and instruments for assessing impairments and competencies in psychosocial functioning (for reviews see Bird, 1999; Canino, Costello, & Angold, 1999; John, 2001). Some of the interviews and ratings scales discussed above include measures of functional impairments and competencies. For example, the CAPA includes a comprehensive assessment of the major areas of child psychosocial functioning (Angold & Costello, 2000); the CBCL (Achenbach & Rescorla, 2001) has a 16-item social competence scale; and the Berkeley Puppet Interview includes scales tapping academic and social competence and peer acceptance (Ablow et al., 1999). In this section, we briefly discuss several additional measures of psychosocial functioning in children and adolescents. For a comprehensive review of scales assessing psychosocial impairment in youth, see Winters, Collett, and Myers (2005).

One group of measures consists of global or unidimensional scales. Global measures of functional impairment provide information on the extent of impairment from the disorder and the severity of the disorder, which influence the choice of treatment setting (e.g., inpatient vs. outpatient), the intensity and duration of treatment, and the treatment modality. Both the Child Global Assessment Scale (C-GAS;

TABLE 4.2 Ratings of Instruments Used for Case Conceptualization and Treatment Planning

Instrument	Norms	Internal Consistency	Inter-Rater Reliability	Test–Retest Reliability	Content Validity	Construct Validity	Validity Generalization	Clinical Utility	Highly Recommended
Depression Severity Rating Scales									
CDRS-R	G	G	G	A	G	G	E	A	✓
CDI	E	G	NA	A	G	G	E	A	✓
MFQ	E	G	NA	A	A	G	E	A	✓
RCDS	E	E	NA	A	G	A	A	A	
RADS	E	E	NA	G	G	G	E	A	✓
Global Scales of Functioning									
C-GAS	E	NA	G	G	A	G	E	A	✓
CIS	E	A	A	A	A	G	E	A	
Multidimensional Scales of Functioning									
CAFAS	G	NA[a]	G	A	G	G	E	A	
SAICA	A	A	A	E	G	G	A	A	

[a] See Bates (2001).

Note: CDRS-R = Children's Depression Rating Scale-Revised; CDI = Children's Depression Inventory; MFQ = Mood and Feelings Questionnaire; RCDS = Reynolds Child Depression Scale; RADS = Reynolds Adolescent Depression Scale; C-GAS = Child Global Assessment Scale; CIS = Columbia Impairment Scale; CAFAS = Child and Adolescent Functional Assessment Scale; SAICA = Social Adjustment Inventory for Children and Adolescents; A = Adequate; G = Good; E = Excellent; NA = Not Applicable.

Shaffer et al., 1983) and the Columbia Impairment Scale (CIS; Bird et al., 1993) are global measures of functional impairment and are included in Table 4.2. The C-GAS, adapted from the Global Assessment Scale for adults (which is also the basis for DSM-IV Axis V), is a single 100-point scale designed for clinicians to rate the severity of symptomatology and functional impairment. The rating is based on information collected through other means (i.e., a diagnostic interview), as the C-GAS does not provide questions. The CIS is a respondent-based interview that consists of 13 items tapping a variety of domains of social functioning and symptomatology that are combined to form a single score. Some findings suggest that the parent versions of the CIS and the C-GAS are more sensitive than the child version (Goodman, Schwab-Stone, Lahey, Shaffer, & Jensen, 2000). The C-GAS and CIS are both economical. They have good convergent validity and differentiate various populations (e.g., clinical vs. community). However, they each yield only one score; hence, they do not provide information on the nature of impairment in specific areas of functioning. In addition, both measures combine symptoms and psychosocial functioning so that a child's score could reflect problems in either or both domains.

Several more extensive instruments are also available. These measures typically assess the youth's functioning across several domains, including academic, family, and peer functioning. This information can be used to select areas to be targeted in therapy and to identify strengths that may be utilized to accelerate progress in treatment. For example, as parent–child conflict predicts lack of recovery from depression after treatment, chronicity of depression, and recurrence of depression (Birmaher et al., 2000), interventions that focus on this conflict may boost treatment response. At present, there is no evidence to recommend family therapy as a first line treatment; however, interventions that incorporate family psychoeducation, parent training, or communication training to reduce expressed emotion and criticism within the family may enhance treatment outcomes (Asarnow, Scott, & Mintz, 2002; Park & Goodyer, 2000). For instance, the Treatment for Adolescents with Depression Study (TADS), which used a manualized CBT protocol, also incorporated a parent psychoeducation component and optional treatment modules on peer relationship problems and family communication deficits (Rohde, Feeny, & Robins,

2005). This provided clinicians with the flexibility to target client-specific mechanisms in the patient's distress. The TADS group contends that targeting these background contexts was integral in treatment delivery and adherence; however, this assertion awaits verification. The measures presented below and in Table 4.2 assess a number of social domains that may be critical to an understanding of the youth's depression and designing his/her treatment plan.

The Child and Adolescent Functional Assessment Scale (CAFAS; Hodges, 1999) is a widely used clinician-rated instrument that takes approximately 30 minutes to administer (see Bates, 2001, for a review). It assesses five domains: Role Performance (including School/Work, Home, and Community), Behavior Towards Others, Moods/Self-Harm, Substance Use, and Thinking. The CAFAS has demonstrated good inter-rater reliability, adequate test–retest reliability, and has correlated well with other measures of impairment (Winters et al., 2005). The CAFAS has differentiated outpatients from inpatients and shows good predictive validity. Overall, this measure has good psychometric properties and has been widely used in mental health settings. The CAFAS assesses symptomatology as well as psychosocial functioning. As these domains are assessed in separate sections, it is possible to obtain information on functioning alone. However, there is considerable overlap between the symptom-focused sections and the interviews and rating scales discussed above, and the symptom sections are not comprehensive enough to substitute for a diagnostic interview or depression rating scale.

Finally, there are several semistructured interviews for psychosocial functioning that were designed to accompany semistructured diagnostic interviews without overlapping with more symptom-focused assessments. The Social Adjustment Inventory for Children and Adolescents (SAICA; John, Gammon, Prusoff, & Warner, 1987) assesses school functioning, peer relations, home life, and spare time activities in youths ages 6 to 18. It takes about 30 minutes and is administered separately to the parent and child. The SAICA has acceptable levels of inter-rater reliability and excellent test–retest reliability and is considered to have good convergent and discriminant validity (Winters et al., 2005). One study has reported that the SAICA performed better than a global functioning scale (i.e., C-GAS) in predicting the course of depression in adolescents (Sanford et al., 1995). The Psychosocial Schedule for School Age Children-Revised (PSS-R;

Puig-Antich, Lukens, & Brent, 1986) was designed to assess school functioning, relationships with parents, siblings, and peers, and the parents' marital relationship in children ages 6 to 16 years. Similar to the SAICA, it is administered separately to the parent and child. The PSS-R has good psychometric properties, including test–retest reliability (Lukens et al., 1983).

Finally, an 11-item interview based on the adult Longitudinal Interval Follow-up Evaluation-Range of Impaired Functioning Tool (LIFE-RIFT; Leon et al., 1999) is currently being developed for children and adolescents (Fisher, Leon, & Coles, 2002). Similar to the SAICA and PSS-R, it assesses school, family, peer, and recreational functioning but is briefer and can be easily incorporated into a more comprehensive evaluation.

In addition to the instruments noted above, there are numerous more focused measures designed to assess specific areas of functioning. For example, there are a number of widely used inventories assessing key dimensions of family functioning (e.g., Epstein, Baldwin, & Bishop, 1983) and parenting behavior (e.g., Schaefer, 1965), laboratory tasks that have been used to examine the interaction patterns of families of depressed children (see Garber & Kaminski, 2000), and interview and laboratory measures of expressed emotion (e.g., Asarnow, Goldstein, Tompson, & Guthrie, 1993). Finally, there are a variety of peer nomination measures and teacher ratings of peer functioning that can be used to assess children's social status in school (e.g., Coie, Dodge, & Coppotelli, 1982; Huesmann, Eron, Guerra, & Crawshaw, 1994). Unfortunately, even though these measures provide valuable information in terms of case conceptualization and treatment planning, these measures are not practical for a clinical setting.

Stressful Life Events

Prospective studies in children have shown that stress, and particularly events related to loss, disappointments, conflict, or rejection, predict the onset and persistence of depressive symptoms (Garber & Horowitz, 2002; Goodyer, 2001). As such, the time course of recent psychosocial stressors should be established as they may be precipitants of depression, and stressors related to the onset and maintenance of the disorder should be addressed in the treatment plan. In addition, it is important to assess whether the stressors are acute or chronic and whether the stressor is independent or dependent of the child's behavior. For example, if a stressor is chronic, such as marital conflict, the clinician may recommend marital counseling for the parents and treatment may incorporate ways to cope with the ongoing source of stress. Furthermore, if the youth's behavior is "generating" life stress, it would be important to focus on changing the youth's problematic behavior patterns that are contributing to the occurrence of life stressors (Hammen, 2006).

Life stress can be assessed through self-administered questionnaires (e.g., Johnson & McCutcheon, 1980) or interviews (e.g., Sandberg et al., 1993; Williamson et al., 2003). Questionnaires are more economical, but semistructured interviews have a number of critical advantages, including the ability to assess the temporal relationship between the stressor and the onset of the depressive episode, distinguish potentially important features of events such as long-term threat and whether the event is independent of, versus dependent on, the child's behavior, and minimize idiosyncratic interpretations of items (Duggal et al., 2000; Williamson et al., 2003).

Family History of Psychopathology

A number of studies have reported elevated rates of depression, and often other forms of psychopathology, in the relatives of depressed children and adolescents (e.g., Klein, Lewinsohn, Seeley, & Rhode, 2001). Clinicians should be particularly cautious in individuals with a family history of bipolar disorder or psychosis, and should be alert to emerging signs of mania, psychosis, or both in their offspring. Furthermore, parental depression has been related to prolonged depressive episodes in their children and poorer treatment response (Brent et al., 1998). Therefore, if a parent is suffering from a psychiatric disorder and is not in treatment, it is advisable to recommend that the parent seek individual psychiatric services. Some evidence suggests that treating maternal depression contributed to reductions in child psychopathology (Weissman et al., 2006).

Family history data can be elicited using diagnostic interviews conducted directly with family members (the family interview method) or by interviewing key informants about the other relatives (the family history method). A number of semistructured interviews for eliciting family history information from informants are available, including the Family History

Research Diagnostic Criteria (Andreasen, Endicott, Spitzer, & Winokur, 1977), the Family Informant Schedule and Criteria (Mannuzza & Fyer, 1990), and a brief family history screening interview developed by Weissman et al. (2000). Family history data collected from informants tend to have high specificity, but only moderate sensitivity. Hence, it is advisable to obtain information from at least two informants when possible in order to increase the probability of detecting psychopathology in relatives.

Overall Evaluation

Assessment for the purpose of case conceptualization and treatment planning requires a combination of measures assessing a variety of social domains (e.g., relationships with family and peers, dating, school work, and activities/hobbies) and factors related to the disorder (i.e., stressful life events, family history of psychopathology), and requires information from multiple informants. It is also important to consider the context of the youth's behavior and the cultural milieu because what is considered maladaptive in one context or culture may be adaptive in another.

First, we recommend multidimensional measures that assess a variety of social domains. The SAICA has been mostly used by clinicians to assess functioning rather than by mental health planners to determine service needs. The CAFAS is a reasonable option for a multidimensional scale to guide selection of the level and types of services. It has been widely used in clinical, research, and administrative work across the country, and is supported by a website. Although these measures are recommended, they were not *highly recommended* in Table 4.2 as they have not yet been specifically examined in many studies of child and adolescent depression.

Next, it is important to assess stressful life events and family history of psychopathology. If time permits, the best option for assessing life events is with an interview that provides qualitative information regarding the stressor (e.g., independence/dependence of stressor, chronic/acute, the stressor's impact on the individual, and timing of the stressor in relation to symptoms). Finally, there are a variety of acceptable methods to assess family history of psychopathology. Although it can be difficult to do, we recommend using multiple informants to increase sensitivity. In summary, assessment for case conceptualization and treatment planning should provide the clinician with

information to determine the severity/prognosis of the disorder, areas of impairment and strength, and factors that are contributing to the onset and maintenance of the disorder.

ASSESSMENT FOR TREATMENT MONITORING AND TREATMENT OUTCOME

To evaluate the assessment tools used in the treatment literature, we examined the various measures' sensitivity to treatment effects (see Table 4.3). This included significant change on depression measures, such as MDD diagnoses and rating scales, as well as change on measures of functional impairment using both global and multidimensional scales. Furthermore, we included only published pharmacological and psychotherapy treatment research that reported at least one significant treatment effect on at least one outcome measure of depression. Otherwise, it is not possible to distinguish the treatment's lack of efficacy from the measure's insensitivity in detecting change.

All studies examined compared depression treatment to a waitlist control or another active treatment. Some treatment studies reported change in MDD diagnoses (i.e., no longer meeting criteria). Each of these reports used the K-SADS, which was sensitive to change in all studies (Clarke et al., 1995; 2001; Clarke, Rohde, Lewinsohn, Hops, & Seeley, 1999; Diamond et al., 2002; Lewinsohn, Clarke, Hops, & Andrews, 1990; Stark, 1990; Vostanis, Feehan, Grattan, & Bickerton, 1996; Wood, Harrington, & Moore, 1996), demonstrating significant between-group treatment effects, within-group treatment change, and posttreatment follow-up effects. A number of depression rating scales have also been shown to be sensitive to treatment effects. The CDRS has detected treatment effects in both psychopharmacology and psychotherapy trials (Brooks & Kutcher, 2001; Myers & Winters, 2002). The CDI has also been widely used and has been shown to be sensitive to change in several treatment studies (Brooks & Kutcher, 2001; Myers & Winters, 2002). One study reported that it was more sensitive in detecting the effects of group CBT in school-aged children than the RCDS was (Stark, Reynolds, & Kaslow, 1987); however, another study found that it was less sensitive to the effects of medication than the CDRS (Emslie et al., 1997). Both the RCDS and RADS have detected treatment effects in controlled clinical trials. The MFQ has been

TABLE 4.3 Ratings of Instruments Used for Treatment Monitoring and Treatment Outcome Evaluation

Instrument	Norms	Internal Consistency	Inter-Rater Reliability	Test–Retest Reliability	Content Validity	Construct Validity	Validity Generalization	Treatment Sensitivity	Clinical Utility	Highly Recommended
K-SADS	NA	U	G	A	G	E	E	E	G	
CDRS-R	G	G	G	A	G	G	G	E	A	✓
CDI	E	G	NA	A	G	G	E	A	A	✓
MFQ	E	E	NA	A	A	G	E	A	A	
RCDS	E	E	NA	A	G	A	A	A	A	
RADS	E	E	NA	G	G	G	E	G	A	✓
C-GAS	E	NA	G	G	A	G	E	E	A	✓
SAICA	A	A	A	E	G	G	A	A	A	

Note: K-SADS = Schedule for Affective Disorders and Schizophrenia in School-Age Children; CDRS-R = Children's Depression Rating Scale-Revised; CDI = Children's Depression Inventory; MFQ = Mood and Feelings Questionnaire; RCDS = Reynolds Child Depression Scale; RADS = Reynolds Adolescent Depression Scale; C-GAS = Child Global Assessment Scale; SAICA = Social Adjustment Inventory for Children and Adolescents; A = Adequate; G = Good; E = Excellent; U = Unavailable; NA = Not Applicable.

used less frequently than the other measures, and it has demonstrated sensitivity to change in some, but not all, clinical trials (Brooks & Kutcher, 2001). Finally, many of the youth self-report rating scales reviewed here (e.g., CDI, RADS, MFQ) have been shown to be more sensitive to treatment effects than the parent versions (Kahn, Kehle, Jenson, & Clark, 1990; Woods et al., 1996).

A few treatment studies included parent versions of the CBCL-Anxious/Depressed scale, CBCL Internalizing scale, and an adapted depression scale from the CBCL. Overall, these studies did not report posttreatment effects using any of these measures even though other youth-reported depression measures demonstrated treatment effects (Clark et al., 1999; Clark et al., 2001; De Cuyper, Timbremont, Braet, Backer, & Wullaert, 2004; Rosello & Bernal, 1999; Stark et al., 1987). Interestingly, however, some of these studies later found posttreatment follow-up effects using parent-report measures (Clark et al., 1999; De Cuyper et al., 2004). This suggests that parents and youths may be focusing on different indicators of improvement (i.e., parents may rely more heavily on behavioral than mood changes). Nevertheless, it appears that parents are less sensitive to the more immediate changes in the youth's depressive symptomatology than the youths themselves.

Finally, it is important to emphasize that treatment monitoring and outcome should include psychosocial functioning in addition to symptom reduction/remission. Unfortunately, few treatment studies have examined improvement in functioning. The C-GAS has been the most widely used functional impairment scale in treatment studies, and has been sensitive to treatment of depression in children and adolescents (Goodman et al., 2000; Muratori, Picchi, Bruni, Patarnello, & Ramagnoli, 2003). The SAICA is one of the few multidimensional measures of social functioning to be used in youth depression treatment studies. It demonstrated sensitivity to posttreatment effects and 9-month follow-up effects (Vostanis et al., 1996). The CAFAS has also been shown to be sensitive to treatment gains (Winters et al., 2005), however, these studies did not focus on depression. Future research should focus on the effects of treatment on adaptive functioning, and determine whether the areas targeted in treatment actually improve.

Overall Evaluation

Determining which measures to use for monitoring and evaluating treatment will depend on a number of

factors, including the nature of the patient's condition and the form of treatment. For patients with diagnoses of MDD, the K-SADS MDD section can be used to assess remission. In addition to the K-SADS, a combination of the clinician-rated CDRS-R, which has been sensitive to both pharmacological and psychotherapy treatment studies, and the youth-rated CDI, which has been sensitive to change and widely used with child and adolescent populations, are highly recommended. However, if a clinician-rating scale is too costly, the CDI, RCDS, RADS, or MFQ is acceptable. These measures have all been shown to be sensitive to psychotherapy, and they are all self-report measures, which appear to be more sensitive than parent-report measures of depression. In Table 4.3, among these self-report measures, only the CDI and RADS are considered *highly recommended* because they have been most widely used and consistently shown to be sensitive to treatment effects.

Parent-report measures may be more useful in assessing and monitoring the youth's functional impairment. In addition, youth and teacher reports on multidimensional measures of functional impairment would also be advisable as multiple informants may be required to get a comprehensive assessment of functioning across different contexts and relationships. We recognize that it is often difficult to obtain information from multiple sources; nevertheless, we strongly recommend that information from multiple informants be obtained during the initial assessment and treatment planning phase and in evaluating treatment outcome. However, it would be acceptable to monitor the youth's functioning over the course of treatment using only parent, youth reports, or both as these are more easily obtainable in clinical settings. We recommend that the C-GAS be used as the global measure of functional impairment. Finally, we suggest that future research examine the clinical utility and sensitivity to change of a number of multidimensional scales, as recommending one over the other for the purpose of assessing treatment monitoring and outcome seems premature at this time.

CONCLUSIONS AND FUTURE DIRECTIONS

In this chapter, we reviewed the major approaches and measures for diagnosing and assessing depression in children and adolescents. In addition, we identified a number of additional variables that should be considered for prognosis, treatment planning, case conceptualization, and treatment monitoring and evaluation, and briefly discussed their assessment.

In summary, a comprehensive assessment of child and adolescent depression should include (a) determining whether criteria are met for MDD or DD; (b) ruling out exclusionary diagnoses such as bipolar disorder and depression due to a general medical condition or substance; (c) assessing key symptoms such as suicidal ideation and psychotic symptoms that might influence treatment decisions; (d) carefully assessing the previous course of the depression (e.g., prior episodes and chronicity); (e) evaluating comorbid psychiatric, developmental, and general medical disorders; (f) assessing family, school, and peer functioning; (g) exploring significant stressors, traumas, and social factors, including ethnicity and culture; and (h) assessing family history of psychopathology.

Our recommendations are as follows. First, the assessment of psychopathology should include a semistructured diagnostic interview as less systematic approaches frequently overlook key areas of psychopathology and as respondent-based interviews pose several limitations, including overdiagnosing, poor discriminant validity, and the inability to clarify questions or responses. Second, data should be obtained from multiple informants, including the child (particularly if the child is over 8 years of age) and primary caregiver. Finally, regular monitoring and evaluation of treatment using clinician, self-rating, and parent-rating scales is important. Although a reduction in test scores when monitoring treatment effects should be viewed cautiously in light of the possibility of attenuation effects, this provides a means of objectively assessing progress and allows for comparison to published treatment benchmarks.

Issues for Future Research

Evaluating empirically supported assessments of child and adolescent depression is a challenging task, and a number of issues must be resolved in order to accomplish this aim. There are a number of significant gaps in the development of empirically supported assessments for youth depression that limit progress but, at the same time, define an agenda for future research.

First, more research into the phenomenology of depression in children and adolescents, including very young children, is needed, specifically addressing defining depression in categorical or dimensional terms, subtypes of youth depression, and where boundaries should be drawn between depression and other conditions.

Second, there is a need for longitudinal studies of the course of mood disorders in children and adolescents that focus specifically on the processes associated with the maintenance, recovery, and recurrence of depression. In addition, there is a need for more research on predictors of differential treatment response. This may provide valuable information regarding potential targets for assessment and treatment, and for choosing between treatment options.

Third, the poor discriminant validity of most youth depression rating scales may be improved by increasing the emphasis on aspects of depression with greater diagnostic specificity, such as anhedonia and low positive affectivity (Clark & Watson, 1991; Chorpita & Daleiden, 2002). Fourth, we need to determine the best method for integrating data from multiple informants for diagnosis and treatment evaluation.

Fifth, there is a need for methodologically rigorous comparisons between different diagnostic interviews or rating scales, and a need to determine the cost-effectiveness and treatment utility of these measures. Hayes, Nelson, and Jarrett (1987) and Nelson-Gray (2003) have described a number of research designs that can be used to test treatment utility, and which are easily implemented.

Finally, the reliability and validity of case formulations and treatment planning is a critical area in which little work has been done for child and adolescent depression. Furthermore, during the treatment monitoring phase of assessment, there are few guidelines regarding whether treatment should be intensified, changed, or discontinued. Fortunately, there are some models in the adult literature that may be useful in beginning to consider this issue (e.g., Jacobson, Roberts, Berns, & McGlinchey, 1999; Lueger et al., 2001). These gaps in the literature present us with many challenging research tasks that will further the development of evidence-based assessment tools for child and adolescent depression and facilitate the development of evidence-based treatments for depressed youth of all ages.

References

Ablow, J. C., Measelle, J. R., Kraemer, H. C., Harrington, R., Luby, J., Smider, N., et al. (1999). The MacArthur

Three-City Outcome Study: Evaluating multi-informant measures of young children's symptomatology. *Journal of the American Academy of Child & Adolescent Psychiatry, 38,* 1580–1590.

Achenbach, T. M., & Rescorla, L. A. (2004). Empirically based assessment and taxonomy: Applications to infants and toddlers. In R. DelCarmen-Wiggins & A. Carter (Eds.), *Handbook of infant, toddler, and preschool mental health assessment* (pp. 161–184). New York: Oxford University Press.

Achenbach, T. M., McConaughy, S. H., & Howell, C. T (1987). Child/adolescent behavioral and emotional problems: Implications of cross-informant correlations for situational specificity. *Psychological Bulletin, 101,* 213–232.

Achenbach, T. M., & Rescorla, L. A. (2001). *Manual for the ASEBA school-age forms & profiles.* Burlington, VT: University of Vermont.

Ambrosini, P. J. (2000). Historical development and present status of the Schedule for Affective Disorders and Schizophrenia for School-Age Children (K-SADS). *Journal of the American Academy of Child & Adolescent Psychiatry, 39,* 49–58.

American Psychiatric Association (2000). *Diagnostic and statistical manual of mental disorders* (4th ed., Text Revision). Washington, DC: Author.

Andreasen, N. C., Endicott, J., Spitzer, R. L., & Winokur, G. (1977). The family history method using diagnostic criteria. *Archives of General Psychiatry, 34,* 1229–1235.

Angold, A., & Costello, E. J. (1995). A test–retest reliability study of child-reported psychiatric symptoms and diagnoses using the Child and Adolescent Psychiatric Assessment (CAPA-C). *Psychological Medicine, 25,* 755–762.

Angold, A., & Costello, E. J. (2000). The Child and Adolescent Psychiatric Assessment (CAPA). *Journal of the American Academy of Child & Adolescent Psychiatry, 39,* 39–48.

Angold, A., Costello, E. J., & Erkanli, A. (1999). Comorbidity. *Journal of Child Psychology & Psychiatry & Allied Disciplines, 40,* 57–87.

Angold, A., Costello, E. J., Messer, S. C., & Pickles, A. (1995). Development of a short questionnaire for use in epidemiological studies of depression in children and adolescents. *International Journal of Methods in Psychiatric Research, 5,* 237–249.

Angold, A., & Fisher, P. W. (1999). Interviewer-based interviews. In D. Shaffer, C. P. Lucas, & J. E. Richters (Eds.), *Diagnostic assessment in child and adolescent psychopathology* (pp. 34–64). New York: Guilford Press.

Angold, A., Prendergast, M., Cox, A., Harrington, R., Simonoff, E., & Rutter, M. (1995). The Child and Adolescent Psychiatric Assessment (CAPA). *Psychological Medicine, 25,* 739–753.

Asarnow, J. R., Goldstein, M. J., Tompson, M., & Guthrie, D. (1993). One-year outcomes of depressive disorders in child psychiatric in-patients: Evaluation of the prognostic power of a brief measure of expressed emotion. *Journal of Child Psychology & Psychiatry & Allied Disciplines, 34,* 129–137.

Asarnow, J. R., Jaycox, L. H., & Thompson, M. C. (2001). Depression in youth: Psychosocial interventions. *Journal of Clinical Child Psychology, 30,* 33–47.

Asarnow, J. R., Scott, C., & Mintz, J. (2002). A combined cognitive-behavioral family education intervention for depression in children: A treatment development study. *Cognitive Therapy and Research, 26,* 221–229.

Bates, M. P. (2001). The Child and Adolescent Functional Assessment Scale (CAFAS): Review and current status. *Clinical Child & Family Psychology Review, 4,* 63–84.

Bird, H. R. (1999). The assessment of functional impairment. In D. Shaffer, C. P. Lucas, & J. E. Richters (Eds.), *Diagnostic assessment in child and adolescent psychopathology* (pp. 209–229). New York: Guilford Press.

Bird, H. R., Shaffer, D., Fisher, P., Gould, M. S., Staghezza, G., Chen, J. Y., et al. (1993). The Columbia Impairment Scale (CIS): Pilot findings on a measure of global impairment for children and adolescents. *International Journal of Methods in Psychiatric Research, 3,* 167–176.

Birmaher, B., Arbelaez, C., & Brent, D. (2002). Course and outcome of child and adolescent major depressive disorder. *Child and Adolescent Clinics of North America, 11,* 619–638.

Birmaher, B., Brent., D., Kolko, D., Baugher, M., Bridge, J., Holder, D., et al. (2000). Clinical outcome after short-term psychotherapy for adolescents with major depressive disorder. *Archives of General Psychiatry, 57,* 29–36.

Boyle, M. H., Offord, D. R., Racine, Y., Sanford, M., Szatmari, P., Fleming, J. E., et al. (1993). Evaluation of the diagnostic interview for children and adolescents for use in general population samples. *Journal of Abnormal Child Psychology, 21,* 663–681.

Brent, D., Kolko, D., Birmaher, B., Baugher, M., Bridge, J., Roth, C., et al. (1998). Predictors of treatment efficacy in a clinical trial of three psychosocial treatments for adolescent depression. *Journal of the American Academy of Child & Adolescent Psychiatry, 37,* 906–909.

Brooks, S. J., & Kutcher, S. (2001). Diagnosis and measurement of adolescent depression: A review of commonly utilized instruments. *Journal of Child & Adolescent Psychopharmacology, 11,* 341–376.

Canino, G., Costello, E. J., & Angold, A. (1999). Assessing functional impairment for mental health services research: A review of measures. *Journal of Mental Health Research, 1,* 93–108.

Chen, I. G., Roberts, E., & Aday, L. A. (1998). Ethnicity and adolescent depression: The case of Chinese Americans. *Journal of Nervous and Mental Disease, 186,* 623–630.

Chorpita, B. F., & Daleiden, E. L. (2002). Tripartite dimensions of emotion in a child clinical sample: Measurement strategies and implications for clinical utility. *Journal of Consulting and Clinical Psychology, 70,* 1150–1160.

Clarke, G. N., Hawkins, W., Murphy, M., Sheeber, L. B., Lewinsohn, P. M., & Seeley, J. R. (1995). Targeted prevention of unipolar depressive disorder in an at-risk sample of high school adolescents: A randomized trial of group cognitive intervention. *Journal of the American Academy of Child & Adolescent Psychiatry, 34,* 312–321.

Clarke, G. N., Hornbrook, M., Lynch, F., Polen, M., Gale, J., Beardslee, W., et al. (2001). A randomized trial of group cognitive intervention for preventing depression in adolescent offspring of depressed parents. *Archives of General Psychiatry, 58,* 1127–1134.

Clarke, G. N., Rhode, P., Lewinsohn, P., Hops, H., & Seeley, J. R. (1999). Cognitive-behavioral treatment of adolescent depression: Efficacy of acute group treatment and booster sessions. *Journal of the American Academy of Child & Adolescent Psychiatry, 38,* 272–279.

Clark, L. A., & Watson, D. (1991). Tripartite model of anxiety and depression: Evidence and taxonomic implications. *Journal of Abnormal Psychology, 100,* 316–336.

Coie, J. D., Dodge, K. A., & Coppotelli, H. (1982). Dimensions and types of social status: A cross-age perspective. *Developmental Psychology, 18,* 557–570.

Cole, D. A., Hoffman, K., Tram, J. M., & Maxwell, S. E. (2000). Structural differences in parent and child reports of children's symptoms of depression and anxiety. *Psychological Assessment, 12,* 174–185.

Costello, A. J., Edelbrock, C., Dulcan, M. K., Kalas, R., & Klaric, S. (1984). *Report on the NIMH Diagnostic Interview Schedule for Children (DISC).* Washington, DC: National Institute of Mental Health.

De Cuyper, S., Timbremont, B., Braet, C., De Backer, V., & Wullaert, R. (2004). Treating depressive symptoms in school children: A pilot study. *Journal of European Child and Adolescent Psychiatry, 13,* 105–114.

Diamond, G. S., Reis, B. F., Diamond, G. M., Siqueland, L., & Isaacs, L. (2002). Attachment-based family therapy for depressed adolescents: A treatment development study. *Journal of the American Academy of Child & Adolescent Psychiatry, 41,* 1190–1196.

Duggal, S., Malkoff-Schwartz, S., Birmaher, B., Anderson, B., Matty, M. K., Houck, P. R., et al. (2000). Assessment of life stress in adolescents: Self-report versus interview methods. *Journal of the American Academy of Child & Adolescent Psychiatry, 39,* 445–452.

Edelbrock, C., Costello, A. J., Dulcan, M. K., Kalas, R., & Conover, N. C. (1985). Age differences in the reliability of the psychiatric interview of the child. *Child Development, 56,* 265–275.

Egger, H. L., & Angold, A. (2004). The Preschool Age Psychiatric Assessment (PAPA): A structured parent interview for diagnosing psychiatric disorders in preschool children. In R. DelCarmen-Wiggins & A. Carter (Eds.), *Handbook of infant, toddler, and preschool mental health assessment* (pp. 223–243). New York: Oxford University Press.

Egger, H. L., & Angold, A. (2006). Common emotional and behavioral disorders in preschool children: Presentation, nosology, and epidemiology. *Journal of Child Psychology and Psychiatry, 47,* 313–337.

Egger, H. L., Erkanli, A., Keeler, G., Potts, E., Walter, B., & Angold, A. (2006). Test–retest reliability of the Preschool Age Psychiatric Assessment (PAPA). *Journal of the American Academy of Child & Adolescent Psychiatry, 45,* 538–549.

Emslie, G. J., Rush, A. J., Weinberg, W. A., Kowatch, R. A., Hughes, C. W., Carmody, T., et al. (1997). Double-blind placebo-controlled trial of fluoxetine in depressed children and adolescents. *Archives of General Psychiatry, 54,* 1031–1037.

Emslie, G. J., Mayes, T. L., Laptook, R. S., & Batt, M. (2003). Predictors of response to treatment in children and adolescents with mood disorders. *Psychiatric Clinics of North America, 26,* 435–456.

Epstein, N. B., Baldwin, L. M., & Bishop, D. S. (1983). The McMaster family assessment device. *Journal of Marital & Family Therapy, 9,* 171–180.

Essex, M. J., Boyce, W. T., Goldstein, L. H., Armstrong, J. M., Kraemer, H. C., & Kupfer, D. J. (2002). The confluence of mental, physical, social, and academic difficulties in middle childhood. II: Developing the MacArthur Health and Behavior Questionnaire. *Journal of the American Academy of Child & Adolescent Psychiatry, 41,* 588–603.

Ezpeleta, L., de la Osa, N., Domenech, J. M., Navarro, J. B., Losilla, J. M., & Judez, J. (1997). Diagnostic agreement between clinicians and the Diagnostic Interview for Children and Adolescents—DICA-R—in an outpatient sample. *Journal of Child Psychology & Psychiatry & Allied Disciplines, 38,* 431–440.

Ferdinand, R. F., Hoogerheide, K. N., van der Ende, J., Visser, J. H., Koot, H. M., Kasius, M. C., et al. (2003). The role of the clinician: Three-year predictive value of parents', teachers', and clincians' judgments of childhood psychopathology. *Journal of Child Psychology and Psychiatry, 44*, 867–876.

Fisher, P., Leon, A. C., & Coles, M. E. (2002). *The Longitudinal Interval Follow-up Evaluation Range of Impaired Functioning Tool (LIFE-RIFT), adapted for children and adolescents.* Unpublished manuscript, New York State Psychiatric Institute, New York.

Gadow, K. D., & Sprafkin, J. (2000). *Early childhood inventory-4: Screening manual.* Stony Brook, NY: Checkmate Plus.

Garber, J., & Horowitz, J. L. (2002). Depression in children. In Gotlib, I. H., & Hammen, C. L. (Eds.), *Handbook of depression* (pp. 510–540). New York: Guilford Press.

Garber, J., & Kaminski, K. M. (2000). Laboratory and performance-based measures of depression in children and adolescents. *Journal of Clinical Child Psychology, 29*, 509–525.

Geller, B., Fox, L. W., & Clark, K. A. (1994). Rate and predictors of prepubertal bipolarity during follow-up of 6- to 12-year-old depressed children. *Journal of the American Academy of Child & Adolescent Psychiatry, 33*, 461–468.

Goodman, S. H., Schwab-Stone, M. D., Lahey, B. B., Shaffer, D., & Jensen, P. S. (2000). Major depression and dysthymia in children and adolescents: Discriminant validity and differential consequences in a community sample. *Journal of the American Academy of Child & Adolescent Psychiatry, 39*, 761–770.

Goodyer, I. M. (2001). Life events: Their nature and effects. In I. M. Goodyer (Ed.), *The depressed child and adolescent* (2nd ed., pp. 204–232). New York: Cambridge University Press.

Goodyer, I. M., Herbert, J., Tamplin, A., Secher, S., & Pearson, J. (1997). Life events, family dysfunction, and friendship difficulties as predictors of persistent depression. *Journal of the American Academy of Child & Adolescent Psychiatry, 36*, 474–477.

Hamilton, J., & Gillham, J. (1999). The K-SADS and diagnosis of major depressive disorder. *Journal of the American Academy of Child & Adolescent Psychiatry, 38*, 1065–1066.

Hammen, C. (2006). Stress generation in depression: Reflections on origins, research, and future directions. *Journal of Clinical Psychology, 62*, 1065–1082.

Hammen, C., Rudolph, K., Weisz, J., Rao, U., & Burge, D. (1999). The context of depression in clinic-referred youth: Neglected areas in treatment. *Journal of the American Academy of Child and Adolescent Psychiatry, 38*, 64–71.

Hankin, B. L., Abramson, L. Y., Moffitt, T. E., Silva, P. A., McGee, R., & Angell, K. E. (1998). Development of depression from preadolescence to young adulthood: Emerging gender differences in a 10-year longitudinal study. *Journal of Abnormal Psychology, 107*, 128–140.

Hart, E. L., & Lahey, B. B. (1999). General child behavior rating scales. In D. Shaffer, C. P. Lucas, & J. E. Richters (Eds.), *Diagnostic assessment in child and adolescent psychopathology* (pp. 65–87). New York: Guilford Press.

Hawley, K. M., & Weisz, J. R. (2003). Child, parent, and therapist (dis)agreement on target problems in outpatient therapy: The therapist's dilemma and its implications. *Journal of Consulting and Clinical Psychology, 71*, 62–70.

Hayes, S. C., Nelson, R. O., & Jarrett, R. B. (1987). The treatment utility of assessment: A functional approach to evaluating assessment quality. *American Psychologist, 42*, 963–974.

Herjanic, B., & Reich, W. (1982). Development of a structured psychiatric interview for children: Agreement between child and parent on individual symptoms. *Journal of Abnormal Child Psychology, 10*, 307–324.

Hodges, K. (1994). Evaluation of depression in children and adolescents using diagnostic clinical interviews. In W. M. Reynolds & H. F. Johnston (Eds.), *Handbook of depression in children and adolescents* (pp. 183–208). New York: Plenum Press.

Hodges, K. (1999). Child and Adolescent Functional Assessment Scale (CAFAS). In M. E. Maruish (Ed.), *The use of psychological testing for treatment planning and outcomes assessment* (2nd ed., pp. 631–664). Mahwah, NJ: Lawrence Erlbaum Associates, Publishers.

Huesmann, L. R., Eron, L. D., Guerra, N. G., & Crawshaw, V. B. (1994). Measuring children's aggression with teachers' predictions of peer nominations. *Psychological Assessment, 6*, 329–336.

Huey, S. J., Henggeler, S., Rowland, M., Halliday-Boykins, C., Cunningham, P., & Pickrel, S. (2005). Predictors of treatment response for suicidal youth referred for emergency psychiatric hospitalization. *Journal of Clinical Child and Adolescent Psychiatry, 34*, 582–589.

Hughes, C. W., Emslie, G. J., Wohlfahrt, H., Winslow, R., Kashner, R. M., & Rush, A. J. (2005). Effect of structured interviews on evaluation time in pediatric community mental health settings. *Psychiatric Services, 56*, 1098–1103.

Ialongo, N. S., Edelsohn, G., & Kellam, S. G. (2001). A further look at the prognostic power of young children's reports of depressed mood. *Child Development, 72,* 736–747.

Jacobson, N. S., Roberts, L. J., Berns, S. B., & McGlinchey, J. B. (1999). Methods for defining and determining the clinical significance of treatment effects: Description, application, and alternatives. *Journal of Consulting and Clinical Psychology, 67,* 300–307.

Jensen P. S., Rubio-Stipec, M., Canino, G., Bird, H. R., Dulcan, M. K., Schwab-Stone, M. E., et al. (1999). Parent and child contributions to diagnosis of mental disorder: Are both informants always necessary? *Journal of the American Academy of Child & Adolescent Psychiatry, 38,* 1569–1579.

John, K. (2001). Measuring children's social functioning. *Child Psychology and Psychiatry Review, 6,* 181–188.

John, K., Gammon, G. D., Prusoff, B. A., & Warner, V. (1987). The Social Adjustment Inventory for Children and Adolescents (SAICA): Testing of a new semistructured interview. *Journal of the American Academy of Child & Adolescent Psychiatry, 26,* 898–911.

Johnson, J. H., & McCutcheon, S. M. (1980). Assessing life stress in older children and adolescents: Preliminary findings with the life events checklist. In I. G. Sarason & C. D. Spielberger (Eds.), *Stress and anxiety* (pp. 111–125). Washington, DC: Hemisphere.

Kahn, J. S., Kehle, T. J., Jenson, W. R., & Clark, E. (1990). Comparison of cognitive-behavioral, relaxation, and self-modeling interventions for depression among middle school students. *School Psychology Review, 19,* 196–211.

Kaslow, N. J., McClure, E. B., & Connell, A. M. (2002). Treatment of depression in children and adolescents. In I. H. Gotlib & C. L. Hammen (Eds.), *Handbook of depression* (pp. 441–464). New York: Guilford Press.

Kaufman, J., Birmaher, B., Brent, D., Rao, U., Flynn, C., Moreci, P., et al. (1997). Schedule for Affective Disorders and Schizophrenia for School-Age Children-Present and Lifetime version (K-SADS-PL): Initial reliability and validity data. *Journal of the American Academy of Child & Adolescent Psychiatry, 36,* 980–988.

Kazdin, A. E. (2003). Delineating mechanisms of change in child and adolescent therapy: Methodological issues and research recommendations. *Journal of Child Psychology and Psychiatry and Allied Disciplines, 44,* 1116–1129.

Kendall, P. C., Cantwell, D. P., & Kazdin, A. E. (1989). Depression in children and adolescents: Assessment issues and recommendations. *Cognitive Therapy and Research, 13,* 109–146.

Kent, L., Vostanis, P., & Feehan, C. (1997). Detection of major and minor depression in children and adolescents: Evaluation of the Mood and Feelings Questionnaire. *Journal of Child Psychology & Psychiatry & Allied Disciplines, 38,* 565–573.

Klein, D. N., Lewinsohn, P. M., Seeley, J. R., & Rhode, P. (2001). A family study of major depressive disorder in a community sample of adolescents. *Archives of General Psychiatry, 58,* 13–20.

Klein, D. N., Ouimette, P. C., Kelly, H. S., Ferro, T., & Riso, L. P. (1994). Test-retest reliability of team consensus best-estimate diagnoses of Axis I and II disorders in a family study. *American Journal of Psychiatry, 151,* 1043–1047.

Klein, D. N., & Riso, L. P. (1993). Psychiatric diagnoses: Problems of boundaries and co-occurrences. In C. G. Costello (Ed.), *Basic issues in psychopathology* (pp. 19–66). New York: Guilford Press.

Klein, D. N., Shankman, S. A., & McFarland, B. (2006). Classification of mood disorders. In D. J. Stein, D. J. Kupfer, & A. F. Schatzberg (Eds.), *The American psychiatric publishing textbook of mood disorders* (pp. 17–32). Washington, DC: American Psychiatric Publishing, Inc.

Kovacs, M. (1986). A developmental perspective on the methods and measures in the assessment of depressive disorders: The clinical interview. In M. Rutter, C. E. Izard, and P. B. Read (Eds.), *Depression in young people: Developmental and clinical perspectives* (pp. 435–465). New York: Guilford Press.

Kovacs, M. (1992, 2003). *Children's depression inventory manual.* North Tonawanda, NY: Multi-Health Systems.

Kovacs, M. (1996). Presentation and course of major depressive disorder during childhood and later years of the life span. *Journal of the American Academy of Child & Adolescent Psychiatry, 35,* 705–715.

Kraemer, H. C., Measelle, J. R., Ablow, J. C., Essex, M. J., Boyce, W. T., & Kupfer, D. J. (2003). A new approach to integrating data from multiple informants in psychiatric assessment and research: Mixing and matching contexts and perspectives. *American Journal of Psychiatry, 160,* 1566–1577.

Leon, A. C., Solomon, D. A., Mueller, T. I., Turvey, C. A., Endicott, J., & Keller, M. B. (1999). The Range of Impaired Functioning Tool (LIFE-RIFT): A brief measure of functional impairment. *Psychological Medicine, 29,* 869–878.

Lewczyk, C. M., Garland, A. F., Hurlbert, M. S., Gearity, J., & Hough, R. L. (2003). Comparing DISC-IV and clinician diagnoses among youths receiving public mental health services. *Journal* of the American Academy of Child & Adolescent Psychiatry, 42, 349–356.

Lewinsohn, P. M., & Essau, C. A. (2002). Depression in adolescents. In I. H. Gotlib & C. L. Hammen (Eds.), Handbook of depression (pp. 541–559). New York: Guilford Press.

Lewinsohn, P., Clarke, G. N., Hops, H., & Andrews, J. (1990). Cognitive-behavioral treatment for depressed adolescents. Behavior Therapy, 21, 385–401.

Luby, J. L., Heffelfinger, A., Measelle, J. R., Ablow, J. C., Essex, M. J., Dierker, L., et al. (2002). Differential performance of the McArthur HBQ and DISC-IV in identifying DSM-IV internalizing psychopathology in young children. Journal of the American Academy of Child & Adolescent Psychiatry, 41, 458–466.

Luby, J. L., Mrakotsky, C., Heffelfinger, A., Brown, K., & Spitznagel, E. (2004). Characteristics of depressed preschoolers with and without anhedonia: Evidence for a melancholic depressive subtype in young children. American Journal of Psychiatry, 161, 1998–2004.

Luby, J. L., Sullivan, J., Belden, A., Stalets, M., Blankenship, S., & Spitznagel, E. (2006). An observational analysis of behavior in depressed preschoolers: Further validation of early-onset depression. Journal of the American Academy of Child & Adolescent Psychiatry, 45, 203–212.

Lucas, C., Fisher, P., & Luby, J. (1998). Young-Child DISC-IV Research Draft. Diagnostic Interview Schedule for Children. New York: Columbia University, Division of Child Psychiatry.

Lueger, R. J., Howard, K. I., Martinovich, Z., Lutz, W., Anderson, E. E., & Grissom, G. (2001). Assessing treatment progress of individual patients using expected treatment response models. Journal of Consulting and Clinical Psychology, 69, 150–158.

Lukens, E., Puig-Antich, J., Behn, J., Goetz, R., Tabrizi, M., & Davies, M. (1983). Reliability of the Psychosocial Schedule for School-Age Children. Journal of the American Academy of Child & Adolescent Psychiatry, 22, 29–39.

Mannuzza, S., & Fyer, A. J. (1990). Family informant schedule and criteria (FISC), July 1990 revision. New York: Anxiety Disorders Clinic, New York State Psychiatric Institute.

Matthey, S., & Petrovski, P. (2002). The Children's Depression Inventory: Error in cutoff scores for screening purposes. Psychological Assessment, 14, 146–149.

Meehl, P. E., & Rosen, A. (1955). Antecedent probability and the efficacy of psychometric signs, patterns, or cutting scores. Psychological Bulletin, 52, 194–216.

Muratori, F., Picchi, L., Bruni, B., Patarnello, M., & Romagnoli, G. (2003). A two-year follow-up of psychodynamic psychotherapy for internalizing disorders in children. Journal of the American Academy of Child & Adolescent Psychiatry, 42, 331–339.

Myers, K., & Winters, N. C. (2002). Ten-year review of rating scales. II: Scales for internalizing disorders. Journal of the American Academy of Child & Adolescent Psychiatry, 41, 634–659.

Nelson-Gray, R. O. (2003). Treatment utility of psychological assessment. Psychological Assessment, 15, 521–531.

Olsson, G., & von Knorring, A. L. (1997). Depression among Swedish adolescents measured by the self-rating scale Center for Epidemiology Studies-Depression Child (CES-DC). European Journal of Child & Adolescent Psychiatry, 6, 81–87.

Park, R. J., & Goodyer, I. M. (2000). Clinical guidelines for depressive disorders in childhood and adolescence. European Child & Adolescent Psychiatry, 9, 147–161.

Poznanski, E. O., Cook, S. C., & Carroll, B. J. (1979). A depression rating scale for children. Pediatrics, 64, 442–450.

Poznanski, E. O., & Mokros, H. B. (1999). Children Depression Rating Scale-Revised (CDRS-R). Los Angeles, CA: Western Psychological Services.

Puig-Antich, J., & Chambers, W. (1978). The Schedule for Affective Disorders and Schizophrenia for School-Age Children. New York: New York State Psychiatric Institute.

Puig-Antich, J., Lukens, E., & Brent, D. (1986). Psychosocial schedule for school-age children-Revised. Pittsburgh, PA: Western Psychiatric Institute and Clinic.

Reich, W. (2000). Diagnostic Interview for Children and Adolescents (DICA). Journal of the American Academy of Child & Adolescent Psychiatry, 39, 59–66.

Reynolds, W. M. (1987). Reynolds adolescent depression scale: Professional manual. Odessa, FL: Psychological Assessment Resources.

Reynolds, W. M. (1989). Reynolds child depression scale: Professional manual. Odessa, FL: Psychological Assessment Resources.

Reynolds, W. M. (2004). The Reynolds Adolescent Depression Scale-Second Edition (RADS-2). In M. J. Hilsenroth & D. L. Segal (Eds.), Comprehensive handbook of psychological assessment, Vol 2: Personality assessment (pp. 224–236). Hoboken, NJ: John Wiley & Sons Inc.

Richters, J. E. (1992). Depressed mothers as informants about their children: A critical review of the evidence for distortion. *Psychological Bulletin, 112*, 485–499.

Roberts, R. E., Lewinsohn, P. M., & Seeley, J. R. (1991). Screening for adolescent depression: A comparison of depression scales. *Journal of the American Academy of Child & Adolescent Psychiatry, 30*, 58–66.

Rohde, P., Feeny, N., & Robins, M. (2005). Characteristics and components of the TADS CBT approach. *Cognitive and Behavioral Practice, 12*, 186–197.

Rosello, J., & Bernal, G. (1999). The efficacy of cognitive-behavioral and interpersonal treatments for depression in Puerto-Rican adolescents. *Journal of Consulting and Clinical Psychology, 67*, 734–745.

Rudolph, K. D., Hammen, C., & Burge, D. (1994). Interpersonal functioning and depressive symptoms in childhood: Addressing the issues of specificity and comorbidity. *Journal of Abnormal Child Psychology, 22*, 355–371.

Sandberg, S., Rutter, M., Giles, S., Owen, A., Champion, L., Nicholls, J., et al. (1993). Assessment of psychosocial experiences in childhood: Methodological issues and some illustrative findings. *Journal of Child Psychology and Psychiatry, 34*, 879–897.

Sanford, M., Szatmari, P., Spinner, M., Munroe-Blum, H., Jamieson, E., Walsh, C., et al. (1995). Predicting the one-year course of adolescent major depression. *Journal of the American Academy of Child & Adolescent Psychiatry, 34*, 1618–1628.

Schaefer, E. S. (1965). Children' reports of parental behavior: An inventory. *Child Development, 36*, 413–424.

Schwab-Stone, M. E., Shaffer, D., Dulcan, M. K., Jensen, P. S., Fisher, P. Bird, H. R., et al., (1996). Criterion validity of the NIMH Diagnostic Interview Schedule for Children (DISC-2.3). *Journal of the American Academy of Child & Adolescent Psychiatry, 35*, 878–888.

Shaffer, D., Fisher, P., Lucas, C., Dulcan, M., & Schwab-Stone, M. (2000). The Diagnostic Interview Schedule for Children Version IV (DISC-IV): Description, differences from previous versions, and reliability of some common diagnoses. *Journal of the American Academy of Child & Adolescent Psychiatry, 39*, 28–38.

Shaffer, D., Gould, M. S., Brasic, J., Ambrosini, P., Fisher, P., Bird, H., et al. (1983) A Children's Global Assessment Scale (CGAS). *Archives of General Psychiatry, 40*, 1228–1231.

Silverman, W. K., & Rabian, B. (1999). Rating scales for anxiety and mood disorders. In D. Shaffer, C. P. Lucas, & J. E. Richters (Eds.), *Diagnostic assessment in child and adolescent psychopathology* (pp. 127–166). New York: Guilford Press.

Sheeber, L., Hops, H., & Davis, B. (2001). Family processes in adolescent depression. *Clinical Child and Family Psychology Review, 4*, 19–35.

Stark, K. D. (1990). *Childhood depression: School-based intervention*. New York: Guilford Press.

Stark, K. D., Reynolds, W. M., & Kaslow, N. J. (1987). A comparison of the relative efficacy of self-control therapy and a behavioral problem-solving therapy for depression in children. *Journal of Abnormal Child Psychology, 15*, 91–113.

Taylor, J., & Turner, R. J. (2002). Perceived discrimination, social stress, and depression in the transition to adulthood: Racial contrasts. *Social Psychology Quarterly, 65*, 213–225.

Thapar, A., & McGuffin, P. (1998). Validity of the shortened Mood and Feelings Questionnaire in a community sample of children and adolescents: A preliminary research note. *Psychiatry Research, 81*, 259–268.

Vasa, R. A., Carlino, A. R., & Pine, D. S. (2006). Pharmacotherapy of depressed children and adolescents: Current issues and potential directions. *Biological Psychiatry, 59*, 1021–1028.

Verhulst, F. C., Dekker, M. C., & van der Ende, J. (1997). Parent, teacher, and self-reports as predictors of signs of disturbance in adolescents: Whose information carries the most weight? *Acta Psychiatrica Scandinavica, 96*, 75–81.

Vostanis, P., Feehan, C., Grattan, E., & Bickerton, W. L. (1996). A randomized controlled outpatient trial of cognitive-behavioral treatment for children and adolescents with depression: 9-month follow-up. *Journal of Affective Disorders, 40*, 105–116.

Wadsworth, M. E., Hudziak, J. J., Heath, A. C., & Achenbach, T. M. (2001). Latent class analysis of Child Behavior Checklist anxiety/depression in children and adolescents. *Journal of the American Academy of Child & Adolescent Psychiatry, 40*, 106–114.

Wamboldt, M. Z., Wamboldt, F. S., Gavin, L., & McTaggart, S. (2001). A parent-child relationship scale derived from the Child and Adolescent Psychiatric Assessment (CAPA). *Journal of the American Academy of Child & Adolescent Psychiatry, 40*, 945–953.

Weersing, V., & Weisz, J. (2002). Community clinic treatment of depressed youth: Benchmarking usual care against CBT clinical trials. *Journal of Consulting and Clinical Psychology, 70*, 299–310.

Weiss, B., & Garber, G. (2003). Developmental differences in the phenomenology of depression. *Development and Psychopathology, 15*, 403–430.

Weissman, M., Pilowsky, D., Wickramaratne, P., Talati, A., Wisniewski, S., Fava, M., et al. (2006). Remissions in maternal depression and child psychopathology: A

STAR*D-Child Report. *Journal of the American Medical Association, 295,* 1389–1398.

Weissman, M. M., Wickramaratne, P., Adams, P., Wolk, S., Verdeli, H., & Olfson, M. (2000). Brief screening for family psychiatric history: The family history screen. *Archives of General Psychiatry, 57,* 675–682.

Weisz, J. R., Chaiyasit, W., Weiss, B., Eastman, K. L., & Jackson, E. W. (1995). A multimethod study of problem behavior among Thai and American children in school: Teacher reports versus direct observations. *Child Development, 66,* 402–415.

Weisz, J. R., McCarty, C. A., & Valeri, S. M. (2006). Effects of psychotherapy for depression in children and adolescents: A meta-analysis. *Psychological Bulletin, 132,* 132–149.

Weller, E. B., Weller, R. A., Fristad, M. A., Rooney, M. T., & Schecter, J. (2000). Children's Interview for Psychiatric Disorders (ChIPS). *Journal of the American Academy of Child & Adolescent Psychiatry, 39,* 76–84.

Wight, R. G., Aneshensel, C. S., Botticello, A. L., & Sepulveda, J. E. (2005). A multilevel analysis of ethnic variation in depressive symptoms among adolescents in the United States. *Social Science & Medicine, 60,* 2073–2084.

Williamson, D. E., Birmaher, B., Ryan, N. D., Shiffrin, T. P., Lusky, J. A., Protopapa, J., et al. (2003). The stressful life events schedule for children and adolescents: Development and validation. *Psychiatry Research, 119,* 225–241.

Winters, N. C., Collett, B. R., & Myers, K. M. (2005). Ten-year review of rating scales. VII: Scales assessing functional impairment. *Journal of the American Academy of Child & Adolescent Psychiatry, 44,* 309–338.

Winters, N. C., Myers, K., & Proud, L. (2002). Ten-year review of rating scales. III: Scales assessing suicidality, cognitive style, and self-esteem. *Journal of the American Academy of Child & Adolescent Psychiatry, 41,* 1150–1181.

Wood, A., Kroll, L., Moore, A., & Harrington, R. (1995). Properties of the Mood and Feelings Questionnaire in adolescent psychiatric outpatients: A research note. *Journal of Child Psychology & Psychiatry & Allied Disciplines, 36,* 327–334.

Wood, A., Harrington, R., & Moore, A. (1996). Controlled trial of a brief cognitive-behavioral intervention in adolescent patients with depressive disorders. *Journal of Child Psychology and Psychiatry, 37,* 737–746.

Youngstrom, E., Izard, C., & Ackerman, B. (1999). Dysphoria-related bias in maternal ratings of children. *Journal of Consulting and Clinical Psychology, 67,* 905–916.

Zimmerman, M. (2003). What should the standard of care for psychiatric diagnostic evaluations be? *Journal of Nervous and Mental Disease, 191,* 281–286.

5

Adult Depression

Jacqueline B. Persons

David M. Fresco

Following a brief overview of the diagnostic criteria and epidemiology of major depressive disorder (MDD), we describe the current major empirically supported theories of depression and the therapies based on them. We begin the discussion of the assessment by describing diagnostic assessment tools. Next, we discuss using the general theories and therapies of depression described in the first part of the chapter to create a conceptualization and treatment plan for a particular patient. We conclude with a review of assessment tools and strategies for monitoring the process and outcome of therapy, and a brief discussion of some future directions of assessment of depression.

We focus this review on MDD, both because space is limited and because the empirical support for the tools we describe is strongest for MDD. However, many other mood disorders (including dysthymic disorder, adjustment disorder with depressed mood, schizoaffective disorder, bipolar disorder, and cyclothymic disorder) share features with MDD, and many of the assessment tools described below will be helpful in those cases. For a discussion of assessment issues related specifically to bipolar disorder, the reader may consult Chapter 6 in this volume by Johnson, Miller, and Eisner.

THE NATURE OF MAJOR DEPRESSIVE DISORDER

Diagnostic Criteria

MDD is an episodic mood disorder characterized by depressed mood or anhedonia (loss of interest and pleasure in life) that has persisted for most of the day,

nearly every day, for at least 2 weeks and is accompanied by five or more of the following symptoms: weight gain or significant weight loss not associated with dieting, decrease or increase in appetite, insomnia or hypersomnia, psychomotor agitation or retardation (observable by others), fatigue or loss of energy, feelings of worthlessness, excessive or inappropriate guilt, diminished ability to think or concentrate, indecisiveness, or suicidality (American Psychiatric Association, 2000). The symptoms cause clinically significant distress or impairment in social, occupational, or other important areas of functioning and are not due to the direct physiological effects of a substance (e.g., a drug of abuse, a medication) or a general medical condition (e.g., hypothyroidism).

Epidemiology of Major Depressive Disorder

MDD is a prevalent and debilitating national health problem. In the National Comorbidity Survey Replication (Kessler, Chiu, Demler, Merikangas, & Walters, 2005), MDD had the highest lifetime and 12-month prevalence (17% and 7%, respectively) estimates of 14 major psychiatric disorders. MDD affects over 13 million individuals per year in the United States (Kessler et al., 2003). Estimates of the monetary cost of MDD exceed $43 billion a year in treatment and lost productivity—a toll slightly greater than the cost of heart disease (Greenberg, 1993; Stewart, Ricci, Chee, Hahn, & Morganstein, 2003). Mintz, Mintz, Arruda, and Hwang (1992) found that a disproportionate number of depressed individuals were unemployed (11%) or experienced profound impairment on the job (44%). According to the World Health Organization,

MDD accounted for the fourth greatest burden of all diseases worldwide and will move into "second place" by 2020 (Lopez & Murray, 1998). MDD is 1.5 times more common in women than men. Mood disorders are significantly less common among individuals of Hispanic and African ethnicity. MDD is associated with high rates of comorbidity with other psychiatric disorders. Comorbid anxiety disorders are common, with rates ranging from 37% with separation anxiety to 62% with generalized anxiety disorder. Other common comorbid conditions include substance abuse, pain, and other somatoform disorders, eating disorders, dementias, and personality disorders. There is a growing consensus that the long-term outcome of MDD is relatively poor (Fava, Rafanelli, Grandi, Conti, & Belluardo, 1998), with the risk of MDD becoming a chronic problem increasing substantially with each episode experienced (Solomon et al., 2000).

Theories of Depression

We describe several of the major behavioral, cognitive, emotion-focused, and interpersonal theories of depression and the therapies based on them. We present theories with a substantial evidence base that have given rise to evidence-based therapies. However, we do not review those evidence bases here. Some recent reviews are provided by Hollon, Stewart, and Strunk (2006) and Nathan and Gorman (2002).

Behavioral Models

Behavioral approaches view depression as resulting from an excess of maladaptive escape or avoidance behaviors and a dearth of behavioral responses capable of producing positive reinforcement (Ferster, 1973). Lewinsohn (1974) posited that depressed individuals lack positive reinforcement, or have experienced life events or stressors that caused them to lose, the ability to obtain positive reinforcers, and that until they learn to obtain positive reinforcement, they will be inactive, withdrawn, and dysphoric. Lewinsohn developed a therapy based on his theory that helps depressed individuals increase the positive reinforcement they experience by learning to identify and carry out positive activities, learn and practice relaxation, and improve their social skills.

Ferster (1973) proposed that depression arises and is maintained because individuals have oriented their lives in service of escape or avoidance instead of the pursuit of positive reinforcement. Ferster proposed a functional analytic approach to depression that focused on decreasing the reliance on escape or avoidance behaviors and expanding an individual's behavioral repertoire to increase the availability of positive reinforcements. Although Ferster never developed a manualized therapy, the essence of his model is well-represented in the work of Jacobson and colleagues who rekindled interest in this behavioral approach by conceptualizing depressed individuals as having developed a narrow repertoire of behavior that predominantly features escape or avoidance of aversive stimuli and consequences (Jacobson, Martell, & Dimidjian, 2001; Martell, Addis, & Jacobson, 2001). In contrast to cognitive theorists (described in the next section), these theorists view the symptom of rumination as an avoidance behavior that prevents adaptive approach behaviors. On the basis of this theory, Jacobson and colleagues developed a treatment for depression called behavioral activation (BA), which strives to promote a broader repertoire of behaviors and to reduce escape and avoidance behaviors, including rumination.

Cognitive Models

Cognitive models of depression include the learned helplessness and hopelessness theories (Abramson, Metalsky, & Alloy, 1989; Abramson, Seligman, & Teasdale, 1978), Beck's cognitive theory (Beck, 1967, 1976), the mindfulness-based model of Segal, Williams, and Teasdale (2002), and the theory of chronic depression developed by McCullough (2000). The reformulated learned helplessness theory (Abramson et al., 1978) and the hopelessness theory (Abramson et al., 1989) are cognitive diathesis-stress models of depression that follow from the original learned helplessness theory (Seligman, 1974). The reformulated helplessness theory and the hopelessness theory propose that individuals become depressed when they experience stressful life events and make internal, stable, and global attributions about the causes of negative events, and/or external, unstable, and specific attributions about the causes of positive events. Although the hopelessness and helplessness theories have not directly led to the development of a particular therapy, these theories certainly suggest interventions that can be imported from cognitive and behavioral therapies and can be useful in the case conceptualization process (i.e., identification of pessimistic causal attributions and the deficits in motivation/onset of depression symptoms that arise).

Beck's (1967, 1976) cognitive theory of depression, like the helplessness and hopelessness theories, is a diathesis-stress theory. That is, it proposes that depression results when a vulnerability factor in an individual (the diathesis) is triggered by a stressor. Beck's theory proposes that individuals who have negative and distorted schemas of the self, world, and future (the "negative cognitive triad") are at increased risk for depression when life events activate those schemas. Beck (1976) describes schemas as organized, enduring representations of knowledge and experience, generally formed in childhood, which guide the processing of current information. Beck's model views symptoms as comprised of emotions, automatic thoughts, and behaviors that are connected and influence one another. Cognitive therapy (CT) of depression (Beck, Rush, Shaw, & Emery, 1979), which was predicated on Beck's theory, is designed to help the patient modify his/her distorted *automatic thoughts* and maladaptive *behaviors* to reduce depressed feelings and emotional states, and to change or replace the problematic *schemas*, to reduce the person's vulnerability to future episodes of depression. The therapist may also help the patient change his/her *life circumstances* so as to reduce activation of problematic schemas.

Mindfulness-based cognitive therapy (MBCT; Segal et al., 2002) is based on the premise that previously depressed individuals are vulnerable for relapse or recurrence because dysphoria can reactivate patterns of thinking that can maintain and intensify the dysphoric states through escalating and self-perpetuating cycles of ruminative cognitive-affective processing (Teasdale, 1997, 1988). MBCT combines elements of traditional cognitive-behavioral therapy (CBT) for depression (Beck et al., 1979) with components of the mindfulness-based stress reduction program (MBSR) developed by Kabat-Zinn and colleagues (e.g., Kabat-Zinn, 1990) to provide individuals with metacognitive awareness of their thoughts, that is, "a cognitive set in which negative thoughts/feelings are experienced as mental events, rather than as the self" (p. 275) and by helping them develop the capacity to *decenter*, that is, to observe their thoughts and feelings as temporary, objective events in the mind rather than as true reflections of the self. (Fresco, Moore, et al., 2007)

McCullough (2000) proposed a cognitive theory of chronic depression that states (as do the learned helplessness and learned hopelessness theories described earlier) that the chronically depressed person lacks "perceived functionality," or "the ability to perceive a contingency relationship between one's behavior and consequences" (p. 71). Without perceived functionality the person loses the motivation to take action, with the result that she or he suffers a dearth of positive reinforcers and an excess of punishers. To address this deficit, McCullough developed the Cognitive-Behavioral Analysis System of Psychotherapy (CBASP). In CBASP, the therapist guides the patient through detailed examinations (assessment) of specific interpersonal interactions, and helps the patient learn to identify and remediate their passive and ineffectual behaviors. The goal is to teach patients that they actually do have the power to get what they want in interpersonal transactions.

Emotion Models

Historically, the prevailing theoretical approaches within clinical psychology, notably the psychodynamic and cognitive-behavioral traditions, viewed emotions in negative terms (cf. Mennin & Farach, 2006). However, clinical psychology is beginning to consider and understand the importance of emotional systems in adaptive human functioning and experience. Contemporary perspectives on emotion posit that there are multiple pathways to emotion generation and expression, including hard-wired or *lower-order* systems, and more controlled, *higher-order* systems. The two systems are viewed as separate but interacting, and responsible for different aspects of emotional experience (Clore & Ortony, 2000). Similarly, Gross (1998, p. 275) defines emotion regulation as "the process by which individuals influence which emotions they have, when they have them, and how they experience and express these emotions." Researchers are also paying more attention to positive emotions, which are hypothesized to widen the array of thoughts and actions that come to mind and help the individual build new approaches to solve problems by helping them generate enduring personal resources (e.g., a social support network; Frederickson, 2001).

We focus here on three applications of emotion theory to depression and its treatment. First, Beevers, Wenzlaff, Hayes, and Scott, (1999) reviewed evidence that depressed individuals use maladaptive emotion regulation strategies (in particular, they over-use suppression), and described strategies, many drawn from current cognitive-behavioral and mindfulness-based therapies, to help depressed individuals improve their emotion regulation abilities.

Second, Gray (1973, 1982) proposed a theory of emotion that accounts for symptoms of depression and anxiety and for positive emotions. He described emotions as resulting from two affective-motivational systems, the Behavioral Activation System (BAS) and the Behavioral Inhibition System (BIS). The BAS responds to signals of reward and nonpunishment (safety signals) by facilitating approach and appetitive behavior, positive affect such as elation, and interest. An underactive approach system is seen as causing depression and anhedonia, and an overactive approach system is seen as causing mania and impulsivity. The BIS responds to stimuli that signify nonreward, punishment, novelty, and danger. It orients the organism's attention toward the stimulus, suppresses ongoing behavior, activates withdrawal behavior, and generates anxiety and other negative affect. Watson, Wiese, Vaidya, and Tellegen (1999) have theorized that the BAS and BIS operate in a mutually inhibitory way, with an underactivation of the BAS typically accompanied by an overactivation in the BIS. Consistent with Gray's two-system dimensional model, Watson and Clark (Watson et al., 1999) proposed that emotional states have two dimensions, which they label positive affect (PA or positive activation) and negative affect (NA or negative activation), where a high degree of positive activation results in states such as active, elated, enthusiastic, and excited, and a high degree of negative activation results in states such as fearful, hostile, distressed, and guilty.

Third, psychotherapy researchers have begun to point to the importance of working in therapy with all patients, including depressed patients, to promote (rather than dampen) emotional arousal. Samoilov and Goldfried (2000) posit that a vital part of psychotherapy is in-session emotional arousal that promotes "reorganization of underlying emotional themes, assimilation of new information, and formation of new implicit meaning structures" (p. 383). Further, this emphasis on emotion is evident and prominent in a variety of empirically supported treatments, including process experiential therapy (cf. Pos, Greenberg, Goldman, & Korman, 2003) and increasingly important from a behavioral (cf. Jacobson et al., 2001) and cognitive-behavioral perspective (cf. Hayes et al., 2007; Samoilov & Goldfried, 2000).

Interpersonal Models

Interpersonal psychotherapy (IPT) was developed by the late Gerald Klerman and Myrna Weissman and their colleagues as a treatment for MDD (Klerman, Weissman, Rounsaville, & Chevron, 1984). The interpersonal model of depression of Klerman et al. emphasizes the reciprocal relations between biological and interpersonal factors in causing and maintaining depression. Problems or deficits in one or more of four areas of interpersonal functioning (unresolved grief, interpersonal disputes, role transitions, and interpersonal deficits, e.g., social skills deficits or social isolation) are conceptualized as contributing to the onset or maintenance of depression, and the IPT therapist intervenes to address the patient's deficits in that area.

PURPOSES OF ASSESSMENT

We will discuss assessment for diagnosis, assessment for case conceptualization and treatment planning, and assessment for treatment monitoring and treatment outcome. Assessment of all of these phenomena can be affected by many factors, including medications or other treatment the patient is receiving, the patient's medical status, life stressors, and even his/her level of emotional arousal. There is some overlap in tools used to assess diagnosis, conceptualization and treatment planning, and treatment monitoring. For example, self-report measures of depressive symptoms are useful for assessing all of these phenomena.

Assessment for Diagnosis

In addition to discussing diagnosis of MDD in this section, we will also briefly discuss diagnosis of other disorders and problems on Axis I, and we will also discuss diagnosis on Axes II, III, IV, and V. We take this approach because all of this information is needed to diagnose MDD (e.g., information about life stressors such as bereavement are needed to determine whether the patient has MDD), and because this information is also needed to develop a case conceptualization and treatment plan and to monitor the process and outcome of treatment.

We encourage clinicians to use the tools described here (and summarized in Table 5.1) to obtain an

TABLE 5.1 Ratings of Instruments Used for Diagnosis

Instrument	Norms	Internal Consistency	Inter-Rater Reliability	Test–Retest Reliability	Content Validity	Construct Validity	Validity Generalization	Clinical Utility	Highly Recommended
Axis I and II Diagnosis									
SCID/SCID-II	A	NA	G	NA	G	G	G	E	✓
ADIS	A	NA	G	NA	G	G	G	E	✓
Depression Severity									
BDI-II	G	E	NA	E	E	E	E	E	✓
QIDS	E	E	NA	E	E	E	E	E	✓
Psychosocial and Environmental Problems									
LES	A	A	NA	G	G	A	A	A	
Functioning									
GAF	A	NA	A	A	G	G	G	G	✓
QOLI	G	E	NA	G	G	G	G	E	✓

Note: SCID = Structured Clinical Interview for DSM-IV; SCID-II = Structured Clinical Interview for DSM-IV Personality Disorders; ADIS = Anxiety Disorders Interview Schedule for DSM-IV Lifetime; BDI-II = Beck Depression Inventory-II; QIDS = Quick Inventory for Depression Severity; LES = Life Experiences Survey; GAF = Global Assessment of Functioning; QOLI = Quality of Life Inventory; A = Adequate; G = Good; E = Excellent; NA = Not Applicable.

accurate diagnosis, because the treatment efficacy, epidemiology, and psychopathology literatures are organized by diagnosis, and the clinician will want to draw on those literatures. In addition, our method for developing an individualized case conceptualization and treatment plan calls for the clinician to begin the process of conceptualizing and planning treatment for any particular case by relying on a template that is based on one or more of the disorder-focused theories of depression that we described earlier in the chapter.

Assessment of Depression

Semistructured Interviews The Structured Clinical Interview for DSM-IV-TR (SCID; First, Spitzer, Gibbon, & Williams, 2002) is the most frequently used instrument for assigning a DSM-IV diagnosis or resolving issues of differential diagnosis. The Axis I SCID requires between 60 and 90 minutes to administer and allows the clinician to identify current and lifetime Axis I disorders. The SCID helps a clinician differentiate between unipolar and bipolar depression because it allows the clinician to assess the lifetime course of the disorder, not just a snapshot at one point in time. The SCID was fashioned after the traditional interview in which clinicians considered and tested several diagnostic hypotheses simultaneously. Each section begins with a YES/NO probe followed by queries that ask for elaborations. This strategy has two main advantages: (1) diagnostic decisions are known to the interviewer during the interview and (2) interviews are shorter, because irrelevant sections are not exhaustively probed. Ventura (1998) reported high inter-rater agreement for current diagnosis based on the SCID, with an overall weighted κ of .82. κ values for MDD are good to excellent (range = .80 to .91; Ventura et al., 1998). A streamlined clinician version of the SCID is available from American Psychiatric Publishing (www.appi.org). The research version is available from the New York State Psychiatric Institute (www.scid4.org) in an unbound hard-copy version, paper version, or electronic version that allows the clinician to evaluate just the diagnostic modules that are most relevant to his or her clinical setting. This Web site also provides citations to published studies attesting to the superior validity of the SCID relative to general clinical interviews.

The Anxiety Disorders Interview Schedule, Lifetime Version for DSM-IV (ADIS-IV-L; Brown, Dinardo, & Barlow, 1994) is a semistructured interview for the diagnosis of DSM-IV anxiety, mood, somatoform, and substance related disorders. A 0 to 8 clinician severity rating (CSR) is assigned for each diagnosis based on the severity of the patient's distress regarding his or her symptoms and the degree of interference in daily functioning related to these symptoms. A CSR of 4 or higher is considered clinically significant. A disorder is designated as the principal diagnosis if it is given a CSR that is at least one point higher than any other clinically significant diagnosis. If the goal of the interview is simply to confirm the presence of current and lifetime diagnoses, the ADIS-IV-L takes roughly the same amount of time to administer as the SCID. However, the clinician may want to make use of the extensive probes for assessing the specific impairment associated with a particular disorder, the client's strengths, hypothesized etiological factors and situational antecedents, and a "Diagnostic Timeline" approach to assist the clinician in tracking the onset, remission, and temporal ordering of diagnoses that are unique features of the ADIS-IV-L. As shown in Table 5.1, the norms are adequate; the inter-rater reliability, content validity, construct validity, and validity generalization are good; and clinical utility is excellent. The ADIS is available from Graywind/Oxford University Press (www.oup.com).

Self-Report Measures Many self-report scales of depression have been developed, but we focus on two: the Beck Depression Inventory because it is so widely used in randomized controlled trials, and the Quick Inventory of Depressive Symptomatology-Self-Rated (QIDS-SR), because it has good psychometric qualities and is easily available.

The Beck Depression Inventory, 2nd Edition (BDI-II; Beck, Steer, & Brown, 1996) is a 21-item self-report instrument that assesses the presence and severity of symptoms of depression. The BDI-II is the successor to the original BDI (Beck et al., 1979). The BDI-II retains the familiar 4-point scale for each item ranging from 0 to 3 used in the original version of the BDI, and retains the scoring system (each of the 21 items corresponding to a symptom of depression is summed to give a single score for the measure). The BDI-II differs from the BDI in that, on two items, there are options to indicate either an increase or decrease of appetite and sleep, and patients are asked to consider each statement as it relates to the way they have felt for the past two weeks, to more accurately correspond to the DSM-IV criteria for MDD. Cut score guidelines for the BDI-II are given with the recommendation that thresholds be adjusted based on sample characteristics and purpose of the assessment. As shown in Table 5.1, the norms of the BDI-II are good, and the reliability and validity are excellent.

The QIDS-SR (Rush et al., 2003) is a 16-item self-report measure that is designed to assess the severity of depressive symptoms. The scale evaluates all the criterion symptom domains in the DSM-IV criteria for MDD. The QIDS-SR is a shortened version of the 30-item Inventory of Depressive Symptomatology (IDS-SR); the IDS-SR, in addition to assessing depressive symptoms, also assesses many symptoms of anxiety. The QIDS-SR and IDS-SR are, in turn, adaptations of clinician-rated versions of the IDS and QIDS. Both the QIDS and the IDS were designed to be maximally sensitive to symptom change. As indicated in Table 5.1, the norming, reliability, and validity of the QIDS-SR are excellent. Lamoureux et al. (2006) conducted receiver operating characteristic (ROC) analysis in a sample of 125 primary care patients who completed the QIDS-SR and the SCID and concluded that a score of 11 on the QIDS-SR provided the best balance of sensitivity ($Sn = .81$) and specificity ($Sp = .72$) and correctly classified 75% of the sample as to their MDD status. The clinician-rated and self-rated versions of the IDS and QIDS as well as copious psychometric information about the scales are available free for download from the Internet (http://www.ids-qids.org). The measures are available in 13 languages.

Assessment of Psychiatric Comorbidity

The SCID and ADIS, described above, are useful for assessing comorbid disorders, and the IDS, described above, assesses some anxiety symptoms. The Mood and Anxiety Symptom Questionnaire-Short Form (MASQ; Clark & Watson, 1991; Watson & Walker, 1996; Watson et al., 1995), described in detail later, assesses depressive symptoms, anxiety symptoms, and positive emotions. Other tools for comorbid disorders and problems are described in other chapters of this volume.

Assessment of Axis II Disorders

Patients with MDD commonly suffer from personality disorders (i.e., Axis II diagnoses), which are discussed by Widiger (Chapter 19, this volume).

Assessment of Medical Comorbidity

Most mental health professionals do not have the training or expertise to directly assess medical problems. However, it is essential to assess them, as they can cause, exacerbate, or result from MDD. We recommend that the clinician asks the patient to obtain a physical examination if she/he has not had one in the last year to be certain that medical conditions that might be causing or contributing to depressive symptoms have been identified and are being treated. In some cases, a written report from the treating physician can be useful in guiding treatment for depression.

Assessment of Psychosocial and Environmental Problems

Axis IV of the DSM-IV-TR is used to identify psychosocial and environmental problems that may play a role "in the initiation or exacerbation of a mental disorder," may "develop as a consequence of a person's psychopathology," or may "constitute problems that should be considered in the overall management plan." (APA, 2000, p. 31). Assessment of these phenomena is particularly important in view of the facts that (a) most of the psychosocial theories described above propose that depression results from the triggering of diatheses by stressful life events and (b) depression often leads to negative psychosocial consequences for patients that are often a focus of treatment and/or can interfere with treatment.

The Life Experiences Survey (LES; Sarason, Johnson, & Siegel, 1978) is a self-report scale listing 57 events, with three blank spaces provided for write-in events. Participants are instructed to circle or write in events that happened to them during the past month, to provide the date on which the event occurred, and to indicate the type and extent of the impact the event had on their life. Impact is rated on a scale ranging from –3 (extremely negative) to 3 (extremely positive). The LES possesses good test–retest reliability (rs = .53 to .88), is not contaminated by social desirability biases, and predicts a number of stress-related dependent measures, including malad-justment (Sarason et al., 1978).

Assessment of Functioning

The Global Assessment of Functioning Scale (GAF, Axis V, DSM-IV-TR; American Psychiatric Association, 2000) is a single rating used to evaluate an individual's overall level of psychological, social, and occupational functioning. Values on the scale range from 1 (lowest level of functioning) to 100 (highest level of functioning) and are divided into ten 10-point intervals. Each interval is anchored with detailed, behaviorally oriented descriptors. Validation studies conducted with both inpatients and outpatients have indicated that the GAF correlates highly with validated measures of overall severity of illness and changes in severity and with therapists' and relatives' ratings of patient's functioning, and has good inter-rater reliability (Endicott, Spitzer, Fleiss, & Cohen, 1976).

The Quality of Life Inventory (QOLI; Frisch, Cornell, Villanueva, & Retzlaff, 1992). The QOLI assesses the degree to which an individual is satisfied with 16 areas of his or her life, including health, standard of living, friendships, relationship with family, and community. Each area is rated once on a 0-to-2 scale of importance to the individual's life and again on a scale of –3 to 3 of how satisfied the individual is in that area. The total score has been shown to be internally consistent, $\alpha = .98$, and has demonstrated good test–retest reliability; rs range from .80 to .91 (Frisch et al., 1992). QOLI scores were also positively correlated with scores on a clinician-administered life satisfaction interview, peer ratings of life satisfaction, and five self-report measures assessing life satisfaction and subjective well being.

Overall Evaluation

Clinicians in practice often neglect diagnosis. We emphasized its importance, especially the importance of a lifetime diagnostic assessment to distinguish between unipolar and bipolar mood disorder. The SCID and ADIS are both useful for this purpose. We also described two self-report measures of depressive symptoms (BDI and QIDS/IDS) that are useful in assessing the severity of depressive symptoms in all psychiatric patients. The BDI is supported by extensive normative and benchmarking data, but the QIDS/IDS are quickly catching up and are available free from the Internet. The psychometric qualities are excellent for the interview measures of diagnosis and the self-report measures of symptom severity, adequate for the measures of life stress, and good to excellent for the measures of functioning.

Assessment for Case Conceptualization and Treatment Planning

Assessment for case conceptualization and treatment planning requires two types of translation. One is from *disorder-level* (and sometimes *symptom-level*) conceptualizations and treatment plans to the *case-level* conceptualization and treatment plan. Most of the models we reviewed above are conceptualizations and therapies for a particular *disorder* (usually MDD). A few of the models also provide conceptualizations and interventions for *symptoms* (e.g., the BA formulation of rumination as avoidance behavior). A conceptualization (or formulation) at the level of the *case* is a hypothesis about the causes of *all* of the patient's symptoms, disorders, and problems and how they are related, and the case-level treatment plan describes all of the therapies the patient is receiving for these symptoms, disorders, and problems. The three levels (symptom, disorder, and case) are nested. A *disorder* consists of a set of *symptoms*, and a *case* consists of one or more disorders and problems. Thus, a case-level formulation generally consists of an extrapolation or extension of one or more disorder- and symptom-level formulations.

The second translation is from *nomothetic* to *idiographic*. A nomothetic formulation and treatment plan is *general* (e.g., that depression results from a dearth of positive reinforcers and can be treated by increasing the positive reinforcers an individual receives (Lewinsohn & Gotlib, 1995). An *idiographic* case formulation and treatment plan describes the mechanisms that are causing and maintaining the symptoms, disorders, and problems, and the plan for treating them in a *particular individual*. For example, the formulation that Joe's depressive symptoms of lack of enjoyment and satisfaction, reduced interest in others, inertia, fatigue, and anorexia result from the loss of intellectual stimulation, respect from clients and colleagues, and income he suffered when he retired from his job as a criminal attorney; accordingly, the plan to treat Joe's depressive symptoms involves helping him identify and access new sources of positive reinforcement.

General Issues about Idiographic Assessment

The psychometric qualities of idiographic assessment tools are rarely studied (Haynes & O'Brien, 2000). Moreover, often these assessments are simply the therapist's observations in the therapy session (e.g., the patient arrives 15 minutes late and does not apologize or explain) or rough-and-ready ratings, such as a count of the number of days that suicidal thoughts occurred, or a rating of intensity of depressed mood using subjective units of distress (SUD) on a scale of 0 to 100. These data might be recorded in the clinician's progress note in the clinical record, on a paper-and-pencil log or in a personal digital assistant (PDA).

We use three strategies to strengthen idiographic assessment tools and strategies. First, as described below, we use evidence-based nomothetic formulations and therapies as templates for the idiographic formulation and treatment plan (Haynes, Kaholokula, & Nelson, 1999); these tell the clinician which phenomena to assess. Second, we recommend that the clinician rely on basic principles of behavioral assessment, including collecting data at multiple time points, from multiple observers, using multiple methods (Haynes & O'Brien, 2000). Finally, we recommend that clinicians work collaboratively with the patient to collect data to monitor the progress and process of treatment, to be sure that the targets of assessment are helpful to the treatment process (Hayes, Nelson, & Jarrett, 1987).

Case Conceptualization

A case conceptualization is a hypothesis about the mechanisms causing and maintaining one or more of a particular patient's symptoms, disorders, and problems; the formulation might also include biological mechanisms. The case-level conceptualization accounts for *all* of the patient's symptoms, disorders, and problems, not just the depressive symptoms or disorders. The formulation describes the *symptoms/disorders/problems*, the *mechanisms* causing them, the *precipitants of the symptoms/disorders/problems*,

and the *origins of the mechanisms*. It also describes the *relationships among the symptoms, disorders, and problems*.

Symptoms/Disorders/Problems   We recommend developing a comprehensive problem list that describes all of a patient's symptoms, disorders, and problems— that is, all of the difficulties and deficits the patient has across these domains: psychological/psychiatric symptoms, interpersonal, occupational, school, medical, financial, housing, legal, leisure, and mental health or medical treatment. We focus primarily on strategies for assessing depression and related problems; the other chapters of this volume describe strategies for assessing other disorders and problems.

The problem list overlaps considerably with Axes I–IV of a DSM diagnosis. It will likely include the Axis I depressive disorders, either stated as the disorder, or by listing its symptoms. The problem list will also include any significant Axis II disorders or symptoms, important Axis III disorders, and problems described in Axis IV. Thus, all the assessment tools described earlier for diagnosis are helpful in formulating a problem list.

However, the problem list differs from diagnosis because, in the problem list, the clinician begins to translate the DSM information into terms that facilitate conceptualization and intervention from the point of view of one or more nomothetic models described earlier. Thus, for example, a cognitive-behavior therapist might describe a patient's symptoms of depression in the problem list by identifying some of their behavioral, cognitive, and emotions aspects. For example, Joan, a patient treated by the first author, reported depressive symptoms that included emotions of sadness, lack of satisfaction in anything, disgust in herself, irritability, and guilt, cognitions that included, "I'm a failure," "I'm a bad mother," "I'm lazy and unproductive," "I'm boring and uninteresting," and behaviors of inactivity, procrastination, and avoidance of social contacts.

The main strategies used to collect a comprehensive problem list are the clinical interview, self-report measures, observations of the patient's behavior, and communications with family members or other treatment providers. A good general strategy is the "funnel" approach (Mash & Hunsley, 1990), in which the clinician begins with a broad-based assessment of all the important domains before obtaining more detailed information about problems and disorders that are identified by the broad-based screen. We focus here on the use of self-report tools and direct observation; Turkat (1987) provides an excellent discussion of the use of the clinical assessment interview to obtain a case conceptualization.

Self-Report Measures   The tension that always confronts the clinician is the pressure to move quickly to address the patient's current concerns while taking the time to obtain the information needed to develop a good formulation and treatment plan. Self-report tools help resolve this tension by allowing the clinician to collect considerable information quickly. The clinician can send these to the patient in the mail before the initial interview and ask the patient to bring the completed materials to the initial interview or send them in advance of the interview. To construct a problem list, the therapist will want to use self-report measures of depression (described above) as well as self-report measures of other problems the patient has described in the telephone contact before the initial interview or that emerge during the initial interview; useful measures are described in other chapters of this volume.

Observation   Direct observation can alert the therapist to problems (e.g., a disheveled appearance, or poor eye contact) that patients may not acknowledge, recognize, or verbalize. For example, the first author observed that a depressed patient, Sam, had a verbal report (of intense distress) that was discrepant from his facial expression (of calm). When the therapist pointed this out, Sam noted that the failure of his facial expression to reflect his internal distress was contributing to his marital problems; he and his wife had had a recent major blowup resulting from her feeling uncared about when he appeared blasé and unconcerned when he said goodbye as she was being wheeled into surgery. In this case, the therapist's observation of the patient's behavior in the therapy session contributed to a conceptualization hypothesis about the relationship between Sam's depressive symptoms and his marital difficulties.

Hypothesized Mechanisms   The decision about what phenomena to assess for case conceptualization purposes flows from the nomothetic model(s) the therapist uses to conceptualize the patient's depression, and the models the therapist uses are typically based on his orientation or training. When the therapist's orientation admits several possible models (e.g., cognitive and behavioral), the decision about

what phenomena to assess may also be based on results of some initial assessments, as in the case of the cognitive-behavioral therapist who elects to first consider using Beck's cognitive model to conceptualize the case of a patient whose chief complaint is, "I have a ton of negative thoughts." Of course, as she/ he collects more assessment data, the clinician may find that another model provides a better fit for the patient's case (Haynes et al., 1999).

We describe measures for assessing the mechanisms of the behavioral, cognitive, emotion-focused, and interpersonal models of depression described above; these measures are summarized in Table 5.2. As already observed, there is quite a bit of overlap among the models. Thus, for example, clinicians who use Beck's cognitive model, the BA model, or Lewinsohn's behavioral model may wish to assess the patient's activity level using the Activity Schedule described in the Behavioral Mechanisms section below. Symptoms and mechanisms also overlap. For example, an Activity Schedule assesses both a symptom (behavioral inactivity) and a mechanism (e.g., pleasant events). We describe assessment of phenomena such as pleasant events and automatic thoughts here in the mechanism section, even though they can also be seen as aspects of symptoms.

Behavioral Mechanisms   The Activity Schedule presented originally by Becket et al. (1979; see also pp. 126–127 of Persons, Davidson, & Tompkins, 2001 for a version that clinicians may reproduce for clinical use) is essentially a calendar that allows the patient to log his or her activities during each day of the week. It is ideal for assessing how the patient spends time and can also be used to track behavioral homework assignments, such as recording pleasant activities. The Activity Schedule can be useful to clinicians who are conceptualizing and treating depression using any of the behavioral, cognitive, emotion-focused or interpersonal models described earlier.

The Pleasant Events Schedule (PES; MacPhillany & Lewinsohn, 1982) published in Lewinsohn, Munoz, Youngren, and Zeiss (1986) is a self-report inventory of 320 potentially reinforcing activities. Respondents assign ratings for each event for the frequency of occurrence over the past 30 days on a 3-point scale ranging from 0 (*not happened*) to 2 (*happened often*; seven or more times) and a pleasantness rating on a 3-point scale ranging from 0 (*not pleasant*) to 2 (*very pleasant*). The PES has been used extensively in research related to the behavioral model of depression with

TABLE 5.2 Ratings for Instruments Used for Case Conceptualization and Treatment Planning

Instrument	Norms	Internal Consistency	Inter-Rater Reliability	Test–Retest Reliability	Content Validity	Construct Validity	Validity Generalization	Clinical Utility	Highly Recommended
Case Conceptualization (Hypothesized Mechanism)									
PES	G	G	NA	G	G	G	A	G	✓
CBAS	A	A	NA	U	A	A	A	A	✓
DAS	A	E	NA	G	G	A	A	G	✓
ASQ	A	A	NA	A	G	G	A	A	
EQ	A	G	NA	U	G	G	A	G	✓
EDCS	A	A	NA	U	A	A	U	A	
ERQ	A	G	NA	U	A	G	A	A	
MASQ	A	G	NA	U	G	G	A	G	✓
SAS-SR	A	A	NA	A	G	A	G	G	
Treatment Planning									
GAS	A	NA	A	A	NA	A	A	E	✓

Note: PES = Pleasant Events Schedule; CBAS = Cognitive and Behavioral Avoidance Scale; DAS = Dysfunctional Attitude Scale; ASQ = Attributional Style Questionnaire; EQ = Experiences Questionnaire; EDCS = Emotion Dysregulation Composite Scale; ERQ = Emotion Regulation Questionnaire; MASQ = Mood and Anxiety Questionnaire; SAS-SR = Social Adjustment Scale-Self Report; GAS = Goal Attainment Scaling; A = Adequate; G = Good; E = Excellent; U = Unavailable; NA = Not Applicable.

generally good reliability and adequate to good validity (e.g., Grosscup & Lewinsohn, 1980; MacPhillamy & Lewinsohn, 1982; Nezu, Ronan, Meadows, & McClure, 2000). The PES and supporting materials can be downloaded free of charge at http://www.ori.org/research/scientists/lewinsohnP.html.

The Cognitive–Behavioral Avoidance Scale (CBAS; Ottenbreit & Dobson, 2004) is a 31-item self-report measure that assesses four first order factors of cognitive and behavioral avoidance that are relevant to behavioral models of depression. The overall measure demonstrates good internal consistency ($\alpha = .91$) and the first order factors of cognitive nonsocial (e.g., "While I know that I have to make some important decisions about school/work, I just do not get down to it."), cognitive social (e.g., "I just wait out tension in my relationships hoping that it will go away."), behavioral nonsocial (e.g., "I avoid trying new activities that hold the potential for failure."), and behavioral social (e.g., "I avoid attending social activities.") have internal consistencies ranging from .75 to .86. The CBAS is a relatively new measure, and thus extensive validity data are not yet available. Until new published studies in clinical samples emerge, the validity is best regarded as adequate.

The therapist who is using Lewinsohn's behavioral theory or BA theory to conceptualize depression will want to collect information about the antecedents and consequences of target behaviors, especially of rumination, depressed mood, withdrawal, and passivity. Tomes have been written on the topic of collecting data about the antecedents and consequences of problem behaviors for behavioral analysis (Haynes & O'Brien, 2000; Kazdin, 2001; Watson & Tharp, 2002). Sometimes the clinician can obtain this information by interview, carefully asking about the target behaviors identified in the case conceptualization, but typically, data must be collected between sessions to flesh out the factors controlling a target behavior. Patients can record this information on a diary card, or log them on their PDA, perhaps even in response to a timer that prompts them to do so. To identify antecedents, the patient can identify the following: where, when, with whom, what was going on, what thoughts were you having, what sensations did you have in your body, what feelings were you having, what were you doing? To identify consequences, the patient can identify: external events that occurred, emotional reactions, valence of the experience, bodily sensations, and behavioral reactions.

Cognitive Mechanisms To assess the automatic thoughts described by Beck's theory, the therapist can use a self-monitoring diary (such as the *Daily Record of Dysfunctional Thoughts*, Beck et al., 1979), forms provided by Greenberger and Padesky (1995), or the *Thought Record* (Persons et al., 2001) that provides places for the depressed patient to identify an activating situation; the emotions, behaviors, and automatic thoughts triggered by that situation; and coping responses (both thoughts and behaviors) that can be used to alleviate distress. Emotions, behaviors, and automatic thoughts are typically obtained by simply asking the patient to report them while recalling the specific concrete event that triggered them. Beck (1995) offers strategies for eliciting this information when a direct and straightforward approach fails, including asking patients to report images and asking them to vividly imagine and recreate the event that triggered negative painful emotions. Research measures of automatic thoughts that may also be useful clinically include the Automatic Thoughts Questionnaire-Negative (ATQ-N; Hollon & Kendall, 1980) and the Automatic Thoughts Questionnaire-Positive (ATQ-P; Ingram & Wisnicki, 1988).

The Dysfunctional Attitude Scale (DAS; Weissman & Beck, 1978) consists of two 40-item, factor-analytically derived questionnaires that tap into the depressed person's unrealistic, distorted, and illogical beliefs about the self, world, and future. It is the most widely used research tool to assess the schemas described in Beck's cognitive theory. Form A of the DAS is the more widely used of the two measures. Weissman and Beck (1978) reported excellent internal consistencies ($\alpha > .90$) across several samples. The content validity of the measure is good, and construct and generalization validities are adequate (Nezu et al., 2000). Two criticisms of the DAS have been raised: first, Hollon, Kendall, & Lumry (1986) reported that DAS scores were elevated in nondepressed psychiatric populations (such as schizophrenia and bipolar patients), suggesting that these cognitions are not specific to unipolar depression and, second, many studies have found that DAS scores of remitted depressed subjects were not different from a nonpsychiatric control group—suggesting that dysfunctional attitudes are mood-state dependent (Persons & Miranda, 1992). Nevertheless, if the clinician is aware of these weaknesses, the measure can be clinically useful.

The Attributional Style Questionnaire (ASQ; Peterson et al., 1982) is a self-report inventory that assesses causal attributions described by the helplessness and hopelessness theories. The scale asks respondents to rate six hypothetical positive and six hypothetical negative events that can be further divided into categories of achievement and interpersonal. Participants are asked to vividly imagine a hypothetical negative or positive event, identify the one major cause if that event were to actually occur, and rate that cause along attributional dimensions. Each dimension is scored on a one to seven Likert-type scale with the higher end representing a response endorsing internal, global, or stable causes and the lower end representing external, specific, and unstable causes. Generally, a Composite Negative (CN) score is computed by summing or averaging the values of the 18 internal, stable, and global items for the negative events. A similar Composite Positive (CP) score from the positive hypothetical event items is also computed. Alternatively, to be more consistent with hopelessness theory (Abramson et al., 1989), a generality score is computed by averaging the values of the 12 stability and globality items across negative events to produce a score that ranges from 1 to 7. The ASQ has demonstrated adequate internal consistency (α = .70 to .75; Sweeney, Anderson, & Bailey, 1986). Recently, Fresco, Alloy, and Reilly-Harrington (2006) assessed a large sample of college students for current and lifetime psychopathology and reported adequate to good internal consistency for CN (α = .79) and CP (α = .82). The CN composite also demonstrates adequate test–retest reliability (r = .70 to .73; Colin, Sweeney, & Schaeffer, 1981; Peterson et al., 1982; Sweeney et al., 1986) in both psychiatric and undergraduate populations. The validity of the measure is adequate (Nezu et al., 2000).

The Experiences Questionnaire (EQ; Fresco, Moore et al., 2007) is an 11-item self-report measure of decentering. Fresco et al. used both exploratory and confirmatory factor analysis techniques to examine the factor structure of the measure in two consecutive large samples of college students and a sample of depressed patients. The measure showed good internal consistency, ranging from α = .81 to .90, and good concurrent and discriminant validity. In a study of patients with MDD randomly assigned to either CT or antidepressant medication treatment (ADM; Fresco, Segal et al., 2007) found that CT responders evidenced significantly greater gains in decentering as compared to CT nonresponders or ADM patients (irrespective of responder status). Further,

among acute treatment responders, high posttreatment decentering, as compared to low posttreatment decentering was associated with a more durable treatment response in the subsequent 18 months.

The Coping Style Questionnaire (CSQ; McCullough, 2001) was developed to facilitate the process of teaching patients in CBASP to learn to identify and make needed behavioral and cognitive changes to achieve the outcomes they desire in their interpersonal interactions. The CSQ is not so much a questionnaire as it is a form the patient completes for a particular unsuccessful (or successful) interpersonal interaction; the CSQ helps the patient and therapist to identify and remediate the patient's maladaptive interpretations and behaviors in the situation.

Emotion-Focused Mechanisms   The Emotion Dysregulation Composite Scale (EDCS; Mennin, Holaway, Fresco, Moore, & Heimberg, 2007) is a 46-item self-report measure assessing the dimensions of heightened intensity of emotions, poor understanding of emotions, negative reactivity to emotions, and maladaptive management of emotions. The EDCS was derived with exploratory and confirmatory factor analysis from several existing self-report measures of emotion regulation and emotional intelligence. Mennin et al. (in press), in a large, unselected sample of college students, found that the subscales had acceptable to good internal consistency and that all four facets of emotion dysregulation significantly predicted concurrent levels of self-report depression symptoms. Further, negative reactivity and poor understanding of emotions remained statistically significant after controlling for concurrent levels of social anxiety and general anxiety.

The Emotion Regulation Questionnaire (ERQ; Gross & John, 2003) is a 10-item rationally derived measure of two aspects of emotion regulation: reappraisal and suppression. The reappraisal subscale, consisting of 6 items, assesses the ability to modify or change the emotions one experiences (e.g., "I control my emotions by changing the way I think about the situation I'm in"). The suppression subscale, consisting of 4 items, assesses the ability to avoid or prevent the expression of emotions (e.g., "I control my emotions by not expressing them"). Fresco, Moore, et al. (in press) reported the internal consistency was good for both the reappraisal subscale (α = .84) and the suppression subscale (α = .82). The reappraisal scale was significantly and positive correlated with decentering

($r = .25$), but was uncorrelated with depression symptoms ($r = .14$) or depressive rumination ($r = .14$). Conversely, the suppression subscale was significantly and negatively correlated with decentering ($r = -.31$) and significantly and positively correlated with depression symptoms ($r = .39$), and depressive rumination ($r = .31$). The ERQ is available free on the Internet (http://www-psych.stanford.edu/~psyphy/).

The MASQ (Clark & Watson, 1991; Watson & Walker, 1996; Watson et al., 1995) is a 62-item instrument designed to assess discrete dimensions of depression and anxiety symptoms as proposed by Clark and Watson's (1991) tripartite model. Items are rated on a 1 ("not at all") to 5 ("extremely") Likert-type scale and are divided into four subscales: General Distress Anxious Symptoms (GDA), General Distress Depressive Symptoms (GDD), Anxious Arousal (AA), and Anhedonic Depression (AD). The GDA subscale comprises 11 items indicative of anxious mood, but provides little discrimination from depressed mood. The GDD subscale comprises 12 items indicative of depressed mood, but provides little discrimination from anxious mood. The AA subscale contains 17 items detailing symptoms of somatic tension and hyperarousal, and the AD subscale contains 8 items assessing depression-specific symptoms, such as a loss of interest in pleasurable activities and low energy, and 14 reverse-coded items assessing positive emotional experiences. The AA and AD subscales evidence relatively low zero-order correlations with one another ($r = .25 = .38$), whereas the GDA and GDD subscales evidence more overlap ($r > .50$; Watson et al., 1995). The MASQ has been used primarily in research contexts. However, we mention it here because it is one of the few measures of positive emotions available that also assesses anxiety and depression in a manner that provides excellent concurrent and discriminant validity (Watson & Walker, 1996). Inquiries about the MASQ can be directed to David B. Watson, PhD (david-watson@uiowa.edu).

Interpersonal Mechanisms Weissman and Bothwell (1976) developed the Social Adjustment Scale-Self-Report (SAS-SR), a 54-item self-report measure that assesses six social role areas. The domains are work/homemaker/student, social and leisure activities, relationships with extended family, marital partner role; parental role, and role within the family unit. Internal consistency of the measure is adequate ($\alpha = .74$). The measure has good known-groups validity, distinguishing samples from the community, of patients with depression, and patients with schizophrenia, from one another on the basis of total score. The SAS-SR is available for purchase from Multi-Health Systems, Inc. (www.mhs.com).

Precipitants Hypothesized precipitants of the current depressive episode are important to assess because most of the nomothetic formulations of depression are diathesis-stress models, proposing that *symptoms* and *problems* result from the activation of psychological and/or biological *diatheses* by one or more *stressors*. Stressors can be internal, external, biological, psychological, or some combination of these. Measures of psychosocial stressors were described above in the section that discusses the assessment of Axis IV of the DSM (Psychosocial and Environmental Problems). In addition, the clinician will want to ask the patient about precipitants of the current and previous depressive episode in the clinical interview, perhaps by conducting a formal illness history timeline to identify triggers of episodes of mood disorder (Frank, 2005).

Origins The *origins* part of the formulation offers a hypothesis about how the patient learned or acquired the hypothesized mechanisms of the formulation. So, for example, within a helplessness theory formulation, origins focus on the events or experiences that taught the patient that outcomes were independent of his behaviors. Origins can be one or more external environmental events (e.g., the death of a parent, or early abuse or neglect), cultural factors, or biological factors (e.g., an unusually short stature that might elicit teasing from peers), including genetics.

To generate hypotheses about how patients acquired the conditioned maladaptive responses, learned the faulty schemas, developed an emotional vulnerability or emotion regulation deficit, and/or acquired a biological or genetic vulnerability, it is essential to collect a family and social history that identifies key events and factors in the patient's upbringing and development, especially a history of early traumas, neglect, and abuse. In addition, the clinician will want to obtain a family history of depression and other psychiatric disorders, which can shed light on both biological and psychosocial causes of the problematic mechanisms in question.

Tying All the Elements Together   After collecting all the information described above, the clinician uses it to lay out a brief formulation that describes what *mechanisms*, activated by what *precipitants*, caused by what *origins*, are causing what *symptoms, disorders, and problems*, and *how all the patient's symptoms, disorders, and problems are related*. The formulation accounts for all of the patient's problems and their relationships in the most parsimonious way, with the fewest mechanisms (Persons, 1989). So, for example, a formulation for a depressed patient, Peter, read:

> As a result of many experiences in childhood and adolescence when he was brutally teased and humiliated by his family, especially his older brother (ORIGINS), Peter learned the schema "I'm inadequate, a loser," and "Others are critical, attacking, and unsupportive of me" (MECHANISM HYPOTHESES). These schema were activated by a recent poor performance evaluation at work (PRECIPITANT). As a result, Peter has experienced symptoms of anxiety and depression at work, with which he has coped by avoiding tackling important work projects and withdrawing from collegial interactions with both peers and superiors at work. The avoidance, although negatively reinforced by the immediate reduction in anxiety it produces, has had some negative consequences, causing Peter to miss some deadlines, which has resulted in criticism from his colleagues and boss, and led to increased symptoms of sadness, feelings of worthlessness, self-criticism and self-blame, low energy, difficulty working, and loss of interest in others. Peter is using drugs and alcohol at home in the evening. This use is negatively reinforced by the immediate reduction in anxiety and depression it produces, but exacerbates Peter's pre-diabetic medical condition" (SYMPTOMS AND PROBLEMS AND HOW THEY ARE RELATED).

Psychometrics of Idiographic Case Conceptualizations   Two studies of the inter-rater reliability of cognitive case formulations of depressed patients showed that clinician raters identified approximately 65% of patient's problems on a criterion problem list developed by the investigator; inter-rater reliability coefficients of schema ratings were .72 to .76 when ratings were averaged over five judges (Persons & Bertagnolli, 1999; Persons, Mooney, & Padesky, 1995). Two uncontrolled trials show that naturalistic (often including adjunct therapy, including pharmacotherapy) cognitive-behavior therapy of depressed (Persons, Bostrom, & Bertagnolli, 1999), and depressed anxious patients (Persons, Roberts, Zalecki, & Brechwald, 2006) guided by a cognitive-behavioral case formulation and weekly progress monitoring produced outcomes similar to those of depressed patients who received CBT or CBT plus pharmacotherapy in the randomized controlled trials.

Treatment Plan

To develop an initial treatment plan, the clinician works with the patient to set treatment goals, develop an intervention plan, and make decisions about treatment modality (e.g., individual vs. group), frequency, and adjuncts.

The Intervention Plan   The heart of the treatment plan is the intervention plan. The intervention plan identifies the changes in the mechanisms described in the case conceptualization that the treatment will attempt to produce. For example, for the case of Peter, described above, the therapy sought to change the negative automatic thoughts, maladaptive behaviors, and schemas that caused his symptoms of depression and anxiety.

Treatment interventions usually focus on symptoms, and are guided by the formulation of the symptoms. Thus, BA identifies the symptom of rumination as avoidance behavior and uses interventions to promote behavioral approach and reengagement with one's environment, whereas Beck's model typically tackles ruminations by helping patients change the content of their thoughts. Thus, often the clinician carries out interventions that target overt symptoms, but interventions are generally guided by and done in the service of changing the underlying mechanisms that are hypothesized to cause and maintain the symptoms.

As this discussion indicates, a good formulation is needed to make a good treatment plan. However, other factors are also important, and we mention them briefly but do not describe details of assessing them because they are not specific to assessment of depression. These factors include the patient's upbringing and personal history, treatment history, strengths and assets, values and preferences, readiness to change, and social supports, as well as the availability and cost of treatment options in the community where the patient lives. We do focus here in some detail on assessment of treatment goals, as good assessment of goals is indispensable to the process of monitoring outcome and progress, which we take up later in the chapter.

Setting Treatment Goals Clinicians who wish to take a systematic approach to assessing idiographic treatment goals can use goal attainment scaling (Kiresuk & Sherman, 1968), which is an appealing measure because it has both nomothetic and idiographic features and allows for assessment of affirmatives (goals and objectives that are positively valued by the patient) rather than negatives (psychopathology). Goal Attainment Scaling (GAS) calls for patient and therapist to identify, at the outset of treatment, 3 to 5 goals that will be the focus of treatment. A 5-point scale is used to define the outcome level for each goal, as follows: −2 (much less than expected), −1 (somewhat less than expected), 0 (expected level of outcome), +1 (somewhat more than expected), or +2 (much more than expected). Before treatment, a behavioral or other specific referent is chosen to define each level of outcome. For example, for Joan's goal to "reduce irritable outbursts toward her daughter," she and her therapist agreed that the expected outcome level (score of 0) was that she reduce the outbursts to once per month. Scores are assigned to each goal, at a predetermined time or at the end of treatment, by the patient and therapist who work together, or, if data are being collected for program evaluation purposes, by an independent evaluator. If needed, a single summary score summarizing the patient's overall progress can be calculated, typically by averaging the scores across all scales. Thus, the GAS does not so much measure absolute change in a content area, but, instead represents a measure of perceived ability to change a particular problem, or, stated a bit differently, the amount of change that occurred relative to what was expected or predicted.

The reliability and validity of the GAS are adequate (see Table 5.2). Cardillo and Smith (1994a, 1994b) reported inter-rater reliability coefficients in the range of $r = .52$ to $.99$ over a range of types of populations and raters (see also a review by Lambert, 1994). In a sample of Veterans Administration hospital patients, Cardillo and Smith (1994b) found that the GAS was related to change during treatment and that the content of goals on the GAS showed good concordance with goals selected by a three-person team who reviewed the patients' clinical records. Haynes and O'Brien (2000, p. 124) described the measure as "informally standardized" because general outlines, but not precise procedures, for obtaining GAS scores

are provided, and variations in the methods can affect the reliability and validity of the scores.

Overall Evaluation

We describe here (and in Table 5.2) measures to assess the psychological mechanisms detailed by the major current evidence-based theories that the therapist can use to aid in the process of case conceptualization. The therapist's choice of measure will generally be dictated by the theory she/he is using to conceptualize the case. However, the psychometrics of individualized case conceptualization (Bieling & Kuyken, 2003; Haynes, Leisen, & Blaine, 1997) and treatment planning are weak, and this is true not only for depression, but for most other disorders and problems. Therefore, we recommend that clinicians rely on basic principles of behavioral assessment, and collect idiographic data (as described in the next section) to test their formulation of hypotheses and monitor treatment progress for each case they treat.

Assessment for Treatment Monitoring and Treatment Outcome

In addition to monitoring *outcome* of therapy (Kazdin, 1993), the therapist also monitors the *process* (i.e., what is going on in the therapy?), and, moreover, monitors process and outcome in a way that allows patient and clinician to test hypotheses about the relationships among them—for example, to test the hypothesis that an increase in the number of a depressed patient's pleasurable activities is associated with a decrease in severity of depressive symptoms (Persons, 2007). The *process* has two parts: *the therapeutic relationship* and *mechanisms of change*. The clinician and patient can monitor outcome and process at three time points: at each therapy session, within the session, and over longer time periods. We discuss each in turn, focusing primarily on monitoring at each therapy session. Measures useful for monitoring outcome and process are summarized in Table 5.3.

In addition, Online Progress Tracking (OPT) is an online tool that helps the therapist administer, in a convenient, secure, and HIPAA-compliant way, measures from a large library of measures, including many of those described here, that assess the outcome and process of psychotherapy. The first author (J. B. P.) is collaborating (disclosure!) with Kelly Koerner and Cannon Thomas on this project, which is in early stages of development and can be accessed at www.onlineprogresstracking.com.

Session-by-Sesssion Monitoring

Assessing Outcome   To monitor idiographic target behaviors and goals, the therapist can give the patient a daily log to track a particular behavior or symptom or problem, such as a bout of depressed mood, arrival on time at work, social activities, crying jags, or the like. This log can be used in conjunction with, or instead of, the GAS. Joan's clinician gave her a form to monitor irritable outbursts with her son, noting the date, time, situation, content, and intensity (scored 1, "a harsh word," to 10, "a full-blown outburst, the worst I've ever had or could imagine having").

As described previously, the QIDS-SR was expressly designed for monitoring change in depressive symptoms across the course of treatment. The two-week reporting interval of the BDI-II, which is ideal for diagnostic assessment of Major Depressive Disorder, makes it less useful for assessing weekly change.

Combined measures of symptoms and functioning have been developed to monitor change during treatment for depressed (and indeed for nearly all psychiatric patients). The three best established and most studied of these are the Outcome Questionnaire-45 (Lambert et al., 1996), the clinical outcomes in Routine Evaluation Outcome Measure (CORE-OM; Barkham et al., 2001), and the Treatment Outcome Package (TOP; Kraus, Seligman, & Jordan, 2005). One of the strongest features of all three measures is that they allow the clinician to compare outcomes of his or her patients to outcomes of large benchmarking samples that have been established for all of the measures. However, although the CORE-OM scales are available on the Internet (www.coreims.co.uk) and can be freely photocopied, the benchmarking feature is not yet available to users in the United States, and therefore we review the OQ-45 and the TOP here.

The OQ-45 (Lambert et al., 1996) is a 45-item self-report scale that assesses four domains: subjective discomfort, interpersonal relations, social role performance, and positive aspects of satisfaction and functioning. Respondents answer each question in the context of their experience over the past week using a 5-point Likert scale. The clinician obtains a total score on the measure and subscale scores on the first three domains listed above, and uses the scoring

manual or software package to classify each client as an improver, nonresponder, or deteriorator on the basis of benchmarking data from a large sample of clients that Lambert and his colleagues have collected. Internal consistency for the undergraduate sample and for a sample of 504 Employee Assistance Program clients was .93 for each sample (Lambert et al., 1996). The total score on the measure has good test–retest reliability (.84) over an interval of 3 weeks for a sample of 157 undergraduates. The measure is sensitive to change in clients and stable in untreated individuals (Vermeersch, Lambert, & Burlingame, 2000). Repeated testing does not, itself, produce changes in scores (Durham et al., 2002). Concurrent validity coefficients for the total score range from .55 to .88 on several measures of psychopathology (Lambert et al., 1996). The measure has good treatment utility, as Lambert and colleagues (Lambert et al., 2003) have shown that psychotherapy patients have better treatment outcome when clinicians use the information to adjust treatment as necessary (i.e., when the patient is classified as a nonresponder or deteriorator). There is also some evidence that obtaining additional data on the therapeutic alliance and the patient's readiness for change can be useful in adjusting treatments to enhance patient outcome (Whipple et al., 2003). The measure is available from the American Professional Credentialing Services LLC.

The TOP is a 93-item scale that assesses functioning, quality of life, and mental health symptoms and is intended to provide a theory-neutral core battery for outcome monitoring in clinical and research settings across all diagnoses and levels of care. Respondents indicate the presence of symptoms in the last month on a 6-point Likert scale. Items are divided into 11 subscales. Psychometrics of the measure was presented by Kraus et al. (2005). Internal consistency for the 11 subscales ranged from .53 (for the mania subscale) to .93 (for the depression subscale) in a sample of psychiatric inpatients. Test–retest reliability over one week in 53 community mental health center clients who provided data before receiving treatment was high, ranging from .87 to .94, except for the mania subscale (where reliability was .76). Validity of the measure is mixed. Convergent validity for some scales is excellent (the depression subscale correlates .92 with the BDI), and poor for others (the psychosis subscale correlates −.28 with the MMPI-2 schizophrenia scale). The measure did a good job of distinguishing patients from nonpatients. In logistic analyses, 80% to 89% of

TABLE 5.3 Ratings of Instruments Used for Treatment Monitoring and Treatment Outcome Evaluation

Instrument	Norms	Internal Consistency	Inter-Rater Reliability	Test–Retest Reliability	Content Validity	Construct Validity	Validity Generalization	Treatment Sensitivity	Clinical Utility	Highly Recommended
Monitoring Outcome										
BDI-II	G	E	NA	E	E	E	E	E	E	✓
QIDS	E	E	NA	E	E	E	E	E	E	✓
OQ-45	G	E	NA	G	A	G	G	G	E	✓
TOP	G	A	NA	G	G	A	E	G	A	✓
GAF	A	NA	A	A	G	G	G	G	G	✓
QOLI	A	G	NA	E	G	G	G	G	E	✓
Monitoring Therapeutic Relationship										
WAI	E	E	NA	A	G	G	G	G	G	✓
HAq-II	E	E	NA	G	G	G	G	G	G	✓

Note: BDI-II = Beck Depression Inventory-II; QIDS = Quick Inventory for Depression Severity; OQ-45 = Outcome Questionnaire-45; TOP = Treatment Outcome Package; GAF = Global Assessment of Functioning; QOLI = Quality of Life Inventory; WAI = Working Alliance Inventory; HAq-II = Helping Alliance Questionnaire-II; A = Adequate; G = Good; E = Excellent; NA = Not Applicable.

participants were correctly classified as patients or members of the general population. The measure's sensitivity to change appears adequate.

The GAF (Endicott et al., 1976) and the QOLI (Frisch et al., 1992) have good treatment sensitivity.

Assessing the Therapeutic Relationship Deteriorations in the quality of the relationship between patient and clinician can be difficult to detect, but they are vital to address, because they can lead to unilateral termination by the patient. Castonguay, Goldfried, Wiser, Raue, and Hayes (1996) found that alliance ruptures were common in CT for depression, especially during sessions in which the clinician focused on challenging negative cognitions of the patient. Safran, Muran, Samstag, and Stevens (2001) suggested that clinicians should be aware that patients often have negative feelings about the therapy, should look for subtle indications of ruptures, and take the initiative to explore what is transpiring.

The CB clinician traditionally informally assesses the quality of the therapeutic relationship at each session by asking the patient for feedback about the session at the end of the session (Beck et al., 1979). Objective scales to measure the therapeutic relationship include the Working Alliance Inventory (WAI; Horvath & Greenberg, 1986; Tracey & Kokotovic, 1989) and the Revised Helping Alliance Questionnaire (HAq-II; Luborsky et al., 1996).

The WAI assesses factors common to all treatments associated with the collaborative efforts of the patient and therapist. The 12-item patient version of the WAI assesses three integrated components: Goals (the outcomes of therapy agreed upon by patient and therapist), Tasks (the therapeutic processes that take place during sessions), and Bond (the key elements of rapport—trust, acceptance, and confidence), as well as a total score (Horvath & Greenberg, 1989). The WAI demonstrates excellent internal consistency ($\alpha = .93$; Horvath & Greenberg, 1989) and good validity (Fischer & Corcoran, 1994), with patient ratings serving as better predictors than therapist ratings (Tryon & Kane, 1990).

The HAq-II is a 19-item self-report scale that measures the alliance between patient and therapist. Internal consistency for the scale is excellent ($\alpha = .90$) and test–retest reliability has been found to be $r = .78$ over three sessions (Luborsky et al., 1996). Concurrent validity demonstrated by correlations between the HAq-II and the California Psychotherapy

Alliance Scale ranged between $r = .59$ and $r = .71$. In a demonstration of the measure's treatment utility, Whipple et al. (2003) showed that outcome of psychotherapy (on the OQ-45) was positively related to the clinician's obtaining weekly feedback of the patient's HAq-II scores. The HAq-II is available for download on the Internet at http://www.uphs.upenn.edu/psycther/HAQ2QUES.pdf.

Assessing Mechanism Here the goal is to measure the treatment targets that are described in the case formulation, such as frequency of pleasant events, distorted thoughts, positive thoughts, use of decentering skills, rumination, activity level, and interpersonal interactions. The measures described in the section titled Mechanisms can be used for this purpose. In addition, simple counts and logs can also be used. For example, when Joan was working in therapy on increasing her positive thoughts about herself and her experience, she tallied them on a golf-score counter each day, and wrote the daily tally on a log that she brought to her therapy session.

Putting It All Together It is daunting to try to monitor outcome, the therapeutic relationship, and mechanisms at each therapy session. Fortunately, these phenomena often overlap. Thus, for example, in Joan's case, the count of positive thoughts was a measure both of mechanism and outcome. To ease the data collection process, patients at the first author's center arrive five minutes early for each session and complete the BDI and other measures relevant to their care (e.g., a self-report measure of anxiety), which are kept in the waiting room, and present them to the clinician, who scores and plots the measure(s) at the beginning of the session. The session-by-session data plot is kept at the front of the clinical record to remind the clinician to review the measure with the patient and plot the score at the beginning of each session; the notion here, of course, is that the outcome data feed into and inform the nature of the session (Persons, 2001). The clinician can ask the patient to bring the alliance scale to the next session, or to leave it in a drop-off box in the waiting room after the session.

Monitoring during the Therapy Session

Most monitoring during the therapy session happens simply by observation (e.g., patient's facial expression, nonverbal behaviors, and emotional arousal (Samoilov & Goldfried, 2000), and even the clinician's emotional responses (e.g., feeling pulled by the patient to step forward and solve a problem, cf. McCullough, 2000). Sometimes more systematic measures can be used, such as collecting a report on a simple 0-to-100 scale of intensity of depressed mood or of the urge to quit therapy. To track *outcome* during the therapy session, the clinician can monitor symptoms that are relevant to the patient's treatment goals, including passivity, assertiveness, personal hygiene, disorganization, irritability, and promptness. These data often complement the patient's self-report. To monitor the *therapeutic relationship*, the clinician carefully monitors the "feel" of the patient–clinician interaction at every moment, attending to the patient's behaviors as well as to the clinician's emotional responses. The clinician can also assess the relationship by asking about it directly: "I'm noticing that about five minutes ago you and I seemed to get into a sort of a tussle. Did you notice that?" Data on *mechanisms* can be collected during the therapy session in several ways, including on some of the intervention forms that are described in the Mechanisms section. For example, during a cognitive restructuring intervention, the therapist can ask the patient to rate his/her degree of belief in his/her automatic thoughts, before and after the intervention, his/her degree of belief in the coping responses, and the intensity of distress before and after the intervention to monitor the process of change. These ratings can readily be recorded with a Thought Record.

Long-Term Monitoring

A long-term progress review can be done at a predetermined time (e.g., after 10 sessions), in response to data generated by the weekly monitoring (e.g., if no progress is being made), or at the end of treatment. In contrast to session-by-session and within-session monitoring, which often focuses in detail on one or two treatment targets or mechanisms, a long-term progress review examines progress on all of the treatment goals and takes account not just of what is going on in the psychotherapy but in the adjunct therapies as well. If GAS (Kiresuk, Smith, & Cardillo, 1994) is being used, the clinician and patient can, together, rate each goal that was set at the beginning of treatment. If weekly outcome or process measures have been collected, they can be reviewed. In conjunction with assessing the degree to which the treatment goals have (or have not) been accomplished, patient and

clinician can also discuss the process: their therapeutic relationship and the mechanism of change (i.e., factors that appear to have played a causal role in any change that has, or has not occurred). The goal of this discussion is to obtain some answers to the questions: Has progress occurred? If so, what produced it? What has impeded progress? What would need to happen to get more progress?

Overall Evaluation

Monitoring outcome and process during treatment is demanding; however, patients generally like doing this task, and Whipple et al. (2003) have shown that therapist's review of weekly outcome and process data improves patient outcomes. If monitoring only one of these, we recommend that clinicians monitor outcome, collecting a weekly score on the QIDS or BDI and plotting the score at each session. A visual record of the data on a plot is a key part of the use of monitoring data. Without it, the therapist can easily accumulate a stack of measures in the clinical record that do not inform the treatment process. Nevertheless, caution is indicated in the frequent use of self-report measures. Longwell and Truax (2005) and Sharpe and Gilbert (1998) have shown that repeated administration of the BDI consistently resulted in a lower score, even when research participants were not depressed and were not receiving treatment. Although the reasons for this drop are unclear (and may include socially desirable responding, mood-state congruent effects, or regression to the mean), clinicians who use the scale repeatedly must be aware of the possibility of measurement reactivity. In addition, the measures are quite transparent, and therefore, the patient who wants to communicate distress, poor progress, or recovery to the clinician can do so without much difficulty. If the scores on self-report measures are surprisingly high or low, the clinician can use the case formulation to aid in interpreting the score (e.g., the patient who is excessively concerned about pleasing the clinician may obtain an unduly low score).

CONCLUSIONS AND FUTURE DIRECTIONS

A rich body of measures is available for the assessment of depression. Nevertheless, there is much room for improvement. Inexpensive Web-based systems of measures with good psychometric properties that are inexpensive and easily available to clinicians are urgently needed and are now being developed (Percevic, Lambert, & Kordy, 2004). In this review, we were often unable to rate assessment tools for treatment sensitivity and clinical utility, as these qualities of assessment tools have not received much attention in the literature (except in Sackett, Richardson, Rosenberg, & Haynes, 1997). However, we expect the field to pay increasing attention to the sensitivity and specificity of assessment tools, which in turn, will increase the clinical utility of the measures. Interest in positive psychology (Seligman, Steen, Park, & Peterson, 2005), as well as a focus on patients' goals and values (see Hayes, Strosahl, & Wilson, 1999; Linehan, 1993), is likely to increasingly influence assessment and treatment of depression. Much more information is needed about idiographic assessment, especially the treatment utility of case conceptualization (Bieling & Kuyken, 2003). Efforts to increase the numbers of clinicians who make daily use of good quality assessment tools are needed. Finally, we need more and better tools to assess mechanism, especially to capture constructs like schema that are not readily available for self-report. Improved tools for measuring underlying processes of change will allow us to improve our understanding of the mechanisms causing depression and thus to improve our treatment of this devastating disorder.

References

Abramson, L. Y., Metalsky, G. I., & Alloy, L. B. (1989). Hopelessness depression: A theory-based subtype of depression. *Psychological Review, 96*, 358–372.

Abramson, L. Y., Seligman, M. E. P., & Teasdale, J. (1978). Learned helplessness in humans: Critique and reformulation. *Journal of Abnormal Psychology, 87*, 49–74.

American Psychiatric Association. (2000). *Diagnostic and statistical manual of mental disorders (DSM-IV-TR)*. Washington, DC: Author.

Barkham, M., Margison, F., Leach, C., Lucock, M., Mellor-Clark, J., Evans, C., et al. (2001). Service profiling and outcomes benchmarking using the CORE-OM: Toward practice-based evidence in the psychological therapies. *Journal of Consulting and Clinical Psychology, 69*, 184–196.

Beck, A. T. (1967). *Depression: Clinical, experimental and theoretical aspects*. New York: Harper & Row.

Beck, A. T. (1976). *Cognitive therapy and the emotional disorders*. New York: International Universities Press.

Beck, A. T., Rush, J. A., Shaw, B. F., & Emery, G. (1979). *Cognitive therapy for depression*. New York: Guilford Press.

Beck, A. T., Steer, R. A., & Brown, G. K. (1996). *Manual for Beck Depression Inventory-II*. San Antonio, TX: Psychological Corporation.

Beck, J. S. (1995). *Cognitive therapy: Basics and beyond*. New York: Guilford Press.

Beevers, C. G., Wenzlaff, R. M., Hayes, A. M., & Scott, W. D. (1999). Depression and the ironic effects of thought suppression: Therapeutic strategies for improving mental control. *Clinical Psychology: Science and Practice, 6*, 133–148.

Bieling, P. J., & Kuyken, W. (2003). Is cognitive case formulation science or science fiction? *Clinical Psychology: Science and Practice, 10*, 52–69.

Brown, T. A., Dinardo, P. A., & Barlow, D. H. (1994). *Anxiety disorders interview schedule for DSM-IV: lifetime version (ADIS-IV-L)*. Albany, NY: Graywind Publications.

Cardillo, J. E., & Smith, A. (1994a). Psychometric issues. In T. J. Kiresuk, A. Smith & J. E. Cardillo (Eds.), *Goal attainment scaling: Applications, theory and measurement* (pp. 173–212). Hillsdale, NJ: Lawrence Erlbaum Associates.

Cardillo, J. E., & Smith, A. (1994b). Reliability of goal attainment scores. In T. J. Kiresuk, A. Smith, & J. E. Cardillo (Eds.), *Goal attainment scaling: Applications, theory, and measurement* (pp. 213–242). Hillsdale, NJ: Lawrence Erlbaum Associates.

Castonguay, L. G., Goldfried, M. R., Wiser, S., Raue, P. J., & Hayes, A. M. (1996). Predicting the effect of cognitive therapy for depression: A study of unique and common factors. *Journal of Consulting and Clinical Psychology, 64*, 497–504.

Clark, L. A., & Watson, D. (1991). Tripartite model of anxiety and depression: Evidence and taxonomic implications. *Journal of Abnormal Psychology, 100*, 316–336.

Clore, G. L., & Ortony, A. (2000). Cognition in emotion: Always, sometimes, or never? In R. D. Lane & L. Nadel (Eds.), *Cognitive neuroscience of emotion* (pp. 24–61). New York: Oxford University Press.

Colin, S., Sweeney, P. D., & Schaeffer, D. E. (1981). The causality of causal attributions in depression: A cross-lagged panel correlational analysis. *Journal of Abnormal Psychology, 90*, 14–22.

Durham, C. J., McGrath, L. D., Burlingame, G. M., Schaajle, G. B., Lambert, M. J., & Davies, D. R. (2002). The effects of repeated administrations on self-report and parent-report rating scales. *Journal of Psychoeducational Assessment, 20*, 240–257.

Endicott, J., Spitzer, R. L., Fleiss, J. L., & Cohen, J. (1976). The Global Assessment Scale: A procedure for measuring overall severity of psychiatric disturbance. *Archives of General Psychiatry, 33*, 766–771.

Fava, G. A., Rafanelli, C., Grandi, S., Conti, S., & Belluardo, P. (1998). Prevention of recurrent depression with cognitive behavioral therapy: Preliminary findings. *Archives of General Psychiatry, 55*, 816–820.

Ferster, C. B. (1973). A functional analysis of depression. *American Psychologist, 28*, 857–870.

First, M. B., Spitzer, R. L., Gibbon, M., & Williams, J. B. W. (2002). *Structured Clinical Interview for DSM-IV-TR Axis I Disorders, Research Version, Patent Edition. (SCID-I/P).* New York: Biometrics Research, New York State Psychiatric Institute.

Fischer, J., & Corcoran, K. (1994). *Measures for clinical practice: A sourcebook (Adults).* (Vol. 2). New York, NY: Free Press.

Frank, E. (2005). *Treating bipolar disorder: A clinician's guide to interpersonal and social rhythm therapy.* New York: Guilford Press.

Frederickson, B. L. (2001). The role of positive emotions in positive psychology: The broaden-and-build theory of positive emotions. *American Psychologist, 56*, 218–226.

Fresco, D. M., Alloy, L. B., & Reilly-Harrington, N. (2006). The association of attributional style for positive and negative events and life stress to depression and anxiety. *Journal of Social and Clinical Psychology, 25*, 975–994.

Fresco, D. M., Moore, M. T., van Dulmen, M., Segal, Z. V., Teasdale, J. D., Ma, H., et al. (2007). Initial psychometric properties of the Experiences Questionnaire: A self-report survey of decentering. *Behavior Therapy, 38*, 234–246.

Fresco, D. M., Segal, Z. V., Buis, T., & Kennedy, S., (2007). Relationship of post treatment decentering and cognitive reactivity to relapse of major depressive disorder. *Journal of Consulting and Clinical Psychology, 27*, 447–455.

Frisch, M. B., Cornell, J., Villanueva, M., & Retzlaff, P. J. (1992). Clinical validation of the Quality of Life Inventory: A measure of life satisfaction for use in treatment planning and outcome assessment. *Psychological Assessment, 4*, 92–101.

Gray, J. A. (1973). Causal theories of personality and how to test them. In J. R. Royce (Ed.), *Multivariate analysis to psychological theory* (pp. 409–463). New York: Academic Press.

Gray, J. A. (1982). *The neuropsychology of anxiety: An enquiry into the functions of the sept-hippocampal system.* Oxford: Clarendon Press.

Greenberg, L. S. (1993). In-session change in emotionally focused therapy. *Journal of Consulting and Clinical Psychology, 61*, 78–84.

Greenberger, D., & Padesky, C. A. (1995). *Mind over mood: A cognitive therapy treatment manual for clients.* New York: Guilford Press.

Gross, J. J. (1998). The emerging field of emotion regulation: An integrative review. *Review of General Psychology, 2*, 271–299.

Gross, J. J., & John, O. P. (2003). Individual differences in two emotion regulation processes: Implications for affect, relationships, and well-being. *Journal of Personality and Social Psychology, 85*, 348–362.

Grosscup, S. J., & Lewinsohn, P. M. (1980). Unpleasant and pleasant events and mood. *Journal of Clinical Psychology, 36*, 252–259.

Hayes, A. M., Feldman, G. C., Beevers, C. G., Laurenceau, J.-P., Cardaciotto, L., & Smith, J. L. (2007). Two patterns of change in the treatment of depression: The rapid response and the depression spike. *Journal of Consulting and Clinical Psychology, 27*, 409–421.

Hayes, S. C., Nelson, R. O., & Jarrett, R. B. (1987). The treatment utility of assessment: A functional approach to evaluating assessment quality. *American Psychologist, 42*, 963–974.

Hayes, S. C., Strosahl, K. D., & Wilson, K. G. (1999). *Acceptance and commitment therapy: An experiential approach to behavior change.* New York: Guilford Press.

Haynes, S. N., Kaholokula, J. K., & Nelson, K. (1999). The idiographic application of nomothetic, empirically based treatments. *Clinical Psychology: Science and Practice, 6*, 456–461.

Haynes, S. N., Leisen, M. B., & Blaine, D. D. (1997). Design of individualized behavioral treatment programs using functional analytic clinical case models. *Psychological Assessment, 9*, 334–348.

Haynes, S. N., & O'Brien, W. H. (2000). *Principles and practice of behavioral assessment.* New York: Kluwer Academic/Plenum Publishers.

Hollon, S. D., & Kendall, P. C. (1980). Cognitive self-statements in depression: Development of an automatic thoughts questionnaire. *Cognitive Therapy and Research, 4*, 383–395.

Hollon, S. D., Kendall, P. C., & Lumry, A. (1986). Specificity of depressogenic cognitions in clinical depression. *Journal of Abnormal Psychology, 95*, 52–59.

Hollon, S. D., Stewart, M. O., & Strunk, D. R. (2006). Enduring effects for cognitive behavior therapy in the treatment of depression and anxiety. *Annual Review of Psychology, 57*, 285–315.

Horvath, A. O., & Greenberg, L. S. (Eds.) (1986). *The working alliance: Theory, research, and practice.* New York: John Wiley & Sons, Inc.

Horvath, A. O., & Greenberg, L. S. (1989). Development and validation of the Working Alliance Inventory. *Journal of Counseling Psychology, 36,* 223–233.

Ingram, R. E., & Wisnicki, K. S. (1988). Assessment of positive automatic cognition. *Journal of Consulting and Clinical Psychology, 56,* 898–902.

Jacobson, N. S., Martell, C. R., & Dimidjian, S. (2001). Behavioral activation treatment for depression: Returning to contextual roots. *Clinical Psychology: Science and Practice, 8,* 255–270.

Kabat-Zinn, J. (1990). *Full catastrophe living: Using the wisdom of your body and mind to face stress, pain, and illness.* New York: Dell.

Kazdin, A. E. (1993). Evaluation in clinical practice: Clinically sensitive and systematic methods of treatment delivery. *Behavior Therapy, 24,* 11–45.

Kazdin, A. E. (2001). *Behavior modification in applied settings* (6th ed.). Belmont: Wadsworth/Thomson Learning.

Kessler, R. C., Berglund, P., Demler, O., Jin, R., Koretz, D., Merikangas, K. R., et al. (2003). The epidemiology of major depressive disorder: Results from the National Comorbidity Survey Replication (NCS-R). *Journal of the American Medical Association, 289,* 3095–3105.

Kessler, R. C., Chiu, W. T., Demler, O., Merikangas, K. R., & Walters, E. E. (2005). Prevalence, severity, and comorbidity of 12-month DSM-IV disorders in the National Comorbidity Survey Replication. *Archives of General Psychiatry, 62,* 617–627.

Kiresuk, T. J., & Sherman, R. E. (1968). Goal Attainment Scaling: A general method for evaluating comprehensive community mental health programs. *Community Mental Health Journal, 4,* 443–453.

Kiresuk, T. J., Smith, A., & Cardillo, J. E. (1994). *Goal Attainment Scaling: Applications, theory, and measurement.* Hillsdale, NJ: Lawrence Erlbaum Associates.

Klerman, G. L., Weissman, M. M., Rounsaville, B. J., & Chevron, E. S. (1984). *Interpersonal psychotherapy for depression.* New York: Basic Books.

Kraus, D. R., Seligman, D. A., & Jordan, J. R. (2005). Validation of a behavioral health treatment outcome and assessment tool designed for naturalistic settings: The treatment outcome package. *Journal of Clinical Psychology, 61,* 285–314.

Lambert, M. J. (1994). Use of psychological tests for outcome assessment. In M. E. Maruish et al. (Eds.), *The use of psychological testing for treatment planning and outcome assessment* (pp. 75–97). Hillsdale, NJ: Lawrence Erlbaum Associates.

Lambert, M. J., Burlingame, G. M., Umphress, V. J., Hansen, N. B., Vermeersch, D. A., Clouse, G., et al. (1996). The reliability and validity of the outcome questionnaire. *Clinical Psychology and Psychotherapy, 3,* 106–116.

Lambert, M. J., Whipple, J. L., Hawkins, E. J., Vermeersch, D. A., Nielsen, S. L., & Smart, D. W. (2003). Is it time for clinicians to routinely track patient outcome?: A meta-analysis. *Clinical Psychology: Science and Practice, 10,* 288–301.

Lamoureux, B. E., Linardatos, E., Haigh, E. A. P., Fresco, D. M., Bartko, D., Logue, E., & Milo, L. (2007, November). *Screening for major depressive disorder in a primary care medical population with the Quick Inventory of Depressive Symptomatology-Self-Report.* Poster presented at the annual meeting of the Association for Behavioral and Cognitive Therapies, Philadelphia, PA.

Lewinsohn, P. M. (1974). A behavioral approach to depression. In R. J. Friedman & M. Katz (Eds.), *The psychology of depression: Contemporary theory and research.* Oxford: John Wiley & Sons.

Lewinsohn, P. M., & Gotlib, I. H. (1995). Behavioral theory and treatment of depression. In E. E. Beckham & W. R. Leber (Eds.), *Handbook of depression* (2nd ed., pp. 352–375). New York: Guilford.

Lewinsohn, P. M., Munoz, R. F., Youngren, M. A., & Zeiss, A. M. (1986). *Control your depression.* New York: Simon and Schuster.

Linehan, M. M. (1993). *Cognitive-behavioral treatment of borderline personality disorder.* New York: Guilford Press.

Longwell, B. T., & Truax, P. (2005). The differential effects of weekly, monthly, and bimonthly administrations of the Beck Depression Inventory-II: Psychometric properties and clinical implications. *Behavior Therapy, 36,* 265–275.

Lopez, A. D., & Murray, C. J. L. (1998). The global burden of disease (1990–2020). *Nature Medicine, 4,* 1241–1243.

Luborsky, L., Barber, J., Siqueland, L., Johnson, S., Najavits, L., Franks, A., et al. (1996). The revised Helping Alliance Questionnaire (HAq-II). *Journal of Psychotherapy Practice and Research, 5,* 260–271.

MacPhillany, D. J., & Lewinsohn, P. M. (1982). The pleasant events schedule: Studies on reliability, validity, and scale intercorrelation. *Journal of Consulting and Clinical Psychology, 50,* 363–380.

Martell, C. R., Addis, M. E., & Jacobson, N. S. (2001). *Depression in context: Strategies for guided action.* New York: W. W. Norton.

Mash, E. J., & Hunsley, J. (1990). Behavioral assessment: A contemporary approach. In A. S. Bellack, M. Hersen, & A. E. Kazdin (Eds.), *International handbook of behavior modification and therapy* (2nd ed., pp. 87–106). New York: Plenum.

McCullough, J. J. P. (2000). *Treatment for chronic depression: Cognitive behavioral analysis system of psychotherapy (CBASP)*. New York: Guilford.

McCullough, J. J. P. (2001). *Skills training manual for diagnosing and treating chronic depression*. New York: Guilford Press.

Mennin, D. S., & Farach, F. J. (2006). *Emotion and evolving treatments for adult psychopathology*. Unpublished manuscript.

Mennin, D. S., Holaway, R. M., Fresco, D. M., Moore, M. T., & Heimberg, R. G. (2007). Delineating components of emotion dysregulation in anxiety and mood psychopathology. *Behavior Therapy, 38,* 284–302.

Mintz, J., Mintz, L. I., Arruda, M. J., & Hwang, S. S. (1992). Treatment of depression and the functional capacity to work. *Archives of General Psychiatry, 49,* 761–768.

Nathan, P. E., & Gorman, J. M. (Eds.) (2002). *A guide to treatments that work* (2nd ed.). New York: Oxford University Press.

Nezu, A. M., Ronan, G. F., Meadows, E. A., & McClure, K. S. (Eds.) (2000). *Practioner's guide to empirically based measures of depression*. New York: Kluwer Academic/Plenum Publishers.

Ottenbreit, N. D., & Dobson, K. S. (2004). Avoidance and depression: The construction of the cognitive-behavioral avoidance scale. *Behavior Research and Therapy, 42,* 293–313.

Percevic, R., Lambert, M. J., & Kordy, H. (2004). Computer-supported monitoring of patient treatment response. *Journal of Clinical Psychology, 60,* 285–299.

Persons, J. B. (1989). *Cognitive therapy in practice: A case formulation approach*. New York: Norton & Company.

Persons, J. B. (2001). Conducting effectiveness studies in the context of evidence-based clinical practice. *Clinical Psychology: Science and Practice, 8,* 168–172.

Persons, J. B. (2007). Psychotherapists collect data during routine clinical work that can contribute to knowledge about mechanisms of change in psychotherapy. *Clinical Psychology: Science and Practice, 14*(3), 244–246.

Persons, J. B., & Bertagnolli, A. (1999). Inter-rater reliability of cognitive-behavioral case formulation of depression: A replication. *Cognitive Therapy and Research, 23,* 271–284.

Persons, J. B., Bostrom, A., & Bertagnolli, A. (1999). Results of randomized controlled trials of cognitive therapy for depression generalize to private practice. *Cognitive Therapy and Research, 23,* 535–548.

Persons, J. B., Davidson, J., & Tompkins, M. A. (2001). *Essential components of cognitive-behavior therapy for depression*. Washington, DC: American Psychological Association.

Persons, J. B., & Miranda, J. (1992). Cognitive theories of vulnerability to depression: Reconciling negative evidence. *Cognitive Therapy and Research, 16,* 485–502.

Persons, J. B., Mooney, K. A., & Padesky, C. A. (1995). Inter-rater reliability of cognitive-behavioral case formulation. *Cognitive Therapy and Research, 19,* 21–34.

Persons, J. B., Roberts, N. A., Zalecki, C. A., & Brechwald, W. A. G. (2006). Naturalistic outcome of case formulation-driven cognitive-behavior therapy for anxious depressed outpatients. *Behaviour Research and Therapy, 44,* 1041–1051.

Peterson, C., Semmel, A., von Baeyer, C., Abramson, L. Y., Metalsky, G. I., & Seligman, M. E. P. (1982). The attributional style questionnaire. *Cognitive Therapy and Research, 6,* 287–299.

Pos, A. E., Greenberg, L. S., Goldman, R. N., & Korman, L. M. (2003). Emotional processing during experiential treatment of depression. *Journal of Consulting and Clinical Psychology, 71,* 1007–1016.

Rush, A. J., Trivedi, M. H., Ibrahim, H. M., Carmody, T. J., Arnow, B., Klein, D. N., et al. (2003). The 16-Item Quick Inventory of Depressive Symptomatology (QIDS), Clinician Rating (QIDS-C), and Self-Report (QIDS-SR): A psychometric evaluation in patients with chronic major depression. *Biological Psychiatry, 54,* 585.

Sackett, D. L., Richardson, W. S., Rosenberg, W., & Haynes, R. B. (1997). *Evidence-based medicine: How to practice and teach EBM*. New York: Churchill Livingstone.

Safran, J. D., Muran, J. C., Samstag, L. W., & Stevens, C. (2001). Repairing alliance ruptures. *Psychotherapy: Theory, Research, Practice, Training, 38,* 406–412.

Samoilov, A., & Goldfried, M. R. (2000). Role of emotion in cognitive-behavior therapy. *Clinical Psychology: Science and Practice, 7,* 373–385.

Sarason, I. G., Johnson, J. H., & Siegel, J. M. (1978). Assessing the impact of life changes: Development of the Life Experiences Survey. *Journal of Consulting and Clinical Psychology, 45,* 932–946.

Segal, Z. V., Williams, M. G., & Teasdale, J. D. (2002). *Mindfulness-based cognitive therapy for depression*. New York: Guilford Press.

Seligman, M. E. P. (1974). Depression and learned helplessness. In R. J. Friedman & M. Katz (Eds.), *The psychology of depression: Contemporary theory and research* (pp. 83–113). New York: Wiley.

Seligman, M. E. P., Steen, T. A., Park, N., & Peterson, C. (2005). Positive psychology progress: Empirical validation of interventions. *American Psychologist, 60,* 410–421.

Sharpe, J. P., & Gilbert, D. G. (1998). Effects of repeated administration of the Beck Depression Inventory and other measures of negative mood states. *Personality and Individual Differences, 24,* 457–463.

Solomon, D. A., Keller, M. B., Leon, A. C., Mueller, T. I., Lavori, P. W., Shea, M. T., et al. (2000). Multiple recurrences of major depressive disorder. *American Journal of Psychiatry, 157,* 229–233.

Stewart, W. F., Ricci, J. A., Chee, E., Hahn, S. R., & Morganstein, D. (2003). Cost of lost productive work time among US workers with depression. *Journal of the American Medical Association, 289,* 3135–3144.

Sweeney, P. D., Anderson, K., & Bailey, S. (1986). Attributional style in depression: A meta-analytic review. *Journal of Personality and Social Psychology, 50,* 974–991.

Teasdale, J. D. (1988). Cognitive vulnerability to persistent depression. *Cognition and Emotion, 2,* 247–274.

Teasdale, J. D. (1997). The relationship between cognition and emotion: The mind-in-place mood disorders. In D. M. Clark & C. G. Fairburn (Eds.), *Science and practice of cognitive behaviour therapy* (pp. 67–93). Oxford: Oxford University Press.

Tracey, T. J., & Kokotovic, A. M. (1989). Factor structure of the working alliance inventory. *Psychological Assessment, 1,* 207–210.

Tryon, G. S., & Kane, A. S. (1990). The helping alliance and premature termination. *Counseling Psychology Quarterly, 3,* 233–238.

Turkat, I. D. (1987). The initial clinical hypothesis. *Journal of Behavior Therapy and Experimental Psychiatry, 18,* 349–356.

Ventura, J., Liberman, R. P., Green, M. F., Shaner, A., & Mintz, J. (1998). Training and quality assurance with the Structured Clinical Interview for DSM-IV (SCID-I/P). *Psychiatry Research, 79,* 163–173.

Vermeersch, D. A., Lambert, M. J., & Burlingame, G. M. (2000). Outcome questionnaire: Item sensitivity to change. *Journal of Personality Assessment, 74,* 242–261.

Watson, D., & Walker, L. M. (1996). The long-term stability and predictive validity of trait measures of affect. *Journal of Personality and Social Psychology, 70,* 567–577.

Watson, D., Weber, K., Smith Assenheimer, J., Clark, L. A., Strauss, M. E., & McCormick, R. A. (1995). Testing a tripartite model: I. Evaluating the convergent and discriminant validity of anxiety and depression symptoms scales. *Journal of Abnormal Psychology, 104,* 3–14.

Watson, D., Wiese, D., Vaidya, J., & Tellegen, A. (1999). The two general activation systems of affect: Structural findings, evolutionary considerations, and psychobiological evidence. *Journal of Personality and Social Psychology, 76,* 820–838.

Watson, D. L., & Tharp, R. G. (2002). *Self-directed behavior: Self-modification for personal adjustment.* Belmont: Wadsworth.

Weissman, A. N., & Beck, A. T. (1978). *Development and validation of the Dysfunctional Attitude Scale: A preliminary investigation.* Paper presented at the American Education Research Association Meeting, Toronto, Canada.

Weissman, M. M., & Bothwell, S. (1976). Assessment of social adjustment by patient self-report. *Archives of General Psychiatry, 33,* 1111–1115.

Whipple, J. L., Lambert, M. J., Vermeersch, D. A., Smart, D. W., Nielsen, S. L., & Hawkins, E. J. (2003). Improving the effects of psychotherapy: The use of early identification of treatment failure and problem solving strategies in routine practice. *Journal of Counseling Psychology, 58,* 59–68.

6

Bipolar Disorder

Sheri L. Johnson

Christopher Miller

Lori Eisner

The goal of this chapter is to review measures that are relevant for the clinical evaluation and treatment of bipolar disorder. More specifically, we will focus on assessment measures relevant to diagnosis, treatment planning, and treatment monitoring. In each area, we will focus on those few assessment measures that have gained at least moderate psychometric support.

Only a small number of measures meet established psychometric criteria, perhaps as a consequence of the limited amount of psychological research on bipolar disorder compared to other psychopathologies. With the advent of lithium treatment and the recognition of the genetic basis of disorder, psychological researchers all but abandoned the study of this disorder for several decades, and the development of new assessment instruments languished. Psychological research on the disorder entered a renewed phase of interest in the 1990s, with the volume of research increasing each year since then. Nonetheless, research on bipolar disorder lags far behind that available on other psychopathologies, and many of the assessment needs for conducting research and clinical work within this field remain relatively unaddressed.

NATURE OF BIPOLAR DISORDER

The *Diagnostic and Statistical Manual* of the American Psychiatric Association (APA, 2000) defines several different forms of bipolar disorders, differentiated by the severity and duration of manic symptoms. Bipolar I disorder is diagnosed on the basis of a single lifetime episode of mania. A manic episode is diagnosed on the basis of euphoric or irritable mood, accompanied by at least three symptoms (four if mood is only irritable), and marked social or occupational impairment. Criteria specify that symptoms must last at least 1 week or require hospitalization. Bipolar II disorder is diagnosed on the basis of hypomania and episodes of major depression. Hypomania is less severe than mania: criteria specify a distinct change in functioning, rather than severe impairment. Hypomanic episodes can be diagnosed with 4 days of symptoms. A third form of bipolar disorder, cyclothymia, is diagnosed based on recurrent mood swings, both high and low, which do not meet the severity of bipolar I or bipolar II disorder. Criteria for cyclothymia specify that numerous mood swings must be present.

Manic symptoms may be secondary to drugs (e.g., cocaine, amphetamines) and medical conditions (e.g., thyroid conditions). The use of antidepressants without mood stabilizing medication can trigger episodes of mania or hypomania, particularly among those with an individual or family history of bipolar disorder (Ghaemi, Lenox, & Baldessarini, 2001). Such episodes are not considered in making a diagnosis of bipolar I or bipolar II disorder, but rather, can contribute to a diagnosis of bipolar disorder not otherwise specified.

Prevalence rates are about 1% for bipolar I disorder, and 3.9% for bipolar I and II disorders combined (Kessler, Berglund, Demler, Jin, & Walter, 2005). Rates of comorbidity within bipolar disorder are quite high, and treatment planning will require consideration of these syndromes. Although not required for diagnosis of bipolar I disorder, as many as 66% to 75% of people with bipolar I disorder in community surveys experience episodes of major depression (Karkowski & Kendler, 1997; Kessler, Rubinow, Holmes, Abelson, &

Zhao, 1997). Similarly, as many as 93% of people with bipolar disorder meet lifetime diagnostic criteria for at least one anxiety disorder (Kessler et al., 1997), and as many as 61% for alcohol or substance abuse (Reigier et al., 1990). Indeed, in a Veterans Administration sample, 78% met criteria for comorbid conditions during their lifetime (Bauer et al., 2005). Hence, initial assessments should consider the possible presence of comorbid syndromes.

Estimates from twin studies suggest that heritability accounts for as much as 93% of the variability in whether or not this disorder develops (Kieseppa, Partonen, Haukka, Kaprio, & Lonnqvis, 2004). For those affected by the disorder, though, psychosocial variables predict the course of symptoms. Depression within bipolar disorder appears triggered by negative life events, deficits in social support, and negative cognitive styles (Johnson & Kizer, 2002), whereas mania has been found to be predicted by sleep dysregulation (Leibenluft, Albert, Rosenthal, & Wehr, 1996) and variables relevant to excessive goal engagement (Johnson, 2005). The evidence for genetic contributions to disorder led to a focus on medication approaches, such as lithium and other mood stabilizing medications (Prien & Potter, 1990). With increased evidence that psychosocial variables influence the course of disorder, adjunctive psychosocial treatments have become more common (Johnson & Leahy, 2004).

ASSESSMENT FOR DIAGNOSIS

There is no biological assay for bipolar disorder, so diagnosis is based entirely on review of symptoms and of potential organic explanations. In practice, most clinicians review the DSM symptoms in an informal manner. It is worth noting, however, that clinicians using unstructured diagnostic interviews tend to miss about half of all diagnoses (Zimmerman & Mattia, 1999).

Even though many people with a history of major depression will meet diagnostic criteria for bipolar disorder, most practitioners report that they do not routinely screen for bipolar disorder among people with depression (Brickman, Johnson, & LoPiccolo, 2002). Perhaps as a consequence of poor screening, participants in one community survey reported that it took an average of 8 years from the time their symptoms began until they received a formal diagnosis (Lish, Dime-Meenan, Whybrow, Price, & Hirschfeld, 1994). Failure to detect this diagnosis can have serious

repercussions, in that antidepressant treatment without mood stabilizing medication can trigger iatrogenic mania (Ghaemi et al., 2001).

In this section, we discuss diagnostic instruments for bipolar disorder (see Table 6.1 for a summary of relevant measures). For adults, two diagnostic instruments are most commonly used: the Structured Clinical Interview for DSM-IV (SCID) and the Schedule for Affective Disorders and Schizophrenia (SADS). Although both interviews are more formal than traditional practice procedures, they provide interview probes, guidelines for symptom thresholds, and information about potential exclusionary criteria (such as medical and pharmacological conditions that could provoke manic symptoms). The SCID is designed to assess DSM-IV diagnoses, whereas the SADS is designed to assess the Research Diagnostic Criteria (RDC). Although the two diagnostic systems are similar for mania, RDC criteria are slightly stricter than the DSM criteria about the nature of psychotic symptoms that can be manifested within bipolar disorder, in that certain psychotic symptoms are considered indicative of schizoaffective rather than bipolar disorder. We begin by describing these measures as tools for assessing bipolar I disorder, and then discuss some concerns regarding the diagnosis of bipolar II disorder. Then, we discuss issues and tools for the diagnosis of child and adolescent bipolar disorder. We conclude our discussion of diagnostic assessment with a description of self-report measures designed to aid diagnostic screening.

Diagnostic Assessment of Bipolar I Disorder in Adults

The Structured Clinical Interview for DSM-IV-TR

The SCID is recommended as a part of clinical intake procedures (Spitzer, Williams, Gibbon, & First, 1992), and a clinician's version is available through American Psychiatric Publishing (First, Spitzer, Gibbon, & Williams, 1997). The clinician's version includes less detail about subtype and course distinctions than is provided within the research version. The SCID is a semistructured interview—probes are provided, but diagnosticians are expected to rephrase probes as needed to determine whether a given criterion is met.

Inter-rater reliability for the SCID has been established in a large international multisite trial

TABLE 6.1 Ratings of Instruments Used for Diagnosis

Instrument	Norms	Internal Consistency	Inter-Rater Reliability	Test–Retest Reliability	Content Validity	Construct Validity	Validity Generalization	Clinical Utility	Highly Recommended
Clinician Rated									
SCID	E	NA	G	G	G	G	E	A	✓
SADS	A	NA	G	G	G	G	E	A	✓
Pediatric Clinician Rated									
K-SADS-PL	A	NA	E	E	A	G	G	A	✓
Self-Report									
GBI	NA	E	NA	A	A	G	NA	NA	
MDQ	NA	G	NA	A	A	A	L	NA	

Note: SCID = Structured Clinical Interview for DSM-IV; SADS = Schedule for Affective Disorders and Schizophrenia; K-SADS-PL = Kiddie Schedule for Affective Disorders and Schizophrenia-Present and Lifetime Version; GBI = General Behavior Inventory; MDQ = Mood Disorder Questionnaire; L = Less Than Adequate; A = Adequate; G = Good; E = Excellent; NA = Not Applicable.

(Williams et al., 1992) and at least 10 other major trials (Rogers, 2001). Initial attempts to test the mania module within a community sample were thwarted by the low base rates of the disorder (Williams et al., 1992). Diagnoses of bipolar disorder based on the SCID, though, were substantially more reliable than those obtained by clinicians who were not using a diagnostic interview, or by paraprofessionals using more structured interviews such as the Composite International Diagnostic Interview (CIDI; WHO, 1990). The SCID has achieved high concordance for bipolar diagnoses between twins and has been validated in a number of countries (Kieseppa et al., 2004).

The Schedule for Affective Disorders and Schizophrenia

Considerable evidence has accrued for the reliability of the Schedule for Affective Disorders and Schizophrenia (SADS; Endicott and Spitzer, 1978) across 21 studies (see Rogers, 2001, for a review). SADS diagnoses of bipolar disorder have been found to robustly correlate with other measures of mania (Secunda et al., 1985), and the SADS appears to validly capture diagnoses across different cultural and ethnic groups within the United States (Vernon & Roberts, 1982). Lifetime mania diagnoses have achieved good test–retest reliability over 5 years among adults (Rice et al., 1986) and adolescents (Strober et al., 1995), as well as 10 years among adults (Coryell et al., 1995).

Diagnostic Assessment of Bipolar II Disorder in Adults

Bipolar II disorder was not recognized within the DSM as a diagnostic category until the fourth edition. It is worth noting that hypomania is the only major syndrome within the DSM in which functional impairment is not a criterion for diagnosis. That is, persons can qualify for hypomanic episodes with a relatively mild shift in functioning. Perhaps because of the minimal severity, bipolar II disorder is not diagnosed unless the person also suffers from episodes of major depression. Intriguingly, considerable debate still exists about the criteria for hypomania; whereas the DSM-IV-TR criteria specify four symptoms with duration of at least 4 days, the RDC criteria are less stringent, specifying three symptoms with duration of at least 2 days. Given the recent addition of

this category to the diagnostic system and ongoing debates about the diagnostic threshold, it is not surprising that assessment tools for bipolar II disorder are less well established.

Despite debate about diagnostic criteria and instruments, though, there is evidence that the diagnosis itself may be important to capture. Diagnoses of bipolar II disorder using the SADS show expected correlations with trait measures of mood lability and energy/activity (Akiskal et al., 1995), as well as family history of bipolar II disorder (Rice et al., 1986). Three studies have also suggested that people with bipolar II disorder are at higher risk for suicide than persons with bipolar I disorder or unipolar depression (Dunner, 1996). Hence, identification of bipolar II disorder may be important in planning treatment.

The lower threshold for this disorder appears to create difficulty in reliably capturing symptoms, an issue that is particularly well documented for the SADS. Even when interviewers rate the same tapes, reliability estimates for bipolar II disorder within the SADS are quite inadequate and much lower than the estimates for bipolar I disorder reflected in Table 6.1 (Keller, Lavori, & McDonald-Scott et al., 1981), although some teams achieved higher estimates (Simpson et al., 2002; Spitzer, Endicott, & Robins, 1978). In addition to poor reliability for the diagnostic category, interviewers also have been found to have very poor agreement on mild symptoms of mania (Andreasen et al., 1981). Test–retest reliability over a 6-month period was quite poor for bipolar II disorder, intraclass $r = .06$, and even poorer for cyclothymia (Andreasen et al., 1981). In a 5-year test–retest study, SADS diagnoses of bipolar II disorder achieved kappa scores of only .09 (Rice et al., 1986), and in a 10-year study, only 40% of persons initially diagnosed with bipolar II disorder on the SADS experienced further episodes of hypomania or mania (Coryell et al., 1995).

Inter-rater reliability can be limited by either a lack of specificity or a lack of sensitivity. Both the SCID and the SADS have been found to have inadequate sensitivity in detecting cases of bipolar II disorder. In one study, about one-third of cases that were diagnosed through expert clinical interview with bipolar II disorder were not identified as such within SCID interviews ($\kappa = .67$), despite evidence for high inter-rater agreement of unstructured clinical interviews (Dunner & Tay, 1993; Simpson et al., 2002). Accordingly, an important goal has been to develop more sensitive interviews for bipolar II disorder.

Akiskal and Benazzi (2005) report that including questions about periods of intense behavioral engagement and goal-directed behavior can help patients and family members recall periods of mood disturbance that may qualify for bipolar II disorder. Caution is warranted, though, as new approaches have not been validated yet.

In sum, a set of issues mar the diagnostic assessment of bipolar II disorder. On the one hand, persons who meet criteria for bipolar II disorder may be at high risk for suicidality. On the other hand, available tools do not produce reliable diagnoses of bipolar II disorder.

Diagnostic Assessment of Bipolar Disorder in Children and Adolescents

Even the most conservative statistics indicate that rates of bipolar I disorder among high school students approximate those shown in adulthood, with a prevalence of approximately 1% (Lewinsohn, Seeley, & Klein, 2003). The DSM-IV-TR diagnostic criteria for juvenile bipolar disorder are the same as those for adult bipolar disorder, with the exception that cyclothymia can be diagnosed within 1 year, rather than 2 years, of symptoms. There is considerable debate in the field about the diagnostic criteria as some researchers have argued many diagnoses of bipolar disorder among children and adolescents are missed because the criteria are too stringent. Some have argued that episodes of shorter duration or diminished symptom severity should be diagnosable, particularly given that children may not have the same opportunities to exhibit symptomatic behavior in domains such as hypersexuality or overspending. Ongoing research is focused on the validity of differing criteria (Nottelmann et al., 2001).

Here, we will focus briefly on the key issues involved in diagnosing bipolar disorder among youth. Readers interested in more detailed coverage of issues involved in assessing bipolar disorder among children and adolescents are referred to a recent overview (Youngstrom, Findling, Youngstrom, & Calabrese, 2005).

In diagnosing juvenile bipolar disorder, there is a movement toward the use of multiple sources of data, including youths, parents, and teachers (Youngstrom, Findling, & Calabrese, 2003). Youths can be poor reporters of hyperactivity, inattention, and oppositional behaviors (Youngstrom, Loeber, & Stouthamer-Loeber, 2000). To the extent that mania involves externalizing symptoms, youths may be poor reporters of manic symptoms. For internalizing problems, youth and caregiver reports are preferable (Loeber, Green, & Lahey, 1990). Teacher reports are often discrepant with the reports of parents and youths (Youngstrom, Loebe, & Stouthamer-Loeber, 2000), as children may show different behaviors across different settings. Given that impairment may not be equal across all settings, averaging scores from different sources appears to enhance reliability (Youngstrom, Gracious, Ranielson, Findling, Calabrese, 2003).

Parent report offers several advantages in making accurate psychiatric diagnoses, especially among younger children. Parents are more psychologically minded than youth (Anastasi & Urbina, 1997), and they are aware of the child's developmental history and family functioning (Richters, 1992), as well as low base rate phenomena (fire setting, suicide attempts; Kazdin & Kagan, 1994). Not surprisingly, then, parent report tends to be more accurate in predicting diagnostic status than either youth or teacher reports (Youngstrom et al., 2004).

Youths should not be discounted in the diagnostic process. Parent and youth reports have been shown to be more discrepant for externalizing disorders than internalizing disorders, for girls than boys, and for older children than younger children (Verhulst & van der Ende, 1992). Adolescents, especially as they grow older, are important informants on their own problem behaviors given that internalizing behaviors and concealed high-risk behaviors may go unnoticed by their parents (Loeber, Green, & Lahey, 1990). One way to approach clinical interviewing with parents and their children is by using diagnostic interviews, described next.

Kiddie Schedule for Affective Disorders and Schizophrenia for School-Age Children— Present and Lifetime Version

Many different versions of the Kiddie Schedule for Affective Disorders and Schizophrenia for School-Age Children (K-SADS) have been developed. The K-SADS-PL, however, is the only instrument that provides global and diagnosis-specific impairment ratings (Kaufman et al., 1997). Excellent inter-rater reliability (98% to 100%) and test–retest reliability (κ for current and lifetime diagnosis both = 1.00) have been documented for bipolar disorders with the K-SADS-PL.

Several groups have attempted to refine the mania section of the K-SADS. Axelson et al. (2003)

developed a Child Mania Rating Scale module that demonstrated excellent inter-rater reliability (intraclass correlation = .97), excellent internal consistency (α = .94), and, using a cutoff score of 12 or higher, demonstrated sensitivity of 87% and specificity of 81% with clinical judgments of mania (Axelson et al., 2003). These results suggest that the K-SADS-MRS holds promise as a rating scale for manic symptoms in children and adolescents.

Geller and colleagues (2001) at Washington University at St. Louis developed a more detailed version of the K-SADS (WASH-U-KSADS). Although the measure has achieved good to excellent interrater reliability for mania symptoms (κ range from .82 to 1.00; Geller et al., 2001), the training and time burdens may be too extensive for general clinical practice.

Self-Report Measures

Detailed assessment by a trained clinician is considered the most reliable and valid way to obtain a diagnosis of bipolar disorder (Akiskal, 2002). Several self-report screeners have been developed, however, to aid in detecting potential diagnoses of bipolar disorder. At this point in their development, information on psychometric adequacy is limited (see Table 6.1).

Of these measures, the one with the most robust psychometric support is the General Behavior Inventory (GBI; Depue et al., 1981). GBI items were designed to cover symptom intensity, duration, and frequency using a response scale that ranges from 1 ("never or hardly ever") to 4 ("very often or almost constantly"). The original GBI consisted of 69 items, chosen to cover the core symptoms of bipolar disorder by the consensus of three item writers. Modified versions have been developed, as well, that tap both the depressed and manic poles of bipolar disorder (e.g., Depue & Klein, 1988; Mallon, Klein, Bornstein & Slater, 1986). The variety of different versions, ranging from 52 to 73 items, makes generalizations regarding psychometric properties difficult.

Normative data have not been reported for the GBI in any large clinical samples, but it has generally demonstrated excellent internal consistency and adequate test–retest reliability. Several studies have assessed the GBI's ability to discriminate bipolar cases from noncases. In general, the GBI has demonstrated sensitivity to bipolar disorder of approximately 75%, and specificity greater than 97% (Depue et al., 1989;

Depue & Klein, 1988; Klein Dickstein, Taylor, & Harding, 1989; Mallon et al., 1986), in both clinical and nonclinical samples. Unfortunately, generalizability is limited because cutoff scores were not consistent across studies, but rather were determined within each study to maximize predictive power.

The GBI has also been adapted for use with parents to capture mood symptoms in children ages 5 to 17 years and has been shown to be diagnostically informative, especially for young children (Findling et al., 2002; Youngstrom, Findling, Danielson, & Calabrese, 2001). Parallel to the original GBI, the Parent GBI (P-GBI) consists of depressive and hypomanic/biphasic subscales both of which demonstrate excellent internal consistency. The scale also demonstrated strong validity in differentiating children with mood disorders from those with disruptive behavior disorders (80.6% accuracy), as well as distinguishing children with bipolar disorder from those with other mood disorders (86.1% accuracy; Youngstrom et al., 2001).

There has also been one study that has examined the validity of youth report on the GBI (Danielson, Youngstrom, Findling & Calabrese, 2003). The GBI depression scale demonstrates good discriminative validity distinguishing between those with Axis I mood disorders and those with disruptive behavior disorders or no diagnosis, and the hypomanic/biphasic scale distinguishes between children with bipolar spectrum diagnoses and those with other disorders (depression, disruptive behavior disorder, and no diagnosis).

Overall, the GBI is a promising screening tool for identifying bipolar disorder among adult and pediatric populations. Nonetheless, more research is needed to establish norms and to evaluate this scale using consistent items and cutoff scores.

One other promising measure that has been subjected to some empirical study is the Mood Disorder Questionnaire (MDQ; Hirschfeld et al., 2000). The first 13 items of the MDQ are yes–no questions covering the full range of manic symptoms; at least seven must be answered "yes" to achieve a positive screen. Additional items query as to whether the symptoms identified co-occurred and caused at least moderate problems. The MDQ has attained good internal consistency ranging from .79 (Isometsa et al., 2003) to .90 (Hirschfeld et al., 2000), adequate 1 month test–retest reliability in clinical samples (Weber Rouget et al., 2005), and fair sensitivity in differentiating bipolar disorder from unipolar disorder clinical samples

(.73 to .90). Nonetheless, specificities have been low in some studies (.47 to .90, Hirschfeld Klugman, Berr, Resenquist, & Ghaemi, 2000, 2003; Isometsa et al., 2003; Miller Klugman, Berv, Rosenquist, & Ghaemi, 2004; Weber Rouget et al., 2005) and the sensitivity in a community sample was only 0.28 (Hirschfeld et al., 2003). Overall, the MDQ is a potentially useful tool in clinical settings that would benefit from additional research regarding norms and applicability to specific populations.

Other scales await more testing. The Hypomanic Personality Scale (HPS; Eckblad & Chapman, 1986) has been found to predict the development of manic episodes at 13-year follow-up in undergraduates (Kwapil et al., 2000) and a Spanish language version is available (Ruggero, Johnson, & Cuellar, 2004), but the scale has not been studied in clinical populations. The Bipolar Spectrum Disorder Scale (BSDS; Ghaemi et al., 2005) and the Mood Spectrum Self-Reports (MOODS-SR; Dell'Osso et al., 2002) have only been tested in a single study each. The Hypomania Checklist (HCL-32; Angst, Adolbsson, et al., 2005) is a new scale that has only been tested in Italy and Sweden. The Temperament Evaluation of Memphis, Pisa, Paris, and San Diego (TEMPS; Akiskal & Akiskal, 2005) is a measure to which an issue of the *Journal of Affective Disorders* was dedicated, but it has not been compared with a diagnostic interview. The Child Mania Rating Scale (Pavuluri, Henry, Devineni, Carbray, & Birmaher, 2006) and the Parent-Young Mania Rating scale (P-YMRS; Gracious, Youngstrom, Findling, & Calabrese, 2002) are both designed to assess current symptoms of mania among youths. Although initial psychometric studies suggest strong reliability and good ability to distinguish between bipolar disorder and other disorders, only one psychometric study is available for each scale.

Overall Evaluation

To date, two measures of diagnosis are dominant in diagnosing bipolar disorder among adults: the SCID and the SADS. Both have excellent psychometric characteristics for the assessment of bipolar I disorder, but function poorly in identifying bipolar II disorder. It is not currently clear whether the limits in detection of bipolar II are strictly a measurement issue, or reflect underlying issues in the definitions of hypomanic episodes.

Although there is much debate regarding the diagnostic criteria for pediatric bipolar disorder,

assessment should include a detailed clinical interview that assesses family history, as well as the intensity and duration of any mood symptoms. The mania modules of the K-SADS have achieved psychometric support.

To aid in diagnostic screening, the best validated scale is the GBI, but caution is warranted regarding the multiple forms of this scale. Several other promising scales await more psychometric development. When considering self-report scales as screening tools, several issues must be kept in mind. For instance, Phelps and Ghaemi (2006) demonstrated that the usefulness of a screening tool varies depending on clinicians' previous estimates of the probability of the disorder in question. Thus, clinician knowledge about a disorder's prevalence in the population of interest may be more important than a screening tool's sensitivity or specificity. Second, different measures have been used as reference standards. Third, several authors have expanded the diagnostic interviews used as a reference standard to capture milder forms of bipolar spectrum disorder, yet provide only vague information about the modifications. Each of these issues complicates comparisons between measures.

ASSESSMENT FOR CASE CONCEPTUALIZATION AND TREATMENT PLANNING

With the discovery of the efficacy of lithium, research on psychosocial treatment approaches to bipolar disorder entered a fairly quiescent period. It was not until 1988 that the National Institute of Mental Health (NIMH) convened a panel of experts on bipolar disorder to review the state of the field, and the panel noted the significant gaps in the efficacy of currently available treatment approaches and the need for adjunctive psychotherapeutic approaches (Prien & Potter, 1990). A set of randomized controlled trials of adjunctive therapy were conducted, and initial results suggested promise for cognitive therapy, family therapy, and interpersonal psychotherapy (Johnson & Leahy, 2004). Since the initial tests of those trials, researchers have begun to assess which persons might be most responsive to given approaches. Nonetheless, treatment research on the predictors of outcome remains in its infancy within bipolar disorder (Miklowitz & Johnson, 2006). Hence, there are few measures available to

TABLE 6.2 Ratings of Instruments Used for Case Conceptualization and Treatment Planning

Instrument	Norm	Internal Consistency	Inter-Rater Reliability	Test–Retest Reliability	Content Validity	Construct Validity	Validity Generalization	Clinical Utility	Highly Recommended
SAI-E	A	A	U	NA	A	A	A	A	

Note: SAI-E = Schedule for Assessment of Insight-Expanded Version; A = Adequate; U = Unavailable; NA = Not Available.

predict response to a given treatment approach (see Table 6.2 for a review of key measures).

Certainly, there is evidence that severity of symptom history, whether defined by multiple episodes per year, earlier age of onset, severity of depressive symptoms during manic periods, or comorbid medical and psychiatric conditions, will predict poorer outcome. Hence, clinicians will do well to gather a good clinical history to document the severity of the manic episodes, as well as the presence of comorbid complications. Reviewing the history of episodes can be somewhat bewildering, as the median time to relapse, even on adequate medication levels, is approximately 1 year (Keller et al., 1992). Hence, most patients will have had many episodes, and the episodes will have varied in their triggers, severity, and consequences. One strategy that can be very helpful in organizing the complex information is the Lifechart (Denicoff et al., 1997), a graphing procedure developed at NIMH, which can provide a collaborative tool for helping a patient describe the pattern of episodes over time, potential triggers, and effectiveness of different treatment approaches. Although frequently used, little psychometric information on the Lifechart is available.

Other measures are relevant for tracking specific dimensions related to outcome. One of the best predictors of poor outcome is treatment nonadherence, with substantial evidence that treatment drop-out increases risk of relapse, suicide, and hospitalization (Keck et al., 1998). It is also well established that treatment nonadherence is normative within bipolar disorder—less than 25% of patients remain continuously adherent with lithium (Weiss et al., 1998). Hence, one would expect that predicting treatment nonadherence would be a primary goal of any baseline assessment. The Scale to Assess Unawareness of Mental Disorder (SUMD; Amador, Strauss, Gorman, Endicott, Yale, & Flaum, 1993), a semistructured interview to assess awareness of symptoms of mental disorder, symptoms, social consequences of disorder, and misattributions for symptoms, has been shown to differentiate people with bipolar disorder from those without bipolar disorder (Varga Magnusson,

Flekkoy, Ronneberg, & Opjordsmoen, 2006), but baseline scores have not been found to predict treatment success over time (Ghaemi, Boiman, & Goodwin, 2000). On the other hand, the Schedule for Assessment of Insight-Expanded Version (SAI-E; Kemp & David, 1996) has been found to predict treatment adherence at 1-year follow-up among people with bipolar disorder (Yen et al., 2005), to differentiate people with and without bipolar disorder (Sanz Constable, Lopez-lbor, Kemp, & David, 1998), and to achieve a cross-sectional correlation of .70 with other indices of treatment adherence (Sanz et al., 1998). Unfortunately, inter-rater reliability of the interview has not been established within bipolar disorder. In sum, no measure of treatment adherence has demonstrated both adequate validity and reliability within bipolar disorder.

Choices regarding which other risk factors to assess will likely depend on the treatment being employed. Hence, if offering cognitive therapy to address maladaptive negative cognitions about the self, clinicians may want to draw from the measures of negative cognition routinely used within the unipolar depression literature (see Chapter 5 in this volume for a review), such as the Dysfunctional Attitudes Scale (DAS; Weissman & Beck, 1978) or the Automatic Thoughts Questionnaire (Hollon & Kendall, 1980). These measures have been extremely well tested in both unipolar depression and general populations. Scores on both measures are elevated compared with healthy control groups during depressive episodes of bipolar disorder (Cuellar, Johnson, & Winters, 2005), and DAS scores have been found to predict increased depressive symptoms over time (Johnson & Fingerhut, 2004). Nonetheless, psychometric data within bipolar disorder is limited to small normative samples. Moreover, the factor structure of the DAS appears to differ among people with bipolar disorder compared with the general population (Lam, Wright, & Smith, 2004).

For clinicians who offer Interpersonal and Social Rhythm Psychotherapy (Frank, 2005), a substantial component of treatment focuses on helping clients develop a more regular schedule of daily activities.

One measure, the social rhythm metric, has been most widely used to test the constancy of the daily schedule (Monk, Flaherty, Frank, Hoskinson, & Kupfer, 1990). The scale has been shown to correlate with indices of sleep (Monk et al., 2003) and to be lower among persons with rapid cycling bipolar disorder (Ashman et al., 1999) compared with healthy controls. Nonetheless, the scale correlates with rather than predicting mania symptom fluctuations disorder over time (Frank et al., 2005), so it is not recommended at this point.

Drawing on expressed emotion (EE) theory, family treatment programs in bipolar disorder aim to help families become less critical of their ill relative (Miklowitz & Goldstein, 1997). The most feasibly administered scale of family criticism is the Perceived Criticism scale (PCS; Hooley & Teasdale, 1989). Patients rate on a scale of 1 to 10 how critical they think they are of their relative and how critical they think their relative is of them. This scale has demonstrated temporal stability as well as concurrent validity with the other validated measures of EE such as the Camberwell Family Interview ($r = .45$, $p < .01$; van Humbeeck et al., 2004). Unfortunately, the scale has not been found to predict outcome of family therapy (Miklowitz, Wisniewski, Miyahara, Otto, & Sachs, 2005).

Overall Evaluation

As clinical severity and comorbidity are important predictors of poorer outcome, clinicians should assess these parameters during intake interviews. The Lifechart provides a way of organizing clinical history. Beyond clinical severity, the SAI-E has been found to predict poorer medication adherence. Assessments to help plan specific psychosocial interventions are lacking, as relatively few clinical trials have been designed to consider the predictors of outcome. Although the present state of research does not offer clinicians much guidance on how to choose treatment predictors, there are some promising developments in measuring constructs relevant to case conceptualization and treatment planning, particularly in the domain of cognitive styles.

ASSESSMENT FOR TREATMENT MONITORING AND TREATMENT OUTCOME

In this section, we consider measures that can be used to track the progress of treatment (see Table 6.3).

At this point, well-validated measures for this purpose exist only for the purpose of documenting changes in symptom levels. The Young Mania Rating Scale and the Bech–Rafaelsen Mania Rating Scale are among the most widely used scales for this purpose.

The Young Mania Rating Scale (YMRS) was designed to be administered by a trained clinician in a 15- to 30-minute patient interview that captures the patient's subjective report of his/her condition over the past 48 hours as well as the clinician's observations during the interview (Young, Biggs, Ziegler, & Meyer, 1978). The 11 items are rated on a scale of 0 to 4, and 4 items are given twice the weight. In the original study, the YMRS showed excellent inter-rater reliability for total scores (intraclass correlation = .93). The YMRS is sensitive to changes in severity. The YMRS (as opposed to the parent-YMRS), has also been used to measure manic symptoms in one small study of hospitalized children. Fristad, Weller, & Weller (1992, 1995) found that the total score and elevated mood item both showed good validity in differentiating children with bipolar disorder from those with attention deficit hyperactivity disorder.

The Bech–Rafaelsen Mania Rating Scale (MAS; Bech, 1979) is an 11-item rating scale. Each item is rated on a 5-point scale (0 to 4), and the total score is obtained by summing the items. The MAS has been used in many different trials of antimanic therapies owing to its strong psychometric characteristics (see Table 6.3). The scale has strong validity in detecting changes with treatment and discriminating between active and placebo therapy groups (Bech, 2002).

The Schedule for Affective Disorders and Schizophrenia-Change Version (SADS-C) for mania is a 5-item interview designed to assess current severity of manic symptoms. Each item is rated on a 6-point scale based on behavioral anchors. Inter-rater reliability has been established in a range of settings, including forensic settings (Rogers, Jackson, Salekin, & Neumann, 2003). One exception to a pattern of good inter-reliability results was found in a sample of patients referred for emergency evaluation (intraclass correlation = .63 for mania; Rogers Jackson, Salekin, & Neumann, 2003). The scale has been found to show expected elevations within a bipolar sample compared to patients with other psychiatric disorders, and robust correlations with another interview to assess manic severity, the MAS ($r = .89$; Johnson, Magaro, & Stern, 1986). In factor analytic studies, all items load on a single scale that is distinct from dysphoria, insomnia, and

TABLE 6.3 Ratings of Instruments Used for Treatment Monitoring and Treatment Outcome Evaluation

Instrument	Norms	Internal Consistency	Inter-Rater Reliability	Test–Retest Reliability	Content Validity	Construct Validity	Validity Generalization	Treatment Sensitivity	Clinical Utility	Highly Recommended
YMRS	A	E	E	NA	A	G	A	G	A	
MAS	A	E	E	NA	A	G	A	G	G	✓
SADS-C	A	NA	G	NA	A	G	G	E	G	✓
Altman	A	A	NA	A	A*	G	A	A	G	
SRMI	A	G	NA	A	G	A	A	A	A	

* But missing grandiosity.

Note: YMRS = Young Mania Rating Scale; MAS = Bech–Rafaelsen Mania Scale; SADS-C = Schedule for Affective Disorders and Schizophrenia-Change Mania Scale; SRMI = Self-Rating Mania Inventory; A = Adequate; G = Good; E = Excellent; NA = Not Applicable.

psychosis (Rogers et al., 2003). Nonetheless, less factor analytic support was obtained in a study that considered the item loadings for the SADS-C and a nurse observation scale for mania (Swann et al., 2001).

Self-Report Measures

Several self-report measures have been used to track patients' symptoms throughout the course of treatment. Of these, only two have a broad range of supporting psychometric evidence: the Altman Self-Rating Mania scale and the Self-Rating Mania Inventory (see Table 6.3). After describing these measures, we briefly discuss other measures that are under development.

The Altman Self-Rating Mania scale (ASRM; Altman, Hedeker, Peterson, & Davies, 1997) consists of five items. For each item, participants choose from a set of five statements to best capture their feelings or behavior over the past week. Each item is scored on a scale of 0 (absent) to 4 (severe), so that total scores on can range from 0 to 20. Additional items assess psychosis and irritability, but are not included in the total score. Grandiosity is not covered. Two studies have reported comparable norms for the ASRM in patient samples (Altman et al., 1997; Altman, Hedeker, Peterson, & Davies, 2001), but little data are available regarding scores for nonpatients.

The ASRM has demonstrated adequate internal consistency and concurrent validity when compared with several different reference standards, including SADS-based diagnoses, Young Mania Rating Scale (YMRS; Young et al., 1978), and Clinician-Administered Rating Scale for Mania (CARS-M; Altman et al., 1997, 2001; Altman, Hedeker, Janicak, Peterson, & Davies, 1994). On the basis of an Area Under the Curve analysis (AUC; Hanley & McNeil, 1982), Altman and colleagues concluded that a cutoff score of 5.5 resulted in an optimal combination of sensitivity and specificity (85% and 86%, respectively), although this cutoff might result in lower specificity (Altman et al., 2001). Finally, the ASRM has demonstrated good sensitivity to treatment, with scores dropping an average of five points after discharge from the hospital in one study (Altman et al., 2001). Overall, the ASRM has demonstrated good psychometric properties. Both of the validation studies, however, have been conducted by the same research group, and the scale covers fewer symptoms than other mania indices.

The Self-Report Manic Inventory (SRMI; Braünig, Shugar & Kruger, 1996; Shugar et al., 1992) is a 47-item true/false inventory covering a range of manic symptoms,

with one additional item covering insight. Expert clinicians reviewed each item during the development phase. In its original design, the time frame for items was the past month; later editions assessed symptoms during the previous week. Normative data have been reported for the SRMI in three small studies of inpatients, and it has demonstrated good internal consistency (Altman et al., 2001; Braünig et al., 1996; Shugar, Schertzer, Toner, & Ri Gasbarro, 1992). Two studies have found that the scale differentiates people with bipolar disorder from those with other psychopathologies (Braünig et al., 1996; Shugar et al., 1992), although one other study found the SRMI to have low concurrent validity (Altman et al., 2001). The scale appears sensitive to change in symptoms, but seven of the SRMI items capture behaviors that would not be possible within a hospital setting (Altman et al., 2001). Hence, it has been argued that the content of the scale may not be well-suited to inpatient assessment.

The Internal State Scale (ISS; Bauer et al., 1991) is a 17-item scale designed to assess the severity of manic and depressive symptoms. Of its four subscales, only the 5-item activation subscale has correlated with mania ratings. These items were designed to cover behavioral activation (e.g., restlessness and impulsivity), but not other mania symptoms (e.g., euphoria). The ISS has demonstrated correlations with other measures of mania ranging from .21 to .60 and rates of correct classification ranging from .55 to .78 (Altman et al., 2001; Bauer et al., 1991; Bauer, Vojta, Kinosian, Altshuler, & Glick, 2000; Cooke Krüger, & Shugar, 1996). The ISS has demonstrated some sensitivity to treatment change, in that scores diminish appreciably posttreatment (Altman et al., 2001; Bauer et al., 1991; Cooke et al., 1996). Despite these strengths, scoring algorithms have varied substantially across studies, as have means and standard deviations (Altman et al., 2001; Bauer et al., 1991; Cooke et al., 1996). The scale has also been found to have a low sensitivity to manic symptoms at the time of hospitalization (Altman et al., 2001). Given these concerns, the ISS is not currently recommended.

Finally, clinicians should bear in mind that naturalistic studies suggest that people with bipolar disorder experience at least some depressive symptoms one-third of the weeks in a year (Judd et al., 2002). Higher risk of suicide has been documented during depression within bipolar disorder (Angst, Angst et al., 2005). Given this, it is recommended that clinicians track not only manic symptoms, but depression and suicidality as well.

Overall Evaluation

Ideally, outcome assessments should incorporate both interview and self-report measures. Clinicians have several interview-based measures available for tracking change in symptoms over time: the SADS-C, the YMRS, and the MAS. Although more data is available to support the YMRS and the MAS, the SADS-C has the advantage of brevity. Self-report measures such as the Altman and the SRMI can also be completed quickly. This brevity and ease-of-use can come with the price, however, of reduced precision. To track progress, many clients find it helpful to create their own self-monitoring forms or to complete brief checklists. Comparing results of the interview with self-reported symptoms can be helpful for clients in building a greater awareness of symptoms. As treatment progresses, clients often find it helpful to begin to attend to smaller fluctuations in symptoms, such that they can implement early intervention strategies to promote calm and good medical care before symptoms intensify (Lam & Wong, 2005). Given the common problems with insight within this disorder, research is needed on how best to integrate self and clinician ratings of manic symptoms.

CONCLUSIONS AND FUTURE DIRECTIONS

In this chapter, we have considered assessment tools that could be helpful in diagnosis, treatment planning, and treatment outcome monitoring of bipolar disorder. In evaluating current measures, the need for ongoing research is quite apparent. In regard to diagnostic assessment, there is ongoing discussion about the requisite severity and duration of symptoms for hypomania. Similarly, substantial debate exists concerning the best criteria for the diagnosis of bipolar disorder among children and adolescents. Hence, diagnostic instruments are likely to be modified over time to increase their applicability for milder forms of the disorder and for younger age groups. Beyond the need for better diagnostic measures, there is a fundamental need for research on the predictors of outcome within psychological forms of treatment. Measures that could help define the best choice of therapy would be extremely helpful for clinicians. Finally, there is a need for measures that are specifically developed to capture the types of social dysfunctions that are most prevalent in bipolar disorder. Although many researchers apply social functioning measures developed for depression and schizophrenia, it will be important to consider ways in which manic symptoms can damage relationships.

At present, though, several excellent resources for assessment of bipolar disorder are available. For diagnosis, the SCID and the SADS allow for reliable and valid diagnosis of bipolar I disorder. For case conceptualization and treatment planning, the SAI-E predicts medication nonadherence in bipolar disorder, and the Lifechart can help assess the history of episodes and triggers. The Sense of Hyper-Positive Self Scale, although relatively new, has predicted outcomes of cognitive therapy in one study. Once treatment commences, interview measures such as the YMRS and the MAS, as well as self-report measures such as the Altman and the SRMI are available for monitoring symptom severity. We hope that this review stimulates clinical use of the available measures and encourages research focused on addressing the gaps in the assessment literature.

References

Akiskal, H. S. (2002). Classification, diagnosis, and boundaries of bipolar disorders: A review. In M. Maj, H. S. Akiskal, J. J. Lopez-Ibor, & N. Sarotius (Eds.), *Bipolar disorder* (pp. 1–52). Chichester: Wiley.

Akiskal, H. S., & Akiskal, K. K. (2005). TEMPS: Temperament evaluation of Memphis, Pisa, Paris and San Diego. *Journal of Affective Disorders, 85,* 1–2.

Akiskal, H. S., & Benazzi, F. (2005). Optimizing the detection of bipolar II disorder in outpatient private practice: Toward a systematization of clinical diagnostic wisdom. *Journal of Clinical Psychiatry, 66,* 914–921.

Akiskal, H. S., Maser, J. D., Zeller, P. J., Endicott, J., Coryell, W., Keller, M., et al. (1995). Switching from 'unipolar' to bipolar II. An 11-year prospective study of clinical and temperamental predictors in 559 patients. *Archives of General Psychiatry, 52,* 114–123.

Altman, E. G., Hedeker, D., Peterson, J. L., & Davis, J. M. (1997). The Altman Self-Rating Mania Scale. *Biological Psychiatry, 42,* 948–955.

Altman, E. G., Hedeker, D., Peterson, J. L., & Davis, J. M. (2001). A comparative evaluation of three self-rating scales for acute mania. *Biological Psychiatry, 50,* 468–471.

Altman, E. G., Hedeker, D. R., Janicak, P., Peterson, J. L., & Davis, J. M. (1994). The Clinician-Administered

Rating Scale for Mania (CARS-M): Development, reliability, and validity. *Biological Psychiatry, 36,* 124–134.

Amador, X. F., Strauss, D. H., Gorman, J. M., Endicott, J., Yale, S. A., & Flaum, M. (1993). The assessment of insight in psychosis. *American Journal of Psychiatry, 150,* 873–879.

American Psychiatric Association. (2000). *Diagnostic and statistical manual of mental disorders* (4th ed., text revision). Washington, DC: Author.

Anastasi, A., & Urbina, S. (1997). *Psychological testing* (7th ed.). New York: MacMillan.

Andreasen, N. C., Grove, W. M., Shapiro, R. W., Keller, M. B., Hirschfeld, R. M., & McDonald-Scott, P. (1981). Reliability of lifetime diagnosis. A multicenter collaborative perspective. *Archives of General Psychiatry, 38,* 400–405.

Angst, J., Adolfsson, R., Benazzi, F., Gamma, A., Hantouche, E., Meyer, T. D., et al. (2005). The HCL-32: Towards a self-assessment tool for hypomanic symptoms in outpatients. *Journal of Affective Disorders, 88,* 217–233.

Angst, J., Angst, F., Gerber-Werder, R., & Gamma, A. (2005). Suicide in 406 mood-disorderd patients with and without long-term medication: A 40 to 44 years' follow-up. *Archives of Suicide Research, 9,* 279–300.

Ashman, S. B., Monk, T. H., Kupfer, D. J., Clark, C. H., Myers, F. S., Frank, E., et al. (1999). Relationship between social rhythms and mood in patients with rapid cycling bipolar disorder. *Psychiatry Research, 86,* 1–8.

Axelson, D., Birmaher, B. J., Brent, D., Wassick, S., Hoover, C., Bridge, J., et al. (2003). A preliminary study of the kiddie schedule for affective disorders and schizophrenia for school-age children mania rating scale for children and adolescents. *Journal of Child and Adolescent Psychopharmacology, 13,* 463–470.

Bauer, M. S., Altshuler, L., Evans, D. R., Beresford, T., Williford, W. O., & Hauger, R. (2005). Prevalence and distinct correlates of anxiety, substance, and combined comorbidity in a multi-site public sector sample with bipolar disorder. *Journal of Affective Disorders, 85,* 301–315.

Bauer, M. S., Crits-Christoph, P., Ball, W. A., Dewees, E., McAllister, T., Alahi, P., et al. (1991). Independent assessment of manic and depressive symptoms by self-rating: Scale characteristics and implications for the study of mania. *Archives of General Psychiatry, 48,* 807–812.

Bauer, M. S., Vojta, C., Kinosian, B., Altshuler, L., & Glick, H. (2000). The Internal State Scale: Replication of its discriminating abilities in a multisite, public sector sample. *Bipolar Disorders, 2,* 340–346.

Bech, P. (2002). The Bech–Rafaelsen Mania Scale in clinical trials of therapies for bipolar disorder. *CNS Drugs, 16,* 47–63.

Bech, P., Bolwig, T. G., Kramp, P., & Rafaelsen, O. J. (1979). The Bech–Rafaelsen Mania Scale and the Hamilton Depression Scale. *Acta Psychiatrica Scandinavica, 59,* 420–430.

Bräunig, P., Shugar, G., & Krüger, S. (1996). An investigation of the Self-Report Mania Inventory as a diagnostic and severity scale for mania. *Comprehensive Psychiatry, 37,* 52–55.

Brickman, A., LoPiccolo, C., & Johnson, S. L. (2002). Screening for bipolar disorder by community providers [Letter to the editor]. *Psychiatric Services, 53,* 349.

Cooke, R. G., Krüger, S., & Shugar, G. (1996). Comparative evaluation of two self-report mania rating scales. *Biological Psychiatry, 40,* 279–283.

Coryell, W., Endicott, J., Maser, J. D., Keller, M. B., Leon, A. C., & Akiskal, H. S. (1995). Long-term stability of polarity distinctions in the affective disorders. *The American Journal of Psychiatry, 152,* 385–390.

Cuellar, A. K., Johnson, S. L., & Winters, R. (2005). Distinctions between bipolar and unipolar depression. *Clinical Psychology Review, 25,* 307–339.

Danielson, C. K., Youngstrom, E. A., Findling, R. L., & Calabrese, J. R. (2003). Discriminative validity of the General Behavior Inventory using youth report. *Journal of Abnormal Child Psychology, 31,* 29–39.

Dell'Osso, L., Armani, A., Rucci, P., Frank, E., Fagiolini, A., & Corretti, G., et al. (2002). Measuring mood spectrum: Comparison of interview (SCI-MOODS) and self-report (MOODS-SR) instruments. *Comprehensive Psychiatry, 43,* 69–73.

Denicoff, K. D., Smith-Jackson, E. E., Disney, E. R., Suddath, R. L., Leverich, G. S., & Post, R. M. (1997). Preliminary evidence of the reliability and validity of the prospective life-chart methodology (LCM-p). *Journal of Psychiatric Research, 31,* 593–603.

Depue, R. A., & Klein, D. N. (1988). Identification of unipolar and bipolar affective conditions in nonclinical and clinical populations by the General Behavior Inventory. In D. L. Dunner, E. S. Gershon, & J. E. Barrett (Eds.), *Relatives at risk for mental disorder,* (pp. 179–204). New York: Raven Press, Ltd.

Depue, R. A., Krauss, S., Spoont, M. R., & Arbisi, P. (1989). General behavior inventory identification of unipolar and bipolar affective conditions in a nonclinical university population. *Journal of Abnormal Psychology, 98,* 117–126.

Depue, R. A., Slater, J. F., Wolfstetter-Kausch, H., Klein, D., Goplerud, E., & Farr, D. (1981). A behavioral paradigm for identifying persons at risk for bipolar depressive disorder: A conceptual framework and five validation studies. *Journal of Abnormal Psychology, 90*, 381–437.

Dunner, D. L. (1996). Bipolar Depression with Hypomania (Bipolar II). In T. A. Widiger, A. J. Frances, H. A. Pincus, R. Ross, M. B. First, & W. W. Davis (Eds.), *DSM-IV sourcebook, Vol. 2* (pp. 53–64), Washington, DC: American Psychiatric Association Press.

Dunner, D. L., & Tay, L. K. (1993). Diagnostic reliability of the history of hypomania in bipolar II patients and patients with major depression. *Journal of Comprehensive Psychiatry, 34*, 303–307.

Eckblad, M., & Chapman, L. J. (1986). Development and validation of a scale for hypomanic personality. *Journal of Abnormal Psychology, 95*, 214–222.

Endicott, J., & Spitzer, R. L. (1978). A diagnostic interview: The schedule for affective disorders and schizophrenia. *Archives of General Psychiatry, 35*, 837–844.

Findling, R. L., Youngstrom, E. A., Danielson, C. K., DelPorto-Bedoya, D., Papish-David, R., Townsend, L., et al. (2002). Clinical decision-making using the General Behavior Inventory in juvenile bipolarity. *Bipolar Disorders, 4*, 34–42.

First, M. B., Spitzer, R. L., Gibbon, M., & Williams, J. B. W. (1997). *Structured Clinical Interview for DSM-IV (SCID)*. Washington, DC: American Psychiatric Press.

Frank, E. (2005). *Treating bipolar disorder: A clinician's guide to interpersonal and social rhythm therapy*. New York: Guilford Press.

Frank, E., Kupfer, D. J., Thase, M. E., Mallinger, A. G., Swartz, H. A., Fagiolini, A. M., et al. (2005). Two-year outcomes for interpersonal and social rhythm therapy in individuals with bipolar I disorder. *Archives of General Psychiatry, 62*, 996–1004.

Fristad, M. A., Weller, E. B., & Weller, R. A. (1992). The Mania Rating Scale: Can it be used in children. *Journal of American Academy of Child and Adolescent Psychiatry, 31*, 252–257.

Fristad, M. A., Weller, E. B., & Weller, R. A. (1995). The Mania Rating Scale (MRS): Further reliability and validity studies with children. *Annals of Clinical Psychiatry, 7*, 127–132.

Geller, B., Zimerman, B., Williams, M., Bolhofner, K., Craney, J. L., DelBello, M. P., et al. (2001). Reliability of the Washington University in St. Louis Kiddie Schedule for Affective Disorders and Schizophrenia (WASH-U-KSADS) mania and rapid cycling sections. *Journal of Academy of Child and Adolescent Psychiatry, 40*, 450–455.

Ghaemi, S. N., Boiman, E., & Goodwin, F., K. (2000). Insight and outcome in bipolar, unipolar and anxiety disorders. *Journal of Comprehensive Psychiatry, 41*, 161–171.

Ghaemi, S. N., Lenox, M. S., & Baldessarini, R. J. (2001). Effectiveness and safety of long-term antidepressant treatment in bipolar disorder. *Journal of Clinical Psychiatry, 62*, 565–569.

Ghaemi, S. N., Miller, C. J., Berv, D. A., Klugman, J., Rosenquist, K. J., & Pies, R. W. (2005). Sensitivity and specificity of a new bipolar spectrum diagnostic scale. *Journal of Affective Disorders, 84*, 273–277.

Gracious, B. L., Youngstrom, E. A., Findling. R. L., & Calabrese, J. R. (2002). Discriminative validity of a parent version of the young mania rating scale. *Journal of the Academy of Child and Adolescent Psychiatry, 41*, 1350–1359.

Hanley, J. A., & McNeil, B. J. (1982). The meaning and use of the area under a receiver operating characteristic (ROC) curve. *Radiology, 143*, 29–36.

Hirschfeld, R. M. A., Holzer, C., Calabrese, J. R., Weissman, M., Reed, M., Davies, M., et al., (2003). Validity of the mood disorder questionnaire: A general population study. *American Journal of Psychiatry, 160*, 178–180.

Hirschfeld, R. M. A., Williams, J. B. W., Spitzer, R. L., Calabrese, J. R., Flynn, L., Keck, P. E. Jr., et al. (2000). Development and validation of a screening instrument for bipolar spectrum disorder: The mood disorder questionnaire. *American Journal of Psychiatry, 157*, 1873–1875.

Hollon, S. D., & Kendall, P. C. (1980). Cognitive self-statements in depression: Development of an automatic thoughts questionnaire. *Cognitive Therapy and Research, 4*, 383–395.

Hooley, J. M., & Teasdale, J. D. (1989). Predictors of relapse in unipolar depressives: Expressed emotion, marital distress, and perceived criticism. *Journal of Abnormal Psychology, 98*, 229–235.

Isometsä, E., Suominen, K., Mantere, O., Valtonen, H., Leppämäki, S., Pippingsköld, M., et al. (2003). The mood disorder questionnaire improves recognition of bipolar disorder in psychiatric care. *BMC Psychiatry, 3*, 8.

Johnson, M. H., Magaro, P. A., & Stern, S. L. (1986). Use of the SADS-C as a diagnostic and symptom severity measure. *Journal of Consulting and Clinical Psychology, 54*, 546–551.

Johnson, S. L. (2005). Mania and dysregulation in goal pursuit. *Clinical Psychology Review, 25*, 241–262.

Johnson, S. L., & Fingerhut, R. (2004). Negative cognitions predict the course of bipolar depression, not mania. *Journal of Cognitive Psychotherapy, 18,* 149–162.

Johnson, S. L., & Kizer, A. (2002). Bipolar and unipolar depression: a comparison of clinical phenomenology and psychosocial predictors. In I. H. Gotlib & C. Hammen (Eds.), *Handbook of depression* (pp. 141–165). New York: Guilford Press.

Johnson, S. L., & Leahy, R. L. (Eds.). (2004). *Psychological treatment of bipolar disorder.* New York: Guilford Press.

Judd, L. L., Akiskal, H. S., Schettler, P. J., Endicott, J., Maser, J., Solomon, D. A., et al. (2002). The long-term natural history of the weekly symptomatic status of bipolar I disorder. *Archives of General Psychiatry, 59,* 530–538.

Karkowski, L. M., & Kendler, K. S. (1997). An examination of the genetic relationship between bipolar and unipolar illness in an epidemiological sample. *Psychiaric Genetics, 7,* 159–163.

Kaufman, J., Birmaher, B., Brent, D., Rao, U., Flynn, C., Moeci, P., et al. (1997). Schedule for Affective Disorders and Schizophrenia for School-Age Children–Present and Lifetime Version (K-SADS-PL): Initial reliability and validity data. *Journal of the American Academy of Child & Adolescent Psychiatry, 36,* 980–988.

Kazdin, A. E., & Kagan, J. (1994). Models of dysfunction in developmental psychopathology. *Clinical Psychology: Science and Practice, 1,* 35–52.

Keck, P. E., McElroy, S. L., Strakowski, S. M., West, S. A., Sax, K. W., Hawkins, J. M., et al. (1998). Twelve-month outcome of patients with bipolar disorder following hospitalization for a manic or mixed episode. *The American Journal of Psychiatry, 155,* 646–52.

Keller, M. B., Lavori, P. W., Kane, J. M., Gelenberg, A. J., Rosenbaum, J. F., Walzer, E. A., et al. (1992). Subsyndromal symptoms in bipolar disorder: A comparison of standard and low serum levels of lithium. *Archives of General Psychiatry, 49,* 371–376.

Keller, M. B., Lavori, P. W., McDonald-Scott, P., Scheftner, W. A., Andreasen, N. C., Shapiro, R. W., et al. (1981). Reliability of lifetime diagnoses and symptoms in patients with current psychiatric disorder. *Journal of Psychiatry Research, 16,* 229–240.

Kemp, R., & David, A. (1996). Insight and compliance. In B. Blackwell (Ed.), *Treatment compliance and the therapeutic alliance.* Newark, NJ: Gordon and Breach.

Kessler, R. C., Berglund, P., Demler, O., Jin, R., & Walters, E. E. (2005). Lifetime prevalence and age-of-onset distributions of DSM-IV disorders in the National Comorbidity Survey replication. *Archives of General Psychiatry, 62,* 593–602.

Kessler, R. C., Rubinow, D. R., Holmes, C., Abelson, J. M., & Zhao, S. (1997). The epidemiology of DSM-III-R bipolar I disorder in a general population survey. *Psychological Medicine, 27,* 1079–1089.

Kieseppa, T., Partonen, T., Haukka, J., Kaprio, J., & Lonnqvis, J. (2004). High concordance of bipolar I disorder in a nationwide sample of twins. *American Journal of Psychiatry, 161,* 1814–1821.

Klein, D. N., Dickstein, S., Taylor, E. B., & Harding, K. (1989). Identifying chronic affective disorders in outpatients: Validation of the general behavior inventory. *Journal of Consulting and Clinical Psychology, 57,* 106–111.

Kwapil, T. R., Miller, M. B., Zinser, M. C., Chapman, L. J., Chapman, J., & Eckblad, M. (2000). A longitudinal study of high scorers on the hypomanic personality scale. *Journal of Abnormal Psychology, 109,* 222–226.

Lam, D., & Wong, G. (2005). Prodromes, coping strategies, and psychological interventions in bipolar disorders. *Clinical Psychology Review, 25,* 1028–1042.

Lam, D., Wright, K., & Smith, N. (2004). Dysfunctional assumptions in bipolar disorder. *Journal of Affective Disorders, 79,* 193–199.

Lam, D., Wright, K., & Sham, P. (2005). Sense of hyperpositive self and response to cognitive therapy in bipolar disorder. *Psychological Medicine, 35,* 69–77.

Leibenluft, E., Albert, P. S., Rosenthal, N. E., & Wehr, T. A. (1996). Relationship between sleep and mood in patients with rapid-cycling bipolar disorder. *Journal of Psychiatric Research, 63,* 161–68.

Lewinsohn, P. M., Seeley, J. R., & Klein, D. N. (2003). Bipolar disorders during adolescence. *Acta Psychiatrica Scandinavica, 108,* 47–50.

Lish, J. D., Dime-Meenan, S., Whybrow, P. C., Price, R. A., & Hirschfeld, R. M. (1994). The National Depressive and Manic-Depressive Association (DMDA) survey of bipolar members. *Journal of Affective Disorders, 31,* 281–294.

Loeber, R., Green, S. M., & Lahey, B. B. (1990). Mental health professionals' perception of the utility of children, mothers, and teachers as informants on childhood psychopathology. *Journal of Clinical Child Psychology, 19,* 136–143.

Mallon, J. C., Klein, D. N., Bornstein, R. F., & Slater, J. F. (1986). Discriminant validity of the General Behavior Inventory: An outpatient study. *Journal of Personality Assessment, 50,* 568–577.

Miklowitz, D. J., & Goldstein, M. J. (1997). *Bipolar disorder: A family-focused treatment approach.* New York: Guilford Press.

Miklowitz, D. J., & Johnson, S. L. (2006). The psychopathology and treatment of Bipolar Disorder. *Annual Review of Clinical Psychology, 2,* 199–235.

Miklowitz, D. J., Wisniewski, S. R., Miyahara, S., Otto, M. W., & Sachs, G. S. (2005). Perceived criticism from family members as a predictor of the one-year course of bipolar disorder. *Psychiatry Research, 136,* 101–111.

Miller, C. J., Klugman, J., Berv, D. A., Rosenquist, K. J., & Ghaemi, S. N. (2004). Sensitivity and specificity of the mood disorder questionnaire for detecting bipolar disorder. *Journal of Affective Disorders, 81,* 167–171.

Monk, T. H., Flaherty, J. F., Frank, E., Hoskinson, K., & Kupfer, D. J. (1990). The social rhythm metric: An instrument to quantify the daily rhythms of life. *The Journal of Nervous and Mental Disease, 178,* 120–126.

Monk, T. H., Reynolds, C. F., III, Buysse, D. J., DeGrazia, J. M., & Kupfer, D. J. (2003). The relationship between lifestyle regularity and subjective sleep quality. *Chronobiology International, 20,* 97–107.

Nottelmann, E., Biederman, J., Birmaher, B., Carlson, G. A., Chang, K. D., Fenton, W. S., et al. (2001). NIMH research roundtable on prepubertal bipolar disorder. *Journal of the American Academy of Child & Adolescent Psychiatry, 40,* 871–878.

Pavuluri, M. N., Henry, D. B., Devineni, B., Carbray, J. A., & Birmaher, B. (2006). Child Mania Rating Scale: Development, reliability, and validity. *Journal of the American Academy of Child & Adolescent Psychiatry, 45,* 550–560.

Phelps, J. R., & Ghaemi, S. N. (2006). Improving the diagnosis of bipolar disorder: Predictive value of screening tests. *Journal of Affective Disorders, 92,* 141–148.

Prien, R. F., & Potter, W. Z. (1990). NIMH workshop report on treatment of bipolar disorder. *Psychopharmacology Bulletin, 26,* 409–427.

Reigier, D. A., Farmer, M. E., Rae, D. S., Locke, B. Z., Keith, S. J., Judd, L. L., et al. (1990). Comorbidity of mental disorders with alcohol and other substance abuse: Results from the Epidemiological Catchment Area (ECA) Study. *Journal of the American Medical Association, 264,* 2511–2518.

Rice, J. P., McDonald-Scott, P., Endicott, J., Coryell, W., Grove, W. M., Keller, M. B., et al. (1986). The stability of diagnosis with an application to bipolar II disorder. *Journal of Psychiatry Research, 19,* 285–296.

Richters, J. E. (1992). Depressed mothers as informants about their children: A critical review of the evidence for distortion. *Psychological Bulletin, 112,* 485–499.

Rogers, R., Jackson R. L., Salekin, K. L., & Neumann, C. S. (2003). Assessing axis I symptomatology on the SADS-C in two correctional samples: The validation of subscales and a screen for malingered presentations. *Journal of Personality Assessment, 81,* 281–290.

Rogers, R., Jackson, R. L., & Cashel, M. (2001). The schedule for affective disorders and schizophrenia (SADS). In R. Rogers (Ed.), *Handbook of diagnostic and structural interviewing* (pp. 84–102). New York: Guilford Press.

Ruggero, C., Johnson, S. L., & Cuellar, A. K. (2004). Spanish language measures for mania and depression. *Psychological Assessment, 16,* 381–385.

Sanz, M., Constable, G., Lopez-Ibor, I., Kemp, R., & David, A. S. (1998). A comparative study of insight scales and their relationship to psychopathological and clinical variables. *Psychological Medicine, 28,* 437–446.

Secunda, S. K., Katz, M. M., Swann, A., Koslow, S. H., Maas, J. W., & Chuang, S. (1985). Mania: Diagnosis, state measurement and prediction of treatment response. *Journal of Affective Disorders, 8,* 113–121.

Shugar, G., Schertzer, S., Toner, B. B., & Di Gasbarro, I. (1992). Development, use, and factor analysis of a self-report inventory for mania. *Comprehensive Psychiatry, 33,* 325–331.

Simpson, S. G., McMahon, F. J., McInnis, M. G., MacKinnon, D. F., Edwin, D., Folstein, S. E., et al. (2002). Diagnostic reliability of bipolar II disorder. *Archives of General Psychiatry, 59,* 746–740.

Spitzer, R. L., Endicott, J., & Robins, E. (1978). Research diagnostic criteria: Rationale and reliablity. *Archives of General Psychiatry, 35,* 773–782.

Spitzer, R. L., Williams, J. B. W., Gibbon, M., & First, M. B. (1992). The structured clinical interview for DSM-III-R (SCID). I. History, rationale, and description. *Archives of General Psychiatry, 49,* 624–629.

Strober, M., Schmidt-Lackner, S., Freeman, R., Bower, S., Lampert, C., & DeAntonio, M. (1995). Recovery and relapse in adolescents with bipolar affective illness: A five-year naturalistic, prospective follow-up. *Journal of the American Academy of Child & Adolescent Psychiatry, 34,* 724–731.

Swann, A. C., Janicak, P. L., Calabrese, J. R., Bowden, C. L., Dilsaver, S. C., Morris, D. D., et al. (2001). Structure of mania: Depressive, irritable, and psychotic clusters with different retrospectively-assessed course patterns of illness in randomized clinical trial participants. *Journal of Affective Disorders, 67,* 123–132.

Van Humbeeck, G., Van Audenhove, C., Storms, G., De Hert, M., Pieters, G., & Vertommen, H. (2004). Expressed emotion in the professional-client dyad: A comparison of three expressed emotion instruments. *European Journal of Psychological Assessment, 20,* 237–246.

Varga, M., Magnusson, A., Flekkoy, K., Ronneberg, U., & Opjordsmoen, S. (2006). Insight, symptoms and neurocognition in bipolar I patients. *Journal of Affective Disorders, 91*, 1–9.

Verhulst, F. C., & Van der Ende., J. (1992). Agreement between parents' reports and adolescents' self-reports of problem behavior. *Journal of Child Psychology and Psychiatry and Allied Disciplines, 33*, 1011–1023.

Vernon, S. W., & Roberts, R. E. (1982). Use of the SADS-RDC in a tri-ethnic community survey. *Archives of General Psychiatry, 39*, 47–52.

Weber Rouget, B., Gervasoni, N., Dubuis, V., Gex-Fabry, M., Bondolfi, G., & Aubry, J. (2005). Screening for bipolar disorders using the French version of the Mood Disorder Questionnaire (MDQ). *Journal of Affective Disorders, 88*, 103–108.

Weiss, R. D., Greenfield, S. F., Najavits, L. M., Soto, J. A., Wyner, D., Tohen, M., et al. (1998). Medication compliance among patients with bipolar disorder and substance use disorder. *Clinical Psychology Review, 59*, 172–174.

Weissman, A., & Beck, A. T. (1978). *Development and validation of the dysfunctional attitude scale: A preliminary investigation.* Paper presented at the annual meeting of the American Educational Research Association, Toronto.

Williams, J. B. W., Gibbon, M., First, M. B., Spitzer, R. L., Davies, M., Borus, J., et al. (1992). The structured clinical interview for the DSM-III-R (SCID). II. Multisite test-retest reliability. *Archives of General Psychiatry, 49*, 630–636.

World Health Organization (1990). *Composite International Diagnostic Interview (CIDI, Version 1.0).* Geneva, Switzerland: World Health Organization.

Yen, C. F., Chen, C. S., Ko, C. H., Yeh, M. L., Yang, S. J., Yen, J. Y., et al. (2005). Relationships between insight and medication adherence in outpatients with schizophrenia and bipolar disorder. *Psychiatry and Clinical Neurosciences, 59*, 403–409.

Young, R. C., Biggs, J. T., Ziegler, V. E., & Meyer, D. A. (1978). A rating scale for mania: Reliability, validity and sensitivity. *British Journal of Psychiatry, 133*, 429–435.

Youngstrom, E. A., Findling, R. L., & Calabrese, J. R. (2003). Who are the comorbid adolescents? Agreement between psychiatric diagnosis, youth, parent, and teacher report. *Journal of Abnormal Child Psychology, 31*, 231–245.

Youngstrom, E. A., Findling, R. L., Calabrese, J. R., Gracious, B. L., Demeter, C., Bedoya, D. D., et al. (2004). Comparing the diagnostic accuracy of six potential screening instruments for bipolar disorder in youths aged 5 to 17 years. *Journal of the American Academy of Child & Adolescent Psychiatry, 43*, 847–858.

Youngstrom, E. A., Findling, R. L., Danielson, C. K., & Calabrese, J. R. (2001). Discriminative validity of parent report of hypomanic and depressive symptoms on the General Behavior Inventory. *Psychological Assessment, 13*, 267–276.

Youngstrom, E. A., Findling, R. L., Youngstrom, J. K., & Calabrese, J. R. (2005). Toward an evidence-based assessment of pediatric bipolar disorder. *Journal of Clinical Child and Adolescent Psychology, 34*, 433–448.

Youngstrom, E. A., Gracious, B. L., Danielson, C. K., Findling, R. L., & Calabrese, J. (2003). Toward an integration of parent and clinician report on the Young Mania Rating Scale. *Journal of Affective Disorders, 77*, 179–190.

Youngstrom, E., Loeber, R., & Stouthamer-Loeber, M. (2000). Patterns and correlates of agreement between parent, teacher, and male adolescent ratings of externalizing and internalizing problems. *Journal of Consulting and Clinical Psychology, 68*, 1038–1050.

Zimmerman, M., & Mattia, J. I. (1999). Psychiatric diagnosis in clinical practice: Is comorbidity being missed? *Comprehensive Psychiatry, 40*, 182–191.

7

Depression in Late Life

Amy Fiske
Alisa A. O'Riley

Assessing depression in older adults presents unique challenges to the clinician for several reasons. First, depression may be underreported in older adults because clients and their families (and, unfortunately, sometimes their physicians) often assume depressive symptoms are normal in late adulthood (Karel, Ogland-Hand, & Gatz, 2002). Second, depression can sometimes be difficult to differentially diagnose in older adulthood because of the prevalence of comorbid physical and cognitive problems. Finally, it may be difficult to diagnose depression in older adulthood because older adults often demonstrate the disorder with symptoms that differ from typical presentations in other age groups (Karel et al., 2002).

Given these challenges, it may be unwise to assess depression in older adults with the same methods and instruments used for younger adults. Even instruments that are well validated and empirically supported for the assessment of depression in younger adults may lack measurement equivalence across the life span (Karel et al., 2002). The present chapter sets out to examine the utility of current measurements of depression for adults over the age of 60. We begin by elaborating on the nature of depression in older adulthood. We then examine depression measurement instruments in terms of their utility for purposes of diagnosis, case conceptualization and treatment planning, and treatment monitoring and outcome measurement for older adults.

THE NATURE OF DEPRESSION
IN LATE LIFE

Depression in late life is commonly defined as meeting diagnostic criteria for one of several mood disorders. Categories within the *Diagnostic and Statistical Manual for Mental Disorders* (4th Edition-Text Revision; DSM-IV-TR; American Psychiatric Association [APA], 2000) include major depressive disorder, dysthymic disorder, and adjustment disorder with depressed mood. The *International Statistical Classification of Diseases* (10th Revision; ICD-10; World Health Organization [WHO], 1992) specifies categories of mild, moderate, and severe recurrent depressive disorders as well as dysthymia. ICD-10 moderate and severe depressive disorders are largely equivalent to DSM-IV-TR major depressive disorder. Bipolar disorder, which is seen infrequently in older adults, and which differs in important ways from unipolar depression (Depp & Jeste, 2004), will not be discussed in this chapter.

The diagnosis of major depressive disorder requires either dysphoria (depressed mood) or anhedonia (diminished interest or pleasure in activities) most of the day, nearly every day, for at least 2 weeks, along with additional symptoms of appetite disturbance, sleep disturbance, low energy, psychomotor retardation or agitation, inability to concentrate, feelings of worthlessness or guilt, or thoughts of death or suicide, for a total of five or more symptoms. Additional criteria require impairment in social, occupational, or other important areas of functioning, and exclude symptoms that can be attributed to recent bereavement, a medical condition, or a substance. Dysthymic disorder is diagnosed when symptoms are present for at least 2 years, without a break of 2 months or more. To meet criteria for dysthymic disorder, symptoms must include pervasive dysphoria plus two additional symptoms from among the following: appetite disturbance, sleep disturbance, low energy, low self-esteem, inability to concentrate, and hopelessness. The diagnosis of adjustment disorder with depressed mood is assigned when symptoms occur in response to a specific stressor if the symptoms cause significant distress or impairment but do not meet the criteria for major depression or dysthymia.

Existing diagnostic criteria may not be appropriate for the classification of depression among older adults, as older adults frequently present a symptom picture that differs from the profiles most often reported by younger and middle aged adults. Although reports vary somewhat regarding specifics, an emerging consensus is that older adults are less likely to report certain ideational symptoms, such as dysphoria (Gallo, Rabins, & Anthony, 1999), guilt (Gallo, Anthony, & Muthén, 1994), and suicidal ideation (Blazer, Bachar, & Hughes, 1987). Exceptions include findings that reports of hopelessness and helplessness (Christensen et al., 1999) and nonsuicidal thoughts about death (Gallo et al., 1994) may be more common in older than in younger adults. In contrast to their general tendency to report fewer ideational symptoms, older adults are more likely to report somatic symptoms, such as fatigue (Gallo et al., 1994), insomnia (Christensen et al., 1999; Gallo et al., 1994), psychomotor retardation (Christensen et al., 1999; Gallo et al., 1994), agitation (Brodaty et al., 1997), or diminished appetite and weight loss (Blazer et al., 1987; Brodaty et al., 1991, 1997). This symptom pattern has been referred to variously as "masked depression" (Blumenthal, 1980) and "depression without sadness" (Gallo et al., 1999)—names that highlight the extent to which these depressive symptoms are likely to be overlooked if using existing diagnostic systems. Yet evidence shows that these somatic symptoms cannot be attributed entirely to increases in physical illness (Nguyen & Zonderman, 2006), and (with the exception of changes in appetite and libido) are indicative of depression in older adults (Norris, Arnau, Bramson, & Meagher, 2004). In addition to these differences, older adults are more likely than younger adults to display cognitive deficits (Rapp et al., 2005). Some reports also indicate that anhedonia is increasingly common with age (Christensen et al., 1999).

Furthermore, the very nature of late adult life may affect diagnostic classification. For example, diagnostic criteria require that impairment be evident in social, occupational, or other important areas of functioning. However, the definition of normal functioning in these domains has not been well determined for older adults, raising the possibility that older adults may be less likely than younger and middle aged adults to be seen as functionally impaired. In addition, exclusionary criteria may lead to underdetection of depression in older adults. Symptoms that can be attributed to physical illness or medication use are not to be considered when diagnosing depression, but distinguishing the cause of these symptoms may not be straightforward. Taken together, these factors suggest that existing diagnostic categories may lack sensitivity for detecting depression among older adults. Numerous new categories have been proposed to classify depressive symptoms that do not meet diagnostic criteria (for a discussion, see Kumar, Lavretsky, & Elderkin-Thompson, 2004), but a single standard has not emerged.

A widely used alternative for identifying cases of depression in older adults is the use of a cutoff score on a depressive symptom checklist to indicate presence of clinically significant depressive symptoms. This dimensional approach identifies older adults who are experiencing an elevated level of depressive symptoms without excluding individuals whose symptoms do not include dysphoria or anhedonia, those without evidence of impaired functioning, or those with comorbid physical illness. Thus, this method overcomes limitations of diagnostic criteria that do not map well onto depressive experience in old age. Because this approach lacks syndromal criteria, however, it lacks specificity for ruling out causes of symptoms that may not represent depression, such as those that are the direct effects of physical illness or recent bereavement.

Cognitive decline may also complicate the measurement of depression in late life. Cognitive deficits are often reported among older adults with depression, and evaluating whether these deficits are symptoms of depression or dementia can be challenging (Schoepflin Sanders, Lyness, Eberly, King, & Caine, 2006). Alexopoulos and colleagues (1997) have proposed that cognitive deficits, primarily deficits in executive functioning, accompanied by cerebrovascular risk factors and a late age of depression onset, may indicate an etiologically distinct form of depression, which they term "vascular depression." A substantial minority of cases meeting proposed criteria for vascular depression go on to develop dementia

(Tuma, 2000). Further, rates of depression are elevated among individuals with dementia (Vilalta-Franch et al., 2006). Thus, cognitive dysfunction may represent a symptom of depression, or depression may be a prodromal symptom of, or reaction to, dementia.

In addition to being aware of the possible coexistence of dementia and depression in older adults, other psychiatric and medical comorbidities should also be taken into account. As at other ages, anxiety is highly comorbid with depression in late life, although there is no evidence that it is more common in depression with late onset (Janssen, Beekman, Comijs, Deeg, & Heeren, 2006). In contrast to other age groups, however, late life depression is more likely to involve comorbid medical or neurological conditions (see Williamson, Shaffer, & Parmelee, 2000). Physical illness may represent a cause of depression (Alexopoulos et al., 1997; Zeiss, Lewinsohn, & Rohde, 1996), an effect of depression (Frasure-Smith, Lesperance, & Talajic, 1993), or simply co-occurrence. Further, illness may lead to depression as a result of organic mechanisms (Alexopoulos et al., 1997) or as a psychological reaction. Zeiss and colleagues (1996) concluded that functional impairment largely mediates the relationship between illness and depression, suggesting that depression is a psychological response to limitations imposed by the illness. Whatever the direction of causation or mechanism, the comorbidity of depression and physical illness makes assessment more challenging since certain symptoms are shared by both.

There is heterogeneity in the prognosis of late life depression. Depressed older adults respond to treatment as quickly as their younger counterparts, but appear to be at risk of earlier relapse (Mueller et al., 2004). Earlier relapse is predicted by residual symptoms following treatment (Chopra, Zubritzky, & Knott, 2005), which suggests that incomplete resolution of a depressive episode may predispose to another episode. Time to relapse is also predicted by presence of executive dysfunction (Alexopoulos et al., 2000), consistent with a neurobiological explanation such as vascular depression (Alexopoulos et al., 1997).

Finally, depression in late life has been linked to many of the same risk and protective factors as at other points in the life span, although the prevalence of these factors, and the strength of their association with depression, may vary by age. Age of depression onset has been examined as a potential marker for an etiologically distinct subtype of the disorder (Alexopoulos et al., 1997). Research in clinical samples suggests that half of older adults with depression experienced the first episode after age 60 (Steingart & Herrmann, 1991). However, much accumulated knowledge regarding depression in older adults, including that reviewed here, is not specific to age of depression onset.

Genetic factors have been implicated in depressive symptoms among older adults. Estimates of heritability range from .16 to .37 (Gatz, Pedersen, Plomin, Nesselroade, & McClearn, 1992). Family studies suggest that genetic influences play a greater role in depression earlier in life (Baldwin & Tomenson, 1995). In contrast, other biological factors, such as cerebrovascular risk factors (Alexopoulos et al., 1997), may be more influential in late life depression.

Stressors also contribute to the risk of depression in older adults, as at other ages (for a meta-analysis, see Kraaij, Arensman, & Sponhoven, 2002). Among the specific stressors most frequently examined in older populations are physical illness and disability (as discussed above), bereavement, and caregiving. Bereavement may be a risk factor for depression in late life, particularly among individuals with a history of depressive episodes (Zisook & Shuchter, 1993). Latham and Prigerson (2004) have argued that abnormal distress following bereavement generally does not resemble depression, and should instead be considered a different syndrome, which they term "complicated grief." Caregiving for someone with dementia or disability is a potentially stressful experience that occurs with greater frequency in late life. High rates of depression among caregivers have been reported (see Schulz & Martire, 2004, for a review). Social factors may act as either protective or risk factors for depression in late life. Perceived social support buffers the effects of stressors in older adults, but support that is too intensive, or perceived as unsupportive, may also contribute to risk (for a review, see Hinrichsen & Emery, 2005).

Thus, depression in late life differs from depression earlier in the life span in terms of presentation, comorbidities, course, and risk factors. These differences imply a need for special care in assessing depression in an older adult. Assessment should consider the possibility of medical comorbidity or declines in cognitive functioning. Furthermore, due to the unique presentation of depression in late life, diagnostic classification may underestimate

TABLE 7.1 Ratings of Instruments Used for Diagnosis

Instrument	Norms	Internal Consistency	Inter-Rater Reliability	Test–Retest Reliability	Content Validity	Construct Validity	Validity Generalization	Clinical Utility	Highly Recommended
Structured Clinical Interviews									
SCID	NA	NA	E	U	A	U	G	A	
SADS	NA	NA	E	U	A	U	G	A	
GMS	NA	NA	G	G	G	G	G	A	✓

Note: SCID = Structured Clinical Interview for DSM; SADS = Schedule for Affective Disorders and Schizophrenia; GMS = Geriatric Mental State Schedule; A = Adequate; G = Good; E = Excellent; U = Unavailable; NA = Not Applicable.

pathology in this group, whereas symptom checklists may overestimate problems, suggesting that categorical and dimensional measurements may both be important.

PURPOSES OF ASSESSMENT

In the following sections, we review assessment instruments with a focus on three specific clinical purposes: diagnosis; case conceptualization and treatment planning; and treatment monitoring and the assessment of treatment outcome. We will not evaluate instruments for use in screening. Much empirical work has focused on the evaluation of instruments to screen for depression in older adults, particularly within primary care settings. For a discussion, the interested reader is referred to Watson and Pignone (2003).

A specialized literature exists with respect to the assessment of depression within dementia. Some individuals with dementia may be able to provide accurate information about their own depressive symptoms, but the validity of self-report varies with the level of awareness of deficits (Snow et al., 2005). As a result, instruments that have been developed specifically for this task are largely observer rated, to be completed by a clinician or lay interviewer, and some incorporate information from a caregiver or other proxy as well. Information on the use of these measures for the assessment purposes discussed above is included in the relevant sections.

Because older adults, particularly older men, are at the highest risk of death by suicide of any age group (Hoyert, Heron, Murphy, & Kung, 2006), a clinician assessing depression among older adults must also be prepared to assess suicide risk. For a review of instruments for assessing suicide risk, see Chapter 8.

ASSESSMENT FOR THE PURPOSE OF DIAGNOSIS

Structured Interviews

Structured clinical interviews address all information needed for a diagnosis. Table 7.1 summarizes the properties of structured clinical interviews when used to diagnose depression in older adults. The primary advantage of structured over unstructured clinical interviews is reliability, as seen in the table. As previously mentioned, however, a consideration when assessing older adults is whether diagnostic criteria themselves may lead to under-detection of depression in this age group.

Lengthy administration represents a challenge with respect to the use of these instruments in clinical settings with older adults. However, that administration time depends on the person's responses. Furthermore, increasingly brief versions have been published in recent years. A further challenge is the extensive training required to reach proficiency in the administration of structured clinical interviews, ranging from days to weeks. Although training requirements may be viewed as a burden, training and experience in using structured interviews can be especially helpful for new clinicians (Segal, Kabacoff, Hersen, Van Hasselt, & Ryan, 1995).

The most widely used structured clinical interview in the United States is the Structured Clinical Interview for DSM (SCID; First, Spitzer, Gibbon, & Williams, 1997) which, in its current revision, yields diagnoses according to DSM-IV criteria. There is evidence, based on an earlier revision of the SCID, that master's level clinicians can be trained on the measure (Segal et al., 1995). The current revision is available in either research or clinical versions, with the clinical version (SCID-CV; First et al., 1997) abbreviated to minimize administration time. The SCID-CV assesses all major DSM-IV Axis I disorders and requires 45 to 90 minutes to administer, but individual modules can be administered separately. Although the current revision of the SCID-CV has not yet been evaluated in older adult samples, the previous form of the SCID, which was based on DSM-III-R diagnostic criteria (American Psychiatric Association, 1987), has been found to have good inter-rater reliability for the diagnosis of major depressive disorder in older adult samples (Segal et al., 1995). Notably, inter-rater reliability appears to be lower for diagnosis of dysthymia (Segal et al., 1995). Extensive pilot and field testing (First et al., 1997) suggest good content validity, but the measure was not developed specifically for use with older adults. There is ample evidence of construct validity for the SCID in mixed-age samples (see First et al., 1997), and available evidence suggests content validity in older adult samples as well (Stukenberg, Dura, & Kiecolt-Glazer, 1990), but data are too sparse to permit conclusions to be drawn. There is evidence from a mixed-age sample that using the SCID (version not specified) improves clinical management of cases (Basco, cited in First et al., 1997). Thus, the SCID-CV may be useful for diagnosing major depressive disorders in older adults, but training and administration requirements are substantial and more empirical work is needed in older adult samples, specifically using the SCID-CV version, before it can be highly recommended for use in this population.

The Schedule for Affective Disorders and Schizophrenia (SADS; Endicott & Spitzer, 1978) yields diagnoses according to the Research Diagnostic Criteria (RDC; Spitzer, Endicott, & Robins, 1978). The SADS requires extensive training ("weeks," according to Dozois & Dobson, 2002) and takes 90 to 120 minutes to administer (Dozois & Dobson, 2002). In mixed-age samples, the SADS demonstrates excellent inter-rater reliability (Endicott & Spitzer, 1978). Although use of the SADS with older adults has not often been evaluated, one study reported excellent inter-rater reliability (Rapp, Smith, & Britt, 1990). As with the SCID, development of the SADS involved thorough evaluation of the content (Endicott & Spitzer, 1978), but the measure was not designed specifically for older adults. The SADS has demonstrated good efficiency in detecting "cases" of depression in older adults as defined by a cutoff score on the Beck Depression Inventory (BDI; Gallagher,

Breckenridge, Steinmetz, & Thompson, 1983), but it has been tested too infrequently in this population to support any conclusions regarding construct validity. Thus, the SADS may be a reliable and valid method of diagnosing depression in older adults, but training and administration costs are high, and further evaluation of its validity in this age group is needed before it can be highly recommended.

Whereas the SCID and SADS were designed for administration by a trained clinician, the Composite International Diagnostic Interview (CIDI; Robins et al., 1988) was initially developed for administration by trained laypersons for use in research and has since been used in clinical settings. The CIDI is a composite of the Diagnostic Interview Schedule (DIS; Robins, Helzer, Croughan, & Ratcliff, 1981) and the Present State Exam (PSE; Wing, Birley, Cooper, Graham, & Isaacs, 1967). It was designed to produce current and lifetime diagnoses according to both DSM-III-R (APA, 1987) and ICD-10 (WHO, 1992) criteria. Although there is little information on the DSM-IV version of the CIDI, the previous version has been extensively validated in mixed-age samples and has some evidence for use with older adults. A stringent test that combined inter-rater and test–retest reliability showed adequate reliability for the detection of major depressive disorder and for any depressive disorder in the elderly (Heun, Müller, Freyberger, & Maier, 1998). Reliability was much lower with respect to diagnosing recurrent brief depression and subthreshold recurrent brief depression. Several short forms of the CIDI have been developed. One short form (UM-CIDI-SF; Kessler & Mroczek, 1993) was evaluated in a large sample of older adults and found to be as strongly related to physician diagnosis as was the CES-D (Turvey, Wallace, & Herzog, 1999). Nonetheless, properties of the CIDI and its various short forms in older adult samples have yet to be well examined and, therefore, it cannot yet be recommended for clinical use with this population.

In contrast to most structured interview protocols, the Geriatric Mental State Schedule (GMS; Copeland et al., 1976) was developed specifically with older adults in mind. A classification system (known as AGECAT) was empirically derived for use with the GMS and is implemented through a computer-based algorithm. The GMS with the AGECAT system assesses eight psychiatric syndromes in older adults, including neurotic and psychotic depression. Ratings indicate level of diagnostic confidence, from

0 to 5, with 3 or greater indicating presence of a case. The GMS has good to excellent inter-rater and test–retest reliability (Copeland et al., 1988). The GMS was derived from previous scales, including the PSE (Wing et al., 1967), in consultation with experts and extensive field testing with older adult samples, suggesting good content validity. Construct validity has been demonstrated with good correspondence with DSM-III diagnosis in community (Copeland, Dewey, & Griffiths-Jones, 1990) and medical samples (Ames Flynn, Tuckwell, & Harrigan, 1994), although GMS/ AGECAT is more inclusive than DSM-IV major or minor depression (Newman, Sheldon, & Bland, 1998). Whereas the GMS has shown validity in US and UK samples (Copeland et al., 1976), a recent study involving 26 sites in India, China, Latin America, and Africa showed that sensitivity to depression varied widely by country (Prince et al., 2004).

The GMS Schedule has been incorporated into a larger instrument, the Comprehensive Assessment and Referral Evaluation (CARE; Gurland et al., 1977–1978), which assesses psychiatric, medical, nutritional, economic, and social problems. The CORE-CARE (Gurland & Wilder, 1984) is a shorter version that takes 45 to 90 minutes to administer and requires a trained interviewer, though not necessarily a clinician. The strength of this measure is the extent to which contextual factors are taken into account. This feature may be especially important when assessing depression in older adults, among whom medical and other problems may be especially likely to confound the diagnosis. The CORE-CARE depression scale has demonstrated good internal consistency (Gurland & Wilder, 1984), good to excellent inter-rater reliability (Gurland et al., 1977–1978), and good convergent and discriminant validity (Golden, Teresi, & Gurland, 1984). A 143-item version, the SHORT-CARE (Gurland, Golden, Teresi, & Challop, 1984), requires 30 to 45 minutes to administer. It has six indicator scales and two diagnostic scales: depression and dementia. Tunstall, Prince, and Mann (1997) reported good inter-rater reliability.

Taken together, these findings indicate that the GMS is a reliable and valid tool for diagnosing depression in older adults, and the related CARE, CORE-CARE, and SHORT-CARE instruments have similar properties and provide additional contextual information. A possible limitation is that these instruments yield diagnoses based on the empirically derived AGECAT diagnostic criteria and not the more widely accepted DSM or ICD criteria.

Overall Evaluation

In summary, structured interviews require more time to administer and a greater investment for training than unstructured interviews, but yield highly reliable diagnoses, and may be particularly useful in the training of new clinicians. In terms of specific instruments, the SCID and the SADS require the most training and are among the lengthiest to administer, but they also yield extremely reliable results. However, neither has been evaluated fully in older adult samples. The CIDI and GMS offer flexibility, as they can be administered by trained interviewers who are not clinicians. Thus, no single structured interview is clearly superior: the choice of a measure should depend on who will administer it and how much time can be invested.

ASSESSMENT FOR CASE CONCEPTUALIZATION AND TREATMENT PLANNING

Self-Report Measures

Several self-report depressive symptom measures may prove useful for the development of case conceptualizations and treatment plans for older adults (see Table 7.2). One of the most well-known depressive symptom measures in use today is the BDI (Beck, Ward, Mendelson, Mock, & Erbaugh, 1961), now in its second edition. The BDI is a 21-item measure, using a 4-point Guttman scale. In terms of case conceptualization and treatment planning, the BDI provides information about somatic, affective, and cognitive symptoms of depression (Arnau, Meagher, Norris, & Bramson, 2001). In mixed-age samples (using participants ages 19 to 69), the BDI has very good internal consistency (Arnau et al., 2001; Beck, Steer, & Brown, 1996), fairly good test–retest reliability (Beck et al., 1961), and is highly correlated with other measures of depression (including the Hamilton Rating Scale for Depression, the Zung Self-rating Depression Scale, and the Minnesota Multiphasic Personality Inventory Depression Scale; Beck et al., 1961).

In terms of its use with older adults, however, results are somewhat mixed. The original norms for the BDI did not include older adults. Some researchers (Gallagher, Nies, & Thompson, 1982) have demonstrated that the BDI has good reliability

TABLE 7.2 Ratings of Instruments Used for Case Conceptualization and Treatment Planning

Instrument	Norms	Internal Consistency	Inter-Rater Reliability	Test–Retest Reliability	Content Validity	Construct Validity	Validity Generalization	Clinical Utility	Highly Recommended
Self-Report Measures									
BDI	A	G	NA	G	A	A	L	A	
CES-D	E	G	NA	G	A	G	G	A	✓
GDS	G	G	NA	G	A	A	A	A	
SDS	A	A	NA	U	A	A	A	A	
Structured Clinical Interviews									
SCID	NA	NA	E	U	A	U	G	A	
SADS	NA	NA	E	U	A	U	G	A	
GMS	NA	NA	G	G	G	G	G	A	
Clinician Rating Scales									
GDRS	A	E	G	U	A	U	A	A	
MADRS	A	A	E	U	A	A	A	A	
Measures to Assess Depression in Dementia									
CSDD	A	G	A	A	G	G	G	A	
DMAS	A	A	A	U	U	A	A	A	

Note: BDI = Beck Depression Inventory; CES-D = Center for Epidemiological Studies-Depression Scale; GDS = Geriatric Depression Scale; SDS = Zung Self-rating Depression Scale; SCID = Structured Clinical Interview for DSM; SADS = Schedule for Affective Disorders and Schizophrenia; GMS = Geriatric Mental State Schedule; GDRS = Geriatric Depression Rating Scale; MADRS = Montgomery–Åsberg Depression Rating Scale; CSDD = Cornell Scale for Depression in Dementia; DMAS = Dementia Mood Assessment Scale; L = Less Than Acceptable; A = Adequate; G = Good; E = Excellent; U = Unavailable; NA = Not Applicable.

and validity in older adults in community psychiatric populations (Olin, Schneider, Eaton, Zemansky, & Pollock, 1992), and hospitalized patients (Clark, Cavanaugh, & Gibbons, 1983). Other researchers, however, have found that the BDI may have poor sensitivity for older males (Allen-Burge, Storandt, Kinscherf, & Rubin, 1994), that older women may be more hesitant to complete the measure (especially a question related to sexual interest) than other measures of depression (Jefferson, Powers, & Pope, 2001), and that the somatic items on the BDI may be confounded with physical illness in older adults (Clark et al., 1983; Zemore & Eames, 1979). In addition, some researchers have suggested that the complexity of the Guttman-type response options may limit the assessment's utility in older adults with any cognitive dysfunction (Clark et al., 1983). Finally, when factor analyses were conducted for older and younger adults, measurement invariance was not obtained (Zemore & Eames, 1979). Given these mixed results, the BDI is not highly recommended for case conceptualization and treatment planning in older adults. It should be noted that the newer version (BDI-II; Beck et al., 1996) included older adults in the normative sample; however, there is not currently enough empirical evidence supporting the use of the BDI-II in older adults

to recommend its use for case conceptualization and treatment planning.

Another self-report measure is the Center for Epidemiological Studies-Depression Scale (CES-D; Radloff, 1977). The CES-D is a 20-item measure where individuals are asked to respond to items on a 4-point Likert-type scale based on how they felt in the last week. In terms of case conceptualization and treatment planning, factor analyses show that the CES-D can provide clinicians information about depressed mood, psychomotor retardation, the absence of well-being, and interpersonal difficulties (Gatz, Johansson, Pederson, Berg, & Reynolds, 1993). The CES-D has good internal consistency, test–retest reliability, and validity (it is correlated with the BDI, the Hamilton Rating Scale for Depression and the State-Trait Anxiety Inventory in mixed-age samples; Radloff, 1977). Many researchers have demonstrated that it has measurement equivalence across the lifespan (e.g., Gatz et al., 1993). Eaton and colleagues (Eaton, Muntaner, Smith, Tien, & Ybarra, 2004) developed a revised version, the CESD-R, that includes several symptoms not included in the CES-D, specifically weight changes, sleeping problems, feelings of worthlessness, and concentration difficulties. The CESD-R also eliminates items in the CES-D not related to the current definition of major depression. The CESD-R has good reliability and some convergent validity (it is highly correlated with the CES-D). This measure has not yet been thoroughly evaluated with older adults.

Despite the strengths of the CES-D (and, possibly, the CESD-R) other researchers have found problems with the use of this measure in older adults. Some investigators have suggested that the measure may contain items that are biased against being older, female, widowed, or having a physical disorder (Grayson, MacKinnon, Jorm, Creasey, & Broe, 2000). Other researchers have demonstrated that the CES-D is only modestly related to symptoms reported in structured interviews and that it often identifies individuals who either do not meet criteria for depression or who meet criteria for other diagnoses (Myers & Weissman, 1980). This last criticism may be reflecting the fact that older adults generally exhibit more subsyndromal rather than syndromal symptoms of depression (Newman, 1989). When examining the criticisms made against this measure, it appears that these issues are most likely problems related to the use of the CES-D as a diagnostic tool. The evidence suggests that the CES-D can be highly recommended as an instrument for case conceptualization and treatment planning, especially as part of a multimethod assessment that also includes a thorough clinical interview.

A widely used self-report measure designed to assess depression in older adults is the Geriatric Depression Scale (GDS; Yesavage et al., 1983). The GDS is a 30-item measure with a yes/no answer format. In response to concerns that depression measures are often confounded by physical illness in older adults, the developers of the GDS intended to exclude somatic items from the scale. In terms of its use for case conceptualization and treatment planning, the measure provides information about unhappiness, apathy, anxiety, loss of hope, and energy loss (Onishi, Suzuki, & Umegaki, 2006). The GDS has good internal consistency (Meeks, 2004; Yesavage et al., 1983), good test–retest reliability (Lesher, 1986), and good convergent validity (it is correlated with the BDI, the Beck Anxiety Inventory, the Zung Self-rating Depression Scale, HRSD, clinician's ratings, and it predicts diagnoses determined by structured interviews; Lesher, 1986; Rapp, Parisi, Walsh, & Wallace, 1988; Yesavage et al., 1983). In terms of its use with older adults, numerous researchers have questioned

the strategy of eliminating somatic items from a depression measure (Karel et al., 2002). As mentioned earlier, older adults tend to endorse cognitive items less frequently than younger adults. Thus, eliminating the somatic items may reduce the sensitivity of the test. Furthermore, when individual somatic items are examined, only appetite disturbance seems to be entirely confounded with age (Norris et al., 2004), which suggests there is no reason to eliminate the valuable information the somatic items on depression scales provide. In addition, there are both strengths and limitations inherent in the yes/no answer format of this measure. On the positive side, the format is not too cognitively demanding. As such, it may be useful for older adults with cognitive dysfunction. On the other hand, in one survey, older adults indicated they did not like the forced-choice aspect of this measure (Fischer, Rolnick, Jackson, Garrard, & Luepke, 1996). Because this measure may not be sensitive to somatic presentations of depression and because there may be some issues with the format of the measure, the GDS should be used with caution for case conceptualization and treatment planning in older adults.

Another self-report measure that might be useful in case conceptualization and treatment planning for older adults is the Zung Self-rating Depression Scale (SDS; Zung, 1965). The SDS is a 20-item measure scored on a 4-point Likert-type scale. The SDS provides information about a lack of well-being and depressive affect (Schafer, 2006). It has good reliability and validity in mixed-age samples, including a normative sample with adults up to age 69 (Zung, 1965). The SDS has adequate internal consistency in older adult samples (Dunn & Sacco, 1989; Rapp et al., 1988), and there is some evidence for its validity in this population, especially as a screening measure (Dunn & Sacco, 1989; Rapp et al., 1988); however, more research is needed before it can be recommended for case conceptualization and treatment planning in older adults.

Structured Interviews

Because evidence suggests that structured interviews may result in a more thorough and comprehensive picture of a client's presenting problem than unstructured interviews (Segal et al., 1995), they may be useful for case conceptualization and treatment planning, especially when used in conjunction with other assessment methods. Structured interviews that could be utilized for this purpose include the clinical version of the SCID (SCID-CV; First et al., 1997), the SADS (Endicott & Spitzer, 1978), and the GMS (Copeland et al., 1976). All of these interviews are described earlier and Table 7.2 summarizes the utility of these measures for the purposes of case conceptualization and treatment planning in older adults. In addition, a version of the GMS developed specifically to assess depression severity (GMS-DS; Ravindran, Welburn, & Copeland, 1994), is particularly promising. It takes only 15 minutes to administer and has high internal consistency, and good convergent validity with respect to self-report and clinician ratings (Ravindran et al., 1994). Replication is needed before the measure can be highly recommended. Overall, all of these interviews have good potential for the purposes of treatment planning and case conceptualization with older adults; however, each needs more empirical evaluation before it can be recommended for this purpose.

Clinician Rating Scales

Clinician rating scales are generally developed to assess severity of depression among individuals who have been diagnosed with the disorder; however, the kinds of questions asked in these scales may also provide useful information for case conceptualization and treatment planning. Table 7.2 summarizes properties of clinician rating scales that may prove useful for the development of case conceptualizations and treatment plans for older adults.

Perhaps the most popular clinician rating scale is the Hamilton Rating Scale for Depression (HRSD; Hamilton, 1960, 1967), which is often utilized in treatment outcome studies. A comprehensive review of the HRSD across a wide range of samples concluded, however, that the measures' weaknesses outweigh its strengths (Bagby, Ryder, Schuller, & Marshall, 2004). In particular, the authors noted that individual items are poorly designed, the total score does not reflect a unidimensional structure, and the measure has not been updated despite numerous revisions in accepted diagnostic criteria for depression. A problem with evaluating the properties of this scale is that multiple versions have appeared, and empirical reports often fail to identify which version was used (Zitman et al., 1990, as cited in Williams, 2001). The versions vary

in length (17 to 27 items) and even what domains of depression are addressed; all versions assess somatic symptoms, whereas only some versions include items to assess cognitive symptoms of helplessness, hopelessness, and worthlessness. The HRSD requires a trained clinician and takes 30 minutes to administer to depressed older adults (Moberg et al., 2001).

In terms of reliability and validity, the HRSD has several problems. Although the measure appears to have good inter-rater reliability (Rapp et al., 1990; Stukenberg et al., 1990; Williams, 1988), the scales have questionable internal consistency in older adults (e.g., Cronbach's α = .46; Hammond, 1998). Reports vary widely with respect to validity. Concurrent validity has been reported to be equivalent to other clinician rating instruments in a sample of depressed older adults (Mottram, Wilson, & Copeland, 2000), but no better than the BDI in a community sample (Stukenberg et al., 1990). Rapp and colleagues (1990) used an extracted version of the HRSD, and reported moderate to high correlations with the BDI, the SDS, and the GDS, and better concurrent validity than these measures in a sample of older male medical inpatients; although Baker and Miller (1991), also using a medical sample, reported that concurrent validity was lower than for the GDS. In a sample of older adults with dementia, validity was particularly problematic (sensitivity was 8% for the HRSD as compared with 82% for the GDS; Lichtenberg, Marcopulos, Steiner & Tabscott, 1992). Indeed, some researchers have suggested that the HRSD does not actually measure depression at all, as factor analysis has shown that the scale may instead measure aspects of anxiety and insomnia (Cole et al., 2004; Hammond, 1998; Stukenberg et al., 1990). Finally, the disproportionate number of somatic items may make the measure especially problematic for use with older adults (Jamison & Scogin, 1992). Given all this, the HRSD is not recommended as a measure for treatment planning or case conceptualization with older adults.

The Geriatric Depression Rating Scale (GDRS; Jamison & Scogin, 1992) was developed in response to problems with the HRSD. It may provide information useful for treatment planning and case conceptualization in older adults as it is based on the GDS with the addition of somatic items that are considered only if responses are not attributable to physical illness. The GDRS is a 35-item measure that requires a trained interviewer and takes 35 minutes to administer. It is internally consistent with fairly high inter-rater reliability. Finally, it has also been found by the developers to have some validity for older adults (it is correlated with the HRSD, BDI, and GDS; Jamison & Scogin, 1992). However, more research must be conducted before this measure can be recommended for case conceptualization and treatment planning.

Another clinician rating scale that may be useful in case conceptualization and treatment planning is the Montgomery–Åsberg Depression Rating Scale (MADRS; Montgomery & Åsberg, 1979). The MADRS is a 10-item clinician rating scale of depression severity. The MADRS has been shown to have good inter-rater reliability (Zimmerman, Posternak, & Chelminski, 2004), and adequate construct validity (correlated with HRSD and has good sensitivity and specificity; Hammond, 1998; Mottram et al., 2000; Zimmerman et al., 2004) in older adult samples. Compared with the HRSD, the MADRS contains fewer somatic items and has a factor structure that more clearly measures aspects of the depression construct (dysphoria and anhedonia; Hammond, 1998). Like the HRSD, however, it has only fair internal consistency in this population (Bent-Hansen et al., 2003; Hammond, 1998). Thus the MADRS may be a better alternative than the HRSD as a clinician rating instrument and, with modification, it could be a useful measure in this population, but it cannot be highly recommended at this time.

The Inventory of Depressive Symptomatology (IDS; Rush et al., 1986) has 28 items rated on a scale of 0 to 3. It provides useful information for case conceptualization and treatment planning in terms of information about severity of symptoms. In younger and mixed-age samples, the IDS is internally consistent (Rush et al., 1986; Rush, Gullion, Basco, Jarrett, & Trivedi, 1996) and has good inter-rater reliability (Rush et al., 1996). Finally the measure demonstrates convergent validity (it is correlated with the HRSD and the BDI; Rush et al., 1986, 1996). Nonetheless, there is not enough information about the use of the IDS in older adults for this scale to be highly recommended.

Measures to Assess Depression in Dementia

Several measures that assess depression in individuals with dementia may be useful for case conceptualization and treatment planning (see Table 7.2). The most frequently used measure of this type is the Cornell Scale for Depression in Dementia (CSDD; Alexopoulos, Abrams, Young, & Shamoian, 1988). The scale includes 19 items that are rated by a mental health professional on a 3-point scale (absent, mild or intermittent, and severe). Ratings are based on observation of the client as well as interviews with the client and a caregiver. Administration requires 30 minutes. The CSDD provides information about general depression, rhythm disturbance (including insomnia), agitation/psychosis, and negative symptoms (Ownby, Harwood, Acevedo, Barker, & Duara, 2001). The scale has good internal consistency and adequate inter-rater reliability (Alexopoulos et al., 1988). It has been shown to distinguish individuals with dementia who meet criteria for depression (Alexopoulos et al., 1988) and is significantly correlated with other measures in the expected directions (Mack & Patterson, 1994). Further, the CSDD is not confounded by cognitive status (Maixner, Burke, Roccaforte, Wengel, & Potter, 1995). Experienced interviewers who evaluated the instrument reported that instructions lack detail in places, and that the focus on behaviors occurring within the last week may limit the measure's sensitivity, but the option to indicate "unable to rate" was particularly helpful (Mack & Patterson, 1994). In summary, the CSDD is a reliable and valid instrument to measure depression severity in individuals with dementia for purposes of conceptualization and treatment planning.

The Dementia Mood Assessment Scale (DMAS; Sunderland et al., 1988) includes 17 items that assess depressive symptoms in the past week in individuals with dementia on a 0-to-6 scale. Administered by a trained clinician, the measure involves a semi-structured interview and observation of the patient, along with input from collateral sources. Factor analyses vary slightly in the domains assessed by the DMAS; in the largest reported study, factors were depressed affect, environmental interaction, diurnal patterns, agitation or suspicion, and somatic indicators (Onega & Abraham, 1997). Adequate internal consistency (Camus, cited in Perrault, Oremus, Demers, Vida, & Wolfson, 2000), inter-rater reliability (Sunderland et al., 1988) and construct validity (Camus, cited in Perrault et al., 2000; Sunderland et al., 1988) have been reported for the measure, but sample sizes have generally been small and little detail has been provided in some of the reports (Sunderland & Minichiello, 1996). Thus, this measure is promising, but more evidence of reliability and validity is needed before it could be highly recommended.

In addition to scales that measure depression specifically, several instruments have been developed to assess for depressive symptoms among other disturbances in persons with dementia. Although these instruments may be useful in case conceptualization and treatment planning, in most cases, psychometric information is not given specifically for the depression subscale. One exception is the Neuropsychiatric Inventory (NPI; Cummings et al., 1994), a semi-structured interview that is conducted with a knowledgeable informant. The measure includes questions to screen for presence of depressed mood, apathy, and ten other psychiatric symptoms. Each screening question is followed by a series of questions to confirm presence or absence of the symptom, along with ratings of symptom frequency and severity. Although psychometric information specific to subscales is limited, the NPI as a whole demonstrates acceptable to good reliability and good validity (Cummings et al., 1994). Employing a version developed for use in nursing homes (NPI-NH), Wood and colleagues (2000) showed that the depression and apathy subscales correlate moderately with research observations. Thus, the NPI or NPI-NH may be useful in detecting depression among individuals with dementia, but further work is needed to establish the validity of the relevant subscales specifically for this purpose.

Overall Evaluation

Formalized assessment can provide clinicians with invaluable information for case conceptualization and treatment planning when working with older adults who are demonstrating symptoms of depression; however, for measurement devices to be useful for this purpose they must be chosen based on reliability, validity, and utility in older adult populations. The preceding section examined several different types of measures commonly used in the assessment of depression in older adults, and, in terms of fulfilling the goal of case conceptualization and treatment planning, several measures stand out as being particularly useful. When using a self-report measure it is recommended that the CES-D (Radloff, 1977) be considered before any other measure, because it is well validated in older adults and it provides information across several domains of depressive symptoms. Several structured clinical interviews may also provide useful information for case conceptualization and treatment planning for older adults with depression. The GMS-DS (Ravindran et al., 1994) is a promising

structured interview, as it was developed specifically for use with older adults, preliminary data show good reliability and validity, and it requires the least time to administer, but further evaluation is needed. Although there are some promising clinician rating scales, at present it is difficult to recommend a specific measure for treatment planning and case conceptualization. Finally, when assessing depression in older adults with dementia, it would be worth considering the CSDD, as it has adequate to good reliability and good validity in this population.

Whether self-report, structured interview, or clinician rating scale is used for treatment planning and case conceptualization, it is important to keep in mind that each type of measure is subject to biases and, therefore, a multimethod approach may be the most effective way to formulate case conceptualizations and treatment plans. In particular, it is important to address other key aspects of case conceptualization within an informal clinical interview. For older adults, it is particularly important to assess general social functioning, medical health and medications, and the ability to perform activities of daily living (e.g., walking, dressing, eating, etc.) and instrumental activities of daily living (e.g., balancing a checkbook, grocery shopping, cooking, etc.; Karel et al., 2002). In addition, it may be useful to utilize a more formal measure of overall functioning. For example, the Short Form Health Survey (SF-36; Ware & Sherbourne, 1992) is a well-validated measure of several components of functioning, including physical function, role limitations, bodily pain, general health, vitality, social functioning, emotional functioning, and mental health. Finally, every evaluation of an older adult client for the purposes of case conceptualization should include some sort of evaluation of cognitive functioning, such as the Mini-Mental State Examination (Folstein, Folstein, & McHugh, 1975) or the Neurobehavioral Cognitive Status Examination (COGNISTAT; Kiernan, Mueller, Langston, & Van Dyke, 1987).

ASSESSMENT FOR TREATMENT MONITORING AND TREATMENT OUTCOME EVALUATION

Self-Report Measures

Because of their efficiency and cost effectiveness, self-report measures can be very useful for treatment monitoring and measuring treatment outcomes. Most self-report measures for depression can be administered in less than 20 minutes and several of the instruments that will be described have shorter versions that can be administered in just a few minutes. Despite the usefulness of self-report measures in terms of their inherent efficiency, there are some limitations to the use of these measures for treatment monitoring and outcome assessment. Specifically, they may be subject to internal validity problems because of carryover effects (Whitley, 2002).

There are several self-report measures that may prove useful for treatment monitoring and measuring treatment outcomes in older adults with depressive symptoms (see Table 7.3). There is some evidence that the BDI (Beck et al., 1996; see above) is a useful measure of change. As mentioned previously, the measure has fairly good test–retest reliability in older adult samples (Gallagher et al., 1982). Also, in terms of maximizing the efficiency of this measure, there is a reliable and valid short form of the BDI (Beck & Beck, 1972). Despite this evidence, it is important to keep in mind that the BDI is not highly recommended for older adults for reasons discussed earlier, including concern that scores may be inflated by the presence of physical illness (Clark et al., 1983) and response format may be confusing, especially for older adults with cognitive deficits (Jefferson et al., 2001; Zemore & Eames, 1979).

Another self-report measure that may prove useful for treatment monitoring and assessing outcomes in older adults is the CES-D (Radloff, 1977; see above). The CES-D may be a particularly advantageous self-report measure because it explicitly instructs respondents to reflect on symptoms over the last week, which may lessen testing effects. In addition, the CES-D may be a useful measure of change because it has demonstrated good test–retest reliability (Radloff, 1977). Researchers have also demonstrated that changes in CES-D scores are significantly related to changes in older patients' self-report ratings of change in their depressive symptoms (Datto, Thompson, Knott, & Katz, 2006). In terms of efficiency, there are several CES-D short forms available. For example, 8- and 10-item versions, respectively known as the Boston and the Iowa forms, have both demonstrated good reliability and validity with older adults (Kohout, Berkman, Evans, & Cornoni-Huntley, 1993). All in all, the CES-D is recommended as a good assessment instrument to use to track treatment progress and outcomes in older adults with depressive symptoms.

The GDS (Yesavage et al., 1983; see above) may also be useful for assessing treatment progress and outcomes in older adults with depression. The GDS has demonstrated good test–retest reliability (Lesher, 1986), which suggests that it may be used to track change over time and, in terms of efficiency, there is a 15-item short form that has demonstrated fairly good reliability and validity (Sheikh & Yesavage, 1986). Despite these advantages, many authors have expressed doubts about the strategy of excluding all somatic symptoms when assessing depression in older adults (Norris et al., 2004; see discussion above). In addition, the individual items on this measure are dichotomous and thus do not have very much clinical utility in terms of measuring change at the symptom level. These limitations should be taken into consideration when selecting a measure for treatment monitoring or assessment of outcomes in older adults with depression.

Structured Interviews

Unlike self-report measures, structured interviews are often time-intensive and require extensive training for administration; as such, they are generally not used for treatment monitoring. However, as noted above, administration times vary and short forms are available. In addition, structured interviews may provide useful information about treatment outcomes.

The structured interview that appears to have the most utility for the assessment of treatment outcomes is the GMS-DS (Ravindran et al., 1994; see above), which was specifically designed to assess changes in depression levels in older adults, although further evaluation is needed. It takes 15 minutes to administer to depressed older adults and has demonstrated good reliability and validity, as mentioned earlier (Ravindran et al., 1994). As a measure of treatment outcomes, the GMS-DS has excellent correlations between before and after scores (Ravindran et al., 1994). Unfortunately, there is little research examining the utility of the GMS-DS, but available evidence suggests it is a promising measure for assessing outcomes in depressed older adults.

Clinician Rating Scales

Several clinician rating scales have been evaluated for the purposes of treatment monitoring and assessment of treatment outcomes in older adults (see Table 7.3).

TABLE 7.3 Ratings of Instruments Used for Treatment Monitoring and Treatment Outcome Evaluation

Instrument	Norms	Internal Consistency	Inter-Rater Reliability	Test–Retest Reliability	Content Validity	Construct Validity	Validity Generalization	Treatment Sensitivity	Clinical Utility	Highly Recommended
Self-Report Measures										
BDI	A	G	NA	G	A	A	L	A	A	
CES-D	E	G	NA	G	A	G	G	G	A	✓
GDS	G	G	NA	G	A	A	A	L	A	
Clinician Rating Scales										
GDRS	A	E	G	U	A	U	A	G	A	
MADRS	A	A	E	U	A	A	A	G	A	
Measures to Assess Depression in Dementia										
CSDD	A	G	A	A	G	G	G	A	A	

Note: BDI = Beck Depression Inventory; CES-D = Center for Epidemiological Studies-Depression Scale; GDS = Geriatric Depression Scale; GDRS = Geriatric Depression Rating Scale; MADRS = Montgomery–Åsberg Depression Rating Scale; CSDD = Cornell Scale for Depression in Dementia; L = Less Than Acceptable; A = Adequate; G = Good; E = Excellent; U = Unavailable; NA = Not Applicable.

The HRSD (Hamilton, 1960; see above) is often touted as a good measure for both treatment monitoring and assessments of outcome, but problems have been noted (Bagby et al., 2004). Investigations using older adult samples show that the HRSD does not have good reliability in this age group and may not actually be measuring depression (Baker & Miller, 1991; Hammond, 1998; Lichtenberg et al., 1992), which makes this measure's usefulness in tracking changes in depression in older adults questionable. Also, some researchers have found that it can be time-consuming and difficult to administer to some populations of older adults (Baker & Miller, 1991), which suggests that this measure may be inconvenient to administer repeatedly. Given these concerns, the HRSD is not recommended for treatment monitoring and assessment of treatment outcome in depressed older adults.

A measure that may prove useful for treatment monitoring and outcome assessments in depressed older adults is the Geriatric Depression Rating Scale (GDRS; Jamison & Scogin, 1992; see above). The GDRS has fairly good inter-rater reliability (Jamison & Scogin, 1992), but test–retest reliability has not been assessed. It is somewhat lengthy to administer (35 minutes), so it may be more appropriate for outcome assessment than for monitoring treatment progress. Although there is not enough empirical support for the GDRS (particularly as a measure of change) to recommend its use at this time, it appears to be promising as an outcome measure.

The MADRS (Montgomery & Åsberg, 1979) was specifically designed to be sensitive to change with treatment. However, is has only fair internal consistency in older adult samples (Bent-Hansen et al., 2003), and thus may not be stable enough to assess change reliably. On the positive side, the measure has very good inter-rater reliability (Zimmerman et al., 2004) and fairly good efficiency (Mottram et al., 2000) when used with older adults. Finally, the measure has been shown to differentiate significantly between placebo and maintenance phase of treatment in older adults (Bent-Hansen et al., 2003). Despite these promising findings, the problems with this measure's reliability and the relative dearth of research examining this measure in older adults suggest that it cannot be recommended for the assessment of progress and outcomes in the treatment of older adults with depression until more research evaluating the MADRS is conducted.

The IDS (Rush et al., 1986; see above) may prove useful for measuring treatment progress and outcomes although it has not yet been empirically examined in older adults. In particular, the measure's fairly good internal consistency (Rush et al., 1996) suggests that it is stable enough to be used as a repeat measure. However, the IDS has not been assessed for test–retest reliability, which is problematic in terms of its use as a measure for treatment monitoring. Despite the promising evidence from research in mixed-age samples, the IDS cannot be recommended for use with older adults until it its properties are evaluated in this population.

Measures to Assess Depression in Dementia

The CSDD (Alexopoulos et al., 1988; see above) may be useful for monitoring the outcome of depression treatment in individuals who have dementia. This rating scale has adequate to good reliability and good validity, as described above, and ability to detect treatment effects has been demonstrated (Mayer et al., 2006). As Perrault and colleagues (2000) caution, however, most evidence for the reliability and validity of this measure comes from inpatient samples and it may not be generalizable to community-dwelling individuals with dementia. The DMAS (Sunderland et al., 1988; see above) has adequate reliability and validity, but test–retest reliability and sensitivity to change have not yet been demonstrated. Consequently, the use of this scale for outcome monitoring is not recommended until further research is conducted.

Overall Evaluation

Given measurement considerations described previously in this section, several measures stand out as potentially useful for treatment monitoring and assessment of treatment outcomes in older adults with depression. Among self-report measures, the CES-D (Radloff, 1977) may be the most useful assessment tool for this purpose. For structured interviews, the GMS-DS (Ravindran et al., 1994) is the most promising assessment tool, but it is not yet supported by sufficient research. In terms of clinician rating scales, several scales appear promising for treatment monitoring and evaluation, but more research is needed before any can be recommended. The CSDD provides a reliable and valid measure of change in depression severity among individuals with dementia. In general, it is important to keep in mind that each type of instrument is vulnerable to testing effects and other threats to internal validity if administered repeatedly. Thus, it would be important to attain data from multiple measures when making decisions about how effective treatment was for a particular client.

CONCLUSIONS AND FUTURE DIRECTIONS

Our examination of the assessment of depression in late life leads to several conclusions. First, assessing depression in older adults poses unique challenges to clinicians. Many older adults suffer from physical illnesses that result in symptoms similar to somatic symptoms of depression. Given this fact, differential diagnosis of depression in this population can be difficult. Failure to account for this difficulty may result in over-identification of depression in this age group. Eliminating somatic symptoms from measures of depression seems less than ideal because somatic symptoms are often prominent in late life depression. It appears that the best solution at this time is to incorporate information from different types of measures.

Another challenge posed when assessing late life depression centers on differentially diagnosing depression and dementia. Cognitive symptoms of depression are prominent in late life, and it can often be difficult to determine if these symptoms are truly reflecting depression or if the patient is experiencing cognitive decline. Again, measures often fail to take this difficulty into account. In addition, some measures of depression can present real difficulties for older adults experiencing mild cognitive decline due to the complexity of their format. This difficulty may limit the validity of such measures in older adults.

A further challenge is that older adults often display symptoms of depression that differ from those presented by younger and middle aged adults; thus measures of depression need to be validated and normed with older adults specifically before they can be considered valid in this population. Unfortunately, this research step has not yet been taken for many measures.

Similarly, different subgroups should be considered when measuring depression in older adults. Although many instruments originally developed for younger adults have demonstrated validity in healthy older adults, it may be imprudent to utilize these same instruments with individuals with either physical illness or cognitive impairment. Before using any measure of depression with an older adult, it is essential to get information about medical illnesses and cognitive functioning and use measures validated specifically with these populations.

A final conclusion that may be drawn from this chapter is the need for more research examining assessment of depression in older adults. Most instruments assessing depression need to be more thoroughly evaluated for their utility with older adult clients. Some instruments that have been designed specifically for this population appear particularly promising, yet they too require further validation. It may be useful, given the challenges of assessing depression in older adulthood, to develop additional measures specifically to assess depression in older adults for the purposes of diagnosis, case conceptualization, treatment planning, treatment monitoring, and the assessment of treatment outcomes. An area that particularly remains to be addressed is the empirical examination of clinical utility. Despite the challenges of assessing depression in older adults, a number of instruments have been developed that show good reliability and validity—it now remains to be established whether their use will improve clinical outcomes.

References

Alexopoulos, G. S., Abrams, R. C., Young, R. C., & Shamoian, C. A. (1988). Cornell scale for depression in dementia. *Biological Psychiatry, 23,* 271–284.

Alexopoulos, G. S., Meyers, B. S., Young, R. C., Campbell, S., Silbersweig, D., & Charlson, M. (1997). "Vascular depression" hypothesis. *Archives of General Psychiatry, 54,* 915–922.

Alexopoulos, G. S., Meyers, B. S., Young, R. C., Kalayam, B., Kakuma, T., Gabrielle, M., et al. (2000). Executive dysfunction and long-term outcomes of geriatric depression. *Archives of General Psychiatry, 57,* 285–290.

Allen-Burge, R., Storandt, M., Kinscherf, D. A., & Rubin, E. H. (1994). Sex differences in the sensitivity of two self-report depression scales in older depressed inpatients. *Psychology and Aging, 9,* 443–445.

American Psychiatric Association. (1987). *Diagnostic and statistical manual for mental disorders* (3rd ed., Rev.). Washington, DC: Author.

American Psychiatric Association. (1994). *Diagnostic and statistical manual for mental disorders* (4th ed.). Washington, DC: Author.

American Psychiatric Association. (2000). *Diagnostic and statistical manual for mental disorders* (4th ed., Text Revision). Washington, DC: Author.

Ames, D., Flynn, E., Tuckwell, V., & Harrigan, S. (1994). Diagnosis of psychiatric disorder in elderly general and geriatric hospital patients: AGECAT and DSM-III-R compared. *International Journal of Geriatric Psychiatry, 9,* 627–633.

Arnau, R. C., Meagher, M. W., Norris, M. P., & Bramson, R. (2001). Psychometric evaluation of the Beck Depression Inventory-II with primary care medical patients. *Health Psychology, 20,* 112–119.

Bagby, R. M., Ryder, A. G., Schuller, D. R., & Marshall, M. B. (2004). The Hamilton Depression Rating Scale: Has the gold standard become a lead weight? *American Journal of Psychiatry, 161,* 2163–2177.

Baker, F. M., & Miller, C. L. (1991). Screening a skilled nursing home population for depression. *Journal of Geriatric Psychiatry and Neurology, 4,* 218–221.

Baldwin, R. C., & Tomenson, B. (1995). Depression in later life: A comparison of symptoms and risk factors in early and late onset cases. *British Journal of Psychiatry, 167,* 649–652.

Beck, A. T., & Beck, R. W. (1972). Screening depressed patients in family practice. *Postgraduate Medicine, 52,* 81–85.

Beck, A. T., Steer, R. A., & Brown, G. K. (1996). Comparison of Beck depression inventories- IA and -II in psychiatric outpatients. *Journal of Personality Assessment, 67,* 588–597.

Beck, A. T., Ward, C. H., Mendelson, M., Mock, J., & Erbaugh, J. (1961). An inventory for measuring depression. *Archives of General Psychiatry, 4,* 53–63.

Bent-Hansen, J., Lunde, M., Klysner, R., Andersen, M., Tanghøj, P., Solstad, K., et al. (2003). The validity of the depression rating scales in discriminating between Citalopram and placebo in depression recurrence in the maintenance therapy of elderly unipolar patients with major depression. *Pharmacopsychiatry, 36,* 313–316.

Blazer, D., Bachar, J. R., & Hughes, D. C. (1987). Major depression with melancholia: A comparison of middle-aged and elderly adults. *Journal of the American Geriatrics Society, 35,* 927–932.

Blumenthal, M. D. (1980). Depressive illness in old age: Getting behind the mask. *Geriatrics, 35,* 34–43.

Brodaty, H., Luscombe, G., Parker, G., Wilhelm, K., Hickie, I., Austin, M.-P., et al. (1997). Increased rate of psychosis and psychomotor change in depression with age. *Psychological Medicine, 27,* 1205–1213.

Brodaty, H., Peters, K., Boyce, P., Hickie, I., Parker, G., Mitchell, P., et al. (1991). Age and depression. *Journal of Affective Disorders, 23,* 137–149.

Chopra, H. P., Zubritsky, C., & Knott, K. (2005). Importance of subsyndromal symptoms of depression in elderly patients. *American Journal of Geriatric Psychiatry, 13,* 597–606.

Christensen, H., Jorm, A. F., MacKinnon, A. J., Korten, A. E., Jacomb, P. A., Henderson, A. S., et al. (1999). Age differences in depression and anxiety symptoms: A structural equation modelling analysis of data from a general population sample. *Psychological Medicine, 29,* 325–339.

Clark, D. C., Cavanaugh, S. V., & Gibbons, R. D. (1983). The core symptoms of depression in medical and psychiatric patients. *Journal of Nervous and Mental Disease, 17,* 705–713.

Cole, J. C., Motivala, S. J., Dang, J., Lucko, A., Lang, N., Levin, M. J., et al. (2004). Structural validation of the Hamilton Depression Rating Scale. *Journal of Psychopathology and Behavioral Assessment, 26,* 241–254.

Copeland, J. R. M., Dewey, M. E., & Griffiths-Jones, H. M. (1990). Dementia and depression in elderly persons: AGECAT compared with DSM III and pervasive illness. *International Journal of Geriatric Psychiatry, 5,* 47–51.

Copeland, J. R. M., Dewey, M. E., Henderson, A. S., Kay, D. W. K., Neal, C. D., Harrison, M. A. M., et al. (1988). The Geriatric Mental State (GMS) used in the community: Replication studies of the computerized diagnosis AGECAT. *Psychological Medicine, 18,* 219–223.

Copeland, J. R. M., Kelleher, M. J., Kellett, J. M., Gourlay, A. J., Gurland, B. J., Fleiss, J. L., et al. (1976). A semi-structured clinical interview for the assessment of diagnosis and mental state in the elderly: The Geriatric Mental State Schedule: I. Development and reliability. *Psychological Medicine, 6,* 439–449.

Cummings, J. L., Mega, M., Gray, K., Rosenberg-Thompson, S., Carusi, D. A., Gornbein, J. (1994). The Neuropsychiatric Inventory: Comprehensive assessment of psychopathology in dementia. *Neurology, 44,* 2308–2314.

Datto, C. J., Thompson, R., Knott, K., & Katz, I. R. (2006). Older adult report of change in depressive symptoms as a treatment decision tool. *Journal of the American Geriatrics Society, 54,* 627–631.

Depp, C. A., & Jeste, D. V. (2004). Bipolar disorder in older adults: A critical review. *Bipolar Disorders, 6,* 343–367.

Dozois, D. J. A., & Dobson, K. S. (2002). Depression. In M. M. Antony & D. H. Barlow (Eds.), *Handbook of assessment and treatment planning for psychological disorders* (pp. 259–299). New York: Guilford.

Dunn, V. K., & Sacco, W. P. (1989). Psychometric evaluation of the Geriatric Depression Scale and the Zung Self-rating Scale using an elderly community sample. *Psychology and Aging, 4*, 125–126.

Eaton, W. W., Muntaner, C., Smith, C., Tien, A., & Ybarra, M. (2004). Center for Epidemiologic Studies Depression Scale: Review and revision (CESD and CESDR). In M. E. Maruish (Ed.), *The use of psychological testing for treatment planning and outcome assessments: Vol. 3: Instruments for adults* (pp. 363–377). Mahwah, NJ: Lawrence Erlbaum Associates.

Endicott, J., & Spitzer, R. L., (1978). A diagnostic interview. The schedule for affective disorders and schizophrenia. *Archives of General Psychiatry, 35*, 837–844.

First, M. B., Spitzer, R. L., Gibbon, M., & Williams, J. B. W. (1997). *User's guide for the structured clinical interview for DSM-IV Axis I disorders—clinician version (SCID-CV)*. Washington, DC: American Psychiatric Press.

Fischer, L. R., Rolnick, S. J., Jackson, J., Garrard, J., & Luepke, L. (1996). The Geriatric Depression Scale: A content analysis of respondent comments. *Journal of Mental Health and Aging, 2*, 125–135.

Folstein, M. F., Folstein, S. E., & McHugh, P. R. (1975). Mini-mental state: A practical method for grading the cognitive state of patients for the clinician. *Journal of Psychiatric Research, 12*, 189–198.

Frasure-Smith, N., Lesperance, F., & Talajic, M. (1993). Depression following myocardial infarction: Impact on 6-month survival. *Journal of the American Medical Association, 270*, 1819–1825.

Gallagher, D., Breckenridge, J. N., Steinmetz, J., & Thompson, L. W. (1983). The Beck Depression Inventory and research diagnostic criteria: Congruence in an older population. *Journal of Consulting and Clinical Psychology, 51*, 945–946.

Gallagher, D., Nies, G., & Thompson, L. W. (1982). Reliability of the Beck Depression Inventory in older adults. *Journal of Consulting and Clinical Psychology, 50*, 152–153.

Gallo, J. J., Anthony, J. C., & Muthén, B. O. (1994). Age differences in the symptoms of depression: A latent trait analysis. *Journal of Gerontology: Psychological Sciences, 49*, P251–P264.

Gallo, J. J., Rabins, P. V., & Anthony, J. C. (1999). Sadness in older persons: 13-year follow-up of a community sample in Baltimore, Maryland. *Psychological Medicine, 29*, 341–350.

Gatz, M., Johansson, B., Pederson, N., Berg, S., & Reynolds, C. (1993). A cross-national self-report measure of depressive symptomatology. *International Psychogeriatrics, 5*, 147–156.

Gatz, M., Pedersen, N. L., Plomin, R., Nesselroade, J. R., & McClearn, G. E. (1992). Importance of shared genes and shared environments for symptoms of depression in older adults. *Journal of Abnormal Psychology, 101*, 701–708.

Golden, R. R., Teresi, J. A., & Gurland, B. J. (1984). Development of indicator scales for the Comprehensive Assessment and Referral Evaluation (CARE) interview schedule. *Journal of Gerontology, 2*, 138–146.

Grayson, D. A., MacKinnon, A., Jorm, A. F., Creasey, H., & Broe, G. A. (2000). Item bias in the center for epidemiologic studies depression scale: Effects of physical disorders and disability in an elderly community sample. *Journal of Gerontology, 55B*, 273–282.

Gurland, B. J., & Wilder, D. E. (1984). The CARE interview revisited: Development of an efficient, systematic clinical assessment. *Journal of Gerontology, 39*, 129–137.

Gurland, B. J., Golden, R. R., Teresi, J. A., & Challop, J. (1984). The SHORT-CARE: An efficient instrument for the assessment of depression, dementia and disability. *Journal of Gerontology, 39*, 166–169.

Gurland, B., Kuriansky, J., Sharpe, L., Simon, R., Stiller, P., & Birkett, P. (1977–1978). The Comprehensive Assessment and Referral Evaluation (CARE): Rationale, development and reliability. *International Journal of Aging & Human Development, 8*, 9–42.

Hamilton, M. (1960). A rating scale for depression. *Journal of Neurology, Neurosurgery, and Psychiatry, 23*, 56–62.

Hamilton, M. (1967). Development of a rating scale for primary depressive illness. *British Journal of Social and Clinical Psychology, 6*, 278–296.

Hammond, M. F. (1998). Rating depression severity in the elderly physically ill patient: Reliability and factor structure of the Hamilton and the Montgomery–Åsberg Depression Rating Scales. *International Journal of Geriatric Psychiatry, 13*, 257–261.

Heun, R., Müller, H., Freyberger, H. J., & Maier, W. (1998). Reliability of interview information in a family study in the elderly. *Social Psychiatry and Psychiatric Epidemiology, 33*, 140–144.

Hinrichsen, G. A., & Emery, E. E. (2005). Interpersonal factors and late-life depression. *Clinical Psychology: Science & Practice, 12*, 264–275.

Hoyert, D. L., Heron, M. P., Murphy, S. L., & Kung, H.-C. (2006). Deaths: Final data for 2003. *National Vital Statistics Report, 54*(13). Hyattsville, MD: National Center for Health Statistics.

Jamison, C., & Scogin, F. (1992). Development of an interview-based Geriatric Depression Rating Scale. *International Journal of Aging and Human Development, 35*, 193–204.

Janssen, J., Beekman, A. T. F., Comijs, H. C., Deeg, D. J. H., & Heeren, T. J. (2006). Late-life depression: The differences between early- and late-onset illness in a community-based sample. *International Journal of Geriatric Psychiatry, 21,* 86–93.

Jefferson, A., L., Powers, D. V., & Pope, M. (2001). Beck Depression Inventory-II (BDI-II) and the Geriatric Depression Scale (GDS) in older women. *Clinical Gerontologist, 22,* 3–12.

Karel, M. J., Ogland-Hand, S., & Gatz, M. (2002). *Assessing and treating late life depression.* New York: Basic Books.

Kessler, R., & Mroczek, D. (1993). *UM-CIDI short-form* [Memo]. Ann Arbor, MI: University of Michigan.

Kiernan, R. J., Mueller, J., Langston, J. W., & Van Dyke, C. (1987). The neurobehavioral cognitive status examination: A brief but quantitative approach to cognitive assessment. *Annals of Internal Medicine, 107,* 481–485.

Kohout, F. J., Berkman, L. F., Evans, D. A., & Cornoni-Huntley, J. (1993). Two shorter forms of the CES-D Depression Symptoms Index. *Journal of Aging and Health, 5,* 179–193.

Kraaij, V., Arensman, E., & Spinhoven, P. (2002). Negative life events and depression in elderly persons: A meta-analysis. *Journal of Gerontology: Psychological Sciences, 57B,* 87–94.

Kumar, A., Lavretsky, H., & Elderkin-Thompson, V. (2004). Nonmajor clinically significant depression in the elderly. In S. P. Roose & H. A. Sackeim (Eds.), *Late-life depression* (pp. 64–80). New York: Oxford.

Latham, A. E., & Prigerson, H. G. (2004). Suicidality and bereavement: Complicated grief as a psychiatric disorder presenting greatest risk for suicidality. *Suicide and Life-Threatening Behavior, 34,* 350–362.

Lesher, E. L. (1986). Validation of the geriatric depression scale among nursing home residents. *Clinical Gerontologist, 4,* 21–28.

Lichtenberg, P. A., Marcopulos, B. A., Steiner, D. A., & Tabscott, J. A. (1992). Comparison of the Hamilton Depression Rating Scale and the Geriatric Depression Scale: Detection of depression in dementia patients. *Psychological Reports, 70,* 515–521.

Mack, J. L., & Patterson, M. B. (1994). The evaluation of behavioral disturbances in Alzheimer's disease: The utility of three rating scales. *Journal of Geriatric Psychiatry and Neurology, 7,* 99–115.

Maixner, S. M., Burke, W. J., Roccaforte, W. H., Wengel, S. P., & Potter, J. F. (1995). A comparison of two depression scales in a geriatric assessment clinic. *American Journal of Geriatric Psychiatry, 3,* 60–67.

Mayer, L. S., Bay, R. C., Politis, A., Steinberg, M., Steele, C., Baker, A. S., et al. (2006). Comparison of three rating scales as outcome measures for treatment trials of depression in Alzheimer disease: Findings from DIADS. *International Journal of Geriatric Psychiatry, 21,* 930–936.

Meeks, S. (2004). Further evaluation of the MDS Depression Scale versus the Geriatric Depression Scale among nursing home residents. *Journal of Mental Health and Aging, 10,* 325–335.

Moberg, P. J., Lazarus, L. W., Mesholam, R. I., Bilker, W., Chuy, I. L., Neyman, I., et al. (2001). Comparison of the standard and structured interview guide for the Hamilton Depression Rating Scale in depressed geriatric inpatients. *American Journal of Geriatric Psychiatry, 9,* 35–40.

Montgomery, S., & Åsberg, M. (1979). A new depression scale designed to be sensitive to change. *British Journal of Psychiatry, 134,* 382–389.

Mottram, P., Wilson, K., & Copeland, J. (2000). Validation of the Hamilton Depression Rating Scale and Montgomery and Åsberg Rating Scales in terms of AGECAT depression cases. *International Journal of Geriatric Psychiatry, 15,* 1113–1119.

Mueller, T. I., Kohn, R., Leventhal, N., Leon, A. C., Solomon, D., Coryell, W., et al. (2004). The course of depression in elderly patients. *American Journal of Geriatric Psychiatry, 12,* 22–29.

Myers, J. K., & Weissman, N. M. (1980). Use of a self-report symptom scale to detect depression in a community sample. *American Journal of Psychiatry, 137,* 1081–1084.

Newman, J. P. (1989). Aging and depression. *Psychology and Aging, 4,* 150–165.

Newman, S. C., Sheldon, C. T., & Bland, R. C. (1998). Prevalence of depression in an elderly community sample: A comparison of GMS-AGECAT and DSM-IV diagnostic criteria. *Psychological Medicine, 28,* 1339–1345.

Nguyen, H. T., & Zonderman, A. B. (2006). Relationship between age and aspects of depression: Consistency and reliability across two longitudinal studies. *Psychology and Aging, 21,* 119–126.

Nock, M. (2007). Self-injurious behavior. In J. D. Hunsley & E. J. Mash (Eds.), *A guide to assessments that work* (pp. 158–177). New York: Oxford University Press.

Norris, M. P., Arnau, R. C., Bramson, R., & Meagher, M. W. (2004). The efficacy of somatic symptoms in assessing depression in older primary care patients. *Clinical Gerontologist, 27,* 43–57.

Olin, J. T., Schneider, L. S., Eaton, E. M., Zemansky, M. F., & Pollock, V. E. (1992). The Geriatric Depression Scale and the Beck Depression Inventory as screening instruments in an older adult outpatient population. *Psychological Assessment, 4,* 190–192.

Onega, L. L., & Abraham, I. L. (1997). Factor structure of the dementia mood assessment scale in a cohort of community-dwelling elderly. *International Psychogeriatrics, 9*, 449–457.

Onishi, J., Suzuki, Y., & Umegaki, H. (2006). A comparison of depressive mood of older adults in a community, nursing home, and a geriatric hospital: Factor analysis of Geriatric Depression Scale. *Journal of Geriatric Psychiatry and Neurology, 19*, 26–31.

Ownby, R. L., Harwood, D. G., Acevedo, A., Barker, W., & Duara, R. (2001). Factor structure of the Cornell Scale for Depression in Dementia for Anglo and Hispanic patients with dementia. *American Journal of Geriatric Psychiatry, 9*, 217–224.

Perrault, A., Oremus, M., Demers, L., Vida, S., & Wolfson, C. (2000). Review of outcome measurement instruments in Alzheimer's disease drug trials: Psychometric properties of behavior and mood scales. *Journal of Geriatric Psychiatry and Neurology, 13*, 181–196.

Prince, M., Acosta, D., Chiu, H., Copeland, J., Dewey, M., Scazufca, M., et al. (2004). Effects of education and culture on the validity of the geriatric mental state and its AGECAT algorithm. *British Journal of Psychiatry, 185*, 429–436.

Radloff, L. S. (1977). The CES-D scale: A self-report depression scale for research in the general population. *Applied Psychological Measurement, 1*, 385–401.

Rapp, M. A., Dahlman, K., Sano, M., Grossman, H. T., Haroutunian, V., & Gorman, J. M. (2005). Neuropsychological differences between late-onset and recurrent geriatric major depression. *American Journal of Psychiatry, 162*, 691–698.

Rapp, S. R., Parisi, S. A., Walsh, D. A., & Wallace, C. E. (1988). Detecting depression in elderly medical inpatients. *Journal of Consulting and Clinical Psychology, 56*, 509–513.

Rapp, S. R., Smith, S. S., & Britt, M. (1990). Identifying comorbid depression in elderly medical patients: Use of the Extracted Hamilton Depression Rating Scale. *Psychological Assessment, 2*, 243–247.

Ravindran, A. V., Welburn, K., & Copeland, J. R. M. (1994). Semi-structured depression scale sensitive to change with treatment for use in the elderly. *British Journal of Psychiatry, 164*, 522–527.

Robins, L. N., Helzer, J. E., Croughan, J., & Ratcliff, K. S. (1981). National Institute of Mental Health Diagnostic Interview Schedule: Its history, characteristics, and validity. *Archives of General Psychiatry, 38*, 381–389.

Robins, L. N., Wing, J., Wittchen, H. U., Helzer, J. E., Babor, T. F., Burke, J., et al. (1988). The Composite International Diagnostic Interview. An epidemiological instrument suitable for use in conjunction with different diagnostic systems and in different cultures. *Archives of General Psychiatry, 45*, 1069–1077.

Rush, A. J., Giles, D. E., Schlesser, M. A., Fulton, C. L., Weissenburger, J. E., & Burns, C. T. (1986). The Inventory for Depressive Symptomatology (IDS): Preliminary findings. *Psychiatry Research, 18*, 65–87.

Rush, A. J., Gullion, C. M., Basco, M. R., Jarrett, R. B., & Trivedi, M. H. (1996). The Inventory of Depressive Symptomatology (IDS): Psychometric properties. *Psychological Medicine, 26*, 477–486.

Schafer, A. B. (2006). Meta-analysis of the factor structures of four depression questionnaires: Beck, CES-D, Hamilton, & Zung. *Journal of Clinical Psychology, 62*, 123–146.

Schoepflin Sanders, M. L., Lyness, J. M., Eberly, S., King, D. A., & Caine, E. D. (2006). Cerebrovascular risk factors, executive dysfunction, and depression in older primary care patients. *American Journal of Geriatric Psychiatry, 14*, 145–152.

Schulz, R., & Martire, L. M. (2004). Family caregiving of persons with dementia: Prevalence, health effects, and support strategies. *American Journal of Geriatric Psychiatry, 12*, 240–249.

Segal, D. L., Kabacoff, R. I., Hersen, M., Van Hasselt, V. B., & Ryan, C. F. (1995). Update on the reliability of diagnosis in older psychiatric outpatients using the Structured Clinical Interview for DSM IIIR. *Journal of Clinical Geropsychology, 1*, 313–321.

Sheikh, J. I., & Yesavage, J. A. (1986). Geriatric Depression Scale (GDS): Recent evidence and development of a shorter version. *Clinical Gerontologist, 5*, 165–173.

Snow, A. L., Kunik, M. E., Molinari, V. A., Orengo, C. A., Doody, R., Graham, D. P., et al. (2005). Accuracy of self-reported depression in persons with dementia. *Journal of the American Geriatrics Society, 53*, 389–396.

Spitzer, R. L., Endicott, J., & Robins, E. (1978). Research Diagnostic Criteria: Rationale and reliability. *Archives of General Psychiatry, 35*, 773–782.

Steingart, A., & Herrmann, N. (1991). Major depressive disorder in the elderly: The relationship between age of onset and cognitive impairment. *International Journal of Geriatric Psychiatry, 6*, 593–598.

Stukenberg, K. W., Dura, J. R., & Kiecolt-Glaser, J. K. (1990). Depression screening scale validation in an elderly, community-dwelling population. *Psychological Assessment, 2*, 134–138.

Sunderland, T., & Minichiello, M. (1996). Dementia Mood Assessment Scale. *International Psychogeriatrics, 8* (Suppl. 3), 329–331.

Sunderland, T., Alterman, I. S., Yount, D., Hill, J. L., Teriot, P. N., Newhouse, P. A., et al. (1988). A new scale for the assessment of depressed mood in demented patients. *American Journal of Psychiatry, 148*, 955–959.

Tuma, T. A. (2000). Outcome of hospital-treated depression at 4.5 years: An elderly and a younger adult cohort compared. *The British Journal of Psychiatry, 176*, 224–228.

Tunstall, N., Prince, M., & Mann, A. (1997). Concurrent validity of a telephone administered version of the Gospel Oak instrument (including the SHORT-CARE). *International Journal of Geriatric Psychiatry, 12*, 1035–1038.

Turvey, C. L., Wallace, R. B., & Herzog, R. (1999). A revised CES-D measure of depressive symptoms and a DSM-based measure of major depressive episodes in the elderly. *International Psychogeriatrics, 11*, 139–148.

Vilalta-Franch, J., Garre-Olmo, J., Lopez-Pousa, S., Turon-Estrada, A., Lozano-Gattego, M., Hernandez-Ferrandiz, M., et al. (2006). Comparison of different clinical diagnostic criteria for depression in Alzheimer disease. *American Journal of Geriatric Psychiatry, 14*, 589–597.

Ware, J. E., & Sherbourne, C. D. (1992). The MOS 36-item Short-Form Health Survey (SF-36): I. Conceptual framework and item selection. *Medical Care, 30*, 473–483.

Watson, L. C., & Pignone, M. P. (2003). Screening accuracy for late-life depression in primary care: A systematic review. *The Journal of Family Practice, 52*, 956–964.

Whitley, B. E. (2002). *Principles of research in behavioral science.* Boston: McGraw Hill.

Williams, J. B. W. (1988). A structured interview guide for the Hamilton Depression Rating Scale. *Archives of General Psychiatry, 45*, 742–747.

Williams, J. B. W. (2001). Standardizing the Hamilton Depression Rating Scale: Past, present, and future. *European Archives of Psychiatry and Clinical Neuroscience, 251* (Suppl. 2), 6–12.

Williamson, G. M., Shaffer, D. R., & Parmelee, P. A. (Eds.). (2000). *Physical illness and depression in older adults: A handbook of theory, research, and practice.* New York: Kluwer Academic/Plenum.

Wing, J. K., Birley, J. L. T., Cooper, J. E., Graham, P., & Isaacs, A. D. (1967). Reliability of procedure for measuring and classifying "Present Psychiatric State." *British Journal of Psychiatry, 113*, 499–515.

Wood, S., Cummings, J. L., Hsu, M.-A., Barclay, R., Wheatley, M. V., Yarema, K. T., et al. (2000). The use of the neuropsychiatric inventory in nursing home residents. *American Journal of Geriatric Psychiatry, 8*, 75–83.

World Health Organization. (1992). *International statistical classification of diseases* (10th rev.). Geneva, Switzerland: Author.

Yesavage, J. A., Brink, T. L., Rose, T. L., Lum, O., Huang, V., Ade, M., et al. (1983). Development and validation of a geriatric screening scale: A preliminary report. *Journal of Psychiatric Research, 17*, 37–49.

Zeiss, A. M., Lewinsohn, P. M., & Rohde, P. (1996). Functional impairment, physical disease, and depression in older adults. In P. M. Kato & T. Mann (Eds.), *Handbook of diversity issues in health psychology* (pp. 161–184). New York: Plenum.

Zemore, R., & Eames, N. (1979). Psychic and somatic symptoms of depression among young adults, institutionalized aged and noninstitutionalized aged. *Journal of Gerontology, 34*, 716–722.

Zimmerman, M., Posternak, M. A., & Chelminski, I. (2004). Derivation of a definition of remission on the Montgomery–Åsberg Depression Rating Scale corresponding to the definition of remission on the Hamilton Rating Scale for depression. *Journal of Psychiatric Research, 38*, 577–582.

Zisook, S., & Shuchter, S. R. (1993). Major depression associated with widowhood. *American Journal of Geriatric Psychiatry, 1*, 316–326.

Zung, W. W. K. (1965). A self-rating depression scale. *Archives of General Psychiatry, 12*, 63–70.

8

Self-Injurious Thoughts and Behaviors

Matthew K. Nock
Michelle M. Wedig
Irene Belle Janis
Tara L. Deliberto

Self-injurious thoughts and behaviors (SITB) are an enormous public health problem around the world. Suicide, the most extreme manifestation of this problem, is a leading cause of death, and nonlethal SITB are common and have a lifetime prevalence of 2% to 15% in the general population (e.g., Kessler, Borges, & Walters, 1999; Nock, Borges, et al., 2007). The majority of those who experience SITB seek treatment (Kessler, Berglund, Borges, Nock, & Wang, 2005). Recent surveys of mental health professionals indicate that 97% of clinical psychologists encounter at least one patient with suicidal thoughts or behaviors by the time they leave graduate school, and 25% of psychologists and 50% of psychiatrists have a patient actually die by suicide during their career (Kleespies & Dettmer, 2000b). The prevalence and dangerousness of SITB, combined with the frequency with which mental health professionals are called upon to provide assessment of such conditions, highlight the importance of using an evidence-based approach to assessment when working with SITB.

The purpose of this chapter is to provide basic information about assessing SITB directly, and to describe the current evidence for measures designed specifically to assess SITB. Comprehensive guidelines for assessing suicide risk—the likelihood of a suicide attempt or suicide death in a particular person at a particular point in time—have been outlined in greater detail elsewhere (AACAP, 2001; APA, 2003; Jacobs, 1999), as have practical recommendations for conducting such

risk assessments in the context of a clinical interview and for the ongoing management of potential suicidal patients (Bryan & Rudd, 2006; Joiner, Walker, Rudd, & Jobes, 1999; Kleespies & Dettmer, 2000a). Given both the likelihood that clinicians and clinical researchers will encounter potentially self-injurious individuals and the limited training in the assessment of SITB currently provided in most training programs (Kleespies et al., 2000), the reader is strongly encouraged to consult these sources on suicide assessment. Each of these sources suggests that clinicians and researchers directly assess the presence and severity of SITB using measures with strong empirical support. This chapter provides detailed information on the evidentiary basis for the various instruments available to assess SITB.

The National Institute of Mental Health recently commissioned two thorough reviews of measures for assessing suicidal behaviors and risk among adults (G. K. Brown, 2000) as well as children and adolescents (Goldston, 2000). The current chapter extends this earlier work by (a) reviewing the evidence for a broader range of SITB, including nonsuicidal self-injury (NSSI); (b) updating the evidentiary base for some of the most promising measures; (c) providing concise and accessible information about the relative strengths and weaknesses of each measure reviewed; and (d) making recommendations about preferred measures for specific assessment purposes based on current evidence. Our goals were to be comprehensive in our coverage but succinct in our presentation,

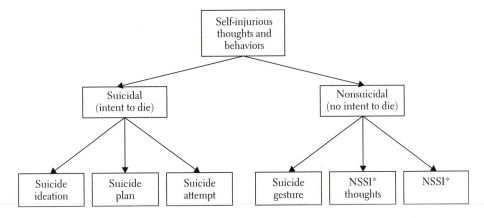

FIGURE 8.1 Classification of self-injurious thoughts and behaviors (SITB). * NSSI = Nonsuicidal self-injury.

and to provide a useful guide for those seeking an evidence-based approach to the assessment of SITB.

We begin with a brief discussion of key issues in the assessment of SITB, including the importance of clear and accurate classification of SITB and the consideration of the prevalence and conditional probabilities of these behaviors. We then provide a review of measures for (a) identifying the presence of SITB, (b) case conceptualization and treatment planning, and (c) treatment monitoring and outcome evaluation. We include measures appropriate for different populations (i.e., adults, children/adolescents), using different formats (e.g., semistructured interviews, structured interviews, self-report scales), and note the extent to which each measure is appropriate for assessing suicide ideation, suicide attempt, and NSSI. We also note the relevant contextual factors on which the evidence is based, and we end with recommendations for clinical and scientific work on the evidence-based assessment of SITB.

NATURE OF SITB

Classification

SITB refer to a broad class of thoughts and behaviors in which a person's primary purpose is direct and deliberate self-injury. One of the biggest problems in the assessment of SITB in both clinical and research contexts is that vague and inconsistent terms and definitions often are used to refer to different forms of SITB. For instance, people commonly refer to "suicidal behaviors" or "suicidality" without specifying whether they

are referring to thoughts, behaviors, or both. Similarly, vague terms such as "deliberate self-harm" have been used to refer to both NSSI (e.g., cutting, burning) and suicidal self-injury (e.g., suicide attempts). The vagueness and inconsistency in the terms and definitions used can introduce problems with reliability and validity, both within and between research and clinical contexts. As such, specific terms and definitions for different forms of SITB have been proposed (Beck et al., 1973; O'Carroll et al., 1996) and subsequent research has supported the distinctions between these different constructs, as they have different base rates and correlates (Kessler et al., 2005; Nock & Kazdin, 2002; Nock & Kessler, 2006), as well as different responsiveness to treatment (G. K. Brown et al., 2005; Linehan, Armstrong, Suarez, Allmon, & Heard, 1991).

A guide for classifying SITB is presented in Figure 8.1. Any assessment of SITB should attend to these distinctions and provide clear information about which type of SITB is present. The first major distinction that should be made is between *suicidal self-injury*, in which the person has some intent to die from their behavior, and *nonsuicidal self-injury* (NSSI), in which there is no intent to die. Suicidal self-injury is typically the higher risk behavior, as death is more likely a direct result of the behavior and those who self-injure with intent to die also are more likely to subsequently die by suicide (Harriss, Hawton, & Zahl, 2005; Hjelmeland, 1996).

Suicidal self-injury can be classified more specifically into three categories: *suicide ideation*, which refers to thoughts of engaging in behavior intended to end one's own life (typically distinguished from passive thoughts of death or dying); *suicide plan*, which refers to the formulation of a specific method through which one intends to die and may include preparation of such methods; and *suicide attempt*, which refers to engagement in potentially self-injurious behavior in which there is at least some intent to die. Clinicians are encouraged to assess intent to die among those who report making a "suicide attempt," as prior work has shown that many who report "suicide attempts" indicate that they actually had no intent to die from their behavior (Nock & Kessler, 2006). *Suicide gesture* is a term used to describe self-injury in which a person has no intent to die but wishes to give the appearance of intending to kill oneself for some purpose, such as to gain attention or communicate with others (see Nock & Kessler, 2006; O'Carroll et al., 1996). As such, they are classified as a form of nonsuicidal SITB, which is a spectrum that also includes categories of NSSI thoughts and actual NSSI.

Prevalence and Conditional Probabilities

The assessment and detection of SITB should be informed by an understanding of the prevalence of each of these behaviors. Recent data from a nationally representative sample of adult U.S. residents have provided information about the estimated prevalence of suicide ideation (13.5%), plans (4.6%), attempts (2.7%), and gestures (1.9%) in the general population (Kessler et al., 1999; Nock & Kessler, 2006). An important concept of potential use to clinicians is the *conditional probability* of each outcome, or the likelihood of its occurrence within the context of existing SITB. For instance, beyond knowing the overall prevalence, it is useful to know that 34% of suicide ideators go on to make a suicide plan, and 72% of those with a plan go on to make a suicide attempt—and the vast majority of these transitions occur within the first year after the first onset of suicide ideation (Kessler et al., 1999). Although the prevalence of each form of SITB varies somewhat cross-nationally (e.g., 3.1% to 15.9% for lifetime suicide ideation and 0.9% to 5.0% for lifetime suicide attempt), the conditional probabilities are quite consistent (Nock, Borges et al., 2007).

The actual prevalence of NSSI is not known, as nationally representative studies have not included assessments of these behaviors. Data on NSSI are available, however, from several smaller studies ($N = 400$ to 2000) of community and clinical samples of children, adolescents, and adults. These data offer fairly consistent estimates of the rate of NSSI: approximately 7.7% of pre-adolescents (Hilt, Nock, Lloyd-Richardson, & Prinstein, in press), 13.9% to 21.4% of adolescents and young adults (Muehlenkamp & Gutierrez, 2004; Ross & Heath, 2002; Zoroglu et al., 2003), and 4% of adults (Briere & Gil, 1998; Klonsky, Oltmanns, & Turkheimer, 2003) report a lifetime history of NSSI. Although NSSI and suicide-related outcomes are distinct constructs, 50% to 75% of those with a history of NSSI make a suicide attempt at some point (Favazza & Conterio, 1988; Nock, Joiner, Gordon, Lloyd-Richardson, & Prinstein, 2006).

Purposes of Assessment

Unlike many of the conditions covered in this volume (e.g., anxiety disorders, schizophrenia), there is no actual diagnosis of SITB. Instead, SITB are behaviors that occur within the context of mental disorders in general, and at a particularly high rate among some disorders in particular (e.g., depressive disorders and borderline personality disorder). As such, rather than focusing on diagnosis, the primary purpose of assessment of SITB is to determine (a) whether or not such conditions are present, (b) what factors influence their onset and maintenance, and (c) if and how they change over time. In the subsequent section of this chapter we present measures with empirical evidence supporting their use for each of these three purposes. In addition to requiring empirical evidence supporting the use of each measure, our inclusion criteria for measures contained in this review were that the measure had to have three or more items and the primary purpose of the measure be focused on the assessment of some form of SITB. So, for instance, diagnostic interviews (e.g., the Structured Clinical Interview for DSM-IV) and rating scales (e.g., Beck Depression Inventory) used primarily for assessing other constructs and including only one or a few items focused on SITB were not included. In each section, summary psychometric information for each measure is presented in tables to provide readers with a brief and accessible view of the relative strengths and weaknesses of the measures so that they may make decisions about which measures may best suit their needs. These ratings follow the guidelines provided by the editors of this volume, are based directly on the papers cited, and provide an overview of the evidence base for each measure of SITB. Measures are considered "Highly Recommended" if they receive ratings of "Good" or "Excellent" on the majority of categories for which data are available.

Assessment for the Identification of SITB

The first purpose of assessment is to determine whether SITB is present. It is recommended that a direct assessment of the presence of SITB be included as part of all comprehensive clinical interviews (e.g., intake interviews, interview prior to change in level of care, discharge interview) and not be confined to interviews with those patients who appear to be at elevated risk for SITB based on the presence of known risk factors (AACAP, 2001; APA, 2003; Jacobs, 1999; Kessler et al., 1999; Nock, Borges, et al., 2007). Indeed, SITB often is present in individuals who lack key risk factors, and many people with multiple risk factors will not engage in SITB. Moreover, it is not recommended that clinicians rely on the presence of the "warning signs" for SITB that often are outlined and disseminated by clinical agencies (e.g., "giving away possessions, sudden improvement in mood"). A recent expert panel that convened to examine the evidence for such factors concluded that most factors appearing on these lists lack empirical support, and only the direct expression of self-injurious thoughts or intentions should be considered warning signs for suicide (Rudd et al., 2006).

One common concern regarding the direct assessment of SITB is that asking a person questions about SITB will actually increase the likelihood that that person will engage in SITB (i.e., that it will give them the idea to do so). Although such a concern is understandable, a recent randomized controlled trial testing this assumption revealed that assessing the presence of suicide ideation and attempts does not increase the subsequent risk of such outcomes or even increase current distress (Gould et al., 2005). Nevertheless, asking a person if she is thinking about killing herself inevitably involves broaching a very personal and sensitive topic, and assessment guidelines commonly recommend beginning an assessment of SITB after less sensitive areas (e.g., depression, anxiety) have been assessed. In addition, it is suggested that the assessment of SITB begin with a focus on less severe constructs such as suicide ideation, and then proceed to increasingly severe ones, such as suicide plans and suicide attempts. A wide range of psychometrically sound measures are available for assessing the presence of SITB. Given the large number of measures

available for this assessment purpose, measures for use with adults (see Table 8.1a) and children/adolescents are presented separately (see Table 8.1b).

MEASURES FOR USE WITH ADULTS

Structured Interviews

The Self-Injurious Thoughts and Behaviors Interview (SITBI; Nock, Holmberg, Photos, & Michel, 2007) is a comprehensive (long form: 169 items; short form: 72 items) structured interview that assesses not only the presence, but also the frequency, age of onset, and other characteristics of suicide ideation, plans, gestures, and attempts, as well as NSSI. The SITBI begins with a screening question that asks about the lifetime presence of each of these thoughts or behaviors which, if endorsed, leads into a longer module. Each module assesses severity, methods used, the self-reported function of each behavior, and the extent to which the respondent believes different factors may have contributed to his or her behavior, including "family," "friends," "relationships," "peers," "work/school," and "mental state." Respondents also are asked about other characteristics of their SITB, including the experience of pain, use of alcohol/ drugs, and impulsiveness of the SITB. Finally, the SITBI assesses respondents' self-reported likelihood that they will engage in each SITB at some time in the future. Administration, which can be done by bachelor's level staff following several hours of training and ongoing supervision, takes approximately 3 to 15 minutes depending on the number of modules administered.

The SITBI has been tested among young adults and adolescents and also includes a parent-report version. In instances in which the parent or guardian is available, they are interviewed separately by the same interviewer and answer each question about their child. Initial testing of the SITBI has revealed excellent inter-rater reliability, adequate test–retest reliability for the presence of each form of SITB assessed over a 6-month period, as well as construct validity via strong correspondence with other measures of suicide ideation and attempt and NSSI (Nock, Holmberg, et al., 2007). The SITBI currently is being used in a variety of settings (i.e., outpatient, inpatient, psychiatric emergency room) and by several different research groups; however, the current

TABLE 8.1a Ratings of Instruments Used for Assessing Adults

Instrument	Norms	Internal Consistency	Inter-Rater Reliability	Test–Retest Reliability	Content Validity	Construct Validity	Validity Generalization	Treatment Sensitivity	Clinical Utility	Highly Recommended
Adults										
Structured Interviews										
SITBI	G	NA	E	A	G	A	G	U	A	
SASII	A	G	E	E	A	G	A	G	G	✓
PSS	U	A	U	U	A	G	G	U	A	✓
Semistructured Interviews										
SSI	U	G	G	U	G	E	E	E	E	✓
SSI-W	U	G	G	A	G	E	G	U	A	✓
MSSI	U	G	E	L	G	E	G	A	E	✓
Self-Report Measures										
BSI	A	E	NA	L	G	E	A	U	G	✓
SMSI	U	U	NA	U	L	A	A	A	A	
SPS	A	G	NA	A	U	E	G	A	A	
PANSI	U	G	NA	U	A	G	E	A	A	
ASIQ	U	E	NA	A	U	E	E	I	A	
SIS	U	G	NA	U	A	A	A	U	A	
SBQ	U	G	NA	A	U	G	A	A	G	
SHBQ	U	G	NA	A	A	G	L	U	G	✓
SHI	A	A	NA	A	A	G	A	U	A	
SIQ	U	G	NA	A	A	G	A	U	A	
DSHI	U	G	NA	G	A	A	A	U	A	
SRS	U	G	NA	U	A	A	A	U	A	

Note: SITBI = Self-Injurious Thoughts and Behaviors Interview; SASII = Suicide Attempt Self-Injury Interview; PSS = Paykel Suicide Scale; SSI = Scale for Suicide Ideation; SSI-W = Scale for Suicide Ideation-Worst; MSSI = Modified Scale for Suicide Ideation; BSI = Beck Scale for Suicide Ideation; SMSI = Self-Monitoring Suicidal Ideation Scale; SPS = Suicide Probability Scale; PANSI = Positive and Negative Suicide Ideation Inventory; ASIQ = Adult Suicide Ideation Questionnaire; SIS = Suicide Ideation Scale; SBQ = Suicidal Behaviors Questionnaire; SHBQ = Self-Harm Behavior Questionnaire; SHI = Self-Harm Inventory; SIQ = Self-Injury Questionnaire; DSHI = Deliberate Self-Harm Inventory; SRS = Suicide Risk Scale; L = Less Than adequate; A = Adequate; G = Good; E = Excellent; U = Unavailable; NA = Not Applicable.

TABLE 8.1b Ratings of Instruments Used for Assessing Children

Instrument	Norms	Internal Consistency	Inter-Rater Reliability	Test–Retest Reliability	Content Validity	Construct Validity	Validity Generalization	Treatment Sensitivity	Clinical Utility	Highly Recommended
Child/Adolescent										
Structured Interviews										
SITBI	G	NA	E	A	G	A	G	U	A	✓
Semistructured Interviews										
SSI	U	G	U	U	E	G	G	U	G	✓
SBI	U	E	E	U	G	A	G	U	A	✓
CSPS	U	A	E	U	A	G	E	U	A	✓
Self-Report Measures										
BSI	A	E	NA	U	E	G	A	A	G	✓
SBQ	U	A	NA	U	U	A	A	U	A	
SBQ-C	U	G	NA	A	U	A	U	U	A	
SIQ	E	G	NA	A	A	G	G	A	G	✓
SIQ-JR	E	G	NA	A	A	G	G	U	G	✓
SPS	A	E	NA	U	U	A	A	U	A	
CSS	A	G	NA	L	U	A	L	U	A	
HASS	U	E	NA	U	A	G	A	U	A	

Note: SITBI = Self-Injurious Thoughts and Behaviors Interview; SSI = Scale for Suicide Ideation; SBI= Suicide Behaviors Interview; CSPS = Child Suicide Potential Scales; BSI = Beck Scale for Suicide Ideation; SBQ = Suicidal Behaviors Questionnaire; SBQ-C = Suicidal Behaviors Questionnaire for Children; SIQ = Suicidal Ideation Questionnaire; SIQ-JR = Suicidal Ideation Questionnaire for Children; SPS = Suicide Probability Scale; CSS = Columbia Suicide Screen; HASS = Harkavy Asnis Suicide Scale; L = Less Than adequate; A = Adequate; G = Good; E = Excellent; U = Unavailable; NA = Not Applicable.

evidence for this measure is from only one study of adolescents and young adults (12 to 19 years), and so further examination is needed.

The Suicide Attempt Self-Injury Interview (SASII; Linehan, Comtois, Brown, Heard, & Wagner, 2006), formerly known as the Parasuicide History Interview (Linehan, Wagner, & Cox, 1989), is a 31-item measure that assesses the topography and intent of each episode of self-injurious behavior in which a person has engaged. Areas assessed for each episode include intent and outcome expectations, method used, lethality of the method, physical condition resulting from the act, medical treatment received, planning and preparations, contextual and behavioral factors, antecedent events, and functional outcomes (Linehan, Comtois, Brown, et al., 2006). The SASII has been used primarily among samples of women with borderline personality disorder (Brown, Comtois, & Linehan, 2002; Koons et al., 2001; Linehan et al., 1991; Linehan, Heard, & Armstrong, 1993).

Given that the SASII assesses each self-injurious episode in detail, it is ideal for situations where a very comprehensive history of SITB is desired. Although the collection of data on each episode may require a significant amount of time for assessment if the person has an extensive self-injury history, a standard short version is available if greater brevity is required, and a computerized scoring version is being made available to make the scoring process less burdensome. In addition, the SASII, like the SITBI, is one of the few measures that assess both suicidal and NSSI, as well as the functions and contextual factors associated with such behaviors. Another strength of the SASII is its attention to the intent and lethality of each behavior. Linehan et al. (2006) found the SASII to have excellent inter-rater reliability and adequate validity. Given this comprehensive focus, as well as the support for the SASII in several different samples, this measure is recommended for clinical and research purposes.

The Paykel Suicide Scale (PSS; Paykel, Myers, Lindenthal, & Tanner, 1974) is a 5-item (yes/no) interview that assesses past history of thoughts of death, suicide ideation, and suicide attempt over the past week, month, year, or lifetime. Administration requires only a few minutes. Although preliminary evidence suggests that the PSS is a useful method for screening purposes, the reliability and validity of this measure have not been extensively documented. Further studies using the PSS are needed before this measure can be considered clinically useful.

Semistructured Interviews

The Scale for Suicide Ideation (SSI; Beck, Kovacs, & Weissman, 1979) is a 21-item semistructured interview that assesses recent thoughts of suicide. The SSI quantifies suicide ideation by measuring its presence, frequency, and severity. Items inquire about passive suicide desire, active suicide desire, and specific plans for suicide. Administration takes approximately 10 minutes. The SSI is widely used in both research and clinical settings and its reliability and validity have been supported with both adults and adolescents (e.g., Clum & Curtin, 1993; Rifai, George, Stack, Mann, & Reynolds, 1994), diverse racial and ethnic groups (e.g., Beck et al., 1979), various clinical populations (e.g., Beck, Brown, & Steer, 1997; Beck, Steer, Kovacs, & Garrison, 1985) and several clinical settings including primary care practices, emergency rooms, rehabilitation programs, and private practice (e.g., Vuorilehto, Melartin, & Isometsä, 2006). The extensive evidence for the reliability, validity, and clinical utility of the SSI makes it an excellent choice for assessing suicide ideation in most research and clinical settings.

Two modified versions of the SSI are available. The Scale for Suicide Ideation-Worst (SSI-W; Beck et al., 1997) is adapted directly from the SSI and assesses suicide ideation at its worst point in the patient's life. The SSI-W has not been evaluated as thoroughly as the original SSI; however, existing data suggest that the SSI-W has good internal consistency and inter-rater reliability, excellent construct validity, and that scores on the SSI-W are predictive of prior suicide attempts and eventual suicide (Beck, Brown, Steer, Dahlsgaard, & Grisham, 1999; Joiner et al., 2003). The Modified Scale for Suicide Ideation (MSSI; Miller, Norman, Bishop, & Dow, 1986) is a revised version of the SSI containing 18 items, 13 of which are taken directly from the SSI. The five new items assess the intensity of ideation as well as courage and competence to attempt, talk, and write about death. Reliability and validity values have generally been good to excellent in samples of inpatients (Miller et al., 1986), outpatients (Rudd, Joiner, & Rajab, 1996), college students seeking treatment (Clum & Yang, 1995), and across several research settings (Joiner et al., 2005).

Self-Report Measures

The Beck Scale for Suicide Ideation (BSI; Beck & Steer, 1991) is a 21-item self-report version of the SSI, reviewed above. The BSI's well-documented reliability, validity, and ease of administration have made it one of the most widely used assessments of suicide ideation. The BSI is appropriate for use across many different clinical and research settings (e.g., Healy, Barry, Blow, Welsh, & Milner, 2006) and cultures (Ovuga, Boardman, & Wassermann, 2005).

The Self-Monitoring Suicidal Ideation Scale (SMSI; Clum & Curtin, 1993) is a 3-item self-report measure adapted from the SSI. Items measure the presence, intensity, and duration of ideation and the level of reported control over making a suicide attempt. The SMSI is intended to be administered daily to track changes in suicide ideation. Reliability and validity data for the scale are limited and, although initial results suggest the SMSI may be a clinically useful measure for tracking regular fluctuations in suicidal ideation, more extensive research evaluation is required at this point.

The Suicide Probability Scale (SPS; Cull & Gill, 1988) is a 36-item measure of current suicide ideation, hopelessness, negative self-evaluation, and hostility designed to assess probability of suicide attempt. Administration takes about 10 minutes. Initial study of the SPS indicates that the scale has adequate reliability and validity; however, there is little evidence that this measure is useful for predicting suicide.

The Positive and Negative Suicide Ideation Inventory (PANSI; Osman et al., 1998) is a 20-item measure of positive and negative thoughts that rests on the assumption that more negative than positive thoughts present a risk for suicide. Negative items include, "Felt so lonely or sad you wanted to kill yourself so you could end your pain?" Positive items include, "Felt confident about your ability to cope with most of the problems in your life?" Administration takes only 5 minutes. The PANSI was initially developed in a college student population where its reliability and validity have been demonstrated; however, psychometric evidence in clinical populations is lacking. The PANSI takes a unique approach to the assessment of thoughts about suicide, but currently is limited by a lack of evidence in clinical populations.

The Adult Suicide Ideation Questionnaire (ASIQ) is a 25-item self-report measure of suicide ideation and planning (Reynolds, 1991a). Responses represent the frequency of each thought or behavior over the past month, and administration takes approximately 5 minutes. The reliability and validity of the ASIQ have been supported among college students (Reynolds,

1991b), adult outpatients (Reynolds, 1991a), adults in the general population (Reynolds, 1991a), and psychiatric patients in long-term care facilities (Osman et al., 1999). The ASIQ also has shown the ability to predict suicide attempts at 3-month follow-up (Osman et al., 1999). The evidence supporting the ASIQ suggests it is a solid choice for clinical and research purposes.

The Suicide Ideation Scale (SIS; Rudd, 1989) is a 10-item measure of the presence and severity of suicide ideation in the past year. Initial study has supported the reliability and validity of this measure in a college student sample (Rudd, 1989); however, it has not been studied in clinical samples.

The Suicidal Behaviors Questionnaire (SBQ; Linehan, 1981) is a 90-item measure that assesses five domains of suicide ideation, suicide attempts, and NSSI including past suicide ideation, future suicide ideation, past suicide threats, future suicide attempts, and the likelihood of dying in a future suicide attempt. The reliability and validity of the SBQ have been demonstrated in hospital settings (Linehan, Camper, Chiles, Strosahl, & Shearin, 1987; Linehan, Chiles, Egan, Devine, & Laffaw, 1986). In addition, a shortened 4-item version has been used among psychiatric outpatients and college students (Cotton, Peters, & Range, 1995; Sabo, Gunderson, Najavits, Chauncey, & Kisiel, 1995). The SBQ is a useful and well-validated self-report measure of behavior and NSSI.

Finally, preliminary information is available for some newly developed measures that appear quite promising but require further evaluation. The Self-Harm Behavior Questionnaire (SHBQ; Gutierrez, Rodriguez, & Garcia, 2001) assesses the presence of suicide ideation, threats, and attempts as well as NSSI, with follow-up questions on frequency, intent, lethality, outcome, age of onset and offset, and whether anyone else knows of the behavior. This measure was developed in a college population and was recently translated into German (Fliege et al., 2006), although further evidence is needed in clinical populations. The Self-Harm Inventory (SHI; Sansone, Wiederman, & Sansone, 1998) is a 41-item measure of suicidal and NSSI that also assesses more general self-destructive behaviors with demonstrated reliability and validity among psychiatric outpatients (Sansone, Pole, Dakroub, & Butler, 2006), psychiatric inpatients (Sansone, Songer, & Miller, 2005), and community samples (Sansone et al., 1998). The Self-Injury Questionnaire (SIQ; Santa Mina et al., 2006) is a 30-item measure of the frequency, type, and functions of self-injurious behaviors that also includes assessment of childhood trauma. The Deliberate Self-Harm Inventory (DSHI; Gratz, 2001), a 17-item measure of the frequency, severity, duration, and method used for NSSI, was developed and has demonstrated reliability and validity among college students (Gratz, 2001) and it has been recently translated into German and shown to be reliable and valid in that language as well (Fliege et al., 2006). However, the DSHI requires examination in clinical samples. Lastly, the Suicide Risk Scale (SRS; Plutchik, van Praag, Conte, & Picard, 1989) is a 26-item (yes/no) measure of suicide ideation and attempt, with the majority of items focused on risk factors for suicide (e.g., depression, marital status, feelings of worthlessness). The reliability and validity of the SRS have been demonstrated among psychiatric inpatients, psychiatric outpatients, college students (Plutchik et al., 1989), and adult sexual offenders in a prison setting (Giotakos, Markianos, & Vaidakis, 2005).

MEASURES FOR USE WITH CHILDREN AND ADOLESCENTS

Several of the measures reviewed above have evidence supporting their use with children and adolescents, and several measures have been developed specifically for this younger population.

Structured and Semistructured Interviews

The SITBI (Nock, Holmberg et al., 2007), reviewed above, has been examined primarily among adolescents and young adults (12 to 19 years) and has demonstrated strong reliability and validity among this population. The SSI (Beck, Schuyler, & Herman, 1974), also reviewed above, has been supported in studies of children and adolescents in psychiatric inpatient settings (e.g., Allan, Kashani, Dahlmeier, Taghizadeh, & Reid, 1997; Nock & Kazdin, 2002). These studies add to the already large evidence base for this measure and indicate the SSI has reliability and validity among child and adolescent clinical samples. The Suicide Behaviors Interview (SBI; Reynolds, 1990) is a 22-item semistructured clinical interview measure of suicidal behaviors designed for use with adolescents. Two items specific to attempted suicide are not scored, but are included to gain clinical insight into suicidal behavior.

The psychometric characteristics of the SBI were derived from a sample of nonclinically referred high school students, but the SBI has also been used with inner city (primarily African American and Hispanic) children and adolescents and with psychiatrically hospitalized adolescents (Reynolds & Mazza, 1999). Though the data to date seem to show strong psychometric properties, there are still few published studies using this measure.

The Child Suicide Potential Scales (CSPS; Pfeffer, Conte, Plutchik, & Jerrett, 1979) includes eight scales measuring suicidal behavior, precipitating events, recent affect and behavior, family background, affect and behavior in the past, the child's concept of death, ego functioning, and ego defense mechanisms. Of these scales, the Spectrum of Suicidal Behavior scale most directly assesses the presence and severity of suicidal behavior. It has been used with children and adolescents, psychiatric inpatients, and nonclinically referred children, and has been translated into Hebrew and used in studies of Israeli adolescents in inpatient, emergency room, and community settings. The CSPS has strong psychometric properties but more research is needed regarding sensitivity to treatment response and clinical utility.

Self-Report Measures

A number of self-report measures, reviewed under the section on assessing adults, have also been evaluated for their use with youth. The BSI (Beck & Steer, 1991) has been used among adolescents and shown to be reliable and valid among adolescent psychiatric inpatients (Steer, Kumar, & Beck, 1993) and outpatients (Rathus & Miller, 2002). The SBQ (Linehan, 1981) has been used in some published studies with adolescents (see Goldston, 2000) and a children's version of the SBQ, simplified to the third-grade level (the SBQ-C), has been developed (Cotton & Range, 1993). However, limited psychometric data are available on these measures. The SIQ (Reynolds, 1988) also has been supported for use with adolescents. Moreover, a shorter version called the SIQ-JR (15 items) has been created and used with children below the 10th grade level. The SIQ and SIQ-JR are widely used and the psychometric properties well supported in both research and clinical contexts. Finally, the SPS (Cull & Gill, 1988) has been used with adolescents. Initial studies have reported higher scores on the SPS for adolescents compared to adults, and a different factor structure has been identified for adolescents (see Range & Knott, 1997 for review).

The Columbia Suicide Screen (CSS; Shaffer et al., 2004) is a brief screening questionnaire intended to identify high school students at risk for suicide. Eleven items assess lifetime suicide attempts and recent suicide ideation, negative mood, and substance abuse. To avoid a specific focus on suicidality, these items are embedded within 32 general health questions and 4 items on relationships and family concerns. Most items are scored along a five-point visual analog scale, with anchors labeled as 1 ("no problem") to 5 ("very bad problem"); however, items for suicide ideation and attempts have a yes/no response. The CSS has good sensitivity and reasonable specificity in identifying students at risk for suicide. Further study is needed to increase the specificity and expand on the known psychometric properties of this measure.

The Harkavy Asnis Suicide Scale (HASS; Harkavy Friedman & Asnis, 1989) assesses current (past 2 weeks) and lifetime suicide plans, suicide attempts, substance use, and exposure to suicidal behavior. The HASS was first used with a high school sample and subsequently has been used with adolescent psychiatric outpatients (Velting & Miller, 1998; Wetzler et al., 1996) as well as in a treatment trial evaluating dialectical behavior therapy with suicidal adolescents (Rathus & Miller, 2002). This measure has shown excellent internal consistency reliability and adequate to good construct validity with various samples.

OVERALL EVALUATION

Overall, there is a fairly broad array of measures for the assessment of SITB. Decisions about which are most appropriate for use in clinical and research settings should be guided primarily by two considerations. First, one should take into account the evidence supporting each measure. Tables 8.1a and 8.1b provide a summary of the evidence and make clear that several measures are especially strong on the criteria examined. It is apparent, however, that much more work is needed on all of these measures. Second, in selecting the best measure clinicians and researchers should carefully consider the purpose of their assessment. For instance, if the purpose is to screen for the presence of each form of SITB and to obtain information about the basic characteristics of each, then the SASII and SITBI are recommended.

However, if the purpose is to obtain a more in-depth assessment of the presence, severity, frequency, and characteristics of a single construct such as suicide ideation, then more focused measures like the SSI or BSI are recommended. Given that different forms of SITB often co-occur, and also that the presence of milder forms of SITB (e.g., suicide ideation, suicide plans) are predictive of more severe forms such as suicide attempts (e.g., Borges et al., 2006; Kessler et al., 1999), it is advisable in most clinical settings and situations to conduct a comprehensive assessment of each form of SITB reviewed here.

Unfortunately, few studies have examined agreement across measurement methods (e.g., interview vs. self-report) or informants (e.g., adolescent- vs. parent-report). Studies that have done so generally have shown higher rates of detecting SITB when using self-report relative to interview or clinician/parent ratings (Kaplan et al., 1994; Klimes-Dougan, 1998; Prinstein, Nock, Spirito, & Grapentine, 2001). Moreover, poor agreement consistently is found across assessment methods and informants (Joiner, Rudd, & Rajab, 1999; Kaplan et al., 1994; Prinstein et al., 2001), raising important questions of how one should integrate information from multiple sources. For instance, if a person denies suicide ideation in the interview, but reports it on a rating scale, what is the clinician to do? Similarly, if a parent reports suicide ideation in their child, but the child herself denies it, who should the clinician believe?

The absence of answers for these questions highlights the imperfect state of the measurement strategies currently available for assessing the presence of SITB and underscores the need, not for additional instruments, but for research on the best methods of integrating information from those currently available. Until such information is available, given the importance of detecting SITB when they are present, it is recommended that clinicians use multiple assessment methods and informants whenever possible in screening for SITB, and that the detection of any SITB during screening should trigger the administration of a more thorough assessment of each form of SITB as well as a risk assessment according to standard guidelines (see AACAP, 2001; APA, 2003; Jacobs, 1999). Once one has assessed the presence and severity of SITB and performed a risk assessment, it is instructive for the purposes of case conceptualization and treatment planning to assess factors that may be influencing the occurrence of SITB.

ASSESSMENT FOR CASE CONCEPTUALIZATION AND TREATMENT PLANNING

A comprehensive evidence-based assessment of SITB can best inform case conceptualization and treatment planning if it goes beyond measuring the presence of a given form of SITB to provide additional information about the factors influencing the occurrence of the SITB. Of course, SITB are complex, multi-determined outcomes that are influenced by a broad range of factors, including sociodemographic factors, the presence and accumulation of mental disorders, geographic region of residence, and even season of the year. Although a review of all of the factors that should be considered in assessing the risk of SITB is beyond the scope of this chapter, several factors consistently shown in the research to increase the risk of SITB warrant brief comment.

In conceptualizing the factors influencing SITB and planning for the treatment of these conditions, prior research points toward several factors that warrant clinical attention. First, decades of research on SITB has consistently demonstrated that most individuals who engage in each form of SITB have a current mental disorder, especially mood disorders, alcohol/substance use disorders, and personality disorders (AACAP, 2001; APA, 2003; Jacobs, 1999). Second, those engaging in SITB report the experience of a greater number of stressors prior to engaging in SITB than do non-self-injurers (Paykel, Prusoff, & Myers, 1975). Third, several specific traits such as hopelessness (Beck, Brown, & Steer, 1989), anhedonia (Fawcett et al., 1990; Nock & Kazdin, 2002), and behavioral impulsiveness (Mann, Brent, & Arango, 2001; Oquendo & Mann, 2000), as well as the presence of acute distress and agitation (Fawcett, Busch, Jacobs, Kravitz, & Fogg, 1997) have been shown to be strongly associated with the occurrence of SITB, especially suicide attempts. It also is notable that the presence of prior SITB is the strongest predictor of subsequent SITB (see Borges et al., 2006), and that the nature of current SITB, such as the presence of suicide plans and intent to die, are strongly predictive of more severe SITB (Borges et al., 2006; Harriss et al., 2005).

It is common for the purposes of case conceptualization and treatment planning to assess and target modifiable factors associated with SITB, such as some of those noted above. However, there is no evidence to date demonstrating that changing any of these factors actually decreases the risk of subsequent SITB. Instead, treatments that target SITB directly have been shown to decrease SITB in randomized clinical trials (G. K. Brown et al., 2005; Linehan, Comtois, Murray et al., 2006; Linehan et al., 1991), and we therefore recommend the use of measures aimed at assessing and understanding the reasons for SITB directly. In this section we review evidence supporting the use of measures designed specifically to assess individuals' understanding of the reasons for their SITB (summarized in Table 8.2). Measures for adults and children/adolescents are presented together given there are far fewer measures for this assessment purpose.

Structured Interviews

Two of the interviews reviewed above, the SITBI and SASII, also collect information likely to be useful for case conceptualization and treatment planning. More specifically, both obtain detailed information about an individual's reason for engaging in SITB, which can be used to understand the function of such behavior. In addition, each includes assessment of contextual factors (i.e., setting events, triggers) reported to influence the occurrence of SITB.

The Functional Assessment of Self-Mutilation (FASM; Lloyd, Kelley, & Hope, 1997) is another interview that assesses an individual's self-reported reasons for engaging in self-injury, though it focuses specifically on NSSI. The FASM assesses the frequency of engagement in 11 methods of NSSI, receipt of medical treatment, impulsiveness of the behavior, the use of alcohol or drugs during NSSI, amount of pain experienced, and age of onset of NSSI. The FASM also assesses 22 possible reasons for engaging in NSSI. Studies have supported the factor structure (Nock & Prinstein, 2004), adequate internal consistency reliability (Guertin, Lloyd-Richardson, Spirito, Donaldson, & Boergers, 2001), and adequate construct validity (Nock & Prinstein, 2005) of the FASM.

Interestingly, factor analyses of the items in the SASII (M. Z. Brown et al., 2002) and FASM (Nock & Prinstein, 2004) have independently yielded similar four-function models of engagement in self-injury that include reinforcement that is either positive or negative and either intrapersonal or interpersonal in nature. Subsequent analyses have supported the construct validity of this model (Nock & Prinstein, 2005).

TABLE 8.2 Ratings of Instruments Used for Case Conceptualization and Treatment Planning

Instrument	Norms	Internal Consistency	Inter-Rater Reliability	Test–Retest Reliability	Content Validity	Construct Validity	Validity Generalization	Treatment Sensitivity	Clinical Utility	Highly Recommended
Interviews										
SITBI	G	NA	E	A	G	A	G	U	A	✓
SASII	A	G	E	E	A	G	A	G	G	✓
FASM	G	A	U	U	A	A	G	U	A	
Self-Report Measures										
RFL	E	E	NA	G	A	E	E	A	G	✓
B-RFL	G	G	NA	U	A	E	G	U	A	✓
RFL-A	G	E	NA	U	A	A	G	U	G	✓
B-RFL-A	G	A	NA	U	A	A	G	U	A	
CSRLI	G	G	NA	U	A	A	E	U	A	
RFL-YA	A	E	NA	U	A	A	A	U	A	
RSAQ	E	A	NA	U	A	A	E	U	A	
MAST	G	G	NA	U	A	G	E	U	A	✓

Notes: SITBI = Self-Injurious Thoughts and Behaviors Interview; SASII = Suicide Attempts Self-Injury Interview; FASM = Functional Assessment of Self-Mutilation; RFL = Reasons for Living Inventory; B-RFL = Brief Reasons for Living Inventory; RFL-A = Reasons for Living for Adolescents; B-RFL-A = Brief Reasons for Living for Adolescents; CSRLI = College Student Reasons for Living Inventory; RFL-YA = Reasons for Living for Young Adult; RSAQ = Reasons for Suicide Attempts Questionnaire; MAST = Multi-Attitude Suicide Tendency Scale for Adolescents; A = Adequate; G = Good; E = Excellent; U = Unavailable; NA = Not Applicable.

Decisions about which of these measures to use for assessing the reasons or functions of SITB should be guided by the goals of assessment in any particular case. For instance, the SASII and SITBI assess a broader range of SITB than the FASM, and scores on the functions of NSSI from the SITBI are significantly correlated with those from the FASM, suggesting it obtains similar information using fewer items (Nock, Holmberg et al., 2007). However, the FASM is a much shorter measure, and therefore if one is interested only in NSSI, this is perhaps the better choice.

Self-Report Measures

The Reasons for Living Inventory (RFL; Linehan, Goodstein, Nielsen, & Chiles, 1983) is a 72-item (long form) or 48-item (Brief-RFL; Ivanoff, Jang, Smyth, & Linehan, 1994) measure assessing an individual's reasons for living when they are considering suicide. The RFL consists of six subscales: Survival and Coping Beliefs, Responsibility to Family, Child Concerns, Fear of Suicide, Fear of Social Disapproval, and Moral Objections. The RFL has been translated into several languages and adapted for assessment of a wide range of populations and settings, including nonclinical (Osman et al., 1996) and inpatient (Goldston, Daniel, Reboussin, Frazier, & Harris, 2000; Pinto, Whisman, & Conwell, 1998) populations. Gender differences in RFL scores have been reported (Pomili, Tatarelli, & Lester, 2006). Although the RFL does not assess the presence or frequency of SITB, it is a novel measure that assesses factors thought to influence the likelihood of SITB. Notably, because the framing of items is positive (i.e., reasons for living) it is unlikely to be distressing for people to complete and some have even suggested that completing the RFL may have a suicide-preventive impact (Range & Knott, 1997).

The Reasons for Living for Adolescents (RFL-A; Osman et al., 1998) is a 32-item adaptation of the RFL. The RFL-A includes five factors: Future Optimism, Suicide-Related Concerns, Family Alliance, Peer Acceptance and Support, and Self-Acceptance. This measure has been tested in high school students (Gutierrez, Osman, Kopper, & Barrios, 2000; Osman et al., 1998) and in an adolescent psychiatric inpatient population (Osman et al., 1998), and support exists for reliability and predictive validity. The Brief RFL-A (Osman et al., 1996) is a 14-item version of the RFL-A for which factor structure, reliability, and construct validity are supported by research.

The College Student Reasons for Living Inventory (CSRLI; Westefeld, Cardin, & Deaton, 1992) is a 46-item measure that assesses perceived reasons to stay alive after the onset of suicide ideation. The CSRLI was inspired by the original RFL but was created using newly generated items. Factor analysis yielded five of the original six factors, with a new one reflecting College and Future-Related Concerns. The CSRLI has been used in samples of nonclinical college students (Westefeld et al., 1992), African American college students (Westefeld, Badura, Kiel, & Scheel, 1996), and college students seeking outpatient counseling (Westefeld, Scheel, & Maples, 1998), with support for reliability and validity.

The Reasons for Living for Young Adults (RFL-YA; Gutierrez et al., 2002) is a 32-item version of the RFL developed specifically for those aged 17 to 30 years. Three initial studies among college students support the reliability and validity of this measure (Gutierrez et al., 2002). It is similar in focus to the CSRLI; however, no direct comparisons have been performed. Clinicians and researchers working in college settings are encouraged to examine both in order to determine which provides the best match with their assessment goals.

The Reasons for Suicide Attempt Questionnaire (RSAQ; Holden, Kerr, Mendonca, & Velamoor, 1998) is a 14-item measure that assesses motivations for suicide. The RSAQ includes two subscales: Extrapunitive/Manipulative Reasons (8 items) and Internal Perturbation Based Motivations (6 items). The psychometric properties of the RSAQ have been supported in multiple populations including adults attending a crisis unit (Holden et al., 1998), males from a maximum security prison in Canada (Holden, 2003), and adult suicide attempters (Holden & DeLisle, 2006).

The Multi-Attitude Suicide Tendency Scale for Adolescents (MAST; Orbach et al., 1991) is a 30-item measure that examines two sets of conflicting attitudes about life and death: attraction to life, repulsion to life, attraction to death, and repulsion to death. The psychometric properties of this measure have been supported in the United States (Osman, Barrios, Grittmann, & Osman, 1993), Israel (Orbach et al., 2006), and China (Wong, 2004). Moreover, research examining differences across White, Black, and Hispanic samples has reported that attitudes toward life and death may differ across these groups (Gutierrez et al., 2001).

Overall Evaluation

Overall, there are many measures from which to choose for the purpose of case conceptualization and treatment planning. Several available measures have significant evidence on their behalf, and one's choice of measures again should be guided by the evidentiary support for each measure and the purposes of the assessment. The SASII, SITBI, and FASM all provide an assessment of the potential functions served by engagement in self-injury, and the relative strengths and weaknesses of these have been described. The RFL measure provides novel and clinically relevant information about factors that may influence the likelihood of engagement in self-injury, and various versions of this measure have been tailored to a broad range of contexts. The assessment of both the functions of self-injury and one's reasons for *not* engaging in self-injury can provide very useful information for conceptualizing the occurrence of self-injury and for planning a course of treatment. For instance, if functional assessment reveals self-injury is being used to regulate emotions, then treatment may be best focused on teaching more adaptive emotion regulation skills or distress tolerance. If assessment reveals self-injury is being used to communicate with others, then training in interpersonal effectiveness or family therapy may be indicated. Although these links may make sense intuitively, the use of these assessment instruments to guide or tailor treatment has not yet been tested, and so these recommendations themselves are not yet evidence-based.

ASSESSMENT FOR TREATMENT MONITORING AND OUTCOME EVALUATION

The prevention and reduction of SITB is the ultimate goal of scientific and clinical work in this area. Recent survey data from nationally representative samples of adults in the United States have revealed both the good and bad news about the impact of treatment efforts on SITB. The good news is that the percentage of people experiencing SITB who receive treatment significantly increased from 1990–1992 to 2001–2003 (Kessler et al., 2005). The bad news is that, despite increased treatment, the rates of SITB did not change over the 10-year study period (Kessler et al., 2005). This may be because although people are receiving

more treatment, the treatments they are receiving are not necessarily evidence-based. Several treatments now exist that have been shown to decrease SITB in randomized controlled trials (e.g., G. K. Brown et al., 2005; Linehan et al., 1991; Linehan, Comtois, Murray et al., 2006); however, it is unlikely that these are available in most community settings.

Given the relative dearth of treatment studies on SITB (Comtois & Linehan, 2006; Linehan, 1997), the evidentiary base supporting measures for treatment monitoring and outcome evaluation is fairly limited. The focus of treatment monitoring and outcome evaluation is on the presence, frequency, and severity of SITB (i.e., the goal of treatment is most often to prevent or reduce SITB). Therefore, measures reviewed above on the identification of SITB (Tables 8.1a and 8.1b) are appropriate for treatment monitoring and outcome evaluation. Of course, measures will only be useful for treatment monitoring and outcome evaluation if they assess constructs that can change over time, so measures/items assessing lifetime history of SITB will not be of use for this assessment purpose. Of the measures listed in Tables 8.1a and 8.1b, less than half of the adult measures and only two of the child/adolescent measures have been used in treatment studies and have demonstrated sensitivity to change in treatment, as has one additional measure from Table 8.2 (i.e., the Reasons for Living Scale). Of greater concern is the lack of information about whether data from these assessment measures can actually improve clinical decision-making or clinical outcomes. This is a question of outstanding importance, but unfortunately one that has not been assessed in a single study, to our knowledge.

Overall Evaluation

Measures are available for identifying SITB and examining the frequency, severity, and characteristics of these constructs. Given that many of these measures have strong psychometric properties and the ability to measure SITB over varying periods of time, one would expect that they would detect changes in treatment, should they occur; however, such information is lacking for most measures reviewed here. When selecting measures for monitoring and evaluating changes in SITB over the course of time, it is important for clinicians and researchers to be sure that the measures selected assess a time period that maps on to the time between each assessment point. Specifically, if one is

TABLE 8.3 Clinical Recommendations and Research Questions for Evidence-Based Assessment of SITB

1. Identification of SITB
   (a) Assess the presence of each type of SITB in all patients
   (b) Use multiple assessment methods (interview, questionnaire) and informants (patient, clinician, parent) whenever possible
   (c) If SITB is identified on any measure, conduct a more thorough SITB evaluation and risk assessment
2. Case Conceptualization and Treatment Planning
   (a) Assess risk and protective factors for future SITB[a]
   (b) Assess the function of SITB
   (c) Treatment should target SITB directly
3. Treatment Monitoring and Outcome Evaluation
   (a) Assessment should begin before treatment and continue as frequently as feasible
   (b) Measure multiple forms of SITB and select measures with evidence of treatment sensitivity
   (c) Examine clinical utility of information gained from SITB assessment

[a] See sources cited in text for detailed guidelines for conducting an SITB risk assessment.

interested in frequency of each type of SITB over the prior month, then the SITBI may be a useful measure to consider; however, if one is interested in measuring daily fluctuations in suicide ideation, than the SMSI is a better choice. Regardless of the lack of information about the treatment sensitivity of any given measure, it is recommended that clinicians follow guidelines for conducting rigorous clinical assessment of the primary outcomes of interest, including completing a comprehensive clinical evaluation before commencing with any intervention, and repeating the assessment of key constructs over the course of treatment. Moreover, the assessment should examine multiple constructs, using a multimethod and multi-informant approach whenever possible. Perhaps most importantly, it is important for clinicians and researchers alike to begin to examine the clinical utility of the information gathered from these various assessment instruments. We assume that they provide a valuable tool for enhancing clinical care, but this remains an open and completely unexplored question.

CONCLUSIONS AND FUTURE DIRECTIONS

We have provided a brief overview of the current state of the evidence for measures designed to assess SITB. Many measures exist for these purposes, and several instruments are specifically recommended given their empirical support. In addition to providing information about specific measures, we have reviewed recent research on the nature and assessment of SITB more generally that can and should

inform assessment in this area. A summary of clinical recommendations based on this information is presented in Table 8.3.

After describing what we know about assessing SITB in an evidence-based manner, we conclude by highlighting a few very important things that we *don't* know about SITB, each of which suggests directions for future scientific work in this area. First, most of the measures reviewed rely on aggregate, retrospective reporting of SITB, introducing well-known problems with memory and recall bias. Real-time data on the actual frequency, duration, and severity of SITB do not currently exist, and this is an important direction for research. Such information would be of clear value for both scientific and clinical purposes. Recent technological advances that are already improving clinical assessment efforts in other areas (e.g., ecological momentary assessment using electronic diaries) could be especially useful in this regard. Second, all of the measures reviewed rely on an individual's explicit self-report of SITB, which is problematic given that there is very often motivation to conceal such thoughts and behaviors. Indeed, reporting of suicidal thoughts or intentions often results in involuntary hospitalization, and so many people may hide such thoughts or desires in order to avoid (or facilitate release from) locked settings. A very important goal for future research in this area is the development of measures that do not rely on explicit self-report, such as performance-based (e.g., measures of implicit cognitions about self-injury) and biologically based measures. Although there have been exciting advances toward this end, these have yet to be translated into a form that is useful for clinical assessment (Mann et al., 2006). An ultimate and perhaps long-term goal for evidence-based assessment is the effective integration of information from multiple sources in a way that detects and predicts SITB more accurately than is currently possible. Until such time, the instruments reviewed here represent those with the strongest empirical support and should be used by researchers and clinicians working with potentially self-injurious individuals.

References

AACAP. (2001). Practice parameter for the assessment and treatment of children and adolescents with suicidal behavior. American Academy of Child and Adolescent Psychiatry. *Journal of the American Academy of Child & Adolescent Psychiatry*, 40(Suppl. 7), 24S–51S.

Allan, W. D., Kashani, J. H., Dahlmeier, J., Taghizadeh, P., & Reid, J. C. (1997). Psychometric properties and clinical utility of the scale for suicide ideation with inpatient children. *Journal of Abnormal Child Psychology, 25,* 465–473.

APA. (2003). Practice guideline for the assessment and treatment of patients with suicidal behaviors. *American Journal of Psychiatry, 160*(Suppl. 11), 1–60.

Beck, A. T., Brown, G., & Steer, R. A. (1989). Prediction of eventual suicide in psychiatric inpatients by clinical ratings of hopelessness. *Journal of Consulting and Clinical Psychology, 57,* 309–310.

Beck, A. T., Brown, G. K., & Steer, R. A. (1997). Psychometric characteristics of the scale for suicide ideation with psychiatric outpatients. *Behaviour Research and Therapy, 35,* 1039–1046.

Beck, A. T., Brown, G. K., Steer, R. A., Dahlsgaard, K. K., & Grisham, J. R. (1999). Suicide ideation at its worst point: A predictor of eventual suicide in psychiatric outpatients. *Suicide and Life-Threatening Behavior, 29,* 1–9.

Beck, A. T., Davis, J. H., Frederick, C. J., Perlin, S., Pokorny, A. D., Schulman, R. E., et al. (1973). Classification and nomenclature. In H. L. P. Resnick & B. C. Hathorne (Eds.), *Suicide prevention in the seventies* (pp. 7–12). Washington, DC: U.S. Government Printing Office.

Beck, A. T., Kovacs, M., & Weissman, A. (1979). Assessment of suicidal intention: The Scale for Suicide Ideation. *Journal of Consulting and Clinical Psychology, 47,* 343–352.

Beck, A. T., Schuyler, D., & Herman, I. (1974). Development of Suicide Intent Scales. In A. T. Beck, H. Resnick, & D. Lettieri (Eds.), *The prediction of suicide,* (pp. 45–46). Bowie, MD: Charles Press.

Beck, A. T., & Steer, R. A. (1991). *Manual for the Beck scale for suicide ideation*. San Antonio, TX: The Psychological Corporation.

Beck, A. T., Steer, R. A., Kovacs, M., & Garrison, B. (1985). Hopelessness and eventual suicide: A 10-year prospective study of patients hospitalized with suicidal ideation. *American Journal of Psychiatry, 142,* 559–563.

Borges, G., Angst, J., Nock, M. K., Ruscio, A. M., Walters, E. E., & Kessler, R. C. (2006). A risk index for 12-month suicide attempts in the National Comorbidity Survey Replication (NCS-R). *Psychological Medicine, 36,* 1747–1757.

Briere, J., & Gil, E. (1998). Self-mutilation in clinical and general population samples: Prevalence, correlates, and functions. *American Journal of Orthopsychiatry, 68,* 609–620.

Brown, G. K. (2000). *A review of suicide assessment measures for intervention research with adults and older adults.* Unpublished manuscript.

Brown, G. K., Ten Have, T., Henriques, G. R., Xie, S. X., Hollander, J. E., & Beck, A. T. (2005). Cognitive therapy for the prevention of suicide attempts: A randomized controlled trial. *Journal of American Medical Association, 294,* 563–570.

Brown, M. Z., Comtois, K. A., & Linehan, M. M. (2002). Reasons for suicide attempts and nonsuicidal self-injury in women with borderline personality disorder. *Journal of Abnormal Psychology, 111,* 198–202.

Bryan, C. J., & Rudd, M. D. (2006). Advances in the assessment of suicide risk. *Journal of Clinical Psychology, 62,* 185–200.

Clum, G. A., & Curtin, L. (1993). Validity and reactivity of a system of self-monitoring suicide ideation. *Journal of Psychopathology and Behavioral Assessment, 15,* 375–385.

Clum, G. A., & Yang, G. (1995). Additional support for the reliability and validity of the Modified Scale for Suicide Ideation. *Psychological Assessment, 7,* 122–125.

Comtois, K. A., & Linehan, M. M. (2006). Psychosocial treatments of suicidal behaviors: A practice-friendly review. *Journal of Clinical Psychology, 62,* 161–170.

Cotton, C., Peters, D. K., & Range, L. M. (1995). Psychometric properties of the Suicide Behaviors Questionnaire. *Death Studies, 19,* 391–397.

Cotton, C., & Range, L. (1993). Suicidality, hopelessness, and attitudes toward life and death in children. *Death Studies, 17,* 185–191.

Cull, J. G., & Gill, W. S. (1988). *Suicide probability scale manual.* Los Angeles, CA: Western Psychological Services.

Favazza, A. R., & Conterio, K. (1988). The plight of chronic self-mutilators. *Community Mental Health Journal, 24,* 22–30.

Fawcett, J., Busch, K. A., Jacobs, D., Kravitz, H. M., & Fogg, L. (1997). Suicide: A four-pathway clinical-biochemical model. *Annals of the New York Academy of Sciences, 836*, 288–301.

Fawcett, J., Scheftner, W. A., Fogg, L., Clark, D. C., Young, M. A., Hedeker, D., et al. (1990). Time-related predictors of suicide in major affective disorder. *American Journal of Psychiatry, 147*, 1189–1194.

Fliege, H., Kocalevent, R., Walter, O. B., Beck, S., Gratz, K. L., Gutierrez, P. M., et al. (2006). Three assessment tools for deliberate self-harm and suicide behavior: Evaluation and psychopathological correlates. *Journal of Psychosomatic Research, 61*, 113–121.

Giotakos, O., Markianos, M., & Vaidakis, N. (2005). Aggression, impulsivity, and plasma sex hormone levels in a group of rapists, in relation to their history of childhood attention-deficit/hyperactivity disorder symptoms. *Journal of Forensic Psychiatry and Psychology, 16*, 423–433.

Goldston, D. (2000). *Assessment of suicidal behaviors and risk among children and adolescents.* Technical report submitted to NIMH under Contract No. 263-MD-909995.

Goldston, D., Daniel, S. S., Reboussin, B., Frazier, P., & Harris, A. (2000). Cognitive risk factors and suicide attempts among formerly hospitalized adolescents: A prospective naturalistic study. *Journal of the American Academy of Child & Adolescent Psychiatry, 40*, 91–99.

Gould, M. S., Marrocco, F. A., Kleinman, M., Thomas, J. G., Mostkoff, K., Cote, J., et al. (2005). Evaluating iatrogenic risk of youth suicide screening programs: A randomized controlled trial. *Journal of the American Medical Association, 293*, 1635–1643.

Gratz, K. L. (2001). Measurement of deliberate self-harm: Preliminary data on the Deliberate Self-Harm Inventory. *Journal of Psychopathology and Behavioral Assessment, 23*, 253–263.

Guertin, T., Lloyd-Richardson, E., Spirito, A., Donaldson, D., & Boergers, J. (2001). Self-mutilative behavior in adolescents who attempt suicide by overdose. *Journal of the American Academy of Child & Adolescent, 40*, 1062–1069.

Gutierrez, P. M., Osman, A., Barrios, F. X., Kopper, B. A., Baker, M. T., & Haraburda, C. M. (2002). Development of the reasons for living inventory for young adults. *Journal of Clinical Psychology, 58*, 339–357.

Gutierrez, P. M., Osman, A., Kopper, B. A., & Barrios, F. X. (2000). Why young people do not kill themselves: The reasons for living inventory for adolescents. *Journal of Clinical Child Psychology, 29*, 177–187.

Gutierrez, P. M., Rodriguez, P. J., & Garcia, P. (2001). Suicide risk factors for young adults: Testing a model across ethnicities. *Death Studies, 25*, 319–340.

Harkavy Friedman, J., & Asnis, G. (1989). Assessment of suicidal behavior: A new instrument. *Psychiatric Annals, 19*, 382–387.

Harriss, L., Hawton, K., & Zahl, D. (2005). Value of measuring suicidal intent in the assessment of people attending hospital following self-poisoning or self-injury. *British Journal of Psychiatry, 186*, 60–66.

Healy, D. J., Barry, K., Blow, F., Welsh, D., & Milner, K. K. (2006). Routine use of the Beck Scale for Suicide Ideation in a psychiatric emergency department. *General Hospital Psychiatry, 28*, 323–329.

Hilt, L. M., Nock, M. K., Lloyd-Richardson, E., & Prinstein, M. J. (in press). Longitudinal study of an interpersonal model of non-suicidal self-injury among preadolescents. *Journal of Early Adolescence,* Manuscript submitted for publication.

Hjelmeland, H. (1996). Verbally expressed intentions of parasuicide: II. Prediction of fatal and nonfatal repetition. *Crisis, 17*, 10–14.

Holden, R. R. (2003). Differentiating suicidal motivations and manifestations in a forensic sample. *Canadian Journal of Behavioral Sciences, 35*, 35–44.

Holden, R. R., & DeLisle, M. (2006). Factor Structure of the Reasons for Attempting Suicide Questionnaire (RSAQ) with suicide attempters. *Journal of Psychopathology and Behavioral Assessment, 28*, 1–8.

Holden, R. R., Kerr, P. S., Mendonca, J. D., & Velamoor, V. R. (1998). Are some motives more linked to suicide proneness than others? *Journal of Clinical Psychology, 54*, 569–576.

Ivanoff, A., Jang, S. J., Smyth, N. J., & Linehan, M. M. (1994). Fewer reasons for staying alive when you are thinking of killing yourself: The brief reasons for living inventory. *Journal of Psychopathology and Behavioral Assessment, 16*, 1–13.

Jacobs, D. G. (Ed.). (1999). *Harvard Medical School guide to suicide assessment and intervention.* San Francisco, CA: Jossey-Bass.

Joiner, T. E., Jr., Conwell, Y., Fitzpatrick, K. K., Witte, T. K., Schmidt, N. B., Berlim, M. T., et al. (2005). Four studies on how past and current suicidality relate even when "everything but the kitchen sink" is covaried. *Journal of Abnormal Psychology, 114*, 291–303.

Joiner, T. E., Jr., Rudd, M. D., & Rajab, M. H. (1999). Agreement between self- and clinician-rated suicidal symptoms in a clinical sample of young adults: Explaining discrepancies. *Journal of Consulting and Clinical Psychology, 67*, 171–176.

Joiner, T. E., Jr., Steer, R. A., Brown, G., Beck, A. T., Pettit, J. W., & Rudd, M. D. (2003). Worst-point suicide plans: A dimension of suicidality predictive of past suicide attempts and eventual death by suicide. *Behaviour Research and Therapy, 41*, 1469–1480.

Joiner, T. E., Jr., Walker, R. L., Rudd, M. D., & Jobes, D. A. (1999). Scientizing and routinizing the assessment of suicidality in outpatient practice. *Professional Psychology: Research and Practice, 30*, 447–453.

Kaplan, M. L., Asnis, G. M., Sanderson, W. C., Keswani, L., De Lecuona, J. M., & Joseph, S. (1994). Suicide assessment: Clinical interview vs. self-report. *Journal of Clinical Psychology, 50*, 294–298.

Kessler, R. C., Berglund, P., Borges, G., Nock, M., & Wang, P. S. (2005). Trends in suicide ideation, plans, gestures, and attempts in the United States, 1990–1992 to 2001–2003. *Journal of American Medical Association, 293*, 2487–2495.

Kessler, R. C., Borges, G., & Walters, E. E. (1999). Prevalence of and risk factors for lifetime suicide attempts in the National Comorbidity Survey. *Archives of General Psychiatry, 56*, 617–626.

Kleespies, P. M., Berman, A. L., Ellis, T. E., McKeon, R., McNeil, D., Resnick, H., et al. (2000). *Report on education and training in behavioral emergencies.* Retrieved from http://www.apa.org/divisions/div12/sections/section7/tfreport.html

Kleespies, P. M., & Dettmer, E. L. (2000a). An evidence-based approach to evaluating and managing suicidal emergencies. *Journal of Clinical Psychology, 56*, 1109–1130.

Kleespies, P. M., & Dettmer, E. L. (2000b). The stress of patient emergencies for the clinician: Incidence, impact, and means of coping. *Journal of Clinical Psychology, 56*, 1353–1369.

Klimes-Dougan, B. (1998). Screening for suicidal ideation in children and adolescents: Methodological considerations. *Journal of Adolescence, 21*, 435–444.

Klonsky, E. D., Oltmanns, T. F., & Turkheimer, E. (2003). Deliberate self-harm in a nonclinical population: Prevalence and psychological correlates. *American Journal of Psychiatry, 160*, 1501–1508.

Koons, C. R., Robins, C. I., Tweed, J. L., Lynch, T. R., Gonzalez, A. M., Morse, J. Q., et al. (2001). Efficacy of dialectical behavior therapy in women veterans with borderline personality disorder. *Behavior Therapy, 32*, 371–390.

Linehan, M. M. (1981). *Suicide behaviors questionnaire.* Unpublished manuscript, University of Washington, Seattle, WA.

Linehan, M. M. (1997). Behavioral treatments of suicidal behaviors. Definitional obfuscation and treatment outcomes. *Annals of the New York Academy of Science, 836*, 302–328.

Linehan, M. M., Armstrong, H. E., Suarez, A., Allmon, D., & Heard, H. L. (1991). Cognitive-behavioral treatment of chronically parasuicidal borderline patients. *Archives of General Psychiatry, 48*, 1060–1064.

Linehan, M. M., Camper, P., Chiles, J. A., Strosahl, K., & Shearin, E. (1987). Interpersonal problem solving and parasuicide. *Cognitive Therapy and Research, 11*, 1–12.

Linehan, M. M., Chiles, J. A., Egan, K. J., Devine, R. H., & Laffaw, J. A. (1986). Presenting problems of parasuicides versus suicide ideators and nonsuicidal psychiatric patients. *Journal of Consulting and Clinical Psychology, 54*, 880–881.

Linehan, M. M., Comtois, K. A., Brown, M. Z., Heard, H. L., & Wagner, A. (2006). Suicide attempt self-injury interview (SASII): Development, reliability, and validity of a scale to assess suicide attempts and intentional self-injury. *Psychological Assessment, 18*, 302–312.

Linehan, M. M., Comtois, K. A., Murray, A. M., Brown, M. Z., Gallop, R. J., Heard, H. L., et al. (2006). Two-year randomized controlled trial and follow-up of dialectical behavior therapy vs. therapy by experts for suicidal behaviors and borderline personality disorder. *Archives of General Psychiatry, 63*, 757–766.

Linehan, M. M., Goodstein, J. L., Nielsen, S. L., & Chiles, J. A. (1983). Reasons for staying alive when you are thinking of killing yourself: The reasons for living inventory. *Journal of Consulting and Clinical Psychology, 51*, 276–286.

Linehan, M. M., Heard, H. L., & Armstrong, H. E. (1993). Naturalistic follow-up of a behavioral treatment for chronically parasuicidal borderline patients. *Archives of General Psychiatry, 50*, 971–974.

Linehan, M. M., Wagner, A. W., & Cox, G. (1989). *Parasuicide history interview: Comprehensive assessment of parasuicidal behavior.* Seattle, WA: University of Washington.

Lloyd, E. E., Kelley, M. L., & Hope, T. (1997). *Self-mutilation in a community sample of adolescents: Descriptive characteristics and provisional prevalence rates.* Paper presented at the Society for Behavioral Medicine, New Orleans, LA.

Mann, J. J., Brent, D. A., & Arango, V. (2001). The neurobiology and genetics of suicide and attempted suicide: A focus on the serotonergic system. *Neuropsychopharmacology, 24*, 467–477.

Mann, J. J., Currier, D., Stanley, B., Oquendo, M. A., Amsel, L. V., & Ellis, S. P. (2006). Can biological tests assist prediction of suicide in mood disorders? *International Journal of Neuropsychopharmacology, 9*, 465–474.

Miller, I. W., Norman, W. H., Bishop, S. B., & Dow, M. G. (1986). The modified scale for suicidal ideation: Reliability and validity. *Journal of Consulting and Clinical Psychology, 54,* 724–725.

Muehlenkamp, J. J., & Gutierrez, P. M. (2004). An investigation of differences between self-injurious behavior and suicide attempts in a sample of adolescents. *Suicide and Life Threatening Behavior, 34,* 12–23.

Nock, M. K., Borges, G., Bromet, E. J., Alonso, J., Angermeyer, M., Beautrais, A., et al. (2007). *Prevalence and risk factors for suicide ideation, plans, and attempts in the WHO World Mental Health Surveys.* Manuscript submitted for publication.

Nock, M. K., Holmberg, E. B., Photos, V. I., & Michel, B. D. (2007). Self-Injurious Thoughts and Behaviors Interview: Development, reliability, and validity in an adolescent sample. *Psychological Assessment, 19,* 309–317.

Nock, M. K., Joiner, T. E., Jr., Gordon, K. H., Lloyd-Richardson, E., & Prinstein, M. J. (2006). Non-suicidal self-injury among adolescents: Diagnostic correlates and relation to suicide attempts. *Psychiatry Research, 144,* 65–72.

Nock, M. K., & Kazdin, A. E. (2002). Examination of affective, cognitive, and behavioral factors and suicide-related outcomes in children and young adolescents. *Journal of Clinical Child and Adolescent Psychology, 31,* 48–58.

Nock, M. K., & Kessler, R. C. (2006). Prevalence of and risk factors for suicide attempts versus suicide gestures: Analysis of the National Comorbidity Survey. *Journal of Abnormal Psychology, 115,* 616–623.

Nock, M. K., & Prinstein, M. J. (2004). A functional approach to the assessment of self-mutilative behavior. *Journal of Consulting and Clinical Psychology, 72,* 885–890.

Nock, M. K., & Prinstein, M. J. (2005). Contextual features and behavioral functions of self-mutilation among adolescents. *Journal of Abnormal Psychology, 114,* 140–146.

O'Carroll, P. W., Berman, A. L., Maris, R. W., Moscicki, E. K., Tanney, B. L., & Silverman, M. M. (1996). Beyond the Tower of Babel: A nomenclature for suicidology. *Suicide and Life Threatening Behavior, 26,* 237–252.

Oquendo, M. A., & Mann, J. J. (2000). The biology of impulsivity and suicidality. *Psychiatric Clinics of North America, 23,* 11–25.

Orbach, I., Gilboa-Schechtman, E., Sheffer, A., Meged, S., Har-Even, D., & Stein, D. (2006). Negative bodily self in suicide attempters. *Suicide and Life Threatening Behavior, 36,* 136–153.

Orbach, I., Milstein, I., Har-Even, D., Apter, A., Tiano, S., & Elizner, A. (1991). A Multi-Attitude Suicide Tendency Scale for adolescents. *Psychological Assessment, 3,* 398–404.

Osman, A., Barrios, F. X., Grittmann, L. R., & Osman, J. R. (1993). The Multi-Attitude Suicide Tendency Scale: Psychometric characteristics in an American sample. *Journal of Clinical Psychology, 49,* 701–708.

Osman, A., Downs, W. R., Kopper, B. A., Barrios, F. X., Baker, M. T., Osman, J. R., et al. (1998). The Reasons for Living Inventory for Adolescents (RFL-A): Development and psychometric properties. *Journal of Clinical Psychology, 54,* 1063–1078.

Osman, A., Kopper, B. A., Barrios, F. X., Osman, J. R., Besett, T., & Linehan, M. M. (1996). The Brief Reasons for Living Inventory for Adolescents (BRFL-A). *Journal of Abnormal Child Psychology, 24,* 433–443.

Osman, A., Kopper, B. A., Linehan, M. M., Barrios, F. X., Gutierrez, P. M., & Bagge, C. L. (1999). Validation of the Adult Suicidal Ideation Questionnaire and the Reasons for Living Inventory in an adult psychiatric inpatient sample. *Psychological Assessment, 11,* 115–123.

Ovuga, E., Boardman, J., & Wassermann, D. (2005). Prevalence of suicide ideation in two districts of Uganda. *Archives of Suicide Research, 9,* 321–332.

Paykel, E. S., Myers, J. K., Lindenthal, J. J., & Tanner, J. (1974). Suicidal feelings in the general population: A prevalence study. *British Journal of Psychiatry, 124,* 460–469.

Paykel, E. S., Prusoff, B. A., & Myers, J. K. (1975). Suicide attempts and recent life events. A controlled comparison. *Archives of General Psychiatry, 32,* 327–333.

Pfeffer, C. R., Conte, H. R., Plutchik, R., & Jerrett, I. (1979). Suicidal behavior in latency-age children. *Journal of the American Academy of Child Psychiatry, 18,* 679–692.

Pinto, A., Whisman, M. A., & Conwell, Y. (1998). Reasons for living in a clinical sample of adolescents. *Journal of Adolescence, 21,* 397–405.

Plutchik, R., van Praag, H. M., Conte, H. R., & Picard, S. (1989). Correlates of suicide and violence risk 1: The suicide risk measure. *Comprehensive Psychiatry, 30,* 296–302.

Pomili, M., Tatarelli, R., & Lester, D. (2006). Sex differences in reasons for living. *Perceptual and Motor Skills, 102,* 321–322.

Prinstein, M. J., Nock, M. K., Spirito, A., & Grapentine, W. L. (2001). Multimethod assessment of suicidality in adolescent psychiatric inpatients: Preliminary results. *Journal of the American Academy of Child & Adolescent Psychiatry, 40,* 1053–1061.

Range, L. M., & Knott, E. C. (1997). Twenty suicide assessment instruments: Evaluation and recommendations. *Death Studies, 21,* 25–58.

Rathus, J. H., & Miller, A. L. (2002). Dialectical behavior therapy adapted for suicidal adolescents. *Suicide and Life Threatening Behavior, 32*, 146–157.

Reynolds, W. M. (1988). *Suicide Ideation Questionnaire: Professional manual.* Odessa, FL: Psychological Assessment Resources.

Reynolds, W. M. (1990). Development of a semistructured clinical interview for suicidal behaviors in adolescents. *Psychological Assessment, 2*, 382–390.

Reynolds, W. M. (1991a). *Adult Suicide Ideation Questionnaire: Professional manual.* Odessa, FL: Psychological Assessment Resources.

Reynolds, W. M. (1991b). Psychometric characteristics of the Adult Suicide Ideation Questionnaire in college students. *Journal of Personality Asessment, 56*, 289–307.

Reynolds, W. M., & Mazza, J. (1999). Assessment of suicidal ideation in inner-city children and young adolescents: Reliability and validity of the Suicidal Ideation Questionnaire-Jr. *School Psychology Review, 28*, 17–30.

Rifai, A. H., George, C. J., Stack, J. A., Mann, J. J., & Reynolds, C. F. (1994). Hopelessness in suicide attempters after acute treatment of major depression in late life. *American Journal of Psychiatry, 151*, 1687–1690.

Ross, S., & Heath, N. (2002). A study of the frequency of self-mutilation in a community sample of adolescents. *Journal of Youth and Adolescence, 31*, 67–77.

Rudd, M. D. (1989). The prevalence of suicidal ideation among college students. *Suicide and Life Threatening Behavior, 19*, 173–183.

Rudd, M. D., Berman, A. L., Joiner, T. E., Jr., Nock, M. K., Silverman, M. M., Mandrusiak, M., et al. (2006). Warning signs for suicide: Theory, research, and clinical applications. *Suicide and Life Threatening Behavior, 36*, 255–262.

Rudd, M. D., Joiner, T., & Rajab, M. H. (1996). Relationships among suicide ideators, attempters, and multiple attempters in a young-adult sample. *Journal of Abnormal Psychology, 105*, 541–550.

Sabo, A. N., Gunderson, J. G., Najavits, L. M., Chauncey, D., & Kisiel, C. (1995). Changes in self-destructiveness of borderline patients in psychotherapy: A prospective follow-up. *Journal of Nervous and Mental Disease, 183*, 370–376.

Sansone, R. A., Pole, M., Dakroub, H., & Butler, M. (2006). Childhood trauma, borderline personality symptomatology, and psychophysiological and pain disorders in adulthood. *Psychosomatics, 47*, 158–162.

Sansone, R. A., Songer, D. A., & Miller, K. A. (2005). Childhood abuse, mental healthcare utilization, self-harm behavior, and multiple psychiatric diagnoses among inpatients with and without a borderline diagnosis. *Comprehensive Psychiatry, 46*, 117–120.

Sansone, R. A., Wiederman, M. W., & Sansone, L. A. (1998). The Self-Harm Inventory (SHI): Development of a scale for indentifying self-destructive behaviors and borderline personality disorder. *Journal of Clinical Psychology, 54*, 973–983.

Santa Mina, E. E., Gallop, R., Links, P., Heslegrave, R., Pringle, D., Wekerle, C., et al. (2006). The Self-Injury Questionnaire: Evaluation of the psychometric properties in a clinical population. *Journal of Psychiatric and Mental Health Nursing, 13*, 221–227.

Shaffer, D., Scott, M., Wilcox, H., Maslow, C., Hicks, R., Lucas, C. P., et al. (2004). The Columbia Suicide Screen: Validity and reliability of a screen for youth suicide and depression. *Journal of the American Academy of Child & Adolescent Psychiatry, 43*, 71–79.

Steer, R. A., Kumar, G., & Beck, A. T. (1993). Self-reported suicidal ideation in adolescent psychiatric inpatients. *Journal of Consulting and Clinical Psychology, 61*, 1096–1099.

Velting, D., & Miller, A. (1998). *Diagnostic risk factors for adolescent parasuicidal behavior.* Presentation at NIMH workshop, "Suicidality in Youth: Developing the Knowledge Base for Youth at Risk," Bethesda, MD.

Vuorilehto, M. S., Melartin, T. K., & Isometsä, E. T. (2006). Suicidal behaviour among primary-care patients with depressive disorders. *Psychological Medicine, 36*, 203–210.

Westefeld, J. S., Badura, A., Kiel, J., & Scheel, K. (1996). Development of the College Student Reasons for Living Inventory with African Americans. *Journal of College Student Psychotherapy, 10*, 61–65.

Westefeld, J. S., Cardin, D., & Deaton, W. L. (1992). Development of the College Student Reasons for Living Inventory. *Suicide and Life Threatening Behavior, 22*, 442–452.

Westefeld, J. S., Scheel, K., & Maples, M. R. (1998). Psychometric analyses of the College Student Reasons for Living Inventory using a clinical population. *Measurement and Evaluation in Counseling and Development, 31*, 86–94.

Wetzler, S., Asnis, G. M., Hyman, R. B., Virtue, C., Zimmerman, J., & Rathus, J. H. (1996). Characteristics of suicidality among adolescents. *Suicide and Life Threatening Behavior, 26*, 37–45.

Wong, W. S. (2004). Attitudes toward life and death among Chinese adolescents: The Chinese version of the multi-attitude suicide tendency scale. *Death Studies, 28*, 91–110.

Zoroglu, S. S., Tuzun, U., Sar, V., Tutkun, H., Savacs, H. A., Ozturk, M., et al. (2003). Suicide attempt and self-mutilation among Turkish high school students in relation with abuse, neglect and dissociation. *Psychiatry and Clinical Neurosciences, 57*, 119–126.

Part IV

Anxiety Disorders

9

Child and Adolescent Anxiety Disorders

Wendy K. Silverman
Thomas H. Ollendick

This chapter summarizes the research evidence supporting psychological assessment strategies for use with children and adolescents with anxiety disorders. The focus is on assessment measures and strategies that are not only evidence based but also clinically relevant and feasible for practitioners. The information provided in this chapter should help the reader determine the suitability and value of each measure for specific clinical and research purposes.

Consistent with the other chapters in this volume, this chapter begins with a description of the disorder. This is followed by a discussion of psychological assessment measures and issues involved in their use for accomplishing three primary purposes of assessment: (1) diagnosis, (2) case conceptualization and treatment planning, and (3) treatment monitoring and evaluation. An "Overall Evaluation" highlighting the scientific suitability and clinical relevance of the measures covered in the chapter concludes each section. The chapter ends with concluding comments and recommendations.

There are additional purposes of assessment that can be achieved using other types of assessment methods that are not covered in this chapter. For example, in research settings, investigators have applied performance-based methods, particularly those emanating from experimental cognitive psychology (e.g., Stroop tests, dot probe tests) to assess cognitive and information biases and processing of threat-related information in youth with anxiety disorders. The interested reader is referred to Vasey, Dalgleish, and Silverman (2003) for summaries and critiques of these methods.

The importance of sympathetic arousal in the experience of anxious emotions also has led investigators to apply methods of psychophysiology to assess youth heart rate, blood pressure, and electrodermal responding (e.g., Beidel, 1991; Carrión et al., 2002; King, 1994). In addition, because levels of negative affect and anxiety have been correlated with amygdala activity in adults (Davidson, Abercrombie, Nitschke, & Putnam, 1999), recent studies have used fMRI to assess amygdala activation in response to emotionally expressive faces in younger anxious individuals. Findings, overall, have been mixed with regard to showing an association between anxiety and amygdala activity. Moreover, the cost and specialized training of the equipment needed to assess physiological and biological indexes serve to reduce the likelihood of their wide adaptation in practice settings. The reader is referred to Pine et al. (2001) for a summary and critique of this work and to Pine (2006) for the use of brain imaging in child and adolescent disorders, including anxiety.

Finally, although projective methods are frequently used in clinical practice, their utility for informing diagnosis, case conceptualization and treatment planning, or treatment monitoring and evaluation has scarce empirical support. Lilienfeld, Wood, and Garb (2000) provide a critical evaluation of the empirical underpinnings of projective techniques; they will not be reviewed in this chapter.

NATURE OF THE DISORDERS

Anxiety problems are among the most common forms of emotional disturbance in children and adolescents (e.g., Ollendick & March, 2004; Silverman & Ginsburg, 1998). Furthermore, although mild anxiety problems are often short-lived, childhood anxiety disorders are often chronic, and they interfere substantially with children's adaptive functioning. Many of them persist into adulthood, and many adult anxiety disorders appear to have their onset in childhood and adolescence (see Ollendick & Seligman, 2006; Saavedra & Silverman, 2002).

As defined most recently in the *Diagnostic and Statistical Manual of Mental Disorders*, 4th Edition (DSM-IV-TR; American Psychiatric Association, 2000), the major subtypes of anxiety disorders include specific phobia (SP; formerly simple phobia), social phobia (SOP), panic disorder (PD) with and without agoraphobia, generalized anxiety disorder (GAD), obsessive compulsive disorder (OCD), and post-traumatic stress disorder (PTSD). Separation anxiety disorder (SAD) is the only anxiety disorder in the DSM-IV-TR that is viewed as specific to childhood. Anxiety disorders of childhood and adolescence that were contained in DSM-III and DSM-III-R, overanxious disorder and avoidant disorder, were subsumed under GAD and SOP, respectively, in DSM-IV-TR. This decision was based largely on the lack of evidence for the validity of overanxious disorder and avoidant disorder as distinct from GAD and SOP.

Epidemiology

The prevalence of anxiety disorders in childhood and adolescence has been ascertained in unselected community and referred clinical samples. Studies of community samples generally find anxiety disorders to be relatively common among children and adolescents, with estimates of overall population prevalence ranging from 12% to 17%, with rates falling from 5% to 10% when minimal requirements for impairment are considered in these nonclinical samples (Anderson, Williams, McGee, & Silva, 1987). Averaged for boys and girls across age, prevalence estimates for unselected community samples range from 0.7% to 12.9% for SAD, 2.7% to 12.4% for GAD, 2.4% to 9.2% for SP, and 1% to 1.1% for SOP (Costello, Egger, & Angold, 2004). Prevalence estimates vary from 0.3% to 3% for OCD (Albano, Chorpita, & Barlow, 1996) and, in studies of adolescents only, vary from 1% to 4.7% for PD (Albano et al., 1996).

Rates for anxiety disorders among clinic-referred samples of anxious children and adolescents vary from 11.4% to 33% for SAD, 15% to 17.5% for GAD, and 15% to 25.3% for SOP (Albano et al., 1996; Costello et al., 2004). Albano et al. (1996) also reported that 13.3% of their sample of 7- to 17-year-olds presented with OCD, 9.6% for specific phobia, and 6% for PD. With respect to prevalence rates by sex, the general pattern across studies is that girls report higher and more intense normative, subclinical, and clinical levels of fear, worry, and anxiety than do boys. Further research is however needed to determine specific patterns (e.g., content) of fear, worry, and anxiety by sex (see Silverman & Carter, 2006). Further, compared to community studies, clinic-based findings regarding youth prevalence rates by sex have been inconsistent and vary by anxiety disorder subtypes (Silverman & Carter, 2006). This inconsistency in clinic-based findings may stem in part from differences in families' perceived need and willingness to seek mental health services for their sons and daughters.

Etiological Factors

This section provides a brief overview of major etiological factors implicated in the development of the various forms of anxiety in childhood and adolescence. Although each factor is discussed separately, there are likely multiple pathways to a given anxiety disorder in youth, reflecting complex transactions among multiple factors (Cicchetti & Cohen, 1995). Similarly, depending on the configuration of other factors with which it occurs, any given pathway may lead to several different anxiety disorders, to other forms of psychopathology, or to no disorder at all. Such a position is consistent with a developmental psychopathology perspective on the development of anxiety disorders (see Silverman & Ollendick, 1999). The reader is referred to Weems and Silverman (in press) for further discussion of each of these etiological factors, including biological factors.

Genetic Factors

Family history studies consistently show substantial familial risk for anxiety disorders (see Eley, 2001; Silverman, & Nelles, 1988). This risk has been reported among children of clinically anxious parents (Turner, Beidel, & Costello, 1987) as well as parents of clinically anxious children (Last, Hersen, Kazdin, Orvaschel, & Perrin, 1991). Although such findings suggest the possibility of genetic influences, they also reflect the influence of the family environment. Although there are no adoption studies relevant to this issue, numerous twin studies of anxiety are available. Twin studies of anxiety disorders among adults generally indicate significant genetic influence with most recent studies suggesting both general and disorder specific genetic risks (e.g., Kendler, Neale, Kessler, Heath, & Eaves, 1992). Twin studies further suggest that about 33% of the variance in measures of childhood anxiety symptoms is accounted for by genetic influences (see Eley, 2001).

Temperamental Factors

Negative affectivity (Watson & Clark, 1984) and similar temperamental dimensions, including neuroticism (Eysenck & Eysenck, 1985) and behavioral inhibition to the unfamiliar (Reznick, Hegeman, Kaufman, Woods, & Jacobs, 1992), have been shown to increase risk for anxiety and to be moderately heritable (see Lonigan, Vasey, Phillips, & Hazen, 2003). Of these overlapping constructs, behavioral inhibition (BI) has received the most attention as a risk factor for childhood anxiety disorders. BI appears to be associated with heightened risk for anxiety disorders in childhood, particularly in that subset of children who show stable BI from infancy through middle childhood and into adolescence (Turner, Beidel, & Wolff, 1996). Because studies also show that many BI children do not develop anxiety disorders and uninhibited children sometimes do, BI can be neither sufficient nor necessary to produce anxiety disorders. Instead, paths to anxiety disorders involving BI or similar anxiety-prone temperamental factors also involve shared and unshared environmental factors (Eley, 2001). It is also unclear whether BI poses a general risk for anxiety or a specific risk for SOP (see Kagan, 1997), or for psychopathology more broadly construed (Muris & Ollendick, 2005).

Exposure to Stressful Events and Uncontrollable Environments

In interaction with other factors, stressful life events appear to be associated with anxiety symptoms and their onset in childhood. The controllability of environmental events, especially early in childhood, may be particularly important in the development of anxiety disorders (see Chorpita & Barlow, 1998; Weems & Silverman, 2006). Early exposure to controllable environments appears to protect against anxiety, whereas uncontrollable environments seem to predispose to anxiety. For example, infant rhesus monkeys exposed to chronically uncontrollable environments responded to novel stimuli with greater fear and less exploration (Mineka, Gunnar, & Champoux, 1986) and higher cortisol levels (Insel, Scanlan, & Champoux, 1988) than do monkeys who had control over their environment. Evidence from studies of children and adolescents also supports the predisposing role of uncontrollability to anxiety (e.g., Weems, Silverman, Rapee, & Pina, 2003) and the protective role of controllable experiences (see Weems & Silverman, 2006).

Learning Influences

The principles of respondent conditioning suggest several mechanisms by which environmental experiences may predispose to, precipitate, or protect against the development of anxiety disorders (Bouton, Mineka, & Barlow, 2001). Consistent with this view, evidence suggests that a substantial percentage of children and adolescents with fears and phobias have a history of direct or indirect conditioning (Ollendick & King, 1991). However, even severely traumatic experiences are not always sufficient to produce phobic anxiety (e.g., Vernberg, La Greca, Silverman, & Prinstein, 1996). Moreover, even traumatic conditioning episodes are not necessary causes in as much as phobic anxiety can develop in their absence (see Menzies & Clarke, 1995).

Traumatic conditioning episodes appear to interact with predisposing factors such as temperament and prior learning history to produce heightened risk for phobic responses in vulnerable individuals. Growing evidence further suggests that direct conditioning experiences may account for only a small percentage of childhood phobias, with observation-based learning and information-processing modes of acquisition being predominant (e.g., Field, 2006; Field & Lawson, 2003).

Social and Interpersonal Processes

Interpersonal theories focus on the interpersonal environment of the child. Research suggests important peer (La Greca, 2001) and familial (Boer & Lindhout, 2001) influences on child and adolescent anxiety. Moreover, social contextual approaches suggest factors such as poverty, parental psychopathology, exposure to trauma, and exposure to violence can exacerbate vulnerability to developing an anxiety disorder (Dick-Niederhauser & Silverman, 2004).

Attachment theory suggests that human infants form enduring emotional bonds with their caregivers (Bowlby, 1977). Warren, Huston, Egeland, and Sroufe (1997) found that children classified as anxious/resistant in their attachment (assessed at 12 months of age) were more likely to have anxiety disorders at age 17 than children classified with other types of attachment, even when controlling for temperament and maternal anxiety. Insecure attachment also has been linked with increased levels of anxiety sensitivity (Weems, Berman, Silverman, & Rodriguez, 2002). The risk associated with insecure attachment status, however, is likely to depend on the co-occurrence of other predisposing factors such as BI temperament.

Overcontrolling parental behavior is also thought to influence childhood anxiety. For example, the presence of anxiety in either member of the mother–child dyad tends to elicit maternal overcontrol during interactions (Whaley, Pinto, & Sigman, 1999). Research, overall, suggests that parents who exhibit overcontrolling, overinvolved, dependent, or intrusive behavior may (a) prevent youth from facing fear-provoking events, a developmentally important task that allows children to develop solutions to face fear; and/or (b) send a message that particular stimuli are threatening or dangerous, which may reinforce youth avoidant behavior (see Silverman et al., 1988; Vasey & Ollendick, 2000).

Cognitive Biases and Distortions

Childhood anxiety disorders appear to be associated with a variety of information-processing biases at various stages in cognition, including encoding, interpretation, and recall (see Vasey et al., 2003). For example, clinically anxious and highly test-anxious youth show an attentional bias in favor of threat-relevant stimuli (Vasey, Daleiden, Williams, & Brown, 1995). Compared to normal controls, clinically anxious and highly test anxious youth also show a bias toward interpreting ambiguous information as threatening (Dadds, Barrett, Rapee, & Ryan, 1996). Whether such cognitive biases predispose one to or result from anxiety, once present, they may foster the maintenance and intensification of anxiety (Vasey et al., 2003). By virtue of their tendency to show attentional biases toward threat cues and to interpret ambiguous

information as threatening, anxious children and adolescents construct their own anxiogenic experiences. Anxiety sensitivity, the belief that anxiety sensations have negative social, psychological, and/or physical consequences, is another cognitive factor that has been implicated in the etiology of anxiety disorders, particularly panic attacks and panic disorder (e.g., Ollendick, 1998; Silverman & Weems 1998).

Summary

Anxiety disorders are among the most common disorders in childhood and adolescence. Prevalence estimates vary considerably, dependent on whether the samples are clinic-referred or community-based as well as the age and gender of the samples studied. The etiologies of anxiety disorders are multiple, complex, and overdetermined. That is, it is likely that there is more than one pathway to any one disorder and that any one pathway can result in any one of the anxiety disorders or, for that matter, other disorders or even no disorder. As a result, the assessment of these related but relatively distinct disorders require specific assessment tools. The specific tools depend on one's assessment purpose. We turn now to one main assessment purpose: diagnosis.

ASSESSMENT FOR PURPOSE OF DIAGNOSIS

This section deals with assessment measures and strategies most useful for formulating anxiety diagnoses in children and adolescents, namely diagnostic interview schedules. Emphasis is placed on the Anxiety Disorders Interview Schedule for Children for DSM-IV: Child and Parent Versions, which has the most research support in terms of utility for formulating reliable and valid diagnoses. The utility of rating scales for the purpose of diagnosis also is covered. Next, a discussion of "best practices" with respect to conceptual and practical issues in diagnosis, including differential diagnosis, is presented. The section concludes with an overall evaluation of available assessment instruments.

Semistructured and Structured Diagnostic Interview Schedules

The use of semistructured and structured interview schedules represents best practices for the purpose of formulating an anxiety disorder diagnosis in children and adolescents. A number of diagnostic interview schedules have been developed to cover the different types of anxiety disorders specified in the DSM-IV-TR. The most widely used interview schedules for diagnosing clinical disorders of childhood and adolescence including the anxiety disorders are presented in Table 9.1. In contrast to the unstructured clinical interview, semistructured and structured interviews are relatively standardized with respect to the types of questions that are asked of informants. This increase in standardization serves to reduce the error or variance attributed to interviewers, usage in diagnostic criteria, or both (Silverman, 1994).

Anxiety Disorders Interview Schedule for Children for DSM-IV: Child and Parent Versions

The Anxiety Disorders Interview Schedule for Children for DSM-IV: Child and Parent Versions (ADIS for DSM-IV: C/P; Silverman & Albano, 1996; Silverman, Saavedra, & Pina, 2001), a downward extension of the adult Anxiety Disorders Interview Schedule for DSM-IV (Brown, Di Nardo, & Barlow, 1994), is most detailed in its coverage of the anxiety disorders, relative to the other interview schedules listed in Table 9.1. The ADIS for DSM-IV: C/P and its previous DSM-III and DSM-III-R versions (Silverman, 1991) also have been used most frequently in the youth anxiety disorders research literature, including randomized clinical trials.

The ADIS for DSM-IV: C/P contains a series of modules that cover all the anxiety disorders described in DSM-IV-TR, as well as sections that cover the most prevalent disorders of childhood and adolescence (e.g., attention-deficit/hyperactivity disorder [ADHD], depressive disorder) and screening questions for most other disorders (e.g., eating disorders, enuresis). Additional questions are included that allow interviewers to obtain information about the history of the problem as well as situational and youth cognitive factors influencing anxiety.

In addition, the ADIS for DSM-IV: C/P contains clinician severity rating scales (ADIS-C/P: CRS) that assess for degree of impairment or interference in youth functioning associated with the specific anxiety disorder endorsed by the youth and parent, respectively. Specifically, based on the information obtained from the child and parent versions of the interview, interviewers assign the degree of distress and interference associated with each disorder (0 = "none" to 8 = "very severely disturbing/impairing") with respect to the youth's peer relationships, school work, family life, and personal distress. Each module in the interview also contains questions that allow interviewers to assign 0-to-8 ratings on the youth's fear and avoidance of diverse situations relevant to a particular disorder (e.g., SOP, SP). Similar to the adult ADIS, clinician severity ratings of 4 ("definitely disturbing/impairing") or higher are viewed as "clinical" diagnoses and those less than four are viewed as "subclinical" or subthreshold.

Reliability of Diagnoses

A number of studies conducted in university-based research clinics have confirmed empirically the reliability of diagnoses formulated using the ADIS for DSM-IV: C/P, including inter-rater reliability (Grills & Ollendick, 2003; Rapee, Barrett, Dadds, & Evans, 1994; Silverman et al., 1988), retest reliability of specific diagnoses (Silverman & Eisen, 1992), and retest reliability of symptom patterns (Silverman & Rabian, 1995).

Validity of Diagnoses

Research has confirmed empirically the validity of diagnoses formulated using the child and parent versions of the ADIS by showing that scores on child and parent rating scales converge in expected ways with diagnoses (e.g., Weems, Silverman, Saavedra, Pina, & Lumpkin, 1999; Wood, Piacentini, Bergman, McCracken, & Barrios, 2002). Wood et al. (2002), for example, evaluated concurrent validity of ADIS-C/P diagnoses of SOP, SAD, GAD, and PD in children and adolescents referred to an outpatient anxiety disorders clinic. In addition to youth and parents being administered their respective versions of the ADIS interviews, they were administered the Multidimensional Anxiety Scale for Children (MASC; March, Parker, Sullivan, Stallings, & Conners, 1997). Strong correspondence was found between ADIS-C/P diagnoses and empirically derived MASC factor scores corresponding to each of these diagnoses, with the exception of GAD.

Additional Diagnostic Interview Schedules

In addition to the ADIS-IV: C/P, other diagnostic interview schedules used to assess the presence of

TABLE 9.1 Ratings of Instruments Used for Diagnosis

Instrument	Norms	Internal Consistency	Inter-Rater Reliability	Test–Retest Reliability	Content Validity	Construct Validity	Validity Generalization	Clinical Utility	Highly Recommended
Diagnostic Interview Schedules									
ADIS C/P-IV	NA	NA	E	E	E	E	E	E	✓
DISC-IV	NA	NA	A	G	G	G	G	G	
DICA	NA	NA	A	G	G	G	G	G	
K-SADS	NA	NA	G	A	A	A	G	A	
Child Self-Rating Scales									
RCMAS	E	G	NA	G	G	E	G	G	
STAIC	G	G	NA	G	G	G	G	A	
FSSC-R	A	E	NA	G	E	G	G	G	✓
MASC	A	G	NA	G	G	E	E	G	✓
SCARED	G	E	NA	G	G	G	E	G	
SCAS	A	G	NA	A	E	E	G	G	
SPAIC	A	G	NA	E	E	G	G	G	✓
SASC-R	A	G	NA	G	G	G	G	G	
CASI	A	G	NA	G	G	G	G	G	

Note: ADIS C/P-IV = Anxiety Disorders Interview Schedule; DISC-IV = Diagnostic Interview Schedule for Children, Version IV; DICA = Diagnostic Interview Schedule for Children and Adolescents; K-SADS = Schedule for Affective Disorders and Schizophrenia for School-Age Children; RCMAS = Revised Children's Manifest Anxiety Scale; STAIC = State-Trait Anxiety Inventory for Children; FSSC-R = Fear Survey Scale for Children-Revised; MASC = Multidimensional Anxiety Scale for Children; SCARED = Screen for Child Anxiety-Related Emotional Disorders; SCAS = Spence Children's Anxiety Scale; SPAIC = Social Phobia and Anxiety Inventory for Children; SASC-R = Social Anxiety Scale for Children-Revised; CASI = Children's Anxiety Sensitivity Index; A = Adequate; G = Good; E = Excellent; NA = Not Applicable.

anxiety disorders in youth include the Diagnostic Interview Schedule for Children (DISC-IV; Shaffer, Fisher, Lucas, Dulcan, & Schwab-Stone, 2000), the Diagnostic Interview for Children and Adolescents (DICA; Herjanic & Reich, 1982; Reich, 2000), and the Schedule for Affective Disorders and Schizophrenia in School-Age Children (K-SADS; Ambrosini, 2000). Similar to the ADIS-IV: C/P, these structured or semistructured interview schedules have child and parent versions, assess most of the DSM-IV disorders of childhood and adolescence, including anxiety disorders, and can be used across a wide age range of children. Diagnoses are formulated upon completion of both the youth and parent interviews, and are determined either by rules derived by the interview developers or by computerized algorithms, depending on the specifications of the interview schedule.

Rating Scales

A host of self-rating scales are available for use in assessing anxiety problems in children and adolescents. The most widely used child anxiety self-ratings scales are presented in Table 9.1; also contained in the table are several additional scales that are not discussed in this narrative section of the chapter. Unfortunately, most of these measures are omnibus measures and do not possess the specificity to identify particular anxiety disorders and may be less useful than interviews for diagnostic purposes. Historically, the Revised Children's Manifest Anxiety Scale (RCMAS; Reynolds & Richmond, 1985) and the State-Trait Anxiety Inventory for Children (STAIC; Spielberger, 1973) have been used to identify the presence of anxiety and to quantify anxiety symptoms in youth (see Myers & Winters, 2002; Silverman & Saavedra, 2004). The RCMAS is a 37-item (28 Anxiety and 9 Lie items) rating scale (yes/no) that contains three subscales: physiological, worry/oversensitivity, and concentration. The STAIC is a 20-item rating scale that assesses the chronic (trait) and acute (state) symptoms of anxiety using a 3-point scale (hardly ever, sometimes, often). The Fear Survey Schedule for Children-Revised (FSSC-R; Ollendick, 1983) has been most widely used to assess fear. Containing 80 items, which are rated along a 3-point scale (none, some, a lot), the factor scales consist of the following: fear of failure and criticism, fear of the unknown,

fear of danger and death, medical fears, and small animals.

Discriminant Validity of Youth Self-Rating Scales

Several studies have examined the ability of the RCMAS and STAIC to discriminate between youth with anxiety disorders and youth with no disorders or youth with other disorders. Mattison, Bagnato, and Brubaker (1988) reported that outpatient boys diagnosed with DSM-III overanxious disorder scored significantly higher than boys with either dysthymia or ADD on the worry/oversensitivity and physiological factor scales of the RCMAS. In another study, Perrin and Last (1992) showed that the total score on the RCMAS, along with each of its three subscale scores, differentiated outpatient children with anxiety disorders from children with no disorders. However, the scales did not differentiate between children with an anxiety disorder and children with ADHD. Moreover, Perrin and Last (1992) showed that the state and trait scales of the STAIC differentiated between youth with an anxiety disorder and youth with no disorder, but again not between youth with an anxiety disorder and youth with ADHD. Finally, Lonigan, Carey, and Finch (1994) reported the total score and the worry/oversensitivity subscale of the RCMAS was able to distinguish between hospitalized youth with pure anxiety disorders and those with pure affective disorders, a distinction that has often proven to be problematic and elusive (Seligman & Ollendick, 1998). Thus, it appears that these "older" instruments are successful in discriminating between youth with an anxiety disorder and those without an anxiety disorder, but are less successful in discriminating between youth with ADHD, and at least in outpatient samples, youth with dysthymia or major depressive disorder.

A meta-analysis of 43 published studies by Seligman, Ollendick, Langley, and Baldacci (2004) supports this conclusion. A large effect size (ES) was found for both the RCMAS (ES = 1.30) and the STAIC (ES = .71) when they were used to compare youth with an anxiety disorder to youth with no disorder, as was initially shown by Mattison et al. (1988) and Perrin and Last (1992). However, when comparing youth with anxiety disorders with those with "other" disorders, the picture was more mixed. The RCMAS and STAIC were found to be useful when discriminating between youth with anxiety disorders and youth with oppositional and conduct problems (ES = .54), but not between youth with ADHD (ES < .25) and youth with an affective disorder (ES < .25). According to Hemphill's (2003) analysis of distribution of effect sizes found in the psychological assessment literature, small effect sizes are those below .43, medium effect sizes between .43 and .70, and large effect sizes above .70. Thus, the discriminant validity of these "older" measures has been only partially supported.

In recent years, several "newer" self-rating scales have been developed in an attempt to differentiate the anxiety disorders from other disorders and to discriminate between the various childhood anxiety disorders, including the MASC (March et al., 1997), the Screen for Child Anxiety-Related Emotional Disorders (SCARED; Birmaher et al., 1997), and the Spence Children's Anxiety Scale (SCAS; Spence, 1997, 1998). The MASC is a 39-item rating scale that assesses anxiety in youth in four areas (i.e., physical symptoms, social anxiety, harm avoidance, and separation anxiety) using a 4-point scale (never, rarely, sometimes, often). The SCARED is a 38-item rating scale that assesses symptoms of SAD, GAD, SOP, and school phobia using a 3-point scale (not true or hardly ever true, sometimes true, and often true). The SCAS is a 44-item rating scale that assesses symptoms of SAD, GAD, SOP, OCD, PD/AG, GAD, and fears of physical injury using a 4-point scale (never, sometimes, often, and always).

Each of these measures has been shown to discriminate between youth with an anxiety disorder and youth without an anxiety disorder. In addition, Muris, Merckelbach, Ollendick, King, and Bogie (2002) demonstrated that each of these newer measures not only possessed high internal consistencies (like their older counterparts) and significant and positive relations to the older more generic measures (RCMAS, STAIC, and FSSC-R), but they were useful in discriminating among various anxiety disorders (e.g., SAD vs. SOP). However, like the older measures, relations with depression (as measured by the Children's Depression Inventory) were also positive and significant in this study. The total scores of the SCARED, SCAS, and MASC correlated near or above .70 with the depression measure, as did the RCMAS and the STAIC. Only the FSSC-R showed clear divergent validity with depression. Thus, although it appears these newer instruments are successful in discriminating between youth with an anxiety disorder and those without an anxiety disorder and in discriminating among the anxiety disorders, they too may be less successful in discriminating between youth with other disorders, especially ADHD and the depressive disorders.

Specificity and Sensitivity of Youth Self-Rating Scales

Data on the sensitivity (the percentage of youth who receive an anxiety diagnosis who have been positively identified by the rating scale; true positives) and specificity (the percentage of youth who do not receive the diagnosis and who are not identified by the rating scale as anxious; true negatives) of rating scales are scarce. Also scarce are data on positive predictive power (the probability that a youth has the disorder given that he or she obtained a positive test result) and negative predictive power (the probability of the youth not having the disorder given a negative test result). Overall, the available rating scales for assessing anxiety in children and adolescents are likely to select more false positives than true positives (Costello & Angold, 1988). That is, youth identified as anxious at an initial screen on a self-report measure are not likely not to be so identified through one of the structured or semistructured interviews. In the Mattison et al. (1988) study cited above, the sensitivity of the RCMAS was found to be less than 50% for diagnoses of DSM-III overanxious disorder.

A potentially useful approach for developing empirically based screening methods is to use receiver operator characteristic (ROC) curves. Studies relying on ROC curves focus on the area under the curve (AUC) to estimate diagnostic accuracy across the range of scores on individual scales. This approach is not dependent on prevalence (as is positive predictive power) or on the cutoff scores (as are sensitivity and specificity; Rey, Morris-Yates, & Stanislaw, 1992). Dierker et al. (2001) used ROC curves to evaluate the RCMAS and the MASC as well as one depression self-rating scale, the Center for Epidemiologic Studies-Depression Scale (CES-D), for detecting anxiety and depressive disorders in a school-based survey of ninth grade children. Youth scoring at or above the 80th percentile on any one or more of the three rating scales and a random sample scoring below this threshold participated in subsequent ADIS-C interviews within 2 months of the screening sessions. Results indicated that MASC scores were only partially successful in identifying certain anxiety disorders, and then only among girls. Specifically, among girls, only GAD was significantly associated with the MASC composite scale. Hence, neither SOP nor SP was significantly associated with the MASC composite scale. The RCMAS was found to be the least successful in identifying anxiety and depression. Thus, the Dierker et al. (2001) findings suggest the MASC holds more promise than the RCMAS as a diagnostic screen, but this is so only for screening of GAD in girls and anxiety comorbidities. All together, the findings of Dierker et al. represent a promising first step in evaluating the MASC as a potential diagnostic screen for youth anxiety disorders.

Additional Rating Scales

In addition to the rating scales described above, several other rating scales are available to assess specific dimensions of anxiety (see Table 9.1). For social anxiety, the most widely used scales are the Social Phobia and Anxiety Inventory for Children (SPAIC; Beidel, Turner, & Morris, 1995, 1999) and Social Anxiety Scale for Children-Revised Version (SASC-R; La Greca & Stone, 1993). The SPAIC is a 26-item rating scale that assesses children's distress to social situations along three factors, assertiveness/general conversation, traditional social encounters, and public performance using a three-point scale (never or rarely, sometimes, and most of the time or always). The SASC-R is a 26-item rating scale that assesses children's experiences of social anxiety along three factors, fear of negative evaluation, social avoidance and distress in new situations, and general social avoidance and distress using a 5-point scale (not at all, hardly ever, sometimes, most of the time, and all of the time). The SASC-R also has an adolescent version (La Greca & Lopez, 1998) that consists of 22 items.

Another youth self-rating scale that assesses a specific dimension of anxiety is the Childhood Anxiety Sensitivity Index (CASI; Silverman, Fleisig, Rabian, & Peterson, 1991). The CASI is an 18-item rating scale that assesses the extent that youth view the experience of anxiety-related physiological symptoms as aversive using a 3-point scale (none, some, and *a lot*). The CASI contains four subscales: disease concerns, unsteady concerns, mental incapacitation concerns, and social concerns.

Conceptual and Practical Issues in Diagnosis

Differential Diagnosis

Because of the overlap that exists among the different DSM-IV-TR anxiety disorder subtypes, differential diagnosis of the anxiety disorders is not necessarily straightforward even when a diagnostic interview schedule is used. It is beyond the scope of this chapter to provide a comprehensive analysis of the main issues involved in the differential diagnosis of each of the anxiety disorders. Instead, for illustrative purposes, the focus below is on formulating diagnoses that are particularly thorny to formulate when working with children and adolescents: GAD, PD, and SOP.

In terms of GAD, because "worry" is a process in which all youth engage (e.g., Silverman, La Greca, & Wasserstein, 1995) and because worry also is a pervasive clinical feature of most anxiety disorder subtypes (Weems, Silverman, & La Greca, 2000) it can be difficult to distinguish GAD from the other anxiety disorders. The differential diagnosis of GAD requires that the youth's excessive worrying, which must be endorsed as "uncontrollable" or "hard to stop," can *not* focus solely on areas of worry that would pertain to the other anxiety disorders. This would include social situations (i.e., SOP), specific objects (i.e., SP), or separation from attachment figures (i.e., SAD). The youth's worries also can not have emerged as a consequence of exposure to a traumatic event (i.e., PTSD). GAD also needs to be distinguished from excessive worrying about having a panic attack (i.e., PD) as well as worrying in the form of obsessions (i.e., OCD).

Just as worry is a pervasive clinical feature of many anxiety disorders, so too is panic a common clinical feature that cuts across the different anxiety disorder subtypes (Ollendick, Mattis, & Birmaher, 2004). However, the differential diagnosis of PD requires that the panic attacks are not cued by a specific object (i.e., SP), an evaluative situation (i.e., SOP), separation from attachment figures (i.e., SAD), a traumatic event (i.e., PTSD), excessive worrying (i.e., GAD), and thoughts about exposure to the object or situation related to an obsession (i.e., OCD).

Finally, SOP in children and adolescents is frequently confused diagnostically with GAD. Unlike GAD, however, in SOP, the youth's worry about social situations or academic tasks stems from a fear of negative evaluation by others. In GAD, the worry about social situations and academic tasks stems typically from a fear of failing by not reaching some self-generated standard. The social avoidance associated with SOP also needs to be distinguished from the social avoidance due to having an unexpected panic attack and not wanting to have this attack in public places (i.e., PD with agoraphobia). Also important is distinguishing SOP from pervasive developmental disorder (PDD): youth with SOP have the capacity for and interest in social relationships, while youth with PDD have a general lack of interest in social relationships.

Dealing With Comorbidity

Comorbidity, or the presence of multiple disorders, tends to occur at high rates among youth with anxiety disorders. Estimated rates of comorbidity among children and adolescents with clinical disorders, in general, run as high as 91% in clinic samples (e.g., Angold & Costello, 1999) and up to 71% in community samples (e.g., Woodward & Fergusson, 2001). Although some of the observed high rates of comorbidity reflect assessment artifacts (or other artifacts, such as referral bias), there is considerable "fact" to the observed comorbidity (e.g., Beiderman, Faraone, Mick, & Lelon, 1995; Seligman & Ollendick, 1998). This underscores the need to carefully assess for different disorders during the diagnostic interview process.

Although the many reasons for comorbidity are not fully understood (Angold & Costello, 1999), evidence suggests that anxious youth who are comorbid with another disorder, especially an affective disorder, are more severely impaired than youth with either disorder alone. That is, their problems are more likely to persist over time and are more likely to be refractory to behavior change (see Saavedra & Silverman, 2002; Seligman & Ollendick, 1998). In a recent study by Franco, Saavedra, and Silverman (2007), for example, children and adolescents (N = 329; mean age = 10.04 years) and their parents were administered the ADIS for DSM-IV: C/P and four groups were formed: "pure" anxiety (i.e., no comorbidity), anxiety + anxiety disorders, anxiety + externalizing disorders, and anxiety + depressive disorders. The groups were compared along four sets of variables: sociodemographics, clinical phenomenology, psychosocial, and family factors. The findings revealed that *all* the comorbid groups were more severe than the pure anxiety group on clinical phenomenology and psychosocial factors. The anxiety + depressive disorders group, however, was most severe on all criteria (except sociodemographics).

From a best-practices perspective, these findings highlight the need to consider carefully the different types of comorbid patterns that often accompany an anxiety disorder in youth and the potential for meaningful distinctiveness with regard to the specific comorbid pattern displayed. The use of a diagnostic interview schedule such as the ADIS for DSM-IV: C/P, which covers the full spectrum of youth psychopathological conditions, provides increased assurance that the diverse comorbid patterns that likely co-occur with anxiety disorders have been assessed carefully and thoroughly.

Handling Discrepant Interview Information From Youth and Parent

A widely made claim in the assessment literature is that agreement between youth and parents in their reporting of the youth's disorders is poor when assessed via diagnostic interview schedules (e.g., Grills & Ollendick, 2003; Silverman & Ollendick, 2005). Poor youth–parent agreement has been noted as "the rule, rather than the exception" (Ferdinand, van der Ende, & Verhulst, 2004, p. 198). Although poor agreement between youth and parent reports using interview schedules has been more commonly found than not for most psychiatric conditions, when it comes to anxiety disorders, studies have *not* found uniformly poor agreement. A recent review of the youth–parent agreement research literature for anxiety diagnoses using structured and semistructured interview schedules revealed that, although it is true that youth–parent agreement tends to be poor for GAD and SP when entire sample data are examined, findings are inconsistent for SAD and SOP (Rey, Silverman, Pina, & Dick-Niederhauser, 2006). Also inconsistent across studies is the extent youth–parent (dis)agreement varies as a function of youth sex and age; and no study has evaluated youth–parent (dis)agreement as a function of ethnicity (e.g., European Americans vs. African Americans; Rey et al., 2007). The literature reveals further inconsistencies with regard to the influence of parental psychopathology, particularly mother versus father anxiety and depression, on youth–parent agreement (e.g., Krain & Kendall, 2000).

Even when low levels of agreement between informants are found, this should not be interpreted as one informant is "right" and the other "wrong." The child's anxiety problems simply may not be directly observable to parents, especially if the child manifests his or her anxiety primarily via the cognitive response system. In addition, anxiety in young people may be manifested in different ways in different settings (e.g., home, school), and thus observed differently by diverse sources. Thus, from a best-practices perspective, the general consensus in the child and adolescent anxiety assessment area (e.g., Comer & Kendall, 2004; de Los Reyes and Kazdin, 2005) is that mothers and their children, and fathers if possible, should be considered in assessing youth symptoms and diagnoses.

Overall Evaluation

For the assessment purpose of diagnosis, interview schedules possess the most empirical evidence with respect to their utility for formulating reliable and valid diagnoses. Among the interview schedules available, the ADIS for DSM-IV: C/P (Silverman & Albano, 1996) has been used in the majority of the youth anxiety research studies, and has been subjected to the most evaluation. Additional research is needed, however, about both the reliability and validity of diagnoses when the interview is used in community settings as well as in formulating diagnoses of disorders with varying base rates. Research on the usefulness of other assessment methods for the purpose of diagnosis and differential diagnosis is limited. Although research is sparse, in comparing the RCMAS and the MASC as a potential diagnostic screen, the MASC has stronger evidence. From an evidence-based practice perspective, we recommend the MASC be used for this purpose. Until more evidence become available, however, we recommend the use of the MASC always be followed with a diagnostic interview schedule, preferably the ADIS for DSM-IV: C/P.

CASE CONCEPTUALIZATION AND TREATMENT PLANNING

This section presents assessment measures and strategies (e.g., prescriptive treatment) for use in arriving at a fuller case conceptualization that, in turn, can be used to guide decisions about treatment planning. The most widely used measures used for this purpose are presented in Table 9.2; also contained in the table are several additional measures that are not discussed in this narrative section of the chapter. The focus is on measures and strategies that have supportive evidence for use in developing (a) a clinically meaningful and useful case conceptualization, and (b) a clinically

sensitive and feasible service/treatment plan. A discussion of "best practices" with respect to conceptual and practical issues in case conceptualization and treatment planning is provided as well. The section concludes with an overall evaluation of instruments. Before proceeding, additional comments are offered below to serve as a backdrop for why there even is a linkage between psychological assessment and case conceptualization as well as treatment planning.

In our view, psychological assessment is a fluid, exploratory, hypothesis-testing process, the goal of which is to understand a given youth, group, family, and/or social ecology, often for purposes of formulating and evaluating specific intervention strategies (Ollendick & Hersen, 1993; Silverman & Saavedra, 2004). A definitive understanding of a youth's psychological problems is difficult to achieve and initial conclusions about how to conceptualize the "case" (i.e., the child and her or his problems) and plan treatment are best viewed as *hypotheses* that await verification based on additional information.

The assessment process ought to continue throughout intervention, which, aside from being an attempt to ameliorate the youth's difficulties, can also serve as an opportunity to obtain additional information based on the youth's response to treatment. Thus, evidence-based assessments de-emphasize quick, definitive conclusions and focus more on obtaining information that unfolds over time and is directly relevant to treatment. "Relevance for treatment" refers to the clinical utility of information in planning the treatment and, in the final analysis, the evaluation of intervention outcomes (see Mash & Terdal, 1988). A related concept is treatment utility, which refers to the degree to which assessment strategies are shown to contribute to beneficial treatment outcomes (Hayes, Nelson, & Jarrett, 1987), a point we return to shortly.

Semistructured and Structured Diagnostic Interview Schedules

The initial set of decisions that need to be made when working with children and adolescents with anxiety disorders is how best to conceptualize the case, to determine whether or not an anxiety disorder exists, and to plan treatment accordingly. Differences between the anxiety disorders of childhood and adolescence and other disorders, as well as differences within the anxiety disorders themselves, constitute the primary reason we believe the use of structured

TABLE 9.2 Ratings of Instruments Used for Case Conceptualization and Treatment Planning

Instrument	Norms	Internal Consistency	Inter-Rater Reliability	Test–Retest Reliability	Content Validity	Construct Validity	Validity Generalization	Clinical Utility	Highly Recommended
Diagnostic Interview Schedules									
ADIS C/P-IV	NA	NA	E	E	E	E	E	E	✓
DISC-IV	NA	NA	A	G	G	G	G	G	
DICA	NA	NA	A	G	G	G	G	G	
K-SADS	NA	NA	G	A	A	A	G	A	
Child Self-Rating Scales									
RCMAS	E	G	NA	G	G	E	G	G	✓
SRAS	A	E	NA	G	G	G	G	E	
MASC	A	G	NA	G	G	E	E	E	✓
SCAS	A	G	NA	A	E	E	G	G	✓
SPAIC	A	G	NA	E	E	G	G	G	✓
Behavioral Observations									
BAT	NA	NA	G	G	G	G	G	G	✓
SET/PYIT	NA	NA	G	G	G	G	G	G	✓
SM	NA	NA	NA	G	G	G	G	G	

Note: ADIS C/P-IV = Anxiety Disorders Interview Schedule; DISC-IV = Diagnostic Interview Schedule for Children and Adolescents; K-SADS = Schedule for Affective Disorders and Schizophrenia for School-Age Children; RCMAS = Revised Children's Manifest Anxiety Scale; SRAS = School Refusal Assessment Scale; MASC = Multidimensional Anxiety Scale for Children; SCAS = Spence Children's Anxiety Scale; SPAIC = Social Phobia and Anxiety Inventory for Children; BAT = Behavioral Avoidance Task; SET/PYIT = Social Evaluative Task/Parent-Youth Interaction Task; SM = Self-Monitoring; A = Adequate; G = Good; E = Excellent; NA = Not Applicable.

and semistructured interview schedules is critical and necessary from an evidence-based perspective.

In addition, the current treatment approach that has the strongest and most consistent research support for ameliorating *any* of the anxiety disorders in young people is the cognitive-behavioral treatments (CBT), which involve exposure-based exercises, both in session and out of session (situational, imaginal, interoceptive, virtual; see Ollendick, King, & Chorpita, 2006; Silverman & Berman, 2001). Westen, Novotny, and Thompson-Brenner (2004) similarly acknowledged that the phobic and anxiety disorders "are the disorders that and treatments that have generated the clearest empirical support using RCT [randomized clinical trial] methodology: exposure-based treatments..." (p. 658). Although Westen et al. (2004) were not referring specifically to the child and adolescent treatment research literature, their statement is true whether one is working with child, adolescent, or adult populations (Ollendick et al., 2006; Silverman & Berman, 2001). Hence, although Westen et al. (2004) and others (e.g., Goldfried & Wolfe, 1998) have criticized the strong linkage between diagnosis and treatments in the evidence-based treatment movement, even among critics, this concern is minimized in the context of phobia and anxiety treatment because of the strong supportive evidence for exposure-based CBT approaches.

Consequently, if one wishes to use the treatment procedure that possesses the most research evidence, it is important to *first* have confidence (i.e., have reliable and valid information) that the youth with whom one is working is indeed suffering primarily from clinical levels of anxiety, rather than some other clinical disorder. Second, it is important to have confidence about the *specific* type(s) of anxiety disorder the youth is primarily presenting in order that the appropriate exposure tasks can be planned for and used in and out of treatment sessions (e.g., exposure to social evaluative situations when working with SOP cases; exposure to separation situations when working with SAD cases).

As discussed in the above section on Assessment for Diagnosis, semistructured and structured diagnostic interviews are useful in the initial stages of formulating diagnoses of anxiety disorders in general and in determining the presence of any one specific anxiety disorder in particular. See Table 9.2 for a listing of these schedules used most in the anxiety field. Diagnoses themselves yield powerful information

about treatment targets and potential treatment plans. For example, the anxiety and worry of GAD is associated with one or more of the following six symptoms (DSM-IV-TR, 2000): being restless, being easily fatigued, having difficulty concentrating, being irritable, having muscle tension, and having difficulty falling or staying asleep. Any one or more of these problems (i.e., symptoms) could lead to highly specific treatment plans designed to address them. Similarly, if the RCMAS were administered to such a child, then one could examine each of the three factors of the RCMAS to determine whether the child's anxiety is primarily cognitive, physiological, or behaviorally avoidant in nature. Such information too might lead to specific or prescriptive interventions. We now turn to this topic.

Prescriptive Treatment Strategies

This approach to "prescriptive" interventions is illustrated in the early work of Eisen and Silverman (1993, 1998) and is captured well in a recent text by Chorpita (2007). Again, the reader is referred to Table 9.2 for a listing of the main measures and strategies, with some additional ones noted in the table that are not discussed in this narrative section of the chapter. In an early study, Eisen and Silverman (1993) showed CBTs were most effective for children with overanxious disorder (i.e., the DSM-III-R precursor to GAD) when they were matched with specific symptoms. For example, children with primary symptoms of worry (as defined by the worry/oversensitivity index of the RCMAS) responded more favorably to a cognitive therapy whereas those children with primary symptoms of somatic complaints (as defined by the physiological arousal index of the RCMAS) responded more favorably to relaxation training aimed at dealing with physiological and somatic complaints.

This early study was replicated by Eisen and Silverman (1998), in which these authors again showed that, although both treatments were generally effective, only the prescriptive treatments produced sufficient improvements for the treated children to meet exacting positive end-state functioning criteria. Similar effects of matching were shown by Ollendick, Hagopian, and Huntzinger (1991) with separation anxious children and by Ollendick (1995) with adolescents with PD with agoraphobia. Thus, in these studies, CBTs were shown to be maximally effective when they were closely matched with the symptom presentation of the individual child or adolescent. That is, specific diagnoses, when supplemented with symptom profiles, led to superior outcomes. Each of these studies used single case multiple baseline designs to illustrate the controlling effects of the matched interventions.

This approach also is illustrated in the treatment of school refusal behavior in children and adolescents. Although not a specific psychiatric diagnosis, such behavior is a common mental, health, and educational problem that refers to child-motivated refusal to attend school and/or difficulties remaining in school for an entire school day (Kearney, 2003). Such children who refuse school frequently meet criteria for one or more of the anxiety disorders in childhood, but might also meet criteria for one of the disruptive behavior disorders (Kearney, 2003).

Kearney and Silverman (1990) proposed a functional model that suggested youth refused school for one of four probable reasons: (1) to avoid stimuli that provoke negative affectivity, (2) to escape aversive social and/or evaluative situations, (3) to seek attention from significant others, and (4) to pursue tangible reinforcers outside of school. To address these disparate functions, they developed the School Refusal Assessment Scale (SRAS, Kearney & Silverman, 1993) and its recent revision (SRAS-R, Kearney, 2002, 2006). The original SRAS was a 16-item instrument that contained four items devoted to each of the four functional conditions. Child and parent versions of the scale were developed. Item means were averaged across functions to derive functional profiles that included the primary and secondary reasons for why a particular child refused school. The original SRAS and its recent revision (24 items with parent and child versions) have been found to be reliable across time and between parent raters (Kearney, 2002, 2006; Kearney & Silverman, 1993; Silverman & Ollendick, 2005).

Relevant here, the scale has been found to be useful in the prescriptive treatment of school refusing children. Prescriptive treatment for negatively reinforced school refusal behavior (Functions 1 and 2) consists of psychoeducation, fear hierarchy development, cognitive therapy, modeling, and behavioral exposures designed to gradually reintroduce the child to school. In contrast, prescriptive treatment for positively reinforced school refusal behaviors (Functions 3 and 4) consists of developing daily routines, escorting the youth to school, contingency contracting, and communications skills training. Treatment outcome studies have indicated that the SRAS and the SRAS-R are useful in determining which prescriptive treatment best fits a particular case, and which treatments may be less effective (Chorpita, Albano, Heimberg, & Barlow, 1996; Kearney, Pursell, & Alvarez, 2001; Kearney & Silverman, 1993, 1999). Again, all of these studies have used single-case experimental designs to illustrate the efficacy of these prescriptive treatments.

Behavioral Observations

Direct behavioral observations can play a particularly helpful role in case conceptualization and treatment planning. Please see Table 9.2 for a summary. Many times the adage "a picture is worth a thousand words" really rings true. One useful role of behavioral observations is for identifying and quantifying specific fear and anxiety symptoms and behaviors, such as avoidance. For example, Ost, Svensson, Hellstrom, and Lindwall (2001) observed youth engage in behavioral avoidance tasks, which consisted of a series of graduated steps, and the percentage of steps the youth accomplished was recorded.

Surprisingly, direct observations have been used most frequently in the child and adolescent anxiety area not as much to assess youth's behavioral avoidance but to assess youth's *subjective* judgments of their levels of fear/anxiety in fear/anxiety provoking situations or tasks, to assess trained observers' *subjective* judgments of the youth's levels of fear/anxiety, or both. In some studies, observers' subjective ratings are obtained only by providing the observers with global rating scales (e.g., a Likert rating scale from 1 to 5). In other studies, observers also are provided with behavioral dimensions to help assist the observers in making their subjective ratings (Silverman & Ollendick, 2005).

Thus, in addition to behavioral avoidance tasks, two other types of tasks have been used in the youth anxiety area: (1) social evaluative tasks, and (2) parent–youth interaction tasks. With regard to social evaluative tasks (Beidel et al., 2000), participants are informed of the evaluative nature of the task and are given standard behavioral assertiveness instructions. For example, Beidel et al. (2000) invited children and adolescents to read aloud a story in front of a small group and were told to "Respond as if the scene were really happening." With regard to parent–youth interaction tasks (e.g., Hudson & Rapee, 2002), parents and youth were observed while engaging in problem-solving situations. Specifically, Hudson and Rapee (2002) conducted observations of "normal" and anxious youths and their siblings while completing a separate set of tangram or puzzle tasks designed to be slightly too difficult to complete in 5 minutes. Of interest was degree of parental involvement during the task (e.g., degree of unsolicited help; degree to which the parent physically touched the tangram piece).

From a best-practices perspective, we believe direct observational procedures have clinical utility when it comes to case conceptualization and treatment planning. They can yield helpful conceptual information about the nature of family interactions among anxious children or just "how far children can go" when it comes to interacting with a feared object or event. Given the potentially useful conceptual information that can be gained from these procedures, we encourage their continued use and evaluation.

Self-Monitoring

Self-monitoring procedures often have been viewed as a more efficient and easier way to accomplish the same goals as direct observations in terms of assisting in case conceptualization and treatment planning. More specifically, self-monitoring data have been used in a number of single case study designs (e.g., Eisen & Silverman, 1998; Ollendick, 1995).

Although self-monitoring is relatively common in practice among behaviorally oriented clinicians, little has been done in the child and adolescent anxiety research area to evaluate its feasibility and psychometric properties. An exception is Beidel, Neal, and Lederer (1991), who devised and evaluated the feasibility (i.e., child compliance), reliability, and validity of a daily diary for use in assessing the range and frequency of social-evaluative anxious events in elementary school children ($N = 57$; $n = 32$, test anxious; $n = 25$, nontest anxious) during a 2-week assessment phase. Relatively structured in nature, the daily diary listed events such as *I had a test* and *The teacher called on me to answer a question*, as well as a list of potential responses to the occurrence of the events, including positive (e.g., *practiced extra hard, told myself not to be nervous and it would be okay*), negative (e.g., *cried, got a headache or stomachache*), and neutral (e.g., *did what I was told*) behaviors. The children also rated the degree of distress they experienced using a

Self-Assessment Manikin, which is a pictorial 5-point rating scale that depicts increasing degrees of anxious arousal.

With regard to feasibility or compliance, with no incentives offered, the mean number of days the diary was completed for the 2 weeks ranged from 7.9 to 11.5 days, though only 31% to 39% of the children complied for the full 2 weeks. Retest reliability was found to be modest, but that is probably because the events listed on the diary likely show true fluctuations. Evidence for validity was demonstrated in that the test-anxious children reported significantly more emotional distress and more negative behaviors such as crying or behavioral avoidance.

Thus, as with direct observation procedures, self-monitoring procedures have clinical utility in terms of yielding helpful conceptual information (e.g., the specific situations that elicit anxiety in a child; the child's cognitions when faced with a specific object or event). We encourage their continued use and evaluation.

Conceptual and Practical Issues in Assessing for Case Conceptualization and Treatment Planning

Demonstrating Treatment Utility

The studies cited in this section regarding prescriptive treatment strategies represent important efforts in demonstrating the treatment utility of assessment. For example, in the Eisen and Silverman (1993, 1998) studies, which showed CBTs were most effective for specific aspects of the treatment (e.g., cognitive therapy, relaxation therapy) when matched with the child's specific symptoms (e.g., worry, physiological arousal), the treatment utility of assessing for these specific symptoms vis-à-vis treatment outcome was empirically shown.

Interestingly, however, when it comes to the treatment utility of arriving at formal DSM diagnoses, formulated using interview schedules, treatment utility has not yet been demonstrated (Nelson-Gray, 2003). For example, it has not been empirically demonstrated whether children who have had their diagnoses assigned with a structured or semistructured diagnostic interview schedule (vs., e.g., a more traditional clinical interview) and are given CBT present results different from a group of children who have *not* been given a diagnostic interview schedule and receive CBT. Although it seems plausible to suspect that the use of semistructured and structured interview schedules would possess treatment utility, especially relative to clinical interviews, rating scales, and so forth, the issue remains to be empirically evaluated.

Considering Impaired but not Diagnosed Children and Adolescents

As noted, the diagnostic interview schedules emphasize DSM symptoms and psychopathology and, thus, are in line with the evidence-based treatment approaches' emphasis on targeting specific DSM symptoms and psychopathology. Research has found, however, that a substantial proportion of children and adolescents who present to community mental health clinics do *not* meet criteria for a DSM disorder, yet they evidence impaired functioning (Angold et al., 1999). Anxiety is a specific problem area that has been found likely to lead to youth impairment, but it is not necessarily a diagnosis (Angold et al., 1999).

Because impairment may not be reported by the parents (and even less likely to be reported by the child), it is important to probe carefully for whether the child or adolescent is mastering expected developmental tasks (e.g., developing peer relationships). If the youth is not mastering expected tasks, then anxiety, though perhaps at a subthreshold diagnostic level, may be deemed as impairing youth functioning. An instrument designed to assess impairment is the clinician rating scale contained on the ADIS for Children for DSM-IV (Silverman & Albano, 1996). Reliability estimates of the ratings obtained on this scale have been found to be satisfactory (e.g., Silverman & Eisen, 1992; Silverman et al., 1988). Although the clinician rating scale contained on the ADIS for Children for DSM-IV was designed to assess for interference of each diagnosis formulated for the child, the scale can be adapted to assess for interference of anxiety symptoms (i.e., even if DSM diagnostic criteria are not met). For example, for a child who does not meet full criteria for SAD but cannot sleep alone at night without her mother, the child could be asked: "You just told me that sometimes you have trouble sleeping alone at night without your mother. How does not being able to go to sleep by yourself mess things up for you in terms of how you now are doing in school? How about in terms of things with your family? And how much does it affect things with friends? And how much does it make you feel very upset (personal distress)?"

More recently, the Pediatric Anxiety Rating Scale (PARS;   Research Units on Pediatric Psychopharmacology [RUPP], 2002), was designed to assess the frequency, severity, and associated impairment across SAD, SOP, and GAD symptoms in children and adolescents (aged 6 to 17 years). This contrasts with assessing impairment of each individual anxiety disorder, as done on the clinician severity rating scale of the ADIS for DSM-IV: C/P; Silverman & Albano, 1996). Although the internal consistency of the PARS has been found to be satisfactory, its retest reliability needs further examination (e.g., *retest reliability* = .55 for the total scale score using a retest interval of a mean of about 3 weeks; though this likely reflects in part the changing nature of children's display of anxiety over time).

Also needing further examination is the scale's convergent and divergent validity. With regard to the latter, although the observed correlations were in the expected directions (in terms of being positively correlated with ratings of internalizing symptoms and negatively correlated with externalizing symptoms), this was more true when the PARS ratings were correlated with other clinician ratings than with other sources' ratings, such as children's ratings on the MASC.

Despite the above gaps in knowledge, best practices would suggest the consideration of impairment when assessing children and adolescents who present with anxiety difficulties. Impairment rating scales provide reliable and valid estimates of the extent of the youth's impairment. For those children and adolescents who show significant impairment in their functioning, though subthreshold in diagnosis, treatment services still could be important to provide.

Overall Evaluation

The field has available some promising assessment measures and strategies to augment information obtained from diagnostic interviews to guide decisions about treatment planning, but it has a long way to go in achieving an evidence base to guide us in these efforts. Although the use of these promising measures can help in arriving at a clinically meaningful and useful case conceptualization and implement a clinically sensitive and feasible service/treatment plan at the *individual* level, these measures have not yet been shown to be useful at the group or nomothetic level. Similarly, despite the preliminary evidence for adopting an idiographic, prescriptive approach to treat anxiety disorders and/or school refusal behavior in children, either through the identification of problematic symptoms or functionally motivating conditions, evidence is needed that the former is *more* efficacious than a nomothetic, statistically based approach (Silverman & Berman, 2001). It would seem important for future research to compare the relative efficacy of an idiographic, prescriptive approach to a standard CBT package. The next generation of studies also will need to establish the clinical utility of these measures in randomized control treatment studies.

ASSESSMENT FOR TREATMENT MONITORING AND TREATMENT OUTCOME

This section deals with assessment measures and strategies most useful for tracking the progress of treatment and evaluating the overall effect of treatment on anxiety symptoms, diagnosis, and general functioning. As noted in the preceding sections, diagnostic interview schedules have been found to provide reliable and valid diagnoses. Thus, diagnoses formulated with interview schedules have been used for treatment evaluation purposes. For example, in a treatment study, 100% of youth participants meet diagnostic criteria at pretreatment. In evaluating treatment outcome, of interest is the diagnostic recovery rate at posttreatment and follow-up; most studies report 60% to 80% of participants as recovered or no longer meeting diagnostic criteria at posttreatment, with maintenance of recovery apparent at 1-year follow-up (Ollendick et al., 2006).

Because interview schedules were discussed above and because self-monitoring procedures have been used mostly in single case design studies, not in randomized trials, emphasis is placed in this section on rating scales and observational methods that have supportive empirical evidence (see Table 9.3). The section also includes a discussion of "best practices" with respect to conceptual and practical issues in assessing for treatment monitoring and treatment outcome. The section, like the others, concludes with an overall evaluation of the assessment tools.

Before proceeding, it should be noted that rating scales and observational methods are rarely administered over the course of a child or adolescent treatment program for the purpose of *tracking* treatment progress. Rather, they are typically administered at pretreatment, posttreatment, and follow-up for the purpose of evaluating treatment outcome. Occasionally, rating scales have been administered at mid-treatment (Kendall et al., 1997). Nevertheless, from an evidence-based perspective, we recommend rating scales be used continuously during the course of treatment for this purpose. We hope such practice will become more widespread in the future. If one is concerned about client burden, one could administer an abridged version of a particular rating scale. For example, if one routinely administers a scale in one's setting, one could determine the three or four items of the scale that correlate most highly with the total score (or total subscale scores) and administer only those items on a weekly or biweekly basis. In addition, because research shows there are fluctuations in rating scale scores irrespective of treatment (Silverman & Ollendick, 2005), it has been recommended the scales be administered at least twice prior to the actual intervention, such as once at the initial intake and again immediately prior to treatment. This recommendation, however, has rarely been followed by researchers.

Rating Scales

The use of rating scales represents best practices for the assessment of treatment progress and treatment outcome, in that they have been found to be sensitive to treatment change. Rating scales, for completion by youth, parents, teachers, or clinicians, are advantageous to use in that they are easy to administer, have relatively low cost, and have objective scoring procedures (Silverman & Rabian, 1999; Silverman & Serafini, 1998). See Table 9.3 for ratings of the most widely used rating scales for this assessment purpose. The most common rating scales used in clinical trials that have shown to be sensitive to treatment effects have been the teacher and parent rating versions of the Child Behavior Checklist (Achenbach, 1991a, 1991b). The CBCL is a 118-item (parent version) and an 120-item (teacher version) behavior checklist that assesses the social competencies and behavior problems of youth using a 3-point scale (not true, somewhat or sometimes true, very true or often True). The CBCL includes broadband subscales (i.e., externalizing and internalizing) and narrowband subscales (i.e., withdrawn, somatic complaints, Anxious/

TABLE 9.3 Ratings of Instruments Used for Treatment Monitoring and Treatment Outcome Evaluation

Instrument	Norms	Internal Consistency	Inter-Rater Reliability	Test–Retest Reliability	Content Validity	Construct Validity	Validity Generalization	Clinical Utility	Highly Recommended
Diagnostic Interview Schedules									
ADIS C/P-IV	NA	NA	E	E	E	E	E	E	✓
DISC-IV	NA	NA	A	G	G	G	G	G	
DICA	NA	NA	A	G	G	G	G	G	
K-SADS	NA	NA	G	A	A	A	G	A	
Rating Scales									
Parent									
CBCL-I	E	G	NA	G	E	E	G	G	✓
Clinician									
ADIS-C/P: CRS	NA	NA	G	E	G	NA	NA	E	✓
Child									
RCMAS	E	G	NA	G	G	E	G	G	✓
STAIC	G	G	NA	G	G	G	G	A	
FSSC-R	A	E	NA	G	E	G	G	G	✓✓
MASC	A	G	NA	G	G	E	E	E	✓
SCAS	A	G	NA	A	E	E	G	G	✓✓
SPAIC	A	G	NA	E	E	G	G	G	
Behavioral Observations									
BAT/SET/PYIT	NA	NA	G	G	G	G	G	G	✓

Note: ADIS C/P-IV = Anxiety Disorders Interview Schedule; DISC-IV = Diagnostic Interview Schedule for Children, Version IV; DICA = Diagnostic Interview Schedule for Children and Adolescents; K-SADS = Schedule for Affective Disorders and Schizophrenia for School-Age Children; CBCL-I = Child Behavior Checklist-Internalizing Scale; ADIS-C/P: CRS = Anxiety Disorders Interview Schedule-Child and Parent Versions: Clinician Rating Scale; RCMAS = Revised Children's Manifest Anxiety Scale; STAIC = State-Trait Anxiety Inventory for Children; FSSC-R = Fear Survey Scale for Children-Revised; MASC = Multidimensional Anxiety Scale for Children; SCAS = Spence Children's Anxiety Scale; SPAIC = Social Phobia and Anxiety Inventory for Children; BAT/SET/PYIT = Behavioral Avoidance Task/Social Evaluative Task/Parent–Youth Interaction Task; A = Adequate; G = Good; E = Excellent; NA = Not Applicable.

depressed, Social problems, Thought problems, Attention problems, Delinquent and Aggressive behavior). The Clinician Rating Scale of the ADIS for DSM-IV: C/P (Silverman & Albano, 1996) also has been used in a number of studies and also has found to be sensitive to treatment effects (see Silverman & Ollendick, 2005).

Behavioral Observations

The use of direct behavioral observations represents another approach for assessing treatment progress and treatment outcome (see Table 9.3). It is important to note, though, that supportive evidence for direct observations in terms of showing sensitivity to change is considerably less than the supportive evidence for interviews (i.e., diagnostic recovery rates) and rating scales (i.e., statistically significant declines in continuous scores). In both Beidel et al. (2000) and Kendall et al. (1997), participants were asked to engage in an evaluative task and were given standard behavioral assertiveness instructions. For example, Beidel et al. invited children and adolescents to read aloud a story in front of a small group and were told to "Respond as if the scene were really happening." Both Kendall et al. and Beidel et al. reported treatment improvements in participants' performance on these tasks. Using a family observation task, however, Barrett et al. (1996) did not find significant pre-to-posttreatment differences between an individual-versus family-based cognitive-behavioral treatment.

Conceptual and Practical Issues in the Assessment of Treatment Progress and Treatment Outcome

On the Problems of Normative Data

Concerns have frequently been expressed about using normative values to assess clinical significance. Norming mainly indicates a youth's relative standing; it still does not indicate a youth's absolute standing on anxiety. More specifically, when the Child Behavior Checklist (CBCL; Achenbach, 1991a, 1991b) is used to assess treatment outcome, "clinically significant improvement" is defined as meeting a minimum criterion T-score on the CBCL Internalizing scale of less than 70 (adjusted according to age norms; Kendall et al., 1997; Silverman et al., 1999). In other words, cases that shift from being above this cutoff value to

being below the cutoff value are said to have shown clinically significant improvement following the treatment (see Kazdin, 1999). There is no evidence that youth who score below 70 have fewer worries or display less avoidant behaviors than youth who score above 70. That is, this shift on the CBCL from pre- to posttreatment does not inform whether the treatment had meaningful impact on the day to day functioning of the treated youth (see Kazdin, 1999). Examples such as meeting role demands, functioning in everyday life, and improvement in the quality of one's life might also be measured.

Reporting Biases on Rating Scales

It is reasonable to presume that some anxious youths might be reluctant to self-disclose their personal anxious reactions, which can influence inferences drawn from rating scale data when assessing treatment outcome. The RCMAS does offer an advantage that sets it apart from the other anxiety rating scales in that it contains not only a Total Anxiety Scale but also a Lie Scale. The RCMAS Lie Scale, a downward extension of the Lie Scale on the adult version of the Manifest Anxiety Scale, was derived from the social desirability/Lie Scale of the MMPI. Containing items such as, "I never get angry," "I like everyone I know," and "I am always kind," the Lie Scale has been used as an indicator of social desirability or defensiveness (Dadds, Perrin, & Yule, 1998; Reynolds & Richmond, 1985), reflecting a tendency to present oneself in a favorable light, and/or deny flaws and weaknesses that others are usually willing to admit.

Research using the RCMAS Lie Scale in unselected school samples (Dadds et al., 1998) and clinic-referred anxious samples (Pina, Silverman, Saavedra, & Weems, 2001), reveals younger children score significantly higher on the Lie Scale than do older children; no significant gender differences have been observed in Lie Scale scores, however. These findings underscore the need for clinicians and researchers to recognize that younger anxious children and adolescents are more likely to evidence social desirability when using anxiety rating scales than are older groups. For example, when assessing a young anxious child, if the child endorses four Lie Scale items (which was the younger children's mean Lie score in Pina et al., 2001), or more, it may be worthwhile to question the validity or accuracy of the child's self-reports of anxiety and consider alternative sources. It further underscores the need to emphasize to anxious youth that there are "no right or wrong answers" during the assessment process. Similar pressure to please and to be seen in a favorable light may be placed on children and adolescents with anxiety disorders during other assessment strategies such as behavioral observations, though the issue has not been studied.

Overall Evaluation

There has been little systematic assessment undertaken over the course of a child or adolescent treatment study for the purpose of tracking treatment progress. It is strongly recommended that such efforts be undertaken. Using abbreviated versions of psychometrically sound measures such as the CBCL (Achenbach, 1991a, 1991b) may represent one important way to begin this type of work. Diagnostic interviews and rating scales have been most widely used for evaluating treatment outcome. Despite the wide usage of rating scales and the fact that in most treatment outcome studies the scales show sensitivity to change, considerably more research is needed to determine the meaning or practical value of a youth's score on these scales, as well as the meaning or practical value of observed changes on these scales during the course of a treatment outcome study.

CONCLUSIONS AND RECOMMENDATIONS

This chapter summarized the research evidence supporting clinically relevant psychological assessment measures for use with child and adolescent anxiety disorders. The focus was on assessment measures that are not only evidence based but also feasible and useful for the needs of the practitioner. Based on the information provided in this chapter, several recommendations can be made.

For the purpose of diagnosis, structured or semi-structured clinical interviews are recommended because they lead to more reliable anxiety diagnoses than unstructured clinical interviews. The interview schedule used most frequently in the youth anxiety area has been the ADIS for DSM-IV: C/P. Although reliability and validity of anxiety diagnoses have been documented using the ADIS for DSM-IV: C/P in clinic settings, further evaluation of the interview schedule is needed in community clinics and with disorders of varying base rates.

To assist in screening for anxiety disorders for later diagnostic workups, it is recommended that scales' factor scale scores be examined, not just total scores, when trying to discriminate anxiety disorders from other disorders. Also relating to screening, in comparisons between the RCMAS and the MASC, the MASC has stronger evidence, though the evidence is limited to screening for GAD in girls and anxiety comorbidities in girls and boys (i.e., specific phobia/social phobia). To discriminate between anxiety and depression, consider using scales specifically designed for this purpose such as the RCADS. Different tripartite-based self-rating scales are not equivalent and each appears to capture differential aspects of the tripartite model.

To assess for the purpose of case conceptualization and treatment formulation, a prescriptive treatment approach represents a potentially useful way to proceed and a fruitful avenue for future research. Also clinically useful for the purpose of case conceptualization and treatment formulation are direct observations and self-monitoring procedures, but questions exist about their feasibility, retest reliability, and incremental validity.

Finally, for the purpose of assessing for treatment outcome, diagnostic recovery rates using the ADIS interviews, the RCMAS, and the CBCL—internalizing scales have been the most widely used measures and they all have been found to be sensitive to change. It is important to consider carefully multiple sources of information, and one should not assume there is a gold standard, as different perspectives likely reflect biases and varying perceptions of what is in the best interest of the child or adolescent. Further work on understanding the meaning of these discrepancies is needed.

ACKNOWLEDGMENT This chapter was funded by National Institute of Mental Health Grant R0163997 to Wendy Silverman and R0151308 to Thomas Ollendick. The authors also would like to thank Yasmin Rey for her assistance in the preparation of this chapter.

References

Achenbach, T. M. (1991a). *Manual for the child behavior checklist 14–18 and 1991 profile.* Burlington: University of Vermont.

Achenbach, T. M. (1991b). *Manual for the teachers report form and 1991 profile.* Burlington: University of Vermont.

Albano, A. M., Chorpita, B. F., & Barlow, D. H. (1996). Anxiety disorders in children and adolescents. In E. J. Mash & R. A. Barkley (Eds.), *Child psychopathology* (pp. 196–241). New York: Guilford.

Ambrosini, P. J. (2000). Historical development and present status of the Schedule for Affective Disorders and Schizophrenia for School-Age Children (K-SADS). *Journal of the American Academy of Child & Adolescent Psychiatry, 39,* 49–58.

American Psychiatric Association. (2000). *Diagnostic and statistical manual of mental disorders* (4th ed., Text Revision). Washington, DC: Author.

Anderson, J. C., Williams, S., McGee, R., & Silva, P. A., (1987). DSM-III disorders in preadolescent children: Prevalence in a large sample from the general population. *Archives of General Psychiatry, 44,* 69–76.

Angold, A., & Costello, E. J. (1999). Comorbidity. *Journal of Child Psychology and Psychiatry and Allied Disciplines, 40,* 57–87.

Beidel, D. C. (1991). Determining the reliability of psychophysiological assessment in childhood anxiety. *Journal of Anxiety Disorders, 5,* 139–150.

Beidel, D. C., Neal, A. M., & Lederer, A. S. (1991). The feasibility and validity of a daily diary for the assessment of anxiety in children. *Behavior Therapy, 22,* 505–517.

Beidel, D. C., Turner, S. M., & Morris, T. L. (1995). A new inventory to assess childhood social anxiety and phobia: The social phobia and anxiety inventory for children. *Psychological Assessment, 7,* 73–79.

Beidel, D. C., Turner, S. M., & Morris, T. L. (1999). Psychopathology of childhood social phobia. *Journal of the American Academy of Child & Adolescent Psychiatry, 38,* 643–650.

Beidel, D. C., Turner, S. M., & Morris, T. L. (2000). Behavioral treatment of childhood social phobia. *Journal of Consulting and Clinical Psychology, 68,* 1072–1080.

Biederman, J., Faraone, S., Mick, E., & Lelon, E. (1995). Psychiatric comorbidity among referred juveniles with major depression: Fact or artifact? *Journal of the American Academy of Child & Adolescent Psychiatry, 34,* 579–590.

Birmaher, B., Khetarpal, S., Brent, D. A., Cully, M., Balach, L., Kaufman, J., et al. (1997). The Screen for Child Anxiety Related Emotional Disorders (SCARED): Scale construction and psychometric characteristics. *Journal of the American Academy of Child & Adolescent Psychiatry, 36,* 545–553.

Boer, F., & Lindhout, I. (2001). Family and genetic influences: Is anxiety 'all in the family'? In W. K. Silverman & P. D. A. Treffers (Eds.), *Anxiety disorders in children and adolescents: Research, assessment, and intervention* (pp. 235–254). Cambridge, UK: Cambridge.

Bouton, M. E., Mineka, S., & Barlow, D. H. (2001). A modern learning theory perspective on the etiology of panic disorder. *Psychological Review, 108,* 4–32.

Bowlby, J. (1977). The making and breaking of affectional bonds: Aetiology and psycho-pathology in the light of attachment theory. *British Journal of Psychiatry, 130,* 201–210.

Brown, T. A., Di Nardo, P. A., & Barlow, D. H. (1994). *Anxiety Disorders Interview Schedule for DSM-IV (ADIS-IV).* San Antonio, TX: Psychological Corporation/Graywind Publications Incorporated.

Carrión, V. G., Weems, C. F., Ray, R. D., Glasser, B., Hessl, D., & Reiss, A. L. (2002). Diurnal salivary cortisol in pediatric Posttraumatic Stress Disorder. *Biological Psychiatry, 51,* 575–582.

Chorpita, B. F. (2007). *Modular cognitive-behavioral therapy for childhood anxiety disorders.* New York: Guilford Press.

Chorpita, B. F., Albano, A. M., Heimberg, R. G., & Barlow, D. H. (1996). A systematic replication of the prescriptive treatment of school refusal behavior in a single subject. *Journal of Behavior Therapy and Experimental Psychiatry, 27,* 281–290.

Chorpita, B. F., & Barlow, D. H. (1998). The development of anxiety: The role of control in the early environment. *Psychological Bulletin, 124,* 3–21.

Cicchetti, D., & Cohen, D. J. (1995). Perspectives on developmental psychopathology. In D. Cicchetti & D. Cohen (Eds.), *Developmental psychopathology: Volume 1. Theory and methods* (pp. 3–20). New York: Wiley.

Comer, J. S., & Kendall, P. C. (2004). A symptom-level examination of parent–child agreement in the diagnosis of anxious youth. *Journal of the American Academy of Child and Adolescent Psychiatry, 43,* 878–886.

Costello, E. J., & Angold, A. (1988). Scales to assess child and adolescent depression: Checklists, screens, and nets. *Journal of the American Academy of Child and Adolescent Psychiatry, 27,* 726–737.

Costello, E. J., Egger, H. L., & Angold, A. (2004). Developmental Epidemiology of Anxiety Disorders. In T. H. Ollendick and J. S. March (Eds.), *Phobic and anxiety disorders in children and adolescents: A clinician's guide to effective psychosocial and pharmacological interventions* (pp. 61–91). New York: Oxford University Press.

Dadds, M., Barrett, P., Rapee, R., & Ryan, S. (1996). Family process and child anxiety and aggression: An observational analysis. *Journal of Abnormal Child Psychology, 24,* 715–734.

Dadds, M. R., Perrin, S., & Yule, W. (1998). Social desirability and self-reported anxiety in children:

An analysis of the RCMAS Lie Scale. *Journal of Abnormal Child Psychology, 26,* 311–317.

Davidson, R. J., Abercrombie, H., Nitschke, J. B., & Putnam, K. (1999). Regional brain function emotion and disorders of emotion. *Current Opinion in Neurobiology, 9,* 228–234.

De Los Reyes, A., & Kazdin, A. E. (2005). Informant discrepancies in the assessment of childhood psychopathology: A critical review, theoretical framework, and recommendations for further study. *Psychological Bulletin, 131,* 483–509.

Dick Niederhauser, A., & Silverman, W. K. (2004). Prevention and early detection in emotional disorders. In H. Remschmidt, M. Belfer, & I. Goodyer (Eds.), *Facilitating pathways: Care, treatment, and prevention in child and adolescent mental health.* (pp. 272–286). Berlin: Springer.

Dierker, L. C., Albano, A. M., Clarke, G. N., Heimberg, R. G., Kendall, P. C., Merikangas, K. R., et al. (2001). Screening for anxiety and depression in early adolescence. *Journal of the American Academy of Child & Adolescent Psychiatry, 40,* 929–936.

Eisen, A. R., & Silverman, W. K. (1993). Should I relax or change my thoughts? A preliminary study of the treatment of Overanxious Disorder in children. *Journal of Cognitive Psychotherapy, 7,* 265–280.

Eisen, A. R., & Silverman, W. K. (1998). Prescriptive treatment for generalized anxiety disorder in children. *Behavior Therapy, 29,* 105–121.

Eley, T. C. (2001). Contributions of behavioral genetics research: Quantifying genetic, shared environmental and nonshared environmental influences. In M. W. Vasey & M. R. Dadds (Eds.), *The developmental psychopathology of anxiety* (pp. 45–59). London: Oxford University Press.

Eysenck, H. J., & Eysenck, M. W. (1985). *Personality and individual differences.* New York: Plenum.

Ferdinand R. F., van der Ende, J., & Verhulst, F. C. (2004). Parent–adolescent disagreement regarding psychopathology in adolescents from the general population as a risk factor for adverse outcome. *Journal of Abnormal Psychology, 113,* 198–206.

Field, A. P. (2006). Watch out for the feast: Fear information and attentional bias in children. *Journal of Clinical Child and Adolescent Psychology, 35,* 431–439.

Field, A. P., & Lawson, J. (2003). Fear information and the development of fears during childhood: Effects on implicit fear responses and behavioural avoidance. *Behaviour Research and Therapy, 41,* 1277–1293.

Franco, X., Saavedra, L., & Silverman, W. K. (2007). External validation of comorbid patterns of anxiety disorders in children and adolescents. *Journal of Anxiety Disorders, 21,* 717–729.

Goldfried, M. R., & Wolfe, B. E. (1998). Toward a more clinically valid approach to therapy research. *Journal of Consulting and Clinical Psychology, 66,* 143–150.

Grills, A. E., & Ollendick, T. H. (2003). Multiple informant agreement and the Anxiety Disorders Interview Schedule for Parents and Children. *Journal of the American Academy of Child & Adolescent Psychiatry, 42,* 30–40.

Hayes, S. C., Nelson, R. O., & Jarrett, R. B. (1987). The treatment utility of assessment: A functional approach to evaluating assessment quality. *American Psychologist, 42,* 963–974.

Hemphill, J. F. (2003). Interpreting the magnitudes of correlation coefficients. *American Psychologist, 58,* 78–79.

Herjanic, B., & Reich, W. (1982). Development of a structured psychiatric interview: Agreement between child and parent on individual symptoms. *Journal of Abnormal Child Psychology, 10,* 307–324.

Hudson, J. L., & Rapee, R. M. (2002). Parent–child interactions in clinically anxious children and their siblings. *Journal of Clinical Child and Adolescent Psychology, 31,* 548–555.

Insel, T. R., Scanlan, J., & Champoux, M. (1988). Rearing paradigm in a nonhuman primate affects response to b-CCE challenge. *Psychopharmacology, 96,* 81–86.

Kagan, J. (1997). Temperament and the reactions to unfamiliarity. *Child Development, 68,* 139–143.

Kazdin, A. E. (1999). The meanings and measurement of clinical significance. *Journal of Consulting and Clinical Psychology, 67,* 332–339.

Kearney, C. A. (2002). Identifying the function of school refusal behavior: A revision of the School Refusal Assessment Scale. *Journal of Psychopathology and Behavioral Assessment, 24,* 235–245.

Kearney, C. A. (2003). Bridging the gap among professionals who address youths with school absenteeism: Overview and suggestions for consensus. *Professional Psychology: Research and Practice, 34,* 57–65.

Kearney, C. A., Pursell, C., & Alvarez, K. (2001). Treatment of school refusal behavior in children with mixed functional profiles. *Cognitive and Behavioral Practice, 8,* 3–11.

Kearney, C. A., & Silverman, W. K. (1993). Measuring the function of school refusal behavior: The School Refusal Assessment Scale. *Journal of Clinical Child Psychology, 22,* 85–96.

Kearney, C. A., & Silverman, W. K. (1999). Functionally based prescriptive and nonprescriptive treatment for children and adolescents with school refusal behavior. *Behavior Therapy, 30,* 673–695.

Kendall, P. C., Flannery-Schroeder, E., Panichelli-Mindel, S. M., Southam-Gerow, M., Henin, A., & Warman, M. (1997). Treatment of anxiety disorders in youth: A second randomized clinical trial. *Journal of Consulting and Clinical Psychology, 65,* 366–380.

Kendler, K. S., Neale, M. C., Kessler, R. C., Heath, A. C., & Eaves, L. J. (1992). The genetic epidemiology of phobias in women: The interrelationship of agoraphobia, social phobia, situational phobia, and simple phobia. *Archives of General Psychiatry, 49,* 273–281.

King, N. J. (1994). Physiological assessment. In T. H. Ollendick, N. J. King, & W. Yule (Eds.), *International handbook of phobic and anxiety disorders in children* (pp. 365–380). New York: Plenum Press.

Krain, A. L., & Kendall, P. C. (2000). The role of parental emotional distress in parent report of child anxiety. *Journal of Clinical Child Psychology, 29,* 328–335.

La Greca, A. M. (2001). Friends or foes? Peer influences on anxiety among children and adolescents. In W. K. Silverman & P. D. A. Treffers (Eds.) *Anxiety disorders in children and adolescents: Research, assessment and intervention* (pp. 159–186) London: Cambridge University Press.

La Greca, A. M., & Lopez, N. (1998). Social anxiety among adolescents: Linkages with peer relations and friendships. *Journal of Abnormal Child Psychology, 26,* 83–94.

La Greca, A. M., & Stone, W. L. (1993). Social Anxiety Scale for Children-Revised: Factor structure and concurrent validity. *Journal of Clinical Child Psychology, 22,* 7–27.

Last, C. G., Hersen, M., Kazdin, A. E., Orvaschel, H., & Perrin, S. (1991). Anxiety disorders in children and their families. *Archives of General Psychiatry, 48,* 928–934.

Lilienfeld, S. O., Wood, J. M., & Garb, H. N. (2000). The scientific status of projective techniques. *Psychological Science in the Public Interest, 1,* 27–66.

Lonigan, C. J., Carey, M. P., & Finch, A. J., Jr. (1994). Anxiety and depression in children and adolescents: Negative affectivity and the utility of self-reports. *Journal of Consulting and Clinical Psychology, 62,* 1000–1008.

Lonigan, C. J., Vasey, M. W., Phillips, B. M., & Hazen, R. A. (2003). Temperament, anxiety, and the processing of threat-relevant stimuli. *Journal of Clinical Child and Adolescent Psychology, 27,* 255–267.

March, J. S., Parker, J. D. A., Sullivan, K., Stallings, P., & Conners, K. (1997). The Multidimensional Anxiety Scale for Children (MASC): Factor, structure, reliability, and validity. *Journal of the American Academy of Child & Adolescent Psychiatry, 36,* 554–565.

Mash, E. J., & Terdal, L. G. (1998). *Behavioral assessment of childhood disorders* (2nd ed.). New York: Guilford Press.

Mattison, R. E., Bagnato, S. J., & Brubaker, B. M. (1988). Diagnostic utility of the Revised Children's Manifest Anxiety Scale in children with DSM-III anxiety disorders. *Journal of Anxiety Disorders, 2,* 147–155.

Menzies, R. G., & Clark, J. C. (1995). The etiology of phobias: A nonassociative account. *Clinical Psychology Review, 15,* 23–48.

Mineka, S., Gunnar, M., & Champoux, M. (1986). Control and early socioemotional development: Infant rhesus monkeys reared in controllable versus uncontrollable environments. *Child Development, 57,* 1241–1256.

Muris, P., Merckelbach, H., Ollendick, T. H., King, N. J., & Bogie, N. (2002). Three traditional and three new childhood anxiety questionnaires: Their reliability and validity in a normal adolescent sample. *Behaviour Research and Therapy, 40,* 753–772.

Muris, P., & Ollendick, T. H. (2005). The role of temperament in the etiology of child psychopathology. *Clinical Child and Family Psychology Review, 8,* 271–289.

Myers, K., & Winters, N. C. (2002). Ten-year review of rating scales II. Scales for internalizing disorders. *Journal of the American Academy of Child & Adolescent Psychiatry, 41,* 634–659.

Nelson-Gray, R. O. (2003). Treatment utility of psychological assessment. *Psychological Assessment, 15,* 521–531.

Ollendick, T. H. (1983). Reliability and validity of the Revised Fear Survey Schedule for Children (FSSC-R). *Behaviour Research and Therapy, 21,* 395–399.

Ollendick, T. H. (1995). Cognitive behavioral treatment of panic disorder with agoraphobia in adolescents: A multiple baseline design analysis. *Behavior Therapy, 26,* 517–531.

Ollendick, T. H. (1998). Panic disorder in children and adolescents: New developments, new directions. *Journal of Clinical Child Psychology, 27,* 234–245.

Ollendick, T. H. (1999). Empirically supported assessment for clinical practice: Is it possible? Is it desirable? *The Clinical Psychologist, 52,* 1–2.

Ollendick, T. H., Hagopian, L. P., & Huntzinger, R. M. (1991). Cognitive-behavior therapy with nighttime fearful children. *Journal of Behavior Therapy and Experimental Psychiatry, 22,* 113–121.

Ollendick, T. H., & Hersen, M. (1993). Child and adolescent behavioral assessment. In T. H. Ollendick & M. Hersen (Eds.), *Handbook of child and adolescent assessment* (pp. 3–14). New York: Pergamon Press.

Ollendick, T. H., & King, N. J. (1991). Origins of childhood fears: An evaluation of Rachman's theory of fear acquisition. *Behaviour Research and Therapy, 29,* 117–123.

Ollendick, T. H., King, N. J., & Chorpita, B. (2006). Empirically supported treatments for children and adolescents. In P. C. Kendall (Ed.), *Child and adolescent therapy* (3rd ed., pp. 492–520). New York: Guilford Press.

Ollendick, T. H., & March, J. S. (Eds.) (2004). *Phobic and anxiety disorders: A clinician's guide to effective psychosocial and pharmacological interventions.* New York: Oxford University Press.

Ollendick, T. H., Mattis, S. G., & Birmaher, B. (2004). Panic disorder. In T. L. Morris & J. S. March (Eds.), *Anxiety disorders in children and adolescents* (2nd Ed., pp. 189–211). New York: The Guilford Press.

Ollendick, T. H., & Seligman, L. D. (2006). Anxiety disorders in children and adolescents. In C. Gillberg, R. Harrington, & H.-C. Steinhausen (Eds.), *Clinician's desk book of child and adolescent psychiatry* (pp. 144–147). Cambridge: Cambridge University Press.

Ost, L. G., Svensson, L., Hellstrom. K., & Lindwall, R. (2001). One-session treatment of specific phobias in youths: A randomized clinical trial. *Journal of Consulting and Clinical Psychology, 69,* 814–824.

Pina, A. A., Silverman, W. K., Saavedra, L. M., & Weems, C. F. (2001). An analysis of the RCMAS lie scale in a clinic sample of anxious children. *Journal of Anxiety Disorders, 15,* 443–457.

Pine, D. S. (2006). A primer on brain imaging in developmental psychopathology: What is it good for? *Journal of Child Psychology and Psychiatry, 47,* 983–986.

Pine, D. S., Fyer, A., Grun, J., Phelps, E. A., Szeszko, P. R., Koda, V., et al. (2001). Methods for developmental studies of fear conditioning circuitry. *Biological Psychiatry, 50,* 225–228.

Rapee, R. M., Barrett, P. M., Dadds, M. R., & Evans, L. (1994). Reliability of the DSM-III-R childhood anxiety disorders using structured interview: Interrater and parent–child agreement. *Journal of the American Academy of Child & Adolescent Psychiatry, 33,* 984–992.

Reich, W. (2000). Diagnostic Interview for Children and Adolescents (DICA). *Journal of the American Academy of Child & Adolescent Psychiatry, 39,* 59–66.

Rey, J. M., Morris-Yates, A., & Stanislaw, H. (1992). Measuring the accuracy of diagnostic tests using receiver operating characteristics (ROC) analysis. *International Journal of Methods in Psychiatric Research, 2,* 39–50.

Rey, Y., Silverman, W. K., Pina, A. A., & Dick-Niederhauser, A. (2007). *Agreement on DSM-IV anxiety diagnoses between anxious youth and their parents.* Manuscript submitted.

Reynolds, C. R., & Richmond, B. O. (1985). *Revised children's manifest anxiety scale: Manual.* Los Angeles, CA: Western Psychological Services.

Reznick, J. S., Hegeman, I. M., Kaufman, E. R., Woods, S. W., & Jacobs, M. (1992). Retrospective and concurrent self-report of behavioral inhibition and their relation to adult mental health. *Development and Psychopathology, 4,* 301–321.

RUPP Anxiety Study Group (2002). The Pediatric Anxiety Rating Scale (PARS): Development and psychometric properties. *Journal of the American Academy of Child & Adolescent Psychiatry, 41,* 1061–1069.

Saavedra, L. M., & Silverman, W. K. (2002). Classification of anxiety disorders in children: What a difference two decades make. *International Review of Psychiatry, 14,* 87–100.

Seligman, L. D., & Ollendick, T. H. (1998). Comorbidity of anxiety and depression in children and adolescents: An integrative review. *Clinical Child and Family Psychology Review, 1,* 125–144.

Seligman, L. D., Ollendick, T. H., Langley, A. K., & Baldacci, H. B. (2004). The utility of measures of child and adolescent anxiety: A meta-analytic review of the RCMAS, STAIC, and CBCL. *Journal of Clinical Child and Adolescent Psychology, 33,* 557–565.

Shaffer, D., Fisher, P., Lucas, C., Dulcan, M. K., & Schwab-Stone, M. E. (2000). NIMH Diagnostic Interview Schedule for Children Version IV (NIMH DISC-IV): Description, differences from previous versions, and reliability of some common diagnoses. *Journal of the American Academy of Child & Adolescent Psychiatry, 39,* 28–38.

Silverman, W. K. (1991). *Anxiety disorders interview schedule for children.* Albany, NY: Graywind Publications.

Silverman, W. K. (1994). Structured diagnostic interviews. In T. H. Ollendick, N. J. King, & W. Yule (Eds.), *International handbook of phobic and anxiety disorders in children and adolescents* (pp. 293–315). New York: Plenum Press.

Silverman, W. K., & Albano, A. M. (1996). *Anxiety Disorders Interview Schedule for Children for DSM-IV: (Child and Parent Versions).* San Antonio, TX: Psychological Corporation/Graywind Publications Incorporated.

Silverman, W. K., & Berman, S. L. (2001). Psychosocial interventions for anxiety disorders in children: Status and future directions. In W. K. Silverman & P. D. A. Treffers (Eds.), *Anxiety disorders in children and adolescents: Research, assessment and intervention* (pp. 313–334). Cambridge, UK: Cambridge University Press.

Silverman, W. K., & Carter, R. (2006). Anxiety disturbance in girls and women. In J. Worell & C. Goodheart (Eds.), *Handbook of girls' and women's psychological health* (pp. 60–68). New York: Oxford University Press.

Silverman, W. K., & Eisen, A. R. (1992). Age differences in the reliability of parent and child reports of child anxious symptomatology using a structured interview. *Journal of the American Academy of Child & Adolescent Psychiatry, 31,* 117–124.

Silverman, W. K., Fleisig, W., Rabian, B., & Peterson, R. A. (1991). Childhood Anxiety Sensitivity Index. *Journal of Clinical Child Psychology, 20,* 162–168.

Silverman, W. K., & Ginsburg, G. S. (1998). Anxiety disorders. In T. H. Ollendick & M. Hersen (Eds.), *Handbook of child psychopathology* (3rd. Ed., 5 pp. 239–268). New York: Plenum.

Silverman, W. K., Kurtines, W. M., Ginsburg, G. S., Weems, C. G., Lumpkin, P. W., & Carmichael, D. H. (1999). Treating anxiety disorders in children with group cognitive behavioral therapy: A randomized clinical trial. *Journal of Consulting and Clinical Psychology, 67,* 995–1003.

Silverman, W. K., La Greca, A. M., & Wasserstein, S. B. (1995). What do children worry about? Worry and its relation to anxiety. *Child Development, 66,* 671–686.

Silverman, W. K., & Nelles, W. B. (1988). The anxiety disorders interview schedule for children. *Journal of the American Academy of Child & Adolescent Psychiatry, 27,* 772–778.

Silverman, W. K., & Ollendick, T. H. (Eds.) (1999). *Developmental issues in the clinical treatment of children.* Needham Heights, MA: Allyn & Bacon.

Silverman, W. K., & Ollendick, T. H. (2005). Evidence-based assessment of anxiety and its disorders in children and adolescents. *Journal of Clinical Child and Adolescent Psychology, 34,* 380–411.

Silverman, W. K., & Rabian, B. (1995). Test-retest reliability of the DSM-III-R childhood anxiety disorders symptoms using the Anxiety Disorders Interview Schedule for Children. *Journal of Anxiety Disorders, 9,* 1–12.

Silverman, W. K., & Rabian, B. (1999). Rating scales for anxiety and mood disorders. In D. Shaffer, C. Lucas, & J. Richters (Eds.), *Diagnostic assessment in child and adolescent psychopathology* (pp. 127–166). New York: Guilford Press.

Silverman, W. K., & Saavedra, L. M. (2004). Assessment and diagnosis in evidence based practice. In P. M. Barrett & T. H. Ollendick (Eds.), *Handbook of interventions that work with children and adolescents: Prevention and treatment* (pp. 49–69). New York: Guilford Press.

Silverman, W. K., Saavedra, L. M., & Pina, A. A. (2001). Test–retest reliability of anxiety symptoms and diagnoses using the Anxiety Disorders Interview Schedule for DSM-IV: Child and Parent Versions (ADIS for DSM-IV: C/P). *Journal of the American Academy of Child & Adolescent Psychiatry, 40,* 937–944.

Silverman, W. K., & Serafini, L. T. (1998). Internalizing disorders. In M. Hersen & A. S. Bellack (Eds.), *Behavioral assessment: A practical handbook* (4th ed., pp. 342–360). Needham Heights, MA: Allyn and Bacon.

Silverman, W. K., & Weems, C. F. (1998). Anxiety sensitivity in children. In S. Taylor (Ed.), *Anxiety sensitivity: Theory, research and the treatment of the fear of anxiety* (pp. 239–268). Mahwah, NJ: Lawrence Erlbaum.

Spence, S. H. (1997). The structure of anxiety symptoms among children: A confirmatory factor analytic study. *Journal of Abnormal Psychology, 106,* 280–297.

Spence, S. H. (1998). A measure of anxiety symptoms among children. *Behaviour Research and Therapy, 36,* 545–566.

Spielberger, C. D. (1973). *Manual for the state-trait anxiety inventory for children.* Palo Alto, CA: Consulting Psychologists Press.

Turner, S. M., Beidel, D. C., & Costello, A. (1987). Psychopathology in the offspring of anxiety disorders patients. *Journal of Consulting and Clinical Psychology, 55,* 229–235.

Turner, S. M., Beidel, D. C., & Wolff, P. L. (1996). Is behavioral inhibition related to the anxiety disorders? *Clinical Psychology Review, 16,* 157–172.

Vasey, M. W., Daleiden, E. L., Williams, L. L., & Brown, L. M. (1995). Biased attention in childhood anxiety disorders: A preliminary study. *Journal of Abnormal Child Psychology, 23,* 267–279.

Vasey, M. W., Dalgleish, T., & Silverman, W. K. (2003). Research on information-processing factors in child and adolescent psychopathology: A critical commentary. *Journal of Clinical Child and Adolescent Psychology, 32,* 81–93.

Vasey, M. W., & Ollendick, T. H. (2000). Anxiety. In A. J. Sameroff, M. Lewis, & S. M. Miller (Eds.),

Handbook of developmental psychopathology (2nd Ed., pp. 511–529). New York: Kluwer Academic/Plenum Publishers.

Vernberg, E. M., La Greca, A. M., Silverman, W. K., & Prinstein, M. J. (1996). Prediction of posttraumatic stress symptoms in children after Hurricane Andrew. *Journal of Abnormal Psychology, 105,* 237–248.

Warren S. L., Huston L., Egeland B., & Sroufe L. A. (1997). Child and adolescent anxiety disorders and early attachment. *Journal of the American Academy of Child & Adolescent Psychiatry, 36,* 637–644.

Watson, D., & Clark, L.A. (1984). Negative affectivity: The disposition to experience aversive emotional states. *Psychological Bulletin, 96,* 465–490.

Weems, C. F., Berman, S. L., Silverman, W. K., & Rodriguez, E. (2002). The relation between anxiety sensitivity and attachment style in adolescence and early adulthood. *Journal of Psychopathology and Behavioral Assessment, 24,* 159–168.

Weems, C. F., & Silverman W. K. (2006). An integrative model of control: Implications for understanding emotion regulation and dysregulation in childhood anxiety. *Journal of Affective Disorders, 91,* 113–124.

Weems, C., & Silverman, W. K. (in press). Anxiety disorders. In T. P. Beauchaine & S. P. Hinshaw (Eds.), *Child and adolescent psychopathology.* New York: Wiley.

Weems, C. F., Silverman, W. K., & La Greca, A. M. (2000). What do youth referred for anxiety problems worry about? Worry and its relation to anxiety and anxiety disorders in children and adolescents. *Journal of Abnormal Child Psychology, 28,* 63–72.

Weems, C. F., Silverman, W. K., Rapee, R. R., & Pina, A. A. (2003). The role of control in childhood anxiety disorders. *Cognitive Therapy and Research, 27,* 557–568.

Weems, C. F., Silverman, W. K., Saavedra, L. M., Pina, A. A., & Lumpkin, P. W. (1999). The discrimination of children's phobias using the Revised Fear Survey Schedule for Children. *Journal of Child Psychology and Psychiatry, 40,* 941–952.

Westen, D., Novotny, C. M., & Thompson-Brenner, H. (2004). The empirical status of empirically supported psychotherapies: Assumptions, findings, and reporting in controlled clinical trials. *Psychological Bulletin, 130,* 631–663.

Whaley, S. E., Pinto, A., & Sigman, M. (1999). Characterizing interactions between anxious mothers and their children. *Journal of Consulting and Clinical Psychology, 67,* 826–836.

Wood, J., Piacentini, J. C., Bergman, R. L., McCracken, J., & Barrios, V. (2002). Concurrent validity of the anxiety disorders section of the anxiety disorders interview schedule for DSM-IV: Child and parent versions. *Journal of Clinical Child and Adolescent Psychology, 31,* 335–342.

Woodward, L. J., & Fergusson, D. M. (2001). Life course outcomes of young people with anxiety disorders in adolescence. *Journal of the American Academy of Child & Adolescent Psychiatry, 40,* 1086–1093.

10

Specific Phobia and Social Phobia

Karen Rowa
Randi E. McCabe
Martin M. Antony

Although it is widely accepted that assessment procedures are an important part of understanding and treating anxiety-based problems, relatively little attention has been paid to developing and studying comprehensive, evidence-based assessment protocols for the anxiety disorders. This is in contrast to the extensive attention that has been paid to empirically supported treatment interventions over the last decade (e.g., Chambless et al., 1998), and to the large number of studies regarding the psychometric properties of particular anxiety measures. Indeed, entire books have been devoted to the review of psychometric properties of these widely used tools (e.g., Antony, Orsillo, & Roemer, 2001). More recently, however, the importance of empirically supported assessment *procedures* for anxiety disorders has become a focus of discussion (e.g., Antony & Rowa, 2005), with the hope that research on these procedures and protocols will add to our growing knowledge regarding the reliability and validity of particular instruments.

Although the empirical literature clearly has room to grow when it comes to validating assessment procedures for anxiety disorders, it is useful to summarize what we do know about commonly used assessment tools and procedures, as this can provide guidance to clinicians and researchers regarding the most appropriate tools for various assessment tasks. The purpose of this chapter is to review the scientific status and clinical utility of the most commonly practiced assessment procedures for two of the anxiety disorders—specific phobia and social phobia.

NATURE OF SPECIFIC PHOBIA AND SOCIAL PHOBIA

Diagnostic Considerations

Specific phobia and social phobia share a number of features, including the presence of excessive fear, anxious apprehension, and avoidance behavior. However, it is the focus of fear that distinguishes between the two anxiety disorders. In specific phobia, the excessive fear is focused on a particular situation or object (e.g., animals or insects, heights, seeing blood or receiving a needle, driving, and enclosed places). In social phobia, the excessive fear is focused on one or more social and performance situations in which the individual fears acting in a way that will be embarrassing or lead to negative evaluation by others (e.g., public speaking, parties, being assertive, making small talk, dating). Often dismissed as extreme shyness, social phobia is commonly unrecognized and undertreated, particularly in primary care settings (Heimberg, 2003; Keller, 2003).

Apart from the defining nature of the two disorders, the diagnostic criteria as outlined in the *Diagnostic and Statistical Manual of Mental Disorders* 4th Edition, Text Revision (DSM-IV-TR; American Psychiatric Association, 2000) are largely the same. Exposure to the feared stimulus typically results in an immediate anxiety response that may escalate into a full-blown panic attack. The individual has insight into the excessive nature of the fear, although this may not be the case for children. Moreover, the symptoms (i.e., fear, anxious apprehension, and avoidance) cause the individual significant distress or impairment in functioning and cannot be better explained by any other mental disorder. In addition, for social phobia, the fear is not due to the physiological effects of a substance or a general medical condition, and if a general medical condition or another mental disorder is present, the fear is unrelated to it (e.g., a fear of shaking in the presence of Parkinson's disease or a fear of eating in public in the presence of an eating disorder would not be indicative of a phobic disorder). When assigning a diagnosis of specific phobia, the category of fear may be specified as one of five types: animal (e.g., dogs, birds, insects), natural environment (e.g., heights, water), blood–injection–injury (e.g., getting a needle, seeing blood), situational (e.g., driving, enclosed places, flying), and others (e.g., fear of choking or vomiting). When assigning a diagnosis of social phobia, the specifier *generalized* may be used in cases where the individual fears most social situations.

Evidence suggests that avoidant personality disorder and social phobia are alternative conceptualizations of the same disorder, with avoidant personality disorder representing a more severe and more generalized form of the condition (Ralevski et al., 2005). Given that a personality disorder diagnosis should not be considered when it includes significant features of an Axis I disorder, the diagnosis of social phobia is preferred to that of avoidant personality disorder (Wittchen & Fehm, 2003). Hofmann, Heinrichs, and Moscovitch (2004) noted that, although individuals meeting symptom criteria for a diagnosis of social phobia share certain specific features, in reality, they are a heterogeneous group that may be better characterized along a dimensional continuum of emotional response and behavioral tendencies encompassing fearfulness, anxiousness, shyness, self-consciousness, submissiveness, and anger.

Epidemiology and Descriptive Psychopathology

Specific phobia is one of the most common anxiety disorders, with a lifetime prevalence estimate of 12.5% (e.g., Kessler et al., 2005). For social phobia, a recent review of studies in community samples revealed a median lifetime prevalence rate of 6.65% (Fehm, Pelissolo, Furmark, & Wittchen, 2005), though the recent replication of the National Comorbidity Survey suggested a lifetime prevalence of 12% (Kessler et al., 2005). Specific phobias are more common in women then in men (e.g., Curtis, Magee, Eaton, Wittchen, & Kessler, 1998), though there is variability across specific phobia types with respect to this issue. Similarly, social phobia is slightly more common in women then men (Fehm et al., 2005).

The majority of specific phobias (animal, blood–injection–injury, natural environment) typically have an onset in childhood. However, situational type phobias (e.g., flying, driving, elevators) have a later age of onset, typically in late adolescence or early adulthood (e.g., Antony, Brown, & Barlow, 1997b; Lipsitz, Barlow, Mannuzza, Hofmann, & Fyer, 2002). Onset of social phobia is typically during childhood and adolescence, with a range of 13 to 24 years in clinical studies and 10 to 16.6 years in epidemiological studies (Wittchen & Fehm, 2003). Later onset of social phobia (after the age of 25) is rare and typically secondary to, or encompassed by, a separate mental disorder (e.g., depression, eating disorder, etc.; Wittchen & Fehm, 2003).

Specific phobias are often comorbid with other specific phobias and other anxiety disorders (Curtis et al., 1998; Sanderson, Di Nardo, Rapee, & Barlow, 1990). However, in the latter case, specific phobia tends to be of lesser severity then the comorbid condition (Sanderson et al., 1990). Social phobia is associated with a high degree of comorbidity. It is estimated that 50% to 80% of the patients with social phobia have at least one other mental disorder, most commonly other anxiety disorders, major depressive disorder, and substance abuse disorders (Fehm et al., 2005; Wittchen & Fehm, 2003).

Examination of the impact of specific phobia on quality of life has received little attention (Mogotsi, Kaminer, & Stein, 2000). However, evidence suggests that specific phobia can be associated with high levels of psychosocial impairment (Essau, Conradt, & Petermann, 2000). Social phobia is associated with significant degree of impairment and disability that increases over the patient's lifespan (e.g., Fehm et al., 2005; Wittchen & Fehm, 2003). One study found that 21% of patients with social phobia had clinically severe impairment (defined as being two or more standard deviations below the community norm) in quality of life (Rapaport, Clary, Fayyad, & Endicott, 2005). In addition, there is some evidence that safety behaviors used by individuals with social phobia cause significant impairment in social performance (e.g., Stangier, Heidenreich, & Schermelleh-Engel, 2006).

Etiology

Genetic factors appear to play a role in the development of both specific and social phobia. First-degree relatives of individuals with specific phobia or social phobia have an increased risk of having the disorder compared with first-degree relatives of never mentally ill controls (Fyer et al., 1990). Whether the genetic contribution is a specific genetic factor influencing risk for a specific anxiety disorder (i.e., specific phobia or social phobia) or a more general genetic factor influencing risk for any anxiety disorder is an issue of ongoing investigation.

Rachman (1977) proposed three pathways to fear development: direct conditioning (being hurt or frightened by the phobic object or situation), vicarious acquisition (witnessing a traumatic event or seeing someone behave fearfully in the phobic situation), and informational transmission (through messages received from others). Numerous studies have found support for this model (for review, see Antony & McCabe, 2003). In addition to learning processes, a fourth nonassociative pathway has been proposed to explain findings that are not accounted for by an associative model (e.g., some fears emerge without any prior associative learning experience). According to Poulton and Menzies (2002), a limited number of fears are innate or biologically determined and are adaptive from an evolutionary perspective. Other factors that may play a role in phobia development include the tendency to experience "disgust" in response to certain stimuli (e.g., disgust sensitivity), cognitive variables (e.g., information processing biases), and environmental factors (e.g., the context of a traumatic event, stress, previous, and subsequent exposure to a phobic stimulus; Antony & McCabe, 2003).

In addition to genetics and learning pathways, research has uncovered a number of specific risk factors associated with increased vulnerability for onset of social phobia, including familial environment (overprotective or rejecting parenting style, parental modeling, degree of exposure to social situations), and behavioral-temperamental style (increased behavioral inhibition as a child; Wittchen & Fehm, 2003). Rapee and Spence (2004) have proposed an etiological model of social phobia that attempts to capture the complexity of the disorder based on available evidence. According to their model, individuals have a "set point" level of social anxiety that is somewhat stable and consistent, and is directed by broad genetic factors (e.g., general emotionality, sociability). The individual's *set point* is altered (up or down) largely due to environmental factors (e.g., parents, peers,

negative life events, culture, interrupted social performance, poor social skill) that may operate as powerful influences due to timing (critical stage of vulnerability), impact (intensity or meaning of the event), or chronicity. For example, a significant portion of individuals with social phobia report a history of being severely teased or bullied (McCabe, Antony, Summerfeldt, Liss, & Swinson, 2003).

PURPOSES OF ASSESSMENT

Antony and Rowa (2005) suggested 10 common purposes for which assessments are used: (1) to establish a diagnosis, (2) to measure the presence, absence, or severity of particular symptoms; (3) to measure features that cannot be assessed directly through an interview or self-report scales (e.g., physiological processes, nonconscious processes); (4) to facilitate the selection of target problems for treatment planning; (5) to measure a phenomenon that is of interest for research; (6) to assess whether a particular treatment is "evidence-based"; (7) to include or exclude participants from a research study; (8) to answer questions of interest for insurance companies (e.g., presence of malingering); (9) to predict future behavior (e.g., treatment compliance); and (10) to evaluate eligibility for employment, benefits, legal status, school placement, and so forth. In order to evaluate whether an assessment procedure is evidence-based, one must ask the question, *for what purpose?* A particular assessment protocol or measure may be empirically supported for some purposes, but not others. In this chapter, we review assessment procedures for specific and social phobias as they are used for three main clinical purposes: (1) diagnosis, (2) case conceptualization and treatment planning, and (3) treatment monitoring and evaluation.

ASSESSMENT FOR DIAGNOSIS

Establishing a diagnosis for people suffering from specific and social phobia is important for a number of reasons. Diagnosis facilitates communication about the presenting problem and the accompanying symptoms, and also allows for the selection of the most appropriate evidence-based treatments, many of which have been developed for particular disorders. Diagnostic clarification also helps clinicians to distinguish among different conditions and to make decisions about whether clinical issues are best conceptualized as separate problems or as different features of the same problem. For example, embarrassment about losing bowel control may lead to avoidance of situations similar to that seen in social phobia, but would often be better accounted for by a diagnosis of panic disorder or agoraphobia. Further, achieving a broad diagnostic picture can also aid a clinician in understanding the impact that comorbid conditions (e.g., substance use disorders, personality disorders) may have on the course and treatment outcome for specific and social phobias. The presence of certain comorbid conditions may influence a client's readiness for treatment and decisions about the order of treatment interventions (e.g., whether to treat the anxiety disorder or the substance issue first) and the treatment process (e.g., the necessity to develop alternative coping strategies for someone who is using substances to manage symptoms of anxiety). More details about the assessment of relevant comorbid conditions such as substance use disorders and depression can be found in other chapters in this volume.

Diagnoses can be established using unstructured clinical interviews, fully structured interviews, or semistructured interviews (for a review, see Summerfeldt & Antony, 2002). The main way in which these approaches differ is in the level of standardization. Unstructured clinical interviews are the least standardized, and are the most commonly used clinical interview format in routine practice. In unstructured interviews clinicians ask whatever questions they see as appropriate for assessing the diagnostic features of particular disorders as well as other clinical characteristics of interest. However, research suggests that rates of diagnostic agreement using clinical interviews are often no better than chance (Spitzer & Fleiss, 1974), rendering the reliability and validity of diagnostic findings suspect.

In contrast, fully structured interviews (e.g., the World Health Organization Composite International Diagnostic Interview or WHO-CIDI; Kessler & Ustun, 2004) are the most standardized format for diagnostic interviews. In these interviews, questions are always asked in the same way, and there is little flexibility to ask follow-up questions or to ask for clarification. These interviews are designed to be used by trained lay interviewers, and are primarily used in large epidemiological studies, rather than by clinicians or clinical researchers. A number of studies

have questioned the validity of anxiety disorders diagnoses as established by fully structured interviews (see Antony, Downie, & Swinson, 1998; Summerfeldt & Antony, 2002).

Semistructured interviews include many of the advantages of both structured and unstructured interviews. Standard questions are asked to assess each of the diagnostic criteria necessary for making a diagnosis, but clinicians are permitted to ask follow-up questions for clarification, and to answer questions that respondents may have about particular questions. Semistructured interviews are the most common type of diagnostic interview used in clinical research, and they are occasionally used in routine clinical practice as well.

Two of the most extensively studied semistructured interviews for diagnosing anxiety-related problems including specific and social phobia are the Anxiety Disorders Interview Schedule for DSM-IV (ADIS-IV; Brown, Di Nardo, & Barlow, 1994; Di Nardo, Brown, & Barlow, 1994) and the Structured Clinical Interview for DSM-IV/Axis I Disorders (SCID-IV; First, Spitzer, Gibbon, & Williams, 1996). Both the ADIS-IV and the SCID-IV provide systematic questions to establish a reliable current diagnosis of specific or social phobia (Brown, Di Nardo, Lehman, & Campbell, 2001; Segal, Hersen, & van Hasselt, 1994). Questions and initial probes are outlined for interviewers, ensuring that all clients receive the same questions, in the same order, using the same terminology. Subsequent follow-up questions may deviate from the structured questions. For example, additional questions may be necessary to differentiate a specific phobia of driving from fears of driving associated with panic disorder (e.g., "What is the focus of your fear when driving? Having a panic attack? Being in an accident?"). These interviews provide decision trees to establish diagnoses once pertinent information is collected. Both the ADIS-IV and SCID-IV have versions for use with children, adolescents, and their parents (see Grills & Ollendick, 2002, for a review). The ADIS-IV and SCID-IV are described below in more detail, and a summary of their psychometric properties can be found in Table 10.1.

Anxiety Disorders Interview Schedule for DSM-IV

The ADIS-IV (Di Nardo et al., 1994) is a clinician-administered semistructured interview that provides

TABLE 10.1 Ratings of Instruments Used for Diagnosis

Instrument	Norms	Internal Consistency	Inter-Rater Reliability	Test–Retest Reliability	Content Validity	Construct Validity	Validity Generalization	Clinical Utility	Highly Recommended
ADIS-IV	NA	NA	G	U	E	G	G	E	✓
SCID-IV	NA	NA	E	U	E	G	G	E	✓

Note: ADIS-IV = Anxiety Disorders Interview Schedule; SCID-IV = Structured Clinical Interview for DSM-IV; G = Good; E = Excellent; U = Unavailable; NA = Not Applicable.

both diagnostic and dimensional information about a range of psychological problems, including anxiety disorders, mood disorders, somatoform disorders, and substance use disorders. Screening questions are provided for psychotic disorders, conversion symptoms, and the presence of a family history of psychiatric illness. Diagnoses are assigned based on criteria from the DSM-IV. Depending on the version of the ADIS-IV used (standard and lifetime versions), current and lifetime diagnoses can be ascertained. Clinicians require extensive training in the administration of this interview, and the interview duration can be lengthy (e.g., several hours). Despite these drawbacks for everyday practice, the ADIS-IV has the benefit of providing clear criteria to help determine the presence or absence of specifitc and social phobia (as well as common comorbid disorders), as well as assessing useful information such as the degree of fear and avoidance in a variety of social settings. Indeed, the ADIS-IV goes well beyond the SCID-IV in terms of screening for a wide variety of social and performance situations in which a person may experience fear, increasing the chance that difficulties with social situations or a specific phobia will be identified. If initial inquiries reveal the possibility of symptoms of specific or social phobia, a number of follow-up questions are asked to assess the intensity of the fear, the frequency and breadth of avoidance, the level of distress and interference caused by symptoms, and other relevant variables.

The ADIS-IV has demonstrated good reliability. A recent study by Brown and colleagues examined the inter-rater reliability of diagnostic decisions made using the ADIS-IV (Brown et al., 2001). Inter-rater reliability was strong for specific and social phobia, both when diagnosed as the principal or additional diagnosis. In fact, agreement between clinicians was good to excellent for most clinical diagnoses. The main source of disagreement for both specific and social phobias involved rating the clinical severity of the disorder, with one clinician concluding that the disorder was clinically significant and another clinician concluding that the disorder severity did not exceed clinical threshold for distress or impairment. This study suggested that there were very few disagreements between clinicians when deciding between social phobia and another disorder. In other words, clinicians appeared to be successful in disentangling symptom presentations to reliably diagnose social phobia.

Studies on the ADIS-R, the precursor to the ADIS-IV, also support the reliability and utility of this earlier version of the interview for diagnosing simple and social phobias (in DSM-III-R, *specific phobias* were referred to as *simple phobias*). A large-scale study of 267 outpatients found good agreement between raters on the diagnoses of simple and social phobia (Di Nardo, Moras, Barlow, Rapee, & Brown, 1993). Another study found that the use of the ADIS-R in a low socioeconomic population identified numerous clients with primary and secondary anxiety disorders (including simple and social phobias) that had not been identified by clinical staff (Paradis, Friedman, Lazar, Grubea, & Kesselman, 1992). The ADIS has also proven reliable when diagnosing childhood anxiety disorders using a parent version of this interview (Silverman & Rabian, 1995). Parent ratings of the symptoms of avoidant personality disorder (similar to social phobia symptoms) demonstrated good test–retest reliabilities across a 10- to 14-day interval, when rating the symptoms of younger children (6–11 years) as well as those of older children (12–17 years). The chapter by Silverman and Ollendick this volume contains more information about assessing child and adolescent anxiety. Thus, the ADIS-IV and its precursors appear to be effective in identifying the presence of specific and social phobia, and in providing reliable diagnoses of these disorders.

Structured Clinical Interview for DSM-IV

The SCID-IV (First et al., 1996) is also a clinician-administered semistructured interview that provides diagnostic decisions about a wide range of psychiatric disorders. Two versions are available—a clinician version (SCID-CV) and a research version (SCID-I). The clinician version was designed for use in clinical settings and has a less extensive coverage of disorders. The research version has a broader focus and provides for assessment of mood disorders, anxiety disorders, somatoform disorders, substance disorders, eating disorders, adjustment disorders, and psychotic disorders. Current and lifetime diagnoses are obtained. Extensive training is also required to administer the SCID-IV, and administration can be lengthy, especially for the research version (i.e., 2 to 3 hours for a typical outpatient administration).

Much of the evidence for the psychometric properties of the SCID-IV is derived from research using an earlier version based on DSM-III-R criteria. However, minimal changes affected the revision of the SCID to its current version, so a review of these studies seems appropriate. Studies suggest that the SCID demonstrates adequate or better reliability (both inter-rater and test–retest) for most diagnoses in patient samples (Williams et al., 1992), but not in nonpatient samples. Symptom agreement and diagnostic accuracy using the SCID is also good (Ventura, Liberman, Green, Shaner, & Mintz, 1998). However, for some populations, reliability of diagnoses may be less robust. For example, a study examining DSM-III-R lifetime diagnoses in a substance abusing population found poorer test–retest reliabilities than other studies (Ross, Swinson, Doumani, & Larkin, 1995). Given the comorbidity between social phobia and substance use issues, this issue is of relevance to consider. A summary of the criterion-related validity of the SCID suggests that there is a high level of correspondence between SCID-derived diagnoses and other variables such as the clinical features of disorders, the course of conditions, and treatment outcome for certain conditions (Rogers, 1995).

Overall Evaluation

Because of their greater reliability, semistructured interviews such as the ADIS-IV or SCID-IV are preferable to either unstructured clinical interviews or fully structured clinical interviews, both in routine clinical practice as well as in clinical research. Although few studies have directly examined the validity of these measures, there is a vast body of research that indirectly supports their validity. For example, studies often compare diagnostic results from the ADIS-IV or the SCID-IV to scores on established questionnaire measures for social or specific phobia, finding strong convergence between the presence of the disorder (based on the interview) and the presence of relevant symptoms (based on self-report scales). For example, the widely used Social Interaction Anxiety Scale (Mattick & Clarke, 1998), a self-report measure of symptoms of social anxiety, demonstrated a 97% correct classification rate when compared with diagnoses of social phobia made using the SCID-IV or ADIS-IV (Rodebaugh, Heimberg, Woods, Liebowitz, & Schneier, 2006). Therefore, it is clearly preferable to use a semistructured interview such as the ADIS-IV or SCID-IV versus unstructured or fully structured interviews when establishing a diagnosis of specific or social phobia.

ASSESSMENT FOR CASE CONCEPTUALIZATION AND TREATMENT PLANNING

An important function of assessment is to gather information for the purpose of case conceptualization and treatment planning. Antony and Rowa (2005) reviewed the most important variables to assess when treating anxiety disorders, including the severity of the fear, degree of avoidance, subtle avoidance and safety behaviors, use of maladaptive coping strategies, anxious cognitions, motivation for treatment, treatment history, suitability for various forms of therapy, and presence of skills deficits. In this section, we review a number of assessment measures designed to provide information on variables that are important to consider when developing an empirically supported treatment plan for an individual. Because empirically supported psychological treatments for specific and social phobias include primarily cognitive and behavioral strategies, treatment planning and conceptualization in this chapter will generally refer to preparing for a course of cognitive-behavioral therapy (CBT). Please see Table 10.2 for summary ratings of the instruments. Also, please note that the diagnostic instruments described earlier may also be useful for gathering information relevant to treatment planning

TABLE 10.2 Ratings of Instruments Used for Case Conceptualization and Treatment Planning

Instrument	Norms	Internal Consistency	Inter-Rater Reliability	Test–Retest Reliability	Content Validity	Construct Validity	Validity Generalization	Clinical Utility	Highly Recommended
FSQ	A	E	NA	A	A	G	G	G	
SNAQ	A	G	NA	E	U	G	E	G	
DAI	A	E	NA	A	A	G	E	G	
SPAI	E	E	NA	A	E	E	E	E	✓
SPIN	E	E	NA	A	G	G	E	E	✓
DS	G	G	NA	U	E	G	A	G	
ASI	E	G	NA	G	E	E	E	E	✓
FMPS	G	G	NA	U	G	G	E	G	
SPRS	G	A	G	U	E	E	E	A	

Note: FSQ = Fear of Spiders Questionnaire; SNAQ = Snake Questionnaire; DAI = Dental Anxiety Inventory; SPAI = Social Phobia and Anxiety Inventory; SPIN = Social Phobia Inventory; DS = Disgust Scale; ASI = Anxiety Sensitivity Index; FMPS = Frost Multidimensional Perfectionism Scale; SPRS = Social Performance Rating Scale; A = Adequate; G = Good; E = Excellent; U = Unavailable; NA = Not Applicable.

and conceptualization, and therefore such information (e.g., avoided situations, coping strategies) may already be known after completing a diagnostic assessment. The measures described in this upcoming section will provide additional, as well as complementary, information to what is already known from a diagnostic assessment.

Self-Report Measures of Severity and Phenomenology—Specific Phobia

To plan an effective program of treatment for specific phobia, it is useful to understand the clinical presentation of the person's fear. Objectively, how severe is the individual's fear compared with others with a similar diagnosis? What situations or objects does the person avoid as a result of his or her fear? What kinds of anxious thoughts or worries does the person have when confronting his or her feared situation?

Owing to the heterogeneity of specific phobia, there are few assessment tools that provide information across the broad range of phobic stimuli. Most measures are aimed at one particular type of specific phobia (e.g., a fear of spiders). The exception is the Fear Survey Schedule (FSS), versions II (Geer, 1965) and III (Wolpe & Lang, 1969). These two versions of the popular self-report measure are designed to assess a broad range of phobic stimuli and objects. Individuals are presented with extensive lists of phobic stimuli and are asked to rate the severity of their fear based on Likert scales. Total severity is scored by adding all ratings together. Although the reliability of these measures is strong (e.g., Arindell, 1980; Geer, 1965), there

are questions about the validity and ultimate utility of the FSS. For example, a study that examined the predictive validity of the FSS-III found relatively low correlations between fear ratings on particular scale items and responses to a behavioral approach task involving exposure to the situation described in the particular item (Klieger & Franklin, 1993). Further, the items on the FSS range from common specific phobia stimuli (e.g., needles, airplanes) to stimuli that are irrelevant to phobic disorders in general (e.g., fear of nude bodies). Thus, scores on the FSS are often indistinguishable between groups of individuals with different anxiety disorders (e.g., Beck, Carmin, & Henninger, 1998). Even though scores on the FSS have been demonstrated to decrease after successful treatment for specific phobias (e.g., Öst, 1989), reasons for using the FSS as a first-line assessment tool for specific phobia are limited. It appears that, if this measure is to be used at all, it may be best used as a screening tool before diagnostic decisions and treatment planning begin.

Once diagnosis of a particular specific phobia has been made, it is likely to be more useful to use a measure designed to assess the clinical features of that disorder. Over the past two decades, researchers have developed a number of self-report scales for measuring symptoms related to fears of snakes, spiders, dogs, heights, blood, needles, dentists, enclosed places, and flying. We review several examples in the following paragraphs and in Table 10.2; however, given the broad range of specific phobia types, a comprehensive review of all relevant measures is not possible. For an extensive review of adult measures, see Antony

(2001a) or McCabe and Antony (2002). For a review of child measures, see Ollendick, Davis, and Muris (2004) or Southam-Gerow and Chorpita (2007).

For a principal diagnosis of a specific phobia, animal type, psychometrically sound measures exist for fear of spiders and snakes, two of the most commonly feared animals. For example, the 18-item Fear of Spiders Questionnaire (Szymanski & O'Donohue, 1995) provides an objective measure of the severity of a person's fear of spiders, with scores clearly distinguishing between phobic and nonphobic participants (Muris & Merckelbach, 1996). This questionnaire seems best able to predict conscious avoidance behaviors (i.e., behaviors available to introspection and verbalization), whereas it is less able to predict automatic fear responses, such as a physiological startle response (Huijding & de Jong, 2006). Therefore, the FSQ is useful for understanding the severity of a person's fear of spiders and for understanding the types of situations a client may avoid because of fears of spiders, though it has less utility for helping understand the role of implicit reactions to spiders when planning treatment.

If a client reports a fear of snakes, the Snake Questionnaire (SNAQ; Klorman, Hastings, Weerts, Melamed, & Lang, 1974) provides a detailed understanding of a person's particular concerns about snakes and the way this fear may affect his or her life. Individuals rate 30 fearful or nonfearful statements about snakes as true or false. Total scores clearly distinguish patient populations from nonclinical groups and from individuals with spider phobias (Fredrikson, 1983). Scores are also sensitive to treatment-related changes (Öst, 1978). However, scores on this questionnaire do not correspond to actual behavioral reactions to a caged snake, suggesting that this measure may have good, but not excellent, construct validity (Klieger, 1987). Once again, as a component of treatment planning, a questionnaire like the SNAQ will provide the clinician with an idea of the types of beliefs the individual holds about snakes and the impact of these beliefs on a person's day-to-day functioning. Strongly held beliefs may become the focus of cognitive restructuring efforts in therapy, they may shape the provision of educational information about snakes, or they may suggest ideas for in vivo exposure exercises. For example, one item on the SNAQ is "The way snakes move is repulsive." If a person endorses this item, it suggests that movement may form an important part of his or her fear, and

that the person might benefit from information about why snakes move the way they do and from exposure exercises that incorporate a snake's movements.

Fear of dental and medical procedures is a common type of specific phobia. There are numerous self-report measures of various dental and medical procedures that can be useful in understanding the severity of a client's fear, the focus of the fear, and the types of situations avoided owing to the fear. Examples of these include the Dental Cognitions Questionnaire (de Jongh, Muris, Schoenmakers, & ter Horst, 1995), the Dental Fears Survey (Kleinknecht, Klepac, & Alexander, 1973), the Medical Fear Survey (Kleinknecht, Thorndike, & Walls, 1996), and the Mutilation Questionnaire (Klorman et al., 1974). One particular example of a useful self-report measure for dental fears is the Dental Anxiety Inventory (DAI; Stouthard, Mellenbergh, & Hoogstraten, 1993). This 36-item measure provides information about the types of dental-related fears a client might have and the severity of the fears. It was designed to provide information about when a person experiences anxiety (e.g., in the dental chair, in the waiting room), the situational aspects of being at the dentist that may bother people (e.g., dental treatments, the interaction between patient and dentist), and the emotional, physical, and cognitive reactions the person has to a dental situation. This measure has been shown to have excellent internal consistency and test–retest reliability (though only over a short interval), and moderate correlations with a dentist's perception about a person's anxiety (Stouthard et al., 1993). An independent test of the DAI's convergent and discriminant validity suggested that this measure is highly related to other measures of dental fears, mildly related to general fear and neuroticism, and not related to scales hypothesized to be unrelated to dental fears (Stouthard, Hoogstraten, & Mellenbergh, 1995). The questionnaire has been translated into multiple languages, increasing its clinical utility. We could find no treatment studies using the DAI and therefore its treatment sensitivity is unknown at present.

Self-Report Measures of Severity and Phenomenology—Social Phobia

As is the case for specific phobias, there are a number of measures that provide useful information about the severity and features of social phobia that can guide treatment planning. Once again, there are too many existing measures to provide comprehensive reviews of all of them, so interested readers are referred to Antony et al. (2001) for a more detailed review. Features of interest found in these measures include severity of social phobia symptoms, fearful cognitions, and avoided situations.

A commonly used self-report measure of social phobia symptoms is the Social Phobia and Anxiety Inventory (SPAI; Turner, Beidel, Dancu, & Stanley, 1989; Turner, Beidel, & Dancu, 1996). This 45-item scale has two subscales: social phobia and agoraphobia. Norms are available for individuals with generalized social phobia, generalized social phobia comorbid with avoidant personality disorder, individuals with public speaking fears, socially anxious college students, nonanxious college students, adolescents, and community samples. Norms are also available across ethnic groups (Gillis, Haaga, & Ford, 1995), and the SPAI has been translated into multiple languages. The reliability of the SPAI is strong, especially for the social phobia subscale (Osman et al., 1996). Evidence for the validity of the social phobia scale of the SPAI is also strong (Orsillo, 2001). It has demonstrated strong correlations with other measures of social phobia as well as with behavioral indicators of anxiety (e.g., time spent speaking in a public-speaking task before escaping; Beidel, Borden, Turner, & Jacob, 1989), and only minimal associations have been found with measures thought to be unrelated to social anxiety. There is a strong relationship between scores on this measure when completed by individuals with social anxiety and informant completion of the measure (Beidel et al., 1989). The use of the SPAI has also been validated in adolescents (Clark et al., 1994), increasing the breadth with which this measure can be used.

A more recently developed measure of social phobia symptoms that shows strong promise is the Social Phobia Inventory (SPIN; Connor et al., 2000). This is a much briefer self-report instrument than the SPAI (17 items) that assesses the severity of social anxiety, fear of a number of social and performance stimuli, degree of avoidance, and physiological discomfort. Norms are available for adults with social phobia, adolescents with social phobia, adults with other anxiety disorders, and community samples of adults and adolescents (Antony, Coons, McCabe, Ashbaugh, & Swinson, 2006; Johnson, Inderbitzen-Nolan, & Anderson, 2006). The measure has generally good to excellent psychometric properties, including internal consistency, test–retest reliability, and convergent and discriminant validity, both in adults (Antony et al.,

2006; Connor et al., 2000) and adolescents (Johnson et al., 2006).

In addition to these two measures, there are a host of other measures of the severity of social phobia symptoms and related constructs that would also be considered useful to be incorporated into an assessment protocol, though their psychometric properties will not be reviewed here, due to space restrictions. Examples include the Social Interaction Anxiety Scale (Mattick & Clarke, 1998), the Social Phobia Scale (Mattick & Clarke, 1998), and the Brief Fear of Negative Evaluation Scale (Leary, 1983; Watson & Friend, 1969).

Self-Report Measures of Related Dimensions in Specific and Social Phobias

There are a number of additional dimensions that need to be addressed in a thorough assessment of specific and social phobia for the purpose of case conceptualization. Examples include disgust sensitivity, anxiety sensitivity, and perfectionism. This section discusses each of these dimensions.

Disgust Sensitivity

Disgust sensitivity is a trait that has been implicated in the etiology and phenomenology of certain specific phobias, especially animal phobias and blood–injury–injection (BII) phobias. For example, disgust sensitivity is elevated in BII fears and phobias, in relation to both general (e.g., rotting food) and phobia-specific (e.g., wounds) indicators of disgust (Sawchuk, Lohr, Tolin, Lee, & Kleinknecht, 2000; Tolin, Lohr, Sawchuk, & Lee, 1997). Disgust sensitivity has also been shown to be elevated in people with spider phobias on both questionnaire measures of disgust (e.g., Merckelbach, de Jong, Arntz, & Schouten, 1993) and physiological indicators of disgust (e.g., de Jong, Peters, & Vanderhallen, 2002). Given the elevation of disgust sensitivity in many specific phobias, this is an important dimension to assess when planning treatment. One of the more commonly used measures of this dimension is the Disgust Scale (DS; Haidt, McCauley, & Rozin, 1994). The 32-item DS covers a broad range of disgust-eliciting stimuli including food, animals, body products, sex, bodily violations (e.g., seeing a man with a fishhook in his eye), death, hygiene, and magical pathways of disgust, making it broadly applicable to many subtypes of specific phobia. The internal consistency of the total scale score is good, though reliabilities for each subscale (i.e., food, animals, body products, sex, body envelope violations, death, and hygiene) are modest. The empirical support for the validity of this instrument is generally good (Haidt et al., 1994).

Anxiety Sensitivity

Anxiety sensitivity (i.e., one's beliefs that the physical sensations of fear and anxiety are dangerous) is another relevant construct when assessing specific and social phobias. Individuals with situational phobias or social phobia may be especially concerned with the physical sensations of fear, focusing on the consequences of anxiety and panic attacks when encountering the phobic stimulus or phobic situation (Antony, Brown, & Barlow, 1997a). Research generally supports this notion, demonstrating that individuals with phobias from the situational type score higher on the Anxiety Sensitivity Index (ASI; Peterson & Reiss, 1993) than do individuals with animal phobias and BII phobias (Antony et al., 1997a). Most people with social phobia are also fearful of physical signs of anxiety (e.g., sweating, blushing, etc.), especially if these symptoms occur in front of others. Indeed, individuals with social phobia show elevations on the ASI in comparison to normal controls (Taylor, Koch, & McNally, 1992). Therefore, it is important to assess an individual's fear of physical sensations. The most commonly used measure for this purpose is the ASI, a 16-item self-report measure that has demonstrated generally excellent psychometric properties (Antony, 2001b). Elevated scores on the ASI suggest that treatment should include a possible focus on the meaning of physical sensations in CBT (i.e., through cognitive restructuring) and the possible inclusion of interoceptive exposure exercises, where an individual engages in exercises to purposely bring about feared physical sensations in a safe environment.

Perfectionism

Research supports the idea that levels of maladaptive perfectionism are elevated in social phobia. For example, people with social phobia appear to believe that other people have high expectations for them (Bieling & Alden, 1997), and show elevated levels of concerns over mistakes, doubts about their actions, and reports of parental criticism (Antony, Purdon,

Huta, & Swinson, 1998). Perfectionism is therefore an important construct to investigate in the conceptualization of an individual with social phobia. A widely used measure of perfectionism is the 35-item Frost Multidimensional Perfectionism Scale (FMPS; Frost, Marten, Lahart, & Rosenblate, 1990). This self-report measure assesses a number of dimensions of perfectionism (e.g., concern over mistakes, personal standards, parental expectations), allowing the clinician to see which aspects of perfectionism are elevated for a particular individual. This measure has demonstrated strong psychometric properties, including good internal consistency and strong relations between the scores on this measure and behavioral indications of perfectionism (e.g., reactions to mistakes made in a task; Frost et al., 1997). There is some question about the appropriate factor structure of this measure, with different studies yielding different factor solutions (e.g., Purdon, Antony, & Swinson, 1999; Stober, 1998).

Behavioral Assessment

Behavioral assessment is an especially useful form of assessment for planning cognitive or behavioral treatments. The most common form of behavioral assessment is the behavioral approach test (BAT). A BAT for a specific phobia may involve seeing how close the person can get to his or her feared stimulus (e.g., an animal or high ledge), how long a person can stay in a feared situation before escaping, or the degree of fear a person experiences in the situation. A BAT for social phobia may involve asking a person to engage in a feared activity (e.g., giving a speech) and measuring the degree of fear experienced during the activity. These tests provide valuable information about the intensity of a person's fear, the cues that affect a person's fear (e.g., size of spider, sex of the conversation partner), the physical sensations a person experiences, the person's fearful thoughts, and the use of avoidance or subtle avoidance strategies when in the feared situation (e.g., avoiding eye contact, leaving the situation).

Research suggests that responses to behavioral challenges such as a BAT are related to responses on self-report measures of social phobia symptoms (e.g., Gore, Carter, & Parker, 2002), supporting the convergent validity for behavioral measures. Analogue behavioral assessment strategies have demonstrated strong discriminative and convergent validity for the assessment of social functioning (Norton & Hope, 2001).

Assessment of Skills Deficits

Individuals with specific and social phobias may have skills deficits that impact on treatment. For example, some people with social phobia appear to have impairment in social skills (e.g., Fydrich, Chambless, Perry, Buergener, & Beazley, 1998; Smari, Bjarnadottir, & Bragadottir, 1998; Spence, Donovan, & Brechman-Toussaint, 1999), and some people with specific phobias of driving may lack adequate driving skills, particularly if they have avoided driving for many years. Although there are no gold standard measures to assess skills deficits, these deficits are important to address when planning for treatment. For example, poor driving skills may necessitate a course of remedial driving instruction either before exposure therapy or concurrent with it. Driving skills are likely best evaluated by a professional driving instructor. Social skills deficits in social phobia may be readily apparent during the course of initial meetings with an individual (e.g., lack of eye contact may be noticeable during a semistructured interview). To assess these deficits more formally, the Social Performance Rating Scale (SPRS) can be used. This behavioral assessment tool was originally developed by Trower, Bryant, and Argyle (1978), modified by Turner, Beidel, Dancu, and Keys (1986), and then further modified by Fydrich and colleagues (1998) to provide a reliable and valid measure of social skill level during video-taped role- plays. The modified SPRS provides information about the following skill areas: gaze, vocal quality, speech length, discomfort, and conversation flow. Although this measure provides broad and useful ratings of behavioral skill deficits, it may not be easily transferred to a clinical setting. For example, the role-plays require the presence of a confederate. Although this may be accomplished easily in the context of a clinic or hospital-based program, it may be near impossible in other clinical settings, such as private practice. Further, the training and time necessary for raters of the role-plays may be difficult to justify in many contexts. Thus, although this measure appears to provide excellent information on skills deficits, it may be more reasonable for most clinicians to use some aspects of this measure. For example, clinicians could use the behavioral anchors provided for this measure to rate the social skills that emerge either in the context of an interview or other assessment protocol, or to conduct analogue role-plays with their clients using themselves as the confederate.

Assessment of Treatment History, Treatment Concerns, and Suitability for CBT

During the course of treatment planning, it is useful to assess an individual's treatment history, any treatment concerns, and suitability for a therapeutic intervention such as CBT. Previous treatment failures may provide useful information about what not to try when treating a particular patient. On the other hand, previous treatment failures may have been the result of receiving inappropriate interventions for a problem like social or specific phobia. Research suggests that individuals seen in a specialty anxiety clinic reported having received a number of nonempirically supported treatments (especially psychological treatments) before receiving cognitive or behavioral interventions for their anxiety disorder (Rowa, Antony, Brar, Summerfeldt, & Swinson, 2000). In cases where past treatment attempts were not successful, it may be important to identify reasons for the negative outcome. For example, treatment noncompliance and lack of acceptance of the treatment rationale are predictors of negative outcome following psychological treatment (e.g., Addis & Jacobson, 2000; Woods, Chambless, & Steketee, 2002). Knowledge of the presence of either of these issues suggests useful pathways the clinician should consider when planning treatment and potential obstacles that may arise. For example, the clinician may consider investing more time at the beginning stages of treatment to help the client fully understand and hopefully accept the rationale underlying treatment interventions. Further, a history of treatment noncompliance may suggest the importance of contracting about the completion of therapy assignments and session attendance in order for therapy to proceed. Unfortunately, there are currently no evidence-based ways to measure previous treatment attempts.

Individuals may have strong fears about treatment, including fears that they will not get better. New measures such as the Treatment Ambivalence Questionnaire (TAQ; Purdon, Rowa, & Antony, 2004) are showing promise for evaluating a host of treatment fears presented by individuals with anxiety disorders. Finally, a clinician may want to consider whether a particular client is a good match for cognitive or behavioral interventions. Even though these techniques are empirically supported for treating specific and social phobias, this does not guarantee that a particular individual is well-suited for a CBT intervention. Clients have to be willing to complete between-session work, confront feared stimuli, and accept a CBT rationale for their difficulties. Suitability interviews for CBT do exist and scores on one suitability instrument have shown moderate correlations with both client and therapist ratings of success in cognitive therapy for depression (Safran & Segal, 1990). However, these interviews are detailed and time-consuming, focus more on suitability for cognitive interventions than behavioral interventions, have not been validated for anxiety disorders, and may not be practical for clinical practice. They may be best used when suitability issues appear to be a potential obstacle in treatment planning.

Assessment of Coping Strategies

A final consideration when conducting assessment for the purpose of treatment planning in specific and social phobia is to ensure a thorough assessment of an individual's use of safety behaviors, subtle avoidance, and maladaptive coping strategies (e.g., alcohol and drug use). Elevated drug and alcohol use has been documented in social phobia (e.g., Van Ameringen, Mancini, Styan, & Donison, 1991) and is often conceptualized as a means of coping with otherwise debilitating levels of anxiety. Other examples of safety behaviors and coping strategies in social phobia include wearing high-necked shirts to cover blushing, over-rehearsing or memorizing presentations, carrying antianxiety medication, and always bringing a "safe other" when attending a social gathering. Safety behaviors or subtle avoidance in specific phobia may include looking away when getting a needle, wearing long sleeves or a hooded shirt to prevent spiders from falling directly on one's skin, holding a railing in a high place, and playing the radio while driving to distract oneself from fear. Although safety behaviors are prevalent and are a crucial aspect of understanding a person's social or specific phobia, the breadth and variety of strategies used by individuals is hard to measure using a particular instrument. Therefore, this information is often gleaned from semistructured interviews, monitoring forms, or direct questioning. Clearly, the value of collecting such information is

apparent, as the elimination of maladaptive coping strategies and safety behaviors is a central part of most CBT protocols for social or specific phobia (e.g., Clark & Wells, 1995). Therefore, the utility of gathering this information outweighs the limited empirically supported means for doing so.

Overall Evaluation

There are a number of topics to cover when using assessment to aid conceptualization and treatment planning for specific and social phobia. We have highlighted a series of variables that we feel are valuable to cover, including symptom severity, relevant cognitions and avoidance behaviors, related constructs, coping strategies, skills deficits, treatment history, and attitudes toward future treatment. When reviewing these topics, it is encouraging that a number of excellent and clinical useful measures exist to assess these areas (see Table 10.2 for a summary). Therefore, at minimum, this stage of assessment should include a well-studied and validated measure such as the SPIN or the FSQ to complement the diagnostic information already provided from a semistructured interview. Please note that some instruments are not designated as "highly recommended" in Table 10.2 simply because evidence of their psychometric properties is good, but not excellent at present. Even without a designation of "highly recommended," we still encourage practitioners to use instruments such as these for the purpose of treatment planning. Further, it also seems reasonable to include well-validated measures of related constructs, such as anxiety sensitivity, disgust, and perfectionism. The questionnaires highlighted to measure these constructs are all quick and straightforward measures whose value clearly exceeds the time taken to complete and score the instruments.

We would also argue that the use of idiographic diaries, questions, or monitoring forms to ascertain coping strategies and safety behaviors, though not empirically validated, is an essential aspect of treatment planning. Similarly, behavioral assessment using a BAT is a useful way to discover a great deal of valuable information for treatment planning. Overlooking this information could have serious implications for treatment outcome (e.g., if the use of maladaptive coping strategies is never targeted). The assessment picture becomes more complicated when evaluating the utility of measuring constructs such as social skills and suitability for CBT in a routine assessment for social phobia. We argue that the lack of quick and easily administered measures limits the feasibility of systematically assessing these features in routine practice, and we know of no data to suggest that not measuring these constructs leads to compromised treatment outcome. Instead, therefore, we would recommend the use of measures specifically designed to assess these topics only in scenarios when these topics appear especially relevant (e.g., if an individual clearly communicates a bad experience with previous CBT and extreme skepticism about its effectiveness; a person who clearly has extreme social skills deficits). Otherwise, the general theme of social skills, suitability for CBT, and treatment fears can be assessed in a less structured way during the course of a diagnostic interview or assessment of these variables.

ASSESSMENT FOR TREATMENT MONITORING AND EVALUATION

The final use of assessment procedures we will cover is assessment for the purpose of evaluating treatment progress and outcome, both for medication and CBT. Clearly, a hallmark feature of CBT interventions is the rigorous evaluation of their effectiveness. This is also true when using these techniques with a particular client. It is essential to understand whether treatment strategies were helpful, in what way they were helpful, and on what dimensions strategies had their impact. In some instances, degree of improvement will have important implications for course and duration of treatment. In other cases, indicators of improvement will have implications for continued funding of treatment (e.g., by insurance companies or third party payers). On a most basic level, it is useful for a client to understand and be aware of the degree of improvement made. Without explicitly assessing these variables, important gains can be ignored or missed. Table 10.3 provides a review of measures that are useful for treatment evaluation.

Self-Report Measures of Severity—Specific and Social Phobia

One important way to assess treatment progress and outcome is to compare self-report questionnaire scores obtained during and at the end of treatment with those obtained at pretreatment. Possible

assessment tools include the self-report measures described earlier (e.g., FSQ, SNAQ, DAI, SPAI, and SPIN). Each of these measures except for the DAI has shown at least adequate treatment sensitivity, in that scores meaningfully decline after successful medication or psychological treatment (see Antony et al., 2001 for a review). For example, Taylor, Woody, McLean, and Koch (1997) found that the SPAI was very sensitive to treatment outcome for generalized social phobia, yielding large effect sizes when compared with other self-report or subjective ratings of social anxiety.

In addition to using empirically validated self-report measures for specific and social phobia, there is also value to using more idiosyncratic self-report instruments to monitor progress in therapy. For example, a widely used tool of symptom progression is the fear and avoidance hierarchy, used in exposure-based treatments of specific and social phobia. Exposure hierarchies are developed either before treatment or near the beginning of treatment, and can be updated by the client on a regular basis (i.e., each session; pre-, mid-, and posttreatment, etc.). Although no studies have examined the predictive value of hierarchy ratings in social or specific phobia, a study by our group on patients with panic disorder provides support for their utility. We found that fear and avoidance ratings on hierarchies yielded large effect sizes for change, even greater than effect sizes obtained from standard outcome measures for panic disorder (McCabe, Rowa, Antony, Swinson, & Ladak, 2001). Valuable information can also be gleaned from monitoring forms and exposure graphs completed by the client. For example, notable shifts in the content of cognitions can be an indicator that the client is benefiting from CBT; hypothesized reductions in peak fear, and the time needed for fear to decrease, can inform the therapist of whether exposure exercises are producing the desired effects.

Interview Measures of Symptom Severity

When evaluating progress and outcome as a result of medication or CBT for social phobia, there are two widely used clinician-rated measures of symptom severity. Clinician-rated measures are a useful addition to self-report measures to broaden the breadth and source of data used to evaluate outcome. One example is the Liebowitz Social Anxiety Scale (LSAS; Liebowitz, 1987). This measure lists

TABLE 10.3 Ratings of Instruments Used for Treatment Monitoring and Treatment Outcome Evaluation

Instrument	Norms	Internal Consistency	Inter-Rater Reliability	Test–Retest Reliability	Content Validity	Construct Validity	Validity Generalization	Treatment Sensitivity	Clinical Utility	Highly Recommended
FSQ	A	E	NA	A	A	G	G	E	G	
SNAQ	A	G	NA	E	U	G	E	E	G	
DAI	A	E	NA	A	A	G	E	U	G	
SPAI	E	E	NA	A	E	E	E	E	E	✓
SPIN	E	E	NA	A	G	G	E	E	E	✓
LSAS	G	E	U	U	G	G	E	E	E	✓
BSPS	A	A	U	A	A	A	A	G	E	
BAT	U	U	NA	U	NA	G	E	E	E	✓
IIRS	E	E	E	G	G	E	E	G	E	✓

Note: FSQ = Fear of Spiders Questionnaire; SNAQ = Snake Questionnaire; DAI = Dental Anxiety Inventory; SPAI = Social Phobia and Anxiety Inventory; SPIN = Social Phobia Inventory; LSAS = Liebowitz Social Anxiety Scale; BSPS = Brief Social Phobia Scale; BAT = Behavioral Approach Test; IIRS = Illness Intrusiveness Rating Scale; A = Adequate; G = Good; E = Excellent; U = Unavailable; NA = Not Applicable.

24 situations that are commonly anxiety-producing for people with social anxiety, and the interviewer rates each situation in terms of fear and avoidance. It is relatively brief, taking approximately 20 minutes to complete. The psychometric properties of the LSAS are good to excellent and it has demonstrated sensitivity to treatment outcome, having been a primary outcome measure in many medication and cognitive-behavioral treatment trials for social phobia. Another widely used clinician-rated measure of social phobia symptoms is the Brief Social Phobia Scale (BSPS; Davidson et al., 1991). This 18-item measure covers symptoms of fear, avoidance, and physiological arousal and can be administered in 5 to 15 minutes. Although it is much briefer than the LSAS, its psychometric properties have not been shown to be as strong.

Behavioral Indicators of Treatment Progress

Behavioral assessment (e.g., a BAT) is also a useful way of monitoring outcome of treatment for specific and social phobias. If an individual with a spider phobia is unable to look at a spider during a pretreatment BAT but can hold a spider comfortably during a posttreatment BAT, the client can be assumed to have improved. Hofmann (2000) used four behavioral tasks both before and after a treatment trial of CBT for social phobia, and measured self-statements made during these tasks. Results suggested that content of self-statements made while anticipating the behavioral tasks changed across successful treatment, with participants endorsing fewer negative self-focused thoughts after treatment. The use of behavioral tests in this example allowed the evaluator to see related changes in cognition across treatment.

Physiological Indications of Treatment Progress

Models of the development and maintenance of social phobia place importance on the physiological manifestations of anxiety, suggesting that people with social phobia experience elevated physical symptoms of anxiety (e.g., blushing, racing heart) and that the anticipation of and reaction to these physical sensations is an important factor in their experience of anxiety (e.g., Clark & Wells, 1995).

Elevated physiological reactivity may also be implicated in specific phobias, with individuals often experiencing cued panic attacks in feared situations. Further, individuals with BII phobias have an elevated risk of fainting when encountering their feared stimuli (Antony & Barlow, 2002), a unique physiological response. Research also suggests that people with situational, as compared with nonsituational phobias have a higher rate of unexpected panic attacks, and people with BII phobias have a greater focus on physical symptoms than on harm or catastrophe (Lipsitz et al., 2002). Thus, particular subtypes of specific phobias may have unique physiological presentations. If this is the case, it might be useful to measure physiological reactivity to behavioral tasks and exposure stimuli as an indication of progress in therapy.

Although it is clear that people with specific and social phobias report greater than normal apprehension about physiological sensations (e.g., Hugdahl & Öst, 1985), research is not clear regarding whether actual physiological differences exist. For example, Edelmann and Baker (2002) found no physiological differences between individuals with generalized social phobia, anxious controls, and nonanxious controls on measures of heart rate, skin conductance, and facial and neck temperatures on a series of behavioral, physical, and imagery tasks. Interestingly, participants with social phobia and other anxiety disorders provided higher subjective ratings of some sensations than nonanxious controls even in the absence of physiological differences. This result is consistent across other anxiety conditions, including panic disorder and generalized anxiety disorder (Hoehn-Saric, McLeod, Funderburk, & Kowalski, 2004). On the other hand, individuals with dental fears demonstrated changes in physiology during exposure to scenes of dental treatment, though this study did not have a comparison group of nonanxious individuals, limiting the conclusions that can be made about unique physiological responses in dental phobias (Johnson et al., 2003). Thus, at the current time, there appears to be limited empirical support for using physiological indicators to measure treatment progress. Given the expense and burden of accurately measuring physiological responses of anxiety, it appears more useful to measure concern over physiological symptoms using validated self-report measures like the ASI, described earlier.

Assessment of Functional Impairment and Quality of Life

Traditionally, treatment outcome research in the area of anxiety disorders has focused on measuring change in symptom severity, paying less attention to whether treatment improves associated distress, functional impairment, and quality of life. There are no assessment tools designed specifically to assess distress, functional impairment, and quality of life in people with anxiety disorders, though a number of more general scales (e.g., Sheehan Disability Scale; Sheehan, 1983) have been used to measure these constructs in this population (e.g., Antony, Roth, Swinson, Huta, & Devins, 1998; Mendlowicz & Stein, 2000; Quilty, van Ameringen, Mancini, Oakman, & Farvolden, 2003). One such scale is the Illness Intrusiveness Rating Scale (IIRS; Devins et al., 1983). Originally developed for use with medical populations, the IIRS has been adapted for use with mental health populations. This brief self-report measure asks people to rate the degree to which their illness (i.e., anxiety disorder) interferes with 13 domains of functioning (e.g., work, sex life, relationships, religious expression). The IIRS has demonstrated strong psychometric properties. Antony et al. (1998) found that individuals with anxiety disorders (including social phobia) reported higher levels of functional impairment than did people with serious medical conditions, including end stage renal disease and multiple sclerosis. Whether this finding reflects the true level of functional impairment in anxiety disorders is unknown because research has not examined the relationship between scores on these scales and more objective indices of impairment (e.g., missed days at work, relationship impairment, etc.) in people with anxiety disorders. However, the IIRS appears sensitive to changes across treatment (e.g., Rowa et al., 2007) and is a straightforward way of measuring subjective changes in impairment as a result of treatment efforts.

Overall Evaluation

Measuring treatment outcome is not only important in the broad sense of validating the use of particular treatment interventions, but it is also useful on an individual basis to quantify changes made by particular clients across particular courses of therapy. Clinically, it is clear that many clients make significant changes across the course of therapy, but do not recognize the magnitude or importance of these changes. Similarly, it is easy for clinicians to "forget" the severity of a client's original fears when they have observed progress on a week-to-week basis. Efficacy data from randomized controlled trials may not mirror effectiveness of the treatment in a particular clinic or with a particular client. For these reasons, it is valuable to measure treatment outcome for individual clients as well as in larger, well-controlled treatment trials. We believe that the measurement of treatment outcome should be multifaceted, ideally including self-report, behavioral, and clinician-rated measures of improvement. In addition, treatment outcome should not only target improvements in symptoms of social or specific phobia, but also improvements in a person's general functioning and quality of life. At minimum, assessment of treatment outcome should involve examining changes on self-report measures with demonstrated treatment sensitivity, on idiographic measures of progress (e.g., hierarchies and monitoring forms), on behavioral indicators of progress (e.g., ability to enter and remain in feared situations), and on measures of everyday life functioning.

CONCLUSIONS AND FUTURE DIRECTIONS

It is clear that assessment plays a crucial role in understanding an individual's presenting problems, making informed decisions about treatment interventions, and evaluating the effectiveness of any such interventions. Within the anxiety disorders, there is a long tradition of ensuring that assessment instruments possess strong psychometric properties and that reliable and valid assessment tools are used to measure the efficacy of treatment interventions. More recently, authors have begun to shift the focus from individual assessment tools to the efficacy of assessment protocols. For example, the National Institutes of Health (NIH) Consensus Development Conference on the Treatment of Panic Disorder recommended a standardized assessment strategy for research on panic disorder (Shear & Maser, 1994), a strategy that has strong implications for the clinical assessment of panic disorder as well. However, these types of recommendations do not yet exist for disorders like specific and social phobia. We have provided a sample assessment strategy for social phobia in Table 10.4. This strategy involves assessment measures for the purpose of diagnosis, measures to assess clinical features of both the disorder and related constructs (e.g.,

TABLE 10.4 Sample Assessment Protocol for Assessing Treatment Outcome in Social Phobia

Domain	Assessment Tools	Type of Tool
Diagnostic features	Structured Clinical Interview for DSM-IV (SCID-IV; First et al., 1996, 1997)	Semistructured interview
	Anxiety Disorders Interview Schedule for DSM-IV (ADIS-IV; Di Nardo, Brown, & Barlow, 1994)	Semistructured interview
Conceptualization		
Severity, situational cues, cognitive features, and avoidance behavior	Social Phobia and Anxiety Inventory (SPAI; Turner, Beidel, Dancu, & Stanley, 1989)	Self-report
	Diaries to record situational fear, avoidance and safety behaviors	Diary
Avoidance	Behavioral approach test	Behavioral assessment
Related constructs	Anxiety Sensitivity Index (ASI; Peterson & Reiss, 1993)	Self report
	Disgust Scale (Haidt, McCauley, & Rozin, 1994)	Self-report
	Frost Multidimensional Perfectionism Scale (FMPS; Frost, Marten, Lahart, & Rosenblate, 1990)	Self-report
Treatment outcome		
Severity, situational cues, cognitive features, and avoidance behavior	Social Phobia and Anxiety Inventory (SPAI; Turner, Beidel, Dancu, & Stanley, 1989)	Self-report
	Diaries to record situational fear, avoidance, and safety behaviors	Diary
	Liebowitz Social Anxiety Scale (LSAS; Liebowitz, 1987)	Interview
Avoidance	Behavioral approach test	Behavioral assessment
Functional impairment	Illness Intrusiveness Rating Scale (IIRS; Devins et al., 1994)	Self-report
	ADIS-IV or SCID-IV	Semistructured interview

perfectionism) for the purpose of treatment planning, and measures that are sensitive to change across treatment. A further concern is that, in recent years, anxiety researchers appear to be using assessment protocols that are less multimodal, relying most often on self-report scales only (Lawyer & Smitherman, 2004). Therefore, despite our strong history of using well-validated tools and interventions, it appears that an increased emphasis on empirically supported, multimodal assessment in specific and social phobia is warranted.

Although research on the incremental validity of multimodal protocols over singular measures in anxiety disorders is just in its inception, it is useful to review what we do know about individual assessment instruments and techniques to make informed judgments about what tools should be considered when assessing social or specific phobias. In this vein, we have provided a review of some individual tools and techniques commonly used in the assessment of specific and social phobia, with the idea that an empirically supported assessment strategy must have its roots in well-validated, psychometrically sound instruments. Further, we have reviewed these instruments and techniques from the perspective of clinical utility as well, with the understanding that there has to exist a crossroads between empirically supported and clinically feasible assessment strategies. From these reviews, we have suggested some possible avenues for combining assessment techniques in a way that will hopefully prove to be useful and valid in our assessment of specific and social phobia. From suggestions such as these, future research can focus on the optimal combination of assessment strategies for different purposes, how different strategies affect the utility and efficacy of others used concurrently, and how to balance clinical feasibility with maximal efficacy.

References

Addis, M. E., & Jacobson, N. S. (2000). A closer look at the treatment rationale and homework compliance in cognitive-behavioral therapy for depression. *Cognitive Therapy and Research, 24,* 313–326.

American Psychiatric Association. (2000). *Diagnostic and statistical manual of mental disorders* (4th ed., Text revision). Washington, DC: Author.

Antony, M. M. (2001a). Measures for specific phobia. In M. M. Antony, S. M. Orsillo, & L. Roemer (Eds.), *Practitioner's guide to empirically based measures of anxiety* (pp. 133–158). New York: Springer.

Antony, M. M. (2001b). Measures for panic disorder and agoraphobia. In M. M. Antony, S. M. Orsillo, & L. Roemer (Eds.), *Practitioner's guide to empirically based measures of anxiety* (pp. 95–125). New York: Springer.

Antony, M. M., & Barlow, D. H. (2002). Specific phobia. In D. H. Barlow (Ed.), *Anxiety and its disorders: The nature and treatment of anxiety and panic* (2nd ed.) (pp. 380–417). New York: Guilford.

Antony, M. M., & McCabe, R. E. (2003). Social and specific phobias. In A. Tasman, J. Lieberman, & J. Kay (Eds.), *Psychiatry* (2nd ed., pp. 1298–1330). London, UK: John Wiley & Sons.

Antony, M. M., & Rowa, K. (2005). Evidence-based assessment of anxiety disorders in adults. *Psychological Assessment, 17,* 256–266.

Antony, M. M., Brown, T. A., & Barlow, D. H. (1997a) Heterogeneity among specific phobia types in DSM-IV. *Behaviour Research and Therapy, 35,* 1089–1100.

Antony, M. M., Brown T. A., & Barlow D. H. (1997b). Response to hyperventilation and 5.5% CO_2 inhalation of subjects with types of specific phobia, panic disorder, or no mental disorder. *American Journal of Psychiatry, 154,* 1089–1095.

Antony, M. M., Coons, M. J., McCabe, R. E., Ashbaugh, A., & Swinson, R. P. (2006). Psychometric properties of the social phobia inventory: Further evaluation. *Behaviour Research and Therapy, 44,* 1177–1185.

Antony, M. M., Downie, F., & Swinson, R. P. (1998). Diagnostic issues and epidemiology in obsessive compulsive disorder. In R. P. Swinson, M. M. Antony, S. Rachman, & M. A. Richter (Eds.). *Obsessive compulsive disorder: Theory, research, and treatment* (pp. 3–32). New York: Guilford.

Antony, M. M., Orsillo, S. M., & Roemer, L. (Eds.) (2001). *Practitioner's guide to empirically based measures of anxiety.* New York: Springer.

Antony, M. M., Purdon, C. L., Huta, V., & Swinson, R. P. (1998). Dimensions of perfectionism among the anxiety disorders. *Behaviour Research and Therapy, 36,* 1143–1154.

Antony, M. M., Roth, D., Swinson, R. P., Huta, V., & Devins, G. M. (1998). Illness intrusiveness in individuals with panic disorder, obsessive compulsive disorder, or social phobia. *Journal of Nervous and Mental Disease, 186,* 311–315.

Arindell, W. A. (1980). Dimensional structure and psychopathology correlates of the Fear Survey Schedule (FSS-III) in a phobic population: A factorial definition of agoraphobia. *Behaviour Research and Therapy, 18,* 229–242.

Beck, J. G., Carmin, C. N., & Henninger, N. J. (1998). The utility of the Fear Survey Schedule-III: An extended replication. *Journal of Anxiety Disorders, 12,* 177–182.

Beidel, D. C., Borden, J. W., Turner, S. M., & Jacob, R. G. (1989). The social phobia and anxiety inventory: Concurrent validity with a clinical sample. *Behaviour Research and Therapy, 27,* 573–576.

Bieling, P. J., & Alden, L. E. (1997). The consequences of perfectionism for patients with social phobia. *The British Journal of Clinical Psychology, 36,* 387–395.

Brown, T. A., Di Nardo, P. A., & Barlow, D. H. (1994). *Anxiety Disorders Interview Schedule for DSM-IV (ADIS-IV).* New York: Oxford.

Brown, T. A., Di Nardo, P. A., Lehman, C. L., & Campbell, L. A. (2001). Reliability of DSM-IV anxiety and mood disorders: Implications for the classification of emotional disorders. *Journal of Abnormal Psychology, 110,* 49–58.

Chambless, D. L., Baker, M. J., Baucom, D. H., Beutler, L. E., Calhoun, K. S., Crits-Christoph, P., et al. (1998). Update on empirically validated therapies, II. *The Clinical Psychologist, 51*(1), 3–14.

Clark, D. B., Turner, S. M., Beidel, D. C., Donovan, J. E., Kirisci, L., & Jacob, R. G. (1994). Reliability and validity of the social phobia and anxiety inventory for adolescents. *Psychological Assessment, 6,* 135–140.

Clark, D. M., & Wells A. (1995). A cognitive model of social phobia. In R. G Heimberg, M. R. Liebowitz, D. A. Hope, & F. R. Schneier (Eds.), *Social phobia: Diagnosis, assessment, and treatment* (pp. 69–93). New York: Guilford.

Connor, K. M., Davidson, J. R. T., Churchill, E., Sherwood, A., Foa, E., & Weisler, R. H. (2000). Psychometric properties of the Social Phobia Inventory (SPIN): New self-rating scale. *British Journal of Psychiatry, 176,* 379–386.

Curtis, G. C., Magee, W. J., Eaton, W. W., Wittchen, H.-U., & Kessler, R. C. (1998). Specific fears and phobias: epidemiology and classification. *British Journal of Psychiatry, 173,* 212–217.

Davidson, J. R. T., Potts, N. L. S., Richichi, E. A., Ford, S. M., Krishnan, R. R., Smith, R. D., et al. (1991). The Brief Social Phobia Scale. *Journal of Clinical Psychiatry, 52*(Suppl. 11), 48–51.

de Jongh, A., Muris, P., Schoenmakers, N., & ter Horst, G. (1995). Negative cognitions of dental phobics: Reliability and validity of the dental cognitions questionnaire. *Behaviour Research and Therapy, 33,* 507–515.

de Jongh, P. J., Peters, M., & Vanderhallen, I. (2002). Disgust and disgust sensitivity in spider phobia: Facial EMG in response to spider and oral disgust imagery. *Journal of Anxiety Disorders, 16*, 477–493.

Devins, G. M., Binik, Y. M., Hutchinson, T. A., Hollomby, D. J., Barré, P. E., & Guttman, R. D. (1983). The emotional impact of end-stage renal disease: Importance of patients' perceptions of intrusiveness and control. *International Journal of Psychiatry in Medicine, 13*, 327–343.

Di Nardo, P., Brown, T. A., & Barlow, D. H. (1994). *Anxiety disorders interview schedule for DSM-IV.* New York: Oxford.

Di Nardo, P., Moras, K., Barlow, D. H., Rapee, R. M., & Brown, T. A. (1993). Reliability of DSM-III anxiety disorder categories. *Archives of General Psychiatry, 50*, 251–256.

Edelmann, R. J., & Baker, S. R. (2002). Self-reported and actual physiological responses in social phobia. *British Journal of Clinical Psychology, 41*, 1–14.

Essau, C. A., Conradt, J., & Petermann, F. (2000). Frequency, comorbidity, and psychosocial impairment of specific phobia in adolescents. *Journal of Clinical Child Psychology, 29*, 221–231.

Fehm, L., Pelissolo, A., Furmark, T., & Wittchen, H. (2005). Size and burden of social phobia in Europe. *European Neuropsychopharmacology, 15*, 453–462.

First, M. B., Spitzer, R. L., Gibbon, M., & Williams, J. B. W. (1996). *Structured clinical interview for axis I DSM-IV disorders—patient edition (SCID-I/P Version 2.0).* New York: Biometrics Research Department, New York State Psychiatric Institute.

Fredrikson, M. (1983). Reliability and validity of some specific fear questionnaires. *Scandinavian Journal of Psychology, 24*, 331–334.

Frost, R. O., Marten, P., Lahart, C., & Rosenblate, R. (1990). The dimensions of perfectionism. *Cognitive Therapy and Research, 14*, 449–468.

Frost, R. O., Trepanier, K. L., Brown, E. J., Heimberg, R. G., Juster, H. R., Makris G. S., et al. (1997). Self-Monitoring of mistakes among subjects high and low in perfectionistic concern over mistakes. *Cognitive Therapy and Research, 21*, 209–222.

Fydrich, T., Chambless, D. L., Perry, K. L., Buergener, F., & Beazley, M. B. (1998). Behavioral assessment of social performance: A rating system for social phobia. *Behaviour Research and Therapy, 36*, 995–1010.

Fyer, A. J., Mannuzza, S., Gallops, M. S., Martin, L. Y., Aaronson, C., Gorman, J. G., et al. (1990). Familial transmission of simple phobias and fears. *Archives of General Psychiatry, 47*, 252–256.

Geer, J. H. (1965). The developmental of a scale to measure fear. *Behaviour Research and Therapy, 3*, 45–53.

Gillis, M., Haaga, D., & Ford, G. (1995). Normative values for the BDI, FQ, PSWQ and SPAI. *Psychological Assessment, 7*, 450–455.

Gore, K. L., Carter, M. M., & Parker, S. (2002). Predicting anxious response to a social challenge: The predictive utility of the social interaction anxiety scale and the social phobia scale in a college population. *Behaviour Research and Therapy, 40*, 689–700.

Grills, A. E., & Ollendick, T. H. (2002). Issues in parent–child agreement: The case of structured diagnostic interviews. *Clinical Child and Family Psychology Review, 5*, 57–83.

Haidt, J., McCauley C., & Rozin, P. (1994). Individual differences in sensitivity to disgust: A scale sampling seven domains of disgust elicitors. *Personality and Individual Differences, 16*, 701–713.

Heimberg, R. G. (2003). Assessment and diagnosis of social phobia in the clinic and the community. *Psychological Medicine, 33*, 583–588.

Hoehn-Saric, R., McLeod, D. R., Funderburk, F., & Kowalski, P. (2004). Somatic symptoms and physiologic responses in generalized anxiety disorder and panic disorder: An ambulatory monitor study. *Archives of General Psychiatry, 61*, 913–921.

Hofmann, S. G. (2000). Self-focused attention before and after treatment of social phobia. *Behaviour Research and Therapy, 38*, 717–725.

Hofmann, S. G., Heinrichs, N., & Moscovitch, D. A. (2004). The nature and expression of social phobia: Toward a new classification. *Clinical Psychology Review, 24*, 769–797.

Hugdahl, K., & Öst, L. G. (1985). Subjectively rated physiological and cognitive symptoms in six different clinical phobias. *Personality and Individual Differences, 6*, 175–188.

Huijding, J., & de Jong, P. J. (2006). Specific predictive power of spider-related affective associations for controllable and uncontrollable fear responses toward spiders. *Behaviour Research and Therapy, 44*, 161–176.

Johnson, B. H., Thayer, J. F., Laberg, J. C., Wormnes, B., Raadal, M., Skaret, E., et al. (2003). Attentional and physiological characteristics of patients with dental anxiety. *Journal of Anxiety Disorders, 17*, 75–87.

Johnson, H. S., Inderbitzen-Nolan, H. M., & Anderson, E. R. (2006). The Social Phobia Inventory: Validity and reliability in an adolescent community sample. *Psychological Assessment, 18*, 269–277.

Keller, M. B. (2003). The lifelong course of social anxiety disorder: A clinical perspective. *Acta Psychiatrica Scandinavica, 108*, 85–94.

Kessler, R. C., & Ustun, T. B. (2004). The World Mental Health (WMH) survey initiative version of the World Health Organization (WHO) Composite International Diagnostic Interview (CIDI). *International Journal of Methods in Psychiatric Research, 13*, 93–121.

Kessler, R. C., Berglund, P., Demler, O., Jin, R., Merikangas, K. R., & Walters, E. E. (2005). Lifetime prevalence and age-of-onset distributions of DSM-III-R disorders in the National Comorbidity Survey Replication. *Archives of General Psychiatry, 62*, 593–602.

Kleinknecht, R. A., Klepac, R. K., & Alexander, L. D. (1973). Origins and characteristics of dental fear. *Journal of the American Dental Association, 86*, 842–848.

Kleinknecht, R. A., Thorndike, R. M., & Walls, M. M. (1996). Factorial dimensions and correlates of blood, injury, injection and related medical fears: Cross validation of the Medical Fear Survey. *Behaviour Research and Therapy, 34*, 323–331.

Klieger, D. M. (1987). The Snake Anxiety Questionnaire as a measure of ophidophobia. *Educational and Psychological Measurement, 47*, 449–459.

Klieger, D. M., & Franklin, M. E. (1993). Validity of the fear survey schedule in phobia research: A laboratory test. *Journal of Psychopathology and Behavioral Assessment, 15*, 207–217.

Klorman, R., Hastings, J. E., Weerts, T. C., Melamed, B. G., & Lang, P. J. (1974). Psychometric description of some specific-fear questionnaires. *Behaviour Therapy, 5*, 401–409.

Lawyer, S. R., & Smitherman, T. A. (2004). Trends in anxiety assessment. *Journal of Psychopathology and Behavioral Assessment, 26*, 101–106.

Leary, M. R. (1983). A brief version of the fear of negative evaluation scale. *Personality and Social Psychology Bulletin, 9*, 371–375.

Liebowitz, M. R. (1987). Social phobia. *Modern Problems in Pharmacopsychiatry, 22*, 141–173.

Lipsitz, J. D., Barlow, D. H., Mannuzza, S., Hofmann, S. G., & Fyer, A. J. (2002). Clinical features of four DSM-IV specific phobia subtypes. *Journal of Nervous and Mental Disease, 190*, 471–478.

Mattick, R. P., & Clarke, J. C. (1998). Development and validation of measures of social phobia scrutiny fear and social interaction anxiety. *Behaviour Research and Therapy, 36*, 455–470.

McCabe, R. E., & Antony, M. M. (2002). Specific and social phobias. In M. M. Antony & D. H. Barlow (Eds.), *Handbook of assessment and treatment planning psychological disorders* (pp. 113–146). New York: Guilford.

McCabe, R. E., Antony, M. M., Summerfeldt, L., Liss, A., & Swinson, R. P. (2003). Preliminary examination of the relationship between anxiety disorders in adults and self-reported history of teasing or bullying experiences. *Cognitive Behaviour Therapy, 32*, 187–193.

McCabe, R. E., Rowa, K., Antony, M. M., Swinson, R. P., & Ladak, Y. (2001, July). *The exposure hierarchy as a measure of cognitive and behavioral change, treatment progress and efficacy.* Paper presented at the World Congress of Behavioral and Cognitive Therapies, Vancouver, British Columbia.

Mendlowicz, M. V., & Stein, M. B. (2000). Quality of life in individuals with anxiety disorders. *American Journal of Psychiatry, 157*, 669–682.

Merckelbach, H., de Jong, P. J., Arntz, A., & Schouten, E. (1993). The role of evaluative learning and disgust sensitivity in the etiology and treatment of spider phobia. *Advances in Behaviour Research and Therapy, 15*, 243–255.

Mogotsi, M., Kaminer, D., & Stein, D. J. (2000). Quality of life in the anxiety disorders. *Harvard Review of Psychiatry, 8*, 273–282.

Muris, P., & Merckelbach, H. (1996). A comparison of two spider phobia questionnaires. *Journal of Behavior Therapy and Experimental Psychiatry, 27*, 241–244.

Norton, P. J., & Hope, D. A. (2001). Analogue observational methods in the assessment of social functioning in adults. *Psychological Assessment, 13*, 59–72.

Ollendick, T., Davis, T., & Muris, P. (2004). Treatment of specific phobia in children and adolescents. In P. Barrett & T. Ollendick (Eds.), *Handbook of interventions that work with children and adolescents: Prevention and treatment* (pp. 273–300). Chichester: Wiley.

Orsillo, S. M. (2001). Measure for social phobia. In M. M. Antony, S. M. Orsillo, & L. Roemer (Eds.), *Practitioner's guide to empirically based measures of anxiety* (pp. 165–187). New York: Springer.

Osman A., Barrios, F. X., Haupt, D., King, K., Osman, J. R., & Slavens, S. (1996). The social phobia and anxiety inventory: Further validation in two nonclinical samples. *Journal of Psychopathology and Behavioral Assessment, 18*, 35–47.

Öst, L.-G. (1978). Fading vs. systematic desensitization in the treatment of snake and spider phobia. *Behaviour Research and Therapy, 16*, 379–389.

Öst, L.-G. (1989). One-session treatment for specific phobias. *Behaviour Research and Therapy, 27*, 1–7.

Paradis, C. M., Friedman, S. Lazar, R. M., Grubea, J., & Kesselman, M. (1992). Use of a structured interview to diagnose anxiety disorders in a minority population. *Hospital and Community Psychiatry, 43*, 61–64.

Peterson, R. A., & Reiss, S. (1993). *Anxiety sensitivity index revised test manual.* Worthington, OH: IDS Publishing Corporation.

Poulton, R., & Menzies, R. G. (2002). Non-associative fear acquisition: A review of the evidence from retrospective and longitudinal research. *Behaviour Research and Therapy, 40,* 127–149.

Purdon, C., Antony, M. M., & Swinson, R. P. (1999). Psychometric properties of the frost multidimensional perfectionism scale in a clinical anxiety disorders sample. *Journal of Clinical Psychology, 55,* 1271–1286.

Purdon, C., Rowa, K., & Antony, M. M. (2004, November). Treatment fears in individuals awaiting treatment for obsessive compulsive disorder. In C. Purdon (Chair), *Treatment ambivalence, readiness, and resistance in obsessive–compulsive disorder.* Symposium presented at the meeting of the Association for Advancement of Behavior Therapy, New Orleans, LA.

Quilty, L. C., van Ameringen, M., Mancini, C., Oakman, J., & Farvolden, P. (2003). Quality of life and the anxiety disorders. *Journal of Anxiety Disorders, 17,* 405–426.

Rachman, S. (1977). The conditioning theory of fear-acquisition: A critical examination. *Behaviour Research and Therapy, 15,* 375–387.

Ralevski, E., Sanislow, C. A., Grilo, C. M., Skodol, A. E., Gunderson, J. G., & Shea, M. T., et al. (2005). Avoidant personality disorder and social phobia: Distinct enough to be separate disorders? *Acta Psychiatrica Scandinavica, 112,* 208–214.

Rapaport, M. H., Clary, C., Fayyad, R., & Endicott, J. (2005). Quality-of-life impairment in depressive and anxiety disorders. *American Journal of Psychiatry, 162,* 1171–1178.

Rapee, R. M., & Spence, S. H. (2004). The etiology of social phobia: Empirical evidence and an initial model. *Clinical Psychology Review, 24,* 737–767.

Rodebaugh, T. L., Heimberg, R. G., Woods, C. M., Liebowitz, M. R., & Schneier, F. R. (2006). The factor structure and screening utility of the social interaction anxiety scale. *Psychological Assessment, 18,* 231–237.

Rogers, R. (1995). *Handbook of diagnostic and structured interviewing.* New York: Guilford.

Ross, H. E., Swinson, R., Doumani, S., & Larkin, E. J. (1995). Diagnosing comorbidity in substance abusers: A comparison of the test–retest reliability of two interviews. *American Journal of Drug and Alcohol Abuse, 21,* 167–185.

Rowa, K., Antony, M. M., Brar, S., Summerfeldt, L. J., & Swinson, R. P. (2000). Treatment histories of patients with three anxiety disorders. *Depression and Anxiety, 12,* 92–98.

Rowa, K., Antony, M. M., Summerfeldt, L. J., Purdon, C., Young, L., & Swinson, R. P. (2007). Office-based vs. home-based behavioral treatment for obsessive compulsive disorder: A preliminary study. *Behaviour Research and Therapy, 45,* 1883–1892.

Safran, J. D., & Segal, Z. V. (1990). *Interpersonal process in cognitive therapy.* New York: Basic Books.

Sanderson, W. C., Di Nardo, P. A., Rapee, R. M., & Barlow, D. H. (1990). Syndrome comorbidity in patients diagnosed with a DSM-III-R anxiety disorder. *Journal of Abnormal Psychology, 99,* 308–312.

Sawchuk, C. N., Lohr, J. M., Tolin, D. F., Lee, T. C., & Kleinknecht, R. A. (2000). Disgust sensitivity and contamination fears in spider and blood-injection-injury phobias. *Behaviour Research and Therapy, 38,* 753–762.

Segal, D. L., Hersen, M., & van Hasselt, V. B. (1994). Reliability of the Structured Clinical Interview for DSM-III-R: An evaluative review. *Comprehensive Psychiatry, 35,* 316–327.

Shear, M. K., & Maser, J. D. (1994). Standardized assessment for panic disorder research: A conference report. *Archives of General Psychiatry, 51,* 346–354.

Sheehan, D. V. (1983). *The anxiety disease.* New York: Charles Scribner and Sons.

Silverman, W. K., & Rabian, B. (1995). Test–retest reliability of the DSM-III-R childhood anxiety disorders symptoms using the anxiety disorders interview schedule for children. *Journal of Anxiety Disorders, 9,* 139–150.

Smari, J., Bjarnadottir, A., & Bragadottir, B. (1998). Social anxiety, social skills and expectancy/cost of negative social events. *Scandinavian Journal of Behaviour Therapy, 27,* 149–155.

Southam-Gerow, M. A., & Chorpita, B. F. (2007). Anxiety disorders. In E. J. Mash & R. A. Barkley (Eds.), *Assessment of childhood disorders* (4th ed., pp. 347–397). New York: Guilford.

Spence, S. H., Donovan, C., & Brechman-Toussaint, M. (1999). Social skills, social outcomes, and cognitive features of childhood social phobia. *Journal of Abnormal Psychology, 108,* 211–221.

Spitzer, R. L., & Fleiss, J. L. (1974). A re-analysis of the reliability of psychiatric diagnosis. *British Journal of Psychiatry, 125,* 341–347.

Stangier, U., Heidenreich, T., & Schermelleh-Engel, K. (2006). Safety behaviors and social performance in patients with generalized social phobia. *Journal of Cognitive Psychotherapy, 20,* 17–31.

Stober, J. (1998). The frost multidimensional perfectionism scale revisited: More perfect with four (instead of six) dimensions. *Personality and Individual Differences, 24,* 481–491.

Stouthard, M. E. A., Hoogstraten, J., & Mellenbergh, G. J. (1995). A study on the convergent and discriminant validity of the Dental Anxiety Inventory. *Behaviour Research and Therapy, 5,* 589–595.

Stouthard, M. E. A., Mellenbergh, G. J., & Hoogstraten, J. (1993). Assessment of dental anxiety: A facet approach. *Anxiety, Stress and Coping, 6,* 89–105.

Summerfeldt, L. J., & Antony, M. M. (2002). Structured and semi-structured diagnostic interviews. In M. M. Antony & D. H. Barlow (Eds.), *Handbook of assessment and treatment planning psychological disorders* (pp. 3–37). New York: Guilford.

Szymanski, J., & O'Donohue, W. (1995). The potential role of state-dependent learning in cognitive therapy with spider phobics. *Journal of Rational-Emotive and Cognitive-Behavior Therapy, 13,* 131–150.

Taylor, S., Koch, W. J., & McNally, R. J. (1992). How does anxiety sensitivity vary across the anxiety disorders? *Journal of Anxiety Disorders, 6,* 249–259.

Taylor, S., Woody, S., McLean, P. D., & Koch, W. J. (1997). Sensitivity of outcome measures for treatments of generalized social phobia. *Assessment, 4,* 181–191.

Tolin, D. F., Lohr, J. M., Sawchuk, C. N., & Lee, T. C. (1997). Disgust and disgust sensitivity in blood-injection-injury and spider phobia. *Behaviour Research and Therapy, 35,* 949–953.

Trower, P., Bryant, B., & Argyle, M (1978). *Social skills and mental health.* Pittsburgh, PA: University of Pittsburgh Press.

Turner, S. M., Beidel, D. C., Dancu, C. V., & Stanley, M. A. (1989). An empirically derived inventory to measure social fears and anxiety: The social phobia and anxiety inventory. *Psychological Assessment, 1,* 35–40.

Turner, S. M., Beidel, D. C., & Dancu, C. V. (1996). *SPAI—Social Phobia & Anxiety Inventory: Manual.* Toronto: Multi-Health Systems.

Turner, S. M., Beidel, D. C., Dancu, C. V., & Keys, D. J. (1986). Psychopathology of social phobia and comparison with avoidant personality disorder. *Journal of Abnormal Psychology, 95,* 389–394.

Van Ameringen, M., Mancini, C., Styan, G., & Donison, D. (1991). Relationship of social phobia with other psychiatric illness. *Journal of Affective Disorders, 21,* 93–99.

Ventura, J., Liberman, R. P., Green, M. F., Shaner, A., & Mintz, J. (1998). Training and quality assurance with the structured clinical interview for DSM-IV (SCID-I/P). *Psychiatry Research, 79,* 163–173.

Watson, D., & Friend, R. (1969). Measurement of social-evaluative anxiety. *Journal of Consulting and Clinical Psychology, 33,* 448–457.

Williams, J. B. W., Gibbon, M., First, M. B., Spitzer, R. L., Davies, M., Borus, J., et al. (1992). The structured clinical interview for DSM-III-R (SCID): Multisite test–retest reliability. *Archives of General Psychiatry, 49,* 630–636.

Wittchen, H.-U., & Fehm, L. (2003). Epidemiology and natural course of social fears and social phobia. *Acta Psychiatrica Scandinavica, 108*(Suppl. 417), 4–18.

Wolpe, J., & Lang, P. J. (1969). *Fear survey schedule.* San Diego, CA: Educational and Industrial Testing Service.

Woods, C. M., Chambless, D. L., & Steketee, G. (2002). Homework compliance and behavior therapy outcome for panic with agoraphobia and obsessive compulsive disorder. *Cognitive Behaviour Therapy, 31,* 88–95.

11

Panic Disorder and Agoraphobia

Melody L. Keller
Michelle G. Craske

In this chapter, we first describe the presenting features and prevailing theories regarding etiology and maintenance factors for panic disorder and agoraphobia (PDA). Next, we describe the diagnostic, treatment conceptualization and planning, and treatment outcome and monitoring assessment methods and strategies specific to PDA.

NATURE OF PANIC DISORDER
AND AGORAPHOBIA

Presenting Features

Panic attacks are brief, discrete episodes of intense dread or fear, accompanied by physical and cognitive symptoms, as listed in the *Diagnostic and Statistical Manual of Mental Disorders* (4th edition, Text Revision; DSM-IV-TR) panic attack checklist (American Psychiatric Association, 2000). Unexpected panic attacks refer to attacks that, from the patient's perspective, happen without an obvious trigger. Panic attacks occur occasionally in approximately 3% to 5% of the general population who do not otherwise meet the criteria for panic disorder (Norton, Cox, & Malan, 1992) and occur across a variety of anxiety and mood disorders (Barlow, Vermilyea, Blanchard, Vermilyea, & Di Nardo, 1985). The defining feature of panic disorder (PD) does not rest on the presence of panic attacks per se but rather on recurrent "unexpected" panic attacks, followed by at least 1 month of persistent concern about their recurrence and their consequences or by a significant change in behavior consequent to the attacks.

Agoraphobia refers to avoidance or endurance with dread of situations from which escape might be difficult or help unavailable in the event of a panic attack, or symptoms that could be incapacitating and embarrassing, such as loss of bowel control or vomiting. Typical agoraphobic situations include shopping malls, waiting in line, traveling by car or bus, and being alone. Not all persons who panic develop agoraphobia, and the extent of agoraphobia that emerges is highly variable (Craske & Barlow, 1988) and unrelated to age of onset, frequency, or intensity of panic (e.g., Craske, Miller, Rotunda, & Barlow, 1990; Kikuchi et al., 2005). On the other hand, concerns about social consequences of panicking may be stronger when agoraphobia is more severe (e.g., Amering et al., 1997), being unemployed predicts agoraphobia (de Jong & Bouman, 1995), and the ratio of males to females shifts dramatically in the direction of female predominance as severity of agoraphobia worsens (e.g., Thyer, Himle, Curtis, Cameron, & Nesse, 1985).

From the latest epidemiological study, the National Comorbidity Survey-Replication (NCS-R), prevalence estimates in the adult American population for panic disorder with or without agoraphobia are 2.7% (12 month) and 4.7% (lifetime; Kessler, Berglund, et al., 2005; Kessler, Chiu, Demler, & Walters, 2005). Individuals with agoraphobia who seek treatment almost always report a history of panic that preceded development of their avoidance (Wittchen, Reed, & Kessler, 1998). In contrast, epidemiological data indicate that a subset of the population experiences agoraphobia without a history of panic disorder: 0.8% in the last 12 months (Kessler, Chiu, et al., 2005) and 1.4% lifetime prevalence (Kessler, Berglund, et al., 2005). The discrepancy between clinical and epidemiological data has been attributed to misdiagnosis in epidemiological studies (Horwath, Lish, Johnson, Hornig, & Weissman, 1993), and to the fact that individuals who panic are more likely to seek help (Boyd, 1986).

Rarely does the diagnosis of PD, with or without agoraphobia, occur in isolation. Commonly co-occurring Axis I conditions include specific phobias, social phobia, dysthymia, generalized anxiety disorder, major depressive disorder, and substance abuse (e.g., Brown, Campbell, Lehman, Grishman, & Mancill, 2001; Kessler, Chiu, et al., 2005). In addition, 25% to 60% of persons with panic disorder meet criteria for a personality disorder, mostly avoidant and dependent personality disorders (e.g., Chambless & Renneberg, 1988).

A substantial proportion of adolescents report panic attacks (e.g., Hayward, Killen, Hammer, Litt, Wilson, et al., 1992) and the modal age of onset for PD is late teenage years and early adulthood (Kessler, Berglund, et al., 2005). However, treatment is usually sought at a much later age, on average around 34 years (e.g., Noyes, Crowe, Harris, Hamra, & McChesney, 1986). Most people with PD report identifiable stressors around the time of their first panic attack commonly related to interpersonal issues or physical well-being (Craske et al., 1990). Approximately one-half of those with PD report having experienced panicky feelings at some time before their first panic, suggesting that onset may be either insidious or acute (Craske et al., 1990).

Finally, PDA tends to be a chronic condition, with severe financial and interpersonal costs. Only one-third of untreated individuals remit without subsequent relapse within a few years (e.g., Katschnig & Amering, 1998). In addition, individuals with PD overutilize medical resources compared to the general public and individuals with other psychiatric disorders (e.g., Roy-Byrne et al., 1999).

Etiological and Maintaining Factors

Several independent lines of research converged in the 1980s on the same basic conceptualization of PD as an acquired fear of bodily sensations, particularly sensations associated with autonomic arousal, which is enhanced in the presence of certain psychological and biological predispositions. The following descriptions draw heavily from a more detailed description presented in Craske and Barlow (2007).

Genetics and Temperament

The temperament most associated with anxiety disorders, including PD, is neuroticism (Eysenck, 1967), or negative affectivity (Watson & Clark, 1984). Neuroticism and its proxy (i.e., emotional reactivity) predict the onset of panic attacks (e.g., Hayward, Killen, Kraemer, & Taylor, 2000) and PD (Craske, Poulton, Tsao, & Plotkin, 2001). Numerous multivariate genetic analyses of human twin samples consistently attribute approximately 30% to 50% of variance in neuroticism to additive genetic factors (e.g., Eley, 2001). In addition, anxiety and depression appear to be variable expressions of the heritable tendency toward neuroticism (Kendler, Heath, Martin, & Eaves, 1987). Symptoms of panic (i.e., breathlessness, heart pounding) may be additionally explained by a unique source of genetic variance that is differentiated from the variance relevant to neuroticism (Martin, Jardine, Andrews, & Heath, 1988). However, there is no evidence at this point for a specific link between genetic markers and temperament, on the one hand, and PD (see Roy-Byrne, Craske, & Stein, 2006). Rather, neurobiological factors seem to comprise a nonspecific biological vulnerability.

Anxiety Sensitivity

Anxiety sensitivity, or the belief that anxiety and its associated symptoms may cause deleterious physical, social, and psychological consequences that extend beyond any immediate physical discomfort during an episode of anxiety or panic (Reiss, 1980), is elevated in PD more than in other anxiety disorders (e.g., Zinbarg & Barlow, 1996). In addition, several longitudinal studies indicate that high scores on the Anxiety Sensitivity Index predict the onset of panic attacks over 1- to 4-year intervals (e.g., Hayward et al., 2000), and spontaneous panic attacks and worry about panic, during an acute military stressor (i.e., 5 weeks of basic training; Schmidt, Lerew, & Jackson, 1999). However, the relationship between anxiety sensitivity and panic attacks in these studies is relatively small, not exclusive to panic, and is weaker than the relationship between panic and neuroticism (Bouton, Mineka, & Barlow, 2001). Thus, the causal significance of anxiety sensitivity for PD remains to be fully understood.

History of Medical Illness and Abuse

Other studies highlight the role of medical illnesses. For example, experience with personal respiratory disturbance (and parental ill health) as a youth predicted PD at the ages of 18 or 21 (Craske et al., 2001). Others report more respiratory disturbance in the history of PD patients compared to other anxiety disordered patients (Verburg, Griez, Meijer, & Pols, 1995), and in first-degree relatives of PD patients compared to first-degree relatives of patients with other anxiety disorders (van Beek, Schruers, & Friez, 2005). Childhood experiences of sexual and physical abuse may also prime PD (Goodwin, Fergusson, & Horwood, 2005). The association with childhood abuse was found to be stronger for PD than for other anxiety disorders (e.g., Safren, Gershuny, Marzol, Otto, & Pollack, 2002). Retrospective reporting, however, limits the findings.

Maintenance Factors

Following the first panic attack, individuals with PD develop an acute fear of bodily sensations associated with panic attacks (e.g., racing heart, dizziness; Barlow, 1988). For example, they are more likely to interpret bodily sensations in a catastrophic fashion (Clark et al., 1988), and to allocate more attentional resources to words that represent physical threat (e.g., Maidenberg, Chen, Craske, Bohn, & Bystritsky, 1996) and heartbeat stimuli (Kroeze & van den Hout, 2000). In addition, they are more anxious in procedures that elicit bodily sensations similar to the ones experienced during panic attacks, such as carbon dioxide inhalations, compared to patients with other anxiety disorders (e.g., Perna, Bertani, Arancio, Ronchi, & Bellodi, 1995). Finally, individuals with PD fear signals that ostensibly reflect heightened arousal and false physiological feedback (e.g., Craske et al., 2002).

Fear of bodily sensations has been attributed to interoceptive conditioning, in which early somatic components of anxiety elicit conditioned bursts of anxiety or panic (Bouton et al., 2001). An extensive body of experimental literature attests to the robustness of interoceptive conditioning (e.g., Sokolowska, Siegel, & Kim, 2002) and its independence from conscious awareness of triggering cues (e.g., Block, Ghoneim, Fowles, Kumar, & Pathak, 1987). Hence, slight changes in relevant bodily functions that are not consciously recognized may elicit conditioned anxiety or fear and panic owing to previous pairings with panic (Bouton et al., 2001). An alternative model offered by Clark (1986) attributes fear of sensations to catastrophic misappraisals (e.g., misinterpretation of sensations as signs of imminent death). Others argue that catastrophic misappraisals become conditioned stimuli that trigger panic (Bouton et al., 2001).

Autonomic arousal generated by fear of sensations is believed to contribute to ongoing panic by intensifying the sensations that are feared, thus creating a reciprocating cycle of fear and sensations. Also, because bodily sensations that trigger panic attacks are not always immediately obvious, panic attacks appear to be unexpected (Barlow, 1988), resulting in even further anxiety (Craske, Glover, & DeCola, 1995). The perceived inability to escape from bodily sensations similarly increases anxiety (e.g., Maier, Laudenslager, & Ryan, 1985). In turn, anxiety increases the likelihood of panic, by directly increasing the availability of sensations that have become conditioned cues for panic and/or by increasing attentional vigilance for these bodily cues. Thus, a maintaining cycle of panic and anxiety develops (Barlow, 1988). In addition, subtle avoidance behaviors (such as holding onto supports for fear of fainting) are believed to maintain negative beliefs about feared bodily sensations (Clark & Ehlers, 1993). Finally, anxiety over specific contexts in which the occurrence of panic would be particularly troubling could contribute to agoraphobia, which in turn maintains distress.

There is no direct evidence that a distinct marital system predisposes one toward agoraphobia. On the other hand, interpersonal discord/dissatisfaction may represent one of several possible stressors that precipitate panic attacks, and interpersonal relations may be negatively impacted by the development of agoraphobia (Buglass, Clarke, Henderson, & Presley, 1977).

PURPOSES OF ASSESSMENT

The focus of this chapter is on assessment for the purpose of (a) diagnosis, (b) case conceptualization and treatment planning, and (c) treatment monitoring and evaluation. Emphasis is given to multiple methodologies and domains, including clinician-administered interviews, self-report questionnaires, behavioral observations, and measures of peripheral physiological functioning. In addition, we include measures of

TABLE 11.1 Ratings of Instruments Used for Diagnosis

Instrument	Norms	Internal Consistency	Inter-Rater Reliability	Test–Retest Reliability	Content Validity	Construct Validity	Validity Generalization	Clinical Utility	Highly Recommended
ADIS	NA	NA	G	A[a]	A	A	G	A	
SCID	NA	NA	G	A[a]	A	A	E	A	
PDSS	A	G	G	A[a]	A	A	G	A	

[a] *Different raters.*

Note: ADIS = Anxiety Disorders Interview Schedule; SCID = Structured Clinical Interview for the DSM; PDSS = Panic Disorder Severity Scale; A = Adequate; G = Good; E = Excellent; NA = Not Applicable.

the constructs relevant to the perpetuation of PDA, including anxiety sensitivity, fear, and catastrophic misappraisals of bodily sensations, and avoidance of not only agoraphobic situations but also bodily sensations. The methods of cognitive-behavioral therapy (CBT) uniquely designed, and highly effective, for PDA (Craske & Barlow, 2007) are derived from models emphasizing these constructs. Hence, changes in measures of these constructs are assumed to be critical indices of therapeutic outcomes. These measures are also relevant indices of the efficacy of pharmacological approaches to treatment, which is the other effective treatment option for PDA (see Roy-Byrne et al., 2006).

ASSESSMENT FOR DIAGNOSIS

As a part of the diagnostic process, medical evaluation is generally recommended to rule out several medical conditions for the diagnosis of PDA. These include thyroid conditions, caffeine or amphetamine intoxication, drug withdrawal, or pheochromocytoma (a rare adrenal gland tumor). Furthermore, certain medical conditions such as mitral valve prolapse, asthma, allergies, and hypoglycemia can exacerbate PDA because they produce sensations that overlap with panic attack symptoms (e.g., shortness of breath); however, these are not rule outs and PDA is likely to continue even when they are under medical control. In addition, for those reporting nocturnal panic attacks, a polysomnographic sleep assessment may be recommended to rule out other sleep-related disorders such as sleep apnea, night terrors, periodic movements, seizures, stage IV night terrors, nonrestorative sleep, sleep hallucinogenesis, and sleep paralysis, all of which are distinct from nocturnal panic (Craske & Tsao, 2005).

Informally generated clinical diagnoses are rarely as reliable as diagnoses obtained from structured diagnostic interviews (e.g., Basco et al., 2000). Given that panic attacks are ubiquitous, differential diagnosis requires carefully structured questioning regarding the degree to which the panic attacks are a source of anxiety or a reason for behavioral changes (as would be characteristic of PDA), or are part of another anxiety disorder. Hence, diagnostic assessment of PDA benefits from structured interviews. However, fully structured diagnostic interviews provide almost no opportunity for probing and may suffer from limited validity. Thus, preference is given to semistructured interviews that involve flexibility in questioning and clinical judgment. The two semistructured interviews used most often for the diagnosis of PDA are the Anxiety Disorders Interview Schedule for DSM-IV (the ADIS-IV; Brown, Di Nardo, & Barlow, 1994) and the Structured Clinical Interview for DSM-IV Axis I Disorders (SCID; First, Spitzer, Gibbon, & Williams, 1994). Ratings of the psychometric properties for these two instruments are shown in Table 11.1.

Anxiety Disorders Interview Schedule

The ADIS (Di Nardo, O'Brien, Barlow, Waddell, & Blanchard, 1983) was developed specifically for the assessment of anxiety disorders and other comorbid disorders such as mood disorders and hypochondriasis, with screens for psychosis and substance abuse or dependence. The ADIS is useful for differentiating among anxiety disorders as well as diagnosing comorbid mood disorders, which may impact treatment planning. Some of the interview questions require a "yes" or "no" response, whereas others involve ratings of fear, avoidance, and control on Likert scales. The PD section of the ADIS assesses full and limited panic attacks, and some versions include a separate section to assess for nocturnal panic attacks. The agoraphobia section includes a list of 23 situations that are each rated in terms of fear and avoidance, as well as related questions such as probes for typical safety signals. In addition to determining diagnostic status, the interviewer rates each diagnosed disorder on a 0-to-8-point rating to reflect overall levels of distress and impairment associated with the disorder. The latter is referred to as a clinical severity rating (CSR), with 4 representing the cutoff for clinical severity (Grisham, Brown, & Campbell, 2004). Thus, the ADIS encourages diagnostic categorization as well as a dimensional approach to understanding sets of symptoms and differentiation between clinical and subclinical levels of anxiety.

The ADIS is administered by a trained clinician. Training typically involves at least three observations of trained interviewers followed by achievement of acceptable inter-rater reliability while being observed by a trained interviewer on at least three consecutive occasions (e.g., Brown et al., 1994). The full ADIS may take several hours to complete, although it can be shortened by excluding nondiagnostic research based questions. Given the modular structure of the ADIS, it is possible to limit its use to the PDA sections, thereby reducing the time investment considerably. However, given the ubiquitous nature of panic attacks and the intricacies of differential diagnosis, completion of the entire ADIS interview is advised. Although this will require more time for the clinician, we believe that an accurate diagnosis of PDA depends on differential diagnosis, and that this should not be compromised.

Versions of the ADIS exist for DSM-III, the DSM-III-R, and currently the DSM-IV (ADIS: Di Nardo et al., 1983; ADIS-R: Di Nardo & Barlow, 1988; ADIS-IV: Brown, Di Nardo, et al., 1994, respectively). Versions exist for current as well as for lifetime psychopathology (ADIS-IV-L; Di Nardo, Brown, & Barlow, 1994), as well as child and parent versions of the ADIS (ADIS-C & ADIS-P, respectively: Silverman & Nelles, 1988; also see Silverman & Ollendick, this volume) that assess for anxiety and related disorders in children and adolescents between 6 and 18 years of age. Versions of the ADIS exist in English, Spanish, Portuguese, and French (Grisham et al., 2004). The following discussion includes references to various versions of the adult version of this interview.

In their college sample, Brown and Deagle (1992) found good inter-rater reliability for "panic classification" when the ADIS-R (Di Nardo & Barlow, 1988) was

rated by two individuals ($\kappa = .83$). In Tsao, Lewin, and Craske's (1998) study, inter-rater reliability was less than adequate to excellent for CSR ratings, dependent on the point of assessment ($r = .68$ to .99). On the whole, the ADIS is judged to have good inter-rater reliability.

The test–retest reliability of PD diagnoses was generally good when diagnoses with and without agoraphobia were combined ($\kappa = .75$ to .79) and adequate to good for diagnoses of PDA ($\kappa = .71$ to .81; Brown, Di Nardo, Lehman, & Campbell, 2001; Di Nardo, Moras, Barlow, Rapee, & Brown, 1993). However, reliability values were not consistent across levels of agoraphobia and most often, less than adequate values were obtained for diagnoses of PD without agoraphobia ($\kappa = .39$ to .72; Brown et al., 2001; Di Nardo et al., 1993). Lastly, Brown et al. (2001) obtained a good rating of CSR test–retest reliability ($r = .83$). Given the variability and short test–retest time intervals (0 to 44 days), the ADIS is judged to have only adequate test–retest reliability.

The ADIS modules were developed to assess the diagnostic criteria as they are stated in the DSM (American Psychiatric Association). However, given that the contents of the interview were not reviewed by outside judges (D. H. Barlow, personal communication, October 26, 2006), the ADIS was rated as demonstrating only adequate content validity. Brown, Chorpita, and Barlow (1998) reported convergent and discriminant validity by showing that symptom measures of anxiety and depression differentially loaded on different diagnostic factors making a PDA diagnosis distinguishable from some other diagnoses. The limitation to only one study led to an assignment of adequate construct validity.

Although the ADIS has been used with various groups of people, no data exist to support its use in different contexts. Thus, it is rated as having only good validity generalization. Though the ADIS is frequently used as a treatment outcome measure, it is rated as having demonstrated only adequate clinical utility because there is no evidence that the use of data obtained with this particular interview results in a better treatment outcome than that which would have occurred by using a different instrument.

Structured Clinical Interview for the DSM

The SCID (First et al., 1994) is administered by a clinician to assess nine areas of psychopathology, including anxiety disorders. Thus, it facilitates differential diagnoses and assessment of comorbid conditions (e.g., mood disorders). In addition to the clinician version of the SCID (SCID-CV; First, Spitzer, Gibbon, & Williams, 1996), several research versions exist, including the most current versions of the SCID-I/P (Patient Edition: First, Spitzer, Gibbon, & Williams, 2002a), SCID-I/NP (Nonpatient Edition: First, Spitzer, Gibbon, & Williams, 2002b), and the SCID-I/P (Patient Edition, with psychotic screening module: First, Spitzer, Gibbon, & Williams, 2002c). In addition, a child version of the SCID, the Structured Clinical Interview for DSM-IV Childhood Diagnoses (KID-SCID; Hien et al., 1994), is available, but has been rarely evaluated in research studies. The SCID is available in many languages, including German, Spanish, Portuguese, French, Italian, Swedish, Greek, Hebrew, Russian, Turkish, Danish, and Dutch (Skodol & Bender, 2000). The focus of our discussion and ratings in Table 11.1 is on the SCID for adults.

The structure of the SCID includes a general probe question at the beginning of each disorder module, followed by other specific questions as deemed appropriate based on answers to the probe question. This interview format is similar to the ADIS. However, inclusion of each diagnostic criterion next to relevant questions makes the SCID more transparent than the ADIS. For each question, the interviewer assesses how consistent the information is with the diagnostic criterion of interest, and gives a rating of 1 (absent/false), 2 (subthreshold), or 3 (threshold/true). According to Spitzer, Williams, Gibbon, and First (1992), SCID training should include becoming familiar with the SCID User's Guide (Spitzer, Williams, Gibbon, & First, 1990), watching videotaped interviews, and achieving acceptable inter-rater and test–retest reliability.

Evidence regarding the inter-rater reliability of PD is mixed. Kappa (κ) values range from .65 to 1.0 (e.g., Dammen, Arnesen, Ekeberg, Husebye, & Friis, 1999; Löwe et al., 2003; Zanarini & Frankenburg, 2001; Zanarini et al., 2000). There is some evidence for adequately reliable agoraphobia diagnoses ($\kappa = .69$; Zanarini & Frankenburg, 2001). Overall, the SCID is judged to have good inter-rater reliability because, amongst the mixed data, there were several excellent values.

Most test–retest data for SCID diagnoses of PD are slightly less than adequate to adequate. In a large study of patients and nonpatients ($N = 592$), Williams, Gibbon, and colleagues (1992) obtained test–retest κ values for panic disorder diagnoses, based on interviews conducted 1 to 14 days apart, ranging from .54 to .65. However, studies with smaller sample sizes obtained κ

values ranging from .61 to .82, dependent on whether subtypes were examined (Williams, Spitzer, & Gibbon, 1992; Zanarini & Frankenburg, 2001; Zanarini et al., 2000). Data for agoraphobia diagnoses are mixed, with κ ranging from .43 to 1.0 (Williams, Gibbon, et al., 1992; Williams, Spitzer, et al., 1992; Zanarini & Frankenburg, 2001). On the basis of the range of findings, a somewhat liberal rating of adequate test–retest reliability was assigned. However, it appears that like the ADIS, diagnoses from the SCID may have some limitations in reliably differentiating panic disorder from agoraphobia.

As with the ADIS, although the SCID is worded to address each of the DSM-IV diagnostic criteria, there is no evidence of its contents being evaluated by outside judges. Hence, it too demonstrates only adequate content validity. Kessler, Berglund, and colleagues (2005) found that anxiety disorder diagnoses generated from the SCID and the World Mental Health Survey Initiative Version of the World Health Organization Composite International Diagnostic Interview (WMH-CIDI; Kessler & Ustun, 2004) "generally were in good concordance" (p. 594). However, as the findings were limited to one study, the SCID was assigned only adequate construct validity.

Evidence of the SCIDs excellent validity generalization lies in the fact that it has been used in more than 1000 studies (First & Gibbon, 2004), and has been administered to coronary heart patients (Bankier, Januzzi, & Littman, 2004), individuals seeking community outpatient treatment (Zimmerman & Mattia, 2000) and primary care patients (e.g., Rodriguez et al., 2004). Furthermore, the SCID has been administered to people of different ethnicities (e.g., African American: Carter, Sbrocco, Gore, Marin, & Lewis, 2003; Chinese: Wilson & Young, 1988).

The SCID allows clinicians and assessors to follow closely the DSM-IV criteria when making diagnoses. It is relatively inexpensive, does not require a scoring program, and is even available for computer administration (Skodol & Bender, 2000). In addition, it may result in more valid diagnoses than those based on a standard clinical interview (Basco et al., 2000). However, since further research is needed on the usefulness of the SCID in assessing PDA specifically, clinical utility is judged to be adequate.

Panic Disorder Severity Scale

Following completion of a diagnostic assessment, a dimensional assessment specifically designed for

PDA, such as the Panic Disorder Severity Scale (PDSS; Shear et al., 1997), may be helpful. This clinician-completed scale rates seven areas of responding using a 0-to-4 severity rating scale: panic attack frequency, distress, anticipatory anxiety, agoraphobic and interoceptive-related fears and avoidant behavior, and work and social impairment. Administration of this instrument requires less than 15 minutes (Antony, 2001).

Internal consistency is adequate to excellent (Cronbach's α ranging from .71 to .92; e.g., Houck, Spiegel, Shear, Rucci, & Stat, 2002; Monkul et al., 2004; Yamamoto et al., 2004), with "adequate" limited to one study (Monkul et al., 2004). Overall, this measure is judged to possess good internal consistency.

Different versions of the PDSS have been found to have adequate to excellent inter-rater reliability ($r = .79$; ICC $= .87$ to .99; Monkul et al., 2004; Shear et al., 1997; Yamamoto et al., 2004), resulting in an averaged rating of good inter-rater reliability. Its test–retest data range from less than adequate to good ($r = .63$ to .71; $ICC = .81$ to .88) over short periods of time (Houck et al., 2002; Monkul et al., 2004; Shear et al., 1997; Shear, Rucci, Williams, Frank, Grochocinski, et al., 2001), resulting in an overall rating of adequate test–retest reliability studies.

The PDSS has only adequate content validity because there is no evidence to indicate that independent judges reviewed this measure. Shear et al. (1997, 2001) found evidence for construct validity in that ADIS-R PD CSRs were strongly related to PDSS total scores ($r = .55$), patients with PDA scored higher on the PDSS than patients with other anxiety or mood diagnoses, and PDSS scores correlated with various anxiety-related questionnaires. However, overall, the construct validity was judged to be adequate rather than good, due to the lack of independently replicated validity findings.

Validity generalization of the PDSS is judged to be good. This measure has been used in samples of varying racial and ethnic backgrounds. Japanese (Yamamoto et al., 2004) and Turkish versions of this measure (Monkul et al., 2004) exist. In addition, a self-report version of this instrument (the PDSS-SR) has been developed that has promising psychometric properties. Although the PDSS may help clinicians assess different aspects of PDA, it has only adequate clinical utility because there is no research to show that the use of its data results in benefits above those seen when data are used from other instruments.

Overall Evaluation

Although semistructured diagnostic interviews may be somewhat time consuming, the data they yield are helpful in making differential diagnoses, which is particularly important given the ubiquitous nature of panic attacks. If time does not permit to complete a full interview, the PDA modules may be complemented by screener questions from the other anxiety disorder modules and/or by self-report questionnaires to gauge whether the use of the term "panic" is related to other disorders. Clinicians should also inquire about medical conditions and stimulant drug use. Additional research is needed for reliably distinguishing amongst levels of agoraphobia, and to compare the clinical utility of the ADIS and the SCID.

ASSESSMENT FOR CASE CONCEPTUALIZATION AND TREATMENT PLANNING

Development of a thorough case conceptualization to guide treatment planning requires assessment of symptoms (including severity and distress), as well as fear of and beliefs about the symptoms, and avoidance of situations and activities. Whenever possible, a variety of assessment methodologies, including self-report, in vivo, and physiological measures is preferred. This section provides clinicians with a number of relevant instruments and methodologies.

Self-Report Instruments

Self-report measures are relatively inexpensive, require only a brief amount of time to complete, are often standardized, and allow for easy comparisons of effect sizes across treatment studies. However, self-report instruments may result in an overestimation of panic attack frequency (e.g., Margraf, Taylor, Ehlers, & Roth, 1987) and physiological symptoms (e.g., Calvo & Eysenck, 1998). Nonetheless, self-report instruments yield useful information and are likely to remain one of the primary methods of assessing PDA.

The following is not intended to be a comprehensive review of all available self-report measures for PDA, but rather covers the self-report instruments that are most helpful for assessing thoughts, feelings, and behaviors as they relate to PDA. The self-report measures

TABLE 11.2 Ratings of Instruments Used for Case Conceptualization and Treatment Planning

Instrument	Norms	Internal Consistency	Inter-Rater Reliability	Test–Retest Reliability	Content Validity	Construct Validity	Validity Generalization	Clinical Utility	Highly Recommended
ASI	G	G	NA	A	A	E	E	A	✓
BSQ	G	G	NA	G	A	G	G	A	✓
ACQ	G	G	NA	A	A	G	G	A	✓
FQ	G	A	NA	G	A	G	E	A	✓
MI	G	E	NA	A	A	A	G	A	
APPQ	A	G	NA	A	A	A	A	A	

Note: ASI = Anxiety Sensitivity Index; BSQ = Body Sensations Questionnaire; ACQ = Agoraphobic Cognitions Questionnaire; FQ = Fear Questionnaire; MI = Mobility Inventory for Agoraphobia; APPQ = Albany Panic and Phobia Questionnaire; A = Adequate; G = Good; E = Excellent; NA = Not Applicable.

to be discussed are Anxiety Sensitivity Index (ASI; Reiss, Peterson, Gursky, & McNally, 1986), Body Sensations Questionnaire (BSQ; Chambless, Caputo, Bright, & Gallagher, 1984), Agoraphobia Cognitions Questionnaire (ACQ; Chambless et al., 1984), Fear Questionnaire (FQ; Marks & Mathews, 1979), Mobility Inventory (MI; Chambless, Caputo, Jasin, Gracely, & Williams, 1985), and Albany Panic and Phobia Questionnaire (APPQ; Rapee, Craske, & Barlow, 1994/1995). Ratings for the psychometric properties of each instrument are shown in Table 11.2. Across measures, we were somewhat liberal in our ratings of the property of norms, such that if there were at least two available studies to cite and data from both clinical and nonclinical samples, the norms were rated as good. In addition, none of the reviewed measures received content validity or clinical utility ratings that were better than adequate. This is because there are no published data to indicate that any of the measures in their entirety were evaluated by independent judges, and no published data to suggest that using results from these self-report measures leads to clinical benefits above those gained by using data obtained from other instruments.

Anxiety Sensitivity Index

The ASI (Reiss et al., 1986) is a 16-item self-report measure that assesses beliefs that anxiety-related symptoms are harmful. Zinbarg, Barlow, and Brown (1997) evaluated the factor structure to find an overall general factor representing level of sensitivity to anxiety, as well as three factors that measure physical concerns (e.g., "It scares me when my heart beats rapidly"), mental incapacitation concerns (e.g., "When I am nervous, I worry that I might be mentally ill"),

and social concerns (e.g., "Other people notice when I feel shaky").

Norms for the ASI exist for nonclinical and clinically anxious individuals (see Peterson & Reiss, 1993; Rapee, Brown, Antony, & Barlow, 1992, respectively). This measure has good internal consistency (Cronbach $\alpha = .84$ to .90) and adequate test–retest reliability over a 2-week period ($r = .75$; see Shear et al., 2000). On the basis of the adjusted item-to-scale correlations and factor loadings, Blais, Otto, Zucker, McNally, Schmidt, et al. (2001) reanalyzed ASI data from three earlier studies with items 1, 5, 7, 8, and 13 removed. In comparison to the original ASI, the data produced by the 11-item version related more specifically to PD than to other psychiatric conditions and were highly correlated with data from the 16-item version ($r > .95$). The 11-item version's two factors are "fears of somatic sensations of anxiety and fears of loss of mental control" (Blais et al., 2001, p. 273).

There is evidence for excellent construct validity for the ASI, including convergent, criterion, construct, predictive, and discriminative validity. For example, as reviewed earlier, longitudinal studies indicate that high scores on the ASI predict the onset of panic attacks and worry about panic. In addition, the ASI discriminates PD from other anxiety disorders (e.g., Zinbarg & Barlow, 1996). In addition, treatment studies have shown that changes in ASI scores partially mediate the effects of CBT on panic attack frequency, anxiety, and agoraphobia (e.g., Smits, Powers, Cho, & Telch, 2004). Thus, construct validity for the ASI was judged to be excellent.

In terms of validity generalization, this measure is available in a variety of languages (see Antony, 2001). It has been administered to samples of various ethnic backgrounds (e.g., native Americans: Zvolensky, McNeil, Porter, & Stewart, 2001; Russians: Kotov, Schmidt, Zvolensky, Vinogradov, & Antipova, 2005), although the ASI's factor structure does not hold true for all populations (e.g., African American college students; Carter, Miller, Sbrocco, Suchday, & Lewis, 1999). In addition, the ASI has been used with anxious patients in primary care settings (Craske, Golinelli, Stein, Roy-Byrne, Bystritsky, et al., 2005). Hence, the overall rating for validity generalization was excellent.

In terms of clinical utility, the ASI is relatively inexpensive, takes only 3 to 5 minutes to complete (Antony, 2001), and can be used as a measure of treatment outcome (e.g., Craske, Farchione, et al., 2007). It is rated as having adequate clinical utility. In summary, the ASI measures a construct believed to be central to the onset and maintenance of PDA, described earlier, and is critical to the measurement of responsiveness to treatment.

Body Sensations Questionnaire

The BSQ (Chambless et al., 1984) assesses level of fear of somatic sensations (e.g., sweating, nausea, and dizziness) experienced during an anxious state. This measure, which can be completed within 5 to 10 minutes, consists of 18 items with ratings based on a Likert scale. The BSQ is available in a variety of languages, including Spanish, Portuguese, French, Greek, German, Swedish, Mandarin, and Dutch (see Antony, 2001)

Norms for the BSQ exist for clinical as well as community samples (see Chambless et al., 1984; Chambless & Gracely, 1989). This measure has good to excellent internal consistency (Cronbach α ranging from .84 to .95; Carlbring, et al., 2007; Chambless et al., 1984; Novy, Stanley, Averill, & Daza, 2001) and its test–retest reliability ranges from below adequate to good (ranging from $r = .67$ over a median of 31 days to a corrected $r = .89$ over a 3-month period; Arrindell, 1993a; Carlbring et al., 2007; Chambless et al., 1984). Thus, an overall rating of good was assigned for test–retest reliability.

The items for the BSQ were developed from discussions and sessions with clients and therapists (Chambless et al., 1984), suggestive of adequate content validity. Evidence for good construct validity derives from correlated scores between the BSQ and the ACQ and other self-report measures of anxiety,

and from the finding that individuals with PDA, other anxiety disorders, and no anxiety disorders score differently on the BSQ (see Arrindell 1993b; Chambless, Beck, Gracely, & Grisham, 2000). Also, Smits et al. (2004) found that BSQ change scores were partial mediators of the effects of group CBT on levels of anxiety, agoraphobia, and frequency of panic attacks.

Because the BSQ has been used with people of different ethnic backgrounds but lacks data to support its use in different settings, it was rated as having good validity generalization. According to Chambless et al. (1984), the BSQ helps clinicians focus on the particular sensations that are of most concern to clients. BSQ responses may be useful in the development of individualized Behavioral Approach Tests (BATs, see below) and effective interoceptive exposures (e.g., Craske, Rowe, Lewin, & Noriega-Dimitri, 1997). Thus, the BSQ has adequate clinical utility.

Agoraphobic Cognitions Questionnaire

The ACQ (Chambless et al., 1984) assesses the frequency of particular thoughts while the respondent is in an anxious state. This measure consists of 15 items with ratings based on a Likert scale and can be completed within 5 to 10 minutes (Antony, 2001). The ACQ generates an overall mean score of the first 14 items, a mean "physical concerns" subscale score, and a mean "loss of control" subscale score. The ACQ is available in a variety of languages, including Spanish, Portuguese, French, Greek, German, Swedish, Mandarin, and Dutch (see Antony, 2001).

Norms for this questionnaire exist for clinical as well as community samples (see Chambless et al., 1984; Bibb, 1988, respectively). In addition, this measure has good internal consistency (Cronbach α ranging from .80 to .87) and adequate test–retest reliability ($r = .86$ to .92, ranging from a nonspecified time period to a 3-month period; see Arrindell, 1993a; Carlbring et al., 2007).

Items on the ACQ were decided upon based on inputs received from clients and therapists (Chambless et al., 1984), suggestive of adequate content validity. The construct validity of the ACQ appears to be good given evidence for correlations with the BSQ and other self-report measures of anxiety, as well as the finding that individuals with PDA, other anxiety disorders, and no anxiety disorders score differently on the ACQ (see Arrindell 1993b; Chambless et al.,

2000). Bouvard and colleagues (1998) found evidence of internal consistency and validity for the French version of the ACQ. The ACQ was rated as exhibiting good validity generalization owing to its use with people of different language backgrounds, but was not rated as excellent owing to the lack of research using the ACQ in different settings.

The clinical utility of the ACQ lies in its identification of anxious thoughts to be targeted through cognitive restructuring and exposures to feared situations and bodily sensations. Thus, it has adequate clinical utility.

Fear Questionnaire

The FQ (Marks & Mathews, 1979) assesses phobic severity and distress, as well as related symptoms of anxiety and depression. For current purposes, the discussion focuses on the agoraphobia subscale. It consists of five situation items for which level of avoidance is rated on a Likert scale. Less than 10 minutes is required to complete the entire 20-item measure. It is available in a variety of languages, including Dutch, French, German, Italian, Catalan, Chinese, and Spanish (Roemer, 2001).

Norms for this measure exist for a clinical sample (Cox, Swinson, & Shaw, 1991), as well as for a normative sample (Gillis, Haaga, & Ford, 1995). Though the agoraphobia subscale had less than adequate internal consistency values in one study (Cronbach α ranging from .59 to .69; Cox et al., 1991), other studies with clinical and nonclinical samples, including a Spanish/English bilingual sample, indicate adequate to good internal consistency (Cronbach α ranging from .76 to .84; e.g., Cox, Swinson, Parker, Kuch, 1993; Novy et al., 2001). Given the variable data, an overall internal consistency rating of adequate, rather than good, was assigned. Test–retest reliability of the FQ agoraphobia subscale has been assessed over different time delays ranging from 1 to 16 weeks (Cronbach $\alpha = .85$ to .89; Marks & Mathews, 1979; Michelson & Mavissakalian, 1983), although with small samples, resulting in an overall assignment of good test–retest reliability.

The items on the FQ were determined through multiple factor analyses (Marks & Mathews, 1979) and appear to represent the constructs of interest, indicative of adequate content validity. The construct validity of the FQ is judged to be good based on correlations with other self-report measures of anxiety,

as well as the finding that FQ agoraphobia subscale scores are higher in individuals with PDA in comparison to other individuals (see Cox, et al., 1991; Oei, Moylan, & Evans, 1991). The FQ has been used with people of different ethnicities, including Spanish-speaking anxious individuals (Novy et al., 2001) and Chinese college students (Lee & Oei, 1994), as well as with primary care and community mental health patients (Craske, Golinelli, et al., 2005; Wade, Treat, & Stuart, 1998). Given the various populations and settings in which the FQ has been studied, it is judged to have excellent validity generalization. The FQ is rated as having adequate clinical utility. The greatest utility of the FQ is that it is a brief index of level of agoraphobic avoidance, to be compared against established norms.

Mobility Inventory for Agoraphobia

The MI (Chambless et al., 1985) assesses degree of avoidance owing to agoraphobia, as well as the frequency and severity of panic attacks. The MI has undergone some changes since its original development (see Antony, 2001). The first part of the MI lists 27 agoraphobic-like situations (including one write-in response). Using a Likert scale, two avoidance ratings are given to each situation, one when accompanied and one when alone. Separate mean values (for accompanied and alone) are calculated for the first 26 items. The respondent also circles the five situations that are most impairing. Three questions, rated on a Likert scale, assess the frequency and severity of panic attacks. Lastly, the respondent is asked about his/her safety zone, including its size and location. This questionnaire can be completed in less than 20 minutes (Chambless et al., 1985) and is available in Spanish, Portuguese, French, Swedish, Dutch, German, and Greek (Antony, 2001).

Norms exist for clinical as well as normal samples (see Chambless et al., 1985) and the MI has been completed by an elderly community sample (Craske, Rachman, & Tallman, 1986). Because item development was informed by exposure session observations and information obtained through client interviews, as well as by items on a measure of fear (Chambless et al., 1985), the MI has adequate content validity. Also, this measure has excellent internal consistency (Cronbach α ranges from .91 to .97) and adequate test–retest reliability ($r = .75$ to $.90$ over a 31-day period; Chambless et al., 1985). The MI has adequate construct validity as evidenced by correlations with other self-report measures of anxiety (e.g., Ehlers, 1995).

Although the MI is available for people from different language backgrounds, there is a lack of research using it in different contexts. Thus, it has only good rather than excellent validity generalization. Regardless, this measure has at least adequate clinical utility because it can be useful in generating a hierarchy of agoraphobic situations to be targeted during in vivo exposures (Chambless et al., 1985).

Albany Panic and Phobia Questionnaire

The APPQ (Rapee et al., 1994/1995) is a 27-item questionnaire that measures degree of fear imagined in a given situation (e.g., "exercising vigorously alone"). Each item is rated from 0 (*no fear*) to 8 (*extreme fear*). Scores are calculated separately for agoraphobia, social phobia, and interoceptive subscales.

Descriptive statistics are available on the APPQ for various anxiety disorders, as well as for a small nonclinical sample (Rapee et al., 1994/1995). However, norms are not available from large samples. The APPQ items were tested in three pilot studies (Rapee et al., 1994/1995), but the measure was not judged independently by others, and hence it was assigned adequate content validity. The internal consistency of its subscales ranges from good to excellent in English and Spanish versions (Cronbach α ranges from .85 to .92; Brown, White, & Barlow, 2005; Novy et al., 2001; Rapee et al., 1994/1995). Overall, its internal consistency appears to be good. There is some evidence of this measure displaying adequate test–retest reliability (r ranging from .68 to .84, mean period of 10.9 weeks; Rapee et al., 1994/1995).

Several studies have found evidence for this measure's construct validity (Brown et al., 2005; Novy et al., 2001; Rapee et al., 1994/1995), including correlations with other self-report measures of anxiety and evidence that the subscale scores differ between groups. Examples include different interoceptive subscale scores for PD groups varying in levels of avoidance, as well as differences in agoraphobia subscale scores between a PD group with varying levels of avoidance and three comparison groups (social phobia, other anxiety, and control; Rapee et al., 1994/1995). Overall, a rating of adequate construct validity was assigned.

There is evidence for the use of the APPQ with two different groups (i.e., English and Spanish-speaking individuals; Novy et al., 2001). However, given the lack of evidence regarding use of the APPQ among other groups and across different clinical settings, validity generalization was judged to be only adequate. Nonetheless, this scale is the only standardized self-report instrument that assesses fears of activities that produce bodily sensations (such as exercising vigorously, or drinking coffee), a type of fear that is central to PDA and is a target of treatment. The instrument is useful for generating a hierarchy of feared activities and is therefore beneficial to treatment planning as well. At this time, the APPQ is judged to have adequate clinical utility.

Behavioral Approach Tests

BATs assess the degree of behavioral approach or avoidance of specific situations or internal stimuli (i.e., bodily sensations). Although degree of avoidance can be *reported upon* during diagnostic interviews or with self-report questionnaires, the BAT provides another modality of assessment that is not constrained by the biases of retrospective judgment that limit verbal reporting.

The BAT can be standardized across patients or individually tailored for a patient. The standardized BAT for agoraphobia usually involves walking or driving a particular route, such as a 1-mile loop around the clinic setting (see Williams & Zane, 1989 for examples). Standardized BATs for physical sensations involve exercises that induce panic-like symptoms, such as spinning in a circle, running in place, hyperventilating, and breathing through a straw (Barlow & Craske, 2006). The disadvantage of standardized BATs is that the specific task may not be relevant to everyone with PDA. Individually tailored BATs usually entail attempts at three to five individualized situations and physical exercises designed to be moderately to extremely anxiety-provoking for a given patient. Individually tailored BATs are more informative for clinical practice, although they confound between-participant comparisons for research purposes.

With both individualized and standardized BATs, anxiety levels are rated at regular intervals throughout, and actual distance or length of time is measured. Ongoing anxiety typically is measured using the Subjective Units of Distress Scale (SUDS; Wolpe, 1958), a verbal or written rating of anxiety, ranging from 0 (no anxiety) to 100 (extreme anxiety). Some prefer to use a smaller range than the original SUDS rating system (e.g., a 9-point scale; Mavissakalian & Michelson, 1982). Computerized technology for BATs now exists (e.g., Meng, Kirkby, Martin, Gilroy, & Daniels, 2004), but more research is needed on its value.

Standardized and individually tailored BATs are each susceptible to demand biases, for distress before treatment and improvement after treatment (Borkovec, Weerts, & Bernstein, 1977). On the other hand, BATs are an important supplement to self-report of agoraphobic avoidance because patients tend to underestimate what they can actually achieve (Craske, Rapee, & Barlow, 1988). In addition, BATs often reveal information of which the individual is not fully aware but that is important for treatment planning. For example, safety signals and safety behaviors, which alleviate distress in the short term but sustain anxiety in the long term (Siddle & Bond, 1988), may not be acknowledged until in the act of attempting to approach a situation or a bodily sensation that had been previously avoided. Typical safety signals include other people and medication bottles. The removal of safety signals and safety behaviors is critical to effective exposure therapy (e.g., Salkovskis, 1991).

Physiological Measures

To date, there have been few practical options available to clinicians for assessing ongoing physiological responses. Such data can, however, provide important information. Ongoing monitoring of heart rate and blood pressure during BATs, for example, may illuminate discrepancies between reports of symptoms and actual physiological arousal (i.e., report of heart rate acceleration in the absence of actual heart rate acceleration), which can serve as a therapeutic demonstration of the role of attention and cognition in symptom production. Similarly, physiological data can disconfirm misappraisals such as "my heart feels like its going so fast that it will explode."

Another option is to record basal peripheral physiology over protracted periods of time, such as 24-hour ambulatory recordings as individuals engage in their normal daily routine. However, the clinical value of such data is not clear, especially because the results are inconsistent (e.g., Bystritsky, Craske,

Maidenberg, Vapnik, & Shapiro, 1995; Shear et al., 1992). Nonetheless, the finding that CBT effects are not limited to self-reported symptoms but extend to shifts in basal levels of physiology (Craske, Lang, Aikins, & Mystkowski, 2005) is useful information for the clinician.

Measures of In Vivo Cognition

In contrast to strong endorsements of perceived dangers on self-report questionnaires in anticipation of feared situations, Williams, Kinney, Harap, and Liebmann (1997) reported a general absence of danger appraisals as patients with PDA and other phobias confronted their most feared driving and claustrophobic situations. That is, patients reported very little anticipation of panic or the situation itself while confronting those situations. Instead, their verbal reports pertained mostly to perceived inability to cope. This suggests that self-report questionnaires tap a different construct than in vivo measures of cognition. Conceivably, endorsements on self-report questionnaires, when *not* faced with an agoraphobic situation, represent a state of anticipatory anxiety whereas reports during in vivo exposures represent the state of fear responding. There is some reason to believe that cognitive functions differ between these two states. That is, whereas anxiety is associated with improved attentional selectivity for threat-relevant stimuli, processing of threatening information may be impeded at the height of intense fear (e.g., Watts, Trezise, & Sharrock, 1986). In addition, Goldsmith (1994) noted that cognitions associated with emotions (e.g., fear) are relatively elementary or automatic, in contrast to the more complex cognitive processing of mood states (e.g., anxiety).

Thus, a more comprehensive assessment of experience when faced with agoraphobic situations or feared bodily sensations would entail behavioral observations, anxiety ratings, physiological measurements, and cognitions in the moment. There is no specific instrument to recommend, however, other than instructing individuals to verbalize their thoughts throughout the BAT.

Overall Evaluation

Several self-report instruments are helpful in the assessment of subjective state (i.e., ASI, BSQ, ACQ, and FQ). SUDS ratings and assessment of cognitions and physiology during BATs can generate a more thorough understanding of the individual's subjective experience and what to target during treatment. A clear case conceptualization necessary for individualizing treatment for PDA warrants gathering information across all of these domains using multiple methodologies.

ASSESSMENT FOR TREATMENT MONITORING AND TREATMENT OUTCOME

Similar to case conceptualization and treatment planning, assessment for treatment monitoring and treatment outcome should include measures of symptom-related misappraisals, fear, and avoidance, as well as cognitions related to control and self-efficacy. Although the evidence to date remains sparse and inconsistent, there is some evidence that measures of catastrophic thinking about panic attacks predict treatment outcome (e.g., Margraf & Schneider, 1991), as well as follow-up status (Clark et al., 1994) for patients with PDA. However, there is other evidence to suggest that measures of self-efficacy and perceived control may be more relevant and telling (e.g., Craske, Farchione, et al., 2007; Williams, Kinney, & Falbo, 1989). In addition to assessing multiple constructs, it is also important that various methodologies be used in treatment monitoring and treatment outcome assessment. Our discussion will include interview, self-report, self-monitoring, and behavioral assessment methodologies.

Interviews

ADIS

In addition to the diagnostic value of the ADIS (Brown et al., 1994), there is evidence that CSRs for the diagnoses of PDA are sensitive to change following CBT (e.g., Craske, Farchione, et al., 2007). The ADIS is rated in Table 11.3 as having good rather than excellent treatment sensitivity because the empirical evidence regarding sensitivity is restricted to only one type of treatment (i.e., CBT).

SCID

The SCID (First et al., 1994) is most often used as a pretreatment diagnostic instrument rather than as an outcome measure. Because we were able to locate only one study in which pre- to posttreatment change was measured through the SCID (Carter, Sbrocco, et al., 2003), treatment sensitivity was judged to be adequate.

PDSS

The PDSS (Shear et al., 1997) has been found to be sensitive to change following treatment (Barlow, Gorman, Shear, & Woods, 2000). This instrument is judged to have excellent treatment sensitivity due to its ability to detect change in PDA following various types of treatment (including pharmacological and CBT).

Self-Report Instruments

Anxiety Sensitivity Index

Administration of the ASI (Reiss et al., 1986) before, during, and after treatment maps the degree to which beliefs about physical symptoms of anxiety have changed over the course of treatment. The ASI is rated as having excellent treatment sensitivity due to the empirical evidence showing change on this instrument following CBT (e.g., Craske, Farchione et al., 2007) and pharmacological treatments (e.g., Simon et al., 2004).

Anxiety Control Questionnaire

The Anxiety Control Questionnaire (ACQ-CON; Rapee, Craske, Brown, & Barlow, 1996), not to be confused with the Agoraphobia Cognitions Questionnaire, is a 30-item self-report instrument that assesses perceived ability to control external events and internal emotional responses. Brown, White, Forsyth, and Barlow (2004) found evidence of three factors (emotion control, stress control, and threat control) and from their item analysis, developed a revised version (known as the ACQ-R) comprised of only 15 of the original 30 items.

ACQ-CON total score norms and ACQ-R subscale norms exist for anxious and nonclinical samples (Brown et al., 2004; Rapee et al., 1996). The internal consistency of the ACQ-CON is generally good (ranging from .81 to .89), though some data on the subscales were in the less than adequate to adequate range (.65 to .74; see Ballash et al., 2006; Brown et al., 2004; Craske, Farchione, et al., 2007; Lang & McNiel, 2006;

TABLE 11.3 Ratings of Instruments Used for Treatment Monitoring and Treatment Outcome Evaluation

Instrument	Norms	Internal Consistency	Inter-Rater Reliability	Test–Retest Reliability	Content Validity	Construct Validity	Validity Generalization	Treatment Sensitivity	Clinical Utility	Highly Recommended
ADIS	NA	NA	G	A[a]	A	A	G	G	A	
SCID	NA	NA	G	A[a]	A	A	E	A	A	
PDSS	A	G	G	A[a]	A	A	G	E	A	
ACQ-CON	G	G	NA	A	A	E	G	A	A	
ASI	G	G	NA	A	A	E	E	E	A	
BSQ	G	G	NA	G	A	G	G	G	A	✓
ACQ	G	G	NA	A	A	G	G	G	A	✓
FQ	G	A	NA	G	A	G	E	E	A	✓
MI	G	E	NA	A	A	A	G	G	A	✓
APPQ	A	G	NA	A	A	A	A	A	A	

[a] Different raters.

Note: ADIS = Anxiety Disorders Interview Schedule; SCID = Structured Clinical Interview for the DSM; PDSS = Panic Disorder Severity Scale; ACQ-CON = Anxiety Control Questionnaire; ASI = Anxiety Sensitivity Index; BSQ = Body Sensations Questionnaire; ACQ = Agoraphobic Cognitions Questionnaire; FQ = Fear Questionnaire; MI = Mobility Inventory for Agoraphobia; APPQ = Albany Panic and Phobia Questionnaire; A = Adequate; G = Good; E = Excellent; NA = Not Applicable.

Rapee et al., 1996; & Zebb & Moore, 1999 to review the various findings). Adequate ACQ-CON test–retest reliability data exist based on 1-week to 1-month periods of time (r ranging from .82 to .88; Rapee et al., 1996).

Although ACQ-CON data from an anxious sample were used in a factor analysis (Rapee et al., 1996), there is no information to suggest that this sample evaluated the items or the measure's instructions, and thus content validity is only adequate. There is evidence of the ACQ-CON's construct validity (Lang & McNiel, 2006; Rapee et al., 1996), including data to support its incremental validity in predicting interpretation biases associated with ambiguous internal and external phenomena (Zvolensky et al., 2001), prediction of a latent factor of anxious arousal (Brown et al., 2004), and its relatedness to trait anxiety (Kashdan, Barrios, Forsyth, & Steger, 2006). Moreover, the threat control factor has been found to be a moderator of the relationship between anxiety sensitivity and agoraphobia (White, Brown, Somers, & Barlow, 2006) and a mediator of the relationship between some aspects of family functioning and anxiety in a nonclinical sample (Ballash et al., 2006). Thus, the construct validity of the ACQ-CON was judged to be excellent.

The ACQ-CON (or ACQ-R) has been used with various samples, including outpatient clinical samples (e.g., White et al., 2006), inpatient clinical samples (Lang & McNiel, 2006), and nonclinical samples (e.g., Kashdan et al., 2006). As a result of its use in more than one setting and with different samples, this measure was given a rating of good validity generalization. Further research is warranted on the use of the ACQ-CON with people from different language backgrounds, as well as in nonoutpatient settings.

ACQ-CON scores (Rapee et al., 1996) have been sensitive to change after CBT for PDA, and able to predict the severity of comorbid diagnoses at follow-up assessment of CBT for PDA (Craske, Farchione, et al., 2007). However, treatment sensitivity was judged to be adequate, rather than good, due to the present lack of research by authors unconnected with the development of the instrument.

Body Sensations Questionnaire

BSQ scores are sensitive to change following short term, intensive exposure treatment for agoraphobia (Chambless et al., 1984), group CBT plus exercise treatment for PDA (Cromarty, Robinson, Callcott, &

Freeston, 2004), and individual CBT for PDA (Carlbring et al., 2005). Thus, the BSQ is judged to have good treatment sensitivity, although not excellent because all of the supporting data were from behavioral or CBT treatments.

Agoraphobic Cognitions Questionnaire

ACQ scores are sensitive to change following short-term, intensive exposure treatment for agoraphobia (Chambless et al., 1984), group CBT plus exercise treatment for PDA (Cromarty et al., 2004), and individual CBT for PDA (Carlbring et al., 2005). Thus, the ACQ is rated as having good treatment sensitivity.

Fear Questionnaire

The FQ has been used as a treatment outcome measure in 41 studies, and a meta-analysis of 56 treatment groups revealed a mean effect size of $d = 1.93$ (Ogles, Lambert, Weight, & Payne, 1990). Thus, the FQ is rated as exhibiting excellent treatment sensitivity.

Mobility Inventory

MI scores change following exposure therapy (Chambless et al., 1985; Ehlers, 1995) and individual CBT for PDA (e.g., Carlbring et al., 2005). Thus, the MI is rated as having good treatment sensitivity.

Albany Panic and Phobia Questionnaire

Rapee et al. (1994/1995) provided some evidence of this measure's treatment sensitivity following a course of CBT, but in the absence of other outcome data, its sensitivity to change following treatment is rated as adequate.

Self-Efficacy to Control a Panic Attack Questionnaire

In anxiety-provoking situations, 15% of the reported thoughts from a sample with agoraphobia were about self-efficacy (Williams et al., 1997). Moreover, research suggests that these judgments help to predict behaviors that are often the target of treatment (e.g., Kinney & Williams, 1988) and mediate the effects of treatment for PDA upon approach behaviors (Williams, Kinney, et al., 1989) and panic severity (Casey, Newcombe, & Oei,

2005). One self-report measure of self-efficacy that is directly relevant to PD is the Self-Efficacy to Control a Panic Attack Questionnaire (SE-CPAQ; Gauthier, Bouchard, Cote, Laberge, & French, 1993). This measure is well suited to be administered along with other measures discussed in this chapter. It is a 25-item measure, consisting of the Self-Efficacy-Cognitions (6 items), Self-Efficacy-Mobility (10 items), and Self-Efficacy-Symptoms (9 items) subscales. Each item is assigned a rating indicative of the respondent's confidence in controlling panic attacks in a given situation (i.e., when experiencing a particular thought in a particular location, or having a particular physiological sensation). The thoughts, locations, and sensations used in the SE-CPAQ were adapted from the ACQ (Chambless et al., 1984), MI (Chambless et al., 1985), and the BSQ (Chambless et al., 1984). There is some evidence of its validity (Gauthier et al., 1993) and sensitivity to treatment-related changes (Bouchard et al., 1996). This is a promising measure, but there is only limited research, at this point, on its psychometric properties.

Self-Monitoring

Ongoing self-monitoring is yet another modality of assessment, albeit one that overlaps with other verbal report measures (i.e., diagnostic instruments and self-report questionnaires). To self-monitor panic attacks, patients typically are given portable paper forms or hand-held computers to record every occurrence of panic (i.e., frequency recording) in terms of time of onset and offset, intensity, symptoms, and location, among other things (e.g., Barlow, Craske, Cerny, & Klosko, 1989; Taylor, Fried, & Kenardy, 1990). Most commonly, self-monitoring continues over consecutive days for 1 to 2 weeks, especially when used to evaluate pre- to posttreatment changes (e.g., Craske et al., 1997). Providing detailed instructions to patients can enhance the consistency and accuracy of data collection. This includes training in the use of rating scales and providing definitions of what constitutes a panic attack (although patients' self-perceptions of panic may be important in their own right; Basoglu, Marks, & Sengün, 1992).

Self-monitoring of agoraphobic avoidance entails monitoring excursions from home, recording the time of beginning and end, whether alone or accompanied, maximum anxiety, destination or purpose, escape behavior, distance traveled, and so on (e.g., Murphy, Michelson, Marchione, Marchione, & Testa, 1998).

This format of self-monitoring may be cumbersome for the mildly agoraphobic person who is relatively mobile. General anxiety and accompanying moods also can be self-monitored (Barlow et al., 1989; Hiebert & Fox, 1981). Hand-held computers offer a particular advantage in that mechanized prompts to enter data at specific points in time may preclude the delay in self-monitoring that probably occurs otherwise. Taylor et al. (1990) used a hand-held computer to collect hourly data (e.g., level of anxiety, sense of control and threat, and likelihood of panic) from patients with PDA.

Self-monitoring strategies represent a quantification of experience at the time of its occurrence (whether it be tied to a specific event, or to a moment in time), whereas self-reported estimates of frequency, duration, or content represent judgments of experience that is retrospective and generalized in nature. Some investigators have attempted to assess the level of agreement between self-monitored and self-estimated data by having the same individuals provide retrospective estimates of panic attacks, and then self-monitor for an interval of time that is equivalent to the interval that was estimated. Using this approach, patients with PDA were found to have endorsed fewer panic symptoms during self-monitoring in comparison to previously collected estimates (Basoglu et al., 1992; Margraf et al., 1987). Similarly, retrospective estimates of the frequency of panic attacks and symptoms collected during diagnostic interviewing have been found to be substantially higher than frequency obtained with self-monitored data (e.g., de Beurs, Lange, & van Dyck, 1992).

There is evidence that anxiety (Hiebert & Fox, 1981) and panic (de Jong & Bouman, 1995) decrease with self-monitoring. Nevertheless, reactivity effects generally are short-lived and subside when self-monitoring discontinues, perhaps because the self-monitoring device becomes a discriminative stimulus controlling the occurrence of the target behavior (Borkovec et al., 1977). Though there are potential problems associated with the self-monitoring methodology, it acts as a very effective means of assessing PDA and is sensitive to change over the course of CBT (e.g., Barlow et al., 1989).

Behavioral Approach Tests

Ogles, Lambert, Weight, and Payne (1990) calculated effect sizes pertaining to BATs from their meta-analysis of 21 treatment studies for agoraphobia. The behavioral score (i.e., duration or amount completed) yielded a mean BAT effect size of $d = 1.15$. The heart rate score during BATs yielded an average effect size of $d = .44$, and the SUDS score yielded a mean effect size of $d = 1.36$. Other individual studies similarly reported large treatment effect sizes from individualized BATs (e.g., Steketee, Chambless, & Tran, 2001). In addition, some individual studies have shown significant reductions in subjective anxiety in response to interoceptive exposures such as hyperventilation (e.g., Craske, Farchione, et al., 2007).

Overall Evaluation

An accurate diagnosis and case conceptualization is only the first step to conducting a thorough assessment as it relates to the treatment of PDA. The measures reviewed in this section gauge the level of symptomatic improvement and shifts in variables considered critical to therapeutic success, such as cognition, self-efficacy and perceived control. Because behaviors and thoughts may arise during fear and anxiety that differ from self-reported estimates, observation and recording of ongoing experience captures another aspect of PDA that is important for measuring treatment change.

CONCLUSIONS AND FUTURE DIRECTIONS

From this review, it should be evident that there are a variety of measures and assessment methodologies to help guide clinicians or researchers in their work with individuals with PDA. Throughout this chapter, we have emphasized the importance of measuring subjective, physiological, and behavioral aspects of this disorder, preferably with multiple methodologies of assessment, including diagnostic interviews, standardized self-report questionnaires, self-monitoring, behavioral observations, and physiological data.

Neither diagnostic interview reviewed in this chapter met the criteria for being highly recommended for several reasons. First, the differentiation between PD with and without agoraphobia is not highly reliable, possibly due to problems inherent in the diagnostic descriptions of DSM (see Brown, Di Nardo, et al., 2001; Di Nardo et al., 1993). Second,

attempts to assess the validity of these interviews cannot be separated from attempts at validating the diagnostic system itself (Grisham et al., 2004), and "a gold standard for psychiatric diagnoses remains illusive" (First & Gibbon, 2004, p. 139). One option suggested by Spitzer (1983) is a method called "LEAD," which involves experts assigning a diagnosis based on a collection of all possible longitudinal data that exist about an individual. Clearly, more research of this nature is needed. Third, since the SCID is rarely used as an index of treatment outcome, data regarding its sensitivity to change as a result of treatment are lacking.

Though diagnostic interviews are generally more time consuming than standard clinical interviews, an assessment that allows for differential diagnosis (such as the ADIS or the SCID) is very important for the diagnosis of PDA. Time and money wasted on an inaccurate diagnosis and inappropriate treatment will be significantly greater than the additional time required to conduct a thorough diagnostic assessment using a standardized instrument. Each interview has its own strengths and weaknesses, and selection can be based on purpose. For purposes of validity generalization, diagnoses being made in atypical settings or with samples with varied ethnicities, the SCID instrument is preferred. When the purpose is to obtain detailed information for treatment planning, the ADIS is preferred.

Of the self-report measures reviewed, four are highly recommended for the assessment of PDA because they were assigned mostly good or excellent ratings: the ASI, BSQ, ACQ, and FQ. Although the remaining measures were not listed as highly recommended, further research could provide additional information and lead to improvements in their psychometric properties.

Self-monitoring and behavioral observational methods, with accompanying measures of physiology and cognition in the moment, cannot easily be reviewed in accordance with the psychometric properties listed for the diagnostic instruments and self-report scales. Nevertheless, given their value in treatment monitoring and treatment outcome, we do judge these methods to be critical to the assessment of PDA.

Directions for future research obviously include more research on those measures that were not rated as highly recommended, especially with respect to adding to or improving their test–retest reliability and evidence of construct validity. Second, although many measures are available in multiple languages, more research is needed on the usefulness of these measures with different populations. Third, because measures may operate differently in different settings (e.g., outpatient vs. inpatient vs. community centers), it is critical that researchers (especially instrument developers) expand the number and variety of settings in which the measures are evaluated. Fourth, many treatment studies (especially pharmacological studies) use diagnostic interviews only in the pretreatment phase. In order to gather additional data on treatment sensitivity, diagnostic assessments are needed both prior to and following a course of treatment. Fifth, given the glaring lack of research on the clinical utility of the measures reviewed in this chapter, more time and energy should be devoted to this area of assessment research.

It is our hope that this chapter will help clinicians choose measures and assessment methodologies that are scientifically sound and that address the various components of PDA (i.e., cognitions, emotional reactions, physiological symptoms, and behavioral avoidance) and how to use PDA assessment data in their treatment planning.

References

American Psychiatric Association (2000). *Diagnostic and statistical manual of mental disorders* (4th ed., Text Revision). Washington, DC: Author.

Amering, M., Katschnig, H., Berger, P., Windhaber, J., Baischer, W., & Dantendorfer, K. (1997). Embarrassment about the first panic attack predicts agoraphobia in disorder patients. *Behaviour Research and Therapy, 35*, 517–521.

Antony, M. M. (2001). Measures for panic disorder and agoraphobia. In M. M. Antony, S. M. Orsillo, & L. Roemer (Eds.), *Practitioner's guide to empirically based measures of anxiety* (pp. 95–125). New York: Kluwer Academic/Plenum Publishers.

Arrindell, W. A. (1993a). The fear of fear concept: Stability, retest artefact and predictive power. *Behaviour Research and Therapy, 31*, 139–148.

Arrindell, W. A. (1993b). The fear of fear concept: Evidence in favor of multidimensionality. *Behaviour Research and Therapy, 31*, 507–518.

Ballash, N. G., Pemble, M. K., Usui, W. M., Buckley, A. F., & Woodruff-Borden, J. (2006). Family functioning, perceived control, and anxiety: A mediational model. *Journal of Anxiety Disorders, 20*, 486–497.

Bankier, B., Januzzi, J. L., & Littman, A. B. (2004). The high prevalence of multiple psychiatric disorders in stable outpatients with coronary heart disease. *Psychosomatic Medicine, 66*, 645–650.

Barlow, D. H. (1988). *Anxiety and its disorders: The nature and treatment of anxiety and panic.* New York: Guilford Press.

Barlow, D. H., & Craske, M. G. (2006). *Mastery of your anxiety and panic: Patient workbook* (4th ed.). New York: Oxford University Press.

Barlow, D. H., Craske, M. G., Cerny, J. A., & Klosko, J. S. (1989). Behavioral treatment of panic disorder. *Behavior Therapy, 20*, 261–282.

Barlow, D. H., Gorman, J. M., Shear, M. K., & Woods, S. W. (2000). Cognitive-behavioral therapy, imipramine, or their combination for panic disorder: A randomized controlled trial. *Journal of the American Medical Association, 283*, 2529–2536.

Barlow, D. H., Vermilyea, J., Blanchard, E. B., Vermilyea, B., Di Nardo, P. A., & Cerny, J. A. (1985). The phenomenon of panic. *Journal of Abnormal Psychology, 94*, 320–328.

Basco, M. R., Bostic, J. Q., Davies, D., Rush, A. J., Witte, B., Hendrickse, W., et al. (2000). Methods to improve diagnostic accuracy in a community mental health setting. *American Journal of Psychiatry, 157*, 1599–1605.

Basoglu, M., Marks, I. M., & Sengün, S. (1992). A prospective study of panic and anxiety in agoraphobia with panic disorder. *British Journal of Psychiatry, 160*, 57–64.

Bibb, J. L. (1988). *Parental bonding, pathological development, and fear of losing control among agoraphobics and normals.* Unpublished doctoral dissertation, American University, Washington, DC.

Blais, M. A., Otto, M. W., Zucker, B. G., McNally, R. J., Schmidt, N. B., Fava, M., et al. (2001). The anxiety sensitivity index: Item analysis and suggestions for refinement. *Journal of Personality Assessment, 77*, 272–294.

Block, R. I., Ghoneim, M. M., Fowles, D. C., Kumar, V., & Pathak, D. (1987). Effects of a subanesthetic concentration of nitrous oxide on establishment, elicitation, and semantic and phonemic generalization of classically conditioned skin conductance responses. *Pharmacology, Biochemistry & Behavior, 28*, 7–14.

Borkovec, T., Weerts, T., & Bernstein, D. (1977). Assessment of anxiety. In A. Ciminero, K. Calhoun, & H. Adams (Eds.), *Handbook of behavioral assessment* (pp. 367–428). New York: John Wiley & Sons.

Bouchard, S., Gauthier, J., Laberge, B., French, D., Pelletier, M., & Godbout, D. (1996). Exposure versus cognitive restructuring in the treatment of panic disorder with agoraphobia. *Behaviour Research and Therapy, 34,* 213–224.

Bouton, M. E., Mineka, S., & Barlow, D. H. (2001). A modern learning-theory perspective on the etiology of panic disorder. *Psychological Review, 108,* 4–32.

Bouvard, M., Cottraux, J., Talbot, F., Mollard, E., Duhem, S., Yao, S., et al. (1998). Validation of the French translation of the agoraphobic cognitions questionnaire. *Psychotherapy and Psychosomatics, 67,* 249–253.

Boyd, J. H. (1986). Use of mental health services for the treatment of panic disorder. *American Journal of Psychiatry, 143,* 1569–1574.

Brown, T. A., Campbell, L. A., Lehman, C. L., Grisham, J. R., & Mancill, R. B. (2001). Current and lifetime comorbidity of the DSM-IV anxiety and mood disorders in a large clinical sample. *Journal of Abnormal Psychology, 110,* 585–599.

Brown, T. A., Chorpita, B. F., & Barlow, D. H. (1998). Structural relationships among dimensions of the DSM-IV anxiety and mood disorders and dimensions of negative affect, positive affect, and autonomic arousal. *Journal of Abnormal Psychology, 107,* 179–192.

Brown, T. A., & Deagle, E. A. (1992). Structured interview assessment of nonclinical panic. *Behavior Therapy, 23,* 75–85.

Brown, T. A., Di Nardo, P. A., & Barlow, D. H. (1994). *Anxiety Disorders Interview Schedule for DSM-IV (ADIS-IV).* San Antonio, TX: Psychological Corporation.

Brown, T. A., Di Nardo, P. A., Lehman, C. L., & Campbell, L. A. (2001). Reliability of DSM-IV anxiety and mood disorders: Implications for the classification of emotional disorders. *Journal of Abnormal Psychology, 110,* 49–58.

Brown, T. A., White, K. S., & Barlow, D. H. (2005). A psychometric reanalysis of the Albany Panic and Phobia Questionnaire. *Behaviour Research and Therapy, 43,* 337–355.

Brown, T. A., White, K. S., Forsyth, J. P., & Barlow, D. H. (2004). The structure of perceived emotional control: Psychometric properties of a revised anxiety control questionnaire. *Behavior Therapy, 35,* 75–99.

Buglass, P., Clarke, J., Henderson, A., & Presley, A. (1977). A study of agoraphobic housewives. *Psychological Medicine, 7,* 73–86.

Bystritsky, A., Craske, M., Maidenberg, E., Vapnik, T., & Shapiro, D. (1995). Ambulatory monitoring of panic patients during regular activity: A preliminary report. *Biological Psychiatry, 38,* 684–689.

Calvo, M. G., & Eysenck, M. W. (1998). Cognitive bias to internal sources of information in anxiety. *International Journal of Psychology, 33,* 287–299.

Carlbring, P., Brunt, S., Bohman, S., Austin, D., Richards, J., Öst, L-G., et al. (2007). Internet vs. paper and pencil administration of questionnaires commonly used in panic/agoraphobia research. *Computers in Human Behavior, 23,* 1421–1434.

Carlbring, P., Nilsson-Ihrfelt, E., Waara, J., Kollenstam, C., Buhrman, M., Kaldo, V. et al. (2005). Treatment of panic disorder: Live therapy vs. self-help via the internet. *Behaviour Research and Therapy, 43,* 1321–1333.

Carter, M. M., Miller, O. J., Sbrocco, T., Suchday, S., & Lewis, E. L. (1999). Factor structure of the anxiety sensitivity index among African American college students. *Psychological Assessment, 11,* 525–533.

Carter, M. M., Sbrocco, T., Gore, K. L., Marin, N. W., & Lewis, E. L. (2003). Cognitive-behavioral group therapy versus a wait-list control in the treatment of African American women with panic disorder. *Cognitive Therapy and Research, 27,* 505–518.

Casey, L. M., Newcombe, P. A., & Oei, T. P. S. (2005). Cognitive mediation of panic severity: The role of catastrophic misinterpretation of bodily sensations and panic self-efficacy. *Cognitive Therapy and Research, 29,* 187–200.

Chambless, D. L., Beck, A. T., Gracely, E. J., & Grisham, J. R. (2000). Relationship of cognitions to fear of somatic symptoms: A test of the cognitive theory of panic. *Depression and Anxiety, 11,* 1–9.

Chambless, D. L., Caputo, G. C., Bright, P., & Gallagher, R. (1984). Assessment of fear of fear in agoraphobics: The body sensations questionnaire and the agoraphobic cognitions questionnaire. *Journal of Consulting and Clinical Psychology, 52,* 1090–1097.

Chambless, D. L., Caputo, G. C., Jasin, S. E., Gracely, E. J., & Williams, C. (1985). The mobility inventory for agoraphobia. *Behaviour Research and Therapy, 23,* 35–44.

Chambless, D. L., & Gracely, E. J. (1989). Fear of fear and the anxiety disorders. *Cognitive Therapy and Research, 13,* 9–20.

Chambless, D. L., & Renneberg, B. (1988, September). *Personality disorders of agoraphobics.* Paper presented at World Congress of Behavior Therapy, Edinburgh, Scotland.

Clark, D. M. (1986). A cognitive approach to panic. *Behaviour Research and Therapy, 24,* 461–470.

Clark, D. M., & Ehlers, A. (1993). An overview of the cognitive theory and treatment of panic disorder. *Applied & Preventive Psychology, 2,* 131–139.

Clark, D. M., Salkovskis, P., Gelder, M., Koehler, C., Martin, M., Anastasiades, P., et al. (1988). Tests of a cognitive theory of panic. In I. Hand & H. Wittchen (Eds.), *Panic and phobias II* (pp. 149–158). Berlin: Springer-Verlag.

Clark, D. M., Salkovskis, P. M., Hackmann, A., Middleton, H., Anastasiades, P., & Gelder, M. (1994). A comparison of cognitive therapy, applied relaxation and imipramine in the treatment of panic disorder. *British Journal of Psychiatry, 164,* 759–769.

Cox, B. J., Swinson, R. P., Parker, J. D., & Kuch, K. (1993). Confirmatory factor analysis of the fear questionnaire in panic disorder with agoraphobia. *Psychological Assessment, 5,* 235–237.

Cox, B. J., Swinson, R. P., & Shaw, B. F. (1991). Value of the Fear Questionnaire in differentiating agoraphobia and social phobia. *British Journal of Psychiatry, 159,* 842–845.

Craske, M. G., & Barlow, D. H. (1988). A review of the relationship between panic and avoidance. *Clinical Psychology Review, 8,* 667–685.

Craske, M. G., & Barlow, D. H. (2007). Panic disorder and agoraphobia. In D. H. Barlow (Ed.), *Clinical handbook of psychological disorders* (4th ed.). New York: Guilford Press.

Craske, M. G., Farchione, T., Allen, L., Barrios, V., Stoyanova, M., & Rose, D. (2007). Cognitive behavioral therapy for panic disorder and comorbidity: More of the same or less of more. *Behaviour Research and Therapy, 45,* 1095–1109.

Craske, M. G., Glover, D., & DeCola, J. (1995). Predicted versus unpredicted panic attacks: Acute versus general distress. *Journal of Abnormal Psychology, 104,* 214–223.

Craske, M. G., Golinelli, D., Stein, M. B., Roy-Byrne, P., Bystritsky, A., & Sherbourne, C. (2005). Does the addition of cognitive behavioral therapy improve panic disorder treatment outcome relative to medication alone in the primary care setting? *Psychological Medicine, 35,* 1645–1654.

Craske, M. G., Lang, A. J., Aikins, D., & Mystkowski, J. (2005). Cognitive behavioral therapy for nocturnal panic. *Behavior Therapy, 36,* 43–54.

Craske, M. G., Lang, A. J., Rowe, M., DeCola, J. P., Simmons, J., Mann, C., et al. (2002). Presleep attributions about arousal during sleep: Nocturnal panic. *Journal of Abnormal Psychology, 111,* 53–62.

Craske, M. G., Miller, P. P., Rotunda, R., & Barlow, D. H. (1990). A descriptive report of features of initial unexpected panic attacks in minimal and extensive avoiders. *Behaviour Research and Therapy, 28,* 395–400.

Craske, M. G., Poulton, R., Tsao, J. C. I., & Plotkin, D. (2001). Paths to panic-agoraphobia: An expolatory analysis from age 3 to 21 in an unselected birth cohort. *American Journal of Child and Adolescent Psychiatry, 40,* 556–563.

Craske, M. G., Rachman, S. J., & Tallman, K. (1986). Mobility, cognitions, and panic. *Journal of Psychopathology and Behavioral Assessment, 8,* 199–210.

Craske, M. G., Rapee, R. M., & Barlow, D. H. (1988). The significance of panic-expectancy for individual patterns of avoidance. *Behavior Therapy, 19,* 577–592.

Craske, M. G., Rowe, M., Lewin, M., & Noriega-Dimitri, R. (1997). Interoceptive exposure versus breathing retraining within cognitive-behavioural therapy for panic disorder with agoraphobia. *British Journal of Clinical Psychology, 36,* 85–99.

Craske, M. G., & Tsao, J. C. I. (2005). Assessment and treatment of nocturnal panic attacks. *Sleep Medicine Reviews, 9,* 173–184.

Cromarty, P., Robinson, G., Callcott, P., & Freeston, M. (2004). Cognitive therapy and exercise for panic and agoraphobia in primary care: Pilot study and service development. *Behavioural and Cognitive Psychotherapy, 32,* 371–374.

Dammen, T., Arnesen, H., Ekeberg, Ø., Husebye, T., & Friis, S. (1999). Panic disorder in chest pain patients referred to cardiological outpatient investigation. *Journal of Internal Medicine, 245,* 497–507.

de Beurs, E., Lange, A., & van Dyck, R. (1992). Self-monitoring of panic attacks and retrospective estimates of panic: Discordant findings. *Behaviour Research and Therapy, 30,* 411–413.

de Jong, G. M., & Bouman, T. K. (1995). Panic disorder: A baseline period. Predictability of agoraphobic avoidance behavior. *Journal of Anxiety Disorders, 9,* 185–199.

Di Nardo, P. A., & Barlow, D. H. (1988). *Anxiety Disorders Interview Schedule-Revised (ADIS-R).* Albany, NY: Phobia and Anxiety Disorders Clinic, State University of New York.

Di Nardo, P. A., Brown, T. A., & Barlow, D. H. (1994). *Anxiety Disorders Interview Schedule for DSM-IV: Lifetime version (ADIS-IV-L).* San Antonio, TX: Psychological Corporation.

Di Nardo, P. A., Moras, K., Barlow, D. H., & Rapee, R. M. (1993). Reliability of DSM-III-R anxiety disorder categories: Using the Anxiety Disorders Interview Schedule-Revised (ADIS-R). *Archives of General Psychiatry, 50,* 251–256.

Di Nardo, P. A., O'Brien, G. T., Barlow, D. H., Waddell, M. T., & Blanchard, E. B. (1983). Reliability of the DSM-III anxiety disorder categories using a new structured interview. *Archives of General Psychiatry*, *40*, 1070–1074.

Ehlers, A. (1995). A 1-year prospective study of panic attacks: Clinical course and factors associated with maintenance. *Journal of Abnormal Psychology*, *104*, 164–172.

Eley, T. C. (2001). Contributions of behavioral genetics research: Quantifying genetic, shared environmental, and nonshared environmental influences. In M. W. Vasey & M. R. Dadds (Eds.), *The developmental psychopathology of anxiety* (pp. 45–59). New York: Oxford University Press.

Eysenck, H. J. (1967). *The biological basis of personality*. Springfield, IL: C. C. Thomas.

First, M. B., & Gibbon, M. (2004). The Structured Clinical Interview for DSM-IV Axis I Disorders (SCID-I) and the Structured Clinical Interview for DSM-IV Axis II disorders (SCID-II). In M. J. Hilsenroth & D. L. Segal (Eds.), *Comprehensive handbook of psychological assessment, Vol. 2: Personality assessment* (pp. 134–143). Hoboken, NJ: John Wiley & Sons, Inc.

First, M. B., Spitzer, R. L., Gibbon, M., & Williams, J. B. W. (1994). *Structured clinical interview for axis 1 DSM-IV disorders*. New York: Biometric Research Department, New York State Psychiatric Institute.

First, M. B., Spitzer, R. L., Gibbon, M., & Williams, J. B. W. (1996). *Structured Clinical Interview for DSM-IV Axis I Disorders, Clinician Version (SCID-CV)*. Washington, DC: American Psychiatric Press, Inc.

First, M. B., Spitzer, R. L., Gibbon, M., & Williams, J. B. W. (2002a). *Structured Clinical Interview for DSM-IV-TR Axis I Disorders, Research Version, Patient Edition (SCID-I/P)*. New York: Biometrics Research, New York State Psychiatric Institute.

First, M. B., Spitzer, R. L., Gibbon, M., & Williams, J. B. W. (2002b). *Structured Clinical Interview for DSM-IV-TR Axis I Disorders, Research Version, Non-patient Edition (SCID-I/NP)*. New York: Biometrics Research, New York State Psychiatric Institute.

First, M. B., Spitzer, R. L., Gibbon, M., & Williams, J. B. W. (2002c). *Structured Clinical Interview for DSM-IV-TR Axis I Disorders, Research Version, Patient Edition With Psychotic Screen (SCID-I/P W/ PSY SCREEN)*. New York: Biometrics Research, New York State Psychiatric Institute.

Gauthier, J., Bouchard, S., Côté, G., Laberge, B., & French, D. (1993). Development of two scales measuring self-efficacy to control panic attacks. *Canadian Psychology*, *30*, 305.

Gillis, M. M., Haaga, D. A. F., & Ford, G. T. (1995). Normative values for the Beck Anxiety Inventory, Fear Questionnaire, Penn State Worry Questionnaire, and Social Phobia and Anxiety Inventory. *Psychological Assessment*, *7*, 450–455.

Goldsmith, H. H. (1994). Parsing the emotional domain from a developmental perspective. In P. Ekman & R. J. Davidson (Eds.), *The nature of emotion: Fundamental questions* (pp. 68–73). New York: Oxford University Press.

Goodwin, R. D., Fergusson, D. M., & Horwood, L. J. (2005). Childhood abuse and familial violence and the risk of panic attacks and panic disorder in young adulthood. *Psychological Medicine*, *35*, 881–890.

Grisham, J. R., Brown, T. A., & Campbell, L. A. (2004). The Anxiety Disorders Interview Schedule for DSM-IV (ADIS-IV). In M. J. Hilsenroth & D. L. Segal (Eds.), *Comprehensive handbook of psychological assessment, Vol. 2: Personality assessment* (pp. 163–177). Hoboken, NJ: John Wiley & Sons, Inc.

Hayward, C., Killen, J. D., Hammer, L. D., Litt, I. F., Wilson, D. M., Simmonds, B., et al. (1992) Pubertal stage and panic attack history in sixth- and seventh-grade girls. *American Journal of Psychiatry*, *149*, 1239–1243.

Hayward, C., Killen, J. D., Kraemer, H. C., & Taylor, C. B. (2000). Predictors of panic attacks in adolescents. *Journal of the American Academy of Child & Adolescent Psychiatry*, *39*, 1–8.

Hiebert, B., & Fox, E. E. (1981). Reactive effects of self-monitoring anxiety. *Journal of Counseling Psychology*, *28*, 187–193.

Hien, D., Matzner, F. J., First, M. B., Spitzer, R. L., Williams, J., & Gibbon, M. (1994). *Structured Clinical Interview for DSM-IV Childhood Diagnoses (KID-SCID)*. New York: Biometrics Research presentation.

Horwath, E., Lish, J. D., Johnson, J., Hornig, C. D., & Weissman, M. M. (1993). Agoraphobia without panic: Clinical reappraisal of an epidemiologic finding. *American Journal of Psychiatry*, *150*, 1496–1501.

Houck, P. R., Spiegel, D. A., Shear, M. K., Rucci, P., & Stat, D. (2002). Reliability of the self-report version of the panic disorder severity scale. *Depression and Anxiety*, *15*, 183–185.

Kashdan, T. B., Barrios, V., Forsyth, J. P., & Steger, M. F. (2006). Experiential avoidance as a generalized psychological vulnerability: Comparisons with coping and emotion regulation strategies. *Behaviour Research and Therapy*, *44*, 1301–1320.

Katschnig, H., & Amering, M. (1998). The long-term course of panic disorder and its predictors. *Journal of Clinical Psychopharmacology, 18*(6 Suppl. 2), 6S–11S.

Kendler, K. S., Heath, A. C., Martin, N. G., & Eaves, L. J. (1987). Symptoms of anxiety and symptoms of depression: Same genes, different environments? *Archives of General Psychiatry, 44,* 451–457.

Kessler, R. C., Berglund, P., Demler, O., Jin, R., Merikangas, K. R., & Walters, E. E. (2005). Lifetime prevalence and age-of-onset distributions of DSM-IV disorders in the National Comorbidity Survey Replication. *Archives of General Psychiatry, 62,* 593–602.

Kessler, R. C., Chiu, W. T., Demler, O., & Walters, E. E. (2005). Lifetime prevalence and age-of-onset distributions of DSM-IV disorders in the National Comorbidity Survey Replication. *Archives of General Psychiatry, 62,* 593–602.

Kessler, R. C., & Ustun, T. B. (2004). The World Mental Health (WMH) survey initiative version of the World Health Organization (WHO) Composite International Diagnostic Interview (CIDI). *International Journal of Methods in Psychiatric Research, 13,* 93–121.

Kikuchi, M., Komuro, R., Hiroshi, O., Kidani, T., Hanaoka, A., & Koshino, Y. (2005). Panic disorder with and without agoraphobia: Comorbidity within a half-year of the onset of panic disorder. *Psychiatry and Clinical Neurosciences, 58,* 639–643.

Kinney, P. J., & Williams, S. L. (1988). Accuracy of fear inventories and self-efficacy scales in predicting agoraphobic behavior. *Behaviour Research and Therapy, 26,* 513–518.

Kotov, R., Schmidt, N. B., Zvolensky, M. J., Vinogradov, A., & Antipova, A. V. (2005). Adaptation of panic-related psychopathology measures to Russian. *Psychological Assessment, 17,* 242–246.

Kroeze, S., & van den Hout, M. A. (2000). Selective attention for cardiac information in panic patients. *Behaviour Research and Therapy, 38,* 63–72.

Lang, A. J., & McNiel, D. E. (2006). Use of the anxiety control questionnaire in psychiatric inpatients. *Depression and Anxiety, 23,* 107–112.

Lee, H. B., & Oei, T. P. S. (1994). Factor structure and reliability of the fear questionnaire in a Hong Kong Chinese population. *Journal of Psychopathology and Behavioral Assessment, 16,* 189–199.

Löwe, B., Gräfe, K., Zipfel, S., Spitzer, R. L., Herrmann-Lingen, C., Witte, S., et al. (2003). Detecting panic disorder in medical and psychosomatic outpatients: Comparative validation of the hospital anxiety and depression scale, the patient health questionnaire, a screening question, and

physicians' diagnosis. *Journal of Psychosomatic Research, 55,* 515–519.

Maidenberg, E., Chen, E., Craske, M., Bohn, P., & Bystritsky, A. (1996). Specificity of attentional bias in panic disorder and social phobia. *Journal of Anxiety Disorders, 10,* 529–541.

Maier, S. F., Laudenslager, M. L., & Ryan, S. M. (1985). Stressor controllability, immune function and endogenous opiates. In F. R. Brush & J. B. Overmeier (Eds.), *Affect, conditioning and cognition: Essays on the determinants of behavior* (pp. 183–201). Hillsdale, NJ: Lawrence Erlbaum.

Margraf, J., & Schneider, S. (1991, November). *Outcome and active ingredients of cognitive-behavioural treatments for panic disorder.* Paper presented at the 25th Annual Meeting of the Association for the Advancement of Behavior Therapy, New York.

Margraf, J., Taylor, C. B., Ehlers, A., & Roth, W. T. (1987). Panic attacks in the natural environment. *Journal of Nervous and Mental Disease, 175,* 558–565.

Marks, I. M., & Mathews, A. M. (1979). Brief standard self-rating for phobic patients. *Behaviour Research and Therapy, 17,* 263–267.

Martin, N. G., Jardine, R., Andrews, G., & Heath, A. C. (1988). Anxiety disorders and neuroticism: Are there genetic factors specific to panic? *Acta Psychiatrica Scandinavica, 77,* 698–706.

Mavissakalian, M., & Michelson, L. (1982). Patterns of psychophysiological change in the treatment of agoraphobia. *Behaviour Research and Therapy, 20,* 347–356.

Meng, C. T. T., Kirkby, K. C., Martin, F., Gilroy, L. J., & Daniels, B. A. (2004). Computer-delivered behavioural avoidance tests for spider phobia. *Behaviour Change, 21,* 173–185.

Michelson, L., & Mavissakalian, M. (1983). Temporal stability of self-report measures in agoraphobia research. *Behaviour Research and Therapy, 21,* 695–698.

Monkul, E. S., Tural, Ü., Onur, E., Fidaner, H., Alkin, T., & Shear M. K. (2004). Panic disorder severity scale: Reliability and validity of the Turkish version. *Depression and Anxiety, 20,* 8–16.

Murphy, M. T., Michelson, L. K., Marchione, K., Marchione, N., & Testa, S. (1998). The role of self-directed in vivo exposure in combination with cognitive therapy, relaxation training, or therapist-assisted exposure in the treatment of panic disorder with agoraphobia. *Behaviour Research and Therapy, 12,* 117–138.

Norton, G. R., Cox, B. J., & Malan, J. (1992). Nonclinical panickers: A critical review. *Clinical Psychology Review, 12,* 121–139.

Novy, D. M., Stanley, M. A., Averill, P., & Daza, P. (2001). Psychometric comparability of English- and Spanish language measures of anxiety and related affective symptoms. *Psychological Assessment, 13,* 347–355.

Noyes, R., Crowe, R. R., Harris, E. L., Hamra, B. J., McChesney, C. M., & Chaudhry, D. R. (1986). Relationship between panic disorder and agoraphobia: A family study. *Archives of General Psychiatry, 43,* 227–232.

Oei, T. P., Moylan, A., & Evans, L. (1991). Validity and clinical utility of the fear questionnaire for anxiety-disorder patients. *Psychological Assessment, 3,* 391–397.

Ogles, B. M., Lambert, M. J., Weight, D. G., & Payne, I. R. (1990). Agoraphobia outcome measurement: A review and meta-analysis. *Psychological Assessment, 2,* 317–325.

Perna, G., Bertani, A., Arancio, C., Ronchi, P., & Bellodi, L. (1995). Laboratory response of patients with panic and obsessive–compulsive disorders to 35% CO2 challenges. *American Journal of Psychiatry, 152,* 85–89.

Peterson, R. A., & Reiss, S. (1993). *Anxiety sensitivity index revised text manual.* Worthington, OH: IDS Publishing Corporation.

Rapee, R. M., Brown, T. A., Antony, M. M., & Barlow, D. H. (1992). Response to hyperventilation and inhalation of 5.5% carbon dioxide-enriched air across the DSM-III-R anxiety disorders. *Journal of Abnormal Psychology, 101,* 538–552.

Rapee, R. M., Craske, M. G., & Barlow, D. H. (1994/1995). Assessment instrument for panic disorder that includes fear of sensation producing activities: The Albany panic and phobia questionnaire. *Anxiety, 1,* 114–122.

Rapee, R. M., Craske, M. G., Brown, T. A., & Barlow, D. H. (1996). Measurement of perceived control over anxiety-related events. *Behavior Therapy, 27,* 279–293.

Reiss, S. (1980). Pavlovian conditioning and human fear: An expectancy model. *Behavior Therapy, 11,* 380–396.

Reiss, S., Peterson, R. A., Gursky, D. M., & McNally, R. J. (1986). Anxiety sensitivity, anxiety frequency and the predictions of fearfulness. *Behaviour Research and Therapy, 24,* 1–8.

Rodriguez, B. F., Weisberg, R. B., Pagano, M. E., Machan, J. T., Culpepper, L., & Keller, M. B. (2004). Frequency and patterns of psychiatric comorbidity in a sample of primary care patients with anxiety disorders. *Comprehensive Psychiatry, 45,* 129–137.

Roemer, L. (2001). Measures for anxiety and related constructs. In M. M. Antony, S. M. Orsillo, & L. Roemer (Eds.), *Practitioner's guide to empirically based measures of anxiety* (pp. 49–83). New York: Kluwer Academic/Plenum Publishers.

Roy-Byrne, P. P., Craske, M. G., & Stein, M. B. (2006). Panic disorder. *The Lancet, 368,* 1023–1032.

Roy-Byrne, P. P., Stein, M. B., Russo, J., Mercier, E., Thomas, R., McQuaid, J., et al. (1999). Panic disorder in the primary care setting: Comorbidity, disability, service utilization, and treatment. *Journal of Clinical Psychiatry, 60,* 492–499.

Safren, S. A., Gershuny, B. S., Marzol, P., Otto, M. W., & Pollack, M. H. (2002). History of childhood abuse in panic disorder, social phobia, and generalized anxiety disorder. *Journal of Nervous and Mental Disease, 190,* 453–456.

Salkovskis, P. M. (1991). The importance of behaviour in the maintenance of anxiety and panic: A cognitive account. *Behavioural Psychotherapy, 19,* 6–19.

Schmidt, N. B., Lerew, D. R., & Jackson, R. J. (1999). Prospective evaluation of anxiety sensitivity in the pathogenesis of panic: Replication and extension. *Journal of Abnormal Psychology, 108,* 532–537.

Shear, M. K., Brown, T. A., Barlow, D. H., Money, R., Sholomskas, D. E., Woods, S. W., et al. (1997). Multicenter collaborative panic disorder severity scale. *American Journal of Psychiatry, 154,* 1571–1575.

Shear, M. K., Feske, U., Brown, C., Clark, D. B., Mammen, O., & Scotti, J. (2000). Anxiety disorders measures. In A. J. Rush, Jr., et al. (Task Force), *Handbook of psychiatric measures* (pp. 549–589). Washington, DC: American Psychiatric Association.

Shear, M. K., Polan, J. J., Harshfield, G., Pickering, T., Mann, J. H., Frances, A., et al. (1992). Ambulatory monitoring of blood pressure and heart rate in panic patients. *Journal of Anxiety Disorders, 6,* 213–221.

Shear, M. K., Rucci, P., Williams, J., Frank, E., Grochocinski, V., Vander Bilt, J., et al. (2001). Reliability and validity of the panic disorder severity scale: Replication and extension. *Journal of Psychiatric Research, 35,* 293–296.

Siddle, D. A., & Bond, N. W. (1988). Avoidance learning, Pavlovian conditioning, and the development of phobias. *Biological Psychology, 27,* 167–183.

Silverman, W. K., & Nelles, W. B. (1988). The anxiety disorders interview schedule for children. *Journal of the American Academy of Child & Adolescent Psychiatry, 27,* 772–778.

Simon, N. M., Otto, M. W., Smits, J. A. J., Nicolaou, D. C., Reese, H. E., & Pollack, M. H. (2004). Changes in anxiety sensitivity with pharmacotherapy for panic disorder. *Journal of Psychiatric Research, 38,* 491–495.

Skodol, A. E., & Bender, D. S. (2000). Diagnostic interviews for adults. In A. J. Rush, Jr., H. A. Pincus, M. B. First, D. Blacker, J. Endicott, & S. J. Keith, (Eds.), Handbook of psychiatric measures (pp. 45–70). Washington, DC: American Psychiatric Association.

Smits, J. A., Powers, M. B., Cho, Y., & Telch, M. J. (2004). Mechanism of change in cognitive-behavioral treatment of panic disorder: Evidence for the fear of fear mediational hypothesis. Journal of Consulting and Clinical Psychology, 72, 646–652.

Sokolowska, M., Siegel, S., & Kim. J. A. (2002). Intraadministration associations: Conditional hyperalgesia elicited by morphine onset cues. Journal of Experimental Psychology: Animal Behavior Processes, 28, 309–320.

Spitzer, R. L. (1983). Psychiatric diagnosis: Are clinicians still necessary? Comprehensive Psychiatry, 24, 399–411.

Spitzer, R. L., Williams, J. B. W., Gibbon, M., & First, M. B. (1990). SCID user's guide for the Structured Clinical Interview for DSM-III-R. Washington, DC: American Psychiatric Press.

Spitzer, R. L., Williams, J. B. W., Gibbon, M., & First, M. B. (1992). The structured clinical interview for DSM-III-R (SCID). I: History, rationale, and description. Archives of General Psychiatry, 49, 624–629.

Steketee, G., Chambless, D. L., & Tran, G. Q. (2001). Effects of axis I and II comorbidity on behavior therapy outcome for obsessive–compulsive disorder and agoraphobia. Comprehensive Psychiatry, 42, 76–86.

Taylor, C. B., Fried, L., & Kenardy, J. (1990). The use of a real-time computer diary for data acquisition and processing. Behaviour Research and Therapy, 28, 93–97.

Thyer, B. A., Himle, J., Curtis, G. C., Cameron, O. G., & Nesse, R. M. (1985). A comparison of panic disorder and agoraphobia with panic attacks. Comprehensive Psychiatry, 26, 208–214.

Tsao, J. C. I., Lewin, M. R., & Craske, M. G. (1998). The effects of cognitive-behavior therapy for panic disorder on comorbid conditions. Journal of Anxiety Disorders, 12, 357–371.

van Beek, N., Schruers, K. R. J., & Friez, E. J. L. (2005). Prevalence of respiratory disorders in first-degree relatives of panic disorder patients. Journal of Affective Disorders, 87, 337–340.

Verburg, K., Griez, E., Meijer, J., & Pols, H. (1995). Respiratory disorders as a possible predisposing factor for panic disorder. Journal of Affective Disorder, 33, 129–134.

Wade, W. A., Treat, T. A., & Stuart, G. L. (1998). Transporting an empirically supported treatment for panic disorder to a service clinic setting: A benchmarking strategy. Journal of Consulting and Clinical psychology, 66, 231–239.

Watson, D., & Clark, L. A. (1984). Negative affectivity: The disposition to experience aversive emotional states. Psychological Bulletin, 96, 465–490.

Watts, F. N., Trezise, L., & Sharrock, R. (1986). Processing of phobic stimuli. British Journal of Clinical Psychology, 25, 253–259.

White, K. S., Brown, T. A., Somers, T. J., & Barlow, D. H. (2006). Avoidance behavior in panic disorder: The moderating influence of perceived control. Behaviour Research and Therapy, 44, 147–157.

Williams, J. B. W., Gibbon, M., First, M. B., Spitzer, R. L., Davies, M., Borus, J. et al. (1992). The Structured Clinical Interview for DSM-III-R (SCID): Multisite test-retest reliability. Archives of General Psychiatry, 49, 630–636.

Williams, J. B. W., Spitzer, R. L., & Gibbon, M. (1992) International reliability of a diagnostic intake procedure for panic disorder. American Journal of Psychiatry, 149, 560–562.

Williams, S. L., Kinney, P. J., & Falbo, J. (1989). Generalization of therapeutic changes in agoraphobia: The role of perceived self-efficacy. Journal of Consulting and Clinical Psychology, 57, 436–442.

Williams, S. L., Kinney, P. J., Harap, S. T., & Liebmann, M. (1997). Thoughts of agoraphobic people during scary tasks. Journal of Abnormal Psychology, 106, 511–520.

Williams, S. L., & Zane, G. (1989). Guided mastery and stimulus exposure treatments for severe performance anxiety in agoraphobics. Behaviour Research and Therapy, 27, 237–245.

Wilson, L. G., & Young, D. G. (1988). Diagnosis of the severely ill inpatients in China: A collaborative project using the Structured Clinical Interview for DSM-III (SCID). Journal of Nervous and Mental Diseases, 176, 585–592.

Wittchen, H.-U., Reed, V., & Kessler, R. C. (1998). The relationship of agoraphobia and panic in a community sample of adolescents and young adults. Archives of General Psychiatry, 55, 1017–1024.

Wolpe, J. (1958). Psychotherapy by reciprocal inhibition. Stanford, CA: Stanford University Press.

Yamamoto, I., Nakano, Y., Watanabe, N., Noda, Y., Furukawa, T. A., Kanai, T. et al. (2004). Crosscultural evaluation of the Panic Disorder Severity Scale in Japan. Depression and Anxiety, 20, 17–22.

Zanarini, M. C., & Frankenburg, F. R. (2001). Attainment and maintenance of reliability of Axis I and Axis II disorders over the course of a longitudinal study. Comprehensive Psychiatry, 42, 369–374.

Zanarini, M. C., Skodol, A. E., Bender, D., Dolan, R., Sanislow, C., & Schaefer, E., et al. (2000). The collaborative longitudinal personality disorders study: Reliability of axis I and II diagnoses. *Journal of Personality Disorders, 14,* 291–299.

Zebb, B. J., & Moore, M. C. (1999). Another look at the psychometric properties of the anxiety control questionnaire. *Behaviour Research and Therapy, 37,* 1091–1103.

Zimmerman, M., & Mattia, J. I. (2000). Principal and additional DSM-IV disorders for which outpatients seek treatment. *Psychiatric Services, 51,* 1299–1304.

Zinbarg, R. E., & Barlow, D. H. (1996). Structure of anxiety and the anxiety disorders: A hierarchical model. *Journal of Abnormal Psychology, 105,* 184–193.

Zinbarg, R. E., Barlow, D. H., & Brown, T. A. (1997). Hierarchical structure and general factor saturation of the Anxiety Sensitivity Index: Evidence and implication. *Psychological Assessement, 9,* 277–284.

Zvolensky, M. J., McNeil, D. W., Porter, C. A., & Stewart, S. H. (2001). Assessment of anxiety sensitivity in young American Indians and Alaska natives. *Behaviour Research and Therapy, 39,* 477–493.

12

Generalized Anxiety Disorder

Nicole J. Gervais

Michel J. Dugas

The main goal of this chapter is to present comprehensive assessment options for clinicians working with individuals suffering from generalized anxiety disorder (GAD). The chapter begins with a discussion of the nature of GAD. Specifically, we review the history of the diagnostic criteria, and then summarize the data on the disorder's onset and course, age and gender differences, prevalence, comorbidity, and associated costs. Subsequently, we provide a detailed description of assessment strategies for diagnosing GAD, assessing for case conceptualization and treatment-planning purposes, and treatment monitoring and outcome evaluation. Finally, we discuss the current status of assessment methods for GAD and suggest ways of enhancing our ability to measure the symptoms and associated features of this prevalent and costly anxiety disorder.

NATURE OF GAD

History of the Diagnostic Criteria

The diagnostic category of GAD has undergone much change since its debut in the third edition of the *Diagnostic and Statistical Manual of Mental Disorders* (DSM-III; American Psychiatric Association [APA], 1980). In DSM-III, GAD was considered a residual disorder characterized by persistent anxiety occurring for at least 1 month and accompanied by symptoms from three out of four categories (i.e., motor tension, autonomic hyperactivity, apprehensive expectation, and vigilance/ scanning). In contrast, in the fourth edition of DSM (DSM-IV, 1994, and DSM-IV-TR, 2000), GAD is now described as a chronic condition (minimum duration of 6 months) involving excessive

and uncontrollable worry and anxiety about a number of events or activities, and leading to significant distress or impairment in important areas of functioning. In addition, the diagnosis of GAD now requires at least three of six somatic symptoms: restlessness or feeling keyed up or on edge, being easily fatigued, difficulty concentrating or mind going blank, irritability, muscle tension, and sleep disturbance. The current definition reflects attempts to identify features that are specific to GAD, including muscle tension and excessive and uncontrollable worry about a number of events or activities. In general, worry is common among individuals with anxiety disorders; however, for those with anxiety disorders other than GAD, the content of their worry tends to be confined to topics related to their specific disorder. For example, someone with social anxiety disorder may worry about how others perceive him/her, and someone with obsessive–compulsive disorder with checking compulsions may worry about whether or not he/she locked the front door.

Onset and Course

Some research suggests that there is an early and a late onset of this disorder, with the early onset occurring between the age of 11 and the early 20s, and the late onset typically occurring in middle adulthood (Blazer, Hughes, & George, 1987; Brown, Barlow, & Liebowitz, 1994). According to these studies, although a significant minority experience a late onset of GAD, an early onset is more common, with approximately two-thirds of individuals with GAD developing the disorder by their early 20s. Recently, however, Kessler and colleagues (2005) reported a slightly different pattern of results. Specifically, the authors found evidence for a steady increase in the onset of GAD during the early 20s (which is consistent with the findings reported above); but rather than finding evidence of a late onset, Kessler and colleagues found moderately lower rates of onset between the ages of 31 and 47, and dramatically lower rates after the age of 47. Therefore, the data presented by Kessler and colleagues support a peak onset age in the early 20s, but find no evidence for a later peak. Irrespective of onset, GAD is a chronic condition, characterized by the fluctuation of symptoms over time in response to life stressors, with episodes of the disorder commonly persisting for over 10 years (Kessler, Keller, & Wittchen, 2001; Stein, 2004).

In addition, symptoms of GAD rarely remit completely without treatment (Stein, 2004). In the Harvard/Brown Anxiety Research Program (HARP), a prospective study examining the course of anxiety disorders, GAD remission rates were examined in a large number of patients. The results show that 15% of patients with GAD remitted after 1 year, 25% after 2 years, and 38% after 5 years (Yonkers, Warshaw, Massion, & Keller, 1996). However, Kessler and colleagues (2001) have suggested that the HARP study underestimates the rate of remission for GAD, as their criteria for full remission were quite conservative (i.e., being symptom free for at least 8 consecutive weeks). Despite these criticisms, the general consensus is that GAD is a chronic condition that is unlikely to remit unless treated.

Etiology

Biological, environmental, and psychological factors all play a role in the development and maintenance of GAD. Biological factors include genetic predisposition and alterations in neurotransmitter function. Genetic predisposition plays a relatively modest role in the development of GAD, with research suggesting that GAD has a heritability of 15% to 30% (Hettema, Prescott, & Kendler, 2001; Kendler, Neale, Kessler, Heath, & Eaves, 1992). However, genetic predisposition appears to be nonspecific in that individuals who are at higher risk of developing GAD are also more likely to develop other anxiety and mood disorders (Andrews, Stewart, Morris-Yates, Holt, & Henderson, 1990). It is likely that genetic predisposition interacts with environmental and psychological factors to determine if a given individual will in fact develop GAD and/or another disorder. Alterations in several neurotransmitters also appear to be involved

in GAD, although their exact role has yet to be clearly understood (Gorman, 2002).

Research into environmental factors indicates that interactions between young children and their parents (or caregivers) also play a role in the later development of GAD. Whereas a number of studies show that children with "insecure" attachments to their parents are at risk of developing GAD (see Hudson & Rapee, 2004, for a review), other studies have found that the childhood experiences of adults with GAD are characterized by high levels of enmeshment (Lichtenstein & Cassidy, 1991; Peasley, Molina, & Borkovec, 1994). In this context, enmeshed relationships refer to the children attending to the needs of their parents, without necessarily having their own needs met. In other words, the parent–child relationship is marked by role reversal with the child "taking care" of the parent.

Many psychological factors also appear to play a role in the development and maintenance of GAD (see e.g., Borkovec, Alcaine, & Behar, 2004; Mennin, Heimberg, Turk, & Fresco, 2002; Wells & Carter, 1999). Our own research group has developed a cognitive model of GAD that has four main features: intolerance of uncertainty, positive beliefs about worry, negative problem orientation, and cognitive avoidance (Dugas, Gagnon, Ladouceur, & Freeston, 1998). According to this model, deep-seated negative beliefs about uncertainty (which manifest as intolerance of uncertainty) lead to biases in cognitive processing, contribute to the other model components, and ultimately lead to the development and maintenance of GAD (Dugas & Koerner, 2005). Research shows that intolerance of uncertainty is not only closely and specifically related to GAD, but that it also appears to play a causal role in GAD (Ladouceur, Gosselin, & Dugas, 2000). Research also shows that although intolerance of uncertainty is the most important cognitive vulnerability factor in our model, all model components nonetheless make significant and unique contributions to the prediction of GAD symptoms (Dugas et al., 1998).

Age and Gender Differences

Epidemiological data suggest that the number of individuals with GAD increases with age, peaking during middle age (Wittchen et al., 2002), with some of the lowest rates in individuals over 65 (Blazer, Hughes, George, Swartz, & Boyer, 1991). However, studies examining GAD in older adults also suggest that it is one of the most prevalent disorders in that population, with some authors reporting a steady increase in the rate of GAD that extends beyond the age of 65 (Beekman et al., 1998; Carter, Wittchen, Pfister, & Kessler, 2001). Dugas and Robichaud (2007) suggest that such discrepancy in the findings can be explained by the many health complications older adults typically experience; as such, these complications can obscure the presence of GAD, especially when symptoms of the health problem are similar to those seen in GAD. Given that GAD is a chronic disorder that typically commences in the early 20s and rarely remits on its own, it seems obvious that middle-aged adults would have a higher likelihood of having GAD than would younger adults. However, more research examining the presence of GAD in adults aged 65 and above is necessary to clarify whether the rates of this disorder continue to increase in this population.

Data also show that GAD is more common among women than men (Blazer et al., 1991; Hunt, Issakidis, & Andrews, 2002; Wittchen, Zhao, Kessler, & Eaton, 1994), which is consistent with most other anxiety disorders (Kessler et al., 1994). For example, Wittchen and colleagues (1994) found that women were about twice as likely as men to have had GAD at some point in their lives, with a reported lifetime prevalence of 6.6% for women and 3.6% for men. Other epidemiological studies have found similar results (e.g., Blazer et al., 1991; Hunt et al., 2002).

Prevalence, Comorbidity, and Cost

GAD is prevalent in the general population, with a point-prevalence rate of nearly 2% and a lifetime prevalence rate varying between 4.1% and 6.6% (Blazer et al., 1991; Hunt et al., 2002; Kessler et al., 2005; Wittchen et al., 1994). In the clinical population, the reported prevalence rate is higher, with nearly 8% of all patients seeking treatment meeting diagnosis for GAD (Maier et al., 2000). Finally, Wittchen and colleagues (2002) argued that there is evidence suggesting that GAD is the most frequent anxiety disorder and the second most frequent of all mental disorders in clinical settings.

Although GAD can present in individuals without other disorders (Wittchen et al., 1994), it is most commonly accompanied by other mental disorders, in particular depressive and anxiety disorders. Carter and colleagues (2001) reported a 12-month prevalence rate of 93% for other Axis I disorders among

individuals from the general population meeting DSM-IV criteria for GAD. This included 71% for any depressive disorder, and 56% for any anxiety disorder. In addition, individuals meeting GAD criteria were more likely to have two or more comorbid conditions, rather than just one comorbid condition. Given its high comorbidity rates, many have suggested that GAD is not a distinct disorder, but rather a condition that promotes the development of anxiety or mood disorders (Akiskal, 1998; Maser, 1998; Roy-Byrne & Katon, 1997). However, this position has essentially been rejected, as there is much evidence supporting the position that GAD is a distinct diagnostic category (e.g., Brown, Chorpita, & Barlow, 1998; Maier et al., 2000). For example, although the comorbidity rates for GAD are quite high, they are in fact comparable to those of other anxiety and mood disorders (Holaway, Rodebaugh, & Heimberg, 2006). In addition, with the exception of depression (Kessler, Walters, & Wittchen, 2004), GAD does not systematically precede or follow the onset of other disorders (although GAD typically precedes depression, it follows depression in a significant minority of cases). Other than anxiety and mood disorders, personality disorders have also been found to occur frequently in individuals with GAD (Grant et al., 2005), with avoidant, obsessive–compulsive, and dependent personality disorders being the most common (Dyck et al., 2001).

Compared to noncomorbid GAD (also referred to as pure GAD), comorbid GAD is associated with a greater likelihood of impairment, help seeking, and medication use (Kessler, DuPont, Berglund, & Wittchen, 1999; Wittchen et al., 1994). However, pure GAD is also associated with significant impairment, which is comparable to the impairment found in major depression (Kessler et al., 1999). Further, GAD is costly not only to the individual, but also to society, as it often leads to decreases in work productivity and higher utilization of health-care services (Wittchen & Hoyer, 2001). Despite the disproportionate use of primary care facilities, many individuals with GAD avoid seeking proper treatment for as long as 25 years (Rapee, 1991). Further, GAD is the anxiety disorder with the lowest diagnostic reliability (Brown, Di Nardo, Lehman, & Campbell, 2001), making this disorder difficult to identify in help-seeking individuals. However, as will be discussed shortly, there have been many recent advances in the diagnostic tools available for the assessment of GAD, which have improved the diagnostic reliability of this disorder.

Summary

GAD is a prevalent, chronic, and disabling disorder that has undergone numerous revisions in definition and diagnostic criteria since its introduction to the DSM. Considering the many factors that can complicate the assessment of GAD, it is imperative that clinicians use a sound assessment strategy for diagnosing this disorder. In addition, it is important to assess for the presence of comorbid conditions (including Axis I disorders, Axis II disorders, and physical conditions), as they can influence diagnostic and treatment decisions that relate to GAD. In the following sections, we first provide a thorough review of the diagnostic tools with the strongest empirical support. Following this, measures commonly used during the case formulation and treatment-planning phase will be presented, followed by a discussion of assessment tools for monitoring treatment progress and outcome.

PURPOSES OF ASSESSMENT OF GAD

For the most part, the measures currently available for the assessment of GAD consist of semistructured interviews and self-report questionnaires. Given that different research groups have developed self-report questionnaires that are specific to their conceptualization of GAD, not all GAD measures are reviewed in this chapter. In the sections on assessment for case conceptualization/treatment planning and treatment monitoring/treatment outcome, we focus our presentation of instruments on (a) constructs common to most models of GAD and (b) specific components of our model of GAD, namely intolerance of uncertainty, positive beliefs about worry, negative problem orientation, and cognitive avoidance (see Dugas & Robichaud, 2007). Validated measures of GAD components are available for other models of GAD, and the interested reader can refer to Borkovec et al. (2004), Mennin et al. (2002) or Wells and Carter (1999), for more information.

ASSESSMENT FOR THE DIAGNOSIS OF GAD

Before conducting the psychological assessment of a client, the clinician should ensure that a medical examination has been conducted by a physician to rule out conditions that can produce symptoms that resemble those of GAD (e.g., hyperthyroidism, hypoglycemia, and anemia). Further, either the physician or clinician should obtain information about family history of both medical problems and mental disorders. Once a complete picture of the client's physical state is obtained, the clinician should then proceed with the psychological assessment for diagnosis. In the following paragraphs, we discuss both self-report measures as well as semistructured interviews that assess for the presence of mental disorders including GAD. The two self-report measures to be presented are screening tools for GAD that can be used prior to conducting a semistructured interview. We recommend using semistructured interviews rather than unstructured clinical interviews, as the former produces diagnoses that are more reliable. Additionally, semistructured interviews encourage clinicians to inquire about a broad range of disorders, thus reducing the risk that they will overlook particular disorders. This is an especially important consideration for individuals with GAD because many present for assessment without realizing that it is worthwhile to mention their excessive and uncontrollable worry. Further, individuals with GAD may be seeking help for problems that are the *result* of their worrying, such as painful muscle tension. However, when they are specifically probed about the experience of worry, these individuals readily acknowledge its importance. There are, however, certain limitations to using semistructured interviews, the most obvious being the time required to conduct them. Further, practice is required before the clinician may feel fully comfortable in the use of such interviews. Despite these limitations, semistructured interviews are clearly superior to unstructured clinical interviews in terms of obtaining reliable information about a broad array of symptom constellations. A summary of the psychometric properties of both the self-report measures and the semistructured interviews reviewed in this section are presented in Table 12.1.

Self-Report Measures

The following two self-report measures can be used to screen for GAD prior to administering a semistructured interview. Given that the two provide similar information, it is recommended that the clinician choose one. The reader should keep in mind that although the symptoms covered by self-report

TABLE 12.1 Ratings of Instruments Used for Diagnosis[a]

Instrument	Norms	Internal Consistency	Inter-Rater Reliability	Test–Retest Reliability	Content Validity	Construct Validity	Validity Generalization	Clinical Utility	Highly Recommended
WAQ	G	U	NA	A	G	A	A	A	✓
GAD-Q-IV	G	E	NA	A	G	A	U	A	
ADIS-IV	NA	NA	A	NA	A	A	G	E	✓
SCID-I/P	NA	NA	A	NA	A	A	G	E	
SCID-II	NA	NA	E	NA	U	U	A	A	

[a] The ratings reported in this table are based on conclusions that the authors derived from the available information on the instruments.

Note: WAQ = Worry and Anxiety Questionnaire; GAD-Q-IV = Generalized Anxiety Disorder Questionnaire for DSM-IV; ADIS-IV = Anxiety Disorders Interview Schedule for DSM-IV; SCID-I/P = Structured Clinical Interview for DSM-IV-TR for Axis I disorders, Patient Edition; SCID-II = Clinical Interview for DSM-IV-TR for Axis II disorders; A = Adequate; G = Good; E = Excellent; U = Unavailable; NA = Not Applicable.

measures are similar to those covered by the semi-structured interviews, they can by no means replace diagnostic interviews. Clearly, semistructured interviews provide the clinician with more comprehensive and reliable information for the formal diagnosis of GAD. However, as mentioned above, self-report questionnaires can be used to screen for the presence of GAD prior to beginning an interview, as it can provide initial information on the presence of GAD.

Worry and Anxiety Questionnaire (WAQ)

The WAQ (Dugas et al., 2001) is an 11-item self-report questionnaire assessing for the presence of DSM-IV/DSM-IV-TR diagnostic criteria for GAD. The WAQ assesses worry themes, the degree of excessiveness and uncontrollability of worry, the length of time that the person has experienced excessive worry, the severity of GAD somatic symptoms, and the degree of interference and distress related to the worry and anxiety. With the exception of the first item, which asks respondents to list their worry themes, items are rated on a 9-point Likert scale. A categorical scoring system for the WAQ is available from the authors (Dugas et al., 2001).

Overall, the WAQ demonstrates adequate to good psychometric properties (Beaudoin et al., 1997; Dugas et al., 2001). For example, Beaudoin and colleagues (1997) found the test–retest reliability of the WAQ at 4 weeks to be adequate ($r = .76$) Further, there is evidence of good content validity and adequate construct validity (Dugas et al., 2001). In addition, there is good normative data available for the WAQ in non-clinical and clinical samples (Buhr & Dugas, 2002; Dugas et al., 2007). Both Buhr and Dugas (2002) and

Dugas and colleagues (2007) report a gender difference, which is not surprising given that women tend to report more worry and anxiety symptoms than men in the general population (Robichaud, Dugas, & Conway, 2003).

Generalized Anxiety Disorder Questionnaire-IV (GAD-Q-IV)

The GAD-Q-IV (Newman et al., 2002) is the most commonly used self-report measure assessing for the presence of DSM-IV diagnostic criteria for GAD. The original questionnaire (GAD-Q; Roemer, Borkovec, Posa, & Borkovec, 1995) was designed to be used as a screening instrument for DSM-III-R GAD, but was later updated to correspond to DSM-IV criteria. The updated GAD-Q-IV consists of nine items, the majority of which inquire about the presence or absence of specific symptoms of GAD (dichotomous response scale), including whether the respondent experiences excessive and uncontrollable worry as well as any of the six GAD somatic symptoms. There are, however, two items on the GAD-Q-IV which are rated on a 9-point Likert scale. These items assess the severity of functional impairment and subjective distress that result from the worry and anxiety. Additionally, the GAD-Q-IV contains one item asking respondents to list their most frequent worry topics.

The GAD-Q-IV total score can be used to screen for GAD, and Newman and colleagues (2002) have suggested a clinical cutoff score. In fact, to screen for the presence of GAD, the authors recommend using the cutoff for the total score rather than the categorical system that was used for the original GAD-Q. For a detailed description of the scoring system for the GAD-Q-IV, please refer to the validation article (Newman et al., 2002).

The GAD-Q-IV has demonstrated adequate to excellent psychometric properties, including excellent internal consistency (α = .93; Luterek, Turk, Heimberg, Fresco, & Mennin, 2002), adequate test–retest reliability at 2 weeks (κ = .64), good content validity, and adequate construct validity (Newman et al., 2002). Further, there is good normative data on the GAD-Q-IV as provided in the Newman and colleagues (2002) article.

Semistructured Interviews

Anxiety Disorders Interview Schedule for DSM-IV (ADIS-IV)

The ADIS-IV is the most commonly used semistructured diagnostic interview for the anxiety disorders. In addition to providing a thorough description of the presence or absence of symptoms for each anxiety disorder, the ADIS-IV contains sections that allow one to screen for mood disorders, somatoform disorders, psychoactive substance use disorders, psychotic disorders, and medical problems. This interview exists in both a current version (ADIS-IV; Brown, Di Nardo, & Barlow, 1994), which assesses for the presence of anxiety disorders, and a lifetime version (ADIS-IV-L; Di Nardo, Brown, & Barlow, 1994), which assesses for the experience of anxiety disorders at any point in the client's lifetime. The lifetime version provides a diagnostic timeline in addition to the assessment of presenting problems, and includes information pertaining to the onset, remission, and temporal sequence of current and lifetime disorders (Brown et al., 2001). Despite the valuable information provided by the lifetime version, the current version of the ADIS-IV provides sufficient information for the diagnosis of anxiety disorders for most clinical purposes. The ADIS-IV has many advantages over other semistructured interviews for the assessment of anxiety disorders. For one, each section begins with a screening question for a particular disorder, followed by questions pertaining to specific symptoms related to that disorder, which are then rated on a 9-point Likert scale (0 to 8). Another advantage of the ADIS-IV over other semistructured interviews is that it contains a Clinical Severity Rating (CSR) scale, which also consists of a 9-point Likert scale (0 to 8).

The CSR allows the clinician to evaluate the severity of each diagnosed condition. A score of 4 or above indicates the presence of a clinically significant disorder. When more than one clinically significant disorder is identified, the disorder with the highest CSR is considered the principal diagnosis and the others are referred to as additional diagnoses. Further, when a client presents with a subclinical form of a particular disorder, the disorder can nonetheless be noted with a CSR ranging from 1 to 3.

Although the ADIS-IV is an attractive measure for the reasons mentioned above, it also has certain limitations. For one, it does not cover all disorders appearing in the DSM-IV, including some that often co-occur with anxiety disorders, such as eating disorders. Further, the evaluation of some disorders, such as substance dependence, is not detailed enough to establish whether or not the client meets criteria. Finally, the ADIS-IV is one of the longest semistructured interviews available, taking as long as 2 hours to administer. Despite these limitations, we recommend the use of the ADIS-IV as there exists adequate empirical support for its use in diagnosing anxiety disorders, including GAD.

In a large reliability study conducted by Brown and colleagues (2001), 362 patients received two independent ADIS-IV-L interviews and κ values were calculated to obtain inter-rater agreement. In this study, GAD demonstrated adequate inter-rater agreement. The rates of agreement were superior to those obtained with the previous version of the ADIS (i.e., the ADIS-R; Di Nardo & Barlow, 1988), although this difference was not statistically significant. Brown and colleagues also found that much of the diagnostic disagreement frequently involved mood disorders, which have considerable symptom overlap with GAD. Further, the ADIS-IV has demonstrated adequate content and construct validity, good validity generalization, and excellent clinical utility.

Structured Clinical Interview for DSM-IV-TR Axis I Disorders, Research Version, Patient Edition (SCID-I/P)

The SCID-I/P (First, Spitzer, Gibbon, & Williams, 2002) is a semistructured interview that includes sections on anxiety disorders, mood disorders, psychotic disorders, substance use disorders, somatoform disorders, eating disorders, and adjustment disorders. The breadth of conditions covered by the

SCID-I/P constitutes a distinct advantage over the ADIS-IV, which does not cover such a wide array of mental disorders. The SCID-I/P, which takes between 45 and 90 minutes to complete, assesses for the presence or absence of symptoms of DSM-IV-TR disorders over the past month and over the client's lifetime. The SCID-I/P is structured quite differently from the ADIS-IV, as each symptom is scored based on whether it is absent (coded as "1"), present at the subclinical level (coded as "2"), or present at the clinical level (coded as "3"). Another advantage of the SCID-I/P is that it is organized into modules, so clinicians can choose to omit sections that are clearly not relevant for a particular client. The clinician may also discontinue a module once enough information has been gathered to conclude that the disorder is absent.

The SCID-I/P also has certain limitations. One limitation of this interview is that it does not include severity ratings for the symptoms; the clinician merely determines whether the symptom is present or not, and if so, whether it is at a level that is considered clinically meaningful. Further, sections pertaining to anxiety disorders, and particularly GAD, are lacking in detail and may result in poor discrimination between such disorders. This is an important limitation, as there are often difficulties encountered in the differential diagnosis of GAD.

To our knowledge, there are no published data on the reliability of the SCID-I/P; therefore, we will discuss the properties of earlier versions of the SCID. The inter-rater reliability of the SCID has been reported as adequate (Williams et al., 1992; Zanarini et al., 2000). Although the results are comparable to those reported for the ADIS-IV (Brown et al., 2001), more research examining the reliability of the SCID-I/P is needed. The SCID-I/P has also demonstrated adequate content and construct validity, good validity generalization, and excellent clinical utility (First & Gibbon, 2004). In addition to the SCID-I/P, there also exists the Structured Clinical Interview for DSM-IV Axis I Disorders, Clinician Version (SCID-CV; First, Spitzer, Gibbon, & Williams, 1996). The SCID-CV, which is much less detailed than the SCID-I/P, is designed for use in clinical settings. However, given that the SCID-CV does not include many important specifiers, subtypes, and even disorders included in the SCID-I/P, we recommend that clinicians use the Patient Edition.

Structured Clinical Interview for DSM-IV Axis II Personality Disorders (SCID-II)

Finally, the SCID-II (First, Spitzer, Gibbon, & Williams, 1997) can be used to assess for the presence of personality disorders. The SCID-II assesses for the presence of DSM-IV Axis II disorders, as well as depressive personality disorder and passive–aggressive personality disorder. This interview allows for either categorical or dimensional scoring, and similar to the SCID-I/P, allows for the administration of only certain sections. The SCID-II is structured in the same way as the SCID-I/P, with the exception of a self-report questionnaire containing screening questions. This questionnaire aids in the administration of the interview, as the interviewer is required to address only those questions that correspond to items the client endorsed on the questionnaire. The SCID-II has demonstrated excellent inter-rater reliability (Maffei et al., 1997) and adequate validity generalization (First & Gibbon, 2004).

Overall Evaluation

As mentioned previously, two self-report measures were described in this section, but only one of the two is required to screen for GAD. Therefore, the clinician must decide which screening tool to use. Despite evidence of similar psychometric properties, we believe that the WAQ is the superior choice as a screening measure for GAD, because it contains ratings for each item (with the exception of the first item, which requires the respondent to list worry topics), whereas the GAD-Q-IV possesses nearly all dichotomous items.

Although there are other semistructured diagnostic interviews that can be used to identify GAD (including briefer interviews), the ADIS-IV and SCID-I/P are excellent choices because they have considerable empirical support. Diagnosing GAD is quite a challenge as many difficulties can be encountered, given its overlapping symptoms with other anxiety and mood disorders, and the high likelihood that it will be comorbid. Semistructured interviews for Axis I disorders such as the two described above are extremely valuable, as they necessitate the clinician going beyond the clients presenting complaints, thus allowing for the possibility that other diagnoses can be made, if warranted. If the most reliable and valid semistructured interviews are utilized, clinicians should find that many difficulties will be considerably reduced. Although they are lengthy, the benefits to using such tools in clinical settings far outweigh the costs. As was recommended above for the self-report measures used to screen for the presence of GAD, the clinician will need to choose which of the two semistructured interviews to administer.

ASSESSMENT FOR CASE CONCEPTUALIZATION AND TREATMENT PLANNING

In this section, we discuss assessment tools for the purposes of case conceptualization and treatment planning. As such, we first present measures designed to assess worry severity, somatic anxiety, depression, and quality of life. As somatic anxiety symptoms, depression, and poor quality of life can negatively impact treatment progression, it is important for the clinician to assess such factors prior to the start of treatment to determine whether they should be targeted during therapy. Subsequently, we present measures of the cognitive processes central to our model of GAD (intolerance of uncertainty, positive beliefs about worry, negative problem orientation, and cognitive avoidance; see Dugas et al., 1998). Assessing these cognitive processes is necessary when clinicians are intending on implementing the treatment protocol based upon that model and described in detail in Dugas and Robichaud (2007). Even if the clinician intends on utilizing another treatment developed for GAD, we believe that it would be useful to assess the level of each cognitive process experienced by the client, as these four cognitive processes have been implicated in the maintenance of GAD. Finally, although the WAQ was described in the previous section as it is a screening measure for GAD, it can also be used to assess the severity of GAD symptoms. Therefore, if the clinician is interested in collecting such data, we would recommend that the WAQ be used. Given that the WAQ was presented in the previous section, and that this measure's psychometric properties do not change depending upon its use as a screening tool or measure of GAD severity, it will not be presented here. Newman and colleagues (2002) recommend that the GAD-Q-IV not be used as a measure of GAD severity, therefore, we also suggest the GAD-Q-IV not be used for such purposes. Ratings of the psychometric properties of the instruments discussed in this section are presented in Table 12.2.

Measure of Worry Severity

Penn State Worry Questionnaire (PSWQ)

The PSWQ (Meyer, Miller, Metzger, & Borkovec, 1990) is the most commonly used measure of pathological worry, the cardinal feature of GAD; in fact, it is widely recognized as the gold standard for the measurement of worry. Given that there is much normative data available for this questionnaire, it is clearly the best choice for clinicians, as clients' scores can be interpreted with relative ease (for a review, see Startup & Erickson, 2006). Although the available data include cutoff scores, we recommend using this questionnaire solely as a measure of the severity of pathological worry. Interestingly, although women report more worry than men in the general population, among GAD patients, there is no such gender difference on the PSWQ. There also seems to be no major difference in PSWQ scores across ethnic or cultural groups. However, age does appear to influence level of worry, as younger individuals have consistently been found to report more worry on the PSWQ than older adults (Startup & Erickson, 2006).

The 16 items from the PSWQ are rated on a 5-point Likert scale. Examples of the items include "My worries overwhelm me" and "I know I shouldn't worry about things but I just can't help it." Five of the items are inverted (e.g., "I find it easy to dismiss worrisome thoughts"). The psychometric properties of the PSWQ range from adequate to excellent. This includes excellent internal consistency, which has been assessed in both clinical and nonclinical samples. In addition, the PSWQ has shown good test–retest reliability over periods of 2 to 10 weeks. Further, the PSWQ has demonstrated good content and good construct validity (Molina & Borkovec, 1994; Startup & Erickson, 2006). Finally, given that there is a lot of data supporting use of this measure with many different groups, and across multiple contexts, this measure demonstrates excellent validity generalization.

Anxiety, Depression, and Quality of Life

In addition to obtaining information about the severity of GAD symptoms, clinicians should also acquire information about somatic anxiety, depression, and quality of life. Although somatic anxiety is more characteristic of panic disorder, it is not uncommon for individuals with GAD to experience panic-like

TABLE 12.2 Ratings of Instruments Used for Case Conceptualization and Treatment Planning

Instrument	Norms	Internal Consistency	Inter-Rater Reliability	Test–Retest Reliability	Content Validity	Construct Validity	Validity Generalization	Clinical Utility	Highly Recommended
Measure of Worry Severity									
PSWQ	E	E	NA	G	G	G	E	A	✓
Measures of Anxiety, Depression, and Quality of Life									
BAI	G	E	NA	A	A	A	G	G	
BDI-II	G	E	NA	A	A	A	G	G	
QLQ	A	G	NA	A	U	U	U	A	✓
QOLI	U	G	NA	A	U	A	U	U	✓
Measures of GAD Cognitive Processes									
IUS	G	E	NA	A	G	G	G	G	✓
WW-II	A	E	NA	A	A	A	G	G	✓
NPOQ	U	E	NA	A	G	G	U	A	✓
CAQ	A	E	NA	A	G	G	A	G	✓

Note. PSWQ = Penn State Worry Questionnaire; BAI = Beck Anxiety Inventory; BDI-II = Beck Depression Inventory-II; QLQ = Quality of Life Questionnaire; QOLI = Quality of Life Inventory; IUS = Intolerance of Uncertainty Scale; WW-II = Why Worry-II; NPOQ = Negative Problem Orientation Questionnaire; CAQ = Cognitive Avoidance Questionnaire; A = Adequate; G = Good; E = Excellent; U = Unavailable; NA = Not Applicable.

symptoms. Therefore, it is important to establish whether a particular GAD client experiences somatic anxiety, as it may need to be addressed during treatment. Further, given that GAD generally has a chronic and unremitting course, it should come as no surprise that many individuals with GAD come to experience symptoms of demoralization and depression. Consequently, it is standard procedure to assess for the presence of depressive symptoms or even depressive disorder in a comprehensive GAD assessment protocol. Finally, individuals with GAD typically experience poor quality of life, which can often be attributed to the distress and interference that result from GAD worry and associated symptoms. As will be discussed in the section on treatment outcome, clinicians should also assess somatic anxiety, depression, and quality of life at the end of treatment, as this can provide additional indices of treatment success.

Beck Anxiety Inventory

Although GAD is not characterized by somatic anxiety (in this case, symptoms of autonomic arousal), the assessment of such symptoms is recommended for treatment planning. In fact, our clinical experience suggests that somatic symptoms of anxiety are more common in GAD clients than is generally acknowledged. The Beck Anxiety Inventory (BAI; Beck, Epstein, Brown, & Steer, 1988) is a 21-item measure that assesses, for the most part, the severity of somatic anxiety symptoms. BAI items are rated on a 4-point scale, with respondents indicating the degree to which they have been bothered by each symptom during the past week. Because the BAI was designed to discriminate anxiety from depressive symptoms, the majority of its items describe symptoms of autonomic arousal and panic (e.g., "heart pounding or racing," or "hands trembling"), as they do not overlap with symptoms of depression. Although these symptoms are not considered to be characteristic of GAD, a significant minority of individuals with GAD experience symptoms of somatic arousal, such as the ones described in the BAI. Thus, the BAI provides information that can prove extremely useful for treatment planning.

Overall, the BAI demonstrates adequate to excellent psychometric properties. The BAI has demonstrated excellent internal consistency (Beck et al., 1988; de Beurs, Wilson, Chambless, Goldstein, & Feske, 1997; Fydrich, Dowdall, & Chambless, 1992). Additionally, the test–retest reliability of this measure is adequate

over a 5-week period (r = .83; de Beurs et al., 1997). Further, adequate content and construct validity, and good validity generalization has been shown for the BAI (Beck et al., 1988; de Beurs et al., 1997; Fydrich et al., 1992; Gillis, Haaga, & Ford 1995). Finally, as the BAI has been widely used in clinical research, it has well-established norms in both clinical and nonclinical samples (Beck & Steer, 1990; Gillis et al., 1995).

Beck Depression Inventory-II

The Beck Depression Inventory-II (BDI-II; Beck, Steer, & Brown, 1996) is a 21-item self-report measure of the severity of depressive symptoms. Each item contains four options referring to the degree to which the symptom is experienced; respondents are asked to indicate which of the options best describes them. For items assessing symptoms involving a change in either direction (e.g., sleep disturbance includes either insomnia or hypersomnia), additional options are included to account for both the increase and decrease in the behavior. The BDI-II assesses all DSM-IV-TR diagnostic criteria for depression and uses a time frame of the past 2 weeks.

As is the case for the BAI, there exist good normative data for the BDI-II (Beck et al., 1996; Steer & Clark, 1997). Further, the BDI-II demonstrates excellent internal consistency and adequate test–retest reliability at 1 week (Beck et al., 1996). In addition, the BDI-II demonstrates adequate content and construct validity, and adequate validity generalization (Beck et al., 1996).

Quality of Life Questionnaire

The Quality of Life Questionnaire (QLQ; Léger, Freeston, Dugas, & Ladouceur, 1998) is a 31-item measure assessing eight quality of life domains. The life domains include health, family, activity, finance, community, work, goals, and security. Each item is rated initially on a 4-point scale assessing level of satisfaction, and then rated on another 4-point scale assessing level of importance placed on each domain. The psychometric properties of this measure include good internal consistency (α = .86) and adequate test–retest reliability at 6 weeks (r = .86; Labrecque, Leblanc, Kirouac, Marchand, & Stephenson, 2001). Additionally, there are some normative data available in both clinical and nonclinical samples (Labrecque et al., 2001). As this is a relatively new measure, further research is necessary to assess its psychometric properties, particularly in a clinical sample.

Quality of Life Inventory

The Quality of Life Inventory (QOLI; Frisch 1994) is a 17-item measure assessing quality of life. Each item refers to a different life domain. Respondents are asked to indicate the level of importance each domain has on their overall happiness and satisfaction using a 3-point Likert scale. The respondents are also asked to rate their overall satisfaction with each life domain using a 7-point scale. The total score is the average of the weighted scores of the life domains deemed to be relevant to the individual. The psychometric properties of the QOLI include good internal consistency, adequate test–retest reliability over 2 to 3 weeks, and adequate construct validity (Frisch, Cornell, Villanueva, & Retzlaff, 1992).

Despite using the QLQ in our clinical research, we equally recommend using the QOLI. Currently, more research is needed to establish the psychometric properties for either measure and so for this reason, we are unable to recommend one over the other.

GAD Cognitive Processes

As mentioned previously, this section focuses on measures of the four cognitive processes identified by our model of GAD (see Dugas et al., 1998). Over the past 15 years, we have developed and validated self-report questionnaires for each of our model's four components (intolerance of uncertainty, positive beliefs about worry, negative problem orientation, and cognitive avoidance). Overall, the measures have proven to be clinically useful, not only in terms of identifying treatment mechanisms but also in terms of predicting the maintenance of treatment gains. The four measures described below are the Intolerance of Uncertainty Scale (IUS), the Why Worry-II (WW-II), the Negative Problem Orientation Questionnaire (NPOQ), and the Cognitive Avoidance Questionnaire (CAQ).

Intolerance of Uncertainty Scale

Intolerance of uncertainty (IU) refers to a dispositional characteristic that arises from a set of negative beliefs about uncertainty and its implications (Dugas & Robichaud, 2007). The negative beliefs include that uncertainty is unacceptable; reflects badly on a person; and leads to feelings of frustration, stress, and the inability to act (Buhr & Dugas, 2002). Within our cognitive model of GAD (see Dugas et al., 1998), IU

is the central component and is believed to contribute to the development and maintenance of GAD both directly and through its impact on the other model components. The Intolerance of Uncertainty Scale (IUS; original French version: Freeston, Rhéaume, Letarte, Dugas, & Ladouceur, 1994; English translation: Buhr & Dugas, 2002) is a 27-item self-report measure that was developed to assess beliefs about uncertainty. Items on the IUS are rated on a 5-point Likert scale; items include "Being uncertain means that a person is disorganized" and "Being uncertain means that I am not first rate." The IUS is an easily administered self-report measure that takes between 5 and 10 minutes to complete.

The English version of the IUS has demonstrated adequate to excellent psychometric properties. The psychometric properties of this version are consistent with those of the original French version of the scale (Freeston et al., 1994). For example, the IUS demonstrated excellent internal consistency ($\alpha = .94$), adequate test–retest reliability at 5 weeks ($r = .74$), good content and construct validity, and good validity generalization (Buhr & Dugas, 2002, 2006; Freeston et al., 1994). Finally, normative data have been presented elsewhere (Buhr & Dugas, 2002; Dugas et al., 2007).

The IUS has been translated into many languages including German, Spanish, Portuguese, and Turkish. A recent article by Norton (2005) provides preliminary evidence for the cross-cultural validity of the IUS, which demonstrated strong and similar evidence of reliability and validity across four racial groups. However, it should be noted that the factor structure of the IUS appears to be somewhat inconsistent across different translations (see Buhr & Dugas, 2002; Freeston et al., 1994) and across different cultural groups for the English version of the questionnaire (see Norton, 2005).

Why-Worry-II

Although other models of GAD include both positive and negative beliefs about worry (i.e., Wells & Carter, 1999), our current treatment protocol (see Dugas & Robichaud, 2007) does *not* directly address negative beliefs about worry (negative beliefs are subsumed under the "cognitive avoidance" component). For this reason, measures of negative beliefs about worry are not presented this section. In terms of positive beliefs about worry, previous research has shown that these

beliefs distinguish patients with GAD from nonclinical individuals (Dugas et al., 1998; Ladouceur et al., 1999). However, positive beliefs about worry do not seem to distinguish patients with GAD from patients with other anxiety disorders (Dugas, Marchand, & Ladouceur, 2005; Ladouceur et al., 1999), suggesting that positive beliefs are not specific to the diagnosis of GAD. Nevertheless, in nonclinical samples, positive beliefs about worry have been found to predict excessive and uncontrollable worry (Laugesen, Dugas, & Bukowski, 2003; Robichaud et al., 2003). Finally, data from a recent treatment study show that the re-evaluation of positive beliefs about worry led to decreases in both positive beliefs and GAD symptoms (Dugas et al., 2004). Thus, although positive beliefs about worry are not specific to GAD, they nevertheless appear to be important targets in the treatment of this anxiety disorder. Therefore, we suggest that clinicians should assess positive beliefs about worry prior to the start of treatment in order to determine appropriate intervention strategies.

The Why Worry-II (WW-II; French version: Gosselin et al., 2003; English translation: Holowka, Dugas, Francis, & Laugesen, 2000) is a revised version of the original Why Worry questionnaire (WW; Freeston et al., 1994). The original version of this measure was revised in order to include five types of positive beliefs about worry that have been identified in the literature as being related to worry. The current WW-II is a 25-item self-report questionnaire that contains five subscales, with each subscale measuring one type of positive belief about worry. The five subscales assess the following beliefs: (1) worry facilitates problem solving (e.g., "The fact that I worry helps me plan my actions to solve a problem"); (2) worry helps motivate (e.g., "The fact that I worry motivates me to do the things I must do"); (3) worrying protects one from difficult emotions in the event of a negative outcome (e.g., "If I worry, I will be less unhappy when a negative event occurs"); (4) the act of worrying itself prevents negative outcomes (e.g., "My worries can, by themselves, reduce the risks of danger"); and (5) worry is a positive personality trait (e.g., "The fact that I worry shows that I am a good person"). Items are rated on a 5-point Likert scale.

The WW-II demonstrates adequate to excellent psychometric properties, including excellent internal consistency for the total score ($\alpha = .93$), adequate test–retest reliability at 6 weeks ($r = .80$), and adequate content and construct validity (Gosselin

et al., 2003; Holowka et al., 2000). Further, normative data is available on the WW-II for both clinical and nonclincial samples (Dugas et al., 2007; Gosselin et al., 2003).

Negative Problem Orientation Questionnaire

The NPOQ (original French version: Gosselin, Ladouceur, & Pelletier, 2005; English translation: Robichaud & Dugas, 2005a) is a 12-item measure of a dysfunctional cognitive set that influences the ability to solve everyday problems effectively. More specifically, negative problem orientation refers to the tendency to view problems as threats, to doubt one's own ability to problem solve, and to be pessimistic about the outcome of problem-solving attempts. Using a 5-point Likert scale, respondents rate their reactions or thoughts when confronted with a problem. Examples include "I see problems as a threat to my well-being" and "I often see problems as bigger than they really are." In nonclinical samples, the English translation of the NPOQ has adequate to excellent psychometric properties, which include excellent internal consistency ($\alpha = .92$), adequate test–retest reliability at 5 weeks ($r = .80$), and good content and construct validity (Gosselin et al., 2005; Robichaud & Dugas, 2005a, 2005b). It should be noted, however, that only normative data from nonclinical samples are currently available (see, Gosselin et al., 2005; Robichaud & Dugas, 2005a) and that clinical data are currently being collected.

Research indicates that although worry and GAD are associated with a negative problem orientation (Dugas et al., 1998; Ladouceur et al., 1999), they are mostly unrelated to knowledge of problem-solving skills (Dugas et al., 1998; Dugas & Robichaud, 2007). In other words, although individuals with GAD tend to know *what they should do* to solve their problems, they have the tendency to view problems as threatening, to doubt their ability to deal with problems, and to view the outcome of problem-solving attempts pessimistically. Given this cognitive set, individuals with GAD typically experience difficulty in solving their problems successfully. Relatedly, negative problem orientation appears to be an important treatment target for individuals with GAD, as this cognitive set has been shown to be sensitive to both the presence and severity of GAD (Dugas et al., 1998; Dugas et al., 2007). For these reasons, we believe that clinicians should assess the problem orientation of their GAD clients prior to beginning treatment.

Cognitive Avoidance Questionnaire

The CAQ (original French version: Gosselin et al., 2002; English translation: Sexton & Dugas, in press) is a 25-item measure of the tendency to use cognitive avoidance strategies when dealing with threatening intrusive thoughts. The process of cognitive avoidance, although not specific to GAD, has been implicated as a contributing process in excessive and uncontrollable worry (Borkovec, Ray, & Stöber, 1998). The CAQ contains five subscales, each of which assesses a different avoidance strategy: (1) suppressing worrisome thoughts (e.g., "There are things I try not to think about"); (2) substituting neutral or positive thoughts for worries (e.g., "I think about trivial details so as not to think about important subjects that worry me"); (3) using distraction as a way to interrupt worrying (e.g., "I often do things to distract myself from my thoughts"); (4) avoiding actions/situations that can lead to worrisome thinking (e.g., "I avoid actions that remind me of things I do not want to think about"); and (5) transforming mental images into verbal-linguistic thoughts (e.g., "When I have mental images that are upsetting, I say things to myself in my head to replace the images"). Items on the CAQ are rated on a 5-point Likert scale. This measure has been shown to have adequate to excellent psychometric properties. For example, the CAQ has demonstrated excellent internal consistency for the total score ($\alpha = .95$), adequate test–retest reliability over a 5-week period ($r = .85$), good content and construct validity, and adequate validity generalization (Gosselin et al., 2002; Sexton & Dugas, in press). Further, adequate normative data on both clinical and nonclinical samples have been described elsewhere (Dugas et al., 2007; Gosselin et al., 2002; Sexton & Dugas, in press).

Overall Evaluation

Most of the questionnaires described in this section have received at least adequate empirical support for their use in clinical settings. The PSWQ, which has the most support, is a widely accepted measure of worry. The BAI and BDI-II have also shown strong support for use in clinical settings. However, to our knowledge, no data have yet been published on the clinical utility of either quality of life measures described above. Despite this lack of information, assessing for quality of life, as well as both somatic anxiety and depression is important during this phase of treatment. As mentioned above, the measures of model-specific components should be used by clinicians intending on using the treatment protocol described in Dugas and Robichaud (2007), as they offer the unique opportunity to assess each component of the underlying cognitive model with a questionnaire that was developed explicitly for that purpose. Even if the clinician were to use an alternative treatment for GAD, assessing for such cognitive processes, especially IU, is important as beliefs about uncertainty play a central role in the maintenance of worry/GAD. Although these measures are relatively new, there is emerging evidence for their applicability to the assessment of GAD in preparation for treatment. However, more research is necessary to further establish their usefulness as assessment tools for use in clinical settings.

ASSESSMENT FOR TREATMENT MONITORING AND TREATMENT OUTCOME

In this section, we present an overview of the measures that can be used to monitor treatment progress and assess treatment outcome. As a rule, the measures described in the previous sections (both semistructured interviews and self-report questionnaires) can be readministered at posttreatment and at follow-up to assess treatment outcome and maintenance. Therefore, the treatment outcome portion of this section will be brief and will focus on the evidence supporting the sensitivity to change of the previously described measures. This section will also present a simple strategy that clinicians can use to determine clinically meaningful change in their clients. A summary of the psychometric properties of the measures presented in this section is provided in Table 12.3.

Treatment Monitoring

Given that excessive and uncontrollable worry is the central feature of GAD, the assessment of the severity of worry on a weekly basis is essential to monitor the progress of clients. For this purpose, we recommend that clinicians use an adapted version of the PSWQ, which was developed to allow for the weekly assessment of excessive and uncontrollable worry. Clinicians

TABLE 12.3 Ratings of Instruments Used for Treatment Monitoring and Treatment Outcome Evaluation[a]

Instrument	Norms	Internal Consistency	Inter-Rater Reliability	Test–Retest Reliability	Content Validity	Construct Validity	Validity Generalization	Treatment Sensitivity	Clinical Utility	Highly Recommended
Treatment Monitoring Measures										
PSWQ-PW	A	E	NA	L	G	G	U	G	A	✓
Self-monitoring booklet	G	NA	NA	NA	U	A	U	A	A	✓
Treatment Outcome Measures										
ADIS-IV	NA	NA	A	NA	A	A	G	E	E	✓
SCID-I/P	NA	NA	A	NA	A	A	G	E	E	
PSWQ	E	E	NA	G	G	G	E	G	A	✓
WAQ	G	U	NA	A	G	A	A	A	A	✓
BAI	G	E	NA	A	A	A	G	A	G	
BDI-II	G	E	NA	A	A	A	G	A	G	
QLQ	A	G	NA	A	U	U	U	U	A	✓
QOLI	U	G	NA	A	U	A	U	U	U	✓
IUS	G	E	NA	A	G	G	G	G	G	✓
WW-II	A	E	NA	A	A	A	G	U	G	✓
NPOQ	U	E	NA	A	G	G	U	U	A	✓
CAQ	A	E	NA	A	G	G	A	U	G	✓

[a] The ratings reported in this table are based on conclusions that the authors derived from the available information on the instruments.
Note: PSWQ-PW = Penn State Worry Questionnaire–Past Week; ADIS-IV = Anxiety Disorders Interview Schedule for DSM-IV; SCID-I/P = Structured Clinical Interview for DSM-IV-TR for Axis I Disorders, Patient Edition; PSWQ = Penn State Worry Questionnaire; WAQ = Worry and Anxiety Questionnaire; BAI = Beck Anxiety Inventory; BDI-II = Beck Depression Inventory-II; QLQ = Quality of Life Questionnaire; QOLI = Quality of Life Inventory; IUS = Intolerance of Uncertainty Scale; WW-II = Why Worry-II; NPOQ = Negative Problem Orientation Questionnaire; CAQ = Cognitive Avoidance Questionnaire; L = Less than Adequate; A = Adequate; G = Good; E = Excellent; U = Unavailable; NA = Not Applicable.

can simply ask clients to complete this questionnaire prior to the start of every therapy session. The Penn State Worry Questionnaire-Past Week (PSWQ-PW; Stöber & Bittencourt, 1998) is a reformulation of the original PSWQ (Meyer et al., 1990). The instructions for the revised version emphasize worry over the past week (rather than trait worry). In addition, each item was rephrased to past tense, with the exception of one item, which was removed because it specifically assessed trait worry ("I've been a worrier all my life"). Therefore, the PSWQ-PW contains 15 items instead of 16. A further change was made to the response scale, which was changed from a 5-point to a 7-point scale. In general, the PSWQ-PW demonstrated excellent internal consistency ($\alpha = 0.91$) and test–retest reliability ($r = .59$) that is appropriate for a measure designed to assess weekly fluctuations in symptoms. The content and construct validity of the PSWQ-PW was found to be good, which is consistent with that of the original PSWQ (Stöber & Bittencourt, 1998). Moreover, the revised questionnaire has shown good sensitivity to treatment-related changes in worry (more so than the original PSWQ).

In addition to the weekly assessment of excessive and uncontrollable worry, clinicians should also obtain daily self-ratings of worry, anxiety, depression, and medication use, if applicable. Not only is daily self-monitoring a helpful tool for helping clients to become more aware of their affective states, it also provides valuable information about client progress. We typically use a self-monitoring booklet that consists of four questions, each of which is responded to at the end of the day (proportion of the day spent worrying, feeling anxious or tense, feeling sad or depressed, and name and quantity of any medication consumed). There is evidence supporting the validity of this type of self-monitoring, which includes good normative data, adequate construct validity, and adequate sensitivity to treatment (for a summary, refer to Table 12.3). For example, one study using daily self-monitoring booklets found that patients with GAD reported significantly more time spent worrying than a nonclinical control group (Dupuy, Beaudoin, Rhéaume, Ladouceur, & Dugas, 2001). However, self-monitoring booklets are not without their limitations. In particular, they would benefit from greater standardization, as different GAD treatment protocols tend to use different self-monitoring booklets. Despite this limitation, self-monitoring booklets remain a useful means of monitoring treatment progress and

assessing treatment outcome (see e.g., Campbell & Brown, 2002).

Treatment Outcome

As mentioned above, the assessment of treatment outcome (and treatment maintenance) involves the readministration of measures described in the previous sections. Following treatment, either the ADIS-IV or the SCID-I/P should be used to assess for the presence of GAD and any comorbid conditions (both interviews have been shown to be sensitive to treatment changes). Of course, the same interview used at pretreatment should be used at posttreatment to allow for direct comparisons of diagnostic conditions. The PSWQ and WAQ should also be readministered at posttreatment and follow-up assessments, as well as the measures of somatic anxiety (BAI), depression (BDI-II), and quality of life (QLQ or QOLI). Likewise, clinicians should readminister the measures of the cognitive processes involved in GAD (IUS, WW-II, NPOQ, and CAQ) immediately following treatment and at all follow-up assessments. In fact, having clients complete the IUS at posttreatment may be particularly important. Data show that changes in IUS scores pre- to posttreatment predict GAD symptoms up to 2 years after treatment completion (Dugas et al., 2003). We recognize that readministering each of these measures at posttreatment is time consuming and would probably take approximately two sessions to complete. Although it is highly recommended to do so, if it is not feasible for the clinician, then the BAI, WW-II, NPOQ, and CAQ may be removed from the assessment protocol. Generally, all measures described above have been shown to be sensitive to treatment changes (see e.g., Borkovec & Costello, 1993; Dugas et al., 1998; Ladouceur et al., 2000).

The information obtained following treatment can be used by the clinician to determine if the client has achieved *clinically significant change*. According to Jacobson and Truax (1991), the clinical significance of change can be estimated by determining whether a client's posttreatment score falls within the range of the general population rather than the range of the clinical population (in this case, GAD). Given that normative data are available for most of the measures presented in this chapter, clinicians will be in a position to assess the clinical significance of change on these measures. Jacobson and Truax (1991) also argued that clinicians should determine the degree of change on each measure for each client, which can be accomplished by calculating the *index of reliable change* (for the formulas for calculating the clinical significance of change and the reliable change index, see Jacobson & Truax, 1991). In addition to the methods described by Jacobson and Truax, some GAD studies have defined treatment response as a 20% reduction from pre- to posttreatment on measures of GAD and associated symptoms (see e.g., Borkovec & Costello, 1993; Dugas et al., 2003; Ladouceur et al., 2000). Other methods also exist for calculating clinically significant change, many of which are more complex than the one described by Jacobson and Truax. However, a study examining the efficacy of different techniques for assessing clinically significant change (Atkins, Bedics, McGlinchey, & Beauchaine, 2005) found that the method described by Jacobson and Truax was comparable to other more complex methods.

Overall Evaluation

Overall, there is considerable support for the use of the measures described in this section (PSWQ-PW and self-monitoring booklets) to assess progress during treatment. Further, the measures that can be used to assess for the presence/absence of GAD (and other disorders), the severity of worry/GAD symptoms, somatic anxiety, depression, quality of life, and cognitive processes implicated in GAD also have empirical support for their use following treatment. What is less clear is *how much* change is sufficient to terminate the therapy. Weighing the advantages and disadvantages for terminating treatment while evaluating the level of clinically significant change will aid the clinician in his/her decision.

CONCLUSIONS AND FUTURE DIRECTIONS

GAD is a relatively new diagnostic category that has undergone much change since its introduction in the DSM-III; thus, the development of adequate assessment options has been a difficult task. However, due to recent developments in our understanding of GAD, there has been considerable improvement in our ability to comprehensively assess GAD for the purposes of treatment. The reader should keep in mind, nonetheless, that some measures described

in this chapter do not yet have sufficient normative data. As such, more information needs to be gathered on these measures.

Additionally, there is currently much reliance on self-report measures for the assessment of GAD, which is problematic because this type of assessment method does not always produce valid and clinically meaningful information. Clearly, more attention needs to be directed at producing more "objective" methods of assessing GAD to complement the interview and self-report methods. For example, psychophysiological measures are used more frequently for other anxiety disorders than for GAD. However, before these measures can be incorporated into an assessment battery for GAD, we need to learn more about the disorder's psychophysiological features. Perhaps future research can investigate whether physiological indices such as heart rate and skin conductance can provide useful information for the differential diagnosis of GAD. Additionally, clarifying the neural circuitry of GAD is another area in need of more attention. Identifying neuroanatomical structures and neural pathways implicated in GAD (and discovering how these structures and pathways influence the development of specific symptoms of GAD) can aid in the identification of GAD-like patterns of brain activity in at-risk or symptomatic individuals.

Despite the challenges that are encountered when assessing individuals with GAD, assessment options have come a long way since GAD was first introduced as a diagnostic category. By presenting the assessment strategies described in this chapter, we hope to help clinicians working with this population to better identify GAD, monitor treatment progress, and assess short- and long-term treatment outcomes. Although the comprehensive assessment of GAD is a work in progress, it can be said that we now possess a variety of measurement instruments that have considerable clinical utility.

References

Akiskal, H. S. (1998). Toward a definition of generalized anxiety disorder as an anxious temperament type. *Acta Psychiatrica Scandinavica, 98*, 66–73.

American Psychiatric Association. (1980). *Diagnostic and statistical manual of mental disorders* (3rd ed.). Washington, DC: Author.

American Psychiatric Association. (1994). *Diagnostic and statistical manual of mental disorders* (4th ed.). Washington, DC: Author.

American Psychiatric Association (2000). *Diagnostic and statistical manual of mental disorders: Text revision* (4th ed.). Washington, DC: Author.

Andrews, G., Stewart, G. W., Morris-Yates, A., Holt, P., & Henderson, A. S. (1990). Evidence for a general neurotic syndrome. *British Journal of Psychiatry, 157,* 6–12.

Atkins, D. C., Bedics, J. D., McGlinchey, J. B., & Beauchaine, T. P. (2005). Assessing clinical significance: Does it matter which method we use? *Journal of Consulting and Clinical Psychology, 73,* 982–989.

Beaudoin, S., Tremblay, M., Carbonneau, C., Dugas, M. J., Provencher, M., & Ladouceur, R. (1997, October). *Validation d'un instrument diagnostique pour le trouble d'anxiété généralisée* [Validation of a diagnostic measure for generalized anxiety disorder]. Poster session presented at the annual meeting for the Société Québecoise pour la Recherche en Psychologie, Sherbrooke, QC, Canada.

Beck, A. T., Epstein, N., Brown, G., & Steer, R. A. (1988). An inventory for measuring clinical anxiety: Psychometric properties. *Journal of Consulting and Clinical Psychology, 56,* 893–897.

Beck, A. T., & Steer, R. A. (1990). *Manual for the Beck Anxiety Inventory.* San Antonio, TX: The Psychological Corporation.

Beck, A. T., Steer, R. A., & Brown, G. K. (1996). *Beck Depression Inventory Manual* (2nd ed.). San Antonio, TX: Psychological Corporation.

Beekman, A. T. F., Bremmer, M. A., Deeg, D. J. H., van Balkom, A. J. L. M., Smit, J. H., de Beurs, E., et al. (1998). Anxiety disorders in later life: A report from the Longitudinal Aging Study Amsterdam. *International Journal of Geriatric Psychiatry, 13,* 717–726.

Blazer, D. G., Hughes, D., & George, L. K. (1987). Stressful life events and the onset of generalized anxiety disorder syndrome. *American Journal of Psychiatry, 144,* 1178–1183.

Blazer, D. G., Hughes, D., George, L. K., Swartz, M., & Boyer, R. (1991). Generalized anxiety disorder. In L. N. Robins & D. A. Reiger (Eds.), *Psychiatric disorders in America: The epidemiologic catchment area study* (pp. 180–203). New York: Free Press.

Borkovec, T. D., Alcaine, O., & Behar, E. (2004). Avoidance theory of worry and generalizaed anxiety disorder. In: R. G. Heimberg, C. L. Turk, & D. S. Mennin (Eds.), *Generalized anxiety disorder: Advances in research and practice* (pp. 77–108). New York: Guilford Press.

Borkovec, T. D., & Costello, E. J. (1993). Efficacy of applied relaxation and cognitive-behavioral therapy in the treatment of generalized anxiety disorder. *Journal of Consulting and Clinical Psychology, 61,* 611–619.

Borkovec, T. D., Ray, W. J., & Stöber, J. (1998). Worry: A cognitive phenomenon intimately linked to affective, physiological, and interpersonal behavioral processes. *Cognitive Therapy and Research, 22,* 561–576.

Brown, T. A., Barlow, D. H., & Liebowitz, M. R. (1994). The empirical basis of generalized anxiety disorder. *American Journal of Psychiatry, 151,* 1272–1280.

Brown, T. A., Chorpita, B. F., & Barlow, D. H. (1998). Structural relationships among dimensions of the DSM-IV anxiety and mood disorders and dimensions of negative affect, positive affect, and autonomic arousal. *Journal of Abnormal Psychology, 107,* 179–192.

Brown, T. A., Di Nardo, P. A., & Barlow, D. H. (1994). *Anxiety Disorders Interview Schedule for DSM-IV (ADIS-IV).* Albany, NY: Graywind.

Brown, T. A., Di Nardo, P. A., Lehman, C. L., & Campbell, L. A. (2001). Reliability of DSM-IV anxiety and mood disorders: Implications for the classification of emotional disorders. *Journal of Abnormal Psychology, 110,* 49–58.

Buhr, K., & Dugas, M. J. (2002). The Intolerance of Uncertainty Scale: Psychometric properties of the English version. *Behaviour Research and Therapy, 40,* 931–945.

Buhr, K., & Dugas, M. J. (2006). Investigating the construct validity of intolerance of uncertainty and its unique relationship with worry. *Journal of Anxiety Disorders, 20,* 222–236.

Campbell, L. A., & Brown, T. A. (2002). Generalized anxiety disorder. In M. M. Antony & D. H. Barlow (Eds.), *Handbook of assessment and treatment planning for psychological disorders* (pp. 147–181). New York: Guilford.

Carter, R. M., Wittchen, H.-U., Pfister, H., & Kessler, R. C. (2001). One-year prevalence of subthreshold and threshold DSM-IV generalized anxiety disorder in a nationally representative sample. *Depression and Anxiety, 13,* 78–88.

de Beurs, E., Wilson, K. A., Chambless, D. L., Goldstein, A. J., & Feske, U. (1997). Convergent and divergent validity of the Beck Anxiety Inventory for patients with panic disorder and agoraphobia. *Depression and Anxiety, 6,* 140–146.

Di Nardo, P. A., & Barlow, D. H. (1988). *Anxiety Disorders Interview Schedule-Revised (ADIS-R).* Albany, NY: Graywind.

Di Nardo, P. A., Brown, T. A., & Barlow, D. H. (1994). *Anxiety Disorders Interview Schedule for DSM-IV: Lifetime Version (ADIS-IV-L).* Albany, NY: Graywind.

Dugas, M. J., Freeston, M. H., Provencher, M. D., Lachance, S., Ladouceur, R., & Gosselin, P. (2001). Le Questionnaire sur l'inquiétude et l'anxiété: Validation dans des échantillons non cliniques et cliniques. [The Worry and Anxiety Questionnaire: Validation in clinical and non-clinical samples]. *Journal de Thérapie Comportementale et Cognitive, 11,* 31–36.

Dugas, M. J., Gagnon, F., Ladouceur, R., & Freeston, H. (1998). Generalized anxiety disorder: A preliminary test of a conceptual model. *Behaviour Research and Therapy, 36,* 215–226.

Dugas, M. J., & Koerner, N. (2005). The cognitive-behavioral treatment for generalized anxiety disorder: Current status and future directions. *Journal of Cognitive Psychotherapy: An International Quarterly, 19,* 61–81.

Dugas, M. J., Ladouceur, R., Légcr, E., Frecston, M. H., Langlois, F., Provencher, M., et al. (2003). Group cognitive-behavioral therapy for generalized anxiety disorder: Treatment outcome and long-term follow-up. *Journal of Consulting and Clinical Psychology, 71,* 821–825.

Dugas, M. J., Marchand, A., & Ladouceur, R. (2005). Further validation of a cognitive-behavioral model of generalized anxiety disorder: Diagnostic and symptom specificity. *Journal of Anxiety Disorders, 19,* 329–343.

Dugas, M. J., & Robichaud, M. (2007). *Cognitive-behavioral treatment for generalized anxiety disorder: From science to practice.* New York: Routledge.

Dugas, M. J., Savard, P., Gaudet, A., Turcotte, J., Brillon, P., Leblanc, R., et al. (2004, November). Cognitive-behavioral therapy versus applied relaxation for generalized anxiety disorder: Differential outcomes and processes. In H. Hazlett-Stevens (Chair), *New advances in the treatment of chronic worry and generalized anxiety disorder.* Symposium conducted at the annual convention of the Association for Advancement of Behavior Therapy, New Orleans, LA.

Dugas, M. J., Savard, P., Gaudet, A., Turcotte, J., Laugesen, N., Robichaud, M., et al. (2007). Can the components of a cognitive model predict the severity of generalized anxiety disorder? *Behavior Therapy, 38,* 165–178.

Dupuy, J.-B., Beaudoin, S., Rhéaume, J., Ladouceur, R., & Dugas, M. J. (2001). Worry: Daily self-report in clinical and non-clinical populations. *Behaviour Research and Therapy, 39,* 1249–1255.

Dyck, I. R., Phillips, K. A., Warshaw, M. G., Dolan, R. T., Shea, T., Stout, R. L., et al. (2001). Patterns of personality pathology in patients with generalized anxiety disorder, panic disorder with and without agoraphobia, and social phobia. *Journal of Personality Disorders, 15,* 60–71.

First, M. B., & Gibbon, M. (2004). The Structured Clinical Interview for DSM-IV Axis I Disorders (SCID-I) and the Structured Clinical Interview for DSM-IV Axis II Disorders (SCID-II). In M. J. Hilsenroth & D. L. Segal (Eds.), *Comprehensive handbook of psychological assessment: Vol 2. Personality assessment* (pp. 134–143). Hoboken, NJ: Wiley.

First, M. B., Spitzer, R. L, Gibbon, M., & Williams, J. B.W. (1996). *Structured Clinical Interview for DSM-IV Axis I Disorders, Clinician Version (SCID-CV).* Washington, DC: American Psychiatric Press, Inc.

First, M. B., Spitzer, R. L., Gibbon, M., & Williams, J. B. W.(1997). *Structured Clinical Interview for DSM-IV Personality Disorders* (SCID-II). Washington, DC: American Psychiatric Press.

First, M. B., Spitzer, R. L, Gibbon, M., & Williams, J. B. W. (2002). *Structured Clinical Interview for DSM-IV-TR Axis I Disorders, Research Version, Patient Edition. (SCID-I/P).* New York: Biometrics Research, New York State Psychiatric Institute.

Freeston, M. H., Rhéaume, J., Letarte, H., Dugas, M. J., & Ladouceur, R. (1994). Why do people worry? *Personality and Individual Differences, 17,* 791–802.

Frisch, M. B. (1994). *Quality of Life Inventory: Manual and treatment guide.* Minneapolis, MN: National Computer Systems.

Frisch, M. B., Cornell, J., Villanueva, M., & Retzlaff, P. J. (1992). Clinical validation of the Quality of Life Inventory: A measure of life satisfaction for use in treatment planning and outcome assessment. *Psychological Assessment, 4,* 92–101.

Fydrich, T., Dowdall, D., & Chambless, D. L. (1992). Reliability and validity of the Beck Anxiety Inventory. *Journal of Anxiety Disorders, 6,* 55–61.

Gillis, M. M., Haaga, D. A. F., & Ford, G. T. (1995). Normative values of the Beck Anxiety Inventory, Fear Questionnaire, Penn State Worry Questionnaire, and Social Phobia and Anxiety Inventory. *Psychological Assessment, 7,* 450–455.

Gorman, J. M., (2002). Treatment of generalized anxiety disorder. *Journal of Clinical Psychiatry, 63*(Suppl. 8), 17–23.

Gosselin, P., Ladouceur, R., Langlois, F., Freeston, M. H., Dugas, M. J., & Bertrand, J. (2003). Développement et validation d'un nouvel instrument évaluant les croyances erronées à l'égard des inquiétudes [Development and validation of a new instrument evaluating erroneous beliefs about worry]. *European Review of Applied Psychology, 53,* 199–211.

Gosselin, P., Ladouceur, R., & Pelletier, O., (2005). Évaluation de l'attitude d'un individu face aux différents problèmes de vie : Le Questionnaire d'Attitude face aux Problèmes (QAP) [Evaluation of an individual's attitude toward daily life problems: The Negative Problem Orientation Questionnaire]. *Journal de Thérapie Comportementale et Cognitive, 15,* 141–153.

Gosselin, P., Langlois, F., Freeston, M. H., Ladouceur, R., Dugas, M. J., & Pelletier, O. (2002). Le Questionnaire d'Évitement Cognitif (QEC): Développement et validation auprès d'adultes et d'adolescents. [The Cognitive Avoidance Questionnaire (CAQ): Development and validation among adult and adolescent samples]. *Journal de Thérapie Comportementale et Cognitive, 12,* 24–37.

Grant, B. F., Hasin, D. S., Stinson, F. S., Dawson, D. A., Chou, S. P., Ruan, W. J., et al. (2005). Co-occurrence of 12-month mood and anxiety disorders and personality disorders in the US: Results from the national epidemiologic survey on alcohol and related conditions. *Journal of Psychiatric Research, 39,* 1–9.

Hettema, J. M., Prescott, C. A., & Kendler, K. S. (2001). A population-based twin study of generalized anxiety disorder in men and women. *Journal of Nervous and Mental Disease, 189,* 413–420.

Holaway, R. M., Rodebaugh, T. M., & Heimberg, R. G. (2006). The epidemiology of worry and generalized anxiety disorder. In G. C. L. Davey & A. Wells (Eds.), *Worry and its psychological disorders: Theory, assessment and treatment* (pp. 3–20). Chichester, UK: Wiley.

Holowka, D. W., Dugas, M. J., Francis, K., & Laugesen, N. (2000, November). *Measuring beliefs about worry: A psychometric evaluation of the Why Worry-II Questionnaire.* Poster session presented at the annual convention of the Association for Advancement of Behavior Therapy, New Orleans, LA.

Hudson, J. L., & Rapee, R. M. (2004). From anxious temperament to disorder: An etiological model. In R. G. Heimberg, C. L. Turk, & D. S. Mennin (Eds.), *Generalized anxiety disorder: Advances in research and practice* (pp. 51–74). New York: Guilford.

Hunt, C., Issakidis, C., & Andrews, G. (2002). DSM-IV generalized anxiety disorder in the Australian National Survey of Mental Health and Well-Being. *Psychological Medicine, 32,* 649–659.

Jacobson, N. S., & Truax, P. (1991). Clinical significance: A statistical approach to defining meaningful change in psychotherapy research. *Journal of Consulting and Clinical Psychology, 59,* 12–19.

Kendler, K. S., Neale, M. C., Kessler, R. C., Heath, A. C., & Eaves, L. J. (1992). Major depression and generalized anxiety disorder: Same genes, (partly) different environments? *Archives of General Psychiatry, 49,* 716–722.

Kessler, R. C., Berglund, P., Demler, O., Jin, R., Merikangas, K. R., & Walters, E. E. (2005). Lifetime prevalence and age-of-onset distributions of DSM-IV disorders in the National Comorbidity Survey Replication. *Archives of General Psychiatry, 62,* 593–603.

Kessler, R. C., DuPont, R. L., Berglund, P., & Wittchen, H. U. (1999). Impairment in pure and comorbid generalized anxiety disorder and major depression at 12 months in two national surveys. *American Journal of Psychiatry, 156,* 1915–1923.

Kessler, R. C., Keller, M. B., & Wittchen, H.-U. (2001). The epidemiology of generalized anxiety disorder. *Psychiatric Clinics of North America, 24,* 19–39.

Kessler, R. C., McGonagle, K. A., Zhao, S., Nelson, C. B., Hugues, M., Eshleman, S., et al. (1994). Lifetime and 12-month prevalence of DSM-III-R psychiatric disorders in the United States. *Archives of General Psychiatry, 51,* 8–19.

Kessler, R. C., Walters, E. E., & Wittchen, H.-U. (2004). Epidemiology. In R. G. Heimberg, C. L. Turk, & D. S. Mennin (Eds.), *Generalized anxiety disorder: Advances in research and practice* (pp. 29–50). New York: Guilford.

Labrecque, J., Leblanc, G., Kirouac, C., Marchand, A., & Stephenson, R. (2001, March). Validation d'un questionnaire mesurant le qualité de vie auprès d'un échantillon étudiant. [Validation of a quality of life questionnaire in a student population]. Poster session presented at the 24th annual congress of La Société Québecoise pour la Recherche en Psychologie, Montréal, QC, Canada.

Ladouceur, R., Dugas, M. J., Freeston, M. H., Léger, E., Gagnon, F., & Thibodeau, N. (2000). Efficacy of a new cognitive-behavioral treatment for generalized anxiety disorder: Evaluation in a controlled clinical trial. *Journal of Consulting and Clinical Psychology, 68,* 957–964.

Ladouceur, R., Dugas, M. J., Freeston, M. H., Rhéaume, J., Blais, F., Boisvert, J.-M., et al. (1999). Specificity of generalized anxiety disorder symptoms and processes. *Behavior Therapy, 30,* 191–207.

Ladouceur, R., Gosselin, P., & Dugas, M. J. (2000). Experimental manipulation of intolerance of uncertainty: A study of a theoretical model of worry. *Behaviour Research and Therapy, 38,* 933–941.

Laugesen, N., Dugas, M. J., & Bukowski, W. M. (2003). Understanding adolescent worry: The application of a cognitive model. *Journal of Abnormal Child Psychology, 31,* 55–64.

Léger, E., Freeston, M. H., Dugas, M. J., & Ladouceur, R. (1998). Behavioural Therapy Laboratory, School of Psychology, Laval University.

Lichtenstein, J., & Cassidy, J. (1991, April). *The inventory of adult attachment (INVAA): Validation of a new measure.*

Paper presented at the biennial meeting of the Society for Research in Child Development, Seattle, WA.

Luterek, J. A., Turk, C. L., Heimberg, R. G., Fresco, D. M., & Mennin, D. S. (2002, November). *Psychometric properties of the GAD-Q-IV among individuals with clinician-assessed generalized anxiety disorder: An update*. Poster session presented at the annual meeting of the Association for the Advancement of Behavior Therapy, Reno, NV.

Maffei, C., Fossati, A., Agostoni, I., Barraco, A., Bagnato, M., Deborah, D., et al. (1997). Interrater reliability and internal consistency of the Structured Clinical Interview for DSM-IV Axis II Personality Disorders (SCID-II), Version 2.0. *Journal of Personality Disorders, 11,* 279–284.

Maier, W., Gansicke, M., Freyberger, H. J., Linz, M., Heun, R., & Lecrubier, Y. (2000). Generalized anxiety disorder (ICD-10) in primary care from a cross-cultural perspective: A valid diagnostic entity? *Acta Psychiatrica Scandinavica, 101,* 29–36.

Maser, J. D. (1998). Generalized anxiety disorder and its comorbidities: Disputes at the boundaries. *Acta Psychiatrica Scandinavica, 98,* 12–22.

Mennin, D. S., Heimberg, R. G., Turk, C. L., & Fresco, D. M. (2002). Applying an emotion regulation framework to integrative approaches to generalized anxiety disorder. *Clinical Psychology: Science and Practice, 9,* 85–90.

Meyer, T. J., Miller, M. L., Metzger, R. L., & Borkovec, T. D. (1990). Development and validation of the Penn State Worry Questionnaire. *Behaviour Research and Therapy, 28,* 487–495.

Molina, S., & Borkovec, T. D. (1994). The Penn State Worry Questionnaire: Psychometric properties and associated characteristics. In G. C. L. Davey. & F. Tallis (Eds.), *Worrying: Perspectives on theory, assessment, and treatment* (pp. 265–283). Chichester, UK: Wiley.

Newman, M. G., Zuellig, A. R., Kachin, K. E., Constantino, M. J., Przeworski, A., Erickson, T., et al. (2002). Preliminary reliability and validity of the Generalized Anxiety Disorder Questionnaire-IV: A revised self-report diagnostic measure of generalized anxiety disorder. *Behavior Therapy, 33,* 215–233.

Norton, P. (2005). A psychometric analysis of the Intolerance of Uncertainty Scale among four racial groups. *Journal of Anxiety Disorders, 19,* 699–707.

Peasley, C. E., Molina, S., & Borkovec, T. D. (1994, November). *Empathy in generalized anxiety disorder*. Poster session presented at the annual meeting of the Association for the Advancement of Behavior Therapy, San Diego, CA.

Rapee, R. M. (1991). Generalized anxiety disorder: A review of clinical features and theoretical concepts. *Clinical Psychology Review, 11,* 419–440.

Robichaud, M., & Dugas, M. J. (2005a). Negative problem orientation (part I): Psychometric properties of a new measure. *Behaviour Research and Therapy, 43,* 391–401.

Robichaud, M., & Dugas, M. J. (2005b). Negative problem orientation (part II): Construct validity and specificity to worry. *Behaviour Research and Therapy, 43,* 403–412.

Robichaud, M., Dugas, M. J., & Conway, M. (2003). Gender differences in worry and associated cognitive-behavioral variables. *Journal of Anxiety Disorders, 17,* 501–516.

Roemer, L., Borkovec, M., Posa, S., & Borkovec, T. D. (1995). A self report diagnostic measure of generalized anxiety disorder. *Journal of Behavior Therapy and Experimental Psychiatry, 26,* 345–350.

Roy-Byrne, P. P., & Katon, W. (1997). Generalized anxiety disorder in primary care: The precursor/modifier pathway to increased healthcare utilization. *Journal of Clinical Psychiatry, 58,* 34–38.

Sexton, K. A., & Dugas, M. J. (in press). The Cognitive Avoidance Questionnaire: Validation of the English translation. *Journal of Anxiety Disorders.*

Startup, H. M., & Erickson, T. M. (2006). The Penn State Worry Questionnaire (PSWQ). In G. C. L. Davey & A. Wells (Eds.), *Worry and its psychological disorders: Theory, assessment and treatment* (pp. 101–119). Chichester, UK: Wiley.

Steer, R. A., & Clark, D. A. (1997). Psychometric properties of the Beck Depression Inventory-II with college students. *Measurement and Evaluation in Counselling and Development, 30,* 128–136.

Stein, M. B. (2004). Public health perspectives on generalized anxiety disorder. *Journal of Clinical Psychiatry, 65,* 3–7.

Stöber, J., & Bittencourt, J. (1998). Weekly assessment of worry: An adaptation of the Penn State Worry Questionnaire for monitoring changes during treatment. *Behaviour Research and Therapy, 36,* 645–656.

Wells, A., & Carter, K. (1999). Preliminary tests of a cognitive model of generalized anxiety disorder. *Behaviour Research and Therapy, 37,* 585–594.

Williams, J. B. W., Gibbon, M., First, M. B., Spitzer, R. L., Davies, M., Borus, J., et al. (1992). The Structured Clinical Interview for DSM-III-R (SCID): II. Multisite test–retest reliability. *Archives of General Psychiatry, 49,* 630–636.

Wittchen, H.-U., & Hoyer, J. (2001). Generalized anxiety disorder: Nature and course. *Journal of Clinical Psychiatry, 62*(Suppl. 11), 15–19.

Wittchen, H.-U., Kessler, R. C., Beesdo, K., Krause, P., Höfler, M., & Hoyer, J. (2002). Generalized anxiety and depression in primary care: Prevalence, recognition, and management. *Journal of Clinical Psychiatry, 63,* 24–34.

Wittchen, H.-U., Zhao, S., Kessler, R. C., & Eaton, W. W. (1994). DSM-III-R generalized anxiety disorder in the National Comorbidity Survey. *Archives of General Psychiatry, 51,* 355–364.

Yonkers, K. A., Warshaw, M. G., Massion, A. O., & Keller, M. B. (1996). Phenomenology and course of generalized anxiety disorder. *British Journal of Psychiatry, 168,* 308–313.

Zanarini, M. C., Skodol, A. E., Bender, D., Dolan, R., Sanislow, C., Schaefer, E., et al. (2000). The Collaborative Longitudinal Personality Disorders Study: Reliability of Axis I and II diagnoses. *Journal of Personality Disorders, 14,* 291–299.

13

Obsessive–Compulsive Disorder

Jonathan S. Abramowitz

This chapter addresses the conceptualization and assessment of obsessive–compulsive disorder (OCD) in order to aid the clinician in the treatment of this condition. After identifying, defining, and describing the nature of OCD, I provide a brief review of empirically based theories and psychological treatments. Next, three sections address assessment for the purposes of (1) establishing a clinical diagnosis of OCD, (2) formulating a treatment plan, and (3) measuring severity and treatment response. Not all of the available measures of OCD are reviewed in this chapter, as some older measures have fallen out of favor as our understanding of this disorder has advanced; other measures have poor psychometric properties or confound important variables. The chapter concludes with a discussion of the strengths and limitations of existing assessment options, as well as future directions in the assessment of OCD.

THE NATURE OF OCD

Definition

OCD is classified in the *Diagnostic and Statistical Manual of Mental Disorders*, 4th Edition, (DSM-IV-TR, APA, 2000) as an anxiety disorder characterized by *obsessions* or *compulsions*. Obsessions are persistent intrusive thoughts, ideas, images, impulses, or doubts that are experienced as unacceptable, senseless, or bizarre. The intrusions also evoke subjective distress (e.g., anxiety, fear, doubt) and are not simply everyday worries about work, relationships, or finances. Common obsessions include ideas of contamination by the AIDS virus, unwanted impulses to harm others, doubts that one is responsible for accidents, and intrusive sacrilegious images. Although

highly individualistic, obsessions typically concern the following general themes: aggression and violence, responsibility for causing harm, contamination, sex, religion, the need for exactness or completeness, and concerns about serious illnesses. Most individuals with OCD evidence multiple types of obsessions.

To control their anxiety, individuals with OCD attempt to avoid stimuli that trigger obsessions (e.g., public restrooms in the case of contamination obsessions). If such stimuli cannot be avoided, however, the person experiences compulsive rituals—urges to perform behavioral or mental acts according to idiosyncratic personal "rules." The rituals are deliberate, yet clearly senseless or excessive in relation to the obsessional fear they are designed to neutralize (e.g., washing one's hands for 30 minutes after using the restroom). As with obsessions, rituals are highly individualized. Common *behavioral* rituals include excessive decontamination (e.g., washing), checking (e.g., locks, the stove), counting, and repeating routine actions (e.g., going through doorways, turning the light switch off and on several times). Examples of *mental* rituals include excessive prayer and using special "safe" numbers or phrases (e.g., "God is great") to neutralize "unsafe" obsessional thoughts or stimuli (e.g., the number "666"). Obsessions and compulsions are functionally related in that obsessions (e.g., images of germs) *increase* subjective distress whereas rituals (e.g., washing) *reduce* obsessional distress.

Individuals with OCD display a range of insight into the senselessness of their symptoms in that some acknowledge the irrationality of their obsessions and compulsions and others are firmly convinced that these symptoms are rational. Often, the degree of insight varies across time and obsessional themes. For example, one person might recognize her obsessional thoughts of harm as senseless, yet have poor insight into the irrationality of her contamination obsessions.

Etiological Models and Treatment

Biological Models

Prevailing neurotransmitter theories posit that abnormalities in the serotonin system underlie OCD (Gross, Sasson, Chorpa, & Zohar, 1998). Results from studies that have directly examined the relationship between serotonin and OCD, however, have been inconsistent. Whereas the preferential response of patients with OCD to serotonergic medication is often championed as supporting the serotonin hypothesis, this argument is of little value since the serotonin hypothesis was initially derived *from* this treatment outcome result (for a discussion of this logical problem with the serotonin hypothesis, see Shafran & Speckens, 2005). Thus, whether serotonin functioning mediates OCD symptoms remains unclear.

Predominant neuroanatomical models of OCD propose that symptoms arise from structural and functional abnormalities in orbitofrontal-subcortical circuits within the brain (Saxena, Bota, & Brody, 2001). These circuits are thought to connect regions of the brain involved in information processing with those involved in the initiation of certain behavioral responses. Although highly interesting, these models are derived from cross-sectional data indicating differences in brain structure and function between people with and without OCD. Because of their correlational nature, however, such data cannot reveal whether OCD is a cause or consequence of the observed brain differences. It is indeed possible that such observations represent the effects of chronic anxiety on normally functioning brain systems.

Psychological Models

Two psychological models are relevant to the effective psychological treatment of OCD: a conditioning approach and a cognitive-behavioral approach. Early conditioning models of OCD proposed that obsessional anxiety is acquired when a previously neutral stimulus (e.g., the floor) becomes associated with fear through classical conditioning. This fear is then maintained by avoidance and the performance of rituals, which prevent the natural extinction of the fear. Avoidance and rituals are also negatively reinforced by the reduction in fear they engender, thus they develop into compulsive-like habits. Contemporary learning models focus on other sources of learning, such as vicarious conditioning and social learning to account for the development of obsessions (e.g., Mineka & Zinbarg, 2006).

Conditioning models form the basis for the most effective treatment for OCD, which includes the behavioral therapy techniques of exposure and response prevention (ERP; Abramowitz, Franklin, & Foa, 2002). Therapeutic exposure aims to extinguish obsessional fear by helping the individual to systematically confront situations and stimuli that evoke obsessions (e.g., touching floors, thinking upsetting thoughts) and remain in the feared situation until anxiety naturally decreases. Response prevention entails refraining from compulsive rituals, with the aim of weakening the association between rituals and anxiety reduction. Exposure exercises are repeated frequently and in multiple contexts, using a hierarchy-driven (i.e., graduated) approach in which less distressing stimuli are confronted and mastered before more difficult stimuli are faced. The details regarding implementation of ERP are beyond the scope of this chapter, but are well described elsewhere (e.g., Abramowitz, 2006a, 2006b). Numerous studies conducted around the world indicate that ERP is highly effective, with the average patient receiving a 60% to 70% reduction in symptoms (e.g., Abramowitz et al., 2002).

Cognitive-behavioral models of OCD (e.g., Salkovskis, 1996; for a review see Shafran, 2005) are derived from Beck's (1976) cognitive specificity hypothesis, which proposes that different types of psychopathology arise from disorder-specific dysfunctional beliefs and appraisals of various stimuli. As applied to OCD, such models consider intrusive thoughts, images, and impulses as normal stimuli that occur from time to time in just about everyone. Salkovskis (1996) proposed that such normal intrusions develop into clinical obsessions when the intrusions are appraised as posing a threat for which the individual is personally responsible.

To illustrate, consider an unwanted intrusive thought of harming an infant. Whereas most people would regard this experience as meaningless ("mental noise"), such an intrusion could develop into a clinical obsession if the person mistakenly appraised it as having serious consequences (e.g., "If I think about this too much I will act on it"). Such appraisals evoke distress and motivate the person to try to suppress or remove the intrusion (e.g., via rituals). The tendency to misappraise intrusive thoughts as having serious consequences is thought to arise from dysfunctional beliefs concerning responsibility, the importance of thoughts, need for perfectionism, overestimation of threat, and need for certainty (Frost & Steketee, 2002). Rituals are conceptualized as efforts to remove obsessional intrusions and to prevent any perceived harmful consequences.

Treatment based on the cognitive-behavioral model incorporates ERP, but emphasizes *cognitive* changes that occur with this treatment. For example, exposure is thought to modify erroneous expectations about the likelihood and severity of feared outcomes. Therapy also includes verbal techniques such as psychoeducation and cognitive restructuring that help the patient to recognize and correct faulty beliefs and appraisals of intrusive thoughts and other feared stimuli (e.g., Clark, 2004; Wilhelm & Steketee, 2006). Research indicates such cognitive approaches can be helpful, yet are best employed as adjuncts to ERP (Abramowitz, 2006a).

Epidemiology, Course, and Prognosis

The lifetime prevalence of OCD in the general adult population is as high as 2.3% (e.g., Kessler et al., 2005). Symptoms typically develop gradually, often beginning in the teenage years. An exception is the abrupt onset sometimes observed following pregnancy (Abramowitz, Schwartz, Moore, & Luenzmann, 2003). Left untreated, the disorder typically runs a chronic course; although symptoms may wax and wane in severity over time, and in some cases improve (often dependent upon levels of psychosocial stress; e.g., Skoog & Skoog, 1999).

Most individuals with OCD suffer for several years before they receive adequate diagnosis and treatment. Factors contributing to the under-recognition of OCD include the failure of patients to disclose symptoms, the failure to assess for obsessions and compulsions during mental status examinations, and difficulties with differential diagnoses. Because OCD represents a seemingly complex set of thinking and behavioral symptoms, its assessment has traditionally been considered highly challenging. This is likely because many clinicians undertake assessment without a theoretical framework to guide the process. The aim of this chapter is to facilitate a theoretically grounded approach to assessing OCD that is also consistent with the empirically supported cognitive and behavioral interventions for this condition.

Associated Features

Most individuals with OCD also suffer from depressive symptoms, which can exacerbate obsessional problems and attenuate response to ERP (e.g., Abramowitz, Franklin, Kozak, Street, & Foa, 2000). Therefore, it is necessary to assess mood state and, in particular, to inquire about the chronological history of mood complaints in order to establish whether such symptoms should be considered as a primary diagnosis (e.g., major depressive disorder) or as secondary to OCD symptoms.

Relatives' emotional and behavioral responses to the patient's OCD symptoms should also be considered. In some instances family members, who wish not to see their loved one suffer, unwittingly contribute to the persistence of OCD symptoms by performing rituals, providing frequent reassurance, and engaging in avoidance to "help the affected relative cope with anxiety." Thus, family accommodation is an important factor to assess. In other families, relatives are highly critical and express hostility toward their loved one with OCD. When relatives meddle or chronically intrude into the patient's daily activities, it can affect course and treatment response. Relatives can be invited to take part in the assessment process, thus providing an opportunity to assess how he or she interacts with the patient. Relatives can be asked about (a) the extent to which they participate in the patient's rituals and avoidance habits, (b) how they respond when repeatedly asked questions for reassurance, (c) what consequences they fear might occur if symptoms are not accommodated, and (d) the extent to which the family's daily activities are influenced by the patient's OCD symptoms.

PURPOSES OF ASSESSMENT

Proper assessment of OCD is guided by conceptual models of phenomenology, etiology, and treatment. As the cognitive-behavioral model has consistent empirical support, this framework is used in this chapter to determine what parameters are necessary to assess. The next sections include a review and discussion of the use of particular instruments and methodologies that clinicians and clinical researchers will find helpful for the purposes of (a) making a diagnosis of OCD, (b) case conceptualization and treatment planning, and (c) evaluating the effects of treatment.

ASSESSMENT FOR DIAGNOSIS

General Description of the Problem

It is useful to begin the diagnostic assessment in an unstructured way by asking the patient to provide a general description of his or her difficulties with obsessions and compulsions. Reviewing a typical day can highlight, for example, the frequency and duration of OCD symptoms, how these symptoms are managed, and the ways in which the person is functionally impaired. Examples of open-ended questions to ask regarding presence of obsessions, compulsions, and related signs and symptoms include the following:

- What kinds of activities or situations trigger anxiety or fear?
- What kinds of upsetting or scary thoughts have you been experiencing?
- What places or situations have you have been avoiding?
- Tell me about any behaviors that you feel compelled to perform over and over.

Information about the onset, historical course of the problem, comorbid conditions, social and developmental history, and personal/family history of mental health treatment should also be obtained. The most common comorbid conditions among individuals with OCD are unipolar mood disorders (see Chapter 5 of this volume) and other anxiety disorders (e.g., generalized anxiety disorder; see Chapter 12 of this volume).

Yale-Brown Obsessive–Compulsive Scale Symptom Checklist

Because OCD is highly heterogeneous in its presentation, a semistructured approach to assessing the topography of a given patient's symptoms is recommended as an initial step. The Yale-Brown Obsessive–Compulsive Scale Symptom Checklist (Y-BOCS-SC; Goodman et al., 1989a, 1989b; reprinted in the *Journal of Clinical Psychiatry*, volume 60 [1999], suppl. 18, pp. 67–77) is the best available instrument for such purposes. The first section of the Y-BOCS-SC provides definitions of obsessions and compulsions that are read to the patient. Next, the clinician reviews a list of over 50 common obsessions and compulsions and asks whether each symptom is currently present or has occurred in the past. Finally, the most prominent obsessions,

compulsions, and OCD-related avoidance behaviors are identified from those endorsed by the patient.

Although it is comprehensive in scope, there are no psychometric studies of the Y-BOCS-SC. Moreover the checklist merely assesses the *form* of the patient's obsessions and rituals without regard for the *function* of these symptoms. That is, there are no questions relating to how rituals are used to reduce obsessional fears (further below, I describe a functional approach to assessing OCD symptoms that has incremental validity over the Y-BOCS-SC for the purpose of developing a treatment plan). Another limitation of the Y-BOCS-SC is that it contains only one item assessing mental rituals. Thus, the clinician must probe in a less structured way for the presence of these covert symptoms (the assessment of mental rituals is also discussed further in the section on case conceptualization and treatment planning). Finally, because of its emphasis on the overt characteristics of obsessions and compulsions—such as their repetitiveness and thematic content (e.g., fears of illness, repetitive counting)—the Y-BOCS-SC offers little help in differentiating OCD symptoms from other clinical phenomena that might also be repetitive or thematically similar. For example, worries might be repetitive and can focus on matters of health and illness, depressive ruminations are repetitive and involve negative thinking, and impulse-control disorders (e.g., trichotillomania) can involve repetitive behaviors. It is therefore necessary to distinguish OCD symptoms from these other entities.

Distinguishing OCD Symptoms from other Phenomena

Whereas obsessions and worries can both involve themes of illness and harm, obsessions focus on doubts about unrealistic disastrous consequences (e.g., "What if I had a hit-and-run automobile accident and didn't realize it?"). Worries, in contrast, concern real life (everyday) situations such as relationships, health and safety, work or school, and finances. In addition, compared with worries, obsessions are experienced as more unacceptable and they evoke greater subjective resistance. Obsessions can be differentiated from depressive ruminations based on content as well as subjective experience. Depressive ruminations typically involve overly general negative thoughts about self, world, and future (e.g., "No one will ever love me"). Moreover, depressive ruminations do not elicit subjective resistance or ritualistic behavior.

Whereas obsessions are experienced as distressing, unwanted, and unacceptable, *fantasies* are experienced as pleasurable and therefore should not be confused with obsessions. For example, the erotic thoughts of individuals with paraphilia lead to sexual arousal (even if the sufferer wishes not to have such thoughts or feels guilty about them). Sexual obsessions in OCD, however, do not lead to sexual arousal (Schwartz & Abramowitz, 2003). Similarly, repetitive "obsessive" thoughts about acquiring psychoactive substances (e.g., drugs, alcohol) are not, in and of themselves, experienced as distressing (although the person might feel guilty about the consequences of their drinking). Finally, whereas obsessions and delusions might both have a bizarre quality, delusions do not evoke anxiety or rituals.

Tics (as in Tourette's syndrome) and compulsive rituals differ primarily in that rituals are usually purposeful, meaningful behaviors that are performed in response to obsessional distress and intended to reduce a obsessional fear. Tics, in contrast, are purposeless behaviors that are not triggered by obsessional thinking or performed to reduce fear. Other repetitive behaviors such as "compulsive" hair-pulling, gambling, excessive sexual behavior, overeating, stealing, and excessive shopping are associated with impulse-control disorders, yet are often mistaken for OCD rituals. These impulsive behaviors, however, are not associated with obsessions and do not serve to reduce anxiety or the probability of feared outcomes. In fact these acts are experienced as pleasurable even if the person wishes he or she did not feel compelled to do these behaviors.

Standardized Diagnostic Assessment

When initial questioning reveals the apparent presence of obsessions and/or compulsions, assessment should include a standardized diagnostic interview to confirm the diagnosis of OCD (as well as other common comorbid anxiety and mood disorders). Two incrementally valid instruments exist for this purpose and these are described below. Table 13.1 shows ratings of various psychometric and practical characteristics of these diagnostic interviews.

Anxiety Disorders Interview Schedule for DSM-IV

The ADIS-IV is a clinician-administered, semistructured, diagnostic interview developed to establish the differential diagnosis among the anxiety disorders based on DSM-IV criteria (ADIS-IV; Di Nardo, Brown, & Barlow, 1994). Compared with other diagnostic interviews, it provides greater detail about anxiety-related problems. The ADIS-IV begins with demographic questions and items about general functioning and life stress. Sections for assessing each anxiety, mood, and somatoform disorder appear next. The OCD section begins with a screening question, a positive answer to which triggers more detailed questions about obsessions and compulsions based on DSM-IV criteria.

In a large reliability study (Brown et al., 2001) the ADIS-IV OCD module evidenced very good inter-rater reliability, with the main sources of unreliability coming from the occasional assignment of a subclinical OCD diagnosis (as opposed to a different anxiety disorder). Although no studies have directly examined the validity of the ADIS-IV OCD section, the many studies showing that OCD samples diagnosed with this instrument have higher scores on measures of OCD severity, when compared with non-OCD samples, provide evidence for its validity. Other advantages of the ADIS-IV include the fact that it contains a semistructured format, which allows the clinician to collect detailed information. It also includes a dimensional rating of symptom severity. One limitation of the ADIS-IV is that administration of the entire instrument can be time consuming, although the OCD module itself is not very long.

Structured Clinical Interview for DSM-IV Axis I Disorders

The SCID is a clinician-administered, semistructured interview developed for the purpose of diagnosing a range of DSM-IV Axis I disorders (SCID; First, Spitzer, Gibbon, & Williams, 2002). Accordingly, it contains a module to assess the presence of OCD. The SCID begins with an open-ended assessment of demographic information and various domains of functioning. The OCD section includes probe questions about the presence of obsessions and compulsions. Next to each probe appear the corresponding DSM-IV diagnostic criteria, which are rated as absent (false), subthreshold, or present (true). Thus, ratings are of diagnostic criteria, not of interviewees' responses. Research on the reliability of the SCID for assessing the presence of OCD has provided mixed results. Whereas some studies report low kappas, others report more acceptable inter-rater reliability (e.g., Williams et al., 1992).

TABLE 13.1 Ratings of Instruments Used for Diagnosis

Instrument	Norms	Internal Consistency	Inter-Rater Reliability	Test–Retest Reliability	Content Validity	Construct Validity	Validity Generalization	Clinical Utility	Highly Recommended
ADIS-IV	NA	NA	E	G	E	E	E	G	✓
SCID-IV	NA	NA	A	A	E	E	E	A	
Y-BOCSC-SC	NA	NA	NA	NA	G	E	NA	A	✓
BABS	A	G	G	A	G	G	G	G	✓

Note: ADIS-IV = Anxiety Disorders Interview Schedule for DSM-IV; SCID-IV = Structured Clinical Interview for DSM-IV; Y-BOCS-SC = Yale-Brown Obsessive Compulsive Scale Symptom Checklist; BABS = Brown Assessment of Beliefs Scale; A = Adequate; G = Good; E = Excellent; NA = Not Applicable.

Assessing Insight Into the Senselessness of OCD Symptoms

The Brown Assessment of Beliefs Scale

The BABS is a brief (seven items) interview that provides a continuous measure of insight into the senselessness of OCD symptoms (BABS; Eisen et al., 1998). Administration begins with the interviewer and patient identifying one or two of the patient's specific obsessional fears that have been of significant concern over the past week. Next, individual items assess the patient's (a) conviction in the validity of this fear, (b) perceptions of how others view the validity of the fear, (c) explanation for why others hold a different view, (d) willingness to challenge the fear, (e) attempts to disprove the fear, (f) insight into whether the fear is part of a psychological/psychiatric problem, and (g) ideas/delusions of reference. Only the first six items are summed to produce a total score.

Norms for OCD samples have been established in several studies (e.g., Eisen, Phillips, Coles, & Rasmussen, 2004). The BABS appears to have good internal consistency and it discriminates OCD patients with good insight from those with poor insight (Eisen et al., 1998). Whereas the BABS is sensitive to treatment-related changes in OCD symptoms, there is mixed evidence regarding whether higher scores are predictive of poorer response to treatment (e.g., Ravie Kishore et al., 2004).

Practical Considerations

People with OCD often have difficulty discussing their obsessions and compulsions. Embarrassment over the theme (e.g., sexual) and senselessness of such symptoms is a primary factor. The interviewer must be sensitive to such concerns and demonstrate appropriate empathy regarding the difficulties inherent in discussing these problems with others. Clearly, the clinician should avoid appearing shocked or disturbed by descriptions of obsessions and compulsions. Semistructured instruments such as the Y-BOCS-SC and BABS help the interviewer normalize such symptoms. Patients also have difficulty describing their symptoms when they are unaware that such thoughts and behaviors represent obsessions and compulsions. Thus, including significant others in the interview can help identify such symptoms.

Occasionally, features of OCD itself—such as indecisiveness, rigidity, and the need for reassurance—attenuate the assessment process. Patients might be highly circumstantial in their responses because of fears that if they do not provide "all the details," they will not benefit from therapy. Such obstacles require the clinician's patience, but can often be managed with persistent gentle, yet firm, reminders of time constraints and the need for short, concise responses.

Overall Evaluation

OCD is a highly heterogeneous condition in which each individual presents with idiosyncratic and personalized symptom content. Thus, the clinician must be flexible and comprehensive, and able to distinguish bona fide OCD symptoms from symptoms of other disorders with topographically similar presentations. Family members, who might play a role in maintaining OCD symptoms, can be a reliable source of information regarding the validity of this diagnosis. Keeping these points in mind and using careful open-ended questioning often leads to correctly identifying whether or not an individual has OCD.

The ADIS-IV and SCID are empirically established and widely used structured interviews for confirming the diagnosis of OCD. Some authors favor the ADIS-IV for its excellent reliability and wider scope of information yielded as compared with the SCID. Both of these instruments, however, require that interviewers be well trained in their administration, although BA- or MA-level training in psychology is often sufficient to achieve good reliability as long as the interviewers are supervised by experienced doctoral-level psychologists. How well the individual recognizes his or her obsessions and compulsions as senseless and excessive is best assessed using the BABS, a continuous measure of insight, as opposed to using the dichotomous DSM-IV specifier ("with poor insight").

ASSESSMENT FOR CASE CONCEPTUALIZATION AND TREATMENT PLANNING

The cognitive-behavioral model, from which effective psychological treatment is derived, provides a framework for collecting patient-specific information and generating an individualized case conceptualization and treatment plan. This framework, referred to as *functional assessment*, is important because identifying the particular stimuli to be confronted during exposure therapy requires detailed knowledge of the patient's idiosyncratic fear triggers and cognitions. Similarly, assisting patients to resist compulsive urges (i.e., response prevention) requires knowing about all ritualistic maneuvers performed in response to obsessive fear. The section below describes the procedures for conducting this type of assessment.

Assessing Obsessional Stimuli

Guided by information already collected, a thorough inventory of external triggers and intrusive thoughts that evoke the patient's obsessional fear is obtained. Some of these stimuli will later be chosen for inclusion as exposure therapy tasks. Because of the idiosyncratic nature of obsessional triggers, there are no psychometrically validated instruments for this purpose. Therefore, the assessor must rely on his or her clinical experience and knowledge of the OCD research literature.

External Triggers

These include specific objects, situations, places, and so on that evoke obsessional fears and urges to ritualize. Examples include toilets, knives, completing paperwork, religious icons, feared numbers (e.g., 13 or 666), leaving the house, and so on. Examples of questions to help the patient describe such triggers include "In what situations do you feel anxious?" "What do you avoid?" and "What triggers your urge to do compulsive rituals?"

Intrusive Thoughts

These include unwanted mental stimuli (e.g., upsetting images) that are experienced as unacceptable, immoral, or repulsive, and that evoke obsessional anxiety. Examples include images of germs, impulses to harm loved ones, doubts about one's sexual preference, and thoughts of loved ones being injured. Examples of questions to elicit this information include "What intrusive thoughts do you have that trigger anxiety?" and "What thoughts do you try to avoid, resist, or dismiss?" Some patients are unwilling to describe their intrusions fearing that the therapist will not understand that these are *unwanted* thoughts. To overcome such reluctance, the assessor can educate the patient about the universality of such intrusions and even self-disclose his or her own senseless intrusions. A list of intrusive thoughts from nonclinical individuals that can be given to patients to demonstrate the universality of such phenomena is published elsewhere (e.g., Abramowitz, 2006a).

Assessing Cognitive Features

Feared Consequences

Information should be obtained about the cognitive basis of obsessional fear; that is, the feared consequences associated with obsessional stimuli (e.g., "If I use a public restroom I will get AIDS," "If my receipt has the number 13, I will have bad luck"). Knowing this information helps the therapist arrange exposure tasks that will disconfirm such exaggerated expectations. Although most patients readily articulate such fears, some do not. When feared disasters cannot be explicitly articulated, the patient might fear that anxiety itself will persist indefinitely (or escalate to "out-of-control" levels) unless a ritual is performed. The following open-ended questions are appropriate for assessing feared consequences: "What is the worst thing that could happen if you are exposed to (obsessional trigger)?" "What do you think might happen if you didn't complete the ritual?" and "What would

TABLE 13.2 Domains of Dysfunctional Beliefs Associated With OCD

Belief Domain	Description
Overestimation of threat and inflated responsibility	Beliefs that negative events are especially likely and would be especially awful. Beliefs that one has the special power to cause, and/or the duty to prevent, negative outcomes.
Overimportance of, and need to control, intrusive thoughts	Beliefs that the mere presence of a thought indicates that the thought is significant. For example, the belief that the thought has ethical or moral ramifications, or that thinking the thought increases the probability of the corresponding behavior or event. Also, beliefs that complete control over one's thoughts is both necessary and possible.
Perfectionism and intolerance for uncertainty	Beliefs that mistakes and imperfection are intolerable. Beliefs that it is necessary and possible to be completely certain that negative outcomes will not occur.

happen if you didn't do anything to reduce your high levels of anxiety?"

Dysfunctional Beliefs

Cognitive therapy techniques (e.g., Wilhelm & Steketee, 2006), which can be used to supplement exposure therapy, require assessment of the patient's dysfunctional thinking patterns that underlie obsessional fear. An international group of researchers, the Obsessive Compulsive Cognitions Working Group (OCCWG), has developed and tested two instruments that provide a comprehensive assessment of the cognitive landscape of OCD: the Obsessive Beliefs Questionnaire (OBQ) and Interpretation of Intrusions Inventory (III; OCCWG, 2005). The reader should note that additional measures for assessing specific OCD-related dysfunctional beliefs are available (e.g., the Thought-Action Fusion Scale; Shafran, Thordarson, & Rachman, 1996). Yet, because the OBQ and III are comprehensive in their coverage of the various domains of dysfunctional beliefs, this chapter focuses on these measures. Information on many of the other measures can be found in Antony, Orsillo, and Roemer (2001).

An initial 87-item version of the OBQ (OCCWG, 2001, 2003) contained six rationally derived and highly correlated subscales. Subsequent research, however, has led to a 44-item version with three empirically derived subscales (OCCWG, 2005), which assess domains of dysfunctional beliefs (termed "obsessive beliefs") thought to increase risk for the development of OCD (e.g., Frost & Steketee, 2002; see Table 13.2). Specifically, obsessive beliefs are considered enduring trait-like cognitive biases that give rise to the misinterpretation of normally occurring intrusive thoughts as highly significant and threatening, leading to obsessional anxiety and compulsive urges (e.g., Taylor, Abramowitz, & McKay, 2007). When completing the measure, respondents rate their agreement with each of the 44 items using a scale from 1 (disagree very much) to 7 (agree very much).

A summary of the psychometric viability of the OBQ appears in Table 13.3. The measure has been studied extensively with clinical and nonclinical samples, and it demonstrates very good internal consistency and test–retest reliability. Items were carefully designed by the OCCWG, and as such, demonstrate excellent content and construct validity. Prospective research also indicates that, to some extent, scores on the OBQ are predictive of the development of obsessive–compulsive symptoms (Abramowitz et al., 2006). The OBQ is quite useful in clinical settings as it identifies patterns of dysfunctional thinking

TABLE 13.3 Ratings of Instruments Used for Case Conceptualization and Treatment Planning

Instrument	Norms	Internal Consistency	Inter-Rater Reliability	Test–Retest Reliability	Content Validity	Construct Validity	Validity Generalization	Clinical Utility	Highly Recommended
OBQ	E	E	NA	G	E	E	G	G	✓
III	E	E	NA	G	E	E	G	G	✓

Note: OBQ = Obsessive Beliefs Questionnaire; III = Interpretation of Intrusions Inventory; G = Good; E = Excellent; NA = Not Applicable.

that can be targeted by cognitive therapy techniques (e.g., Wilhelm & Steketee, 2006).

The III is a semi-idiographic measure designed to assess negative appraisals of intrusive thoughts. The respondent first reads a set of instructions that includes examples of cognitive intrusions (e.g., "an impulse to do something shameful or terrible") and then is asked to identify one or two examples of his or her specific intrusions. He or she next indicates the extent of agreement with the scale's 31 items that concern various erroneous appraisals of intrusions (e.g., "I would be a better person if I didn't have this thought"). Although three theoretically derived subscales were initially proposed, further psychometric analyses indicate that only a single III factor exists (OCCWG, 2005).

As with the OBQ, the III has been studied in clinical and nonclinical samples, and it shows good to excellent reliability (see summary in Table 13.3). It also shows excellent construct validity and predicts, in a prospective fashion, the persistence of obsessional symptoms (Abramowitz et al., 2007). The III is well-suited for clinical practice as it is fairly brief and provides valuable information regarding how the patient negatively appraises the presence and meaning of his or her own intrusive thoughts. The clinician can use this information to illustrate how such faulty appraisals lead to obsessional anxiety, and how such interpretations can be modified (e.g., "It's no wonder you spend so much time trying to fight your unwanted thoughts about accidents. It looks like you're convinced that just by *thinking* these thoughts you will *cause* innocent people to have accidents. I wonder if that's how our thoughts really work").

Assessing Responses to Obsessional Distress

As discussed previously, avoidance and compulsive rituals performed in response to obsessional stimuli serve to reduce anxiety in the short term, but they paradoxically maintain OCD symptoms by preventing the natural extinction of fear and by interfering with the disconfirmation of fears of disastrous consequences. Accordingly, one must ascertain the specifics of such behaviors so that they can be treatment targets.

Passive Avoidance

Most individuals with OCD avoid situations and stimuli associated with their obsessions in order to prevent obsessional thoughts, anxiety, or feared disastrous outcomes. Avoidance might be overt, such as the evasion of certain people (e.g., cancer patients), places (e.g., public washrooms, places of worship), situations (e.g., using pesticides), and certain words (e.g., "murder"). It might also be subtle, such as staying away from the most often touched part of the door handle and refraining from listening to loud music while driving. The assessor should also ascertain the cognitive basis for avoidance (e.g., "If I listen to music, I might not realize it if I hit a pedestrian"). Examples of questions to elicit this information about avoidance include, "What situations do you avoid because of obsessional fear and why?" and "What would happen if you couldn't avoid this situation?"

Behavioral Rituals

Because the external stimuli and intrusive thoughts that evoke obsessional fear are often ubiquitous (i.e., using the bathroom, intrusive thoughts), they might be difficult to avoid successfully. Patients use rituals, therefore, as "active avoidance" strategies that serve as an escape from obsessional fear, which could not be avoided in the first place. Some rituals could be called "compulsive" in that they are performed repetitively and in accordance with certain self-prescribed rules (e.g., checking an even number of times, washing for 40 seconds). Other rituals, however, would not be classified as compulsive since they might be subtle, brief, or performed only once at a time (e.g., holding the steering wheel tightly, using a shirtsleeve to open a door).

Topographically similar rituals can serve very different functions. For example, many patients engage in hand washing rituals to decontaminate themselves. Such washing rituals are typically evoked by thoughts and images of germs, or by doubts of whether one has had contact with a feared contaminant. Some individuals with OCD, however, engage in washing rituals in response to feelings of "mental pollution" evoked by unwanted disturbing intrusive thoughts of a sexual or otherwise immoral nature (e.g., Fairbrother, Newth, & Rachman, 2005). A functional assessment, therefore, is necessary to elucidate how rituals are linked to obsessions and feared consequences, for example, checking the stove to prevent fires, or using a certain type of soap because it specifically targets certain sorts of germs. Examples of probes to elicit this information include "What do you do when you can't avoid the word 'cancer'?" "What do you do to reduce your fears of being responsible for accidents" "Why does this ritual reduce your discomfort?" "What could happen if you didn't engage in this ritual?"

Mental Rituals

The function of mental rituals is the same as behavioral rituals (de Silva, Menzies, & Shafran, 2003)—to reduce anxiety and prevent feared outcomes. Mental rituals typically take the form of silently repeating special "safe" words (e.g., "life"), images (e.g., of Jesus Christ), or phrases (e.g., prayers) in a set manner to neutralize or "deal with" unwanted obsessional thoughts. Other common presentations include thought suppression, privately reviewing one's actions over and over (e.g., to reassure oneself that he or she did not do something terrible), and mental counting. Many clinicians fail to assess mental rituals, or confuse them for obsessions. Although mental rituals and obsessions are both cognitive events, they can be differentiated by careful questioning and by keeping in mind that the former are unwanted, intrusive, and anxiety-evoking, whereas the latter are deliberate attempts to neutralize obsessional intrusions and as such, they function to reduce anxiety. Examples of questions to elicit information about mental rituals include, "Sometimes people with OCD have mental strategies that they use to manage obsessional thoughts. What kinds of mental strategies do you use to dismiss unwanted thoughts?" and "What might happen if you didn't use the strategy?"

Self-Monitoring

Self-monitoring, in which the patient records the occurrence of obsessive–compulsive symptoms in "real-time," provides data to complement the functional assessment. Patients can be instructed to log the following parameters of each symptomatic episode (i.e., using a form with corresponding column headers): (a) date and time of the episode, (b) situation or thought that triggered obsessional fear, and (c) rituals and the length of time spent engaged. The task of self-monitoring should be introduced as a vehicle by which the assessor and patient can gain

a highly accurate picture of the time spent engaged in, and situations that lead to, rituals. It also helps to identify symptoms that might have gone unreported in the assessment sessions. The patient should be instructed that, rather than guessing, he or she should use a watch to determine the exact amount of time spent ritualizing. Moreover, to maximize accuracy, each entry should be recorded immediately after it occurs (as opposed to waiting until the end of the day).

Case Conceptualization

The functional assessment described above yields the information necessary to construct an individualized conceptualization of the patient's idiosyncratic OCD symptoms. This formulation serves as a "road map" for cognitive-behavioral therapy and is synthesized by listing the obsessional stimuli (external cues and intrusive thoughts), cognitive appraisals of these stimuli (e.g., "I will get sick", "I will be responsible for"), and the avoidance and ritualistic strategies used to reduce obsessional anxiety. Arrows are then drawn to show the links between stimuli, cognitions, emotions, and behavior as specified by the cognitive-behavioral model. An example of a patient's individualized model appears in Figure 13.1. The model suggests that the modification of faulty beliefs and interpretations is required to reduce obsessional anxiety, and that the cessation of avoidance and ritualistic behavior is necessary for being able to modify the faulty cognitions. As discussed earlier, this leads to the use of exposure therapy, cognitive techniques, and response prevention in the treatment of OCD (e.g., Abramowitz 2006a, 2006b; Salkovskis, 1996).

Practical Considerations

As with the diagnostic assessment, patients may seem hesitant to self-disclose some of the details of their OCD symptoms. Explaining the purpose and importance of such an in-depth analysis of obsessions and compulsions might be helpful in this regard. One tactic that often works well in building rapport and camaraderie (and thus, more self-disclosure) is to describe the functional assessment phase as an exchange of information between two "experts." The patient, who is an expert on his or her

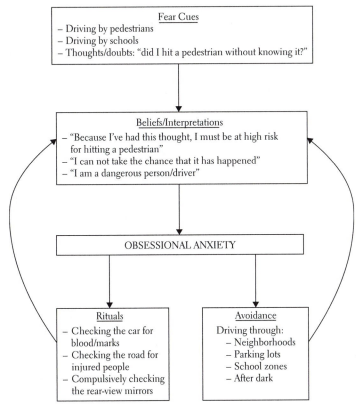

Fear Cues
– Driving by pedestrians
– Driving by schools
– Thoughts/doubts: "did I hit a pedestrian without knowing it?"

Beliefs/Interpretations
– "Because I've had this thought, I must be at high risk for hitting a pedestrian"
– "I can not take the chance that it has happened"
– "I am a dangerous person/driver"

OBSESSIONAL ANXIETY

Rituals
– Checking the car for blood/marks
– Checking the road for injured people
– Compulsively checking the rear-view mirrors

Avoidance
Driving through:
– Neighborhoods
– Parking lots
– School zones
– After dark

FIGURE 13.1 Example of a cognitive-behavioral case formulation for a patient with OCD.

particular OCD symptoms, must help the therapist to understand these symptoms so that an effective treatment plan can be drawn up. Simultaneously, the therapist, an expert on conceptualizing OCD *in general*, must help the patient learn to think about his or her symptoms from a cognitive-behavioral perspective so that the patient can get the most out of treatment.

Sometimes, the patient is afraid to mention certain symptoms due to dysfunctional beliefs about the consequences of saying certain things. For example, one individual was reluctant to describe his unwanted blasphemous images of Jesus having sexual intercourse with Mary because he feared that discussing these ideas (i.e., thinking about them) would invite divine punishment. In such instances, gentle, but firm, encouragement to openly discuss the obsession in the spirit of reducing old avoidance habits is the recommended course of action. As mentioned previously, to avoid reinforcing the patients' fears, the interviewer should be sure to react in a calm and

understanding manner when even the most unpleasant obsessions are self-disclosed.

Overall Evaluation

Because of the idiographic nature of functional assessment, evaluation of the psychometric properties of this approach is difficult. The goals of functional assessment, however, include (a) the identification of target behaviors and the processes that maintain these behaviors and (b) the selection of appropriate interventions (Follette, Naugle, & Linnerooth, 2000). Therefore, given consistent evidence that ERP—which can only be implemented with data derived from a functional assessment—is often highly successful in reducing OCD symptoms when assessed in this manner, it can be indirectly concluded that functional assessment is a valid and highly clinically useful tool. Incorporation of the psychometrically sound OBQ and III can add to the functional assessment by providing additional data regarding the cognitive basis of obsessional fears and compulsive urges. Recent advances in cognitive therapy for OCD (e.g., Wilhelm & Steketee, 2006) include the development of specific cognitive techniques to target the types of cognitive distortions measured by these instruments. Despite these advances, the patient-specific nature and vast heterogeneity of OCD symptoms (and associated cognitive distortions) can present challenges for even the most skilled clinicians.

ASSESSMENT FOR TREATMENT MONITORING AND TREATMENT OUTCOME

Continually assessing the nature and severity of OCD and related symptoms throughout the course of treatment assists the therapist in evaluating whether, and in what ways, the patient is responding. This is consistent with the empirical demonstration of treatment effectiveness. It is not sufficient for the clinician simply to think that the patient seems to be less obsessed or even for the patient (or an informant) to report that he or she "feels better." Instead, progress should be measured systematically by comparing current functioning against the baseline obtained at the outset of treatment. Thus, periodic assessment using the instruments described in this section should be conducted to objectively clarify in what ways treatment has been helpful and what work remains to be done. A multimethod approach is suggested, involving the use of clinician-administered interview and self-report instruments that tap into various facets of OCD and related symptoms (i.e., depression, general anxiety, and functional disability). Table 13.4 shows ratings of various psychometric and practical characteristics of instruments developed to measure the severity of OCD symptoms. The individual measures are described below. As indicated previously, additional chapters in this volume provide guidance in selecting appropriate tools for evaluating and monitoring the symptoms of comorbid conditions.

Interview Measures

Y-BOCS Severity Scale

The Y-BOCS severity scale (Goodman et al., 1989a, 1989b) was designed as a semistructured interview consisting of 10 items that assess five parameters of obsessions (items 1–5) and compulsions (items 6–10) identified using the Y-BOCS-SC. These parameters are (a) time/frequency, (b) related interference in functioning, (c) associated distress, (d) attempts to resist, and (e) degree of control. Each item is rated from 0 (no symptoms) to 4 (extreme), and the 10 items are summed to produce a total score ranging from 0 to 40. In most instances, Y-BOCS scores of 0 to 7 represent subclinical OCD symptoms, those from 8 to 15 represent mild symptoms, scores of 16 to 23 relate to moderate symptoms, scores of 24 to 31 suggest severe symptoms, and scores of 32 to 40 imply extreme symptoms. A strength of the Y-BOCS is that it measures symptom severity independent of the *number* or *types* of different obsessions and compulsions. In fact, it is the only measure of OCD that assesses symptoms in this way. A limitation is that it can take 30 minutes or longer to administer, especially if used together with the Y-BOCS-SC.

Numerous studies have established clinical and nonclinical norms and psychometric properties of the Y-BOCS. The scale has adequate internal consistency, and good inter-rater reliability and test–retest reliability over a period of several weeks (e.g., Goodman et al., 1989a). The Y-BOCS differentiates people with OCD from nondisordered individuals and those with other anxiety disorders (e.g., Rosenfeld, Dar, Anderson, Kobak, & Griest, 1992). Finally, it is also sensitive to changes that occur as a result of treatment (for a review see Taylor, Thordarson & Sochting, 2002).

Self-Report Measures

Some researchers and clinicians use the Y-BOCS severity scale as a self-report measure; however, relatively few studies have evaluated the psychometric properties of the instrument when used in this way. Steketee, Frost, and Bogert (1996) found that the self-report version tends to yield higher scores than the interview version. This might occur if respondents confuse other phenomena (e.g., worries, depressive ruminations, impulsive behaviors) for obsessions and compulsions. An advantage to using the Y-BOCS as a self-report measure, however, is that it can be administered more quickly and, therefore, more regularly during a course of treatment. Many additional self-report inventories, however, have been developed to assess the main symptoms of OCD. The sections below focus on the most promising of these instruments.

TABLE 13.4 Ratings of Instruments Used for Treatment Monitoring and Treatment Outcome Evaluation

Instrument	Norms	Internal Consistency	Inter-Rater Reliability	Test–Retest Reliability	Content Validity	Construct Validity	Validity Generalization	Treatment Sensitivity	Clinical Utility	Highly Recommended
Y-BOCS interview	E	G	G	A	G	E	E	E	A	✓
PI-R	E	E	NA	G	G	E	G	NA	A	
OCI-R	E	G	NA	A	G	G	A	A	A	✓
VOCI	G	E	NA	A	G	A	A	NA	G	✓
SCOPI	G	G	NA	G	G	A	A	NA	A	

Note: Y-BOCS = Yale-Brown Obsessive Compulsive Scale; PI-R = Padua Inventory-Revised Version; OCI-R = Obsessive Compulsive Inventory-Revised; VOCI = Vancouver Obsessional Compulsive Inventory; SCOPI = Schedule of Compulsions, Obsessions, and Pathological Impulses; A = Adequate; G = Good; E = Excellent; NA = Not Applicable.

Revised Padua Inventory (PI-R)

There are several available versions of the Padua Inventory. Because the most recent revision (PI-R; Burns, Keortge, Formea, & Sternberger, 1996) is also the most widely used, it is described here. The PI-R is a 39-item measure that contains five subscales: (1) contamination and washing, (2) dressing and grooming compulsions, (3) checking, (4) obsessional thoughts of harm, and (5) obsessional impulses to harm. Agreement with each item is rated from 0 (not at all) to 4 (very much), thus the total score ranges from 0 to 156. The scale, which requires about 10 minutes to complete, demonstrates at least adequate reliability and validity. It also differentiates between OCD symptoms and worry, although PI-R scores are significantly correlated with scores on measures of worry. Although the van Oppen et al. (1995) revision has been shown to have good sensitivity to treatment, this characteristic has not been formally investigated for the Burns et al. (1996) version.

Revised Obsessive Compulsive Inventory (OCI-R)

There are two versions of the OCI. The original (Foa, Kozak, Salkovskis, Coles, & Amir, 1998) contains 42 items that assess the frequency and distress associated with a wide range of obsessional and compulsive symptoms. Items, each of which is rated on two scales (frequency and distress) from 0 (not at all) to 4 (extremely), are organized into the following seven subscales: washing, checking, obsessing, hoarding, mental neutralizing, ordering, doubting. The original OCI, however, has a number of psychometric and practical liabilities (e.g., the doubting and checking subscales appear to measure the same construct: Wu & Watson, 2003).

A revision of the measure (the OCI-R; Foa et al., 2002) has addressed these limitations. The OCI-R consists of only 18 items (Foa et al., 2002) and six subscales. Each subscale contains three items which are rated on a single 5-point scale (0 to 4) of distress associated with that particular symptom. The OCI-R subscales include washing, checking, ordering, obsessing, hoarding, and neutralizing. A total score may be calculated by summing all 18 items, and subscale scores can be calculated from the three items within each subscale. Research suggests that the OCI-R and its subscales have adequate convergent

validity, although divergent validity of some of the subscales is suspect (e.g., Abramowitz & Deacon, 2006). The neutralizing subscale has been specifically criticized because the three items on this subscale all pertain to counting symptoms (e.g., Abramowitz & Deacon, 2006). Abramowitz, Tolin, and Diefenbach (2005) found that the OCI-R is useful for measuring response to treatment. Moreover, a cutoff score of 21 can differentiate OCD patients from nonpatients (Foa et al., 2002).

Vancouver Obsessive Compulsive Inventory

The Vancouver Obsessive Compulsive Inventory (VOCI; Thordarson et al., 2004) is a 55-item measure that represents an update of the 30-item Maudsley Obsessional Compulsive Inventory (MOCI; Hodgson & Rachman, 1977). Although MOCI has sound psychometric properties and was once widely used, it has largely fallen out of favor due to two factors. First, it has poor sensitivity to treatment due to its true–false response format and inclusion of items assessing past and permanent events (as opposed to current behaviors). Second, the MOCI mainly measures the severity of washing and checking concerns but not other symptoms of OCD such as obsessions and mental rituals. Though the VOCI is a lengthier instrument than its predecessor, items assess a broader range of OCD symptoms and are rated on a Likert-type scale from 0 (not at all true of me) to 4 (very much true of me). The VOCI's six empirically derived subscales include contamination, checking, obsessions, hoarding, just right, and indecisiveness. Thordarson et al. (2004) examined the factor structure and psychometric properties of the scale and found evidence of internal consistency, test–retest reliability, construct validity, and known groups validity of the subscales. The sensitivity to treatment of the VOCI has yet to be examined.

Schedule of Compulsions, Obsessions, and Pathological Impulses

The Schedule of Compulsions, Obsessions, and Pathological Impulses (SCOPI) is a 47-item self-report scale that is designed to measure the presence of OCD symptoms, while also assessing a number of impulse-control phenomena (e.g., "I sometimes feel a sudden urge to play with fire"; Watson & Wu, 2005). The impulse-control focus was included on the basis of evidence that there are links between impulse control and OCD symptoms. Respondents rate their degree of agreement with each item from 1 (disagree strongly) to 6 (agree strongly) and the scale contains five factors that correspond with empirically identified OCD symptom dimensions: obsessive checking (14 items), obsessive cleanliness (12 items), compulsive rituals (8 items), hoarding (5 items), and pathological impulses (8 items). The SCOPI was developed empirically from a large item pool that sampled a broad range of OCD and impulsive symptoms, which was subjected to a series of factor analyses.

In the only study evaluating the SCOPI, Watson and Wu (2005) found evidence that the various subscales are internally consistent, are stable over a 2-month interval, and show adequate convergent and discriminant validity. In particular, the SCOPI converges well with the OCI-R. Although the measure is fairly easy to administer, the impulse-control items do not assess whether these impulses (e.g., to steal, to act violently) are *unwanted* intrusive urges (i.e., obsessions), or actual impulses that the person acts upon (i.e., premonitory urges). Indeed, such impulses might occur among individuals with OCD and those with impulse-control disorders. Yet they are experienced in very different ways depending on which disorder the individual has. This could lead to difficulties when interpreting responses to such items.

Practical Considerations

In addition to some of the practical issues raised in the previous sections, a few considerations regarding ongoing assessment deserve comment. First, patients sometimes attempt to either minimize their OCD symptoms or make themselves look worse off than they truly are. Self-report measures provide an easy vehicle for doing so. Such behavior might be motivated by either resistance to beginning treatment or the fear of ending treatment and terminating the therapeutic relationship. If this is suspected, it might be helpful to gain observations from significant others to provide additional data regarding symptom severity and current functioning. A separate issue is that individuals with contamination fears might report concern with handling self-report questionnaires, and therefore have difficulty completing such tasks. Gentle, yet firm, encouragement to complete these forms for the purpose of providing important clinical information often helps. Patients can also be reminded that they

can engage in washing or cleaning rituals once they have completed the paperwork.

Overall Evaluation

There exists a wide array of interview and self-report measures of OCD. In most instances scale items have been carefully written, submitted to appropriate statistical procedures, and examined for psychometric viability using clinical or nonclinical samples. Some of these measures are "global" in that they aim to assess the broad range of OCD symptoms, whereas others focus on individual symptom dimensions such as scrupulosity (e.g., Abramowitz et al., 2002) and symmetry/ordering concerns (e.g., Coles, Frost, Heimberg, & Rhéaume, 2003). The Y-BOCS severity scale is unique in that it measures the severity of OCD independent of symptom theme or the number of symptoms. Owing to space limitations, the review of self-report instruments above was restricted to global measures of OCD that have the greatest potential (from a practical and scientific standpoint) for use in clinical and research settings. The heterogeneity of obsessions and rituals presents a major challenge to developing a concise global OCD self-report symptom measure. Authors of such scales must strike a balance between (a) including enough items to comprehensively assess the various sorts of OCD phenomena and (b) constructing a scale that is manageable in length and therefore practical for widespread use. Whereas each of the measures discussed in the previous section provides an adequate self-reported assessment of OCD, the VOCI appears to most optimally achieve this balance.

CONCLUSIONS AND FUTURE DIRECTIONS

This chapter provides the reader with a practical guide for the comprehensive clinical evaluation of patients with obsessions, compulsions, and related phenomena. Advances in how we conceptualize OCD have been paralleled by improvements in the methods for assessment and treatment of this disorder. Although there are numerous valid and reliable instruments for assessing the signs and symptoms of OCD, I wish to underscore that the proper assessment and treatment of this condition requires more than simply administering empirically supported tools. The assessment should be guided by a cognitive-behavioral theoretical framework in which the numerous sorts of obsessions and compulsions are conceptualized in terms of their *function* (i.e., antecedents and consequences) as opposed to their *topography* (form or frequency). Clinicians should avoid the temptation to become sidetracked by the often remarkably senseless and bizarre symptom presentation, and instead keep in mind the truly essential features of OCD, which are that (a) obsessional thoughts and images evoke anxiety and distress, and (b) avoidance and rituals serve to reduce or neutralize this distress. The successful implementation of empirically supported treatment (i.e., ERP) hinges on an assessment strategy grounded within this model.

A multitrait-multimethod approach to assessment will yield the most comprehensive data regarding an individual's symptom presentation and related difficulties. Although I have reviewed both self-report and interview measures of OCD, this chapter has not focused on the measurement of traits or domains *related to* OCD, such as depression, general anxiety, quality of life, and global functional impairment. Nevertheless, such parameters are important to assess during the initial interview and functional assessment, and when measuring treatment outcome. Several sources detail the assessment of OCD-related phenomena (e.g., Abramowitz, 2006a and other chapters in the current volume on mood and anxiety disorders) and can be consulted for suggestions regarding specific measures to use.

Certainly there is room for the development of additional measures of OCD. As research continues to support the idea that OCD symptoms can be distilled into a finite number of dimensions, scales capable of properly assessing dimension-specific symptom severity would be desirable. Our research group is currently developing such a dimensional obsessive–compulsive scale. The development of standardized functional assessment techniques would also be advantageous as long as these could remain flexible enough to accommodate the heterogeneity of OCD. Finally, the assessment of children continues to lag behind advances in the assessment of adults. Although the age-downward extensions of several measures discussed here (e.g., OBQ, OCI-R) have been discussed, little empirical work has appeared in the literature.

References

Abramowitz, J. (2006a). *Understanding and treating obsessive–compulsive disorder: A cognitive-behavioral approach*. Mahwah, NJ: Erlbaum.

Abramowitz, J. S. (2006b). *Obsessive–compulsive disorder: Advances in psychotherapy—evidence based practice*. Cambridge, MA: Hogrefe & Huber.

Abramowitz, J. S. & Deacon, B. J. (2006). Psychometric properties and construct validity of the obsessive–compulsive inventory-revised: Replication and extension with a clinical sample. *Journal of Anxiety Disorders, 20*, 1016–1035.

Abramowitz, J. S., Franklin, M. E., & Foa, E. B. (2002). Empirical status of cognitive-behavioral methods in the treatment of OCD. *Romanian Journal of Cognitive Behavioral Therapy, 2*, 89–104.

Abramowitz, J. S., Franklin, M. E., Kozak, M. J., Street, G. P., & Foa, E. B. (2000). The effects of pretreatment depression on cognitive-behavioral treatment outcome in OCD clinic patients. *Behavior Therapy, 31*, 517–528.

Abramowitz, J. S., Huppert, J. D., Cohen, A. B., Tolin, D. F., & Cahill, S. P. (2002). Religious obsessions and compulsions in a non-clinical sample: The penn inventory of scrupulosity (PIOS). *Behaviour Research and Therapy, 40*, 825–838.

Abramowitz, J. S., Khandker, M., Nelson, C. A., Deacon, B. J., & Rygwall, R. (2006). The role of cognitive factors in the pathogenesis of obsessions and compulsions: A prospective study. *Behaviour Research and Therapy, 44*, 1361–1374.

Abramowitz, J. S., Nelson, C. A., Rygwall, & Khandker, M. (2007). The cognitive mediation of obsessive-compulsive symptoms: A longitudinal study. *Journal of Anxiety Disorders, 21*, 91–104.

Abramowitz, J. S., Schwartz, S. A., Moore, K. M. & Luenzmann, K. R., (2003). Obsessive–compulsive symptoms in pregnancy and the puerperium: A review of the literature. *Journal of Anxiety Disorders, 17*, 461–478.

Abramowitz, J. S., Tolin, D. F., & Diefenbach, G. J. (2005). Measuring change in OCD: Sensitivity of the obsessive compulsive inventory-revised. *Journal of Psychopathology and Behavioral Assessment, 27*, 317–324.

American Psychiatric Association (2000). *Diagnostic and statistical manual of mental disorders (DSM-IV-TR)* (4th ed., Text Revision). Washington, DC: Author.

Antony, M., Orsillo, S., & Roemer L. (Eds.) (2001). *Practitioner's guide to empirically based measures of anxiety*. New York: Kluwer Academic/Plenum Publishers.

Beck, A. T. (1976). *Cognitive therapy of the emotional disorders*. New York: International Universities Press.

Brown, T., Di Nardo, P., Lehman, C., & Campbell, L. (2001). Reliability of DSM-IV anxiety and mood disorders: Implications for the classification of emotional disorders. *Journal of Abnormal Psychology, 110,* 49–58.

Burns, G. L., Keortge, S., Formea, G., & Sternberger, L. (1996). Revision of the Padua Inventory of obsessive-compulsive disorder: Distinctions between worry, obsessions, and compulsions. *Behaviour Research and Therapy, 34,* 163–173.

Clark, D. A. (2004). *Cognitive-behavioral treatment of OCD.* New York: Guilford Press.

Coles, M., Frost, R., Heimberg, R., & Rhéaume, J. (2003). "Not just right experiences": Perfectionism, obsessive–compulsive features and general psychopathology. *Behaviour Research and Therapy, 41,* 681–700.

De Silva, P., Menzies, R. G., & Shafran, R. (2003). Spontaneous decay of compulsive urges: The case of covert compulsions. *Behaviour Research and Therapy, 41,* 129–137.

Di Nardo, P., Brown, T., & Barlow, D. (1994). *Anxiety Disorders Interview Schedule for DSM-IV: Lifetime Version (ADIS-IV-LV).* San Antonio, TX: The Psychological Corporation.

Eisen, J. L., Phillips, K. A., Baer, L., Beer, D. A., Atala, K. D., & Rasmussen, S. A. (1998). The Brown Assessment of Beliefs Scale: Reliability and validity. *American Journal of Psychiatry, 155,* 102–108.

Eisen, J., Phillips, K., Coles, M. E., & Rasmussen, S. A. (2004). Insight in obsessive compulsive disorder and body dysmorphic disorder. *Comprehensive Psychiatry, 45,* 10–15.

Fairbrother, N., Newth, S., & Rachman, S. (2005). Mental pollution: Feelings of dirtiness without physical contact. *Behaviour Research and Therapy, 43,* 121–130.

First, M. B., Spitzer, R. L., Gibbon, M., & Williams, J. (2002). *Structured Clinical Interview for the DSM-IV Axis 1 Disorders.* New York: Biometrics Research Department, New York State Psychiatric Institute.

Foa, E. B., Huppert, J. D., Leiberg, S., Langner, R., Kichic, R., Hajcak, G., et al. (2002). The Obsessive-Compulsive Inventory: Development and validation of a short version. *Psychological Assessment, 14,* 485–496.

Foa, E. B., Kozak, M. J., Salkovskis, P. M., Coles, M. E., & Amir, N. (1998). The validation of a new obsessive-compulsive disorder scale: The obsessive–compulsive inventory. *Psychological Assessment, 10,* 206–214.

Follette, W., Naugle, A., & Linnerroth, P. (2000). Functional alternatives to traditional assessment and diagnosis. In Dougher, M. J. (Ed.), *Clinical behavior analysis* (pp. 99–125). Reno, NV: Context Press.

Frost, R. O., & Steketee, S. (2002). *Cognitive approaches to obsessions and compulsions: Theory, assessment, and treatment.* Oxford: Elsevier.

Goodman, W. K., Price, L. H., Rasmussen, S. A., Mazure, C., Delgado, P., Heninger, G. R., & Charney, D. S. (1989a). The Yale-Brown Obsessive Compulsive Scale: Validity. *Archives of General Psychiatry, 46,* 1012–1016.

Goodman, W. K., Price, L. H., Rasmussen, S. A., Mazure, C., Fleischmann, R. L., Hill, C. L., Heninger, G. R., & Charney, D. S. (1989b). The Yale-Brown Obsessive Compulsive Scale: Development, use, and reliability. *Archives of General Psychiatry, 46,* 1006–1011.

Gross, R. C., Sasson, Y., Chorpa, M., & Zohar, J. (1998). Biological models of obsessive–compulsive disorder: The serotonin hypothesis. In R. P. Swinson, M. Antony, S. Rachman, & M. Richter (Eds.), *Obsessive–compulsive disorder: Theory, research, and treatment* (pp. 141–153). New York: Guilford.

Hodgson, R., & Rachman, S. (1977). Obsessive compulsive complaints. *Behaviour Research and Therapy, 15,* 389–395.

Kessler, R., Berglund, P., Demler, O., Jin, R., Merikangas, K. R., & Walters, E. E. (2005). Lifetime prevalence and age-of-onset distributions of DSM-IV disorders in the National Comorbidity Survey Replication. *Archives of General Psychiatry, 62,* 593–602.

Mineka, S., & Zinbarg, R. (2006). A contemporary learning theory perspective on the etiology of anxiety disorders. *American Psychologist, 61,* 10–26.

Obsessive Compulsive Cognitions Working Group. (2001). Development and initial validation of the Obsessive Beliefs Questionnaire and the Interpretations of Intrusions Inventory. *Behaviour Research & Therapy, 39,* 987–1006.

Obsessive Compulsive Cognitions Working Group. (2003). Psychometric validation of the Obsessive Beliefs Questionnaire and the Interpretation of Intrusions Inventory: Part I. *Behaviour Research & Therapy, 41,* 863–878.

Obsessive Compulsive Cognitions Working Group. (2005). Psychometric Validation of the Obsessive Belief Questionnaire and Interpretation of Intrusions Inventory: Part 2, Factor Analyses and Testing of a Brief Version. *Behaviour Research & Therapy, 43,* 1527–1542.

Ravie Kishore, V., Samar, R., Janardhan Reddy, Y., Chandrasekhar, C., & Thennarasu, K. (2004). Clinical characteristics and treatment response in poor and good insight obsessive–compulsive compulsive disorder. *European Psychiatry, 19,* 202–208.

Rosenfeld, R., Dar, R., Anderson, D., Kobak, K., & Greist, J. (1992). A computer-administered version of the Yale-Brown obsessive compulsive scale. *Psychological Assessment, 4,* 329–332.

Salkovskis, P. M. (1996). Cognitive-behavioral approaches to the understanding of obsessional problems. In R. Rapee (Ed.), *Current controversies in the anxiety disorders* (pp. 103–133). New York: Guilford.

Saxena, S., Bota, R. G., & Brody, A. L. (2001). Brain-behavior relationships in obsessive–compulsive disorder. *Seminars in Clinical Neuropsychiatry, 6,* 82–101.

Schwartz, S. A., & Abramowitz, J. S. (2003). Are non-paraphilic sexual addictions a variant of obsessive–compulsive disorder? A pilot study. *Cognitive and Behavioral Practice, 10,* 373–378.

Shafran, R. (2005). Cognitive-behavioral models of OCD. In J. S. Abramowitz & A. C. Houts (Eds.), *Concepts and controversies in obsessive–compulsive disorder* (pp. 229–252). New York: Springer.

Shafran, R., & Speckens, A. (2005) Biological versus psychological approaches to OCD: War or peace? In J. S. Abramowitz & A. C. Houts (Eds.), *Concepts and controversies in obsessive–compulsive disorder* (pp. 255–260). New York: Springer.

Shafran, R., Thordarson, D. S., & Rachman, S. (1996). Thought-action fusion in obsessive compulsive disorder. *Journal of Anxiety Disorders, 10,* 379–391.

Skoog, G., & Skoog, I. (1999). A 40-year follow-up of patients with obsessive–compulsive disorder. *Archives of General Psychiatry, 56,* 121–127.

Steketee, G., Frost, R., & Bogart, K. (1996). The Yale-Brown obsessive–compulsive scale: Interview versus self-report. *Behaviour Research and Therapy, 34,* 675–684.

Taylor, S., Abramowitz, J. S., & McKay, D. (2007). Cognitive-behavioral models of obsessive-compulsive disorder.

In M. M. Antony, C. Purdon, & L. Summerfeldt (Eds.), *Psychological treatment of obsessive-compulsive disorder: Fundamentals and beyond* (pp. 9–29). Washington, DC: American Psychological Association Press.

Taylor, S., Thordarson, D., & Sochting, I. (2002). Obsessive-compulsive disorder. In M. Antony & D. H. Barlow (Eds.), *Handbook of Assessment and Treatment Planning for Psychological Disorders* (pp. 182–214). New York, NY: Guilford.

Thordarson, D., Radomsky, A., Rachman, S., Shafran, R., Sawchuck, C., & Hakstain, A. (2004). The Vancouver Obsessional Compulsive Inventory. *Behaviour Research and Therapy, 42,* 1289–1314,

van Oppen, P., Hoekstra, J., & Emmelkamp P. (1995). The structure of obsessive–compulsive symptoms. *Behaviour Research and Therapy, 33,* 15–23.

Watson, D., & Wu, K. (2005). Development and validation of the Schedule of Compulsions, Obsessions, and Pathological Impulses (SCOPI). *Assessment, 12,* 50–65.

Wilhelm, S., & Steketee, G. (2006). *Cognitive therapy for obsessive–compulsive disorder.* Oakland: New Harbinger.

Williams, J., Gibbon, M., First, M., Spitzer, R., Davies, M., Borus, J., et al. (1992) The Structured Clinical Interview for DSM-III-R (SCID) II. Multisite test–retest reliability. *Archives of General Psychiatry, 49,* 630–636.

Wu, K., & Watson, D. (2003). Further investigation of the obsessive compulsive inventory: Psychometric analysis in two nonclinical samples. *Journal of Anxiety Disorders, 17,* 305–319.

14

Post-traumatic Stress Disorder

Terence M. Keane

Amy K. Silberbogen

Mariann R. Weierich

Post-traumatic stress disorder (PTSD) was first introduced as a diagnosis in the *Diagnostic and Statistical
Manual of Mental Disorders*, 3rd Edition (DSM-III;
American Psychiatric Association, 1980) and was conceptualized as a relatively rare response to extraordin-
ary and severe stressors, such as war, violent acts,
vehicular or industrial accidents, sexual assault, and
other disasters or events that are outside the range of
usual human experience. Today, traumatic events and
PTSD are viewed as worldwide phenomena that are
prevalent and cross all subgroups of the population.
Epidemiological studies have documented the prevalence of PTSD, providing information on rates of
exposure to trauma, the distribution of PTSD within
different segments of the population (e.g., adults and
children, males and females, etc.), and those factors
that affect the onset and course of PTSD.

Recent events, including the terrorist attacks on
September 11, 2001, and Hurricane Katrina's landfall
in Louisiana, Mississippi, and Texas in August 2005,
emphasize the importance of arriving at best practices for the management of disasters and violence on
humanity. It is essential for clinicians to utilize gold
standard methods to diagnose PTSD and related psychiatric conditions, monitor progress made throughout treatment, and measure treatment outcomes.
A multitude of PTSD measures is available; a clinician seeking a tool to assess PTSD may find this array
of measures overwhelming. Therefore, the purpose of
the present chapter is to examine and discuss available methods for assessing PTSD and make recommendations regarding their suitability in a clinical
context with a variety of populations. Our hope is that

clinicians will adopt the use of state-of-the-art methods
of diagnosing and monitoring PTSD and trauma
symptoms in their work with traumatized adults. To
provide a context for this discussion, we begin with
a brief review of diagnostic considerations related to
PTSD, the epidemiology of trauma, comorbid conditions, etiology, and prognosis.

NATURE OF PTSD

Diagnostic Considerations and Associated Features

Individuals who are diagnosed with PTSD have
experienced or witnessed a traumatic event to which
they responded with fear, helplessness, horror, and
other intense emotional distress. In addition, PTSD
is defined by three symptom clusters as outlined in
the DSM-IV-TR (American Psychiatric Association,
2000). First, those with PTSD reexperience or relive
some, or all, of the traumatic event through vivid and
intrusive nightmares and flashbacks, as if they were
experiencing the event all over again. When reliving
the trauma, the individual is likely to feel those strong
and unpleasant emotions (e.g., fear, horror, anger)
that were originally experienced when the trauma
occurred. The second symptom cluster involves avoidance of stimuli (including people, places, cognitions,
etc.) that are associated with and remind the individual of the traumatic event. Consequently, the lives
of those with PTSD can become increasingly con-
stricted as they withdraw from relationships, routine

activities, or contexts that spark unpleasant memories. In addition, many people experience emotional restriction, known as numbing, in which there is a decreased interest in others, a sense of estrangement, and an inability to feel positive emotions, such as love or happiness. This emotional numbing can interfere with the maintenance or development of interpersonal relationships. The third cluster involves hyperarousal symptoms and can include such symptoms as impaired concentration and memory, difficulty sleeping, physiological reactivity, an exaggerated startle response, and hypervigilance. People with PTSD also often have a sense that their future will be abbreviated, which can impair their ability to live in the present and make healthy decisions for themselves.

Symptoms of PTSD must be present for longer than 1 month and cause clinically significant distress or impairment in functioning. A diagnosis of acute PTSD is given when the duration of symptoms is less than 3 months, whereas a diagnosis of chronic PTSD is assigned when the symptoms last more than 3 months. Occasionally, symptoms emerge months after the traumatic event; in this case, a diagnosis of PTSD with delayed onset is conferred.

The emotional, societal, interpersonal, and psychosocial costs of PTSD are substantial, making PTSD a major public health issue. Individuals diagnosed with PTSD are at an increased risk of developing chronic medical conditions and are more likely to be noncompliant with their physicians' recommendations, practice poor self-care, and use medical services inappropriately (Friedman & Schnurr, 1995). In addition, people with PTSD have lower incomes, divorce more frequently than the general population, and are more likely to become involved with the legal system, change their jobs frequently, and report a decreased quality of life (Koss, Koss, & Woodruff, 1991; Kulka et al., 1990). Undoubtedly, functional impairments associated with PTSD are extensive.

Epidemiological Evidence

When PTSD initially was conceptualized, both exposure to traumatic events and the disorder were considered relatively rare. However, researchers have reported that exposure to a traumatic event is not uncommon (Kessler et al., 1995). A number of epidemiological studies have documented the rates of exposure to traumatic events and the prevalence of PTSD within the general population. The National Comorbidity Survey, the first nationally representative assessment of PTSD in the general population, found that 60% of men and 51% of women have experienced a traumatic event (Kessler et al., 1995). Breslau, Davis, Andreski, and Peterson (1991) reported similar findings, reporting that 39% of their sample had experienced one or more traumatic events. Clearly, exposure to traumatic events is not as rare or unusual as originally believed.

The literature suggests that a trauma can activate PTSD in individuals who are psychologically vulnerable, but that, fortunately, the majority of people who survive a traumatic event will not develop PTSD or any other form of psychopathology (e.g., depression, anxiety, substance abuse disorder). Nonetheless, the likelihood of developing PTSD increases as a traumatic event becomes more frequent, gruesome, or severe, regardless of personal resources or emotional stability (Sutker & Allain, 1996).

Overall lifetime prevalence rates for PTSD in the general population range from 6.8% to 9.5% (Breslau et al., 1991; Kessler et al., 2005), with PTSD being more prevalent in women (rates range from 10.4% to 12%) than in men (5.0% to 9.5%; cf. Resnick, Kilpatrick, Dansky, Saunders, & Best, 1993).

Certain subgroups within the population, including combatants, are at increased risk for exposure to trauma. Researchers have examined the impact of war on the psychological functioning of soldiers since deployment, combat, physical injury, and readjustment to civilian life can be intensely stressful. The National Vietnam Veterans Readjustment Study (NVVRS; Kulka et al., 1990) was the first systematic study of combat-related PTSD, and its findings were striking. The authors reported that 64% of Vietnam veterans were exposed to one or more traumatic events in their lives. More than 15% of males and 9% of females serving in Vietnam met the criteria for current PTSD. More importantly, these rates were 5 to 10 times higher than found for Vietnam-era veteran and civilian comparison subjects, highlighting the psychological toll of war. Skeptics, however, have argued that these results are inflated. In response, Dohrenwend et al. (2006) reanalyzed a sample of the NVVRS data and found little evidence of malingering; according to their results, 9.1% of the veterans met criteria for current PTSD and 18.7% met criteria for lifetime PTSD when using the most stringent criteria for confirming traumatic war experiences.

The current involvement of the United States in Iraq and Afghanistan has placed PTSD in the national spotlight as reports of soldiers returning from deployment reveal significant mental health problems, including PTSD. Hoge et al. (2004) reported that between 11.5% and 19.9% of US infantry met diagnostic criteria for PTSD after their return home from combat duty in Iraq or Afghanistan. More recently, Hoge, Auchterlonie, and Milliken (2006) reported that 9.8% of veterans deployed to Iraq and 4.7% of veterans who served in Afghanistan met screening criteria for PTSD. These studies are among the first to assess the impact of war on psychological functioning while military operations are ongoing.

The impact of the terrorist attacks on September 11, 2001, on psychological functioning also has been examined. Schlenger et al. (2002) assessed symptoms of PTSD through self-report in a nationally representative cross-sectional sample and found that the prevalence of PTSD was significantly higher in the New York area (11.2%) than the rest of the country (4.0%) in the first months following the attacks.

Heightened rates of PTSD can also be found in the wake of natural disasters. Norris et al. (2002) reviewed the extant epidemiological research on disaster victims and reported heightened rates of PTSD following such events. Norris, Perilla, Riad, Kaniasty, and Lavizzo (1999) reported that 25% of their sample of Hurricane Andrew survivors met criteria for PTSD 6 months after the disaster struck and that levels of PTSD did not change 30 months after the hurricane. In 2005, Hurricane Katrina struck the Gulf Coast leaving hundreds of thousands of individuals homeless and displaced. The psychological impact of this disaster was also great, with rates of serious psychological problems essentially doubling from the predisaster levels (Kessler, Galea, Jones, & Parker, 2006).

Comorbidity

Exposure to a traumatic event is a risk factor for a number of mental health problems, including PTSD (Keane & Wolfe, 1990). Kessler, Sonnega, Bromet, Hughes, and Nelson (1995) found that almost half of the individuals in their sample who met criteria for PTSD also had three or more additional comorbid psychiatric diagnoses. The most commonly diagnosed comorbid diagnoses are affective disorders, other anxiety disorders, and substance misuse (Brown et al., 2001; Kessler et al., 1994, 1995). In his sample of 1,126

community outpatients, Brown et al. (2001) reported that the most frequent co-occurring disorders were major depressive disorder (77%), generalized anxiety disorder (38%), and alcohol abuse or dependence (31%). The study by Bollinger et al. (2002) of inpatient veterans with PTSD found that 79% of the sample met criteria for an Axis II disorder, including avoidant (47%), paranoid (46%), obsessive–compulsive (28%), and antisocial (15%) personality disorder. Other co-occurring difficulties include deficits in coping skills, relational issues, and medical issues (Southwick, Yehuda, & Giller, 1993).

The presence of one or multiple comorbid conditions with PTSD complicates the assessment process and can negatively affect treatment outcomes. Individuals diagnosed with PTSD and a comorbid psychiatric condition were shown to present with more severe PTSD symptoms (e.g., Back et al., 2003; Brady & Clary, 2003; Zayfert et al., 2002), greater impairment in functioning (Ouimette, Finney, & Moos, 1999), and poorer response to treatment (e.g., Cloitre & Koenen, 2001; Zlotnick et al., 1999). Thus, a sound understanding of these co-occurring psychiatric conditions and their manifestation in the presence of PTSD is essential when working with this population (see Miller, Kaloupek, Dillon, & Keane, 2004; Miller & Resick, 2007, for a fuller discussion).

Etiology

PTSD emerges from a complex chain of events that begins with psychological and biological predispositions and follows a precipitating traumatic event that leaves an individual with intense and distressing emotions (Keane & Barlow, 2002; Keane, Marshall, & Taft, 2006). Classical conditioning appears to be important in the development and maintenance of PTSD (Keane, Fairbank, Caddell, Zimering, & Bender, 1985). A learned emotional response develops that is similar to the initial intense and distressing emotions that occurred immediately following the traumatic event. This learned response is activated during exposure to situations that symbolize or resemble the traumatic event, including cognitions, feelings, and memories of the actual traumatic event. Wirtz and Harrell (1987) provided support for the process of classical conditioning in PTSD. They found that survivors of assault were less distressed 6 months after the assault if they had experienced exposure to contexts that were similar to the original assault; extinction of the learned distress response apparently occurred with repeated exposure to contexts in the absence of threat. On the other hand, individuals who had not had any exposure to trauma-relevant contexts maintained high levels of distress at the 6-month point. In addition to conditioning processes, psychological and biological vulnerabilities, as well as poor coping skills or inadequate social supports, contribute to the development of PTSD.

Prognosis

Treatment programs to address symptoms of PTSD were developed in response to the influx of returning Vietnam veterans with psychological difficulties. Treatments have continued to be refined throughout the years to include both behavioral and cognitive components. Exposure therapies and cognitive restructuring are among the most widely recommended and studied today. However, there is a need for additional work from perspectives other than cognitive-behavioral ones, including interpersonal and psychodynamic interventions (Kudler, Blank, & Krupnick, 2000). Similarly, there is a need to develop psychopharmacological interventions further so they can be compared with effective psychological methods. Nevertheless, PTSD is often a chronic condition, as more than one-third of those diagnosed with PTSD still meet diagnostic criteria 5 years later (Kessler et al., 1995).

ASSESSMENT OF PTSD

Clinicians are interested in the accurate assessment of patients with PTSD, as many of their patients have experienced traumatic events and present with PTSD symptoms as either primary or secondary diagnoses. PTSD can be assessed for many different purposes, and the goals of a particular assessment determine the approach selected by the clinician. The objective of many mental health clinicians is to diagnose a patient by conducting an evaluation that includes a differential diagnosis, a functional assessment, and the collection of other related data that can be helpful in case conceptualization, as well as treatment planning. Other practitioners may be involved in forensic assessments or compensation evaluations where diagnostic accuracy is paramount. Researchers involved in epidemiological or prevalence studies may be interested in the rate of the occurrence of

PTSD, the risk factors associated with the condition, and the occurrence of comorbid psychiatric conditions. Clearly, different assessment contexts require different assessment approaches, depending upon the particular assessment goals of the professional (see Wilson and Keane, 2004, for reviews of available techniques for the assessment of PTSD within a variety of contexts).

Since the first mention of PTSD in the DSM, there has been excellent progress in developing sound measures to assess trauma symptoms and PTSD in adults (Keane & Barlow, 2002; Keane, Weathers, & Foa, 2000; Weathers, Keane, & Davidson, 2001). A multimethod approach to the assessment of PTSD has been recommended (Keane et al., 1985). This approach may include a structured diagnostic interview to assess PTSD and other comorbidities, self-report psychological questionnaires, and psychophysiological measures.

Structured diagnostic interviews are considered extremely valuable tools for assessing PTSD symptoms (Keane et al., 1996). Although it is standard practice in research settings to employ structured diagnostic interviews, the use of structured interviews in the clinical setting is less common, except in a clinical forensic practice (Keane, 1995; Keane, Buckley, & Miller, 2003). This is likely due to time and cost burdens, as well as the need for specialized training to administer many of these interviews. Nonetheless, the use of structured diagnostic interviews for PTSD in clinical settings has been recommended to improve diagnostic accuracy and aid in treatment planning (Litz & Weathers, 1994). In the following text, we will provide information on several structured interviews that were developed to measure PTSD symptoms, either as modules of comprehensive diagnostic assessment tools or as independent PTSD measures.

Self-report measures provide information on the presence or absence of PTSD, trauma symptoms, and their severity. Several measures provide specific cutoffs that are indicative of a diagnosis of PTSD, whereas the majority incorporates continuous indicators of symptom severity. In general, self-report measures are more time and cost efficient than diagnostic interviews and are of particular utility in clinical settings in which a structured interview is not feasible or practical. To maximize accuracy and efficiency, clinicians are encouraged to use those measures that have been normed in the population for which they will be employed (Keane & Barlow, 2002). We will highlight those self-report measures that we recommend.

We wish to emphasize that the generalizability of methods used to assess PTSD is a function of several features of the assessment setting. Culture, language, race, age, and gender are factors that might influence the use and the interpretation of psychological instruments, whether they are structured diagnostic interviews or self-report measures. Attention to these variables is essential to discerning the presence or absence of PTSD.

We recommend that clinicians consider the populations on which an assessment instrument for PTSD was validated when selecting a measure. The need to develop instruments that are culturally sensitive has been of great interest for many years as a result of documentation of ethnocultural-specific responses to traumatic events. For example, researchers have provided evidence of differences in the reported severity of PTSD symptoms in Caucasians and ethnic minorities following a traumatic event (e.g., Frueh, Brady, & Arellano, 1998; Green, Grace, Lindy, & Leonard, 1990; Kulka et al., 1990). The need for culturally sensitive instruments is further emphasized by the growing awareness that developing countries have a higher prevalence of PTSD than industrialized nations (De Girolamo & McFarlane, 1996).

To date, evidence-based psychological assessment of PTSD has evolved primarily within the context of Western, developed, and industrialized countries. Thus, PTSD assessment may be limited by a lack of culturally sensitive measures and by the tremendous diversity among cultural groups of interest (Marsella, Friedman, Gerrity, & Scurfield, 1996). However, there is progress in developing culturally sensitive measures. A good example of a measure that possesses culturally relevant features is the Harvard Trauma Questionnaire (HTQ; Mollica et al., 1992), which is widely used in refugee and internally displaced samples. The HTQ assesses a range of potentially traumatic events and trauma-related symptoms. The assessment of trauma includes events to which refugees from war-torn countries may have been exposed, including exposure to torture, brainwashing, and deprivation of food or water. Originally, developed in English, the HTQ has been translated and validated in Vietnamese, Laotian, and Khmer. The HTQ possesses linguistic equivalence across the many cultures and languages with which it has been used thus far. Mollica et al. (1992) have reported good reliability for the HTQ.

In addition, the Clinician-Administered PTSD Scale (CAPS; described in detail below) has been studied among culturally different groups with excellent success. As one example, Charney and Keane (2007) recently examined the psychometric properties of the CAPS after it was adapted for use among Bosnian refugees. They applied contemporary methods for translation, back translation, and then qualitative approaches for reconciling any differences in meaning that might have arisen as a function of this process. The researchers found that the CAPS-Bosnian translation was comparable in its psychometric properties to earlier versions of the instrument. This indicates that the CAPS, when properly adapted, can be successfully used to measure PTSD symptoms in culturally diverse populations and that PTSD secondary to war in civilians appears to be comparable in nature to other forms of PTSD.

Over the past 10 years, research on biologically based measures of PTSD has established a foundation for a psychobiological description of PTSD (Orr, Metzger, Miller, & Kaloupek, 2004). Researchers have found that PTSD alters a wide range of physiological functions (Yehuda, 1997) and may affect structural components of the brain, particularly the hippocampus (Bremner et al., 1995). Overall, the most consistent finding in this area is that psychophysiological reactivity to trauma-specific cues is elevated in individuals with PTSD, but not in trauma-exposed individuals without PTSD (for reviews see Orr et al., 2004; Prins, Kaloupek, & Keane, 1995). Although psychophysiological assessment can provide unique information, widespread use of this approach in a clinical environment is not anticipated, as it is expensive and requires equipment and specialized training. In the majority of cases, more time and cost efficient methods of assessment, such as diagnostic interviews or self-report measures, are more than adequate. As psychophysiological methods are not accessible to the majority of clinicians, we refer the interested reader to Orr et al. (2004) for an excellent review.

In addition to the above, the clinician may want to review medical records and interview collateral sources regarding the patient's behavior and experiences, particularly when the accuracy of self-report is questioned or there is suspicion of malingering (e.g., during a compensation evaluation). In this chapter, we review measures of PTSD and their utility for diagnostic purposes, case conceptualization, treatment planning, and treatment monitoring and outcome.

TABLE 14.1 Ratings of Instruments Used for Diagnosis

Instrument	Norms	Internal Consistency	Inter-Rater Reliability	Test–Retest Reliability	Content Validity	Construct Validity	Validity Generalization	Clinical Utility	Highly Recommended
CAPS	E	E	E	E	E	E	E	E	✓
SCID-IV	E	E	A	A	G	G	E	G	✓
PSS-I	G	G	E	G	G	G	G	G	
SIP	G	G	E	A	G	G	G	G	
ADIS	G	G	G	A	G	G	G	G	
PTSD-I	A	E	G	G	E	G	G	G	
IES-R	G	G	NA	A	G	G	G	G	
Mississippi	E	E	NA	G	E	E	G	G	
PK Scale	E	E	NA	G	G	E	E	E	
PDS	E	E	NA	G	G	E	E	G	✓ᵃ
PCL	G	E	NA	G	G	E	E	G	✓ᵃ
LASC	G	E	NA	G	G	G	E	G	

ᵃ Self-report measures used as diagnostic instruments should include explicit assessment of the Criterion A event in addition to assessment of current DSM-IV symptoms.

Note: CAPS = Clinician-Administered PTSD Scale; SCID-IV = Structured Clinical Interview for DSM-IV; PSS-I = PTSD Symptom Scale Interview; SIP = Structured Interview for PTSD; ADIS = Anxiety Disorders Interview Schedule for DSM-IV; PTSD-I = Posttraumatic Stress Disorder Interview; IES-R = Impact of Event Scale-Revised; Mississippi = Mississippi Scale for Combat-Related PTSD; PK Scale = Keane PTSD Scale of the MMPI-2; PDS = Posttraumatic Diagnostic Scale; PCL = PTSD Checklist; LASC = Los Angeles Symptom Checklist; A = Adequate; G = Good; E = Excellent; NA = Not Applicable.

ASSESSMENT FOR A PTSD DIAGNOSIS

It is fundamental to case conceptualization and treatment planning for clinicians to determine the appropriate psychological diagnosis or diagnoses for their patients. Paramount to a diagnosis of PTSD is the clear identification of a Criterion A event, to which subsequent symptoms are linked. Therefore, when selecting diagnostic measures, clinicians should consider whether or not the measure assesses the presence of a traumatic event, in addition to ensuring that the measure is psychometrically sound. We review methods of assessing PTSD for diagnostic purposes, commenting on their comprehensiveness, their utility within a clinical context, and their psychometric properties in the subsequent text. Table 14.1 contains ratings of those instruments currently available for making diagnoses of PTSD.

Structured Diagnostic Interviews

Clinician-Administered PTSD Scale

Developed by the National Center for PTSD (Blake et al., 1990), the CAPS is one of the most widely used structured interviews for diagnosing and measuring the severity of PTSD (Weathers et al., 2001). The CAPS assesses all DSM-IV (American Psychiatric

Association, 1994) diagnostic criteria for PTSD, as well as the associated symptoms of guilt and dissociation. Importantly, the CAPS contain separate ratings for the frequency and intensity of each symptom; this permits flexibility in scoring and analyses. The CAPS also promotes uniform administration and scoring through carefully phrased prompt questions and explicit rating scale anchors with clear behavioral referents. There is also flexibility built into the administration of the CAPS. Interviewers can administer only the 17 core symptoms, all DSM-IV criteria, and/or the associated symptoms. Administration time is approximately 30 minutes to 1 hour, depending on those sections the interviewer chooses to utilize. Once trained, interviewers are able to ask their own follow-up questions and use their clinical judgment in arriving at the best ratings.

Weathers et al. (1999) examined the reliability and validity data of the CAPS across five samples of male Vietnam veterans collected at the National Center for PTSD in Boston. Robust estimates were found for inter-rater reliability over a 2-to-3-day interval for each of the three symptom clusters and all 17 symptoms. Test–retest reliability for a CAPS-based PTSD diagnosis was excellent, as was internal consistency across all 17 items in both research and clinical samples. Weathers et al. (1999) reported strong evidence for validity of the CAPS: the CAPS total severity score correlated highly with other measures of PTSD, such as the Mississippi Scale, the MMPI-PTSD Scale, the number of PTSD symptoms endorsed on the SCID, and the PTSD Checklist (PCL; Weathers, Litz, Herman, Huska, & Keane, 1993). They also found strong evidence for the diagnostic utility of the CAPS using three different CAPS scoring rules for predicting a SCID-based PTSD diagnosis.

The CAPS has been used successfully in a wide variety of trauma populations (e.g., combat veterans, Cambodian and Bosnian refugees, and victims of rape, crime, motor vehicle accidents, incest, the Holocaust, torture, and cancer), has served as the primary diagnostic or outcome measure in more than 200 empirical studies on PTSD, and has been translated into at least 12 languages (Hinton et al., 2006; Weathers et al., 2001). Thus, the existing data strongly support its continued use across clinical and research settings.

STRUCTURED CLINICAL INTERVIEW FOR DSM-IV

The Structured Clinical Interview for DSM-IV (SCID-IV; First et al., 2000) assesses a broad range of Axis I and II psychiatric conditions. It is divided into separate modules corresponding to DSM-IV diagnostic criteria, with each module providing the interviewer with prompts and follow-up inquiries intended to be read verbatim to respondents. The SCID can be administered by clinicians and highly trained interviewers. Although the administration of the full SCID-IV can be time consuming, the modular structure allows clinicians to tailor their assessment appropriately. Within the context of a trauma clinic, it is recommended that the anxiety disorders, affective disorders, and substance use disorder modules be administered to rule out any comorbid diagnoses. Administration of the psychotic screen will also help to rule out psychiatric conditions that require a different set of treatment interventions (Keane & Barlow, 2002).

The SCID-PTSD module is considered psychometrically sound. Keane et al. (1998) reported that the SCID-PTSD had adequate reliability, and McFall, Smith, Roszell, Tarver, and Malas (1990) reported evidence of convergent validity, finding significant correlations between the SCID-PTSD and other measures of PTSD including the Mississippi Scale (Keane et al., 1988) and the MMPI-PTSD Scale (Keane, Malloy, & Fairbank, 1984). The SCID-PTSD

module also had good diagnostic utility (Kulka et al., 1988). Although the SCID is a good diagnostic tool, several limitations exist. First, the SCID permits only a dichotomous rating of PTSD (e.g., presence or absence of symptoms), whereas most clinicians agree that psychological symptoms occur in a dimensional rather than dichotomous fashion (Keane et al., 2000). Second, the SCID does not assess for the frequency or severity of symptoms. Finally, only those symptoms associated with the "worst event" are assessed; the effects of other traumas are not evaluated.

PTSD Symptom Scale Interview

Developed by Foa, Riggs, Dancu, and Rothbaum (1993), the PTSD Symptom Scale Interview (PSS-I) is a structured interview designed to assess symptoms of PTSD. Using a Likert scale, interviewers rate the severity of 17 symptoms corresponding to the DSM-III-R (APS, 1987) criteria for PTSD. One limitation of the PSS-I is that it measures symptoms over the past 2 weeks, rather than 1 month, which the DSM criteria specify as necessary for a diagnosis of PTSD (Cusack et al., 2002). The PSS-I is brief (administration time is approximately 20 minutes) and can be administered by lay interviewers who are trained to work with trauma patients. The PSS-I was originally tested in a sample of women with a history of rape and nonsexual assault and was found to have good internal consistency, test–retest reliability over a 1-month period, and inter-rater agreement for a PTSD diagnosis (Foa et al., 1993). The PSS-I is significantly correlated with other measures of traumatic stress, such as the Impact of Events Intrusion score (Horowitz, 1979) and the Rape Aftermath Symptom Test total score (Kilpatrick, 1988). In addition, it has demonstrated good diagnostic utility when compared to a SCID-PTSD diagnosis. The PSS-I appears to possess many strong features that warrant its consideration for clinical use, especially with sexual assault survivors.

Structured Interview for PTSD

Developed by Davidson, Smith, and Kudler (1989), the Structured Interview for PTSD (SIP) is designed to diagnose PTSD and measure symptom severity. It includes 17 items focused on the DSM-IV criteria for PTSD as well as two items focused on survivor and behavior guilt. Each item is rated by the interviewer on a Likert scale. There are initial probe questions and follow-up questions to promote a more thorough understanding of the respondent's symptom experiences. It can be administered by clinicians or appropriately trained paraprofessionals. The SIP takes 10 to 30 minutes to administer, depending on the symptoms present. Psychometric data for the SIP are good. In a sample of combat veterans, Davidson et al. (1989) reported excellent inter-rater reliability on total SIP scores and perfect agreement on the presence or absence of PTSD across raters. High alpha coefficients have also been reported in both veteran samples and for PTSD patients enrolled in a clinical trial (Davidson et al., 1989; Davidson, Malik, & Travers, 1997). With respect to validity, the SIP was significantly correlated with other measures of PTSD, but not with measures of combat exposure (Davidson et al., 1989, 1997, cited in Orsillo, 2001, p. 291). Davidson et al. (1989) compared the SIP scores of current and remitted SCID-defined PTSD cases and reported good diagnostic utility. Overall, the SIP appears to be a sound diagnostic instrument.

Anxiety Disorders Interview Schedule for DSM-IV

Developed by DiNardo, O'Brien, Barlow, Waddell, and Blanchard (1983), the Anxiety Disorders Interview Schedule-Revised (ADIS) was designed to permit differential diagnoses among the DSM-III anxiety disorder categories. The interview was revised to correspond to DSM-IV criteria (ADIS-IV; DiNardo, Brown, & Barlow, 1994). The ADIS-IV also includes an assessment of affective disorders, substance use disorders, and selected somatoform disorders; a diagnostic timeline; and a dimensional assessment of the key and associated features of the disorders. The provision of a dimensional as well as a categorical assessment allows the clinician to describe subthreshold manifestations of each disorder, allowing for better case conceptualization. Results from psychometric studies on the ADIS-PTSD module are mixed. Originally, tested in a small sample of Vietnam combat veterans, the ADIS-PTSD module yielded strong agreement with interview-determined diagnoses (Blanchard, Gerardi, Kolb, & Barlow, 1986). However, DiNardo, Moras, Barlow, Rapee, and Brown (1993) tested the reliability of the ADIS in a community sample recruited from an anxiety disorders clinic and found only adequate agreement between two independent raters when PTSD was the principal diagnosis or an additional diagnosis. In a

test of the ADIS-IV, the inter-rater reliability across two interviews given 10 days apart was also fair for current diagnoses (Brown, DiNardo, Lehman, & Campbell, 2001) but slightly improved for lifetime diagnoses. Provision of additional reliability and validity data on the ADIS-IV is needed to insure its continued use in clinical settings.

Self-Report Measures

PTSD-Interview

Developed by Watson, Juba, Manifold, Kucala, and Anderson (1991), the PTSD-Interview (PTSD-I) is based on DSM-III-R and is completed with the clinician. Patients are provided a copy of the scale to read along with the interviewer and are asked to provide a rating for each of the symptoms based on a Likert scale. The PTSD-I yields both dichotomous and continuous information and is designed to be used by lay interviewers. Although it was initially developed for use in a veteran population, it has been used in a variety of trauma populations (including those in automobile accidents and victims of sexual assault). It has also been translated into French and Spanish. Psychometric data on the PTSD-I are excellent. Watson et al. (1991) administered the PTSD-I to a sample of veteran outpatients and found high test–retest reliability for the PTSD-I total score over a 1-week interval and high inter-rater reliability for a PTSD diagnosis. A high α coefficient indicated good internal consistency. With regard to validity, the total score of the PTSD-I has been shown to correlate highly with other measures of PTSD, such as the PTSD section of the Diagnostic Interview Schedule and the Impact of Events Scale (IES; Robins & Helzer, 1985; Watson et al., 1991; Wilson, Tinker, Becker & Gillette, 1994).

Impact of Event Scale-Revised

Developed by Horowitz, Wilner, and Alvarez (1979), the IES is one of the most widely used self-report measures to assess psychological responses to a traumatic event. The initial 15-item questionnaire, which focused only on intrusion and avoidance symptoms, was derived from a model of traumatic stress developed by Horowitz (1976). A revised 22-item version was developed to accommodate the DSM-IV criteria, containing items on hyperarousal symptoms and flashback experiences (IES-R; Weiss & Marmar, 1997). Respondents complete the measure by rating on a Likert scale "how distressed or bothered" they were by each symptom during the past week. The IES has been translated into several languages, has been used with many different trauma populations, and takes approximately 10 minute to complete.

Data on the psychometric properties of the revised IES-R are preliminary in nature. In the two studies that incorporated four samples of emergency workers and earthquake survivors, Weiss and Marmar (1997) reported satisfactory internal consistency for each of the subscales, whereas test–retest reliability data from two samples yielded a range of reliability coefficients. Weiss and Marmar (1997) suggested that the shorter interval between assessments and the greater recency of the traumatic event for one sample contributed to higher coefficients of stability for that sample. Still, it remains difficult to make determinations regarding reliability. Convergent and discriminant validity data are not yet available for the IES-R. There were many questions raised about the validity of the original scale, in part because it did not assess all DSM criteria for PTSD (see Joseph, 2000; Weathers et al., 1996). Although it now more closely parallels DSM-IV, items measuring numbing are considered limited by some investigators (Foa, Cashman, Jaycox, & Perry, 1997). In a review of psychometric studies on the IES, Sundin and Horowitz (2002) report a wide range of correlations between the IES subscales and other self-report measures and diagnostic interviews (McFall, Smith, Roszell, et al., 1990; Neal et al., 1994). Additional studies with the revised instrument are clearly needed to establish its reliability and validity.

Mississippi Scale for Combat-Related PTSD

Developed by Keane et al. (1988), the 35-item Mississippi Scale is widely used to assess combat-related PTSD symptoms. The scale items were selected from an initial pool of 200 items generated by experts to match the DSM-III criteria for the disorder. The Mississippi Scale has been updated and now assesses the presence of symptoms reflecting the DSM-IV criteria for PTSD and several associated features. Respondents are asked to rate, on a Likert scale, the severity of symptoms over the time period occurring "since the event." The Mississippi Scale yields a continuous score of symptom severity as well as diagnostic information. It is available in several languages and takes 10 to 15 minutes to administer.

The Mississippi Scale has excellent psychometric properties. In Vietnam-era veterans seeking treatment, Keane et al. (1988) reported high internal consistency and test–retest reliability over a 1-week time interval. In a subsequent validation study, the authors found an overall hit rate of 90% when the scale was used to differentiate between a PTSD group and two non-PTSD comparison groups. McFall, Smith, Mackay, and Tarver (1990) replicated these findings, and further demonstrated that PTSD patients with and without substance use disorders did not differ on the Mississippi Scale. Given the high comorbidity between PTSD and substance use disorders, the authors felt it was important to demonstrate that the test assesses PTSD symptoms rather than effects associated with alcohol and drug use. McFall, Smith, Mackay, et al. (1990) also obtained information on convergent validity, finding significant correlations between the Mississippi Scale and other measures of PTSD, including the total number of SCID-PTSD symptoms, total IES score, and degree of traumatic combat exposure on the Vietnam Era Stress Inventory (Wilson & Krauss, 1984). These findings suggest that the Mississippi Scale is a valuable self-report tool in settings where assessment of combat-related PTSD is needed.

More recently, Orazem, Charney, and Keane (2006) examined the psychometric properties of the Mississippi Scale in over 1,200 cases of Vietnam War veterans participating in a multisite study of the psychophysiology of PTSD (Keane et al., 1998). Results indicated that the Mississippi Scale possessed excellent internal consistency and was highly correlated with the Keane PTSD Scale of the MMPI-2 (PK). Using the SCID-PTSD module as the diagnostic gold standard, the Mississippi Scale possessed excellent diagnostic utility, suggesting strong support for the use of this test when assessing combat-related PTSD.

Keane PTSD Scale of the MMPI-2 (PK)

Originally derived from the MMPI Form R (Keane et al., 1984), the PK Scale now consists of 46 items empirically drawn from the MMPI-2 (Lyons & Keane, 1992). The items are answered in a true–false format. The scale is typically administered as part of the full MMPI-2, but it can be useful as a stand-alone scale. The embedded and stand-alone versions are highly correlated (.90; Herman, Weathers, Litz, & Keane,

1996). The PK Scale yields a total score that reflects the presence or absence of PTSD. The stand-alone scale takes 15 minutes to administer.

Psychometric data on the embedded and stand-alone versions of the PK Scale are excellent. Herman et al. (1996) reported evidence from a veteran sample of strong internal consistency of the embedded and stand-alone versions of the PK Scale, and high test–retest reliability coefficients for the stand-alone version over 2 to 3 days. With regard to validity, the embedded and stand-alone versions of the PK Scale were correlated with other self-report measures of PTSD, including the Mississippi Scale, IES, and PCL, and a diagnostic interview (CAPS). The embedded and stand-alone versions differed slightly in their optimally efficient cutoff score, but both demonstrated good clinical utility as compared to a CAPS diagnosis. More research is needed to determine the generalizability of the findings with veterans to other populations, as well as the optimal cutoff scores (Foa et al., 1997; Watson et al., 1986). Although only a few studies have been conducted on the PK Scale in nonveteran populations, the data present appear to be promising (Koretzky & Peck, 1990; Neal et al., 1994). The PK may be particularly useful in the area of forensic psychology, where the MMPI-2 is often employed because of its validity indexes.

Posttraumatic Diagnostic Scale

Developed by Foa et al. (1997), the Posttraumatic Diagnostic Scale (PDS) is a 49-item scale designed to measure DSM-IV PTSD criteria and symptom severity. The PDS is a revised version of an earlier self-report scale based on DSM-III-R, referred to as the PTSD Symptom Scale-Self-Report Version (PSS-SR; Foa et al., 1993). The PDS reviews trauma exposure and identifies the most distressing trauma. It also assesses Criterion A2 (physical threat or helplessness), Criterion B–D (intensity and frequency of all 17 symptoms), and functional impairment (Criterion F). This scale has been used with several populations, including combat veterans, accident victims, and sexual and nonsexual assault survivors, and has been validated in other languages (e.g., German; Griesel, Wessa, & Flor, 2006). The PDS can be administered in 10 to 15 minutes.

The psychometric properties of the PDS were evaluated among 264 volunteers recruited from several PTSD treatment centers as well as from nontreatment seeking populations at high risk for trauma

(Foa et al., 1997). Investigators reported high internal consistency for the PTSD total score and subscales and adequate test–retest reliability coefficients for the total PDS score and for the symptom cluster scores. With regard to validity, the PDS total score correlated highly with other scales that measure traumatic responses, such as the IES. In addition, the measure yielded high levels of diagnostic agreement with a SCID diagnosis. Most recently, Griffin, Uhlmansiek, Resick, and Mechanic (2004) compared the PDS to the CAPS in a population of female survivors of domestic violence. They found strong intercorrelations between the two measures, although the PDS tended to overdiagnose PTSD. These findings suggest that the PDS might serve as an acceptable screening device for identifying cases of PTSD in this population, but that clinicians should be aware of elevated false positive rates.

PTSD Checklist

Developed by researchers at the National Center for PTSD (Weathers et al., 1993), the PCL is a 17-item self-report measure of PTSD symptoms. Different scoring procedures may be used to yield either a continuous measure of symptom severity or a dichotomous indicator of diagnostic status. Dichotomous scoring methods include either an overall cutoff score or a symptom cluster scoring approach. The original scale was based on the DSM-III-R criteria for PTSD and has been updated to reflect the 17 diagnostic criteria outlined in DSM-IV. Respondents are asked to rate, on a Likert scale, "how much each problem has bothered them" during the past month. The time frame can be adjusted as needed to suit the goals of the assessment. There is a civilian (PCL-C) and a military version (PCL-M) of the measure. On the PCL-C, re-experiencing and avoidance symptoms apply to any lifetime stressful event, whereas for the PCL-M, re-experiencing and avoidance symptoms apply to stressful events that are military-related only. The PCL has been used extensively in both research and clinical settings and takes 5 to 10 minutes to administer. If needed, a 17-item Life Events Checklist developed as a companion to the CAPS to identify potentially traumatic experiences, can be used with the PCL.

The PCL was validated in a sample of Vietnam and Persian Gulf War veterans and found to have strong psychometric properties (Weathers et al., 1993). Keen, Kutter, Niles, and Krinsley (2004) examined the psychometric properties of the updated PCL in veterans with both combat and noncombat traumas and found evidence for high internal consistency. Test–retest reliability was not examined, but the original study suggested this was robust over a 2-to-3-day interval. Other investigators have also documented adequate test–retest reliability of this measure over a 2-week time frame (Ruggiero, Del Ben, Scotti, & Rabalais, 2003). With respect to validity, Keen et al. (2004) found that the scale was highly correlated with other measures of PTSD including the Mississippi Scale and the CAPS, and had good diagnostic power. In addition, using the CAPS as the gold standard, Dobie et al. (2002) reported that the PCL had good diagnostic utility.

Several studies provide evidence for the reliability and validity of the PCL in nonveteran samples (e.g. primary care patients, severely mentally ill adults), although the optimal cutoff score varies across samples (Cook, Elhai, & Arean, 2005; Grubaugh, Elhai, Cusack, Wells, & Frueh, 2006; Walker, Newman, Dobie, Ciechanowski, & Katon, 2002). The many possible reasons for these discrepancies (e.g., gender, recency of trauma, severity of trauma, and treatment seeking status; Manne, DuHamel, Gallelli, Sorgen, & Redd, 1998) warrant further investigation. In addition, there is evidence that different scoring options for the PCL (e.g., an absolute cutoff score vs. symptom cluster scoring) yield differences in sensitivity, specificity, and diagnostic efficiency. The selection of a scoring routine should, therefore, depend on the goal of the assessment (Keen et al., 2004).

Los Angeles Symptom Checklist

Developed by King, King, Leskin, and Foy (1995), the Los Angeles Symptom Checklist (LASC) is a 43-item scale used to diagnose PTSD and describe symptom severity. The original scale was referred to as the PTSD Symptom Checklist (Foy, Sipprelle, Rueger, & Carroll, 1984); it was designed to adhere closely to DSM-III criteria and has now been updated to correspond to DSM-IV. The LASC includes an assessment of B, C, and D criteria (17 items). Respondents are asked to rate, on a Likert scale, "how much of a problem" each symptom is for them. There is also a global assessment of distress and adjustment problems related to trauma exposure. No time frame is established for rating symptoms. Originally validated on a veteran sample, the LACS has now been used to assess trauma symptoms in several other traumatized groups (see King et al., 1995 for details). It takes approximately 15 minutes to administer.

Psychometric data on the LASC are strong. King et al. (1995) combined data from 10 studies that used the LASC with clinical samples derived from a diverse set of populations (i.e., Vietnam veterans, battered women, adult survivors of childhood abuse, psychiatric outpatients, and high-risk adolescents). Evidence was provided for high internal consistency among veterans and women. Test–retest reliability was found to be stable over a 2-week period. With respect to validity, LASC scores correlate to varying degrees with measures of combat exposure (Foy et al., 1984) and traumatic stress (Astin, Lawrence, & Foy, 1993). Results obtained by using either of two scoring schemes provide an acceptable level of precision in classifying PTSD and non-PTSD patients.

Overall Evaluation

Efforts to diagnose and assess patients for PTSD symptoms should include a range of standardized assessment methods in addition to reviewing medical records, accessing collateral sources, and taking a thorough history. Earlier, we reviewed the use of structured diagnostic interviews and self-report measures as primary methods for diagnosing PTSD in a clinical context. In making choices about measures, it is important to consider utility within a clinical context (e.g., are the measures time- and cost-effective?), as well as psychometric properties. Using these guidelines, the gold standard in PTSD assessment is the CAPS structured interview, given that it is a sound measure with excellent psychometric properties. As an adjunct, or in cases when administering a structured interview is not feasible or practical, we recommend the use of self-report measures that explicitly assess the Criterion A event, or that are administered with the instruction to anchor all symptom endorsement to the index Criterion A event. Many of the self-report measures described earlier can be used interchangeably; however, we recommend that clinicians consider the available psychometric data for the instrument for the population on which it is to be used. In doing this, clinicians are maximizing the accuracy and efficiency of the selected measure.

TABLE 14.2 Ratings of Instruments Used for Case Conceptualization and Treatment Planning

Instrument	Norms	Internal Consistency	Inter-Rater Reliability	Test–Retest Reliability	Content Validity	Construct Validity	Validity Generalization	Clinical Utility	Highly Recommended
BTQ	A	NA	NA	A	A	NA	G	A	
LEC	G	NA	NA	G	G	NA	G	A	
LSC-R	A	NA	NA	A	A	NA	G	A	
SLESQ	A	NA	NA	A	A	NA	G	A	
TEQ	A	NA	NA	A	A	NA	G	A	
TLEQ	E	NA	NA	E	E	NA	E	A	✓
TSS	G	NA	NA	A	A	NA	G	A	

Note: BTQ = Brief Trauma Questionnaire; LEC = Life Events Checklist; LSC-R = Life Stressor Checklist-Revised; SLESQ = Stressful Life Events Screening Questionnaire; TEQ = Traumatic Events Questionnaire; TLEQ = Traumatic Life Events Questionnaire; TSS = Traumatic Stress Schedule; A = Adequate; G = Good; E = Excellent; NA = Not Applicable.

ASSESSMENT FOR CASE CONCEPTUALIZATION AND TREATMENT PLANNING

On completion of a comprehensive diagnostic assessment of PTSD that includes identification of the Criterion A event and related symptoms, the clinician will have a considerable amount of information regarding the index trauma and the severity of its psychological sequelae. This obviously is a necessary first step to case conceptualization and treatment planning; however, selection of a particular treatment and specific initial targets of treatment require additional information. The augmentation of diagnostic measures with more idiographic assessment of trauma-related symptoms, as well as the assessment of comorbid conditions (e.g., Keane, Solomon, Maser, & Gerrity, 1995), provides an excellent foundation for treatment planning. We confine our discussion here primarily to case conceptualization and treatment planning specific to PTSD symptoms. Assessment for case conceptualization and treatment planning incorporates the influence of contextual factors that may or may not be revealed during the diagnostic procedure. We will focus on how to address these contextual factors in this section and refer the reader to Table 14.2 for a review of instruments available for this purpose.

Type of Trauma

There is a considerable range of traumatic events that occur, and there are multiple ways in which to categorize these events. For example, involvement in a combat situation, a sexual assault, or a motor vehicle accident all qualify as potential Criterion A events, given the likelihood of intense fear or horror during the events, as well as significant threat to personal integrity. However, these traumatic events may vary on dimensions that are of particular salience in case conceptualization and treatment planning. For example, emotions and beliefs secondary to the trauma might differ in ways related to the trauma type. For example, guilt may be prominent for a combat veteran, dissociation might be more likely for a sexual assault victim, and conditioned fear of driving might be the most serious problem for an individual involved in a motor vehicle accident. Earlier we discussed the availability of assessment components of diagnostic measures that target associated features, such as survivor guilt and dissociation, in addition to the core 17 DSM-IV symptoms. These elements of the diagnostic assessment are particularly valuable in the initial identification of idiographic factors that aid in case conceptualization. In addition, although many of the available diagnostic measures provide only assessment of the presence or absence of the core symptoms, continuous measures of symptom frequency and severity also provide valuable information for case conceptualization and treatment planning in the areas of greatest distress and impairment. Measures that include the assessment of the frequency and severity of clinical features associated with PTSD are the CAPS, the SIP, and the Mississippi Scale for Combat-Related PTSD.

Single Versus Multiple Trauma

Although the diagnostic assessment includes an index trauma as the Criterion A event to which all other symptoms are presumed to be secondary, a striking percentage of individuals with PTSD have experienced multiple traumas during their lifetimes (e.g., Kessler et al., 1995). Indeed, past trauma has been shown to be a risk factor for the development of PTSD in response to a subsequent traumatic event (e.g., Breslau, Chilcoat, Kessler, & Davis, 1999). Generally, the index trauma (i.e., the identified Criterion A event) is the event that prompted the patient to seek treatment, and sequelae of that event often are the primary targets of treatment. It follows that the identification of additional events that may have contributed to maladaptive functioning in response to the Criterion A event can aid in treatment planning. Numerous checklists have been developed to assess the experience of various traumatic events. These measures can be used as an initial PTSD screen for the experience of traumatic events, and they also can be used to identify additional traumatic experiences following a comprehensive diagnostic assessment of the index trauma.

Five brief measures assess exposure to a variety of different DSM-IV-TR Criterion A events, although they do not provide an assessment of Criterion A2, and therefore should not be used as diagnostic measures. The Life Events Checklist (LEC; National Center for PTSD) is embedded in the CAPS interview and has been used as an initial screen for potentially traumatic events. The LEC lists 17 types of traumatic events that may have been experienced, as well as levels of exposure (i.e., happened to me, witnessed event, learned about event). The LEC demonstrates adequate test–retest reliability over 1 week for endorsement of direct exposure to five of the listed events in a nonclinical sample, although reliability was lower for the remaining items, perhaps due to low base rates of those events (Gray, Litz, Hsu, & Lombardo, 2004). The Traumatic Stress Schedule (TSS; Norris, 1990) is a 10-item measure that has demonstrated good reliability ($r = .88$) with multicultural samples. The Traumatic Events Questionnaire (TEQ; Vrana & Lauterbach, 1994) similarly assesses the experience of eleven potential Criterion A events; this measure also demonstrates excellent reliability. The Stressful Life Events Screening Questionnaire (SLESQ; Goodman, Corcoran, Turner, Yuan, & Green, 1998) demonstrates good reliability in the assessment of 13 potentially traumatic events, and the questionnaire also incorporates age at the time of trauma. The last Criterion A1 checklist is the Brief Trauma Questionnaire (BTQ; Schnurr, Vielhauer, Weathers, & Findler, 1999), which assesses the experience of 10 potentially traumatic events. This measure is explicit in its requirement that individuals respond to each item as Criterion A1; respondents are asked if they thought their lives were in danger or if they thought they were injured or could be injured during the event.

In addition to the five measures designed to identify a range of potential Criterion A events, two checklist-type measures are designed also to assess Criterion A2. These measures include a greater number of items that may be helpful in case conceptualization and treatment planning. The Traumatic Life Events Questionnaire (TLEQ; Kubany et al., 2000) assesses exposure to 23 events; this measure expands on the lists employed by the aforementioned Criterion A1 measures by breaking down a generally traumatic experience (e.g., unwanted sexual experience), into more specific items that include contextual factors (e.g., childhood sexual touching, adolescent sexual touching). Test–retest reliability was shown to be good. This measure includes assessment of both Criterion A1 and Criterion A2, although we also note that some items on the checklist may not qualify as Criterion A events (e.g., sexual harassment). In addition, the Life Stressor Checklist-Revised (LSC-R; Wolfe, Kimerling, Brown, Chrestman, & Levin, 1996) assesses Criterion A1 and Criterion A2 for 30 events. The checklist also includes follow-up questions including age at trauma and degree of event-related distress during the last year. Item reliability ranges from good to excellent in a large sample of women (McHugo et al., 2005). Also of note is the inclusion of stressful events that may be of particular relevance for women, such as abortion and miscarriage. In general, checklists that identify exposure to various traumatic events allow the clinician a more comprehensive picture of client experiences for case conceptualization and treatment planning.

Chronicity of PTSD

Although many individuals who experience trauma-related symptoms present themselves for treatment relatively soon after the traumatic event, many others experience symptoms for years before seeking treatment. In its chronic form, PTSD often pervades an individual's life and has a deleterious impact in multiple domains, including occupational functioning, social functioning, and marital relationships. Assessment of maladaptive functioning in the relevant areas begins with a thorough patient history. In addition, the impact of the traumatic event on particular areas of functioning can be assessed using a number of measures available to monitor a wider range of functional difficulty. For example, two particularly useful measures of functioning across multiple domains, including physical and psychiatric functioning, are the SF-36 Health Survey (Ware & Kosinski, 2001) and the BASIS-32 (Eisen, Wilcox, Leff, Schaefer, & Culhane, 1999). Instruments are also available to measure dimensions relevant to marital difficulty (e.g., Conflict Tactics Scale—Revised; Straus et al., 1996) and quality of life (e.g., Quality of Life Inventory; Frisch, Cornell, Villanueva, & Retzlaff, 1992). A comprehensive listing and discussion of these measures is beyond the scope of the current chapter, although we note the importance of such adjunct assessment in case conceptualization and treatment planning, and we suggest that, at a minimum, the patient history incorporates multiple functional domains.

Developmental Factors Related to Age at Trauma

Patient age at which the trauma occurred does not appear to predict treatment outcome (e.g., Foa, Keane, Friedman, 2000). Despite the absence of evidence for treatment effects specific to age, age variables are important for case conceptualization and treatment planning. A 30-year-old adult seeking treatment related to childhood sexual trauma that occurred at age 10 is likely to present very differently from a 40-year-old who seeks treatment for a sexual assault that occurred at age 20. In both cases, 20 years have passed since the trauma; however, the 10-year-old victim presumably coped using strategies that were developmentally appropriate for a child, whereas the 20-year-old victim presumably coped using strategies that were developmentally appropriate for a young adult. Thus, developmental factors have significant potential impact on the manner in which each individual initially processed the difficulty related to the event and how he/she continues to experience it. Given that children have a less mature grasp of the concept of "bad things happening to good people," the patient who experienced childhood trauma may be more likely, for example, to have developed self-blame in response to the event.

Patient age (or approximate age) at the time of the index trauma should be included in the patient history, and, as noted, specifically is requested by several of the Criterion A assessment measures. In addition, an idiographic approach to the identification of beliefs resulting from the traumatic event(s) can incorporate developmental factors, and can be valuable in planning targets for treatment. One such idiographic approach is employed within the Cognitive Processing Therapy manualized treatment for PTSD (Resick & Schnicke, 1993). Patients are instructed to write an "impact statement," which is their own account of how their beliefs about themselves, others, and the world have changed owing to the traumatic event. This procedure often provides detailed information about potentially maladaptive beliefs related to safety, intimacy, control, and so forth, and it provides the initial foundation for cognitive restructuring, should such techniques be utilized in the treatment. We note that this particular measure is completely idiographic, as the format is open-ended and qualitative; we suggest that such an addition to a comprehensive quantitative assessment offers important adjunct data that is useful in treatment planning.

Comorbidity

As observed earlier, several Axis I disorders, including major depression and substance dependence, are frequent concomitants of PTSD. A comprehensive discussion of assessment measures of comorbid conditions is beyond the scope of the current chapter, although we note the importance of screening for the most common co-occurring disorders, at a minimum, during the diagnostic assessment process, as treatment of PTSD often is more effective when the comorbid conditions are also addressed (e.g. Shalev, Friedman, Foa, & Keane, 2000). Comprehensive Axis I diagnostic assessment measures, such as the SCID interview, facilitate identification and diagnosis of comorbid conditions that can be incorporated into the therapeutic plan. We note that rigorous assessment and ongoing monitoring of substance abuse or dependence is extremely important in planning for trauma-focused treatment; if an individual is using substances to self-medicate for PTSD symptoms, that individual might be at greater risk for increased substance misuse in response to distress related to therapy content or process. See the chapters on substance abuse and depression in this volume for a more thorough discussion on how to efficiently measure these conditions when they occur.

Overall Evaluation

In conjunction with a comprehensive diagnostic strategy, assessment for case conceptualization and treatment planning broadens the scope of relevant data available to the clinician. Measures that take into account contextual factors that are relevant to PTSD, such as exposure to multiple traumatic events or presence of comorbid conditions, provide detailed information that can be helpful in deciding on the therapeutic approach and the specific targets of treatment. A variety of psychometrically sound measures are available for these purposes, and we have focused on those with the greatest clinical relevance. Table 14.2 presents our general recommendations for tools that should be considered for use.

ASSESSMENT FOR TREATMENT MONITORING AND OUTCOME

Monitoring the outcome of psychological treatment is essential to help providers demonstrate the effectiveness of their treatments to patients and service payers. In an early example of such monitoring, Keane and Kaloupek (1982) presented the first empirical evidence that cognitive-behavioral treatments for PTSD had promise. Within a single-subject design, they assessed clients' subjective units of distress (SUD) ratings from 0 to 10 within treatment sessions to monitor changes in the response to traumatic memories in a prolonged exposure treatment paradigm. In addition, they utilized the Spielberger State Anxiety Inventory (STAI; Spielberger, Gorsuch, Lushene, Vagg, & Jacobs, 1983) to monitor between-session levels of anxiety and distress throughout the course of the nineteen treatment sessions.

Currently, the use of sound psychometric instruments has become an important part of monitoring outcomes of PTSD treatment, regardless of whether the intervention is psychopharmacological, psychological, or both (e.g., Keane & Kaloupek, 2002). In addition to the provision of a measurement of change within and between sessions for a given individual, such measurements ideally present normative information against which the individual's presentation and progress can be compared either to the general population or target populations of interest (cf. Kraemer, 1992). It follows that clinicians would do well to utilize tests or questionnaires with sound

psychometric properties when deciding how best to monitor the outcomes of their interventions (Keane & Kaloupek, 1997). Table 14.3 provides an analysis of our perspective on a variety of treatment monitoring and outcome measures for use in PTSD work.

When monitoring outcomes, clinicians are also encouraged to consider outcomes at several levels. These would include the symptom level, the individual level, the system level, and the social and contextual level. All are important and can provide valuable information for both clinician and client (Keane & Kaloupek, 1997, 2002). Numerous measures are available to measure psychopathology, and clinicians are encouraged to look for the measures that are most appropriate for their circumstances and settings. Use of these measures at regular intervals (e.g., daily, weekly, monthly, quarterly, etc.) during the course of treatment will provide knowledge of the client's status and communicate to the clinician the extent to which the patient is demonstrating change in the desired directions.

At the symptom level, regular assessment of PTSD symptom frequency and severity can provide the clinician with useful information regarding within- and between-session change over the course of treatment. For example, it may be that some clients experience clinically significant symptom reduction in some symptoms early in treatment, whereas other symptoms persist; frequent assessment can help the clinician target particular problem areas while continually monitoring less problematic symptoms that may not be addressed specifically in session owing to time constraints. In general, regular administration of symptom checklists can provide ongoing feedback to the clinician and the client. The brief PTSD symptom checklists discussed earlier in this chapter can be quite useful for this purpose. In particular, the PTSD Checklist, the Impact of Events Scale-Revised, and the PTSD Interview can be completed quickly, are anchored to the index trauma, and assess symptoms during a specific timeframe relevant to treatment monitoring (e.g., during the past week). Also at the symptom level, comorbid conditions such as major depression similarly can be assessed easily using brief symptom measures (e.g., Beck Depression Inventory; Beck, Brown, & Steer, 1996). There are also a number of measures available for the purpose of monitoring a wider range of outcomes on the systems, social, and contextual levels of clients' lives. Selection of the most appropriate measures of outcome is fundamentally a clinical decision

TABLE 14.3 Ratings of Instruments Used for Treatment Monitoring and Treatment Outcome Evaluation

Instrument	Norms	Internal Consistency	Inter-Rater Reliability	Test–Retest Reliability	Content Validity	Construct Validity	Validity Generalization	Treatment Sensitivity	Clinical Utility	Highly Recommended
CAPS	E	E	E	E	E	E	E	E	E	✓
IES-R	G	G	NA	A	G	G	G	G	G	
PCL	G	E	NA	G	G	E	E	E	G	✓
PDS	E	E	NA	G	G	E	E	E	G	✓
PTSD-I	A	E	NA	G	E	G	G	G	G	
SCID-IV	E	E	A	A	G	G	E	G	G	
TOP-8	G	G	G	G	A	E	E	G	A	

Note: CAPS = Clinician-Administered PTSD Scale; IES-R = Impact of Events Scale; PCL = PTSD Checklist; PDS = Posttraumatic Diagnostic Scale; PTSD-I = PTSD Interview; SCID-IV = Structured Clinical Interview for DSM-IV; TOP-8 = Treatment Outcome PTSD Scale; A = Adequate; G = Good; E = Excellent; NA = Not Applicable.

that should be determined by the provider in consultation with the client. In the context of PTSD, we recommend the use of the World Health Organizations Disability Adjustment Scale (WHODAS) in an effort to arrive at a systematic understanding of the impact of any single disorder or the presence of concurrent disorders.

Assessment of outcomes at termination of treatment should bring the clinician and the client full circle, by again assessing diagnostic and functional status to examine change from pre- to post-treatment and identifying remaining problem areas. Ideally, the clinician and the client will repeat the initial diagnostic interview (e.g., CAPS, PDS) to determine change in symptom frequency and severity, as well as collateral change in other areas of functioning. Owing to clinicians' time constraints, it may not be feasible to repeat an entire structured interview; in such cases, the self-report symptom measures outlined in the "Assessment for A PTSD Diagnosis" section of this chapter may provide an adequate substitute.

In addition, one brief measure was designed specifically to assess core symptoms of PTSD in treatment outcome studies (Davidson & Colket, 1997) and would also be useful in the clinical setting. Derived from the 19-item SIP discussed earlier, the Treatment Outcome PTSD Scale (TOP-8) includes 8 items that are thought to occur most frequently in PTSD and demonstrate the maximum change in response to treatment. Item selection was drawn from a sample of patients with chronic PTSD. Using a Likert scale, interviewers rate the extent to which each symptom has "troubled the person" during the past week. Administration requires 5 to 10 minutes. Initial data on the TOP-8 indicates that it has good psychometric properties, including adequate internal consistency and excellent reliability. The developers suggest that the advantages of the TOP-8 include the reduced administration time compared to other structured interviews, elimination of items that are endorsed infrequently or are resistant to change, and reduction of counter-therapeutic effects caused by lengthy interviews. They also acknowledge disadvantages; some clinically important or distressing symptoms are not assessed, and the brevity of the measure limits its ability to explore properties of treatment. However, it should be noted that the methodological strategies employed in the development and validation of this scale are not commonly accepted in the psychometric literature. Accordingly, independent replication is necessary before endorsement of the measure, and

we suggest that clinicians utilize this interview only in conjunction with other clinical measures.

Overall Evaluation

The most thorough assessment for PTSD treatment monitoring incorporates regular measurement of PTSD symptoms, symptoms of comorbid conditions, and indices of functional domains such as marital relationships. In the clinical setting, this task is best accomplished using brief instruments that are relatively easy to administer and score. Treatment outcome measurement should, at a minimum, include brief assessment of symptoms, although the readministration of diagnostic measures (e.g., structured interview) allows the most comprehensive assessment of change during treatment. We suggest that each of the measures recommended in Table 14.3 have psychometric properties appropriate for these purposes.

CONCLUSIONS AND FUTURE DIRECTIONS

We have discussed the assessment of PTSD for the purposes of diagnosis, case conceptualization, treatment planning, and treatment monitoring and outcome, with emphasis on the most psychometrically sound measures available. We also have attempted to consider clinical feasibility in the use of these measures. We are confident that the available assessment options can be easily incorporated into clinical practice.

With respect to assessment for diagnosis, we emphasize the importance of the clear identification of a Criterion A event, to which subsequent symptom endorsements are linked. We also recommend structured interviews when possible, in particular those which assess frequency and intensity of symptoms. For the purposes of case conceptualization and treatment planning, a broader assessment of contextual factors, including psychiatric comorbidity and exposure to other potentially traumatic events, provides valuable adjunct information. We further recommend regular brief assessments of symptoms for the purposes of treatment monitoring and a repeated diagnostic assessment to determine diagnostic status and functional change at treatment or protocol termination.

Clearly, the present review is not intended to be comprehensive in its evaluation of all instruments available for the assessment of PTSD. The intent of the review has been to provide a heuristic structure that clinicians might employ when selecting a particular instrument for their clinical purposes. By carefully examining the psychometric properties of a measure, the clinician can make an informed decision about the appropriateness of a particular instrument for the task at hand (e.g., diagnosis, case conceptualization, treatment planning, monitoring outcomes). In addition to the psychometric properties of a measure, instruments that are developed and evaluated on multiple trauma populations and culturally diverse populations are highly desirable. Future efforts are needed to establish the reliability and validity of new instruments on a wider range of populations for clinicians' use with diverse patients. The quality of our measures will ultimately determine our understanding of PTSD and will yield improved treatment of patients suffering from this condition.

References

American Psychiatric Association. (1980). *Diagnostic and statistical manual of mental disorders* (3rd ed.). Washington, DC: Author.

American Psychiatric Association (1987). *Diagnostic and statistical manual of mental disorders* (3rd ed., revised). Washington, DC: Author.

American Psychiatric Association (1994). *Diagnostic and statistical manual of mental disorders* (4th ed.). Washington, DC: Author.

American Psychiatric Association (2000). *Diagnostic and statistical manual of mental disorders* (4th ed., text revision). Washington, DC: Author.

Astin, M. C., Lawrence, K. J., & Foy, D. W. (1993). Posttraumatic stress disorder among battered women: Risk and resiliency factors. *Violence and Victims, 8*, 17–28.

Back, S. E., Sonne, S. C., Killeen, T., Dansky, B. S., & Brady, K. T. (2003). Comparative profiles of women with PTSD and comorbid cocaine or alcohol dependence. *American Journal of Drug and Alcohol Abuse, 29*, 169–189.

Beck, A. T., Brown, G., & Steer, R. A. (1996). *Beck depression inventory II manual.* San Antonio, TX: The Psychological Corporation.

Blake, D. D., Weathers, F. W., Nagy, L. M., Kaloupek, D. G., Charney, D. S., & Keane, T. M. (1990). *The clinician administered PTSD scale-IV.* Boston: National Center for PTSD, Behavioral Sciences Division.

Blanchard, E. B., Gerardi, R. J., Kolb, L. C., & Barlow, D. H. (1986). The utility of the Anxiety Disorders Interview Schedule (ADIS) in the diagnosis of Post-Traumatic Stress Disorder (PTSD) in Vietnam Veterans. *Behaviour Research & Therapy, 24*, 577–580.

Bollinger, A., Riggs, D., Blake, D., & Ruzek, J. (2000). Prevalence of personality disorders among combat veterans with posttraumatic stress disorder. *Journal of Traumatic Stress, 13*, 255–270.

Brady, K. T., & Clary, C. M. (2003). Affective and anxiety comorbidity in post-traumatic stress disorder treatment trials of sertraline. *Comprehensive-Psychiatry, 44*, 360–369.

Bremner, J. D., Randall, T. M., Scott, T. M., Bronen, R. A., Seibyl, J. P., Southwick, S. M., et al. (1995). MRI-based measures of hippocampal volume in patients with combat-related PTSD. *American Journal of Psychiatry, 152*, 973–981.

Breslau, N., Chilcoat, H. D., Kessler, R. C., & Davis, G. C. (1999) Prior trauma and the issue of sensitization in posttraumatic stress disorder: Results from the Detroit Area Survey of Trauma. *American Journal of Psychiatry, 156*, 902–907.

Breslau, N., Davis, G. C., Andreski, P., & Peterson, E. (1991). Traumatic events and posttraumatic stress disorder in an urban population of young adults. *Archives of General Psychiatry, 48*, 216–222.

Brown, T. A., DiNardo, P. A., Lehman, C. L., & Campbell, L. A. (2001). Reliability of DSM-IV anxiety and mood disorders: Implications for the classification of emotional disorders. *Journal of Abnormal Psychology, 110*, 49–58.

Charney, M. E. & Keane, T. M. (2007). Psychometric analysis of the Clinician Administered PTSD Scale (CAPS)—Bosnian Translation. *Cultural and Ethnic Minority Psychology, 13*, 161–168.

Cloitre, M., & Koenen, K. C. (2001). The impact of borderline personality disorder on process group outcome among women with posttraumatic stress disorder related to childhood abuse. *International Journal of Group Psychotherapy, 51*, 379–398.

Cook, J. M., Elhai, J. D., & Arean, P. A. (2005). Psychometric properties of the PTSD Checklist with older primary care patients. *Journal of Traumatic Stress, 18*, 371–376.

Cusack, K., Falsetti, S., & de Arellano, M. (2002). Gender considerations in the psychometric assessment of PTSD. In R. Kimerling, P. Ouimette, & J. Wolfe (Eds.), *Gender and PTSD* (pp. 150–176). New York: Guilford Press.

Davidson, J., & Colket, J. T. (1997). The eight-item treatment-outcome post-traumatic stress disorder scale: a brief measure to assess treatment outcome in post-traumatic stress disorder. *International Clinical Psychopharmacology, 12*, 41–45.

Davidson, J. R. T., Malik, M. A., & Travers, J. (1997). Structured Interview for PTSD (SIP): Psychometric validation for DSM-IV criteria. *Depression and Anxiety, 5,* 127–129.

Davidson, J. R. T., Smith, R., & Kudler, H. (1989). Validity and reliability of the DSM-III criteria for posttraumatic stress disorder: Experience with a structured interview. *Journal of Nervous and Mental Disease, 177,* 336–341.

De Girolamo, G., & McFarlane, A. C. (1996). Epidemiology of Posttraumatic Stress Disorder among victims of intentional violence: A review of the literature. In F. L. Mak & C. C. Nadelson (Eds.), *International Review of Psychiatry: Vol. 2.* Washington, DC: American Psychiatric Press.

DiNardo, P. A., Brown, T. A., & Barlow, D. H. (1994). *Anxiety disorders interview schedule for DSM-IV: Lifetime version (ADIS-IV-L).* San Antonio, TX: Psychological Corporation.

DiNardo, P. A., Moras, K., Barlow, D. H., Rapee, R. M., & Brown, T. A. (1993). Reliability of DSM-III-R anxiety disorder categories: Using the Anxiety Disorders Interview Schedule-Revised (ADIS-R). *Archives of General Psychiatry, 50,* 251–256.

DiNardo, P. A., O'Brien, G. T., Barlow, D. H., Waddell, M. T., & Blanchard, E. B. (1983). Reliability of DSM-III anxiety disorder categories using a new structured interview. *Archives of General Psychiatry, 40,* 1070–1074.

Dobie, D. J., Kivlahan, D. R., Maynard, C., Bush, K. R., McFall, M., Epler, A. J., et al. (2002). Screening for post-traumatic stress disorder in female Veteran's Affairs patients: Validation of the PTSD Checklist. *General Hospital Psychiatry, 24,* 367–374.

Dohrenwend, B. P., Turner, J. B., Turse, N. A., Adams, B. G., Koenen, K. C., & Marshall, R. (2006). The psychological risks of Vietnam for U.S. veterans: A revisit with new data and methods. *Science, 313,* 979–982.

Eisen, S. V., Wilcox, M., Leff, H. S., Schaefer, E., & Culhane, M. A. (1999) Assessing behavioral health outcomes in outpatient programs: Reliability and validity of the BASIS-32. *Journal of Behavioral Health Services and Research, 26,* 5–17.

First, M., Spitzer, R., Williams, J., & Gibbon, M. (2000). Structured Clinical Interview for DSM-IV AXIS I Disorders (SCID-I). In A. John Rush (Ed.), *Handbook of Psychiatric Measures* (pp. 49–53). Washington, DC: American Psychiatric Association.

Foa, E. B., Cashman, L., Jaycox, L., & Perry, K. (1997). The validation of a self-report measure of posttraumatic stress disorder: The Posttraumatic Diagnostic Scale. *Psychological Assessment, 9,* 445–451.

Foa, E. B., Keane, T. M., & Friedman, M J. (2000). *Effective treatments for PTSD: Practice guidelines from the International Society for Traumatic Stress Studies.* New York: Guilford Press.

Foa, E. B., Riggs, D. S., Dancu, C. V., & Rothbaum, B. O. (1993). Reliability and validity of a brief instrument for assessing post-traumatic stress disorder. *Journal of Traumatic Stress, 6,* 459–474.

Foy, D. W., Sipprelle, R. C., Rueger, D. B., & Carroll, E. M. (1984). Etiology of posttraumatic stress disorder in Vietnam veterans: Analysis of premilitary, military, and combat exposure influences. *Journal of Consulting and Clinical Psychology, 52,* 79–87.

Friedman, M. J., & Schnurr, P. P. (1995). The relationship between trauma, post-traumatic stress disorder, and physical health. In M. J. Friedman, D. S. Charney, & A. Y. Deutch (Eds.), *Neurobiological and clinical consequences of stress: From normal adaptation to PTSD* (pp. 507–524). Philadelphia, PA: Lippincott-Raven.

Frisch, M. B., Cornell, J., Villañueva, M., & Retzlaff, P. J. (1992). Clinical validation of the quality of life inventory: A measure of life satisfaction for use in treatment planning and outcome assessment. *Psychological Assessment, 4,* 92–101.

Frueh, B. C., Brady, K. L., & Arellano, M. A. (1998). Racial differences in combat-related PTSD: Empirical findings and conceptual issues. *Clinical Psychology Review, 18,* 287–305.

Goodman, L., Corcoran, C., Turner, K., Yuan, N., & Green, B. (1998). Assessing traumatic event exposure: General issues and preliminary findings for the stressful life events screening questionnaire. *Journal of Traumatic Stress, 11,* 521–542.

Gray, M. J., Litz, B. T., Hsu, J. L., & Lombardo, T. W. (2004). Psychometric properties of the life events checklist. *Assessment, 11,* 330–341.

Green, B. L., Grace, M. C., Lindy, J. D., & Leonard, A. C. (1990). Race differences in response to combat stress. *Journal of Traumatic Stress, 3,* 379–393.

Griesel, D., Wessa, M., & Flor, H. (2006). Psychometric qualities of the German version of the Posttraumatic Diagnostic Scale (PTDS). *Psychological Assessment, 18,* 262–268.

Griffin, M. G., Uhlmansiek, M. H., Resick, P. A., & Mechanic, M. B. (2004). Comparison of the posttraumatic stress disorder scale versus the clinician-administered posttraumatic stress disorder scale in domestic violence survivors. *Journal of Traumatic Stress, 17,* 497–503.

Grubaugh, A. L., Elhai, J. D., Cusack, K. J., Wells, C., & Frueh, B. C. (2006). Screening for PTSD in public-sector mental health settings: The diagnostic utility of the PTSD Checklist. *Depression and Anxiety, 24,* 124–129.

Herman, D. S., Weathers, F. W., Litz, B. T., & Keane, T. M. (1996). Psychometric properties of the embedded and stand-alone versions of the MMPI-2 Keane PTSD Scale. *Assessment, 3,* 437–442.

Hinton, D. E., Chhean, D., Pich, V., Pollack, M. H., Orr, S. P., & Pitman, R. K. (2006). Assessment of posttraumatic stress disorder in Cambodian refugees using the Clinician-Administered PTSD Scale: Psychometric properties and symptom severity. *Journal of Traumatic Stress, 19*, 405–409.

Hoge, C. W., Auchterlonie, J. L., & Milliken, C. S. (2006). Mental health problems, use of mental health services, and attrition from military service after returning from deployment to Iraq or Afghanistan. *Journal of the American Medical Association, 295*, 1023–1032.

Hoge, C. W., Castro, C. A., Messer, S. C., McGurk, D., Cotting, D. I., & Koffman, R. L. (2004). Combat duty in Iraq and Afghanistan, mental health problems, and barriers to care. *New England Journal of Medicine, 351*, 13–22.

Horowitz, M. J. (1976). *Stress response syndromes.* Northvale, NJ: Aronson.

Horowitz, M. J., Wilner, N., & Alvarez, W. (1979). Impact of event scale: A measure of subjective stress. *Psychosomatic Medicine, 41*, 209–218.

Joseph, S. (2000). Psychometric evaluation of Horowitz's impact of event scale: A review. *Journal of Traumatic Stress, 13*, 101–113.

Keane, T. M. (1995). Guidelines for the forensic psychological assessment of posttraumatic stress disorder claimants. In R. I. Simon (Ed.), *Posttraumatic stress disorder in litigation: Guidelines for forensic assessment* (pp. 99–115). Washington, DC: American Psychiatric Press, Inc.

Keane, T. M., & Barlow, D. H. (2002). Posttraumatic stress disorder. In D. H. Barlow (Ed.), *Anxiety and its disorders: The nature and treatment of anxiety and panic* (2nd ed., pp. 418–453). New York: Guilford Press.

Keane, T. M., Buckley, T., & Miller, M. (2003). Guidelines for the forensic psychological assessment of posttraumatic stress disorder claimants. In R. I. Simon (Ed.), *Posttraumatic stress disorder in litigation: Guidelines for forensic assessment* (2nd ed., pp. 119–140). Washington, DC: American Psychiatric Association Press, Inc.

Keane, T. M., Caddell, J. M., & Taylor, K. L. (1988). Mississippi Scale for combat-related posttraumatic stress disorder: Three studies in reliability and validity. *Journal of Consulting and Clinical Psychology, 56*, 85–90.

Keane, T. M., Fairbank, J. A., Caddell, J. M., Zimering, R. T., & Bender, M. E. (1985). A behavioral approach to assessing and treating post-traumatic stress disorder in Vietnam veterans. In C. R. Figley (Ed.), *Trauma and its wake* (pp. 257–294). New York: Brunner/Mazel.

Keane, T. M., & Kaloupek, D. G. (1982). Imaginal flooding in the treatment of posttraumatic stress disorder. *Journal of Consulting and Clinical Psychology, 50*, 138–140.

Keane, T. M., & Kaloupek, D. G. (1997) Comorbid psychiatric disorders in post-traumatic stress disorder: Implications for research. In R. Yehuda & A. McFarlane (Eds.), *Psychobiology of posttraumatic stress disorder.* New York: Annals of New York Academy of Science.

Keane, T. M., & Kaloupek, D. G. (2002) Posttraumatic stress disorder: Diagnosis, assessment, and monitoring outcomes. In R. Yehuda (Ed.), *Clinical assessment and treatment of PTSD.* Washington: American Psychiatric Press.

Keane, T. M., Kolb, L. C, Kaloupek, D. G., Orr, S. P., Blanchard, E. B., Thomas, R. G., et al. (1998). Utility of psychophysiology measurement in the diagnosis of posttraumatic stress disorder: Results from a department of Veterans Affairs cooperative study. *Journal of Consulting and Clinical Psychology, 66*, 914–923.

Keane, T. M., Malloy, P. F., & Fairbank, J. A. (1984). Empirical development of an MMPI subscale for the assessment of combat-related posttraumatic stress disorder. *Journal of Consulting and Clinical Psychology, 52*, 888–891.

Keane, T. M., Marshall, A., & Taft, C. (2006) *Posttraumatic stress disorder: Etiology, epidemiology, and treatment outcome. Annual review of clinical psychology.* Washington, DC: APA Press.

Keane, T. M., Solomon, S., Maser, J., & Gerrity, E. (1995, November). *Assessment of PTSD.* National Institute of Mental Health-National Center for PTSD Consensus Conference on Assessment of PTSD, Boston, MA.

Keane, T. M., Weathers, F. W., & Foa, E. B. (2000). Diagnosis and assessment. In E. B., Foa, T. M. Keane, & M. J. Friedman, (Eds.), *Effective treatments for PTSD* (pp. 18–36). New York: Guilford Press.

Keane, T. M., & Wolfe, J. (1990). Comorbidity in posttraumatic stress disorder: An analysis of community and clinical studies. *Journal of Applied Social Psychology, 20*, 1776–1788.

Keen, S. M., Kutter, C. J., Niles, B. L., & Krinsley, K. E. (2004, November). Psychometric properties of the PTSD Checklist. Poster presented at the annual meeting of the International Society for Traumatic Stress Studies, New Orleans, LA.

Kessler, R. C., Berglund, P., Demler, O., Jin, R., Walters, E. (2005) Lifetime prevalence and age of onset distributions of DSM-IV disorders in the National Comorbidity Survey-Replication. *Archives of General Psychiatry, 62*, 593–602.

Kessler, R. C., Galea, S., Jones, R. T., & Parker, H. A. (2006). Mental illness and suicidality after Hurricane Katrina. *Bulletin of the World Health Organization, 84*, 930–939.

Kessler, R. C., Sonnega, A., Bromet, E., Hughes, M., & Nelson, C. B. (1995). Posttraumatic stress disorder in the National Comorbidity Survey. *Archives of General Psychiatry, 52*, 1048–1060.

Kessler, R. C., McGonagle, K. A., Zhao, S., Nelson, C. B., Hughes, M., Eshleman, S., et al. (1994). Lifetime and 12-month prevalence of DSM-III-R psychiatric disorders in the United States: Results from the National Comorbidity Survey. *Archives of General Psychiatry, 51*, 8–19.

Kilpatrick, D. G. (1988). Rape aftermath symptom test. In M. Hersen & A. S. Bellack, (Eds.), *Dictionary of behavioral assessment techniques* (pp. 658–669). Oxford, England: Pergamon Press.

King, L. A., King, D. W., Leskin, G., & Foy, D. (1995). The Los Angeles Symptom Checklist: A self-report measure of Posttraumatic Stress Disorder, *Assessment, 2*, 1–17.

Koretzky, M. B., & Peck, A. H. (1990). Validation and cross-validation of the PTSD Subscale of the MMPI with civilian trauma victims. *Journal of Clinical Psychology, 46*, 296–300.

Koss, M. P., Koss, P. G., & Woodruff, M. S. (1991). Deleterious effects of criminal victimization on women's health and medical utilization. *Archives of Internal Medicine, 151*, 342–347.

Kraemer, H. C. (1992). *Evaluating medical tests: Objective and quantitative guidelines.* Newbury Park, CA: Sage Publications.

Kubany, E., Haynes, S., Leisen, M., Owens, J., Kaplan, A., Watson, S., & Burns, K. (2000). Development and preliminary validation of a brief broad-spectrum measure of trauma exposure: The traumatic life events questionnaire. *Psychological Assessment, 12*, 210–224.

Kubany, E. S., Leisen, M. B., Kaplan, A. S., & Kelly, M. P. (2000). Validation of a brief measure of posttraumatic stress disorder: The Distressing Event Questionnaire (DEQ). *Psychological Assessment, 12*, 197–209.

Kudler, H. S., Blank, A. S., & Krupnick, J. L. (2000). Psychodynamic therapy. In E. B. Foa, T. M. Keane, & M. J. Friedman (Eds.), *Effective treatments for PTSD* (pp. 339–341). New York: Guilford Press.

Kulka, R. A., Schlenger, W. E., Fairbank, J. A., Hough, R. L., Jordan, B. K., Marmar, C. R., et al. (1988). *National Vietnam Veterans Readjustment Study (NVVRS): Design, current status, and initial PTSD prevalence estimates.* Research Triangle Park, NC: Research Triangle Park Institute.

Kulka, R. A., Schlenger, W. E., Fairbank, J. A., Jordan, B. K., Hough, R. L., Marmar, C. R., et al. (1990). *Trauma and the Vietnam war generation: Report of findings from the National Vietnam Veterans Readjustment Study.* New York: Brunner/Mazel.

Litz, B. T., & Weathers, F. (1994). The diagnosis and assessment of post-traumatic stress disorder in adults. In M. B. Williams & J. F. Sommer (Eds.), *The handbook of post-traumatic therapy* (pp. 20–37). Westport, CT: Greenwood Press.

Lyons, J. A., & Keane, T. M. (1992). Keane PTSD scale: MMPI and MMPI-2 update. *Journal of Traumatic Stress, 5*, 111–117.

Manne, S. L., DuHamel, K., Gallelli, K., Sorgen, K., & Redd, W. H. (1998). Posttraumatic stress disorder among mothers of pediatric cancer survivors: Diagnosis, comorbidity, and utility of the PTSD Checklist as a screening instrument. *Journal of Pediatric Psychology, 23*, 357–366.

Marsella, A. J., Friedman, M. J., Gerrity, E. T., & Scurfield, R. M. (Eds.) (1996). *Ethnocultural aspects of posttraumatic stress disorder.* Washington, DC: American Psychological Association.

McFall, M. E., Smith, D. E., Mackay, P. W., & Tarver, D. J. (1990). Reliability and validity of Mississippi Scale for combat-related posttraumatic stress disorder. *Journal of Consulting and Clinical Psychology, 2*, 114–121.

McFall, M. E., Smith, D., Roszell, D. K., Tarver, D. J., & Malas, K. L. (1990). Convergent validity of measures of PTSD in Vietnam combat veterans. *American Journal of Psychiatry, 147*, 645–648.

McHugo, G., Caspi, Y., Kammerer, N., Mazelis, R., Jackson, E., Russell, L., et al. (2005). The assessment of trauma history in women with co-occurring substance abuse and mental disorders and a history of interpersonal violence. *Journal of Behavioral Health Sciences and Research, 32*, 113–127.

Miller, M. W., Kaloupek, D. G., Dillon, A. L., & Keane, T. M. (2004). Externalizing and internalizing subtypes of combat-related PTSD: A replication and extension using the PSY-5 scales. *Journal of Abnormal Psychology, 113*, 636–645.

Miller, M. W., & Resick, P. A. (2007). Internalizing and externalizing subtypes in female sexual assault survivors: Implications for the understanding of complex PTSD. *Behavior Therapy, 38*, 58–71.

Mollica, R. F., Caspi-Yavin, Y., Bollini, P., Truong, T., Tor, S., & Lavelle, J. (1992). The Harvard Trauma Questionnaire: Validating a cross-cultural instrument for measuring torture, trauma, and post-traumatic stress disorder in Indochinese refugees. *Journal of Nervous and Mental Disease, 180*, 111–116.

Neal, L. A., Busuttil, W., Rollins, J., Herepath, R., Strike, P., & Turnbull, G. (1994). Convergent validity of measures of post-traumatic stress disorder in a mixed military and civilian population. *Journal of Traumatic Stress, 7*, 477–455.

Norris,'F. (1990). Screening for traumatic stress: A scale for use in the general population. *Journal of Applied Social Psychology, 20*, 1704–1718.

Norris, F. H., Friedman, M. L., Watson, P. J., Byrne, C. M., Diaz, E., & Kaniasty, K. (2002). 60,000 disaster victims speak: Part I. An empirical review of the empirical literature, 1981–2001. *Psychiatry: Interpersonal and Biological Processes, 65*, 207–239.

Norris, F. H., Perilla, J. L., Riad, J. K., Kaniasty, K., & Lavizzo, E. A. (1999). Stability and change in stress, resources, and psychological distress following natural disaster: Findings from Hurricane Andrew. *Anxiety, Stress, & Coping, 12*, 363–396.

Orazem, R. J., Charney, M. E., & Keane, T. M. (2006, March). *Mississippi Scale for Combat-Related PTSD: Analysis of reliability and validity*. Poster session presented at the annual meeting of the Anxiety Disorders Association of America, Miami, FL.

Orsillo, S. M. (2001). Measures for acute stress disorder and posttraumatic stress disorder. In M. M. Antony, S. M. Orsillo, & L. Roemer (Eds.), *Practitioner's guide to empirically based measures of anxiety* (pp. 255–307). New York: Kluwer Academic/Plenum Publishers.

Orr, S. P., Metzger, L. J., Miller, M. W., & Kaloupek, D. G. (2004). Psychophysiological assessment of PTSD. In J. P. Wilson & T. M. Keane (Eds.), *Assessing psychological trauma and PTSD* (2nd ed.). Guilford Press, New York.

Ouimette, P. C., Finney, J. W., & Moos, R. H. (1999). Two-year posttreatment functioning and coping of substance abuse patients with posttraumatic stress disorder. *Psychology of Addictive Behaviors, 13*, 105–114.

Prins, A., Kaloupek, D. G., & Keane, T. M. (1995). Psychophysiological evidence for autonomic arousal and startle in traumatized adult populations. In M. J. Friedman, D. Charney, & A. Deutch (Eds.), *Neurobiological and clinical consequences of stress: From normal adapatation to PTSD*. New York: Raven Press.

Resick, P. A., & Schnicke, M. K. (1993). *Cognitive processing therapy for rape victims: A treatment manual*. Newbury Park, CA: Sage Publications.

Resnick, H. S., Kilpatrick, D. G., Dansky, B. S., Saunders, B. E., & Best, C. L. (1993). Prevalence of civilian trauma and PTSD in a representative national sample of women. *Journal of Clinical and Consulting Psychology, 61*, 984–991.

Robins, L. H., & Helzer, J. E. (1985). *Diagnostic Interview Schedule (DIS Version III-A)*. St. Louis, MO: Washington University, Department of Psychiatry.

Ruggiero, K. J., Del Ben, K., Scotti, J. R., & Rabalais, A. E. (2003). Psychometric properties of the PTSD Checklist-Civilian Version. *Journal of Traumatic Stress, 16*, 495–502.

Schlenger, W. E., Caddell, J. M., Ebert, L., Jordan, B. K., Rourke, K. M., Wilson, D., et al. (2002). Psychological reactions to terrorist attacks: Findings from the National Study of Americans' reactions to September 11. *Journal of the American Medical Association, 288*, 581–588.

Schnurr, P., Vielhauer, M., Weathers, F., & Findler, M. (1999). *The brief trauma questionnaire*. White River Junction, VT: National Center for PTSD.

Shalev, A. Y., Friedman, M. J., Foa, E. B., & Keane, T. M. (2000). Integration and summary. In E. B. Foa, T. M. Keane, & M. J. Friedman (Eds.), *Effective treatments for PTSD: Practice guidelines from the International Society for Traumatic Stress Studies*. New York: Guilford Press.

Southwick, S. M., Yehuda, R., & Giller, E. L. (1993). Personality disorders in treatment-seeking combat veterans with post-traumatic stress disorder. *American Journal of Psychiatry, 150*, 1020–1023.

Spielberger, C. S., Gorsuch, R. L., Lushene, R., Vagg, P. R., & Jacobs, G. A. (1983). *Manual for the State-Trait Anxiety Inventory (Form Y)*. Palo Alto, CA: Mind Garden.

Straus, M. A., Hamby, S. L., Boney-McCoy, S., & Sugarman, D. B. (1996). The revised Conflict Tactics Scales (CTS2): Development and preliminary psychometric data. *Journal of Family Issues, 17*, 283–316.

Sundin, E. C., & Horowitz, M. J. (2002). Impact of event scale: Psychometric properties. *British Journal of Psychiatry, 180*, 205–209.

Sutker, P. B., & Allain, A. N. (1996). Assessment of PTSD and other mental disorders in World War II and Korean Conflict POW survivors and combat veterans. *Psychological Assessment, 8*, 18–25.

Vrana, S., & Lauterbach, D. (1994). Prevalence of traumatic events and posttraumatic psychological symptoms in a nonclinical sample of college students. *Journal of Traumatic Stress, 7*, 289–302.

Walker, E. A., Newman, E., Dobie, D. J., Ciechanowski, P., & Katon, W. (2002). Validation of the PTSD Checklist in an HMO sample of women. *General Hospital Psychiatry, 24*, 375–380.

Ware, J. E., & Kosinski, M. (2001). *SF-36 Physical and mental health summary scales: A manual for users of version 1* (2nd ed.). Lincoln, RI: QualityMetric Incorporated.

Watson, C. G., Juba, M. P., Manifold, V., Kucala, T., & Anderson, P. E. D. (1991). The PTSD interview: Rationale, description, reliability, and concurrent validity of a DSM-III based technique. *Journal of Clinical Psychology, 47*, 179–188.

Watson, C. G., Kucala, T., & Manifold, V. (1986). A cross-validation of the Keane and Penk MMPI scales as measure of posttraumatic stress disorder. *Journal of Clinical Psychology, 42,* 727–732.

Weathers, F. W., Keane, T. M., & Davidson, J. R. T. (2001). The clinician administered PTSD scale (CAPS): A review of the first ten years of research. *Depression and Anxiety, 13,* 132–156.

Weathers, F. W., Keane, T. M., King, L. A., & King, D. W. (1996). Psychometric theory in the development of posttraumatic stress disorder assessment tools. In J. P. Wilson & T. M. Keane (Eds.), *Assessing psychological trauma and PTSD* (pp. 98–135). New York: Guilford Press.

Weathers, F. W., Litz, B. T., Herman, D. S., Huska, J. A., & Keane, T. M. (1993, October). *The PTSD checklist (PCL): Reliability, validity, and diagnostic utility.* Poster presented at the 9th annual meeting of the International Society for Traumatic Stress Studies, San Antonio, TX.

Weathers, F. W., Ruscio, A. M., & Keane, T. M. (1999). Psychometric properties of nine scoring rules for the clinician-administered PTSD scale (CAPS). *Psychological Assessment, 11,* 124–133.

Weiss, D., & Marmar, C. (1997). The impact of event scale-revised. In J. P. Wilson & T. M. Keane (Eds.), *Assessing psychological trauma and PTSD* (pp. 399–411). New York: Guilford Press.

Wilson, J. P., & Keane, T. M. (2004). *Assessing psychological trauma and PTSD* (2nd ed.). New York: Guilford Press.

Wilson, J. P., & Krauss, G. E. (1984, September). *The Vietnam Era Stress Inventory: A scale to measure war stress and post-traumatic stress disorder among Vietnam veterans.* Paper presented at the 3rd National Conference on Posttraumatic Stress Disorder, Baltimore, MD.

Wilson, S. A., Tinker, R. H., Becker, L. A., & Gillette, C. S. (1994, November). *Using the PTSD-I as an outcome measure.* Poster presented at the annual meeting of the International Society for Traumatic Stress Studies, Chicago, IL.

Wolfe, J., Brown, P., & Kelley, J. M. (1993). Reassessing war stress: Exposure and the Gulf War. *Journal of Social Issues, 49,* 15–31.

Wolfe, J., Kimerling, R., Brown, P. J., Chrestman, K. R., & Levin, K. (1996). Psychometric review of the life stressor checklist-revised. In B. H. Stamm (Ed.), *Measurement of stress, trauma, and adaptation* (pp. 198–201). Lutherville, MD: Sidran Press.

Wirtz, P., & Harrell, A. (1987). Effects of exposure to attack-similar stimuli on long-term recovery of victims. *Journal of Consulting and Clinical Psychology, 55,* 10–16.

Yehuda, R. (1997). Sensitization of the hypothalamic-pituitary-adrenal axis in PTSD. In R. Yehuda & A. McFarlane (Eds.) *Psychobiology of posttraumatic stress disorder* (pp. 57–75). New York: Annals of the New York Academy of Sciences.

Zayfert, C., Becker, C. B., Unger, D. L., & Shearer, D. K. (2002). Comorbid anxiety disorders in civilians seeking treatment for posttraumatic stress disorder. *Journal of Traumatic Stress, 15,* 31–38.

Zlotnick, C., Warshaw, M., Shea, T. M., Allsworth, J., Pearlstein, T., & Keller, M. B. (1999). Chronicity in posttraumatic stress disorder (PTSD) and predictors of course of comorbid PTSD in patients with anxiety disorders. *Journal of Traumatic Stress, 12,* 89–100.

Part V

Substance Use and
Gambling Disorders

15

Substance Use Disorders

Damaris J. Rohsenow

Clinicians working with substance use disorders (SUDs) need good tools to help them evaluate patient needs, plan treatment strategies tailored to these individual needs, and monitor progress in treatment. This chapter provides an overview of the most widely used, psychometrically sound instruments that are potentially useful for clinicians working with clients with SUDs. Instruments that would probably only be used by researchers and commonly used, but psychometrically weak, instruments are not included. Accordingly, this chapter is not intended to provide an exhaustive list of available instruments, and someone's preferred instrument may well be omitted. Nevertheless, most of the best instruments that are likely to be clinically useful are reviewed in the chapter. Additional instruments used in research are described by Donovan and Marlatt (2005).

THE NATURE OF SUBSTANCE ABUSE AND DEPENDENCE

Whether called addiction, abuse, or dependence, patients with SUDs generally show a combination of physical indicators (generally an abstinence syndrome), a variety of serious or ongoing negative consequences of drug use that affect significant areas of their lives (including financial, employment, health, family, social relationships, psychological function), and an apparent compulsion to seek and use drugs despite ongoing negative consequences. Many of the behaviors involved in getting the drugs also lead to victimization of others in terms of crime (usually committed to obtain funds to buy drugs) or physical victimization (e.g., gunshot wounds). As such, addiction has individual effects (physical, psychological, family), community effects (social, employment,

financial burdens), and societal effects (crime, legal system, politics, societal costs). However, for the practitioner, the primary focus is the individual drug abuser (using the term in a broad sense), along with the consequences to that person and the effects of his/her drug use on his/her own network. The diagnostic criteria for substance abuse and dependence will be described below, but it should be noted that the terms "abuse" or "addiction" are often used in the literature in a looser manner to refer to the person who continues to have ongoing use despite serious problems, regardless of whether formal diagnostic criteria for abuse or dependence are met.

Comorbidity

Because this chapter is oriented toward the clinical assessment of SUDs, information on comorbidity derived from clinical samples will be emphasized as more relevant than community samples, to the extent that they differ. Abuse of or dependence on one substance is often comorbid with abuse of or dependence on a second substance, with about half of treatment admissions to substance treatment programs reporting more than one substance of abuse (Substance Abuse and Mental Health Services Administration [SAMSHA], 2003). The most common additional substance of abuse or dependence for patients with opiate use disorders is marijuana, alcohol, and/or cocaine; for injecting drug abusers it is alcohol, benzodiazepines, cannabis, and/or amphetamines; and for patients with cocaine use disorders it is marijuana or alcohol (SAMSHA, 2003). Patients with more than one drug of abuse are less likely to achieve remission and have more relapse after intensive treatment than patients abusing a single drug (Ritsher, Moos, & Finney, 2002; Walton, Blow, & Booth, 2000).

Cluster B personality disorders (i.e., antisocial, borderline, narcissistic, histrionic) occur more frequently in people with SUDs than in those with other disorders (Mors & Sorenson, 1994), occurring in almost half of SUD patients. The most common comorbid personality disorders are antisocial personality (27%) and borderline personality (18%; Rounsaville et al., 1998). Comorbid Axis I disorders are most commonly affective disorders and anxiety disorders (Acosta, Haller, & Schnoll, 2005). Among cocaine abusers, the rates for depressive disorders range from 11% to 55% (with depression usually preceding the SUD by about 7 years) and for bipolar disorder are about 42%; panic disorder is a common result of cocaine abuse; and the prevalence of post-traumatic stress disorder among those with SUDs is 10 times higher than among those who do not have an SUD (Acosta et al., 2005). Axis I comorbidities for individuals with opioid use disorders are most commonly bipolar or anxiety disorders (Dilts & Dilts, 2005), with the prevalence of current mood and/or anxiety disorder among heroin injectors with multiple substances of abuse being about 55%, and with 25% having both a mood and anxiety disorder (Darke & Ross, 1997). An excellent clinical guide to treatment issues involved with psychiatric comorbidity in those with SUDs is provided by Busch, Weiss, and Najavits (2005).

Prevalence

The National Comorbidity Survey (Kessler et al., 2005; Kessler, Chiu, et al., 2005) showed that the lifetime prevalence of drug dependence in the United States was about 3.0% of the adult population, with another 7.9% having had drug abuse without dependence; about 1.8% have a current abuse or dependence diagnosis (past 12 months). Only about 1 in 12 people with lifetime SUD ever received treatment in substance abuse facilities (Kessler et al., 1994). While diagnostic information is generally not available by specific drug, cocaine was currently used in 2001 by 0.7 % of people aged 12 years and up (SAMSHA, 2001), and the National Institute on Drug Abuse estimates that 5% of people who try cocaine develop addiction (Gawin & Ellinwood, 1988). African Americans have a lower prevalence of SUDs than do people of other ethnic groups in the United States (Kessler et al., 2005). The geographic distribution of people in the United States with SUD in the population is fairly even, but with somewhat higher rates in the west and northeast than

in the south; most were 25 to 34 years old, 40% were women, and they were predominantly white (81%; 6% African American, 11% Hispanic American; Kessler et al., 1994). Treatment seekers may have somewhat different demographics from those with SUDs in the general population. In the nationwide Drug Abuse Treatment Outcome Study (e.g., Hubbard, Craddock, Flynn, Anderson, & Etheridge, 1997) of over 10,000 clients from 96 programs in 11 U.S. cities, about 65% were male, 59% were African American, and 61% were more than 30 years old. However, because the surveyed treatment programs were not sampled randomly, these figures may not be representative of all SUD treatment seekers.

The Addiction Career

There is little agreement on the etiology of substance dependence, a topic difficult to study given that not all substances of abuse are similar in mechanism or effects, leading to possibly different determinants (Anthenelli & Schuckit, 1992). Etiology of drug dependence cannot be studied for each drug of abuse completely separately, given the fact that people may use various substances at different times or the same time. For this reason, there has been almost no work done on possible genetic factors (Anthenelli & Schuckit, 1992). Studies of sociocultural factors do little to explain who specifically will develop drug dependence given that such a small number of people affected by these influences develop drug dependence (Johnson & Muffler, 1992). There is no one psychological or sociopsychological theory that is generally accepted as explanatory (e.g., Schulenberg, Maggs, Steinman, & Zucker, 2001). Adolescent substance abuse is highest for those who have high novelty seeking combined with low harm avoidance and low reward dependence personality traits (Wills, Vaccaro, & McNamara, 1994). These scales were correlated with other measures of behavioral undercontrol such as risk-taking, impulsivity, anger, independence, tolerance for deviance, and sensation seeking (Wills et al., 1994). A childhood pattern of behavioral undercontrol often leads to early onset of cigarette use which in turn increases the probability of the onset of drug use (e.g., Brown, Gleghorn, Schuckit, Myers, & Mott, 1996; Farrell, Danish, & Howard, 1992; USDHHS, 1989). However, the etiology of this pattern of behavioral undercontrol itself is unknown and this may not be the only pathway to substance dependence. For a good review of the concept and evidence for and against behavioral undercontrol as a mechanism, see Smith and Anderson (2001).

A large study of the natural history of 581 people with narcotic addictions tracked the course of events over the 30-year period from 1956 to 1986 (Anglin et al., 2001). There were several notable findings. First, 5 years after starting narcotics use (about age 17), most were daily users, with few remaining as occasional users. Second, daily use peaked at about age 30, decreased a little as people entered into methadone maintenance, then remained stable. Third, incarceration rates were highest between ages 20 and 30 (about 60% of group) then dropped off to 11% for the last decade. Fourth, deaths started occurring within 10 years, with a mortality rate of 27% of the group at the end of 30 years. Fifth, for the last 10 to 15 years of the study period, about 22% of the people were abstinent. Others have summarized the course of opiate addiction more simply: first use is usually in the teens or 20s, most active opiate users are 20 to 50 years old, the addiction abates slowly and spontaneously in middle age, with 9 years being the estimated average duration of active addiction (Dilts & Dilts, 2005; Jaffe, 1989). Anglin et al. (2001) concluded that substance abuse treatment is needed much earlier in the addiction careers because treatment interrupts the typical progression of addiction careers. The national Drug Abuse Treatment Outcome Study showed that, overall, treatment does work, with the greatest reductions in drug use occurring with treatments that last 3 or more months (Hubbard et al., 1997).

PURPOSES OF ASSESSMENT

Three specific assessment purposes of most relevance for clinical assessment are emphasized in this chapter: (1) diagnosis, (2) case conceptualization and treatment planning, and (3) treatment monitoring and outcome evaluation. The emphasis in the case conceptualization and treatment planning section will be on problem severity. This section also includes assessment of expectancies, high-risk situations, self-efficacy in handling risk, and coping skills, because these can be useful in planning motivational interventions, relapse prevention, and coping skills training specific to individual needs. Measures of overall functioning/impairment or functioning in interpersonal, family, psychiatric, medical, and employment domains can be useful in evaluating need for family or couples therapy, employment assistance, legal or medical services, social services, and so forth. The focus in this chapter will be on the assessment of substance abuse and dependence in general, with less focus on measures that were developed for use with only one substance. The assessment of other behaviors which are sometimes seen as addictive, such as gambling or sexual offending, will not be discussed here as they are covered in other chapters in this volume. An excellent text that covers an array of substance-specific assessment measures, addictive behaviors not involving chemical substance, and measures designed for use in research studies is the one by Donovan and Marlatt (2005).

ASSESSMENT FOR DIAGNOSIS

The diagnostic criteria of the *Diagnostic and Statistical Manual for Mental Disorders*, 4th Edition, Text Revision (DSM-IV-TR; American Psychiatric Association, 2000) are the most widely used in clinical practice. Although revisions are currently underway that will make abuse and dependence fall more on a continuum than is currently the case (thus preventing people from falling in the gap between abuse and dependence criteria), this distinction is made in the current set of criteria. The intention of the distinction was for dependence to capture more of the sense of a compulsion to use, as opposed to problematic use without this underlying compulsion.

Substance dependence, in brief, is defined as a maladaptive pattern of substance use leading to clinically significant impairment or distress as indicated by three or more of the following occurring within the same 12-month period: tolerance (increased amount needed for same effect or markedly less effect with same amount of use); withdrawal (either the characteristic withdrawal syndrome or using the substance or a closely related substance to prevent/relieve withdrawal); amount or duration of substance use that is greater than intended; repeated unsuccessful attempts to cut down or control substance use; much time spent in activities needed to obtain, use, or recover from the substance; important activities stopped or reduced due to substance use; substance use continues despite knowledge of a persistent or recurrent physical or psychological problem caused or exacerbated by the substance.

TABLE 15.1 Ratings of Instruments Used for Screening and Diagnosis

Instrument	Norms	Internal Consistency	Inter-Rater Reliability	Test–Retest Reliability	Content Validity	Construct Validity	Validity Generalization	Clinical Utility	Highly Recommended
Screening for SUDs									
DAST	NA	E	NA	U	A	A	E	A	
DUSI-R	NA	G	NA	U	A	A	E	A	✓
Diagnostic Instruments									
SCID	NA	NA	G	G	G	A	E	A	
CIDI	NA	NA	G	G	G	A	E	A	
DIS-DSM-IIIR	NA	NA	G	G	G	A	E	A	
SDSS	NA	G	NA	G	G	G[a]	G	A	
GAIN-I	A	G	NA	G	G	G	E	A	✓

[a] Good except for ICD-10 harmful use and cocaine dependence diagnoses which were less than adequate.

Note: DAST = Drug Abuse Screening Test; DUSI-R = Drug Use Screening Inventory-Revised; SCID = Structured Clinical Interview for DSM-IV Axis I Disorders-Patient Version; CIDI = Composite International Diagnostic Interview; DIS-DSM-IIIR = Diagnostic Interview Schedule for DSM-III-R; SDSS = Substance Dependence Severity Scale section on diagnoses; GAIN-I = Global Appraisal of Individual Needs-Initial Interview, section on diagnoses; A = Adequate, G = Good, E = Excellent; U = Unavailable; NA = Not Applicable.

If criteria for dependence have never been met, substance abuse is diagnosed based on a maladaptive pattern of substance use resulting in clinically significant impairment or distress, indicated by one of the following within a 12-month period: failure to fulfill major role obligations at work, school, or home due to recurrent substance use; recurrent use in physically hazardous situations; recurrent legal problems from substance use, or continuing substance use despite persistent or recurrent social or interpersonal problems caused or exacerbated by the substance.

Screening Measures

Screening measures are generally used in settings such as general medical settings or employee assistance programs to identify or rule out probable substance abuse or dependence without providing a diagnosis. These are brief measures that can be quickly administered to identify people who may be in need of further evaluation or assistance. Cutoff points for screening measures can be set to err on the side of false positives or false negatives, depending on the purpose of the assessment. However, any positives should be followed up with further evaluation rather than being considered indicative of an SUD per se. The best known screening measures are rated in Table 15.1 and described in the following paragraphs.

Drug Abuse Screening Test

This brief (28-item) self-report test and a 10-item short form (DAST-10) provide an indicator of who might have an SUD and need further evaluation, with excellent internal reliability and good validity (DAST; Skinner, 1982; Gavin, Ross, Skinner, 1989). Data on test–retest reliability are unavailable. Both ask about drug abuse in the past year, rather than over the lifetime. The DAST is composed of five factors (early psychosocial complications with problem recognition, late onset serious social consequences, treatment/help-seeking, illegal activities, and inability to control drug use) but because psychometric properties of the separate factors were not investigated (Staley & El-Guebaly, 1990), only the total score should be used. Both the DAST and DAST-10 focus on negative consequences of use rather than quantity or frequency of use.

Drug Use Screening Inventory

This somewhat longer self-report measure (140 yes/no items), with both adult and teen versions, assesses problem severity in 10 domains, including substance use preferences and consequences, behavioral maladjustment, health, psychiatric disorder (depression, anxiety, antisocial, and psychotic), school adjustment, work adjustment, social competence, peer relationships (e.g., antisocial, substance involvement), family dysfunction/conflict, and recreation (DUSI; Tarter, 1990). It takes about 20 minutes to complete via paper or computer and is easy to manually score. Efforts were made to ensure items are free of cultural bias and at a fifth-grade reading level. The revised version (DUSI-R) has a validity check and Lie scale, adequate or better psychometric qualities, and cutoff scores to indicate a probable diagnosis (Tarter & Kirisci, 1997). This measure is more highly recommended than the DAST and DAST-10 because it provides more information.

Diagnostic Instruments

In clinical settings, diagnosis is often conducted without a formal structured set of specific questions. When a formal system is needed to ensure accuracy of diagnosis (such as for research or clinical statistics), the instruments rated in Table 15.1 and described next are the best validated structured systems available.

The Structured Clinical Interview for DSM-IV Axis I Disorders-Patient Version (SCID; First, Spitzer, Gibbon, & Williams, 1996) and the Composite International Diagnostic Interview (CIDI; WHO, 1997) both are validated directly against both the DSM-IV and ICD diagnostic criteria. These interviews are considered the most valid methods for determining Axis I psychiatric diagnoses. These structured interviews are very lengthy (an hour or more for the full interview) and require formal training in administration and scoring; as such, they may not be cost-effective for some treatment agencies because the resulting data provides diagnostic information, but no other information necessary for treatment planning. It should be noted, however, that although the SCID should be administered by clinicians, the CIDI was designed to be administered by trained interviewers who were not clinicians. The Diagnostic Interview Schedule (DIS; Robins, Helzer, Cottler, & Golding, 1989; Robins, Helzer, Croughan, & Ratcliff, 1981), designed for epidemiological research, also provides reliable and valid SUD diagnoses based on DSM-III or DSM-III-R using a less lengthy format designed to involve fewer clinical judgment calls so it can be administered by a trained technician. Although it has been updated for DSM-IV (Robins et al., 2000), including a computerized version known as CDIS-IV, no published information could be found using this version (except for one tobacco study without psychometric information on this measure) so the information in Table 15.1 applies to the earlier versions and, therefore, the measure cannot be highly recommended. All three instruments are used to diagnose any Axis I disorder, not just SUDs, and all diagnose SUDs for the separate substances.

Some substance-specific measures of withdrawal have been developed. For assessing withdrawal aspects specific to cannabis abuse, it is preferable to use one of the measures based on recent empirical work that established the cannabis withdrawal syndrome. Budney, Moore, Vandrey, and Hughes's (2003) work demonstrated a unique pattern of withdrawal symptoms, including aggression, anger, anxiety, decreased appetite, decreased body weight, irritability, restlessness, shakiness, sleep problems, and stomach pain. A measure designed to assess this pattern, the Marijuana Withdrawal Checklist (MWC; Budney et al., 2003) is a self-report measure that has some initial evidence supporting its validity. After original work indicated 10 reliable items (Budney, Novy, & Hughes, 1999), the 10-item version (plus 16 unscored additional symptoms as filler items) was evaluated in a second study (Budney, Hughes, Moore, & Novy, 2001), and a 15-item version administered by telephone using an interactive voice-response system (plus 13 unscored additional symptoms) found that 12 items were supported (Budney et al., 2003). Both versions had good internal consistency reliability and validity. However, only seven of the original items were validated (craving, irritability, anger, restlessness, decreased appetite, sleep disturbance, strange dreams) in the two subsequent studies in which change was observed during withdrawal and a new item (aggression) was validated in both the studies in which it was used. Because it is not clear that the final version and its psychometric properties have been established, this instrument was not rated in the table.

Two reliable and valid instruments for assessing opiate withdrawal include the Subjective Opiate Withdrawal Scale (16 items, self-administered) and the Objective Opiate Withdrawal Scale (13 items, interviewer-administered), both developed by Handelsman et al. (1987). For cocaine dependence, withdrawal is an infrequently endorsed symptom. These measures are not rated in Table 15.1 because there is only limited evidence as yet concerning their psychometric properties.

The Substance Dependence Severity Scale (SDSS: Miele et al., 2000a) is a semistructured clinical interview that takes about 40 minutes and requires extensive training. Part of it results in diagnoses for DSM-IV and ICD-10 (WHO, 1997) substance abuse/dependence/harmful use disorders by operationalizing every criterion used in diagnosis. The SDSS scales demonstrate good to excellent test–retest reliability (except for cannabis, which was fair to poor), internal consistency, and validity for the DSM-IV items (Miele et al., 2000a, 2000b). Percent agreement with DSM-IV diagnoses was 83% to 92% for alcohol, cocaine, heroin, sedatives, and cannabis (the only diagnoses checked).

The test–retest reliability and internal consistencies for the ICD-10 dependence scales of alcohol, heroin, and cocaine were excellent, but the ICD-10 harmful use scales mostly had unacceptably poor test–retest and/or internal consistency reliabilities. Percent agreement with ICD-10 dependence diagnoses was good to excellent for alcohol, heroin, and cannabis but only fair for cocaine, and for harmful use diagnoses were only fair (unacceptable) for heroin, cocaine, and cannabis. Therefore, as long as ICD-10 harmful use or cocaine dependence diagnostic information is not needed, this instrument will produce valid diagnoses for alcohol, cocaine, heroin, sedatives, and cannabis use disorders.

The Global Appraisal of Individual Needs (GAIN; Dennis, 1999; Dennis, Scott, & Funk, 2003; Dennis, Titus, White, Unsicker, & Hodgkins, 2003) is a semistructured interview designed to obtain comprehensive information about the functioning of adult or adolescent patients (see further description below). The Initial Interview version includes a diagnostic section, and the diagnoses of SUDs as well as other Axis I or II disorders have good test–retest reliability and concordance with independently obtained diagnoses (Dennis, 1999; Shane, Jasiukaitis, & Green, 2003). There is a 2–5 minutes Short Screener (GAIN-SS) available for rapidly identifying those who are likely to have an SUD.

Overall Evaluation

The above screening and diagnostic measures have all demonstrated scientific adequacy as screening or diagnostic measures. Screening measures such as the DAST are not relevant for SUD treatment programs, but are useful in other settings to identify people probably in need of further assessment or treatment. The GAIN's Short Screener version is useful for identifying people who need full diagnostic assessment for certain diagnoses (SUD or other) but psychometric information about this screener was not available. The DUSI, although a screening measure, is actually also a useful way to screen for a number of areas of life function in a way comparable to the ASI but with easier administration and scoring; for this reason it is highly recommended. The diagnostic measures are relevant only if accurate formal diagnoses are needed. As many SUD treatment programs treat anyone who presents with substance-related problems or concerns, having access to accurate diagnoses is unlikely to affect treatment planning. The GAIN's diagnostic section was most highly recommended as the least time-intensive

way to obtain the most diagnoses with good psychometric support; the others were not recommended due to the lengthy time and training needed (SCID, CIDI, SDSS), limited number of diagnoses (SDSS), or paucity of information about the DSM-IV version (DIS).

ASSESSMENT FOR CASE CONCEPTUALIZATION AND TREATMENT PLANNING

Rationale for Instrument Selection

A number of assessment instruments are commonly used to provide clinicians with guidance for case conceptualization and treatment planning. Some measures include severity of drug use and problems specific to the drugs per se; others address the severity of problems in related aspects of life functioning (e.g., employment, legal, family), whether or not drugs are perceived as the cause of the problems, thus allowing for the determination of areas of life functioning in need of improvement and for additional specialized services such as social services, employment assistance, or marital or family therapy. Assessment of the patient's anticipated positive and negative consequences of drug use is sometimes used in developing motivational interviewing treatment plans by investigating sources of and barriers to motivation. Relapse prevention training involves assessing high-risk situations for relapse so as to prepare patients to cope with their own "Achilles' heel" situations. Assessment of coping skills can provide information about skills and resources that can already be drawn on, maladaptive skills that need to be replaced, and skills and resources that are lacking. Skills training for substance abusers has focused either on making general lifestyle changes consistent with sobriety or on developing skills for coping with immediate urges to use in the presence of situations that pose a high risk for relapse (Monti, Kadden, Rohsenow, Cooney, & Abrams, 2002). In most cases, both types of skills need to be assessed.

Some potential assessment domains are not addressed in the chapter, based on either clinical or scientific reasons. First, measures of craving are not included both because it is not clear that degree of craving per se can be useful in treatment planning (as opposed to identifying situations or events that trigger craving) and because evidence for the reliability and validity of available craving measures is severely limited.

TABLE 15.2 Ratings of Instruments Used for Case Conceptualization and Treatment Planning

Instrument	Norms	Internal Consistency	Inter-Rater Reliability	Test–Retest Reliability	Content Validity	Construct Validity	Validity Generalization	Clinical Utility	Highly Recommended
Severity of Drug Use and Psychosocial Functioning									
SDSS	NA	E	NA	E	E	E	E	A	
ASI	NA	L[a]	L[a]	NA	A	A	G	A	
GAIN-I	NA	G	NA	NA	G	G	A	A	✓
Negative Consequences and Expected Effects									
IDUC	NA	E	NA	G	G	A	A	A	✓
SIP-AD	NA	E	NA	G	G	A	A	A	✓
Substance-Specific Tools									
MPS	NA	E	NA	NA	U	A	U	A	
CNCC-87	NA	G	NA	NA	G	G	A	A	
CEQ	NA	G	NA	NA	G	G	A	A	
Assessment for Relapse Prevention									
IDTS	A	G	NA	NA	G	G	G	A	✓
DTCQ	NA	G	NA	NA	A	A	G	A	✓
POC-10 items	NA	A	NA	NA	A	A	U	A	
USS/GCS	NA	G	NA	NA	G	G	A	A	✓

[a] Unacceptable with original scoring, acceptable to excellent with five-factor scoring of just 65 items.

Notes: Test–retest reliability is generally not applicable because clients in treatment are unstable in these areas and are expected to have variability over short periods of time. SDSS = Substance Dependence Severity Scale; ASI = Addiction Severity Index; GAIN-I =Global Appraisal of Individual Needs-Initial Interview, subtstance use scales; IDUC = Inventory of Drug Use Consequences, four scales (excluding intrapersonal); SIP-AD = Short Inventory of Problems-Alcohol and Drugs; MPS = Marijuana Problems Scale; CNCC-87 = Cocaine Negative Consequences Checklist; CEQ = Cocaine Effects Questionnaire; IDTS = Inventory of Drug-Taking Situations; DTCQ = Drug-Taking Confidence Questionnaire; POC-10 = 10 Items extracted from the Processes of Change Questionnaire for a study with opiate-using patients; USS/GCS = Urge-Specific Strategies Questionnaire and General Change Strategies Questionnaire; L = Less than Adequate, A = Adequate, G = Good, E = Excellent; U = Unavailable; NA = Not Applicable.

Second, although numerous studies have shown that having social networks that include substance users (particularly one's partner) poses a serious risk for continued drug use (see review by Westphal, Wasserman, Masson, & Sorenson, 2005), this risk is easy to assess without any formal assessment tool. Furthermore, measures of social support that are not abstinence-specific have not predicted treatment outcome, and no measure of abstinence-specific structural or functional support currently has enough psychometric evidence with SUDs to be recommended for clinical use. Therefore, this section focuses on tools that have adequate psychometric information and that could be useful in treatment planning. Detailed ratings of their psychometric properties can be found in Table 15.2.

disapproval), (b) assurances of confidentiality, (c) breath alcohol testing at the interview to ensure the person is alcohol-free during the interview, and (d) interviewee awareness that their reports will be corroborated by urine screens and/or reports of family members or close friends (Ehrman & Robbins, 1994; Sobell et al., 1996; Sobell & Sobell, 1986). Patients become dishonest in their reporting when expecting scolding, lectures, disappointing the therapist, changes in treatment, or reporting to others who may impose consequences as a result of disclosing use. Thus, the interviewer set is particularly important both with interviews and self-report measures: knowing that there will be no negative consequences or disapproval for reporting substance use removes the primary disincentive to honesty.

INCREASING HONEST REPORTING

Structured interviews with individuals with SUDs about their drinking or substance use have been found to be sensitive and reliable when there is (a) an interviewer and clinical set that encourages honest reporting (i.e., no unpleasant consequences, including interviewer

SEVERITY OF DRUG USE AND PSYCHOSOCIAL FUNCTIONING

Substance Dependence Severity Scale (SDSS; Miele et al., 2000a). This semistructured clinical interview assesses the severity of every symptom of both DSM-IV and ICD-10 (WHO, 1997) substance abuse/

dependence/harmful use disorders. Substance-specific questions assess frequency, recency, and amount of use in the past 30 days, as well as severity of diagnostic symptoms using both severity and frequency dimensions. These questions cover a wide range of abused substances, including alcohol, cocaine, heroin, stimulants, licit opiates, sedatives, methadone, cannabis, hallucinogens, and two "other" categories covering drugs such as inhalants. (The cannabis items omit withdrawal, which was only found to be a valid symptom after this measure was developed.) The SDSS takes specialized training and can require as much as 40 minutes to administer.

The SDSS scales demonstrate good to excellent test–retest reliability (except for cannabis which was fair to poor), internal consistency, and validity for the use (quantity/frequency) items and DSM-IV severity items (Miele et al., 2000a, 2000b). Patients reporting more days that symptoms were present returned to drug use more quickly, suggesting that this frequency scale predicts need for more intensive care (Miele et al., 2001). On the other hand, greater usual severity of dependence symptoms predicted slower return to drug use (Miele et al., 2001), consistent with more serious problems or concern about consequences of drug use making people more motivated for change. Therefore, this instrument has generally excellent psychometric properties (except for ICD-10 diagnoses, as reviewed in the section on Assessing for Diagnosis) and can be a useful way to assess recent use and severity of specific SUD symptoms.

Addiction Severity Index (ASI)—5th edition

This structured interview has become the most widely used instrument for assessing both SUD severity and severity of other life problems in SUD treatment settings (McLellan, Luborsky, O'Brien, & Woody, 1980; McLellan et al., 1992). The ASI provides severity scores for drug use (not specific to any one drug), alcohol use, and five life areas: medical, employment, legal, psychological, and social/family functioning. The drug and alcohol use sections ask about past 30 days and lifetime frequency of use of each of a number of drugs, and a number of consequences of drug or alcohol use. Each section includes an overall clinical rating of severity, but a composite index (adding the weighted value of certain items) or T-score using a standardized score (based on the mean and standard deviation of the population) can also be generated (Alterman et al., 1998; McGahan, Griffith, & McLellan, 1986). However, whether or not a summary rating or score

is desired, the specific information derived from the interview provides the clinician with a wealth of useful information. The ASI requires specialized training offered by the authors in Philadelphia, requires computerized scoring of the composite indices or T-scores, and the 133 items can require about 40 to 60 minutes to administer. A computer-administered version eases some of the burden.

Validity of the severity ratings in each area scales was shown by correlations with other indicators of problems in each of the life areas (McLellan et al., 1980). However, the interviewer severity ratings are not acceptably reliable in terms of inter-rater reliabilities or internal consistency reliability, a problem that is intended to be solved by using the composite indices or T-scores (Alterman, Brown, Zaballero, & McKay, 1994; Alterman et al., 1998). When the psychometric properties of these indices were checked with 1,008 patients with SUDs (64% primarily opiate dependent, 19% primarily cocaine dependent, 17% alcohol dependent), reliability of the seven indices was not always adequate, especially for the employment, legal, and drug indices (reviewed in Alterman et al., 1998). Therefore, psychometric work was done to improve the reliability, resulting in reducing the measure to 65 items falling on five highly reliable and stable scales: drug, alcohol, psychiatric/psychological, family, and legal problems (Alterman et al., 1998), scored using T-scores, with good to excellent validity. When the predictive validity of these intake ASI T-scores were examined among 308 patients (44% opioid, 34% alcohol, 22% cocaine dependent), elevated drug T-scores and lower alcohol T-scores prospectively predicted urine screens at 6-month follow-up that were more often positive for amphetamines, benzodiazepines, barbiturates, and cocaine use, but did not predict opiate use (Alterman et al., 1998). In our own work with cocaine dependent patients, we did not find the drug composite index to predict 3- or 6-month drug use outcomes after treatment for 119 patients (Martin, Rohsenow & Monti, 2006). However, using a revised index in which each of the items used in the composite was asked again specific to cocaine effects (ASI Cocaine Index), higher index scores predicted higher rates of relapse to cocaine at 3 months (not at 6 months) and were also correlated with a number of cocaine-specific measures of consequences and cravings, unlike the ASI Drug composite (Martin et al., 2006). This suggests that drug-specific severity ratings may be more heuristic at times in identifying those who might be in need of more intensive or extensive treatment.

Version 6 of the ASI is now under development and is designed to improve the instrument in a number of ways (John Cacciola & Arthur Alterman, University of Pennsylvania, personal communication). First, the authors will remove items with low reliability (including interviewer ratings), improve the structure, and give better operational definitions of many items. These changes should improve reliability and decrease training time. Second, a 6-month time frame will be included in addition to the 30-day and lifetime questions to provide a more adequate baseline and to monitor change over longer intervals. Third, questions were added to cover important omitted areas (e.g., age of occurrence in various sections; housing; HIV; pregnancy; treatment services utilization) and to coincide with questions used in national databases. Psychometric analyses of the full and briefer versions are now underway.

Global Appraisal of Individual Needs (GAIN). The GAIN's (Dennis, 1999; Dennis, Scott, & Funk, 2003; Dennis, Titus, et al., 2003; http://www.chestnut.org/li/gain/) semistructured interview has sections on family/living arrangement, substance use, physical health, risk behaviors, mental health, environment, legal, and vocational aspects. As such, it can provide comprehensive background information on patients similar to that obtained by the ASI. It can be used for ASAM-based (American Society of Addiction Medicine) level of care placement, JCAHO-based (Joint Committee on Accreditation of Hospital Organization) treatment planning, and DOMS-based (Drug Outcome Monitoring Study) outcome monitoring. The GAIN can be administered by paper or computer and takes 60 to 120 minutes for the initial evaluation. The substance use section, in addition to providing diagnostic information (as previously described), asks for self-reported frequency of use in the past month for categories of drugs or any substance, recency of use of each of these categories, peak quantity of use of each category, frequency (days) of use of each, number of days with problems from substance use, number of past-month SUD diagnostic symptoms, and a current withdrawal scale, all with excellent reliability and validity (Dennis, Titus, et al., 2003). In a comparison of biometric data (hair and urine) and three self-report measures (recency, quantity, frequency) of use of marijuana, cocaine, opioids, and other substance, the GAIN's Substance Frequency Scale performed as well or better than other measures or methods of combining measures (Lennox, Dennis, Scott, & Funk, 2006). Other scales

in the GAIN, all with at least adequate reliability and validity, include number of days of past treatment, environmental risks for relapse, illegal activities, emotional problems, and employment activities.

Negative Consequences and Expected Effects

Although the assessment of negative consequences of substance abuse overlaps with material addressed in the preceding section, the measures just described either focused on severity of diagnostic symptoms alone or on life functioning (whether or not problems in life functioning could be directly attributed to substance use). Assessment of a range of consequences perceived by patients to be due to substance use can be useful for treatment planning in two ways: First, it provides an overview of areas of functioning that should improve as a result of abstinence and treatment. Second, the information can be useful in motivational interviewing (Miller & Rollnick, 1991) by increasing the patient's awareness of areas of life that could be improved via abstinence. In addition to assessing past consequences, the assessment of positive and negative effects expected acutely from substance use can also be used as feedback in motivational interviewing or in functional analysis based coping skills training (Rohsenow, Monti, et al., 2004).

The Inventory of Drug Use Consequences (IDUC; Tonigan & Miller, 2002) is a 50-item self-report measure of the consequences of drug or alcohol use (not differentiated from each other). There are separate versions for lifetime and the past 3 months of use, and each of these has a version worded in the third person that can be completed by a family member or friend. The IDUC was developed to provide clinicians with a relatively brief (about 10 to 15 minutes) and easy tool that is in the public domain. Four of the five scales have excellent internal consistency reliability: physical problems, social relationships, interpersonal problems, and impulse control, and a confirmatory factor analysis showed that these same four scales adequately represent a larger domain of negative consequences and correlate with other measures other negative consequences (Tonigan & Miller, 2002). Further work produced a 15-item Short Inventory of Problems—Alcohol and Drugs (SIP-AD; Blanchard, Morgenstern, Morgan, Labouvie, & Bux, 2003). The items all load on one reliable and valid scale to give a total indicator of degree of adverse consequences that significantly correlates with other measures of alcohol and drug severity, dependence symptoms, substance use frequency, and psychiatric severity. Although both versions have good to excellent reliability and at least adequate validity (see Table 15.2), the long version (excluding the intrapersonal section) would be more useful in treatment planning because it provides reliable indices of problems in four different life areas that can be targeted for coping skills training or motivational approaches.

Substance-Specific Tools

The Marijuana Problems Scale (MPS; Stephens, Roffman & Curtin, 2000) assesses 19 recent and life-time problems that patients attribute to marijuana use that are summed to provide an index of problem severity. This self-report measure was derived from a 26-problem measure based in part on rewording many DAST items for marijuana, deleting the treatment items, and adding some other consequences (Stephens, Wertz, & Roffman, 1993), sometimes called the Marijuana Consequences Questionnaire (e.g., Budney, Higgins, Radonovich, & Novy, 2000). Domains include psychological, social, legal, and occupational consequences (examples include memory problems, family problems, procrastination). The 26-item version is a checklist, but the 19-item version asks patients to rate each item as a mild or major problem versus no problem. There is limited psychometric information available on either version of this measure. For the 19-item version, one study reports very high reliability (Stephens et al., 2000) and showed change in problems over a 4-month period among marijuana dependent patients in active treatment versus a delayed-treatment condition that paralleled changes reported for frequency of marijuana use and number of dependence symptoms (Stephens et al., 2000). However, no other forms of validity analyses have been conducted as yet. Although the 26-item measure has been used in more studies, there is virtually no supporting psychometric information for this version as yet, with one report of high internal consistency reliability at follow-up (Stephens et al., 1993) but no reported reliability pretreatment, no concurrent correlations reported to support its validity, and no differences between pretreatment abstainers and users of marijuana in scores (Moore & Budney, 2002). Therefore, the 19-item MPS is a brief and valid measure of degree of initial problems but further psychometric information is needed and psychometric properties of the 26-item version are unknown.

The Cocaine Negative Consequences Checklist (CNCC; Michalec et al., 1996) assesses long-term negative life events resulting from their own cocaine use as perceived by cocaine abusers. The items all fall on a highly reliable single scale but can be scored also for four reliable content area scales: physical health, emotional/psychological, social/relationship, and legal problems. The scales correlated significantly with other measures of use and severity in two samples, and were found to predict which cocaine users would seek help (Varney et al., 1995). An expanded second edition, with 87 items (CNCC-87) that added financial and vocational items, has equally high reliability and predicts cocaine use outcomes after treatment.

The Cocaine Effects Questionnaire for Patient Populations (CEQ; Rohsenow, Sirota, Martin, & Monti, 2004) is a 33-item self-report instrument assessing seven factors of fairly immediate positive and negative effects expected from cocaine use. Reliability and validity have been found to be good, with several subscales correlated with amount of cocaine use and with urge to use cocaine. This information was used in coping skills treatment planning by helping patients identify alternative nondrug ways to obtain desired positive effects and to remind patients of negative experiences they wish to avoid (Rohsenow, Monti, Martin, Michalec, & Abrams, 2000), and was used in motivational interviewing as a way to augment discussion of pros and cons of cocaine use (Rohsenow, Monti, et al., 2004). Other cocaine expectancy measures and a parallel measure for marijuana expectancies have been developed on college populations, many or most of whom did not use cocaine/marijuana, much less meet criteria for SUD, so are not described here.

Unfortunately, there are no psychometrically sound and clinically relevant opiate-specific measures of consequences or expectancies. In one study of self-reported expected pros and cons specific to opiate use, rather unusual findings were obtained: expected negative consequences did not correlate with treatment outcome, whereas expected positive consequences predicted better outcomes (Powell et al., 1993). However, the measure was not developed empirically and had fairly few items, so it cannot be recommended until further psychometric work is completed.

Assessment for Relapse Prevention

According to social learning models of relapse prevention (e.g., Monti et al., 2002), some of the most important areas to assess include (a) situations (interpersonal, emotional/cognitive, and environmental) that increase risk of relapse; (b) self-efficacy about staying abstinent (both in general and in specific high-risk situations; and (c) types of coping skills available to use and/or actually used when in high-risk situations or in general to prevent relapse. If initiation of abstinence in treatment seekers who are not abstinent is the goal, these same domains are important to target. The use of other substances is another source of relapse risk, but methods of monitoring these are covered in other sections of the chapter.

The Inventory of Drug Taking Situations (IDTS; Annis & Martin, 1985; Turner, Annis, & Sklar, 1997) assesses high-risk situations for relapse based on common domains of relapse risk situations. The categories were derived from analyses of alcohol dependent patients' relapse risk situations and therefore omit some triggers relevant to people with drug dependence (such as the presence of money or ATM cards, Rohsenow et al., 2000; Rohsenow, Monti, et al. 2004), but the measure was normed on 364 drug dependent patients with primary cocaine ($n = 159$), cannabis ($n = 98$) or alcohol disorders ($n = 76$). Factor structure and reliability have been shown to be good, but there is no simple way to validate items on actual risk situations. The 50 self-report items fall into factors of unpleasant emotions, pleasant emotions, physical discomfort, testing personal control, urges/temptations to use, conflict with others, social pressure to use, and pleasant times with others. These factors can be grouped into three second-order factors (with good psychometric model fit): negative situations, positive situations, and urges and testing personal control. Although the reliability (internal consistency) was poor for the physical discomfort scale, all other scales have adequate to good reliability. For each situation described, patients report how often they have used drugs in that situation in the past. The information can be used to design personalized relapse prevention training by emphasizing skills needed for handling the situations a person has actually most often associated with drug use.

For identifying highly idiosyncratic relapse risk situations, the Drinking Triggers Inventory (DTI; Monti et al., 2002; Rohsenow et al. 2001), a structured interview developed to identify highly personal relapse risk situations for use in cue exposure therapy, is easily adapted for use with any drug of abuse, as was done in identifying personal high-risk situations of cocaine dependent patients as the basis of functional analysis based cocaine-specific coping skills training

(Monti, Rohsenow, Michalec, Martin, & Abrams, 1997; Rohsenow et al., 2000). However, there is insufficient psychometric information to allow this instrument to be rated in the table.

Self-efficacy can be assessed with several measures. First, the Drug-Taking Confidence Questionnaire (DTCQ; Sklar, Annis, & Turner, 1997) is a 50-item measure that uses the same list of situations as in the IDTS to assess self-efficacy. It requires respondents to rate how confident they are that they would be able to resist the urge to use drugs in that situation. Thus, the IDTS is behavioral but past-oriented whereas the DTCQ is more subjective, but future-oriented. This measure also was developed on people with a range of types of SUDs. The confirmatory factor analysis supported essentially the same three high-order factors as the IDTS: positive situations, negative situations, and temptation situations. An eight-item short form also has generally good psychometric properties (Sklar & Turner, 1999). Second, the Alcohol Abstinence Self-Efficacy Scale (AASE; DiClemente, Carbonari, Rosario, Montgomery, & Hughes, 1994) has been adapted for use with drug abusers. This measure has patients rate 20 situations for how confident they are that they would not use in those situations; four subscales using 15 of the items provided a good fit to the data with drug abusers (Hiller, Broome, Knight, & Simpson, 2000). The four subscales are negative affect, social/positive situations, physical and other concerns, and withdrawal and urges. Third, a simple four-point rating of confidence that the person would not use drugs again over a specific period of time predicts treatment outcome for opiate addicts (Gossop, Green, Phillips, & Bradley, 1990). However, there is insufficient information on these two measures to rate them in the table, and the broader situation-specific measures are preferable because they can be used to individualize relapse prevention and/or coping skills training by focusing on the types of situations in which the patient would be most tempted to use or least confident about abstaining from use.

Coping Skills Inventories

Only a few studies investigating coping to predict outcome for opiate abusers used reliable and valid measures. In one such study, 10 items were selected from the psychometrically sound Processes of Change questionnaire (POC; Prochaska, Velicer, DiClemente, & Fava, 1988); among opiate dependent individuals abstinence was related to an increase in the 10 processes of change assessed (POC-10; Gossop, Stewart, Browne, & Marsden, 2002). These items were categorized into Avoidance (remove things from my home that remind me of drugs; stay away from people who remind me of drugs; stay with people who remind me not to use), Cognitive (I tell myself I can choose not to use drugs; I can keep from using if I try hard enough; I am able to avoid using if I want to; I must not use to be content with myself), and Distraction (physical activity; do something to help me relax; think about something else when tempted to use). These three categories had adequate to good internal consistency reliability in this study, and all three types of coping were significantly greater in abstainers, suggesting that only these 10 items are needed for use with opiate dependent patients.

Because existing measures tapped only a limited number of the specific skills taught in many treatment programs, we developed measures of coping skills to be used in high-risk situations, the Urge-Specific Strategies (USS) questionnaire, and of lifestyle change skills designed to maintain abstinence, the General Change Strategies (GCS) questionnaire. Although originally developed and validated with alcohol dependent patients in treatment (Monti et al., 2001), the measure was adapted for use with cocaine dependent patients in treatment (Rohsenow, Martin, & Monti, 2005). The cocaine versions assess 21 strategies in each measure and each formed reliable and valid scales. They were used to determine the specific skills that were correlated with less cocaine use at 3 and 6 months posttreatment, with results indicating that 13 of the USS and 12 of the GCS were effective in this regard. Thus, the measure was found to be heuristic across two types of dependence. The open-ended section can be used to elicit patients' free recall of all the strategies they plan to use and the frequency ratings are used to assess how often they say they have used each strategy. By identifying the skills the patients already know or use, gaps in knowledge or use of effective skills can be targeted for treatment.

Overall Evaluation

There are a variety of clinically useful instruments that can be used in treatment planning. There is a choice of scientifically sound measures that provide an evaluation of the patient's ability to function across major life areas. Whether or not problems in some of these areas result from drug use, these areas may need to be addressed in treatment so as to maximize the individual's structural and functional support for abstinence, motivation to stay clean and sober, and quality of life. Drug-specific consequences can be particularly useful in sustaining or increasing the person's motivation to become or stay abstinent from drugs by highlighting what he or she has to gain from abstinence. The measures of situations in which the patient would be more tempted to use or have less confidence about staying abstinent are sound and can target some aspects of treatment into helping the patient learn to better avoid or cope with the high-risk situations without using. Few measures of coping skills have as yet been developed for people with SUDs to assess the range of coping skills available, and none that can be used in the field to assess quality of coping responses. One coping measure has mostly adequate psychometric properties but assessed very few skills and the other has demonstrated good psychometric properties but has only been evaluated with alcohol or cocaine dependent patients so far (but is easily adapted). Good measures of social support for abstinence have not been developed, but may not be needed because such support is easy to evaluate by the way that predicts outcome (e.g., number of people in one's network and number of abstinent people in one's network predict outcome for cocaine dependent patients; Zywiak, Rohsenow, Martin, Eaton, & Neighbors, 2004).

The measures selected for inclusion in this section are all ones that could be good clinical tools, although some require considerably more training and time than others, and time is often of short supply in many treatment contexts. Some of the measures in Table 15.2 with good psychometric properties are not highly recommended due to the amount of time and training required for administration and the complexity of the scoring (i.e., SDSS, ASI). Other measures were not highly recommended because they were specific to only one substance (e.g., CNCC-87, CEQ). The ones rated as highly recommended are the ones with good psychometric qualities and seeming utility for treatment planning that are also relatively easy to administer.

ASSESSMENT FOR TREATMENT MONITORING AND EVALUATION OF TREATMENT OUTCOME

There are several assessment measures and strategies that can be used to track the effects of treatment on substance use and problem severity. In addition to the

IDUC, SIP-AD, and MPS described above, the main options are indices of symptom severity and toxicology analyses. Details of the psychometric properties of these measures are presented in Table 15.3.

Addiction Severity Index Scales

A briefer (102-item) form of the ASI (ASI-30 day; described previously) that omits the lifetime questions is commonly used for tracking progress. This form asks about drug use and other life areas over the 30 days prior to the interview, with good reliability of the five final indices (drug, alcohol, family, legal, psychiatric; Alterman et al., 1998). However, there are very little psychometric data on the value of using the ASI to track progress. Also, there are no data on ASI scales at any follow-up time point being investigated for correlations with other measures of outcome at the same time point. Using the revised scoring, the ASI drug index at 6 months after treatment start was investigated as a predictor of 2-year outcomes; although the drug index did not predict future drug use, increases from baseline to 6 months in the alcohol index combined with increases in the family problems index and decreases in legal problems index predicted a future decrease in opiate use and increase in cocaine use (Alterman et al., 1998). Complex results such as these make it hard to use these scales to predict whether drug outcomes are likely to improve. Thus, this measure can be used to track changes in functioning on a monthly basis but it is unclear the extent to which changes in ASI scores correlate with changes in drug use during the same time period. It would be expected that changes in life functioning could be somewhat independent from changes in substance use, depending on the extent to which these are direct targets of treatment. However, increase in future crime at 2 years was predicted by change in alcohol use from 0 to 6 months, not by the legal, drug, or other ASI scores (Alterman et al., 1998), contrary to what one would expect.

The GAIN Monitoring 90-Day version (Dennis, Scott, Godley & Funk, 1999; http://www.chestnut.org/li/gain/) is designed to evaluate change over time in living arrangements, substance use (frequency, situational antecedents, withdrawal, problematic consequences), treatment (use, satisfaction, medications), physical health, risk behaviors, emotional health, legal system events, vocation, and finances. The full measure takes 60 minutes and core questions take 25 minutes, with a 10-minute Quick Monitoring version available. The measure has excellent data on change over time in the most relevant areas across a variety of types of substance treatment settings.

Timeline Followback

Although this method of asking about daily drug or alcohol use is used primarily in research, when retrospective self-report of days of use is desired, this method has been found to be the least subject to memory problems (Cooney, Kadden & Steinberg, 2005). The timeline followback (TLFB; Sobell & Sobell, 1980) is a calendar-assisted structured interview which provides a way to cue memory so that recall is more accurate. For the period of time of interest, the person is asked to fill in all days with special events such as holidays, birthdays, and days in jail or hospital. The person is then asked about drug use on those days and the days immediately before and after those days, with other days gradually filled in from there. The TLFB has good to excellent reliability and validity (Ehrman & Robbins, 1994; Sobell et al., 1996) when the caveats above about self-report measures of substance use (see the section on Increasing Honest Reporting) are taken into account. This method has been found to be sensitive to treatment effects across a great many studies (e.g., McKay et al, 1997; Rohsenow, Monti, et al., 2004).

The IDUC (Tonigan & Miller, 2002), a 50-item self-report measure of the consequences of drug or alcohol use, has a version asking about the past 3 months that can be used for tracking progress using the four reliable scales (physical problems, social relationships, interpersonal problems, and impulse control). These scales were sensitive to changes in drug use behavior over 3 months, so that a 40% decrease in drug use was paralleled by a 33% decrease in drug-related consequences (Tonigan & Miller, 2002). The short form reviewed above, the SIP-AD (Blanchard et al., 2003), is sensitive to treatment change, decreasing from pre to posttreatment, and with posttreatment SIP-AD scores correlating as expected ($r = -.43$) with posttreatment number of substance use days (Blanchard et al., 2003). Both measures are rated in Table 15.3. Because of the demonstrated sensitivity of these measures to change combined with ease of administration, they are highly recommended.

The Marijuana Problems Scale (MPS; Stephens et al., 2000), in the 19-item 90-day version, may be used to track change in marijuana-related problems. The MPS was sensitive to change in problems over a 4-month period among marijuana dependent patients in active treatment versus delayed-treatment

TABLE 15.3 Ratings of Instruments Used for Treatment Monitoring and Treatment Outcome Evaluation

Instrument	Norms	Internal Consistency	Inter-Rater Reliability	Test–Retest Reliability	Content Validity	Construct Validity	Validity Generalization	Treatment Sensitivity	Clinical Utility	Highly Recommended
ASI-30 Day	NA	U	L[a]	NA	A	G	G	U	U	
TLFB	NA	NA	G	G	NA	E	E	E	A	
IDUC	NA	E	NA	G	G	A	A	A	A	✓
SIP-AD	NA	E	NA	G	G	A	A	A	A	
MPS	NA	U	NA	U	U	A	U	A	U	
GAIN 90-Day M	NA	G	NA	NA	G	G	A	A	A	
Urine Screens	U	NA	NA	NA	NA	A	A	L	A[b]	✓
Urinalyses	G	NA	NA	NA	NA	G	E	E	E[b]	✓

[a] Unacceptable with original scoring, acceptable to excellent with five-factor scoring.

[b] Utility is excellent during the time a program requires 3 to 7 days/week of attendance, but with high cost.

Note: ASI-30 Day = Addiction Severity Index 30-Day Form; TLFB = Timeline Followback Interview; IDUC = Inventory of Drug Use Consequences, four scales; SIP-AD = Short Inventory of Problems-Alcohol and Drugs; MPS = Marijuana Problems Scale; GAIN-90 Day M = Global Appraisal of Individual Needs-90-Day Monitoring Version; Urine Screens = drug screening with onsite test kits; Urinalyses = urine drug toxicology analyses using standard commercial laboratory methods such as EMIT or gas chromatography; L = Less Than Adequate; A = Adequate; G = Good; E = Excellent; U = Unavailable; NA = Not Applicable.

condition that paralleled changes reported for frequency of marijuana use and number of dependence symptoms (Stephens et al., 2000). The 26-item version, the Marijuana Consequences Questionnaire, has inconsistent results: it showed no effects of treatment in one study (Budney et al., 2000), but showed a significant decrease from before to after treatment independent of type of treatment in two other studies (Budney, Moore, Rocha, & Higgins, 2006; Stephens, Roffman, & Simpson, 1994). Although change over time paralleled change in frequency of use, no attempt was made to validate the measure in terms of change in other measures of problems. Therefore, the 19-item measure may provide a basis for seeing reduction over time in problems as a function of treatment, but replication in a second study and information on correlations of change in this measure to change in other indicators is needed before the actual value of this measure is known. The limited psychometric information prevents a high recommendation for this measure at this time.

Urine and Hair Toxicology Analyses

Urine toxicology drug analyses for drugs of abuse other than alcohol are the gold standard for monitoring patients, but require that patients still be enrolled in a program that provides them with some reason to come in for such testing 3 to 7 days per week. Urine screens and toxicology analyses test for the presence of the drugs themselves and/or of the metabolites of the drugs (for longer detection). The drugs most commonly screened for include benzodiazepines, cocaine, opiates, amphetamines, phencyclidine, and cannabinoids. Commercial laboratories usually provide a standard panel of substances to be analyzed and the option of testing for other drugs upon request. The assay methodologies used in most laboratory testing methods (such as Enzyme-Multiplied Immunoassay Technique [EMIT] or gas chromatography-mass spectrometry [GC-MS]) are highly reliable and valid. Onsite screening tests (strips or cups with detection strips built in) are far less expensive and agree 97% of the time with GC-MS results. They do, however, have increased false positives, so positive readings generally should be confirmed with a laboratory test. A comparison of laboratory-analyzed urine toxicology data and self-reports of days of use 12 months after treatment entry for 337 patients with SUDs found that neither urine tests nor self-reports

were without their problems as a method of detection (Lennox et al., 2006). Higher validity was seen, in general, for self-reported recency of use of cocaine, opioid, and marijuana use (Lennox et al., 2006), indicating that it is of value also simply to ask patients how recently they used drugs when monitoring their use (when using the guidelines described under Increasing Honest Reporting, above).

There are problems that can be encountered with urine drug testing. One such problem pertains to the window of detection. For example, although methadone programs routinely require daily testing, most drugs of abuse can be detected with certainty over a 2 or 3 day window even with qualitative methods of detection (just a positive or negative answer, as opposed to quantitative methods that give the amount detected). However, because most drugs can stay in the tissues for 7 or so days after abstinence begins, and marijuana can be detectable (50 ng/L) for 2 weeks after heavy use (Hawks & Chiang, 1986), readings may be positive for some time after abstinence begins. Therefore, programs often allow an initial washout period for the urine to become clean before imposing any consequences or before contingency management programs start voucher reinforcement based on abstinent readings (e.g., Budney et al., 2006). A second problem is the potential for false positive test results. The methodologies involved in most laboratory tests greatly decrease the chance of false positives, yet a person can still have reason to claim that a test showed a false positive for opiates if, for example, they had eaten a large amount of poppy seeds. When not used for legal purposes, it may be enough to require that patients avoid all nonillicit sources of positive readings. A third problem is related to the introduction of contaminants by patients. Patients who expect unpleasant consequences from positive readings may go to great lengths to "beat" the test. This can include bringing a hidden sample of urine from a clean person, adding contaminants (such as soap, vinegar, lemon juice, salt, or bleach) to invalidate the test, or drinking large quantities of water before giving a sample to make the sample too dilute for a valid test. Other evasion methods have been developed, including an artificial penis or hidden plastic tubing and an IV bag with heating strips. Some of these can be overcome by requiring carefully monitored testing and requiring some hours at the site without drinking before obtaining the sample.

Testing hair for the presence of drugs of abuse has raised some interest, because hair will contain residue of drugs over the length of the hair, thus providing a detection window of months or years, depending on the length of the hair. Drugs enter the hair at the follicle level via blood, sebum (from glands in the scalp), and sweat (Huestis, 2001). However, two serious problems limit the adoption of this method more widely to date: hair color bias and environmental factors. First, drugs are more strongly detectable in darker hair than lighter hair (Joseph, Tsai, Tsao, Su, & Cone, 1997), leading to more false negatives among blond or white-haired people than people with brown or black hair. The concern that this would lead to racial or ethnic differences in detection has raised serious concerns. Second, drugs also can be absorbed into the hair via environmental exposure, especially smoke, and repeated shampoo treatments or solvent washes do not completely remove environmental cocaine from the hair (e.g., Wang, Darwin, & Cone, 1994). Therefore, someone can test positive despite remaining abstinent. A third problem is that there are few places where hair testing for drugs is available. A fourth is that hair testing is less sensitive to detecting marijuana than is urine toxicology analysis and there is great individual variability in the sweat that affects hair testing (Baron, Baron, & Baron, 2005). Therefore, hair analysis has more pitfalls than advantages at the present time. Given that urine detection is highly reliable and fully adequate for within-treatment monitoring, it remains the preferred method.

Overall Evaluation

For monitoring of progress in terms of drug use, urine drug analyses at least three times per week remain the gold standard. Although urine drug screens are poor at detecting alcohol use, due to the rapid metabolism of alcohol, these are excellent for monitoring all other drugs of abuse when the precautions described above are taken. For monitoring of monthly change in problems resulting from drug or alcohol use or function in terms of family, legal and psychological problems, the GAIN-90-Day M is developed for this purpose and is scientifically sound. Both methods can identify when the person might be using substances and, therefore, be in need of some additional booster counseling. The IDUC is effective in showing change in problems that result from drug use over time and so is recommended for this purpose.

CONCLUSIONS AND FUTURE DIRECTIONS

The clinician treating patients with SUD disorders has a number of tools available for screening, diagnosis, assessment of problem severity, assessment of risk factors for relapse to address in treatment, and monitoring of treatment progress and outcomes. Some of the tools (particularly the diagnostic and some problem severity tools) are time-consuming and require extensive training: these may be more difficult to adopt into clinic practices that are short on time. Other tools are quicker and/or easier to administer and score for rapid use in treatment planning or monitoring of progress. Hopefully future work will focus more on developing instruments that clinicians can use easily and with minimal time to provide useful guidance for treatment planning and evaluation.

Future development work with assessment instruments needs to include more of a focus on determining validity and treatment sensitivity, in particular. For example, although the ASI is widely used for monitoring treatment progress, there is very little information to demonstrate that it validly tracks changes in other indicators of progress. Given such a widely used a face-valid instrument, such information would be valuable. Future work should also focus on devising instruments that do not require extensive training, long administration time, and complex scoring procedures. Not only do these factors drive up costs; when extensive training is needed it is too easy for assessors' abilities to drift over time unless regular retraining or testing of their abilities is conducted. A number of instruments in the future will probably not only be available via computer but also via Web-based applications, allowing interactive responses with patients, computerized scoring, and access to expert help at the touch of a mouse.

References

Acosta, M. C., Haller, D. L., & Schnoll, S. H. (2005). Cocaine and stimulants. In R. J. Frances, S. I. Miller, & A. H. Mack (Eds.), *Clinical textbook of addictive disorders* (3rd ed., pp. 184–218). New York: Guilford.

Alterman, A. I., Brown, L. S., Zaballero, A., & McKay, J. R. (1994). The interviewer severity ratings and composite scores of the ASI: A further look. *Drug & Alcohol Dependence, 34*, 201–209.

Alterman, A. I., McDermott, P. A., Cook, T. G., Metzger, D., Rutherford, M. J., Cacciola, J. S., et al.

(1998). New scales to assess change in the addiction severity index for the opioid, cocaine, and alcohol dependent. *Psychology of Addictive Behaviors, 12,* 233–246.

American Psychiatric Association. (2000). *Diagnostic and statistical manual of mental disorders* (4th ed., Text Revision). Washington, DC: Author.

Anglin, M. D., Hser, Y. I., Grella, C. E., Longshore, D., & Prendergast, M. L. (2001). Drug treatment careers: conceptual overview and clinical, research, and policy applications. In F. M. Tims, C. G. Leukefeld, & J. J. Platt (Eds.), *Relapse and recovery in addictions* (pp. 18–39). New Haven: Yale University Press.

Annis, H. M., & Martin, G. (1985). *Inventory of drug-taking situations.* Toronto, Ontario, Canada: Addiction Research Foundation.

Anthenelli, R. M., & Schuckit, M. A. (1992). Genetics. In J. H. Lowinson, P. Ruiz, & R. B. Millman (Eds.), *Substance abuse: A comprehensive textbook* (2nd ed., pp. 56–69). Baltimore, MD: Williams & Wilkins.

Baron, D. A., Baron, D. A., & Baron, S. H. (2005). Laboratory testing for substances of abuse. In R. J. Frances, S. I. Miller, & A. H. Mack (Eds.), *Clinical textbook of addictive disorders* (3rd ed., pp. 63–71). New York: Guilford.

Blanchard, K. A., Morgenstern, J., Morgan, T. J., Labouvie, E. W., & Bux, D. A. (2003). Assessing consequences of substance use: Psychometric properties of the inventory of drug use consequences. *Psychology of Addictive Behaviors, 17,* 328–331.

Brown, S., Gleghorn, A., Schuckit, M., Myers, M., & Mott, M. (1996). Conduct disorder among adolescent alcohol and drug abusers. *Journal of Studies on Alcohol, 57,* 314–324.

Budney, A. J., Higgins, S. T., Radonovich, K. J., & Novy, P. L. (2000). Adding voucher-based incentives to coping skills and motivational enhancement improves outcomes during treatment for marijuana dependence. *Journal of Consulting and Clinical Psychology, 68,* 1051–1061.

Budney, A. J., Hughes, J. R., Moore, B. A., & Novy, P. L. (2001). Marijuana abstinence effects in marijuana smokers maintained in their home environment. *Archives of General Psychiatry, 58,* 917–924.

Budney, A. J., Moore, B. A., Rocha, H. L., & Higgins, S. T. (2006). Clinical trial of abstinence-based vouchers and cognitive-behavioral therapy for cannabis dependence. *Journal of Consulting and Clinical Psychology, 74,* 307–316.

Budney, A. J., Moore, B. A., Vandrey, R. G., & Hughes, J. R. (2003). The time course and significance of cannabis withdrawal. *Journal of Abnormal Psychology, 112,* 393–402.

Budney, A. J., Novy, P. L., & Hughes, J. R. (1999). Marijuana withdrawal among adults seeking treatment for marijuana dependence. *Addiction, 94,* 1311–1321.

Busch, A. B., Weiss, R. D., & Najavits, L. M. (2005). Co-occurring substance use disorders and other psychiatric disorders. In R. J. Frances, S. I. Miller, & A. H. Mack (Eds.), *Clinical textbook of addictive disorders* (3rd ed., pp. 271–302). New York: Guilford.

Cooney, N. L., Kadden, R. M., & Steinberg, H. R. (2005). Assessment of alcohol problems. In D. M. Donovan & G. A. Marlatt (Eds.), *Assessment of addictive behaviors* (2nd ed., pp. 71–112). New York: Guilford.

Darke, S., & Ross, J. (1997). Polydrug dependence and psychiatric comorbidity among heroin injectors. *Drug and Alcohol Dependence, 48,* 135–141.

Dennis, M. L. (1999). *Global Appraisal of Individual Needs (GAIN): Administration guide for the GAIN and related measures* (Version 1299). Bloomington, IL: Chestnut Health Systems.

Dennis, M. L., Scott, C. K., & Funk, R. (2003). An experimental evaluation of recovery management checkups (RMC) for people with chronic substance use disorders. *Evaluation and Program Planning, 26,* 339–352.

Dennis, M. L., Scott, C. K., Godley, M. D., & Funk, R. (1999). *Comparison of adolescents and adults by ASAM profile using GAIN data from the Drug Outcome Monitoring Study (DOMS): Preliminary data tables.* Bloomington, IL: Chestnut Health Systems.

Dennis, M. L., Titus, J. C., White, M., Unsicker, J., & Hodgkins, D. (2003). *Global Appraisal of Individual Needs (GAIN): Administration guide for the GAIN and related measures* (Version 1299). Bloomington, IL: Chestnut Health Systems. Retrieved January 20, 2005, from http://www.chestnut.org/li/gain.

DiClemente, C. C., Carbonari, J. P., Rosario, P. G., Montgomery, M. A., & Hughes, S. O. (1994). The alcohol abstinence self-efficacy scale. *Journal of Studies on Alcohol, 55,* 141–148.

Dilts, S. L., Jr., & Dilts, S. L. (2005). Opioids. In R. J. Frances, S. I. Miller, & A. H. Mack (Eds.), *Clinical textbook of addictive disorders* (3rd ed., pp. 138–156). New York: Guilford.

Donovan, D. M., & Marlatt, G. A. (Eds.) (2005). *Assessment of addictive behaviors* (2nd ed.). New York: Guilford.

Ehrman, R. N. & Robbins, S. J. (1994). Reliability and validity of 6-month timeline reports of cocaine and heroin use in a methadone population. *Journal of Consulting and Clinical Psychology, 62,* 843–850.

Farrell, A., Danish, S., & Howard, C. (1992). Relationship between drug use and other problem behaviors in urban adolescents. *Journal of Consulting and Clinical Psychology, 60,* 705–712.

First, M. B., Spitzer, R. L., Gibbon, M., & Williams, J. B. (1996). *Structured Clinical Interview for DSM-IV, Axis I Disorders-Patient Edition (SCID-I/P, Version 2.0)*. New York: Biometrics Research Department, New York State Psychiatric Institute.

Gavin, D. R., Ross, H. E., & Skinner, H. A. (1989). Diagnostic validity of the Drug Abuse Screening Test in the assessment of DSM-III drug disorders. *British Journal of Addiction, 84*, 301–307.

Gawin, F. H., & Ellinwood, E. H., Jr. (1988). Cocaine and other stimulants: Actions, abuse, and treatment. *New England Journal of Medicine, 318*, 1173–1182.

Gossop, M., Green, L., Phillips, G., & Bradley, B. (1990). Factors predicting outcome among opiate addicts after treatment. *British Journal of Clinical Psychology, 29*, 209–216.

Gossop, M., Stewart, D., Browne, N., & Marsden, J. (2002). Factors associated with abstinence, lapse, or relapse to heroin use after residential treatment: Protective effect of coping responses. *Addiction, 97*, 1259–1267.

Handelsman, L., Cochrane, K. J., Aronson, M. J., Ness, R., Rubinstein, K. J., & Kanof, P. D. (1987). Two new rating scales for opiate withdrawal. *American Journal of Drug and Alcohol Abuse, 13*, 293–308.

Hawks, R. L., & Chiang, C. N. (1986). Examples of specific drugs. In R. L. Hawks & C. N. Chiang (Eds.), *Urine testing for drugs of abuse* (NIDA Research Monograph No. 73, pp. 84–112). Washington, DC: US Government Printing Office.

Hiller, M. L., Broome, K. M., Knight, K., & Simpson, D. D. (2000). Measuring self-efficacy among drug-involved probationers. *Psychological Reports, 86*, 529–538.

Hubbard, R. L., Craddock, S. G., Flynn, P. M., Anderson, J., & Etheridge, R. M. (1997). Overview of 1-year follow-up outcomes in the drug abuse treatment outcome study (DATOS). (1997). *Psychology of Addictive Behaviors, 11*, 261–278.

Huestis, M. A. (2001, February 28). *Monitoring drug exposure with alternative matrices*. Presentation to the NIDA-E Treatment Research Review Committee, Bethesda, MD.

Jaffe, J. H. (1989). Psychoactive substance abuse disorders. In H. I. Kaplan & B. J. Sadock (Eds.), *Comprehensive textbook of psychiatry* (5th ed., pp. 642–698). Baltimore, MD: Williams & Wilkins.

Johnson, B. D., & Muffler, J. (1992). Sociocultural aspects of drug use and abuse in the 1990s. In J. H. Lowinson, P. Ruiz, & R. B. Millman (Eds.), *Substance abuse: A comprehensive textbook* (2nd ed., pp. 56–69). Baltimore, MD: Williams & Wilkins.

Joseph, R. E., Jr., Tsai, W. J., Tsao, L. I., Su, T. P., & Cone, E. J. (1997). In vitro characterization of cocaine binding site in human hair. *Journal of Pharmacology and Experimental Therapeutics, 282*, 1228–1241.

Kessler, R., Berglund, P., Demler, O., Jin, R., Merikangas, K. R., & Walters, E. E. (2005). Lifetime prevalence and age-of-onset distributions of DSM-IV disorders in the National Comorbidity Survey Replication. *Archives of General Psychiatry, 62*, 593–602.

Kessler, R., Chiu, W. T., Demler, O., Merikangas, K. R., & Walters, E. E. (2005). Prevalence, severity, and comorbidity of the 12-month DSM-IV disorders in the National Comorbidity Survey Replication. *Archives of General Psychiatry, 62*, 617–627.

Kessler, R. C., McGonagle, K. A., Zhao, S., Nelson, C. B., Hughes, M., Eshleman, S., et al. (1994). Lifetime and 12-month prevalence of DSM-III-R psychiatric disorders in the United States. *Archives of General Psychiatry, 51*, 8–19.

Lennox, R., Dennis, M. L., Scott, C. S., & Funk, R. (2006). Combining psychometric and biometric measures of substance use. *Drug and Alcohol Dependence, 83*, 95–103.

Martin, R. A., Rohsenow, D. J., Monti, P. M. (2006, June). *Advantage of a drug-specific ASI drug composite index: Validity of an ASI cocaine index for cocaine dependence*. Poster presented at the annual meeting of the College on Problems of Drug Dependence, Scottsdale, AZ.

McGahan, P. L., Griffith, J. A., & McLellan, A. T. (1986). *Composite scores from the Addiction Severity Index: Manual and computer software*. Philadelphia VA Medical Center, Philadelphia, PA: Veterans Administration Press.

McKay, J. R., Alterman, A. I., Cacciola, J. S., Rutherford, M. J., O'Brien, C. P., & Koppenhaver, J. (1997). Group counseling versus individualized relapse prevention aftercare following intensive outpatient treatment for cocaine dependence: Initial results. *Journal of Consulting and Clinical Psychology, 65*, 778–788.

McLellan, A. T., Kushner, H., Metzger, D., Peters, R., Smith, I., Grissom, G., et al. (1992). The fifth edition of the Addiction Severity Index. *Journal of Substance Abuse Treatment, 9*, 199–213.

McLellan, A. T., Luborsky, L., O'Brien, C. P., & Woody, G. E. (1980). An improved diagnostic instrument for substance abuse patients: The Addiction Severity Index. *Journal of Nervous and Mental Disease, 168*, 26–33.

Michalec, E. M., Rohsenow, D. J., Monti, P. M., Varney, S. M., Martin, R. A., Dey, A. N., et al. (1996). A cocaine negative consequences checklist: Development and validation. *Journal of Substance Abuse, 8*, 181–193.

Miele, G. M., Carpenter, K. M., Cockerham, M. S., Trautman, K. D., Blaine, J., & Hasin, D. S. (2000a). Substance Dependence Severity Scale (SDSS): Reliability and validity of a clinician-administered interview for DSM-IV substance use disorder. *Drug and Alcohol Dependence, 59,* 63–75.

Miele, G. M., Carpenter, K. M., Cockerham, M. S., Trautman, K. D., Blaine, J., & Hasin, D. S. (2000b). Concurrent and predictive validty of the Substance Dependence Severity Scale (SDSS). *Drug and Alcohol Dependence, 59,* 77–88.

Miele, G. M., Carpenter, K. M., Cockerham, M. S., Trautman, K. D., Blaine, J., & Hasin, D. S. (2001). Substance Dependence Severity Scale reliability and validity for ICD-10 substance use disorders. *Addictive Behaviors, 26,* 601–612.

Miller, W. R., & Rollnick, S. (1991). *Motivational interviewing: Preparing people to change addictive behavior.* New York: Guilford.

Monti, P. M., Kadden, R., Rohsenow, D. J., Cooney, N. & Abrams, D. B. (2002). *Treating alcohol dependence: A coping skills training guide* (2nd ed.). New York: Guilford Press.

Monti, P. M., Rohsenow, D. J., Michalec, E., Martin, R. A., & Abrams, D. B. (1997). Brief coping skills treatment for cocaine abuse: Substance use outcomes at 3 months. *Addiction, 92,* 1717–1728.

Monti, P. M., Rohsenow, D. J., Swift, R. M, Gulliver, S. B., Colby, S. M., Mueller, T. I., et al. (2001). Naltrexone and cue exposure with coping and communication skills training for alcoholics: Treatment process and one-year outcomes. *Alcoholism: Clinical and Experimental Research, 25,* 1634–1647.

Moore, B. A., & Budney, A. J. (2002). Abstinence at intake for marijuana dependence treatment predicts response. *Drug and Alcohol Dependence, 67,* 249–257.

Mors, O., & Sorenson, L. V. (1994). Incidence and comorbidity of personality disorders among first ever admitted psychiatric patients. *European Psychiatry: The Journal of the Association of European Psychiatrists, 9,* 175–184.

Powell, J., Dawe, S., Richards, D., Gossop, M., Marks, I, Strang, J., et al. (1993). Can opiate addicts tell us about their relapse risk? Subjective predictors of clinical prognosis. *Addictive Behaviors, 18,* 473–490.

Prochaska, J. O., Velicer, W. F., DiClemente, C. C., & Fava, J. S. (1988). Measuring process of change: Applications to the cessation of smoking. *Journal of Consulting and Clinical Psychology, 56,* 520–528.

Ritsher, J. B., Moos, R. H., & Finney, J. W. (2002). Relationship of treatment orientation and continuing care to remission among substance abuse patients. *Psychiatric Services, 53,* 595–601.

Robins, L. N., Cottler, L. B., Bucholz, K. K., Compton, W. M., North, C. S., & Rourke, K. M. (2000). *Diagnostic Interview of Schedule for the DSM-IV (DIS-IV).* St. Louis, MO: Washington University School of Medicine.

Robins, L. N., Helzer, J. E., Cottler, L., & Golding, E. (1989). *National Institute of Mental Health Diagnostic Interview Schedule* (3rd ed.). St Louis, MO: Washington University Press.

Robins, L. N., Helzer, J. E., Croughan, J., & Ratcliff, K. S. (1981). National Institute of Mental Health Diagnostic Interview Schedule: Its history, characteristics, and validity. *Archives General Psychiatry, 38,* 381–389.

Rohsenow, D. J., Martin, R. A., & Monti, P. M. (2005). Urge-specific and lifestyle coping strategies of cocaine abusers: Relationships to treatment outcomes. *Drug and Alcohol Dependence, 78,* 211–219.

Rohsenow, D. J., Monti, P. M., Martin, R. A., Colby, S. M., Myers, M. G., Gulliver, S. B., et al. (2004). Motivational enhancement and coping skills training for cocaine abusers: Effects on substance use outcomes. *Addiction, 99,* 862–874.

Rohsenow, D. J., Monti, P. M., Martin, R. A., Michalec, E., & Abrams, D. B. (2000). Brief coping skills treatment for cocaine abuse: 12-month substance use outcomes. *Journal of Consulting and Clinical Psychology, 68,* 515–520.

Rohsenow, D. J., Monti, P. M., Rubonis, A. V., Gulliver, S. B., Colby, S. M., Binkoff, J. A., et al. (2001). Cue exposure with coping skills training and commuication skills training for alcohol dependence: Six and twelve month outcomes. *Addiction, 96,* 1161–1174.

Rohsenow, D. J., Sirota, A. D., Martin, R. A., & Monti, P. M. (2004). The Cocaine Effects Questionnaire for patient populations: Development and psychometric properties. *Addictive Behaviors, 29,* 537–553.

Rounsaville, B. J., Kranzler, H. R., Ball, S., Tennen, H., Poling, J., & Triffleman, E. (1998). Personality disorders in substance abusers: Relation to substance use. *Journal of Nervous and Mental Disease, 186,* 87–95.

Schulenberg, J., Maggs, J. L., Steinman, K. J., & Zucker, R. A. (2001). Development matters: Taking the long view on substance abuse etiology and intervention during adolescence. In P. M. Monti, S. M. Colby, & T. A. O'Leary (Eds.), *Adolescent, alcohol and substance use* (pp. 109–141). New York: Guilford.

Shane, P., Jasiukaitis, P., & Green, R. S. (2003). Treatment outcomes among adolescents with substance abuse problems: The relationship between comorbidities and post-treatment substance involvement. *Evaluation and Program Planning, 26,* 393–402.

Skinner, H. A., (1982). The Drug Abuse Screening Test. *Addictive Behaviors, 7,* 363–371.

Sklar, S. M., Annis, H. M., & Turner, N. E. (1997). Development and validation of the drug-taking confidence questionnaire: A measure of coping self-efficacy. *Addictive Behaviors, 22,* 655–670.

Sklar, S. M., & Turner, N. E. (1999). A brief measure for the assessment of coping self-efficacy among alcohol and other drug users. *Addiction, 94,* 723–729.

Smith, G. T., & Anderson, K. G. (2001). Personality and learning factors combine to create risk for adolescent problem drinking. In P. M. Monti, S. M. Colby, & T. A. O'Leary (Eds.), *Adolescents, alcohol and substance use* (pp. 109–141). New York: Guilford.

Sobell, L. C., Buchan, G., Cleland, P., Sobell, M. B., Fedoroff, I., & Leo, G. I. (1996, November). *The reliability of the timeline followback (TLFB) method as applied to drug, cigarette and cannabis use.* Paper presented at the 30th meeting of the Association for Advancement of Behavior Therapy, New York, NY.

Sobell, L. C., & Sobell, M. B. (1980). Convergent validity: An approach to increasing confidence in treatment outcome conclusions with alcohol and drug abusers. In L. C. Sobell, M. B. Sobell, & E. Ward (Eds.), *Evaluating alcohol and drug abuse treatment effectiveness: Recent advances* (pp. 177–183). Elmsford, NY: Pergamon Press.

Sobell, L. C., & Sobell, M. B. (1986). Can we do without alcohol abusers' self-reports? *Behavior Therapist, 7,* 141–146.

Staley, D., & El-Guebaly, N. (1990). Psychometric properties of the Drug Abuse Screening Test in a psychiatric patient population. *Addictive Behaviors, 15,* 257–264.

Stephens, R. S., Roffman, R. A., & Curtin, L. (2000). Comparison of extended versus brief treatments for marijuana use. *Journal of Consulting and Clinical Psychology, 68,* 898–908.

Stephens, R. S., Roffman, R. A., & Simpson, E. E. (1994). Treating adult marijuana dependence: A test of the relapse prevention model. *Journal of Consulting and Clinical Psychology, 62,* 92–99.

Stephens, R. S., Wertz, J. S., & Roffman, R. A. (1993). Predictors of marijuana treatment outcomes: The role of self-efficacy. *Journal of Substance Abuse, 5,* 341–353.

Substance Abuse and Mental Health Services Administration (SAMSHA). (2001). *National household survey* [Data file]. Rockville, MD: Author.

Substance Abuse and Mental Health Services Administration (SAMSHA), Office of Applied Studies. (2003). *Treatment Episode Data Set (TEDS): 1992–2001* [National Admissions to Substance Abuse Treatment Services, DASIS Series: S-20, DHHS Publication No. (SMA) 03–3778]. Rockville, MD: U.S. Department of Health and Human Services.

Tarter, R. (1990). Evaluation and treatment of adolescent substance abuse: A decision tree method. *American Journal of Drug and Alcohol Abuse, 16,* 1–46.

Tarter, R., & Kirisci, L. (1997). The Drug Use Screening Inventory for adults: Psychometric structure and discriminative sensitivity. *American Journal of Drug and Alcohol Abuse, 23,* 207–219.

Tonigan, J. S., & Miller, W. S. (2002). The inventory of drug use consequences (InDUC): Test–Retest stability and sensitivity to detect change. *Psychology of Addictive Behaviors, 16,* 165–168.

Turner, N. E., Annis, H. M., & Sklar, S. M. (1997). Measurement of antecedents to drug and alcohol use: Psychometric properties of the Inventory of Drug-Taking Situations (IDTS). *Behaviour Research and Therapy, 35,* 465–483.

United States Department of Health and Human Services (USDHHS). (1989). *Reducing the health consequences of smoking : 25 years of progress. A report of the surgeon general.* [DHHS Publication No. (CDC) 89-8411. Centers for Disease Control, Center for Chronic Disease Prevention and Health Promotion, Office on Smoking and Health: U.S. Department of Health and Human Services, Public Health Service.

Varney, S. M., Rohsenow, D. J., Dey, A. N., Myers, M. G., Zwick, W. R., & Monti, P. M. (1995). Factors associated with help seeking and perceived dependence among cocaine users. *American Journal of Drug and Alcohol Abuse, 21,* 81–91.

Walton, M. A., Blow, F. C., & Booth, B. M. (2000). A comparison of substance abuse patients' and counselors' perceptions of relapse risk: Relationship to actual relapse. *Journal of Substance Abuse Treatment, 19,* 161–169.

Wang, W. L., Darwin, W. D., & Cone, E. J. (1994). Simultaneous assay of cocaine, heroin and metabolites in hair, plasma, saliva and urine by gas chromatography-mass spectrometry. *Journal of Chromatography, B, Biomedical Applications, 660,* 279–290.

Westphal, J., Wasserman, D. A., Masson, C. L., & Sorenson, J. L. (2005). Assessment of opioid use. In D. M. Donovan & G. A. Marlatt (Eds.) *Assessment of addictive behaviors* (2nd ed., pp. 215–247). New York: Guilford.

Wills, T. A., Vaccaro, D., & McNamara, G. (1994). Novelty seeking, risk taking, and related constructs as predictors of adolescent substance use: An application of Cloninger's theory. *Journal of Substance Abuse, 6,* 1–20.

World Health Organization (WHO). (1997). *Composite international diagnostic interview* (Core Version 2.1, 12 Month Version). Geneva: Author.

Zywiak, W. H., Rohsenow, D. J., Martin, R. A., Eaton, C. A., & Neighbors, C. (2004, June). *Internal consistency and validity of the drug and alcohol version of the IPA measure.* Poster presented at the annual meeting of the College on Problems in Drug Dependence, San Juan, Puerto Rico.

16

Alcohol Use Disorders

Kelly Green

Blaise Worden

David Menges

Barbara McCrady

Alcohol use disorders (AUDs) are complex problems that may involve all aspects of human functioning, including the physical, psychological, social-interpersonal, legal, environmental, and occupational realms. Treatment planning requires careful attention to each of these domains, thus requiring a comprehensive approach to assessment that provides the clinician with sufficient information to determine the nature and extent of the problems the client is facing and to understand the factors that control and maintain the individual's drinking. Our approach to assessment in this chapter takes account of the complexity of AUDs and provides our review of a comprehensive set of measures to assist the clinician in the diagnostic, treatment planning, and treatment evaluation processes.

GENERAL DIAGNOSTIC CONSIDERATIONS

Prevalence/Incidence

AUDs are among the most frequently occurring psychiatric diagnoses in the United States. According to the National Epidemiologic Survey on Alcohol and Related Conditions (NESARC; National Institute on Alcohol Abuse and Alcoholism [NIAAA], 2003), approximately 65% of Americans are current drinkers. Among drinkers, 62% are light drinkers (i.e., they consume three or fewer standard drinks per week), 21% are moderate drinkers (3 to 14 drinks/week for males; 3 to 7 drinks/week for females), and 17% are heavy

drinkers (>14 drinks/week for males; >7 drinks/week for females).

Just over 8% of the general population meets the criteria for a diagnosis of either alcohol abuse (4.7%) or alcohol dependence (3.8%; NIAAA, 2003). Among those who drink, prevalence rates of abuse and dependence increase to 7.1% and 5.8%, respectively. Other epidemiological data on incidence rates indicate that within a given year approximately 5.7% of the general population and 19.1% of current problem drinkers will meet the criteria for alcohol dependence (Crum, Chan, Chen, Storr, & Anthony, 2005).

The prevalence of AUDs among current drinkers differs in different sociodemographic groups (NIAAA, 2003). Rates of alcohol dependence are greater among men (7.9%) than women (3.9%) and greater among Native Americans (10.9%) than African Americans (6.7%), Asians (4.9%), Hispanics (6.6%), and Caucasians (5.5%). Age also affects the prevalence of alcohol dependence; rates are significantly higher among Americans in the 18–24 age group than among those in all other age groups combined.

Course/Prognosis

Research on the natural course of AUDs suggests that the average individual with alcohol dependence begins drinking more than intended at age 21, develops tolerance at 23, recognizes his or her drinking as excessive at 26, and makes an initial attempt at abstinence at 28 (Schuckit, Anthenelli, Bucholz, Hesselbrock, & Tipp, 1995). For women, the onset of heavier use, problems, and attempts at abstinence occurs at a somewhat older age. Although the course of untreated alcohol dependence varies greatly, the average annual rate of natural remission in community samples is approximately 3% (Finney, Moos, & Timko, 1999). The rate of annual remission increases to an average of 4.8% among those who receive treatment, suggesting that alcohol interventions positively impact the prognosis of dependence. In relation to longevity, at-risk drinkers have been shown to have rates of mortality as much as 20% higher than not-at-risk drinkers (Moore et al., 2006).

Comorbidity

Alcohol dependence is highly comorbid with other psychiatric disorders (Grant et al., 2004a, 2004b). For example, 20.5% of individuals with alcohol dependence also meet the criteria for major depression, a 1-year prevalence rate much higher than that in the general population. In fact, the odds ratio (OR) between alcohol dependence and major depression is 3.7, meaning that an individual with alcohol dependence is almost four times as likely to experience comorbid depression as someone without alcohol dependence. Odds ratios and prevalence rates for other Axis I disorders such as dysthymia (OR = 2.8, 4.6%), mania (OR = 5.7, 7.6%), social phobia (OR = 2.5, 6.3%), and generalized anxiety disorder (OR = 3.1, 5.7%) as well as Axis II disorders such as paranoid personality disorder (PD; OR = 4.6, 15.8%), histrionic PD (OR = 7.5, 10.3%), and antisocial PD (OR = 7.1, 18.3%) underscore the highly comorbid nature of alcohol dependence.

In population samples, approximately 13.05% of those with alcohol dependence also are dependent on another drug of abuse (Stinson et al., 2005). Rates of comorbidity between alcohol and other substance use disorders may be as high as 50% in clinical samples. Alcohol dependent individuals are many times more likely than those without alcohol dependence to be dependent on other substances, including cocaine (OR = 43.0), amphetamines (OR = 20.3), opioids (OR = 12.9), and cannabis (OR = 3.9). In addition to high rates of comorbid drug dependence, rates of nicotine dependence and pathological gambling among those with alcohol dependence are significantly greater than among those in the general population (Grant, Hasin, Chou, Stinson, & Dawson, 2004; Petry, Stinson, & Grant, 2005).

Etiology

The etiology of AUDs has been proposed to be complex, involving genetic, biological, psychosocial, and environmental influences. The literature on AUD etiology has placed substantial emphasis on genetic influences. Relatives of individuals with AUDs are more likely to have AUDs themselves. Studies of dizygotic twins and adopted individuals have suggested that much of this influence is genetic. However, it is unknown what exactly is being inherited. It is possible that the child inherits a biological vulnerability. For example, some research has suggested that children of parents with AUD inherit a susceptibility in which they are more responsive to the more rewarding effects of alcohol. It has also been suggested that cognitive deficits are more likely to be present in children of parents with AUD, which may be placing them at higher risk for later development of AUDs. Other hypotheses surrounding genetic transmission suggest that the child inherits a temperament that places them at increased risk. One hypothesis is that these individuals have an increased tendency to approach more high-risk environments than individuals without this genetic background. This hypothesis is supported by much research that has suggested that a variety of "externalizing" behavior problems in both childhood and adulthood, such as aggression, conduct disorder, and antisocial personality disorder, tend to be associated with later development of problematic alcohol use (Hesselbrock, Hesselbrock, & Epstein, 1999; Polcin, 1997).

There are also psychosocial models of the development of AUDs. Most of these models propose that AUDs are developed through a process of conditioning. In such an instance, the individual learns that alcohol can be an effective reward, through experiencing alcohol's initial arousal and euphoria; or that it can function as a negative reinforcer by removing negative affect. Other theories build on this conditioning model. Social learning and cognitive-behavioral formulations typically add that social influences and alcohol expectancies have a powerful influence on shaping behavior. Many researchers have pointed to interactions with family members as a crucial mechanism that may contribute to the development of later AUDs; many theorists have suggested that AUDs are a "family disease" in which family behavior patterns contribute to the development of the disorder (Hesselbrock et al., 1999).

It also is likely that there are cultural and socioeconomic factors that contribute to the development of AUDs. For example, certain social environments, such as areas of high crime and poverty, tend to be correlated with high rates of development of substance use disorders (Hesselbrock et al., 1999). However, it is unknown to what degree these factors are contributing to the disorder, rather than being a consequence of high rates of the disorder or being due to other variables.

Contextual Information

AUDs occur within the context of complex interpersonal and intrapersonal relationships. Not only do individuals' alcohol problems interact with other aspects of their personal lives, the drinking affects the lives of those close to them. Relationship distress nearly always accompanies AUDs, and peer or family encouragement or demand is a common reason for treatment-seeking (e.g., Duckert, 1987). Romantic partners of alcoholics tend to have poorer communication and problem-solving skills, express more negativity (e.g., unhappiness, anger, guilt) and have lower levels of marital satisfaction compared to partners of nonalcoholics (for review, see Marshal, 2003). In addition, incidents of domestic violence have been linked to alcohol use (Cunradi, Caetano, Clark, & Schafer, 1999; Leonard & Roberts, 1998b; Quigley & Leonard, 1999). Research has clearly established that the drinking habits of spouses affect each other and that new marriages are often accompanied by the formation of "drinking partnerships," whereby partners' drinking habits become more similar and they spend less time drinking without each other. During this time, newlyweds typically decrease the time they spend drinking and limit their extramarital drinking buddies (Demers, Bisson, & Palluy, 1999; Leonard & Eiden, 1999; Leonard & Mudar, 2003; Leonard & Rothbard, 1999; Roberts & Leonard, 1997, 1998).

It is important to note that the relationship between relationship distress and alcohol use is reciprocal. Research has shown that women, in particular, report that reasons for drinking frequently are related to relationship issues (e.g., Lammers, Schippers, & van der Staak, 1995). Clinically, this relationship is important because drinkers often report that they drink in response to partner stress, whereas partners report that they experience stress because of the drinker's drinking. This is the classic "I drink because she nags—I nag because he drinks" argument. When assessing the role of alcohol in a client's life, it is critical that clinicians assess the interpersonal and social consequences of drinking and abstinence. In addition, the context of drinking episodes (e.g., alone/with others, at home/out of home) and the contributions of social network drinking and support for abstinence are important domains of assessment. In fact, lack of support for abstinence and social network drinking have been linked to poorer treatment outcomes (e.g., Longabaugh, Wirtz, Zweben, & Stout, 1998; Mohr et al., 2001).

PURPOSES OF ASSESSMENT

This chapter focuses on three major functions of assessment: assessment for diagnosis, case conceptualization and treatment planning, and treatment monitoring and treatment evaluation. These are discussed in detail below. Alcohol-related assessments may serve other important functions beyond the scope of this book. First, heavy drinking and alcohol use disorders play an important role in the criminal justice system, with individuals using an AUD as either a defense during a trial or as a mitigating circumstance in sentencing hearings. Reliable and valid assessments provide important information about an individual's drinking, blood alcohol level at the time of a crime, and presence of an AUD. After conviction for driving while intoxicated (DWI), standardized assessments are used to determine whether a convicted DWI offender requires treatment for an AUD. Second, a mandated assessment of alcohol use and AUDs often is required in custody hearings related to divorce proceedings. Third, assessment of drinking may play an important role in medical settings in which determinations about the course of treatment may be affected by the nature of the patient's drinking. Thus, the drinking of patients in need of liver transplants will be assessed; physical trauma patients may be assessed to determine the role of drinking in the original accident; and the accurate assessment of a patient's drinking is important to planning for anesthesia and to predict the possibility of alcohol withdrawal when a patient is hospitalized. The instruments described in this chapter represent the most reliable and valid approaches to the identification and assessment of heavy drinking and AUDs, and can be used appropriately for these other purposes, as well as for the three major purposes that are the focus of this chapter.

With these purposes in mind, we followed a systematic methodology to identify domains for assessment and instruments within those domains. We began by brainstorming areas for assessment on the basis of our own knowledge of the clinical and clinical research literature. We then presented our initial list to a larger group of clinicians and clinical researchers at the Rutgers University Center of Alcohol Studies for additional input and comment. We also reviewed three major sources of information about alcohol-related assessment: (1) a major NIAAA publication on the assessment of alcohol problems (Allen & Wilson, 2003); (2) two major websites that provide lists of and links to major assessment instruments—those at the Center on Alcoholism, Substance Abuse and Addiction (CASAA) at the University of New Mexico (http://casaa.unm.edu/) and at the University of Washington Alcohol and Drug Abuse Institute (http://depts.washington.edu/adai/); and (3) major review chapters and books on assessment of alcohol use and AUDs. Following the development of a comprehensive list of domains and instruments to measure each domain, we conducted searches of PsycInfo and Medline using the name of each instrument and several modifying search terms, including "psychometrics," "reliability," "validity," and "internal consistency." Studies were limited to published English language studies on English-speaking populations. Unpublished dissertations were not included. Ratings are based on the data culled from the references identified through this search process, and, when possible, review of the administration and scoring manual for the instrument.

Settings for Assessment

Assessment can occur in a wide range of settings. Because individuals who drink heavily may be unaware of the extent or severity of their drinking or may be reluctant to reveal their drinking as a problem, screening to identify persons with an at-risk drinking pattern or an AUD occurs in settings that do not provide specialty treatment for AUDs, such as hospitals, emergency rooms, physician offices, mental health clinics, and private therapists' offices. Assessment also may occur in specialty treatment settings that provide various levels of care for the treatment for persons with AUDs, as well as in settings providing only one level of care, such as a detoxification center, intensive outpatient program, or outpatient clinic. The purposes and focus of assessment in each of these settings may differ.

Treatment Models and Assessment

Three major psychological models of treatment have strong evidence to support the effectiveness of the treatment—Cognitive-Behavioral Treatments (CBT), Motivational Enhancement Therapies (MET), and Twelve-Step Facilitation Treatment (TSF; McCrady & Nathan, 2005). Each is based on a different set of assumptions about the etiology and maintenance of AUDs, and each posits different mechanisms of change. Despite these rather disparate models, certain aspects of assessment are appropriate to any model of treatment. These include screening for case identification; assessment for diagnosis; medical and health screening; assessment of the need for detoxification and determination of level of care; assessment of quantity and frequency of drinking, drinking and treatment history, and adverse consequences of use; and assessment to monitor progress in treatment and treatment outcome. Each of these areas of assessment is reviewed in detail. Other aspects of assessment are specific to different treatment models, such as assessment of motivation; high-risk situations for drinking and coping skills to deal with these high-risk situations; cognitive variables such disease model beliefs, expectancies about the effects of alcohol on the individual, self-efficacy, and craving; and the functioning of the social network. We have focused largely on the assessment domains necessary to develop a CBT plan, and do not provide extensive coverage of more nuanced aspects of assessment for treatment planning for other approaches. Generally, however, CBT has a heavier emphasis on initial assessment for case conceptualization and more detailed monitoring of response to treatment than other treatment models, so our focus on CBT-related assessment provides the reader with information about most of the major measures and domains with reasonable empirical support.

Domains of Assessment and Roles for Assessment in Treatment

Screening for heavy drinking and AUDs are viewed as a necessary component of assessment for any health or mental health treatment setting. The prevalence of AUDs in medical and mental health settings ranges from 20% (in community hospitals) to greater than 60% of patients (in U.S. Veterans Administration facilities; e.g., Niles & McCrady, 1991). If an individual is identified with a possible AUD, further assessment to diagnose the disorder is appropriate, and is necessary for documentation of treatment and authorization of payment for treatment for individuals presenting for AUD treatment in a specialty setting. Substantial evidence now suggests that the selection of an appropriate level of intensity of treatment is an important predictor of treatment outcome (Magura et al., 2003; Rychtarik, et al., 2000), and individuals who are undertreated relative to treatment needs and individuals given more intensive treatment than is warranted by the severity of their problems both have poorer outcomes than individuals whose level of care matches the treatment setting in which they receive services. Coincident with the level of care determination should be an assessment of complicating medical and psychological conditions, which will contribute to the level of care determination, and an assessment of the specific need for medically supervised detoxification.

Once a client is placed in an appropriate level of care and, if necessary, stabilized in terms of acute medical and/or psychologically complicating conditions, the clinician can then begin the process of assessment for treatment planning. This phase of assessment also has therapeutic benefits, as the client is engaged in a comprehensive review of his/her drinking and negative consequences of the drinking, as well as his/her overall life functioning. The assessment process itself provides inherent feedback to the client, and accumulating evidence suggests that clients react to assessment by changing their drinking before any formal treatment interventions (e.g., Epstein et al., 2005). Clinicians also may use the results of the initial assessment to provide systematic feedback to the client about his/her drinking relative to national norms, the blood alcohol levels the client is achieving when drinking and risks associated with those blood alcohol levels, and the unique problems that have occurred as a result of the client's drinking. This kind of feedback has demonstrable effects on motivation and subsequent drinking (Baer, Kivlahan, Blume, McKnight, & Marlatt, 2001; Miller, Sovereign, & Krege, 1988) and is particularly important for clients who have mixed motivation for change.

Assessment helps the clinician in developing a plan to guide the balance of treatment. Consistent evidence suggests poorer outcomes for clients with low self-efficacy for change and very strong expectancies about the positive effects of alcohol (e.g., Bates, Pawlak, Tonigan, & Buckman, 2006; Brown, 1985),

so assessment of client beliefs in these domains is particularly important. CBT models also focus on situations that are perceived as high risk for drinking, and help clients develop coping skills to cope with these situations. Other treatment models also seem to be effective in helping clients develop such coping skills (Morgenstern & Longabaugh, 2000), so the identification of high-risk situations and an assessment of the client's ability to cope with these situations may guide the clinician in determining the focus of coping skills training.

Strong evidence also supports the importance of the social network in the change process (reviewed in McCrady, 2004). The presence of others who support client efforts at abstinence and who provide general social support to the client are predictive of positive outcomes. Similarly, the presence of a social network that is strongly supportive of the client's continued drinking is a negative prognostic indicator (Longabaugh et al., 1998), so a careful assessment of sources of support as well as individuals who may be invested in the client's continued drinking also will help the clinician to plan a maximally effective course of treatment.

ASSESSMENT FOR CASE IDENTIFICATION AND DIAGNOSIS

Case Identification

Heavy drinking places individuals at-risk for physical, psychological, and social problems. Heavy drinking also may interfere with treatments for other psychological problems such as anxiety and mood disorders because of the impact of alcohol on affect, and the use of alcohol as a maladaptive coping strategy to deal with anxiety or depression. Because of the negative social stigma associated with heavy drinking and AUDs (e.g., Shober & Annis, 1996), memory problems associated with chronic heavy drinking (e.g., Parsons, 1998), and difficulties in recognizing that drinking has become problematic, it is incumbent on health and mental health professionals to take active steps to identify clients and patients whose drinking places them at risk or whose pattern and consequences of drinking constitutes an AUD.

Screening tests generally are evaluated by somewhat different criteria than tests of psychological characteristics. The *sensitivity* of a test refers to the ability of a screening test to correctly identify individuals with the targeted problem. The *specificity* refers to the ability of a screening test to correctly identify individuals without the targeted problem. The *positive predictive value* (PPV) refers to the probability that an individual who screens positive actually has the targeted problem. The *negative predictive value* refers to the probability that an individual who screens negative does not have the targeted problem. Cutoffs for screening tests are selected to maximize these four variables. Decisions about cutoffs are based on the primary purpose of the screening test, and the consequences for falsely identifying versus missing positive cases. The purpose of screening generally is to identify individuals for further evaluation; high sensitivity is a cardinal characteristic of good screening measures. In our evaluation of screening tests, we recommend those that generally have sensitivity and specificity of at least 70%.

A second important dimension to consider in evaluating screening measures is the ease of administration. If all medical patients or patients presenting to a community mental health clinic are to be screening for heavy drinking or AUDs, the time and cost of administering the test is important. Our recommendations favor tests that are brief, easily administered with minimal training, and easy to incorporate into other evaluation procedures.

Table 16.1 summarizes screening and diagnostic measures. There are three major approaches to screening and case identification: laboratory tests, self-report questionnaires, and brief screening interviews. Laboratory tests are particularly valuable in medical settings if the tests are administered routinely and are readily available for a medical professional to review. A large range of laboratory measures has been examined for their statistical association with heavy drinking or AUD. Gamma Glutamyl Transpeptidase (GGT; e.g., Bell, Tallaksen, Try, & Haug, 1994) is included in most standard comprehensive blood testing profiles and is elevated by recent heavy drinking, but also is elevated by a range of medical conditions. It is sensitive to change with abstinence, and has been studied across a wide range of populations. Sensitivity of GGT is better for detecting AUDs than heavy drinking. Mean Corpuscular Volume (MCV; e.g., Wetterling, Kanitz, Rumpf, Hapke, & Fisher, 1998) is a measure of the size of red blood vessels. Sensitivity of MCV is not as high as that of GGT, but MCV has a particularly high PPV—MCV is elevated primarily in patients with anemias and bleeding disorders, so if a patient does not have one of these conditions, the probability of an AUD is very high. Carbohydrate Deficient Transferrin (CDT; e.g., Reynaud et al., 1998) is a newer blood test that has good sensitivity, excellent specificity, is very sensitive to changes in drinking, and has been studied across a wide range of populations. Cutoffs for a positive CDT are higher for women than men, and the sensitivity is somewhat lower for women even with the higher cutoff value for a positive test. Although we are recommending CDT as a screening measure, it is not part of routine blood profiles, and therefore is costly and more complex to administer and less useful as a routine screening tool in medical settings. Looking at the joint performance of GGT and CDT together provides greater sensitivity and specificity than any individual lab test (Mundle, Munkes, Ackermann, & Mann, 2000). Other laboratory tests, such as Serum Glutamic Oxaloacetic Transaminase/Aspartate Amineotransferase (SGOT/AST) and Serum Glutamic Pyruvic Transaminase/Alanine Aminotransferase (SGPT/ALT) have been studied extensively as potential screening measures, but we judged their clinical utility to be insufficient to recommend them for standard use.

Among self-report screening measures, the Alcohol Use Disorders Identification Test (AUDIT; Babor, Biddle-Higgins, Saunders, & Monteiro, 2001) is the most efficient and psychometrically adequate measure, includes 10 items and takes about 2 minutes to administer, but the Michigan Alcoholism Screening Test (MAST; Selzer, 1971; 25 items, 8 minutes) and the Self-Administered Alcoholism Screening Test (SAAST; 35 items, 5 minutes; Swenson & Morse, 1975) also have good psychometric properties, and good sensitivity and specificity. All three have been used across a range of clinical populations. Among these, the AUDIT is the most effective in identifying heavy drinkers at risk for problems; the other two are effective primarily in identifying individuals with AUDs.

Three interviews are particularly effective and have been used across a range of populations, and require minimal training to administer. The CAGE (Ewing, 1984) has four questions related to the desire to *c*ut down on drinking, feeling *a*nnoyed by others' comments related to drinking, feeling *g*uilty about drinking, or drinking at the start of the day (*eye-opener*), and takes less than a minute to administer. The originally recommended cutoff for the CAGE was two positive responses, but most sensitivity and

TABLE 16.1 Ratings of Instruments Used for Case Identification and Diagnosis

Instrument	Norms	Internal Consistency	Inter-Rater Reliability	Test–Retest Reliability	Content Validity	Construct Validity	Validity Generalization	Clinical Utility	Highly Recommended
Screening and Case Identification Laboratory Tests									
GGT	E	NA	NA	NA	NA	G	E	A	✓
MCV	E	NA	NA	NA	NA	A	G	G	✓
CDT	E	NA	NA	NA	NA	G	E	G	✓
Self-Reports/Screening Interviews									
AUDIT	E	G	U	A	A	G	E	G	✓
MAST	E	G	U	A	A	G	E	A	✓
SAAST	E	E	U	A	A	G	E	A	✓
CAGE	E	G	G	U	A	A	E	G	✓
TWEAK	G	U	U	U	A	A	G	A	✓
FAST	A	U	U	U	A	A	L	A	✓
RAPS	G	U	U	U	A	A	G	A	✓
CRAFFT	A	G	U	U	A	A	A	A	✓
AAS	G	L	U	A	A	A	A	A	
DUSI	G	G	G	A	A	A	G	A	
MacAndrew scale	A	L	U	A	L	A	E	A	
Assessment for Diagnosis									
SCID	E	NA	E	E	A	E	E	E	✓
CIDI-SAM	G	NA	U	E	A	G	G	E	✓
ADS	E	E	NA	E	A	E	E	G	✓
LDQ	E	E	NA	U	E	E	U	G	✓
DIS	E	NA	E	G	A	L	U	G	
DUSI	A	A	NA	U	U	A	L	G	
SSAGA	A	U	U	U	A	U	U	G	
Diagnosis with Age-Limited Populations									
SCID—adapted for adolescents	G	U	E	U	A	A	U	E	✓
T-ASI	U	L	G	A	A	G	U	A	

Note: GGT = Gamma Glutamyl Transpeptidase; MCV = Mean Corpuscular Volume; CDT = Carbohydrate-Deficient Transferrin; AUDIT = Alcohol Use Disorders Identification Test; MAST = Michigan Alcoholism Screening Test; SAAST = Self-Administered Alcoholism Screening Test; AAS = Addiction Acknowledgment Scale; RAPS = Rapid Alcohol Problems Screen; DUSI = Drug Use Screening Inventory. Note that CAGE, TWEAK, FAST, and CRAFFT are not acronyms—the letters cue the questions that compose the screening interviews; Diagnosis: SCID = Structured Clinical Interview for DSM-IV; CIDI-SAM = Composite International Diagnostic Interview-Substance Abuse Module; ADS = Alcohol Dependence Scale; LDQ = Leeds Dependence Questionnaire; DIS = Diagnostic Interview Schedule; DUSI = Drug Use Screening Inventory; SSAGA = Semistructured Assessment for the Genetics of Alcoholism; T-ASI = Teen Addiction Severity Index. L = Less Than Adequate; A = Adequate; G = Good; E = Excellent; U = Unavailable; NA = Not Applicable.

specificity studies suggest that that one positive reply is a better cut score to use. The TWEAK (Russell, 1994) is the CAGE with an additional question about increased tolerance, and takes less than 2 minutes to administer. Some data suggest that the TWEAK may be a better screening interview than the CAGE for women. The FAST (Hodgson, Alwyn, John, Thom, & Smith, 2002) is the shortest interview with good psychometric properties. It is a two-step screening procedure, with 60% of patients correctly screened out by the first question, thus making it particularly effective for situations with a high volume of patients or very limited clinical resources. Finally, the Rapid Alcohol Problems Screen (RAPS; Cherpitel, 2000) is a four-item measure that has extensive validation data across multiple ethnic and racial groups, but has been tested largely in emergency room settings, so its value in mental health settings is less clear. Other screening measures listed in Table 16.1 have adequate psychometric properties, but are lengthier (e.g., the Drug Use Screening Inventory [DUSI]), or have less generalizability across settings and populations.

Diagnosis

There are two disorders that constitute AUDs: alcohol abuse and alcohol dependence. According to the Diagnostic and Statistical Manual of Mental Disorders (DSM-IV; American Psychiatric Association, 1994), both alcohol abuse and dependence are defined as maladaptive patterns of alcohol use leading to clinically significant impairment or distress. To receive a diagnosis of alcohol abuse, an individual must have never been diagnosed with alcohol dependence and in the previous 12 months the individual's alcohol use must have interfered with their responsibilities, be considered hazardous, caused recurrent legal problems, or the individual must have continued drinking despite negative consequences related to their drinking. To receive a diagnosis of alcohol dependence, an individual must exhibit three of the following seven symptoms in a 12-month period: tolerance to the effects of alcohol; withdrawal symptoms or drinking to prevent withdrawal; desire or effort to cut down; drinking larger amounts or over longer periods of time than desired; reduction in activities due to drinking; significant time spent in drinking-related activities; and continued drinking despite negative consequences. An alcohol dependence diagnosis must be designated as with or without physiological

dependence (presence of either tolerance or withdrawal). In addition, alcohol dependence has a set of remission qualifiers used for clients who have ever in their lifetime had a diagnosis of alcohol dependence (APA, 1994).

Diagnosis of AUDs according to established criteria is a fundamental part of alcohol treatment and research. In clinical settings, a diagnosis is not only necessary to obtain insurance reimbursement, but careful diagnosis of AUDs can provide a wealth of clinically useful material. Careful diagnosis also provides a common language for clinicians to discuss treatment planning and outcome. For example, individuals with alcohol abuse, as opposed to alcohol dependence, may not require as intense treatment. Similarly, individuals diagnosed with alcohol dependence with physiological dependence would need to be assessed on need for detoxification whereas those without physiological dependence would not need such an assessment. Though many clinicians assess diagnostic criteria based on information gathered during initial sessions, more formal and structured assessment can improve the validity of diagnoses and provide information useful to treatment planning.

Table 16.1 summarizes the psychometric properties of instruments used for diagnosis of AUDs. The most highly recommended diagnostic interviews are the Structured Clinical Interview for DSM-IV (SCID; First, Spitzer, Gibbon, & Williams, 1996, 2002) and the Composite International Diagnostic Interview-Substance Abuse Module (CIDI-SAM; Cottler, 2000). The SCID comes in clinical and research versions and assesses DSM-IV criteria for alcohol abuse and dependence. The clinical version uses an administration booklet and score sheet and is not as comprehensive as the research version. The research version includes the questions and scoring on the same page and includes all diagnostic criteria, subtypes and specifiers, whereas the clinical version is streamlined and includes only subtypes and specifiers necessary for DSM diagnosis. In terms of AUDs, the clinical version does not yield remission specifiers or the subtypes of with/without physiological dependence. The SCID takes 60 to 90 minutes to administer, is a reliable and valid measure of AUD, and has been validated in inpatient, outpatient, nontreatment, and correctional populations. The SCID also has been modified to assess adolescent substance abuse and is reliable and valid in that population (Martin, Kaczynski, Maisto, Bukstein, & Moss, 1995). The

CIDI-SAM interviewer and computer administered versions assess DSM and ICD diagnostic criteria for tobacco, alcohol, drugs, and caffeine. It yields a diagnosis, age of onset and recency of symptoms, quantity and frequency of heaviest use in the past year, and physical/social/psychological consequences of use. It also assesses treatment seeking and level of impairment. The CIDI-SAM takes 30 to 45 minutes to administer, is reliable and valid for the purpose of diagnosing AUDs and has been used in both adult and adolescent samples.

The most highly recommended self-report measures for diagnosis are the Alcohol Dependence Scale (ADS; Skinner & Allen, 1982; Skinner & Horn, 1984) and the Leeds Dependence Questionnaire (LDQ; Raistrick, Bradshaw, Tober, Weiner, Allison, & Healey, 1994). The 25-item ADS assesses the alcohol dependence syndrome by measuring tolerance, withdrawal, impaired control over drinking, awareness of compulsion to drink, and salience of drink-seeking behavior in the previous year. The ADS takes about 5 minutes for the client to complete and yields a quantitative measure of severity of alcohol dependence. It has excellent reliability and validity and has been evaluated in inpatient, outpatient, and correctional and medical samples. The ADS is a useful tool for assessing severity of alcohol dependence, however recent research suggests that it may detect physiological withdrawal less reliably(Saxon, Kivlahan, Doyle, & Donovan, 2007). The 10-item LDQ assesses psychological aspects of tolerance and withdrawal and changes in such dependence. The LDQ takes less than 5 minutes for the client to complete and can be used with abstinent clients to assess changes in the psychological aspects of alcohol and drug dependence. It has excellent reliability and validity and has been evaluated in inpatient, outpatient, college, and nontreatment seeking samples. It is important to note that, although the ADS and LDQ yield quantitative measures of alcohol dependence, scores do not generate a DSM-IV diagnosis.

Overall Evaluation

In summary, there is a good set of instruments to identify and diagnose AUDs. For the purpose of screening, the most highly recommended laboratory tests are GGTP, MCV, and CDT. The most highly recommended self-report measures are the AUDIT, MAST, SAAST, CAGE, TWEAK, FAST, and RAPS.

For the purpose of diagnosis, the most highly recommended instruments are the SCID, CIDI-SAM, ADS, and LDQ. For diagnosis, the benefits of interviews are that they allow clinicians to use their judgment about the severity of symptoms and probe for additional information when ambiguity exists. The primary weaknesses are that diagnostic interviews are time-consuming and require specialized training for proper administration. The benefits of self-reports questionnaires are that they require minimal clinician involvement and often have published representative norms by which to interpret the scores. The primary weaknesses are that clients may misinterpret items and clients may over- or under-endorse, thereby decreasing the validity of their scores. It is suggested that a clinician use a diagnostic interview, either the SCID or the CIDI-SAM, to make a reliable diagnosis and use either the ADS or the LDQ self-report measures to track changes in the severity of dependence over time.

ASSESSMENT FOR CASE CONCEPTUALIZATION AND TREATMENT PLANNING

Table 16.2 summarizes all measures for case conceptualization and treatment planning.

Need for Detoxification

Alcohol withdrawal can be a simple but unpleasant experience for a person with physiological dependence on alcohol; it also can be a dangerous or life-threatening condition that must be managed with appropriate medical care. The clinician conducting an initial interview with a potential client should assess the potential for complicated alcohol withdrawal as part of determining the initial course of treatment. Clinicians typically make determinations of withdrawal potential through a clinical interview, determining the pattern of drinking (daily drinking placing the person at the highest risk for drinking), volume of drinking (achieving blood alcohol levels above 150 mg% being risky), and past history of attempts to stop drinking. Studies of the predictive validity of such clinician judgments are lacking. We reviewed three potential measures to assess withdrawal potential. The two self-report measures are good measures of the alcohol dependence syndrome (Edwards & Gross, 1976), but neither has specific

TABLE 16.2 Ratings of Instruments Used for Case Conceptualization and Treatment Planning

Instrument	Norms	Internal Consistency	Inter-Rater Reliability	Test–Retest Reliability	Content Validity	Construct Validity	Validity Generalization	Clinical Utility	Highly Recommended
Need for Detoxification									
CIWA-AR	NA	NA	E	NA	A	G	A	A	✓
Medical/Health Screening									
LISRES	G	NA	NA	G	G	U	G	A	✓
Form 90	A	NA	A	A	L	U	A	A	✓
ASI	A	G	A	L	A	A	G	A	
GAIN	A	A	A	A	A	A	A	A	
SF-12	E	A	NA	A	A	G	G	A	
SF-36	E	G	NA	A	G	E	E	A	
Level of Care Determination									
ASAM PPC	NA	NA	G	NA	A	G	A	A	
RAATE	A	A	A	A	A	A	A	A	✓
Drinking Patterns									
TLFB	E	NA	NA	A	A	E	E	E	✓
Form-90	E	NA	G	E	G	E	U	E	✓
QFI	E	NA	NA	A	A	E	E	E	✓
DSML	U	NA	NA	NA	A	E	E	E	✓
AUI	E	G	NA	A	U	E	E	E	
Consequences of Drinking									
SIP	G	A	NA	A	G	G	G	A	✓
DrInC	A	A	NA	G	G	A	G	A	✓
CAPS-r	G	G	U	U	G	G	A	A	
DPI	G	G	NA	A	A	G	A	A	
RAPI	A	A	NA	G	A	A	G	A	✓
Family History									
FTQ	U	NA	E	E	A	U	G	A	✓
Motivation									
URICA	E	G	NA	U	U	G	E	A	
RTCQ-CV/TV	A	G	L	A	E	A	L	A	
SOCQ	A	G	NA	U	G	U	L	A	
SOCRATES	E	E	NA	E	E	A	E	A	✓
CMRS	A	G	NA	U	E	A	A	A	

Measure									
Treatment History									
Form-90	E	NA	E	G	E	U	NA	E	
TLFB	U	NA	U	U	A	U	NA	E	✓
Craving									
AUQ	G	E	A	G	G	A	NA	A	✓
PACS	A	G	U	A	G	A	NA	A	✓
OCDS	A	A	A	A	G	A	NA	A	✓
A-OCDS	G	G	U	G	G	A	NA	A	
ACQ-NOW	A	G	U	A	A	A	NA	A	
Y-BOCS-hd	G	A	U	A	A	G	NA	A	
High-Risk Situations									
IDS	G	E	G	G	G	G	NA	A	✓
IDS-42	G	G	U	G	G	G	NA	A	✓
DCS	A	G	U	G	A	A	NA	A	
DPQ	A	A	U	G	G	A	NA	A	
RFDQ	A	U	U	A	G	G	NA	A	
Cognitive, Affective, and Behavioral Dimensions									
CEOA	E	G	G	A	A	A	NA	A	✓
AEQ	E	G	L	G	G	E	NA	A	
AEQ-A	E	A	G	A	G	G	NA	A	
DEQ	A	G	U	U	G	L	NA	A	
DRSEQ	E	E	U	E	G	E	NA	A	✓
SCQ	E	E	U	U	A	E	NA	A	✓
ASPRT	G	A	U	G	A	A	E	A	✓
CBI	A	A	U	A	A	L	NA	A	✓
ARCQ	A	A	U	A	A	L	NA	A	

(continued)

TABLE 16.2 (Continued)

Instrument	Norms	Internal Consistency	Inter-Rater Reliability	Test–Retest Reliability	Content Validity	Construct Validity	Validity Generalization	Clinical Utility	Highly Recommended
AACRI	A	G	NA	U	L	A	A	A	
TCQ	A	G	NA	U	A	G	A	A	
Social Network									
IPA	A	NA	U	A	A	A	G	G	✓

Note: CIWA-AR = Clinical Institute Withdrawal Assessment for Alcohol; LISRES = Life Stressors and Social Resources Inventory; ASI = Addiction Severity Index; GAIN = Global Appraisal of Individual Needs; SF-12 and SF-36 = Short-Form Health Survey Questionnaire; ASAM PPC = American Society of Addiction Medicine – Patient Placement Criteria; RAATE = Recovery Attitude and Treatment Evaluator; TLFB = Timeline Followback; QFI = Quantity-Frequency Index; DSML = Daily Self-Monitoring Logs; AUI = Alcohol Use Inventory; SIP = Short Inventory of Problems; DrInC = Drinker Inventory of Consequences; CAPS-r = College Alcohol Problems Scale-Revised; DPI = Drinking Problems Index; RAPI = Rutgers Alcohol Problems Index; FTQ = Family Tree Questionnaire; URICA = University of Rhode Island Change Assessment; RTCQ-CV/TV = Readiness to Change Questionnaire-Clinician Version/Treatment Version; SOCQ = Stages of Change Questionnaire; SOCRATES = Stages of Change Readiness and Treatment Eagerness Scale; CMRS = Circumstances, Motivation, Readiness, and Suitability Scale; AUQ = Alcohol Urge Questionnaire; PACS = Penn Alcohol Craving Scale; OCDS = Obsessive–Compulsive Drinking Scale; A-OCDS = Adolescent Obsessive–Compulsive Drinking Scale; ACQ-NOW = Alcohol Craving Questionnaire; Y-BOCS-hd = Yale-Brown Obsessive Compulsive Scale for Heavy Drinking; IDS and IDS-42 = Inventory of Drinking Situations; DCS = Drinking Context Scale; DPQ = Drinking Patterns Questionnaire; RFDQ = Reasons for Drinking Questionnaire; CEOA = Comprehensive Effects of Alcohol Scale; AEQ = Alcohol Expectancies Questionnaire; AEQ-A = Alcohol Expectancies Questionnaire-Adolescent; DEQ = Drinking Expectancies Questionnaire; DRSEQ = Drinking Refusal Self-Efficacy Questionnaire; SCQ = Situational Confidence Questionnaire; ASPRT = Alcohol-Specific Role-Play Test; CBI = Coping Behaviours Inventory; ARCQ = Adolescent Relapse Coping Questionnaire; AACRI = Alcohol Abuse Coping Response Inventory; TCQ = Temptation Coping Questionnaire; IPA = Important People and Activities Interview; L = Less Than Adequate; A = Adequate; G = Good; E = Excellent; U = Unavailable; NA = Not Applicable.

data to suggest its value in predicting alcohol withdrawal syndrome. The Clinical Institute Withdrawal Assessment for Alcohol (CIWA-AR; Sullivan, Sykora, Schneiderman, Naranjo, & Sellers, 1989) is an observational checklist of current withdrawal symptoms and has good psychometric properties, including strong concurrent and predictive validity. However, it has not been tested as a measure of withdrawal potential in patients who are not currently experiencing alcohol withdrawal. Thus, there is no well-validated measure to predict alcohol withdrawal potential. Studies are lacking on the predictive validity of the physiological dependence items on structured diagnostic instruments, but would provide a logical avenue for future research.

Medical/Health Screening

In addition to determining need for detoxification, comprehensive assessment for case conceptualization and treatment planning should include screening for medical and/or physical health problems. AUDs are highly comorbid with a variety of medical problems that, if present, may influence case formulation and change treatment priorities, such as: hypertension, cardiovascular disease, pancreatitis, liver cirrhosis, and certain cancers (Corrao, Bagnardi, Zambon, & La Vecchia, 2004). The presence of other less life-threatening health problems, such as chronic pain, back pain, arthritis, and poor overall health-related quality of life, may contribute to the maintenance of AUDs and should be screened for as well. A final consideration in this type of screening is medication use; consideration of how a client's particular constellation of medications may interact with both pharmacological and nonpharmacological treatment interventionsis also necessary.

The Physical Health Status (PHS) subscale of the Life Stressors and Social Resources Inventory (LISRES; Moos & Moos, 1988) is recommended for the assessment of medical and physical health problems among individuals with AUD. Part of a larger self-report measure of global life functioning, the PHS subscale consists of 27 items assessing the past-year presence and onset of 12 major medical problems and 12 common physical health problems, as well as the occurrence of hospitalization. Two items present open-ended questions and allow for the identification of medical and health problems not included within the measure. Although the LISRES has been validated using AUD samples and is well suited to quickly screen for physical health problems in this population, it does not include an assessment of current medication use. This gap may be filled by an informal query by the clinician or by using an instrument that includes medication assessment, such as the Form 90 (Tonigan, Miller, & Brown, 1997). Other measures appropriate for medical/health screening among individuals with AUDs include the Medical Subscale of the Addiction Severity Index (ASI; McLellan, Luborsky, O'Brien, & Woody, 1980), Health Distress and Health Problem Indexes of the Global Appraisal of Individual Needs (GAIN; Dennis, 1998), SF-12 Health Survey (SF-12; Jenkinson et al., 1997), and SF-36 Health Survey (SF-36; Ware, Snow, & Kosinski, 1993).

Comorbid Psychopathology

In both community and treatment-seeking samples, substance use disorders in men and women are highly comorbid with mood disorders and personality disorders (Rosenthal & Westreich, 1999). Up to 59% of treatment-seeking substance abusers report current psychopathology (Bennett & McCrady, 1993) . In a sample of alcohol-dependent inpatients, 24% had additional Axis I disorders, 16% had Axis II disorders, and 17.2% had concurrent Axis I and Axis II disorders (Driessen et al., 1998). Women with AUD are more likely than men to have affective disorders and borderline personality disorder. On the other hand, men with AUDs are more likely to have antisocial personality disorders (Compton et al., 2000; Ross, Glaser, & Stiasny, 1998). Because comorbid psychopathology can influence treatment decisions, it is important to consider both Axis I and Axis II disorders when evaluating clients with AUDs. Though there are some standardized questionnaires that have considerable empirical support in general populations, the psychometric properties of most have not been investigated in alcoholic samples. This does not mean, however, that they are not reliable or valid for the alcoholic population, just that the research has not been conducted to verify their psychometric properties. Because of the lack of psychometric data on these instruments with alcohol-dependent samples, no ratings of these instruments are provided in Table 16.2.

The most highly recommended interviews are the SCID-I (for Axis I disorders) and the SCID-II (for Axis-II disorders). If complex comorbidity is suspected or sequencing of comorbid diagnosis is necessary, then the Semistructured Assessment for the Genetics of Alcoholism (SSAGA; Bucholz et al., 1994; Hesselbrock,

Easton, Bucholz, et al., 1999) should be considered because it was developed specifically to address comorbidity. The reliability and validity of the SCID-I and SCID-II have been established in numerous clinical trials, and there is no evidence that they are less reliable or valid in alcohol-dependent populations. Among questionnaires that have been validated in alcoholic samples are the Inventory to Diagnose Depression (IDD; Zimmerman & Coryell, 1987), the Symptom Checklist-90-R (SCL-90-R; Derogatis, 1977; Derogatis, Rickels, & Rock, 1976) and its short form the Brief Symptom Inventory (BSI; Derogatis & Melisaratos, 1983), the Beck Depression Inventory (BDI; Beck & Steer, 1996; Beck, Steer, & Brown, 1996), and the State-Trait Anxiety Inventory (STAI; Spielberger & Gorsuch, 1983). The 22-item IDD yields a severity of depression score and a DSM-IV diagnosis. It is a reliable and valid tool for screening for depression, but has been shown to be somewhat less reliable for the diagnosis of major depressive disorder than the SCID in drinking individuals (Hodgins, Dufour, & Armstrong, 2000). The 90-item SCL-90-R and 53-item BSI assess severity of recently experienced physical and psychological distress on nine dimensions. They can be useful tools to identify areas for further evaluation or targets of intervention, but it should be noted that the factor structure is unstable in clinical populations. The BDI has evidence of validity in alcoholic populations, and the BDI-II is commonly used in research trials of treatment for AUDs, so pre- and posttreatment norms are available in the literature. Questionnaires that have not been evaluated in alcoholic populations to date but have clinical utility for assessing Axis I psychopathology include the Beck Anxiety Inventory (Beck & Steer, 1990) and the Outcome Questionnaire-45 (Lambert et al., 1996).

Overall, there is a good set of interviews and questionnaires to evaluate comorbid psychopathology and psychological distress in alcohol-dependent individuals. Though many clinically useful measures have not been evaluated in alcoholic samples, there is no reason to suspect that their psychometric properties are less adequate in such samples. Interviews such as the SCID-I and II should be used when reliable diagnoses are needed, but self-reports are suggested to track changes in symptom severity over time.

Level of Care Determination

Treatment for persons with AUDs occurs in a range of settings such as medically supervised inpatient hospital settings, inpatient and intensive outpatient rehabilitation programs, outpatient therapy settings, and brief interventions provided in the context of other medical or psychological treatments at any level of care. Clients have poorer outcomes when provided with an insufficiently intense treatment, and also have poorer outcomes when they are provided with treatment that is too intense for the severity of their drinking problems (Rychtarik et al., 2000). Consequently, initial decisions about the appropriate level of care are important determinants of the outcome of treatment. The American Society of Addiction Medicine (ASAM, 1996) proposed a set of patient placement criteria (PPC) to determine level of care, suggesting that patients should be evaluated in six domains: need for supervised withdrawal; medical conditions that might require monitoring; comorbid psychiatric conditions; motivation for change and degree of treatment acceptance or resistance; relapse potential; and nature of the individual's social environment. The ASAM criteria map onto four major levels of care, ranging from medically managed inpatient treatment to outpatient care. The RAATE (Recovery Attitude and Treatment Evaluator; Mee-Lee, 1988) is a clinical interview designed to make level of care determinations based on the ASAM PPC. The RAATE includes 35 questions, and takes about 30 minutes to complete. Psychometric properties are adequate across all domains, and the RAATE is our recommended instrument for level of care determination. A group of investigators (e.g., Magura et al., 2003) has been developing and evaluating a computer-guided interview to make more precise level of care determinations, and initial testing has yielded promising results. However, the computer-guided interview is not yet available, requires significant training, and takes almost an hour to administer, and so is not yet a measure that is recommended for general clinical practice. If the computer-guided interview becomes available and if it can be administered efficiently and includes valid measures of all six ASAM domains of assessment, it has the potential in the future to be a useful assessment device that would cover six major areas addressed separately in assessment currently.

Treatment Preference

Another area of assessment that is potentially helpful in case formulation is an examination of the client's treatment preference. A complete assessment of treatment preference should examine several dimensions, including the client's preference for program orientation (e.g., CBT vs. a 12-step approach), preferences about the degree of family involvement, and preferences about level of care and treatment goals.

Unfortunately, there are no psychometrically validated measures that thoroughly examine the above treatment preference variables. It is likely that most discussions of treatment preference are conducted informally between the client and therapist, and that subsequent decisions on level of care are made by the therapist without a formal assessment of the client's preferences.

Consumption Patterns

Understanding a client's typical pattern of alcohol consumption is critical to treatment planning and evaluating the success of interventions. In clinical settings, understanding pretreatment drinking patterns can help clinicians identify high-risk situations and skill deficits to be targets of intervention. In addition, there are several useful quantitative variables that can be derived from data about consumption patterns: percent drinking days; percent days abstinent; mean drinks per drinking day; typical blood alcohol level; peak blood alcohol level; and percent low/moderate/heavy drinking days. These variables can provide useful feedbacks to clients on the potential consequences of their drinking patterns and can provide information about the success or failure of interventions. Some instruments provide necessary information to compute all of these variables whereas others permit the derivation of only some of them.

The most highly recommended interviews are the Timeline Followback Interview (TLFB; Sobell & Sobell, 1992, 1995) and the Form-90 (Tonigan, Miller, & Brown, 1997). Both methods provide information on daily drinking to calculate the above mentioned quantitative variables, but there are subtle differences in how the information is gathered. The TLFB was the first interview to incorporate calendars as memory aids to assess daily drinking and gathers standard drinks consumed for each day during the assessment period (from 30 days to 1 year). The Form-90 also uses calendars, but looks for common drinking patterns and isolates drinking episodes. This information is then extrapolated to provide an estimate of drinking for each day during the assessment period. An advantage to the Form-90 is that it also

assesses medical, social, and treatment variables. In addition, the Form-90 family of instruments includes versions for collateral informants, follow-up periods, and telephone administration. The primary limitations of these interviews are that they are time-consuming (depending on time frame and complexity of drinking pattern) and they require specialized training to be reliable.

The most highly recommended self-report questionnaires are Quantity-Frequency Indexes (QFI) and Daily Self-monitoring Logs (DSML). Various forms of QFI exist and the most reliable and valid forms are beverage specific in that they assess beer, wine, and liquor consumption rates separately (Russell et al., 1991). All forms assess first the frequency of use and then the quantity of typical consumption on days of use. DSML resemble daily diaries and can be used to collect a variety of treatment-relevant information including number of drinks, time consumed, context of drinking, presence and strength of urges, relationship satisfaction, stress levels, and so forth. These logs are extremely useful to track changes in drinking behaviors and identifying high-risk situations and skills deficits that can be targets for intervention.

It is important to note that QFI methods often yield underestimates of drinking when compared to TLFB or DSML, possibly due to an averaging heuristic used by clients when completing QFI. One promising new method to avoid this problem is the Daily Drinking Questionnaire-Revised (DDQ-R; Collins, Parks, & Marlatt, 1985; Kruse, Corbin, & Fromme, 2005). The DDQ-R resembles validated retrospective interviews (e.g., TLFB, Form 90) and attempts to disaggregate the quantity and frequency indices to yield more accurate estimates of drinking frequency and intensity. The DDQ-R first assesses frequency of alcohol consumption on each day of the week during the past 3 months, and then assesses typical consumption levels for days of the week when any drinking was reported.

Overall, there are excellent measures to assess patterns of alcohol consumption. When selecting an instrument to assess alcohol consumption patterns, one must weigh the relative importance of type of information, accuracy of information, and administration time. In research settings where type of information and accuracy are more important than time, interviews such as the TLFB or the Form-90 is the preferred instrument. However, in clinical practice when time may be more important than depth and accuracy, then quantity-frequency methods may be preferable. Daily self-monitoring logs should be used throughout treatment to track changes in drinking and urges to drink.

Consequences of Drinking

Although assessment of consumption provides important objective information that often is predictive of the severity of alcohol's functional impact, it should not serve as a proxy for assessing negative consequences of drinking. The same amount of alcohol may have a greater impact on one individual than on another, and a separate assessment of adverse alcohol-related consequences is therefore recommended. A discrepancy between a client's perceived negative consequences and his or her actual negative consequences often exists, and use of a standardized instrument can serve to highlight this discrepancy. In addition to informing case conceptualization, identifying negative consequences can help enhance and maintain motivation in treatment. When used in a decisional balance sheet or a similar clinician-guided discussion, negative consequences may be translated into the "cons" of continuing to drink and the "pros" of abstinence, underscoring reasons for change.

Among the assessment instruments currently available to identify adverse consequences, the Short Inventory of Problems (SIP; Miller, Tonigan, & Longabaugh, 1995) is recommended. The SIP provides a quick and easy, yet comprehensive assessment of consequences experienced as a result of alcohol abuse in a variety of domains, including physical, social, intrapersonal, impulse and interpersonal. A shortened version of the 50-item Drinker Inventory of Consequences (DrInC; Miller, Tonigan, & Longabaugh, 1995), the SIP contains 15 items and can be administered in less than 5 minutes. Sound psychometric properties, strong clinical utility, and ease of administration and scoring make the SIP a valuable tool in assessing consequences of drinking.

Family History of Alcoholism

Research has established that there is a genetic vulnerability to AUDs. The heritability (h^2) of AUDs is .57, and there is a seven-times-greater risk of alcohol dependence among first-degree relatives of individuals with AUD than in the general population (Goldman et al., 2005). Assessment of family history of alcoholism is,

therefore, an important component of assessment for clients who report any level of drinking. A simple way to do this is to simply ask the question, "Does or has anyone in your immediate or extended family had a drinking problem?" and then follow up with questions about the relationship to that person, severity of the problem, and treatment history. The clinician also may use the Family Tree Questionnaire (FTQ; Mann, Sobell, Sobell, & Sobell, 1985), a reliable and valid measure of family history of alcoholism. The FTQ takes about 5 minutes to complete and uses a family tree diagram to gather information on first- and second-degree relatives. It can be administered by an interviewer or self-administered by the client. It provides information about the presence and severity of alcohol problems in a client. Other measures of family history have not been empirically validated in alcoholic populations, and the FTQ is therefore the recommended instrument to assess this domain. Although there are not many options for the clinician, the FTQ is a reliable, valid, and user-friendly measure of family history of AUDs and can be modified to assess family history of drug use or other psychopathology.

Motivation for Change

Some of the motivation measures, particularly the University of Rhode Island Change Assessment (URICA; DiClemente & Hughes, 1990), Readiness to Change Questionnaire (RTCQ; Rollnick, Heather, Gold, & Hall, 1992) and Stages of Change Questionnaire (SOC; McConnaughy, Prochaska, & Velicer, 1983), are based on Prochaska and DiClemente's (1983) model of stages of change. The stages of change are typically conceptualized as precontemplation, contemplation, decision making, action, and maintenance. Some proponents of the stages of change conceptualization assert that knowledge of the client's motivational stage is necessary in order to match appropriate interventions to the client's stage of readiness (e.g., an alcohol-dependent client in a stage of contemplation will presumably be resistant to taking "action" steps such as reducing their access to alcohol). The other measures, including the Stages of Change Readiness and Treatment Eagerness Scale (SOCRATES; Miller & Tonigan, 1996) and the Circumstances, Motivation, Readiness, & Suitability Scales (CMRS; DeLeon, Melnick, Kressel & Jainchill, 1994) measure the client's recognition of the drinking problem, and motivation to change it.

Low motivation on these measures may suggest the need for additional motivational interventions.

Of the motivational measures, the SOCRATES is highly recommended. The SOCRATES examines three dimensions of motivation, namely, problem recognition, ambivalence, and whether the client has already taken steps to change drinking-related behaviors. This self-report measure has excellent psychometrics based on several large clinical samples. The SOCRATES does not require training for administration, is available at no cost, and typically takes only a few minutes to complete.

Drinking Goals

In addition to assessing the client's motivation to change his or her drinking, it is important to understand what type of change the client is interested in making. Despite the fact that many alcohol treatment programs are abstinence-based, many clients may not want to stop drinking altogether. Pursuing an abstinence-based program with these clients may alienate them or leave them without the appropriate skills to be able to moderate their drinking. In addition, although some clients may wish to become abstinent immediately, some are more successful when they can gradually reduce their drinking (King & Tucker, 2000).

Unfortunately, there are no psychometrically validated measures of drinking goals. Similar to treatment preference, it is likely that any assessment of the client's preference for drinking goal is done informally or not at all. Most studies involving drinking goals do not report how the drinking goal selection was assessed. Given the importance of assessing the client's personal goals and how these goals are consonant with the goals of the program or treatment approach, the development of measures in this area is encouraged.

Treatment History

AUDs are chronic and relapsing conditions that often require multiple treatment episodes. In addition, comorbid psychopathology is more the rule than the exception when it comes to individuals with AUDs. Therefore, many clients seeking treatment for a drinking problem will have some previous experience with psychotherapy and it is important for a clinician to know what has and has not worked for the client in the past. One way to accomplish this is to simply inquire about previous treatment when conducting an intake interview or during the first session of therapy. The duration

and type of treatment (e.g., self-help, group, outpatient, and residential) are important, but understanding the client's response to and personal attitudes towards previous treatment efforts is critical for treatment planning.

Several instruments gather information about treatment during finite time periods (e.g., Form 90), but there also are assessment instruments developed specifically for this purpose. The Teen Treatment Services Review (T-TSR; Kaminer, Blitz, Burleson, & Sussman, 1998) was developed to assess frequency of in-program and out-of-program services received by adolescents with alcohol and drug abuse problems. It can be administered as a self-report or interview and uses the same subscales as the Addiction Severity Index. The T-TSR also could be used with adult populations. The Center on Alcoholism, Substance Abuse, and Addictions (CASAA) provides a useful tool for assessing number of previous treatment episodes called the Lifetime Treatment History Interview (CASAA, 1994). Overall, there is not a psychometrically strong set of measures to assess treatment history. The psychometric properties of the measures have not been studied adequately and the instruments focus on frequency of treatment episodes and type of services rather than the client's perception of their usefulness. Therefore, it is recommended that clinicians gather information about lifetime treatment episodes (alcohol, drug, and other) and then follow-up that assessment with questions about which aspects of each episode were and were not helpful.

Craving

Another important domain of assessment during case conceptualization and treatment planning is the measurement of craving. Although a clear consensus on the definition of this construct has not been reached, craving is broadly conceptualized as an acute urge or strong subjective desire to drink. As a phenomenon closely tied to maladaptive drinking behavior, craving has received a great deal of attention in the addictive behaviors literature and has been found to be strongly associated with the quantity and frequency of past drinking (Yoon, Kim, Thuras, Grant, & Westermeyer, 2006), risk of and latency to relapse after treatment (Bottlender & Soyka, 2004), and quantity and frequency of future drinking (Flannery, Poole, Gallop, & Volpicelli, 2003). In clinical settings, craving is assessed either for a client's current state of craving or to characterize and quantify a client's recent or typical levels of craving. These two methods yield different data and serve distinct purposes. Although state craving assessment instruments can be used to measure reactivity to alcohol cues (a variable predictive of relapse risk) or to monitor urge in behavioral interventions (e.g., cue-exposure treatment), measures of recent/typical craving determine the extent to which drinking is accompanied and influenced by craving. In cases where craving typically plays a prominent role, the development of craving-specific coping skills may be called for.

Among those measures that assess current/state craving, the Alcohol Urge Questionnaire (AUQ; Bohn, Krahn, & Staehler, 1995) is recommended. The AUQ is an 8-item self-report questionnaire that assesses a client's agreement with various statements describing a strong current desire to drink. Both short and easy to administer and score, the AUQ provides an efficient way to capture state-dependent craving for alcohol. When the clinical context calls for a measure of recent craving, however, use of the Penn Alcohol Craving Scale (PACS; Flannery, Volpicelli, & Pettinati, 1999) is suggested. A 5-item, computer-based instrument, the PACS measures the past-week frequency, duration, and intensity of craving, and can be completed by clients in approximately 2 minutes. Although its electronic format may represent an advantage to some clinicians, the PACS may not be suitable for those without computer access. In this case, the Obsessive–Compulsive Drinking Scale (OCDS; Anton, Moak, & Latham, 1995) is recommended. Other measures of craving include the Adolescent Obsessive Compulsive Drinking Scale (A-OCDS; Deas, Roberts, Randall, & Anton, 2001), Alcohol Craving Questionnaire (ACQ-NOW; Singleton, Tiffany, & Henningfield, 1995) and Yale-Brown Obsessive Compulsive Scale for Heavy Drinking (Y-BOCS-hd; Modell, Glaser, Mountz, Schmaltz, & Cyr, 1992).

High-Risk Situations

In addition to measuring overall level of craving, it also is important to identify particular situations in which clients are likely to have a strong desire to drink. The risk of relapse increases when abstinent individuals encounter cues that previously have been associated with drinking. Known as contextual triggers (Marlatt, 1996) or proximal precipitating factors for relapse (Donovan, 1996), these cues may take the form of people, places, events, or feelings that have preceded or accompanied previous drinking episodes. These triggers are able to subsequently evoke a variety of cognitive, behavioral, and affective responses within abstinent individuals, responses that ultimately increase the likelihood of drinking. It follows that the prediction of future high-risk drinking situations and the related development of targeted relapse-prevention interventions ought to be guided by an analysis of previous drinking antecedents. Toward this end, numerous assessment techniques have been developed to identify an individual's particular high-risk drinking situations.

Among self-report instruments, the Inventory of Drinking Situations (IDS; Annis, 1982) has enjoyed the most widespread use and empirical support. Available in both paper-and-pencil and computerized versions, the IDS is a 100-item questionnaire that assesses the frequency of past-year drinking in eight situations proposed by Marlatt (1978): unpleasant emotions, physical discomfort, pleasant emotions, testing personal control, urges or temptations to drink, conflict with others, social pressure to drink, and pleasant times with others. Although the IDS provides a comprehensive assessment of high-risk situations, time constraints may call for a shorter measure, in which case the 42-item short form (IDS-42; Isenhart, 1991) is recommended. Both the IDS and the IDS-42 are strongly recommended as clinical tools to identify high-risk drinking situations. Other measures of high-risk situations include the Drinking Patterns Questionnaire (DPQ; Zitter & McCrady, 1979), Drinking Context Scale (*DCS; O'Hare, 1997) and Reasons for Drinking Questionnaire (RFDQ; Zywiak, Connors, Maisto, & Westerberg, 1996).

Cognitive, Affective, and Behavioral Dimensions

Alcohol Expectancies

Research has suggested that more positive alcohol expectancies are associated with heavy drinking and more alcohol-related problems (Fromme, Stroot, & Kaplan, 1993). Measures of alcohol expectancies can provide enhanced knowledge of the client's motives for drinking and for not drinking.

Of the expectancy questionnaires, the Comprehensive Effects of Alcohol Scale (CEOA; Fromme et al., 1993) is highly recommended. The Alcohol

Expectancy Questionnaire (AEQ; Brown, Christiansen, & Goldman, 1987) also has excellent psychometric properties and is one of the most frequently used measures of alcohol expectancies. However, the AEQ has 120 items, making it lengthy to use in clinical practice, whereas the CEOA has only 38. In addition, the CEOA measures both positive and negative alcohol expectancies, whereas the AEQ measures only positive expectancies. In addition, the AEQ questions focus on moderate drinking, for example, "a few drinks," "a couple of drinks," and therefore the measure is somewhat inappropriate for most dependent drinkers.

Another measure of expectancies is the Negative Alcohol Expectancy Questionnaire (NAEQ; McMahon & Jones, 1993). The NAEQ focuses on negative alcohol expectancies, that is, the beliefs in what negative effects or consequences can result from alcohol consumption. However, this is a comparatively new instrument and its psychometric properties still are being investigated. Preliminary research by the developers of the NAEQ has suggested that negative expectancies may be better predictors of drinking quantity and frequency than positive expectancies (McMahon, Jones, & O'Donnell, 1994).

Self-Efficacy

Many researchers (e.g., Miller & Rollnick, 2002) suggest that, in addition to measuring a client's motivation and the client's willingness to change, it is important to measure a third variable, the client's perceived ability to change. A client may voice being both ready and motivated to change, but at the same time feel as if he or she does not have the skills to do so. It is unlikely that clients with low self-efficacy for change will be willing to take substantial behavioral steps towards change. A treatment focus on increasing confidence for reducing drinking may be helpful for clients whose self-efficacy is low.

Of the self-efficacy measures, the Drinking Refusal Self-Efficacy Questionnaire (DRSEQ; Young, Oei, & Crook, 1991) and the Situational Confidence Questionnaire (SCQ; Annis, & Graham, 1988) are highly recommended. The DRSEQ and the SCQ are similar—both are self-report measures that list several situations considered by many drinkers to be "high-risk" situations, and both ask clients to rate their level confidence in being able to avoid drinking in the situation. The DRSEQ and SCQ have 31 and 39 items, respectively, and both typically take 10 minutes or less to complete, making them easy to use in a clinical setting. The DRSEQ categorizes self-efficacy for reducing drinking into three categories: social situations, opportunistic situations, and emotional relief.

A brief version of the SCQ (SCQ-Brief; Breslin, Sobell, Sobell, & Agrawal, 2000) has eight items. Although the psychometric properties of the brief version have not been investigated as thoroughly as those of the full version, the SCQ-Brief has acceptable norms and good construct validity. Its subscales also have high correlations with the subscales of the SCQ, with correlations ranging from .57 to .81 (Breslin et al., 2000).

Coping Skills

The relationship between high-risk situations, craving, and relapse is believed to be mediated by the availability and accessibility of coping skills. From a cognitive-behavioral perspective on relapse, it is not the mere exposure to high-risk situations or the experience of craving, but rather the inability of an abstinent individual to cope adequately with the events that precipitate relapse. Possession of a diverse coping repertoire from which a variety of skills may be readily retrieved bolsters abstinence self-efficacy and reduces the likelihood of relapse. Careful assessment of a client's coping repertoire can serve to identify existing strengths and to highlight particular deficits or areas of weakness. Armed with this information, relapse prevention interventions may be tailored to capitalize on a client's existing skills and to develop those that are lacking.

Two types of assessment instruments are available to facilitate the identification of alcohol-related coping skills: clinician-guided role-plays and self-report questionnaires. Unlike self-reports, the Alcohol-Specific Role Play Test (ASRPT; Monti et al., 1993) requires that clients go beyond reporting the perceived availability of coping skills and actually retrieve and implement them in a variety of interpersonal and intrapersonal high-risk situations. Although the ASRPT provides perhaps the most ecologically valid assessment of a client's coping repertoire, it also requires substantial clinician training and detailed behavioral coding of taped sessions, requirements that limit its clinical utility. For those seeking a quicker and easier assessment of coping skills, the Coping Behaviors Inventory (CBI; Litman, Stapleton, Oppenheim, & Peleg, 1983) is recommended. A 36-item self-report questionnaire, the CBI assesses the frequency with which a varieties of cognitive and behavioral coping skills are typically utilized to combat one's desire to drink. Adequate psychometric properties, fast administration, and easy scoring make the CBI a useful tool for evaluating clients' coping repertoires. Other measures of coping skills include the Adolescent Relapse Coping Questionnaire (ARCQ; Myers & Brown, 1990), Alcohol Abuse Coping Response Inventory (AACRI; Humke & Radnitz, 2005), and Temptation Coping Questionnaire (TCQ; Myers & Wagner, 1995).

Social Network

The social network can provide tangible support, emotional support, and guidance to an individual. For persons with AUDs, the social network may provide general support to the person in his or her daily life, or specific support for changes in drinking. The social network also can be a source of stress, and the behavior of individuals in the social network may cue or reinforce drinking. A large number of measures are available to measure general social support, and several have been used in treatment outcome studies for persons with AUDs. However, their general psychometric properties have not been evaluated with AUD samples.

The Important People and Activities (IPA) interview (Longabaugh & Zywiak, 1999) is recommended to assess the characteristics of the social networks of persons with AUDs. The IPA is a 19-item interview that begins by having the individual name important people in the social network. Research studies have constrained the number of important persons identified to keep the interview relatively brief; administration time is approximately 20 minutes. Follow-up questions are asked about each person, related to their own drinking or drug use, general support for the identified patient, the degree to which the individual supports drinking, drug use, abstinence, and help-seeking. A number of specific variables can be derived from the IPA for research purposes, but for clinical practice the instrument can guide the clinician's focus on the necessity of interventions to modify the client's social network. Although psychometric studies are limited, data to date support the reliability and validity of the instrument.

Overall Evaluation

In summary, there are measures with adequate to good psychometric properties for the assessment of most dimensions needed for case formulation and treatment planning. The CIWA may be used to determine present withdrawal symptoms, and the Physical Health Status scale of the LISRES provides a good medical/health screening measure. The RAATE can be used to make a determination of the appropriate initial level of care for a client. The strongest measures of drinking pattern are the TLFB interview, or the Form 90, with the QFI and DSML providing similar data through self-report measures. Consequences of drinking can best be measured using the SIP, and the FTQ can assist the clinician in determining any family history of AUDs. The SOCRATES is recommended for determination of motivation to change; there are no established measures to assess client's treatment preferences or drinking goals. Current craving is best measured with the AUQ, and the PACS is a good measure of recent drinking. Specific measures to help formulate a cognitive-behavioral treatment plan include the IDS or the IDS-42 to identify high-risk situations for drinking, the CEAS is a good measure of alcohol expectancies, the DRSEQ and the SCQ are good measures of self-efficacy, and the ASPRT and the CBI are good measures of behavioral coping skills, although the ASPRT is not practical for clinical practice settings.

TREATMENT MONITORING AND TREATMENT EVALUATION

Assessments throughout treatment and follow-up are necessary to determine the effectiveness of an intervention. Important information to consider when monitoring treatment outcome include current patterns of consumption, information from collaterals, biological measures, drinking consequences, AA involvement or 12-step program affiliation, and overall quality of life. These dimensions and recommended measures are summarized in Table 16.3.

Consumption Patterns

Client Reports

The measurement of drinking quantity, frequency, and patterns over follow-up is one of the most important measurement domains, as drinking behavior itself is the most frequently used outcome measure in both research and clinical alcohol treatment settings. It is recommended that clinicians assess these

TABLE 16.3 Ratings of Instruments Used for Treatment Monitoring and Treatment Outcome Evaluation

Instrument	Norms	Internal Consistency	Inter-rater Reliability	Test–Retest Reliability	Content Validity	Construct Validity	Validity Generalization	Treatment Sensitivity	Clinical Utility	Highly Recommended
Drinking Patterns										
TLFB	G	NA	NA	U	U	A	E	E	A	✓
Form-90-C	A	NA	NA	U	U	A	E	G	A	✓
5-HTOL	A	NA	NA	NA	NA	NA	A	A	A	
ASI	A	G	A	L	A	A	G	G	A	
GGT	E	NA	NA	NA	NA	G	E	E	A	✓
CDT	E	NA	NA	NA	NA	G	E	E	A	✓
Ethyl Glucuronide	A	NA	NA	NA	NA	NA	A	A	A	
Serum beta Hexosaminidase	A	NA	NA	NA	NA	U	A	G	A	
Sialic acid	A	NA	NA	NA	NA	U	A	G	A	
Consequences of Drinking										
DrInC	G	G	NA	A	A	G	E	E	A	✓
RAPI	A	G	NA	G	A	A	G	G	A	
Motivation										
SOCRATES	E	E	NA	E	E	A	E	G	A	✓
URICA	E	G	NA	U	U	G	E	A	A	
AA Involvement										
AA affiliation scale	G	G	NA	U	G	A	G	U	A	
AA involvement scale	G	G	NA	A	U	U	G	A	A	
B-PRPI	A	G	NA	U	E	A	A	A	A	
Steps questionnaire	A	L	NA	U	G	A	A	U	A	
Quality of Life										
LSS	G	G	NA	U	G	A	G	G	A	✓

Note: TLFB = Timeline Followback; Form-90-C = Form-90-Collateral; 5-HTOL = 5-Hydroxytryptophol Level; ASI = Addiction Severity Index; GGT = Gamma Glutamyl transferase; CDT = Carbohydrate-Deficient Transferrin; DrInC = Drinker Inventory of Consequences; RAPI = Rutgers Alcohol Problem Index; SOCRATES = Stages of Change Readiness and Treatment Eagerness Scale; URICA = University of Rhode Island Change Assessment; B-PRPI = Brown-Peterson Recovery Progress Inventory; LSS = Life Situation Survey; L = Less Than Adequate; A = Adequate; G = Good; E = Excellent; U = Unavailable; NA = Not Applicable.

dimensions at the beginning of treatment, and compare pretreatment scores with scores throughout treatment to assess treatment progress.

Of the measures listed, the TLFB is highly recommended. This measure is recommended because of its thoroughness—the TLFB results in an estimate of drinking for each day in the past 90 days. The TLFB has been thoroughly validated, has excellent reliability, and has been shown to be sensitive to progress in treatment. However, despite the TLFB's excellent psychometrics, it can be somewhat unwieldy in clinical practice. It is lengthier to administer than other measures of quantity and frequency, and requires training for administration. Unfortunately, there are few measures of drinking quantity or frequency that are short enough in length to administer frequently. If the clinician desires to administer a brief questionnaire more frequently, then the AUDIT is recommended. However, there is currently little evidence that the AUDIT is sensitive to treatment progress. Another option for assessing quantity and frequency of drinking is self-monitoring. For this purpose, the Daily Drinking Log is recommended.

Collateral Reports

Most studies comparing reports of clients with those of collateral informants (e.g., Breslin et al., 1996; Chermack, Singer, & Beresford, 1998) have suggested that collateral reports are highly correlated with self-reports of the drinker. Given this correlation, some researchers (e.g., Babor, Steinberg, Anton, & Del Boca, 2000) have suggested that investing resources in obtaining collateral reports is not worth the effort. However, most of these reports are obtained in research settings, with the purpose of corroborating diagnostic information at baseline. Some studies that obtain collateral information throughout follow-up have informally asked collaterals for an estimate of the client's drinking quantity and frequency (e.g., Heather, Rollnick, Bell, & Richmond, 1996; Sanchez-Craig, Davila, & Cooper, 1996), or have not reported the measure by which collateral information was collected (e.g., Schmidt et al., 1997; Smith, Hodgson, Bridgeman, & Shepherd, 2003; Tucker, Vuchinich, & Rippens, 2004). Others, however, have used standardized measures to assess collaterals' perceptions of the client's drinking during follow-up. The utility of obtaining collateral reports in addition to self-reports throughout follow-up remains largely unknown.

Much information can be asked of collaterals. The most common information obtained from collateral informants for the purpose of treatment outcome monitoring is estimates of the client's drinking quantity and frequency. The TLFB, which asks the participant to provide retrospective estimates of drinking from anywhere over the past 30 days to over the past year, is highly recommended if the clinician wishes to obtain accurate and detailed estimations of quantity and frequency of drinking. The TLFB is one of the most commonly used quantity-frequency measures in research settings, and has been shown to have high treatment sensitivity. However, the TLFB can be lengthy to administer in a clinical setting (takes about 15 minutes to complete) and requires training for use.

If the clinician wishes to obtain information regarding alcohol-related consequences (such as missed work, hospitalizations, etc.) the Form-90-Collateral (Miller & Del Boca, 1994) assesses these dimensions. However, the Form-90 has similar drawbacks to the TLFB in terms of length of administration and training is necessary for use. If a shorter measure is needed, the AUDIT also has been used as a collateral measure. Donovan, Dunn, Rivara, Jurkovich, Ries, and Gentilello (2004) found that AUDITs completed by the client are highly correlated with scores from AUDITs completed by collaterals. There have not been many studies confirming that AUDIT scores are sensitive to treatment change, however, so the AUDIT needs to be used with caution.

Biological Measures

When used as a measure of treatment outcome, biological measures can corroborate self-reports, or can be used to detect possible relapse. Although biological measures are used infrequently in clinical settings, they are widely available in medical settings (Conigrave, Davies, Haber, & Whitfield, 2003). Of the biological measures, both GGT and CDT are highly recommended. GGT and CDT are frequently used in research settings. Both GGT and CDT have been shown to have adequate sensitivity in detecting relapse after abstinence; although estimates of the rates of accurate relapse detection have ranged widely, estimates have been around 80% for GGT (Salaspuro, 1999) and 76% for CDT (Schmidt et al., 1997). In addition to the limitations listed in the earlier section on biological measures, there are additional limitations when the biological measures are used for treatment outcome and monitoring. Tests such as GGT and CDT tend to detect only heavy levels or continuous drinking and therefore will not detect more sporadic, lighter drinking patterns (Neumann & Spies, 2003).

Consequences of Drinking

Some researchers (e.g., Kadden & Litt, 2004) have suggested that a thorough assessment of treatment outcome should include measures of drinking quantity and frequency, as well as drinking-related consequences. Drinking-related consequences can be legal, physical, or social-psychological. Some therapies for AUDs, such as harm-reduction therapy (Marlatt & Witkiewitz, 2002), focus specifically on the reduction of such alcohol-related consequences. Therefore, particularly for harm-reduction type therapies, it is important to have standardized measurements to evaluate this primary outcome. Of the two measures of drinking-related consequences, the Drinker's Inventory of Consequences (DrInC; Miller, Tonigan, & Longabaugh, 1995) is highly recommended. In research settings, the DrInC is currently the most commonly used outcome measure of drinking consequences. The DrInC evaluates five alcohol-related problem areas: physical, intrapersonal, social responsibility, interpersonal, and impulse control. The DrInC asks about both lifetime consequences and consequences over the past 3 months. The DrInC has 50 items, but typically takes a short time to complete (about 10 minutes).

Motivation

Motivation is a variable that changes throughout treatment. Even when a client reports high levels of motivation and readiness to change at the beginning of treatment, motivation to change may wax and wane. Therefore, it is important to continue to monitor motivation, readiness, and willingness to change throughout the course of treatment and any follow-up.

There are two measures that have available evidence of treatment sensitivity. These are the Stages of Change Readiness and Treatment Eagerness Scale (SOCRATES) and the University of Rhode Island Change Assessment (URICA). Both of these measures have shown adequate treatment sensitivity. However, the SOCRATES is highly recommended because of its excellent psychometrics.

AA Involvement/12-Step Affiliation

This set of questionnaires focuses on measuring the client's level of participation in Alcoholics Anonymous (AA), and/or the degree to which they endorse a philosophy of recovery based on the 12 steps. Examining the degree to which a client endorses a 12-step philosophy can help determine whether the client is compatible with program orientation; measuring affiliation over time provides the clinician with information about the degree to which the client is participating in the program of AA, rather than simply assessing the number of meetings the client is attending.

Many research studies (e.g., Moos & Moos, 2006) have asked participants to report on the number of days that they attended AA meetings. Many studies use estimates obtained from other questionnaires, such as the Form-90 (Miller & Del Boca, 1994), which ask for the frequency of AA meeting attendance. However, some researchers (e.g., Thomassen, 2002; Tonigan, Connors, & Miller, 1996) have argued that AA attendance should not be equated with affiliation and the "dose" of AA as a therapy. Therefore, it may be appropriate to get a more comprehensive measure of AA or 12-step participation and or/beliefs.

Two of the measures in this area, the AA Affiliation Scale (Humphreys, Kaskutas, & Weisner, 1998) and the AA Involvement Scale (Tonigan, Connors, & Miller, 1996), ask about the client's level of participation in the AA program specifically and are highly recommended. Both scales are brief (19 and 13 items, respectively) and ask about the client's level of participation in AA, not only assessing the frequency of attendance at meetings, but also asking about AA-related activities such as working the steps and having a sponsor. The AA Affiliation Scale has questions about both the past 30 days and the past year, whereas the AA Involvement Scale does not specify a time period. The Steps Questionnaire (Gilbert, 1991) and the Brown-Peterson Recovery Inventory (Brown & Peterson, 1991) are similar to each other, measuring cognitions and behaviors more broadly related to a 12-step philosophy, such as spirituality, accepting powerlessness, and resisting manipulating others. A limitation of both questionnaires is their length (42 and 53 items, taking about 15 minutes to complete).

There have been several other questionnaires that have been used to measure the extent of AA involvement or 12-step affiliation, such as the General Alcoholics Anonymous Tools of Recovery Scale (GAATOR; Montgomery, Tonigan, & Miller, 1991) and the Recovery Interview (Morgenstern, Kahler, Frey, & Labouvie, 1996), but these questionnaires currently do not have sufficient psychometric data to determine whether they are appropriate for use in a clinical setting.

Quality of Life

Alcohol abuse and dependence often have many related consequences, such as legal, social, and health consequences. Treatments administered to problem drinkers should seek to address and improve these life areas. Most quality-of-life measures have been developed for other populations, primarily for individuals with chronic illnesses. However, the Life Situation Survey (LSS; Chabon, 1987) has published psychometric data for alcoholic, English-speaking populations. However, the Medical Outcome Study Health-Related Survey Short Form (MOS-SF-36; Ware & Sherbourne, 1992) and the World Health Organization Quality of Life Survey (WHOQOL-BREF; WHOQOL Group, 1998) have been used in research on alcoholic populations. Because of its published psychometrics, the LSS is recommended as a measure of quality of life. This measure is brief (20 questions) and spans several areas of life quality. Each question in the LSS asks about a different domain, including work, leisure, nutrition, sleep, social nurturance, earnings, health, love/affection, environment, self-esteem, security, public support, stress, mobility, autonomy, energy level, social support, mood/affect, outlook, and egalitarianism (Chabon, 1987). In research on problematic drinking, the MOS-SF-36 is the most widely used measure of quality of life. However, published norms that are specific to drinking populations could not be located. A limitation of the MOS-SF-36 is that it only measures health-related quality of life.

Overall Evaluation

Many measures that are used at baseline or intake also are suitable for assessing treatment progress and outcome, but there have been few formal investigations of the treatment sensitivity of the measures. Although this substantially limits the number of measures that can be chosen for clinical use, there are many instruments that have been found to be valid for these purposes. In this section, we described measures that have established evidence of treatment sensitivity, most of which have excellent psychometric properties. For accurate treatment outcome monitoring, it is important to measure drinking behaviors and related consequences directly. The TLFB is recommended as a measure of quantity and frequency, along with the DrInC as a measure of drinking-related consequences. Obtaining corroborating information can also be useful; one can use the TLFB-Collateral for this purpose, or one can use biological measures—recommended tests include GGT or CDT. Not only should drinking-related behavior be examined but adequate treatment should increase quality of life as well. The LSS is recommended as a measure to examine quality of life following treatment. It also may be important to determine whether the participant is involved in other types of treatment, or whether the client has shown changes in the degree to which he/she has adopted a 12-step philosophy. For this purpose, any of the above measures related to AA or 12-step involvement (AA Affiliation Scale, AA Involvement Scale, BPRI, and Steps Questionnaire) are adequate.

CONCLUSIONS AND FUTURE DIRECTIONS

Assessment related to heavy drinking and AUDs is complex, comprehensive, and requires the clinician to consider cognitive, affective, and behavioral domains and to address multiple areas of life functioning. The complexity of AUD assessment, though, places a time burden on the clinician and client to complete a comprehensive assessment, and we have tried to identify the most efficient measures in each domain to decrease the time burden. A thorough initial evaluation can easily take 3 hours, and the length of assessment may serve as a deterrent to some clients. In addition, some of the measures with the most clinical applicability require substantial training to administer, and the need for training may deter busy clinicians from using the best available measures.

The research literature is rich in the number of assessment measures that have been developed specifically for AUD populations, and many of these instruments have extensive research to support their use. However, we found a notable lack of standardized assessment measures in several areas known to be clinically important to treatment planning and treatment outcome. These include measures of treatment preferences, client drinking goals, and prediction of alcohol withdrawal. Future research could profitably address instrument development in these areas.

Future research also should consider the linkages between assessment and treatment outcome. Assessment may serve as an intervention in its own right (Epstein et al., 2005), and there may be ways to structure the assessment process to further enhance its positive impacts on treatment retention and outcomes. Research also is lacking on the process by which clinicians use assessment data to guide AUD treatment, and means to translate assessment data into a treatment plan. Finally, future research could profitably address what types of assessment are necessary and sufficient to yield positive treatment outcomes.

References

Allen, J. P., & Wilson, V. B. (2003). *Assessing alcohol problems: A guide for clinicians and researcher* (2nd ed.). NIH Publication No. 03–3745. Bethesda, MD: National Institute on Alcohol Abuse and Alcoholism.

American Psychiatric Association. (1994). *Diagnostic and statistical manual of mental disorders* (4th ed.). Washington, DC: Author.

American Society of Addiction Medicine (ASAM). (1996). *Patient placement criteria for the treatment of psychoactive substance use disorders*. Chevy Chase: Author.

Annis, H. M., & Graham, J. M. (1988) Situational Confidence Questionnaire (SCQ 39): User's Guide. Addiction Research Foundation, Toronto.

Annis, H. M. (1982). *Inventory of drinking situations*. Toronto: Addictions Research Foundation of Ontario.

Anton, R. F., Moak D. H., & Latham, P. (1995). The obsessive compulsive drinking scale: A self-rated instrument for the quantification of thoughts about alcohol and drinking behavior. *Alcoholism: Clinical and Experimental Research, 19*, 92–99.

Babor, T. F., Biddle-Higgins, J. C., Saunders, J. B., & Montiero, M. G. (2001). *AUDIT: The alcohol use disorders identification test: Guidelines for use in primary health care*. Geneva, Switzerland: World Health Organization.

Babor, T. F., Steinberg, K., Anton, R., & Del Boca, F. (2000). Talk is cheap: Measuring drinking outcomes in clinical trials. *Journal of Studies on Alcohol, 61*, 55–63.

Baer, J. S., Kivlahan, D. R., Blume, A. W., McKnight, P., & Marlatt, G. A. (2001). Brief intervention for heavy-drinking college students: 4-year follow-up and natural history. *American Journal of Public Health, 91*, 1310–1316.

Bates, M. E., Pawlak, A. P., Tonigan, J. S., & Buckman, J. F. (2006). Cognitive impairment influences drinking outcome by altering therapeutic mechanisms of change. *Psychology of Addictive Behaviors, 20*, 241–253.

Beck, A. T., & Steer, R. A. (1990). *Manual for the Beck anxiety inventory*. San Antonio, TX: Psychological Corporation.

Beck, A. T., & Steer, R. A. (1996). *Manual for the Beck depression inventory*. San Antonio, TX: Psychological Corporation.

Beck, A. T., Steer, R. A., & Brown, G. K. (1996). *Manual for the Beck depression inventory-II*. San Antonio, TX: Psychological Corporation.

Bell, H., Tallaksen, C. M. E., Try, K., & Haug, E. (1994). Carbohydrate-deficient transferring and other markers of high alcohol consumption: A study of 502 patients admitted consecutively to a medical department. *Alcoholism: Clinical and Experimental Research, 18*, 1103–1108.

Bennett, M. E., & McCrady, B. S. (1993). Subtype by comorbidity in young adult substance abusers. *Journal of Substance Abuse, 5*, 365–378.

Bohn, M. J., Krahn, D. D., & Staehler, B. A. (1995). Development and initial validation of a measure of drinking urges in abstinent alcoholics. *Alcoholism: Clinical and Experimental Research, 19*, 600–606.

Bottlender, M., & Soyka, M. (2004). Impact of craving on alcohol relapse during, and 12 months following, outpatient treatment. *Alcohol and Alcoholism, 39*, 357–361.

Breslin, C., Sobell, L. C., Sobell, M. B., Buchan, G., & Kwan, E. (1996). Aftercare telephone contacts with problem drinkers can serve a clinical and research function. *Addiction, 91*, 1359–1364.

Breslin, F. C., Sobell, L. C., Sobell, M. B., & Agrawal, S. (2000). A comparison of a brief and long version of the situational confidence questionnaire. *Behaviour Research and Therapy, 38*, 1211–1220.

Brown, H. P., & Peterson, J. H. (1991). Assessing spirituality in addiction treatment and follow-up: Development of the Brown-Peterson Recovery Progress Inventory (B-PRPI). *Alcoholism Treatment Quarterly, 8* (2), 21–50.

Brown, S. A. (1985). Reinforcement expectancies and alcoholism treatment outcome after a one-year follow-up. *Journal of Studies on Alcohol, 46*, 304–308.

Brown, S. A., Christiansen, B. A., & Goldman, M. S. (1987). The alcohol expectancy questionnaire: An instrument for the assessment of adolescent and adult alcohol expectancies. *Journal of Studies on Alcohol, 48*, 483–491.

Bucholz, K. K., Cadoret, R., Cloninger, C. R., Dinwiddie, S. H., Hesselbrock, V. M., Nurnberger, J. I. Jr., et al. (1994). Semi-structured psychiatric interview for use in genetic linkage studies: A report on the reliability of the SSAGA. *Journal of Studies on Alcohol, 55*, 149–158.

Center on Alcoholism Substance Abuse and Addictions Research Division. (1994). Lifetime Treatment

History Interview. Retrieved September 25, 2007, from, http://casaa.unm.edu/inst/Lifetime%20Treatment%20History%20Interview.pdf.

Chabon, R. A. (1987). Development of a quality-of-life rating scale for use in health-care evaluation. *Evaluation in the Health Professions, 10*, 186–200.

Chermack, S. T., Singer, K., & Beresford, T. P. (1998). Screening for alcoholism among medical inpatients: How important is corroboration of patient self-report? *Alcoholism: Clinical and Experimental Research, 22*, 1393–1398.

Cherpitel, C. (2000). A brief screening instrument for alcohol dependence in the emergency room: The RAPS 4. *Journal of Studies on Alcohol, 61*, 447–449.

Collins, R. L., Park, G. E., & Marlatt, G. A. (1985). Social determinants of alcohol consumption: The effects of social interaction and model status on the self-administration of alcohol. *Journal of Consulting and Clinical Psychology, 53*, 189–200.

Compton, W.M., Cottler, L.B., Abdallah, A.B., Phelps, D.L., Spitznagel, E.L., & Horton, J.C. (2000). Substance dependence and other psychiatric disorders among drug dependent subjects: Race and gender correlates. *The American Journal on Addictions, 9*, 113–125.

Conigrave, K. M., Davies, P., Haber, P., & Whitfield, J. B. (2003). Traditional markers of excessive alcohol use. *Addiction, 98*(S2), 31–43.

Corrao, G., Bagnardi, V., Zambon, A., & La Vecchia, C. (2004). A meta-analysis of alcohol consumption and the risk of 15 diseases. *Preventive Medicine: An International Journal Devoted to Practice and Theory, 38*, 613–619.

Cottler, L. B. (2000). *Composite international diagnostic interview—Substance Abuse Module (SAM)*. St. Louis, MO: Department of Psychiatry, Washington University School of Medicine.

Crum, R., Chan, Y., Chen, L., Storr, C., & Anthony, J. (2005). Incidence rates for alcohol dependence among adults: Prospective data from the Baltimore epidemiologic catchment area follow-up survey, 1981-1996. *Journal of Studies on Alcohol, 66*, 795–805.

Cunradi, C. B., Caetano, R., Clark, C. L., & Schafer, J. (1999). Alcohol-related problems and intimate partner violence among White, Black, & Hispanic couples in the U. S. *Alcoholism: Clinical and Experimental Research, 23*, 1492–1501.

Deas, D., Roberts, J., Randall, C., & Anton, R. (2001). Adolescent obsessive–compulsive drinking scale: An assessment tool for problem drinking. *Journal of the National Medical Association, 93*, 92–103.

DeLeon, G., Melnick, G., Kressel, D., & Jainchill, N. (1994). Circumstances, motivation, readiness, and suitability (the CMRS scales): Predicting retention in therapeutic community treatment. *American Journal of Drug and Alcohol Abuse, 20*, 495–515.

Demers, A., Bisson, J., & Palluy, J. (1999). Wives' convergence with their husbands' alcohol use: Social conditions as mediators. *Journal of Studies of Alcohol, 60*, 368–377.

Dennis, M. (1998). *Global appraisal of individual needs*. Bloomington, IL: Chestnut Health Systems.

Derogatis, L. R. (1977). Symptom Checklist-90 Manual. Baltimore, MD: Johns Hopkins University Press.

Derogatis, L. R., & Melisaratos, N. (1983). The Brief Symptom Inventory: An introductory report. *Psychological Medicine, 13*, 595–605.

Derogatis, L. R., Rickels, K., & Rock, A. F. (1976). The SCL-90 and the MMPI: A step in the validity of a new self-report scale. *British Journal of Psychiatry, 128*, 280–289.

DiClemente, C. C., & Hughes, S. O. (1990). Stages of change profiles in outpatient alcoholism treatment. *Journal of Substance Abuse, 2*, 217–235.

Donovan, D. M. (1996). Assessment issues and domains in the prediction of relapse. *Addiction, 91*(Suppl.), S29–S36.

Donovan, D. M., Dunn, C. W., Rivara, F. P., Jurkovich, G. J., Ries, R. R., & Gentilello, L. M. (2004). Comparison of trauma center patient self-reports and proxy reports on the Alcohol Use Identification Test (AUDIT). *Journal of Trauma-Injury Infection & Critical Care, 56*, 873–882.

Driessen, M., Veltrup, C., Wetterling, T., John, U., & Dilling, H. (1998). Axis I and Axis II comorbidity in alcohol dependence and the two types of alcoholism. *Alcoholism: Clinical & Experimental Research, 22*, 77.

Duckert, F. (1987). Recruitment into treatment and effects of treatment for female problem drinkers. *Addictive Behaviors, 12*, 137–150.

Edwards, G., & Gross, M. M. (1976). Alcohol dependence: Provisional description of a clinical syndrome. *British Medical Journal, 1*, 1058–1061.

Epstein, E. E., Drapkin, M. L., Yusko, D. A., Cook, S. M., McCrady, B. S. & Jensen, N. K. (2005). Is alcohol assessment therapeutic? Pretreatment change in drinking among alcohol dependent females. *Journal of Studies on Alcohol, 66*, 369–378.

Ewing, J. A. (1984). Detecting alcoholism: The CAGE questionnaire. *Journal of the American Medical Association, 252*, 1905–1907.

Finney, J. W., Moos, R. H., & Brennan, P. L. (1991).The drinking problems index: A measure to assess alcohol-related problems among older adults. *Journal of Substance Abuse, 3*, 395–404.

Finney, J. W., Moos, R. H., & Timko, C. (1999). The course of treated and untreated substance use disorders: Remission and resolution, relapse and mortality. In B. S. McCrady & E. E. Epstein (Eds.), *Addictions: A comprehensive guidebook* (pp. 30–49). New York: Oxford University Press.

First, M. B., Gibbon, M., Spitzer, R. L., & Williams, J. B. W. (1996b). *User's guide for the Structured Clinical Interview for DSM IV Axis II personality disorders— research version.* New York: Biometrics Research Department, New York State Psychiatric Institute.

First, M. B., Spitzer, R. L, Gibbon M., & Williams, J. B. W. (2002). *Structured Clinical Interview for DSM-IV-TR Axis I Disorders, Research Version, Non-patient Edition. (SCID-I/NP).* New York: Biometrics Research, New York State Psychiatric Institute.

Flannery, B. A., Poole, S. A., Gallop, R. J., & Volpicelli, J. R. (2003). Alcohol craving predicts drinking during treatment: An analysis of three assessment instruments. *Journal of Studies on Alcohol, 64*, 120–126.

Flannery, B. A., Volpicelli, J. R., Pettinati, H. M. (1999). Psychometric properties of the Penn Alcohol Craving Scale. *Alcoholism: Clinical and Experimental Research, 23*, 1289–1295.

Fromme, K., Stroot, E. A., & Kaplan, D. (1993). Comprehensive effects of alcohol: Development and psychometric assessment of a new expectancy questionnaire. *Psychological Assessment, 5*, 19–26.

Gilbert, F. S. (1991). Development of a "Steps Questionnaire." *Journal of Studies on Alcohol, 52*, 353–360.

Goldman, D., Oroszi, G., & Ducci, F. (2005). The genetics of addictions: Uncovering the genes. *Nature Reviews Genetics, 6*, 521–532.

Grant, B. F., Hasin, D. S., Chou, S. P., Stinson, F. S., & Dawson, D. A. (2004). Nicotine dependence and psychiatric disorders in the United States. *Archives of General Psychiatry, 61*, 1107–1115.

Grant, B. F., Stinson, F. S., Dawson, D. A., Chou, P., Dufour, M. C., Compton, W., et al. (2004a). Prevalence and co-occurrence of substance use disorders and independent mood and anxiety disorders: Results from the National Epidemiologic Survey on Alcohol and Related Conditions. *Archives of General Psychiatry, 61*, 807–816.

Grant, B. F., Stinson, F. S., Dawson, D. A., Chou, S. P., Ruan, W. J., & Pickering, R. P. (2004b). Co-occurrence of 12-month alcohol and drug use disorders and personality disorders in the United States: Results from the National Epidemiologic Survey on Alcohol and Related Conditions. *Archives of General Psychiatry, 61*, 361–368.

Heather, N., Rollnick, S., Bell, A., & Richmond, R. (1996). Effects of brief counseling among male heavy drinkers identified on general hospital wards. *Drug and Alcohol Review, 15*, 29–38.

Hesselbrock, M., Easton, C., Bucholz, K. K., Schuckit, M., & Hesselbrock, V. (1999). A validity study of the SSAGA—a comparison with the SCAN. *Addiction, 94*, 1361–1370.

Hesselbrock, M., Hesselbrock, V. M., & Epstein, E. E. (1999). Theories of etiology of alcohol and other drug use disorders. In B. S. McCrady & E. E. Epstein (Eds.), *Addictions: A comprehensive guidebook* (pp. 50–72). New York: Oxford.

O'Hare, T. (1997). Measuring excessive alcohol use in college drinking contexts: The Drinking Context Scale. *Addictive Behaviors, 22*, 469–477.

Hodgins, D.C., Dufour, M., & Armstrong, S. (2000). The reliability and validity of the inventory to diagnose depression in alcohol-dependent men and women. *Journal of Substance Abuse, 11*, 369–78.

Hodgson, R., Alwyn, T., John, B., Thom, B., & Smith, A. (2002). The fast alcohol screening test. *Alcohol and Alcoholism, 37*, 61–66.

Humphreys, K., Kaskutas, L., & Weisner, C. (1998). The alcoholism anonymous affiliation scale: Development, reliability, and norms for diverse treated and untreated populations. *Alcoholism: Clinical and Experimental Research, 22*, 974–978.

Isenhart, C. E. (1991). Factor structure of the inventory of drinking situations. *Journal of Substance Abuse, 3*, 59–71.

Jenkinson, C., Layte, R., Jenkinson, D., Lawrence, K., Petersen, S., Paice, C., & Stradling, J. (1997). A shorter form health survey: Can the SF-12 replicate results from the SF-36 in longitudinal studies? *Journal of Public Health Medicine, 19*, 179–186.

Kadden, R. M., & Litt, M. D. (2004). Searching for treatment outcome measures for use across trials. *Journal of Studies on Alcohol, 65*, 145–152.

Kaminer, Y., Blitz, C., Burleson, J. A., & Sussman, J. (1998). The Teen Treatment Services Review (T-TSR). *Journal of Substance Abuse Treatment, 15*, 291–300.

King, M. P., & Tucker, J. A. (2000). Behavior change patterns and strategies distinguishing moderation drinking and abstinence during the natural resolution of alcohol problems without treatment. *Psychology of Addictive Behaviors, 14*, 48–55.

Kruse, M. I., Fromme, K., & Corbin, W. R. (2005). Improving the accuracy of self-report measures of drinking: Disaggregating quantity and frequency indices of alcohol consumption. *Alcoholism: Clinical and Experimental Research, 29* (Suppl.), 118A.

Lambert, M. J., Burlingame, G. M., Umphress, V., Hansen, N. B., Vermeersch, D. A., Clouse, G. C., et al. (1996). The reliability and validity of the Outcome Questionnaire. *Clinical Psychology and Psychotherapy, 3*, 249–258.

Lammers, S. M. M., Schippers, G. M., van der Staak, C. P. F. (1995). Submissions and rebellion: Excessive drinking of women in problematic heterosexual partner relationships. *International Journal of Addictions, 30*, 901–917.

Leonard, K. E., & Das Eiden, R. D. (1999). Husband's and wife's drinking: Unilateral or bilateral influences among newlyweds in a general population sample. *Journal Studies on Alcohol, 13*, 130–138.

Leonard, K. E., & Mudar, P. (2003). Peer and partner drinking and the transition to marriage: A longitudinal examination of the selection and influence processes. *Psychology of Addictive Behaviors, 17*, 115–125.

Leonard, K. E., & Roberts, L. J. (1998). Marital aggression, quality, and stability in the first year of marriage: Findings from the Buffalo newlywed study. In T. N. Bradbury (Ed.), *The developmental course of marital dysfunction* (pp. 44–73). New York: Cambridge University Press.

Leonard, K. E., & Rothbard, J. C. (1999). Alcohol and the marriage effect. *Journal of Studies on Alcohol, 13*(Suppl.), 139–146.

Litman, G. K., Stapleton, J., Oppenheim, A. N., & Peleg, M. (1983). An instrument for measuring coping behaviors in hospitalized alcoholics: Implications for relapse prevention treatment. *British Journal of Addiction, 78*, 269–276.

Longabaugh, R., Wirtz, P. W., Zweben, A., & Stout, R. L. (1998). Network support for drinking, Alcoholics Anonymous and long-term matching effects. *Addiction, 93*, 1313–1333.

Longabaugh, R., & Zywiak, W. (1999). *Manual for the administration of the Important People Instrument adapted for use by Project COMBINE.* Providence, RI: Center for Alcohol and Addiction Studies, Brown University.

Magura, S., Staines, G., Kosanke, N., Rosenblum, A., Foote, J., DeLuca, A., et al. (2003). Predictive validity of the ASAM Patient Placement Criteria for naturalistically matched vs. mismatched alcoholism patients. *American Journal on Addictions, 12*, 386–397.

Mann, R. E., Sobell, L. C., Sobell, M. B., & Sobell, D. P. (1985). Reliability of a family tree questionnaire for assessing family history of alcohol problems. *Drug and Alcohol Dependence, 15*, 61–67.

Marlatt, G. A., & Witkiewitz, K. (2002). Harm reduction approaches to alcohol use: Health promotion, prevention, and treatment. *Addictive Behaviors, 27*, 867–886.

Marlatt, G. A. (1978). Craving for alcohol, loss of control, and relapse: A cognitive-behavioral analysis. In P. E. Nathan, G. A. Marlatt, & T. Loberg (Eds.), *Alcoholism: New directions in behavioral research and treatment* (pp. 271–314). New York: Plenum Press.

Marlatt, G. A. (1996). Taxonomy of high-risk situations for alcohol relapse: Evolution and development of a cognitive-behavioral model. *Addiction, 91*(Suppl.), S37–S49.

Marshal, M. P. (2003). For better or worse? The effects of alcohol use on marital functioning. *Clinical Psychology Review, 23*, 959–997.

Martin, C., Kaczynski, M., Maisto, S., Bukstein, O., & Moss, H. (1995). Patterns of DSM-IV alcohol abuse and dependence symptoms in adolescent drinkers. *Journal of Studies on Alcohol, 56*, 672–680.

McConnaughy, E. A., Prochaska, J. O., & Velicer, W. F. (1983). Stages of change in psychotherapy: Measurement and sample profiles. *Psychotherapy: Theory, Research & Practice, 20*, 368–375.

McCrady, B. S. (2004). To have but one true friend: Implications for practice of research on alcohol use disorders and social networks. *Psychology of Addictive Behaviors, 18*, 113–121.

McCrady, B. S., & Nathan, P. E. (in press). Impact of treatment factors on outcomes of treatment for substance use disorders. In L. E. Beutler & L. G. Castonguay (Eds.), *Integrating theories and relationships in psychotherapy.* New York: Oxford University Press.

McLellan, A. T., Luborsky, L., O'Brien, C. P., & Woody, G. E. (1980). An improved diagnostic instrument for substance abuse patients: The Addiction Severity Index. *Journal of Nervous Mental Disorders, 168*, 26–33.

McMahon, J., & Jones, B. T. (1993). The negative alcohol expectancy questionnaire. *Journal of the Association of Nurses on Substance Abuse, 12*, 17.

McMahon, J., Jones, B. T., & O'Donnell, P. (1994). Comparing positive and negative alcohol expectancies in male and female social drinkers. *Addiction Research, 1*, 349–365.

Mee-Lee, D. (1988). An instrument for treatment progress and matching: The recovery attitude and treatment evaluator (RAATE). *Journal of Substance Abuse Treatment, 5*, 183–186.

Miller, W. R., & Del Boca, F. K. (1994). Measurement of drinking behavior using the Form 90 family of instruments. *Journal of Studies on Alcohol, S12*, 112–118.

Miller, W. R., & Rollnick, S. (2002). *Motivational interviewing: Preparing people for change* (2nd ed.). New York: Guilford Press.

Miller, W. R., Sovereign, R. G., & Krege, B. (1988). Motivational interviewing with problem drinkers: II. The Drinker's Check-up as a preventive intervention. *Behavioural Psychotherapy, 16*, 251–268.

Miller, W. R., & Tonigan, J. S. (1996) Assessing drinkers' motivations for change: The SOCRATES. *Psychology of Addictive Behaviors, 10*(2), 81–89.

Miller W. R., Tonigan, J. S., & Longabaugh, R. (1995). *The Drinker Inventory of Consequences (DrInC): An* instrument for assessing adverse consequences of alcohol abuse (Project MATCH Monograph Series) (NIH Publication No. 95-3911). Vol 4. US Department of Health and Human Services, Public Health Service, National Institutes of Health, National Institute on Alcohol Abuse and Alcoholism, Rockville, MD.

Modell, J. G., Glaser, F. B., Mountz, J. M., Schmaltz, S., & Cyr L. (1992). Obsessive and compulsive characteristics of alcohol abuse and dependence: Quantification by a newly developed questionnaire. *Alcoholism: Clinical and Experimental Research*, 16, 266–271.

Mohr, C. D., Averna, A., Kenny, D. A., & Del Boca, F. K. (2001). Getting by (or getting high) with a little help from my friends: An examination of adult alcoholics; friendships. *Journal of Studies on Alcohol*, 62, 637–646.

Montgomery, H. A., Tonigan, J. S., & Miller, W. R. (1991). *The General Alcoholics Anonymous Tools of Recovery Scale (GAATOR)*. Unpublished instrument, University of New Mexico, Center on Alcoholism, Substance Abuse, and Addictions (CASAA).

Monti, P. M., Rohsenow, D. J., Abrams, D. B., & Zwick, W. R. (1993). Development of a behavior analytically derived alcohol-specific role-play assessment instrument. *Journal of Studies on Alcohol*, 54, 710–721.

Moore, A. A., Giuli, L., Gould, R., Hu, P., Zhou, K., Reuben, D., et al. (2006). Alcohol use, comorbidity, and mortality. *Journal of the American Geriatrics Society*, 54, 757–762.

Moos, R. H., & Moos, B. S. (1988). *Life stressors and social resources inventory: Adult form manual*. Palo Alto, CA: Center for Health Care Evaluation.

Moos, R. H., & Moos, B. S. (2006). Participation in treatment and alcoholics anonymous: A 16-year follow-up of initially untreated individuals. *Journal of Clinical Psychology*, 62, 735–750.

Morgenstern, J., Kahler, C., Frey, R., & Labouvie, E. (1996). Modeling therapeutic responses to 12-step treatment: Optimal responders, non-responders and partial responders. *Journal of Substance Abuse*, 8, 45–59.

Morgenstern, J., & Longabaugh, R. (2000). Cognitive-behavioral treatment for alcohol dependence: A review of evidence for its hypothesized mechanisms of action. *Addiction*, 95, 1475–1490.

Mundle, G., Munkes, J., Ackermann, K, & Mann, K. (2000). Sex differences of carbohydrate-deficient transferrin, gamma-glutamyltransferase, and mean corpuscular volume in alcohol-dependent patients. *Alcoholism: Clinical and Experimental Research*, 24, 1400–1405.

Myers, M. G., & Brown S. A. (1990). Coping and appraisal in potential relapse situations among adolescent substance abusers following treatment. *Journal of Adolescent Chemical Dependency*, 1, 95–115.

Myers, M. G., & Wagner, E. F. (1995). The Temptation-Coping Questionnaire: Development and validation. *Journal of Substance Abuse*, 7, 463–479.

Neumann, T., & Spies, C. (2003). Use of biomarkers for alcohol use disorders in clinical practice. *Addiction*, 98(S2), 81–91.

National Institute on Alcohol Abuse and Alcoholism. (2003). *National Epidemiologic Survey on Alcohol and Related Conditions (NESARC)*. Bethesda, MD.

Niles, B., & McCrady, B. S. (1991). Detection of alcohol problems in a hospital setting. *Addictive Behaviors*, 16, 223–233.

O'Hare T. (1997). Measuring excessive alcohol use in college drinking contexts: The Drinking Context Scale. Addictive Behaviors, 22, 469–477.

Rosenthal, R.N., & Westreich, L. (1999). Treatment of persons with dual diagnoses of substance use disorder and other psychological problems. In B.S. McCrady & E. E. Epstein (Eds.), *Addictions: A Guidebook for Professionals* (pp. 439–476). New York: Oxford University Press.

Parsons, O. A. (1998). Neurocognitive deficits in alcoholics and social drinkers: A continuum? *Alcoholism: Clinical and Experimental Research*, 22, 954–961.

Petry, N. M., Stinson, F. S., & Grant, B. F. (2005). Comorbidity of DSM-IV pathological gambling and other psychiatric disorders: Results from the National Epidemiologic Survey on Alcohol and Related Conditions. *Journal of Clinical Psychiatry*, 66, 564–574.

Polcin, D. L. (1997). The etiology and diagnosis of alcohol dependence: Differences in the professional literature. *Psychotherapy: Theory, Research, Practice, Training*, 34, 297–306.

Prochaska, J. O., & DiClemente, C. C. (1983). Stages and processes of self-change of smoking: Toward an integrative model of change. *Journal of Consulting and Clinical Psychology*, 51, 390–395.

Quigley, B. M., & Leonard, K. E. (1999). Husband alcohol expectancies, drinking, and marital conflict styles as predictors of severe marital violence among newlywed couples. *Psychology of Addictive Behaviors*, 13, 49–59.

Raistrick, D. S., Bradshaw, J., Tober, G., Weiner, J., Allison, J., & Healey, C. (1994). Development of the leads dependence questionnaire. *Addiction*, 89, 563–572.

Reynaud, M., Hourcade, F., Planche, F., Albuisson, E., Meunier, M. N., & Planceh, R. (1998). Useful ness of carbohydrate-deficient transferring in alcoholic patients with normal gamma-glutamyltranspeptidase. *Alcoholism: Clinical and Experimental Research*, 22, 615–618.

Roberts, L. J., & Leonard, K. E. (1997). Gender differences and similarities in the alcohol and marriage relationship. In R. W. Wilsnack & S. C. Wilsnack (Eds.), *Gender and alcohol. Individual and social perspectives* (pp. 289–311). New Brunswick, NJ: Alcohol Research Documentation, Inc., Rutgers University.

Roberts, L. J., & Leonard, K. E. (1998). An empirical typology of drinking partnerships and their relationships to marital functioning and drinking consequences. *Journal of Marriage and the Family, 60,* 515–526.

Rollnick, S., Heather, N., Gold, R., & Hall, W. (1992). Development of a short "readiness to change" questionnaire for use in brief, opportunistic interventions among excessive drinkers. *British Journal of Addiction, 87,* 743–754.

Rosenthal, R.N., & Westreich, L. (1999). Treatment of persons with dual diagnoses of substance use disorder and other psychological problems. In B. S. McCrady & E. E. Epstein (Eds.), *Addictions: A Guidebook for Professionals* (pp. 439–476). New York: Oxford University Press.

Ross, H.E., Glaser, F.B., & Stiasny, S. (1988). Sex differences in the prevalence of psychiatric disorders in patients with alcohol and drug problems. *Addiction, 83,* 1179–1192.

Russell, M. (1994). New assessment tools for drinking in pregnancy: T-ACE, TWEAK, and others. *Alcohol, Health and Research World, 18,* 55–61.

Russell, M., Welte, J. W., & Barnes, G. M. (1991). Quantity-frequency measures of alcohol consumption: Beverage-specific vs global questions. *British Journal of Addiction, 86,* 409–417.

Rychtarik, R. G., Connors, G. J., Whitney, R. B., McGillicuddy, N. B., Fitterling, J. M., & Wirtz, P. W. (2000). Treatment settings for persons with alcoholism: Evidence for matching clients to inpatient versus outpatient care. *Journal of Consulting and Clinical Psychology, 68,* 277–289.

Salaspuro, M. (1999). Carbohydrate-deficient transferrin as compared to other markers of alcoholism: A systematic review. *Alcohol, 19,* 261–271.

Sanchez-Craig, M., Davila, R., & Cooper, G. (1996). A self-help approach for high-risk drinking: Effect of an initial assessment. *Journal of Consulting and Clinical Psychology, 64,* 694–700.

Saxon, A. J., Kivlahan, D. R., Doyle, S., & Donovan, D. M. (2007). Further validation of the alcohol dependence scale as and index of severity. *Journal of Studies on Alcohol and Drugs, 68,* 149–156.

Schmidt, L. G., Schmidt, K., Dufeu, P., Ohse, A., Rommelspacher, H., & Müller, C. (1997). Superiority of carbohydrate-deficient transferrin to gamma-glutamyltransferase in detecting relapse in alcoholism. *American Journal of Psychiatry, 154,* 75–80.

Schuckit, M. A., Anthenelli, R. M., Bucholz, K. K., Hesselbrock, V. M., & Tipp, J. (1995). The time course of development of alcohol-related problems in men and women. *Journal of Studies on Alcohol, 56,* 218–224.

Schober, R., & Annis, H. M. (1996). Barriers to help-seeking for change in drinking: A gender-focused review of the literature. *Addictive Behaviors, 21,* 81–92.

Selzer, M. (1971). The Michigan Alcoholism Screen Test (MAST): The quest for a new diagnostic instrument. *American Journal of Psychiatry, 127,* 1653–1658.

Singleton, E. G., Tiffany, S. T., & Henningfield, J. E. (1995). Development and validation of a new questionnaire to assess craving for alcohol. *Problems of Drug Dependence, 1994: Proceeding of the 56th Annual Meeting, The College on Problems of Drug Dependence, Inc., Volume II: Abstracts* (p. 289). NIDA Research Monograph 153, Rockville, MD: National Institute on Drug Abuse.

Skinner, H. A., & Allen, B. A. (1982). Alcohol dependence syndrome: Measurement and validation. *Journal of Abnormal Psychology, 91,* 199–209.

Skinner, H. A., & Horn, J. L. (1984). *Alcohol dependence scale: Users guide.* Toronto, Canada: Addiction Research Foundation.

Smith, A. J., Hodgson, R. J., Bridgeman, K., & Shepherd, J. P. (2003). A randomized controlled trial of a brief intervention after alcohol-related facial injury. *Addiction, 98,* 43–52.

Sobell, L. C., & Sobell, M. B. (1992). Timeline followback: A technique for assessing self-reported alcohol consumption. In R. Litten & J. Allen (Eds.), *Measuring alcohol consumption* (pp. 41–69). Totowa, NJ: Humana Press.

Sobell, L. C., & Sobell, M. B. (1995). *Alcohol timeline followback users' manual.* Toronto, Canada: Addiction Research Foundation.

Spielberger, C. D., & Gorsuch, R. L. (1983). *Manual for the state-trait anxiety inventory: form Y: Self-evaluation questionnaire.* Palo Alto, CA: Consulting Psychologists Press.

Stinson, F. S., Grant, B. F., Dawson, D. A., Ruan, W. J., Huang, B., & Saha, T. (2005). Comorbidity between DSM-IV alcohol and specific drug use disorders in the United States: Results from the National Epidemiologic Survey on Alcohol and Related Conditions. *Drug and Alcohol Dependence, 80,* 105–116.

Sullivan, J. T., Sykora, K., Schneiderman, J., Naranjo, C. A., & Sellers, E. M. (1989). Assessment of alcohol withdrawal: The revised Clinical Institute Withdrawal Assessment for Alcohol scale (CIWA-AR). *British Journal of Addiction, 84,* 1353–1357.

Swenson, W. M., & Morse, R. M. (1975). The use of a self-administered alcoholism screening test (SAAST) in a medical center. *Mayo Clinical Proceedings, 50,* 204–208.

Thomassen, L. (2002). AA utilization after introduction in outpatient treatment. *Substance Use & Misuse, 37,* 239–253.

Tonigan, J. S., Connors, G. J., & Miller, W. R. (1996). Alcoholics Anonymous Involvement (AAI) scale: Reliability and norms. *Psychology of Addictive Behaviors, 10,* 75–80.

Tonigan, J. S., Miller, W. R., & Brown, J. M. (1997). The reliability of the Form 90: An instrument for assessing alcohol treatment outcome. *Journal of Studies on Alcohol, 58,* 358–364.

Tucker, J. A., Vuchinich, R. E., & Rippens, P. D. (2004). Different variables are associated with help-seeking patterns and long-term outcomes among problem drinkers. *Addictive Behaviors, 29,* 433–439.

Ware, J. E., & Sherbourne, C. D. (1992.) The MOS 36-item short-form health survey (SF-36). I. Conceptual framework and item selection. *Medical Care, 30,* 473–483.

Ware, J. E., Snow, K. K., & Kosinski, M. (1993). *SF-36 Health Survey: Manual and interpretation guide.* Boston, MA: Health Institute, New England Medical Center.

Wetterling, T., Kanitz, R., Rumpf, H., Hapke, U., & Fischer, D. (1998). Comparison of CAGE and MAST with the alcohol marker CDT, gamma-GT, ALAT, ASAT, and MCV. *Alcohol and Alcoholism, 33,* 424–430.

White, H. R., & Labouvie, E. W. (1989). Towards the assessment of adolescent problem drinking. *Journal of Studies on Alcohol, 50,* 30–37.

WHOQOL Group. (1998). Development of the World Health Organization WHOQOL-BREF quality of life assessment. *Psychological Medicine, 28,* 551–558.

Yoon, G., Kim, S. W., Thuras, P., Grant, J. E., & Westermeyer, J. (2006). Alcohol craving in outpatients with alcohol dependence: Rate and clinical correlates. *Journal of Studies on Alcohol, 67,* 770–777.

Young, R. M., Oei, T. P., & Crook, G. M. (1991). Development of a drinking self-efficacy questionnaire. *Journal of Psychopathology and Behavioral Assessment, 13,* 1–15.

Zimmerman, M., & Coryell, W. (1987) The Inventory to Diagnose Depression (IDD): A self-report scale to diagnose major depressive disorder. *Journal of Consulting and Clinical Psychology, 55,* 55–59.

Zywiak, W. H., Connors, G. J., Maisto, S. A., & Westerberg, V. S. (1996). Relapse research and the Reasons for Drinking Questionnaire: A factor analysis of Marlatt's relapse taxonomy. *Addiction, 91,* 121–130.

Zitter, R., & McCrady, B. S. (1979). The Drinking Patterns Questionnaire. Unpublished manuscript.

17

Gambling Disorders

David C. Hodgins

Randy Stinchfield

Gambling is defined as wagering money or something else of value on an outcome that is partially or primarily determined by chance. This broad definition comprises a wide range of activities including the purchase of raffle tickets for a local charity, playing the animal lottery in Sao Paulo, betting on the outcome of a weekly golf game in Los Angeles, dog track betting in Miami, or playing casino games at the Grand Casino in Ashgabat, Turkmenistan, or Pachinko in a parlor in Tokyo. People can become overinvolved in any of these activities, although certain types of gambling appear to be more likely to lead to problems. Types of gambling such as slot machines and other electronic formats that provide relatively quick feedback are considered most risky for the development of problematic gambling. These formats are typically relatively inexpensive, easy to learn and play, and are often widely available both inside and outside casinos, which also contributes to the risk associated with them. Although the financial cost of limited social play is small, uncontrolled involvement leads to overwhelmingly large expenditures. Although gambling problems have been recognized for centuries, and have been described in the *Diagnostic and Statistical Manual of Mental Disorders* (DSM) since 1980, their prevalence and visibility have increased significantly since gambling has become broadly available over the past two decades (Shaffer & Hall, 2001). Currently, online gambling is mushrooming in popularity, which may lead to even further growth in the prevalence of gambling problems.

Clinicians from both the mental health and addiction communities have begun to respond to the need for treatment for gambling disorders. This chapter briefly describes the nature of gambling disorders and then reviews the various assessment instruments that are available to help clinicians with diagnosis, case conceptualization and treatment planning, and treatment monitoring and evaluation. The psychometric research for each type of assessment instrument is summarized and instruments are rated in terms of their clinical utility.

THE NATURE OF GAMBLING DISORDERS

The Diagnostic and Statistical Manual of Mental Disorders, 4th Edition, Text Revision (DSM-IV-TR; American Psychiatric Association, 2000) provides diagnostic criteria for Pathological Gambling, a disorder characterized by impaired control over gambling activities. As these criteria are unchanged from the DSM-IV (1994), we make reference throughout the chapter to the DSM-IV criteria. Most general population prevalence surveys, in contrast, describe two levels of problems, pathological gambling, which roughly corresponds to the DSM-IV category, and problem gambling, which is a significant but less severe type of problem. Local prevalence surveys have been conducted worldwide, mostly using random digit telephone dialing methodologies. Shaffer and colleagues have summarized these survey results (Shaffer & Hall, 2001; Shaffer, Hall, & Vander Bilt, 1999) and report average adult lifetime problem gambling rates of 3% to 5% and pathological gambling rates of 1% to 2%. More recent face-to-face diagnostic past-year assessments have reported DSM-IV pathological rates of 0.4% in the United States (Welte, Barnes, Wieczorek, Tidwell, & Parker, 2001) and problem gambling rates of 2.0% in Canada (Cox, Yu, Afifi, &

Ladouceur, 2005). These rates are highest in geographic areas with more gambling availability (Cox et al., 2005; Volberg, 2001).

Although gambling disorders can affect anyone, younger people, males, and individuals with lower socioeconomic status have higher rates (Petry, 2005). Gambling disorders are associated with significant distress and social and family impairment. Huge financial debts contribute to high level of stress and pressure to be less than honest with family members, friends, colleagues and even with themselves. Nongambling leisure activities are curtailed and increasing time and energy goes into gambling or obtaining the money for gambling. Sometimes checks are knowingly cashed without sufficient money in the bank to cover them and not infrequently funds are embezzled from employers. Rates of suicidal ideation, attempts, and completed attempts are high among individuals with gambling disorders (Hodgins, Mansley, & Thygesen, 2006).

Other mental health diagnoses are highly comorbid with gambling disorders, especially substance use, mood, and anxiety disorders (Crockford & el-Guebaly, 1998). For example, a community survey of over 43,000 Americans revealed that almost three quarters of pathological gamblers had a lifetime alcohol use disorder, 38% had a lifetime drug use disorder, 50% had a mood disorder, and 41% had an anxiety disorder (Petry, Stinson, & Grant, 2005). Our understanding of the temporal onset and patterning of pathological gambling and other mental health disorders is limited, but the relationship appears to vary by disorder. Substance abuse tends to precede pathological gambling (e.g., Cunningham-Williams, Cottler, Compton, Spitznagel, & Ben-Abdallah, 2000). On the other hand, the onset of major depression was found to be equally likely to precede or to follow the development of pathological gambling in one study (Hodgins, Peden, & Cassidy, 2005), and more often followed the onset of pathological gambling in others (Taber, McCormick, Russo, Adkins, & Ramirez, 1987).

A variety of psychological treatment approaches have been offered, including mutual support groups such as Gamblers Anonymous, psychodynamic therapies, behavioral and cognitive-behavioral treatments, and brief motivational treatments. Cognitive-behavioral and brief motivational treatments have the most empirical support to date (Hodgins & Petry, 2004). Pharmacological trial results generally have been disappointing, with high placebo response and high drop-outs, and are not, therefore, recommended as first line treatment (Petry, 2005). Natural or non-treatment-assisted recovery rates are also sizeable. Surveys that report past-year prevalence as well as lifetime prevalence consistently indicate recovery rates of about 40%, with the vast majority of these recovered individuals reporting never having accessed treatment (Hodgins, Wynne, & Makarchuk, 1999; Slutske, 2006).

ASSESSMENT FOR DIAGNOSIS

There has been a proliferation of disordered gambling assessment instruments over the past decade and the majority of them fall into the area of interview or self-report diagnostic instruments. The preponderance of measures has been developed for use in prevalence surveys and their design reflects the need to balance maximal reliability and validity with the brevity that is required in such research. Some of these diagnostic instruments have only had psychometric properties assessed in community samples and, therefore, will not be reviewed in this chapter. However, as discussed below and shown in Table 17.1, a number have also been validated in clinical populations and are becoming widely used by clinicians.

The DSM-IV conceptualization of pathological gambling is currently the predominant diagnostic model (National Research Council, 1999). A number of the diagnostic instruments are based upon either DSM-IV criteria or criteria from earlier versions of the DSM. Although Pathological Gambling is contained in the impulse disorder section of the DSM, the diagnostic criteria are modeled after the substance dependence criteria. The criteria include items such as tolerance (escalating gambling activities over time), withdrawal-like symptoms (restlessness and irritability), attempts to control one's gambling, impaired control ("chasing losses") and continuing to gamble despite negative consequences. Generally, the criteria are behavioral and objective in nature. An individual receives a diagnosis if five or more of the ten criteria are met (criterion A) and the gambling behavior is not better accounted for by a manic episode (criterion B).

The problem gambling category that is often reported in prevalence surveys, but not included in the DSM, is typically conceptualized as subthreshold

TABLE 17.1 Ratings of Instruments Used for Diagnosis

Instrument	Norms	Internal Consistency	Inter-Rater Reliability	Test–Retest Reliability	Content Validity	Construct Validity	Validity Generalization	Clinical Utility	Highly Recommended
SOGS	E	E	G	A	A	E	E	G	✓
SOGS-R	E	G	U	A	A	E	A	G	✓
NODS	U	A	U	A	A	G	A	G	
GAMTOMS-DSM	A	A	U	G	A	G	A	A	
DIGS-DSM	U	E	U	U	A	A	U	G	
SCI-PG	U	U	E	A	A	G	U	G	
GBI	A	E	U	U	A	G	U	A	
CPGI–PGSI	A	G	U	A	L	A	A	A	

Note: SOGS = South Oaks Gambling Screen; SOGS-R = SOGS past-year version; NODS = National Opinion Research Center DSM-IV Screen for Gambling Problems; GAMTOMS = Gambling Treatment Outcome Monitoring System; DIGS = Diagnostic Interview for Gambling Schedule; SCI-PG = Structured Clinical Interview for Pathological Gambling; GBI = Gambling Behavior Inventory; CPGI PGSI = Canadian Problem Gambling Index–Problem Gambling Severity Index; L = Less Than Adequate; A = Adequate; G = Good; E = Excellent; U = Unavailable.

pathological gambling. Many of the diagnostic instruments reviewed below and summarized in Table 17.1 provide a lower cut-off for determining problem gambling and some instruments provide one or two additional "at risk" categories that reflect even lower levels of problem severity.

The medically based conceptualization of pathological gambling in the DSM has been criticized as ignoring the role of the social and environmental context of gambling disorders. In response, broader "harm-based" models of gambling problems have been proposed in which problems are defined as gambling that creates negative consequences for the gambler, others in the social network, or the community (Ferris & Wynne, 2001; Ferris, Wynne, & Single, 1998). The final instrument reviewed below, the Problem Severity Index of the Canadian Problem Gambling Index (Ferris & Wynne, 2001) was developed from this alternative conceptualization and has been popular in Canada as well as some other areas of the world (e.g., Australia, New Zealand).

South Oaks Gambling Screen

The most well-known instrument is the South Oaks Gambling Screen (SOGS; Lesieur & Blume, 1987). The SOGS, developed in the 1980s to screen clinical populations, was based upon the DSM-III and III-R criteria. It subsequently became the most widely used instrument in general population prevalence surveys (Shaffer et al., 1999) and has been translated into French, Spanish, Italian, Swedish, Lao, Vietnamese, and Cambodian. The original SOGS consisted of

20 true/false self-completion items that reflect lifetime gambling involvement, although a parallel past-year version was subsequently developed (Lesieur & Blume, 1993); most recently, a 3-month version has also undergone preliminary assessment of its psychometric properties (Wulfert et al., 2005). This latter version is potentially useful in evaluating outcome and will be discussed in the treatment monitoring section below. The SOGS can be administered either in self-report format or via face-to-face or telephone interview. Although the original scale was designed to identify pathological gambling, a lower cut-off score for problem gambling has been established and the SOGS total score is also used as an indicator of gambling problem severity.

The content of the SOGS includes items that inquire about hiding evidence of gambling, spending more time or money gambling than intended, arguing with family members about gambling, and borrowing money from a variety of sources to gamble or to pay gambling debts. Each of these sources of money is scored as a separate item, which weights this criterion very heavily. Because the SOGS items were developed from DSM-III criteria, there is some concern regarding its content validity for DSM-IV assessments. A number of criteria have been changed significantly in the DSM revisions and the DSM-IV requires that the individual meet 5 of 10 criteria in comparison to the DSM-III that required 4 of 9 criteria. Nonetheless, the recent investigation of the psychometric properties of the past-year self-report version of the SOGS in three large clinical samples suggested that it is has good internal reliability and concurrent validity compared with DSM-IV assessments (Stinchfield, 2002). Classification accuracy overall was good (.96) with better sensitivity (.99) than specificity (.75). Regarding specificity, the SOGS appears to be a liberal measure of DSM-IV pathological gambling. In general population samples, the SOGS identifies a greater number of pathological gamblers than do DSM-IV-oriented measures (Cox et al., 2005; Stinchfield, 2002). Fewer comparative data are available for clinical samples, although the same concern about false positives exists (Grant, Steinberg, Kim, Rounsaville, & Potenza, 2004; Hodgins, 2004).

Test–retest reliability was acceptable with the original interview version (Lesieur & Blume, 1987) and the past-year self-report version in a clinical sample (Stinchfield, Winters, Botzet, Jerstad, & Breyer, 2007). The self-report SOGS often acts as the comparison standard in the assessment of other measures, so evidence of concurrent validity of both past-year and lifetime versions across a variety of clinical and non-clinical samples is available and is generally positive (see Table 17.1; Grant et al., 2004; Hodgins, 2004; Lesieur & Blume, 1987; Stinchfield, Govoni, & Frisch, 2005; Wulfert et al., 2005). Ladouceur and colleagues (Ladouceur et al., 2000) investigated validity at the item level and reported that most respondents in a community sample misinterpreted one or more items. Because all the true–false items are keyed in the true direction (true reflecting a problem), community respondents were more likely to over report than under report symptoms—clarification of item meaning reduced the number of individuals classified as pathological gamblers. Similar research has not been conducted with clinical samples but clearly interpretation at the item level is likely to be unreliable for any scale.

National Opinion Research Center DSM-IV Screen for Gambling Problems (NODS)

The NODS was originally developed for a U.S. national gambling telephone survey as a past-year and lifetime diagnostic measure based on DSM-IV diagnostic criteria (Gerstein et al., 1999). As well as being designed for use in an interview format, it is also used as a self-report instrument although no psychometric information is available for the self-report version. Seventeen true–false items measure the 10 DSM-IV diagnostic criteria and the past-year items are asked only if the lifetime item is answered with a positive response. The NODS total score is used to identify pathological gambling but also lower cut-offs indicate problem and low-risk gamblers. A number of the DSM criteria are operationalized with the use of time periods (e.g., past 2 weeks) and frequency parameters (e.g., three or more times) in order to increase the item reliability. Because these changes represent a tightening of these criteria relative to their description in the DSM-IV, the NODS may under identify pathological gamblers. Consistent with this concern, in the U.S. national sample, the estimated prevalence was lower than found in other surveys (Gerstein et al., 1999). However, without a gold standard for comparison, it is unclear that this lower estimate is less valid. There have not been published comparisons of the NODS compared with other DSM-IV measures in either general or clinical populations.

This relatively new scale has less supporting psychometric research than the SOGS and therefore received mostly adequate ratings in Table 17.1. In terms of additional indicators of validity, during the scale development phase the NODS was administered to a small sample of individuals in outpatient problem gambling treatment programs. Of the 40, 38 scored 5 or more on the lifetime NODS and 2 obtained scores of 4. Retest reliability over 2 to 4 weeks in an overlapping sample of 44 gamblers in treatment was high ($r = .99$ and $r = .98$ for lifetime and past year, respectively). The authors did not report internal consistency coefficients, although alpha coefficients in treatment samples were reported to be adequate in the past-year version administered via telephone (Hodgins, 2004) and good in the past-year and lifetime versions administered face to face (Wulfert et al., 2005).

The validity of the lifetime and past-year total scores was also assessed in these clinical samples. Using a variety of discriminant and convergent measures, good validity results were generally obtained (Hodgins, 2004; Wulfert et al., 2005). Hodgins (2004) also reported the validity of the categorical cut-points compared with the SOGS pathological and problem categories. Agreement was poor, with most NODS problem gamblers categorized as pathological on the SOGS (i.e., more severe). As it is unclear which categorization is more valid in the absence of a gold standard indicator, clinicians should be cautious about relying too much on cut-off scores to indicate the presence or absence of a diagnosable condition.

In summary, the NODS appears to identify fewer individuals as pathological gamblers in both general population and treatment samples. It is a brief scale that provides a DSM-IV diagnosis plus a subclinical problem gambling category. To date, positive, but limited, psychometric research is available for the interview version.

GAMTOMS-DSM-IV Measure

The Gambling Treatment Outcome Monitoring System (GAMTOMS; Stinchfield et al., 2007) is a multidimensional self-report or interview assessment tool designed for outcome assessment. It is described in detail in the sections on other assessment purposes. However, it also contains a 10-item true/false DSM-IV measure relevant for diagnostic purposes. Both the self-report and interview versions of the GAMTOMS have been subjected to a number of psychometric evaluations in clinical samples (Stinchfield et al., 2007). The DSM-IV total score showed good internal reliability in one treatment sample but less than adequate reliability in two other samples. Retest reliability over 1 week was good in the three samples but slightly lower than the SOGS retest estimate in the same samples. The total scores showed good convergent and discriminant validity with a variety of criteria, including the SOGS. The categorical diagnosis of pathological gambling showed good sensitivity (.96) and specificity (.95) identifying clinical from nonclinical individuals and good sensitivity (.97) and specificity (1.0) using SOGS classification as the criterion (Stinchfield, 2003; Stinchfield et al., 2005).

Other DSM-IV Measures

A number of additional DSM-IV-based measures have been developed but, to date, have had limited psychometric evaluation. For example, a brief gambling module of the Diagnostic Interview Schedule (DIS; Robins, Cottler, Bucholz, & Compton, 1996) has been used in a number of investigations (e.g., Cunningham-Williams, Cottler, Compton, & Spitznagel, 1998; Welte et al., 2001) although no psychometric data have been reported. A revised and more extensive DIS and Composite International Diagnostic Interview module, the Gambling Assessment Module, is currently under development at Washington University, St. Louis.

Two other diagnostic assessment measures are appealing because they allow the clinician to probe responses to determine whether each diagnostic criterion is passed. The Diagnostic Interview

for Gambling Schedule-DSM-IV Diagnosis (DIGS-DSM-IV; Winters, Specker, & Stinchfield, 2002) is a structured clinical interview for assessment and treatment planning that contains a 20-item assessment of the DSM-IV criteria for the past-year and lifetime timeframes. Psychometric data were assessed in only one treatment sample but were positive (Winters et al., 2002). Grant and colleagues describe a similar measure, the Structured Clinical Interview for Pathological Gambling (SCI-PG) that is modeled after the Structured Clinical Interview for the DSM-IV (SCID; Spitzer, Williams, Gibbon, & First, 1990), which is widely used for assessment of DSM disorders but does not include a pathological gambling module. In a SCID assessment, trained clinicians use a series of probe questions to determine whether each of the 10 criteria has been met over the lifetime and currently. If the gambling module is used in conjunction with the full SCID, then the clinician can assess the DSM exclusion criteria for pathological gambling, the gambling behaviors are not better accounted for by a manic episode (Criterion B). In a small clinical sample, inter-rater reliability and retest reliability over a 1-week period were excellent and sensitivity was .88 and specificity was 1.00 assessed against clinical ratings.

A final DSM alternative is the Gambling Behavior Inventory (GBI; Stinchfield, 2003; Stinchfield et al., 2005), which is a 76-item structured interview that includes a 10-item past-year DSM scale. The DSM scale has shown excellent internal reliability in two treatment samples as well as convergent and discriminant validity with a variety of measures (Stinchfield, 2003; Stinchfield et al., 2005, 2007). The categorical diagnosis of pathological gambling showed good sensitivity (.91), but lower specificity (.83), in identifying clinical from nonclinical individuals (Stinchfield et al., 2005). Sensitivity and specificity improved using a cutoff of four versus five criteria.

Canadian Problem Gambling Index–Problem Gambling Severity Index

The Canadian Problem Gambling Index (CPGI; Ferris & Wynne, 2001) is an interview tool assessing gambling involvement and social context designed for prevalence surveys. It has been used in surveys in most Canadian provinces and nationally, which provides a large normative database (Cox et al., 2005).

The CPGI contains a nine-item Problem Gambling Severity Index (PGSI) which has a past-year time-frame. The PGSI total score indicates low-risk, moderate-risk, and problem gambling. The total score has demonstrated good internal reliability and adequate test–retest reliability over a 4-week period in the general population. It also shows good convergent validity with the SOGS, DSM-IV, and clinical ratings in a treatment sample. Classification accuracy of the problem gambling category showed adequate sensitivity (.83) and excellent specificity (1.0) using DSM-IV classification as the criterion (Ferris & Wynne, 2001) Although the large normative database is a strength for use of the scale in Canada, there is a need for independent evaluations of the psychometric properties of the PGSI and more attention to evaluating the validity of the instrument's cut-off scores.

Overall Evaluation

As gambling disorders are a relatively new area of investigation, there is a lack of consensus about the gold standard diagnostic instruments. Indeed, the DSM-IV criteria were primarily based upon expert consensus and not empirical research (Lesieur & Rosenthal, 1991; Stinchfield et al., 2005) and their validity continues to be debated. In terms of instruments, the SOGS was almost unanimously used until it was eclipsed by the desire for a DSM-IV-based instrument. Because of its lengthy history, sufficient psychometric support is available for both the lifetime and past-year versions to describe them as highly recommended in Table 17.1. More recently, a number of DSM-IV alternatives have been developed, but none has the extensive psychometric database of the SOGS and none has become universally used in either research or clinical contexts. Although the SOGS and DSM-IV measures generally appear to assess the same construct, it also appears that the SOGS pathological and problem gambling categories represent a lower threshold for the disorders than the DSM-IV measures. The SOGS also lacks content validity with respect to the DSM-IV criteria.

All of the proposed DSM-IV measures have positive preliminary psychometric support and, not surprisingly, the items on the various scales are quite similar. In fact, even the CPGI–PGSI, which was not derived from a DSM conceptualization, has eight of nine items that overlap with either the SOGS or DSM-IV items. The measures vary in other ways.

The NODS and GAMTOMS DSM are the only self-completion options, although all of the psychometric evaluation of the NODS has been on the interview format. The interview options include the GAMTOMS, NODS, GBI, DIGS, and SCI-PG. The NODS and GBI can be administered via telephone as well as face to face. The GAMTOMS, NODS, and GBI can be administered by lay persons and the DIGS and SCI-PG require clinical training and experience. These latter two measures are, arguably, true diagnostic measures because interviewers probe to ensure that each criterion is reached whereas the others can be better viewed as screening measures. Nonetheless, further psychometric evaluation is required before any of these instruments can be highly recommended for routine use (see Table 17.1). In the meantime, the information available for each instrument is generally supportive and clinicians are advised to use the instrument that best fits their purpose from a practical perspective.

ASSESSMENT FOR CASE CONCEPTUALIZATION AND TREATMENT PLANNING

Table 17.2 outlines important domains in case conceptualization and treatment planning for gambling disorders. Together the domains provide a comprehensive description of the severity and consequences of the problem. These factors point to potential treatment targets. It is also recommended that some type of functional analysis of the precipitants of gambling be performed. This type of information is particularly relevant for cognitive-behavioral therapy but can also inform the therapeutic direction in other treatment models. Assessment of comorbidity serves a similar purpose and also may provide information about etiology (as does family history). A clear understanding of the client's treatment goal, previous treatment experience, and motivation is also essential.

Limited instrumentation exists for many of these areas and, in fact, research regarding the specifics of the construct is also limited in some instances. A good example is the first domain in Table 17.2, Severity/Impaired Control. An issue exists in the field that parallels a long-standing debate in the alcohol field—the advisability of gambling moderation goals versus complete abstinence from gambling (Ladouceur, 2005). The issue in gambling is complicated by the

TABLE 17.2 Important Domains in Case Conceptualization and Treatment Planning for Gambling Disorders

General Dimension	Specific Construct	Standardized Tools
Severity/Impaired Control	Impaired control?	SOGS, NODS, CPGI–PGSI
Gambling Quantity	Lifetime history	
	Recent (past month)	Timeline follow-back method
Consequences	Health (e.g., gastrointestinal, insomnia)	ASI–GSI, GAMTOMS, DIGS
	Family	
	Social relationships	
	Employment	
	Financial	
	Emotional (self-esteem)	
	Legal	
Association/Circumstances of Gambling	Functional analysis	IGS, TGS
Comorbid Psychiatric Disorders	DSM Axis I and II	SCID, DIS, CIDI
Other Drug Use	Prescription and illicit drugs	AUDIT, DAST
	Nicotine, caffeine	
Family History	Biological and family exposure to gambling	
Treatment History	Programs started and completed	GAMTOMS
	Twelve-step involvement	
	Periods of abstinence or nonproblematic gambling	
Treatment Goal	Goal (abstinence or moderation)	GASS, SCQG
	Self-efficacy	
Motivation	Readiness to change	GAMTOMS
	Reasons to change	
	Family and social support	

Notes: SOGS = South Oaks Gambling Screen; SOGS-R = SOGS past-year version; NODS = National Opinion Research Center DSM-IV Screen for Gambling Problems; CPGI–PGSI = Canadian Problem Gambling Index–Problem Gambling Severity Index; ASI-GSI = Addiction Severity Index–Gambling Severity Index; GAMTOMS = Gambling Treatment Outcome Monitoring System; DIGS =Diagnostic Interview for Gambling Schedule; IGS = Inventory of Gambling Situations; TGS = Temptation to Gamble Scale; SCID = Structured Clinical Interview for the DSM-IV; DIS = Diagnostic Interview Schedule; CIDI = Composite International Diagnostic Interview; AUDIT = Alcohol Use Disorders Identification Test; DAST = Drug Abuse Screening Test; GASS = Gambling Abstinence Self-Efficacy Scale; SCQG = Situational Confidence Questionnaire for Gambling.

possibility that gambling abstinence can be narrowly defined as quitting the types of gambling that have caused problems for the individual or broadly defined as all types of gambling even if they have never caused problems.

In the alcohol field, the most robust clinical indicator of the likelihood of the success of moderation versus abstinence from alcohol is the degree of alcohol dependence (Rosenberg, 1993). Efforts are underway to delineate a similar construct in the gambling field, impairment of control over gambling, although efforts to develop a reliable measurement tool have yielded mixed results (Dickerson & O'Connor, 2006). Kyngdon (2004) described a 12-item unifactorial scale that, in preliminary studies, correlated highly with measures of severity, such as the SOGS, which suggests that, until measurement of impaired control further develops, severity of problem can be used

as a proxy. Problem severity has been shown to be related to natural versus treatment assisted recovery (Hodgins & el-Guebaly, 2000) and response to brief interventions (Diskin, 2006), and it is used by clinicians to help determine the optimal treatment goal (Robson, Edwards, Smith, & Colman, 2002). Table 17.2 provides a number of suggestions for standardized tools to assess *severity of problem* and these tools are described in detail in the preceding diagnostic section. As outlined previously, psychometric research has focused on the validity of these scales as indicators of pathological gambling and little work has assessed the validity of these scales as indicators of lower degree of problem severity. DSM-based measures are designed to have items that measure severe pathology. For example, an examination of the SOGS with a Rasch model of measurement (Strong, Breen, Lesieur, & Lejuez, 2003) found that SOGS items

TABLE 17.3 Ratings of Instruments Used for Case Conceptualization and Treatment Planning

Instrument	Norms	Internal Consistency	Inter-Rater Reliability	Test–Retest Reliability	Content Validity	Construct Validity	Validity Generalization	Clinical Utility	Highly Recommended
SOGS	E	E	G	E	A	E	E	G	✓
NODS	U	A	U	A	A	G	A	G	
CPGI–PGSI	A	G	U	A	L	A	A	A	
GAMTOMS	U	G	U	G	G	G	U	G	✓
ASI–GSI	U	A	U	A	A	G	G	G	✓
DIGS	U	A	U	U	A	A	U	G	
TLFB	U	NA	A	A	A	A	E	G	
IGS	A	E	NA	U	G	G	A	A	✓
TGS	U	E	NA	A	G	A	U	A	
GASS	A	E	NA	A	G	G	U	A	✓
SCQG	U	E	NA	A	G	A	U	A	

Note: SOGS = South Oaks Gambling Screen; NODS = National Opinion Research Center DSM-IV Screen for Gambling Problems; CPGI–PGSI = Canadian Problem Gambling Index–Problem Gambling Severity Index; GAMTOMS = Gambling Treatment Outcome Monitoring System; DIGS = Diagnostic Interview for Gambling Schedule; TLFB = Timeline followback; ASI–GSI = Addiction Severity Index–Gambling Severity Index; IGS = Inventory of Gambling Situations; TGS = Temptations to Gamble Scale; GASS = Gambling Abstinences Self-Efficacy Scale; SCQG = Situational Confidence Questionnaire for Gambling; L = Less than Adequate; A = Adequate; G = Good; E = Excellent; U = Unavailable; NA = Not Applicable.

could be ordered in terms of their level of gambling problem severity, similar to a Guttman scale, but that the scale is comprised of mostly items reflecting severe gambling problems and that more low- and moderate-severity items would be necessary to obtain an optimal measure of the entire continuum of problem severity. In contrast to DSM-based scales, the CPGI–PGSI was specifically designed to assess the full range of severity, although the low- and moderate-risk interpretation categories also have not been validated for the CPGI–PGSI.

There are several omnibus instruments that cover a number of the remaining relevant assessment domains outlined in Table 17.2. The first is an adapted version of the Addiction Severity Index (ASI; McLellan, Kushner, Metzger, & Peters, 1992). The ASI is among the most widely used and validated tools for assessing and monitoring substance abuse patients. It provides assessment of the severity and need for treatment in the medical, employment, family-social, psychiatric, legal and substance abuse domains, which are all relevant for individuals with gambling disorders. The ASI was developed as an interview although computerized and self-completion versions are also available. The ASI–Gambling Severity Index (Lesieur & Blume, 1991) is a supplemental module that uses five items to assess gambling severity and need for treatment. It was initially validated in the interview format with inpatients in a substance abuse and gambling program (Lesieur & Blume, 1991) and later with a

large sample drawn from four different populations, pathological gamblers in outpatient treatment, pathological gamblers participating in a treatment study, community problem gamblers, and substance abusers (Petry, 2003). In the first study, internal reliability was adequate and some evidence of convergent validity was presented. The second study was more comprehensive revealing strong internal reliability and good test–retest reliability over a 1-month period as well as convergent and discriminant validity across a range of external variables, including collateral and clinical ratings. The ASI, together with the ASI gambling module, can provide a profile of the treatment needs of an individual, although the composite severity scores for each of the domains are difficult to compute by hand. As indicated below, each index is responsive to change, which makes it a useful tool for monitoring outcome but its value for treatment planning is limited by lack of interpretation guidelines and norms (see Table 17.3).

A second omnibus instrument is the Gambling Treatment Outcome monitoring System (GAMTOMS; Stinchfield et al., 2007) which is a self-report or interview instrument that takes about 30 to 45 minutes to complete. As shown in Table 17.3, the GAMTOMS receives generally good psychometric ratings although information is unavailable in three areas. The latest version of the GAMTOMS includes, in addition to the DSM-IV measure described above, scales assessing gambling frequency, mental health, financial problems, legal problems, and stage of change. The GAMTOMS also incorporates the SOGS scale. Content validity for assessing outcome was confirmed by an expert panel of gambling treatment professionals. Gambling quantity is measured by items enquiring about the frequency of gambling for 14 specific types of gambling. These items in both the interview and self-administered versions generally show good test–retest reliability over a week period as well as convergent validity with a timeline interview of gambling behavior described below (Stinchfield et al., 2007). Mental health is measured with Addiction Severity Index Psychiatric composite severity score described above. The ASI psychiatric score had inadequate internal reliability but good retest reliability over 1 week (ICC = 0.83) and good convergent validity with the BASIS-32 (Eisen, Dill, & Grob, 1994), a self-report instrument validated with psychiatric outpatients. The 23-item financial consequences scale and the 7-item legal consequences scale had good internal reliability and retest reliability as well as convergent and discriminant validity with other GAMTOMS scales and with federal bankruptcy and court records and collateral reports (Stinchfield et al., 2007). Finally, the GAMTOMS includes a single item assessing stage or readiness to change according to the Prochaska and DiClemente model (Prochaska, DiClemente, & Norcross, 1992). The item showed poor retest reliability over a 1-week period although it was sensitive to change and showed good convergent validity with gambling items (Stinchfield et al., 2007).

In summary, the GAMTOMS covers a number of important content domains for treatment planning and for monitoring treatment outcome. Psychometric evidence for both the self-report and interview versions is accumulating and is generally positive. To date, as with the ASI, interpretation norms for the various scales have not been published, which limits its value for clinicians assessing individual clients.

The DIGS (Winters et al., 2002) is a third omnibus instrument, previously described, designed to assess numerous dimensions relevant to case conceptualization and treatment planning. The DIGS assesses demographics, gambling involvement and history, legal problems, other impulse disorders, medical status, and family and social functioning and also includes a mental health screen. These domains represent the majority of the relevant assessment areas but, as mentioned above, the DIGS has had limited psychometric evaluation although the available data are positive.

These three omnibus instruments collect basic *gambling frequency* information. More detailed descriptions of gambling frequency, expenditures, time spent gambling, and monthly patterns can be assessed using the timeline followback (TLFB) methodology, adapted from the alcohol field. The TLFB has been shown to provide reliable and valid gambling reports, at least in the research context (Hodgins & Makarchuk, 2003; Weinstock, Whelan, & Meyers, 2004). The method involves providing the individuals with a calendar, reviewing with them personal and public events to cue memories and having them reconstruct their daily gambling over a period of 1 to 6 months. Frequency and expenditure information can be summarized into reliable indices for weekly or monthly time periods but clinically rich information about patterns of gambling can also emerge.

Table 17.2 lists the assessment of the *associations and circumstances associated with gambling behavior* as a third important domain. Prospective research examining the process of relapse in pathological gamblers seeking abstinence (Hodgins & el-Guebaly, 2004) has revealed that individuals are most likely to be alone and thinking about finances, but that a positive mood state is as likely as a negative mood state to precede the initiation of gambling. A relapse associated with social pressure to participate or a desire to fit in socially typically led to a relatively minor relapse, whereas gambling associated with a false optimism about winning or a feeling of financial pressure was more serious. Women were more likely to relapse in response to feelings of depression, whereas men described gambling in response to being bored or having unstructured time or in response to the need to make money (Hodgins & el-Guebaly, 2004). A detailed assessment of these potential high-risk situations at the individual level is important for treatment planning and can be accomplished by conducting an informal functional analysis of recent heavy gambling situations.

The Inventory of Gambling Situations has been developed to provide a reliable assessment of these factors (IGS; Littman-Sharp, Turner, Stirpe, Toneatto, & Liu, in press). The self-report scale contains 63 items that are scored into 10 subscales: Negative Emotions, Conflict with Others, Urges and Temptations, Testing Personal Control, Pleasant Emotions, Social Pressure, Need for Excitement, Worried about Debts, Winning and Chasing, and Confidence in Skill. The IGS scales show excellent internal reliability and the factor structure was confirmed in two clinical samples. Preliminary evidence of discriminant and convergent validity is also offered. The subscales all correlate highly with the SOGS and DSM-IV criteria and the pattern of correlations with a group of external measures such as depression, impulsivity, and cognitive errors conformed to expectation. The scale has good potential for clinical use although it is lengthy and a computer scoring program is recommended because it is difficult to score by hand.

An alternative and briefer option is the Temptations to Gamble Scale (TGS; Holub, Hodgins, & Peden, 2005), which has 21 items scored into four subscales: Negative Affect, Positive Mood/Impulsivity, Seeking Wins, and Social Factors. The TGS has good content validity and strong internal and test–retest reliability over a 3-week period in a sample of pathological gamblers.

Table 17.2 also lists routinely assessing *comorbid psychiatric disorders* and substance use and abuse. A number of well-validated structured assessment instruments are available for psychiatric disorders (e.g., SCID; First, Spitzer, Gibbon, & Williams, 1997). The Alcohol Use Disorders Inventory (AUDIT; Babor, de la Fuente, Saunders, & Grant, 1992) provides a brief, 10-item, self-report assessment of alcohol problems. The AUDIT is most easily administered in a self-report version but it can also be administered orally or via computer. The AUDIT covers three domains: alcohol consumption, alcohol dependence, and alcohol-related problems. It was developed for a six-nation World Health Organization study on brief interventions and was designed to be appropriate for use in a number of cultures and languages. The psychometric properties of this scale, including the validation of cut-points for identifying high-risk and abusive drinking, have been assessed in a broad range of populations (e.g., primary care, students, emergency room patients; see Reinert & Allen, 2002 for a review), although not specifically with pathological gamblers. Less well validated but also widely used is a similar self-completion measure for other drug use, the Drug Abuse Screening Test (DAST; Skinner, 1982). There are 28-, 20-, and 10-item versions of the DAST with interpretation guidelines although the majority of the psychometric data were derived from the longest version (Cocco & Carey, 1998). Studies with gambling samples have not been reported.

Treatment history and experience, treatment goals, and motivation are also important assessment domains that are identified in Table 17.2. As standardized tools to assess these domains are not available, they are typically assessed through clinical interview. It is recommended that treatment goals be assessed in clear behavioral terms in which the person identifies a goal of abstinence or moderation for each type of gambling and that moderation goals be specified in terms of frequency and expenditure limits (Hodgins & Makarchuk, 2002). The setting of specific goals also facilitates the task of monitoring treatment progress.

There are two self-completion measures available to assess self-efficacy: the Gambling Abstinence Self-efficacy Scale (GASS; Hodgins, Peden, & Makarchuk, 2004) and the Situational Confidence Questionnaire for Gambling (SCQG; May, Whelan, Steenbergh, & Meyers, 2003). The GASS has 21 items that parallel the temptation items of the TGS (described above) and which are scored into the same four subscales. A sample of pathological gamblers revealed strong internal and test–retest reliability over a 3-week period (ICC = 0.86) and also showed evidence of predictive validity over 12 months. Higher GASS scores predicted less gambling, which is consistent with self-efficacy theory. The SCQG has 16 items, similar to the GASS items, and yields a single score. Psychometric properties of the SCQG have not been assessed in clinical samples although internal reliability in a community sample of gamblers ($\alpha = 0.96$) and test–retest reliability over 2 weeks with a college sample were good ($r = 0.86$) yielding adequate ratings in Table 17.3.

Overall Evaluation

Substantial progress has been made in the development of gambling treatment planning assessment tools over a short period of time although many gaps remain as shown in Tables 17.2 and 17.3. Table 17.3 identifies recommended instruments that have mostly good or excellent psychometric support for these purposes, albeit based on limited research. These include the SOGS, GAMTOMS, ASI–GSI, IGS, and the GASS. The omnibus instruments, the ASI–GSI and GAMTOMS, provide much potentially useful clinical information for individual clients, although the initial phases of measurement development have focused on their utility in outcome monitoring where scores are aggregated over groups of individuals.

Interpretation guidelines and norms for individual scores are necessary for these scales to be optimally useful to clinicians.

The gambling field has benefited from a long history of measurement in alcohol, other drug, and mental health disorders although we need to exert caution when adopting tools from these areas, such as the AUDIT and DAST. It is also important that we establish psychometric properties and collect norms from gambling samples.

ASSESSMENT FOR TREATMENT MONITORING AND EVALUATION

There is considerable variability in the focus of outcome measurement in the small, but growing, body of disordered gambling treatment efficacy trials. Some investigators include behavioral measures of gambling, such as frequency and expenditure (Hodgins, Currie, el-Guebaly, & Peden, 2004). Others, in addition or instead, report the effect of treatment on craving or urges to gamble, or focus on the consequences of gambling. Some studies use DSM-based measures and report changes in a total summed score or the numbers of individuals who no longer meet diagnostic criteria (Ladouceur et al., 2001). Pharmacological trials often use the pathological gambling modification of the Yale-Brown Obsessive Compulsive Scale (Hollander et al., 1998) or the Gambling Symptom Assessment Scale (G-SAS; Kim, Grant, Adson, & Shin, 2001), scales that include a mixture of craving, behavioral, and consequence items.

In response to this wide variability of assessment targets, which makes comparison of trials challenging, an expert panel of outcome researchers recently provided a set of recommendations on outcome measurement (Walker et al., 2006). The panel identified three important elements in determining the effectiveness of treatment interventions: reduction in the frequency or intensity of gambling behavior, reduction in gambling-related consequences, and evidence that the reduction in gambling behavior results from the hypothesized therapeutic mechanism. As well as being helpful to treatment researchers, the "Banff framework" is instructive for clinicians, as it clearly identifies two readily measured domains: gambling behavior and gambling-related consequences. The third element, measurement of process variables,

will vary in focus depending upon the type of intervention.

Measurement of Gambling Behavior

The Banff framework noted that the wide individual variation in types, frequency, and intensity of gambling means that any single measurement of gambling involvement is unable to capture all relevant aspects. At minimum, two specific indicators of gambling behavior are recommended for evaluation: financial losses and gambling frequency. Financial losses should be reported as net expenditure (i.e., the amount of money that the individual brought to or accessed during the gambling session minus the amount left at the end of the session). Asking how much an individual "spent gambling" leads to inconsistent responses depending upon the pattern of wins and losses during the gambling session, which is typically quite lengthy. Disordered slot machine gamblers, for example, report gambling sessions that are typically 5 to 8 hours in length. Net expenditure, in contrast, ignores any wins that are subsequently lost during the session. It is further recommended in the Banff framework that money lost not be normed against total personal or family income or expendable income. It is true that the same monetary loss will have different consequences for individuals of different financial means, but it is also true that individuals do not easily provide reliable reports of their financial means (Walker et al., 2006). The attempt to normalize loss reports with financial means is apt to lead to an overall less reliable expenditure index. Because the focus in outcome monitoring is individual change over the course of time or treatment, the expenditure information does not require this adjustment in order to monitor change. Per session expenditures need to be averaged over a monthly or longer time period to reduce the variability in gambling that results from variability in access to money and gambling opportunities. Gambling behavior often varies according to employment pay schedules, for example, which can be weekly, biweekly, or monthly. The optimal timeframe for summarizing expenditures has not yet been identified, although a 3-month period is often reported in efficacy studies (e.g., Petry et al., 2006). Future research will help establish the benefits of this timeframe versus a shorter (e.g., 1 month) or longer period (e.g., 6 months). Finally, the framework recommended that the expenditure measure include only forms of gambling that are causing the individual problems in order to minimize error variance. Monitoring involvement in nonproblematic types of gambling is also advisable, but should be reported as a separate factor.

The second critical indicator of gambling behavior is gambling frequency. Frequency can be measured in a variety of metrics such as hours, number of sessions, time spent thinking about gambling, and so forth, although days of gambling appears to be the easiest for individuals to recall reliably (Hodgins & Makarchuk, 2003). As with expenditures, days are typically averaged over a time period of 1 to 3 months. The timeline follow-back interview is one procedure for eliciting reliable expenditure and frequent reports, and it is rated as highly recommended in Table 17.4. The use of other methodologies, such as daily diaries or quantity-frequency summary measures, has not yet been evaluated.

Measurement of Gambling-Related Consequences

Table 17.2 outlined specific gambling-related consequences that are relevant for outcome monitoring as well as treatment planning. We have already reviewed two omnibus instruments, the ASI and the GAMTOMS, which cover some of these consequences. Table 17.4 provides ratings of psychometric research for purposes of outcome monitoring. The ASI provides composite scores in each of the eight assessment areas that are responsive to change and are often used in substance abuse efficacy research (McLellan et al., 1992). The composite scales, including the ASI-GSI, assess frequency of behavior, related problems, and perceived need for treatment in a 30-day window using a 0-to-1 range. Ideal outcome would involve a score of zero on the scale indicating no problems (McLellan et al., 1992) although more typically statistically significant pre and posttreatment differences are used to demonstrate improvement. Because the scores are not pure measures of behavior, related problems, or a therapeutic mechanism, interpretation of specific scores is problematic. A score of .5, for example, could indicate a number of different problems. There are no interpretation guidelines for specific nonzero values, which limit the usefulness of these scores for clinicians.

The GAMTOMS includes a treatment discharge and a treatment follow-up questionnaire or interview

to complement the intake assessment. The questionnaire version has been used to evaluate outcome in Minnesota state treatment programs and its content validity for this purpose has been assessed positively by an expert panel. Psychometric evaluation of these scales is promising, albeit limited to date. The discharge questionnaire (88 items, 30 minutes) provides outcome indices in six areas: gambling frequency, stage of change, efforts at recovery, psychiatric symptoms, treatment component helpfulness, and client satisfaction. In support of construct validity, principal component analyses of the latter four of these scales, which are designed to be summed total scores, confirmed that they are unifactorial in a treatment sample who completed the self-report version and one that completed the interview version (Stinchfield et al., 2007). Internal reliability in these same samples varied from unacceptable to excellent, but overall is rated good (see Table 17.4).

The follow-up assessment is designed to be administered after 6 to 12 months (95 items, 30 to 45 minutes) and provides a broader range of indicators: gambling frequency, gambling debt, stage of change, alcohol, tobacco and other drug use frequency, posttreatment service utilization, gambling-related illegal activities, occupational problems, problem gambling severity (DSM and SOGS), financial problems, psychiatric symptoms, and general treatment outcome. Principal component analyses of the five of these scales, which are designed to be summed total scores, confirmed that they are unifactorial in a treatment sample completing the interview version. Overall, the internal reliability for these scales was good (Stinchfield et al., 2007).

As with the ASI, norms are not provided to facilitate interpretation of these scores, although scores of zero indicate optimal functioning. The GAMTOMS incorporates both the SOGS and the DSM-IV measure as outcome indicators. Continuously scored data from these diagnostic scales are often reported in efficacy trials and could serve as benchmarks against which to compare the progress of individual patients. The Banff framework cautions against the use of these severity measures as primary outcome measures because of the ambiguity in meaning of low, but nonzero, scores. Nonetheless, these measures can act as useful secondary indicators of outcome. Most of these measures were developed to assess lifetime and past-year functioning (Hodgins, 2004) and, therefore, cannot be used for treatment monitoring with follow-up

TABLE 17.4 Ratings of Instruments Used for Treatment Monitoring and Treatment Outcome Evaluation

Instrument	Norms	Internal Consistency	Inter-Rater Reliability	Test–Retest Reliability	Content Validity	Construct Validity	Validity Generalization	Treatment Sensitivity	Clinical Utility	Highly Recommended
GAMTOMS-D	U	G	U	U	G	G	U	A	G	✓
GAMTOMS-F	U	G	U	U	G	G	U	A	G	✓
TLFB	NA	NA	G	A	G	G	E	E	G	✓
ASI–GSI	U	A	U	G	A	A	G	G	A	
GASS	U	G	NA	A	E	G	A	A	G	✓
SOGS-3	U	G	U	U	A	A	U	G	G	✓
NODS-3	U	G	U	A	A	A	U	A	G	
GBQ	U	G	U	A	U	A	U	U	G	
GCQ	U	E	U	A	A	A	U	U	G	
PG-YBOCS	U	U	G	U	L	A	U	G	G	

Notes: GAMTOMS = Gambling Treatment Outcome Monitoring System, D = discharge questionnaire, F = follow-up questionnaire; TLFB = Timeline followback; ASI–GSI = Addiction Severity Index–Gambling Severity Index; GASS = Gambling Abstinence Self-Efficacy Scale; SOGS-3 = 3-Month Version South Oaks Gambling Screen; NODS-3 = 3-Month Version–National Opinion Research Center DSM-IV Screen for Gambling Problems; GBQ= Gamblers' Beliefs Questionnaire; GCQ = Gambling Cognitions Questionnaire; PG-YBOCS = Yale-Brown Obsessive–Compulsive Scale Pathological Gambling Modification; L = Less Than Adequate; A = Adequate; G = Good; E = Excellent; U = Unavailable; NA = Not Applicable.

time periods shorter than one year. However, Wulfert et al. (2005) has examined the reliability and validity of 3-month versions of the SOGS and NODS and concluded that they are potentially useful for outcome evaluation. The 3-month versions showed good internal reliability and convergent validity with gambling frequency and expenditure in a treatment sample (Wulfert et al., 2005), as well as sensitivity to change in an efficacy study (Wulfert, Blanchard, Freidenberg, & Martell, 2006). The SOGS-3 has been shown to be sensitive to change in other treatment studies so it currently is recommended over the NODS-3 (see Table 17.4).

Measurement of Therapeutic Mechanisms

The measurement of therapeutic variables, the third element recommended in the Banff framework, will vary in focus depending upon the type of intervention. However, based upon the growing empirical support of cognitive-behavioral treatments (Hodgins & Petry, 2004) and the interest in pharmacological efficacy, measurement in four process domains is reviewed in this chapter. Reduction of gambling in cognitive-behavioral therapy is hypothesized to be mediated by reductions in cognitive errors, increases in coping skills, and increases in self-efficacy. Reduction of gambling related to pharmacological agents (e.g., Naltrexone) is thought to be related to reductions in urges to gamble.

Measurement of Cognitive Distortions, Coping Skills, and Self-Efficacy

Cognitive-behavioral therapy targets, in part, changes in cognitive distortions, coping skills and self-efficacy. Assessment of self-efficacy was addressed previously in relation to general treatment planning; additionally, the GASS has been shown to be sensitive to change and to mediate improvement in gambling (Peden, 2004; see Table 17.4 for relevant ratings for this purpose). To date, we are not aware of any established measures of coping skills that have been validated for gambling, although a number of similar behavioral role play and self-completion measures are available in the alcohol field (Finney, 1995). Content validity may be an issue if these measures are adapted to gambling, given that they assess methods for coping with typical drinking situations. The coping skills targeted in cognitive-behavioral therapy for gambling disorders are overlapping, but not identical to, those targeted in alcohol use disorders.

Assessment of cognitive distortions is relevant for both treatment planning for this type of therapy as well as outcome monitoring, but is a challenge because these distortions are thought to operate outside of conscious awareness (Toneatto, 1999). Theoretically, a number of assessment options exist. It is possible to observe gambling behavior to assess underlying cognitions. For example, throwing dice vigorously when a high number is desired and lightly when a lower number is desired is indicative of an illusion of control over the outcome. However, this assessment depends upon an inference concerning the cognition underlying the behavior, which may limit the reliability and validity of this technique. The think-aloud method (Ericsson & Simon, 1980) provides a more direct assessment of cognitions. It requires that, after a brief training, gamblers verbalize their thoughts while they are engaged in a gambling activity. These verbalizations are typically recorded, transcribed, and then examined for the presence of irrational statements. This method has been effectively used in research paradigms and trained raters can provide reliable categorizations of cognitive distortions (Ladouceur, Gaboury, Bujold, Lachance, & Tremblay, 1991). However, reactivity is an issue that compromises validity: once voiced, a certain statement may sound dubious or surprising to the participant, and therefore influence his or her subsequent thoughts and actions (Steward & Jefferson, 2007). The verbalization requirement has also been criticized as "unnatural," not reflecting cognitions but rather self-descriptions of behavior (Delfabbro & Winefield, 1999). More research is required concerning validity and practicality of the paradigm is necessary prior to clinical use.

Finally, cognitions can be assessed directly with self-report scales, which is a practical method but one that also requires individuals to report on a process that is assumed to be unconscious (Holub, 2003). Steenbergh and colleagues developed a 21-item self-report scale measuring two factors: luck/perseverance and illusion of control. The Gamblers' Beliefs Questionnaire showed factorial validity, good internal and test–retest reliability, and some evidence of discriminative and convergent validity within student and community samples (Steenbergh, Meyers, May, & Whelan, 2001). The scale has not been validated in clinical samples and has not been shown to be sensitive to change. Holub (2003; Holub, Hodgins, & Rose, 2007) described the Gambling Cognitions Questionnaire, a 40-item self-report scale that measures four categories of cognitive distortions: probability errors, magical thinking/luck, information processing biases, and illusion of control. The scale is unifactorial and the total scores showed excellent internal reliability in student and pathological gambling samples, as well as some evidence of convergent validity. The total score was not, however, related to the number of cognitive errors during a think-aloud task, which supports the need for more research on the validity of different assessment approaches. This scale also has not been shown to be sensitive to change related to improvement in cognitive-behavioral treatment.

Measurement of Urges

Pharmacological trials often target urges to gamble (Hollander, Begaz, & DeCaria, 1998) and these studies often include measures of overall outcome that mix urge items with behavior items (e.g., Gambling Symptom Assessment Scale, Kim et al., 2001). The Pathological Gambling Modification of the Yale-Brown Obsessive–Compulsive Scale (PG-YBOCS; Hollander et al., 1998), however, is a widely used scale that provides separate behavior and urge scores, as well as a total score. The PG-YBOCS interview includes five urge and five behavior items that are clinician-rated. To date, psychometric study has been very limited but the two subscales show good interrater reliability and the total score shows convergent validity with the SOGS and another clinical rating scale in a small clinical sample. The PG-YBOCS is also sensitive to change, as shown in a number of efficacy trials (Grant et al., 2003).

Overall Evaluation

The outcome monitoring area is more advanced than the treatment planning area because of the strong interest in the field of developing evidence-based treatments. The Banff framework is designed to encourage increased consistency among studies by recommending basic measures of gambling behavior, related problems and therapeutic mechanisms. These same dimensions are important for clinicians. Measurement of gambling behavior (frequency and expenditure) can be done easily, reliably, and validly

using the timeline interview method. Alternative methods, such as diaries and retrospective quantity-frequency reports, may also be feasible although they have not been assessed. Measurement of gambling-related problems is less advanced, although the ASI and GAMTOMS are promising omnibus measures. On the basis of the available psychometric research, the GAMTOMS is recommended for use in Table 17.4. Omnibus measures have appeal to clinicians because they are comprehensive and do not require compiling a battery of individual measures to cover the important domains to be assessed.

Two additional instruments are highly recommended in Table 17.4. The SOGS-3 provides a brief measure of severity of problems using a 3-month window. The GASS is the only instrument that measures a therapeutic mechanism that currently meets the criteria for recommendation.

CONCLUSIONS AND FUTURE DIRECTIONS

It is exciting to work in a nascent and expanding clinical area where policy makers and treatment providers are thirsty for new information and novel ideas about organizing and delivering effective treatment. The clear advances, made in assessment and treatment of gambling problems over the past few years, reflect this attention.

The DSM-IV conceptualization underpins much of the clinical research that is conducted. The criteria were developed based on expert opinion and have not been subjected to extensive psychometric study to evaluate the validity of the criteria. For example, the cut-off of four or more criteria in the DSM-III-R was raised to five for the DSM-IV based upon expert opinion, not empirical data (Lesieur & Rosenthal, 1991). Zimmerman, Chelminski, and Young (2006) recently examined the sensitivity and specificity of each DSM criterion in an outpatient mental health sample. Although the base rate of gambling problems was low in the sample, they proposed that two criteria, committing illegal acts and reliance on others for financial bailouts, could be eliminated without reducing diagnostic accuracy. However, this study also showed that these criteria are particularly good indicators of extreme pathology, at least in a mental health population, which suggests that they are valuable when a DSM symptom count is used to measure severity on a continuum. Items that are ideal for a diagnostic classification measure may be different than those that are ideal for a continuous severity measure, so it may be helpful to develop content and construct valid measures of severity that are independent from the DSM criteria. Item selection would be based upon the ability to discriminate different levels of severity versus using a DSM diagnosis or DSM-based continuous measure as the gold standard.

One of the issues that have not been addressed in this area is the heavy reliance on information obtained from the individual with the gambling problem. All of the measures identified as promising are self-report or interview measures. There is evidence that pathological gamblers provide accurate self-reports in the research context where confidentiality is emphasized and the information provided does not have personal consequences for the individual (Hodgins & Makarchuk, 2003). However, little is known about accuracy in clinical settings where the implications of honesty are more variable. Lying to "family members, therapist or others to conceal the extent of involvement with gambling" is one of the DSM-IV criteria (American Psychiatric Association, 2000) and should be expected to be the norm among individuals in treatment. Certainly such individuals are likely to withhold sensitive information until trust is established with the treatment provider (Stinchfield, Govoni, & Frisch, 2007). Multimethod assessment, which is advisable with all clinical assessment, seems even more important with gambling disorders, although this has received little attention in the assessment literature. In the research context, family members and friends are sometimes used as collateral reporters (e.g., Hodgins, Currie, & el-Guebaly, 2001) but family members, even if more honest, typically have less complete information than the identified gambler about his or her behavior (Hodgins & Makarchuk, 2003). Other sources of collateral information, such as bank or court records, are impractical for routine clinical use. Assessment techniques such as the "think-aloud" procedure for cognitive distortions have potential, but are not yet sufficiently developed for clinical use.

We have noted that measurement in the field is advancing rapidly (cf. Smith, 2007). It is imperative that we take the steps to "do it right" and set a solid empirical measurement foundation upon which to conduct meaningful research and provide effective intervention. Although rapid progress has been made

and a number of assessment tools are promising in terms of their diagnostic, treatment planning and monitoring ability, very few were rated as highly recommended. In many instances, the only psychometric information that is available for other promising instruments is based on the development sample, that is, the sample used to derive the instrument. Accuracy in measurement in this field will require not only the development of new instruments but also further psychometric research on existing instruments.

References

American Psychiatric Association. (2000). *Diagnostic and statistical manual of mental disorders, text revision.* (4th ed.) Washington, DC: Author.

Babor, T., de la Fuente, J. R., Saunders, J., & Grant, M. (1992). *The alcohol use disorders identification test: Guidelines for use in primary health care.* Geneva: World Health Organization.

Cocco, K. M., & Carey, K. B. (1998). Psychometric properties of the drug abuse screening test in psychiatric outpatients. *Psychological Assessment, 10,* 408–414.

Cox, B. J., Yu, N., Afifi, T. O., & Ladouceur, R. (2005). A national survey of gambling problems in Canada. *Canadian Journal of Psychiatry—Revue Canadienne de Psychiatrie, 50,* 213–217.

Crockford, D. N., & el-Guebaly, N. (1998). Psychiatric comorbidity in pathological gambling: A critical review. *Canadian Journal of Psychiatry, 43,* 43–50.

Cunningham-Williams, R. M., Cottler, L. B., Compton, W. M., & Spitznagel, E. L. (1998). Taking chances: problem gamblers and mental health disorders— results from the St. Louis epidemiologic catchment area study. *American Journal of Public Health, 88,* 1093–1096.

Cunningham-Williams, R. M., Cottler, L. B., Compton, W. M., Spitznagel, E. L., & Ben-Abdallah, A. (2000). Problem gambling and comorbid psychiatric disorders among drug users recruited from drug treatment and community settings. *Journal of Gambling Studies, 16,* 347–376.

Delfabbro, P. H., & Winefield, A. H. (1999). Poker-machine gambling: An analysis of within session characteristics. *British Journal of Psychology, 90,* 425–439.

Dickerson, M., & O'Connor, J. (2006). *Gambling as an addictive behaviour. Impaired control, harm minimisation, treatment and prevention.* Cambridge: Cambridge University Press.

Diskin, K. M. (2006). *Effect of a single session motivational intervention on gambling.* Unpublished doctoral dissertation University of Calgary, Calgary, Alberta, Canada.

Eisen, S. V., Dill, D. L., & Grob, M. C. (1994). Reliability and validity of a brief patient-report instrument for psychiatric outcome evaluation. *Hospital and Community Psychiatry, 45,* 242–247.

Ericsson, K. A., & Simon, H. A. (1980). Verbal reports as data. *Psychological Review, 87,* 215–251.

Ferris, J., & Wynne, H. (2001). *The Canadian problem gambling index: Final report.* Ottawa. Ontario: Canadian Centre on Substance Abuse.

Ferris, J., Wynne, H., & Single, E. (1998). *Measuring problem gambling in Canada: Interim report to the inter-provincial task force on problem gambling.* Toronto: Canadian Interprovincial Task force on Problem Gambling.

Finney, J. W. (1995). Assessing treatment and treatment processes. In J. P. Allen & M. Columbus (Eds.), *Assessing alcohol problems. A guide for clinicians and researchers* (pp. 123–142). Washington, DC: U.S. Department of Health and Human Services.

First, M. B., Spitzer, R. L., Gibbon, M., & Williams, J. B. W. (1997). *Structured clinical interview for DSM-IV Axis I Disorders-Clinician Version (SCID-CV).* Washington, DC: American Psychiatric Press.

Gerstein, D., Murphy, S., Toce, M., Hoffman, J., Palmer, A., Johnson, R. et al. (1999). *Gambling impact and behaviour study: Report of the national gambling impact study commission.* Retrieved from http://www2.norc.org/new/gamb-fin.htm.

Grant, J. E., Kim, S. W., Potenza, M. N., Blanco, C., Ibanez, A., Stevens, L. et al., (2003). Paroxetine treatment of pathological gambling: A multi-centre randomized controlled trial. *International Clinical Psychopharmacology, 18,* 243–249.

Grant, J. E., Steinberg, M. A., Kim, S. W., Rounsaville, B. J., & Potenza, M. A. (2004). Preliminary validity and reliability testing of a structured clinical interview for pathological gambling. *Psychiatry Research, 128,* 79–88.

Hodgins, D. C. (2004). Using the NORC DSM Screen for Gambling Problems (NODS) as an outcome measure for pathological gambling: Psychometric evaluation. *Addictive Behaviors, 29,* 1685–1690.

Hodgins, D. C., & el-Guebaly, N. (2000). Natural and treatment-assisted recovery from gambling problems: A comparison of resolved and active gamblers. *Addiction, 95,* 777–789.

Hodgins, D. C., & el-Guebaly, N. (2004). Retrospective and prospective reports of precipitants to relapse in pathological gambling. *Journal of Consulting and Clinical Psychology, 72,* 72–80.

Hodgins, D. C., & Makarchuk, K. (2002). *Becoming a winner. Defeating problem gambling.* Edmonton: AADAC.

Hodgins, D. C., & Makarchuk, K. (2003). Trusting problem gamblers: Reliability and validity of self-reported gambling behavior. *Psychology of Addictive Behaviors, 17,* 244–248.

Hodgins, D. C., & Petry, N. M. (2004). Cognitive and behavioral treatments. In J. E. Grant & M. N. Potenza (Eds.), *Pathological gambling. A clinical guide to treatment* (pp. 169–188). New York: American Psychiatric Association Press.

Hodgins, D. C., Currie, S. R., & el-Guebaly, N. (2001). Motivational enhancement and self-help treatments for problem gambling. *Journal of Consulting and Clinical Psychology, 69,* 50–57.

Hodgins, D. C., Currie, S. R., el-Guebaly, N., & Peden, N. (2004). Brief motivational treatment for problem gambling: A 24-month follow-up. *Psychology of Addictive Behaviors, 18,* 293–296.

Hodgins, D. C., Mansley, C., & Thygesen, K. (2006). Risk factors for suicide ideation and attempts among pathological gamblers. *The American Journal of Addiction, 15,* 303–310.

Hodgins, D. C., Peden, N., & Cassidy, E. (2005). The association between comorbidity and outcome in pathological gambling: A prospective follow-up of recent quitters. *Journal of Gambling Studies, 21,* 255–271.

Hodgins, D. C., Peden, N., & Makarchuk, K. (2004). Self-efficacy in pathological gambling treatment outcome: Development of a gambling abstinence self-efficacy scale (GASS). *International Gambling Studies, 4,* 99–108.

Hodgins, D. C., Wynne, H., & Makarchuk, K. (1999). Pathways to recovery from gambling problems: Follow-up from a general population survey. *Journal of Gambling Studies, 15,* 93–104.

Hollander, E., Begaz, T., & DeCaria, C. M. (1998). Pharmacologic approaches in the treatment of pathological gambling. *CNS Spectrums, 3,* 72–82.

Hollander, E., DeCaria, C. M., Mari, E., Wong, C. M., Mosovich, S., Grossman, R., et al., (1998). Short-term single-blind fluvoxamine treatment of pathological gambling. *American Journal of Psychiatry, 155,* 1781–1783.

Holub, A. (2003). *Construction of the gambling cognitions inventory.* Unpublished master's thesis University of Calgary, Calgary, Alberta, Canada.

Holub, A., Hodgins, D. C., & Peden, N. E. (2005). Development of the temptations for gambling questionnaire: A measure of temptation in recently quit gamblers. *Addiction Research and Theory, 13,* 179–191.

Holub, A., Hodgins, D. C., & Rose, K. (2007). *Validation of the gambling cognitions inventory on a pathological gambling sample. Final report for the Alberta*

Gaming Research Institute. Calgary: University of Calgary.

Kim, S. W., Grant, J. E., Adson, D. E., & Shin, Y. C. (2001). Double-blind naltrexone and placebo comparison study in the treatment of pathological gambling. *Biological Psychiatry, 49*, 914–921.

Kyngdon, A. (2004). Comparing factor analysis and the Rasch model for ordered response categories: An investigation of the scale of gambling choices. *Journal of Applied Measurement, 5*, 398–418.

Ladouceur, R. (2005). Controlled gambling for pathological gamblers. *Journal of Gambling Studies, 21*, 49–57.

Ladouceur, R., Bouchard, C., Rheaume, N., Jacques, C., Ferland, F., Leblond, J., et al. (2000). Is the SOGS an accurate measure of pathological gambling among children, adolescents and adults? *Journal of Gambling Studies, 16*, 1–24.

Ladouceur, R., Gaboury, A., Bujold, A., Lachance, N., & Tremblay, S. (1991). Ecological validity of laboratory studies of videopoker gaming. *Journal of Gambling Studies, 7*, 109–116.

Ladouceur, R., Sylvain, C., Boutin, C., Lachance, S., Doucet, C., Leblond, J., et al. (2001). Cognitive treatment of pathological gambling. *Journal of Nervous and Mental Disease, 189*, 774–780.

Lesieur, H. R., & Blume, S. B. (1987). The south oaks gambling screen (SOGS): A new instrument for the identification of pathological gamblers. *American Journal of Psychiatry, 144*, 1184–1188.

Lesieur, H. R., & Blume, S. B. (1991). Evaluation of patients treated for pathological gambling in a combined alcohol, substance abuse and pathological gambling treatment unit using the addiction severity index. *British Journal of Addiction, 86*, 1017–1028.

Lesieur, H. R., & Blume, S. B. (1993). Revising the South Oaks gambling screen in different settings. *Journal of Gambling Studies, 9*, 213–223.

Lesieur, H. R., & Rosenthal, R. J. (1991). Pathological gambling: A review of the literature (Prepared for the American Psychiatric Association task force on DSM-IV committee on disorders of impulse control not elsewhere classified). *Journal of Gambling Studies, 7*, 5–39.

Littman-Sharp, N., Turner, N., Stirpe, T., Toneatto, T., & Liu, E. (in press). *The inventory of gambling situations: Reliability, factor structure, and validity. Technical manual*. Toronto: Centre for Addiction and Mental Health.

May, R. K., Whelan, J. P., Steenbergh, T. A., & Meyers, A. W. (2003). The gambling self-efficacy questionnaire: An initial psychometric evaluation. *Journal of Gambling Studies, 19*, 339–357.

McLellan, A. T., Kushner, H., Metzger, D., & Peters, R. (1992). The fifth edition of the Addiction Severity Index. *Journal of Substance Abuse Treatment, 9*, 199–213.

National Research Council (1999). *Pathological gambling: A critical review*. Washington, DC: National Academy Press.

Peden, N. (2004). *Construct validity of self-efficacy in problem gambling*. Calgary: University of Calgary.

Petry, N. M. (2003). Validity of a gambling scale for the addiction severity index. *Journal of Nervous and Mental Disease, 191*, 1–9.

Petry, N. M. (2005). *Pathological gambling: Etiology, comorbidity, and treatment*. Washington, DC: American Psychological Association.

Petry, N. M., Ammerman, Y., Bohl, J., Doersch, A., Gay, H., Kadden, R., et al. (2006). Cognitive-behavioral therapy for pathological gamblers. *Journal of Consulting and Clinical Psychology, 74*, 555–567.

Petry, N. M., Stinson, F. S., & Grant, B. F. (2005). Comorbidity of DSM-IV pathological gambling and other psychiatric disorders: Results from the national epidemiological survey on alcohol and related conditions. *Journal of Clinical Psychiatry, 66*, 564–574.

Prochaska, J. O., DiClemente, C. C., & Norcross, J. C. (1992). In search of how people change. Applications to addictive behaviors. *American Psychologist, 47*, 1102–1114.

Reinert, D. F., & Allen, J. P. (2002). The Alcohol use disorders identification test (AUDIT): A review of recent research. *Alcoholism: Clinical and Experimental Research, 26*, 272–279.

Robins, L., Cottler, L. B., Bucholz, K., & Compton, W. M. (1996). *Diagnostic interview schedule, fourth version (DISIV)*. Saint Louis, MO: Washington University Press.

Robson, E., Edwards, J., Smith, G., & Colman, I. (2002). Gambling decisions: An early intervention program for problem gamblers. *Journal of Gambling Studies, 18*, 235–255.

Rosenberg, H. (1993). Prediction of controlled drinking by alcoholics and problem drinkers. *Psychological Bulletin, 113*, 129–139.

Shaffer, H. J., & Hall, M. N. (2001). Updating and refining prevalence estimates of disordered gambling and behaviour in the United States and Canada. *Canadian Journal of Public Health, 92*, 168–172.

Shaffer, H. J., Hall, M. N., & Vander Bilt, J. (1999). Estimating the prevalence of disordered gambling behavior in the United States and Canada: A research synthesis. *American Journal of Public Health, 89*, 1369–1376.

Skinner, H. (1982). The Drug Abuse Screening Test. *Addictive Behaviors, 7*, 363–371.

Slutske, W. S. (2006). Natural recovery and treatment-seeking in pathological gambling: Results of two U.S. national surveys. *American Journal of Psychiatry, 163*, 297–302.

Smith, G. (2007). Preface. In G. Smith, D. C. Hodgins, & R. J. Williams (Eds.), *Research and measurement issues in gambling research* (pp. xxvii–xxxiv). New York: Elsevier.

Spitzer, R. L., Williams, J. B., Gibbon, M., & First, M. B. (1990). *Structured clinical interview for DSM-III-R.* Washington, DC: American Psychiatric Press.

Steenbergh, T. A., Meyers, A. W., May, R. K., & Whelan, J. P. (2001). Development and validation of the gamblers' beliefs questionnaire. *Psychology of Addictive Behaviors, 16*, 143–149.

Steward, S. H., & Jefferson, S. (2007). Experimental methodologies. In G. Smith, D. C. Hodgins, & R. J. Williams (Eds.), *Research and measurement issues in gambling research* (pp. 88–111). New York: Elsevier.

Stinchfield, R. (2002). Reliability, validity, and classification accuracy of the South Oaks gambling screen (SOGS). *Addictive Behaviors, 27*, 1–19.

Stinchfield, R. (2003). Reliability, validity, and classification accuracy of a measure of DSM-IV diagnostic criteria for pathological gambling. *American Journal of Psychiatry, 160*, 180–182.

Stinchfield, R., Govoni, R., & Frisch, G. R. (2005). DSM-IV diagnostic criteria for pathological gambling: Reliability, validity, and classification accuracy. *American Journal of Addictions, 14*, 73–82.

Stinchfield, R., Govoni, R., & Frisch, G. R. (2007). A review of screening and assessment instruments for problem and pathological gambling. In G. Smith, D. C. Hodgins, & R. J. Williams (Eds.), *Research and measurement issues in gambling research* (pp. 180–217). New York: Elsevier.

Stinchfield, R., Winters, K. C., Botzet, A., Jerstad, S., & Breyer, J. (2007). Development and psychometric evaluation of the gambling treatment outcome monitoring system (GAMTOMS). *Psychology of Addictive Behaviors, 21*, 174–184.

Strong, D. R., Breen, R. B., Lesieur, H. R., & Lejuez, C. W. (2003). Using the Rasch model to evaluate the South Oaks gambling screen for use with nonpathological gamblers. *Addictive Behaviors, 28*, 1465–1472.

Taber, J. I., McCormick, R. A., Russo, A. M., Adkins, B. J., & Ramirez, L. F. (1987). Follow-up of pathological gamblers after treatment. *American Journal of Psychiatry, 144*, 757–761.

Toneatto, T. (1999). Cognitive psychopathology of problem gambling. *Substance Use and Misuse, 34*, 1593–1604.

Volberg, R. A. (2001). *When the chips are down: Problem gambling in America.* New York: The Century Foundation Press.

Walker, M., Toneatto, T., Potenza, M., Petry, N. M., Ladouceur, R., Hodgins, D. C., et al. (2006). A framework for reporting outcomes in problem gambling treatment research: The Banff, Alberta Consensus. *Addiction, 101*, 504–511.

Weinstock, J., Whelan, J. P., & Meyers, A. W. (2004). Behavioral assessment of gambling: An application of the timeline followback method. *Psychological Assessment, 16*, 72–80.

Welte, J., Barnes, G., Wieczorek, W., Tidwell, M., & Parker, J. (2001). Alcohol and gambling pathology among U.S. adults: Prevalence, demographic patterns and comorbidity. *Journal of Studies on Alcohol, 62*, 706–712.

Winters, K. C., Specker, S., & Stinchfield, R. (2002). Measuring pathological gambling with the Diagnostic Interview for Gambling Severity (DIGS). In J. J. Marotta, J. A. Cornelius, & W. R. Eadington (Eds.), *The downside: Problem and pathological gambling* (pp. 143–148). Reno, NV: University of Nevada, Reno.

Wulfert, E., Blanchard, E. B., Freidenberg, B., & Martell, R. (2006). Retaining pathological gamblers in cognitive-behavioral therapy through motivational enhancement. *Behavior Modification, 30*, 315–340.

Wulfert, E., Hartley, J., Lee, M., Wang, N., Franco, C., & Sodano, R. (2005). Gambling screens: Does shortening the time frame affect their psychometric properties? *Journal of Gambling Studies, 21*, 521–536.

Zimmerman, M., Chelminski, I., & Young, D. (2006). A psychometric evaluation of the DSM-IV pathological gambling diagnostic criteria. *Journal of Gambling Studies, 22*, 329–337.

Part VI

Schizophrenia & Personality Disorders

18

Schizophrenia

Kim T. Mueser

Shirley M. Glynn

Schizophrenia is a major mental illness characterized by psychosis, apathy and social withdrawal, and cognitive impairment, which results in impaired functioning in the areas of work, school, parenting, self-care, independent living, interpersonal relationships, and leisure time. Among psychiatric disorders, schizophrenia is the most disabling and its treatment requires a disproportionate share of mental health services. For example, people with schizophrenia occupy approximately 25% of all psychiatric hospital beds (Terkelsen & Menikoff, 1995) and, due to the episodic but chronic nature of the disorder, represent 50% of inpatient admissions (Geller, 1992). The combined economic and social costs of schizophrenia place it among the world's top 10 causes of Disability Adjusted Life Years (Murray & Lopez, 1996), accounting for an estimated 2.3% of all burdens in developed countries, and 0.8% in developing economies (U.S. Institute of Medicine, 2001).

Because of the pervasive impact of schizophrenia across the full range of life domains, comprehensive assessment is necessarily broad, ranging from basic psychopathology to cognitive functioning to social and community functioning. In this chapter we describe standardized assessment instruments for diagnosis, treatment planning, and monitoring outcomes of persons with schizophrenia-spectrum disorders, including schizoaffective disorder and schizophreniform disorder. We begin with a brief description of schizophrenia, including diagnosis, clinical presentation and associated features, epidemiology, and etiology. This is followed by discussion of the purposes of assessment, and then consideration of specific instruments for assessing diagnosis and

specific domains of functioning commonly impaired in schizophrenia.

THE NATURE OF SCHIZOPHRENIA

Modern conceptualizations of schizophrenia are based on the work of Kraepelin (1919–1971), who focused on the long-term deteriorating course of the illness, and Bleuler (1911–1950), who emphasized the core symptoms of the disorder as difficulties in thinking straight (loosening of associations), incongruous or flattened affect, loss of goal-directed behavior or ambivalence due to conflicting impulses, and retreat into an inner world (autism). The two major diagnostic systems for schizophrenia in common use are the 10th Revision of the *International Classification of Diseases* (ICD-10; World Health Organization [WHO], 1992) and the *Diagnostic and Statistical Manual of Mental Disorders*, 4th Edition (DSM-IV; American Psychiatric Association, 1994, 2000). Both systems objectively define symptoms and characteristic impairments of schizophrenia in a similar fashion, and have improved the reliability of diagnostic assessments over more subjectively based approaches. The major differences between the systems are the DSM-IV requirements of social or occupational dysfunction (not included in ICD-10) and the 6-month duration of illness (vs. 1 month for ICD-10), resulting in a somewhat narrower definition of the disorder in *DSM-IV*. Reliability of diagnoses between the two systems is high (Peralta & Cuesta, 2003). The stability of diagnosis over time is moderate, with most variability immediately following onset of the disorder; 21% to 30% of people treated for a

391

first episode have no symptom relapses over the next 5 years (Häfner & an der Heiden, 2003).

Symptoms and Associated Impairments

Schizophrenia is characterized by three broad types of symptoms, including psychotic symptoms, negative symptoms, and cognitive impairment (Liddle, 1987). *Psychotic symptoms* involve the loss of contact with reality, including false beliefs (*delusions*), perceptual experiences not shared by others (*hallucinations*), or bizarre behaviors. A variety of different types of hallucinations occur in schizophrenia, including auditory, visual, olfactory, gustatory, or tactile hallucinations, with auditory hallucinations most common. Common delusions in schizophrenia include persecutory delusions, delusions of control (e.g., the belief that others can interfere with one's thoughts), grandiose delusions (e.g., the belief that one is Jesus Christ), and somatic delusions (e.g., the belief that one's brain is rotting away). The presence and severity of psychotic symptoms tend to be episodic over time.

Negative symptoms are deficit states in which basic emotional and behavioral processes are diminished or absent. Common negative symptoms include *blunted affect* (e.g., immobile facial expression, monotonous voice tone), *anhedonia* (lack of pleasure), *avolition* or *apathy* (diminished ability to initiate and follow through on plans), and *alogia* (reduced quantity or content of speech). Negative symptoms are more pervasive and fluctuate less over time than psychotic symptoms (Fenton & McGlashan, 1991), and are strongly associated with poor psychosocial functioning (Sayers, Curran, & Mueser, 1996). Because it is less readily apparent to others that negative symptoms are manifestations of a psychiatric illness, people are often perceived by relatives and others to be lazy and wilfully unengaged in bettering their lives (Weisman, Nuechterlein, Goldstein, & Snyder, 1998).

Cognitive impairment in schizophrenia includes problems in *attention* and *concentration, psychomotor speed, learning and memory,* and *executive functions* (e.g., abstract thinking, problem solving). A decline in cognitive abilities compared to premorbid functioning is present in most individuals with schizophrenia, with cognitive functioning after onset of the illness relatively stable over time (Heaton et al., 1994). Despite this decline, some clients' cognitive functioning is in the normal range. Similar to negative symptoms, cognitive impairment is strongly associated

with functional impairment, including community living and work (McGurk & Mueser, 2004; Mueser, 2000).

Impaired role functioning or significant change in personal behavior is also included as diagnostic criteria for schizophrenia. Problems in these areas include reduced ability to work, attend school, or parent, to have close relationships, to take care of oneself, and to enjoy one's leisure time, with difficulties often emerging several years before psychotic symptoms (Häfner, Löffler, Maurer, Hambrecht, & an der Heiden, 1999). Impairment in functioning can be profound, resulting in the need for disability entitlements and assistance in getting basic living needs met, such as housing, medical care, food, and clothing. Improving functioning remains the single most important challenge for the management of schizophrenia. Impairment in functioning tends to be relatively stable over time in schizophrenia, with some improvements over the long run, including partial or complete symptom remissions (Harding & Keller, 1998).

In addition to symptoms and impaired role functioning, schizophrenia affects many other areas of living. People with schizophrenia are at increased risk for alcohol and drug problems (Kavanagh et al., 2004), infectious diseases (e.g., hepatitis C, HIV infection; Rosenberg et al., 2001), violent victimization (Bebbington et al., 2004) and posttraumatic stress disorder (PTSD; Mueser, Rosenberg, Goodman, & Trumbetta, 2002), housing instability and homelessness (Susser, Struening, & Conover, 1989), smoking-related and other illnesses (de Leon et al., 1995), and negative emotions, such as anxiety (Huppert & Smith, 2001), depression (Addington, Addington, & Patten, 1998), and hostility (Bartels, Drake, Wallach, & Freeman, 1991) The net result of exposure to these risks is a sharply increased rate of premature mortality (Miller, Paschall, & Svendsen, 2006) due mainly to diseases (Brown, 1997), but also including an increased risk of suicide, estimated to be about 5% (Inskip, Harris, & Barraclough, 1998).

Epidemiology

The annual incidence of schizophrenia is .2 to .4 per 1000, with lifetime prevalence (risk) of approximately 1% (Jablensky, 1997). The incidence of schizophrenia is the same across genders, although women tend to have a later age of onset than men (Murray & Van Os, 1998), and a more benign course of illness, including fewer hospitalizations and better social functioning (Angermeyer, Kuhn, & Goldstein, 1990). The later age of onset in women is associated with higher attainment of preillness social role functioning, which confers a better outcome (Häfner, 2000).

Significant variations in the prevalence and incidence of schizophrenia across different countries and cultural groups have been reported (U.S. Institute of Medicine, 2001). However, these differences are minimized when stricter diagnostic criteria for schizophrenia are used (Jablensky, 1997). In a WHO study, the incidence of schizophrenia was quite similar across 10 countries (Jablensky et al., 1992). Research by the WHO across multiple countries also indicates that the clinical syndrome of schizophrenia is similar across a wide range of cultures and countries, including in developed and developing nations (Jablensky et al., 1992; WHO, 1979).

Etiology

Both genetic and environmental factors appear to play a role in the etiology of schizophrenia. Rates of schizophrenia are higher among relatives of those with schizophrenia than in the general population. Adoption and twin studies have shown that this increased risk is genetic, with a 10-fold increase in risk associated with the presence of an affected first-degree family member. This genetic risk increases with each affected relative, to nearly 50% when both parents are affected (McGuffin, Owen, & Farmer, 1996), and 60% to 84% when a monzygotic twin is affected (Cardno et al., 1999). The genetic transmission does not appear to follow simple Mendelian single-gene inheritance patterns. More likely, there are multiple susceptibility genes, each with small effect and acting in concert with epigenetic and environmental factors. At least seven genes have shown association with schizophrenia (Harrison & Owen, 2003; Thaker & Carpenter, 2001).

Environmental risks for schizophrenia include biological and psychosocial factors. The risk for development of schizophrenia is increased by pre/perinatal events including maternal influenza, rubella, malnutrition, diabetes mellitus, and smoking during pregnancy, and obstetric complications (Susser & Lin, 1992; Takei et al., 1996; Thomas et al., 2001). Obstetric complications associated with hypoxia are particularly related to increased risk for the development of schizophrenia, with the risk perhaps mediated by excitotoxic effects of hypoxia on the fetal neonatal brain (Cannon, Jones, & Murray, 2002). It has been suggested that, because most cases of obstetric complications do not lead to schizophrenia, such complications interact with genetic vulnerability to increase risk of schizophrenia (Cannon et al., 2000). However, it is not yet known whether the high frequency of obstetric complications in schizophrenia is the result of abnormal brain development associated with genetic vulnerability, or an additive environmental factor toward the development of schizophrenia.

Several sociodemographic factors are associated with increased risk of schizophrenia (van Os & Marcelis, 1998). Poverty and lower social class have long been linked to higher rates of schizophrenia (Bruce, Takeuchi, & Leaf, 1991). Individuals born in urban areas are more likely to develop schizophrenia than those in rural areas (Peen & Dekker, 1997). Although the incidence of schizophrenia is similar across different racial/ethnic groups (Jablensky, 1999), increased rates are present in some ethnic minority populations, such as second generation Afro Caribbeans in the United Kingdom (Boydell et al., 2001), Dutch Antillean and Surinamese immigrants in Holland (Selten, Slaets, & Kahn, 1997), and African Americans (Rabkin, 1979). These differences may reflect the stressful effects of being an ethnic minority in a social environment, which may increase vulnerability to schizophrenia in biologically predisposed individuals, as hypothesized in the *stress-vulnerability model* (Nuechterlein & Dawson, 1984; Zubin & Spring, 1977).

PURPOSES OF ASSESSMENT

Assessment in schizophrenia serves a number of distinct purposes. First, as the diagnosis of a schizophrenia-spectrum disorder can have important treatment implications, especially with regard to pharmacological management, a careful assessment is necessary to ensure an accurate diagnosis. Aside from undetected substance abuse or medical conditions that can lead to common symptoms of schizophrenia, there is a great overlap with the symptoms of bipolar disorder and major depression. The primary distinction between schizophrenia and mood disorders is made based on the course and co-occurrence of different symptoms (e.g., the absence of psychotic symptoms in people with a mood disorder when depression or mania are absent), which requires accurate historical information and sound clinical judgment.

Second, assessment serves a critical purpose in identifying treatment needs and informing treatment planning. Although it was once thought that schizophrenia led to irreversible deterioration (Kraepelin, 1919–1971), it is now clear that comprehensive interventions, grounded in a wide-ranging and thorough assessment, can dramatically improve outcomes. In addition to the complex of symptoms present in schizophrenia, and its impact on role functioning, social relationships, and self-care, other comorbidities are often present, including psychiatric, substance abuse, and medical comorbidity. In this chapter we will focus mainly on the assessment of symptoms and functioning for treatment planning, with only brief attention to comorbid substance abuse.

Third, assessment is necessary in order to monitor the effects of treatments. Ongoing evaluation of targeted areas for treatment is critical in order to know whether alternative approaches are necessary, and when treatment goals have been achieved. Numerous different treatments may impact on specific symptoms and areas of functioning, and thus many alternatives exist if treatment targets have not improved sufficiently.

In light of the pervasive nature of the deficits in schizophrenia, it is not surprising to observe that assessment of many other domains may be critical to the development of an accurate diagnosis and treatment plan in schizophrenia. Although important, they are beyond the scope of the chapter here. For example, we will not cover the assessment of cognitive impairment (Sharma & Harvey, 2000), but at a minimum recommend employing a brief cognitive screen to evaluate cognitive functioning (Gold, Queern, Iannone, & Buchanan, 1999; Keefe et al., 2004), followed up by a more comprehensive neuropsychological assessment if prominent deficits are identified. We also will not describe the assessment of medical disorders, but considering the high rates of medical comorbidity in schizophrenia (Dixon, Postrado, Delahanty, Fischer, & Lehman, 1999) we recommend arranging for all clients to have a physical examination. Similarly, we will not address the assessment of health risk behaviors, such as smoking (Zammit et al., 2003) and unprotected sex (Carey, Carey, Maisto, Gordon, & Vanable, 2001), but due to the high rate of nicotine addiction and infectious diseases in this population we recommend routine assessment of these and other health related behaviors (e.g., diet) in all clients using standard approaches developed for the general population. Finally, we will not describe the assessment of trauma history and PTSD, despite their high prevalence in this population (Mueser et al., 2002). Although treatment models for PTSD and related disorders have recently been articulated for persons with severe mental illness (Frueh et al., 2004; Harris, 1998; Mueser, Rosenberg, Jankowski, Hamblen, & Descamps, 2004), this work is still in its early phases and treatment implications remain to be established. For information on the assessment of trauma and PTSD in schizophrenia, see Mueser, Salyers, et al. (2001) and Rosenberg, Mueser, Jankowshi, and Hamblen (2002).

ASSESSMENT FOR DIAGNOSIS

Diagnostic assessment for schizophrenia-spectrum disorders involves obtaining a broad range of information that includes subjective states (e.g., hallucinations, delusions), behavioral observation (e.g., blunted affect, bizarre behavior), and reports about functioning in areas such as social relationships, work or school, and self-care. As the diagnosis of schizophrenia in DSM-IV requires ascertaining whether the duration of impaired functioning has been 6 months or longer, historical information must also be obtained. Although much of the information required to establishing a diagnosis can be obtained by directly interviewing the client, the lack of insight characteristic of the illness (Amador & Gorman, 1998) often necessitates obtaining supplementary information. Such information can be usually obtained from relatives, other treatment providers, and medical records, and is most useful for determining the presence of psychotic symptoms or problems in functioning.

Historically, the diagnosis of schizophrenia was unreliable (Matarazzo, 1983) before objective criteria were established by DSM-III (American Psychiatric Association, 1980), and the disorder was frequently overdiagnosed (Kuriansky, Deming, & Gurland, 1974). With the clearer specification of diagnostic criteria for schizophrenia in the DSM series, more reliable diagnostic assessment became possible. However, even with these objective criteria, the reliability of diagnoses is greatest when it is established using a structured clinical interview to probe for symptoms in a systematic fashion.

TABLE 18.1 Ratings of Instruments Used for Diagnosis

Instrument	Norms	Internal Consistency	Inter-Rater Reliability	Test–Retest Reliability	Content Validity	Construct Validity	Validity Generalization	Clinical Utility	Highly Recommended
DIS	E	NA	E	E	E	G	G	A	
PSE	E	NA	E	E	E	E	E	A	✓
SCID	E	NA	E	E	E	E	E	A	✓

Note: DIS = Diagnostic Interview Schedule; PSE = Present-State Examination; SCID = Structured Clinical Interview for DSM-IV; A = Adequate; G = Good; E = Excellent; NA = Not Applicable.

In the United States, the most widely used standardized instrument for diagnostic interviewing is the Structured Clinical Interview for DSM-IV (SCID; First, Spitzer, Gibbon, & Williams, 1996; Sbrana et al., 2005; Ventura, Liberman, Green, Shaner, & Mintz, 1998), and in the United Kingdom it is the Present State Examination (PSE; Luria & Berry, 1979; Wing, 1970). As indicated in Table 18.1, both of these instruments have excellent reliability and validity for the diagnosis of schizophrenia, although considerable training and clinical interviewing experience are required to use either instrument, and they are time-consuming to conduct, often requiring one to two or more hours to complete. The Diagnostic Interview Schedule (DIS; Robins, 1995) was designed primarily for use by lay interviewers in large-scale epidemiological research studies, and it lacks the sensitivity and specificity necessary for use in clinical settings. The DIS requires less training to learn than the SCID or PSE, and can usually be administered in under an hour, but it also has lower reliability and validity (Malgady, Lloyd, & Tryon, 1992). Briefer versions of the SCID have been developed, such as the PRIME MD (Spitzer et al., 1994), but their reliability and validity for assessing relatively low frequency disorders such as schizophrenia remain uncertain.

Overall Evaluation

Schizophrenia is a complex illness to diagnose that overlaps with many other major mental illnesses, especially major mood disorders. Highly reliable and well-validated measures for determining a diagnosis of schizophrenia include the SCID and PSE. Although these measures are time-consuming to administer in routine clinical settings, the importance of establishing an accurate diagnosis of schizophrenia, and the poorer reliability of briefer diagnostic instruments for

schizophrenia, makes the increased time and effort to administer these measures a worthwhile investment.

ASSESSMENT FOR CASE CONCEPTUALIZATION AND TREATMENT PLANNING

In this section we describe the assessment of symptoms, medication adherence, community functioning, subjective appraisal, family attitudes, and comorbid substance abuse for the purposes of case conceptualization and treatment planning. The ratings of the psychometric properties of these tools are presented in Table 18.2. As we describe subsequently, many of these same assessment tools can also be used for symptom monitoring and determining treatment outcomes.

Symptoms

Three semistructured interview instruments with well-established reliability and validity are widely used for the assessment of symptoms of schizophrenia, including the Brief Psychiatric Rating Scale (BPRS; Hafkenscheid, 1993; Hedlund & Vieweg, 1980; Lukoff, Nuechterlein, & Ventura, 1986; Overall & Gorham, 1962), the Positive and Negative Syndrome Scale (PANSS; Kay, Opler, & Fiszbein, 1987), and the Scale for the Assessment of Negative Symptoms (SANS; Andreasen, 1981, 1984; Mueser, Sayers, Schooler, Mance, & Haas, 1994; Vadhan, Serper, Harvey, Chou, & Cancro, 2001). The BPRS and PANSS cover a broad range of symptoms commonly present in schizophrenia, whereas the SANS focuses exclusively on negative symptoms. All three instruments include specific interview probes, clearly elucidated descriptions of target symptoms, and behaviorally anchored 5- to 7-point rating scales for scoring the presence and severity of

TABLE 18.2 Ratings of Instruments Used for Case Conceptualization and Treatment Planning

Instrument	Norms	Internal Consistency	Inter-Rater Reliability	Test–Retest Reliability	Content Validity	Construct Validity	Validity Generalization	Clinical Utility	Highly Recommended
Symptoms									
BPRS	A	G	E	A	A	G	E	A	✓
PANSS	A	G	E	A	A	E	E	A	✓
SANS	A	G	E	A	A	E	E	A	
Medication Adherence									
ROMI	A	A	G	A	A	A	A	A	✓
Community Functioning									
CASIG	A	A	E	A	E	A	G	A	✓
ILSS	A	G	G	A	G	A	A	A	✓
MCAS	A	A	G	A	A	G	G	A	✓
QLS	A	G	E	A	A	G	E	A	
SAFE	A	G	G	A	A	A	E	A	
SAS-II	A	G	E	A	A	G	E	A	
SBS	A	A	G	A	A	A	A	A	
SFS	A	G	E	A	G	G	E	A	✓
SF-36	E	G	NA	A	A	G	E	A	
Subjective Appraisal									
MHRM	A	G	NA	A	A	A	A	A	
QOLI	E	G	NA	A	G	E	E	A	✓
RAS	A	G	NA	A	G	A	E	A	✓
TL-30S	A	G	NA	A	A	A	E	A	
Family Attitudes									
PRS	A	G	NA	A	A	A	A	A	
Substance Abuse									
ASI	E	G	E	A	E	E	E	A	✓
AUDIT	E	G	NA	A	G	G	E	A	
DALI	A	A	NA	A	A	G	G	A	
DAST	E	G	NA	A	A	A	E	A	
MAST	E	G	NA	A	A	A	E	A	
SATS	A	NA	E	A	A	G	G	A	✓
TLFB	E	NA	E	A	A	G	E	A	✓

Note: BPRS = Brief Psychiatric Rating Scale; PANSS = Positive and Negative Syndrome Scale; SANS = Scale for Assessment of Negative Symptoms; ROMI = Rating of Medication Influences; CASIG = Client's Assessment of Strengths, Interests, and Goals (both client and informant versions); ILSS = Independent Living Skills Survey (both client and informant versions); MCAS = Multnomah Community Ability Scale; QLS = Quality of Life Scale; SAFE = Social-Adaptive Functioning Evaluation; SAS-II = Social Adjustment Scale-II SBS = Social Behavior Scale; SFS = Social Functioning Scale; SF-36 = Short-Form-36 Health Survey; MHRM = Mental Health Recovery Measure; QOLI = Quality of Life Interview; RAS = Recovery Assessment Scale; TL-30S = The Lehman Quality of Life Interview Short Form; PRS = Patient Rejection Scale; ASI = Alcohol Severity Inventory; AUDIT = Alcohol Use Disorder Identification Test; DALI = Dartmouth Assessment of Lifestyle Instrument; DAST = Drug Abuse Screening Test; MAST = Michigan Alcoholism Screening Test; SATS = Substance Abuse Treatment Scale; TLFB = Timeline Followback Calendar; A = Adequate; G = Good; E = Excellent; NA = Not Applicable.

symptoms. The PANSS includes 30 items, of which the first 18 were drawn from the original version of the BPRS (Overall & Gorham, 1962). Following the development of the PANSS, an additional six items were developed for the BPRS, which is often referred to as the Expanded BPRS (Lukoff et al., 1986). Each of these measures requires 25 to 40 minutes to complete.

The BPRS was designed as a general psychiatric rating scale for the broad range of symptoms present in severe mental illnesses, whereas the PANSS and SANS were developed to more specifically tap the symptoms of schizophrenia. Factor analyses of the BPRS have most frequently identified either four or five symptom dimensions (Long & Brekke, 1999; Mueser, Curran, & McHugo, 1997; Shafer, 2005), corresponding to thought disorder, anergia (negative symptoms), anxiety–depression, disorganization, and activation. As expected, because of the overlap in symptoms between the BPRS and PANSS, very similar factor structures have been identified for the PANSS (van der Gaag, Cuijpers, et al., 2006; van der Gaag, Hoffman, et al., 2006; White et al., 1994). For the SANS, one large factor analysis indicated a three-factor solution comprised of blunted affect, apathy-anhedonia, and alogia-inattention (Sayers et al., 1996).

The symptom assessments mentioned in the preceding two paragraphs are labor intensive to implement, as they require the interviewer be trained to adequate levels of reliability and the scales themselves can often require over a half hour to administer. More recently, health services researchers have addressed these impediments by designing broad symptom self-report measures intended for use with general psychiatric populations (e.g., the BASIS-R; Eisen, Normand, Belanger, Spiro, & Esch, 2004), and even evaluating whether computer administration of such self-report measures can yield useful results (Chinman, Young, Schell, Hassell, & Mintz, 2004), Initial data are promising, in so far as subscales on the BASIS-R discriminate psychotic from nonpsychotic groups in outpatient and inpatient samples, and some of the subscales indicate sensitivity to change (Jerrell, 2005). Furthermore, Chinman et al. (2004) have reported that comparisons of results on BASIS-R computer-administered assessments and interviews were highly correlated.

Three caveats are warranted in considering the use of self-report and/or computer administration of symptom measures such as the BASIS-R in persons with schizophrenia, however. First, these measures have not been widely used in typical clinical settings, so their day-to-day use may require some revision of procedures or interpretation of data. Second, even with self- or computer-administration, professional efforts are required to orient clients to the assessment, answer questions, and assure that individuals comprehend the task sufficiently to respond accurately. Third, many people with schizophrenia lead economically disadvantaged lives and may have limited prior experience with computers. Thus, orienting them to the computer assessment of symptoms in the office may entail teaching them how to work the computer (e.g., how to use a mouse, what to do if the monitor screen freezes, etc.) and being available while the assessment is being conducted. The professional time and effort required to assure the respondent can complete the task successfully should not be underestimated; of course, personnel assisting with these tasks do not require graduate training.

Medication Adherence

For most people with schizophrenia, adequate symptom control necessitates regular medication taking, and monitoring adherence with prescribed medication regimens is a critical aspect of treatment. Although noncompliance with antipsychotic medication is often identified as a problem (Dolder et al., 2004), it is important to note that reviews of prescription studies with nonpsychiatric populations report noncompliance rates of at least 30%. Not taking medications as prescribed is a common problem, regardless of medical condition.

Clinicians working with persons with schizophrenia should assess at least two dimensions of compliance: (1) actual level of medication taking, and (2) reasons for any noncompliance, as they may lend themselves to different interventions. Unfortunately, assessing medication taking behavior accurately is notoriously difficult across medical populations (Osterberg & Blaschke, 2005). Although pill counts and electronic pill bottles with cap sensors have been used in scientific investigations as the "gold standard" for assessing adherence, at this point, the norm in nonresearch settings is still to rely on client self-report based on questions asked frequently and nonjudgmentally, beginning with statements such as "I know it must be difficult to take all your medications regularly. How often do you miss taking them?" (Osterberg & Blaschke, 2005). Reports of noncompliance can be followed up with the administration of the Rating of Medication Influences (ROMI) Scale (Weiden et al., 1994), which includes self-report items assessing reasons for nonadherence that have been prospectively linked to nonadherence (Yamada et al., 2006). Specific responses will likely lead to different interventions—someone reporting he/she has a hard time physically obtaining the medication likely needs a different kind of assistance than someone acknowledging he/she feels embarrassed about taking the medication. Research indicates that both self-reports and collateral reports of medication adherence are not especially accurate (Pratt, Mueser, Driscoll, Wolfe, & Bartels, 2006). Clinically, reports of nonadherence are typically assumed to be more accurate than reports of adherence.

Community Functioning

Impaired adjustment in the areas of social, role, and self-care functioning are the hallmarks of schizophrenia, and an accurate assessment is critical to treatment planning. Unfortunately, assessment of each of these functioning domains presents challenges to the clinician in terms of both precise definitions of adequate "adjustment" and the use of clients as informants of their own functioning. For example, the domain of social functioning is complex, and may include a broad range of only weakly intercorrelated dimensions, such as number of regular social contacts, number of "friends," satisfaction with friendships, reciprocity of friendships, initiation of social contacts, romantic involvement, degree of contact and satisfaction with family relationships, social skills, and leisure and recreational activities. Aside from the sheer number of potentially important dimensions of social functioning, clients are not always accurate in their perceptions of how well they function compared to others, necessitating collateral reports from others who know the client, such as relatives or (for clients with frequent contact with professional or paraprofessional staff) mental health workers (Bowie, Reichenberg, Patterson, Heaton, & Harvey, 2006). Furthermore, the definition of "adequate" social adjustment is elusive, even in nonpsychiatric populations. In a society that values independent functioning, are adult offspring who continue to live with their parents less socially adjusted? What about persons who are divorced or never married—are their community-functioning levels necessarily less?

Most measures of community functioning used with persons with schizophrenia are dimensional, with one to several items assessing different domains of functioning (e.g., social support, independent living). The scales vary in their length (from as few as 12 to as many as 70 items with multiple prompts for each one), level of training required for the assessment administrator, relative emphasis on global life domains (e.g., social support) versus specific instrumental skills (e.g., ability to do laundry or ride the bus), whether original development of the scale was directed more for researchers (e.g., the Social Adjustment Scale-II) or practitioners (e.g., the Client Assessment of Strengths, Interests, and Goals [CASIG]), and whether the scales emphasize objective or subjective aspects of functioning. There is no one scale which will meet every need. Clinicians will do best to review the scales discussed below and determine which assess the domains of most interest for a particular client.

Scales of wide use in the assessment of community functioning in schizophrenia include the Social Adjustment Scale-II (SAS-II), the Quality of Life Scale (QLS), the Social Functioning Scale (SFS),

the Independent Living Scale Survey (ILSS), the CASIG, the Short-Form-36 (SF-36), the Multnomah Community Ability Scale (MCAS), the Social Behavior Schedule (SBS), and the Social-Adaptive Functioning Evaluation (SAFE).

The SAS-II is a semistructured client interview, which is a schizophrenia-specific modification of an instrument widely used in depressive samples (Weissman & Bothwell, 1976). The validity of the SAS-II for use with outpatients with schizophrenia has been previously demonstrated (Jaeger, Berns, & Czobor, 2003; Schooler, Hogarty, & Weissman, 1979). Measures of global adjustment in work/student role, household functioning, extended kin role, social and leisure activities, intimate relationships, well-being and overall adjustment are rated on a 1-to-7 scale, based on specific responses to a series of questions in each domain. The SAS-II was primarily designed as a research interview, and thus substantial training is required to administer it with high reliability.

The QLS (Heinrichs, Hanlon, & Carpenter, 1984) contains 21 items and is designed to assess the deficit syndrome concept in individuals with schizophrenia. It assesses four domains—interpersonal functioning, instrumental role functioning, intrapsychic factors (e.g., motivation, curiosity), and possession of common objects/participation in common activities—and also yields a total score. It has been found to be sensitive to change from participating in psychosocial interventions (Glynn et al., 2002). Two abbreviated versions of the QLS have been developed that include five (Ritsner, Kurs, Ratner, & Gibel, 2005) and seven (Bilker et al., 2003) items, which have been found to be strongly correlated with the total QLS score. Similar to the SAS-II, the QLS was designed as a research interview, and is not practical for use in most routine clinical settings.

The SFS (Birchwood, Smith, Cochrane, Wetton, & Copestake, 1990) is a 20-minute interview assessing the following domains of functioning: social engagement and withdrawal, interpersonal communication, independent living skills, socially appropriate behaviors, independence competence, and occupation. Scales are normed in each of the categories and the breadth of topics contains most of the items relevant to psychiatric populations.

The ILSS (Cyr, Toupin, Lesage, & Valiquette, 1994; Wallace, Liberman, Tauber, & Wallace, 2000) is an interview including 70 items asked of the client assessing a range of instrumental skills required for independent living—appearance and clothing, personal hygiene, care of personal possessions, food preparation and storage, health maintenance, money management, transportation, leisure and community, and job seeking and job maintenance. Both client- (self-) rated and staff-rated versions of the scale exist. It is particularly targeted at identifying specific skills required for community functioning (e.g., doing laundry, managing money).

The CASIG (Lecomte, Wallace, Caron, Perreault, & Lecomte, 2004; Wallace, Lecomte, Wilde, & Liberman, 2001) is also available in both client and informant interview formats. Nine areas of social and independent living skills (money management, food preparation, vocational transportation, friends, leisure, personal hygiene, and care of personal possessions) are assessed from four to nine dichotomous items. Items assess performance rather than ability or motivation. The informant and client version are fairly well correlated.

The RAND Short Form-36 Health Survey (SF-36; http://www.rand.org/health/surveys_tools/mos/mos_core_36item.html) is a modification of the SF-36 (Ware, Kosinski, & Keller, 1994) and is designed to assess functioning in a broad range of medical and psychiatric populations. It can be administered by interviews in person or over the phone. The RAND-36-Item Health Survey tapes eight health concepts: physical functioning, bodily pain, role limitations due to physical health problem, roles limitations due to personal or emotional problems, emotional well-being, social functioning, energy/fatigue, and general health perceptions. It also includes a single item that provides an indication of perceived change in health. Scores can be summed for both a total and within specific domains. Note that the scale does not specifically address instrumental skills that might be related to capacity to functioning independently in a psychiatric population (e.g., skill in riding the bus).

The MCAS (Barker, Barron, & McFarlane, 1994; Corbiere et al., 2002; Hendryx, Dyck, McBride, & Whitbeck, 2001) is an informant-based scale designed to be completed by a staff member who is familiar with the client's functioning in the community. The scale includes 17 items rated on 5-point Likert scales, covering the domains of interference with functioning, adjustment to living, social competence, and community integration. A recent modification of this scale has been developed with interview probes (Dickerson, Origoni, Pater, Friedman, & Kordonski, 2003).

The SBS (Lima, Goncalves, Pereira, & Lovisi, 2006; Wykes & Sturt, 1986) is an informant-rated instrument designed for the inpatient setting to be completed by staff members. The SBS contains 30 items, most rated on 5-point or 6-point Likert scales, pertaining to dimensions of adjustment in an intensive treatment setting, such as communication skills, symptomatic behavior, and self-harming behavior. The SBS can also be used with outpatients, as long as an informant who is knowledgeable about the person's day-to-day functioning can be identified.

The SAFE (Harvey et al., 1997) is an informant-rated instrument that is completed by staff members who are familiar with the client's daily functioning. The scale includes 17 items rated on 5-point Likert scales, with subscales corresponding to instrumental and self-care, impulse control, and social functions. The SAFE was originally developed for older persons with severe mental illness, although most of the items are applicable to younger clients.

Subjective Appraisal

In addition to obtaining expert assessments, there is an increasing interest in the field in measuring the client's own attitude toward his/her illness, as well as the individual's subjective appraisal of the his/her circumstances (e.g., living situation, safety, budget, etc.). In many ways, this focus reflects the growing influence of the recovery movement in mental health. Recovery from a serious and persisting psychiatric illness has been defined by the President's New Freedom Commission on Mental Health (2003) as "the process by which people are able to live, work, learn, and participate fully in their communities. For some individuals, recovery is the ability to live a fulfilling and productive life despite a disability. For others, recovery implies the reduction or complete remission of symptoms.... Science has shown that having hope plays an integral role in an individual's recovery" (p. 7). With regard to assessment, this recovery focus highlights two necessary domains of measurement—recovery attitudes and satisfaction with life circumstances.

In a factor analysis of clients' responses to a series of items reflecting recovery orientations, Resnick, Rosenheck, and Lehman (2004) identified four domains that can be seen as aspects of this process: life satisfaction, hope and optimism, knowledge of mental illness, and empowerment. Assessing recovery attitudes is a new area of investigation, but one of the most widely used measures is the Mental Health Recovery Measure (MHRM; Young & Bullock, 2005). The MHRM is a behaviorally anchored self-report measure designed for use with persons who have serious and persistent mental illnesses such as recurrent major depression, bipolar disorder, or schizophrenia. The item content of the MHRM and its subscales are based upon a specific conceptual model of mental health recovery that is grounded in the experiences of persons with psychiatric disabilities (Young & Ensing, 1999). The 30-item version of the MHRM contains the following subscales: overcoming, self-empowerment, learning and self-redefinition, basic functioning, overall well-being, new potentials, advocacy/enrichment, spirituality in the recovery process, and higher order activities, including advocacy, coping with stigma, and financial quality of life. Items are rated on 5-point Likert scales.

Another widely used measure of recovery is the Recovery Assessment Scale (RAS; Giffort, Schmook, Woody, Vollendorf, & Gervain, 1995; Ralph, Kidder, & Phillips, 2000). The RAS includes 41 items, each rated on a 5-point Likert scale, pertaining to different dimensions of recovery. A factor analysis indicated that the RAS taps the following factors: hope, meaningful life, quality of life, symptoms, and empowerment (Corrigan, Salzer, Ralph, Sangster, & Keck, 2004). There is limited evidence suggesting some sensitivity of the RAS to treatment-related change (Corrigan, 2006). A variety of other recovery-oriented measures have been developed (Campbell-Orde, Chamberlin, Carpenter, & Leff, 2005; Ralph et al., 2000) but are not covered here as their psychometric properties are still being evaluated.

A complementary aspect of subjective appraisal is the client's own evaluation of his/her satisfaction with the circumstances of his/her life in areas such as living situation, family relations, and so forth. The original widely used instrument for this type of assessment was the Lehman Quality of Life Interview (Lehman, Kernan, & Postrado, 1995), a 183-item instrument requiring 45-minutes to administer which asks participants to rate their satisfaction with various facets of their life on a scale from 1 to 7. The TL-30S is a validated briefer (30-item) 15-minute version, based on correlation coefficients between the brief and full version scales (Lehman, 2006). The brief version provides measures for satisfaction with living situation, social relations/network, finances, and employment,

and includes both objective and subjective items; the subjective appraisal items are of most interest here.

Family Attitudes

Work conducted in England in the 1950s–1970s (Brown, Birley, & Wing, 1972; Brown, Monck, Carstairs, & Wing, 1962) demonstrated that family attitudes reflective of high levels of distress measured at the time of a loved one's psychotic relapse tended to predict greater rates of subsequent relapse, especially if the relative and client had more than 35 hours of contact per week. This high level of family distress has been labeled "high expressed emotion" (EE), and the relationship between high EE and subsequent relapse is among the most potent predictors of outcome in schizophrenia (Butzlaff & Hooley, 1998). EE is reflected in critical comments or tone or reported extreme self-sacrificing behavior during a semistructured interview (the Camberwell Family Interview [CFI]) at the time of the initial relapse (Leff & Vaughn, 1985), and is likely evidenced in actual interactions with the client (Mueser et al., 1993; Strachan, Leff, Goldstein, Doane, & Burtt, 1986).

The measurement of EE requires an extensive research assessment and scoring procedure, which is outside the time capacities of most clinicians. However, clinicians can be alert to signs of extreme distress, criticism, and self-sacrificing behavior on the part of the relative at the time of a relapse and consider a referral for an evidence-based family intervention if these are observed. These might be reflected, for example, in frequent calls to the clinic for assistance, repeated complaints about the client, or tearfulness in a relative. Hooley and Parker (2006) have suggested that one feasible method for assessing EE is to ask clients how critical their relative is of them. In a sample of clients with depression, Hooley and Teasdale (1989) simply asked clients to rate how critical they thought their relative was of them using a 10-point Likert-type scale. Clients' perceptions of their partner's criticism level (assessed during the index hospitalization) was highly predictive ($r = -.64$) of client relapse over the course of a 9-month follow-up. Although this result has not been replicated in schizophrenia, the method warrants more consideration and may have special utility for busy clinicians.

An alternative measure to ratings of perceived criticism is the Patient Rejection Scale (PRS; Kreisman et al., 1988; Kreisman, Simmens, & Joy, 1979). This

24-item scale consists of both positively and negatively worded items reflecting feelings of love and acceptance, criticism, disappointment, and rejection; it can be considered an analog of the critical comments and hostility factors composing the concept of EE. Presumably, families high in rejecting attitudes would benefit from participation in targeted interventions such as education or stress management. However, clinicians using the PRS should be aware that some of the items may be distressing for relatives to rate (e.g., "I wish (the patient) had never been born") and that a short debriefing with relatives after they complete the scale may be in order.

Comorbid Substance Abuse

The assessment of co-occurring substance use disorders may have important treatment planning implications for clients with schizophrenia. About 50% of persons with schizophrenia develop either substance abuse or dependence at some point in their illness (Regier et al., 1990), and most estimates of the point prevalence of substance use disorders range between 25% and 35% (Mueser, Bennett, & Kushner, 1995). The treatment of co-occurring substance abuse is important because of its deleterious effects on the course and outcome of schizophrenia (Drake & Brunette, 1998), and the emergence of effective treatment models that integrated services for the two disorders (Drake & O'Neal, in press; Mueser, Noordsy, Drake, & Fox, 2003).

A number of brief screening instruments may be used to detect substance abuse problems in schizophrenia (Carey, 2002). Although some research suggests that instruments developed for measuring substance abuse in the general population may be insensitive to it in people with schizophrenia (Corse, Hirschinger, & Zanis, 1995; Wolford et al., 1999), several measures have demonstrated acceptable reliability and validity, including the Alcohol Use Disorder Identification Test (Dawe, Seinen, & Kavanagh, 2000; Maisto, Carey, Carey, Gordon, & Gleason, 2000; Saunders, Aasland, Babor, de la Fuente, & Grant, 1993; Seinen, Dawe, Kavanagh, & Bahr, 2000), the Michigan Alcoholism Screening Test (McHugo, Paskus, & Drake, 1993; Searles, Alterman, & Purtill, 1990; Selzer, 1971; Wolford et al., 1999), and the Drug Abuse Screening Test (Maisto et al., 2000; Skinner, 1982; Wolford et al., 1999). In addition, the Dartmouth Assessment of Lifestyle Instrument was developed specifically to

detect alcohol, cannabis, and cocaine use disorders in persons with severe mental illness, and has shown good reliability and validity in this population (Ford, 2003; Rosenberg et al., 1998).

Diagnoses of substance abuse and dependence in clients with schizophrenia can also be reliably measured with the SCID (First et al., 1996). Although there is a tendency for clients with schizophrenia to have low subscale scores on the Addiction Severity Index, which was developed for the general population (McLellan et al., 1992), valid and reliable measures of the consequences of substance use can nevertheless be obtained with it (Corse et al., 1995). Limited work has been conducted indicating that measures of expectancies and reasons for substance use developed for the general population may be valid in persons with schizophrenia (Carey & Carey, 1995; Laudet, Magura, Vogel, & Knight, 2004; Mueser, Nishith, Tracy, DeGirolamo, & Molinaro, 1995), although at this point the research is too preliminary to make firm recommendations. Mueser and colleagues (2003) provide detailed standardized assessment tools of substance use in persons with severe mental illness for treatment planning purposes, although rigorous psychometric evaluation remains to be conducted.

The Substance Abuse Treatment Scale (SATS; McHugo, Drake, Burton, & Ackerson, 1995; Mueser, Drake, et al., 1995; Mueser et al., 2003) is an 8-point behaviorally anchored scale designed to measure motivation for substance abuse treatment in persons with severe mental illness. The SATS is based on the stages of treatment model (Mueser et al., 2003; Osher & Kofoed, 1989), which was adapted from the transtheoretical stages of change model (Prochaska & DiClemente, 1984). The stages of treatment include *engagement* (establishing a therapeutic relationship with the client), *persuasion* (motivating the person to work on substance abuse problems), *active treatment* (helping the person reduce substance use and/or attain abstinence), and *relapse prevention* (helping the client prevent substance abuse relapses). As the client's stage of treatment has implications for treatment planning (e.g., in the engagement stage the clinician focuses on establishing rapport and meeting with the client regularly, whereas in active treatment stage the focus is on changing substance use behavior), the SATS is clinically useful.

The Timeline Followback (TLFB) Calendar (Sobell & Sobell, 1992) is an instrument for quantifying substance use over the past 6 months, and obtaining information about patterns of use that can be useful in treatment planning. The primary dependent variable studied has been the number of days of drinking to intoxication and the number of days of drug use. The TLFB has been adapted for use with persons with severe mental illness (Mueser, Drake, et al., 1995; Mueser et al., 2003), with research supporting its reliability and validity (Carey, Carey, Maisto, & Henson, 2004).

Overall Evaluation

A wide range of validated instruments have been developed for case conceptualization and treatment planning regarding the domains of symptoms, community functioning, and comorbid substance abuse in schizophrenia. The most strongly validated measures for each of these areas involve either semistructured interviews or informant-based ratings, which is consistent with the poor insight many clients with schizophrenia have into their illness (Amador & Gorman, 1998). There are fewer choices for treatment planning-related assessment of medication adherence, subjective appraisal, and family attitudes, but there is at least one validated instrument for each domain that is practical for use in clinical settings.

ASSESSMENT FOR TREATMENT MONITORING AND TREATMENT OUTCOME

Symptoms

The BPRS, PANSS, and SANS administered by interview have demonstrated sensitivity to change following treatment, and are suitable for monitoring the effects of interventions on symptoms. Many research studies have utilized the BPRS and PANSS as frequently as every 2 weeks during times of psychotic exacerbation to determine when symptoms return to baseline. Self-reported symptoms on scales such as the BASIS-R tend to measure global distress, and not specific dimensions of symptoms as with interview measures, and therefore their clinical utility for monitoring the effects of treatment on symptoms is not established (see Table 18.3).

The Clinical Global Impression Scale (Guy, 1976; Haro et al., 2003) has been widely used to assess symptom change, especially in pharmaceutical studies.

The scale has three items, the first two being rated on seven-point Likert scales and of most relevance here. These items assess severity of illness (from "normal" to "extremely ill") and global improvement from baseline ("very much improved" to "very much worse"). There is a third efficacy item, typically referring to the hypothesized effect of a pharmaceutical agent, which is rated on a 4-point scale. Although the three ratings are brief, they are typically made after extended clinical assessments and/or contact with clients and require that assessors have known the client since the baseline period.

Medication Adherence

Although a range of instruments have been developed to measure medication adherence, none has a consistent track record for demonstrating sensitivity to change. Most interventions that have been evaluated in research trials for improving medication adherence employ either pill counts or electronic pill bottles with cap sensors (Zygmunt, Olfson, Boyer, & Mechanic, 2002).

Community Functioning

The Global Assessment of Functioning (GAF; American Psychiatric Association, 2000), based on the widely used Global Assessment Scale (Endicott, Spitzer, Fleiss, & Cohen, 1976), is a single rating scale for evaluating a person's psychological, social, and occupational functioning on a hypothetical continuum of mental illness—mental health, which ranges from 1 (most ill) to 100 (most healthy). The scale provides defining characteristics, including both symptoms and functioning, for each 10-point interval between 1 and 100. Scores are reliable and correlated with symptom measures, especially with repeated assessments, and have been found to have high interrater reliability (Pedersen, Hagtvet, & Karterud, 2007; Söderberg, Tungström, & Armelius, 2005; Startup, Jackson, & Pearce, 2002).

The client-based interview instruments of community functioning reviewed in the previous section on assessment for treatment planning (including the SAS-II, QLS, ILSS, SFS, and CASIG) are sensitive to change and suitable for the purposes of monitoring treatment effects. Similarly, the informant-based instruments have demonstrated sensitivity to change and are appropriate for treatment monitoring

TABLE 18.3 Rating of Instruments Used for Treatment Monitoring and Treatment Outcome Evaluation

Instrument	Norms	Internal Consistency	Inter-Rater Reliability	Test–Retest Reliability	Content Validity	Construct Validity	Validity Generalization	Treatment Sensitivity	Clinical Utility	Highly Recommended
Symptoms										
BPRS	A	G	E	A	A	G	E	E	A	✓
CGI	A	NA	E	A	A	A	E	E	A	✓
PANSS	A	G	E	A	A	E	E	E	A	✓
SANS	A	G	E	A	A	E	E	A	A	✓
Community Functioning										
CASIG	A	A	E	A	E	A	G	G	A	✓
ILSS	A	G	G	A	G	A	A	G	A	✓
MCAS	A	A	G	A	A	G	G	G	A	✓
QLS	A	G	E	A	A	G	E	E	A	
SAFE	A	G	G	A	A	A	E	G	A	
SAS-II	A	G	E	A	A	G	E	E	A	
SBS	A	A	G	A	A	A	A	G	A	
SFS	A	G	E	A	G	G	E	G	A	✓
SF-36	E	G	NA	A	A	G	E	A	A	
Subjective Appraisal										
MHRM	A	G	NA	A	A	A	A	A	A	
QOLI	E	G	NA	A	G	E	E	A	A	
RAS	A	G	NA	A	G	A	E	A	A	✓
TL-30S	A	G	NA	A	A	A	G	A	A	
Family Attitudes										
PRS	A	G	NA	A	A	A	A	A	A	
Substance Abuse										
ASI	E	G	E	A	E	E	E	G	A	✓
AUS	A	NA	E	A	A	A	E	E	A	✓
DUS	A	NA	E	A	A	A	E	E	A	✓
SATS	A	NA	E	A	A	A	E	E	A	✓
TLFB	E	NA	E	A	A	G	E	E	A	

Note: BPRS = Brief Psychiatric Rating Scale; CGI = Clinical Global Impression Scale; PANSS = Positive and Negative Syndrome Scale; SANS = Scale for Assessment of Negative Symptoms; CASIG = Client's Assessment of Strengths, Interests, and Goals (both client and informant versions); ILSS = Independent Living Skills Survey (both client and informant versions); MCAS = Multnomah Community Ability Scale; QLS = Quality of Life Scale; SAFE = Social-Adaptive Functioning Evaluation; SAS-II= Social Adjustment Scale-II SBS = Social Behavior Scale; SFS = Social Functioning Scale; SF-36 = Short-Form-36 Health Survey; MHRM = Mental Health Recovery Measure; QOLI = Quality of Life Interview; RAS = Recovery Assessment Scale; PRS = Patient Rejection Scale; ASI = Alcohol Severity Inventory; AUS =Alcohol Use Scale; DUS = Drug Use Scale; SATS = Substance Abuse Treatment Scale; TLFB = Timeline Followback Calendar; A = Adequate; G = Good; E = Excellent; NA = Not Applicable.

(including SAS-II, CASIG, MCAS, SBS, and SAFE). However, these measures would rarely be used more frequently than quarterly, as changes in social and community functioning typically lag behind symptom changes and require relatively long periods of time to occur (e.g., to find a job, an apartment, develop a friendship, etc.).

Subjective Appraisal

The three measures discussed in the treatment planning section (MHRM, RAS, and TL-30S) have been proposed for ongoing monitoring and assessment of treatment outcomes, although data on their use in this way are limited. As subjective appraisal and quality of life tend to be stable over relatively long periods of time, and their sensitivity to change is uncertain, they would best be administered no more frequently than once every 6 months.

Family Attitudes

The CFI was developed primarily as a measure of negative family affect for clients who have recently experienced a symptom relapse, and has been evaluated as predictor of subsequent relapse and rehospitalization (Butzlaff & Hooley, 1998). Research evaluating changes in negative family affect measured on the CFI indicate modest sensitivity to treatment-related change (Hogarty et al., 1991). However, the extensive time required to administer the CFI makes it impractical for monitoring the effects of family intervention in clinical settings. Reports of client measures of perceived relative criticism have not been reported in schizophrenia to date. The PRS has been found to be predictive of relapse in schizophrenia (Kreisman et al., 1988) and is sensitive to the effects of participation in family interventions (Mueser, Sengupta, et al., 2001).

Substance Abuse

The Alcohol Use Scale (AUS) and Drug Use Scale (DUS) are 5-point rating scales completed by clinicians to rate substance abuse problems over the past 6 months, based on all available information (Drake et al., 1990; Mueser, Drake, et al., 1995; Mueser et al., 2003). For each scale, 1 = no substance use, 2 = use but not abuse, 3 = abuse, 4 = dependence, and 5 = dependence and substance-use-related institutionalization (e.g., hospitalizations, incarcerations).

The AUS and DUS have high sensitivity to change and are appropriate for monitoring treatment outcomes. Similarly, the SATS and TLFB have demonstrated sensitivity to treatment-related change. The Alcohol Severity Inventory (ASI) is also sensitive to change following treatment, although clients with moderate substance abuse severity tend to have floor effects (Corse et al., 1995).

Overall Evaluation

Similar to assessment for the purposes of treatment planning, a wide range of validated instruments are available for monitoring and evaluating the effects of treatment on symptoms, community functioning, and comorbid substance abuse in schizophrenia. In contrast, there are more limited, but nevertheless clinically suitable, choices for measuring family attitudes. Measures of subjective appraisal and quality of life appear to be less sensitive to treatment-related change, although it is not clear that this reflects limitations in the measures or the high stability of these appraisals over time. At this point, there are no scientifically validated (and hence recommended) measures of medication adherence that can be used for the purposes of treatment monitoring, and clinicians are advised to combine client self-report with observational measures such as pill counts or use of electronic pill bottles with cap sensors.

CONCLUSIONS AND FUTURE DIRECTIONS

Because schizophrenia can affect so many different areas of life functioning, assessment is necessarily complex and spans a broad range of different domains. Furthermore, because impaired insight into the illness is a common feature of schizophrenia, the most sensitive measures of functioning usually require either standardized interviews or informant ratings. With these considerations, well-validated measures have been developed for diagnosing schizophrenia, and for both treatment planning and monitoring treatment effects in the domains of symptoms, community functioning, family attitudes, and substance abuse. More work is needed to develop and evaluate instruments of subjective appraisal and medication adherence that are sensitive to the effects of treatment.

In addition to the importance of developing measures for some domains that are more sensitive to change, there is a strong need for measures that can be implemented in routine clinical settings by competent clinicians without requiring extensive training. With the exception of self-report measures of subjective appraisal, the strongest measures for assessment in schizophrenia have been developed in the context of research studies and validated with trained clinicians. Only limited evidence supports the utility of these instruments in the routine practice of treating clients with schizophrenia, and time constraints often prevent a thorough assessment that would lead to comprehensive treatment.

A related problem is the absence of measures that provide a comprehensive, integrated assessment across the broad range of domains of functioning that are often impaired, or for which there are often needs, in schizophrenia. For example, Mueser and Gingerich (2006) identified 10 different areas of potential treatment need, including managing symptoms, emotional well-being, role functioning, social relationships, leisure activities, self-care and independent living, physical health, substance use, and spirituality. Instead, clinicians must select among the variety of different instruments that are available, with the net result that many domains are never assessed, and treatment fails to address many needs. The development of more fully integrated measures that cover a broader range of functioning in schizophrenia could improve the comprehensiveness of assessment, and effectiveness of treatment planning.

Finally, there is a need to develop assessment and treatment planning methods that strive to reconcile and integrate the perspectives of treatment providers and clients with schizophrenia. Shared decision-making between clients and providers has been growing in mental health services (Fenton, 2003; Hamann, Leucht, & Kissling, 2003) and is an important value espoused by the President's New Freedom Commission on Mental Health (2003). Models of shared decision-making have recently been proposed for prescribing medication (Deegan & Drake, 2006), and there is a need for further work to develop such approaches that span the full range of functioning in schizophrenia. Shared decision-making approaches have the potential to both integrate different perspectives on functioning, and to set informed treatment priorities based on client preferences. Such approaches are critical considering the ever-growing array of effective medications and rehabilitation approaches for schizophrenia.

References

Addington, D., Addington, J., & Patten, S. (1998). Depression in people with first-episode schizophrenia. *British Journal of Psychiatry, 172*(Suppl. 33), 90–92.

Amador, X. F., & Gorman, J. M. (1998). Psychopathologic domains and insight in schizophrenia. *The Psychiatric Clinics of North America, 21,* 27–42.

American Psychiatric Association. (1980). *Diagnostic and statistical manual of mental disorders* (3rd ed.). Washington, DC: Author.

American Psychiatric Association. (1994). *Diagnostic and statistical manual of mental disorders* (4th ed.). Washington, DC: Author.

American Psychiatric Association. (2000). *Diagnostic and statistical manual of mental disorders* (4th ed., text revision). Washington, DC: Author.

Andreasen, N. C. (1981). *Scale for the assessment of negative symptoms (SANS).* Iowa City: University of Iowa.

Andreasen, N. C. (1984). *Modified scale for the assessment of negative symptoms.* Bethesda, MD: U.S. Department of Health and Human Services.

Angermeyer, M. C., Kuhn, L., & Goldstein, J. M. (1990). Gender and the course of schizophrenia: Differences in treated outcome. *Schizophrenia Bulletin, 16,* 293–307.

Barker, S., Barron, N., & McFarlane, B. (1994). *Multnomah community ability scale: Users manual.* Portland, OR: Western Mental Health Research Center, Oregon Health Sciences University.

Bartels, S. J., Drake, R. E., Wallach, M. A., & Freeman, D. H. (1991). Characteristic hostility in schizophrenic outpatients. *Schizophrenia Bulletin, 17,* 163–171.

Bebbington, P. E., Bhugra, D., Brugha, T., Singleton, N., Farrell, M., Jenkins, R., et al. (2004). Psychosis, victimisation and childhood disadvantage: Evidence from the second British National Survey of Psychiatric Morbidity. *British Journal of Psychiatry, 185,* 220–226.

Bilker, W. B., Brensinger, C. M., Kurtz, M. M., Kohler, C. G., Gur, R. C., Siegel, S. J., et al. (2003). Development of an abbreviated schizophrenia Quality of Life Scale using a new method. *Neuropsychopharmacology, 28,* 773–777.

Birchwood, M., Smith, J., Cochrane, R., Wetton, S., & Copestake, S. (1990). The Social Functioning Scale: The development and validation of a new scale of social adjustment for use in family intervention programmes with schizophrenic patients. *British Journal of Psychiatry, 157,* 853–859.

Bleuler, E. (1911/1950). *Dementia praecox or the group of schizophrenias.* New York: International Universities Press.

Bowie, C. R., Reichenberg, A., Patterson, T. L., Heaton, R. K., & Harvey, P. D. (2006). Determinants of real-world functional performance in schizophrenia subjects: Correlations with cognition, functional capacity, and symptoms. *American Journal of Psychiatry, 163,* 418–425.

Boydell, J., van Os, J., McKenzie, K., Allardyce, J., Goel, R., McCreadie, R., et al. (2001). Incidence of schizophrenia in ethnic minorities in London: Ecological study into interactions with environment. *British Medical Journal, 323,* 1336–1338.

Brown, G. W., Birley, J. L. T., & Wing, J. K. (1972). Influence of family life on the course of schizophrenic disorders: A replication. *British Journal of Psychiatry, 121,* 241–258.

Brown, G. W., Monck, E. M., Carstairs, G. M., & Wing, J. K. (1962). Influence of family life on the course of schizophrenic illness. *British Journal of Preventive and Social Medicine, 16,* 55–68.

Brown, S. (1997). Excess mortality of schizophrenia: A meta-analysis. *British Journal of Psychiatry, 171,* 502–508.

Bruce, M. L., Takeuchi, D. T., & Leaf, P. J. (1991). Poverty and psychiatric status: Longitudinal evidence from the New Haven Epidemiologic Catchment Area Study. *Archives of General Psychiatry, 48,* 470–474.

Butzlaff, R. L., & Hooley, J. M. (1998). Expressed emotion and psychiatric relapse. *Archives of General Psychiatry, 55,* 547–552.

Campbell-Orde, T., Chamberlin, J., Carpenter, J., & Leff, H. S. (Eds.). (2005). *Measuring the promise: A compendium of recovery measures.* (Vol. II). Cambridge, MA: Evaluation Center at Human Services Research Institute.

Cannon, T. D., Jones, P. B., & Murray, R. M. (2002). Obstetric complications and schizophrenia: Historical and meta-analytic review. *American Journal of Psychiatry, 159,* 1080–1092.

Cannon, T. D., Rosso, I. M., Hollister, J. M., Bearden, C. E., Sanchez, L. E., & Hadley, T. (2000). A prospective cohort study of genetic and perinatal influences in the etiology of schizophrenia. *Schizophrenia Bulletin, 26,* 351–366.

Cardno, A., Marshall, E., Coid, B., Macdonald, A., Ribchester, T., Davies, N., et al. (1999). Heritability estimates for psychotic disorders: The Maudsley twin psychosis series. *Archives of General Psychiatry, 56,* 162–168.

Carey, K. B. (2002). Clinically useful assessments: Substance use and comorbid psychiatric disorders. *Behaviour Research and Therapy, 40,* 1345–1361.

Carey, K. B., & Carey, M. P. (1995). Reasons for drinking among psychiatric outpatients: Relationship to drinking patterns. *Psychology of Addictive Behaviors, 9,* 251–257.

Carey, K. B., Carey, M. P., Maisto, S. A., & Henson, J. M. (2004). Temporal stability of the timeline followback interview for alcohol and drug use with psychiatric outpatients. *Journal of Studies on Alcohol, 65,* 774–781.

Carey, M. P., Carey, K. B., Maisto, S. A., Gordon, C. M., & Vanable, P. A. (2001). Prevalence and correlates of sexual activity and HIV-related risk behavior among psychiatric outpatients. *Journal of Consulting and Clinical Psychology, 69,* 846–850.

Chinman, M., Young, A. S., Schell, T., Hassell, J., & Mintz, J. (2004). Computer-assisted self-assessment in persons with severe mental illness. *Journal of Clinical Psychiatry, 65,* 1343–1351.

Corbiere, M., Crocker, A. G., Lesage, A. D., Latimer, E., Ricard, N., & Mercier, C. (2002). Factor structure of the Multnomah Community Ability Scale. *Journal of Nervous and Mental Disease, 190,* 399–406.

Corrigan, P. W. (2006). Impact of consumer-operated services on empowerment and recovery of people with psychiatric disabilities. *Psychiatric Services, 57,* 1493–1496.

Corrigan, P. W., Salzer, M., Ralph, R., Sangster, Y., & Keck, L. (2004). Examining the factor structure of the Recovery Assessment Scale. *Schizophrenia Bulletin, 30,* 1035–1041.

Corse, S. J., Hirschinger, N. B., & Zanis, D. (1995). The use of the Addiction Severity Index with people with severe mental illness. *Psychiatric Rehabilitation Journal, 19,* 9–18.

Cyr, M., Toupin, J., Lesage, A. D., & Valiquette, C. A. (1994). Assessment of independent living skills for psychotic patients. Further validity and reliability. *Journal of Nervous and Mental Disease, 182,* 91–97.

Dawe, S., Seinen, A., & Kavanagh, D. J. (2000). An examination of the utility of the AUDIT in people with schizophrenia. *Journal of Studies on Alcohol, 61,* 744–750.

Deegan, P. E., & Drake, R. E. (2006). Shared decision making and medication management in the recovery process. *Psychiatric Services, 57,* 1636–1639.

de Leon, J., Dadvand, M., Canuso, C., White, A. O., Stanilla, J. K., & Simpson, G. M. (1995). Schizophrenia and smoking: An epidemiologial survey at a state hospital. *American Journal of Psychiatry, 152,* 453–455.

Dickerson, F. B., Origoni, A. E., Pater, A., Friedman, B. K., & Kordonski, W. M. (2003). An expanded version of the Multnomah Community Ability Scale: Anchors and interview probes for the assessment of adults with serious mental illness. *Community Mental Health Journal, 39*, 131–137.

Dixon, L., Postrado, L., Delahanty, J., Fischer, P. J., & Lehman, A. (1999). The association of medical comorbidity in schizophrenia with poor physical and mental health. *The Journal of Nervous and Mental Disease, 187*, 496–502.

Dolder, C. R., Lacro, J. P., Warren, K. A., Golshan, S., Perkins, D. O., & Jeste, D. V. (2004). Brief evaluation of medication influences and beliefs: Development and testing of a brief scale for medication adherence. *Journal of Clinical Psychopharmacology, 24*, 404–409.

Drake, R. E., & Brunette, M. F. (1998). Complications of severe mental illness related to alcohol and other drug use disorders. In M. Galanter (Ed.), *Recent developments in alcoholism: Consequences of alcoholism* (Vol. 14, pp. 285–299). New York: Plenum Publishing Company.

Drake, R. E., & O'Neal, E. (in press). A systematic review of research on interventions for people with co-occurring severe mental and substance use disorders. *Journal of Substance Abuse Treatment.*

Drake, R. E., Osher, F. C., Noordsy, D. L., Hurlbut, S. C., Teague, G. B., & Beaudett, M. S. (1990). Diagnosis of alcohol use disorders in schizophrenia. *Schizophrenia Bulletin, 16*, 57–67.

Eisen, S., Normand, S. L., Belanger, A. J., Spiro, A., & Esch, D. (2004). The Revised Behavior and Symptom Identification Scale (BASIS-R): Reliability and validity. *Medical Care, 42*, 1230–1241.

Endicott, J., Spitzer, R. L., Fleiss, J. L., & Cohen, J. (1976). The Global Assessment Scale: A procedure for measuring overall severity of psychiatric disturbance. *Archives of General Psychiatry, 33*, 766–771.

Fenton, W. S. (2003). Shared decision making: A model for the physician–patient relationship in the 21st century? *Acta Psychiatrica Scandinavica, 107*, 401–402.

Fenton, W. S., & McGlashan, T. H. (1991). Natural history of schizophrenia subtypes: II. Positive and negative symptoms and long term course. *Archives of General Psychiatry, 48*, 978–986.

First, M. B., Spitzer, R. L., Gibbon, M., & Williams, J. B. W. (1996). *Structured clinical interview for DSM-IV axis-I disorders-Patient edition* (SCID-I/P, Version 2.0). New York: Biometrics Research Department, New York State Psychiatric Institute.

Ford, P. (2003). An evaluation of the Dartmouth Assessment of Lifestyle Inventory and the Leeds Dependence Questionnaire for use among detained psychiatric inpatients. *Addiction, 98*, 111–118.

Frueh, B. C., Buckley, T. C., Cusack, K. J., Kimble, M. O., Grubaugh, A. L., Turner, S. M., et al. (2004). Cognitive-behavioral treatment for PTSD among people with severe mental illness: A proposed treatment model. *Journal of Psychiatric Practice, 10*, 26–38.

Geller, J. L. (1992). An historical perspective on the role of state hospitals viewed from the "revolving door." *American Journal of Psychiatry, 149*, 1526–1533.

Giffort, D., Schmook, A., Woody, C., Vollendorf, C., & Gervain, M. (1995). *Construction of a scale to measure consumer recovery.* Springfield, IL: Illinois Office of Mental Health.

Glynn, S. M., Marder, S. R., Liberman, R. P., Blair, K., Wirshing, W. C., Wirshing, D. A., et al. (2002). Supplementing clinic-based skills training with manual-based community support sessions: Effects on social adjustment of patients with schizophrenia. *American Journal of Psychiatry, 159*, 829–837.

Gold, J. M., Queern, C., Iannone, V. N., & Buchanan, R. W. (1999). Repeatable battery for the Assessment of Neuropsychological Status as a screening test in schizophrenia, II: Convergent/discriminant validity and diagnostic group comparisons. *American Journal of Psychiatry, 156*, 1944–1950.

Guy, W. (1976). *ECDEU assessment manual for psychopharmacology* (revised, DHEW Publication No ADM 76-338). Rockville, MD: U.S. Department of Health and Human Services.

Hafkenscheid, A. (1993). Reliability of a standardized and expanded Brief Psychiatric Rating Scale: A replication study. *Acta Psychiatrica Scandinavica, 88*, 305–310.

Häfner, H. (2000). Onset and early course as determinants of the further course of schizophrenia. *Acta Psychiatrica Scandinavica, 102*(Suppl. 407), 44–48.

Häfner, H., & an der Heiden, W. (2003). Course and outcome of schizophrenia. In S. R. Hirsch & D. R. Weinberger (Eds.), *Schizophrenia* (2nd ed., pp. 101–141). Oxford: Blackwell Scientific.

Häfner, H., Löffler, W., Maurer, K., Hambrecht, M., & an der Heiden, W. (1999). Depression, negative symptoms, social stagnation and social decline in the early course of schizophrenia. *Acta Psychiatrica Scandinavica, 100*, 105–118.

Hamann, J., Leucht, S., & Kissling, W. (2003). Shared decision making in psychiatry. *Acta Psychiatrica Scandinavica, 107*, 403–409.

Harding, C. M., & Keller, A. B. (1998). Long-term outcome of social functioning. In K. T. Mueser & N. Tarrier (Eds.), *Handbook of social functioning in schizophrenia* (pp. 134–148). Boston: Allyn & Bacon.

Haro, J. M., Kamath, S. A., Ochoa, S., Novick, D., Rele, K., Fargas, A., et al. (2003). The Clinical Global

Impression-Schizophrenia scale: A simple instrument to measure the diversity of symptoms present in schizophrenia. *Acta Psychiatrica Scandanavia, 416*(Suppl.), 16–23.

Harris, M. (1998). *Trauma recovery and empowerment: A clinician's guide for working with women in groups.* New York: The Free Press.

Harrison, P. J., & Owen, M. J. (2003). Genes for schizophrenia: Recent findings and their pathophysiological implications. *The Lancet, 361,* 417–419.

Harvey, P. D., Davidson, M., Mueser, K. T., Parrella, M., White, L., & Powchik, P. (1997). Social-Adaptive Functioning Evaluation (SAFE): A rating scale for geriatric psychiatric patients. *Schizophrenia Bulletin, 23,* 131–145.

Heaton, R., Paulsen, J. S., McAdams, L. A., Kuck, J., Zisook, S., Braff, D., et al. (1994). Neuropsychological deficits in schizophrenics: Relationship to age, chronicity, and dementia. *Archives of General Psychiatry, 51,* 469–476.

Hedlund, J. L., & Vieweg, B. W. (1980). The Brief Psychiatric Rating Scale (BPRS): A comprehensive review. *Journal of Operational Psychiatry, 11*(1), 48–65.

Heinrichs, D. W., Hanlon, T. E., & Carpenter, W. T. J. (1984). The Quality of Life Scale: An instrument for rating the schizophrenia deficit syndrome. *Schizophrenia Bulletin, 10,* 388–396.

Hendryx, M., Dyck, D. G., McBride, D., & Whitbeck, J. (2001). A test of the reliability and validity of the Multnomah Community Ability Scale. *Community Mental Health Journal, 37,* 157–168.

Hogarty, G. E., Anderson, C. M., Reiss, D. J., Kornblith, S. J., Greenwald, D. P., Ulrich, R. F., et al. (1991). Family psychoeducation, social skills training, and maintenance chemotherapy in the aftercare treatment of schizophrenia, II: Two-year effects of a controlled study on relapse and adjustment. *Archives of General Psychiatry, 48,* 340–347.

Hooley, J. M., & Parker, H. A. (2006). Measuring expressed emotion: An evaluation of the shortcuts. *Journal of Family Psychology, 20,* 386–396.

Hooley, J. M., & Teasdale, J. D. (1989). Predictors of relapse in unipolar depression: Expressed emotion, marital quality, and perceived criticism. *Journal of Abnormal Psychology, 98,* 229–235.

Huppert, J. D., & Smith, T. E. (2001). Longitudinal analysis of subjective quality of life in schizophrenia: Anxiety as the best symptom predictor. *Journal of Nervous and Mental Disease, 189,* 669–675.

Inskip, H. M., Harris, E. C., & Barraclough, C. (1998). Lifetime risk of suicide for alcoholism, affective disorder and schizophrenia. *British Journal of Psychiatry, 172,* 35–37.

Jablensky, A. (1997). The 100-year epidemiology of schizophrenia. *Schizophrenia Research, 28,* 111–125.

Jablensky, A. (1999). Schizophrenia: Epidemiology. *Current Opinion in Psychiatry, 12,* 9–28.

Jablensky, A., Sartorius, N., Ernberg, G., Anker, M., Korten, A., & Cooper, J. E. (1992). Schizophrenia: Manifestations, incidence, and course in different cultures: A World Health Organization ten-country study. *Psychological Medicine, 20*(Suppl.), 1–97.

Jaeger, J., Berns, S. M., & Czobor, P. (2003). The multidimensional scale of independent functioning: A new instrument for measuring functional disability in psychiatric populations. *Schizophrenia Bulletin, 29,* 153–168.

Jerrell, J. M. (2005). Behavior and symptom identification scale 32: Sensitivity to change over time. *Journal of Behavioral Health Services & Research, 20,* 341–346.

Kavanagh, D. J., Waghorn, G., Jenner, L., Chant, D. C., Carr, V., Evans, M., et al. (2004). Demographic and clinical correlates of comorbid substance use disorders in psychosis: Multivariate analyses from an epidemiological sample. *Schizophrenia Research, 66,* 115–124.

Kay, S. R., Opler, L. A., & Fiszbein, A. (1987). The Positive and Negative Syndrome Scale (PANSS) for schizophrenia. *Schizophrenia Bulletin, 13,* 261–276.

Keefe, R. S., Goldberg, T. E., Harvey, P. D., Gold, J. M., Poe, M. P., & Coughenour, L. (2004). The Brief Assessment of Cognition in Schizophrenia: Reliability, sensitivity, and comparison with a standard neurocognitive battery. *Schizophrenia Research, 68,* 283–297.

Kraepelin, E. (1919/1971). *Dementia praecox and paraphrenia* (R. M. Barclay, Trans.). New York: Krieger.

Kreisman, D., Blumenthal, R., Borenstein, M., Woerner, M., Kane, J., Rifkin, A., et al. (1988). Family attitudes and patient social adjustment in a longitudinal study of outpatient schizophrenics receiving low-dose neuroleptics: The family's view. *Psychiatry, 51,* 3–13.

Kreisman, D. E., Simmens, S. J., & Joy, V. D. (1979). Rejecting the patient: preliminary validation of a self-report scale. *Schizophrenia Bulletin, 5,* 220–222.

Kuriansky, J. B., Deming, W. E., & Gurland, B. J. (1974). On trends in the diagnosis of schizophrenia. *American Journal of Psychiatry, 131,* 402–408.

Laudet, A. B., Magura, S., Vogel, H. S., & Knight, E. L. (2004). Perceived reasons for substance misuse among persons with a psychiatric disorder. *American Journal of Orthopsychiatry, 74,* 365–375.

Lecomte, T., Wallace, C. J., Caron, J., Perreault, M., & Lecomte, J. (2004). Further validation of the Client

Assessment of Strengths Interests and Goals. *Schizophrenia Research, 66,* 59–70.

Leff, J., & Vaughn, C. (Eds.). (1985). *Expressed emotion in families.* New York: Guilford Publications.

Lehman, A. F. (2006). *Quality of life interview: Self-administered short form* (TL-30S Version). Baltimore: Center for Mental Health Services Research, Department of Psychiatry, University of Maryland.

Lehman, A. F., Kernan, E., & Postrado, L. (1995). *Toolkit for evaluating quality of life for persons with severe mental illness.* Baltimore, MD: The Evaluation Center at HSRI.

Liddle, P. F. (1987). The symptoms of chronic schizophrenia: A re-examination of the positive-negative dichotomy. *British Journal of Psychiatry, 151,* 145–151.

Lima, L. A., Gonçalves, S., Pereira, B. B., & Lovisi, G. M. (2006). The measurement of social disablement and assessment of psychometric properties of the Social Behaviour Schedule (SBS-BR) in 881 Brazilian long-stay psychiatric patients. *International Journal of Social Psychiatry, 52,* 101–109.

Long, J. D., & Brekke, J. S. (1999). Longitudinal factor structure of the Brief Psychiatric Rating Scale in schizophrenia. *Psychological Assessment, 11,* 498–506.

Lukoff, D., Nuechterlein, K. H., & Ventura, J. (1986). Manual for the Expanded Brief Psychiatric Rating Scale (BPRS). *Schizophrenia Bulletin, 12,* 594–602.

Luria, R. E., & Berry, R. (1979). Reliability and descriptive validity of PSE syndromes. *Archives of General Psychiatry, 36,* 1187–1195.

Maisto, S. A., Carey, M. P., Carey, K. B., Gordon, C. M., & Gleason, J. R. (2000). Use of the AUDIT and the DAST-10 to identify alcohol and drug use disorders among adults with a severe and persistent mental illness. *Psychological Assessment, 12,* 186–192.

Malgady, R., Lloyd, H., & Tryon, W. (1992). Issues of validity in the Diagnostic Interview Schedule. *Journal of Psychiatric Research, 26,* 59–67.

Matarazzo, J. D. (1983). The reliability of psychiatric and psychological diagnosis. *Clinical Psychology Review, 3,* 103–145.

McGuffin, P., Owen, M. J., & Farmer, A. E. (1996). Genetic basis of schizophrenia. *Lancet, 346,* 678–682.

McGurk, S. R., & Mueser, K. T. (2004). Cognitive functioning, symptoms, and work in supported employment: A review and heuristic model. *Schizophrenia Research, 70,* 147–174.

McHugo, G. J., Drake, R. E., Burton, H. L., & Ackerson, T. H. (1995). A scale for assessing the stage of substance abuse treatment in persons with severe mental illness. *Journal of Nervous and Mental Disease, 183,* 762–767.

McHugo, G. J., Paskus, T. S., & Drake, R. E. (1993). Detection of alcoholism in schizophrenia using the MAST. *Alcoholism: Clinical and Experimental Research, 17,* 187–191.

McLellan, A. T., Kushner, H., Metzger, D., Peters, R., Smith, I., Grissom, G., et al. (1992). The fifth edition of the Addiction Severity Index: Historical critique and normative data. *Journal of Substance Abuse Treatment, 9,* 199–213.

Miller, B. J., Paschall, C. B. I., & Svendsen, D. P. (2006). Mortality and medical comorbidity among patients with serious mental illness. *Psychiatric Services, 57,* 1482–1487.

Mueser, K. T. (2000). Cognitive functioning, social adjustment and long-term outcome in schizophrenia. In T. Sharma & P. Harvey (Eds.), *Cognition in schizophrenia: Impairments, importance, and treatment strategies* (pp. 157–177). Oxford: Oxford University Press.

Mueser, K. T., Bellack, A. S., Wade, J. H., Sayers, S. L., Tierney, A., & Haas, G. (1993). Expressed emotion, social skill, and response to negative affect in schizophrenia. *Journal of Abnormal Psychology, 102,* 339–351.

Mueser, K. T., Bennett, M., & Kushner, M. G. (1995). Epidemiology of substance abuse among persons with chronic mental disorders. In A. F. Lehman & L. Dixon (Eds.), *Double jeopardy: Chronic mental illness and substance abuse* (pp. 9–25). New York: Harwood Academic Publishers.

Mueser, K. T., Curran, P. J., & McHugo, G. J. (1997). Factor structure of the Brief Psychiatric Rating Scale in schizophrenia. *Psychological Assessment, 9,* 196–204.

Mueser, K. T., Drake, R. E., Clark, R. E., McHugo, G. J., Mercer-McFadden, C., & Ackerson, T. (1995). *Toolkit for evaluating substance abuse in persons with severe mental illness.* Cambridge, MA: Evaluation Center at HSRI.

Mueser, K. T., & Gingerich, S. (2006). *The complete family guide to schizophrenia: Helping your loved one get the most out of life.* New York: Guilford Press.

Mueser, K. T., Nishith, P., Tracy, J. I., DeGirolamo, J., & Molinaro, M. (1995). Expectations and motives for substance use in schizophrenia. *Schizophrenia Bulletin, 21,* 367–378.

Mueser, K. T., Noordsy, D. L., Drake, R. E., & Fox, L. (2003). *Integrated treatment for dual disorders: A guide to effective practice.* New York: Guilford Press.

Mueser, K. T., Rosenberg, S. D., Goodman, L. A., & Trumbetta, S. L. (2002). Trauma, PTSD, and the course of schizophrenia: An interactive model. *Schizophrenia Research, 53,* 123–143.

Mueser, K. T., Rosenberg, S. D., Jankowski, M. K., Hamblen, J., & Descamps, M. (2004). A cognitive-behavioral treatment program for posttraumatic stress disorder in severe mental illness. *American Journal of Psychiatric Rehabilitation, 7,* 107–146.

Mueser, K. T., Salyers, M. P., Rosenberg, S. D., Ford, J. D., Fox, L., & Carty, P. (2001). A psychometric evaluation of trauma and PTSD assessments in persons with severe mental illness. *Psychological Assessment, 13,* 110–117.

Mueser, K. T., Sayers, S. L., Schooler, N. R., Mance, R. M., & Haas, G. L. (1994). A multisite investigation of the reliability of the Scale for the Assessment of Negative Symptoms. *American Journal of Psychiatry, 151,* 1453–1462.

Mueser, K. T., Sengupta, A., Schooler, N. R., Bellack, A. S., Xie, H., Glick, I. D., et al. (2001). Family treatment and medication dosage reduction in schizophrenia: Effects on patient social functioning, family attitudes, and burden. *Journal of Consulting and Clinical Psychology, 69,* 3–12.

Murray, C. J. L., & Lopez, A. D. (Eds.). (1996). *The global burden of disease: A comprehensive assessment of mortality and disability from diseases, injuries, and risk factors in 1990 and projected to 2020.* Cambridge, MA: Harvard School of Public Health on behalf of the World Health Organization and the World Bank, Harvard University Press.

Murray, R. M., & Van Os, J. (1998). Predictors of outcome in schizophrenia. *Journal of Clinical Psychopharmacology, 18,* 2S–4S.

New Freedom Commission on Mental Health. (2003). *Achieving the promise: Transforming mental health care in America. Final Report* (DHHS Pub. No. SMA-03-3832). Rockville, MD: Substance Abuse and Mental Health Services Administration.

Nuechterlein, K. H., & Dawson, M. E. (1984). A heuristic vulnerability/stress model of schizophrenic episodes. *Schizophrenia Bulletin, 10,* 300–312.

Osher, F. C., & Kofoed, L. L. (1989). Treatment of patients with psychiatric and psychoactive substance use disorders. *Hospital and Community Psychiatry, 40,* 1025–1030.

Osterberg, L., & Blaschke, T. (2005). Adherence to medication. *New England Journal of Medicine, 353,* 487–497.

Overall, J. E., & Gorham, D. R. (1962). The Brief Psychiatric Rating Scale. *Psychological Reports, 10,* 799–812.

Pedersen, G., Hagtvet, K. A., & Karterud, S. (2007). Generalizability studies of the Global Assessment of Functioning-Split version. *Comprehensive Psychiatry, 48,* 88–94.

Peen, J., & Dekker, J. (1997). Admission rates for schizophrenia in The Netherlands: An urban/rural comparison. *Acta Psychiatrica Scandinavica, 96,* 301–305.

Peralta, V., & Cuesta, M. J. (2003). The nosology of psychotic disorders: A comparison among competing classification systems. *Schizophrenia Bulletin, 29,* 413–425.

Pratt, S. I., Mueser, K. T., Driscoll, M., Wolfe, R., & Bartels, S. J. (2006). Medication nonadherence in older people with serious mental illness: Prevalence and correlates. *Psychiatric Rehabilitation Journal, 29,* 299–310.

Prochaska, J. O., & DiClemente, C. C. (1984). *The transtheoretical approach: Crossing the traditional boundaries of therapy.* Homewood, IL: Dow-Jones/Irwin.

Rabkin, J. (1979). Ethnic density and psychiatric hospitalization: Hazards of minority status. *American Journal of Psychiatry, 136,* 1562–1566.

Ralph, R. O., Kidder, K., & Phillips, D. (2000). *Can we measure recovery? A compendium of recovery and recovery-related instruments.* Cambridge, MA: The Evaluation Center at Human Services Research Institute.

Regier, D. A., Farmer, M. E., Rae, D. S., Locke, B. Z., Keith, S. J., Judd, L. L., et al. (1990). Comorbidity of mental disorders with alcohol and other drug abuse: Results from the Epidemiologic Catchment Area (ECA) study. *Journal of the American Medical Association, 264,* 2511–2518.

Resnick, S. G., Rosenheck, R. A., & Lehman, A. F. (2004). An exploratory analysis of correlates of recovery. *Psychiatric Services, 55,* 540–547.

Ritsner, M., Kurs, R., Ratner, Y., & Gibel, A. (2005). Condensed version of the Quality of Life Scale for schizophrenia for use in outcome studies. *Psychiatry Research, 135,* 65–75.

Robins, L. N. (1995). *Diagnostic interview schedule (Version IV).* St. Louis, MO: Washington School of Medicine.

Rosenberg, S. D., Drake, R. E., Wolford, G. L., Mueser, K. T., Oxman, T. E., Vidaver, R. M., et al. (1998). The Dartmouth Assessment of Lifestyle Instrument (DALI): A substance use disorder screen for people with severe mental illness. *American Journal of Psychiatry, 155,* 232–238.

Rosenberg, S. D., Goodman, L. A., Osher, F. C., Swartz, M., Essock, S. M., Butterfield, M. I., et al. (2001). Prevalence of HIV, hepatitis B and hepatitis C in people with severe mental illness. *American Journal of Public Health, 91,* 31–37.

Rosenberg, S. D., Mueser, K. T., Jankowski, J. K., & Hamblen, J. (2002). Trauma exposure and PTSD in people with severe mental illness. *PTSD Research Quarterly, 13*(3), 1–7.

Saunders, J. B., Aasland, O. G., Babor, T. F., de la Fuente, J. R., & Grant, M. (1993). Development of the Alcohol Use Disorders Identification Test (AUDIT): WHO Collaborative Project on Early Detection of Persons with Harmful Alcohol Consumption II. *Addiction, 88,* 791–804.

Sayers, S. L., Curran, P. J., & Mueser, K. T. (1996). Factor structure and construct validity of the Scale for the Assessment of Negative Symptoms. *Psychological Assessment, 8,* 269–280.

Sbrana, A., Dell'Osso, L., Benvenuti, A., Rucci, P., Cassano, P., Banti, S., et al. (2005). The psychotic spectrum: Validity and reliability of the Structured Clinical Interview for the Psychotic Spectrum. *Schizophrenia Research, 75,* 375–387.

Schooler, N., Hogarty, G., & Weissman, M. (1979). Social Adjustment Scale II (SAS-II). In W. A. Hargreaves, C. C. Atkisson, & J. E. Sorenson (Eds.), *Resource materials for community mental health program evaluations* (pp. 290–303). Rockville, MD: NIMH.

Searles, J. S., Alterman, A. I., & Purtill, J. J. (1990). The detection of alcoholism in hospitalized schizophrenics: A comparison of the MAST and the MAC. *Alcoholism: Clinical and Experimental Research, 14,* 557–560.

Seinen, A., Dawe, S., Kavanagh, D. J., & Bahr, M. (2000). An examination of the utility of the AUDIT in people diagnosed with schizophrenia. *Journal of Studies on Alcohol, 61,* 744–750.

Selten, J. P., Slaets, J., & Kahn, R. S. (1997). Schizophrenia in Surinamese and Dutch Antillean immigrants to the Netherlands: Evidence of an increased incidence. *Psychological Medicine, 27,* 807–811.

Selzer, M. L. (1971). The Michigan Alcoholism Screening Test: The quest for a new diagnostic instrument. *American Journal of Psychiatry, 127,* 1653–1658.

Shafer, A. (2005). Meta-analysis of the Brief Psychiatric Rating Scale factor structure. *Psychological Assessment, 17,* 324–335.

Sharma, T., & Harvey, P. (Eds.). (2000). *Cognition in schizophrenia: Impairments, importance and treatment strategies.* New York: Oxford University Press.

Skinner, H. A. (1982). The Drug Abuse Screening Test. *Addictive Behaviors, 7,* 363–371.

Sobell, L. C., & Sobell, M. B. (1992). Timeline followback: A technique for assessing self-reported alcohol consumption. In R. Z. Litten & J. Allen (Eds.), *Measuring alcohol consumption: Psychosocial and biological methods* (pp. 41–72). Totowa, NJ: Humana Press.

Söderberg, P., Tungström, S., & Armelius, B. A. (2005). Special section on the GAF: Reliability of Global Assessment of Functioning ratings made by clinical psychiatric staff. *Psychiatric Services, 56,* 434–438.

Spitzer, R., Williams, J., Kroenke, K., Linzer, M., deGruy, F. V. III, Hahn, S., et al. (1994). Utility of a new procedure for diagnosing mental disorders in primary care: The PRIME-MD 1000 Study. *Journal of the American Medical Association, 272,* 1749–1756.

Startup, M., Jackson, M., & Pearce, E. (2002). Assessing therapist adherence to cognitive-behaviour therapy for psychosis. *Behavioural and Cognitive Psychotherapy, 30,* 329–339.

Strachan, A. M., Leff, J. P., Goldstein, M. J., Doane, J. A., & Burtt, C. (1986). Emotional attitudes and direct communication in the families of schizophrenics: A cross-national replication. *British Journal of Psychiatry, 149,* 279–287.

Susser, E., & Lin, S. (1992). Schizophrenia after prenatal exposure to the Dutch Hunger Winter of 1944–1945. *Archives of General Psychiatry, 49,* 983–988.

Susser, E., Struening, E. L., & Conover, S. (1989). Psychiatric problems in homeless men: Lifetime psychosis, substance use, and current distress in new arrivals at New York City shelters. *Archives of General Psychiatry, 46,* 845–850.

Takei, N., Mortensen, P. B., Klaening, U., Murray, R. M., Sham, P. C., O'Callaghan, E., et al. (1996). Relationship between in utero exposure to influenza epidemics and risk of schizophrenia in Denmark. *Biological Psychiatry, 40,* 817–824.

Terkelsen, K. G., & Menikoff, A. (1995). Measuring costs of schizophrenia: Implications for the post-institutional era in the U.S. *Pharmacoeconomics, 8,* 199–222.

Thaker, G. K., & Carpenter, W. T., Jr. (2001). Advances in schizophrenia. *Nature Medicine, 7,* 667–671.

Thomas, H. V., Dalman, C., David, A. S., Gentz, J., Lewis, G., & Allebeck, P. (2001). Obstetric complications and risk of schizophrenia: Effect of gender, age at diagnosis and maternal history of psychosis. *British Journal of Psychiatry, 179,* 409–414.

U.S. Institute of Medicine. (2001). *Neurological, psychiatric, and developmental disorders: Meeting the challenges in the developing world.* Washington, DC: National Academy of Sciences.

Vadhan, N. P., Serper, M. R., Harvey, P. D., Chou, J. C., & Cancro, R. (2001). Convergent validity and neuropsychological correlates of the Schedule for the Assessment of Negative Symptoms (SANS) attention subscale. *Journal of Nervous and Mental Disease, 189,* 637–641.

van der Gaag, M., Cuijpers, A., Hoffman, T., Remijsen, M., Hijman, R., de Haan, L., et al. (2006). The five-factor model of the Positive and Negative Syndrome Scale I: Confirmatory factor analysis fails to confirm 25 published five-factor solutions. *Schizophrenia Research, 85,* 273–279.

van der Gaag, M., Hoffman, T., Remijsen, M., Hijman, R., de Haan, L., van Meijel, B., et al. (2006).

The five-factor model of the Positive and Negative Syndrome Scale II: A ten-fold cross-validation of a revised model. *Schizophrenia Research, 85,* 280–287.

van Os, J., & Marcelis, M. (1998). The ecogenics of schizophrenia: A review. *Schizophrenia Research, 32,* 127–135.

Ventura, J., Liberman, R. P., Green, M. F., Shaner, A., & Mintz, J. (1998). Training and quality assurance with the Structured Clinical Interview for DSM-IV (SCID-I/P). *Psychiatry Research, 79*(2), 163–173.

Wallace, C. J., Lecomte, T., Wilde, J., & Liberman, R. P. (2001). CASIG: A consumer-centered assessment for planning individualized treatment and evaluating program outcomes. *Schizophrenia Research, 50,* 105–109.

Wallace, C. J., Liberman, R. P., Tauber, R., & Wallace, J. (2000). The Independent Living Skills Survey: A comprehensive measure of the community functioning of severely and persistently mentally ill individuals. *Schizophrenia Bulletin, 26,* 631–658.

Ware, J. E., Kosinski, M., & Keller, S. D. (1994). *SF-36 physical and mental health summary scales: A user's manual.* Boston, MA: Health Assessment Lab.

Weiden, P., Rapkin, B., Mott, T., Zygmunt, A., Goldman, D., Horvitz-Lennon, M., et al. (1994). Rating of Medication Influences (ROMI) Scale in schizophrenia. *Schizophrenia Bulletin, 20,* 297–310.

Weisman, A. Y., Nuechterlein, K. H., Goldstein, M. J., & Snyder, K. S. (1998). Expressed emotion, attitudes, and schizophrenic symptom dimensions. *Journal of Abnormal Psychology, 107,* 355–359.

Weissman, M. M., & Bothwell, S. (1976). Assessment of social adjustment by patient self-report. *Archives of General Psychiatry, 33,* 1111–1115.

White, L., Harvey, P. D., Parella, M., Knobler, H., Powchik, P., & Davidson, M. (1994). Empirical assessment of the factorial structure of clinical symptoms in schizophrenic patients: Symptom structure in geriatric and nongeriatric samples. *New Trends in Experimental and Clinical Psychiatry, 10,* 75–83.

Wing, J. K. (1970). A standard form of psychiatric Present-State Examination and a method for standardizing the classification of symptoms. In E. H. Hare & J. K. Wing (Eds.), *Psychiatric epidemiology: An international symposium* (pp. 93–108). London: Oxford University Press.

Wolford, G. L., Rosenberg, S. D., Drake, R. E., Mueser, K. T., Oxman, T. E., Hoffman, D., et al. (1999). Evaluation of methods for detecting substance use disorder in persons with severe mental illness. *Psychology of Addictive Behaviors, 13,* 313–326.

World Health Organization. (1979). *Schizophrenia: An international follow-up study.* Chichester: John Wiley & Sons.

World Health Organization. (1992). *The ICD-10 classification of mental and behavioural disorders: Clinical descriptions and diagnostic guidelines.* Geneva: World Health Organization.

Wykes, T., & Sturt, E. (1986). The measurement of social behaviour in psychiatric patients: An assessment of the reliability and validity of the SBS Schedule. *British Journal of Psychiatry, 148,* 1–11.

Yamada, K., Watanabe, K., Nemoto, N., Fujita, H., Chikaraishi, C., Yamauchi, K., et al. (2006). Prediction of medication noncompliance in outpatients with schizophrenia: 2-year follow-up study. *Psychiatry Research, 141,* 61–69.

Young, S. L., & Bullock, W. A. (2005). Mental Health Recovery Measure (MHRM). In T. Campbell-Orde, J. Chamberlin, J. Carpenter, & H. S. Leff (Eds.), *Measuring the promise: A compendium of recovery measures* (Vol. II, pp. 36–41). Cambridge, MA: Evaluation Center at Human Services Research Institute.

Young, S. L., & Ensing, D. S. (1999). Exploring recovery from the perspective of people with psychiatric disabilities. *Psychiatric Rehabilitation Journal, 22,* 219–231.

Zammit, S., Allebeck, P., Dalman, C., Lundberg, I., Hemmingsson, T., & Lewis, G. (2003). Investigating the association between cigarette smoking and schizophrenia in a cohort study. *American Journal of Psychiatry, 160,* 2216–2221.

Zubin, J., & Spring, B. (1977). Vulnerability: A new view of schizophrenia. *Journal of Abnormal Psychology, 86,* 103–126.

Zygmunt, A., Olfson, M., Boyer, C. A., & Mechanic, D. (2002). Interventions to improve medication adherence in schizophrenia. *American Journal of Psychiatry, 159,* 1653–1664.

19

Personality Disorders

Thomas A. Widiger

This chapter is concerned with an evidence-based assessment of individuals with personality disorder. It is organized into three sections: instruments for the diagnosis of personality disorder, for case conceptualization and treatment planning, and for treatment monitoring and outcome. Particular attention is given to instruments for the diagnosis of personality disorder because, as yet, little to no systematic research has been conducted on the assessment of treatment planning and outcome for personality disorders. The chapter will begin with a brief discussion of the nature of personality disorder.

NATURE OF THE DISORDER

Personality is one's characteristic manner of thinking, feeling, behaving, and relating to others. Everybody has a personality. Some persons are typically introverted and withdrawn; others are more extraverted and outgoing. Some persons are invariably conscientiousness and efficient, whereas other persons might be consistently undependable and negligent. Some persons are characteristically anxious and apprehensive, whereas others are typically relaxed and unconcerned. These personality traits are typically perceived to be integral to each person's sense of self, as they involve what persons value, what they do, and what they are like most every day throughout much of their lives. It is "when personality traits are inflexible and maladaptive and cause significant functional impairment or subjective distress [that] they constitute Personality Disorders" (American Psychiatric Association [APA], 2000, p. 686).

The APA's *Diagnostic and Statistical Manual of Mental Disorders* (DSM-IV-TR; APA, 2000) provides diagnostic criteria for 10 personality disorders: the paranoid, schizoid, and schizotypal (identified as being within an odd-eccentric cluster); the histrionic, antisocial, borderline, and narcissistic (within a dramatic-emotional cluster); and the avoidant, dependent, and obsessive–compulsive (within an anxious-avoidant cluster). Clinicians can also diagnose a patient with personality disorder, not otherwise specified (PDNOS). Clinicians provide the PDNOS diagnosis when they determine that a personality disorder is present but the symptomatology fails to meet the criterion set for one of the 10 provided diagnoses. In general clinical practice, PDNOS is often one of the more commonly provided diagnoses (Verheul & Widiger, 2004).

By definition, personality disorders must be evident since adolescence or young adulthood and have been relatively chronic and stable throughout adult life. As such, they often predate the occurrence of other mental disorders, such as a mood, anxiety, or substance use disorder. Personality disorders are diagnosed on a separate axis of DSM-IV-TR (i.e., Axis II), whereas most other mental disorders are diagnosed on Axis I (APA, 2000). They were provided this special status to encourage clinicians to consider the presence of a personality disorder even though the clinical attention was naturally being directed to a more immediate concern regarding anxiety, mood, or substance use (Frances, 1980). The authors of DSM-III (APA, 1980) recognized that the presence of a personality disorder might provide a partial explanation for the occurrence of the Axis I disorder (e.g., substance use could be due in part to antisocial personality traits, and a depressive episode could be due in part to dependent personality traits), and there was also considerable empirical support for the concern that the presence of a personality disorder can have a significant impact on the course and treatment of the Axis I disorder (Frances, 1980).

Approximately, 10% to 15% of the general population would be diagnosed with one of the 10 DSM-IV-TR personality disorders, excluding PDNOS (Mattia & Zimmerman, 2001; Torgesen, Kringlen, & Cramer, 2001). Estimates of the prevalence of DSM-IV-TR personality disorder within clinical settings are typically above 50% (Mattia & Zimmerman, 2001). As many as 60% of inpatients within some clinical settings would be diagnosed with borderline personality disorder (APA, 2000; Gunderson, 2001), and as many as 50% of inmates within a correctional setting could be diagnosed with antisocial personality disorder (Derefinko & Widiger, in press). These rates are rather high but consistent with the perspective that many, if not most, persons will have at least one maladaptive personality trait. Although the comorbid presence of a personality disorder is likely to have an important impact on the course and treatment of an Axis I disorder (Dolan-Sewell, Krueger, & Shea, 2001), the prevalence of personality disorder is generally underestimated in clinical practice owing in part to the failure to provide systematic or comprehensive assessments of personality disorder symptomatology (Zimmerman & Mattia, 1999).

Personality disorders are highly comorbid with one another (Bornstein, 1998). Patients who meet the DSM-IV-TR diagnostic criteria for one personality disorder are likely to meet the diagnostic criteria for another. DSM-IV-TR instructs clinicians that all diagnoses should be recorded because it can be important to consider, for example, the presence of antisocial traits in someone with a borderline personality disorder or the presence of paranoid traits in someone with a dependent personality disorder. However, the extent of diagnostic co-occurrence is at times so extensive that many researchers prefer a more dimensional description of personality (Clark, 2007; Livesley, 2003; Oldham & Skodol, 2000; Widiger & Trull, 2007).

There are a wide variety of theoretical models for the etiology and pathology of the DSM-IV-TR personality disorders, including psychodynamic, cognitive-behavioral, interpersonal, and neurobiological (Lenzenweger & Clarkin, 2005). A primary purpose of a diagnosis is to lead to scientific knowledge concerning the etiology for a patient's condition and the identification of a specific pathology for which a particular treatment (e.g., medication) would ameliorate the condition (Frances, First, & Pincus, 1995). However, many of the mental disorders in DSM-IV-TR,

including the personality disorders, may not in fact have single etiologies or even specific pathologies (Rutter, 2003). There is considerable effort to determine a specific etiology and pathology for individual disorders, such as the antisocial (Derefinko & Widiger, in press), the borderline (Gunderson, 2001), and the narcissistic (Zanarini, 2005), but research suggests that the etiology is more likely to involve a complex array of multiple genetic dispositions interacting with a variety of detrimental environmental experiences (Paris, 2005; Rutter, 2003; Widiger & Trull, 2007).

Personality disorders can be among the most difficult of mental disorders to assess, due in large part to the unique qualities of a personality disorder. Personality includes one's characteristic sense of self, and personality disorders can include significant distortions in self-image (Millon et al., 1996). Dependent persons can be excessively self-effacing and even self-denigrating, narcissistic persons can be grandiose and arrogant, and paranoid persons can be highly suspicious and mistrustful. As a result, simply seeking self-reported information from persons who are characterized, in part, by distortions in self-image is unlikely to provide a valid assessment (Westen, 1997; Widiger & Samuel, 2005).

In addition, because personality disorders, by definition, have an age of onset that "can be traced back at least to adolescence or early adulthood" (APA, 2000, p. 689) their assessment should include a consideration of the patients' characteristic manner of thinking, feeling, and relating throughout their adult life. Most mental disorders would be diagnosed simply through an assessment of current functioning. One need not inquire as to the person's functioning 15 years ago to assess whether or not the person currently has a major depressive disorder. However, an assessment of current functioning can be highly misleading when diagnosing a personality disorder, particularly if the person is currently suffering from, or is in treatment for, an Axis I mental disorder. One needs to distinguish the effect of the Axis I mental disorder on the patient's current functioning from the characteristic manner of thinking, feeling, and relating to others that predated the onset of the current Axis I disorder.

By definition, personality disorders are pervasive in their effects, including cognition, affect, impulse control, and many aspects of everyday behavioral functioning. Among the general diagnostic criteria for a DSM-IV-TR personality disorder is the requirement that "the enduring pattern leads to clinically significant distress or impairment in social, occupational, or other important areas of functioning" (APA, 2000, p. 689). Some theoretical models for personality disorder place particular importance on social functioning (Lenzenweger & Clarkin, 2005), but it is evident that there is hardly an aspect of everyday life that cannot be effected by at least one personality disorder.

ASSESSMENT FOR DIAGNOSIS

The most commonly used method for the diagnosis of a personality disorder in general clinical practice is an unstructured clinical interview (Westen, 1997). However, studies have consistently indicated that assessments based on unstructured clinical interviews do not consider all of the necessary or important diagnostic criteria (Garb, 2005; Zimmerman & Mattia, 1999). Personality disorder assessments based on unstructured clinical interviews are often unreliable (Garb, 2005; Mellsop, Varghese, Joshua, & Hicks, 1982); moreover, clinicians tend to diagnose personality disorders hierarchically, failing to assess additional symptoms once they reach a conclusion that a particular personality disorder is present (Blashfield & Flanagan, 1998). The identified personality disorder may even be governed by the particular theoretical interests of the clinician (Mellsop et al., 1982).

The preferred method for diagnosing personality disorders in research is the semistructured interview (Rogers, 2001; Segal & Coolidge, 2003; Zimmerman, 2003). Semistructured interviews have several advantages over unstructured interviews (Kaye & Shea, 2000; Rogers, 2003). Semistructured interviews ensure and document that a systematic and comprehensive assessment of each personality disorder diagnostic criterion has been made. This documentation can be particularly helpful in situations in which the credibility or validity of the assessment might be questioned, such as forensic or disability evaluations. Semistructured interviews also increase the likelihood of reliable and replicable assessments (Rogers, 2001, 2003; Segal & Coolidge, 2003; Wood, Garb, Lilienfeld, & Nezworski, 2002). Semistructured interviews provide specific, carefully selected questions for the assessment of each diagnostic criterion, the application of which increases the likelihood that assessments will be consistent across interviewers. In addition, the manuals that often accompany a semistructured interview frequently provide a considerable amount of helpful information for understanding the rationale of each diagnostic criterion, for interpreting vague or inconsistent symptoms, and for resolving diagnostic ambiguities (e.g., Loranger, 1999; Widiger, Mangine, Corbitt, Ellis, & Thomas, 1995).

A significant problem for semistructured clinical interviews within clinical practice, however, is the amount of time it takes to administer them. The complete administration of a semistructured personality disorder interview (PDI) generally requires 1 to 2 hours, with some as long as 4 hours (e.g., Loranger, 1999). Hence, it is understandable that clinicians are reluctant to administer an entire semistructured interview. It is therefore recommended that one first administer a self-report inventory to identify the principle areas of abnormal (and perhaps normal) personality functioning that warrant additional consideration with a subsequent semistructured interview (Widiger & Samuel, 2005).

Quite a few inventories and interviews that would be useful to clinicians for assessing normal and abnormal personality functioning have been developed. A complete summary of all of these potential instruments is beyond the scope of this chapter, but several extensive reviews exist (e.g., Clark & Harrison, 2001; Kaye & Shea, 2000; McDermut & Zimmerman, 2005; Rogers, 2001; Segal & Coolidge, 2003; Widiger, 2002; Widiger & Coker, 2002).

There are five semistructured interviews for the assessment of the 10 DSM-IV-TR (APA, 2000) personality disorders: (1) Diagnostic Interview for Personality Disorders (DIPD; Zanarini, Frankenburg, Chauncey, & Gunderson, 1987); (2) International Personality Disorder Examination (IPDE; Loranger, 1999); (3) Personality Disorder Interview-IV (PDI-IV; Widiger, et al., 1995); (4) Structured Clinical Interview for DSM-IV Axis II Personality Disorders (SCID-II; First & Gibbon, 2004); and (5) Structured Interview for DSM-IV Personality Disorders (SIDP-IV; Pfohl, Blum, & Zimmerman, 1997). In addition, the Shedler–Westen Assessment Procedure-200 (SWAP-200) is a clinician rating form of 200 items, drawn from the psychoanalytic and personality disorder literature (Shedler, 2002; Westen & Shedler, 1999a). SWAP-200 items are not ranked on the basis of an administration of a series of questions; instead, the SWAP-200 relies on the judgments of "the empathically attuned and dynamically sophisticated clinician given free rein to practice his or her craft" (Shedler, 2002, p. 433).

TABLE 19.1 Ratings of Instruments used for Diagnosis

Instrument	Norms	Internal Consistency	Inter-Rater Reliability	Test–Retest Reliability	Content Validity	Construct Validity	Validity Generalization	Clinical Utility	Highly Recommended
Semistructured Interviews									
DIPD	L	G	E	A	E	G	G	L	✓
IPDE	A	G	E	A	E	E	G	L	✓
PDI-IV	L	G	E	A	E	A	G	L	✓
SCID-II	L	G	E	A	E	E	G	L	✓
SIDP-IV	L	G	E	A	E	E	G	L	✓
Clinician Ratings									
SWAP-200	L	G	A	U	A	U	U	A	
Self-Report Inventories									
CATI	A	G	NA	A	A	A	U	G	
MCMI-III	E	G	NA	L	A	A	L	L	
MMPI-2	E	G	NA	A	A	A	L	G	
OMNI	G	G	NA	A	A	A	U	G	
PAI	E	G	NA	A	L	A	U	L	
PDQ-4	L	A	NA	A	G	L	A	G	
SNAP	A	G	NA	A	A	A	U	G	
WISPI	A	G	NA	A	A	A	U	G	

Note: DIPD = Diagnostic Interview for Personality Disorders; IPDE = International Personality Disorders Examination; PDI-IV = Personality Disorder Interview-IV; SCID-II = Structured Clinical Interview for DSM-IV Axis II Personality Disorders; SIDP-IV = Structured Interview for DSM-IV Personality Disorders; SWAP-200 = Shedler–Westen Assessment Procedure; CATI = Coolidge Axis II Inventory; MCMI-III = Millon Clinical Multiaxial Inventory-III; MMPI-2 = Minnesota Multiphasic Personality Inventory-2; OMNI = Omni Personality Inventory; PAI = Personality Assessment Inventory; PDQ-4 = Personality Diagnostic Questionnaire-4; SNAP = Schedule for Nonadaptive and Adaptive Personality; WISPI = Wisconsin Personality Disorders Inventory; L = Less Than Adequate; A = Adequate; G = Good; E = Excellent; U = Unavailable; NA = Not Applicable.

There are also eight inventories for the assessment of the DSM-IV-TR personality disorders: (1) Minnesota Multiphasic Personality Inventory-2 (MMPI-2) personality disorder scales developed originally by Morey, Waugh, and Blashfield (1985) but revised for the MMPI-2 by Colligan, Morey, and Offord (1994); (2) Millon Clinical Multiaxial Inventory-III (Millon, Millon, & Davis, 1997); (3) OMNI Personality Inventory (OMNI; Loranger, 2001); (4) Personality Diagnostic Questionnaire-4 (PDQ-4; Bagby & Farvolden, 2004); (5) Personality Assessment Inventory (PAI; Morey & Boggs, 2004); (6) Schedule for Nonadaptive and Adaptive Personality Functioning (SNAP; Clark, Simms, Wu, & Casillas, in press); (7) Wisconsin Personality Disorders Inventory (WISPI; Klein et al., 1993); and (8) Coolidge Axis II Inventory (CATI; Coolidge & Merwin, 1992).

Table 19.1 provides a comparative listing of these instruments, using the rating system of this text. The first five instruments in the table (i.e., DIPD, IPDE, PDI-IV, SCID-II, and SIDP-IV) are the five semistructured interviews, presented in alphabetical order and followed by the SWAP-200 rating form. The next eight instruments are the self-report inventories (i.e., CATI, MCMI-III, MMPI-2, OMNI, PAI, PDQ-4, SNAP, and WISPI), again presented in alphabetical order. Rather than provide summary details on each of these measures in turn, the following sections focus on the psychometric properties rated in the table and provide comparisons among instruments for each property.

Norms

Four of the five semistructured interviews and the SWAP-200 were rated as less than adequate with respect to normative data, as normative data have not been provided within their test manuals (Kaye & Shea, 2000; Rogers, 2001). Normative data have not been obtained for semistructured interviews (nor for the SWAP-200), in part, because of the substantial cost in conducting an epidemiological study with a semistructured interview administered by professional clinicians. There are published studies in which mean values and prevalence rates have been provided, and one can then compare one's findings with these published values (e.g., see Westen & Shedler, 2003, for mean SWAP-200 scores obtained in a clinical data set). However, these values vary considerably across clinical settings and one cannot consider these findings to actually represent norma-tive data (i.e., a representative sample obtained from a designated population; Clark, 2007). The one possi-ble exception might be the IPDE, a version of which was administered in 14 mental health centers located in 11 different countries of North America, Europe, Africa, and Asia (Loranger, 1999). However, even in this instance the individual results across countries for each disorder have not been published.

With regard to self-report inventories, the test manuals for the MCMI-III (Millon et al., 1997) and PAI (Morey, 1991) provide substantial information concerning normative data. The study of Colligan et al. (1994) provides substantial information con-cerning the normative data for the MMPI-2 personal-ity disorder scales, although for unclear reasons test manuals for the MMPI-2 refer, at best, only in passing to the Morey et al. (1985) personality disorder scales (e.g., Derksen, 2006). Normative data for the CATI, OMNI, SNAP, and WISPI personality disorder scales have been published, but not with as much diverse sampling and detail as has been obtained for the MCMI-III, PAI, or MMPI-2. A rating of less than adequate for normative data was provided for the PDQ-4 because the PDQ-4 has been treated in a manner comparable to the semistructured interviews (i.e., little attention given to providing normative information; Bagby & Farvolden, 2004).

Reliability

All of the instruments were rated as good to adequate with respect to internal consistency. The PDQ-4 was rated as only adequate as it does tend to obtain rela-tively lower internal consistency coefficients owing in large part to the brevity of its scales (Bagby & Farvolden, 2004). It should be noted, though, that the internal consistency of an instrument is also a reflec-tion of the construct being assessed. The DSM-IV-TR personality disorders involve constellations of mal-adaptive personality traits and they vary in the extent to which they obtain high levels of internal consist-ency coefficients. For example, paranoid personality disorder is a more narrowly defined construct than antisocial personality disorder (Westen & Shedler, 1999b).

All five of the semistructured interviews were rated as excellent with respect to inter-rater reliability (inter-rater reliability is irrelevant to the self-report inven-tories). The major strength of these instruments is

their provision of explicit and systematic assessments of each personality disorder diagnostic criterion con-tributing to their obtainment of good to excellent inter-rater reliability in most studies (Rogers, 2001). Nevertheless, it is also worth noting that the reliability data that are reported in most studies have been con-fined to the agreement in the coding of respondents' answers to interview questions. This might not be the more important or fundamental concern with respect to the reliability of a personality disorder assessment (Clark & Harrison, 2001). As the structure of an inter-view increases, the reliability of response coding can be no more demanding than obtaining agreement as to whether respondents said "yes" or "no" in response to a straightforward question. Of greater importance would be studies addressing whether semistructured interviews are being administered reliably (Segal & Coolidge, 2003). For example, are the questions being administered by different interviewers in a consistent manner? Are some interviewers providing substan-tially more follow-up queries than other interviewers? Do patients respond to the same open-ended questions in a consistent manner over time? Sophisticated reli-ability studies are being conducted (e.g., Trull, 2001; Zanarini et al., 2002) but further research is needed on the agreement between independent administra-tions of the same interview to the same patient.

Inter-rater reliability for the administration of the SWAP-200 is rated as adequate, as there has been one published study in which different persons provided a SWAP-200 assessment of the same patient (Westen & Muderrisoglu, 2003). The findings of this study were encouraging. However, additional research by inde-pendent investigators is needed to determine more confidently whether different persons will describe a patient in a sufficiently similar manner in terms of the 200 SWAP-200 items.

An acceptable level of test–retest reliability has been provided for all but one of the instruments. A less than adequate rating was provided for the MCMI-III due to a replicated finding that it lacks adequate test–retest reliability among persons within clinical treatment. Piersma (1987, 1989) reported sub-stantial changes in MCMI assessments across brief inpatient hospitalizations. Test–retest kappa was only .11 for the borderline diagnosis, .09 for compulsive, .01 for passive–aggressive, and .27 for schizotypal. One could conclude on the basis of this study that clinical treatment resulted in significant changes to personality functioning, as personality disorders are responsive to treatment (Leichsenring & Leibing, 2003; Perry & Bond, 2000). However, inconsistent with this explanation is the fact that the treatment was quite brief and was focused on mood, anxiety, and other forms of psychopathology. Perhaps most problematic to the hypothesis of a valid change in personality was the additional finding of significant increases in the histrionic and narcissistic personality disorder scales (Piersma, 1989). If the inpatient hospitalization did, in fact, contribute to a remission of borderline and compulsive symptoms, it should perhaps take responsibility as well for contributing to the creation of histrionic and narcissistic personality disorders. Piersma (1989) concluded, instead, that the self-report inventory assessment "is not able to measure long-term personality characteristics ('trait' characteristics) independent of symptomatology ('state' characteristics)" (p. 91).

It is perhaps unfair though to single out the MCMI-III with respect to this problem, as it is possible, if not likely, that comparable results would occur for the other self-report inventories and even the semistructured interviews. A significant problem for all of the self-report inventories is the absence of directions, within the instructions to the respondents, to describe one's characteristic manner of functioning before the occurrence of any current Axis I disorder. The instructions for the MCMI-III even refer explicitly to describing one's current problems. As a result, many respondents are probably answering personality disorder items with respect to their current mood, anxiety, or other Axis I disorder.

Semistructured interviews have the potential of being relatively less susceptible to confusing an Axis II disorder with an Axis I disorder than self-report inventories (Rogers, 2001; Segal & Coolidge, 2003; Widiger & Coker, 2002) but they are not immune. An interviewer can easily fail to appreciate the extent to which patients' self-descriptions are being distorted by mood, anxiety, distress, or other situational factors. In fact, results equivalent to those reported by Piersma (1987, 1989) were obtained in a study that was purportedly documenting the resilience of semistructured interviews to mood state distortions. Loranger et al. (1991) compared IPDE assessments obtained at the beginning of an inpatient admission to those obtained 1 week to 6 months later and reported "a significant reduction in the mean number of criteria met on all of the personality disorders except schizoid and antisocial" (p. 726). Loranger et al. argued that the

reduction was not due to an initial inflation of scores secondary to depressed or anxious mood, on the basis of the finding that the changes in personality disorder scores were not correlated with changes in anxiety or depression. However, an alternative perspective is that the study lacked sufficiently sensitive or accurate measures to provide any meaningful explanation for why there was a substantial decrease on 10 of the 12 personality disorder scales (the change scores also failed to correlate with length of treatment). It is unlikely that 1 week to 6 months of treatment that was focused largely on mood, anxiety, and other forms of psychopathology resulted in the extent of changes to personality that were obtained. In fact, comparable to the findings of Piersma (1989), twice as many patients (eight) were diagnosed with a histrionic personality disorder at discharge than were diagnosed with this personality disorder at admission.

Content Validity

A rating of excellent was provided for all five of the semistructured interviews with respect to content validity. Strength of all five semistructured interviews is their explicit effort to obtain a systematic and comprehensive assessment of the DSM-IV-TR criterion sets. The manuals that accompany a semistructured interview may even provide a considerable amount of helpful information for understanding the rationale of each diagnostic criterion, for interpreting vague or inconsistent symptomatology, and for resolving diagnostic ambiguities (e.g., Loranger, 1999). The PDI-IV manual even provides the history of each diagnostic criterion (Widiger et al., 1995).

Age of Onset

An important limitation, however, of the semistructured interviews is the extent to which they adhere to the requirement that the personality disorder symptomatology has an age of onset in late adolescence or young adulthood. All of the interviews focus their initial, if not their entire, assessment on 2 to 5 preceding years. The SCID-II (First & Gibbon, 2004) requires that each diagnostic criterion be evident over a 5-year period, whereas the DIPD (Zanarini et al., 1987) focuses its assessment on the earlier 2 years (Widiger, 2005). The PDI-IV (Widiger et al., 1995), in contrast, encourages the interviewer to document that each diagnostic criterion has been evident since young adulthood but does not provide an explicit set of questions to do so. The IPDE (Loranger, 1999) is the most explicit in its requirements, but it is also more liberal, as it requires that only one diagnostic criterion for a respective personality disorder be present since the age of 25, all of the others can be evident only within the past few years.

The assumption with the DIPD, for example, is that if the behavior has been evident over the previous 2 years, then it's likely to have been present before the onset of a current Axis I disorder and evident since young adulthood. However, this can often be a false and highly problematic assumption. For example, the DIPD is being used in the widely published Collaborative Longitudinal Personality Disorders Study (CLPS; Gunderson et al., 2000). One of the more intriguing findings of this project has been the extent to which persons fail to maintain a personality disorder diagnosis over time. For example, 23 of 160 persons (14%) diagnosed with borderline personality disorder (BPD) at the study's baseline assessment met criteria for two or fewer of the nine diagnostic criteria 6 months later (Gunderson et al., 2003). Eighteen sustained this reduction from 6 months to 1 year. Gunderson et al. (2003) concluded that only one of these 18 persons had been inaccurately diagnosed at baseline, the rest were considered to be valid instances of sudden and dramatic remission. However, it is difficult to imagine so many persons who met the diagnostic criteria for BPD since late childhood and who continued to manifest these symptoms throughout their adult life, experienced, apparently for the first time, dramatic changes in personality functioning soon after the onset of the study. For example, the purportedly valid diagnoses include one person whose original symptoms were determined to be secondary to the use of a stimulant for weight reduction: "the most dramatic improvement following a treatment intervention occurred when a subject discontinued a psychostimulant she had used the year before baseline for purposes of weight loss… Discontinuation was followed by a dramatic reduction of her depression, panic, abandonment fears, and self-destructiveness" (Gunderson et al., 2003, p. 116). For other cases, "the changes involved gaining relief from severely stressful situations they were in at or before the baseline assessment" (p. 115), including the resolution of a traumatic divorce or custody battle. To the extent that these cases of remission represent invalid baseline assessments, the test–retest reliability

of the interview assessments should perhaps be rated as less than adequate.

DSM-IV-TR Criterion Sets

Whereas all five of the semistructured interviews are coordinated explicitly with the respective DSM-IV-TR diagnostic criterion sets, this is not the case for the SWAP-200 or for most of the self-report inventories. These instruments vary considerably in the extent to which they are coordinated with DSM-IV-TR. Many of the SWAP-200 items concern symptoms, features, or traits that are outside of the respective DSM-IV-TR criterion sets, which might, of course, be considered a strength of the SWAP-200 (Shedler, 2002; Westen & Shedler, 1999b) if it then provides a more valid personality disorder assessment. The CATI (Coolidge & Merwin, 1992), the PAI (Morey & Boggs, 2004), and the WISPI (Klein et al., 1993) were constructed in reference to the DSM-III-R criterion sets (APA, 1987) and have not since been revised to be compatible with DSM-IV. The Morey et al. (1985) MMPI-2 personality disorder scales were not even constructed to assess the DSM-IV-TR personality disorders. The authors simply selected the previously existing MMPI(-2) items that appeared to be best suited for the assessment of each respective personality disorder, and it is certainly questionable whether the MMPI(-2) item pool, despite its size, would have items that could adequately assess each of the DSM-IV-TR personality disorder diagnostic criteria. In addition, the original Morey et al. (1985) scales were selected on the basis of the DSM-III criterion sets (APA, 1980). MMPI-2 personality disorder scales coordinated with DSM-IV-TR have since been developed by Ben-Porath (Hicklin & Widiger, 2000; Jones, 2005). It is interesting to note in this regard that Ben-Porath selected quite a number of different items from the original item pool than were selected by Morey et al. (Hicklin & Widiger, 2000). Nevertheless, many researchers and clinicians continue to use the original Morey et al. DSM-III scales.

Even instruments that are coordinated with DSM-IV-TR criteria vary in the theoretical perspectives underlying item content. WISPI items and many of the SWAP-200 items emphasize an object-relational, psychodynamic perspective (Klein et al., 1993; Shedler, 2002). Many of the PAI items emphasize an interpersonal model (Morey & Boggs, 2004). Some of the MCMI-III personality disorder scales are slanted somewhat toward the theoretical model of Millon et al. (1996). In fact, the MCMI-III obsessive–compulsive personality disorder scale often correlates negatively with the respective scale from other self-report inventories (Widiger & Coker, 2002) owing perhaps to its inclusion of adaptive, as well as maladaptive, components of obsessive–compulsive personality traits (Haigler & Widiger, 2001).

The content validity of the PDQ-4 was rated as good because its items were written explicitly to assess the DSM-IV-TR diagnostic criterion sets. However, it provides only one item for each diagnostic criterion and thereby fails to provide adequate coverage of each respective criterion. The content validity of the PAI is rated as less than adequate because it actually includes only two personality disorder scales: antisocial and borderline. Items were not written to assess the eight other personality disorders. An algorithm is provided within the test manual to obtain a score for the other personality disorders (based on combining scores from Axis I and other personality scales), but the validity of these scales has not been adequately tested.

Construct Validity

Ratings of construct validity (Smith, 2005), for this text, are based on the extent to which there is replicated evidence of various aspects of construct validity, such as predictive validity, concurrent validity, and convergent and discriminant validity. The IPDE, SCID-II, and SIDP-IV were provided with excellent ratings for construct validity, in part because these three instruments have been used most extensively in personality disorder research. Much of what is published concerning the etiology, pathology, course, and treatment of personality disorders has been based on studies using one of these three instruments. The DIPD is the instrument being used in the heavily published CLPS project (Gunderson et al., 2000). The PDI-IV has been used in a number of studies but not nearly as frequently as the other four semistructured interviews.

Most of the instruments have demonstrated inadequate discriminant validity, but this probably reflects the absence of adequate discriminant validity of the personality disorder constructs (Bornstein, 1998; Clark, 2007; Lynam & Widiger, 2001; Trull & Durrett, 2005). A valid assessment of an individual personality disorder should perhaps obtain weak discriminant

validity with respect to its near neighbor diagnostic constructs. To the extent that borderline personality disorder does in fact overlap substantially with dependent personality disorder (e.g., both involve fears of separation and abandonment), then scales that assess borderline personality disorder should correlate with scales that assess dependent personality disorder. The scales of some personality disorder self-report inventories (e.g., the MCMI-III and MMPI-2) in fact have substantial item overlap in order to compel the obtainment of a particular degree and direction of co-occurrence that would be consistent with theoretical expectations.

SWAP-200 assessments have consistently obtained better discriminant validity than personality disorder semistructured interviews (Shedler & Westen, 2004), but this could simply reflect the fact that clinicians administering the SWAP-200 are required to provide a distribution of ratings that diminishes substantially the likelihood of obtaining diagnostic co-occurrence (Wood, Garb, Nezworski, & Koren, in press). For example, in Westen and Shedler (1999b), the clinicians were required to identify half of the personality disorder symptoms as being absent and only eight SWAP-200 items could be given the highest rankings, no matter the actual opinions of the clinicians or the symptoms that were in fact present (similar constraints were placed on the other ratings). Discriminant validity of a semistructured interview would also be improved dramatically if the interviewers were instructed to code half of the diagnostic criteria as absent and were instructed to provide only a few of the diagnostic criteria with the highest ratings.

Only three studies have provided data concerning the convergent validity among the personality disorder semistructured interviews (O'Boyle & Self, 1990; Pilkonis et al., 1995; Skodol, Oldham, Rosnick, Kellman, & Hyler, 1991); of these studies, only two involved the administration of interview schedules to the same patients (O'Boyle & Self, 1990; Skodol et al., 1991), and all three were confined to just two of the five semistructured interviews. The most comprehensive study was conducted by Skodol et al. (1991). They administered the IPDE and SCID-II to 100 inpatients of a personality disorders treatment unit. Both interviews were administered blind to one another on the same day (one in the morning, the other in the afternoon). Order of administration was counterbalanced. Kappa for individual diagnoses ranged from .14 (schizoid) to .66 (dependent), with a median kappa of .53 (borderline). The authors considered the agreement for some of the categorical diagnoses to be discouraging. "It is fair to say that, for a number of disorders (i.e., paranoid, schizoid, schizotypal, narcissistic, and passive–aggressive) the two [interviews] studied do not operationalize the diagnoses similarly and thus yield disparate results" (Skodol et al., 1991, p. 22). However, the median agreement does appear to be consistent with rates obtained for many Axis I disorders when their assessments are conducted blind to one another (Loranger, 1992). In addition, agreement with respect to a more quantitative assessment of the extent to which each personality disorder was present was considerably better than the agreement for categorical diagnoses, with correlations ranging from .58 (schizoid) to .87 (antisocial). Skodol et al. (1991) concluded that "the greater agreement shown by comparing dimensions of disorder than by comparing strict categorical diagnoses suggests that patients are providing interviewers with reliable information about areas of difficulty in personality functioning and interviewers are able to judge when at least some of these reports indicate clinically significant psychopathology" (p. 22).

There has only been one published study relating empirically derived SWAP-200 personality disorder assessments with the assessments provided by another personality or personality disorder instrument. Marin-Avellan et al. (2005) examined the relationship of the SWAP-200 with the SCID-II (First & Gibbon, 2004). SCID-II ratings correlated significantly with most of the SWAP-200 PD scores. The highest correlation was obtained for antisocial ($r = .73$); the lowest was for schizotypal (–.07); the others ranged from .33 (narcissistic) to .52 (schizoid). It should be noted, though, that two of the three SCID-II interviewers also provided the SWAP-200 ratings.

Several studies have been published on the convergent validity of personality disorder semistructured interviews with self-report inventories, as well as the convergent validity among self-report inventories. Widiger and Coker (2002) tabulated the findings from 41 of these studies. Convergent validity was adequate to good for all but two of the instruments. The PDQ-4 appears to obtain the weakest convergent validity coefficients, owing perhaps to the fact that it is the briefest of the instruments (99 items) and the items are more behaviorally specific in their content. As noted earlier, the MCMI-III obsessive–compulsive

personality disorder scale tends to correlate negatively with other measures of this personality disorder (Widiger & Coker, 2002). It is problematic enough to fail to obtain convergent validity, but the MCMI-III obsessive–compulsive scale appears to be assessing something that is inversely related to the construct assessed by other personality disorder scales.

Validity Generalization

Validity generalization concerns whether the instrument has been shown to be equally valid across different populations. Considered in this chapter is generalization across age, gender, and culture/ethnicity.

Age

Westen, Shedler, Durrett, Glass, and Martens (2003) diagnosed adolescents with personality disorders using the SWAP-200. However, clinicians are discouraged from assessing personality disorders in adolescents or children, due to the questionable validity of a personality disorder diagnosis in someone this young (APA, 2000). Temporal stability of normal personality traits is generally only .31 in childhood, increasing to .54 during years of college, to .64 at age 30 and then appearing to plateau at .74 between ages of 50 and 70 (Roberts & DelVecchio, 2000). Temporal stability of maladaptive personality traits is likely to be lower, particularly in childhood and adolescence. In addition, the DSM-IV-TR criterion sets were written for adults, and it is not at all clear whether they translate well to children. For example, many children will act in a dependent fashion that will have little to do with a personality disorder, and some adolescents will display borderline personality disorder symptomatology that should perhaps be understood as part of a normative identity crisis rather than a personality disorder.

The same point can be made for the assessment of personality disorders within the elderly. Quite a bit of research has been conducted on personality disorders among the elderly (Abrams & Horowitz, 1999), but this research has also been shown to be rather problematic. For example, estimates of the prevalence of personality disorders among the elderly are generally higher than is obtained within the middle-aged (Abrams & Horowitz, 1999), which is simply inconsistent with the DSM-IV-TR diagnostic system. It is quite possible that maladaptive personality change does, in fact, develop as one ages (Widiger & Seidlitz,

2002; Agronin, 1998), but DSM-IV-TR does not currently recognize the occurrence of an adult onset for a personality disorder; therefore, the prevalence rate should in fact decrease as the population ages (unless those with personality disorders have a much lower rate of mortality). The difficulty perhaps lies, again, with the failure (discussed earlier) of the existing instruments to adequately address age of onset and temporal stability throughout adult life (Agronin, 1998; Segal et al., 1996; Widiger & Seidlitz, 2002). In addition, some of the diagnostic criteria may again have a different meaning within an elderly population. For example, the dependent personality disorder diagnostic criteria of being unrealistically preoccupied with fears of being left to care for oneself, or feeling uncomfortable or helpless when alone because of exaggerated fears of being unable to care for oneself, were written to assess dependency in middle-aged persons who are otherwise fully capable of caring for themselves. They would clearly have a much different meaning for a person who is becoming incapacitated due to aging.

Gender

There has been considerable research on the impact of gender on the assessment of personality disorders (Morey, Alexander, & Boggs, 2005; Widiger, 1998). Many of the personality disorders have a differential sex prevalence rate, and some appear to involve maladaptive variants of gender-related personality traits. The suggestion that these differential sex prevalence rates reflect gender biases has been among the more difficult and heated diagnostic issues (Ross, Frances, & Widiger, 1995).

There are a number of different methods for detecting gender bias within a personality disorder assessment instrument, including differential item functioning across gender using item response theory analyses and differential item validity across gender (Boggs et al., 2005; Oltmanns, Jane, South, & Turkheimer, in press). Studies have indicated that the failure of clinicians to assess diagnostic criterion sets in a thorough or systematic manner has contributed to excessive diagnoses of histrionic personality disorder in females (Garb, 2005). When more systematic assessments of diagnostic criteria sets are provided, as occurs with the administration of a semistructured interview, there appears to be a considerable decrease in gender-biased assessments (Widiger, 1998). It was,

in part, for this reason that the semistructured interviews are provided with an adequate rating (i.e., offsetting to some extent the concern of an inadequate addressing of age of onset). The SWAP-200 was provided a rating of unavailable, as no studies have been conducted on the potential presence of gender bias with SWAP-200 ratings. The SWAP-200 has been confined largely to clinicians providing ratings, and a number of studies have indicated that, in the absence of using a structured interview, clinicians are prone to over-estimating dependent and histrionic traits in females, and under-estimating the presence of antisocial traits (Garb, 2005).

Studies have also suggested that some self-report inventories are providing gender-biased assessments (Lindsay, Sankis, & Widiger, 2000). The MMPI-2 and the MCMI-III personality disorder inventories include gender-related items that are keyed in the direction of adaptive rather than maladaptive functioning. An item need not assess for dysfunction to contribute to a valid assessment of personality disorders. For example, items assessing for gregariousness can identify histrionic persons, items assessing for confidence can identify narcissistic persons, and items assessing conscientiousness can identify obsessive–compulsive persons (Millon et al., 1997). Items keyed in the direction of adaptive, rather than maladaptive, functioning can be helpful in countering the tendency of some respondents to deny or minimize personality disorder symptomatology. However, these items will not be useful in differentiating abnormal from normal personality functioning and they are likely to contribute to an over-diagnosis of personality disorders in normal or minimally dysfunctional populations, such as encountered in student counseling centers, child custody disputes, or personnel selection (Boyle & Le Dean, 2000). When these items are related to the sex or gender of respondents, as many are in the case of the histrionic, dependent, narcissistic, and obsessive–compulsive personality disorder scales of the MCMI-III (Millon et al. (1997) and the MMPI-2 (Colligan et al., 1994), they may contribute to gender biased assessments (Lampel, 1999; Lindsay et al., 2000). It is for this reason that the MCMI-III and MMPI-2 are rated as less than adequate for validity generalization in Table 19.1. The PDQ-4 was provided an adequate rating because all of its items are keyed in a maladaptive direction and therefore do not demonstrate the gender bias evident within the MMPI-2 and the MCMI-III (Lindsay et al., 2000).

The CATI, OMNI, PAI, SNAP, and WISPI are rated as unclear (or unavailable) in part because studies on gender bias have not yet been conducted with these measures.

Culture and Ethnicity

One might expect considerable variation in the diagnosis and assessment of personality disorders across different cultural and ethnic groups (Alarcon, 1996). DSM-IV-TR narcissistic personality disorder is not even included within the World Health Organization's (1992) international classification of mental disorders. However, there has been relatively little research on the impact of culture and ethnicity on the diagnosis or assessment of personality disorders (Alarcon, 1996; Cooke, 1996).

Items within self-report inventories are generally written from the perspective of a member of the dominant ethnic, cultural group, and such items may not have the same meaning or implications when provided to members of a minority ethnic group (Okazaki, Kallivayalil, & Stanley, 2002). Hindering the effort of psychologists to identify (a) the cultural contexts in which assessment techniques should be interpreted differently or (b) the adjustments in test interpretation that should be made across different ethnic groups, is the absence of sufficient research on the mechanisms for cultural or ethnic group differences. Much of the existing research has been confined to the reporting of group differences, without an assessment of the purported mechanism by which the differences could be explained or understood (Okazaki et al., 2002).

As an example of this line of research, studies have reported the obtainment of significantly higher scores by African Americans (compared with Caucasian Americans) on the paranoid personality disorder scales of the MCMI-III (e.g., Frue, Smith, & Libet, 1996), but there has not yet been any published research that has attempted to explain or account for these group differences. One possible social–cultural explanation for the different elevations is the presence of racial discrimination and prejudice (Whaley, 1997). Clark, Anderson, Clark, and Williams (1999) documented well the importance of considering racism as a stressor on the psychological functioning of African Americans. Membership within a minority ethnic group that has historically been severely mistreated and exploited, and still experiences prejudicial,

discriminatory, or antagonistic behaviors from members of the majority ethnic group, would understandably contribute to feelings of mistrust, skepticism, and suspicion that would not be shared by members of the majority ethnic group. African Americans who have experienced a history of racial discrimination might respond differently than Caucasian Americans to such paranoid personality disorder items as "I am sure I get a raw deal from life," or "The people I work with are not sympathetic with my problems" (Colligan et al., 1994; Millon et al., 1997). Similar hypotheses might be generated for the interpretation of personality disorder test items by members of other ethnic/cultural groups.

Clinical Utility

The DIPD, PDI-IV, SCID-II, and SIDP-IV semistructured interviews were all rated as less than adequate for clinical utility as they require, on average, 2 hours to be administered. The IPDE may require up to 4 hours to be administered. Loranger et al. (1991) recommends that the IPDE be administered on two separate occasions in order to minimize fatigue. The administration of a semistructured interview will be advantageous in clinical situations in which the credibility or validity of the assessment might be questioned (e.g., forensic or disability evaluations), because the administration of the interview will document that the assessment was reasonably comprehensive, replicable, and objective (Rogers, 2003; Zimmerman, 2003). Nevertheless, the routine administration of a semistructured interview is simply impractical for general clinical practice.

The SWAP-200 requires considerably less time to complete than does a semistructured interview, as its items are rated on the basis of whatever information is available to the clinician. No questions are required to be administered to rank the items. It was for this reason that the SWAP-200 was provided a rating of adequate for clinical utility. However, the SWAP-200 includes twice as many items (i.e., 200) as the entire set of DSM-IV-TR personality disorder diagnostic criteria (i.e., 96). If clinicians routinely fail to consider systematically the diagnostic criteria currently included within DSM-IV-TR (Blashfield & Flanagan, 1998; Zimmerman & Mattia, 1999), it might not be realistic to expect them to assess systematically or carefully a patient with a set of items that is twice as long. The clinicians participating in the SWAP-200 studies appear to complete the SWAP-200 faithfully (requiring approximately one half hour or more to complete), but it should be noted that these research participants are paid by the investigators for their effort.

The amount of time required for the administration of a semistructured interview can be reduced considerably by first administering and scoring a self-report inventory (Widiger & Samuel, 2005). The interview could then be confined to the personality disorder scales that were significantly elevated on the self-report inventory. In fact, the SCID-II (First & Gibbon, 2004) and the IPDE (Loranger, 1999) include screening measures precisely for this purpose. However, if a self-report inventory is to be administered, it is probably preferable to administer one that was constructed to provide a comprehensive and valid assessment (e.g., PDQ-4), and for which there is empirical support for its validity, rather than a brief screening measure.

The CATI, MMPI-2, OMNI, PDQ-4, SNAP, and WISPI self-report inventories all received a rating of good with respect to clinical utility. Self-report inventories can be very useful in alerting a clinician to maladaptive personality functioning that might otherwise have been missed owing to false expectations or assumptions, such as failing to notice antisocial personality traits in female patients (Widiger, 1998). As self-report inventories, they also require little time on the part of the clinician to administer, although they do vary in the amount of time it can take to score them. The CATI, MMPI-2, PDQ-4, SNAP, and WISPI must be scored by hand, (computer scoring systems for the MMPI-2 do not include the Morey et al., 1985, scales). One can purchase a computer scoring system for the OMNI, but this entails an additional expense. The PDQ-4 is the briefest of these self-report inventories, consisting of only 99 items, and there is even a format in which the pages of the PDQ-4 are organized with respect to each diagnostic criterion set. It is perhaps the most frequently used self-report inventory in clinical research because it is so much shorter than the alternative measures. The MCMI-III, in contrast, is exceedingly difficult to score by hand, as it includes quite a number of moderating scores and adjustments based on demographic variables and other scale elevations. Hand scoring an MCMI-III can require up to 45 minutes; there is a computer scoring system for the MCMI-III, but it is relatively expensive (Kaye & Shea, 2000).

A concern, however, for the self-report inventories is the inadequate basis for their cutoff scores. Colligan et al. (1994), for example, recommend using the MMPI-2 normative data to provide personality disorder diagnoses, but using cutoff points set at 1.5 standard deviations from a population mean for each personality disorder would have little apparent relationship with a DSM-IV-TR diagnosis. The cutoff points for the PAI are also based on statistical deviance from a population mean, yet it is not at all clear that a diagnosis of personality disorder should be governed primarily by statistical deviance, let alone using the same degree of statistical deviance for the diagnosis of each personality disorder. Cutoff scores that are coordinated with the actual base rate of a disorder will provide more accurate diagnoses (Meehl & Rosen, 1955). "An important feature that distinguishes the MCMI from other inventories is its use of actuarial base rate data rather than normalized standard score transformations" (Millon et al., 1997, p. 5). However, the advantages of using base rates to set cutoff points can be undermined if they are not adjusted for changes in the base rates across different settings and patient groups. The MCMI-III cutoff points are coordinated with the total set of inpatient and outpatient settings that provided the normative clinical pool. Clinicians will find that the MCMI-III cutoff points result in many false positive assessments when applied to populations that do not include many individuals with personality disorder pathology, such as college counseling centers, introductory psychology pools, or child custody and divorce mediation evaluations (King, 1994; Lampel, 1999). This was one reason that the MCMI-III was rated as less than adequate for clinical utility.

An additional concern for the MCMI-III is that it appears to provide an excessive number of false positive diagnoses for the histrionic, narcissistic, dependent, and obsessive–compulsive personality disorders within nonclinical settings (King, 1994; Lampel, 1999), not only because of the use of diagnostic thresholds that are inappropriate for nonclinical populations, but also because, as indicated earlier, these scales include items that are keyed in the direction of normal psychological functioning. Persons without maladaptive personality functioning will endorse the item in the direction of normal psychological functioning, and yet be given points toward the presence of a histrionic or narcissistic personality disorder. The inclusion of such items provides partial explanation for why Piersma (1987, 1989) found MCMI-III scale scores increasing after successful treatment of an Axis I disorder (e.g., persons endorses narcissistic items describing normal self-esteem after the remission of a depression). Similar problems are likely to occur for some MMPI-2 scales that include items keyed in the direction of normal psychological functioning (particularly the narcissistic and histrionic scales) but this has not yet been tested empirically.

The PAI was scored as less than adequate for clinical utility because it includes only two scales for the assessment of personality disorders (i.e., borderline and antisocial). The manual for the PAI does provide algorithms that use scores from other scales to derive a measure of the other personality disorders, but these algorithms are somewhat cumbersome to use and there is not yet compelling research to indicate that they have sufficient validity. In addition, no cutoff points are provided for the interpretation of the resulting score.

Overall Evaluation

The strongest statement that can be made in a review of instruments for the diagnosis of personality disorder is that there are clearly quite a number of alternative measures. Regrettably, no single measure stands out as being clearly preferable to all others. Semistructured interviews are strongly preferred over self-report inventories in research owing to their relatively greater resilience to distortions secondary to comorbid Axis I disorders (Widiger & Samuel, 2005), but there appears to be no clear advantage of one semistructured interview relative to another. The IPDE has more international application, but its clinical value is limited by the fact that it requires considerably more time to administer. The SCID-II and DIPD are relatively more straightforward to administer, relative to the SIDP-IV and the PDI-IV, but the latter could be said to be more sophisticated in their assessment. Researchers are recommended to obtain copies of at least three of the existing semistructured interviews and base their selection, in part, on which instrument appears to be best suited for their particular research needs and interests. Some researchers actually use more than one instrument. For example, Oltmanns et al. (in press) used the SIDP-IV for the assessment of personality disorders but the PDI-IV manual to train and guide the interviewers administering the SIDP-IV.

Clinicians are generally recommended to administer a self-report inventory first as a screening measure, identifying which one to four personality disorders should be emphasized during a subsequent follow-up interview and which can be safely ignored. Brief screening measures can be used for this purpose (the PDQ-4 is the briefest of the measures) but there might be little advantage in using a screening instrument in preference to an inventory that was constructed to provide a comprehensive and valid assessment. Most of the self-report inventories listed in Table 19.1 can be used for this purpose. None of the self-report inventories can be said to be highly recommended. The PAI is limited by the absence of scales for all of the personality disorders, quite a number of problems occur for the MCMI-III with respect to test–retest reliability, gender bias, problematic cutoff points, and cost, the PDQ-4 is less than adequate for construct validity, and validity generalization is unavailable or less than adequate for the others.

ASSESSMENT FOR CASE CONCEPTUALIZATION AND TREATMENT PLANNING

The personality disorder diagnostic measures covered in the earlier section could be used for case conceptualization and treatment planning. There are numerous texts with suggestions for the treatment of personality disorders (e.g., Gunderson & Gabbard, 2000; Millon et al., 1996; Oldham, Skodol, & Bender, 2005; Paris, 1998; Stone, 1993). Case conceptualization and treatment planning with these texts are guided by the presence of personality disorders diagnosed with one or more of the instruments discussed earlier. These texts, though, are based largely on clinical experiences and theoretical speculations. There are few empirically validated manuals for the treatment of personality disorders. The American Psychiatric Association has published empirically based guidelines for the treatment of individual mental disorders. Guidelines, however, have been published for only one personality disorder: borderline (APA, 2001), due in large part to the fact that there is currently insufficient research to develop empirically based guidelines for the treatment of the dependent, avoidant, obsessive–compulsive, and the other personality disorders.

TABLE 19.2 Ratings of Instruments Used for Case Conceptualization and Treatment Planning

Instrument	Norms	Internal Consistency	Inter-Rater Reliability	Test–Retest Reliability	Content Validity	Construct Validity	Validity Generalization	Clinical Utility	Highly Recommended
NEO PI-R	E	E	NA	E	E	E	E	U	✓
IIP	G	E	NA	G	E	G	A	G	
TCI	G	G	NA	G	G	L	G	U	

Note: NEO PI-R = NEO Personality Inventory-Revised; IIP = Inventory of Interpersonal Problems; TCI = Temperament and Character Inventory; G = Good; A = Adequate; L = Less Than Adequate; E = Excellent; U = Unavailable; NA = Not Applicable.

This section is, in any case, for assessment measures that could be used to augment diagnostic information to yield a psychological case conceptualization that can be used to guide decisions on treatment planning beyond that which is provided simply by a personality disorder diagnosis. A general recommendation in this regard is to obtain an assessment of general personality structure, including both normal and abnormal personality functioning. One potentially useful instrument in this respect is the NEO Personality Inventory-Revised (NEO PI-R; Costa & McCrae, 1992). The NEO PI-R is a self-report measure of the five-factor model (FFM) of general personality structure. The FFM is the predominant model of general personality structure within psychology, with considerable support for its construct validity (Mullins-Sweatt & Widiger, 2006). The five broad domains of the FFM include extraversion versus introversion, agreeableness versus antagonism, conscientiousness (or constraint), neuroticism (emotional instability or negative affectivity), and openness (or unconventionality). The NEO PI-R further differentiates each of these five broad domains into underlying facets. For example, the facets of agreeableness versus antagonism are trust versus mistrust, straightforwardness versus deception, self-sacrifice versus exploitation, compliance versus aggression, modesty versus arrogance, and tender-mindedness versus tough-mindedness.

Ratings of the psychometric properties of the NEO PI-R are presented in Table 19.2. The NEO PI-R comes in both self-report and informant report versions, as well as an abbreviated version consisting of just 60 items (Costa & McCrae, 1992). There has been extensive research conducted with the NEO PI-R, including test–retest reliability over 6 years, norms for different age and gender groups, and cross-cultural validation for both the self-report and informant report versions in over 40 different countries (Allik, 2005; Costa & McCrae, 1992). The NEO PI-R

is being included within the CLPS longitudinal study and existing research suggests that its scales demonstrate better temporal stability than scales assessing the DSM-IV-TR personality disorders (Warner et al., 2004).

Conceptualization of a patient in terms of the FFM would augment a personality disorder diagnosis by providing a more comprehensive and individualized description of the patient's general personality structure (Widiger & Lowe, 2007). One can bring to one's understanding of the personality disorder what is known about the etiology, course, and life outcomes (e.g., occupational, personal, social, and marital implications) that have been documented empirically for elevations on the domains and facets of the FFM (e.g., Costa & McCrae, 1992; Ozer & Benet-Martinez, 2006). Much more is known empirically about the genetics, the developmental antecedents, the course, and the outcome of FFM general personality structure than is known about the DSM-IV-TR personality disorders (Widiger & Trull, 2007). One would also have information concerning both adaptive, as well as maladaptive, personality traits that would have treatment implications (Widiger & Lowe, 2007). Elevations on a respective domain can have specific implications for treatment engagement and responsivity. For example, high scores in conscientiousness are likely to be predictive of completing the demanding rigor of dialectical behavioral therapy, whereas high openness to experience would predict engagement within the specific treatment technique of mindfulness (Sanderson & Clarkin, 2002). An FFM description may even have more utility for treatment planning than the existing diagnostic categories (Samuel & Widiger, 2006). The DSM-IV-TR diagnostic categories involve overlapping constellations of an array of maladaptive personality traits (Lynam & Widiger, 2001), contributing to a lack of clarity or specificity in treatment planning (Verheul, 2005). The FFM, in contrast, has a more coherent and distinctive structure that could yield more distinct treatment implications. For example, the domains of extraversion and introversion concern matters of interpersonal relatedness, neuroticism is the domain of personality concerning emotional dysregulation, conscientiousness involves matters of impulse dyscontrol at the low end and excessive constraint, perfectionism, and workaholism at the high end, and openness involves cognitive-perceptual aberrations at the high end and closed-minded stubbornness and rigidity at the low end. A rating of unclear or unavailable, however, was provided for clinical utility, as there is limited research on the clinical application of the FFM for treatment planning.

The Inventory of Interpersonal Problems (IIP-64; Horowitz, Alden, Wiggins, & Pincus, 2000) also provides information that is relevant to case conceptualization and treatment planning. The IIP is a self-report measure designed to screen for interpersonal problems and the level of distress associated with them. This measure was guided by the interpersonal circumplex (IPC) model of general personality structure (Wiggins, 2003). The IPC relates closely to the extraversion and agreeableness domains of the FFM: these respective FFM domains can, in fact, be understood as 45° rotations of the two agency (dominance vs. submission) and communion (love vs. hate) dimensions of the IPC (Wiggins & Pincus, 1989). All matter of interpersonal relatedness can be located along or around the interpersonal circumplex, and some suggest that the primary, if not the sole, pathology of personality disorder involves maladaptive interpersonal relatedness (Benjamin, Rothweiler, & Critchfield, 2006; Pincus, 2005). The IIP provides a reasonably comprehensive and differentiating measure of the fundamental ways in which a person can relate dysfunctionally with another person. The IPC organizes this interpersonal realm of personality functioning by eight scales selected to be equidistant from one another around the circumplex. Maladaptive variants of the eight basic styles of interpersonal relatedness could be said to be domineering, intrusive (histrionic), excessively attached, dependent, submissive, introverted, callous, or antagonistic.

Psychometric ratings for the IIP are provided in Table 19.2. There has been considerably less psychometric study of the IIP in comparison to the NEO PI-R. Nevertheless, existing research does suggest excellent internal consistency, good temporal stability, excellent coverage of the full range of interpersonal

problems as specified within the IPC and adequate generalization across different age and gender groups (Horowitz et al., 2000). A rating of good was provided for clinical utility owing to the importance some theorists place on interpersonal relatedness for understanding the pathology of personality disorder (Benjamin et al., 2006; Pincus, 2005). A rating of excellent was not provided owing to the concern that personality disorders may also involve excessive constraint, impulsivity, and emotional dysregulation.

Another measure of general personality structure that has been related to personality disorder is the Temperament and Character Inventory (TCI) of Cloninger (2000). Cloninger developed a seven-factor model of personality structure consisting of four fundamental temperaments and three character styles. The four temperaments reflect innate dispositions to respond to stimuli in a consistent manner; the character dimensions are considered to be individual differences that developed through a nonlinear interaction of temperament, family environment, and life experiences (Svrakic et al., 2002). The four temperaments are novelty seeking (behavioral activation: exhilaration or excitement in response to novel stimuli or cues for potential rewards or potential relief from punishment), harm avoidance (behavioral inhibition: intense response to signals of aversive stimuli), reward dependence (behavioral maintenance: response to signals of reward or to resist extinction of behavior that has been previously reinforced), and persistence. The first three are hypothesized to be associated with a particular monoamine neuromodulator (i.e., dopamine, serotonin, and norepinephrine, respectively). The three character dimensions are self-directedness (responsible, goal-directed vs. insecure, inept), cooperativeness (helpful, empathic vs. hostile, aggressive), and self-transcendence (imaginative, unconventional vs. controlling, materialistic).

Table 19.2 provides a summary of the psychometric properties of the TCI. Quite a few studies have been conducted with the TCI, documenting well a strong normative foundation, the adequacy of the internal consistency of its scales, temporal stability, and generalization across age and different cultural groups (Svrakic et al., 2002). Content validity for the assessment of the constructs as identified by Cloninger (2000) is good but construct validity is less than adequate (Clark, 2007). Efforts to validate the seven-factor structure have not been successful (Gana & Trouillet, 2003), nor does there appear to be support for the temperament and character distinction (Ando et al., 2004; Herbst et al., 2000). The four temperament scales also do not appear to be well tied to the existing literature on childhood temperaments (Caspi, Roberts, & Shiner, 2005) and current understanding of neurobiology appears to be inconsistent with the theoretical model (Paris, 2005). It was for this reason that the rating for clinical utility was unclear or unavailable, as it is not yet clear that the suggested pharmacotherapy implications for elevations on the temperament scales (e.g., pharmacotherapy specific to norepinephrine for elevations on reward dependence) will in fact prove to be valid.

Overall Evaluation

Recommendations for instruments that would augment treatment planning and case conceptualization are hindered by the absence of much controlled clinical trials of manually guided treatment programs for personality disorders. The general recommendation is for the use of measures of general personality structure that could thereby provide a more comprehensive description of both normal and abnormal personality functioning, allowing for the application of basic science research on one's understanding of the personality disorder and the consideration of personality traits that might facilitate, as well as hinder, treatment response. The NEO PI-R is highly recommended as it has considerably more empirical support as a measure of general personality structure than does either the IIP or the TCI.

ASSESSMENT FOR TREATMENT MONITORING AND TREATMENT OUTCOME

This section presents assessment measures and strategies that can be used to (a) track the progress of treatment and (b) evaluate the overall effect of treatment on symptoms, diagnosis, and general functioning. The semistructured interviews and self-report inventories considered within the first section could, again, provide a natural choice as treatment outcome measures. However, a significant disadvantage of most of the personality disorder semistructured interviews and self-report inventories is that they were constructed to assess long-term functioning, including functioning before the onset of treatment. For this reason, these instruments are not included in Table 19.3.

Each of the instruments could, hypothetically, be modified to assess only current or recent functioning, specifying, for instance, that the persons should describe their characteristic manner of thinking, feeling, and relating to others only with respect to the previous week or month. A limitation of this proposal, however, is that it is not really clear what period of time should be specified to accurately document that a maladaptive personality trait is now within remission or no longer present. Personality traits vary in the frequency with which they are evident within any particular period of time. Borderline self-destructiveness must be evident for at least 5 years to indicate its presence on the SCID-II, but it is unclear how long it should not be present to indicate its absence. Simply because a person does not report being suicidal at the end of treatment does not necessarily suggest that, the self-destructiveness of borderline personality disorder is no longer present. The suicidality of an untreated person with borderline personality disorder will not be evident every day, week, or even every month of the year (Gunderson, 2001). One month of no suicidal ideation may indicate an improvement in functioning during that period of time, but it may not indicate an actual or sustained change to personality functioning. If persons must evidence self-destructiveness over a 5-year period to indicate the presence of borderline suicidality, perhaps they should also evidence the absence of self-destructiveness over a 5-year period to indicate the successful treatment of this borderline suicidality. Fortunately, one of the specific aims of the CLPS project (Gunderson et al., 2000) is an exploratory study of the concept of remission for maladaptive personality traits. The DIPD has been modified to obtain "follow-along" assessments of personality functioning and future reports from the project will provide a more accurate understanding of the frequency of each diagnostic criterion in persons with the diagnosis as well as in persons judged to be in remission.

An additional limitation of most of the existing personality disorder semistructured interviews and self-report inventories, including the DIPD, for the purpose of treatment monitoring and outcome assessment, is that they are not well differentiated with respect to the facets or components of each personality disorder. What is evident from the limited amount of research on the treatment of personality disorders is that this treatment rarely involves a comprehensive or complete cure of the personality disorder (Leichsenring & Leibing,

TABLE 19.3 Ratings of Instruments Used for Treatment Monitoring and Treatment Outcome Evaluation

Instrument	Norms	Internal Consistency	Inter-Rater Reliability	Test–Retest Reliability	Content Validity	Construct Validity	Validity Generalization	Treatment Sensitivity	Clinical Utility	Highly Recommended
DAPP-BQ	G	E	NA	G	E	E	E	E	E	✓
SNAP	E	E	NA	G	E	G	G	E	E	✓

Note: DAPP-BQ = Dimensional Assessment of Personality Psychopathology-Basic Questionnaire; SNAP = Schedule for Nonadaptive and Adaptive Personality; G = Good; E = Excellent; NA = Not Applicable.

2003; Perry & Bond, 2000), nor does the treatment itself focus on the entire personality structure (Paris, 2006). It appears to be the case, for example, that clinicians treat the affective instability, the fears of abandonment, the behavioral dyscontrol, or the self-mutilation of persons diagnosed with borderline personality disorder. Effective change occurs with respect to the components, rather than with the entire, global construct. One of the empirically supported treatments for borderline personality disorder (APA, 2001) is dialectical behavior therapy (DBT). Research has demonstrated that DBT is an effective treatment for many of the components of this personality disorder, but it is evident to even the proponents of this clinical approach that the treatment is not entirely comprehensive in its effectiveness (Linehan, 2000). DBT has been particularly effective with respect to decreasing parasuicidal behavior and angry hostility, but not with other aspects of borderline psychopathology, such as hopelessness (Linehan, 2000; Scheel, 2000).

Measures of treatment monitoring and outcome should, therefore, include assessments of the specific components, rather than simply the global construct. In this regard, a unique advantage of the PAI assessment of the antisocial and borderline personality disorders is the inclusion of subscales. The PAI antisocial scale includes subscales for antisocial behaviors, egocentricity, and stimulus seeking; the PAI borderline scale includes subscales for affective instability, identity problems, negative relationships, and self-harm. All of the other diagnostic measures reviewed in this chapter provide only an assessment of the overall antisocial and borderline constructs. However, the PAI has this potential clinical utility only for the antisocial and borderline personality disorders.

Perhaps the most clinically useful measures of specific components of personality disorder are provided by the Dimensional Assessment of Personality Pathology-Basic Questionnaire (DAPP-BQ; Livesley, 2003) and/or the Schedule for Nonadaptive and Adaptive Personality (SNAP; Clark et al., in press). The DAPP and the SNAP were constructed in a similar

manner to provide assessments of the fundamental dimensions of maladaptive personality functioning that cut across and define the existing diagnostic categories. Livesley (2003) obtained personality disorder symptoms and features from a thorough content analysis of the personality disorder literature. An initial list of criteria was then coded by clinicians with respect to their prototypicality for respective personality disorders. One hundred scales (each with 16 items) were submitted to a series of factor analyses to derive a set of 18 fundamental dimensions (e.g., anxiousness, self-harm, intimacy problems, social avoidance, passive opposition, and interpersonal disesteem). These 18 dimensions are subsumed within four higher order constructs of emotional dysregulation, dissocial, inhibitedness, and compulsivity that align well with the neuroticism, antagonism, introversion, and conscientiousness domains of the FFM, respectively (Clark & Livesley, 2002; Livesley, 2001).

The approach of Clark et al. (in press) was quite similar to that of Livesley (2003). The DSM-III-R personality disorder criteria, along with trait-like manifestations of anxiety and mood disorders, were sorted by clinicians into 22 conceptually similar symptom clusters. Factor analyses of these 22 symptom clusters yielded 12 dimensions of maladaptive personality functioning (e.g., self-harm, entitlement, eccentric perceptions, workaholism, detachment, and manipulation). These 12 dimensions of abnormal personality functioning are related conceptually to three higher-order factors of general personality hypothesized by Watson and Tellegen (Watson, Clark, & Harkness, 1994): negative affectivity, positive affectivity, and constraint, which again align well with the neuroticism, extraversion, and conscientiousness domains of the FFM (Watson et al., 1994). However, factor analyses of the 12 SNAP scales do not appear to yield a three-factor structure consistent with the three temperaments of Tellegen. Joint factor analyses of the DAPP and the SNAP yield the four-factor structure (Clark, Livesley, Schroeder, & Irish, 1996).

Overall Evaluation

The primary goal for the treatment of a personality disorder would naturally be the remission of the personality disorder. As such, the appropriate treatment outcome measure might then be a diagnostic measure. However, the existing instruments, with the exception of the DIPD, are limited in this regard, as they have not yet been modified to assess change in long-standing personality traits. An additional limitation is that treatment of personality disorders does not appear to address the global personality structure, focusing instead on more specific personality traits and components of the personality disorders. In this regard, the DAPP-BQ and the SNAP are likely to be better suited as treatment outcome measures.

Table 19.3 provides a summary of the psychometric properties of the DAPP-BQ and SNAP, and their overall evaluation. Both are provided high ratings for treatment sensitivity (and clinical utility) as the scales concern specifically that which is typically the focus of personality disorder treatment (e.g., mistrusts, self-harm, manipulativeness, insecure attachment, identity problems, affective liability, and self-harm). A preference for either the DAPP-BQ or the SNAP is not clear, as they have very similar psychometric properties (see Table 19.3). The decision could be based on coverage. For example, the DAPP-BQ does not include a scale for workaholism, whereas the SNAP does not include a scale for identity problems. Clinicians should consider both instruments and select which appears to be best suited to their particular clinical population. The SNAP does appear to have better normative support (Clark et al., in press), whereas the DAPP-BQ appears to have better support for its higher order factor structure (Livesley, 2003) and a greater cross-cultural application. Both of these instruments are considered to be highly recommended.

CONCLUSIONS AND FUTURE DIRECTIONS

A considerable amount of attention and research has been devoted to the assessment and diagnosis of the DSM-IV personality disorders. It is striking that this chapter identifies 14 distinct instruments developed that provide assessments of these personality disorders.

This is both a testament to the complexity and interest in personality disorder assessment and, regrettably perhaps, the inadequacy of each of the existing instruments. If one instrument was clearly preferable to another, there would be no need or interest in so many alternative measures. It is perhaps time to devote research attention to more direct comparisons of the reliability and validity of the alternative measures in order to begin to separate the wheat from the chaff. However, in the absence of a gold standard for what constitutes an unambiguously valid criterion, comparative research can be difficult to conduct.

It will also be important for future studies to devote more attention to the construction of measures that could be used to augment diagnostic information that can be used to guide decisions on treatment planning and treatment outcome assessment beyond that which is provided simply by a personality disorder diagnosis. Progress in such research is hindered, in large part, by the virtual absence of studies devoted to the development and validation of empirically supported treatments for specific personality disorders. Systematic studies have been conducted on manualized treatment protocols for borderline personality disorder (APA, 2001), but currently little can be said regarding the empirically guided treatment of the obsessive–compulsive, avoidant, dependent, paranoid, schizoid, narcissistic, or histrionic personality disorders.

Hand in hand with the development of such treatments, it will be necessary to (a) tackle the thorny issue of what constitutes successful treatment of personality disorders and (b) develop, based on this formulation, measures that are designed to be sensitive to treatment effects. The successful treatment of a personality disorder will not be the construction of an ideal personality structure. One is unlikely to change a "Theodore Bundy" into a "Mother Teresa." On the other hand, given the substantial public health care costs that can be associated with some of the more dysfunctional personality disorders (e.g., costs to victims and to law enforcement agencies of persons with an antisocial personality disorder, the costs of the many brief hospitalizations of persons with borderline personality disorder), even moderate improvements in personality functioning can have substantial personal, social, and public health care benefits (Linehan, 2000). Measures more specifically suited to these important benefits of personality disorder treatment need to be developed.

References

Abrams, R. C., & Horowitz, S. V. (1999). Personality disorders after age 50: A meta-analytic review of the literature. In E. Rosowsky, R. C. Abrams, & R. A. Zweig (Eds.), *Personality disorders in older adults: Emerging issues in diagnosis and treatment* (pp. 55–68). Mahwah, NJ: Erlbaum.

Agronin, M. E. (1998). Personality and psychopathology in late life. *Geriatrics, 53*, 35–40.

Alarcon, R. D. (1996). Personality disorders and culture in DSM-IV: A critique. *Journal of Personality Disorders, 10*, 260–270.

Allik, J. (2005). Personality dimensions across cultures. *Journal of Personality Disorders, 19*, 212–232.

American Psychiatric Association (1980). *Diagnostic and statistical manual of mental disorders* (3rd ed.). Washington, DC: American Psychiatric Association.

American Psychiatric Association (1987). *Diagnostic and statistical manual of mental disorders* (3rd ed., rev. ed.). Washington, DC: American Psychiatric Association.

American Psychiatric Association (2000). *Diagnostic and statistical manual of mental disorders* (4th ed., text rev.). Washington, DC: Author.

American Psychiatric Association. (2001). *Practice guidelines for the treatment of patients with borderline personality disorder*. Washington, DC: Author.

Ando, J., Suzuki, A., Yamagata, S., Kijima, N., Maekawa, H., Ono, Y., et al. (2004). Genetic and environmental structure of Cloninger's temperament and character dimensions. *Journal of Personality Disorders, 18*, 379–393.

Bagby, R. M., & Farvolden, P. (2004). The Personality Diagnostic Questionnaire-4 (PDQ-4). In M. J., Hilsenroth, D. L. Segal, & M. Hersen (Eds.), *Comprehensive handbook of psychological assessment, Vol. 2. Personality assessment* (pp. 122–133). New York: John Wiley.

Benjamin, L. S., Rothweiler, J. C., & Critchfield, K. L. (2006). The use of structural analysis of social behavior (SASB) as an assessment tool. *Annual Review of Clinical Psychology, 2*, 83–110.

Blashfield, R. K., & Flanagan, E. (1998). A prototypic nonprototype of a personality disorder. *Journal of Nervous and Mental Disease, 186*, 244–246.

Boggs, C. D, Morey, L. C, Skodol, A. E., Shea, M. T., Sanislow, C. A., Grilo, C. M., et al. (2005). Differential impairment as an indicator of sex bias in DSM-IV criteria for four personality disorders. *Psychological Assessment, 17*, 492–496.

Bornstein, R. F. (1998). Reconceptualizing personality disorder diagnosis in the DSM-V: The discriminant validity challenge. *Clinical Psychology: Science and Practice, 5*, 333–343.

Boyle, G. J., & Le Dean, L. (2000). Discriminant validity of the Illness Behavior Questionnaire and Millon Clinical Multiaxial Inventory-III in a heterogeneous sample of psychiatric outpatients. *Journal of Clinical Psychology, 56*, 779–791.

Caspi, A., Roberts, B. W., & Shiner, R. L. (2005). Personality development: Stability and change. *Annual Review of Psychology, 56*, 453–484.

Clark, L. A. (2007). Assessment and diagnosis of personality disorder: Perennial issues and an emerging reconceptualization. *Annual Review of Psychology, 58*, 227–257.

Clark, L. A., & Harrison, J. A. (2001). Assessment instruments. In W. J. Livesley (Ed.), *Handbook of personality disorders. Theory, research, and treatment* (pp. 277–306). New York: Guilford.

Clark, L. A., & Livesley, W. J. (2002). Two approaches to identifying the dimensions of personality disorder: Convergence on the five-factor model. In P. T. Costa & T. A. Widiger (Eds.), *Personality disorders and the five-factor model of personality* (2nd ed., pp. 161–176). Washington, DC: American Psychological Association.

Clark, L. A., Livesley, W. J., Schroeder, M. L., & Irish, S. L. (1996). Convergence of two systems for assessing personality disorder. *Psychological Assessment, 8*, 294–303.

Clark, L. A., Simms, L. J., Wu, K. D., & Casillas, A. (in press). *Manual for the Schedule for Nonadaptive and Adaptive Personality (SNAP-2)*. Minneapolis, MN: University of Minnesota Press.

Clark, R., Anderson, N. B., Clark, V. R., & Williams, D. R. (1999). Racism as a stressor for African Americans. *American Psychologist, 54*, 805–816.

Cloninger, C. R. (2000). A practical way to diagnosis personality disorders: A proposal. *Journal of Personality Disorders, 14*, 99–108.

Colligan, R. C., Morey, L. C., & Offord, K. P. (1994). MMPI/MMPI-2 personality disorder scales. Contemporary norms for adults and adolescents. *Journal of Clinical Psychology, 50*, 168–200.

Cooke, D. J. (1996). Psychopathic personality in different cultures: What do we know? What do we need to find out? *Journal of Personality Disorders, 10*, 23–40.

Coolidge, F. L., & Merwin, M. M. (1992). Reliability and validity of the Coolidge Axis II Inventory: A new inventory for the assessment of personality disorders. *Journal of Personality Assessment, 59*, 223–238.

Costa, P. T., & McCrae, R. R. (1992). *Revised NEO Personality Inventory (NEO PI-R) and NEO Five-Factor Inventory (NEO-FFI) professional manual*. Odessa, FL: Psychological Assessment Resources.

Derefinko, K. J., & Widiger, T. A. (in press). Antisocial personality disorder. In S. H. Fatemi & P. Clayton (Eds.), *The medical basis of psychiatry* (3rd ed.). Totowa, NJ: The Humana Press.

Derksen, J. J. (2006). The contribution of the MMPI-2 to the diagnosis of personality disorder. In J. N. Butcher (Ed.), *MMPI-2: A practitioner's guide* (pp. 99–120). Washington, DC: American Psychological Association.

Dolan-Sewell, R. G., Krueger, R. F., & Shea, M. T. (2001). Co-occurrence with syndrome disorders. In W. J. Livesley (Ed.), *Handbook of personality disorders* (pp. 84–104), New York: Guilford.

First, M. B., & Gibbon, M. (2004). The Structured Clinical Interview for DSM-IV Axis I Disorders (SCID-I) and the Structured Clinical Interview for DSM-IV Axis II Disorders (SCID-II). In M. J., Hilsenroth, D. L. Segal, & M. Hersen (Eds.), *Comprehensive handbook of psychological assessment, Vol. 2. Personality assessment* (pp. 134–143). New York: John Wiley & Sons.

Frances, A. J. (1980). The DSM-III personality disorders section: A commentary. *American Journal of Psychiatry, 137*, 1050–1054.

Frances, A. J., First, M. B., & Pincus, H. A. (1995). *DSM-IV guidebook*. Washington, DC: American Psychiatric Press.

Frueh, B. C., Smith, D. W., & Libet, J. M. (1996). Racial differences on psychological measures in combat veterans seeking treatment for PTSD. *Journal of Personality Assessment, 66*, 41–53.

Gana, K., & Trouillet, R. (2004). Structural invariance of the Temperament and Character Inventory (TCI). *Personality and Individual Differences, 35*, 1483–1495.

Garb, H. (2005). Clinical judgment and decision making. *Annual Review of Clinical Psychology, 1*, 67–89.

Gunderson, J. G. (2001). *Borderline personality disorder: A clinical guide*. Washington, DC: American Psychiatric Press.

Gunderson, J. G., & Gabbard, G. O. (Eds.). (2000). *Psychotherapy for personality disorders*. Washington, DC: American Psychiatric Press.

Gunderson, J. G., Bender, D., Sanislow, C., Yen, S., Rettew, J. B., Dolan-Sewell, R., et al. (2003). Plausibility and possible determinants of sudden "remissions" in borderline patients. *Psychiatry, 66*, 111–119.

Gunderson, J. G., Shea, M. T., Skodol, A. E., McGlashan, T. H., Morey, L. C., Stout, R. L., et al. (2000). The Collaborative Longitudinal Personality Disorders Study, I: Development, aims, design, and sample characteristics. *Journal of Personality Disorders, 14*, 300–315.

Haigler, E. D., & Widiger, T. A. (2001). Experimental manipulation of NEO PI-R items. *Journal of Personality Assessment, 77*, 339–358.

Herbst, J. H., Zonderman, A. B., McCrae, R. R., & Costa, P. T. (2000). Do the dimensions of the temperament and character inventory map a simple genetic architecture? Evidence from molecular genetics and factor analysis. *American Journal of Psychiatry, 157*, 1285–1290.

Hicklin, J., & Widiger, T. A. (2000). Convergent validity of alternative MMPI-2 personality disorder measures. *Journal of Personality Assessment, 75*, 502–518.

Horowitz, L. M., Alden, L. E., Wiggins, J. S., & Pincus, A. L. (2000). *Inventory of Interpersonal Problems manual*. Odessa, FL: The Psychological Corporation.

Jones, A. (2005). An examination of three sets of MMPI-2 personality disorder scales. *Journal of Personality Disorders, 19*, 370–385.

Kaye, A. L., & Shea, M. T. (2000). Personality disorders, personality traits, and defense mechanisms measures. *Handbook of psychiatric measures* (pp. 713–749). Washington, DC: American Psychiatric Association.

King, R. E. (1994). Assessing aviators for personality pathology with the millon clinical multiaxial inventory (MCMI). *Aviation, Space, and Environmental Medicine, 65*, 227–231.

Klein, M. H., Benjamin, L. S., Rosenfeld, R., Treece, C., Husted, J., & Greist, J. H. (1993). The Wisconsin personality disorders inventory: I. Development, reliability, and validity. *Journal of Personality Disorders, 7*, 285–303.

Lampel, A. K. (1999). Use of the Millon Clinical Multiaxial Inventory-III in evaluating child custody litigants. *American Journal of Forensic Psychology, 17*, 19–31.

Leichsenring, F., & Leibing, E. (2003). The effectiveness of psychodynamic therapy and cognitive behavior therapy in the treatment of personality disorders: A meta-analysis. *American Journal of Psychiatry, 160*, 1223–1232.

Lenzenweger, M., & Clarkin. J. (Eds.). (2005). *Major theories of personality disorder*. New York: Guilford.

Lindsay, K. A., Sankis, L. M., & Widiger, T. A. (2000). Gender bias in self-report personality disorder inventories. *Journal of Personality Disorders, 14*, 218–232.

Linehan, M. (2000). The empirical basis of dialectical behavior therapy: Development of new treatments versus evaluation of existing treatments. *Clinical Psychology: Science and Practice, 7*, 113–119.

Livesley, W. J. (2001). Conceptual and taxonomic issues. In W. J. Livesley (Ed.), *Handbook of personality disorders. Theory, research, and treatment* (pp. 3–38). New York: Guilford.

Livesley, W. J. (2003). Diagnostic dilemmas in classifying personality disorder. In K. A. Phillips, M. B. First, & H. A. Pincus (Eds.), *Advancing DSM. Dilemmas in psychiatric diagnosis* (pp. 153–190). Washington, DC: American Psychiatric Association.

Loranger, A. W. (1992). Are current self-report and interview methods adequate for epidemiological studies of personality disorders? *Journal of Personality Disorders, 6,* 313–325.

Loranger, A. W. (1999). *International personality disorder examination (IPDE).* Odessa, FL: Psychological Assessment Resources.

Loranger, A. W. (2001). *OMNI Personality inventories. Professional manual.* Odessa, FL: Psychological Assessment Resources.

Loranger, A. W., Lenzenweger, M. F., Gartner, A. F., Susman, V. L., Herzig, J., Zammit, G. K., et al. (1991). Trait-state artifacts and the diagnosis of personality disorders. *Archives of General Psychiatry, 48,* 720–729.

Lynam, D. R., & Widiger, T. A. (2001). Using the five factor model to represent the DSM-IV personality disorders: An expert consensus approach. *Journal of Abnormal Psychology, 110,* 401–412.

Marin-Avellan, L. E., McGauley, G., Campbell, C., & Fonagy, P. (2005). Using the SWAP-200 in a personality-disordered forensic population: Is it valid, reliable, and useful? *Criminal Behaviour and Mental Health, 15,* 28–45.

Mattia, J. I., & Zimmerman, M. (2001) Epidemiology. In W. J. Livesley (Ed.), *Handbook of personality disorders* (pp. 107–123). New York: Guilford.

McDermut, W., & Zimmerman, M. (2005). Assessment instruments and standardized evaluation. In J. Oldham, A. Skodol, & D. Bender (Eds.), *Textbook of personality disorders* (pp. 89–101). Washington, DC: American Psychiatric Press.

Meehl, P. E., & Rosen, A. (1955). Antecedent probability and the efficiency of psychometric signs, patterns, or cutting scores. *Psychological Bulletin, 52,* 194–216.

Mellsop, G., Varghese, F. T. N., Joshua, S., & Hicks, A. (1982). The reliability of Axis II of DSM-III. *American Journal of Psychiatry, 139,* 1360–1361.

Millon, T., Davis, R. D., Millon, C. M., Wenger, A. W., Van Zuilen, M. H., Fuchs, M., et al. (1996). *Disorders of personality. DSM-IV and beyond.* New York: John Wiley & Sons.

Millon, T., Millon, C., & Davis, R. (1997). *MCMI-III manual* (2nd ed.). Minneapolis, MN: National Computer Systems.

Morey, L. C. (1991). *The personality assessment inventory professional manual.* Odessa, FL: Psychological Assessment Resources.

Morey, L. C., & Boggs, C. (2004). The personality assessment inventory (PAI). In M. J. Hilsenroth, D. L. Segal, & M. Hersen (Eds.), *Comprehensive handbook of psychological assessment, Vol. 2. Personality assessment* (pp. 15–29). New York: John Wiley.

Morey, L. C., Alexander, G. M., & Boggs, C. (2005). Gender and personality disorder. In J. Oldham, A. Skodol, & D. Bender (Eds.), *Textbook of personality disorders* (pp. 541–554). Washington, DC: American Psychiatric Press.

Morey, L. C., Waugh, M. H., & Blashfield, R. K. (1985). MMPI scales for DSM-III personality disorders: Their derivation and correlates. *Journal of Personality Assessment, 49,* 245–251.

Mullins-Sweatt, S. N., & Widiger, T. A. (2006). The five-factor model of personality disorder: A translation across science and practice. In R. F. Krueger & J. L. Tackett (Eds.), *Personality and psychopathology* (pp. 39–70). New York: Guilford.

O'Boyle, M., & Self, D. (1990). A comparison of two interviews for DSM-III-R personality disorders. *Psychiatry Research, 32,* 85–92.

Okazaki, S., Kallivayalil, D., & Sue, S. (2002). Clinical personality assessment with Asian Americans. In J. T. Butcher (Ed.), *Clinical personality assessment: Practical approaches* (2nd ed., pp. 135–153). London: Oxford University Press.

Oldham, J. M., & Skodol, A. E. (2000). Charting the future of Axis II. *Journal of Personality Disorders, 14,* 17–29.

Oldham, J. M., Skodol, A. E., & Bender, D. S. (Eds.). (2005). *Textbook of personality disorders.* Washington, DC: American Psychiatric Publishing.

Oltmanns, T., Jane, J., South, S., & Turkheimer, E. (in press). Gender bias in diagnostic criteria for personality disorders: An item response theory analysis. *Journal of Abnormal Psychology.*

Ozer, D. J., & Benet-Martinez, V. (2006). Personality and the prediction of consequential outcomes. *Annual Review of Psychology, 57,* 401–421.

Paris, J. (1998). *Working with traits: Psychotherapy of personality disorders.* Northvale, NJ: Jason Aronson.

Paris, J. (2005). A current integrative perspective on personality disorders. In J. M. Oldham, A. E. Skodol, & D. S. Bender (Eds.), *Textbook of personality disorders* (pp. 119–128). Washington, DC: American Psychiatric Publishing.

Paris, J. (2006, May). *Personality disorders: Psychiatry's stepchildren come of age.* Invited lecture presented at the 159th Annual Meeting of the American Psychiatric Association, Toronto, Canada.

Perry, J. C., & Bond, M. (2000). Empirical studies of psychotherapy for personality disorders. In J. G. Gunderson & G. O. Gabbard (Eds.), *Psychotherapy for personality disorders* (pp. 1–31). Washington, DC: American Psychiatric Press.

Pfohl, B., Blum, N., & Zimmerman, M. (1997). *Structured interview for DSM-IV personality.* Washington, DC: American Psychiatric Press.

Piersma, H. L. (1987). The MCMI as a measure of DSM-III Axis II diagnoses: An empirical comparison. *Journal of Clinical Psychology, 43,* 478–483.

Piersma, H. L. (1989). The MCMI-II as a treatment outcome measure for psychiatric inpatients. *Journal of Clinical Psychology, 45,* 87–93.

Pilkonis, P. A., Heape, C. L., Proietti, J. M., Clark, S. W., McDavid, J. D., & Pitts, T. E. (1995). The reliability and validity of two structured diagnostic interviews for personality disorders. *Archives of General Psychiatry, 52,* 1025–1033.

Pincus, A. L. (2005). A contemporary integrative interpersonal theory of personality disorders. In J. Clarkin & M. Lenzenweger (Eds.), *Major theories of personality disorder* (2nd ed., pp. 282–331). New York: Guilford.

Roberts, B. W., & DelVecchio, W. F. (2000). The rank-order consistency of personality traits from childhood to old age: A quantitative review of longitudinal studies. *Psychological Bulletin, 126,* 3–25.

Rogers, R. (2001). *Diagnostic and structured interviewing. A handbook for psychologists.* New York: Guilford.

Rogers, R. (2003). Standardizing DSM-IV diagnoses: The clinical applications of structured interviews. *Journal of Personality Assessment, 81,* 220–225.

Ross, R., Frances, A. J., & Widiger, T. A. (1995). Gender issues in DSM-IV. In J. M. Oldham & M. B. Riba (Eds.), *Review of psychiatry* (Vol. 14, pp. 205–226). Washington, DC: American Psychiatric Press.

Rutter, M. (2003, October). *Pathways of genetic influences on psychopathology.* Zubin Award address at the 18th Annual Meeting of the Society for Research in Psychopathology, Toronto, Canada.

Samuel, D. B., & Widiger, T. A. (2006). Clinicians' judgments of clinical utility: A comparison of the DSM-IV and five factor models. *Journal of Abnormal Psychology, 115,* 298–308.

Sanderson, C., & Clarkin, J. F. (2002). Further use of the NEO PI R personality dimensions in differential treatment planning. In P. T. Costa, Jr. & T. A. Widiger (Eds.), *Personality disorders and the five factor model of personality* (2nd ed., pp. 351–375). Washington, DC: American Psychological Association.

Scheel, K. R. (2000). The empirical basis of dialectical behavior therapy: Summary, critique, and implications. *Clinical Psychology: Science Practice, 7,* 68–86.

Segal, D. L., & Coolidge, F. L. (2003). Structured interviewing and DSM classification. In M. Hersen & S. Turner (Eds.), *Adult psychopathology and diagnosis* (4th ed., pp. 72–103). New York: John Wiley & Sons.

Segal, D. L., Hersen, H., Van Hasselt, V. B., Silberman, C. S., & Roth, L. (1996). Diagnosis and assessment of personality disorders in older adults: A critical review. *Journal of Personality Disorders, 10,* 384–399.

Shedler, J. (2002). A new language for psychoanalytic diagnosis. *Journal of the American Psychoanalytic Association, 50,* 429–456.

Shedler, J., & Westen, D. (2004). Refining personality disorder diagnosis: Integrating science and practice. *American Journal of Psychiatry, 161,* 1350–1365.

Skodol, A. E., Oldham, J. M., Rosnick, L., Kellman, H. D., & Hyler, S. E. (1991). Diagnosis of DSM-III-R personality disorders: A comparison of two structured interviews. *International Journal of Methods in Psychiatric Research, 1,* 13–26.

Smith, G. T. (2005). On construct validity: Issues of method and measurement. *Psychological Assessment, 17,* 396–408.

Stone, M. H. (1993). *Abnormalities of personality. Within and beyond the realm of treatment.* New York: W.W. Norton and Company.

Svrakic, D. M., Draganic, S., Hill, K., Bayon, C., Przybeck, T. R., & Cloninger, C. R. (2002). Temperament, character, and personality disorders: Etiologic, diagnostic, and treatment issues. *Acta Psychiatrica Scandinavica, 106,* 189–195.

Torgesen, S., Kringlen, E., & Cramer, V. (2001). The prevalence of personality disorders in a community sample. *Archives of General Psychiatry, 58,* 590–596.

Trull, T. J. (2001). Structural relations between borderline personality disorder features and putative etiological correlates. *Journal of Abnormal Psychology, 110,* 471–481.

Trull, T. J., & Durrett, C. A. (2005). Categorical and dimensional models of personality disorder. *Annual Review of Clinical Psychology, 1,* 355–380.

Verheul, R. (2005). Clinical utility for dimensional models of personality pathology. *Journal of Personality Disorders, 19,* 283–302

Verheul, R., & Widiger, T. A. (2004). A meta-analysis of the prevalence and usage of the personality disorder not otherwise specified (PDNOS) diagnosis. *Journal of Personality Disorders, 18,* 309–319.

Warner, M. B., Morey, L. C., Finch, J. F., Gunderson, J. G., Skodol, A. E., Sanislow, C. A., et al. (2004). The longitudinal relationship of personality traits and disorders. *Journal of Abnormal Psychology, 113,* 217–227.

Watson, D., Clark, L. A., & Harkness, A. R. (1994). Structures of personality and their relevance to psychopathology. *Journal of Abnormal Psychology, 103,* 18–31.

Westen, D. (1997). Divergences between clinical and research methods for assessing personality disorders: Implications for research and the evolution of Axis II. *American Journal of Psychiatry, 154,* 895–903.

Westen, D. & Shedler, J. (2003). *SWAP-200 instructions for use.* Boston, MA: Department of Psychology and Center for Anxiety and Related Disorders.

Westen, D., & Muderrisoglu, S. (2003). Assessing personality disorders using a systematic clinical interview: Evaluation of an alternative to structured interviews. *Journal of Personality Disorders, 17,* 351–369.

Westen, D., & Shedler, J. (1999a). Revising and assessing Axis II, Part I: Developing a clinically and empirically valid assessment method. *American Journal of Psychiatry, 156,* 258–272.

Westen, D., & Shedler, J. (1999b). Revising and assessing Axis II, Part II: Toward an empirically based and clinically useful classification of personality disorders. *American Journal of Psychiatry, 156,* 273–285.

Westen, D., Shedler, J., Durrett, C., Glass, S., & Martens, A. (2003). Personality diagnoses in adolescence: DSM-IV Axis II diagnosis and an empirically derived alternative. *American Journal of Psychiatry, 160,* 952–966.

Whaley, A. L. (1997). Ethnicity/race, paranoia, and psychiatric diagnoses: Clinician bias versus sociocultural differences. *Journal of Psychopathology and Behavioral Assessment, 19,* 1–20.

Widiger, T. A. (1998). Sex biases in the diagnosis of personality disorders. *Journal of Personality Disorders, 12,* 95–118.

Widiger, T. A. (2002). Personality disorders. In M. M. Antony & D. H. Barlow (Eds.), *Handbook of assessment, treatment planning, and outcome for psychological disorders* (pp. 453–480). New York: Guilford.

Widiger, T. A. (2005). CIC, CLPS, and MSAD. *Journal of Personality Disorders, 19,* 586–593.

Widiger, T. A., & Coker, L. A. (2002). Assessing personality disorders. In J. N. Butcher (Ed.), *Clinical personality assessment. Practical approaches* (2nd ed., pp. 407–434). New York: Oxford University Press.

Widiger, T. A., & Lowe, J. (2007). Five factor model assessment personality disorder. *Journal of Personality Assessment, 89,* 16–29.

Widiger, T. A., & Samuel, D. B. (2005). Evidence based assessment of personality disorders. *Psychological Assessment, 17,* 278–287.

Widiger, T. A., & Seidlitz, L. (2002). Personality, psychopathology, and aging. *Journal of Research in Personality, 36,* 335–362.

Widiger, T. A., & Trull, T. J. (2007). Plate tectonics in the classification of personality disorder: Shifting to a dimensional model. *American Psychologist, 62,* 71–83.

Widiger, T. A., Mangine, S., Corbitt, E. M., Ellis, C. G., & Thomas, G. V. (1995). *Personality disorder interview-IV. A semistructured interview for the assessment of personality disorders. Professional manual.* Odessa, FL: Psychological Assessment Resources.

Wiggins, J. S. (2003). *Paradigms of personality assessment.* New York: Guilford.

Wiggins, J. S., & Pincus, H. A. (1989). Conceptions of personality disorder and dimensions of personality. *Psychological Assessment, 1,* 305–316.

Wood, J. M., Garb, H. N., Lilienfeld, S. O., & Nezworski, M. T. (2002). Clinical assessment. *Annual Review of Psychology, 53,* 519–543.

Wood, J. M., Garb, H. N., Nezworski, M. T., & Koren, D. (in press). The Shedler–Westen Assessment Procedure-200 as a basis for modifying DSM personality disorder categories. *Journal of Abnormal Psychology.*

World Health Organization. (1992). *The ICD-10 classification of mental and behavioural disorders. Clinical descriptions and diagnostic guidelines.* Geneva, Switzerland: Author.

Zanarini, M. (Ed.). (2005). *Borderline personality disorder.* Boca Raton, FL: Taylor & Francis.

Zanarini, M. C., Frankenburg, F. R., Chauncey, D. L., & Gunderson, J. G. (1987). The diagnostic interview for personality disorders: Interrater and test–retest reliability. *Comprehensive Psychiatry, 28,* 467–480.

Zanarini, M. C., Frankenburg, F. R., & Vujanovic, A. A. (2002). Inter-rater and test–retest reliability of the Revised Interview for Borderlines. *Journal of Personality Disorders, 16,* 270–276.

Zimmerman, M. (2003). What should the standard of care for psychiatric diagnostic evaluations be? *Journal of Nervous and Mental Disease, 191,* 281–286.

Zimmerman, M., & Mattia, J. I. (1999). Differences between clinical and research practices in diagnosing borderline personality disorder. *American Journal of Psychiatry, 156,* 1570–1574.

Part VII

Couple Distress and Sexual Problems

20

Couple Distress

Douglas K. Snyder
Richard E. Heyman
Stephen N. Haynes

Assessment of couple distress shares basic principles of assessing individuals—namely, that (a) the content of assessment methods be empirically linked to target problems and constructs hypothesized to be functionally related; (b) selected assessment methods demonstrate evidence of reliability, validity, and cost-effectiveness; and (c) findings be linked within a theoretical or conceptual framework of the presumed causes of difficulties, as well as to clinical intervention or prevention. However, couple assessment differs from individual assessment in that couple assessment strategies (a) focus specifically on relationship processes and the interactions between individuals, (b) provide an opportunity for direct observation of target complaints involving communication and other interpersonal exchange, and (c) must be sensitive to potential challenges unique to establishing a collaborative alliance when assessing highly distressed or antagonistic partners, particularly in a conjoint context. Similar to the assessment process itself, our discussion of strategies for assessing couple distress is necessarily selective—emphasizing dimensions empirically related to couple distress, identifying alternative methods and strategies for obtaining relevant assessment data, and highlighting specific techniques within each method.

We begin this chapter by defining couple distress and noting its prevalence and comorbidity with emotional, behavioral, and physical health problems of individuals in both clinical and community populations. Both brief screening measures and clinical methods are presented for diagnosing couple distress in clinical as well as research applications. The bulk

of the chapter is devoted to conceptualizing and assessing couple distress for the purpose of planning and evaluating treatment. Toward this end, we review empirical findings regarding behavioral, cognitive, and affective components of couple distress and specific techniques derived from clinical interview, behavioral observation, and self-report methods. In most cases, these same assessment methods and instruments are relevant to evaluating treatment progress and outcome. We conclude with general recommendations for assessing couple distress and directions for future research.

CONCEPTUALIZING COUPLE RELATIONSHIP DISTRESS

Defining Couple Distress

The fourth edition of the *Diagnostic and Statistical Manual of Mental Disorders-Text Revision* (DSM-IV-TR; American Psychiatric Association, 2000) defines a "partner relational problem" as a pattern of interaction characterized by negative or distorted communication, or "noncommunication (e.g., withdrawal)" that is associated with clinically significant impairment in individual or relationship functioning or the development of symptoms in one or both partners. The acknowledgment of relational problems as a "frequent focus of clinical attention," but their separation from other emotional and behavioral disorders, amounts to only a marginal improvement over earlier versions of the DSM that all but ignored the interpersonal context of distressed lives.

What are the limitations to this conceptualization of partner relational problems? First is an almost exclusive emphasis on the etiological role of communication in the impairment of functioning or development of symptoms in one or both partners. Although group comparisons document differences in communication between clinic versus community couples (Heyman, 2001), and "communication problems" is the most frequent presenting complaint of couples (Geiss & O'Leary, 1981), evidence that communication differences precede, rather than follow, relationship distress is weak or nonexistent. Moreover, research with community samples indicates that some forms of "negative" communication predict *better* rather than worse relationship outcomes longitudinally (Gottman, 1993). In addition, positive changes in relationship satisfaction following couple therapy correspond only weakly or nonsignificantly with actual changes in communication behavior (Jacobson, Schmaling, & Holtzworth-Munroe, 1987; Sayers, Baucom, Sher, Weiss, & Heyman,1991). Even the distinction between communication and "noncommunication" seems flawed, in that most couple and family theorists would argue that all behavior (including withdrawal) is communicative (Fraenkel, 1997).

In proposing a broadened conceptualization of relationship disorders for the DSM-V, First et al. (2002, p. 161) defined relational disorders as "persistent and painful patterns of feelings, behavior, and perceptions involving two or more partners in an important personal relationship…marked by distinctive, maladaptive patterns that show little change despite a great variety of challenges and circumstances." Still lacking in this conceptualization (as well as in the DSM-IV-TR) is a recognition of "nonsymptomatic" deficiencies that couples often present as a focus of concern, including those that detract from optimal individual or relationship well-being. These include deficits in feelings of security and closeness, shared values, trust, joy, love, and similar positive emotions that individuals typically value in their intimate relationships. Not all such deficits reflect communication difficulties, nor do they necessarily culminate in "clinically significant" impaired functioning or emotional and behavioral symptoms as traditionally conceived; yet, frequently, these deficits are experienced as significant concerns that may culminate in partners' disillusion or their dissolution of the relationship. The most positive features of the DSM's conceptualization of partner relational problems are its emphasis on the interactions between partners and its recognition that relational problems are frequently associated with individual symptoms in one or both partners.

Prevalence and Comorbid Conditions

Clinical interventions targeting couple distress continue to gain in stature as vital components of mental health services. Three factors contribute to this growing recognition: (1) the prevalence of couple distress in both community and clinic samples; (2) the impact of couple distress on both the emotional and physical well-being of adult partners and their offspring; and (3) increased evidence of the effectiveness of couple therapy, not only in treating couple distress and related relationship problems but also as a primary or adjunct treatment for a variety of individual emotional, behavioral, or physical health disorders (Snyder, Castellani, & Whisman, 2006).

Couple distress is prevalent in both community epidemiological studies and in research involving clinical samples. In the United States, the most salient indicator of couple distress remains a divorce rate of approximately 50% among married couples (Kreider & Fields, 2002), with about half of these occurring within the first 7 years of marriage. Independent of divorce, the research literature suggests that many, if not most, marriages experience periods of significant turmoil that place partners at risk for dissatisfaction, dissolution, or symptom development (e.g., depression or anxiety). Data on the effects of stigma, prejudice, and multiple social stressors experienced by lesbian, gay, and bisexual populations suggest that same-sex couples may experience additional challenges (Meyer, 2003).

In a previous national survey, the most frequently cited causes of acute emotional distress were relationship problems including divorce, separation, and other marital strains (Swindle, Heller, Pescosolido, & Kikuzawa, 2000). Other studies have indicated that maritally discordant individuals are overrepresented among individuals seeking mental health services, regardless of whether or not they report marital distress as their primary complaint (Lin, Goering, Offord, Campbell, & Boyle, 1996). In a study of 800 employee assistance program (EAP) clients, 65% rated family problems as "considerable" or "extreme" (Shumway, Wampler, Dersch, & Arredondo, 2004).

Data from the National Comorbidity Survey indicated that, in comparison to happily married persons, maritally distressed partners are three times more likely to have a mood disorder, two and a half times more likely to have an anxiety disorder, and two times more likely to have a substance use disorder (Whisman, 1999). Additional findings from an epidemiological survey in Ontario showed that, even when controlling for distress in other relationships with relatives and close friends, marital distress was significantly correlated with major depression, generalized anxiety disorder, social and simple phobia, panic disorder, and alcohol dependence or abuse (Whisman, Sheldon, & Goering, 2000). Moreover, couple distress—particularly negative communication—has direct adverse effects on cardiovascular, endocrine, immune, neurosensory, and other physiological systems that, in turn, contribute to physical health problems (Kiecolt-Glaser & Newton, 2001). Nor are the effects of couple distress confined to the adult partners. Gottman (1999) cites evidence indicating that "marital distress, conflict, and disruption are associated with a wide range of deleterious effects on children, including depression, withdrawal, poor social competence, health problems, poor academic performance, a variety of conduct-related difficulties, and markedly decreased longevity" (p. 4).

In brief, couple distress has a markedly high prevalence, has a strong linkage to emotional, behavioral, and health problems in the adult partners and their offspring, and is among the most frequent primary or secondary concerns reported by individuals seeking assistance from mental health professionals.

Etiological Considerations and Implications for Assessment

Both the aforementioned comorbidity findings and clinical observations suggest that couple distress likely results from, as well as contributes to, emotional and behavioral problems in one or both partners as well as their children. However, as a relational (vs. individual) disorder, understanding a given couple's distress requires extending beyond individual considerations to pursue a broader assessment of the relational and socioecological context in which couple distress emerges. Snyder, Cavell, Heffer, and Mangrum (1995) proposed a multitrait, multilevel assessment model for assessing couple and family distress comprising five overlapping construct domains (cognitive, affective, behavioral, interpersonal, and structural/developmental) operating at five system levels (individuals, dyads, the nuclear family, the extended

family, and community/cultural systems). Table 20.1 (from Snyder & Abbott, 2002) provides a modest sampling of specific constructs relevant to each domain at each system level.

The relevance of any specific facet of this model to relationship distress for either partner varies dramatically across couples; hence, although providing guidance regarding initial areas of inquiry from a nomothetic perspective, the relation of any specific component to relationship distress for a given individual or couple needs to be determined from a functional-analytic approach and applied idiographically (Cone, 1988; Haynes, Leisen, & Blaine, 1997; Haynes & O'Brien, 2000). Moreover, interactive effects occur within domains across levels, within levels across domains, and across levels and domains. For example, individual differences in emotion regulation could significantly impact how partners interact when disclosing personal information or attempting to resolve conflict. Later in this chapter, we highlight more salient components of this assessment model operating primarily at the dyadic level as they relate to case conceptualization and treatment planning.

ASSESSMENT FOR DIAGNOSIS

A diagnosis of *couple distress* is based on the subjective evaluation of dissatisfaction by one or both partners with the overall quality of their relationship. By comparison, *relationship dysfunction* may be determined by external evaluations of partners' objective interactions. Although subjective and external evaluations frequently converge, partners may report being satisfied with a relationship that—by outsiders' evaluations—would be rated as dysfunctional due to observed deficits in conflict resolution, emotional expressiveness, management of relationship tasks involving finances or children, interactions with extended family, and so forth; similarly, partners may report dissatisfaction with a relationship that to outsiders appears characterized by effective patterns of interacting in these and other domains. Discrepancies between partners' subjective reports and outside observers' evaluations may result, in part, from raters' differences in personal values, gender, ethnicity, or cultural perspectives (Tanaka-Matsumi, 2004).

For screening purposes, a brief structured interview may be used to assess overall relationship distress and partner violence. Heyman, Feldbau-Kohn,

TABLE 20.1 Sample Assessment Constructs Across Domains and Levels of Couple and Family Functioning

	Individual	Dyad (Couple, Parent–Child)	Nuclear Family System	Extended System (Family of Origin, Friends)	Culture/Community
Cognitive	Intelligence; memory functions; thought content; thought quality; analytic skills; cognitive distortions; schemas; capacity for self-reflection and insight.	Cognitions regarding self and other in relationship; expectancies, attributions, attentional biases, and goals in the relationship.	Shared or co-constructed meanings within the system; family ideology or paradigm; thought sequences between members contributing to family functioning.	Intergenerational patterns of thinking and believing; co-constructed meaning shared by therapist and family or other significant friends or family.	Prevailing societal and cultural beliefs and attitudes; ways of thinking associated with particular religious or ethnic groups that are germane to the family or individual.
Affective/emotional	Mood; affective range, intensity, and valence; emotional lability and reactivity.	Predominant emotional themes or patterns in the relationship; cohesion; range of emotional expression; commitment and satisfaction in the relationship; emotional content during conflict; acceptance and forgiveness.	Family emotional themes of fear, shame, guilt, or rejection; system properties of cohesion or emotional disaffection; emotional atmosphere in the home—including humor, joy, love, and affection as well as conflict and hostility.	Emotional themes and patterns in extended system; intergenerational emotional legacies; patterns of fusion or differentiation across generations.	Prevailing emotional sentiment in the community, culture, and society; cultural norms and mores regarding the expression of emotion.
Behavioral	Capacity for self-control; impulsivity; aggressiveness; capacity to defer gratification; substance abuse; overall health, energy, and drive.	Recursive behavioral sequences displayed in the relationship; behavioral repertoire; reinforcement contingencies; strategies used to control other's behavior.	Repetitive behavioral patterns or sequences used to influence family structure and power; shared recreation and other pleasant activities.	Behavioral patterns displayed by the extended system (significant friends, family of origin, therapist) used to influence the structure and behaviors of the extended system.	Cultural norms and mores of behavior; behaviors which are prescribed or proscribed by the larger society.

Domain	Individual	Dyadic/couple	Family	Community/extrafamilial	Cultural/societal
Interpersonal/ communication	Characteristic ways of communicating and interacting across relationships or personality (e.g. shy, gregarious, narcissistic, dependent, controlling, avoidant).	Quality and frequency of the dyad's communication; speaking and listening skills; how couples share information, express feelings, and resolve conflict.	Information flow in the family system; paradoxical messages; family system boundaries, hierarchy, and organization; how the family system uses information regarding its own functioning; family decision-making strategies.	Degree to which information is shared with and received from significant others outside the nuclear family system or dyad; the permeability of boundaries and the degree to which the family or couple is receptive to outside influences.	Information that is communicated to the family or individual by the community or culture in which they live; how the family or individual communicates their needs and mobilizes resources.
Structural/ developmental	All aspects of physiological and psychosocial development; personal history that influences current functioning— including psychosocial stressors; intrapersonal consistency of cognitions, affect, and behavior.	History of the relationship and how it has evolved over time; congruence of partners' cognitions, affect, and behavior.	Changes in the family system over time; current stage in the family life cycle; stressors related to childrearing; congruence in needs, beliefs, and behaviors across family members.	Developmental changes across generations; significant historical events influencing current system functioning (e.g. death, illness, divorce, abuse); congruence of beliefs and values across extended social support systems.	The cultural and political history of the society in which the family or individual lives; current political and economic changes; congruence of the individual's or couple's values with those of the larger community.

Source: From D. K. Snyder and B. V. Abbott (2002). Couple distress. In M. M. Antony & D. H. Barlow (Eds.), *Handbook of Assessment and Treatment Planning for Psychological Disorders* (pp. 341–374). New York: Guilford Press. Copyright 2002 by Guilford Press. Reprinted with permission.

TABLE 20.2 Ratings of Instruments Used for Screening and Diagnosis

Instrument	Norms	Internal Consistency	Inter-Rater Reliability	Test–Retest Reliability	Content Validity	Construct Validity	Validity Generalization	Clinical Utility	Highly Recommended
SDI-MD-PA	U	NA	E	U	G	G	G	G	✓
DAS	A	G	NA	G	A	A	G	A	✓
DAS-7	U	A	NA	U	G	G	U	G	
KMSS	A	G	NA	U	A	G	U	G	
CSI	A	E	NA	U	E	G	U	A	
RMICS	E	E	A	U	A	G	G	A	✓
RCISS	E	U	A	U	A	G	G	A	

Note: SDI-MD-PA = Structured Diagnostic Interview for Marital Distress and Partner Aggression; DAS = Dyadic Adjustment Scale; DAS-7 = Dyadic Adjustment Scale-7 item version; KMSS = Kansas Marital Satisfaction Scale; CSI = Couple Satisfaction Index Scales; RMICS = Rapid Marital Interaction Coding System; RCISS = Rapid Couples Interaction Scoring System; A = Adequate; G = Good; E = Excellent; U = Unavailable; NA = Not Applicable.

Ehrensaft, Langhinrichsen-Rohling, and O'Leary (2001) developed a structured diagnostic interview to provide an initial assessment of marital distress and partner aggression (SDI-MD-PA), patterned after the Structured Clinical Interview for the DSM (First, Gibbon, Spitzer, & Williams, 1997). An initial evaluation of this structured interview demonstrated high inter-rater reliability; moreover, partners' responses to items presented in this interview showed a high correspondence with the same items given in the form of a questionnaire (see Table 20.2).

The emphasis on partners' subjective evaluations of couple distress has led to development of numerous self-report measures of relationship satisfaction and global affect. There is considerable convergence across measures purporting to assess such constructs as marital "quality," "satisfaction," "adjustment," "happiness," "cohesion," "consensus," "intimacy," and the like, with correlations between measures often approaching the upper bounds of their reliability. Differentiation among such constructs at a theoretical level often fails to achieve the same operational distinction at the item-content level (cf., Fincham & Bradbury, 1987, for an excellent discussion of this issue). Hence, selection among such measures should be guided by careful examination of item content (i.e., content validity) and empirical findings regarding both convergent and discriminant validity.

Relatively short measures of overall relationship satisfaction may be useful as diagnostic and screening strategies for couple distress. The most frequently used global measure of relationship satisfaction in couple research is the Dyadic Adjustment Scale (DAS; Spanier, 1976), a 32-item instrument purporting to differentiate among four related subscales reflecting cohesion, satisfaction, consensus, and affectional expression. For abbreviated screening measures of couple distress, several alternatives are available—including a brief (7-item) version of the DAS (Hunsley, Best, Lefebvre, & Vito, 2001). An even briefer measure, the Kansas Marital Satisfaction Scale (KMSS; Schumm et al., 1986), includes three Likert items assessing satisfaction with marriage as an institution, the marital relationship, and the character of one's spouse. New global measures of relationship sentiment continue to be developed for both research and clinical purposes—including a new set of three Couple Satisfaction Index (CSI) scales constructed using item response theory (IRT) and comprising 32, 16, and 4 items each (Funk & Rogge, in press).

Despite its widespread use, a review of psychometric properties reveals important limitations to the DAS. Factor analyses have failed to replicate its four subscales (Crane, Busby, & Larson, 1991), and the reliability of the affectional expression subscale is weak. There is little evidence that the full-length DAS and similar longer global scales offer incremental validity above the 3-item KMSS—although preliminary evidence suggests that the new CSI scales may offer higher precision of measurement and greater sensitivity for detecting differences in relationship satisfaction.

Because partners frequently present for treatment together, clinicians have the rare opportunity to observe the reciprocal social determinants of problem behaviors without venturing outside the therapy office. Structured observations constitute a useful assessment method because they minimize inferences needed to assess behavior, can facilitate formal or informal functional analysis, can provide an additional method of assessment in a multimethod strategy (e.g., integrated with interview and questionnaires), and can facilitate the observation of otherwise difficult to observe behaviors (Haynes & O'Brien, 2000; Heyman & Slep, 2004). We discuss analog behavioral observation of couple interactions and describe specific observational coding systems at greater length in the following section on case conceptualization and treatment planning. However, for purposes of initial screening and diagnosis, we advocate two approaches to assessing partners' descriptions of relationship problems, expression of positive and negative feelings, and efforts to resolve conflicts and reach decisions—specifically, the Rapid Marital Interaction Coding System (RMICS; Heyman, 2004), and the Rapid Couples Interaction Scoring System (RCISS; Krokoff, Gottman, & Hass, 1989). Even when not formally coding couples' interactions, clinicians' familiarity with the behavioral indicators for specific communication patterns previously demonstrated to covary with relationship accord or distress should facilitate empirically informed screening of partners' verbal and nonverbal exchanges.

When a couple presents for therapy with primary complaints of dissatisfaction in their relationship, screening for the mere presence of couple distress is unnecessary. However, there are numerous other situations in which the practitioner may need to screen for relationship distress as a contributing or exacerbating factor in patients' presenting complaints—including mental health professionals treating individual emotional or behavioral difficulties; physicians evaluating the interpersonal context of such somatic complaints as fatigue, chronic headaches, or sleep disturbance, or emergency room personnel confronting persons with severe relationship distress culminating in physical violence and injuries. We advocate a sequential strategy of progressively more detailed assessment when indicators of relationship distress emerge (cf., Snyder & Abbott, 2002, pp. 366–367):

1. Clinical inquiry as to whether relationship problems contribute to individual difficulties such as feeling depressed or anxious, having difficulty sleeping, abusing alcohol or other substances, or feeling less able to deal with such stresses as work, children and family, or health concerns.

2. Alternatively, use of an initial brief screening measure (e.g., the KMSS or DAS-7) having evidence of both internal consistency and construct validity.

3. For individuals reporting moderate to high levels of global relationship distress, following up with more detailed assessment strategies such as semistructured interviews, analog behavioral observation, and multidimensional relationship satisfaction questionnaires to differentiate among levels and sources of distress.

Overall Evaluation

When screening for either clinical or research purposes, we advocate assessment strategies favoring sensitivity over specificity to minimize the likelihood of overlooking potential factors contributing to individual or relationship distress. This implies the initial use of broad screening items in clinical inquiry or self-report measures such as the DAS-7 or the KMSS—along with direct observation of partner interactions whenever possible—and subsequent use of more extensive narrow-band or multidimensional measures described in the following section on treatment planning to pinpoint specific sources of concern. Initial assessment findings indicating overall relationship distress need to be followed by functional-analytic assessment strategies to delineate the manner in which individual and relationship concerns affect each other and relate to situational factors (Floyd, Haynes, & Kelly, 1997).

ASSESSMENT FOR CASE CONCEPTUALIZATION AND TREATMENT PLANNING

Conceptualizing couple distress for the purpose of planning treatment requires extending beyond global sentiment to assess specific sources and levels of relationship difficulties, their individual and broader socioecological determinants, and their potential responsiveness to various clinical interventions. We begin our consideration of assessing couple relationships for case conceptualization and treatment planning with a discussion of construct domains particularly relevant to couple distress—including relationship behaviors, cognitions, and affect—as well as individual and broader cultural factors. We follow this with a discussion of various assessment strategies and techniques for evaluating specific constructs in these domains.

Domains to Target When Evaluating Couple Distress

Relationship Behaviors

Research examining behavioral components of couple distress has emphasized two domains: the rates and reciprocity of positive and negative behaviors exchanged between partners, and communication behaviors related to both emotional expression and decision-making. Regarding the former, distressed couples are distinguished from nondistressed couples by (a) higher rates of negative verbal and nonverbal exchanges (e.g., disagreements, criticism, hostility); (b) higher levels of reciprocity in negative behavior (i.e., the tendency for negativity in partner A to be followed by negativity in partner B); (c) lengthier chains of negative behavior once initiated; (d) higher ratios of negative to positive behaviors, independent of their separate rates; and (e) lower rates of positive verbal and nonverbal behaviors (e.g., approval, empathy, smiling, positive touch; Weiss & Heyman, 1997). Findings suggest a stronger linkage for negativity, compared to positivity, to overall couple distress.

Given the inevitability of disagreements arising in long-term relationships, numerous studies have focused on specific communication behaviors that exacerbate or impede the resolution of couple conflicts. Most notable among these are difficulties in articulating thoughts and feelings related to specific relationship concerns and deficits in decision-making strategies for containing, reducing, or eliminating conflict. Gottman (1994) observed that expression of criticism and contempt, along with defensiveness and withdrawal, predicted long-term distress and risk for relationship dissolution. Christensen and Heavey (1990) found that distressed couples were more likely than nondistressed couples to demonstrate a demand → withdraw pattern in which one person attempts to engage the partner in relationship exchange and that partner withdraws, with respective approach and retreat behaviors progressively intensifying.

Given findings regarding the prominence of negativity, conflict, and ineffective decision-making strategies as correlates of relationship distress, couple assessment must address specific questions regarding relationship behaviors—especially communication behaviors. We list these below, along with sample assessment methods; in subsequent sections specifying interview, observational, and self-report strategies for assessing couple distress, we describe these and related methods in greater detail.

1. How frequent and intense are the couple's conflicts? How rapidly do initial disagreements escalate into major arguments? For how long do conflicts persist without resolution? Both interview and self-report measures may yield useful information regarding rates and intensity of negative exchanges as well as patterns of conflict engagement. Commonly used self-report measures specific to communication include the Communication Patterns Questionnaire (CPQ; Christensen, 1987; see Table 20.3). Couples' conflict-resolution patterns may be observed directly by instructing partners to discuss problems of their own choosing representative of both moderate and high disagreement, and then either formally or informally coding these interactions using one of the behavioral coding systems described later in this chapter.

2. What are common sources of relationship conflict? For example, interactions regarding finances, children, sexual intimacy, use of leisure time, or household tasks; involvement with others including extended family, friends, or coworkers; differences in preferences or core values? In addition to the clinical interview, numerous self-report measures sample sources of distress across a variety of relationship domains. Among those having evidence of both reliability and construct validity are the Frequency and Acceptability of Partner Behavior Inventory (FAPBI; Doss & Christensen, 2006) and the Marital Satisfaction Inventory-Revised (MSI-R; Snyder, 1997)—both of which are described in greater detail later along with other self-report measures.

3. What resources and deficits do partners demonstrate in problem-identification and conflict-resolution strategies? Do they engage couple issues at adaptive levels (i.e., neither avoiding nor dwelling on relationship concerns)? Do partners balance their expression of feelings with decision-making strategies? Are problem-resolution efforts hindered by inflexibility or imbalances in power? Do partners offer each other support when confronting stressors from within or outside their relationship? As noted by others (e.g., Bradbury, Rogge, & Lawrence, 2001; Cutrona, 1996), most of the interactional tasks developed for use in couple research have emphasized problem-solving and conflict-resolution to the exclusion of tasks designed to elicit more positive relationship behaviors such as emotional or strategic support. Hence, when designing interaction tasks for couples, both clinicians and researchers should include tasks specifically designed to sample potential positive, as well as negative exchanges. For example, couples might be asked to discuss a time when one partner's feelings were hurt by someone outside the relationship (e.g., a friend or coworker), in order to assess behaviors expressing understanding and caring—although few templates with these foci have been developed and psychometrically evaluated.

TABLE 20.3 Ratings of Instruments Used for Case Conceptualization and Treatment Planning

Instrument	Norms	Internal Consistency	Inter-Rater Reliability	Test–Retest Reliability	Content Validity	Construct Validity	Validity Generalization	Clinical Utility	Highly Recommended
Self-Report Measures									
Specific Relationship Behaviors									
FAPBI	A	G	NA	U	E	G	A	A	
CPQ	U	G	NA	A	U	G	G	G	
CTS	E	A	NA	A	A	A	A	G	
CTS2	U	G	NA	A	A	A	A	G	✓
Relationship Cognitions									
RAM	U	G	NA	G	A	G	U	G	
Multidimensional Inventories									
MSI-R	E	G	NA	G	E	E	G	E	✓
ENRICH	G	G	NA	A	G	A	A	A	
Observational Measures									
Affect									
BARS	A	U	A	U	A	A	U	A	
SPAFF	G	U	A	G	A	G	G	A	✓
Communication (Demand/Withdraw)									
CRS	G	A	G	U	A	G	G	A	
Communication (Affect)									
CRAC	G	G	G	A	A	G	G	A	✓
IDCS	U	U	A	U	A	G	A	A	
KPI	G	U	G	U	A	G	E	A	
Communication (Problem-Solving)									
COMFI	U	U	A	U	A	A	A	A	
CST	G	U	G	U	A	G	E	A	✓
DISC	U	U	A	U	A	U	A	A	
LIFE	G	U	G	U	A	G	A	A	
VTCS	U	U	A	U	A	G	A	A	
Communication (Power/Affect)									
SCID	U	U	A	U	A	A	G	A	✓
Support/intimacy									
SSICS	U	U	G	U	A	G	A	A	✓

Notes: FAPBI = Frequency and Acceptability of Partner Behavior Inventory; CPQ = Communication Patterns Questionnaire; CTS = Conflict Tactics Scale; CTS2 = Conflict Tactics Scale-Revised; RAM = Relationship Attribution Measure; MSI-R = Marital Satisfaction Inventory-Revised; ENRICH = Evaluating and Nurturing Relationship Issues, Communication, Happiness; BARS = Behavioral Affective Rating System; SPAFF = Specific Affect Coding System; CRS = Conflict Rating System; CRAC = Clinical Rating of Adult Communication Scale; IDCS = Interactional Dimensions Coding System; KPI = Kategoriensystem für Partnerschaftliche Interaktion; COMFI = Codebook of Marital and Family Interaction; CST = Communication Skills Test; DISC = Dyadic Interaction Scoring Code; LIFE = Living In Family Environments Coding System; VTCS = Verbal Tactics Coding Scheme; SCID = System for Coding Interactions in Dyads; SSICS = Social Support Interaction Coding System; A = Adequate; G = Good; E = Excellent; U = Unavailable; NA = Not applicable.

Relationship Cognitions

Social learning models of couple distress have expanded to emphasize the role of cognitive processes in moderating the impact of specific behaviors on relationship functioning (Baucom, Epstein, & LaTaillade, 2002). Research in this domain has focused on such factors as selective attention, attributions for positive and negative relationship events, and specific relationship assumptions, standards, and expectancies. For example, findings indicate that distressed couples often exhibit a bias toward selectively attending to negative partner behaviors and relationship events and ignoring or minimizing positive events (Sillars, Roberts, Leonard, & Dun, 2000). Compared to non-distressed couples, distressed partners also tend to blame each other for problems and to attribute each other's negative behaviors to broad and stable traits (Bradbury & Fincham, 1990). Distressed couples are also more likely to have unrealistic standards and assumptions about how relationships should work, and lower expectancies regarding their partner's willingness or ability to change their behavior in some desired manner (Epstein & Baucom, 2002). Based on these findings, assessment of relationship cognitions should emphasize the following questions:

1. Do partners demonstrate an ability to accurately observe and report both positive and negative relationship events? For example, partners' descriptions and interpretations of couple interactions observed directly in therapy can be compared to the clinician's own assessment of these same exchanges. Partners' response-sets when completing self-report relationship measures can also be assessed; for example, the Conventionalization (CNV) scale on the MSI-R (Snyder, 1997) assesses the tendency to distort relationship appraisals in an overly positive direction.

2. What interpretation or meaning do partners impart to relationship events? Clinical interviews are particularly useful for eliciting partners' subjective interpretations of their own and each other's behaviors; such interpretations and attributions also frequently are expressed during conflict-resolution or other interactional tasks. To what extent are partners' negative relationship behaviors attributed to stable, negative aspects of the partner versus external or transient events? Self-report measures assessing relationship attributions include the Relationship Attribution Measure (RAM; Fincham & Bradbury, 1992).

3. What beliefs and expectancies do partners hold regarding both their own and the other person's ability and willingness to change in a manner anticipated to be helpful to their relationship? What standards do they hold for relationships generally?

Relationship Affect

Similar to findings regarding behavior exchange, research indicates that distressed couples are distinguished from nondistressed couples by higher overall rates, duration, and reciprocity of negative relationship affect and, to a lesser extent, by lower rates of positive relationship affect. Nondistressed couples show *less reciprocity* of positive affect, reflecting partners' willingness or ability to express positive sentiment spontaneously independent of their partner's affect (Gottman, 1999). By contrast, partners' influence on each other's negative affect has been reported for both proximal and distal outcomes. For example, Pasch, Bradbury, and Davila (1997) found that partners' negative mood prior to discussion of a personal issue predicted lower levels of emotional support they provided to the other

during their exchange. From a longitudinal perspective, couples who divorce are distinguished from those who remain married by partners' initial levels of negative affect and by a stronger linkage of initial negativity to the other person's negative affect over time (Cook et al., 1995). Gottman (1999) determined that the single best predictor of couples' eventual divorce was the amount of contempt partners expressed in videotaped interactions. Hence, assessment of couple distress should evaluate the following:

1. To what extent do partners express and reciprocate negative and positive feelings about their relationship and toward each other? Partners' reciprocity of affect is best evaluated using either structured or unstructured interactions and coded (either formally or informally) using one of the behavioral observation systems described later in this section. Although much of the couple literature emphasizes negative emotions, positive emotions such as smiling, laughter, expressions of appreciation or respect, comfort or soothing, and similar expressions are equally important to assess through observation or clinical inquiry.

2. What ability does each partner have to express his or her feelings in a modulated manner? Problems with emotion self-regulation may be observed either in overcontrol of emotions (e.g., an inability to access, label, or express either positive or negative feelings) or in undercontrol of emotions (e.g., the rapid escalation of anger into intense negativity approaching rage, progression of tearfulness into sobbing, or deterioration in quality of thought secondary to emotional overload). Unregulated negativity culminating in either verbal or physical aggression can be assessed through self- or partner report using either the original or revised versions of the Conflict Tactics Scale (CTS/CTS2; Straus, 1979; Straus, Hamby, Boney-McCoy, & Sugarman, 1996).

3. To what extent does partners' negative affect generalize across occasions? Generalization of negative affect, or "negative sentiment override" (Weiss, 1980), can be observed in partners' inability to shift from negative to either neutral or positive affect during the interview or in interactional tasks, or in reports of distress across most or all domains of relationship functioning assessed using self-report. In research applications, ratings of affect by partners observing their videotaped interactions may provide an additional means of assessing sentiment override. For example, in a study of the effects of relationship sentiment override on couples' perceptions, partners used an affect-rating dial to indicate how positively

or negatively they felt during a previously video-taped interaction and how they thought their partner felt during the interaction (Hawkins, Carrère, & Gottman, 2002).

Comorbid Individual Distress

As noted earlier when discussing comorbid conditions, there is growing evidence that relationship difficulties covary with, contribute to, and result from individual emotional and behavioral disorders (Snyder & Whisman, 2003). Both clinician reports and treatment outcome studies suggest that individual difficulties render couple therapy more difficult or less effective (Allgood & Crane, 1991; Northey, 2002; Sher, Baucom, & Larus, 1990; Snyder, Mangrum, & Wills, 1993; Whisman, Dixon, & Johnson, 1997). Hence, when evaluating couple distress, additional attention should be given to disorders of individual emotional or behavioral functioning to address the extent to which either partner exhibits individual emotional or behavioral difficulties potentially contributing to, exacerbating, or resulting in part from couple distress. Given the association of couple distress with affective disorders and alcohol use, initial interviews of couples should include questions regarding suicidality and alcohol or other substance use—as well as brief screening for previous treatment of emotional or behavioral disorders.

When clinical interview suggests potential interaction of relationship and individual dysfunction, focused and brief measures (e.g., the Beck Depression Inventory-II [BDI-II]; Beck, Steer, & Brown, 1996, or the Symptom Checklist-90-Revised [SCL-90-R]; Derogatis & Savitz, 1999) should be considered. It is equally important to assess couples' strengths and resources across intrapersonal, relationship, and broader social system levels. These include partners' ability to limit the impact of individual or couple dysfunction despite overwhelming stressors, or containing the generalization of distress to other family members.

Finally, establishing the direction and strength of causal relations among individual and relationship disorders, as well as their linkage to situational stressors or buffers, is crucial for determining both the content and sequencing of clinical interventions. In many cases, such functional relations are reciprocal—supporting interventions at either end of the causal chain.

Cultural Differences in Couple Distress

Consistent with our conceptual framework, cultural differences in the development, subjective experience, overt expression, and treatment of couple distress are critical to evaluate. By this we refer not only to cross-national differences in couples' relationships, but also to cross-cultural differences within nationality and consideration of nontraditional relationships including gay and lesbian couples. There are important differences among couples as a function of their culture, religious orientation, economic level, and age. These dimensions can affect the importance of the couple relationship to a partner's quality of life, their expectancies regarding marital and parenting roles, typical patterns of verbal and nonverbal communication and decision-making within the family, the behaviors that are considered distressing, sources of relationship conflict, the type of external stressors faced by a family, and the ways that partners respond to couple distress and divorce (e.g., Diener, Gohm, Suh, & Oishi, 2000; Gohm, Oishi, Darlington, & Diener, 1998; Jones & Chao, 1997). For example, Haynes et al. (1992) found that parenting, extended family, and sex were less strongly related to marital satisfaction whereas health of the spouse and other forms of affection were more important factors in marital satisfaction in older (i.e., over 55 years) compared to younger couples. Similarly, Bhugra and De Silva (2000) suggested that relationships with extended family members might be more important in some cultures. Also, when partners are from different cultures, cultural differences and conflicts can be a source of relationship dissatisfaction (e.g., Baltas & Steptoe, 2000). An important implication of such findings is that measures shown to be valid for one population may be less so for another.

Assessment Strategies and Specific Techniques for Evaluating Couple Distress

Assessment strategies for evaluating relationships vary across the clinical interview, observational methods, and self- and other-report measures. In the sections that follow, we discuss empirically supported techniques within each of these assessment strategies. Although specific techniques within any method could target diverse facets of individual, dyadic, or broader system functioning, we emphasize those more commonly used when assessing couple distress.

The Clinical Interview

The pretreatment clinical interview is the first step in assessing couples. It can aid in identifying a couple's behavior problems and strengths, help specify a couple's treatment goals, and be used to acquire data that are useful for treatment outcome evaluation. The assessment interview can also serve to strengthen the client–clinician relationship, identify barriers to treatment, and increase the chance that the couple will participate in subsequent assessment and treatment tasks. Furthermore, it is the primary means of gaining a couple's informed consent about the assessment–treatment process. Data from initial assessment interviews also guide the clinician's decisions about which additional assessment strategies may be most useful; for example, Gordis, Margolin, and John (2001) used an interview to select topics for discussion during an analog behavioral observation of couple communication patterns. Perhaps most importantly, the assessment interview can provide a rich source of hypotheses about factors that may contribute to the couple's distress. These hypotheses contribute to the case formulation which, in turn, affects decisions about the best treatment strategy for a particular couple.

The interview can also be used to gather information on multiple levels, in multiple domains, and across multiple response modes in couple assessment. It can provide information on the specific behavioral interactions of the couple, including behavioral exchanges and violence; problem-solving skills, sources of disagreement, areas of satisfaction and dissatisfaction, each partner's thoughts, beliefs, and attitudes; and their feelings and emotions regarding the partner and relationship. The couple assessment interview can also provide information on cultural and family system factors and other events that might affect the couple's functioning and response to treatment. These factors might include interactions with extended family members, other relationship problems within the nuclear family (e.g., between parents and children), economic stressors, and health challenges. The initial assessment interview can also provide information on potentially important causal variables for couple distress at an individual level, such as a partner's substance use, mood disorder, or problematic personality traits.

Moreover, the clinical interview can be especially useful in identifying *functional relations* that may account for relationship difficulties. The functional relations of greatest interest in couple assessment are those that are relevant to problem behaviors, feelings, and relationship enhancement. Identifying functional relations allows the assessor to hypothesize about "why" a partner is unhappy or what behavioral sequences lead to angry exchanges. Clinicians are interested, for example, in finding out what triggers a couple's arguments and what communication patterns lead to their escalation. What does one partner do, or not do, that leads to the other partner to feel unappreciated or angry?

In the previous section on screening and diagnosis, we identified a brief structured interview for identifying overall relationship distress and partner aggression. Various formats for organizing and conducting more extensive assessment interviews with couples have been proposed (cf., Epstein & Baucom, 2002; Gottman, 1999; Karpel, 1994; L'Abate, 1994; Snyder & Abbott, 2002). For example, Karpel (1994) suggested a four-part evaluation that includes an initial meeting with the couple together, followed by separate sessions with each partner individually, and then an additional conjoint meeting with the couple. Snyder and Abbott (2002) recommended an extended initial assessment interview lasting about 2 hours in which the following goals are stated at the outset: (a) first getting to know each partner as an individual separate from the marriage; (b) understanding the structure and organization of the marriage; (c) learning about current relationship difficulties, their development, and previous efforts to address these; and (d) reaching an informed decision together about whether to proceed with couple therapy and, if so, discussing respective expectations.

However, none of the comprehensive interview structures proposed for couples has been subjected to the rigorous development and psychometric evaluation that have characterized other couple assessment methods such as self-report questionnaires or behavioral observation techniques. Moreover, the limited research on couple-based interviews has shown lower rates of endorsement for sensitive or socially undesirable behaviors (e.g., infidelity) when assessed by interview in comparison to alternative self-report methods (Whisman & Snyder, 2007).

The clinical literature reflects considerable divergence on the issue of whether initial assessment of couple distress should be conducted with partners conjointly or should also include individual interviews with partners separately. Arguments for the latter include considerations of both veridicality and safety—particularly when assessing such sensitive issues as partner violence, substance abuse, or sexual interactions (Haynes, Jensen, Wise, & Sherman, 1981). Research indicates that couples experiencing domestic violence often do not disclose a partner's violent behavior in early interviews due to embarrassment, minimization, or fear of retribution (Ehrensaft & Vivian, 1996). Moreover, risks of retaliatory aggression against one partner by disclosing the other's violence in conjoint interview argue for the importance of conducting inquiries concerning partner violence in individual interviews.

Arguments against individual interviews when assessing couple distress emphasize potential difficulties in conjoint therapy if one partner has disclosed information to the therapist about which the other partner remains uninformed. Of particular concern are disclosures regarding partner violence (Aldarondo & Straus, 1994; Rathus & Feindler, 2004) and sexual infidelity (Snyder & Doss, 2005; Whisman & Wagers, 2005). Hence, if separate interviews are conducted with partners as a prelude to conjoint couple therapy, the interviewing clinician needs to be explicit with both partners ahead of time regarding conditions under which information disclosed by one partner will be shared with the other, and any criteria for selecting among individual, conjoint, or alternative treatment modalities.

Observational Methods

As noted previously in this chapter, couple assessment offers the unique opportunity to observe partners' complaints involving communication and other interpersonal exchanges directly. Like interviews and self-report methods, analog behavioral observation (ABO) describes a method of data collection; specifically, it involves a situation designed, manipulated, or constrained by a clinician that elicits both verbal and nonverbal behaviors of interest such as motor actions, verbalized attributions, and observable facial reactions (Heyman & Slep, 2004, p. 162). We earlier identified both the RMICS and RCISS as rapid observational methods particularly useful for initial screening and diagnosis of couple distress. Detailed descriptions and psychometric reviews of additional couple coding systems have been published previously (cf., Heyman, 2001; Kerig & Baucom, 2004). Although these systems vary widely, in general they reflect six major a priori classes of targeted behaviors:

1. Affect (e.g., humor, affection, anger, criticism, contempt, sadness, anxiety). Examples include the Behavioral Affective Rating System (BARS; Johnson, 2002) and the Specific Affect Coding System (SPAFF; Gottman, McCoy, Coan, & Collier, 1996; Shapiro & Gottman, 2004).
2. Behavioral engagement (e.g., demands, pressures for change, withdrawal, avoidance). An example is the Conflict Rating System (CRS; Heavey, Christensen, & Malamuth, 1995).
3. General communication skills (e.g., involvement, verbal and nonverbal negativity and positivity, information and problem description). Examples include the Clinician Rating of Adult Communication (CRAC; Basco, Birchler, Kalal, Talbott, & Slater, 1991), the Interactional Dimensions Coding System (IDCS; Kline et al., 2004), and the Kategoriensystem für Partnerschaftliche Interaktion (KPI; Hahlweg, 2004).
4. Problem-solving (e.g., self-disclosure, validation, facilitation, interruption). Examples include the Codebook of Marital and Family Interaction (COMFI; Notarius, Pellegrini, & Martin, 1991), the Communication Skills Test (CST; Floyd, 2004), the Dyadic Interaction Scoring Code (DISC; Filsinger, 1983), the Living in Family Environments (LIFE) coding system (Hops, Davis, & Longoria, 1995), and the Verbal Tactics Coding Scheme (VTCS; Sillars, 1982).
5. Power (e.g., verbal aggression, coercion, attempts to control). An example is the System for Coding Interactions in Dyads (SCID; Malik & Lindahl, 2004).
6. Support/intimacy (e.g., emotional and tangible support, attentiveness). An example is the Social Support Interaction Coding System (SSICS; Pasch, Harris, Sullivan, & Bradbury, 2004).

Psychometric characteristics for the 15 couple coding systems summarized in Tables 20.2–20.4 indicate considerable variability in the extent to which information regarding reliability, validity, and treatment sensitivity for each system has been accrued. For example, only 3 of 15 coding systems report data concerning internal consistency—although this likely reflects systems' emphasis on specific behaviors rather than broader constructs. When superordinate classes of behavior (e.g., positive or negative) are of interest, internal consistency should be evaluated by using either Cronbach's alpha or indices derived from factor analysis (Heyman, Eddy, Weiss, & Vivian,

TABLE 20.4 Ratings of Instruments Used for Treatment Monitoring and Treatment Outcome Evaluation

Instrument	Norms	Internal Consistency	Inter-Rater Reliability	Test–Retest Reliability	Content Validity	Construct Validity	Validity Generalization	Treatment Sensitivity	Clinical Utility	Highly Recommended
KMSS	A	G	U	A	G	U	A	A	G	
DAS	A	G	NA	G	A	A	G	G	A	✓
MSI-R	E	G	NA	G	E	E	G	G	E	✓
RMICS	E	E	A	U	A	G	G	A	A	✓
GAS	NA	A	NA	U	G	G	U	A	A	

Note: KMSS = Kansas Marital Satisfaction Scale; DAS = Dyadic Adjustment Scale; MSI-R = Marital Satisfaction Inventory-Revised; RMICS = Rapid Marital Interaction Coding System; GAS = Goal Attainment Scaling; A = Adequate; G = Good; E = Excellent; U = Unavailable; NA = Not applicable.

1995). Stable estimates of behavioral frequencies may require extended observation depending on the base-rate of their occurrence—for example, as few as 2 minutes for frequent behaviors, but 30 minutes or longer for infrequent behaviors (Heyman et al., 2001). Inter-rater reliability for nearly all coding systems reviewed here was adequate or better following coder training—although the more comprehensive or complicated the system, the more difficult it is to obtain high inter-rater reliability. Few studies have been conducted on the temporal stability of observed couple behaviors across tasks or settings. However, the limited evidence suggests that couples' interactions likely vary across topic (e.g., high- vs. low-conflict), setting (e.g., home vs. clinic or research laboratory), and length of marriage (with longer married couples exhibiting more enduring patterns; Gottman & Levenson, 1999; Lord, 1999; Wieder & Weiss, 1980).

Although varying in their emphasis, each of the couple coding systems reviewed here clearly assesses constructs related to communication and other domains of partner interaction relevant to relationship functioning and couple distress. Many of the coding systems can trace their origins to the Family Interaction Coding System (Patterson, Ray, Shaw, & Cobb, 1969; Reid, 1978) that was developed from naturalistic observations of family members' behaviors in the home. Nearly all coding systems have accrued evidence of discriminative validity and relatedness to independent measures of similar constructs, and only the most recently developed systems have yet to accrue evidence of validity generalization. Pre and posttreatment data for couple behavioral coding systems are limited, in part because of fewer funded clinical trials of couple therapy during recent years in which these systems were developed. However, the Marital Interaction Coding System (MICS) and Couples Interaction Scoring System (CISS) have evidence of

treatment sensitivity; it is reasonable to infer that their quicker versions (RMICS and RCISS) and coding systems that measure similar constructs (i.e., most of the communication-oriented systems) would demonstrate similar levels of treatment sensitivity.

Concerns have been raised about the clinical utility of analog behavioral observations (e.g., Mash & Foster, 2001), because nearly all coding systems require extensive observer training to reach adequate levels of inter-observer agreement. Even after observers are certified as reliable, a great deal of energy is required to maintain reliability (e.g., weekly meetings with regular feedback on agreement). Thus, even if clinicians expended a great deal of time learning a system to the point of mastery (i.e., meeting the reliability criterion), their reliability would naturally decay without ongoing efforts to maintain agreement. Such a requirement is likely not reasonable for most clinicians.

However, even if not striving to code behavioral observations in the manner required for scientific study of couple interactions, the empirically informed use of behavioral observations should be standard in clinicians' assessment of couple distress. That is, collecting communication samples is an important part of couple clinical assessment because "communication is the common pathway to relationship dysfunction because it is the common pathway for getting what you want in relationships. Nearly all relationship-relevant conflicts, emotions, and neuroses are played out via observable communication—either verbally or nonverbally" (Heyman, 2001, p. 6).

If questionnaire or interview assessments suggest that an interactive task may place one or both partners in danger (e.g., if there is a history of serious physical or emotional abuse, indications of severe power or control dynamics, or threats conveyed to the assessor), analog behavioral observation would be contraindicated. However, if it seems reasonable that it is safe to proceed, then the clinician should hypothesize which classes of behaviors seem most highly connected to the target problems. Wherever possible, analog behavioral observations should be video-recorded so that the sample can be reviewed later with an eye toward a class of behaviors other than what was the assessor's primary focus during the *in vivo* ABO. Furthermore, unless the clinician can rule out a plausible connection between conflict communication and the couple's problems, we recommend that a conflict communication ABO be collected. Based on findings from observational research with couples, Heyman (2001) suggested that clinicians use behavioral observations in assessing couple distress to address the following:

1. How does the conversation start? Does the level of anger escalate? What happens when it does? Does the couple enter repetitive negative loops?
2. Do partners indicate afterward that what occurred during the conversations is typical? Is their behavior stable across two or more discussions?
3. Do partners' behaviors differ when it is her topic versus his? Do they label the other person or the communication process as the problem?
4. What other communication behaviors—either positive (e.g., support, empathic reflection) or negative (e.g., criticism, sneers, turning away)—appear functionally related to partners' ability to discuss relationship issues effectively?

Self- and Other-Report Methods

The rationale underlying self-report methods in couple assessment is that such methods (a) are convenient and relatively easy to administer, (b) are capable of generating a wealth of information across a broad range of domains and levels of functioning germane to clinical assessment or research objectives including those listed in Table 20.1, (c) lend themselves to collection of data from large normative samples which can serve as a reference for interpreting data from individual respondents, (d) allow disclosure about events and subjective experiences respondents may be reluctant to discuss with an interviewer or in the presence of their partner, and (e) can provide important data concerning internal phenomena opaque to observational approaches including thoughts and feelings, values and attitudes, expectations and attributions, and satisfaction and commitment.

However, the limitations of traditional self-report measures also bear noting. Specifically, data from self-report instruments can (a) reflect bias in self- and other-presentation in either a favorable or unfavorable direction, (b) be affected by differences in stimulus interpretation and errors in recollection of objective events, (c) inadvertently influence respondents' nontest behavior in unintended ways, and (d) typically provide few fine-grained details concerning moment-to-moment interactions compared to analog behavioral observations. Because of their potential advantages and despite their limitations, self-report techniques of couple and family functioning have proliferated—with published measures numbering well over 1000 (Touliatos, Perlmutter, Straus, & Holden, 2001). However, relatively few of these measures have achieved widespread adoption. Chun, Cobb, and, French (1975) found that 63% of measures they reviewed had been used only once, with only 3% being used 10 times or more. Fewer than 40% of marital and family therapists regularly use *any* standardized instruments (Boughner, Hayes, Bubenzer, & West, 1994). Contributing to these findings is the inescapable conclusion that the majority of measures in this domain demonstrate little evidence regarding the most rudimentary psychometric features of reliability or validity, let alone clear evidence supporting their clinical utility (Snyder & Rice, 1996).

We describe below, and summarize in Table 20.3, a small subset of self-report instruments selected on the basis of their potential clinical utility and at least moderate evidence of their reliability and validity. In some domains (e.g., relationship cognitions and affect), well-validated measures are few. Additional measures identified in previous reviews (cf., Epstein & Baucom, 2002; Sayers & Sarwer, 1998; Snyder, Heyman, & Haynes, 2005) or in comprehensive bibliographies of self-report couple and family measures (e.g., Corcoran & Fischer, 2000; Davis, Yarber, Bauserman, Schreer, & Davis, 1998; Fredman & Sherman, 1987; Grotevant & Carlson, 1989; Jacob & Tennenbaum, 1988; L'Abate & Bagarozzi, 1993; Touliatos et al., 2001) may be considered as additional clinical resources; however, the data they generate should generally be regarded as similar to other self-reports derived from interview—namely, as subject to various biases of observation, recollection, interpretation, and motivations to present oneself or one's partner in a favorable or unfavorable light.

A variety of self-report measures has been developed to assess couples' behavioral exchanges including communication, verbal and physical aggression, and physical intimacy. The Frequency and Acceptability of Partner Behavior Inventory (FAPBI; Doss & Christensen, 2006) assesses 20 positive and negative behaviors in 4 domains (affection, closeness, demands, and relationship violations) and possesses excellent psychometric characteristics. As a clinical tool, the FAPBI has the potential to delineate relative strengths and weaknesses in the relationship—transforming diffuse negative complaints into specific requests for positive change.

Among self-report measures specifically targeting partners' communication, one that demonstrates good reliability and validity is the Communication Patterns Questionnaire (CPQ; Christensen, 1987). The CPQ was designed to measure the temporal sequence of couples' interactions by soliciting partners' perceptions of their communication patterns before, during, and following conflict. Scores on the CPQ can be used to assess characteristics of the demand $\rightarrow$ withdraw pattern frequently observed among distressed couples.

Assessing relationship aggression by self-report measures assumes particular importance because of some individuals' reluctance to disclose the nature or extent of such aggression during an initial conjoint interview. By far the most widely used measure of couples' aggression is the Conflict Tactics Scale (CTS). The original CTS (Straus, 1979) included 19 items assessing three modes of conflict resolution including reasoning, verbal aggression, and physical aggression. The revised instrument (CTS2; Straus, Hamby, Boney-McCoy, & Sugarman, 1996) adds scales of sexual coercion and physical injury as well as additional items to better differentiate between minor and severe levels of verbal and physical aggression. An additional measure of relationship aggression, the Aggression (AGG) scale of the Marital Satisfaction Inventory-Revised (MSI-R; Snyder, 1997), comprises 10 items reflecting psychological and physical aggression experienced from one's partner. Advantages of the AGG scale as a screening measure include its relative brevity and its inclusion in a multidimensional measure of couples' relationships (the MSI-R) described below.

Earlier we noted the importance of evaluating partners' attributions for relationship events. The Relationship Attribution Measure (RAM; Fincham & Bradbury, 1992) presents hypothetical situations and asks respondents to generate responsibility attributions indicating the extent to which the partner intentionally behaved negatively, was selfishly motivated, and was blameworthy for the event. Both causal and responsibility attributions assessed by the RAM have evidence of good internal consistency and test–retest reliability, as well as convergence with partners' self-reported overall relationship satisfaction and observed affect.

For purposes of case conceptualization and treatment planning, well-constructed multidimensional measures of couple functioning are useful for discriminating among various sources of relationship strength, conflict, satisfaction, and goals. Widely used in both clinical and research settings is the MSI-R-(Snyder, 1997), a 150-item inventory designed to identify both the nature and intensity of relationship distress in distinct areas of interaction. The MSI-R includes two validity scales, one global scale, and ten specific scales assessing relationship satisfaction in such areas as affective and problem-solving communication, aggression, leisure time together, finances, the sexual relationship, role orientation, family of origin, and interactions regarding children. More than 20 years of research have supported the reliability and construct validity of the MSI-R scales (cf., Snyder & Aikman, 1999). The instrument boasts a large representative national sample, good internal consistency and test–retest reliability, and excellent sensitivity to treatment change. The Global Distress Subscale (GDS) of the MSI-R has been shown to predict couples' likelihood of divorce 4 years following therapy (Snyder, 1997). A validation study using a national sample of 60 marital therapists supported the overall accuracy and clinical utility of the computerized interpretive report for this instrument (Hoover & Snyder, 1991). Recent studies suggest the potential utility of Spanish and German adaptations of the MSI-R for cross-cultural application with both clinic and community couples (Snyder et al., 2004), as well as use of the original English version with nontraditional (e.g., gay and lesbian) couples (Means-Christensen, Snyder, & Negy, 2003).

Additional multidimensional measures obtaining fairly widespread use are the PREPARE and ENRICH inventories (Fowers & Olson, 1989, 1992; Olson & Olson, 1999), developed for use with premarital and married couples, respectively. Both of these measures include 165 items in 20 domains reflecting personality (e.g., assertiveness, self-confidence), intrapersonal issues (e.g., marriage expectations, spiritual beliefs), interpersonal issues (e.g., communication, closeness), and external issues (e.g., family and friends). A computerized interpretive report identifies areas of "strength" and "potential growth" and directs respondents to specific items reflecting potential concerns. The ENRICH inventory has a good normative sample and has ample evidence supporting both its reliability and validity.

Overall Evaluation

Couples presenting for therapy vary widely in both the content and underlying causes of their individual and relationship problems. Conceptualizing partners' distress and planning effective treatment requires careful assessment of behavioral, cognitive, and affective components of relationship functioning conducted across multiple modalities including interview, analog behavioral observation, and self-report measures. Effective intervention depends upon assimilating assessment findings within an overarching theoretical framework linking individual and relationship difficulties to presumed etiologies as well as to clinical intervention. Toward this end, assessment of couple distress requires going beyond nomothetic conclusions derived from standardized measures of relationship functioning to integrate idiographic findings from clinical interview and behavioral observation in a functional-analytic approach (Floyd et al., 1997; Haynes et al., 1997).

ASSESSMENT FOR TREATMENT MONITORING AND TREATMENT OUTCOME

In principle, assessment strategies relevant to case conceptualization and treatment planning are also germane to monitoring treatment progress and evaluating outcome. It would be difficult to imagine adequate assessment of partners' changes in individual and relationship functioning *not* including clinical inquiry about alterations in behavioral, cognitive, and affective domains outside of treatment sessions; repeated analog behavioral observations to track the acquisition and use of targeted communication skills; and integration of self-report measures profiling changes across diverse domains and providing information in sensitive areas.

Several caveats moderate this general conclusion. First, the use of repeated assessments to evaluate changes attributable to treatment requires measures demonstrating temporal reliability in the absence of clinical intervention. Although obvious as a precondition for interpreting change, information regarding the temporal reliability of couple-based assessment techniques is remarkably sparse. Second, treatment effects are best assessed by using measures both relevant and specific to aspects of individual and relationship functioning targeted by clinical interventions. Finally, treatment monitoring across sessions imposes pragmatic constraints on measures' length, thus suggesting enhanced utility for reliable and valid measures distinguished by their brevity (e.g., the KMSS as a measure of global affect or the FAPBI to assess more specific dyadic behaviors). Table 20.4 provides ratings on several relevant instruments.

Changes in individualized treatment goals can be quantified using *goal attainment scaling* (GAS; Kiresuk, Smith, & Cardilo, 1994) as described previously for use in couple therapy by Whisman and Snyder (1997). When adopting the GAS method, the issues that will be the focus of treatment are first identified, and then each problem is translated into one or more goals. The expected level of outcome is then specified for each goal, along with the "somewhat more" and "much more" than expected levels of outcome, as well as the "somewhat less" and "much less" expected levels. Each level of outcome is assigned a value on a 5-point measurement scale ranging from –2 for much less than expected level of outcome, to +2 for much more than expected level of outcome. Levels of outcome can then be rated during or following treatment, and the ratings across goals can be averaged to provide a summary score for evaluating the degree to which treatment helped the couple attain their own individualized goals.

Overall Evaluation

Gains or deterioration in individual and relationship functioning should be evaluated using techniques sensitive and specific to treatment effects across assessment modalities incorporating interview, behavioral observation, and self-report methods. Conclusions drawn from nomothetic approaches (such as the DAS or MSI-R) should be complemented by idiographic methods, ideally incorporating observational assessment as well as goal attainment scaling or similar procedures.

CONCLUSIONS AND FUTURE DIRECTIONS

Recommendations for Assessing Couple Distress

Assessment strategies and specific methods for assessing couple distress will necessarily be tailored to partners' unique constellation of presenting difficulties, as well as specific resources of both the couple and the clinician. However, regardless of the specific context, the following recommendations for assessing couple distress will generally apply.

1. Given empirical findings linking couple distress to individual disorders and their respective impact in moderating treatment outcome, assessment of couple functioning should be standard practice when treating individuals. Screening for couple distress when assessing individuals may involve a brief interview format shown to relate to relevant indicators of couple interactions (e.g., the SDI-MD-PA; Heyman et al., 2001) or a brief self-report measure exhibiting prior evidence of discriminative validity (e.g., the KMSS or short-form DAS). Similarly, when treating couples, partners should be screened for individual emotional or behavioral difficulties potentially contributing to, exacerbating, or resulting in part from couple distress.

2. Assessment foci should progress from broad to narrow—first identifying relationship concerns at the broader construct level and then examining more specific facets of couple distress and its correlates using a finer-grained analysis. The specific assessment methods described in this review vary considerably in their overall breadth or focus within any specific construct domain and, hence, will vary both in their applicability across couples and their placement in a sequential exploratory assessment process.

3. Within clinical settings, certain domains should always be assessed with every couple either because of their robust linkage to relationship difficulties (e.g., communication processes involving emotional expressiveness and decision-making) or because the specific behaviors, if present, have particularly adverse impact on couple functioning (e.g., physical aggression or substance abuse).

4. Couple assessment should integrate findings across multiple assessment methods. Self- and other-report measures may complement findings from interview or behavioral observation in generating data across diverse domains both central or conceptually related to the couple's difficulties, or across those domains potentially more challenging to assess because of their sensitive nature or their not being amenable to direct observation. However, special caution should be exercised when adopting self- or other-report measures in assessing couple distress. Despite their proliferation, most measures of couple functioning described in the literature have not undergone careful scrutiny of their underlying psychometric features. Among those instruments for which some evidence concerning reliability and validity has been garnered, evidence often exists only for overall scores and not at the level of subscales or smaller units of analysis at which interpretations may be made.

5. At the same time, assessment of couple distress should be parsimonious. This objective can be facilitated by choosing evaluation strategies and modalities that complement each other and by following a sequential approach that uses increasingly narrowband measures to target problem areas that have been identified by other assessment techniques.

6. Psychometric characteristics of any assessment technique—whether from interview, analog behavioral observation, or self-report measure—are conditional upon the specific population and purpose for which that assessment method was developed. Given that nearly all measures of couple distress were developed and tested on white, middle-class, married couples, their relevance to and utility for assessing ethnic couples, gay and lesbian couples, and low-income couples is unknown. This caveat extends to content- as well as criterion-related validity. Hence, any assessment measure demonstrating evidence of validity with some couples may not be valid, in part or in whole, for any given couple, thus further underscoring the importance of drawing upon multiple indicators across multiple methods for assessing any specific construct.

Recommendations for Further Research

Future directions for assessment research germane to the field generally also apply to research in assessing couple distress specifically, including the need for greater attention to (a) psychometric underpinnings of various measurement methods and instruments, (b) factors moderating reliability and validity across populations differing in sociocultural characteristics as well as in clinical functioning, (c) the assessment process including initial articulation of assessment goals, selection of assessment method and instruments, and methods of interpreting data and providing feedback, and (d) the functional utility of assessment findings in enhancing treatment effectiveness (Hayes, Nelson, & Jarrett, 1987).

In considering the implications of these directives for assessing couple distress, considerably more research is needed before a comprehensive, empirically based couple assessment protocol can be advocated. For example, despite the ubiquitous use of couple assessment interviews, virtually no research has been conducted to assess their psychometric features. Observational methods, although a rich resource for generating and testing clinical hypotheses, are less frequently used and present significant challenges to their reliable and valid application in everyday practice. Questionnaires—despite their ease of administration and potential utility in generating a wealth of data—frequently suffer from inadequate empirical development and, at best, comprise only part of a multimethod assessment strategy.

We would recommend, as a research roadmap, that clinical researchers consider adapting the Institute of Medicine stages of intervention research cycle (Mrazek & Haggerty, 1994). Stage 1 involves identifying the disorder and measuring its prevalence. Despite being so basic a need, there currently exists no gold standard for discriminating distressed from nondistressed couples; the questionnaires typically used for such classifications are of limited sensitivity and specificity (Heyman et al., 2001). Stage 2 involves delineating specific risk and protective factors. As noted above, some replicated factors have been identified, although this research could be sharpened by defining groups more carefully (via Stage 1 above). Stage 3 (efficacy trials) would involve tightly controlled trials of the efficacy of a multimethod assessment in clinical practice. Stage 4 (effectiveness trials) would involve controlled trials of the outcome of this assessment in more real-world clinical environments. Only then would testing broad-scale dissemination (Stage 5) of empirically based couple assessment be appropriate.

This research roadmap reflects an ambitious agenda unlikely to be met by any single investigator or group of investigators. However, progress toward evidence-based assessment of couple distress will be enhanced by research on specific components targeting more notable gaps in the empirical literature along the lines recommended below.

1. Greater attention should be given to expanding the empirical support for promising assessment instruments already detailed in the literature than to the initial (and frequently truncated) development of new measures. Proposals for new measures should be accompanied by compelling evidence for their incremental utility and validity and a commitment to programmatic research examining their generalizability across diverse populations and assessment contexts.

2. Research needs to delineate optimal structured and semistructured interview formats for assessing couples. Such research should address (a) issues of content validity across populations and settings, (b) organizational strategies for screening across diverse system levels and construct domains relevant to couple functioning (similar to branching strategies for the Structured Clinical Interview for the DSM [First et al., 1997] and related structured interviews for individual disorders), (c) relative strengths and limitations to assessing partners separately versus conjointly, (d) factors promoting the disclosure and accuracy of verbal reports, (e) relation of interview findings to complementary assessment methods (as in generating relevant tasks for analog behavioral observation), and (f) the interview's special role in deriving functional-analytic case conceptualization.

3. Although laboratory-based behavioral observation of couple interaction has considerably advanced our understanding of couple distress, generalization of these techniques to more common clinical settings has lagged behind. Hence, researchers should develop more macro-level coding systems for quantifying observational data that promote their routine adoption in clinical contexts while preserving their psychometric fidelity.

4. Research needs to attend to the influences of culture at several levels. First, there has been little attention to developing measures directly assessing domains specific to relationship functioning at the community or cultural level (e.g., cultural standards or norms regarding emotional expressiveness, balance of decision-making influence, or boundaries governing the interaction of partners with extended family or others in the community). Hence, assessment of such constructs currently depends almost exclusively on the clinical interview, with no clear guidelines regarding either the content or format of questions. Second, considerably more research needs to examine the moderating effects of sociocultural factors on measures of couple functioning, including the impact of such factors as ethnicity, age, socioeconomic status, or sexual orientation. Third, work needs

to proceed on adapting established measures to alternative languages. In the United States, the failure to adapt existing instruments to Spanish or to examine the psychometric characteristics of extant adaptations is particularly striking given that (a) Hispanics are the largest and fastest-growing ethnic minority group, and (b) among U.S. Hispanic adults age 18 to 64, 28% have either limited or no ability to speak English (Snyder et al., 2004).

Adapting existing measures to alternative contexts (i.e., differing from the original development sample in language, culture, or specific aspects of the relationship such as sexual orientation) should proceed only when theoretical or clinical formulations suggest that the construct being measured does not differ substantially across the new application. Detailed discussions of both conceptual and methodological issues relevant to adapting tests to alternative languages or culture exist elsewhere (e.g., Butcher, 1996; Geisinger, 1994). Because clinicians and researchers may fail to recognize the inherent cultural biases of their conceptualization of couple processes, the appropriateness of using or adapting tests cross-culturally should be evaluated following careful empirical scrutiny examining each of the following:

- Linguistic equivalence including grammatical, lexical, and idiomatic considerations.
- Psychological equivalence of items across the source and target cultures.
- Functional equivalence indicating the congruence of external correlates in concurrent and predictive criterion-related validation studies of the measure across applications.
- Scalar equivalence ensuring not only that the slope of regression lines delineating test–criterion relations be parallel (indicating functional equivalence) but also that they have comparable metrics and origins (zero points) in both cultures.

Finally, research needs to examine the process, as well as the content, of couple assessment. For example, little is known regarding the impact of decisions about the timing or sequence of specific assessment methods, the role of the couple in determining assessment objectives, or the provision of clinical feedback on either the content of assessment findings or their subsequent effect on clinical interventions.

Although assessment of couples has shown dramatic gains in both its conceptual and empirical underpinnings over the past 25 years, much more remains to be discovered. Both clinicians and researchers need to avail themselves of recent advances in assessing couple distress and collaborate in promoting further development of empirically based assessment methods.

ACKNOWLEDGMENTS Portions of this chapter were adapted from Snyder, Heyman, and Haynes (2005). Richard Heyman's work on this chapter was supported by National Institute of Child Health and Human Development grant R01 HD046901-01. The authors express their appreciation to Brian Abbott, Danielle Provenzano, and Dawn Yoshioka for their contributions to Tables 20.1–20.4.

References

Aldarondo, E., & Straus, M. (1994). Screening for physical violence in couple therapy: Methodological, practical, and ethical considerations. *Family Process, 33,* 425–439.

Allgood, S. M., & Crane, D. R. (1991). Predicting marital therapy dropouts. *Journal of Marital and Family Therapy, 17,* 73–79.

American Psychiatric Association. (2000). *Diagnostic and statistical manual of mental disorders* (4th ed., text rev.). Washington, DC: Author.

Baltas, Z., & Steptoe, A. (2000). Migration, culture conflict and psychological well being among Turkish-British married couples. *Ethnicity & Health, 5,* 173–180.

Basco, M. R., Birchler, G. R., Kalal, B., Talbott, R., & Slater, A. (1991). The Clinician Rating of Adult Communication (CRAC): A clinician's guide to the assessment of interpersonal communication skill. *Journal of Clinical Psychology, 47,* 368–380.

Baucom, D. H., Epstein, N., & LaTaillade, J. J. (2002). Cognitive-behavioral couple therapy. In A. S. Gurman & N. S. Jacobson (Eds.), *Clinical handbook of couple therapy* (3rd ed., pp. 26–58). New York: Guilford Press.

Beck, A. T., Steer, R. A., & Brown, G. K. (1996). *Manual for the Beck Depression Inventory-II.* San Antonio, TX: Psychological Corporation.

Bhugra, D., & De Silva, P. (2000). Couple therapy across cultures. *Sexual & Relationship Therapy, 15,* 183–192.

Boughner, S. R., Hayes, S. F., Bubenzer, D. L., & West, J. D. (1994). Use of standardized assessment instruments by marital and family therapists: A survey. *Journal of Marital and Family Therapy, 20,* 69–75.

Bradbury, T. N., & Fincham, F. D. (1990). Attributions in marriage: Review and critique. *Psychological Bulletin, 107,* 3–33.

Bradbury, T. N., Rogge, R., & Lawrence, E. (2001). Reconsidering the role of conflict in marriage. In A. Booth, A. C. Crouter, & M. Clements (Eds.), *Couples in conflict* (pp. 59–81). Mahwah, NJ: Erlbaum.

Butcher, J. N. (1996). Translation and adaptation of the MMPI-2 for international use. In J. N. Butcher (Ed.), *International adaptations of the MMPI-2: A handbook of research and clinical applications* (pp. 26–43). Minneapolis, MN: University of Minnesota Press.

Christensen, A. (1987). Detection of conflict patterns in couples. In K. Hahlweg & M. J. Goldstein (Eds.), *Understanding major mental disorder: The contribution of family interaction research* (pp. 250–265). New York: Family Process Press.

Christensen, A., & Heavey, C. L. (1990). Gender and social structure in the demand/withdraw pattern of marital conflict. *Journal of Personality and Social Psychology, 59,* 73–81.

Chun, K., Cobb, S., & French, J. R. P. (1975). *Measures for psychological assessment: A guide to 3,000 original sources and their applications.* Ann Arbor, MI: University of Michigan, Survey Research Center of the Institute for Social Research.

Cone, J. D. (1988). Psychometric considerations and the multiple models of behavioral assessment. In A. S. Bellack & M. Hersen (Eds.), *Behavioral assessment: A practical handbook* (3rd ed., pp. 42–66). New York: Pergamon Press.

Cook, J., Tyson, R., White, J., Rushe, R., Gottman, J. M., & Murray, J. (1995). The mathematics of marital conflict: Qualitative dynamic mathematical modeling of marital interaction. *Journal of Family Psychology, 9,* 110–130.

Corcoran, K., & Fischer, J. (2000). *Measures for clinical practice: A sourcebook. Vol. 1. Couples, families, and children.* New York: Free Press.

Crane, D. R., Busby, D. M., & Larson, J. H. (1991). A factor analysis of the Dyadic Adjustment Scale with distressed and nondistressed couples. *American Journal of Family Therapy, 19,* 60–66.

Cutrona, C. (1996). *Social support in couples: Marriage as a resource in times of stress.* Thousand Oaks, CA: Sage.

Davis, C. M., Yarber, W. L., Bauserman, R., Schreer, G., & Davis, S. L. (1998). *Handbook of sexuality-related measures.* Thousand Oaks, CA: Sage.

Derogatis, L. R., & Savitz, K. L. (1999). The SCL-90-R, Brief Symptom Inventory, and matching clinical rating scales. In M. E. Maruish (Ed.), *The use of psychological testing for treatment planning and outcomes assessment* (2nd ed., pp. 679–724). Mahway, NJ: Erlbaum.

Diener, E., Gohm, C. L., Suh, E., & Oishi, S. (2000). Similarity of the relations between marital status and subjective well-being across cultures. *Journal of Cross-Cultural Psychology, 31,* 419–436.

Doss, B. D., & Christensen, A. (2006). Acceptance in romantic relationships: The frequency and acceptability of partner behavior inventory. *Psychological Assessment, 18,* 289–302.

Ehrensaft, M., & Vivian, D. (1996). Spouses' reasons for not reporting existing physical aggression as a marital problem. *Journal of Family Psychology, 10,* 443–453.

Epstein, N. B., & Baucom, D. H. (2002). *Enhanced cognitive-behavioral therapy for couples: A contextual approach.* Washington, DC: American Psychological Association.

Filsinger, E. E. (1983). A machine-aided marital observation technique: The dyadic interaction scoring code. *Journal of Marriage and the Family, 45,* 623–632.

Fincham, F. D., & Bradbury, T. N. (1987). The assessment of marital quality: A reevaluation. *Journal of Marriage and the Family, 49,* 797–809.

Fincham, F. D., & Bradbury, T. N. (1992). Assessing attributions in marriage: The relationship attribution measure. *Journal of Personality and Social Psychology, 62,* 457–468.

First, M. B., Bell, C. C., Cuthbert, B., Krystal, J. H., Malison, R., Offord, D. R., et al. (2002). Personality disorders and relational disorders: A research agenda for addressing crucial gaps in DSM. In D. J. Kupfer, M. B. First, & D. A. Regier (Eds.), *A research agenda for DSM-V* (pp. 123–199). Washington, DC: American Psychiatric Association.

First, M. B., Gibbon, M., Spitzer, R. L., & Williams, J. B. W. (1997). *Structured clinical interview for DSM-IV axis I disorders—Clinician version.* Washington, DC: American Psychiatric Association.

Floyd, F. J. (2004). Communication Skills Test (CST): Observational system for couples' problem-solving skills. In P. K. Kerig & D. H. Baucom (Eds.), *Couple observational coding systems* (pp. 143–158). Mahwah, NJ: Erlbaum.

Floyd, F. J., Haynes, S. N., & Kelly, S. (1997). Marital assessment: A dynamic and functional analytic perspective. In W. K. Halford & H. J. Markman (Eds.), *Clinical handbook of marriage and couples intervention* (pp. 349–378). New York: Guilford Press.

Fowers, B., & Olson, D. (1989). ENRICH marital inventory: A discriminant validity study. *Journal of Marital and Family Therapy, 15,* 65–79.

Fowers, B., & Olson, D. (1992). Four types of premarital couples: An empirical typology based on PREPARE. *Journal of Family Psychology, 6,* 10–12.

Fraenkel, P. (1997). Systems approaches to couple therapy. In W. K. Halford & H. J. Markman (Eds.), *Clinical handbook of marriage and couples interventions* (pp. 379–413). New York: John Wiley & Sons.

Fredman, N., & Sherman, R. (1987). *Handbook of measurements for marriage and family therapy.* New York: Brunner/Mazel.

Funk, J., & Rogge, R. (in press). Testing the ruler with item response theory: Increasing precision of measurement for relationship satisfaction with the Couples Satisfaction Index. *Journal of Family Psychology.*

Geisinger, K. F. (1994). Cross-cultural normative assessment: Translation and adaptation issues influencing the normative interpretation of assessment instruments. *Psychological Assessment, 6,* 304–312.

Geiss, S. K., & O'Leary, D. (1981). Therapist ratings of frequency and severity of marital problems: Implications for research. *Journal of Marital and Family Therapy, 7,* 515–520.

Gohm, C. L., Oishi, S., Darlington, J., & Diener, E. (1998). Culture, parental conflict, parental marital status, and the subjective well-being of young adults. *Journal of Marriage and the Family, 60,* 319–334.

Gordis, E. B., Margolin, G., & John, R. S. (2001). Parents' hostility in dyadic marital and triadic family settings and children's behavior problems. *Journal of Consulting and Clinical Psychology, 69,* 727–734.

Gottman, J. M. (1993). The roles of conflict engagement, escalation, and avoidance in marital interaction: A longitudinal view of five types of couples. *Journal of Consulting and Clinical Psychology, 61,* 6–15.

Gottman, J. M. (1994). *What predicts divorce? The relationship between marital processes and marital outcomes.* Hillsdale, NJ: Erlbaum.

Gottman, J. M. (1999). *The marriage clinic: A scientifically-based marital therapy.* New York: Norton.

Gottman, J. M., & Levenson, R. W. (1999). How stable is marital interaction over time? *Family Process, 38,* 159–165.

Gottman, J. M., McCoy, K., Coan, J., & Collier, H. (1996). The specific affect coding system (SPAFF). In J. M. Gottman (Ed.), *What predicts divorce? The measures* (pp. 1–169). Hillsdale, NJ: Erlbaum.

Grotevant, H. D., & Carlson, C. I. (1989). *Family assessment: A guide to methods and measures.* New York: Guilford.

Hahlweg, K. (2004). Kategoriensystem für Partnerschaftliche Interaktion (KPI): Interactional Coding System (ICS). In P. K. Kerig & D. H. Baucom (Eds.), *Couple observational coding systems* (pp. 127–142). Mahwah, NJ: Erlbaum.

Hawkins, M. W., Carrère, S., & Gottman, J. M. (2002). Marital sentiment override: Does it influence couples' perceptions? *Journal of Marriage and Family, 64,* 193–201.

Hayes, S. C., Nelson, R. O., & Jarrett, R. B. (1987). The treatment utility of assessment: A functional approach to evaluating assessment quality. *American Psychologist, 42,* 963–974.

Haynes, S. N., Floyd, F. J., Lemsky, C., Rogers, E., Winemiller, D., Heilman, N., et al. (1992). The Marital Satisfaction Questionnaire for older persons. *Psychological Assessment, 4,* 473–482.

Haynes, S. N., Jensen, B., Wise, E., & Sherman, D. (1981). The marital intake interview: A multimethod criterion validity evaluation. *Journal of Consulting and Clinical Psychology, 49,* 379–387.

Haynes, S. N., Leisen, M. B., & Blaine, D. D. (1997). Design of individualized behavioral treatment programs using functional analytic clinical case models. *Psychological Assessment, 9,* 334–348.

Haynes, S. N., & O'Brien, W. H. (2000). *Principles and practice of behavioral assessment.* New York: Kluwer.

Heavey, C. L., Christensen, A., & Malamuth, N. M. (1995). The longitudinal impact of demand and withdrawal during marital conflict. *Journal of Consulting and Clinical Psychology, 63,* 797–801.

Heyman, R. E. (2001). Observation of couple conflicts: Clinical assessment applications, stubborn truths, and shaky foundations. *Psychological Assessment, 13,* 5–35.

Heyman, R. E. (2004). Rapid Marital Interaction Coding System (RMICS). In P. K. Kerig & D. H. Baucom (Eds.), *Couple observational coding systems* (pp. 67–94). Mahwah, NJ: Erlbaum.

Heyman, R. E., Chaudhry, B. R., Treboux, D., Crowell, J., Lord, C., Vivian, D., et al. (2001). How much observational data is enough? An empirical test using marital interaction coding. *Behavior Therapy, 32,* 107–123.

Heyman, R. E., Eddy, J. M., Weiss, R. L., & Vivian, D. (1995). Factor analysis of the Marital Interaction Coding System (MICS). *Journal of Family Psychology, 9,* 209–215.

Heyman, R. E., Feldbau-Kohn, S. R., Ehrensaft, M. K., Langhinrichsen-Rohling, J., & O'Leary, K. D. (2001). Can questionnaire reports correctly classify relationship distress and partner physical abuse? *Journal of Family Psychology, 15,* 334–346.

Heyman, R. E., & Slep, A. M. S. (2004). Analogue behavioral observation. In E. M. Heiby & S. N. Haynes (Eds.), *Comprehensive handbook of psychological assessment: Vol. 3. Behavioral assessment* (pp. 162–180). New York: John Wiley & Sons.

Hoover, D. W., & Snyder, D. K. (1991). Validity of the computerized interpretive report for the Marital Satisfaction Inventory: A customer satisfaction study. *Psychological Assessment, 3,* 213–217.

Hops, H., Davis, B., & Longoria, N. (1995). Methodological issues in direct observation: Illustrations with the Living in Family Environments (LIFE) coding system. *Journal of Clinical Child Psychology, 24,* 193–203.

Hunsley, J., Best, M., Lefebvre, M., & Vito, D. (2001). The seven-item short form of the Dyadic Adjustment Scale: Further evidence for construct validity. *American Journal of Family Therapy, 29,* 325–335.

Jacob, T., & Tennenbaum, D. L. (1988). *Family assessment: Rationale, methods, and future directions.* New York: Plenum.

Jacobson, N. S., Schmaling, K. B., & Holtzworth-Munroe, A. (1987). Component analysis of behavioral marital therapy: 2-year follow-up and prediction of relapse. *Journal of Marital and Family Therapy, 13,* 187–195.

Johnson, M. D. (2002). The observation of specific affect in marital interactions: Psychometric properties of a coding system and a rating system. *Psychological Assessment, 14,* 423–438.

Jones, A. C., & Chao, C. M. (1997). Racial, ethnic and cultural issues in couples therapy. In W. K. Halford & H. J. Markman (Eds.), *Clinical handbook of marriage and couples interventions* (pp. 157–176). New York: John Wiley & Sons.

Karpel, M. A. (1994). *Evaluating couples: A handbook for practitioners.* New York: Norton.

Kerig, P. K., & Baucom, D. H. (Eds.) (2004). *Couple observational coding systems.* Mahwah, NJ: Erlbaum.

Kiecolt-Glaser, J. K., & Newton, T. L. (2001). Marriage and health: His and hers. *Psychological Bulletin, 12,* 472–503.

Kiresuk, T. J., Smith, A., & Cardillo, J. E. (Eds.). (1994). *Goal attainment scaling: Applications, theory, and measurement.* Hillsdale, NJ: Erlbaum.

Kline, G. H., Julien, D., Baucom, B., Hartman, S., Gilbert, K, Gonzalez, T., et al. (2004). The Interactional Dimensions Coding System (IDCS): A global system for couple interactions. In P. K. Kerig & D. H. Baucom (Eds.), *Couple observational coding systems* (pp. 113–126). Mahwah, NJ: Erlbaum.

Kreider, R. M., & Fields, J. M. (2002). Number, timing, and duration of marriages and divorces: 1996. *Current Population Reports P70–80.* Washington, DC: U. S. Census Bureau.

Krokoff, L. J., Gottman, J. M., & Hass, S. D. (1989). Validation of a global rapid couples interaction scoring system. *Behavioral Assessment, 11,* 65–79.

L'Abate, L. (1994). *Family evaluation: A psychological approach.* Thousand Oaks, CA: Sage.

L'Abate, L., & Bagarozzi, D. A. (1993). *Sourcebook of marriage and family evaluation.* New York: Brunner/Mazel.

Lin, E., Goering, P., Offord, D. R., Campbell, D., & Boyle, M. H. (1996). The use of mental health services in Ontario: Epidemiologic findings. *Canadian Journal of Psychiatry, 41,* 572–577.

Lord, C. C. (1999). *Stability and change in interactional behavior in early marriage.* Unpublished doctoral dissertation, State University of New York, Stony Brook, New York.

Malik, N. M., & Lindahl, K. M. (2004). System for Coding Interactions in Dyads. In P. K. Kerig & D. H. Baucom (Eds.), *Couple observational coding systems* (pp. 173–190). Mahwah, NJ: Erlbaum.

Mash, E. J., & Foster, S. L. (2001). Exporting analogue behavioral observation from research to clinical practice: Useful or cost-defective? *Psychological Assessment, 13,* 86–98.

Means-Christensen, A. J., Snyder, D. K., & Negy, C. (2003). Assessing nontraditional couples: Validity of the Marital Satisfaction Inventory-Revised (MSI-R) with gay, lesbian, and cohabiting heterosexual couples. *Journal of Marital and Family Therapy, 29,* 69–83.

Meyer, I. (2003). Prejudice, social stress, and mental health in lesbian, gay, and bisexual populations: Conceptual issues and research evidence. *Psychological Bulletin, 129,* 674–697.

Mrazek, P. J., & Haggerty, R. J. (Eds.). (1994). *Reducing risks for mental disorders: Frontiers for preventive intervention research.* Washington, DC: National Academy Press.

Northey, W. F., Jr. (2002). Characteristics and clinical practices of marriage and family therapists: A national Survey. *Journal of Marital and Family Therapy, 28,* 487–494.

Notarius, C. I., Pellegrini, D., & Martin, L. (1991). *Codebook of Marital and Family Interaction (COMFI).* Unpublished manuscript, Catholic University of America, Washington, DC.

Olson, D. H., & Olson, A. K. (1999). PREPARE/ENRICH program: Version 2000. In R. Berger & M. T. Hannah (Eds.), *Preventive approaches in couples therapy* (pp. 196–216). Philadelphia, PA: Brunner/Mazel.

Pasch, L. A., Bradbury, T. N., & Davila, J. (1997). Gender, negative affectivity, and observed social support behavior in marital interaction. *Personal Relationships, 4,* 361–378.

Pasch, L. A., Harris, K. W., Sullivan, K. T., & Bradbury, T. N. (2004). The social support interaction coding system. In P. K. Kerig & D. H. Baucom (Eds.), *Couple observational coding systems* (pp. 319–334). Mahwah, NJ: Erlbaum.

Patterson, G. R., Ray, R. S., Shaw, D. A., & Cobb, J. A. (1969). *Manual for coding of family interactions.* Unpublished coding manual. New York: Microfiche Publications.

Rathus, J. H., & Feindler, E. L. (2004). *Assessment of partner violence: A handbook for researchers and practitioners.* Washington, DC: American Psychological Association.

Reid, J. B. (Ed.). (1978). *A social learning approach, Vol. 2: Observation in home settings.* Eugene, OR: Castalia.

Sayers, S. L., Baucom, D. H., Sher, T. G., Weiss, R. L., & Heyman, R. E. (1991). Constructive engagement, behavioral marital therapy, and changes in marital satisfaction. *Behavioral Assessment, 13,* 25–49.

Sayers, S. L., & Sarwer, D. B. (1998). Assessment of marital dysfunction. In A. S. Bellack & M. Hersen (Eds.), *Behavioral assessment: A practical handbook* (4th ed., pp. 293–314). Boston, MA: Allyn and Bacon.

Schumm, W. R., Paff-Bergen, L. A., Hatch, R. C., Obiorah, F. C., Copeland, J. M., Meens, L. D., et al. (1986). Concurrent and discriminant validity of the Kansas Marital Satisfaction Scale. *Journal of Marriage and the Family, 48,* 381–387.

Shapiro, A. F., & Gottman, J. M. (2004). The Specific Affect Coding System (SPAFF). In P. K. Kerig & D. H. Baucom (Eds.), *Couple observational coding systems* (pp. 191–208). Mahwah, NJ: Erlbaum.

Sher, T. G., Baucom, D. H., & Larus, J. M. (1990). Communication patterns and response to treatment among depressed and nondepressed maritally distressed couples. *Journal of Family Psychology, 4,* 63–79.

Shumway, S. T., Wampler, R. S., Dersch, C., & Arredondo, R. (2004). A place for marriage and family services in employee assistance programs (EAPs): A survey of EAP client problems and needs. *Journal of Marital and Family Therapy, 30,* 71–79.

Sillars, A. L. (1982). *Verbal Tactics Coding Scheme: Coding manual.* Unpublished manuscript, Ohio State University, Columbus, OH.

Sillars, A., Roberts, L. J., Leonard, K. E., & Dun, T. (2000). Cognition during marital conflict: The relationship of thought and talk. *Journal of Social and Personal Relationships, 17,* 479–502.

Snyder, D. K. (1997). *Manual for the marital satisfaction inventory-revised.* Los Angeles, CA: Western Psychological Services.

Snyder, D. K., & Abbott, B. V. (2002). Couple distress. In M. M. Antony & D. H. Barlow (Eds.), *Handbook of assessment and treatment planning for psychological disorders* (pp. 341–374). New York: Guilford Press.

Snyder, D. K., & Aikman, G. G. (1999). The marital satisfaction inventory—revised. In M. E. Maruish (Ed.), *Use of psychological testing for treatment planning and outcomes assessment* (2nd ed., pp. 1173–1210). Mahwah, NJ: Erlbaum.

Snyder, D. K., Castellani, A. M., & Whisman, M. A. (2006). Current status and future directions in couple

therapy. *Annual Review of Clinical Psychology, 57,* 317–344.

Snyder, D. K., Cavell, T. A., Heffer, R. W., & Mangrum, L. F. (1995). Marital and family assessment: A multi-faceted, multilevel approach. In R. H. Mikesell, D. D. Lusterman, & S. H. McDaniel (Eds.), *Integrating family therapy: Handbook of family psychology and systems theory* (pp. 163–182). Washington, DC: American Psychological Association.

Snyder, D. K., Cepeda-Benito, A., Abbott, B. V., Gleaves, D. H., Negy, C., Hahlweg, K., et al. (2004). Cross-cultural applications of the Marital Satisfaction Inventory—Revised (MSI-R). In M. E. Maruish (Ed.), *Use of psychological testing for treatment planning and outcomes assessment* (3rd ed., pp. 603–623). Mahwah, NJ: Erlbaum.

Snyder, D. K., & Doss, B. D. (2005). Treating infidelity: Clinical and ethical directions. *Journal of Clinical Psychology, 61,* 1453–1465.

Snyder, D. K., Heyman, R. E., & Haynes, S. N. (2005). Evidence-based approaches to assessing couple distress. *Psychological Assessment, 17,* 288–307.

Snyder, D. K., Mangrum, L. F., & Wills, R. M. (1993). Predicting couples' response to marital therapy: A comparison of short- and long-term predictors. *Journal of Consulting and Clinical Psychology, 61,* 61–69.

Snyder, D. K., & Rice, J. L. (1996). Methodological issues and strategies in scale development. In D. H. Sprenkle & S. M. Moon (Eds.), *Research methods in family therapy* (pp. 216–237). New York: Guilford Press.

Snyder, D. K., & Whisman, M. A. (Eds.). (2003). *Treating difficult couples: Helping clients with coexisting mental and relationship disorders.* New York: Guilford Press.

Spanier, G. B. (1976). Measuring dyadic adjustment: New scales for assessing the quality of marriage and similar dyads. *Journal of Marriage and the Family, 38,* 15–28.

Straus, M. A. (1979). Measuring intrafamily conflict and violence: The Conflict Tactics (CT) scales. *Journal of Marriage and the Family, 41,* 75–88.

Straus, M. A., Hamby, S. L., Boney-McCoy, S., & Sugarman, D. B. (1996). The revised Conflict Tactics Scales (CTS2): Development and preliminary psychometric data. *Journal of Family Issues, 17,* 283–316.

Swindle, R., Heller, K., Pescosolido, B., & Kikuzawa, S. (2000). Responses to nervous breakdowns in America over a 40-year period: Mental health policy implications. *American Psychologist, 55,* 740–749.

Tanaka-Matsumi, J. (2004). Individual differences and behavioral assessment. In S. N. Haynes & E. M. Heiby (Eds.), *Comprehensive handbook of psychological assessment (Vol. 3): Behavioral assessment* (pp. 128–139). Hoboken, NJ: John Wiley & Sons.

Touliatos, J., Perlmutter, B. F., Straus, M. A., & Holden, G. W. (Eds.). (2001). *Handbook of family measurement techniques* (Vol. 1–3). Thousand Oaks, CA: Sage.

Weiss, R. L. (1980). Strategic behavioral marital therapy: Toward a model for assessment and intervention. In J. P. Vincent (Ed.), *Advances in family intervention, assessment, and theory* (Vol. 1, pp. 229–271). Greenwich, CT: JAI Press.

Weiss, R. L., & Heyman, R. E. (1997). A clinical-research overview of couples interactions. In W. K. Halford & H. J. Markman (Eds.), *Clinical handbook of marriage and couples intervention* (pp. 13–41). New York: John Wiley & Sons.

Whisman, M. A. (1999). Marital dissatisfaction and psychiatric disorders: Results from the National Comorbidity Survey. *Journal of Abnormal Psychology, 108*, 701–706.

Whisman, M. A., Dixon, A. E., & Johnson, B. (1997). Therapists' perspectives of couple problems and treatment issues in couple therapy. *Journal of Family Psychology, 11*, 361–366.

Whisman, M. A., Sheldon, C. T., & Goering, P. (2000). Psychiatric disorders and dissatisfaction with social relationships: Does type of relationship matter? *Journal of Abnormal Psychology, 109*, 803–808.

Whisman, M. A., & Snyder, D. K. (1997). Evaluating and improving the efficacy of conjoint couple therapy. In W. K. Halford & H. J. Markman (Eds.), *Clinical handbook of marriage and couples interventions* (pp. 679–693). New York: Wiley.

Whisman, M. A., & Snyder, D. K. (2007). Sexual infidelity in a national survey of American women: Differences in prevalence and correlates as a function of method of assessment. *Journal of Family Psychology, 21*, 147–154.

Whisman, M. A., & Wagers, T. P. (2005). Assessing relationship betrayals. *Journal of Clinical Psychology, 61*, 1383–1391.

Wieder, G. B., & Weiss, R. L. (1980). Generalizability theory and the coding of marital interactions. *Journal of Consulting and Clinical Psychology, 48*, 469–477.

21

Sexual Dysfunction

Marta Meana
Yitzchak M. Binik
Lea Thaler

The question of assessment in sexuality has always been a complex one. Arguably more than with other phenomena covered in the *Diagnostic and Statistical Manual of Mental Disorders* (DSM), the classification of sexuality has been complicated by changing notions of normality, the subjective nature of the sexual experience, gender differences, and significant social, economic, and political investment from parties with opposing ideologies. The last decade has evidenced a series of challenges to extant definitions of sexual dysfunction in general and, more specifically, to the legitimacy of certain dysfunctions. The current DSM-IV-TR (American Psychiatric Association [APA], 2000) classification has been critiqued for (a) medicalizing sexuality by discounting the diversity of sexual expression in favor of categorical distinctions between health and disorder (Tiefer, 2002), (b) using an androcentric conceptualization of the sexual response that inadequately accounts for female sexuality (Basson et al., 2004), (c) ignoring questions of sexual and relationship satisfaction (Byers, 1999), and (d) decontextualizing the sexual experience (Laumann & Mahay, 2002). The validity of specific dysfunctions has also been questioned with recent theoretical and empirical challenges to the diagnoses of Hypoactive Sexual Desire Disorder (HSDD; Basson, 2002), Dyspareunia (Binik, 2005), and Vaginismus (Reissing, Binik, Khalife, Cohen, & Amsel, 2004).

Our aim in this chapter is not to determine what rises to the level of a disorder and what does not. Rather, we aim to describe and discuss different ways of measuring subjective and physiological

sexual phenomena related to global sexual function as well as to the nine sexual dysfunctions defined in the DSM-IV-TR: HSDD, Sexual Aversion Disorder (SAD), Female Sexual Arousal Disorder (FSAD), Male Erectile Disorder (ED), Female and Male Orgasmic Disorders, Premature Ejaculation (PE), Dyspareunia, and Vaginismus. After a brief description of the nature of these sexual problems, we will describe global sexual function measures suitable for the purposes of diagnosis, case conceptualization and treatment planning, and treatment monitoring and outcome. A description of assessments specific to each of the aforementioned sexual dysfunctions will follow, concluding with a discussion of future directions.

THE NATURE OF SEXUAL DYSFUNCTION

One of the reasons clinicians and researchers debate the very notion of sexual dysfunction is the ubiquity of sexual complaints in our society. Despite wide variation in prevalence rates for all sexual dysfunctions depending on the population and methodology in question (Simons & Carey, 2001), the numbers remain staggering. With general prevalence figures for sexual dysfunction in the United States estimated at 43% in women and 31% in men (Laumann, Paik, & Rosen, 1999), sexual difficulties seem close to normative. Once relegated strictly to sex therapists and sexologists, the assessment of sexual function is increasingly considered an integral part of an overall health assessment (Parish, 2006). However, it is important to distinguish a fleeting sexual complaint from a more pervasive problem. Most people will experience difficulty with sex at some point in their lives. The DSM-IV-TR restricts diagnosis to cases characterized by a persistence of the problem and significant associated distress for the individual or couple. The DSM-IV-TR further classifies sexual dysfunctions as (a) generalized or situational, (b) lifelong or acquired, and (c) due to psychological or combined factors. Exclusion criteria are other Axis I disorders other than another sexual dysfunction (except dyspareunia for which vaginismus is an exclusion criterion), medical conditions and/or use of substances that could account for or induce the dysfunction.

The exact determination of the DSM-IV-TR inclusion/exclusion criterion relating specifically to etiology is particularly complicated in any individual case. It is often difficult to determine whether the sexual problem emanates from psychological disturbances alone or whether there is organic involvement. Considering the sexual response necessarily involves both peripheral and central nervous system activity, one could argue that every sexual problem either originates or is perpetuated by both psychological and physiological factors. Clearly, a degree of dualism persists in the DSM-IV-TR, with its insistence on the distinction between physical and psychological etiologies, despite its nod to the possibility of combined effects.

The overall organization of the sexual dysfunctions in the DSM-IV-TR integrates seven of the nine dysfunctions within three phases of the sexual response cycle (desire, arousal, and orgasm), concluding with the sexual pain disorders. There are no dysfunctions listed that relate to the resolution phase of the cycle. This may change in future editions given recent support for the existence of Persistent Sexual Arousal Syndrome in women (Goldmeier & Leiblum, 2006; Leiblum & Nathan, 2001). The comorbidity of sexual dysfunctions other than the presenting one is almost a given. A problem at any stage of the sexual response cycle is likely to engender difficulties at other stages. In the absence of much sound data on comorbidity, we must remain cognizant of the close relationship of all phases of the sexual response cycle and the possible effects of deficits in one phase on other phases. A brief description of the known features of each of the sexual dysfunctions listed in the DSM-IV-TR follows.

Hypoactive Sexual Desire Disorder

Defined by the DSM-IV-TR as an absence or deficiency of sexual fantasies and desire for sexual activity, HSDD is the most common presenting problem in couples seeking help for sexual difficulties and far more prevalent in women than in men (Seagraves & Seagraves, 1991). The best estimate of the prevalence rate of HSDD in the general population is 5% of men and 22% of women, with rates and gender ratios varying with age (Laumann et al., 1999).

Considering the large gender ratios, it is imperative to tease apart true HSDD from desire that fails to rise to a partner's wishes or to a societal, oppressive ideal. Barring medical conditions, pain syndromes, or medication side-effects, the most oft-cited biological factor implicated in HSDD has been hormones. Administration of exogenous testosterone has shown effects in the desire of hypo- and eugonadal men with erectile dysfunction (Carani et al., 1990; Schiavi, White, Mandeli, & Levine, 1997) and there is accumulating evidence that androgen replacement increases sexual desire in many surgically postmenopausal women (Sherwin, 1988; Shifren et al., 2000). Psychosocially, many negative emotional states and life experiences have been linked to low desire, including stress, depression, anxiety, cognitive set, self-esteem, trauma, and relational and financial difficulties (for reviews, see Beck, 1995; Wincze & Carey, 2001).

Sexual Aversion Disorder

Individuals with SAD experience extreme aversion to sexual activity and generally avoid genital sexual contact with a partner. Although some consider SAD and HSDD to exist on a continuum of desire (e.g., Winzce & Carey, 2001), the DSM-IV-TR makes a categorical distinction between the indifference of HSDD and the phobic nature of SAD. Its prevalence is unknown, but SAD is believed to be more common in women than in men. Although questions of etiology are largely unanswered (Crenshaw, 1985), SAD appears to be related to state and trait anxiety, fear of negative evaluation, and number and intensity of fears (Katz & Jardine, 1999). The more severe psychosocial factors associated with HSDD (e.g., sexual trauma) are likely to be implicated in SAD. Biologically, it has been linked to the neurochemistry of anxiety and panic disorder (Figueira, Possidente, Marques, & Hayes, 2001).

Female Sexual Arousal Disorder

FSAD is defined as the persistent or recurrent inability to attain or maintain an adequate lubrication-swelling response of sexual excitement during sexual activity. Without teasing apart comorbidity, the prevalence of FSAD is approximately 14% (Laumann et al., 1999; Rosen, Taylor, Leiblum, & Bachman, 1993). Biologically, FSAD has been most often been linked to aging (Laumann et al., 1999), vascular and neurological impairments (Wincze & Carey, 2001), and treatments for reproductive cancers (Jensen et al., 2004), all processes that interfere with hormone availability. Similar to HSDD, negative mood states (e.g., Dunn, Croft, & Hackett, 1999), negative expectancies, relationship factors (e.g., McCabe & Cobain, 1998), and sexual trauma (Loeb et al., 2002; van Berlo & Ensink, 2000) have been linked to arousal problems.

Male Erectile Disorder

The persistent or recurrent, partial or complete inability to attain or maintain an erection sufficient for penetration is how arousal problems generally manifest themselves in men. A prevalence rate of 5% was found by Laumann and colleagues (1999) in men under 60, while others have found rates of 17% for moderate erectile difficulties at age 40 and 34% at age 70 (Feldman, Goldstein, Hatzichristou, Krane, & McKinlay, 1994). Biologically, the role of testosterone remains unclear as the administration of testosterone has often proven ineffective in enhancing erectile function (e.g., Schiavi, et al., 1997). Vascular and neurological diseases or damage are associated with ED as are lifestyle behaviors (e.g., smoking, alcohol abuse, inactivity) that affect the vascularization and innervation necessary for erection and/or the stamina necessary to sustain the physical exertion of penetration (Wincze & Carey, 2001). Some antidepressants, antihypertensives, and drugs that block the conversion of testosterone into dihydro-testosterone (DHT), commonly used to treat male pattern hair loss and benign prostatic hyperplasia (Ekman, 1999; Papatsoris & Korantzopoulos, 2006; Weiner & Rosen, 1997), have also been implicated. Psychosocially, performance demands, arousal underestimation, negative affect during sex, self-critical attributions, depressive symptoms, and relationship problems have all been linked to ED (Araujo, Durante, Feldman, Goldstein, & McKinlay, 1998; Barlow, 1986; McCabe & Cobain, 1998; Weisberg, Brown, Wincze, & Barlow, 2001).

Female Orgasmic Disorder

As per the DSM-IV-TR, a diagnosis of female orgasmic disorder (FOD) requires a persistent or recurrent delay in, or absence of, orgasm following a normal sexual excitement phase. Because of the wide variation in the type or intensity of stimulation that triggers orgasm, clinicians are left to judge that the woman's orgasmic capacity be less than expected for her age, sexual experience, and stimulation received. North American prevalence estimates range from 10% in women ages 51 to 61 (Johannes & Avis, 1997) to 24% in women under 60 (Laumann et al., 1999). Endocrine disruptions have been associated to FOD, albeit unreliably (e.g., Davis, Davison, Donath, & Bell, 2005). Neurophysiological and vascular disruptions, as well as side effects from serotonin reuptake inhibitors have also been implicated (Goldstein & Berman, 1998; Heiman, 2000; Margolese & Assalian, 1996). It is, however, more common that women with FOD have none of these factors present. Psychosocial etiologic factors mirror those associated with HSDD, including personality, relationship quality, and socioeconomic status and educational level (Meston, Levin, Sipski, Hull, & Heiman, 2004).

Male Orgasmic Disorder

Orgasm difficulties in men present as delayed, absent, incomplete (emission or contractile phase disorders such as squirtless seminal dribble and retrograde ejaculation; Kothari, 1984) and anaesthetic response (Dekker, 1993). General population prevalence estimates in recent studies range from 0% to 8%, with significantly higher estimates in homosexual samples (for a review, see Richardson, Nalabanda, & Goldmeier, 2006). The most common physiological etiologies are select disease processes associated with aging, such as heart disease, and benign prostatic hyperplasia/lower urinary tract symptoms, although pelvic surgeries, diabetes, neurological disturbances, and antidepressants and alpha blockers have been linked to MOD. Theorized psychosocial etiologic pathways include fear, performance anxiety, hostility, guilt, low desire for the partner, and inadequate stimulation (Richardson et al., 2006).

Premature Ejaculation

The most common of the male dysfunctions with a North American prevalence rate of 29% (Laumann, Gagnon, Michael, & Michaels, 1994), PE is defined in the DSM-IV-TR as persistent or recurrent ejaculation with minimal sexual stimulation before, on, or shortly after penetration and before the person wishes it. The onus is on the clinician to judge whether conditions described are adequate for most men to delay ejaculation until desired. Waldinger, Zwinderman, Berend, and Schweitzer (2005) have suggested intravaginal ejaculatory latency times (IELT; stopwatch measured) of less than 1 minute for a diagnosis of "definite" PE and 1 to 1.5 minutes for "probable" PE. In addition to innate physiological predispositions to ejaculate quickly, genitourinary, cardiovascular, and neurologic diseases have also been implicated (Metz & Pryor, 2000). Psychosocial factors hypothesized to contribute to PE include negative mood states, unrealistic expectancies, sexual misinformation, poor sexual skills and sensory awareness, maladaptive arousal patterns, and relational problems (Metz & Pryor, 2000; Perelman, 2006).

Dyspareunia

Primarily a female sexual dysfunction, dyspareunia is currently defined in the *DSM-IV-TR* as recurrent or persistent genital pain associated with sexual intercourse that is not caused exclusively by vaginismus or lack of lubrication. General North American prevalence rates in women have been estimated at 14%, whereas in men they are approximately 3% (Laumann et al., 1999). Higher rates have been reported in men who engage in receptive anal intercourse (Rosser, Metz, Bockting, & Buroker, 1997). There is considerable debate as to whether dyspareunia is better characterized as a disorder of sexual function or as a pain syndrome that interferes with sexual functioning only incidentally (Binik, 2005; Binik, Meana, Berkley, & Khalife, 1999; Meana, Binik, Khalife, & Cohen, 1997a). Biologically, dyspareunia can arise from (a) congenital malformations of the genital tract, (b) acute and chronic diseases, (c) nonspecific inflammatory or nerve dysfunction processes, such as vestibulodynia, (d) postmenopausal decreases in estrogen, and (e) iatrogenic damage from genital surgeries/procedures (Meana & Binik, 1994). Until recently, there was a robust tendency to attribute the etiology of dyspareunia directly to psychogenic factors of a developmental, traumatic, or relational nature. There is, however, slim support for the primacy of any one psychosocial etiology as most women with dyspareunia do not differ from controls on psychosocial factors (Meana, Binik, Khalife, & Cohen, 1997b), with the possible exception of a hypersensitivity and hypervigilance to pain in general (Payne, Binik, Amsel, & Khalife, 2005).

Vaginismus

Vaginismus might simply be the severe, phobic end of the dyspareunia continuum (Meana & Binik, 1994; Reissing, et al., 2004), as it is difficult to distinguish between painful intercourse and vaginismus (van Lankveld et al., 2006). The DSM-IV-TR, however, makes a categorical distinction between the two sexual pain disorders by attributing the interference in vaginismus to a spasm of the outer third of the vagina. Either way, vaginismus is characterized by a fear that rises to the level of a phobia (Reissing et al., 2004) and population-based estimates have been reported at 1% or less (Fugl-Meyer & Sjogren Fugl-Meyer, 1999). Although vaginismus is primarily associated with a psychosocial etiology, biological factors implicated in some cases are essentially similar to those hypothesized for dyspareunia. The very same anatomic, disease, or iatrogenic factors may instate a conditioning process complete with classical processes (intercourse paired with pain) and operant ones (avoidance reinforced by relief of anticipatory anxiety). More purely psychological etiologies proposed have included religiously based inhibitions, sexual trauma, partner dysfunction, and relational problems. Fear, however, appears to be the defining characteristic rather than pain itself (Reissing, Binik, Khalife, Cohen, & Amsel, 2003).

PURPOSES OF ASSESSMENT

The latest edition of the Handbook of Sexuality-Related Measures (Davis, Yarber, Bauserman, Schreer, & Davis, 1998) contains 214 self-administered questionnaires that relate to sexuality. The comprehensiveness of this reference text is deceiving, however, as it creates the impression that the field of human sexuality is rich in assessment tools. In terms of sexual function and its clinical assessment, quite the opposite

TABLE 21.1 Ratings of Instruments Used for Diagnosis

Instrument	Norms	Internal Consistency	Inter-Rater Reliability	Test–Retest Reliability	Content Validity	Construct Validity	Validity Generalization	Clinical Utility	Highly Recommended
Global Sexual Function									
For Use With Men, Women, and Couples									
DISF	L	A	G	A	A	A	A	A	
GRISS	G	A	NA	A	A	G	G	A	
For Use With Women Only									
BISF-W	A	A	NA	A	A	A	A	A	
FSFI	G	E	NA	A	G	G	G	A	✓
MFSQ	G	A	NA	A	G	G	G	A	✓
SFQ	G	G	NA	A	E	G	G	A	✓
SDM	A	NA	L	U	A	A	U	A	
For Use With Men Only									
BSFI-M	A	G	NA	A	G	A	A	A	
IIEF	G	G	NA	A	G	G	G	A	✓
MSHQ	G	G	NA	A	G	A	U	A	
Dysfunction-Specific									
SAS	L	G	NA	A	A	U	U	A	
IIEF	G	A	NA	A	G	G	A	A	✓

Note: DISF = Derogatis Interview for Sexual Functioning; GRISS = Golombok–Rust Inventory of Sexual Satisfaction; BISF-W= Brief Index of Sexual Functioning for Women; FSFI = Female Sexual Function Index; MFSQ = McCoy Female Sexuality Questionnaire; SFQ = Sexual Function Questionnaire; SDM = Structured Diagnostic Method; BSFI-M = Brief Sexual Function Inventory-Male; IIEF = International Index of Erectile Function; MSHQ = Male Sexual Health Questionnaire; SAS = Sexual Aversion Scale; L = Less Than Adequate; A = Adequate; G = Good; E = Excellent; U = Unavailable; NA = Not Applicable.

is true. Only a small subset of the measures in the *Handbook* focuses on sexual function and possesses adequate psychometric properties. The assessment of sexual function using extensively validated instruments is actually in its infancy, although growing at an unprecedented rate in the last decade as a consequence of the emerging need to assess outcomes in pharmaceutical clinical trials (Daker-White, 2002).

This chapter is limited to the description and evaluation of measures that (a) aim to assess sexual function in clinically useful ways and (b) have adequate or better psychometric properties. The list of measures covered could arguably have been longer, as the multifactorial conceptualization of sexual problems could conceivably include assessments of myriad aspects of an individual's life. On the other hand, the list could have been shorter, as many of the measures included are in the preliminary stages of validation. Our choice was guided by objective indices of reliability and validity and by our subjective assessment of a measure's promise of clinical utility. We first present multidimensional measures of global sexual function or related constructs (satisfaction, distress, relationship adjustment) adequate for diagnosis, case conceptualization, and treatment monitoring.

This will be followed by a discussion of assessment tools specific to each of the nine sexual dysfunctions. Some of the measures selected are applicable to men, women, and/or couples, whereas others are gender-specific. Critical evaluations of the psychometric properties of all measures (global and dysfunction-specific) by assessment purpose (diagnosis, case conceptualization, treatment monitoring) are provided in Tables 21.1–21.3 and listed in the order in which they appear in the text.

GLOBAL ASSESSMENT OF SEXUAL FUNCTION

Concerns about the growing medicalization of the field have engendered appeals to integrative conceptualizations of sexual dysfunctions that encompass individual, family of origin, relational, social, and cultural factors (Leiblum & Rosen, 2000; Weeks, 2005). This multifactorial approach, however, represents a daunting challenge to assessment and treatment, as it requires the simultaneous consideration of multiple factors. It also calls for assessment of other Axis I and II disorders that may impact on sexual function and

TABLE 21.2 Ratings of Instruments Used for Case Conceptualization and Treatment Planning

Instrument	Norms	Internal Consistency	Inter-Rater Reliability	Test–Retest Reliability	Content Validity	Construct Validity	Validity Generalization	Clinical Utility	Highly Recommended
Global sexual function									
For use with men, women, and couples									
DAS	G	G	NA	A	G	G	G	A	✓
DISF	A	A	G	A	A	A	A	A	
GRISS	G	A	NA	A	G	G	G	A	✓
DSFI	G	A	NA	A	A	G	G	A	
ISS	G	E	NA	A	A	A	A	A	
SII	A	G	NA	A	A	A	A	A	
For use with women only									
FSDS	G	G	NA	A	G	G	A	A	✓
SSS-W	G	G	NA	A	C	A	U	A	
Dysfunction-specific									
SDI	A	G	NA	A	G	A	A	A	
SIDI-F	G	E	U	U	G	A	U	A	
PFSF	G	G	NA	A	G	A	G	A	✓
MSIQ	G	G	NA	A	G	A	U	A	
SAS	L	G	NA	A	A	U	U	A	

Note: Abbreviations for instruments in alphabetical order; DAS = Dyadic Adjustment Scale; DISF = Derogatis Interview for Sexual Functioning; GRISS = Golombok-Rust Inventory of Sexual Satisfaction; DSFI = Derogatis Sexual Functioning Inventory; ISS = Index of Sexual Satisfaction; SII = Sexual Interaction Inventory; FSDS = Female Sexual Distress Scale; SSS-W = Sexual Satisfaction Scale for Women; SDI = Sexual Desire Inventory; SIDI-F = Sexual Interest and Desire Inventory; PFSF = Profile of Female Sexual Function; MSIQ = Menopausal Sexual Interest Questionnaire; SAS = Sexual Aversion Scale.
A = Adequate; G = Good; E = Excellent; NA = Not Applicable; L = Less Than Adequate; U = Unavailable.

for assessment of the comorbidity of other sexual dysfunctions in the client and his or her partner.

The assessment of global sexual function generally involves a clinical interview and/or self-administered questionnaires, depending on the context of the evaluation. General practitioners who want to screen for sexual dysfunction in the context of a busy medical practice will depend primarily on brief screening questionnaires. Sex therapists and other mental health professionals more directly involved in the treatment of sexual dysfunction will almost invariably start with an extended clinical interview, possibly followed by questionnaires.

Assessment for Diagnosis

As there is no diagnostic category of global sexual dysfunction, there is no such diagnosis. The "diagnostic" assessment of global sexual function is thus conducted for one of two reasons: to get a general sense of the person's sexual adjustment multidimensionally defined as function, satisfaction, distress, and relationship quality, or as a screen for the existence of a specific dysfunction which will then be investigated further. Because the DSM-IV-TR criteria depend heavily on clinician judgment rather than on operationalizations of dysfunction, the clinical interview is the main diagnostic tool. Self-report measures of global sexual function and specific dysfunctions are generally considered diagnostic adjuncts.

Clinical Interview

The clinical interview remains the mainstay of sexual dysfunction diagnostic assessment. Clinician judgment is central to the determination of whether a client meets DSM-IV-TR criteria for sexual dysfunction. However, there is no widely used, standardized interview that has been psychometrically validated, as is the case for other Axis I and Axis II disorders. Neither the extensively tested Diagnostic Interview Schedule (DIS) nor the Structured Clinical Interview for DSM-IV Disorders (SCID) covers the sexual dysfunctions (Compton & Cottler, 2004; First & Gibbon, 2004). Several authors have proposed clinical interview outlines and recommendations about coverage of topics and process (e.g., see Bach, Wincze, & Barlow, 2001; Maurice, 1999; McConaghy, 2003; Wincze & Carey,

TABLE 21.3 Ratings of Instruments Used for Treatment Monitoring and Treatment Outcome Evaluation

Instrument	Norms	Internal Consistency	Inter-Rater Reliability	Test–Retest Reliability	Content Validity	Construct Validity	Validity Generalization	Treatment Sensitivity	Clinical Utility	Highly Recommended
Global Sexual Function										
For Use With Men, Women, and Couples										
DISF	A	A	G	A	A	A	A	A	A	
GRISS	G	A	NA	A	G	G	G	G	A	✓
ISS	G	E	NA	A	A	A	A	A	A	
SII	A	G	NA	A	A	A	A	A	A	
CSFQ/CSFQ-14	G	A	NA	A	A	G	G	A	A	✓
For Use With Women Only										
BISF-W	A	A	NA	A	A	A	A	A	A	
FSDS	G	G	NA	A	G	G	A	A	A	
FSFI	G	E	NA	A	G	G	G	A	A	✓
MFSQ	G	A	NA	A	G	G	G	A	A	✓
For Use With Men Only										
IIEF	G	G	NA	A	G	G	G	G	A	✓
Dysfunction-Specific										
SDI	A	G	NA	A	G	A	A	A	A	
MSIQ	G	G	NA	A	G	A	U	A	A	
IIEF-5	G	G	NA	A	G	G	A	A	A	

Note: DISF = Derogatis Interview for Sexual Functioning; GRISS = Golombok-Rust Inventory of Sexual Functioning; ISS = Index of Sexual Satisfaction; SII = Sexual Interaction Inventory; CSFQ = Changes in Sexual Function Questionnaire; BISF-W = Brief Index of Sexual Functioning for Women; FSDS = Female Sexual Distress Scale; FSFI = Female Sexual Function Index; MFSQ = McCoy Female Sexuality Questionnaire; IIEF/IIEF-5 = International Index of Erectile Function; SDI = Sexual Desire Inventory; MSIQ = Menopausal Sexual Interest Questionnaire; A = Adequate; G = Good; E = Excellent; U = Unavailable; NA = Not Applicable.

2001). Briefly, the clinical interview typically starts with the individual describing the nature of the problem and the reasons for seeking treatment at the time. Following an open-ended characterization of the difficulty, the clinician then might start asking more operationally specific questions about the extent of the problem and the conditions under which it occurs. This is ideally followed by questions covering the myriad biological, psychological, and social problems that might be implicated.

From a broadly biological perspective, it is important to assess and take into account age, general health status (e.g., body-mass index, energy levels, sense of physical well-being), lifestyle factors (e.g., diet, cigarette smoking, alcohol use, exercise), hormone levels, chronic pain syndromes (e.g., vulvodynia, interstitial cystitis), vascular diseases (e.g., hypertension, atherosclerosis, impaired cardiac function), conditions that affect nervous system function (e.g., diabetes, neuropathy), and pelvic or perineum trauma. It is also important to assess for the potentially iatrogenic influence of surgeries that may interfere with the musculature and innervation of the genital area, as well as its cosmetic appearance. Antidepressants, antipsychotics, and antihypertensives can also have a deleterious effect on desire, arousal, and orgasm and should be inquired about. Often, assessment of many of these factors will require referral to the appropriate medical professional.

In terms of individual psychological factors, depression and anxiety are often comorbid with sexual dysfunction. Treatment for sexual difficulties that does not simultaneously target mood disturbances and anxiety is unlikely to meet with much success. Substance abuse disorders can also have a major impact on sexual functioning, as can certain maladaptive cognitive sets and negative emotional reactions that interfere with sexual function, although they may not rise to the level of a disorder. These may arise from past trauma, negative experiences, or learned sexual scripts. Often individuals simply lack knowledge of physiology or of sexual techniques.

From a relational/social perspective, family of origin attitudes regarding sexuality can be instated early on and create the conditions for the development of sexual dysfunction. Assessing the quality of the individual's current relationship cannot be stressed enough. Although sexual difficulties can occur in the happiest of relationships, couple disharmony can be a cause and/or consequence of sexual problems and

needs to be addressed. Relational issues important to assess include anger, distrust, discrepancies in drive and preferences, communication, and physical attraction. It is usually recommended that both partners be interviewed together and/or separately to gather as much information as possible. The comorbidity of partner sexual dysfunction is common and crucial to assess. Finally, ethnocultural and religious attitudes and beliefs are important as they can be implicated in the development and maintenance of sexual difficulties. Also, these beliefs need to be respected in order to successfully treat the individual or the couple.

In summary, the presence of any one or combination of the aforementioned factors does not necessarily result in dysfunction. Failing to assess for them, however, may interfere with otherwise reasonable treatment efforts. Although the unstructured clinical interview undeniably provides maximum flexibility to explore the specifics of an individual's sexual problem and profile, the addition of a shorter, structured interview and/or self-administered questionnaires is likely to enhance the accuracy and utility of the overall assessment.

Self-Report Measures of Global Sexual Function

Table 21.1 provides a listing of self-report measures of global sexual function helpful in diagnostic assessment. The first two of these measures are designed to be applicable to men, women, and couples, whereas the rest are gender-specific. A description of these measures follows.

The Derogatis Interview for Sexual Functioning (DISF/DISF-R; Derogatis, 1997, 1998) is a 26-item interview designed to assess sexual functioning multidimensionally as a whole and in terms of each of five domains: sexual cognition/fantasy, sexual arousal, sexual behavior/experience, orgasm, and sexual drive/relationship. There is also a distinct self-report version (DISF-R) consisting of 26 items. Items are responded to on 9- and 5-point adjectival scales and both formats take 15 to 20 minutes to complete, with the DISF-R taking a few minutes less than the interview version. Both formats have separate gender-keyed versions for men and women and were designed to be administered repeatedly to monitor treatment outcome or solely at pre and postintervention. Standard scores allow for meaningful comparisons with the normative community sample. There are, however, no clinical norms at this time. This limits its use for diagnostic purposes, although there is some evidence that scores distinguish between groups with and without dysfunction. The measure has been translated and is available in eight languages other than English.

The Golombok-Rust Inventory of Sexual Satisfaction (GRISS; Rust & Golombok, 1985, 1986, 1998) is a 56-item self-report measure of sexual function and of relationship quality in heterosexual relationships. With 28 items specific to men and 28 specific to women, the GRISS yields scores on five dimensions for women, five for men, and two common dimensions. Female-specific dimensions pertain to orgasmic difficulties, vaginismus, nonsensuality, avoidance, and dissatisfaction. Male-specific dimensions pertain to erectile dysfunction, PE, nonsensuality, avoidance and dissatisfaction. The two common dimensions pertain to infrequency and noncommunication. Items are responded to on 5-point adjectival scales. Scores on the 12 dimensions are transformed into standardized scores and can be plotted to provide a profile. The GRISS also provides a global score indicative of overall relationship quality and the couple's sexual function that can be useful in case conceptualization and treatment planning. Although there is some support for its use as a diagnostic tool, the GRISS was designed primarily as an evaluation tool for sex and marital therapy and for cross-treatment efficacy comparisons. Its clinical utility lies in its ease of administration (approximately 10 minutes to complete) and its simultaneous assessment of both sexual function and relationship quality.

The Brief Index of Sexual Functioning for Women (BISF-W; Rosen, Taylor, & Leiblum, 1998; Taylor, Rosen, & Leiblum, 1994) is a 22-item scale developed to measure global sexual function for the purposes of large-scale clinical trials. A scoring algorithm provides an overall score for sexual function and on seven dimensions: thoughts/desire, arousal, frequency of sexual activity, receptivity/initiation, pleasure/orgasm, relationship satisfaction, and problems affecting sexual function. Items are responded to in a variety of formats from adjectival frequency scales, to multiple choice, to yes/no options. It takes 15 to 20 minutes to administer and some dimensions and overall score have been shown to be sensitive to treatment targeted at women (transdermal testosterone) and their partners (sildenalfil; Rosen et al., 2006; Shifren et al, 2000).

The Female Sexual Function Index (FSFI; Rosen et al., 2000) is a brief, 19-item self report measure of female sexual function yielding a total score, as well as scores on five domains: desire, arousal, lubrication, orgasm, satisfaction, and pain. Items are responded to on 5- to 6-point adjectival scales and in reference to the past 4 weeks. The FSFI takes approximately 15 minutes to administer and is scored such that higher scores denote more difficulty. Cross-validation of this instrument has supported its use as a screening tool or diagnostic aid, but not as the sole basis of diagnosis (Meston, 2003; Wiegel, Meston, & Rosen, 2005). Because it does not address questions of onset, duration, etiological or maintaining factors, or situational specifics, it is not as useful in the conceptualization of cases and treatment planning as in screening and measurement of treatment outcome. There are some data to suggest that it can detect treatment-related changes (e.g., Nappi et al., 2003).

The McCoy Female Sexuality Questionnaire (MFSQ; McCoy & Matyas, 1998) is a 19-item measure that assesses a woman's general level of sexual interest and response in the preceding 4 weeks. It was designed to serve as a diagnostic aid and as an assessment capable of measuring changes in sexual functioning over time. The first 11 questions relate to general sexual enjoyment, arousal, interest, satisfaction with partner, and feelings of attractiveness; the remaining 8 questions cover intercourse frequency and enjoyment, orgasm frequency and pleasure, lubrication, pain with intercourse, and the impact of partner's erectile difficulties. With the exception of one item inquiring about overall frequency of heterosexual intercourse, all items are answered on a 7-point adjectival scale. Time to administer is approximately 10 minutes. Although in its current form the measure is intended for women in heterosexual relationships, the authors suggest removal of the intercourse items to make the measure applicable to lesbian women. It has not, however, been validated with that population. Until recently, the MFSQ had only been used with menopausal women, but an Italian translation of the measure has provided support for its use as a valid measure of dysfunction in women ages 18 to 65 (Rellini et al., 2005).

The Sexual Function Questionnaire (SFQ; Quirk et al., 2002; Quirk, Haughie, & Symonds, 2005) is a 34-item self-report instrument developed to assess multiple dimensions of female sexual function and sexual satisfaction for women in sexual pharmacology clinical trials. The eight specific dimensions targeted are desire, arousal-sensation, arousal-lubrication, subjective arousal, enjoyment, orgasm, pain, and partner relationship. The SFQ specifically distinguishes between subjective and genital aspects of FSAD. It takes 15 to 20 minutes to complete, with items answered in reference to the preceding 4 weeks on 5-point adjectival scales. The intention of the authors was that the SFQ be used diagnostically to determine the likelihood of a sexual problem and the phases of the sexual response cycle (and/or pain) affected. The 4-week reference period also makes the measure suitable for the tracking of treatment progress, although no data supporting its use for treatment outcome has yet been made available. The SFQ has been developed and validated in 16 languages.

The Structured Diagnostic Method (SDM; Utian et al., 2005) is a novel method designed to aid healthcare providers who are not sexuality experts determine a diagnosis of female sexual dysfunction in postmenopausal women. The SDM consists of four self-report measures, followed by a clinical interview. The four questionnaires administered in the order that follows are the Life Satisfaction Checklist (Fugl-Meyer, Lodnert, Branholm, & Fugl-Meyer, 1997), the first seven of the nine questions of the sexual component of the Medical History Questionnaire (Pfeiffer & Davis, 1972), the Female Sexual Distress Scale (FSDS ; Derogatis, Rosen, Leiblum, Burnett, & Heiman, 2002), and the SFQ (Quirk et al., 2002). The combination covers overall life satisfaction (including sexual), decline in sexual function as well as its onset, sexually related distress, and sexual function. The measures are followed by a structured interview based on a guide to diagnostic assignment outlined by Utian and colleagues (2005). The administration of the SDM is lengthy and not suitable for primary care clinic use, but it can be clinically useful in both clinical trials and sex therapy practice. The authors have not provided an algorithm or guidelines to combine results from the measures and interview to arrive at a diagnosis.

The Brief Sexual Function Inventory-M (BSFI-M; O'Leary et al., 1995) is an 11-item measure of male sexual function covering sexual drive, erection, ejaculation, subjective problem assessment of drive, erection and ejaculation, and overall satisfaction. Responses are given on 5-point adjectival scales with higher scores indicating better function. The reference period for responses is the last 30 days. Although the

initial intent was for this measure to provide a multidimensional measure of sexual function in men, more recent validation of the measure suggests that it is most efficacious as a unidimensional tool for general screening purposes (Mykletun, Dahl, O'Leary, & Fossa, 2005). The measure was intended to be suitable whether partners of the male respondents were male or female.

The International Index of Erectile Function (IIEF; Rosen et al., 1997) is a brief self-administered measure of erectile function designed to detect treatment-related changes in patients with erectile dysfunction, although it is also a useful diagnostic adjunct. The 15 items address 5 domains of sexual function: erectile function, orgasmic function, sexual desire, intercourse, and overall satisfaction. Response options consist of 5- or 6-point adjectival scales and the time reference is the prior 4 weeks. It takes less than 15 minutes to complete and is easy to administer in most settings. The IIEF has been validated linguistically in many languages.

The Male Sexual Health Questionnaire (MSHQ; Rosen, Catania, et al., 2004) is a 25-item self-administered measure designed specifically to assess sexual function and satisfaction in aging men with urogenital concerns often associated with heart disease, prostate cancer, benign prostatic hyperplasia/lower urinary tract symptoms. Disorders of ejaculation are common in men with these age-related physical problems, yet erectile function measures such as the IIEF do not focus specifically on problems such as delayed or retrograde ejaculation and diminished sensation, force, or pleasure. The MSHQ thus addresses three domains of sexual function: erection, ejaculation, and satisfaction with the sexual relationship. The questionnaire is suitable for both heterosexual and homosexual men as it does not assume heterosexual intercourse to be the sole or even central sexual activity. Although initial reliability and validity for this measure is promising, it is new and requires further validation.

Assessment for Case Conceptualization and Treatment Planning

Again, the richest tool for case conceptualization and treatment planning is the clinical interview, with its capacity to investigate multiple areas of functioning both in the client and in their partner. One important area to assess in the formulation of a treatment plan is the existence of other Axis I and Axis II disorders, if these are suspected to be present. Other chapters in this text elaborate on the assessment of these and thus these assessment tools will not be covered here. The other area crucial to case conceptualization and treatment planning is the assessment of the nonsexual aspects of the client's primary relationship. Table 21.2 provides a listing of self-report measures suitable as adjuncts in case conceptualization and treatment planning.

Ideally, the assessment of sexual function should include the client's partner if he/she has one and if they are willing to participate. There are multiple functions to partner assessment, including a general assessment of relationship adjustment, the partner's perception of the sexual difficulty, and the presence of partner sexual dysfunction. This couple assessment can be enhanced with self-administered measures of marital adjustment.

The Dyadic Adjustment Scale (DAS; Spanier, 1976), is the most widely used instrument for the measurement of relationship quality. It consists of 32 items in a variety of response formats that are summed to create a total score ranging from 0 to 151, with higher scores indicating better dyadic adjustment. The items also break down into four subscales which can be used independently as they have also shown good reliability and validity: Dyadic Consensus (13 items), Dyadic Satisfaction (10 items), Dyadic Cohesion (5 items), and Affective expression (4 items). Total DAS scores have been shown to discriminate between distressed and nondistressed couples and to identify at-risk marriages. The measure has also been used with gay and lesbian couples (Kurdek, 1992). It is easy to administer (10 to 15 minutes) and provides information about the marital context within which the sexual dysfunction exists.

Because of the multidimensionality of most measures of global sexual function, many are appropriate for use in case conceptualization and treatment planning. Of the measures already covered in the preceding diagnosis section, both the DISF and the GRISS can be useful as they cover corollary cognitions and behaviors, as well as satisfaction and relationship quality. Other measures include:

The Derogatis Sexual Functioning Inventory (DSFI; Derogatis, 1998; Derogatis & Melisaratos, 1979) is a multidimensional measure that assesses constructs associated with sexual functioning and general well-being. It consists of 254 items and arranged into 10 subscales. The response format is a mixture of yes/no answers and multipoint adjectival scales. The 10 dimensions addressed by the scales are information, experiences, drive, attitudes, psychological symptoms, affect, gender role definition, fantasy, body image, and sexual satisfaction. Each scale provides a separate score and the linear combination of the 10 scales yields the Sexual Functioning Index. A second global score, The Global Sexual Satisfaction Score, assesses the individual's subjective perception of their sexual function. The psychometric soundness of the measure varies by subscale.

The Index of Sexual Satisfaction (ISS; Hudson, 1998; Hudson, Harrison, & Crossup, 1981) is a 25-item self-report measure of dissatisfaction in the sexual aspects of a couple's relationship from the perspective of the respondent. In the original measure items were responded to on 5-point adjectival scales describing relative frequency. The newer version has seven-point scales and minor item revisions. The measure takes 5 to 7 minutes to complete.

The Sexual Interaction Inventory (SII; LoPiccolo & Steger, 1974; Reinhardt, 1998) is a self-report inventory designed to assess the heterosexual couple's sexual relationship with regard to functioning and satisfaction. Unlike most other measures designed for one respondent, the SII requires responses from both partners. It is a lengthy measure, with 102 questions covering 17 heterosexual behaviors, and is divided into 11 scales: Frequency Dissatisfaction—Male, Female; Self Acceptance—Male, Female; Pleasure—Male, Female; Perceptual Accuracy—Male of Female, Female of Male; Mate Acceptance—Male of Female, Female of Male; Total Disagreement. The item scales are 6-point adjectival with some items inquiring about frequency and others about pleasure. The inventory is completed in approximately 30 minutes.

The Female Sexual Distress Scale (FSDS; Derogatis et al., 2002) is designed to measure sexually related distress in women. Although the FSDS requires additional independent testing, it shows significant promise. Initially a 20-item measure with frequency and intensity versions, analyses of pilot studies reduced it to one 12-item measure with four-point adjectival scales. The ascertainment of distress over sexual difficulties can be integral to case conceptualization and treatment planning and the FSDS has been shown to be sensitive to treatment changes. It has also demonstrated reliability and validity with different populations (Dennerstein, Alexander, & Kotz, 2003; ter Kuile, Brauer, & Laan, 2006).

The Sexual Satisfaction Scale for Women (SSS-W; Meston & Trapnell, 2005) is a promising new measure of sexual satisfaction in women along personal and relational dimensions. The 30 items in the scale are responded to on 5-point scales anchored at "strongly agree" and "strongly disagree" in reference to the respondent's situation at the time of administration. It consists of five domains of satisfaction (communication, compatibility, contentment, relational concern, and personal concern) with 6 items relating to each. Despite its brevity, it provides the most detailed breakdown available of satisfaction into separate components. This may be particularly helpful in clarifying the sometimes confusing relationship between satisfaction/distress and sexual difficulties in women. Clearly not intended as a diagnostic measure, the SSS-W could prove invaluable in case conceptualization and the holistic measurement of treatment outcome, regardless of the presenting sexual dysfunction.

Assessment for Treatment Monitoring and Treatment Outcome

Treatment monitoring and outcome is the one assessment purpose for which the clinical interview is not optimal. This assessment purpose requires the quantification that only standardized measurement can provide. The recent explosion in clinical trials for pharmacotherapeutic agents targeting sexual dysfunction has happily resulted in the development of a number of measures designed specifically for the assessment of treatment monitoring and outcome. The validation of treatment sensitivity in these measures is in its infancy but finally there are actually measures to validate. Table 21.3 provides a listing of measures suitable to treatment monitoring and the assessment of treatment outcome.

In terms of measures applicable to men, women, and couples, there is data to support that the DISF, GRISS, ISS, and SII can detect changes attributable to treatment effects. Additionally there is one other instrument specifically designed to measure changes in sexual function associated with psychiatric illness and medication effects.

The Changes in Sexual Functioning Questionnaire (CSFQ, CSFQ-14: Clayton, McGarvey, & Clavet, 1997; Clayton, McGarvey, Clavet, & Piazza, 1997; Keller, McGarvey, & Clayton, 2006) can be clinician-administered as a structured interview (CSFQ-I) or self-administered as a gender-specific questionnaire (CSFQ-F or CSFQ-M). It measures five dimensions of sexual functioning (frequency of sexual activity, sexual desire, pleasure, arousal, orgasmic capacity), as well as comorbid conditions, current medications, alcohol and substance use, and relationship status. The first 21 items of the questionnaire apply to both men and women and are followed by 36 male-specific and 35 female-specific items, answered primarily on 5-point Likert-type scales. The CSFQ has been found more valid and reliable in female than in male samples and most of the psychometric data available emanates from the self-administered version. Recently abbreviated into a Short Form, the CSFQ-14 also has gender-specific versions and is self-administered. It yields scores for three scales corresponding to desire, arousal, and orgasm, as well as for the five scales in the original long form. The available psychometric data for the newly introduced CSFQ-14 are very promising and appear to improve on the reliability and validity of the long form, especially with regard to men. The addition of a short form enhances its clinical utility, as it can be administered quickly in busy practices and is amenable to immediate clinician feedback. Although designed with psychiatric patients in mind, the CSFQ has also been tested in nonclinical populations and been found suitable for general use.

In terms of measures specific to female sexual dysfunction, the BISF-W, FSDS, FSFI, and the MSFQ have all been found sensitive to treatment effects. Far more data is needed to raise confidence about the use of these measures for treatment monitoring and outcome, but they are promising and represent a significant advance from a decade ago when none existed. In terms of measures specific to male sexual dysfunction, the IIEF has demonstrated treatment sensitivity and the MSHQ requires further validation but was designed for this purpose and is a promising new measure specifically for older men.

DYSFUNCTION-SPECIFIC ASSESSMENT

The assessment of any one sexual dysfunction is largely dependent on the clinical interview. However, the administration of one or more of the aforementioned self-administered measures of global sexual function that contain a domain pertinent to the dysfunction in question can be a useful adjunct. Dysfunction-specific measures will be described in the following section and they are included in Tables 21.1 to 21.3 as appropriate. As those tables illustrate at a glance, there are very few such dysfunction-specific measures and diagnosis is still almost completely dependent on the clinical interview. When a client presents with symptoms of a specific dysfunction, assessment is more likely to involve physiological assessment strategies than self-report measures. Although few of these psychophysiological measures have been validated for the assessment of sexual dysfunction, they will be discussed briefly in the following section to introduce the reader to promising additions to the multidisciplinary assessment toolkit.

Hypoactive Sexual Desire Disorder

HSDD is perhaps the most difficult sexual dysfunction to diagnose in both men and women as it is not anchored in the absence or disturbance of an expected discrete event (e.g., erection, lubrication, orgasm) or in the presence of an unexpected one (pain during intercourse). Diagnostic assessment is usually based on the presenting complaint of distress about desire level, taking into account natural discrepancies between members of a couple. In addition to the clinical interview, an operationalization of the severity of the problem can be facilitated by self-administered measures. Global sexual function measures for use with either men or women that have domains specific to desire are the CFSQ, DISF, DSFI, and the GRISS. Female-specific global measures that address desire levels are the BISF-W, FSFI, MFSQ, SFQ, and, for postmenopausal women, the SDM. Male-specific measures with desire scales are the BSFI-M and the IIEF. The advantage of these multidimensional measures of desire is that they may also be helpful for the purpose of case conceptualization as they provide information on the existence of comorbid sexual dysfunctions, can also be administered to the partner, and, in some cases, provide information about relationship quality and satisfaction. There are, however, only a handful of desire-specific self-administered measures with acceptable psychometric properties and clinical utility. All of them are more applicable to case conceptualization than to diagnosis and two of them were designed to track treatment progress although we await data to validate their use for this purpose.

The Sexual Desire Inventory (SDI; Spector, Carey, & Steinberg, 1996) is a 14-item self-report measure of dyadic and solitary desire for use with men and women. Its focus is primarily on cognitive rather than behavioral dimensions of desire. Each item is responded to according to the intensity of feeling or frequency of occurrence on seven- or eight-point adjectival scales and yields scores for dyadic desire, solitary desire, as well as a total score. It has been validated in a handful of studies (e.g., Conaglen & Evans, 2006) and has been found sensitive to treatment effects in women with HSDD (van Anders, Chernick, Chernick, Hampson, & Fisher, 2005). Because of its cognitive emphasis, it can be particularly useful in cognitive-behavioral case conceptualizations.

The Sexual Interest and Desire Inventory (SIDI-F; Clayton et al., 2006; Sills et al., 2005;) is a new, 13-item clinician-administered instrument designed to quantify the severity of symptoms in premenopausal women diagnosed with HSDD and to track symptom changes in response to treatment. The 13 items cover the following areas: relationship-sexual, receptivity, initiation, desire-frequency, affection, desire-satisfaction, desire-distress, thoughts-positive, erotica, arousal–frequency, arousal-ease, arousal-continuation, orgasm. Based on the client's response, the clinician chooses among four, five, or six possible answers for most questions, but six of the questions use a grid system that simultaneously rates both intensity and frequency, allowing up to thirteen possible responses. Although more validation is needed, this scale shows higher specificity than the FSFI and CSFQ in assessing the severity of HSDD symptoms. Yet to be tested for inter-rater or test–retest reliability, it holds promise as a brief measure of HSDD severity.

The Profile of Female Sexual Function (PFSF; Derogatis et al., 2004; McHorney et al. 2004) is a new 37-item self-report instrument designed specifically for the measurement of sexual desire and associated symptoms in naturally and surgically menopausal women with HSDD. The aim of the measure was to capture the experience of HSDD in this population by inquiring about its effects on the woman's feelings, thoughts, and behavior. It covers seven domains of sexual function as follows: desire, arousal, orgasm, pleasure, sexual concerns, responsiveness, and self-image. It has been used internationally, although little data are available on its sensitivity to treatment effects.

The Menopausal Sexual Interest Questionnaire (MSIQ; Rosen, Lobo, Block, Yang, Zipfel, 2004) is a 10-item scale designed to assess sexual function in postmenopausal women in three domains: desire, responsiveness and satisfaction. Prior to the administration of these items, there are four questions assessing whether the woman perceives a decline in her level of sexual desire as a consequence of menopause. The MSIQ is meant to be administered at the start of treatment and repeatedly thereafter to track treatment-related changes. Questions are asked in reference to the present or the week preceding and are responded to on 7-point adjectival scales. The construct validity of this measure looks very promising but awaits independent validation.

In the absence of psychological, relational, situational, or disease-related factors that could account for a decline in desire, clinicians are increasingly turning to the assessment of sex hormone levels as aids in the case conceptualization and treatment planning of HSDD. The link between testosterone and sexual desire is stronger than that of estrogen (Bachman et al., 2002) and there is accumulating evidence that androgens impact sexual desire in surgically menopausal women (Shifren et al., 2000). It is important to note that no single estrogen or androgen level has been found predictive of low desire in either sex (Davis et al., 2005; Schiavi et al., 1997).

Sexual Aversion Disorder

Although some clients will disguise their phobic reactions to sex as disinterest, the aversion usually surfaces early in the process of any standard treatment for HSDD, especially once exposure to sexual situations is introduced. In terms of self-report measures, clients with SAD will register disturbances of desire on the desire-specific domains of the global sexual function measures or in the unidimensional desire measures, but it is unlikely that these will detect the severity of the problem. There is only one self-administered measure directly designed to assess sexual fear and avoidance.

The Sexual Aversion Scale (SAS; Katz, Gipson, Kearly, & Kriskovich, 1989; Katz, Gipson, & Turner, 1992) is a 30-item questionnaire designed to assess fears and phobic avoidance of sexual contact theorized by the authors to be associated to sexual trauma, guilt, social inhibitions, and fear of sexually transmitted diseases (STDs). The 30 items are responded to on

four-point adjectival scales. Although this instrument has been used primarily for research purposes, it could be useful in the diagnosis of SAD, despite the fact that it has only been normed with college samples. It might reduce delays in the discovery that what presented as low desire is actually something more intense. It could also prove useful in conceptualization of a case as it can identify the source of the aversion.

Female Sexual Arousal Disorder

In terms of self-administered measures, the CSFQ, BISF-W, and MFSQ all inquire about arousal in general terms and in terms of lubrication, but the inquiry is limited to one or two questions. Arousal questions can also be found in desire-specific measures such as the PFSF and the SIDI-F, but the assessment of sexual arousal remains relatively brief. The two measures that engage in a more detailed assessment of arousal are the FSFI and the SFQ. The FSFI has four questions about general sexual arousal and four about lubrication. The SFQ also has eight questions devoted to arousal, and it distinguishes between genital and subjective arousal.

Unlike the clinical assessment of male erectile dysfunction which has long made use of physiological measures, the assessment of female sexual arousal has relied almost exclusively on self-report, despite evidence that women are relatively unaware of their genital arousal (Laan, Everaerd, van der Velde, & Geer, 1995). After years of relative neglect, there is now a flurry of investigative activity on objective genital arousal assessment instruments, with some of these instruments holding as yet unfulfilled promise for clinical use.

Attempts to measure lubrication, clitoral engorgement, and uterine contractions have met with little success for a variety of reasons (see Meston, 2000; Prause & Janssen, 2006). Vaginal blood flow has been most amenable to measurement, and the most frequently used instrument is the vaginal photoplethysmograph (VPP), a tampon-like, light-emitting device that measures vasocongestion via the amount of light reflected back from the vaginal walls. Pulsed-wave Doppler clitoral ultrasonography appears to distinguish between women with and without sexual dysfunction, although questions as to its specificity to sexual arousal remain (Bechara et al., 2003; Kukkonen et al., 2006; Nader, Maitland, Munarriz, &

Goldstein, 2006). The *heated oxygen electrode* measures blood flow as a function of the power necessary to keep a heated oxygen electrode placed on the vaginal wall by suction at a constant temperature (Levin, 2006). The *vaginal thermistor* measures changes in blood flow via a thermoconductive probe mounted on a diaphragm ring which telemetrically sends a signal to a receiver outside the body (Meston, 2000). The *labial thermistor clip* is a surface temperature probe fastened to the labia minora and it has been found to correlate with VPP results while improving correlations with subjective arousal (Janssen, 2001; Payne & Binik, 2006). *Thermal imaging* technology produces thermal images indicating the average temperature of less than a millimeter of skin with a precision of .07°C rapidly (Kukkonen, Binik, Amsel, & Carrier, 2007). *Magnetic resonance imaging* is now also being applied to the measurement of genital vasocongestion, as well as brain activation during sexual arousal (Maravilla, 2006). These psychophysiological instruments lack validation and their clinical utility is constrained by the necessity of sexual arousal induction, equipment, trained technicians, and interpretive problems. However, these limitations have not hampered the clinical use of similar techniques in the clinical assessment of male erectile dysfunction (Levin, 2004).

Male Erectile Disorder

The comprehensive assessment of ED requires a thorough clinical interview that includes both medical and psychosexual history, physical examination, and laboratory testing. More specialized diagnostic tests may be indicated in some cases and these may include Doppler ultrasound and nocturnal penile tumescence tests (NPT). Self-report measures may be helpful in the diagnosis of the problem, although they are rarely sufficient. General sexual function measures that inquire about ED are CSFQ, DISF-R, and GRISS. Male-specific measures that explore the existence of ED in more detail are the BSFI-M and the IIEF and IIEF-5.

The International Index of Erectile Function-5 (IIEF-5; Rosen, Cappelleri, Smith, Lispky, & Pena, 1999) consists of five items from the IIEF that specifically measure erectile function and intercourse satisfaction. It is easy to administer in the context of busy general practices, although it does not provide information about other aspects of the patient's sexual function. It was designed to tag erectile difficulties and track treatment-related changes. The response options are on 5-point adjectival scales and the reference period is 6 months.

Specialized techniques to assess for ED include NPT, penile strain gauges, the RigiScan Monitor and the Doppler ultrasound. The most commonly used psychophysiologic procedure in the diagnosis of ED is NPT, based on the assumption that the erections during the REM phase of the sleep cycle rule out substantial organic etiology. Usually measured in sleep labs with penile strain gauges that measure circumferential changes, NPT has demonstrated both validity and clinical utility (Shvartzman, 1994). The RigiScan Monitor, a small computerized device, improves on NPT by addressing the issue of rigidity, in addition to tumescence and duration of erectile episodes (Ackerman & Carey, 1995). Finally, intracavernosal injection testing and penile duplex ultrasonography have been found clinically useful in the detection of arterial inflow abnormalities and veno-occlusions (Goldstein, 2004).

Once ED has been adequately diagnosed, case conceptualization can be greatly enhanced by a sexual, medical, and psychosocial history to assess for general sexual functioning, medical, pharmacologic, surgical, and lifestyle risk factors, as well relationships and general psychological well-being. The physical examination should focus on genitourinary, neurologic, and vascular systems with laboratory tests focused on endocrine dysfunction (Goldstein, 2004).

Female Orgasmic Disorder

Within a clinical interview, women with lifelong orgasmic difficulty will typically report either never having had an orgasm or difficulty attaining one. Alternately, they may complain of having lost orgasmic capacity over time or a lack of pleasure or intensity during orgasm or even not knowing whether or not they have had an orgasm. Almost all of the self-administered measures of general and female-specific sexual function covered in this chapter inquire directly about orgasm. Although these measures can be helpful in indicating a potential problem, the questions embedded in these global sexual function questionnaires are not sufficient to establish a nuanced clinical picture of the many variations possible in female orgasmic difficulty. The clinical interview remains the best diagnostic tool for the assessment of orgasmic difficulties in women. Mah and Binik's (2002) Orgasm Rating Scale (ORS) is an interesting recent addition to the assessment of orgasm for both men and women. It is not designed to assess anorgasmia per se, but rather the cognitive-affective and sensory components of orgasm. Although it needs further validation, this measure may be useful in identifying determinants of orgasmic pleasure as part of a treatment program for women or men who are not completely anorgasmic.

Male Orgasmic Disorder

Most global sexual function measures inquire about the occurrence of orgasm and satisfaction with ejaculatory latency and sensation, but instruments designed specifically for male sexual dysfunction tend to more adequately investigate the range of problems that fall under MOD. The IIEF and the BSFI contain one question addressing the occurrence of and difficulty with ejaculation; the IIEF adds one more item on the pleasurable sensation of orgasm and the BSFI-M asks directly about satisfaction with the amount of ejaculate emitted. The best coverage of orgasmic problems in men, however, is provided by the MSHQ which has seven questions devoted to ejaculation, its occurrence, delay, volume, force, pain or discomfort, and pleasure, as well as the occurrence of retrograde ejaculation. Although the MSHQ was designed for aging men, it can be useful for patients of any age who report orgasm problems.

Retrograde ejaculation and emission phase disorders will likely have a physiological cause and, thus, a careful medical history and referral to a physician is important to assess for potential disease or other biological processes (see Segraves & Segraves, 1993, for a list of these). Whether or not biological factors are implicated, a psychosexual history is necessary to assess psychological and relational factors contributing to the problem or consequential to it as this can be helpful for the purpose of case conceptualization and treatment planning.

Premature Ejaculation

The assessment of PE has been complicated by variations in what is considered a normal ejaculatory latency by expert opinions and by the patient himself. In clinical trials, IELT is usually assessed by means of a stopwatch; however, this is not a viable assessment technique in clinical practice. Because PE

depends not only on objective measurement but also on patient distress, most clinicians do not use IELT cutoff points to assess for PE. Assessment usually relies more on clinical impression and patient distress gathered from the clinical interview (Perelman, 2006). There is no self-administered measure that taps directly into PE in sufficient detail to be helpful in assessment.

The clinical interview should assess whether the PE is likely to be attributable to neurologic factors, psychological traits, distress, psychosexual skills deficits, relationship problems, physical illness or injury, and/or medication side effects (Metz & Pryor, 2000). Metz and Pryor (2000) provided a useful decision tree for the aforementioned classifications and potential etiologic pathways. Perelman (2006) stressed the importance of assessing whether the patient is able to detect premonitory sensations (bodily changes reflecting arousal/impending ejaculation), as this is necessary in order to choose to ejaculate or to delay ejaculation.

Dyspareunia and Vaginismus

An understanding of both dyspareunia and vaginismus requires the assessment of sexual function and of pain. A number of self-administered sexual function measures, such as the CSFQ, GRISS, MFSQ, and the BISF-W, contain one question to assess the existence and frequency of pain with intercourse. The SFQ and the FSFI have questions related to frequency and intensity of the pain and the FSFI has been found to have good discriminant validity in the assessment of chronic vulvar pain (Masheb, Lozano-Blanco, Kohorn, Minkin, & Kerns, 2004).

Pain measures found to be useful in the conceptualization and treatment planning of dyspareunia are the McGill Pain Questionnaire (MPQ; Melzak, 1975), the Pain Catastrophizing Scale (PCS; Sullivan, Bishop, & Pivik, 1995), as well as visual analog scales and pain diaries (Payne, Bergeron, Khalife, & Binik, 2006). In addition to a large number of studies attesting to the reliability and validity of the MPQ for a wide range of pain experiences, it has been shown to distinguish between different subtypes of dyspareunia (Meana et al., 1997a). The PCS, another widely validated general pain measure, is useful for determining the amount of distress incurred by intercourse pain and in formulating cognitive treatment strategies. Pain-related distress is particularly germane to women with vaginismus as they recall past intercourse attempts with significant distress (Reissing et al., 2004), and to those with vestibulodynia (VVS) who catastrophize intercourse pain (Pukall, Binik, Khalife, Amsel, & Abbott, 2002).

The clinical interview for dyspareunia should contain questions on the history, onset, location, quality, duration, and intensity of the pain, as these pain characteristics have been found to have discriminant validity in the differentiation of different dyspareunia subtypes (Meana et al., 1997a). Impact of the pain on sexual activity, relationships, and psychological functioning are also important to cover (Meana et al., 1997b). A physical examination that aims to replicate the pain experienced with attempts at intercourse is a necessary component of assessment. The physical examination should include a cotton-swab palpation of the vulva and a pelvic examination. Pukall, Binik, and Khalife (2004) recently introduced an instrument called the vulvalgesiometer to standardize palpation pressure. The palpation serves to both locate the pain precisely and establish the sensitivity of the hyperalgesic area, if one is identified. Assessment of vulvar or pelvic diseases is another important goal of medical referral. Recently, the assessment of pelvic floor tonicity has gained wider acceptance, as it has been shown to discriminate between women with and without vestibulodynia (Reissing, Brown, Lord, Binik, & Khalife, 2005). Pelvic floor physiotherapy has shown promising outcomes in women with sexual pain (Bergeron et al., 2002; Rosenbaum, 2005) and women with vaginismus have been found to have higher vaginal/pelvic muscle tonicity and lower muscle strength (Reissing et al., 2004).

CONCLUSIONS AND FUTURE DIRECTIONS

The multidimensionality of sexual function and its problems poses a formidable challenge to both research and clinical practice. With lengthy laundry lists of potential etiologies for all of the nine sexual dysfunctions, the isolation of any one predominating factor or even of a reasonably articulated system of interdependent factors is exceedingly difficult. It is against this backdrop of complexity that clinicians are left to diagnose, conceptualize, and treat. No single measure of sexual function can provide sufficient information regarding the affective, cognitive,

behavioral, relational, and social contexts within which the sexual difficulties have arisen or are perpetuated. Only the clinical interview has the flexibility to encompass an individual client's specific circumstances, yet it is compromised by reliability and validity deficiencies and by the fact that instrumental details affecting the sexual difficulties tend to trickle out long after the initial intake. For this reason, assessment needs to be an integrated component of treatment at all stages, to track efficacy and to revise strategies as information and conditions change.

Despite their limitations, self-administered measures and psychophysiological tests can be useful in diagnosis, case conceptualization, and the monitoring of treatment progress. The clinical interview does not lend itself well to readministration or to the operationalization of changes in sexual function. Regardless of complexities in the etiology and maintenance of sexual difficulties, simple measures of drive, frequency, pleasure, or pain can tag improvement, stasis, or deterioration. Elaboration on the meaning of the changes can follow, but their quantification is essential to the client's and clinician's evaluation of progress. Self-administered measures are also integral to screening of sexual function in health-care settings. After decades of urging the medical profession to attend to sexual health as a primary component of an overall health assessment, it is up to sex researchers to provide them with the tools to do so accurately.

And therein lies the rub. The majority of sexual function measures require additional psychometric validation. There is a paucity of independent validation and data supporting long-term test–retest reliability, validity generalization, treatment sensitivity, and clinical benefit. Achieving high psychometric standards is an important research goal that will increase our confidence in the continued use of these measures and encourage other disciplines to engage in the assessment of sexual function. There is currently a very encouraging trend toward the sound development and validation of clinically useful measures. The concerning move toward medicalization has had the unexpected benefit of promoting the development of measures for use in clinical trials. We must remain vigilant that the originating drive for the development of these measures does not result in reductionist assessment tools that miss the forest for the trees, or that neglect to address the specific concerns of minority populations. As we endeavor to expand and refine our assessment toolbox, it is important that we also turn our attention to the traditionally neglected issues of sexual orientation, disability, and ethnocultural diversity.

Most sexual function measures are penile–vaginal intercourse centered and validated with predominantly Caucasian, heterosexual, abled populations. There is little research on culturally informed assessment and treatment for sexual difficulties over and above concerns about high-risk behaviors (Lewis, 2004). Cultural norms are important to prevent sexual function measures from pathologizing groups that fall outside of mainstream expectations. The recent cross-national validation of some sexual function measures designed for clinical trials, as well as Laumann et al.'s (2006) recent foray into the sexual well-being of older adults in 29 countries are good examples of this culturally informed direction. Despite the occasional mention that a questionnaire could be applicable to sexual minorities, little data supports the generalizability of any of these self-administered assessment tools. Additionally, the sexual health of individuals with disabilities or chronic illness has also been neglected. The norming of existing measures, as well as the development and validation of measures specific to ethnocultural groups, sexual minorities, and individuals with disabilities is long overdue.

Finally, it should be noted that the much needed corrective trend toward the investigation of female sexual dysfunction may now need to be matched by one that revisits the complexity of male sexual function. There are now many more measures for the assessment of female than of male sexual function. The "age of Viagra" may have reduced male sexual function to a medically produced erection. Although the male sexual response may be more predictable than the female one, we risk simplifying and doing a disservice to male sexual function.

In conclusion, sexual health as defined by the World Health Organization (WHO) is a state of physical, emotional, mental, and social well-being related to sexuality, which is respectful and free of coercion and discrimination (Edwards & Coleman, 2004). Clearly, this encompasses much more than the absence of dysfunction but it includes it. Our endeavors to develop effective assessment strategies are instrumental in the promotion of sexual health. We cannot address problems without the proper tools to identify them. Insuring that these strategies are both accurate and inclusive is essential.

References

Ackerman, M. D., & Carey, M. P. (1995). Psychology's role in the assessment of erectile dysfunction: Historical precedents, current knowledge, and methods. *Journal of Consulting and Clinical Psychology, 63,* 862–876.

American Psychiatric Association (2000). *Diagnostic and statistical manual of mental disorders* (4th ed., text revision). Washington, DC: Author.

Araujo, A. B., Durante, R., Feldamn, H. A., Goldstein, I., & McKinlay, J. B. (1998). The relationship between depressive symptoms and male erectile dysfunction: Cross-sectional results from the Massachusetts Male Aging Study. *Psychosomatic Medicine, 60,* 458–465.

Bach, A. K., Wincze, J. P., & Barlow, D. H. (2001). Sexual dysfunction. In D. H. Barlow (Ed.), *Clinical handbook of psychological disorders: A step-by-step treatment manual* (3rd ed., pp. 562–608). New York: Guilford Press.

Bachman, G., Bancroft, J., Braunstein, G., Burger, H., Davis, S., Dennerstein, I., et.al. (2002). Female androgen insufficiency: The Princeton consensus statement on definition, classification, and assessment. *Fertility and Sterility, 77,* 660–665.

Barlow, D. H. (1986). Causes of sexual dysfunction: The role of anxiety and cognitive interference. *Journal of Consulting and Clinical Psychology, 24,* 321–332.

Basson, R. (2002). Women's sexual desire—disordered or misunderstood? *Journal of Sex and Marital Therapy, 28*(Suppl. 1), 17–28.

Basson, R., Leiblum, S., Brotto, L., Derogatis, L., Fourcroy, J., Fugl-Meyer, K., et al. (2004). Revised definitions of women's sexual dysfunction. *Journal of Sexual Medicine, 1,* 40–48.

Bechara, A., Bertolino, M. V., Casabe, A., Munarriz, R., Goldstein, I., Morin, A., et al., (2003). Duplex Doppler ultrasound assessment of clitoral hemodynamics after topical administration of alprostadil in women with arousal and orgasmic disorders. *Journal of Sex and Marital Therapy, 29*(Suppl. 1), 1–10.

Beck, J. G. (1995). Hypoactive sexual desire disorder: An overview. *Journal of Consulting and Clinical Psychology, 65,* 919–927.

Bergeron, S., Brown, C., Lord, M. J., Oala, M., Binik, Y. M., & Khalife, S. (2002). Physical therapy for vulvar vestibulitis syndrome: A retrospective study. *Journal of Sex and Marital Therapy, 28,* 183–192.

Binik, Y. M. (2005). Should dyspareunia be retained as a sexual dysfunction in DSM-V? A painful classification decision. *Archives of Sexual Behavior, 34,* 11–21.

Binik, Y. M., Meana, M., Berkley, K., & Khalife, S. (1999). The sexual pain disorders: Is the pain sexual or the sex painful? *Annual Review of Sex Research, 10,* 210–235.

Byers, E. S. (1999). The Interpersonal Exchange Model of Sexual Satisfaction: Implications for sex therapy with couples. *Canadian Journal of Counselling, 33,* 95–111.

Carani, C., Zini, D., Baldini, A., Della Casa, L., Ghizzani, A., & Marrama, P. (1990). Effects of androgen treatment in impotent men with normal and low levels of free testosterone. *Archives of Sexual Behavior, 19,* 223–234.

Clayton, A. H., McGarvey, E. L., & Clavet, G. J. (1997). The Changes in Sexual Functioning Questionnaire (CSFQ): Development, reliability, and validity. *Psychopharmacology Bulletin, 33,* 731–745.

Clayton, A. H., McGarvey, E. L., Clavet, G. J., & Piazza, L. (1997). Comparison of sexual functioning in clinical and nonclinical populations using the Changes in Sexual Functioning Questionnaire (CSFQ). *Psychopharmacology Bulletin, 33,* 747–753.

Clayton, A. H., Seagraves, R. T., Leiblum, S., Basson, R., Pyke, R., Cotton, D., et al. (2006). Reliability and validity of the Sexual Interest and Desire Inventory-Female (SIDI-F), a scale designed to measure severity of female Hypoactive Sexual Desire Disorder. *Journal of Sex and Marital Therapy, 12,* 115–135.

Compton, W. M., & Cottler, L. B. (2004). The Diagnostic Interview Schedule (DIS). In M. Hersen (Ed.-in-Chief), M. J. Hilsenroth, & D. L. Segal (Vol. Eds.), *Comprehensive handbook of psychological assessment: Vol. 2. Personality assessment* (pp. 153–162). New York: Wiley.

Conaglen, H. M., & Evans, I. A. (2006). Pictorial cues and sexual desire: An experimental approach. *Archives of Sexual Behavior, 35,* 201–216.

Crenshaw, T. (1985). The sexual aversion syndrome. *Journal of Sex and Marital Therapy, 11,* 285–292.

Daker-White, G. (2002). Reliable and valid self-report outcome measures in sexual (dys)function: A systematic review. *Archives of Sexual Behavior, 31,* 197–209.

Davis, C. M., Yarber, W. L., Bauserman, R., Schreer, G., & Davis, S. L. (Eds.). (1998). *Handbook of sexuality-related measures.* Thousand Oaks, CA: Sage Publications.

Davis, S. R., Davison, S. L., Donath, S., & Bell, R. J. (2005). Circulating androgen levels and self-reported sexual function in women. *Journal of the American Medical Association, 294,* 91–96.

Dekker, J. (1993). Inhibited male orgasm. In W. O'Donohue, & J. H. Geer (Eds.). *Handbook of sexual dysfunctions: Assessment and treatment* (pp. 279–301). Massachusetts: Allyn & Bacon.

Dennerstein, L., Alexander, J. L., & Kotz, K. (2003). The menopause and sexual functioning: A review of population-based studies. *Annual Review of Sex Research, 14,* 64–82.

Derogatis, L. R. (1997). The Derogatis Interview for Sexual Functioning (DISF/DISF-SR): An introductory report. *Journal of Sex and Marital Therapy, 23,* 291–304.

Derogatis, L. R. (1998). The Derogatis Interview for Sexual Functioning. In C. M. Davis, W. L. Yarber, R. Bauserman, G. Schreer, & S. L. Davis (Eds.), *Handbook of sexuality-related measures* (pp. 268–271). Thousand Oaks, CA: Sage Publications.

Derogatis, L. R., & Melisaratos, N. (1979). The DSFI: A multidimensional measure of sexual functioning. *Journal of Sex and Marital Therapy, 5,* 244–248.

Derogatis, L. R., Rosen, R., Leiblum, S., Burnett, A., & Heiman, J. (2002). The Female Sexual Distress Scale (FSDS): Initial validation of a standardized scale for assessment of sexually related personal distress in women. *Journal of Sex and Marital Therapy, 28,* 317–330.

Derogatis, L. R., Rust, J., Golombok, S., Bouchard, C., Nachtigall, L., Rodenberg, C., et al. (2004). Validation of the Profile of Female Sexual Function (PFSF) in surgically and naturally menopausal women. *Journal of Sex and Marital Therapy, 30,* 25–36.

Dunn, K. M., Croft, P. R., & Hackett, G. I. (1999). Association of sexual problems with social, psychological and physical problems in men and women: A cross sectional population survey. *Journal of Epidemiology and Community Health, 53,* 144–148.

Edwards, W. M., & Coleman, E. (2004). Defining sexual health: A descriptive overview. *Archives of Sexual Behavior, 33,* 189–195.

Ekman, P. (1999). Finasteride in the treatment of benign prostatic hypertrophy: An update. New indications for finasteride therapy. *Scandinavian Journal of Urology and Nephrology, 203,* 15–20.

Feldman, H. A., Goldstein, I., Hatzichristou, D. G., Krane, R. J., & McKinlay, J. B. (1994). Impotence and its medical and psychological correlates: Results of the Massachusetts Male Aging Study. *Journal of Urology, 151,* 54–61.

Figueira, I., Possidente, E., Marques, C., & Hayes, K. (2001). Sexual dysfunction: A neglected complication of panic disorder and social phobia. *Archives of Sexual Behavior, 30,* 369–377.

First, M. B., & Gibbon, M. (2004). The Structured Clinical Interview for DSM-IV Axis I Disorders (SCID-I) and the Structured Clinical Interview for DSM-IV Axis II Disorders (SCID-II). In M. Hersen (Ed.-in-Chief), M. J. Hilsenroth, & D. L. Segal (Vol. Eds.), *Comprehensive handbook of psychological assessment: Vol. 2. Personality assessment* (pp. 134–143). New York: Wiley.

Fugl-Meyer, A. R., Lodnert, G., Banholm, I. B., & Fugl-Meyer, K. S. (1997). On life satisfaction in male erectile dysfunction. *International Journal of Impotence Research, 9,* 141–148.

Fugl-Meyer, A. R., & Sjogren Fugl-Meyer, K. (1999). Sexual disabilities, problems and satisfaction in 18–74 year old Swedes. *Scandinavian Journal of Sexology, 3,* 79–105.

Goldmeier, D., & Leiblum, S. R. (2006). Persistent genital arousal in women—a new syndrome entity. *International Journal of STD and AIDS, 17,* 215–216.

Goldstein, I. (2004). Diagnosis of erectile dysfunction. *Sexuality and Disability, 22,* 121–130.

Goldstein, I., & Berman, J. R. (1998). Vasculogenic female sexual dysfunction: Vaginal engorgement and clitoral erectile insufficiency syndromes. *International Journal of Impotence Research, 10,* 584–590.

Heiman, J. (2000). Orgasmic disorders in women. In S. R. Leiblum & R. C. Rosen (Eds.), *Principles and practice of sex therapy* (3rd ed., pp. 118–153). New York: Guilford Press.

Hudson, W. W. (1998). Index of Sexual Satisfaction. In C. M. Davis, W. L. Yarber, R., Bauserman, G. Schreer, & S. L. Davis (Eds.), *Handbook of sexuality-related measures* (pp. 512–513). Thousand Oaks, CA: Sage Publications.

Hudson, W. W., Harrison, D. F., & Crossup, P. C. (1981). A short form scale to measure sexual discord in dyadic relationships. *Journal of Sex Research, 17,* 157–174.

Janssen, E. (2001). Psychophysiological assessment of sexual arousal. In M. W. Wiederman & B. E. Whitley (Eds.), *Handbook for conducting research on human sexuality* (pp. 139–171). New Jersey: Lawrence Erlbaum Associates, Inc.

Jensen, P. T., Groenvold, M., Klee, M. C., Thranov, I., Petersen, M. A., & Machin, D. (2004). Early stage carcinoma, radical hysterectomy, and sexual function: A longitudinal study. *Cancer, 100,* 97–106.

Johannes, C. B., & Avis, N. E. (1997). Gender differences in sexual activity among mid-aged adults in Massachusetts. *Maturitas, 26,* 175–184.

Katz, R. C., Gipson, M. T., Kearly, A., & Kriskovich, M. (1989). Assessing sexual aversion in college students: The Sexual Aversion Scale. *Journal of Sex and Marital Therapy, 15,* 135–140.

Katz, R. C., Gipson, M. T., & Turner, S. (1992). Brief report: Recent findings on the Sexual Aversion Scale. *Journal of Sex and Marital Therapy, 18,* 141–146.

Katz, R. C., & Jardine, D. (1999). The relationship between worry, sexual aversion, and low sexual desire. *Journal of Sex and Marital Therapy, 25,* 293–296.

Keller, A., McGarvey, E. L., & Clayton, A. H. (2006). Reliability and construct validity of the Changes in Sexual Functioning Questionnaire Short-Form (CSFQ-14). *Journal of Sex and Marital Therapy, 32,* 43–52.

Kothari, P. (1984). For discussion: Ejaculatory disorders—a new dimension. *British Journal of Sexual Medicine, 11,* 205–209.

Kukkonen, T. M., Binik, Y. M., Amsel, R., & Carrier, S. (2007). Thermography as a physiological measure of sexual arousal in both men and women. *Journal of Sexual Medicine, 4,* 93–105.

Kukkonen, T. M., Paterson, L., Binik, Y. M., Amsel, R., Bouvier, F., & Khalife, S. (2006). Convergent and discriminant validity of clitoral color Doppler ultrasonography as a measure of female sexual arousal. *Journal of Sex and Marital Therapy, 32,* 281–287.

Kurdek, L. A. (1992). Dimensionality of the Dyadic Adjustment Scale: Evidence from heterosexual and homosexual couples. *Journal of Family Psychology, 6,* 22–35.

Laan, E., Everaerd, W., van der Velde, J., & Geer, J. H. (1995). Determinants of subjective experience of sexual arousal in women: Feedback from genital arousal and erotic stimulus content. *Psychophysiology, 32,* 444–451.

Laumann, E. O., & Mahay, J. (2002). The social organization of women's sexuality. In M. Wingood & R. J. DiClemente (Eds.), *Handbook of women's sexual and reproductive health* (pp. 43–70). New York: Kluwer Academic/Plenum Publishers.

Laumann, E. O., Paik, A., Glasser, D. B., Kang, J.-H., Wang, T., Levinson, B., et al. (2006). A cross-national study of subjective sexual well-being among older women and men: Findings from the global study of sexual attitudes and behaviors. *Archives of Sexual Behavior, 35,* 145–161.

Laumann, E. O., Paik, A., & Rosen, R. C. (1999). Sexual dysfunction in the US: Prevalence and predictors. *Journal of the American Medical Association, 281,* 537–544.

Laumann, E. O., Gagnon, J. H., Michael, R. T., & Michaels, S. (1994). *The Social Organization of Sexuality: Sexual Practices in the United States.* Chicago: University of Chicago Press.

Leiblum, S. R., & Nathan, S. (2001). Persistent sexual arousal syndrome: A newly discovered pattern of female sexuality. *Journal of Sex and Marital Therapy, 27,* 365–380.

Leiblum, S. R., & Rosen, R. C. (2000). Introduction: Sex therapy in the age of Viagra. In S. R. Leiblum & R. C. Rosen (Eds.), *Principles and practice of sex therapy* (3rd ed., pp. 1–13). New York: Guilford Press.

Levin, R. J. (2004). Measuring female genital functions—a research essential but still a clinical luxury? *Sex and Relationship Therapy, 19,* 191–200.

Levin, R. J. (2006). Blood flow: heated electrodes. In I. Goldstein, C. M. Meston, S. R. Davis, & A. M. Traish (Eds.), *Women's sexual function and dysfunction: Study, diagnosis and treatment* (pp. 391–398). Abingdon, Oxon: Taylor & Francis.

Lewis, L. J. (2004). Examining sexual health discourses in a racial/ethnic context. *Archives of Sexual Behavior, 33,* 223–234.

Loeb, T. B., Williams, J. K., Carmona, J. V., Rivkin, I., Wyatt, G. E., Chin, D., et al. (2002). Child sexual abuse: Associations with the sexual functioning of adolescents and adults. *Annual Review of Sex Research, 13,* 307–345.

LoPiccolo, J., & Steger, J. C. (1974). The Sexual Interaction Inventory: A new instrument for assessment of sexual dysfunction. *Archives of Sexual Behavior, 3,* 585–595.

Mah, K., & Binik, Y. M. (2002). Do all orgasm feel alike? Evaluating a two-dimensional model of the orgasm. *Journal of Sex Research, 39,* 104–113.

Maravilla, K. R. (2006). Blood flow: Magnetic resonance imaging and brain imaging for evaluating sexual arousal in women. In I. Goldstein, C. M. Meston, S. R. Davis, & A. M. Traish (Eds.), *Women's sexual function and dysfunction: Study, diagnosis and treatment* (pp. 368–382). Abingdon, Oxon: Taylor & Francis.

Margolese, H., & Assalian, P. (1996). Sexual side effects of antidepressants: A review. *Journal of Sex and Marital Therapy, 22,* 209–217.

Masheb, R. M., Lozano-Blanco, C., Kohorn, E. I., Minkin, M. J., & Kerns, R. D. (2004). Assessing sexual function and dyspareunia with the Female Sexual Function Index (FSFI) in women with volvodynia. *Journal of Sex and Marital Therapy, 30,* 315–324.

Maurice, W. L. (1999). *Sexual medicine in primary care.* St. Louis: C.V. Mosby Co.

McCabe. M. P., & Cobain, M. J. (1998). The impact of individual and relationship factors on sexual dysfunction among males and females. *Sexual and Marital Therapy, 13,* 131–143.

McConaghy, N. (2003). Sexual dysfunctions and deviations. In M. Hersen & S. M. Turner (Eds.), *Diagnostic Interviewing* (3rd ed., pp. 315–341). New York: Kluwer Academic Publishers.

McCoy, N. L., & Matyas, J. R. (1998). McCoy Female Sexuality Questionnaire. In C. M. Davis, W. L. Yarber, R. Bauserman, G. Schreer, & S. L. Davis (Eds.), *Handbook of sexuality related measures* (pp. 249–251). Thousand Oaks, CA: Sage Publications.

McHorney, C. A., Rust, J., Golombok, S., Davis, S., Bouchard, C., Brown, C., et al. (2004). Profile of Female Sexual Function: A patient-based, international, psychometric instrument for the assessment of hypoactive sexual desire disorder in oopherectomized women. *Menopause, 11,* 474–483.

Meana, M., & Binik, Y. M. (1994). Painful coitus: A review of female dyspareunia. *Journal of Nervous and Mental Disease, 182,* 264–272.

Meana, M., Binik, Y. M., Khalife, S., & Cohen, D. (1997a). Dyspareunia: Sexual dysfunction or pain syndrome? *Journal of Nervous and Mental Disease, 185,* 561–569.

Meana, M., Binik, Y. M., Khalife, S., & Cohen, D. (1997b) Biopsychosocial profile of women with dyspareunia: Searching for etiological hypotheses. *Obstetrics and Gynecology, 90,* 583–589.

Melzack, R. (1975) The McGill Pain Questionnaire: Major properties and scoring methods. *Pain, 1,* 277–299.

Meston, C. M. (2000). The psychophysiological assessment of female sexual function. *Journal of Sex Education and Therapy, 25,* 6–16.

Meston, C. M. (2003). Validation of the Female Sexual Function Index (FSFI) in women with Female Orgasmic Disorder and in women with Hypoactive Sexual Desire Disorder. *Journal of Sex and Marital Therapy, 29,* 39–46.

Meston, C. M., Levin, R. J., Sipski, M. L., Hull, E., & Heiman, J. R. (2004). Women's orgasm. *Annual Review of Sex Research, 15,* 173–257.

Meston, C. M., & Trapnell, P. (2005). Development and validation of a five-factor sexual satisfaction and distress scale for women: The Sexual Satisfaction Scale for women. *Journal of Sexual Medicine, 2,* 66–81.

Metz, M. E., & Pryor, J. L. (2000). Premature ejaculation: A psychophysiological approach for assessment and management. *Journal of Sex and Marital Therapy, 26,* 293–320.

Mykletun, A., Dahl, A. A., O'Leary, M. P., & Fossa, S. D. (2005). Assessment of male sexual function by the Brief Sexual Function Inventory. *British Journal of Urology International, 97,* 316–323.

Nader, S. G., Maitland, S. R., Munarriz, R., & Goldstein, I. (2006). Blood flow: Duplex Doppler ultrasound. In I. Goldstein, C. M. Meston, S. R. Davis, & A. M. Traish (Eds.), *Women's sexual function and dysfunction: Study, diagnosis and treatment* (pp. 383–390). Abingdon, Oxon: Taylor & Francis.

Nappi, R. E., Ferdeghini, F., Abbiati, I., Vercesi, C., Farina, C., & Polatti, F. (2003). Electrical stimulation (ES) in the management of sexual pain disorders. *Journal of Sex and Marital Therapy, 29*(Suppl. 1), 103–110.

O'Leary, M. P., Fowler, F. J., Lenderking, W. R., Barber, B., Sagnier, P. P., Guess, H. A., et al. (1995). A brief male sexual function inventory for urology. *Urology, 46*, 697–706.

Papatsoris, A. G., & Korantzopoulos, P. G. (2006). Hypertension, antihypertensive therapy, and erectile dysfunction. *Angiology, 57*, 47–52.

Parish, S. J. (2006). Role of the primary care and internal medicine clinician. In I. Goldstein, C. M. Meston, S. R. Davis, & A. M. Traish (Eds.), *Women's sexual function and dysfunction: Study, diagnosis and treatment* (pp. 689–695). Abingdon, Oxon: Taylor & Francis.

Payne, K. A., Bergeron, S., Khalife, S., & Binik, Y. M. (2006). Assessment, treatment strategies and outcome results: Perspective of pain specialists. In I. Goldstein, C. M. Meston, S. R. Davis, & A. M. Traish (Eds.), *Women's sexual function and dysfunction: Study, diagnosis and treatment* (pp. 471–479). Abingdon, Oxon: Taylor & Francis.

Payne, K. A., & Binik, Y. M. (2006). Reviving the labial thermistor clip. [Letter to the Editor]. *Archives of Sexual Behavior, 35*, 111–113.

Payne, K. A., Binik, Y. M., Amsel, R., & Khalife, S. (2005). When sex hurts, anxiety and fear orient toward pain. *European Journal of Pain, 9*, 427–436.

Perelman, M. A. (2006). A new combination treatment for premature ejaculation: A sex therapist's perspective. *Journal of Sexual Medicine, 3*, 1004–1012.

Pfeiffer, E., & Davis, G. C. (1972). Determinants of sexual behavior in middle and old age. *Journal of the American Geriatric Society, 20*, 151–158.

Prause, N., & Janssen, E. (2006). Blood flow: Vaginal photoplethysmography. In I. Goldstein, C. M. Meston, S. R. Davis, & A. M. Traish (Eds.), *Women's function and dysfunction: Study, diagnosis and treatment* (pp. 359–365). Abingdon, Oxon: Taylor & Francis.

Pukall, C. F., Binik, Y. M., & Khalife, S. (2004). A new instrument for pain assessment in vulvar vestibulitis syndrome. *Journal of Sex and Marital Therapy, 30*, 69–78.

Pukall, C. F., Binik, Y. M., Khalife, S., Amsel, R., & Abbott, F. V. (2002). Vestibular tactile and pain thresholds in women with vulvar vestibulitis syndrome. *Pain, 96*, 163–175.

Quirk, F. H., Haughie, S., & Symonds, T. (2005). The use of the Sexual Function Questionnaire as a screening tool for women with sexual dysfunction. *Journal of Sexual Medicine, 2*, 469–477.

Quirk, F. H., Heiman, J. R., Rosen, R. C., Laan, E., Smith, M. D., & Boolell, M. (2002). Development of a sexual function questionnaire for clinical trials of female sexual dysfunction. *Journal of Women's Health and Gender-Based Medicine, 11*, 277–289.

Reinhardt, R. N. (1998). The Sexual Interaction Inventory. In C. M. Davis, W. L. Yarber, R. Bauserman, G. Schreer, & S. L. Davis (Eds.), *Handbook of sexuality-related measures* (pp. 278–280). Thousand Oaks, CA: Sage Publications.

Reissing, E. D., Binik, Y. M., Khalife, S., Cohen, D., & Amsel, R. (2003). Etiological correlates of vaginismus: Sexual and physical abuse, sexual knowledge, sexual self-schema and relationship adjustment. *Journal of Sex and Marital Therapy, 29*, 47–59.

Reissing, E. D., Binik, Y. M., Khalife, S., Cohen, D., & Amsel, R. (2004). Vaginal spasm, pain, and behavior: An empirical investigation of the diagnosis of vaginismus. *Archives of Sexual Behavior, 33*, 5–17.

Reissing, E. D., Brown, C., Lord, M. J., Binik, Y. M., & Khalife, S. (2005). Pelvic floor muscle functioning in women with vulvar vestibulitis syndrome. *Journal of Psychosomatic Obstetrics and Gynecology, 26*, 107–113.

Rellini, A. H., Nappi, R. E., Vaccaro, P., Ferdeghini, F., Abbiati, I., & Meston, C. M. (2005). Validation of the McCoy Female Sexuality Questionnaire in an Italian sample. *Archives of Sexual Behavior, 34*, 641–647.

Richardson, D., Nalabanda, A., & Goldmeier, D. (2006). Retarded ejaculation—a review. *International Journal of STD and AIDS, 17*, 143–150.

Rosen, R., Brown, C., Heiman, J., Leiblum, S., Meston, C., Shabsigh, R., et al. (2000). The Female Sexual Function Index (FSFI): A multidimensional self-report instrument for the assessment of female sexual function. *Journal of Sex and Marital Therapy, 26*, 191–208.

Rosen, R. C., Cappelleri, J. C., Smith, M. D., Lipsky, J., & Pena, B. M. (1999). Development and evaluation of an abridged, 5-item version of the International Index of Erectile Function (IIEF-5) as a diagnostic tool for erectile dysfunction. *International Journal of Impotence Research, 11*, 319–326.

Rosen, R. C., Catania, J., Pollack, L., Althof, S., O'Leary, M., & Seftel, A. D. (2004). Male Sexual Health Questionnaire (MSHQ): Scale development and psychometric validation. *Urology, 64*, 777–782.

Rosen, R. C., Janssen, E., Wiegel, M., Bancroft, J., Althof, S., Wincze, J., et al. (2006). Psychological and interpersonal correlates in men with erectile dysfunction and their partners: A pilot study of treatment outcome with sildenafil. *Journal of Sex and Marital Therapy, 32*, 215–234.

Rosen, R. C., Lobo, R. A., Block, B. A., Yang, H.-M., & Zipfel, L. M. (2004). Menopausal Sexual Interest Questionnaire (MSIQ): A unidimensional scale for the assessment of sexual interest in postmenopausal women. *Journal of Sex and Marital Therapy, 30*, 235–250.

Rosen, R. C., Riley, A., Wagner, G., Osterloh, I. H., Kirkpatrick, J., & Mishra, A. (1997). The International Index of Erectile Function (IIEF): A multidimensional scale for assessment of erectile dysfunction. *Urology, 49*, 822–830.

Rosen, R. C., Taylor, J. E., & Leiblum, S. (1998). Brief Index of Sexual Functioning for Women. In C. M. Davis, W. L. Yarber, R. Bauserman, G. Schreer, & S. L. Davis (Eds.), *Handbook of sexuality-related measures* (pp. 251–255). Thousand Oaks, CA: Sage Publications.

Rosen, R. C., Taylor, J. E., Leiblum, S. R., & Bachman, G. (1993). Prevalence of sexual dysfunction in women: Results of a survey study in 329 women in an outpatient gynecological clinic. *Journal of Sex and Marital Therapy, 19*, 171–188.

Rosenbaum, T. Y. (2005). Physiotherapy treatment of sexual pain disorders. *Journal of Sex and Marital Therapy, 31*, 329–340.

Rosser, B. R., Metz, M. E., Bockting, W. O., & Buroker, T. (1997). Sexual difficulties, concerns, and satisfaction in homosexual men: An empirical study with implications for HIV prevention. *Journal of Sex and Marital Therapy, 23*, 61–73.

Rust, J., & Golombok, S. (1985). The Golombok-Rust Inventory of Sexual Satisfaction (GRISS). *British Journal of Clinical Psychology, 24*, 63–64.

Rust, J., & Golombok, S. (1986). The GRISS: A psychometric instrument for the assessment of sexual dysfunction. *Archives of Sexual Behavior, 15*, 157–165.

Rust, J., & Golombok, S. (1998). The GRISS: A psychometric scale and profile of sexual dysfunction. In C. M. Davis, W. L. Yarber, R. Bauserman, G. Schreer, & S. L. Davis (Eds.), *Handbook of sexuality-related measures* (pp. 192–194). Thousand Oaks, CA: Sage Publications.

Schiavi, R. C., White, D., Mandeli, J., & Levine, A. C. (1997). Effect of testosterone administration on sexual behavior and mood in men with erectile dysfunction. *Archives of Sexual Behavior, 26*, 231–241.

Segraves, K., & Segraves, R. T. (1991). Hypoactive sexual desire disorder: Prevalence and comorbidity in 906 subjects. *Journal of Sex and Marital Therapy, 17*, 55–58.

Segraves, K., & Segraves, R. T. (1993). Medical aspects of orgasm disorders. In W. O'Donohue & J. H. Geer (Eds.), *Handbook of sexual dysfunctions: Assessment and treatment* (pp. 225–252). Massachusetts: Allyn & Bacon.

Sherwin, B. (1988). A comparative analysis of the role of androgen in human male and female sexual behavior: Behavioral specificity, critical thresholds, and sensitivity. *Psychobiology, 16*, 416–425.

Shifren, J. L., Braunstein, G. D., Simon, J. A., Casson, P. R., Buster, J. E., Redmond, G. P., et al. (2000). Transdermal testeosterone treatment in women with impaired sexual function after oopherectomy. *New England Journal of Medicine, 343*, 682–688.

Shvartzman, P. (1994). The role of nocturnal penile tumescence and rigidity monitoring in the evaluation of impotence. *The Journal of Family Practice, 39*, 279–282.

Sills, T., Wunderlich, G., Pyke, R., Segraves, R. T., Leiblum, S., Clayton, A., et al. (2005). The Sexual Interest and Desire Inventory—Female (SIDI-F): Item response analyses of data from women diagnosed with hypoactive sexual desire disorder. *Journal of Sexual Medicine, 2*, 801–818.

Simons, J. S., & Carey, M. P. (2001). Prevalence of the sexual dysfunctions: Results from a decade of research. *Archives of Sexual Behavior, 22*, 51–58.

Spanier, G. B. (1976). Measuring dyadic adjustment: New scales for assessing the quality of marriage and similar dyads. *Journal of Marriage and Family, 38*, 15–28.

Spector, I. P., Carey, M. P., & Steinberg, L. (1996). The Sexual Desire Inventory: Development, factor structure, and evidence of reliability. *Journal of Sex and Marital Therapy, 22*, 175–190.

Sullivan, M. J. L., Bishop, S. R., & Pivik, J. (1995). The Pain Catastrophizing Scale: Development and validation. *Psychological Assessment, 7*, 524–532.

Taylor, J. F., Rosen, R. C., & Leiblum, S. R. (1994). Self-report assessment of female sexual function: Psychometric evaluation of the Brief Index of Sexual Functioning for Women. *Archives of Sexual Behavior, 23*, 627–643.

ter Kuile, M., Brauer, M., & Laan, E. (2006). The Female Sexual Function Index (FSFI) and the Female Sexual Distress Scale (FSDS): Psychometric properties within a Dutch population. *Journal of Sex and Marital Therapy, 32*, 289–304.

Tiefer, L. (2002). Beyond the medical model of women's sexual problems: A campaign to resist the promotion of "female sexual dysfunction." *Sexual and Relationship Therapy, 17*, 127–135.

Utian, W. H., McLean, D. B., Symonds, T., Symons, J., Somayaji, V., & Sisson, M. (2005). A methodology study to validate a structured diagnostic method used to diagnose female sexual dysfunction and its subtypes in postmenopausal women. *Journal of Sex and Marital Therapy, 31*, 271–283.

van Anders, S. M., Chernick, A. B., Chernick, B. A., Hampson, E., & Fisher, W. A. (2005). Preliminary clinical experience with androgen administration for pre- and postmenopausal women with hypoactive sexual desire. *Journal of Sex and Marital Therapy, 31,* 173–185.

van Berlo, W., & Ensink, B. (2000). Problems with sexuality after sexual assault. *Annual Review of Sex Research, 11,* 235–258.

van Lankveld, J. J. D. M., ter Kuile, M. M., de Groot, H. E., Melles, R., Nefs, J., & Zandbergen, M. (2006). Cognitive-behavioral therapy for women with lifelong vaginismus: A randomized waiting-list controlled trail of efficacy. *Journal of Consulting and Clinical Psychology, 74,* 168–178.

Waldinger, M. D., Zwinderman, A. H., Berend, O., & Schweitzer, D. H. (2005). Proposal for a definition of lifelong premature ejaculation based on epidemiological stopwatch data. *Journal of Sexual Medicine, 2,* 498–507.

Weeks, G. R. (2005). The emergence of a new paradigm in sex therapy: Integration. *Sexual and Relationship Therapy, 20,* 89–103.

Weiner, D. N., & Rosen, R. C. (1997). Medications and their impact. In M. L. Sipski & C. J. Alexander *and chronic illness: A health professional's guide* (pp. 85–114). Gaithersburg, MD: Aspen Publishers Inc.

Weisberg, R. B., Brown, T. A., Wincze, J. P., & Barlow, D. H. (2001). Causal attributions and male sexual arousal: The impact of attributions for a bogus erectile difficulty on sexual arousal, cognitions, and affect. *Journal of Abnormal Psychology, 110,* 324–334.

Wiegel, M., Meston, C., & Rosen, R. (2005). The Female Sexual Function Index (FSFI): Cross-validation and development of clinical cutoff scores. *Journal of Sex and Marital Therapy, 31,* 1–20.

Wincze, J. P., & Carey, M. P. (2001). *Sexual dysfunction: A guide for assessment and treatment.* New York: Guilford Press

22

Paraphilias

Michael C. Seto
Carolyn S. Abramowitz
Howard E. Barbaree

This chapter provides an overview of methods for assessing paraphilias. Paraphilias are intense and persistent sexual interests in atypical targets or activities; thus, the focus of a person's sexual thoughts, fantasies, urges, and arousal are targets other than sexually mature humans, or activities that are highly unusual among individuals who prefer sexually mature partners. Better known examples of target paraphilias include pedophilia (prepubescent children), fetishism (nonliving objects), or partialism (body parts such as hands or feet); examples of activity paraphilias include sadism (physical or psychological suffering of others), masochism (being humiliated, bound, or otherwise made to suffer), exhibitionism (exposing one's genitals to an unsuspecting stranger), or voyeurism (observing an unsuspecting stranger engaged in normally private activities). Other paraphilias are extremely rare, and have only been described in case reports. A target or activity is considered to be an exclusive paraphilia when it is essential for someone to be sexually gratified (e.g., First, 2004; Moser & Levitt, 1987).

Money (1984) has described a complex descriptive typology of paraphilias, and Freund (1990) proposed that certain activity paraphilias—exhibitionism, voyeurism, frotteurism, and preferential rape—reflected disturbances in the species-typical male courtship process. Money's typology and Freund's notion of courtship disorder are descriptive rather than explanatory. We do not have a satisfactory theory to explain why some targets and activities appear to be more likely to become the focus of paraphilias than other targets or activities. For example, fetishistic interest in synthetic materials such as rubber or vinyl is much more likely to occur than fetishism for natural materials such as wood or feathers. Mason (1997) has observed that fetish categories may be stable, but the objects in those categories change (e.g., a fetishistic interest in clothing materials has been observed for more than a hundred years, but interests in velvet or silk in the 19th century have largely been displaced by interests in vinyl, rubber, or leather).

The majority of this review deals with pedophilia, which has received the most research attention because of public and professional concerns about sexual offenses committed against children. Individuals with other paraphilias that lead to criminal behavior if acted upon, such as exhibitionism, voyeurism, or nonconsensual sadism, are also more likely to be referred to clinical or forensic settings than individuals with other paraphilias and therefore more likely to be studied by researchers. Clinicians are unlikely to see other paraphilias in their practices unless the person is greatly troubled by their paraphilic sexual interests or it causes relationship or other personal difficulties.

Reliable and valid assessment methods are needed for effective clinical practice and for scientific research. In this chapter, we review empirically supported methods for assessing paraphilias, including self-report through interview or questionnaire; behavioral history, including sexual offense history; and laboratory tasks involving viewing time or the assessment of penile response (phallometry).

NATURE OF THE DISORDER

In the most recent edition of the *Diagnostic and Statistical Manual of Mental Disorders* (DSM-IV-TR; American Psychiatric Association [APA], 2000), the primary nosological system used by mental health professionals in North America, the diagnostic criteria for paraphilias are (a) recurrent and intense sexual fantasies, urges, or behaviors directed toward body parts or nonhuman objects, suffering or humiliation of either partner in a sexual situation, or sexual activity with a nonconsenting person; and (b) these fantasies, urges, or behaviors cause clinically significant distress or impairment in functioning. The DSM-IV-TR specifically mentions a number of the more commonly known paraphilias. The paraphilias listed in the 10th revision of the *International Classification of Mental and Behavioural Disorders* (ICD-10: World Health Organization, 1997) are generally quite similar in content to the DSM-IV-TR.

Paraphilic individuals are a heterogeneous group and there is little evidence to suggest they differ from nonparaphilic individuals in most sociodemographic characteristics. However, no large-scale comparative studies have been conducted. The prevalence of paraphilias is unknown, as epidemiological surveys regarding persistence and intensity of sexual interests have not been conducted. It is generally accepted, however, that paraphilias are much more likely to manifest in males. Retrospective studies suggest that paraphilias emerge in early adolescence. Phenomenologically, the experience may be similar to the emerging awareness of one's sexual orientation around the time of puberty; this awareness typically precedes identifying oneself as heterosexual or homosexual, and also typically precedes engaging in sexual behavior with opposite-sex or same-sex persons, respectively (McClintock & Herdt, 1996; Remafedi et al., 1992; Savin-Williams & Diamond, 2000).

Abel, Becker, Mittelman, and Cunningham (1987) found that one quarter to one half of their groups of sex offenders with child victims reported an onset of sexual interests in children before the age of 18. Freund and Kuban (1993) surveyed 76 adult sex offenders with child victims who admitted being sexually interested in children and recalled that they were first aware of a curiosity to see nude children as young adolescents. Zolondek, Abel, Northey, and Jordan (2001) reported data from 485 adolescent males between the ages of 11 and 17 referred for assessment or treatment of possibly paraphilic interests or behavior. The adolescents completed a questionnaire about their sexual interests and experiences as part of their evaluation. Of these 26% acknowledged engaging in fetishistic behavior, 17% acknowledged voyeuristic behavior, and 12% acknowledged exhibitionistic behavior. The average age of onset across these paraphilic behaviors was between 10 and 12.

There is evidence that paraphilias are comorbid with mood disorders, so nonforensic practitioners who specialize in seeing clients with mood disorders may occasionally see individuals with paraphilias in their practice. For example, Dunsieth et al. (2004) reported high prevalence rates for mood and anxiety disorders in a sample of 113 male sex offenders seen at a residential treatment facility; 58% met diagnostic criteria for a mood disorder and 23% met diagnostic criteria for an anxiety disorder. The paraphilic sex offenders, half of whom were pedophiles, were more likely to have been diagnosed for any mood disorder, anxiety disorder, or impulse control disorder than the nonparaphilic sex offenders. Kafka (1997, 2003) has argued that paraphilias and mood disorders share an underlying deficit in serotonin regulation, and thus antidepressant medications that increase serotonin may have positive effects on both mood and paraphilic sexual fantasies, thoughts, urges, and behavior.

In addition to complaints of mood problems, paraphilic individuals may come to the attention of clinicians because of relationship difficulties, which can result if the person cannot confide in their partner (e.g., if they have a stigmatized paraphilia such as pedophilia) or if the person's partner is aware and distressed by the paraphilic interest (e.g., a transvestic fetishist whose spouse is upset about his cross-dressing or a masochist whose spouse does not want to engage in sadomasochistic activities).

There is evidence from several studies that paraphilic behaviors tend to co-occur, for example, some pedophiles have also engaged in exhibitionistic behavior, or some voyeurs have also engaged in fetishistic or sadistic behavior (Abel, Becker, Cunningham-Rathner, Mittelman, & Rouleau, 1988; Bradford, Boulet, & Pawlak, 1992; Freund & Seto, 1998; Freund, Seto, & Kuban, 1997; Smallbone & Wortley, 2004). Thus, clients referred because of concerns about one paraphilia should also be assessed regarding their sexual interests in other atypical targets or activities.

PURPOSES OF ASSESSMENT

In the following sections, we focus our review on assessments for the purpose of (a) diagnosis, (b) case conceptualization and treatment planning, and (c) treatment monitoring and evaluation. See Seto (2008) for a review of cognitive science and neuroimaging paradigms adapted to the assessment of sexual interests, particularly pedophilia, in research.

ASSESSMENT FOR DIAGNOSIS

We expect most practitioners will conduct assessments for paraphilias in one of two clinical contexts. First, evaluators will use these assessments in forensic settings where the suspected paraphilia is associated with criminal conduct (e.g., pedophilia and sexual offenses against children, sexual sadism and rape, exhibitionism and indecent exposure). The individual will have criminal charges or convictions for sexual crimes, and the main clinical questions will be about the presence or absence of paraphilias, given the implications of this diagnosis for treatment, management, and risk to sexually offend again. Referrals may come from the courts upon sentencing, parole boards considering a release from custody, or treatment providers considering a candidate for participation in a sex offender treatment program.

The second context involves nonforensic clinical settings where paraphilias that are not usually associated with criminal conduct are encountered. For example, clinicians may be asked to assess someone for paraphilias because that person is distressed about his or her sexual thoughts, fantasies, urges, or behavior, whereas sex or marital therapists may see someone because his or her sexual interests are causing difficulties in relationships or other aspects of interpersonal functioning. Clinicians in settings providing care to individuals with obsessive–compulsive disorder (OCD) may be asked to conduct these assessments with individuals who have obsessive thoughts about atypical targets or activities, for example, reporting recurring and seemingly uncontrollable thoughts about molesting a child (Freeman & Leonard, 2000; Gordon, 2002). Usually, these assessments are done to rule out a paraphilia and to reassure the OCD client concerning the unlikelihood of their acting upon their thoughts. The differential diagnosis is made by determining if the person's thoughts are associated

with sexual arousal or pleasure, instead of anxiety or disgust, and by inquiring about other symptoms of obsessive–compulsive disorder.

There is often a substantial difference in the quality and breadth of information that is available in forensic versus nonforensic evaluations of paraphilias. Forensic evaluators benefit from the availability of justice records regarding criminal sexual behavior (e.g., previous allegations and charges of sexual offenses), previous assessment reports, and information from health and school authorities. At the same time, individuals facing criminal sanctions may be understandably reluctant to disclose paraphilic thoughts, fantasies, urges, or behavior, and thus the information that can be obtained through self-report may be limited or invalid. Nonforensic evaluators do not usually have access to the same breadth of collateral information as their forensic counterparts, but they can often obtain more information through self-report as the client is self-referred and presumably more willing to talk about potentially paraphilic sexual interests, though still very reluctant to disclose highly stigmatized paraphilias (e.g., someone complaining of their masochistic sexual interests because it causes relationship difficulties may not be willing to disclose sexual thoughts, fantasies, or urges regarding prepubescent children). Table 22.1 summarizes the psychometric properties of a selection of relevant measures used for the purpose of diagnosis.

Self-Report

Sexual histories are typically obtained through clinical interview. Respondents are asked questions pertaining to their sexual thoughts, interests, and behaviors, as well as relationship history. Comprehensive interviews also include questions to help clinicians rule out other explanations for potentially paraphilic sexual thoughts, urges, or behavior. No validated semistructured or structured interviews are available.

Interviews can be quite informative, but there are potential problems with recall and other report biases in gathering data on sexual behavior in this way (see Wiederman, 2002, for a review of research on the impact of self-report methods to study sexuality). Another limitation is the face validity of interview questions (e.g., "Do you ever have sexual fantasies about hurting someone?" "Are you sexually attracted to children?"). Individuals may understandably lie because of embarrassment about sexual matters,

TABLE 22.1 Ratings of Instruments Used for Diagnosis

Instrument	Norms	Internal Consistency	Inter-Rater Reliability	Test–Retest Reliability	Content Validity	Construct Validity	Validity Generalization	Clinical Utility	Highly Recommended
Self-Report									
SICQ	A	E	NA	U	G	E	G	G	
MASA	A	G	NA	G	G	G	G	A	
MSI	G	G	NA	E	A	E	E	E	✓
Behavioral History									
SSPI	A	U	A	U	A	A	G	E	✓
Behavioral Measures									
Viewing Time	U	G	NA	U	A	A	G	G	
Phallometry	U	A	NA	L	G	E	G	A	✓

Note: SICQ = Sexual Interest Cardsort Questionnaire; MASA = Multidimensional Assessment of Sex and Aggression; MSI = Multiphasic Sex Inventory; SSPI = Screening Scale for Pedophilic Interests; L = Less Than Adequate; A = Adequate; G = Good; E = Excellent; U = Unavailable; NA = Not Applicable.

or concerns about the legal or social sanctions they could face in acknowledging illegal sexual behavior.

One way to reduce the reluctance of individuals to disclose paraphilic sexual interests or behavior in face-to-face interviews is to administer questionnaires. A number of questionnaires have been developed to assess paraphilias, for example, the Multiphasic Sex Inventory (MSI: Nichols & Molinder, 1984), and the Multidimensional Assessment of Sex and Aggression (MASA: Knight, Prentky, & Cerce, 1994). Manuals are available for these two questionnaires; the first is commercially available and the second is available from the lead developer.

The MSI contains 200 items, organized into 20 scales, tapping different aspects of conventional and paraphilic sexuality, including six validity scales and a scale assessing attitudes regarding treatment. A number of studies have reported on its psychometric properties, which appear to be good to excellent in terms of the internal consistency of scales and test–retest reliability (Day, Miner, Sturgeon, & Murphy, 1989; Kalichman, Henderson, Shealy, & Dwyer, 1992; Simkins, Ward, Bowman, & Rinck, 1989). A revised version of this measure, the MSI-II, has been developed but there is only one peer-reviewed study of this version, and its scoring algorithms cannot be independently verified because tests must be submitted to a scoring service. Thus, we include only the MSI in this review. Day et al. (1989) reported that MSI scores explained more of the variance in past criminal sexual behavior than phallometrically assessed sexual arousal, and several studies have shown that MSI scores can distinguish between types or subgroups of sex offenders (Baldwin & Roy, 1998; Barnard,

Robbins, Tingle, Shaw, & Newman, 1987; Craig et al., 2006; Kalichman et al., 1989).

The MASA has undergone repeated evaluation and revision. It was developed to assess adult male sex offenders, but recent studies have examined its performance in the assessment of adolescent male sex offenders (e.g., Daversa, 2005). It contains items drawn from existing questionnaires and generated by a panel of clinicians, assessing domains such as antisocial behavior, social competence, anger and aggression, paraphilias, sexual preoccupation and compulsivity, offense planning, sexual attitudes, and pornography use. Of most relevance to the current chapter are the items pertaining to sadism and other paraphilias. The sadism and paraphilias scales have good internal consistencies and good test–retest reliabilities, and the sadism items have figured in the testing of theoretical models of sexual offending against women (Knight & Sims-Knight, 2003).

The Sexual Interest Cardsort Questionnaire (SICQ; Holland, Zolondek, Abel, Jordan, & Becker, 2000) contains 75 descriptions of explicit sexual acts that are relevant to different paraphilia diagnoses. Respondents rate each description on a seven-point scale in terms of their sexual interest. The measure is called a cardsort because it was originally developed as a set of cards that were sorted by respondents. Holland et al. (2000) reported that SICQ responses were significantly correlated with group classification made by clinicians in a sample of 371 males seeking assessment or treatment because of their paraphilic interests or sexual offending. Holland et al. also reported on the development of a shorter version of the SICQ that contains only 45 descriptions. Laws,

Hanson, Osborn, and Greenbaum (2000) reported that the SICQ could distinguish between offenders who victimized only boys from offenders who victimized only girls. Hunter, Becker, and Kaplan (1995) reported on the administration of a modification of the SICQ to 38 adolescent sex offenders, but no other published data are available on this adolescent version.

Several promising measures are not included in Table 22.1. The Clarke Sexual History Questionnaire-Revised (SHQ-R: Langevin & Paitich, 2002) is intended for adults and contains 508 items divided into 17 sections, tapping different aspects of conventional and paraphilic sexuality, including early childhood experiences, sexual dysfunction, fantasies, exposure to pornography, and behavior. Langevin, Lang, and Curnoe (1998) compared 201 male sex offenders to 72 controls (50 nonsex offenders and 22 heterosexual volunteers) and found that only one third of the sex offenders admitted to having paraphilic sexual fantasies, and in fact were less likely to report having fantasies of any kind than the controls. Curnoe and Langevin (2002) found that the SHQ-R could be used to distinguish sex offenders who admit to having paraphilic sexual fantasies from those who do not. The SHQ-R was not included in Table 22.1 because it has poor test–retest reliability, and similar measures are available.

The Sexual Fantasy Questionnaire was developed for adolescents and contains items about sexual fantasies involving sex with children under the age of 12, as well as items about other atypical sexual fantasies. The Sexual Fantasy Questionnaire is promising because it is suitable for adolescents and assesses a variety of paraphilic interests, but it has only been examined in a single peer-reviewed article so far (Daleiden, Kaufman, Hilliker, & O'Neil, 1998).

Finally, the Wilson Sexual Fantasy Questionnaire is a 40-item questionnaire that includes a scale assessing sadomasochistic sexual fantasies (other scales assess the frequency of fantasies with intimate, exploratory, or impersonal themes). This questionnaire is distinguished from many of the other measures we have listed because it has been used with both men and women (e.g., Baumgartner, Scalora, & Huss, 2002; Gosselin, Wilson, & Barrett, 1991). Gosselin et al. found that a group of 87 sadomasochistic women scored higher on the items pertaining to sadomasochistic fantasies than a comparison group of 50 nonparaphilic women. Other researchers have examined the Wilson Sexual Fantasy Questionnaire in samples of male sex offenders. Thornton and Mann (1997) found that sex offenders who scored higher on the questionnaire also scored higher on measures of attitudes and beliefs tolerant of sexual offending. Smith, Wampler, Jones, and Reifman (2005) found that 114 adolescent sex offenders rated as high risk because of their criminal histories and antisocial behavior also scored higher on all four scales of the Wilson Sexual Fantasy Questionnaire.

Like interviews, questionnaires are vulnerable to self-report biases because many of their items are face valid, although both the Clarke SHQ-R and the MSI contain validity scales to detect lying. It is worth noting here that the SICQ study reported by Holland et al. (2000) excluded men who denied their sexual offenses. One would expect that men who denied their sexual offenses would not admit to any paraphilic sexual interests, rendering their responses invalid. Because of concerns about the limitation of self-reports, especially in forensic evaluations, there is a great deal of clinical and research interest in measures that draw on other sources of information. In some cases, useful information can be obtained from other sources, such as a past or current sexual partner. Questions can be asked of partners about the client's sexual behavior and what he has disclosed in the past about his sexual thoughts, fantasies, and urges.

Behavioral History

Clinicians have used information about sexual victim characteristics that are empirically related to pedophilic sexual interests to make the diagnosis of pedophilia. Among adult sex offenders with child victims, those who have multiple victims, very young victims, boy victims, or victims outside the offender's immediate family are more likely to be pedophilic than those who do not. This information has typically been combined in a subjective and unstructured fashion in clinical judgments. In response, Seto and Lalumière (2001) developed a 4-item scale, the Screening Scale for Pedophilic Interests (SSPI), to summarize an offender's sexual victim characteristics and identify those who were more likely to be pedophilic in their sexual arousal in terms of their penile responses to depictions of children relative to their responses to depictions of adults.

The SSPI was developed in a large sample of primarily adult men who had been convicted of at least one sexual offense against a child (total N = 1,113 offenders, including 40 adolescent sex offenders). Four major correlates of pedophilia identified from the empirical literature independently contributed to the prediction of phallometrically assessed sexual arousal to children. Having boy victims explained approximately twice the variance of sexual arousal, and, thus, was given twice the weight of the other variables. These four variables were scored as present or absent, using all available information about sexual offenses: having any male victims, having more than one victim, having a victim aged 11 or younger, and having an unrelated victim. Total SSPI scores range from 0 to 5. File information such as police synopses or probation/parole reports are preferred over self-report as a means of obtaining information about sexual offense history, unless the individual reported sexual offenses that were not previously known.

Sex offenders who have higher scores on the SSPI are much more likely to be pedophilic than are sex offenders with lower scores. Approximately one in five sex offenders with a score of zero showed greater sexual arousal to children than to adults when assessed phallometrically, whereas approximately three in four sex offenders with a score of five showed this pattern of sexual arousal. Recent studies have demonstrated that the SSPI is also valid for adolescent sex offenders with child victims (Madrigano, Curry, & Bradford, 2003; Seto, Murphy, Page, & Ennis, 2003). Moreover, SSPI scores predict new serious (nonsexually violent or sexual) offenses among adult male sex offenders with child victims (Seto, Harris, Rice, & Barbaree, 2004).

A disadvantage of the SSPI is that it requires a history of sexual contact with a child, thus a pedophile who has never acted upon his sexual attraction to children cannot be scored. On the other hand, the SSPI does not rely on self-report. Similar behavioral history scales have not yet been developed for other paraphilias.

Viewing Time or Visual Reaction Time

Unobtrusively recorded viewing time of pictures of children and adults is correlated with self-reported sexual interests and phallometric responding in samples of nonoffending male volunteers recruited from the community (Quinsey, Ketsetzis, Earls, & Karamanoukian, 1996; Quinsey, Rice, Harris, & Reid, 1993; but not Gaither, 2001). The basic viewing time or visual reaction time procedure for assessing age preferences involves showing a series of pictures depicting girls, boys, women, or men; these pictures can depict clothed, semiclothed, or nude figures. Respondents are either asked to examine the pictures to answer later questions, or they are asked to rate each picture on certain attributes (e.g., how attractive the person is, how sexually interesting he or she is). Respondents are instructed to proceed to the next picture at their own pace and are supposed to be unaware that the key dependent measure is the amount of time they spend looking at each picture.

Several studies have shown that adult sex offenders with child victims can be distinguished from other men by the amount of time they spend looking at pictures of children relative to pictures of adults (Harris, Rice, Quinsey, & Chaplin, 1996) or by a combination of viewing time and self-reported sexual interests, arousal, and behavior (Abel, Jordan, Hand, Holland, & Phipps, 2001; Abel, Lawry, Karlstrom, Osborn, & Gillespie, 1994). Viewing time can also distinguish sex offenders with boy victims from those with only girl victims (Abel, Huffman, Warberg, & Holland, 1998; Abel et al., 2004; Worling, 2006).

However, Smith and Fischer (1999) were not able to demonstrate discriminative validity in a study of adolescent sex offenders and nonoffenders using the viewing time component of the Abel Assessment of Sexual Interest (AASI), a commercially available measure of paraphilas. The AASI includes both a viewing time component and a computer-administered questionnaire that is completed by clients (see www. abelscreen.com, retrieved on March 1, 2007). No published studies have yet demonstrated that scores on viewing time measures, whether alone or in combination with self-report ratings, predict recidivism among sex offenders.

A potential problem for viewing time measures is that they may become vulnerable to faking once the client learns that viewing time is the key variable of interest (e.g., see www.innocentdads.org/abel.htm, retrieved on March 1, 2007). No published studies have reported on the ability of participants to manipulate their responses on viewing time measures or the ability of examiners to detect such efforts at deception. Normative data are available for the AASI-2, but the algorithms are considered to be proprietary knowledge and thus test results must be submitted to a scoring service (see Abel et al., 1994). The AASI developers claim their measure combining viewing time and self-report can assess other paraphilias, such as fetishism and sadism, but there are no published data regarding this claim, and this claim cannot be verified by independent researchers. Other viewing time measures that allow users to score responses are available (e.g., Harris et al., 1996; Worling, 2006).

Phallometry

Phallometry involves the measurement of penile responses to stimuli that systematically vary on the dimensions of interest, such as the age and sex of the figures in a set of pictures. Phallometry was developed as an assessment method by Kurt Freund, who first showed that it could reliably discriminate between homosexual and heterosexual men (Freund, 1963), and then showed it could distinguish between sex offenders against children and other men (Freund, 1967). Greater detail is provided in this chapter about phallometry because of the clinical utility of phallometry in the assessment of paraphilias among sex offenders, and because several decades of research is available.

Phallometric responses are recorded as increases in either penile circumference or penile volume; bigger increases in circumference or volume reflect greater sexual arousal to the presented stimulus. Circumferential gauges, typically a mercury-in-elastic strain gauge placed over the mid-shaft of the penis, are the most commonly used phallometric devices. Although volumetric devices are more sensitive than circumferential gauges at very low levels of arousal, they show very high agreement above a threshold of approximately 10% of full erection (Kuban, Barbaree, & Blanchard, 1999). Changes in the electrical conductance of the mercury represent changes in penile circumference and can be calibrated to give a precise measure of penile erection. Erectile response (except for erections that occur during sleep) is specifically sexual, unlike other psychophysiological responses such as pupillary dilation, heart rate, and skin conductance (Zuckerman, 1971). Phallometric responses correlate positively and significantly with viewing time and self-report among nonoffenders (Harris et al., 1996) and with AASI scores among sex offenders (Letourneau, 2002).

Phallometric data are optimally reported as the relative response to the category of interest, for example, penile response to pictures of prepubescent children minus penile response to pictures of adults; more positive scores indicate greater sexual interest in children. Relative responses are more informative than absolute penile responses because the former take individual differences in responsivity into account. Responsivity can vary for a variety of reasons, including the man's age (Blanchard & Barbaree, 2005), health, and the amount of time since he last ejaculated. To illustrate the value of relative response scoring, the observation that an individual exhibits a 10 mm increase in penile circumference in response to pictures of children is more interpretable when we know whether he exhibits a 5 mm or 20 mm increase in response to pictures of adults. The first pattern of responses indicates someone who is more sexually aroused by pictures of children compared to pictures of adults, indicating a sexual preference for children; the second pattern of responses indicates someone who is relatively more responsive in the laboratory, but who is more sexually aroused by pictures of adults relative to pictures of children, indicating a sexual preference for adults.

Discriminative Validity

Indices of relative phallometric responding can discriminate sex offenders against children from other men. Sex offenders with child victims respond relatively more to stimuli depicting children than men who have not committed such sexual offenses, including sex offenders with adult victims, nonsex offenders (e.g., men convicted of nonsexual assault), and nonoffenders (e.g., Barbaree & Marshall, 1989; Freund & Blanchard, 1989; Quinsey, Steinman, Bergersen, & Holmes, 1975). Moreover, phallometric responses are associated with victim choice, such that men who have offended against girls tend to respond relatively more to stimuli depicting girls, and those who have offended against boys tend to respond relatively more to stimuli depicting boys (Harris et al., 1996; Quinsey et al., 1975). Rapists respond relatively more to depictions of sexual aggression than nonrapists (see Lalumière & Quinsey, 1994, for a quantitative review; see Lalumière, Quinsey, Harris, Rice, & Trautrimas, 2003, for a recent update), and other investigators have shown that phallometric test results can distinguish men who admit to sadistic fantasies, men who cross-dress, or men expose their genitals in public from other groups of men (Freund, Seto, & Kuban, 1995; Marshall, Payne, Barbaree, & Eccles, 1991; Seto & Kuban, 1996).

The discriminative validity of phallometry can be improved in several ways. Using standardized scores to calculate indices of relative responding and using indices based on differences in the responses to different stimulus categories increases discrimination between male sex offenders and other men (Earls, Quinsey, & Castonguay, 1987; Harris, Rice, Quinsey, Chaplin, & Earls, 1992). The addition of a tracking task in which participants push buttons when they see or hear violent or sexual content increases their attention to the stimuli and subsequently increases the discriminative validity of phallometry for sex offenders (Harris, Rice, Chaplin, & Quinsey, 1999; Proulx, Côté, & Achille, 1993; Quinsey & Chaplin, 1988). Response artifacts can also be used to detect attempts to manipulate test results (Freund, Watson, & Rienzo, 1988). Tactics to reduce faking are important in phallometry because some men can voluntarily control their penile responses during sessions (Quinsey & Bergersen, 1976; Quinsey & Carrigan, 1978). The use of audiotaped descriptions of sexual scenarios also yields very good discrimination (e.g., Chaplin, Rice, & Harris, 1995; Quinsey & Chaplin, 1988).

At the level of individual diagnosis, the sensitivity of phallometric tests, defined as the proportion of paraphilic individuals identified as such on the basis of their phallometric responses, can be calculated after setting a suitable cutoff score (e.g., showing greater arousal to an atypical target or activity than to depictions of sexual intercourse with adults). Given the potentially negative consequences of being identified as a paraphilic individual, cutoff scores providing high specificities are typically used in clinical settings. Specificity is defined as the percentage of nonparaphilic controls who are identified as not being sexually interested in an atypical target or activity. In a sample of 147 sex offenders with unrelated child victims, using a cutoff score that produced 98% specificity, sensitivity was 50% in Freund and Watson (1991). In a sample of sex offenders with child victims who denied being sexually interested in children, Blanchard, Klassen, Dickey, Kuban, and Blak (2001) reported that sensitivity was 61% among men with many child victims, and specificity was 96% among men with many adult victims and/or adult sexual partners. The average sensitivity across the studies reviewed by Lalumière et al. (2003) was 63% (63% of rapists showed greater sexual arousal to depictions of rape than to mutually consenting sex) with a corresponding specificity of 87% (87% of volunteers

showed greater sexual arousal to depictions of mutually consenting sex than to depictions of rape).

If one considers admission of pedophilia to be a suitable standard, then the sensitivity of phallometry is very high. In a series of three studies, Freund and his colleagues reported on the results of phallometric testing for a total of 137 sex offenders with child victims who admitted to having pedophilia; the sensitivity of phallometric testing in this group of self-admitted pedophiles was 92% (Freund & Blanchard, 1989; Freund, Chan, & Coulthard, 1979; Freund & Watson, 1991).

Predictive Validity

Phallometry has good predictive validity. A recent meta-analysis of 10 studies, with a combined sample size of almost 1278 sex offenders, found that phallometrically measured sexual arousal to children was one of the single best predictors of sexual recidivism among sex offenders (Hanson & Morton-Bourgon, 2004, 2005); its correlation with sexual recidivism was similar to the correlations obtained by measures of psychopathy or prior criminal history, and both psychopathy and prior criminal history are strong and robust predictors of recidivism across types of offenders (Gendreau, Little, & Goggin, 1996; Hanson & Morton-Bourgon, 2004; Hare, 2003).

Reliability

Phallometric testing has been criticized for its lack of reliability. Traditional internal consistency and test–retest analyses suggest the reliability of phallometric testing is acceptable, at best (Barbaree, Baxter, & Marshall, 1989; Davidson & Malcolm, 1985; Fernandez, 2002; but see Gaither, 2001). The validity of a test is constrained by its reliability, yet the discriminative and predictive validities of phallometric testing are quite good, suggesting that it must be reliable. This apparent contradiction in test properties suggests the discriminative and predictive effect sizes that have been obtained for phallometry are conservative estimates of its validity and would be even higher if reliability were higher.

One possible explanation for phallometry's low test–retest reliability is that individuals become familiar with the procedure and use tactics to voluntarily control their sexual arousal over sessions. Evidence for this comes from Rice, Quinsey, and Harris (1991), who found that initial phallometric test results were more strongly related to recidivism than subsequent phallometric test results, and Barbaree et al.'s (1989) finding that nonrapist controls showed a signficant change in their responses from the first to second session. Freund et al. (1988) discussed signs of attempts to manipulate penile response and Quinsey and Chaplin (1988) described a method for reducing faking. Because of phallometry's clinical utility in the assessment of paraphilias and sex offenders, it is included in Table 22.1 despite its relatively low test–retest reliability. The purposeful modification of sexual arousal patterns is discussed later in this chapter when we consider the use of phallometry to assess treatment change.

Criticisms

Despite the consistent evidence supporting the clinical and research use of phallometry to assess paraphilias, there is disagreement about the utility of this assessment method, and the number of phallometric laboratories has declined over the past 10 to 15 years (Howes, 1995; McGrath, Cumming, & Burchard, 2003). Critics such as Launay (1999) and Marshall and Fernandez (2000) have discussed their practical and ethical objections to phallometry. One of the main criticisms of phallometric testing is its lack of standardization in stimuli, procedures, and data analysis (though it seems to us that this is more a criticism of how phallometric testing is conducted in practice than the methodology itself). Howes (1995) identified a great deal of heterogeneity in methodologies in a survey of 48 phallometric laboratories operating in Canada and the United States. For example, laboratories vary on the number and nature of stimuli they present, duration of stimulus presentations, and the minimum arousal level accepted for clinical interpretation of individual response profiles. Unfortunately, many phallometric laboratories do not use validated procedures and scoring methods.

Standardization of procedures is needed because some phallometric testing procedures have been validated, but others that are currently in use have not been subjected to empirical scrutiny. Standardization would also facilitate the production of normative data and thereby aid in the interpretation and reporting of phallometric test results. Unfortunately, repeated calls for standardization in the field have resulted in very little progress. Progress on standardization has been slowed by ethical and legal concerns regarding the production and distribution of stimulus material that may constitute child pornography, and other nonscientific reasons. There is empirical evidence to guide decisions about these methodological issues, such as the number and kinds of stimuli to present, the use of circumferential or volumetric devices, and the optimal transformations of data for interpretation (see Lalumière & Harris, 1998; Quinsey & Lalumière, 2001).

Inter-Rater Reliability and Diagnostic Agreement Between Methods

Other issues that need to be addressed in the assessment of paraphilias is the inter-rater reliability of paraphilia diagnoses, and agreement between diagnostic measures. As this review has shown, there are reliable and valid methods for assessing paraphilias, especially pedophilia, yet the diagnostic criteria of paraphilias have been challenged. O'Donohue, Regev, and Hagstrom (2000) and Marshall (2006) have pointed out problems with DSM-IV diagnostic criteria for paraphilias such as pedophilia and sadism, including the absence of data on inter-rater reliability (the extent to which two clinicians would agree in assigning the diagnosis) and test–retest reliability (whether someone diagnosed as having a paraphilia at Time 1 would continue to be identified as such at Time 2). Consistent with these critiques, Levenson (2004) reported diagnostic reliability in a sample of 295 adult male sex offenders (three quarters of the sample had committed sexual offenses against minors) and found that the inter-rater reliability for a diagnosis of pedophilia was only acceptable. Wilson, Abracen, Picheca, Malcolm, and Prinzo (2003) compared the classification provided by different measures of pedophilia—sexual history, strict application of DSM-IV criteria, phallometric responding, and an expert's diagnosis—and found that scores on these measures were not highly correlated in a sample of sex offenders against children, suggesting each was identifying different groups of pedophiles.

Though the criteria seem straightforward, the inter-rater reliability of the diagnosis of pedophilia is constrained because of the subjective way in which information about sexual interests is typically combined; in addition, this information is usually inferred from behavior, because many individuals are unwilling to admit to sexual thoughts, fantasies, or urges regarding prepubescent children. Thus, one of the complications in reviewing the literature on pedophilia is the fact that different assessment methods (and operational definitions of pedophilia) have been used, and thus the groups that have been studied are not equivalent.

An unpublished analysis of the data reported in Seto, Cantor, and Blanchard (2006) found that self-reported sexual interests, sexual history, and possession of child pornography independently contributed to the prediction of phallometric responding. These results suggest that the most accurate identification of pedophiles would come from using multiple sources of information. Given the challenges in subjectively combining different pieces of information, creating an algorithm that incorporates various valid measures of pedophilia—self-report, sexual history, and phallometric responding—might be the best approach (Grove, Zald, Lebow, Snitz, & Nelson, 2000; Ægisdóttir, Spengler, & White, 2006).

Overall Evaluation

The above review suggests that assessments of paraphilia (predominantly pedophilia) can be ranked according to their level of empirical support and their practical utility. The assessment approach that has the greatest amount of empirical support in the literature is phallometry. The disadvantages of phallometry include the need for expensive equipment and its intrusiveness. The assessment approach that uses official offence history data has less empirical support, but the support that is available is encouraging. Potential advantages of the behavioral history over phallometry are that the measure is not intrusive and it is not subject to faking by the individual being assessed (unless they are able to falsify official records).

Assessments based on viewing time are accumulating empirical support in terms of their reliability and validity, but seems to be weakened by the potential that the individual being assessed will discover or discern the purpose of the assessment and thereafter be able to fake their responses. Finally, some self-report measures have adequate empirical support regarding their reliability and validity, but suffer from a lack of confidence in forensic assessment due to the ease with which the individual can fake their responses.

Further research should focus on developing reliable and valid structured or semistructured interviews, gathering further psychometric evaluations of self-report questionnaires such as the SHQ-R and MSI,

developing behavioral history measures for paraphilias other than pedophilia, and further phallometric research on paraphilias other than pedophilia and sadism. More research is also needed on the assessment of paraphilias among women, including female sex offenders. Most of the research cited in this chapter has been drawn from research on male samples. There have been case reports of female sex offenders who clearly meet diagnostic criteria for a paraphilia; for example, Chow and Choy (2002) described the case of a female pedophile who admitted to sexual fantasies about sex with prepubescent children and committed sexual offenses against two young children. Wiegel, Abel, and Jordan (2003) analyzed questionnaire data from a sample of 242 women who admitted to committing a sexual offense. The majority (70%) had sexually offended against a child, and the rest had engaged in obscene telephone calls, or acts of bestiality, exhibitionism, or voyeurism. Approximately a third of the women reported being sexually aroused by male or female children, with slightly more admitting to an interest in boys than in girls.

It remains to be seen if laboratory measures of paraphilic sexual arousal can be developed for women, given recent results reported by Chivers, Rieger, Latty, and Bailey (2004). These investigators found that, unlike men, women could not be accurately classified according to their sexual orientation on the basis of their genital responses to sexual stimuli depicting males or depicting females. Similarly, Gaither (2005) found that, unlike men, women could not be accurately classified according to their sexual orientation on the basis of the time they spent looking at pictures of men and women.

ASSESSMENT FOR CASE CONCEPTUALIZATION AND TREATMENT PLANNING

Once a paraphilia diagnosis has been made, clinicians will need to assess other factors for the purposes of case conceptualization and treatment planning. There is a widely (though not universally) held assumption that paraphilias are stable preferences, akin to sexual orientation, that cannot be changed or that are highly unlikely to change (see Seto, 2004). Thus, the focus of case conceptualization and treatment planning is to assist the person in better managing his or her paraphilia. Factors to be considered in case conceptualization and treatment planning include (a) antisocial tendencies; (b) denial or minimization of personal responsibility for sexual offenses, when applicable; (c) attitudes and beliefs that are supportive of sexual offending; (d) sexual and general self-regulation skills; and (e) risk to sexually reoffend among identified sex offenders. A brief overview of these related assessment domains is provided below.

Although an exhaustive review of measures in each domain is far beyond the scope of this chapter, Table 22.2 summarizes the psychometric properties of a selection of measures of relevant domains. These measures include self-report questionnaires assessing denial or minimization of responsibility (Facets of Sex Offender Denial, FoSOD), attitudes and beliefs tolerant of sexual offending (MSI, Abel and Becker Cognitions Scale, Bumby MOLEST scale), phallometric assessment of sexual arousal patterns, and measures of static (PCL family, Static-99, and SSPI) or dynamic risk (Stable-2000).

Validated measures of risk to reoffend are available for adult male sex offenders (see Doren, 2002, and Hanson et al., 2003, for reviews). There is some encouraging work on risk instruments for adolescent sex offenders (e.g., Parks & Bard, 2006), but similar measures are not yet available for female sex offenders or paraphilic individuals with no known history of sexual offending.

Antisocial Tendencies

Antisocial tendencies are important to assess because of their robust association with criminal behavior across different demographic groups; individuals who score higher on measures of antisocial tendencies are more likely to offend, whether based on self-report or official records (Lalumière, Harris, Quinsey, & Rice, 2005; Quinsey, Book, & Skilling, 2004; Quinsey, Harris, Rice, & Cormier, 2006). Paraphilic sex offenders who score higher in antisocial personality traits, antisocial attitudes and beliefs, and associations with criminal peers are more likely to offend again than those who do not (Hanson & Morton-Bourgon, 2004, 2005).

Many reliable and valid measures of antisocial tendencies are available, including measures of antisocial personality traits, antisocial attitudes and beliefs, and associations with criminal peers. Of particular relevance is psychopathy, a condition characterized by a lack of empathy or conscience, manipulativeness, deceitfulness, and impulsive and irresponsible

behavior. One of the Psychopathy Checklist family of measures (PCL-R for offenders and forensic patients, PCL-SV for nonoffenders and civil psychiatric patients, and PCL-YV for adolescent offenders) can be rated by a clinician on the basis of an interview and file information, and psychopathy scores are robustly associated with future criminal behavior, including violent or sexual offending (Hare, 2003).

Denial or Minimization of Personal Responsibility for Sexual Offending

Among sex offenders, denial or minimization of responsibility can be a problem in treatment planning because an individual who denies committing the offense, or greatly minimizes his responsibility for the offense, may not be able to participate meaningfully in treatment designed to teach him how to refrain from future offending by analyzing past offenses and the sequences of events that lead up to them. (This does not mean denial or minimization of personal responsibility is a risk factor for recidivism, however, because studies have not found such a relationship; see Hanson & Bussière, 1998).

Measures of denial or minimization include scales of the MSI, the Denial and Minimization Checklist (Barbaree, 1991) and the Facets of Sex Offender Denial measure (FoSOD: Schneider & Wright, 2001). These measures assess different aspects of denial or minimization, which can include denial that a sexual offense ever occurred (e.g., claiming there was no sexual contact), denial of personal responsibility (e.g., claiming the victim initiated the sexual contact), and minimization of different aspects of the sexual offense, such as victim impact, planning, paraphilia as a motive, and potential for reoffense. The FoSOD is a 65-item questionnaire completed by offenders against children. Schneider and Wright reported that the questionnaire was significantly correlated with other measures of denial, and was also significantly associated with treatment progress, in that sex offenders in an advanced stage of treatment had lower scores than those in an early stage of treatment (Schneider & Wright, 2001; Wright & Schneider, 2004).

Attitudes and Beliefs Tolerant of Sexual Offending

Cognitions are considered to be important because individuals who espouse tolerant attitudes (e.g., that

TABLE 22.2 Ratings of Instruments Used for Case Conceptualization and Treatment Planning

Instrument	Norms	Internal Consistency	Inter-Rater Reliability	Test–Retest Reliability	Content Validity	Construct Validity	Validity Generalization	Clinical Utility	Highly Recommended
Self-report									
MSI (CDI & J scales)	G	G	NA	E	A	E	E	E	✓
Abel & Becker cognition scale	A	G	NA	A	A	G	G	A	
Bumby MOLEST & RAPE scales	A	E	NA	A	A	A	A	G	
FoSOD (denial)	A	E	NA	E	G	A	A	G	
Behavioral measures									
Phallometry	U	A	NA	L	G	E	G	A	
Rating scales (static risk)									
PCL Family of assessments	E	G	G	G	G	E	E	E	✓
Static-99	E	NA	E	U	A	E	G	G	✓
SSPI	A	NA	A	U	A	A	G	E	
Rating scales (dynamic risk)									
Stable-2000	A	NA	E	NA	A	A	A	G	

Note: MSI = Multiphasic Sex Inventory; CDI = Cognitive Distortion and Immaturity Scale; J = Justification Scale; FoSOD = Facets of Sexual Offender Denial; PCL = Psychopathy Checklist; SSPI = Screening Scale for Pedophilic Interests; L = Less Than Adequate; A = Adequate; G = Good; E = Excellent; U = Unavailable; NA = Not Applicable.

children can benefit from sexual contacts with adults, that women secretly enjoy being sexually dominated) may be more likely to commit sexual offenses (Hanson & Harris, 2000). A variety of measures of attitudes and beliefs about sexual offending are available, but most have not been evaluated or have only been evaluated in only one or two relatively small-scale studies. Measures of attitudes and beliefs tolerant of sexual offending with adequate empirical support are the Cognitive Distortion and Immaturity scale and Justification scale of the MSI, the Abel and Becker Cognitions Scale (Abel, Becker, & Cunningham-Rathner, 1984), and the Bumby MOLEST scale (Bumby, 1996). The MOLEST scale was adapted from the Abel and Becker Cognitions Scale, has excellent internal consistency and acceptable test–retest reliability, and was only modestly correlated with a measure of social desirability. Two studies have shown that the MOLEST scale can distinguish sex offenders from children from groups of other offenders or nonoffending men (Arkowitz & Vess, 2003; Marshall, Marshall, Sachdev, & Kruger, 2003). However, a companion measure, the RAPE scale, did not discriminate rapists from other groups of men.

Attitudes and beliefs tolerant of sexual offending can also be assessed through a single three-point rating on the Stable-2000, a dynamic measure of risk to reoffend developed for adult male sex offenders as part of the Sex Offender Need Assessment Rating (Hanson & Harris, 2000). Men who reoffended during the follow-up period received a higher rating on this item, indicating they endorsed many attitudes and beliefs tolerant of sexual offending.

Sexual and General Self-Regulation

Difficulties with sexual and general self-regulation have been identified as a risk factor for sexual offending by different theorists (e.g., Bickley & Beech, 2002; Ward, Hudson, & Keenan, 1998). The logic is that individuals who are less able to control their sexual impulses are more likely to act upon their paraphilia.

The Stable-2000 includes an item pertaining to sexual self-regulation deficits; sex offenders receive a higher rating if they make statements or engage in behavior indicating they have a high sex drive, feel entitled to sex, or they are preoccupied with paraphilic thoughts or fantasies. Similarly, the Stable-2000 contains an item pertaining to general self-regulation deficits; sex offenders receive a higher rating if they are not

compliant with supervision or treatment requirements, or engaging in other antisocial behavior. Hanson and Harris (2000) found that men who violently or sexually reoffended had a higher rating on these two items. One could also measure general self-regulation through measures of personality traits such as impulsivity, risk-taking, and sensation seeking.

Assessment of Risk to Sexually Offend

For some paraphilic individuals, case conceptualization and treatment planning will focus on risk for future sexual offending. Risk is an important concern because the intensity of interventions should match the risk posed by the individual, with more expensive, higher-intensity interventions reserved for higher-risk individuals (Andrews & Bonta, 2006).

Static and Dynamic Risk

A distinction is made in sex offender risk assessments between static and dynamic risk factors. Actuarial risk instruments such as the Static-99 are comprised of static risk factors, meaning the factors are historical and therefore cannot change (e.g., prior criminal history, history of alcohol abuse) or they are highly stable and very unlikely to change, if they can be modified at all (e.g., having a diagnosis of paraphilia, psychopathy). In contrast, dynamic risk factors are, in principle, changeable (e.g., attitudes and beliefs tolerant of sex with children) or temporally fluctuating (e.g., level of alcohol intoxication), and could therefore be targets of intervention. Another example of a dynamic risk factor would be access to potential victims (Hanson & Harris, 2000).

Paraphilia and Risk

Unfortunately, little is known about the risk posed by individuals with a paraphilia but no history of sexual offending involving some kind of contact with victims. A relevant study was reported by Seto and Eke (2005), who followed a sample of men convicted of child pornography offenses to determine how many of these men would later commit sexual offenses involving children. Seto, Cantor, and Blanchard (2006) demonstrated that a majority of child pornography offenders are likely to be pedophiles on the basis of their phallometrically assessed sexual arousal. As predicted by Seto and Eke, criminal history was a risk factor: child pornography offenders with a history of other kinds of offenses were significantly more likely to commit a contact sexual offense. However, this study was of individuals who had already come into contact with the criminal justice system for possession or distribution of child pornography. No published studies have examined the risk posed by self-identified pedophiles, or individuals who admit to other paraphilias, without any known history of sexual offending.

A paraphilia diagnosis is important to consider when assessing sex offenders because of the evidence that paraphilic sex offenders are at higher risk to reoffend than nonparaphilic sex offenders (Hanson & Bussière, 1998; Hanson & Morton-Bourgon, 2005). In particular, there is strong and consistent data that pedophilia is associated with risk to offend among sex offenders. Many diagnostic indicators of pedophilia predict sexual recidivism, including phallometrically assessed sexual arousal to children, having a boy victim, and having unrelated victims. In fact, these paraphilia-related variables are among the strongest predictors of sexual recidivism studied so far (Hanson & Bussière, 1998; Hanson & Morton-Bourgon, 2004).

Phallometric responding to depictions of children predicts sexual offending against children in groups of sex offenders other than those who have already victimized children. Rabinowitz, Firestone, Bradford, and Greenberg (2002) followed a sample of 221 men who had been criminally charged and who met diagnostic criteria for exhibitionism. None of these offenders were known to have committed a contact sexual offense at the time they were assessed. Nonetheless, among this group of exhibitionistic offenders, phallometrically assessed sexual arousal to children distinguished those who subsequently committed contact sexual offenses from those who committed noncontact sexual offenses again during the average follow-up of almost 7 years.

Actuarial Risk Assessment

Perhaps the most significant advance in sex offender risk during the past 20 years has been the development and dissemination of actuarial instruments that can significantly predict violent or sexual offending among adult male sexual offenders (Doren, 2002; Hanson, 1998; Quinsey, Harris, Rice, & Cormier, 2006). In a recent meta-analysis of sex offender recidivism studies, Hanson and Morton-Bourgon (2004) identified four commonly used actuarial instruments:

the Sex Offender Risk Appraisal Guide (SORAG; Quinsey, et al., 2006), the Rapid Risk Assessment of Sexual Offense Recidivism (RRASOR; Hanson, 1997), the Static-99 (Hanson & Thornton, 1999), and the Minnesota Sex Offender Screening Tool-Revised (MnSOST-R; Epperson et al., 1998).

These four risk instruments incorporate paraphilia-related variables (e.g., the RRASOR, Static-99, MnSOST-R, and SORAG all contain items regarding the age and gender of sexual victims and the SORAG has an item pertaining to phallometrically assessed sexual arousal). These instruments are referred to as actuarial risk instruments because they include a set of empirically identified risk factors that are objectively scored and provide probabilistic estimates of risk based on the established empirical relationships between the individual items and the outcome of interest. Only items that independently contribute to the prediction of recidivism, in combination with the other instrument items, are retained. Probabilistic estimates indicate the proportion of people with the same score who reoffend during a specified period of opportunity.

Actuarial assessments of risk are well established in such disparate areas of practice as determining insurance premiums and predicting survival times for progressive stages of cancers. In a similar vein, the SSPI is an actuarial measure for determining the likelihood that a sex offender with child victims will show a sexual preference for children over adults when assessed phallometrically (and, serendipitously, the SSPI is a significant predictor of recidivism among adult male sex offenders with child victims; Seto et al., 2004).

Because the sex offender risk assessment literature has grown so large over the past 15 years, we focus on one actuarial instrument, the Static-99, in Table 22.2. We chose the Static-99 because it is relatively easy to score given adequate records, its predictive validity has been independently replicated numerous times, and it has the largest number of peer-reviewed studies supporting it among the most common actuarial instruments (see Hanson, Morton, & Harris, 2003). The Static-99 was developed for adult males who are known to have committed at least one sexual offense, and was designed to predict violent or specifically sexual recidivism. Clinicians or other professionals rate 10 items, each of which was selected to independently contribute to the prediction of new offenses. Individual scores range from 0 to 12, and sex offenders are assigned to one of seven risk categories based on their score (individuals with scores of six or more are combined into one group because of the small frequencies of offenders with such scores in the development sample). Static-99 scores consistently produce accurate predictions regarding future sexual offending (e.g., Barbaree, Seto, Langton, & Peacock, 2001).

Overall Evaluation

Measures of additional domains other than paraphilias become more salient when assessment of paraphilias addresses case conceptualization and treatment planning. In this section, we identified antisocial personality traits and other antisocial tendencies, denial or minimization of personal responsibility for sexual offending, attitudes and beliefs tolerant of sexual offending, sexual and general self-regulation, and assessments of risk to violently or sexually reoffend as important to assess when there is concern about someone engaging in paraphilic behavior that is illegal (e.g., having sexual contacts with children, sexual assaults of nonconsenting persons).

ASSESSMENT FOR TREATMENT MONITORING AND TREATMENT OUTCOME EVALUATION

As we noted in the previous section, there is a widely held assumption among clinical sexologists and forensic practitioners that paraphilias cannot be changed. Thus, the focus of treatment and other interventions is to assist the individual in managing their paraphilic sexual interests, to reduce personal distress, improve relationship and other functioning, and refrain from engaging in illegal sexual behavior.

In cases where the paraphilia is particularly strong, distressing, or likely to place the person at risk of engaging in criminal behavior (e.g., frequent and intense sadistic fantasies that the person feels he cannot control), anti-androgen medications such as cyproterone acetate may be prescribed to reduce sex drive (for reviews, see Gijs & Gooren, 1996; Seto, 2008). Changes in sex drive can be assessed through self-report and by interviewing others, whereas changes in sexual responsivity can be assessed using phallometry.

In other cases, it may be possible to teach individuals how to change their attitudes and beliefs about sexual offending, gain voluntary control over their sexual arousal, and regulate their sexual behavior, and thereby refrain from engaging in problematic paraphilic behavior. Thus, measures of attitudes and beliefs tolerant of sexual offending, sexual arousal patterns, and sexual and general self-regulation, and antisocial tendencies can be valuable in monitoring treatment change and evaluating treatment outcome. All of these domains are relevant for both nonforensic and forensic assessments, though not all of these measures have been evaluated for nonforensic clients. Among sex offenders, denial or minimization of personal responsibility for their sexual offenses may interfere with treatment compliance, and thus may be an initial treatment target.

Table 22.3 summarizes the psychometric properties of measures that may be sensitive to treatment change. These include self-report measures of attitudes and beliefs tolerant of sexual offending (all but one already mentioned in Table 22.2), clinician rating scales of changes on dynamic risk factors (SOTRS and Stable-2000), and phallometric assessment of changes in sexual arousal patterns.

Attitudes and Beliefs Tolerant of Sexual Offending

A number of studies have shown that some MSI scales can distinguish sex offenders who admit responsibility for their crimes from those who deny responsibility, and sex offenders who complete treatment from those who do not (Simkins et al., 1989; Waysliw, Haywood, Grossman, Johnson, & Liles, 1992). Simkins et al., for example, reported that MSI scales could explain between 30% and 47% of treatment response. Marques, Wiederanders, Day, Nelson, and van Ommeren (2005) reported that sex offenders who completed treatment had lower scores on MSI items pertaining to attitudes and beliefs about sexual offending (Cognitive Distortions and Immaturity scale).

Hanson and Harris (2000) compared the records of 208 sex offenders who committed another violent or sexual offense while under community supervision and 201 sex offenders who did not violently or sexually reoffend. Those who reoffended were distinguished by more expressions of antisocial attitudes and association with criminal peers, intimacy deficits, endorsement of attitudes and beliefs tolerant of sexual offending, and problems with sexual and general self-regulation.

TABLE 22.3 Ratings of Instruments Used for Treatment Monitoring and Treatment Outcome Evaluation

Instrument	Norms	Internal Consistency	Inter-Rater Reliability	Test–Retest Reliability	Content Validity	Construct Validity	Validity Generalization	Treatment Sensitivity	Clinical Utility	Highly Recommended
Self-report										
MSI (CDI & J Scales)	G	G	NA	E	A	G	E	A	E	✓
MSI (SO Scale)	G	A	NA	G	A	G	E	A	G	
Abel & Becker cognition scale	A	G	NA	A	A	G	G	A	A	
Bumby MOLEST & RAPE scales	A	E	NA	A	A	A	A	A	G	
FoSOD	A	E	NA	E	G	A	A	G	G	
Rating scale										
SOTRS	A	E	A	NA	A	A	U	U	A	✓
Stable-2000	A	NA	E	NA	A	A	A	U	G	
Behavioral measures										
Phallometry (Δ in sexual arousal)	U	A	NA	NA	G	E	G	E	A	✓

Note: MSI = Multiphasic Sex Inventory; CDI = Cognitive Distortion and Immaturity Scale; J Scale = Justification Scale; SO Scale = Sexual Obsession Scale; FoSOD = Facets of Sexual Offender Denial; SOTRS = Sex Offender Treatment Rating Scale; A = Adequate; G = Good; E = Excellent; NA = Not Applicable; U = Unavailable.

Changes in Sexual Arousal

In the behavioral treatment of paraphilias, aversion techniques are used to suppress sexual arousal to atypical targets or activities, whereas masturbatory reconditioning techniques are used to increase sexual arousal to sexual activities involving consenting adults. Treatment progress is monitored through self-report and phallometry. In aversive conditioning procedures, unpleasant stimuli such as mild electric shock or ammonia are paired with repeated presentations of sexual stimuli depicting children. Aversive conditioning techniques were used as early as the 1950s and 1960s for the treatment of paraphilias such as fetishism and transvestic fetishism (e.g., Marks & Gelder, 1967; Raymond, 1956). The efficacy of behavioral approaches for changing sexual arousal patterns has been reviewed in detail by Barbaree, Bogaert, and Seto (1995) and Barbaree and Seto (1997). In sum, the research suggests that behavioral techniques can have an effect on sexual arousal patterns, as assessed by phallometry, but it is unclear how long these changes are maintained and whether they result in actual changes in interests, as opposed to greater voluntary control over paraphilic sexual arousal (e.g., Lalumière & Earls, 1992).

Sexual Self-Regulation

Hanson and Harris (2000) found that sex offenders who committed a violent or sexual reoffense while under community supervision differed from those who did not violently or sexually reoffend by being more likely to view themselves as having a strong sex drive, entitled to sex, and likely to become frustrated or feel deprived if they were not able to satisfy their sexual urges. Similarly, Craig et al. (2006) found that the Sexual Obsessions scale of the MSI distinguished sex offenders who reoffended from those who did not.

Relapse prevention is currently a popular approach for teaching individuals how to regulate their sexual behavior. This approach is cognitive-behavioral in orientation and is adapted from the addictions field (Marlatt & Gordon, 1985). It is currently the most common psychological treatment provided to adult sex offenders (McGrath et al., 2003). The relapse prevention strategy involves (a) identifying situations in which the individual is at high risk for relapse; (b)

identifying lapses, that is, behaviors that do not constitute full-fledged relapses but do constitute approximations to the problem behavior; (c) developing strategies for avoiding high-risk situations; and (d) developing coping strategies which are used in high-risk situations that cannot be avoided and in responding to lapses that do occur. As applied to paraphilias, lapses could include masturbating to paraphilic sexual fantasies, viewing pornography depicting paraphilic content, or engaging in paraphilic activity once, whereas relapses would be a full return to paraphilic activity. High-risk situations could include stressful situations in which paraphilic thoughts and fantasies are more likely to occur as a means of coping.

Whether sex offender treatment is effective in reducing recidivism is hotly debated (e.g., Hanson et al., 2002; Rice & Harris, 2003). Several studies have examined the relationship between treatment performance and outcomes among sex offenders participating in programs espousing cognitive-behavioral and relapse prevention principles. Marques et al. (2005) conducted the largest and most relevant randomized clinical trial comparing the reoffense rates of offenders treated in an inpatient relapse prevention program with the rates of untreated control groups. No significant differences were found in their rates of sexual or violent reoffending over an 8-year follow-up period. However, post hoc analyses suggested that high-risk sex offenders against children who met the treatment goals were less likely to reoffend than high-risk sex offenders who did not meet these goals (10% vs. 50%).

Marques et al. (2005) assessed treatment goals using multiple measures: (a) scores on questionnaire scales pertaining to attitudes and beliefs about sexual offending; (b) changes in phallometrically assessed sexual arousal to children or to coercive sex; and (c) ratings of written homework exercises regarding the offender's understanding of the costs and benefits of offending versus abstaining, the sequence of cognitions and behaviors that preceded their sexual offenses, and the strategies they could use to intervene in this offense sequence. However, two additional studies of sex offenders participating in cognitive-behavioral treatment programs did not find a significant and positive relationship between ratings of relapse prevention knowledge and skills (in addition to other treatment goals) and recidivism (Barbaree, 2005; Looman, Abracen, Serin, & Marquis, 2005; see also Seto, 2003).

General Self-Regulation and Antisocial Tendencies

There is good evidence that certain kinds of cognitive-behavioral treatments are effective in reducing reoffending among offenders in general (see Andrews & Bonta, 2006). These treatments are matched to offenders according to their risk to reoffend and focus on dynamic risk factors, including self-regulation in areas such as anger management, problem-solving, and substance use. Thus, treatments that strengthen self-regulation skills and reduce exposure to disinhibiting influences such as alcohol or other drugs might be very helpful in assisting paraphilic sex offenders from sexually reoffending, and assisting paraphilic individuals from engaging in illegal sexual behavior.

Assessing Treatment Outcome

Research on treatment outcome for individuals with paraphilias and for paraphilic sex offenders would be boosted by the development of psychometrically sound measures of treatment change. Specific measures for paraphilias are not available, other than self-reported changes in paraphilic thoughts, fantasies, urges, or behavior, and self-reported and phallometrically assessed changes in sexual arousal. Among sex offenders, treatment change has been assessed using specific measures of relapse prevention knowledge and skills, such as the Relapse Prevention Knowledge Questionnaire (Beckett, Fisher, Mann, & Thornton, 1997) and Sex Offender Treatment Rating Scale (SOTRS: Anderson, Gibeau, & D'Amora, 1995), and using general measures of treatment change adapted for this purpose, such as Goal Attainment Scaling (Barrett, Wilson, & Long, 2003; Stirpe, Wilson, & Long, 2001).

As an example of a measure developed for sex offenders, Anderson et al. (1995) developed the 54-item SOTRS as a therapist-rated measure of six aspects of treatment performance: (1) insight into their offending in terms of motives and underlying attitudes and beliefs; (2) atypical sexual fantasies and urges; (3) awareness of situational risk factors; (4) motivation for personal change through treatment; (5) empathy for sexual victims; and (6) disclosure of offending patterns and details. In a sample of 122 adult male sex offenders, Anderson et al. reported the SOTRS had excellent internal consistencies, and good inter-rater reliability and test–retest reliability.

Levenson and Macgowan (2004) found that SOTRS ratings were significantly and inversely correlated with offender denial of responsibility for his offenses, and positively correlated with a measure of group therapy engagement in a sample of 61 offenders against children. Ricci, Clayton, and Shapiro (2006) found the SOTRS could detect significant changes over the course of treatment in a small group of 10 offenders against children; moreover, changes on the scales assessing atypical sexual fantasies, motivation for change, and victim empathy were positively correlated with changes on phallometrically assessed sexual arousal.

As an example of a general measure adapted for use with sex offenders, Barrett et al. (2003) used Goal Attainment Scaling to assess the following aspects of motivation to change in a sample of 101 sex offenders: acceptance of guilt for the offense, acceptance of personal responsibility for the offense, disclosure of personal information, motivation to change behavior, and participation in treatment. Motivation to change significantly increased from an intake assessment and following institutional treatment, but then decreased upon release to the community and did not recover following 12 weeks of treatment in the community. Stirpe et al. (2001) monitored treatment progress using GAS scores. Offenders were classified as low, moderate, or high in risk for recidivism. Low- and moderate-risk offenders received better GAS scores, and only low- and moderate-risk offenders showed a steady improvement in ratings of relapse prevention targets and motivation to change from pretreatment to release to the community.

Demonstrating that treatment can have an impact on these targets does not mean that the treatment is effective in reducing sexual offending, which is the ultimate goal of treatments for (paraphilic) sex offenders or paraphilic individuals who are considered to be at great risk of acting upon their interests and thereby committing sexual crimes. Thus, assessment of treatment outcome should ideally include the recording of new offenses, which can be obtained through self-report and through official records of new arrests, charges, and convictions.

Overall Evaluation

Some of the paraphilia measures identified in the diagnosis section are also useful in the assessment of treatment change and outcome. Focusing on the paraphilia, changes in the frequency or intensity of paraphilic thoughts, fantasies, urges, arousal, and behavior can be assessed through self-report, either by interview or through questionnaires. When appropriate, treatment change can be corroborated by interviewing others (e.g., the client's sexual partner) and objective assessment of sexual arousal patterns using phallometry.

For some paraphilic individuals, assessment of treatment change and outcome should also focus on potentially changeable factors associated with risk to offend (dynamic risk factors) if the paraphilia is acted upon. These dynamic risk factors include attitudes and beliefs tolerant of sexual offending, sexual and general self-regulation, and general antisocial tendencies such as antisocial attitudes and beliefs and association with criminal peers. Paraphilias of particular concern are pedophilia and sadism because they are associated with sexual offenses against children and violent sexual offenses, respectively, but frotteurism, exhibitionism, and voyeurism are also of concern. Other paraphilias—though distressing to the client or disruptive to his or her relationships and other functioning—are unlikely to involve criminal behavior if acted upon.

OVERALL SUMMARY AND FINAL COMMENTS

As demonstrated in this review, a number of reliable and valid measures are available for the diagnosis of paraphilias, but more research is needed. No standardized semistructured or structured interview formats for assessing specific paraphilias have been developed and validated, and interview questions and questionnaire items are mostly face valid and therefore vulnerable to socially desirable responding. Questionnaires such as the MSI or SHQ-R contain validity scales, but more studies are needed on the ability of these validity scales to detect socially desirable or exaggerated responding. In addition, the majority of measures that have been developed focus on paraphilias that result in criminal conduct if acted upon, particularly pedophilia and sadism, and to a lesser extent exhibitionism and voyeurism. More work is needed on self-report measures of other paraphilias, particularly those that are not usually associated with criminal conduct.

As we have already mentioned, it would be very beneficial to develop behavioral history measures similar to the SSPI, but designed to assess other

paraphilias. Development of these measures will require a better understanding of the behavioral correlates of these other paraphilias, just as research on sexual offending against children has identified having boy victims, multiple victims, younger victims, and unrelated victims as being associated with pedophilia. Of particular interest would be behavioral correlates among nonoffending individuals with paraphilias. There is a great deal of support for the use of phallometry in the assessment of paraphilias. However, more research is needed to develop valid stimulus sets for paraphilias other than pedophilia and biastophilia (a sexual preference for rape), as only a limited number of studies have examined exhibitionism, transvestism, and fetishism. Finally, more work is needed on the development of reliable and valid assessment methods—self-report, behavioral history, and behavioral testing—for women, and age-appropriate measures for adolescents.

Nonforensic evaluators are likely to rely on self-report for assessment of paraphilias, but can benefit from objective measures when they are available. The Association for the Treatment of Sexual Abusers, a large international organization of professionals who assess and treat sex offenders, maintains a membership directory and can identify laboratories that use viewing time or phallometry to assess sexual interests (see www.atsa.com). Some of these laboratories accept referrals of nonoffending individuals who may have paraphilias. Training is required to conduct such assessments in a reliable and valid fashion. Forensic evaluators will use both self-report and objective methods, and will also be able to draw upon information they obtain regarding sexual offense histories.

Measures that do not rely on self-report but are less intrusive than genital assessment—including viewing time, adaptations of other cognitive science paradigms such as choice reaction time, evoked potential recordings, and brain imaging—would be particularly useful for both clinical and research purposes. Research on paraphilias would also benefit from the development of scales suitable for large-scale epidemiological surveys, in order to address fundamental questions about paraphilias with regard to prevalence, biographic correlates, and developmental course.

Some of the assessment measures used in the diagnosis of paraphilias are suitable for case conceptualization, treatment planning, and monitoring of treatment change and outcome, particularly certain MSI scales and phallometry. Because there is no evidence that paraphilic sexual interests can be altered, treatment planning and monitoring focuses on related factors that are believed to be associated with the likelihood of paraphilic sexual behavior, though changes in the frequency and intensity of paraphilic thoughts, fantasies, urges, arousal, and behavior should also be assessed. Some of the related factors are relevant for both nonforensic and forensic evaluations, such as antisocial tendencies, attitudes and beliefs tolerant of sexual offending, and sexual self-regulation problems. Factors associated with risk to reoffend—as represented in items of actuarial risk scales such as the Static-99—are particularly germane for men who are already known to have committed sexual offenses.

References

Abel, G. G., Becker, J. V., & Cunningham-Rathner, J. (1984). Complications, consent, and cognitions in sex between children and adults. *International Journal of Law and Psychiatry, 7,* 89–103.

Abel, G. G., Becker, J. V., Cunningham-Rathner, J., Mittelman, M., & Rouleau, J. L. (1988). Multiple paraphilic diagnoses among sex offenders. *Bulletin of the American Academy of Psychiatry and the Law, 16,* 153–168.

Abel, G. G., Becker, J. V., Mittelman, M., & Cunningham, J. (1987). Self-reported sex crimes of nonincarcerated paraphiliacs. *Journal of Interpersonal Violence, 2,* 3–25.

Abel, G. G., Huffman, J., Warberg, B., & Holland, C. L. (1998). Visual reaction time and plethysmography as measures of sexual interest in child molesters. *Sexual Abuse: A Journal of Research and Treatment, 10,* 81–95.

Abel, G. G., Jordan, A., Hand, C. G., Holland, L. A., & Phipps, A. (2001). Classification models of child molesters utilizing the Abel Assessment For Sexual Interest. *Child Abuse and Neglect, 25,* 703–718.

Abel, G. G., Jordan, A., Rouleau, J. L., Emerick, R., Barboza-Whitehead, S., & Osborn, C. (2004). Use of visual reaction time to assess male adolescents who molest children. *Sexual Abuse: A Journal of Research and Treatment, 16,* 255–265.

Abel, G. G., Lawry, S. S., Karlstrom, E., Osborn, C. A., & Gillespie, C. F. (1994). Screening tests for pedophilia. *Criminal Justice and Behavior, 21,* 115–131.

Ægisdóttir, S., Spengler, P. M., & White, M. J. (2006). Should I pack my umbrella? Clinical versus statistical prediction of mental health decisions. *The Counseling Psychologist, 34,* 410–419.

American Psychiatric Association (2000). *Diagnostic and statistical manual of mental disorders* (4th ed., text rev.). Washington, DC: Author.

Anderson, R. D., Gibeau, D., & D'Amora, D. A. (1995). The Sex Offender Treatment Rating Scale: Initial reliability data. *Behavioral Science, 7,* 221–227.

Andrews, D. A., & Bonta, J. (2006). *The psychology of criminal conduct* (4th ed.). Cincinnati, OH: Anderson.

Arkowitz, S., & Vess, J. (2003). An evaluation of the Bumby RAPE and MOLEST scales as measures of cognitive distortions in civilly committed sexual offenders. *Sexual Abuse: A Journal of Research and Treatment, 15,* 237–250.

Baldwin, K., & Roys, D. T. (1998). Factors associated with denial in a sample of alleged adult sexual offenders. *Behavioral Science, 10,* 211–226.

Barbaree, H. E. (1991). Denial and minimization among sex offenders: Assessment and treatment outcome. *Forum on Corrections Research, 3,* 30–33.

Barbaree, H. E., (2005). Psychopathy, treatment behavior, and recidivism. *Journal of Interpersonal Violence, 20,* 1115–1131.

Barbaree, H. E., Baxter, D. J., & Marshall, W. L. (1989). Brief research report: The reliability of the rape index in a sample of rapists and nonrapists. *Violence and Victims, 4,* 299–306.

Barbaree, H. E., Bogaert, A. F., & Seto, M. C. (1995). Sexual reorientation therapy: Practices and controversies. In L. Diamant & R. D. McAnulty (Eds.), *The psychology of sexual orientation, behavior, and identity: A handbook* (pp. 357–383). Westport, CT: Greenwood.

Barbaree, H. E., & Marshall, W. L. (1989). Erectile responses among heterosexual child molesters, father–daughter incest offenders, and matched non-offenders: Five distinct age preference profiles. *Canadian Journal of Behavioural Science, 21,* 70–82.

Barbaree, H. E., & Seto, M. C. (1997). Pedophilia: Assessment and treatment. In D. R. Laws & W. T. O'Donohue, (Eds.), *Sexual deviance: Theory, assessment and treatment* (pp. 175–193). New York: Guilford.

Barbaree, H. E., Seto, M. C., Langton, C. M., & Peacock, E. J. (2001). Evaluating the predictive accuracy of six risk assessment instruments for adult sex offenders. *Criminal Justice and Behavior, 28,* 490–521.

Barnard, G. W., Robbins, L., Tingle, D., Shaw, T., & Newman, G. (1987). Development of a computerized sexual assessment laboratory. *Bulletin of the American Academy of Psychiatry and Law, 15,* 339–347.

Barrett, M., Wilson, R. J., & Long, C. (2003). Measuring motivation to change in sexual offenders: From institutional intake to community treatment. *Sexual Abuse: A Journal of Research and Treatment, 15,* 269–283.

Baumgartner, J. V., Scalora, M. J., & Huss, M. T. (2002). Assessment of the Wilson Sex Fantasy Questionnaire among child molesters and nonsexual forensic offenders. *Behavioral Science, 14,* 19–30.

Beckett, R. C., Fisher, D., Mann, R. E., & Thornton, D. (1997). The Relapse Prevention Questionnaire and interview. In H. Eldridge (Ed.), *Therapists' guide for maintaining change: Relapse prevention manual for adult male perpetrators of child sexual abuse.* Thousand Oaks, CA: Sage.

Bickley, J. A., & Beech, A. R. (2002). An investigation of the Ward and Hudson Pathways Model of the sexual offense process with child abusers. *Journal of Interpersonal Violence, 17,* 371–393.

Blanchard, R., & Barbaree, H. E. (2005). The strength of sexual arousal as a function of the age of the sex offender: Comparisons among pedophiles, hebephiles, and teleiophiles. *Sexual Abuse: A Journal of Research and Treatment, 17,* 441–456.

Blanchard, R., Klassen, P., Dickey, R., Kuban, M. E., & Blak, T. (2001) Sensitivity and specificity of the phallometric test for pedophilia in nonadmitting sex offenders. *Psychological Assessment, 13,* 118–126.

Bradford, J. M., Boulet, J., & Pawlak, A. (1992). The paraphilias: A multiplicity of deviant behaviours. *Canadian Journal of Psychiatry, 37,* 104–108.

Bumby, K. M. (1996). Assessing the cognitive distortions of child molesters and rapists: Development and validation of the MOLEST and RAPE scales. *Sexual Abuse: A Journal of Research and Treatment, 8,* 37–54.

Chaplin, T. C., Rice, M. E., & Harris, G. T. (1995). Salient victim suffering and the sexual responses of child molesters. *Journal of Consulting and Clinical Psychology, 63,* 249–255.

Chivers, M. L., Rieger, G., Latty, E., & Bailey, J. M. (2004). A sex difference in the specificity of sexual arousal. *Psychological Science, 15,* 736–744.

Chow, E. W. C., & Choy, A. L. (2002). Clinical characteristics and treatment response to SSRI in a female pedophile. *Archives of Sexual Behavior, 31,* 211–215.

Craig, L. A., Browne, K. D., Beech, A., & Stringer, I. (2006). Psychosexual characteristics of sexual offenders and the relationship to sexual reconviction. *Psychology, Crime & Law, 12,* 231–243.

Curnoe, S., & Langevin, R. (2002). Personality and deviant sexual fantasies: An examination of the MMPIs. *Journal of Clinical Psychology, 58,* 803–815.

Daleiden, E. L., Kaufman, K. L., Hilliker, D. R., & O'Neil, J. N. (1998). The sexual histories and fantasies of youthful males: A comparison of sexual offending, nonsexual offending, and nonoffending groups. *Sexual Abuse: A Journal of Research and Treatment, 10,* 195–209.

Daversa, M. (2005). Early caregiver instability and maltreatment experiences in the prediction of age of victims of adolescent sexual offenders. *Dissertation Abstracts International, 65(08-B),* 4319.

Davidson, P. R., & Malcolm, P. B. (1985). The reliability of the rape index: A rapist sample. *Behavioral Assessment, 7,* 283–292.

Day, D. M., Miner, M. H., Sturgeon, V. H., & Murphy, J. (1989). Assessment of sexual arousal by means of physiological and self-report measures. In D. R. Laws (Ed.), *Relapse prevention with sex offenders* (pp. 115–123). New York: Guilford.

Doren, D. M. (2002). *Evaluating sex offenders: A manual for civil commitments and beyond.* Thousand Oaks, CA: Sage.

Dunsieth, N., Nelson, E., Brusman-Lovins, L., Holcomb, J., Beckman, D., & Welga, J. (2004) Psychiatric and legal features of 113 men convicted of sexual offenses. *Journal of Clinical Psychiatry, 65,* 293–300.

Earls, C. M., Quinsey, V. L., & Castonguay, L. G. (1987). A comparison of three methods of scoring penile circumference changes. *Archives of Sexual Behavior, 16,* 493–500.

Epperson, D. L., Kaul, J. D., Huot, S. J., Hesselton, D., Alexander, W., & Goldman, R. (1998). *Minnesota Sex Offender Screening Tool-Revised (MnSOST-R).* St. Paul, MN: Minnesota Department of Corrections.

Fernandez, Y. M. (2002). Phallometric testing with sexual offenders against female victims: An examination of reliability and validity issues. *Dissertation Abstracts International, 62(12–B),* 6017.

First, M. B. (2004). Desire for amputation of a limb: Paraphilia, psychosis, or a new type of identity disorder. *Psychological Medicine, 35,* 919–928.

Freeman, J. B., & Leonard, H. L. (2000). Sexual obsessions in obsessive–compulsive disorder. *Journal of the American Academy of Child & Adolescent Psychiatry, 39,* 141–142.

Freund, K. (1967). Diagnosing homo- or heterosexuality and erotic age-preference by means of a psychophysiological test. *Behavior Research and Therapy, 5,* 209–28.

Freund, K., Chan, S., & Coulthard, R. (1979). Phallometric diagnosis with "nonadmitters". *Behavior Research and Therapy, 17,* 451–457.

Freund, K. (1963). A laboratory method for diagnosing predominance of homo or hetero-erotic interest in male. *Behavior Research and Therapy, 1,* 85–93.

Freund, K. (1990). Courtship disorder. In W. L. Marshall, D. R. Laws, & H. E. Barbaree (Eds.), *Handbook of sexual assault: Issues, theories, and treatment of the offender* (pp. 195–207). New York: Plenum.

Freund, K., Watson, R., & Rienzo, D. (1988). Signs of feigning in the phallometric test. *Behavior Research and Therapy, 26,* 105–112.

Freund, K., & Blanchard, R. (1989). Phallometric diagnosis of pedophilia. *Journal of Consulting and Clinical Psychology, 57,* 100–105.

Freund, K., & Kuban, M. (1993). Deficient erotic gender differentiation in pedophilia: A follow-up. *Archives of Sexual Behavior, 22,* 619–628.

Freund, K., & Seto, M. C. (1998). Preferential rape in the theory of courtship disorder. *Archives of Sexual Behavior, 27,* 433–443.

Freund, K., & Watson, R. J. (1991). Assessment of the sensitivity and specificity of a phallometric test: An update of phallometric diagnosis of pedophilia. *Psychological Assessment, 3,* 254–260.

Freund, K., Seto, M. C., & Kuban, M. (1995) Masochism: A multiple case study. *Sexuologie, 2,* 313–324.

Freund, K., Seto, M. C., & Kuban, M. (1997). Frotteurism and the theory of courtship disorder. In D. R. Laws & W. T. O'Donohue (Eds.), *Sexual deviance: Theory, assessment and treatment* (pp. 111–130). New York: Guilford.

Gaither, G. A. (2001). The reliability and validity of three new measures of male sexual preferences. *Dissertation Abstracts International, 61*(9-B), 4981.

Gaither, G. A. (2005, March). *Gender differences in sexual interest specificity: Results from viewing time and choice reaction time research.* Paper presented at the Kinsey Institute Interdisciplinary Seminar Series, Bloomington, IN.

Gendreau, P., Little, T., & Goggin, C. (1996). A meta-analysis of the predictors of adult offender recidivism: What works! *Criminology, 34,* 575–608.

Gijs, L. G., & Gooren, L. (1996). Hormonal and psychopharmacological interventions in the treatment of paraphilias: An update. *Journal of Sex Research, 33,* 273–290.

Gordon, W. M. (2002). Sexual obsessions and OCD. *Sexual and Relationship Therapy, 17,* 343–354.

Gosselin, C. C., Wilson, G. D., & Barrett, P. T. (1991). The personality and sexual preferences of sadomasochistic women. *Personality and Individual Differences, 12,* 11–15.

Grove, W. M., Zald, D. H., Lebow, B. S., Snitz, B. E., & Nelson, C. (2000). Clinical versus mechanical prediction: A meta-analysis. *Psychological Assessment, 12,* 19–30.

Hanson, R. K. (1997). *The development of a brief actuarial risk scale for sexual offense recidivism* (User Report 97–04). Ottawa: Public Safety Canada. Retrieved online on March 20, 2007, from http://ww2.ps-sp.gc.ca/publications/corrections/199704_e.pdf

Hanson, R. K. (1998). What do we know about sex offender risk assessment? *Psychology, Public Policy, and Law, 4,* 50–72.

Hanson, R. K., & Thornton, D. (1999). *Static 99: Improving actuarial risk assessments for sex offenders.* Ottawa, ON: Public Safety Canada. Retrieved online on March 20, 2007, from http://ww2.ps-sp.gc.ca/publications/corrections/199902_e.pdf

Hanson, R. K., & Bussière, M. T. (1998). Predicting relapse: A meta-analysis of sexual offender recidivism studies. *Journal of Consulting and Clinical Psychology, 66,* 348–362.

Hanson, R. K., Gordon, A., Harris, A. J. R., Marques, J. K., Murphy, W., Quinsey, V. L., et al. (2002). First report of the Collaborative Outcome Data Project on the effectiveness of psychological treatment for sex offenders. *Sexual Abuse: A Journal of Research and Treatment, 14,* 169–194.

Hanson, R. K., & Harris, A. (2000). *The Sex Offender Need Assessment Rating (SONAR): A method for measuring change in risk levels* (Report No. 2000–1). Ottawa, Ontario: Public Safety Canada. Retrieved online on March 20, 2007, from http://ww2.ps-sp.gc.ca/publications/corrections/pdf/200001b_e.pdf

Hanson, R. K., Morton, K. E., & Harris, A. J. R. (2003). Sexual offender recidivism risk: What we know and what we need to know. *Annals of the New York Academy of Sciences, 989,* 154–166.

Hanson, R. K., & Morton-Bourgon, K. E. (2004). *Predictors of sexual recidivism: An updated meta-analysis.* Ottawa, ON: Public Safety Canada. Retrieved online on March 20, 2007, from http://ww2.ps-sp.gc.ca/publications/corrections/pdf/200001b_e.pdf

Hanson, R. K., & Morton-Bourgon, K. E. (2005). The characteristics of persistent sexual offenders: A meta-analysis of recidivism studies. *Journal of Consulting and Clinical Psychology, 73,* 1154–1163.

Hare, R. D., (2003). *Hare Psychopathy Checklist—Revised* (2nd ed.). Toronto: Multi-Health Systems.

Harris, G. T., Rice, M. E., Chaplin, T. C., & Quinsey, V. L. (1999). Dissimulation in phallometric testing of rapists' sexual preferences. *Archives of Sexual Behavior, 28,* 223–232.

Harris, G. T., Rice, M. E., Quinsey, V. L., & Chaplin, T. C. (1996). Viewing time as a measure of sexual interest among child molesters and normal heterosexual men. *Behavior Research and Therapy, 34,* 389–394.

Harris, G. T., Rice, M. E., Quinsey, V. L., Chaplin, T. C., & Earls, C. (1992). Maximizing the discriminant validity of phallometric assessment data. *Psychological Assessment, 4,* 502–511.

Haywood, T. W., Grossman, L. S., Kravitz, H. M., & Wasyliw, O. E. (1994). Profiling psychological distortion in alleged child molesters. *Psychological Reports, 75,* 915–927.

Holland, L. A., Zolondek, S. C., Abel, G. G., Jordan, A. D., & Becker, J. V. (2000). Psychometric analysis of the Sexual Interest Cardsort Questionnaire. *Sexual Abuse: A Journal of Research and Treatment, 12,* 107–122.

Howes, R. J. (1995). A survey of plethysmographic assessment in North America. *Sexual Abuse: A Journal of Research and Treatment, 7,* 9–24.

Hunter, J. A., Becker, J. V., & Kaplan, M. S. (1995). The Adolescent Sexual Interest Card Sort: Test–retest reliability and concurrent validity in relation to phallometric. *Archives of Sexual Behavior, 24,* 555–561.

Kafka, M. P. (1997). A monoamine hypothesis for the pathophysiology of paraphilic disorders. *Archives of Sexual Behavior, 26,* 343–358.

Kafka, M. P. (2003). The monoamine hypothesis for the pathophysiology of paraphilic disorders: An update. In R. A. Prentky, E. S. Janus, & M. C. Seto (Eds.), *Annals of the New York Academy of Sciences* (pp. 86–94). New York: New York Academy of Sciences.

Kalichman, S. C., Craig, M., Shealy, L., Taylor, J., Szymanowski, D., & McKee, G. (1989). An empirically derived typology of adult sex offenders based on the MMPI: A cross-validation study. *Journal of Psychology and Human Sexuality, 2,* 165–182.

Kalichman, S. C., Henderson, M. C, & Shealy, L. S., & Dwyer, S. M. (1992). Psychometric properties of the Multiphasic Sex Inventory in assessing sex offenders. *Criminal Justice and Behavior, 19,* 384–396.

Knight, R. A., Prentky, R. A., & Cerce, D. D. (1994). The development, reliability, and validity of an inventory for the Multidimensional Assessment of Sex and Aggression. *Criminal Justice and Behavior, 21,* 72–94.

Knight, R. A., & Sims-Knight, J. E. (2003). The developmental antecedents of sexual coercion against women: Testing alternative hypotheses with structural equation modeling. *Annals of the New York Academy of Sciences, 989,* 72–85.

Kuban, M., Barbaree, H. E., & Blanchard, R. (1999). A comparison of volume and circumference phallometry: Response magnitude and method agreement. *Archives of Sexual Behavior, 28,* 345–359.

Lalumière, M. L., & Earls, C. M. (1992). Voluntary control of penile responses as a function of stimulus duration and instructions. *Behavioral Assessment, 14,* 121–132.

Lalumière, M. L., & Harris, G. T. (1998). Common questions regarding the use of phallometric testing with sexual offenders. *Sexual Abuse: A Journal of Research and Treatment, 10,* 227–237.

Lalumière, M. L., Harris, G. T., Quinsey, V. L., & Rice, M. E. (2005). *The causes of rape: Understanding individual differences in male propensity for sexual aggression.* Washington, DC: American Psychological Association.

Lalumière, M. L., & Quinsey, V. L. (1994). The discriminability of rapists from non-sex offenders using phallometric measures: A meta-analysis. *Criminal Justice and Behavior, 21,* 150–175.

Lalumière, M. L., Quinsey, V. L., Harris, G. T., Rice, M. E., & Trautrimas, C. (2003). Are rapists differentially aroused by coercive sex in phallometric assessments? *Annals of the New York Academy of Sciences, 989,* 211–224.

Langevin, R., Lang, R. A., & Curnoe, S. (1998). The prevalence of sex offenders with deviant fantasies. *Journal of Interpersonal Violence, 13,* 315–327.

Langevin, R., & Paitich, D. (2002). *Clarke Sex History Questionnaire for Males—Revised technical manual.* Toronto: Multi-Health Systems.

Launay, G. (1999). The phallometric measurement of offenders: An update. *Criminal Behaviour and Mental Health, 9,* 254–274.

Laws, D. R., Hanson, R. K., Osborn, C. A., & Greenbaum, P. E. (2000). Classification of child molesters by plethysmographic assessment of sexual arousal and a self-report measure of sexual preference. *Journal of Interpersonal Violence, 15,* 1297–1312.

Letourneau, E. J. (2002). A comparison of objective measures of sexual arousal and interest: Visual reaction time and penile plethysmography. *Sexual Abuse: A Journal of Research and Treatment, 14,* 207–223.

Levenson, J. S. (2004). Reliability of sexually violent predator civil commitment criteria in Florida. *Law and Human Behavior, 28,* 357–368.

Levenson J. S., & Macgowan, M. J. (2004). Engagement, denial, and treatment progress among sex offenders in group therapy. *Sexual Abuse: A Journal of Research and Treatment, 16,* 49–63.

Looman, J., Abracen, J., Serin, R., & Marquis, P. (2005). Psychopathy, treatment change, and recidivism in high-risk, high-need sexual offenders. *Journal of Interpersonal Violence, 20,* 549–568.

Madrigano, G., Curry, S., & Bradford, J. M. W. (2003, May). *Sexual arousal of juvenile sex offenders: How do they compare to adult sex offenders?* Paper presented at the 3rd Annual Canadian Conference on Specialized Services for Sexually Abusive Youth, Toronto, Canada.

Marks, I. M., & Gelder, M. G. (1967). Transvestism and fetishism: Clinical and psychological changes during faradic aversion. *British Journal of Psychiatry, 113,* 711–729.

Marlatt, G. A., & Gordon, J. R. (1985). *Relapse prevention: Maintenance strategies in the treatment of addictive behaviors.* New York: Guilford.

Marques, J. K., Wiederanders, M., Day, D. M., Nelson, C., & van Ommeren, A. (2005). Effects of a relapse prevention program on sexual recidivism: Final results from California's Sex Offender Treatment and Evaluation Project (SOTEP). *Sexual Abuse: A Journal of Research and Treatment, 17,* 79–107.

Marshall, W. L. (2006). Diagnosis and treatment of sexual offenders. In I. B. Weiner & A. K. Hess (Eds.), *The handbook of forensic psychology* (3rd ed., pp. 790–818). Hoboken, NJ: Wiley & Sons.

Marshall, W. L., & Fernandez, Y. M. (2000). Phallometric testing with sexual offenders: Limits to its value. *Clinical Psychology Review, 20,* 807–822.

Marshall, W. L., Marshall, L. E., Sachdev, S., & Kruger, R. L. (2003). Distorted attitudes and perceptions, and their relationship with self-esteem and coping in child molesters. *Sexual Abuse: A Journal of Research and Treatment, 15,* 171–181.

Marshall, W. L., Payne, K., Barbaree, H. E., & Eccles, A. (1991). Exhibitionists: Sexual preferences for exposing. *Behavior Research and Therapy, 29,* 37–40.

Mason, F. L. (1997). Fetishism: Psychopathology and theory. In D. R. Laws & W. T. O'Donohue (Eds.), *Sexual deviance: Theory, assessment, and treatment* (pp. 75–91). New York: Guilford.

McClintock, M. K., & Herdt, G. (1996). Rethinking puberty: The development of sexual attraction. *Current Directions in Psychological Science, 5,* 178–183.

McGrath, R. J., Cumming, G. F., & Burchard, B. L. (2003). *Current practices and trends in sexual abuser management: The Safer Society 2002 nationwide survey.* Brandon, VT: Safer Society Foundation.

Money, J. (1984). Paraphilias: Phenomenology and classification. *American Journal of Psychotherapy, 38,* 164–79.

Moser, C., & Levitt, E. E. (1987). An exploratory-descriptive study of a sadomasochistically oriented sample. *Journal of Sex Research, 23,* 322–337.

Nichols, H. R., & Molinder, I. (1984). *Multiphasic Sex Inventory manual.* Tacoma, WA: Nichols & Molinder Assessments. Retrieved on September 17, 2007, from www.nicholsandmolinder.com

O'Donohue, W., Regev, L. G., & Hagstrom, A. (2000). Problems with the DSM-IV diagnosis of pedophilia. *Sexual Abuse: A Journal of Research and Treatment, 12,* 95–105.

Parks, G. A., & Bard, D. E. (2006). Risk factors for adolescent sex offender recidivism: Evaluation of predictive factors and comparison of the three groups based upon victim type. *Sexual Abuse: A Journal of Research and Treatment, 18,* 319–342.

Proulx, J., Côté, G., & Achille, P. A. (1993). Prevention of voluntary control of penile response in homosexual pedophiles during phallometric testing. *Journal of Sex Research, 30,* 140–147.

Quinsey, V. L., & Bergersen, S. G. (1976). Instructional control of penile circumference in assessments of sexual preference. *Behavior Therapy, 7,* 489–493.

Quinsey, V. L., Book, A. S., & Skilling, T. A. (2004). A follow-up of deinstitutionalized men with intellectual disabilities and histories of antisocial behavior. *Journal of Applied Research in Intellectual Disabilities, 17,* 243–254.

Quinsey, V. L., & Carrigan, W. F. (1978). Penile responses to visual stimuli: Instructional control with and without auditory sexual fantasy correlates. *Criminal Justice and Behavior, 5,* 333–342.

Quinsey, V. L., & Chaplin, T. C. (1988). Preventing faking in phallometric assessments of sexual preference. *Annals of the New York Academy of Sciences, 528,* 49–58.

Quinsey, V. L., Harris, G. T., Rice, M. E., & Cormier, C. A. (2006). *Violent offenders: Appraising and managing risk* (2nd ed.). Washington, DC: American Psychological Association.

Quinsey, V. L., Ketsetzis, M., Earls, C., & Karamanoukian, A. (1996). Viewing time as a measure of sexual interest. *Ethology and Sociobiology, 17,* 341–354.

Quinsey, V. L., & Lalumière, M L. (2001). *Assessment of sexual offenders against children* (2nd ed.). Thousand Oaks, CA: Sage.

Quinsey, V. L., Rice, M. E., Harris, G. T., & Reid, K. S. (1993). The phylogenetic and ontogenetic development of sexual age preferences in males: Conceptual and measurement issues. In H. E. Barbaree, W. L. Marshall, & S. M. Hudson (Eds.), *The juvenile sex offender* (pp. 143–163). New York: Guilford.

Quinsey, V. L., Steinman, C. M., Bergersen, S. G., & Holmes, T. F. (1975). Penile circumference, skin conductance, and ranking response of child molesters and "normals" to sexual and nonsexual visual stimuli. *Behavior Therapy, 6,* 213–219.

Rabinowitz, S. R., Firestone, P., Bradford, J. M., & Greenberg, D. M. (2002). Prediction of recidivism in exhibitionists: Psychological, phallometric, and offense factors. *Sexual Abuse: A Journal of Research and Treatment, 14,* 329–347.

Raymond, M. J. (1956). Case of fetishism treated by aversion therapy. *British Medical Journal, 2,* 854–857.

Remafedi, G., Resnick, M., Blum, R., & Harris, L. (1992). Demography of sexual orientation in adolescents. *Pediatrics, 89,* 714–721.

Ricci, R. J., Clayton, C. A., & Shapiro, F. (2006). Some effects of EMDR on previously abused child molesters: Theoretical reviews and preliminary findings. *The Journal of Forensic Psychiatry & Psychology, 17,* 538–562.

Rice, M. E., & Harris, G. T. (2003). The size and signs of treatment effects in sex offender therapy. In R. A. Prentky, E. S. Janus, & M. C. Seto (Eds.), *Annals of the New York Academy of Sciences* (pp. 428–440). New York: New York Academy of Sciences.

Rice, M. E., Quinsey, V. L., & Harris, G. T. (1991). Sexual recidivism among child molesters released from a maximum security psychiatric institution. *Journal of Consulting and Clinical Psychology, 59,* 381–386.

Savin-Williams, R. C., & Diamond, L. M. (2000). Sexual identity trajectories among sexual-minority youths: Gender comparisons. *Archives of Sexual Behavior, 29,* 607–627.

Schneider, S. L., & Wright, R. C. (2001). The FoSOD: A measurement tool for reconceptualizing the role of denial in child molesters. *Journal of Interpersonal Violence, 16,* 545–564.

Seto, M. C. (2001). The value of phallometry in the assessment of male sex offenders. *Journal of Forensic Psychology Practice, 1,* 65–75.

Seto, M. C. (2003). Interpreting the treatment performance of sex offenders. In A. Matravers (Ed.), *Managing sex offenders in the community: Contexts, challenges, and responses* (pp. 125–143), Cambridge Criminal Justice Series. London: Willan.

Seto, M. C. (2004). Pedophilia and sexual offenses against children. *Annual Review of Sex Research, 15,* 321–361.

Seto, M. C. (2008). *Pedophilia and sexual offending against children: Theory, assessment, and intervention.* Washington, DC: American Psychological Association.

Seto, M. C., Cantor, J. M., & Blanchard, R. (2006). Child pornography offenses are a valid diagnostic indicator of pedophilia. *Journal of Abnormal Psychology, 115,* 610–615.

Seto, M. C., & Eke, A. W. (2005). The criminal histories and later offending of child pornography offenders. *Sexual Abuse: A Journal of Research and Treatment, 17,* 201–210.

Seto, M. C., Harris, G. T., Rice, M. E., & Barbaree, H. E. (2004). The Screening Scale for Pedophilic Interests predicts recidivism among adult sex offenders with child victims. *Archives of Sexual Behavior, 33,* 455–466.

Seto M. C., & Kuban, M. (1996). Criterion-related validity of a phallometric test for paraphilic rape and sadism. *Behavior Research and Therapy, 34,* 175–183.

Seto, M. C., & Lalumière, M. L. (2001). A brief screening scale to identify pedophilic interests among child molesters. *Sexual Abuse: A Journal of Research and Treatment, 13,* 15–25.

Seto, M. C., Murphy, W. D., Page, J., & Ennis, L. (2003). Detecting anomalous sexual interests in juvenile sex offenders. *Annals of the New York Academy of Sciences, 989,* 118–130.

Simkins, L., Ward, W., Bowman, S., & Rinck, C. M. (1989). The Multiphasic Sex Inventory: Diagnosis and prediction of treatment response in child sexual abusers. *Annals of Sex Research, 2,* 205–226.

Smallbone, S. W., & Wortley, R. (2004). Criminal diversity and paraphilic interests among adult males convicted of sexual offenses against children. *International Journal of Offender Therapy and Comparative Criminology, 48,* 175–188.

Smith, G., & Fischer, L. (1999). Assessment of juvenile sexual offenders: Reliability and validity of the Abel Assessment for Interest in Paraphilias. *Sexual Abuse: A Journal of Research and Treatment, 11,* 207–216.

Smith, S., Wampler, R., Jones, J., & Reifman, A. (2005). Differences in self-report measures by adolescent sex offender risk group. *International Journal of Offender Therapy and Comparative Criminology, 49,* 82–106.

Stirpe, T. S., Wilson, R. J., & Long, C. (2001). Goal attainment scaling with sexual offenders: A measure of clinical impact at posttreatment and at community follow-up. *Sexual Abuse: A Journal of Research and Treatment, 13,* 65–77.

Thornton, D., & Mann, R. (1997). Sexual masochism: Assessment and treatment. In D. R. Laws & W. O'Donohue (Eds.), *Sexual deviance: Theory, assessment, and treatment* (pp. 240–252). New York: Guilford.

Ward, T., Hudson, S. M., & Keenan, T. (1998). A self-regulation model of the sexual offense process. *Sexual Abuse: A Journal of Research and Treatment, 10,* 141–157.

Wasyliw, O. E., Haywood, T. W., Grossman, L. S., Johnson, S., & Liles, S. (1992). *Measures of denial and cognitive distortions in alleged child molesters.* Paper presented at the Annual Convention of the American Psychological Association, Washington, DC.

Wiederman, M. W. (2002). Reliability and validity of measurement. In M. W. Wiederman & B. E. Whitley (Eds.), *Handbook for conducting research on human sexuality* (pp. 25–50). Mahwah, NJ: Erlbaum.

Wiegel, M., Abel, G. G., & Jordan, A. (2003, October). *The self-reported behaviors of female child abusers.* Paper presented at the 22nd Annual Conference of the Association for the Treatment of Sexual Abusers, St. Louis, MO.

Wilson, R. J., Abracen, J., Picheca, J. E., Malcolm, B., & Prinzo, M. (2003, October). *Pedophilia: An evaluation of diagnostic and risk management methods.* Poster presented at the annual conference of the Association for the Treatment of Sexual Abusers, St. Louis, MO.

World Health Organization. (1992). *The ICD-10 classification of mental and behavioural disorders: Clinical descriptions and diagnostic guidelines.* Geneva, Switzerland: World Health Organization.

Worling, J. R. (2006). Assessing sexual arousal with adolescent males who have offended sexually: Self-report and unobtrusively measured viewing time. *Sexual Abuse: A Journal of Research and Treatment, 18,* 383–400.

Wright, R. C., & Schneider, S. L. (2004). Mapping child molester treatment progress with the FoSOD: Denial and explanations of accountability. *Sexual Abuse: A Journal of Research and Treatment, 16,* 85–105.

Zolondek, S., Abel, G., Northey, W., & Jordan, A. (2001). The self-reported behaviors of juvenile sex offenders. *Journal of Interpersonal Violence, 16,* 73–85.

Zuckerman, M. (1971). Physiological measures of sexual arousal in the human. *Psychological Bulletin, 75,* 297–329.

Part VIII

Health-Related Problems

23

Eating Disorders

Robyn Sysko

This chapter presents the most commonly used and well-validated eating disorder assessments for the purposes of diagnosis, case conceptualization and treatment planning, and treatment monitoring and treatment outcome. General information is also discussed briefly as an introduction to the topic of assessment, including the criteria for an eating disorder diagnosis, prevalence and incidence of eating disorders, common comorbidities, treatment outcomes, and etiology of the disorders. Although structured or semistructured interviews or self-report questionnaires are often used in research studies, and have demonstrated their value for studying the nature of eating disorders in research, the assessments also have promise as clinical tools. As such, this chapter will provide information for practitioners interested in using these measures in clinical practice.

NATURE OF EATING DISORDERS

The fourth edition of the *Diagnostic and Statistical Manual for Mental Disorders* (DSM-IV; American Psychiatric Association, 1994) describes two main eating disorder diagnoses, anorexia nervosa (AN) and bulimia nervosa (BN). The hallmark of AN is the presence of low body weight (e.g., a body weight of less than 85% of expected weight); patients also endorse (a) a fear of gaining weight or becoming fat despite being underweight, (b) describe significant disturbances in the perception of body weight or shape on self-evaluation, or the undue influence of shape or weight on self-evaluation, or a denial of the seriousness of low weight, and in postmenarchal women, amenorrhea is experiencd for a period of 3 months. Individuals who do not regularly engage in binge eating or purging behaviors (i.e., self-induced vomiting and laxative or diuretic abuse) are classified

as having AN-restricting type (AN-R), and patients reporting binge eating or purging are diagnosed with AN-binge-eating/purging (AN-B/P) type. Patients with BN typically are at a normal body weight and report recurrent episodes of binge eating and inappropriate compensatory behavior (e.g., self-induced vomiting, fasting, excessive exercise) at least twice weekly over a 3-month period, and experience an undue influence of shape and weight on their self-evaluation. According to the DSM-IV, an episode of binge eating is characterized by consuming a large amount of food and the experience of a loss of control over eating.

A third, residual, category of Eating Disorder not Otherwise Specified (EDNOS) is provided by the DSM-IV for all other patients with clinically significant eating pathology. The majority of individuals who present for treatment of an eating disorder do not meet full criteria for either AN or BN and are therefore diagnosed with an EDNOS (Fairburn & Bohn, 2005; Fairburn & Harrison, 2003; Turner & Bryant-Waugh, 2004). Despite the substantial proportion of individuals with a clinically meaningful eating disorder classified as EDNOS, little is known about this diagnosis (Fairburn & Bohn, 2005). Criteria for an additional eating disorder, binge-eating disorder (BED), are proposed as a specific example of EDNOS in an appendix of DSM-IV. Patients with BED experience recurrent episodes of binge eating, at least twice weekly over a 6-month period, in the absence of compensatory behaviors. To be diagnosed with BED, patients must experience distress over their binge-eating episodes, have binge-eating episodes characterized by eating large amounts of food during a short time and a sense of loss of control during the episode, and report three of the following: eating until feeling uncomfortably full, eating large amounts of food when not physically hungry, eating much more rapidly than normal, eating alone because of embarrassment, feeling disgusted, depressed, or guilty after overeating. Obesity, or the presence of excess body weight, is listed as a general medical condition and not an eating disorder within the DSM-IV system.

In comparison to other psychiatric diagnoses, such as major depression or substance abuse, eating disorders are relatively rare among the population. The prevalence of AN is approximately 0.28%, and the incidence of AN ranges between 0.42% and 0.81% in Western countries among young women (Hoek, 2002). Among young females, the prevalence of BN is 1.0%, and the incidence ranges between 1.14% and 1.35% in Western countries (Hoek, 2002). Few studies have documented the rates of prevalence and incidence of eating disorders among men, but the available epidemiological data suggest that one male case of AN or BN is seen for every six female cases, and for clinical samples, 10% to 20% of patients with AN are male, and males with BN may be even more uncommon (Andersen, 2002).

Although eating disorders are often considered to be culturally bound syndromes, AN has been documented in every region of the world (Keel & Klump, 2003). In addition, the prevalence of AN is similar in Western and non-Western countries and, therefore, AN does not appear to occur solely, or even more frequently, in Western countries (Keel & Klump, 2003). Although BN has been observed outside of Western countries, Western cultural influences appear to play a more significant role in the development of this disorder, and an increase in the incidence of BN was also observed during the latter half of the twentieth century (Keel & Klump, 2003). Because BED has only been considered as a separate diagnostic category since the development of DSM-IV, fewer epidemiological studies have documented the prevalence and incidence of this diagnosis. Estimates of the prevalence of binge-eating disorder among the general population are typically higher than those of AN, and similar to estimates for BN (Striegel-Moore & Franko, 2003). However, among samples of obese individuals, prevalence estimates can reach up to 8% (Striegel-Moore & Franko, 2003).

Cases of DSM-IV eating disorders are predominantly diagnosed among women, with men representing only 5% to 10% of observed cases (Hoek, 2002). At this time, research on men with eating disorders is limited, and it is not known whether the expression of eating disorders between genders is the same.

Men may experience core disturbances in shape and weight and eating pathology differently than women, such as through muscle dysmorphia, where the defining feature is a drive for leanness and muscularity and not a desire for thinness (Hildebrandt Schlundt, Langenbucher, & Chung, 2006; Pope, Gruber, Choi, Olivardia, & Phillips, 1997). Additional research is needed to evaluate the suitability of the current DSM-IV diagnostic criteria for describing symptoms of disturbed eating in men.

The etiology of eating disorders is complex; however, some biological, environmental, and psychosocial factors may increase an individual's risk for developing these disorders. The interaction of biological (e.g., hormones) and psychological changes around the time of adolescence likely influence the development of these disorders, as the majority of individuals experience the onset of eating disorders near puberty, and a greater proportion of young women are affected by eating disorders (Commission on Adolescent Eating Disorders, 2005). In addition, social influences, such as peers, can affect beliefs about shape and weight or dieting (Jones & Crawford, 2006) and cultural influences, including the influence of mass media, can produce increases in body dissatisfaction and eating disturbances (Becker, Burwell, Gilman, Herzog, & Hamburg, 2002). Genetic factors may also predispose individuals to the development of eating disorders; however, there are currently no specific genes that are identified as specific to patients with AN or BN (Commission on Adolescent Eating Disorders, 2005). Thus, biological, social, cultural, genetic, and other variables likely influence the etiology of eating disorders, but it is not known whether different factors are responsible for the development of these disorders and maintenance of symptoms, or the way in which the factors interact.

Comorbid psychiatric diagnoses are common among treatment-seeking patients with eating disorders. Prevalence rates of a lifetime anxiety disorders range from approximately 33% to 72% of patients with AN-R, 55% of patients with AN-B/P, 41% to 75% of patients with BN (Godart, Flament, Perdereau, & Jeammet, 2002), and 29% of patients with BED (Wilfley, Friedman, et al., 2000). Rates of lifetime major depressive disorder range from 9.5% to 64.7% in AN-R, 50% to 71.3% in AN-B/P, 20% to 80% of patients with BN (Godart et al., 2007) and 58% in BED (Wilfley, Friedman, et al., 2000). Some data suggest that comorbid depressive symptoms improve with successful treatment, as statistically significant improvements in mood symptoms have been observed among inpatients with AN receiving nutritional rehabilitation and psychotherapy after weight restoration (Meehan, Loeb, Roberto, & Attia, 2006) and patients with BN after treatment with cognitive-behavioral therapy (CBT; Wilson & Fairburn, 2002).

The prognosis for individuals with eating disorders varies across diagnostic categories. Anorexia nervosa has the highest mortality rate of all psychiatric disorders, and few treatments, psychological or pharmacological, have been found to be effective for patients with AN (Walsh et al., 2006). A recent review documented the course and outcome of patients with AN 12 years after inpatient treatment and found that 27.5% of patients experienced a good outcome, 25.3% had an intermediate outcome, 39.6% had a poor outcome, and 7.7% had died (Fichter, Quadflieg, & Hedlund, 2006). Patients with AN who are younger or receive treatment after a short duration of illness may experience better treatment outcomes than adults with a longer course of illness (Commission on Adolescent Eating Disorders, 2005; Herpertz-Dahlmann et al., 2001).

Two forms of treatment, CBT and antidepressant medication, have been found to be helpful for the treatment of BN. Patients treated with CBT typically experience a reduction in binge eating and purging of 80% or more, and approximately 30% of patients are abstinent from binge eating and purging at the end of treatment (National Institute of Clinical Excellence, 2004). Antidepressant medications are consistently superior to placebo in pharmacological treatment studies for BN, and median reductions of up to 70% have been observed for symptoms of binge eating and vomiting (Agras, 1997). Despite the availability of effective treatments, the symptoms of BN can be chronic for some individuals, with approximately 30% of patients with BN experiencing recurrent episodes of binge eating and purging more than a decade after presentation for their disorder (Keel, Mitchell, Miller, Davis, & Crow, 1999).

The data suggest more encouraging outcomes among patients with BED, as reductions in binge eating are observed in response to a variety of treatments (CBT, Interpersonal Psychotherapy, Behavioral Weight Loss; Wilson & Fairburn, 2002), which are maintained over at least 1 year (Ricca et al., 2001). CBT is currently considered to be the treatment of choice for BED, but questions remain as to the specificity of this form of treatment (Grilo & Masheb, 2005). Although psychological treatments for BED

have been shown to successfully reduce binge eating and associated psychological symptoms, no significant degree of weight loss is observed among these patients either in the short or long term (Wonderlich, de Zwaan, Mitchell, Peterson, & Crow, 2003). For individuals with BED, a majority of whom are overweight or obese, this failure to achieve weight loss can be associated with significant morbidity and mortality (National Task Force on the Prevention and Treatment of Obesity, 2000).

PURPOSES OF ASSESSMENT

Regardless of the particular purpose for a clinical evaluation, assessments for eating disorders must consider the wide range of symptoms experienced by patients with AN, BN, and BED. These symptoms can include restraint over eating, binge eating and purging, concerns about shape and weight, and obsessions and compulsions about food, eating, shape, and weight. In the following paragraphs, a number of the challenges involved in accurately and fully assessing an individual with an eating disorder are described.

The assessment of binge eating, which is a core eating disturbance experienced by individuals with AN-B/P, BN, and BED, is perhaps the most difficult construct to measure accurately. To receive a diagnosis of BN or BED, an individual must describe binge episodes in which they consume an objectively large amount of food and experience a sense of loss of control over eating (objective bulimic episode; OBE; see description of the Eating Disorder Examination below). This definition of binge eating used by DSM-IV was partially derived from eating behavior experiments conducted in laboratory settings, where patients with BN were asked to binge eat and were provided with a large multi-item meal. The patients demonstrated a significant disturbance in the total amount of calories consumed during the binge episode (mean of between 3,352 and 4,477 kcal), as opposed to a specific type of food, or a specific macronutrient group (Kissileff, Walsh, Kral, & Cassidy, 1986; Walsh, Kissileff, Cassidy, & Dantzic, 1989). Similarly, more recent studies have observed disturbances in total consumption during a binge episode for individuals with BED, although BED patients generally consume fewer calories than do patients with BN (Walsh & Boudreau, 2003).

Thus, although laboratory data helps provide some objective measure of binge eating among patients with BN and BED, there are no explicit criteria for the amount of food needed to constitute a binge episode in the DSM-IV (e.g., consumption of >1,500 calories per sitting). As a result, many of the assessments described in the chapter employ standards stemming from judgments of experts in the field (e.g., Eating Disorder Examination), the judgment of the interviewer (e.g., Structured Clinical Interview for DSM-IV), or the self-report of the patient (e.g., Eating Disorder Diagnostic Scale). The way in which an instrument assesses binge eating will be described throughout the chapter, so that the reader can weigh the pros and cons of each method for determining the presence of absence of binge episodes.

In addition, caution should be exercised when selecting measures to use with a specific patient or a sample of individuals with eating disorders. Many measures of eating disorder symptoms or body image do not assess issues relevant to men (Thompson, Roehrig, Cafri, & Heinberg, 2005). Thus, men may report that commonly used measures ask questions that are not applicable to their experience of shape or weight disturbance (e.g., Have you felt excessively large and rounded?). Some measures have been developed specifically for the purpose of assessing men with eating disorders, including the Male Body Attitudes Scale (Tylka, Bergeron, & Schwartz, 2005), the Muscle Dysmorphic Disorder Inventory (Hildebrandt, Langenbucher, & Schlundt, 2004), and the Muscle Dysmorphia Inventory (Rhea, Lantz, & Cornelius, 2004). As the focus of this chapter is on the routine clinical assessment of eating disorders, and the prevalence of eating disorders among men is so low, measures such as these are not covered here in detail. Second, professionals utilizing the measures described in this chapter should be aware that not all assessments are validated for children or adolescents (Thompson et al., 2005). Thus, in the chapter, information is provided about assessments that have been developed specifically for children or adolescents.

The assessments described in the following three sections focus specifically on eating disorder symptoms. Other features have been shown to be either risk factors for the development of eating disorders or otherwise associated with eating disorders, including perfectionism, body dissatisfaction, impulse regulation, and thin-ideal internalization, and assessments exist to measure these constructs (e.g., Body Esteem Scale, Franzoi & Shields, 1984; Eating Disorder Inventory-2, Garner, 1991; Ideal-Body Stereotype

Scale-Revised, Stice & Bearman, 2001; Satisfaction and Dissatisfaction with Body Parts Scale, Berscheid, Walster, & Bohmstedt, 1973).

Clinicians may also be interested in measuring the general psychological or psychosocial functioning of eating disorder patients, interpersonal functioning, or the patient's family context. A number of treatment studies (Agras, Crow, et al., 2000; Agras, Walsh, Fairburn, Wilson, & Kraemer, 2000; Halmi et al., 2005; Wilfley et al., 2002) assessed general psychological functioning pre- and posttreatment using the Social Adjustment Scale (SAS; Weissman & Bothwell, 1976), others (Agras, Walsh, et al., 2000; Walsh, Fairburn, Mickley, Sysko, & Parides, 2004; Wilfley et al., 2002) employed the Symptom Checklist (53 or 90 items; Derogatis, Lipman, & Covi, 1973), and yet others (Walsh et al., 2006) used the Quality of Life Enjoyment and Satisfaction Questionnaire (QLESQ; Endicott, Nee, Harrison, & Blumenthal, 1993). Interpersonal functioning has been frequently measured using the Inventory of Interpersonal Problems (IIP; Horowitz, Rosenberg, Baer, Ureno, & Villasenor, 1988) in treatment studies for BN (Agras, Crow, et al., 2000; Agras, Walsh, et al., 2000; Carter et al., 2003) or BED (Devlin et al., 2005; Wilfley et al., 2002). Studies of the Maudsley form of family therapy (Lock, Agras, Dare, & Le Grange, 2002), a promising treatment for adolescents with anorexia nervosa, have measured family functioning in a number of ways. Le Grange and colleagues (1992) employed the Standardized Clinical Family Interview (SCFI; Kinston & Loader, 1984), made video recordings of interviews to rate Expressed Emotion (EE; Vaughn & Leff, 1976), and administered the Family Adaptability and Cohesion Evaluation Scales (FACES-III; Olson, Sprenkle, & Russell, 1979; Olson, Portner, & Lavee, 1985), Lock, Agras, Bryson, & Kraemer (2005) used the Family Environment Scale (Moos, 1974; Moos and Moos, 1994), and Robin and colleagues (1999) assessed family conflict with the Parent Adolescent Relationship Questionnaire (PARQ; Robin, Koepke, & Moye, 1990)

Although data on the aforementioned related constructs can provide useful information about patients with eating disorders, the most salient aspect of diagnosis, case conceptualization and treatment planning, and treatment outcome is knowledge of a patient's eating disorder symptoms. Only the assessment of specific eating disorder symptoms can generate DSM-IV diagnoses, and the diagnosis assigned to a given patient subsequently helps determine the most effective treatments for that patient. The research evaluating eating disorder treatments to date has stratified patients on the basis of their diagnosis, and therefore these studies allow clinicians to use empirically supported treatments in routine practice when eating disorder symptoms are measured.

ASSESSMENT FOR DIAGNOSIS

This portion of the chapter focuses on assessment tools used to formulate eating disorder diagnoses, including AN, BN, BED, or EDNOS. One important measurement issue relevant to the diagnosis of eating disorders, regardless of assessment method, is the measurement of body weight. Weight is crucial in differentiating between the diagnoses of AN-B/P versus BN, as similar bulimic symptoms are present in both disorders. To assign the diagnosis of AN-B/P, the individual must be underweight (e.g., at a body weight ≤85% than ideal, or body mass index <18.5; APA, 1994 Expert Panel on the Identification, Evaluation, and Treatment of Overweight in Adults, 1998), and this requires obtaining the patient's weight and, subsequently, using either tables of ideal body weight (e.g., Metropolitan Life Insurance, 1959) or a calculation of BMI (weight in kg/height in m²). Thus, in conjunction with any data from interviews or self-report questionnaires, a measurement of weight must be obtained to assign an accurate eating disorder diagnosis.

Both semistructured interviews and self-report questionnaires are available for use in formulating a diagnosis. Perhaps the most commonly used assessment instrument is the Eating Disorder Examination (EDE; Cooper & Fairburn, 1987; Fairburn & Cooper, 1993), a semistructured interview that is considered to be the "gold standard" of measurement for eating disorders (Wilson, 1993). The EDE provides a comprehensive description of the psychopathology associated with AN, BN, and BED, and allows for DSM-IV eating disorder diagnoses to be assigned. Wilfley, Schwartz, Spurrell, & Fairburn (1997) developed a module that can be added to the EDE to diagnose BED. The BED module extends the timeframe of the standard EDE interview from 3 to 6 months, and includes questions based on the preliminary BED criteria listed in the Appendix of DSM-IV. As the 12th edition of the EDE (Fairburn & Cooper, 1993) is the most recent published version of the instrument, it is described here; however, newer unpublished versions

of the EDE are currently being used in research studies (e.g., Wilfley, 2006), and should be available for clinical use in the future.

The format of the EDE is investigator-based, such that consistent scoring of the EDE items is achieved by a synthesis of information provided by the interviewee and the assessors' understanding of the terms and constructs as defined by the assessment (Fairburn & Cooper, 1993; Wilson, 1993). To become proficient in administering the interview, it is necessary to complete comprehensive training. Training includes mastery of the interview format, corating interviews of trained EDE assessors, and receiving supervision from an individual previously trained in administering the EDE. Trained EDE interviewers make determinations about the severity of eating disorder symptoms and rate the amounts of food that qualify for different types of overeating (see four types of overeating below), which is particularly important for diagnosing BN and BED.

As the EDE assesses eating disorder symptoms over a significant period of time (3 or 6 months), the Timeline Followback (TLFB) method is used. For the EDE TLFB, the interviewer presents the patient with a calendar showing the 3- or 6-month period covered by the EDE, and with the patient, identifies events in each month that might have disrupted the patient's normal eating routine and other notable events (e.g., vacations, birthdays, parties). These events are written on the calendar so that the patient can refer back to them throughout the interview. The TLFB procedure was originally developed to retrospectively measure alcohol consumption (Maisto, Sobell, Cooper, & Sobell, 1982), and helps orient patients to the time period being assessed and provides contextual information during the interview.

The EDE has four subscales (Restraint, Eating Concern, Shape Concern, and Weight Concern) and a global score, and includes items with either frequency or severity ratings. Severity items on the EDE are rated on a scale from 0 to 6, where a 1 is assigned if the feature is "barely present," a 5 is assigned when the symptom does not qualify for the most severe rating (6), and a 3 is used as the midpoint between 0 and 6 (Fairburn & Cooper, 1993). Four different types of overeating are assessed by the EDE, including (1) objective bulimic episodes, or the consumption of an objectively large amount of food while experiencing a sense of loss of control, (2) subjective bulimic episodes, or experiencing loss of control while consuming smaller amounts of food that are viewed by the individual as excessive, (3) objective overeating, or eating an objectively large amount of food without loss of control, and (4) subjective overeating, or eating a small amount of food without a sense of loss of control, which the individual believes is excessive (Fairburn & Cooper, 1993). The designation of an amount of food that constitutes an "objectively large" amount of food during a binge episode is determined by the EDE interviewer; however, an appendix to the EDE was developed by experts in the field to standardize amounts constituting Objective Bulimic Episodes (OBEs). For example, the consumption of two full meals (each with two or more courses), or three main courses (e.g., three Big Macs), or more than 1 pint of ice cream, or 5 donuts would all be considered large when rating OBEs on the EDE.

A version of the EDE suitable for the assessment of children and adolescents (child EDE; ChEDE) has been developed by Bryant-Waugh, Cooper, Taylor, and Lask (1996), and a few studies have evaluated this form of the measure (e.g., Decaluwe & Braet, 2004 Tanofsky-Kraff et al., 2003; Watkins, Frampton, Lask, & Bryant-Waugh, 2005). To make the assessment more appropriate for younger children, the ChEDE uses modified language and a sort task to evaluate the importance of shape and weight (Bryant-Waugh et al., 1996). Clinicians who are trained in the use of the EDE can use the ChEDE to diagnose DSM-IV eating disorders among younger patients (aged 7 to 14 years).

Whereas the EDE is used in numerous treatment studies to diagnose patients with eating disorders, only a few studies have examined the validity of EDE diagnoses. The EDE does successfully distinguish between patients with BN and individuals without BN who are preoccupied with shape and weight (Wilson & Smith, 1989). Comparisons of the diagnoses generated by the EDE and the self-report version of the EDE (EDE-Q) are described in the following paragraphs. Summary psychometric data for the use of the EDE for diagnostic purposes are provided in Table 23.1; comparable data on the EDE for other assessment purposes are reported in subsequent tables. In addition to articles referenced above, data for ratings made in Table 23.1 were obtained from the following studies: Grilo, Masheb, Lozano-Blanco, and Barry (2004), Rizvi, Peterson, Crow, and Agras (2000), Rosen, Vara, Wendt, and Leitenberg (1990), and Wilfley, Schwartz, Spurrell, and Fairburn (2000).

Despite being the gold standard, there are many obstacles in using the EDE in routine clinical

practice. Clinicians may not have completed the extensive training required to administer the EDE, and the amount of time needed to administer the EDE (approximately 1 to 2 hours) is significant, which makes the EDE less practical for private practice settings. However, the EDE can be clinically useful for developing a detailed understanding of a range of eating disorder symptoms (Wilson, 1993), and is also helpful for case conceptualization and monitoring of treatment outcome, issues that are discussed subsequently.

The Structured Clinical Interview for DSM-IV (SCID; First, Spitzer, Gibbon, & Williams, 2002) also generates diagnoses for AN, BN, and BED. The SCID is used in numerous studies of eating disorders, in some cases to diagnose comorbid Axis I psychopathology (e.g., Agras, Crow, et al., 2000), and in others to provide eating disorder diagnoses (e.g., Engel et al., 2005; Grilo & Masheb, 2005). When using the SCID, the clinician must determine what constitutes a large amount of food to classify binge-eating episodes. Although the SCID is employed frequently in research on eating disorders, there are limited data specifically examining the psychometric properties of the version of the instrument for DSM-IV diagnoses. Previous versions of the SCID (SCID for DSM-III-R) found acceptable kappa coefficients and test–retest reliabilities for the eating disorder modules (Segal, Hersen, & van Hasselt, 1994). The data for the inter-rater reliability of DSM-IV eating disorder diagnoses are consistent with previous versions, with a good κ value (= .77); however, the test–retest reliability for DSM-IV eating disorder diagnoses (correlation = .64) are not consistent with a rating of acceptable (minimum correlation over several days or weeks = .70; Zanarini et al., 2000). The most recent version of the SCID does have at least acceptable psychometric data for norms, and construct validity for eating disorder diagnoses, and is thus included in Table 23.1. Additional data on the reliability and validity of the instrument are also available on the SCID website (www.scid4.org).

The SCID, like the EDE, requires significant training for interviewers, and can be time-consuming to complete the entire instrument. However, the SCID only assesses the diagnostic criteria for eating disorders and not associated eating disorder pathology. As such, administering only the SCID eating disorder modules to generate diagnoses is not time-consuming, and could easily be incorporated into routine clinical practice.

TABLE 23.1 Ratings of Instruments Used for Diagnosis

Instrument	Norms	Internal Consistency	Inter-Rater Reliability	Test–Retest Reliability	Content Validity	Construct Validity	Validity Generalization	Clinical Utility	Highly Recommended
EDE	G	A	E	A	E	A	E	A	✓
SCID	A	NA	G	L	E	A	E	A	✓
EDE-Q	E	G	NA	L	E	U	E	A	
EDDS	G	G	NA	A	G	A	A	A	✓

Note: EDE = Eating Disorder Examination; SCID = Structured Clinical Interview for DSM-IV; EDE-Q = Eating Disorder Examination Questionnaire; EDDS = Eating Disorder Diagnostic Scale; L=Less Than Adequate; A = Adequate; G = Good; E = Excellent; U = Unavailable; NA = Not applicable.

Two additional interview measures are available for generating eating disorder diagnoses, the Interview for Diagnosis of Eating Disorders (IDED; Kutlesic, Williamson, Gleeves, Barbin, & Murphy-Eberenz, 1998) and the Structured Interview for Anorexic and Bulimic Syndromes for DSM-IV and ICD-10 (SIAB-EX; Fichter, Herpertz, Quadfleig, & Herpertz-Dahlmann, 1998). As these measures are not yet widely used in research studies, the psychometric data for both interviews are limited, but promising. Both instruments currently lack sufficient data evaluating test–retest reliability, validity generalization, and treatment sensitivity. Thus, future research should further evaluate the psychometric properties of these instruments, which will also help inform whether these measures should be employed clinically.

Several self-report questionnaires are also available to provide clinicians with a means for assigning eating disorder diagnoses. These measures were developed in an effort to generate eating disorder diagnoses while circumventing the need for costly or time-consuming interviews (Stice, Telch, & Rizvi, 2000). However, although self-report measures are brief and do not require specific clinician training, there are also some issues that clinicians should consider before utilizing these assessments, including the need to obtain scoring algorithms and the costs of the questionnaires (Peterson & Mitchell, 2005).

The Eating Disorder Examination Questionnaire (EDE-Q; Fairburn & Beglin, 1994) is a 38-item self-report version of the EDE designed to be completed in 15 minutes. Similar to the EDE, the EDE-Q includes four subscales (Restraint, Eating Concern, Shape Concern and Weight Concern), and uses a combination of frequency items (e.g., objective bulimic episodes, vomiting) and severity items rated on a scale of 0 to 6 to assess the 28-day period before the completion of the questionnaire (Fairburn & Beglin, 1994). A child version of the EDE-Q has also been developed

(ChEDE-Q; Decaluwe, 1999). The EDE-Q is listed in Table 23.1, although the data on test–retest reliability are less than acceptable. However, this questionnaire has acceptable treatment sensitivity and clinical utility, good internal consistency, and excellent norms, content validity, and validity generalization.

A recent study compared the EDE and EDE-Q for diagnosing AN in comparison to clinical interview, which was considered to be the standard for diagnosis (Wolk, Loeb, & Walsh, 2005). By clinical interview, 100% of patients were diagnosed with AN and 66.7% of these patients were diagnosed with AN-B/P, with corresponding percents for the EDE and EDE-Q of 71.7% and 86.7% of patients diagnosed with AN, and 79% and 71% of the subsample with AN-B/P, respectively (Wolk et al., 2005). As all of the patients in the study met criteria for low weight and amenorrhea, the authors indicated that the discrepancies between the diagnosis of AN with the EDE and with the EDE-Q were related to the severity items, and specifically Criterion B of the AN diagnostic criteria, or the fear of gaining weight or becoming fat (Wolk et al., 2005). Thus, to better evaluate this criterion, clinicians interested in using either the EDE or EDE-Q to diagnose AN should consider gathering additional data from patients about the fear of gaining weight or becoming fat. For example, patients may deny fears of gaining weight, but also describe multiple recent therapy experiences where they were unable to comply with the treatment recommendations necessary for weight gain, which a clinician could infer is an endorsement of Criterion B. The EDE-Q should not be used as the only method of diagnosing BN. In a study of women seeking treatment for substance abuse, the EDE-Q under assessed the rate of BN when strict DSM-IV criteria were applied, but overdiagnosed individuals as having BN when the criteria were slightly relaxed (Black & Wilson, 1996).

The Eating Disorder Diagnostic Scale (EDDS; Stice et al., 2000) is a 22-item self-report scale that can generate possible diagnoses for AN, BN, and BED, and an overall composite score for eating disorder symptoms. The EDDS was developed for the purposes of diagnosing eating disorders in etiological research, for use in research that requires frequent measurements, or for identification of individuals with eating disorders in clinical practice (e.g., primary care; Stice et al., 2000), and includes questions rated on a Likert scale, dichotomous response questions, questions about symptom frequency, and open ended questions. In addition, to improve on some of the difficulties inherent in assessing binge eating by self-report, the EDDS does not include the word "binge" and, instead, binge eating is described solely in behavioral terms (Peterson & Mitchell, 2005). Two studies have examined the reliability and validity of the EDDS (Stice et al., 2000; Stice, Fisher, & Martinez, 2004), other studies have used the EDDS to measure treatment sensitivity (Stice, Orjada, & Tristan, 2006; Stice & Ragan, 2002), and information about psychometric properties of the scale is provided in Table 23.1. The EDDS is not only psychometrically sound, but is also a straightforward instrument appropriate for clinical practice. In addition, the measure is brief and can be completed quickly; the EDDS can, therefore, also be helpful in evaluating of patients with other psychiatric disorders for which eating disorders are likely to co-occur (e.g., major depression, anxiety disorders, substance use disorders).

The final self-report questionnaire suitable for use in evaluating the presence of eating disorder diagnoses is the Patient Health Questionnaire (PHQ; Spitzer, Kroenke, & Williams, 1999). The PHQ is a 26-item self-report questionnaire based on the Primary Care Evaluation of Mental Disorders (PRIME-MD), a clinician-administered instrument to diagnose psychiatric disorders in primary care. The PHQ assesses five common groups of disorders, including depressive, anxiety, alcohol, somatoform, and eating disorders. The PHQ is designed as a screening tool for patients presenting in primary care and is, therefore, specifically intended for use by clinicians. Currently, although the criterion validity for the questionnaire is good, data for reliability and validity of eating disorder diagnoses generated by the PHQ are limited.

Overall Evaluation

Only two assessment tools, the EDE and EDDS, have consistently strong supporting psychometric data for use in the diagnosis of eating disorders. However, clinicians should consider confirming diagnoses generated by the EDDS to ensure that the patient has binge-eating episodes that satisfy the DSM-IV criteria. Other measures, such as the SCID and EDE-Q, are widely used in eating disorders research, but have not been found to have acceptable test–retest reliability. Because of their ease of use, self-report measures hold some promise for being used in clinical settings, but current psychometric evidence is limited. The scarcity of instruments with adequate test–retest reliability and possible reasons for difficulties in assessing eating disorder symptoms over time are discussed in the conclusions/future direction section below.

ASSESSMENT FOR CASE CONCEPTUALIZATION AND TREATMENT PLANNING

Assessment instruments can also provide clinically meaningful information for clinicians to guide case conceptualization and treatment planning. Some of the aforementioned instruments (e.g., EDE, EDE-Q) measure a broad spectrum of symptoms, which can allow the clinician to determine the severity of a patient's eating disorder. A significant amount of treatment planning is dependent on the eating disorder and type of treatment to be delivered and, therefore, careful consideration must be given to the choice of assessments for this purpose. In addition, as described earlier in the chapter, many patients with eating disorders experience comorbid Axis I or Axis II disorders. As such, screening assessments for depression, anxiety, and substance use should also be considered for eating-disordered patients. The data from these measures and the presence or absence of co-occurring psychiatric symptoms should then be used in the development of a case formulation. Readers are encouraged to refer to the chapters on assessments for depression, anxiety, and substance abuse in this volume to determine the most clinically relevant and psychometrically sound measures to evaluate comorbid symptoms.

The measurement of body weight is an essential element of case conceptualization and treatment planning because, as described earlier, body weight differentiates patients with AN-B/P from individuals with BN, and informs clinicians about the type of treatment that will be most effective. For example, for individuals with BN, fluoxetine at 60 mg is an effective treatment, and produces significant reductions in binge eating and purging behaviors (Fluoxetine Bulimia Nervosa Collaborative Study Group, 1992; Goldstein, Wilson, Thompson, Potvin, & Rampey, 1995). Conversely, no significant benefits have been observed for individuals with AN-B/P receiving fluoxetine at 60 mg in comparison to placebo for the acute treatment of AN (Attia, Haiman, Walsh, & Flater, 1998) or for preventing relapse (Walsh et al., 2006).

Patients with AN, BN, or BED should be referred for a medical evaluation before the start of treatment, and at regular intervals throughout the course of treatment. The medical assessments described below are based on the recommendations of experts in the field (e.g., Crow & Swigart, 2005; National Task Force on the Prevention and Treatment of Obesity, 2000). Patients at a low weight (e.g., AN-R, AN-B/P) should receive a complete blood count, an electrolyte battery, an electrocardiogram, liver function tests, and a dual-energy x-ray absorptiometry (DEXA; Crow & Swigart, 2005) to evaluate risk for complications associated with low body weight (e.g., low heart rate, hypotension, hyponatremia; Commission on Adolescent Eating Disorders, 2005). Inpatient treatment may be necessary for individuals with AN at a low weight in order to restore body weight and allow for the close monitoring of medical complications that may emerge during the refeeding process. For patients with binge eating and purging behaviors (e.g., AN-B/P, BN), an electrolyte battery and a dental evaluation should be completed, as individuals who purge are at risk for electrolyte disturbances, including potassium depletion (Crow & Swigart, 2005). The majority of individuals presenting with BED are at a weight classified as overweight (body mass index [BMI] > 25 kg/m^2) or obese (BMI > 30 kg/m^2). As such, patients with BED should be assessed for the serious medical sequelae (e.g., type 2 diabetes) associated with higher body weights as outlined by the National Task Force on the Prevention and Treatment of Obesity (2000).

In this chapter, assessments for treatment planning and case conceptualization for individuals with eating disorders will be discussed in the context of empirically supported treatments (ESTs), and specifically CBT. Continuing assessment and evaluation of progress throughout treatment are essential components of CBT, as adjustments can be made by the clinician based on the data provided

by the measures. Research studies of CBT for BN (Fairburn, Marcus, & Wilson, 1993) have not only used assessments to guide treatment, but also to better understand mechanisms of change during treatment. Thus, the remainder of this section will present measures that can be employed during the delivery of CBT for eating disorders.

As described in the earlier section, the EDE and EDE-Q measure a wide range of eating disorder symptoms. These instruments are particularly helpful in case conceptualization for CBT because they assess dietary restraint, bulimic behaviors (binge eating and purging), and shape and weight concerns, all of which are targets of CBT (see Table 23.2 for summary psychometric ratings). The utility of the EDE and EDE-Q are particularly relevant in the delivery of CBT for BN, where patients need to eliminate binge eating and purging behaviors, establish a pattern of regular eating, identify alternative activities, and learn problem-solving strategies. In addition, dietary restraint is addressed through the development of regular eating and exposure to forbidden foods, and shape and weight concerns are targeted through cognitive restructuring and behavioral experiments. Research has demonstrated that the reduction in dietary restraint as early as the fourth week of CBT for BN mediates posttreatment reductions in binge eating and vomiting (Wilson, Fairburn, Agras, Walsh, & Kraemer, 2002), and change in purging behavior after 4 weeks of CBT predicts symptom levels at 8-month follow-up (Fairburn, Agras, Walsh, Wilson, & Stice, 2004). Thus, clinicians could use the EDE-Q during the first month of CBT for BN to monitor levels of dietary restraint and frequency of purging, which would provide important information about whether improvements should be expected with continued CBT. The clinician would then have objective data informing the decision to continue delivering CBT for BN, or to begin using another treatment strategy (e.g., switching to IPT or beginning antidepressant medication).

Another important means of assessment throughout CBT is self-monitoring, which is an integral part of CBT for eating disorders. Patients begin self-monitoring after the first session of CBT, and as such, the monitoring records can help with case conceptualization or treatment planning because they provide information about the patient's baseline eating disorder symptoms. The monitoring typically involves recording circumstances associated with binge eating

TABLE 23.2 Ratings of Instruments Used for Case Conceptualization and Treatment Planning

Instrument	Norms	Internal Consistency	Inter-Rater Reliability	Test–Retest Reliability	Content Validity	Construct Validity	Validity Generalization	Clinical Utility	Highly Recommended
EDE	G	A	E	A	E	A	E	A	✓
EDE-Q	E	G	NA	L	E	U	E	A	
BSQ	A	E	NA	A	G	A	A	A	
BCQ	A	E	NA	A	G	A	A	A	

Note: EDE = Eating Disorder Examination; EDE-Q = Eating Disorder Examination Questionnaire; BSQ = Body Shape Questionnaire; BCQ = Body Checking Questionnaire; L = Less Than Adequate; A = Adequate; G = Good; E = Excellent; U = Unavailable; NA = Not Applicable.

and purging, such as antecedent and consequent events, and general descriptions of food intake. Self-monitoring can also focus on other behaviors typical of patients with eating disorders, including body checking or avoidance (Fairburn, Cooper, & Shafran, 2003). Wilson and Vitousek (1999) reviewed research on self-monitoring in the treatment of eating disorders, and identified a number of important advantages to this form of measurement. As these records are completed closer to the time when the behaviors occur, the likelihood that the records are affected by problems of retrospective recall is reduced (Wilson & Vitousek, 1999). Thus, assessing eating disorder symptoms immediately after they occur may increase the accuracy of self-reported binge eating or restricting behaviors on self-monitoring records in comparison to other forms of assessment (e.g., EDE).

The possibility that symptoms can be measured more accurately without a time delay has recently begun to be explored using ecologic momentary assessment (EMA; Farchaus & Corte, 2003; Smyth et al., 2001). In general, EMA involves recording events multiple times during a day on monitoring records or a handheld computer, and patients can be instructed to record at specific times of day (e.g., just after waking), when signaled by a pager, alarm on a watch, or handheld computer, or when a specific event occurs (e.g., binge eating; Farchaus & Corte, 2003). In the assessment of eating disorders, EMA has been used to measure mood, stressors, eating behavior, dietary restraint, binge eating, antecedents of binge eating, exercise and inappropriate compensatory behaviors among individual with eating disorders (Farchaus & Corte, 2003; Le Grange, Gorin, Catley, & Stone, 2001; Smyth et al., 2001). Ecological momentary assessment has also been examined as an alternative to self-monitoring in CBT for binge-eating disorder, where patients record mood, events, thoughts, and eating behaviors; however, the use of EMA did not

provide any additional benefit to standard CBT (Le Grange, Gorin, Dymek, & Stone, 2002). Thus, like self-monitoring, EMA may be useful in treatment planning and conceptualization, but additional data are needed.

Self-monitoring also provides information about the temporal pattern of eating behaviors, such as the observation that binge eating is more likely to occur during the afternoon or evening, and that episodes of binge eating are often preceded by negative mood states, which can be used to inform the therapeutic process (Wilson & Vitousek, 1999). For example, if the monitoring records indicate that a patient is experiencing difficulties with binge eating in the afternoons, after avoiding eating during the morning, the CBT therapist will help the patient consume additional meals or snacks earlier in the day and schedule activities that are inconsistent with binge eating during the afternoon. Self-monitoring may also serve a crucial role in the process of early response observed among patients with BN treated with CBT (Wilson et al., 1999), as some of the improvements observed in the first few weeks of CBT for BN (e.g., Fairburn et al., 2004; Wilson et al., 2002) may be attributable to the awareness of eating behavior and patterns of eating through self-monitoring. Although self-monitoring records are very useful clinically, this form of measurement is not included in Table 23.2 because studies have not established norms for self-monitoring, it is not possible to measure internal consistency, content validity is not applicable, and inter-rater reliability is not helpful in clinical practice. In addition, test–retest reliability of self-monitoring records is difficult to establish because patterns of eating behavior are constantly changing among individuals with eating disorders (Hildebrandt & Latner, 2006).

Thus, self-monitoring is an integral and useful part of behavioral interventions for eating disorders. However, even when patients are instructed in the appropriate methods for completing self-monitoring records, there are indications that self-monitoring may not provide entirely accurate information about the amount of food consumed. Patients have been shown to report similar meal patterns on 24-hour self-report interviews and the EDE (Bartholome, Raymond, Lee, Peterson, & Warren, 2006); however, patients may exaggerate the size of binge episodes when self-monitoring (Hadigan, Walsh, Devlin, LaChaussee, & Kissileff, 1992). Therefore, when evaluating monitoring records, clinicians should attend to the overall pattern of meals, snacks, and binge episodes, rather than the total amount of food eaten.

The diagnostic criteria for both AN and BN include specific disturbances in body image, which can also be observed among individuals with BED or EDNOS. The Body Shape Questionnaire (BSQ; Cooper, Taylor, Cooper, & Fairburn, 1987) is a 34-item self-report questionnaire that provides an overall measure of concerns about shape, weight, and body image. The BSQ allows clinicians the to assess the need for interventions addressing distortions in the perception of shape or weight among individuals with AN, BN, EDNOS, or BED. Although there are many existing assessments measuring body image concerns (see Thompson et al., 2005 for more information), the BSQ is highly recommended, as it is both psychometrically sound (see Table 23.2) and straightforward for patients to complete. In addition to articles referenced in the text, data for ratings in Table 23.2 for the BSQ were obtained from Evans and Dolan (1993) and Rosen, Jones, Ramirez, and Waxman (1996).

The BSQ also includes two questions that specifically assess body checking and avoidance behaviors. The behaviors measured by the BSQ are avoiding wearing clothes that make the patient particularly aware of the shape of their body and pinching areas of the body to see how much fat there is. Williamson, Muller, Reas, and Thaw (1999) suggested that preoccupation with shape and weight is increased by the selective attention focused on a disliked part of the body that occurs in body checking and avoidance. A study by Shafran, Fairburn, Robinson, and Lask (2004) supported this hypothesis by demonstrating increases in preoccupation with shape and weight after body checking. Thus, checking and avoidance can be important targets for treatment, as these behaviors reinforce negative beliefs about shape and weight and may also maintain eating disorder symptoms. The most recent version of CBT for eating disorders (Fairburn et al., 2003) asks patients to monitor these behaviors during treatment and the clinician intervenes to reducing body checking and avoidance (Fairburn, 2006). The Body Checking Questionnaire (BCQ; Reas, Whisenhunt, Netemeyer, & Williamson, 2002) is a recently developed 23-item measure designed to assess body checking behaviors. Although only a few studies have evaluated this measure to date, the importance of body checking in the maintenance of symptoms of AN (Fairburn, Shafran, & Cooper, 1999) and the psychometric soundness of the measure justifies its inclusion in this chapter. Information about the BCQ is provided in Table 23.2, including data from Calugi, Dalle Grave, Ghisi, and Sanavio (2006) and Reas, White and Grilo (2006).

CBT for eating disorders involves the use of assessments to determine whether the areas of interpersonal functioning, perfectionism, core low self-esteem, or mood intolerance, should be addressed during treatment. Fairburn et al. (2003) proposed that, for some patients, these areas are barriers to change because they serve as additional maintaining processes that interact with the eating disorder maintaining mechanisms usually targeted by CBT for BN (Fairburn et al., 1993; e.g., overevaluation of shape and weight, dietary restraint, and binge eating and compensatory behavior). A number of measures can be used by clinicians to gather data about these areas to inform treatment. Examples of relevant instruments include the Beck Depression Inventory-II (BDI-II; Beck, Steer, & Brown, 1996), Rosenberg Self-Esteem Scale (RSE; Rosenberg, 1979), Inventory of Interpersonal Problems (IIP; Horowitz et al., 1988), and the Dysfunctional Attitude Scale (DAS; Weissman & Beck, 1978).

Overall Evaluation

Similar to what was observed for the assessments used to diagnose eating disorders, there are a handful of measures specific to eating disorders that have sufficient empirical support to allow them to serve as clinical tools for treatment conceptualization and planning. These measures are especially appropriate for treatment planning in CBT, as the CBT model includes strategies designed to affect the areas assessed by these measures (e.g., dietary restraint, overvaluation of shape and weight). However, these instruments are also likely to be of use for other treatment approaches that have the goal of achieving reductions in eating disorder symptoms (e.g., Maudsley family therapy, psychopharmacological treatment).

ASSESSMENT FOR TREATMENT MONITORING AND TREATMENT OUTCOME

Very few measures have been designed and used for tracking and evaluating the impact of treatments for eating disorders. The EDE is the most commonly used assessment for measuring treatment outcome for patients with eating disorders, including studies of AN (e.g., Pike, Walsh, Vitousek, Wilson, & Bauer, 2003; Walsh et al., 2006), BN (e.g., Agras, Crow, et al., 2000; Agras, Walsh, et al., 2000; Walsh et al., 2004), and BED (e.g., Devlin et al., 2005; Wilfley et al., 2002). However, as described earlier, the EDE is time-consuming and requires extensive training of interviewers, which make the instrument less practical for multiple assessments of outcome. As such, a number of studies have investigated whether the EDE-Q can be substituted for the EDE in measuring treatment outcome for patients with eating disorders.

The first comparison of the EDE and EDE-Q (Fairburn & Beglin, 1994) examined the agreement between the measures among a sample of women from the community ($n = 243$) and a sample of women with eating disorders ($n = 23$ patients with BN, $n = 13$ patients with AN). Across the two instruments, OBEs, self-induced vomiting, and laxative misuse were highly correlated, with the data on self-induced vomiting being the most highly correlated between EDE and EDE-Q for both samples. When comparing the scores obtained for the EDE and EDE-Q subscales, the agreement was greatest for the restraint and weight concern subscales. A number of studies have since compared the EDE and EDE-Q in women seeking treatment for substance abuse (Black & Wilson, 1996), obese patients with BED (Wilfley et al., 1997), obese bariatric surgery candidates (Kalarchian, Wilson, Brolin, & Bradley, 2000), patients with BED (Grilo, Masheb, & Wilson, 2001a; 2001b), women with AN (Wolk et al., 2005), and women with BN (Carter, Aime, & Mills, 2001; Sysko, Walsh, & Fairburn, 2005). A general pattern of results have emerged among these studies, in which the behavioral features (e.g., self-induced vomiting) and clearly defined concepts (e.g., dietary restraint) are most highly correlated between EDE and EDE-Q (Black & Wilson, 1996; Wilfley et al., 1997; Wolk et al., 2005). Greater discrepancies have been observed between the EDE and EDE-Q for complex concepts like binge eating (Black & Wilson, 1996; Carter et al., 2001; Grilo et al., 2001a; Wilfley et al., 1997), and significantly higher

levels of pathology have been observed on the EDE-Q subscales in comparison to the EDE (Kalarchian et al., 2000; Wilfley et al., 1997). High levels of convergence between the EDE and EDE-Q for the assessment of binge eating can be produced with the addition of a brief (one page) instruction sheet to the EDE-Q providing detail definitions and examples of binge eating (Goldfein, Devlin, & Kamenetz, 2005). The results of two studies examining the ChEDE and ChEDE-Q among obese children and adolescents with AN found a similar pattern of results, with higher levels of eating disorder pathology observed on the questionnaire measure (Decaluwe & Braet, 2004; Passi, Bryson, & Lock, 2003).

When the EDE and EDE-Q were compared for the measurement of change in a study of patients with BN, the change in compensatory behaviors over the course of the study was highly correlated, but the change in binge eating (OBE and SBE) and attitudinal features (e.g., importance of shape and weight) were more discrepant (Sysko, Walsh, & Fairburn, 2005). The authors concluded that, although both instruments assess change, it is not possible to evaluate which measure provides greater validity in assessing eating disorder pathology. In light of all the evidence available to date, Sysko, Walsh, & Fairburn (2005) recommended that clinicians and researchers should consistently use one measure (EDE or EDE-Q) consistently, rather than switching back and forth between measures or seeing the measures as interchangeable.

As patients with AN often experience obsessive thoughts and compulsions related to eating disorder symptoms, a number of studies evaluating treatments for AN have evaluated change using the Yale-Brown-Cornell Eating Disorder Scale (YBC-EDS; Attia et al., 1998; Kaye et al., 2001; Mazure, Halmi, Sunday, Romano, & Einhorn, 1994; Walsh et al., 2006). The YBC-EDS includes a 65-item symptom checklist assessing 18 categories (e.g., food/eating/weight and shape/clothing/hoarding/exercise preoccupations, eating/food/binge eating/purging/somatic rituals). In addition, 19 questions measuring specific symptoms are asked and a total score is calculated by summing eight items assessing preoccupations and rituals. Summary psychometric information about the YBC-EDS is provided in Table 23.3.

Any of the three measures described above in the context of measuring overall treatment outcome can also be used to evaluate progress during treatment. As the EDE and EDE-Q both assess eating-disordered

TABLE 23;3 Ratings of Instruments Used for Treatment Monitoring and Treatment Outcome Evaluation

Instrument	Norms	Internal Consistency	Inter-Rater Reliability	Test–Retest Reliability	Content Validity	Construct Validity	Validity Generalization	Treatment Sensitivity	Clinical Utility	Highly Recommended
EDE	G	A	E	A	E	A	E	A	A	
EDE-Q	E	G	NA	L	E	U	E	A	A	✓
YBC-EDS	A	G	E	U	G	A	G	G	A	

Note: EDE = Eating Disorder Examination; EDE-Q = Eating Disorder Examination Questionnaire; YBC-EDS = Yale-Brown-Cornell Eating Disorder Scale; L=Less Than Adequate; A = Adequate; G = Good; E = Excellent; U= Unavailable; NA = Not Applicable.

behaviors over a 28-day period, these measures are ideal for evaluating change on a monthly basis. Clinicians interested in changes in symptoms on a weekly basis can use self-monitoring records to determine progress in treatment.

Overall Evaluation

The overall evaluation of measures assessing treatment monitoring and treatment outcome is consistent with the conclusions of the two previous sections. Only the EDE and YBC-EDS can be included in Table 23.3 as assessments that work and, although these instruments are widely used in research, they may be less practical for use by clinicians. Both are semistructured interviews that require extensive training and the amount of time needed to administer the EDE or YBC-EDS can be considerable. Thus, the development of more efficient assessment tools is an important goal for furthering the assessment of treatment monitoring and outcome evaluation.

CONCLUSIONS AND FUTURE DIRECTIONS

In conclusion, the assessments described in this chapter are among the most widely used in the field of eating disorders. However, only a small number of measures can be classified as having extensive supporting psychometric evidence. Commonly used research strategies, such as the use of laboratory meal situations, can provide an objective measure of eating behavior, but are simply not feasible in clinical practice (Wilson, 1993).

Although some variability in symptoms over time is to be expected, none of the instruments described in this chapter have more than an acceptable rating for test–retest reliability. Mond and colleagues (2004) conducted the longest evaluation of the stability of eating disorder assessment over time, giving the EDE-Q a mean of 303.2 days apart. The authors found that "although the cognitive and personality dimensions of eating disorder psychopathology are relatively stable, eating-disordered behaviors such as binge eating and use of exercise as a means of weight control are liable to fluctuate considerably in intensity and severity over time" (Mond, Hay, Rodgers, Owen, & Beaumont, 2004, p. 200). Symptom reactivity in eating-disordered behaviors has also been observed with other forms of assessment, with a study by Hildebrandt and Latner (2006) demonstrating a significant decrease in OBEs and a concurrent increase in SBEs among women with BN and BED after 7 days of self-monitoring and no additional treatment intervention. These studies suggest that the core eating-disordered behavior of binge eating may oscillate and be significantly reactive to nonspecific interventions, rendering the evaluation of binge eating over a long period of time quite difficult.

One measurement issue that affects the accuracy and reliability of most eating disorder instruments is the frequent reliance on a single questionnaire or interview item to assess a particular behavior or symptom. For example, most measures have only one question for quantifying the number of binge-eating episodes during a specified period. This can provide important and meaningful information for the purpose of diagnosis (e.g., whether a patient meets criteria for BN), treatment conceptualization (e.g., are binge-eating episodes decreasing over time), and treatment outcome (e.g., has a clinically meaningful change been observed). However, the reliance on a single item increases measurement error and decreases the overall statistical power to detect changes across time or between groups (Viswanathan, 2005). Given the poor test–retest reliability observed for some measures, it may be useful to determine if reliability could be improved by using multiple indicators for each behavior or symptom. Beyond this, future research should focus on attempting to design new measures and refine existing measures in order to provide scientifically sound assessment tools available to clinicians.

ACKNOWLEDGMENT   I would like to thank G. Terence Wilson, PhD, who served as a consultant on this chapter and provided guidance about the content of the chapter and evaluated earlier drafts of the manuscript.

References

Agras, W. S. (1997). Pharmacotherapy of bulimia nervosa and binge eating disorder: Longer-term outcomes. *Psychopharmacology Bulletin, 33,* 433–436.

Agras, W. S., Crow, S. J., Halmi, K. A., Mitchell, J. E., Wilson, G. T., & Kraemer, H. C. (2000). Outcome predictors for the cognitive behavior treatment of bulimia nervosa: Data from a multisite study. *American Journal of Psychiatry, 157,* 1302–1308.

Agras, W. S., Walsh, B. T., Fairburn, C. G., Wilson, G. T., & Kraemer, H. C. (2000). A multicenter comparison of cognitive-behavioral therapy and interpersonal psychotherapy for bulimia nervosa. *Archives of General Psychiatry, 57,* 459–466.

American Psychiatric Association. (1994). *Diagnostic and statistical manual of mental disorders* (4th ed.). Washington, DC: Author.

American Psychiatric Association. (2000). *Diagnostic and statistical manual of mental disorders* (4th ed., text rev). Washington, DC: Author.

Andersen, A. E. (2002). Eating disorders in males. In C. G. Fairburn & K. D. Brownell (Eds.), *Eating disorders and obesity: A comprehensive handbook* (pp. 233–237). New York: The Guilford Press.

Attia, E., Haiman, C., Walsh, B. T., & Flater, S. (1998). Does fluoxetine augment the inpatient treatment of anorexia nervosa? *American Journal of Psychiatry, 155,* 548–551.

Bartholome, L. T., Raymond, N. C., Lee, S. S., Peterson, C. B., & Warren, C. S. (2006). Detailed analysis of binges in obese women with binge eating disorder: Comparisons using multiple methods of data collection. *International Journal of Eating Disorders, 39,* 685–693.

Beck, A. T., Steer, R. A., & Brown, G. K. (1996). *Manual for the Beck Depression Inventory* (2nd ed.). San Antonio, TX: The Psychological Corporation, Harcourt Brace & Co.

Becker, A., Burwell, R., Gilman, S., Herzog, D., & Hamburg, P. (2002). Eating behaviors and attitudes following prolonged exposure to television among ethnic Fijian adolescent girls. *British Journal of Psychiatry, 180,* 509–514.

Berscheid, E., Walster, E., & Bohmstedt, G. (1973). The happy American Body: A survey report. *Psychology Today, 7,* 119–131.

Black, C. M. D., & Wilson, G. T. (1996). Assessment of eating disorders: Interview versus questionnaire. *International Journal of Eating Disorders, 20,* 43–50.

Bryant-Waugh, R. J., Cooper, P. J., Taylor, C. L., & Lask, B. D. (1996). The use of the eating disorder examination with children: A pilot study. *International Journal of Eating Disorders, 19,* 391–397.

Calugi, S., Dalle Grave, R., Ghisi, M., & Sanavio, E. (2006). Validation of the Body Checking Questionnaire (BCQ) in an eating disorders population. *Behavioural and Cognitive Psychotherapy, 34,* 233–242.

Carter, J. C., Aime, A. A., & Mills, J. S. (2001). Assessment of bulimia nervosa: A comparison of interview of self-report questionnaire methods. *International Journal of Eating Disorders, 30,* 187–192.

Carter, J. C., Olmsted, M. P., Kaplan, A. S., McCabe, R. E., Mills, J. S., & Aime, A. (2003). Self-help for bulimia nervosa: A randomized controlled trial. *American Journal of Psychiatry, 160,* 973–978.

Commission on Adolescent Eating Disorders. (2005). Eating disorders. In D. L. Evans, E. B. Foa, R. E. Gur, H. Hendin, C. P. O'Brien, M. E. P. Seligman, et al. (Eds.), *Treating and preventing adolescent mental health disorders: What we know and what we don't know.* New York: Oxford University Press, The Annenberg Foundation Trust at Sunnylands, and the Annenberg Public Policy Center of the University of Pennsylvania.

Cooper, Z., & Fairburn, C. (1987). The eating disorder examination: A semi-structured interview for the assessment of the specific psychopathology of eating disorders. *International Journal of Eating Disorders, 6,* 1–8.

Cooper, P. J., Taylor, M. J., Cooper, Z., & Fairburn, C. G. (1987). The development and validation of the Body Shape Questionnaire. *International Journal of Eating Disorders, 6,* 485–494.

Crow, S., & Swigart, S. (2005). Medical assessment. In J. E. Mitchell & C. B. Peterson (Eds.), *Assessment of eating disorders* (pp. 120–128). New York: Guilford Publications.

Decaluwe, V. (1999). *Child Eating Disorder Examination-Questionnaire. Dutch translation and adaptation of the Eating Disorder Examination-Questionnaire, authored by C. G. Fairburn & S. J. Beglin.* Unpublished manuscript.

Decaluwe, V., & Braet, C. (2004). Assessment of eating disorder psychopathology in obese children and adolescents: Interview versus self-report questionnaire. *Behaviour Research and Therapy, 42,* 799–811.

Derogatis, L. R., Lipman, R. S., & Covi, L. (1973). SCL-90: An outpatient psychiatric rating scale-preliminary report. *Psychopharmacology Bulletin, 9,* 13–28.

Devlin, M. J., Goldfein, J. A., Petkova, E., Jiang, H., Raizman, P. S., Wolk, S., et al. (2005). Cognitive behavioral therapy and fluoxetine as adjuncts to group behavioral therapy for binge eating disorder. *Obesity Research, 13,* 1077–1088.

Endicott, J., Nee, J., Harrison, W., & Blumenthal, R. (1993). Quality of life enjoyment and satisfaction questionnaire: A new measure. *Psychopharmacology Bulletin, 29,* 321–326.

Engel, S. G., Corneliussen, S. J., Wonderlich, S. A., Crosby, R. D., Le Grange, D., Crow, S. et al. (2005). Impulsivity and compulsivity in bulimia nervosa. *International Journal of Eating Disorders, 38,* 244–251.

Evans, C., & Dolan, B. (1993). Body Shape Questionnaire: Derivation of shortened "alternate forms." *International Journal of Eating Disorders, 13,* 315–321.

Expert Panel on the Identification, Evaluation, and Treatment of Overweight in Adults. (1998). Clinical guidelines on the identification, evaluation, and treatment of overweight and obesity and adults: Executive Summary. *American Journal of Clinical Nutrition, 68,* 899–917.

Fairburn, C. G. (2006). *Body checking, body avoidance and "feeling fat."* Workshop presented at the 17th International Conference on Eating Disorders, Barcelona, Spain.

Fairburn, C. G., Agras, W. S., Walsh, B. T., Wilson, G. T., & Stice, E. (2004). Early change in treatment predicts outcome in bulimia nervosa. *American Journal of Psychiatry, 161,* 2322–2324.

Fairburn, C. G., & Beglin, S. J. (1994). Assessment of eating disorders: Interview or self-report questionnaire? *International Journal of Eating Disorders, 16,* 363–370.

Fairburn, C. G., & Bohn, K. (2005). Eating disorder NOS (EDNOS): An example of the troublesome "not otherwise specified" (NOS) category in DSM-IV. *Behavior Research and Therapy, 43,* 691–701.

Fairburn, C. G., & Cooper, Z. (1993). The eating disorder examination. In C. G. Fairburn & G. T. Wilson (Eds.), *Binge eating: Nature, assessment, and treatment* (12th ed., pp. 317–360). New York: Guilford Press.

Fairburn, C. G., Cooper, Z., & Shafran, R. (2003). Cognitive behavior therapy for eating disorders: A "transdiagnostic" theory and treatment. *Behaviour Research and Therapy, 41,* 509–528.

Fairburn, C. G., & Harrison, P. J. (2003). Eating disorders. *The Lancet, 361,* 407–416.

Fairburn, C. G., Marcus, M. D., & Wilson, G. T. (1993). Cognitive-behavioral therapy for binge eating and bulimia nervosa: A comprehensive treatment manual. In C. G. Fairburn & G. T. Wilson (Eds.), *Binge eating: Nature, assessment, and treatment* (pp. 361–404). New York: Guilford Press.

Fairburn, C. G., Shafran, R., & Cooper, Z. (1999). A cognitive behavioural theory of anorexia nervosa. *Behaviour Research and Therapy, 37,* 1–13.

Farchaus, S., K., & Corte, C. M. (2003). Ecologic momentary assessment of eating-disordered behaviors. *International Journal of Eating Disorders, 34,* 349–360.

Fichter, M. M., Herpertz, S., Quadflieg, N., & Herpertz-Dahlmann, B. (1998). Structured Interview for Anorexic and Bulimic Disorders for DSM-IV and ICD-10: Updated (Third) Revision. *International Journal of Eating Disorders, 24,* 227–249.

Fichter, M. M., Quadflieg, N., & Hedlund, S. (2006). Twelve-year course and outcome predictors of anorexia nervosa. *International Journal of Eating Disorders, 39,* 87–100.

First, M. B., Spitzer, R. L, Gibbon M., & Williams, J. B. W. (2002). Structured Clinical Interview for DSM-IV Axis I Disorders, Research Version, Patient Edition. (SCID-I/P) New York: Biometrics Research, New York State Psychiatric Institute.

Fluoxetine Bulimia Nervosa Collaborative Study Group. (1992). Fluoxetine in the treatment of bulimia nervosa: A multicenter, placebo-controlled, double-blind trial. *Archives of General Psychiatry, 49,* 139–147.

Franzoi, S. L., & Shields, S. A. (1984). The body esteem scale: Multidimensional structure and sex differences in a college population. *Journal of Personality Assessment, 48,* 173–178.

Garner, D. M. (1991). *Eating Disorder Inventory 2, Professional Manual.* Psychological Assessment Resources, Odessa, FL.

Godart, N. T., Flament, M. F., Perdereau, F., & Jeammet, P. (2002). Comorbidity between eating disorders and anxiety disorders: A review. *International Journal of Eating Disorders, 32,* 253–270.

Godart, N. T., Perdereau, F., Rein, Z., Berthoz, S., Wallier, J., Jeammet, P., et al. (2007). Comorbidity studies of eating disorders and mood disorders: Critical review of the literature. *Journal of Affective Disorders, 97,* 37–49.

Goldfein, J. A., Devlin, M. J., & Kamenetz, C. (2005). Eating Disorder Examination-Questionnaire with and without instruction to assess binge eating in patients with binge eating disorder. *International Journal of Eating Disorders, 37,* 107–111.

Goldstein, D. J., Wilson, M. G., Thompson, V. L., Potvin, J. H., Rampey, A. H. & Fluoxetine Bulimia Nervosa Research Group (1995). Long-term fluoxetine treatment of bulimia nervosa. *British Journal of Psychiatry, 166,* 660–666.

Grilo, C. M., & Masheb, R. M. (2005). A randomized controlled comparison of guided self-help cognitive behavioral therapy and behavioral weight loss for binge eating disorder. *Behavior Research and Therapy, 43,* 1509–1525.

Grilo, C. M., Masheb, R. M, Lozano-Blanco, C., & Barry, D. T. (2004). Reliability of the Eating Disorder Examination in patients with binge eating disorder. *International Journal of Eating Disorders, 35,* 80–85.

Grilo, C. M., Masheb, R. M., & Wilson, G. T. (2001a). Different methods for assessing the features of eating disorders in patients with binge eating disorder: A replication. *Obesity Research, 9,* 418–422.

Grilo, C. M., Masheb, R. M., & Wilson, G. T. (2001b). A comparison of different methods for assessing the features of eating disorders in patients with binge eating disorder. *Journal of Consulting and Clinical Psychology, 69,* 317–322.

Hadigan, C. M., Walsh, B. T., Devlin, M. J., LaChaussee, J. L., & Kissileff, H. R. (1992).

Behavioral assessment of satiety in bulimia nervosa. *Appetite, 18,* 233–241.

Halmi, K. A., Agras, W. S., Crow, S., Mitchell, J., Wilson, G. T., Bryson, S. W., et al. (2005). Predictors of treatment acceptance and completion in anorexia nervosa: Implications for future study designs. *Archives of General Psychiatry, 62,* 776–781.

Herpertz-Dahlmann, B., Muller, B., Herpertz, S., Heussen, N., Hebebrand, J., & Remschmidt, H. (2001). Prospective 10-year follow-up in adolescent anorexia nervosa: Course, outcome, psychiatric comorbidity, and psychosocial adaptation. *Journal of Child Psychology and Psychiatry and Allied Disciplines, 42,* 603–162.

Hildebrandt, T., Langenbucher, J., & Schlundt, D. G. (2004). Muscularity concerns among men: development of attitudinal and perceptual measures. *Body Image, 1,* 169–181

Hildebrandt, T., & Latner, J. (2006). Effect of self-monitoring on binge eating: Treatment response or binge drift? *European Eating Disorders Review, 14,* 17–22.

Hildebrandt, T., Schlundt, D., Langenbucher, J., & Chung, T. (2006). Presence of muscle dysmorphia symptomology among male weightlifters. *Comprehensive Psychiatry, 47,* 127–135.

Hoek, H. W. (2002). Distribution of eating disorders. In C. G. Fairburn & K. D. Brownell (Eds.), *Eating Disorders and Obesity: A Comprehensive Handbook* (pp. 233–237). New York: The Guilford Press.

Horowitz, L., Rosenberg, S. E., Baer, B. A., Ureno, G., & Villasenor, V. S. (1988). Inventory of interpersonal problems: Psychometric properties and clinical applications. *Journal of Consulting and Clinical Psychology, 56,* 885–892.

Jones, D. C., & Crawford, J. K. (2006). The peer appearance culture during adolescence: Gender and body mass variations. *Journal of Youth and Adolescence, 35,* 243–255.

Kalarchian, M. A., Wilson, G. T., Brolin, R. E., & Bradley, L. (2000). Assessment of eating disorders in bariatric surgery candidates: Self-report questionnaire versus interview. *International Journal of Eating Disorders, 28,* 465–469.

Kaye, W. H., Nagata, T., Weltzin, T. E., Hsu, L. K. G., Sokol, M. S., McConaha, C., et al. (2001). Double-blind placebo-controlled administration of fluoxetine in restricting- and restricting-purging type anorexia nervosa. *Biological Psychiatry, 49,* 644–652.

Keel, P. K., & Klump, K. L. (2003). Are eating disorders culture-bound syndromes? Implications for conceptualizing their etiology. *Psychology Bulletin, 129,* 747–769.

Keel, P. K., Mitchell, J. E., Miller, K. B., Davis, T. L., & Crow, S. J. (1999). Long-term outcome of bulimia nervosa. *Archives of General Psychiatry, 56,* 63–69.

Kissileff, H. R., Walsh, B. T., Kral, J. G., & Cassidy, S. M. (1986). Laboratory studies of eating behavior in women with bulimia. *Physiology and Behavior, 38,* 563–570.

Kinston, W., & Loader, P. (1984). Eliciting whole-family interaction with a standardized clinical interview. *Journal of Family Therapy, 6,* 347–334.

Kutlesic, V., Williamson, D. A., Gleaves, D. H., Barbin, J. M., & Murphy-Eberenz, K. P. (1998). The interview for the diagnosis of eating disorders IV: Application to DSM-IV diagnostic criteria. *Psychological Assessment, 10,* 41–48.

Le Grange, D., Eisler, I., Dare, C., & Russell, G. F. M. (1992). Evaluation of family treatments in adolescent anorexia nervosa: A pilot study. *International Journal of Eating Disorders, 12,* 347–357.

Le Grange, D., Gorin, A., Catley, D., & Stone, A. (2001). Does momentary assessment detect binge eating in overweight women that is denied at interview? *European Eating Disorders Review, 9,* 1–16.

Le Grange, D., Gorin, A., Dymek, M., & Stone, A. (2002). Does ecological momentary assessment improve cognitive behavioral therapy for binge eating disorder: A pilot study. *European Eating Disorders Review, 10,* 316–328.

Lock, J., Agras, W. S., Bryson, S., & Kraemer, H. C. (2005). A comparison of short- and long-term family therapy for adolescent anorexia nervosa. *Journal of the American Academy of Child & Adolescent Psychiatry, 44,* 632–639.

Lock, J. E., Agras, W. S., Dare, C., & Le Grange, D. (2002). *Treatment manual for anorexia nervosa: A family-based approach.* New York: Guilford Press.

Maisto, S. A., Sobell, L. C., Cooper, A. M., & Sobell, M. B. (1982). Comparison of two techniques to obtain retrospective reports of drinking behavior from alcohol abusers. *Addictive Behaviors, 7,* 33–38.

Mazure, C. M., Halmi, K. A., Sunday, S. R., Romano, S. J., & Einhorn, A. M. J. (1994). The Yale-Brown-Cornell Eating Disorder Scale: Development, use, reliability and validity. *Journal of Psychiatric Research, 28,* 425–445.

Meehan, K. G., Loeb, K. L., Roberto, C. A., & Attia, E. (2006). Mood change during weight restoration in patients with anorexia nervosa. *International Journal of Eating Disorders, 39,* 587–589.

Metropolitan Life Insurance. (1959). New weight standards for men and women. *Statistical Bulletin, 40,* 1–4.

Moos, R. (1974). *The Family Environment Scale. Form R.* Palo Alto, CA: Consulting Psychologists Press.

Moos, R., & Moos, B. (1994). *Family Environment Scale Manual.* Palo Alto, CA: Consulting Psychologists Press.

Mond, J. M., Hay, P. J., Rodgers, B., Owen, C., & Beaumont, P. J. V. (2004). Temporal stability of the Eating

Disorder Examination Questionnaire. *International Journal of Eating Disorders, 36*, 195–203.

National Institute for Clinical Excellence. (2004). *Eating disorders. Core interventions in the treatment and management of eating disorders in primary and secondary care.* London: National Institute for Clinical Excellence.

National Task Force on the Prevention and Treatment of Obesity (2000). Dieting and the development of eating disorders in overweight and obese adults. *Archives of Internal Medicine, 160*, 2581–2589.

Olson, D. H., Portner, L., & Lavee, Y. (1985). *FACES III.* Minnesota: Family Social Science, University of Minnesota.

Olson, D. H., Sprenkle, D. H., & Russell, C. S. (1979). Circumplex Model of marital and family systems: I. Cohesion and Adaptability dimensions, family types and clinical applications. *Family Process, 18*, 3–28.

Passi, V. A., Bryson, S. W., & Lock, J. (2003). Assessment of eating disorders in adolescents with anorexia nervosa: Self-report questionnaire versus interview. *International Journal of Eating Disorders, 33*, 45–54.

Peterson, C. B., & Mitchell, J. E. (2005). Self-report measures. In J. E. Mitchell & C. B. Peterson (Eds.), *Assessment of eating disorders* (pp. 98–119). New York: Guilford Press.

Pike, K. M., Walsh, B. T., Vitousek, K. B., Wilson, G. T., & Bauer, J. (2003). Cognitive behavioral therapy in the post-hospital treatment of anorexia nervosa. *American Journal of Psychiatry, 160*, 2046–2049.

Pope, H. G., Gruber, A. J., Choi, P., Olivardia, R., & Phillips, K. A. (1997). Muscle dysmorphia. An underrecognized form of body dysmorphic disorder. *Psychosomatics, 38*, 548–557.

Reas, D. L., White, M. A., & Grilo, C. M. (2006). Body Checking Questionnaire: Psychometric properties and clinical correlates in obese men and women with binge eating disorder. *International Journal of Eating Disorders, 39*, 326–331.

Reas, D. L., Whisenhunt, B. L., Netemeyer, R., & Williamson, D. A. (2002). Development of the body checking questionnaire: A self-report measure of body checking behaviors. *International Journal of Eating Disorders, 31*, 324–333.

Rhea, D. J., Lantz, C. D., & Cornelius, A. E. (2004). Development of the Muscle Dysmorphia Inventory (MDI). *Journal of Sports Medicine and Physical Fitness, 44*, 428–435.

Ricca, V., Mannucci, E., Mezzani, B., Di Bernardo, M., Zucchi, T., Paionni, A., et al. (2001). Psychopathological and clinical features of outpatients with an eating disorder not otherwise specified. *Eating and Weight Disorders, 6*, 157–165.

Rizvi, S. L., Peterson, C. B., Crow, S. J., & Agras, W. S. (2000). Test-retest reliability of the Eating Disorder Examination. *International Journal of Eating Disorders, 28*, 311–316.

Robin, A. L., Koepke, T., & Moye, A. (1990). Multidimensional assessment of parent–adolescent relations. *Psychological Assessment, 2*, 451–459.

Robin, A. L., Siegel, P. T., Moye, A. W., Gilroy, M., Baker-Dennis, A., & Sikand, A. (1999). A controlled comparison of family versus individual therapy for adolescents with anorexia nervosa. *Journal of the American Academy of Child & Adolescent Psychiatry, 38*, 1482–1489.

Rosen, J. C., Jones, A., Ramirez, E., & Waxman, S. (1996). Body Shape Questionnaire: Studies of validity and reliability. *International Journal of Eating Disorders, 20*, 315–319.

Rosen, J. C., Vara, L., Wendt, S., & Leitenberg, H. (1990). Validity studies of the Eating Disorder Examination. *International Journal of Eating Disorders, 9*, 519–528.

Rosenberg, M. (1979). *Conceiving the self.* New York: Basic Books.

Segal, D. L., Hersen, M., & Van Hasselt, V. B. (1994). Reliability of the structured clinical interview for DSM-III-R: An evaluative review. *Comprehensive Psychiatry, 35*, 316–327.

Shafran, R., Fairburn, C. G., Robinson, P., & Lask, B. (2004). Body checking and its avoidance in eating disorders. *International Journal of Eating Disorders, 35*, 93–101.

Smyth, J., Wonderlich, S., Crosby, R., Miltenberger, R., Mitchell, J., & Rorty, M. (2001). The use of ecological momentary assessment approaches in eating disorder research. *International Journal of Eating Disorders, 30*, 83–95.

Spitzer, R. L., Kroenke, K., & Williams, J. B. W. (1999). Validation and utility of a self-report version of the PRIME-MD: The PHQ primary care study. *Journal of American Medical Association, 282*, 1737–1744.

Stice, E., & Bearman, S. K. (2001). Body image and eating disturbances prospectively predict increases in depressive symptoms in adolescent girls: A growth curve analysis. *Developmental Psychology, 37*, 597–607.

Stice, E., Fisher, M., & Martinez, E. (2004). Eating disorder diagnostic scale: Additional evidence of reliability and validity. *Psychological Assessment, 16*, 60–71.

Stice, E., Orjada, K., & Tristan, J. (2006). Trial of a psychoeducational eating disturbance intervention for college women: A replication and extension. *International Journal of Eating Disorders, 39,* 233–239.

Stice, E., & Ragan, J. (2002). A preliminary controlled evaluation of an eating disturbance psychoeducational intervention for college students. *International Journal of Eating Disorders, 31,* 159–171.

Stice, E., Telch, C. F., & Rizvi, S. L. (2000). Development and validation of the eating disorder diagnostic scale: A brief self-report measure of anorexia, bulimia, and binge-eating disorder. *Psychological Assessment, 12,* 123–131.

Striegel-Moore, R. H., & Franko, D. L. (2003). Epidemiology of binge eating disorder. *International Journal of Eating Disorders, 34,* S19–S29.

Sysko, R., Walsh, B. T., & Fairburn, C. G. (2005). Eating Disorder Examination-Questionnaire as a measure of change in patients with bulimia nervosa. *International Journal of Eating Disorders, 37,* 100–106.

Sysko, R., Walsh, B. T., Schebendach, J., & Wilson, G. T. (2005). Eating behavior among women with anorexia nervosa. *American Journal of Clinical Nutrition, 82,* 296–301.

Thompson, J. K., Roehrig, M., Cafri, G., & Heinberg, L. J. (2005). Assessment of body image disturbance. In J. E. Mitchell & C. B. Peterson (Eds.), *Assessment of eating disorders* (pp. 175–202). New York: Guilford Press.

Tanofsky-Kraff, M., Morgan, C. M., Yanovski, S. Z., Marmarosh, C., Wilfley, D. E., & Yanovski, J. A. (2003). Comparison of assessments of children's eating-disordered behaviors by interview and questionnaire. *International Journal of Eating Disorders, 33,* 213–224.

Turner, H., & Bryant-Waugh, R. (2004) Eating disorder not otherwise specified (EDNOS): Profiles of clients presenting at a community eating disorders service. *European Eating Disorders Review, 12,* 18–26.

Tylka, T. L., Bergeron, D., & Schwartz, J. P. (2005). Development and psychometric evaluation of the Male Body Attitudes Scale (MBAS). *Body Image, 2,* 161–175.

Vaughn, G. E., & Leff, J. (1976). The influence of family and social factors on the course of psychiatric illness: A comparison of schizophrenic and depressed neurotic patients. *British Journal of Psychiatry, 129,* 125–137.

Viswanathan, M. (2005). *Measurement error and research design: A practical approach to the intangibles of research design.* Thousand Oaks, CA: Sage Publications.

Walsh, B. T., & Boudreau, G. (2003). Laboratory studies of binge eating disorder. *International Journal of Eating Disorders, 34,* S30–S38.

Walsh, B. T., Fairburn, C. G., Mickley, D., Sysko, R., & Parides, M. K. (2004) Treatment of Bulimia Nervosa in a primary care setting. *American Journal of Psychiatry, 161,* 556–561.

Walsh, B. T., Kaplan, A. S., Attia, E., Olmsted, M., Parides, M., Carter, J. C., et al. (2006). Fluoxetine after weight restoration in anorexia nervosa: A randomized controlled trial. *Journal of American Medical Association, 295,* 2605–2612.

Walsh, B. T., Kissileff, H. R., Cassidy, S. M., & Dantzic, S. (1989). Eating behavior of women with bulimia. *Archives of General Psychiatry, 46,* 54–58.

Watkins, B., Frampton, I., Lask, B., & Bryant-Waugh, R. (2005). Reliability and validity of the child version of the Eating Disorder Examination: A preliminary investigation. *International Journal of Eating Disorders, 38,* 183–187.

Weissman, A. N., & Beck, A. T. (1978). *Development and validation of the Dysfunctional Attitude Scale: A preliminary investigation.* Paper presented at the 86th annual convention of the American Psychological Association, Toronto, Ontario, Canada, August–September.

Weissman, M. M., & Bothwell, S. (1976). Assessment of social adjustment by patient self-report. *Archives of General Psychiatry, 33,* 1111–1115.

Wilfley, D. E. (2006). *Short-term outcome of three psychological treatments for binge eating disorder.* Paper presented at the 40th Annual Conference of the Association for the Advancement of Cognitive-Behavior Therapy, Chicago, IL.

Wilfley, D. E., Friedman, M. A., Dounchis, J. Z., Stein, R. I., Welch, R. R., & Ball, S. A. (2000). Comorbid psychopathology in binge eating disorder: Relation to eating disorder severity at baseline and following treatment. *Journal of Consulting and Clinical Psychology, 68,* 641–9.

Wilfley, D. E., Schwartz, M. B., Spurrell, E. B., & Fairburn, C. G. (2000). Using the Eating Disorder Examination to identify the specific psychopathology of binge eating disorder. *International Journal of Eating Disorders, 27,* 259–269.

Wilfley, D. E., Schwartz, M. B., Spurrell, E. B., & Fairburn, C. G. (1997). Assessing the specific psychopathology of binge eating disorder patients: Interview or self-report? *Behaviour Research and Therapy, 35,* 1151–1159.

Wilfley, D. E., Welch, R. R., Stein, R. I., Spurrell, E. B., Cohen, L. R., Saelens, B. E., et al. (2002). A randomized comparison of group cognitive-behavioral therapy and group interpersonal psychotherapy for the treatment of overweight individuals with binge-eating disorder. *Archives of General Psychiatry, 59,* 713–721.

Williamson, D. A., Muller, S. L., Reas, D. L., & Thaw, J. M. (1999). Cognitive bias in eating disorders: Implications for theory and treatment. *Behavior Modification, 23,* 556–577.

Wilson, G. T. (1993). Assessment of binge eating. In C. G. Fairburn & G. T. Wilson (Eds.), *Binge eating: Nature, assessment, and treatment* (pp. 227–249). New York: Guilford Press.

Wilson, G. T., & Fairburn, C. G. (2002). Treatments for eating disorders. In P. E. Nathan & J. M. Gorman (Eds.), *A guide to treatments that work* (2nd ed., pp. 559–592). New York: Oxford University Press.

Wilson, G. T., Fairburn, C. G., Agras, W. S., Walsh, B. T., & Kraemer, H. (2002). Cognitive-behavioral therapy for bulimia nervosa: Time course and mechanisms of change. *Journal of Consulting and Clinical Psychology, 70,* 267–274.

Wilson, G. T., Loeb, K. L., Walsh, B. T., Labouvie, E., Petkova, E., Liu, X., et al. (1999). Psychological versus pharmacological treatments for bulimia nervosa: Predictors and processes of change. *Journal of Consulting and Clinical Psychology, 67,* 451–459.

Wilson, G. T., & Smith, D. (1989). Assessment of bulimia nervosa: An evaluation of the Eating Disorder Examination. *International Journal of Eating Disorders, 8,* 173–179.

Wilson, G. T., & Vitousek, K. M. (1999). Self-monitoring in the assessment of eating disorders. *Psychological Assessment, 11,* 480–489.

Wolk, S. L., Loeb, K. L., & Walsh, B. T. (2005). Assessment of patients with anorexia nervosa: Interview versus self-report. *International Journal of Eating Disorders, 37,* 92–99.

Wonderlich, S. A., de Zwaan, M., Mitchell, J. E., Peterson, C., & Crow, S. (2003). Psychological and dietary treatments of binge eating disorder: Conceptual implications. *International Journal of Eating Disorders, 34,* S58–S73.

Zanarini, M. C., Bender, D., Sanislow, C., Morey, L. C., Shea, M. T., & Gunderson, J. G. (2000). The collaborative longitudinal personality disorders study: Reliability of Axis I and II diagnoses. *Journal of Personality Disorders, 14,* 291–299.

24

Sleep Disorders

Shawn R. Currie

This chapter will provide the reader with a review of empirically supported assessment methods in the field of sleep disorders. Because insomnia is the most frequently encountered sleep disorder by mental health clinicians, the focus of the chapter will be on the assessment of primary and secondary insomnia. A wide range of assessment tools will be reviewed, including interviews, self-report scales, bed partner reports, sleep diaries, and objective sleep measures. The goal of the chapter is to provide clinicians without a background in sleep medicine with the basic knowledge on how to screen for sleep disorders, diagnose insomnia, develop a case conceptualization, and monitor response to treatment.

NATURE OF SLEEP DISORDERS

Sleep Disorder Types

The over 50 sleep disorder types described in medical and psychology textbooks can be placed into two broad categories: dyssomnias and parasomnias. Dyssomnias are disorders that result in either too little or too much sleep (Thorpy, 2005). Insomnia and sleep apnea are the most common dyssomnias. Hypersomnia and narcolepsy are dyssomnia conditions characterized by an excess of sleep. Parasomnias are conditions in which the sleep process is largely normal but undesirable physical phenomena occur during the sleep period. Sleep bruxism (teeth grinding) and enuresis (bed-wetting) are types of parasomnias. The etiology of most sleep disorders can be primary or secondary in nature. A primary sleep disorder exists when no other cause of the sleep problem can be identified. When the sleep problem is deemed the result of another conditions—for example, substance misuse, medication, neurological disorder,

neoplasms, pain, or another psychiatric condition—the disorder is said to be secondary in nature.

Prevalence of Disturbed Sleep

Insomnia

Physical and mental well being are both impacted by inadequate or poor sleep. Disturbed sleep is also one of the most common complaints of clients in both mental health and primary care service settings (Ohayon, 2002; Partinen & Hublin, 2005; Üstün et al., 1996). General population surveys suggest an overall prevalence rate of 15.3% for adults with insomnia (Lichstein, Durrence, Reidel, Taylor, & Bush, 2004). The range of estimates across studies is actually quite broad owing to the inconsistent use of strict diagnostic criteria for defining insomnia (Ancoli-Israel & Roth, 1999; Ohayon, 2002; Partinen & Hublin, 2000). Using the *Diagnostic and Statistical Manual of Mental Disorders* (DSM-IV; American Psychiatric Association [APA], 1994) criteria for primary insomnia, Ohayon (2002) estimated a prevalence of 6% in the general population. An additional 25% to 30% of adults complain of occasional or transient insomnia (Ancoli-Israel, & Roth, 1999; Ohayon, 2002). Significant health care costs are associated with insomnia. About $1.7 billion is spent annually in the United States on medications and other sleep-promoting aids, with other health-care costs (physician visits, sleep medicine consultations) directly attributed to insomnia, amounting to an estimated $12 billion annually (Morin, Bastien, & Savard, 2003). Furthermore, indirect costs, including lost work time, reduced productivity, and fatigue-related accidents, are estimated at $30 billion to $35 billion per year in the United States (Chilcott & Shapiro, 1996).

Female gender and advancing age are the most robust demographic risk factors for insomnia, with the prevalence within the elderly reaching as high as 50% in some studies (Lichstein et al., 2004; Ohayon 2002). Insomnia is frequently comorbid with another medical or psychiatric disorder (Balter & Uhlenhuth, 1992; McCall & Reynolds, 2000; Lichstein, McCrae, & Wilson, 2003). Epidemiological studies indicate that about 40% to 65% of individuals with insomnia have a history of at least one other psychiatric disorder (Lichstein, McCrae, et al., 2003; Ohayon, 2002). Certain client groups are particularly vulnerable to sleep disturbances: for example, up to 70% of treatment-seeking individuals with chronic pain reported significant insomnia (Pilowsky, Crettenden, & Townley, 1985). High rates of insomnia are also associated with major depression, anxiety disorders (Lichstein, McCrae, et al., 2003) and alcohol dependence (Brower, 2001; Currie, Clark, Rimac, Malhotra, 2003). Insomnia is a criterion for diagnosing several psychological disorders (e.g., major depression, generalized anxiety disorder; APA, 2000), hence one possible explanation for the high degree of comorbidity in symptom overlap with other conditions. Historically, disturbed sleep in these populations has been considered a consequence or symptom of the primary disorder. However, insomnia often persists after the primary disorder resolves (Currie et al., 2003; Lichstein, McCrae, et al., 2003). Therefore, if the marker of a primary disorder is that its successful treatment automatically leads to remission of the secondary disorder, there is little evidence to suggest that insomnia is necessarily a secondary disorder (Harvey, 2001). Other evidence points to insomnia being a risk factor for the later development of major depression, anxiety disorders, and alcohol abuse (Ford & Kamerow, 1989; Weissman, Greenwald, Nino-Murcia, & Dement, 1997; Wong, Brower, Fitzgerald, & Zucker, 2004).

Noninsomnia Disorders

After insomnia, the most common sleep disorder is sleep apnea (known as a breathing-related sleep disorder in the DSM-IV-TR; APA, 2000) characterized by the cessation of airflow through the mouth and nose at night. About 2% of adult women and 4% of adult males have sleep apnea (Partinen & Hublin, 2005). Unfortunately, because people with sleep apnea generally breathe normally during the day, this very serious disorder is often undetected. Restless legs syndrome (defined as the presence of a creeping, crawling, or uncomfortable feeling in the legs that is relieved by moving them) and periodic limb movement (repeated arm or leg movements at night that are in excess of normal movement during the sleep period) occur in the general population with about the same frequency as sleep apnea. Functional impairment associated with restless legs and periodic limb movements is often minimal and so only those with severe symptoms tend to seek medical treatment (Montplaisir, Nicolas, Godbout, & Walters, 2005). The other noninsomnia sleep disorders are typically rare (e.g., sleep terrors) or occur primarily in children (e.g., enuresis; Partinen & Hublin, 2005). Most of these disorders require assessment procedures that are beyond the scope of practice for most mental health clinicians. Therefore, the primary focus in this chapter will be on the assessment of primary and secondary insomnia.

Theoretical Underpinnings

The etiology of insomnia is thought to be multifactorial, and several predisposing risk factors have been identified. For example, individuals with a high basal level of physiological arousal are at risk for insomnia. Compared to good sleepers, those with insomnia show higher metabolic rates, muscle tension, cardiovascular activity, and cortical activation (Bonnet & Arand, 1997; Morin, 1993). Cognitive arousal is also strongly implicated in the etiology of poor sleep. Compared to good sleepers, individuals with insomnia demonstrate excessive cognitive activity such as racing thoughts and intrusive cognitions during the presleep period (Harvey, 2002). Familial risk factors are also evident. Individuals with insomnia are more likely to have a family history of sleep disorders than are those not suffering from insomnia (Bastien & Morin, 2000). Genetics have also been implicated in the etiology of insomnia (Ohayon, 2002).

The cognitive-behavioral model of insomnia is the predominant theoretical framework guiding modern psychological assessment and treatment (Harvey, 2002; Morin, 1993). Although predisposing factors are an acknowledged influence, a central tenet of the model is that insomnia is maintained by maladaptive sleep activities (Espie, 1991). These activities can be cognitive (covert) or behavioral (overt) in nature (Morin, 1993). Overt maladaptive behaviors would include using the bedroom for activities other than sleep or sex (e.g., watching TV, reading), engaging in stimulating activities before bedtime (e.g., problem solving with spouse, drinking coffee, exercise, working on the computer), and remaining in bed for long periods when not able to sleep. Incompatible cognitive activities could include using the presleep period for rehashing the day's events, excessive mental focus on insomnia and its consequences, and trying to force the sleep process. A pure conditioning model of insomnia proposes that when sleep-incompatible behaviors are repeated over time, a mental association is formed between the bedroom and a state of arousal. Accordingly, the bedroom environment and usual temporal cues to sleep (i.e., the bedtime hour) lose their sleep-inducing properties. Additional cognitive responses (e.g., performance anxiety or apprehension while trying to fall asleep) may be formed as a consequence of repeated sleep-incompatible activities. The cognitive and behavioral facets maintaining an individual's insomnia can be elucidated in the functional analysis, described later in the chapter.

ASSESSMENT FOR DIAGNOSIS

Nosological Systems

The diagnosis of insomnia is made complicated by the existence of two parallel diagnostic schemes for categorizing sleep disorders. The most widely used diagnostic system, the DSM-IV-TR (American Psychiatric Association, 2000) is actually not preferred by specialists in the field of sleep medicine owing to the purely descriptive nature of the criteria. Notably, the atheoretical approach of the DSM-IV-TR does not identify etiological markers in the criteria for insomnia. Primary insomnia in the DSM-IV-TR is defined as at least 1 month of persistent difficulty initiating or maintaining sleep, or nonrestorative sleep that also interferes with the individual's ability to function during the day or cause clinically significant distress. The International Classification of Sleep Disorders' (ISCD; American Sleep Disorders Association, 1997) definition of psychophysiological insomnia is comparable to the DSM system in terms of the symptom severity, but also specifies that the condition is maintained by learned cognitive and emotional arousal over the sleep experience. In this conceptual framework, insomnia is described as a condition of somatized tension and conditioned arousal leading to distress and decreased daytime functioning. Although there is often a precipitating event, many learned behaviors manifest in clients over time and are believed to play a dominant role in sustaining the insomnia (Harvey, 2002).

Unfortunately, neither classification scheme provides quantitative criteria for distinguishing normal from abnormal sleep based on severity of symptoms. Disturbed sleep exists on a continuum of severity and transient symptoms of insomnia are quite common among mentally healthy adults. To differentiate between normal and abnormal sleep, researchers have adopted a quantitative criteria set to identify those suffering from insomnia. Specifically, the individual must have reported either sleep onset latency (SOL) or a time awake after sleep onset (WASO) greater than 30 minutes for a minimum of three nights per week. These criteria were validated by Lichstein, Durrence, Taylor, Bush, and Riedel (2003); however, a more recent investigation by Lineberger, Carney, Edinger, and Means (2006) indicated a more conservative criteria of 20 minutes maximizes sensitivity and specificity in discriminating normal and abnormal sleep. Despite the value of these criteria in identifying abnormal sleep, their adoption outside of the research context appears to be limited.

An important criterion for the clinical diagnosis of insomnia is evidence of compromised daytime functioning. Many individuals complain of poor sleep but report no distress or consequences to their daytime functioning (Fichten et al., 1995). In both the ISCD and DSM diagnostic schemes, such individuals would not be classified as having insomnia. Hence, identifying the consequences of sleep dysfunction in terms of work performance, vigor, mood, cognitive functioning, reliance on sleep medication, and overall quality of life is an important area of assessment. Roth (2004) recently reviewed the evidence that total sleep time (TST) and measures of sleep continuity are correlated with alertness, memory, psychomotor performance, risk of car accidents, and pain threshold. Insomnia is also associated with increased depression, (Breslau, Roth, & Rosenthal, 1996; Chang, Ford, & Mead, 1997; Ford & Kamerow, 1989), absenteeism (Zammitt, Weinera, & Damato, 1999), accidents (Balter & Uhlenhuth, 1992), and increased health care utilization (Simon & Von Korff, 1997). A variety of instruments are available to assist in the diagnosis of insomnia and related disorders (Chervin,

TABLE 24.1 Ratings of Instruments Used for Diagnosis

Instrument	Norms	Internal Consistency	Inter-rater Reliability	Test–Retest Reliability	Content Validity	Construct Validity	Validity Generalization	Clinical Utility	Highly Recommended
SIS-D	NA	G	E	G	E	A	A	G	✓
PSG	E	NA	A	A	NA[a]	NA[a]	NA[a]	A	

[a] PSG is considered the gold standard for assessing sleep disorders.

Note: SIS-D = Structured Interview for Sleep Disorders for DSM-III-R; PSG = Polysomnography; A = Adequate; G = Good; E = Excellent; NA = Not Applicable.

2005). The main instruments and their psychometric properties are shown in Table 24.1. It is worth noting that symptoms of insomnia are routinely assessed in mental health settings, as disturbed sleep is a common marker for psychiatric illness. Hence, general questions concerning sleep quality (e.g., "How are you sleeping?") are often asked in the context of a structured or semistructured interview for most mental disorders. The global, retrospective assessment of sleep is not necessarily inaccurate, but it lacks the depth of information necessary for properly diagnosing a sleep disorder. To assess insomnia and rule out other causes of disturbed sleep, a more detailed interview is required.

Interviews

Surprisingly, commonly used structured psychiatric interviews such as the Structured Clinical Interview for DSM-IV (First, Spitzer, Gibbon, & Williams, 1995) do not include a sleep disorder module. The Structured Interview for Sleep Disorders (SIS-D), based on DSM-III-R criteria, was developed by Schramm et al. (1993). The SIS-D consists of a structured inquiry about specific symptoms of sleep disorders as defined by the DSM classification scheme. Originally developed for DSM-III-R criteria (American Psychiatric Association, 1987), it has been adapted to include DSM-IV criteria (Currie et al., 2003; Currie, Wilson, Pontefract, & deLaplante, 2000). The criteria for insomnia did not change with the DSM-IV-TR. The SIS-D has strong psychometric properties, but it is rarely used outside of research studies. Although the SIS-D is useful to establish the diagnosis of insomnia, it does not provide the depth of information needed to fully understand the nature of disturbed sleep from the client's perspective.

Morin (1993) has developed a detailed semistructured interview that includes a functional analysis of the sleep problems. Unfortunately, no psychometric evaluation of this interview schedule has been conducted. At present, the options for clinicians to use psychometrically sound interviews are limited. As a result, the depth of content and level of detail obtained in the clinical interview will ultimately depend on the experience of the interviewer and the time available. At a minimum, the clinical interview should collect sufficient information to make a preliminary diagnosis, screen for noninsomnia sleep disorders, and rule out other causes of the individual's sleep complaint. Ideally, the clinician should also strive to complete a comprehensive evaluation of the history of the client's sleep problem including, but not limited to, impact on daytime functioning, current sleeping habits, health behaviors (diet, exercise, and substance use), medical history and medication use, history of psychopathology, and past treatment for sleep problems, including attempts at self-management. The latter information is necessary to determine if the insomnia complaint is primary or secondary in nature.

Objective Sleep Assessment

Sleep is one of the few areas in mental health where standardized physiological assessment protocols are available. Polysomnography (PSG) is a structured assessment procedure involving the simultaneous overnight recording of multiple physiological signals (brain activity, respiratory function, eye movements, muscle activity) using a prescribed set of protocols (Rechtschaffen & Kales, 1968). Although considered the gold standard for sleep assessment, PSG is rarely used in the routine evaluation of insomnia and most clients presenting with the symptoms of primary insomnia do not require PSG to confirm the diagnosis. The symptoms and characteristics of insomnia do not lend themselves to accurate assessment using PSG (Morin, 2000; Reite, Buysse, Reynolds, & Mendelson, 1995; Smith, Smith, Nowakowski, & Perlis et al., 2003). In addition, PSG is an inconvenient, expensive procedure that is usually only available in large urban centers with a dedicated sleep medicine clinic. The Practice Parameters for the Evaluation of Chronic Insomnia from the American Academy of Sleep Medicine (AASM; Chesson et al., 2000) state that PSG is unnecessary for the routine evaluation of insomnia. On the other hand, the diagnosis of the noninsomnia sleep disorders typically necessitates the use of PSG. Initial screening for the noninsomnia disorders can usually be achieved in a clinical interview, but a firm diagnosis for most noninsomnia disorders such as sleep apnea cannot be made without overnight PSG. The AASM therefore recommends PSG for individuals with symptoms of insomnia when (a) another sleep disorder is the suspected cause of poor sleep, (b) an underlying neurological disorder is suspected, or (c) the client has shown to be refractory to all treatment for insomnia (Chesson et al., 2000).

If objective sleep data are available, clinicians should be aware that the severity of sleep dysfunction revealed might disagree with the self-reported severity of the client. Carskadon et al.'s highly cited 1976 study reported that clients with insomnia overestimated time to fall asleep and underestimated sleep duration by approximately 30 minutes each (Carskadon et al., 1976). Similar studies conducted over the past 25 years have produced the same pattern of results (Edinger & Fins, 1995; Rosa & Bonnet, 2000). Good sleepers also overestimate SOL and underestimate TST by about 15 minute each (Lacks, 1987).

It is important to prioritize the subjective perception of inadequate sleep over any objective assessment results (Edinger & Fins, 1995; Rosa & Bonnet, 2000). Although self-report and PSG tend to produce different absolute sleep estimates, both will generally indicate that a sleep problem exists. Furthermore, diary and PSG measures tend to correlate highly with one another (Currie, 2006; Lacks, 1988). Clinicians need be concerned when the severity of self-reported insomnia seems extreme or highly improbable (e.g., claims of sleeping only 2 to 4 hours per night). With such extreme cases, a referral for overnight PSG can be useful, both diagnostically and for case conceptualization. The objective feedback may help to correct clients' misperceptions about sleep duration and they may obtain some relief knowing that they are getting more sleep than originally estimated. In addition, continued self-monitoring through the sleep diary can provide clients with empirical data that some

variation in sleep pattern, including good nights of sleep, will occur during a typical week.

Psychiatric Comorbidity

Comorbidity among mental disorders is common (Kaplan & Sadock, 2002) and sleep disorders are no exception to this pattern (Buysse, Germain, Moul, & Nofzinger, 2005; Ohayon, 2002). The presence of other mental health problems can complicate the assessment of sleep disorders. Clinicians may find themselves unable to direct a focused discussion on sleep when the client seems overwhelmed with other mental health concerns. The diagnosis of primary or psychophysiological insomnia is often made by exclusion of other causes of the client's sleep disturbance. In many cases, however, insomnia coexists as a distinct, but functionally related, condition to another psychiatric disorder, making differential diagnosis more difficult. Disentangling the source of overlapping symptoms can be assisted by ascertaining (a) the onset of insomnia in relation to the onset of psychiatric illness, (b) whether symptoms of insomnia persist during periods of full or partial remission of the psychiatric disorder, (c) how the client distinguishes between disorders, and (d) assessing the relative severity of the psychiatric and insomnia disorders. The use of standardized instruments such as the Beck Depression Inventory-II (Beck, Brown, & Steer, 1996), Beck Anxiety Inventory (Beck, Epstein, Brown, & Steer, 1988), and a brief diagnostic interview can assist in both diagnosing and quantifying the severity of comorbid psychiatric symptoms.

Overall Evaluation

Disturbed sleep is a common complaint of individuals seeking mental health treatment. The diagnosis of insomnia is challenging when numerous secondary causes of sleep problems are possible. Indeed, most clinicians begin their assessment with the assumption that the client's sleep complaint is a symptom of another mental health concern. The diagnosis of primary insomnia is most often made by ruling out other causes. The primary tool for making a firm diagnosis is the structured clinical interview. Although a SIS-D has been validated, it is infrequently used in clinical settings. A semistructured interview, if properly aligned with either DSM-IV-TR or ICSD diagnostic criteria, can be used to confirm diagnosis as well as provide a rich base of contextual information on the

TABLE 24.2 Ratings of Instruments Used for Case Conceptualization and Treatment Planning

Instrument	Norms	Internal Consistency	Inter-Rater Reliability	Test–Retest Reliability	Content Validity	Construct Validity	Validity Generalization	Clinical Utility	Highly Recommended
Sleep Diary	E	G	NA	A	A	G	G	E	✓
PSQI	E	G	NA	A	E	G	G	E	✓
DBAS	NA	G	NA	G	G	G	A	G	✓
SII (S)	NA	NA	A	A	A	A	A	A	

Note: PSQI = Pittsburgh Sleep Quality Index; DBAS = Dysfunctional Beliefs and Attitudes about Sleep Scale; SII (S) = Sleep Impairment Instrument (spouse ratings); A = Adequate; G = Good; E = Excellent; NA = Not Applicable.

individual. PSG is not needed in the routine assessment of primary and secondary insomnia but is necessary to rule out another sleep disorder if it is the suspected cause of disturbed sleep in the individual.

ASSESSMENT FOR CASE CONCEPTUALIZATION AND TREATMENT PLANNING

Following a confirmation of diagnosis, the assessment of insomnia should determine the severity of insomnia and identify specific learned behaviors that can be targets for change during treatment. Insomnia severity can be quantified in several ways. A profile of insomnia severity can be attained by examining the portion of the sleep period that is most disturbed. An individual's overnight sleep profile is generally quantified in terms of his or her time to fall asleep (SOL), frequency of awakenings, total time WASO, TST (in minutes or hours), sleep efficiency (SEF; the ratio of hours slept to time in bed up to a maximum of 100%), and overall satisfaction with his or her sleep, which is generally referred to as sleep quality (usually assessed with a numerical rating scale such as 0 to 10, with 0 being "extremely poor" and 10 being "extremely good"). A self-monitoring instrument, the sleep diary, includes items for recording all of these parameters and is recommended for obtaining these data.

Sleep Diary

Although it may not be practical in all settings, a self-monitoring period of 2 weeks through a sleep diary is the preferred method to quantify the severity of insomnia and to develop a detailed profile of the individual's sleep habits (Lacks & Morin, 1992; Smith, Smith, et al., 2003). The information collected on each sleep

parameter (SOL, SEF, etc.) can be condensed into averages to determine overall insomnia severity and identify treatment targets for improvement. The range of values can also be informative to determine the extremes of good and bad sleep across a typical 2-week period. Diaries can also include items for the client to record naps, consumption of caffeinated beverages, the use of sleep aids, daytime fatigue or feelings of restfulness, and application of sleep hygiene principals (Bouchard, Bastien, & Morin, 2003; Morin, 1993). The latter items would include the number of times the client leaves the bed when unable to sleep and the use of any strategies to relax. Normative sleep diary data for good and bad sleepers are available to determine the severity of a client's insomnia symptoms in terms of statistical variations from age and gender consistent averages (Lichstein et al. 2004).

The psychometric properties of the sleep diary have been well documented (Bootzin & Engle-Friedman, 1981; Coates et al., 1982; Currie et al., 2000; Currie, Malhotra, & Clark, 2004; Haythornthwaite, Hegel, & Kerns, 1991). An overview of its psychometric strengths is provided in Table 24.2. Despite the strong empirical basis and clinical benefits of regular self-monitoring of sleep, compliance with the daily logs remains a big issue. Stone, Shiffman, Schwartz, and Hufford (2002) reported a large discrepancy between clients' self-reported compliance with paper logs and actual compliance assessed through an electronic monitor of which clients were unaware. It is important, therefore, for clinicians to routinely inquire about the frequency and time of day that a client actually completes the sleep diary.

Self-Report Measures

Several retrospective sleep questionnaires have been developed for clinical and research applications.

These multiitem instruments ask clients about their sleep habits over a specified time frame, typically 2 to 4 weeks. Sleep questionnaires have several advantages over other methods of assessing sleep: (a) ease of administration in most clinical settings; (b) inexpensive and, therefore, convenient for mass screening situations; (c) provision of detail on a client's sleep behavior to make a preliminary evaluation of whether a sleep problem exists; (d) retrospective data correlates well with prospective sleep diaries (Smith, Nowakowski, Soeffing, Orff, & Perlis, 2003); and (e) sensitivity to treatment effects (Currie, Clark, et al., 2004; Edinger, Wohlgemuth, Radtke, Marsh, & Quillian, 2001; Mimeault & Morin, 1999). The 19-item Pittsburgh Sleep Quality Index (PSQI; Buysse, Reynolds, Monk, Berman, & Kupfer, 1989) is a brief, self-rated questionnaire that inquires about the individual's sleep for the past month. The PSQI has strong psychometric properties across a variety of medical, psychiatric, and ethnic populations (Backhaus, Junghanns, Broocks, Riemann, & Hohagen, 2002; Beck, Schwartz, Towsley, Dudley, & Barsevick, 2004; Carpenter & Andrykowski, 1998; Tsai et al., 2005). In addition to a total score, there are seven component scales on the PSQI that are scored on a 4-point ordinal scale: (1) subjective sleep quality; (2) sleep latency; (3) sleep duration; (4) habitual SEF; (5) sleep disturbances; (6) use of sleeping medication; and (7) daytime dysfunction. The global index score is the most commonly used in research applications. The PSQI also has five questions for a bed partner to complete to provide a collateral assessment of sleep problems, although these responses are not included in the total score.

One of the disadvantages of retrospective questionnaires such as the PSQI is that a single sample method of data collection is used (Smith, Nowakowski, et al., 2003). Clients are asked to make broad judgments about their sleep quantity and quality using a long period of reference (e.g., 30 nights of sleep). Clients may selectively report on their most recent night of sleep or focus exclusively on the bad nights when making judgments rather than make a true personal average (Gehrman, Matt, Turigan, Dinh, & Ancoli-Israel, 2002). Furthermore, sleep questionnaires lack sufficient specificity concerning sleep disorders. Insomnia symptoms (e.g., poor sleep quality) overlap substantially with other sleep disorders. A high score can indicate that a sleep disorder exists, but not the type of sleep disorder.

Another useful questionnaire for case conceptualization is the Dysfunctional Beliefs and Attitudes about Sleep Scale (DBAS; Morin, 1993). The DBAS assesses negative thoughts and unrealistic expectations about sleep, insomnia, and the consequences of sleep loss. A popular instrument in research (Espie, Inglis, Tessier, & Harvey, 2001), it is also effective as a clinical tool for identifying specific dysfunctional thoughts that may be maintaining sleep-incompatible behaviors. An examination of the highest scores across the five subscales (misconceptions about the causes of insomnia, need for control over insomnia, magnifying consequences, unrealistic sleep expectations, and faulty beliefs about sleep-promoting practices) can help to formulate an understanding of the behavioral impact of retaining such beliefs. Although the DBAS has strong psychometric properties, the use of a visual analogue scale, which requires a ruler to score for each of the 30 items, can be a deterrent for some clinicians who may prefer an easier numerical scale. Smith and Trinder (2001) identified 35 mm as the optimal cutoff to identify dysfunctional thoughts that are consistent with insomnia.

Self-report instruments are available for measuring other facets of disturbed sleep. For example, the Stanford Sleepiness Scale (SSS; Hoddes, Zarcone, Smythe, Phillips, & Dement, 1973) and Epworth Sleepiness Scale (ESS; Johns, 1991) assess subjective propensity to fall asleep. Although daytime sleepiness is a common symptom of insomnia, several studies have found no significant differences between overall sleepiness ratings in those with and without insomnia (Sateia, Doghramji, Hauri, & Morin, 2000). Reporting on a sample of over 700 good and bad sleepers, Lichstein et al. (2004) found that the SSS and ESS scores correlated higher with ratings of sleep quality than quantitative sleep measures such as SOL and TST. The ESS has a stronger research base than the SSS (Baker & Sederer, 2002) and is considered better at distinguishing tiredness from sleepiness. The ESS has good discriminant validity in terms of distinguishing sleep apnea clients from normal sleepers and also correlates with PSG measures of sleepiness (Baker & Sederer, 2002).

Functional Analysis

The initial interview used to determine diagnosis can also be used to initiate the functional analysis, an integral component to any behavioral assessment

(Ollendick, Alvarez, & Greene, 2004). A functional analysis should encompass a detailed evaluation of the precipitants, antecedents, possible secondary gains (e.g., sick role), and perpetuating factors functionally related to the individual's disturbed sleep. In clinical practice, a functional analysis should be initiated when the sleep complaint is felt by the clinician to be symptomatic of insomnia disorder rather than a sign of another condition. This portion of the assessment is used to identify the key maintenance factors in the client's insomnia—staying in bed when unable to fall asleep, for example—that may become the focal point of change during treatment. Key areas of the functional assessment would include (a) characteristics of the client's bedtime routine, (b) client's response when unable to fall asleep or return to sleep, (c) factors that exacerbate insomnia, (d) factors that improve sleep, (e) impact of insomnia on the individual's daytime functioning (mood, alertness, performance), (f) coping strategies and their effectiveness, and (g) change in sleep problems over time.

Inadequate coping attempts may further reinforce the persistence of insomnia. In many cases, the coping strategies that individuals with insomnia develop serve to maintain, rather than ameliorate, the sleep disorder. For example, napping in response to a poor night's sleep can lead to additional sleep fragmentation at night. In response to daytime fatigue, those with insomnia may consume excess caffeine and curtail daytime activities. Lack of regular exercise can further perpetuate poor sleep. People with insomnia often resort to sedative medications, both prescription and over-the-counter, in an attempt to improve their sleep. Pharmacological sleep aids have limited empirical evidence of long-term efficacy and are thought to maintain insomnia if taken for extended periods (Smith, Smith, et al., 2003). Clients are often reluctant to abandon coping responses, even ones that seem to be incompatible with good sleep hygiene. Harvey's (2002) notion of a concept of sleep "safety behavior" refers to maladaptive response to the anxiety caused by chronic insomnia. For example, the fearful thought that a poor night of sleep will impair performance at work may lead to the client calling in sick and trying to recover lost sleep by napping during the day.

Collateral Reports

A spouse or roommate can provide invaluable information on a client's sleep pattern that can assist in both diagnosis and treatment planning. The observations of a bed partner can be especially helpful in ruling out noninsomnia causes of the client's poor sleep. A directed inquiry can help determine if the sleep complaint is caused by sleep apnea, restless legs syndrome, periodic limb movements, or parasomnia. Specific questions to ask those providing collateral information include the following:

- Does he or she snore loudly, gasp, choke, or stop breathing at night (symptoms of sleep apnea)?
- Does he or she complain of a creeping, crawling, or uncomfortable feeling in his or her limbs that is relieved by moving them (restless legs syndrome)?
- Do your spouse's legs or arms jerk repeatedly during sleep? Are you kicked in bed throughout the night (periodic limb movement)?
- Does he or she wake up during the night in a terrified state and have no memory of the event in the morning (night terrors)?

Informants can also corroborate the severity of primary insomnia symptoms. People suffering from insomnia are known to overestimate sleep onset and underestimate sleep duration (Carskadon et al., 1976). In extreme cases, it is helpful to obtain a bed partner's estimate of time to fall asleep, sleep duration, and awakenings to assess whether the client is misperceiving the state of sleep. Finally, the informant's assessment of lifestyle factors (caffeine use, alcohol consumption, exercise) and the impact of insomnia on the client (e.g., daytime fatigue) may assist in the overall evaluation and treatment planning.

As noted earlier, the PSQI includes a set of questions for bed partners to complete. Research has generally suggested that bed partner's estimates of sleep behaviors have satisfactory reliability and validity (Coates et al., 1982; Domino, Blair, & Bridges, 1984; Lacks, 1988). In research applications, the spousal version of the Sleep Impairment Index (SII; Morin, 1993) is recommended for collateral observations of insomnia. In research studies, the concordance between client and spousal ratings on the SII has ranged from very good (Bastien, Vallieres, & Morin, 2001) to poor (Currie, Malhotra, et al., 2004; Kump, Whalen, & Tishler, 1994). Currie et al. (2004) found better agreement on the SII items pertaining to sleep behaviors (e.g., time to fall asleep, frequency of awakenings), than on items assessing the consequences of insomnia (e.g., daytime fatigue). In other words, collateral informants are better at approximating the severity of nocturnal insomnia symptoms than they are with the associated daytime impairment and distress caused by the insomnia. The spousal version of the SII is sensitive to change following treatment (Currie et al., 2004; Mimeault & Morin, 1999; Morin, Colecchi, Stone, Sood, & Brink, 1999).

Determining Treatment Priorities

The treatment of insomnia should not take precedence over treating another mental disorder, particularly one that is untreated or significantly under-treated. In assigning treatment priority, it is important to consider the client's preference, the stability of the comorbid condition, and his or her ability to fully engage in behavioral treatment for insomnia. On the other hand, medical or psychiatric comorbidity does not preclude focused treatment of insomnia. Nonpharmacological treatment for insomnia can be initiated concurrently, assuming the other disorder is stable and the client is motivated to address the sleep disorder. Recent research suggests that targeting insomnia in treatment can alleviate depressive symptoms in the absence of any specific interventions for depression (Morawetz, 2003). Similarly, there is now ample evidence of efficacy in the cognitive-behavioral treatment (CBT) of secondary insomnia (Currie et al., 2000, 2004; Lichstein, McCrae, et al., 2003). If sleep-focused treatment is to be initiated, the goals of therapy and the role of the therapist should be unambiguously conveyed. Most important, treatment should be coordinated with the client's other health-care providers to avoid duplication of services.

Overall Evaluation

In contrast to the diagnostic assessment, which produces a simple dichotomous outcome (i.e., presence or absence of a sleep disorder), the case conceptualization places greater emphasis on understanding the individual's unique situation regarding the presentation and consequences of the sleep disorder. The main objective of case conceptualization is to put the sleep disorder into context by considering all of the relevant psychosocial and biological influences that may impact the presentation of disturbed sleep in the individual. All of the assessment tools described in this section should therefore be used in

an idiographic manner. Because every case is different, the functional analysis should produce a highly individualized case profile with the major precipitants and maintenance factors operating within the individual. The sleep diary is a well-regarded, evidence-based methodology that can greatly enhance the clinician's understanding of the nightly variations in sleep pattern and provide insight into factors maintaining the client's insomnia. Collateral reports provide a third party, observational perspective on the individual's habits in their natural sleep environment, affording the clinician additional insight into what is typically a private activity.

ASSESSMENT FOR TREATMENT MONITORING AND TREATMENT OUTCOME EVALUATION

The need for reliable, sensitive measures to monitor response to interventions is important in all areas of mental health, but is especially critical in the field of sleep disorders. Insomnia is often a long-standing condition that can be difficult to treat. Although CBT has been shown to be effective in treating insomnia (Morin, Hauri, et al., 1999; Sivertsen et al., 2006), very few individuals with insomnia, particularly those with other health problems, become normal sleepers following treatment (Currie, Wilson, & Curran, 2002). In general, about 40% to 50% of clients treated with behavior therapy show a clinically significant improvement in SOL (Morin et al. 1999; Murtagh & Greenwood, 1995). Hence, roughly half of treated clients continue to experience some degree of sleep impairment. Treatment outcomes require assessment instruments that can quantify severity of insomnia as a continuous variable. Instruments with the most empirical support for monitoring treatment response are detailed in Table 24.3.

Sleep Diary

Researchers and clinicians generally agree the optimal instrument for monitoring response to treatment is the sleep diary (Baker & Sederer, 2002; Chervin, 2005; Morin, 1993). This conclusion is also consistent with the AASM recommendations (Chesson et al., 2000). The sleep diary is highly sensitive to sleep interventions, including both psychological and pharmacological therapies. It also has the advantage of providing

TABLE 24.3 Ratings of Instruments Used for Treatment Monitoring and Treatment Outcome Evaluation

Instrument	Norms	Internal Consistency	Inter-Rater Reliability	Test–Retest Reliability	Content Validity	Construct Validity	Validity Generalization	Treatment Sensitivity	Clinical Utility	Highly Recommended
Sleep Diary	E	G	NA	A	A	G	E	E	E	
PSQI	G	G	NA	A	E	G	G	E	E	✓
SII	NA	G	NA	A	E	G	A	E	E	✓
Actigraph	G	G	NA	A	A	G	A	A	A	✓

Note: PSQI = Pittsburgh Sleep Quality Index; SII = Sleep Impairment Instrument (self-rated version); A = Adequate; G = Good; E = Excellent; NA = Not Applicable.

data across several dimensions of sleep behaviors. The sleep diary is highly cost-effective and is considered an integral part of CBT itself. Throughout the assessment, and certainly during treatment, clients should be asked to bring their completed diaries for review and discussion with the clinician. Regular completion of the sleep diary during treatment can potentially augment therapeutic gains, as feedback on the diary values (e.g., weekly averages for sleep measures) can be a powerful incentive for clients when making changes in their sleep habits. Clients are more motivated to implement sleep improvement techniques when they can observe improvements in their sleep. As mentioned earlier, data derived from the sleep diary has proven to be both reliable and valid (Currie, 2006; Lacks, 1988; Smith, Nowakowski, et al., 2003).

Self-Report Measures

The PSQI has been employed as an outcome measure in several insomnia treatment trials (Currie et al., 2000, 2004; Mimeault & Morin, 1999). It is sensitive to treatment effects and can be used to determine the extent of clinically significant changes in treated individuals by using a score of 6 or less on the global index as indicative of normal sleep (Currie et al., 2002). The SII (Morin, 1993) is a 7-item scale that covers similar dimensions of insomnia as the PSQI. Similar to the PSQI, the SII is also psychometrically strong (Bastien, Vallieres, & Morin, 2001) and highly sensitive to change following treatment (Morin, Colecchi, et al., 1999; Currie et al., 2004). Smith and Trinder (2001) evaluated the SII for assessing sleep in a young adult population and found that the total score correlated highly with other self-report measures and differentiated those with insomnia from good sleepers. Smith and Trinder (2001) empirically determined the optimal cutoff score (14) for identifying clinically significant insomnia. This cutoff has been used in outcome research to determine the proportion of treated people with insomnia who no longer met criteria for insomnia (Morin et al., 1999). The SII has a clinician-rated version that has also proven internally reliable and responsive to treatment effects (Currie et al., 2004).

Portable Sleep Assessment Devices

Actigraphs and similar movement-based sleep devices have become a popular alternative to PSG in research studies to assess response to treatment. The actigraph unit is a small device worn on the nondominant wrist that provides continuous recording of movement across one or more nights (Tyron, 2006). Studies have shown that low activity levels and prolonged episodes of uninterrupted immobility are associated with deep sleep, whereas high activity levels and prolonged episodes of movement are associated with intermittent wakefulness (Middlekoop, van Hilton, Kramer, & Kamphuisen, 1993; Tyron, 2006). Actigraphy provides clinicians and researchers with the means to detect and quantify human movement with the purpose of inferring states of wake or sleep from the specific pattern of movement (Smith, Smith, et al., 2003). Although information on sleep stages is not provided, the technology has an advantage over PSG in cases of insomnia because many aspects of sleep behavior can be studied unobtrusively in the client's natural sleep environment (Brooks, Friedman, Bliwise, & Yesavage, 1993; Currie et al., 2000; Sadeh, Hauri, Kripke, & Lavie, 1995). Internally, reliable estimates of common indices of insomnia severity can be produced (Sadeh et al., 1995), and these estimates are sensitive to change after treatment (Brooks et al., 1993; Currie et al., 2000). When compared to the gold standard of PSG, however, the movement-based sleep estimates from the actigraph are prone to large measurement errors. In cases of insomnia, the disagreement between actigraph and PSG estimates of sleep duration can vary from only a few minutes to well over an hour (Sadeh et al. 1995; Tyron, 2006). Actigraphs have limited value in diagnosing insomnia and their real value is the assessment of overall sleep patterns over several days and documenting change following treatment.

Actigraphs and other portable sleep assessment devices are intended to augment, rather than replace, the data from a sleep diary and other self-report measures used to monitor treatment response. The cost of the technology ($500 to $2,000 per unit depending on the vendor) is out of reach for the average mental health clinician and is rarely used by nonsleep researchers. This fact, combined with the poor concordance with other objective sleep measures, make it difficult to recommend actigraphs for routine treatment monitoring of insomnia outside of a research trial.

Overall Evaluation

Of the measures reviewed in this section, the sleep diary emerges as the method of choice for assessing response to treatment. It provides detailed, reliable data on changes following the initiation of an intervention. Daily self-monitoring can also be therapeutic on its own. During CBT for insomnia, weekly review of the sleep diary is a central component of therapy, not unlike weekly review of a thought log in CBT for depression. Clients often obtain insight into ways to improve their sleep by relating daytime routines and sleep habits to nightly variations in sleep quality and quantity. Sleep questionnaire (SII and PSQI) and portable sleep devices are also recommended assessment tools to augment data provided by a sleep diary. These instruments can also be used to determine the impact of treatment in a global fashion when sleep diary data is not available.

CONCLUSIONS AND FUTURE DIRECTIONS

Trouble sleeping is a common mental health concern. Although dozens of sleep disorders have been described in the literature, insomnia is the most prevalent among the general population. It is also one of the most challenging to assess and accurately diagnose. Insomnia can encompass a wide range of symptoms, varying degrees of functional impairment, and often co-occurs with numerous other mental and physical disorders. Determining whether a client's insomnia is a primary or secondary disorder is complicated when other mental health problems are present.

There is no literature that relates evaluation procedures for insomnia with actual outcomes of treatment (Chervin, 2005; Chesson et al., 2000). Theoretically, a better assessment protocol using valid and reliable instruments will lead to more accurate diagnosis, case conceptualization, and ultimately better treatment response (Hunsley & Mash, 2006). However, there is no systematic data comparing the impact of different assessment procedures (e.g., minimal vs. comprehensive) on outcomes. Hence, the choice of instruments can only be guided by consensus statements of experts in the field and the limitations of experience and resources facing the clinician conducting the assessment.

The practice parameters for the Evaluation of Chronic Insomnia (Chesson et al., 2000) constitutes the best advice in the field regarding evidence-based assessment of insomnia. The practice parameters are presented as general guidelines and identify few

specific instruments. Some practical advice on the use of instruments will therefore be offered. A minimal sleep assessment for clinicians who are not specialists in the field should include the use of a screening tool such as the PSQI. Clients with a high score (e.g., exceeding the cutoff of 6 for the PSQI) should be interviewed regarding the nature and severity of their sleep problems. The presentation of breathing-related symptoms, or features that are not typical of insomnia would be an indication for further assessment by a specialist in sleep disorders (PSG may be indicated in such cases). The optimal assessment procedure for clients presenting with symptoms consistent with insomnia would be the PSQI or SII, a detailed clinical interview including a functional analysis, and 2 weeks of self-monitoring using a sleep diary. Such an assessment would provide sufficient information to confirm a diagnosis of insomnia, identify the precipitating and perpetuating psychological factors, identify targets for behavior change, and establish a baseline of sleep habits before any interventions are initiated. Use of the sleep diary should continue throughout treatment to monitor improvements following interventions.

References

American Psychiatric Association (1987). *Diagnostic and statistical manual of mental disorders* (3rd ed., revised). Washington, DC: Author.

American Psychiatric Association (1994). *Diagnostic and statistical manual of mental disorders* (4th ed.). Washington, DC: Author.

American Psychiatric Association (2000). *Diagnostic and statistical manual of mental disorders* (4th ed., text revision). Washington, DC: Author.

American Sleep Disorders Association (1997). *International classification of sleep disorders: Diagnostic and coding manual.* Lawrence, KS: Allen Press Inc.

Ancoli-Israel, S., & Roth, T. (1999). Characteristics of insomnia in the United States: Results of the 1991 National Sleep Foundation Survey I. *Sleep,* 22(Suppl. 2), S347–S353.

Backhaus, J., Junghanns, K., Broocks, A., Riemann, D., & Hohagen, F. (2002). Test–retest reliability and validity of the Pittsburgh Sleep Quality Index in primary insomnia. *Journal of Psychosomatic Research, 53,* 737–740.

Baker, H., & Sederer, L. I. (2002). Outcome measurement in sleep disorders. [References]. In W. W. IsHak, T.Burt, & L. Sederer (Eds.), *Outcome measurement in psychiatry: A critical review* (pp. 259–271). Washington, DC American Psychiatric Publishing, Inc.

Balter, M. B., & Uhlenhuth, E. (1992). New epidemiologic findings about insomnia and its treatment. *Journal of Clinical Psychiatry, 53,* 34–39.

Bastien, C. H., & Morin, C. M. (2000). Familial incidence of insomnia. *Journal of Sleep Research, 9,* 49–54.

Bastien, C. H., Vallieres, A., & Morin, C. M. (2001). Validation of the Insomnia Severity Index as an outcome measure for insomnia research. *Sleep Medicine, 2,* 297–307.

Beck, A. T., Brown, G., & Steer, R. A. (1996). *Beck Depression Inventory II manual.* San Antonio, TX: The Psychological Corporation.

Beck, A. T., Epstein, N., Brown, G., & Steer, R. (1988). An inventory for measuring clinical anxiety: Psychometric properties. *Journal of Consulting and Clinical Psychology, 56,* 893–897.

Beck, S. L., Schwartz, A. L., Towsley, G., Dudley, W., & Barsevick, A. (2004). Psychometric Evaluation of the Pittsburgh Sleep Quality Index in Cancer Patients. *Journal of Pain and Symptom Management, 27,* 140–148.

Bonnet, M. H., & Arand, D. L. (1997). Physiological activation in patients with sleep state misperception. *Psychosomatic Medicine, 59,* 533–540.

Bootzin, R. R., & Engle-Friedman, M. E. (1981). The assessment of insomnia. *Behavioral Assessment, 3,* 107–126.

Bouchard, S., Bastien, C. H., & Morin, C. M. (2003). Self-efficacy and adherence to cognitive-behavioural treatment of insomnia. *Behavioural Sleep Medicine, 1,* 187–199.

Breslau, N., Roth, T., & Rosenthal, L. (1996). Sleep disturbance and psychiatric disorders: A longitudinal epidemiological study of young adults. *Biological Psychiatry, 39,* 411–418.

Brooks, J. O., Friedman, L., Bliwise, D. L., & Yesavage, J. A. (1993). Use of wrist actigraphs to study insomnia in older adults. *Sleep, 16,* 151–155.

Brower, K. J. (2001). Alcohol's effects on sleep in alcoholics. *Alcohol Health and Research World, 25,* 110–125.

Buysse, D. J., Germain, A., Moul, D., & Nofzinger, E. A. (2005). Insomnia. In D. Buysse (Ed.), *Sleep disorders and psychiatry* (pp. 29–75). Washington, DC: American Psychiatric Publishing, Inc.

Buysse, D. J., Reynolds, C. F., Monk, T. H., Berman, S. R., & Kupfer, D. J. (1989). The Pittsburgh Sleep Quality Index: A new instrument for psychiatric practice and research. *Psychiatry Research, 28,* 193–213.

Carpenter, J. S., & Andrykowski, M. A. (1998). Psychometric evaluation of the Pittsburgh Sleep Quality Index. *Journal of Psychosomatic Research, 45,* 5–13.

Carskadon, M. A., Dement, W. C., Mitler, M. M., Guilleminault, C., Zarcone, V. P., & Spiegel, R. (1976). Self-reports versus sleep laboratory findings in 122 drug-free subjects with complaints of chronic insomnia. *American Journal of Psychiatry, 133,* 1382–1388.

Chang, P., Ford, D. E., & Mead, L. A. (1997). Insomnia in young men and subsequent depression: The Johns Hopkins Precursors Study. *American Journal of Epidemiology, 146,* 105–114.

Chervin, R. D. (2005). Use of clinical tools and tests in sleep medicine. In M. H. Kryger, T. Roth, & W. C. Dement (Eds.), *Principles and practice of sleep medicine* (4th ed., pp. 602–614). Toronto: W. B. Saunders Company.

Chesson, A., Hartse, K., Anderson, W. M., Davila, D., Johnson, S., Littner, M., et al. (2000). Practice parameters for the evaluation of chronic insomnia. *Sleep, 23,* 237–241.

Chilcott, L. A., & Shapiro, C. M. (1996). The socioeconomic impact of insomnia: An overview. *PharmacoEconomics, 10,* 1–14.

Coates, T. J., Killen, J. D., George, J., Marchini, E., Silverman, S., & Thoresen, C. (1982). Estimating sleep parameters: A multitrait-multimethod analysis. *Journal of Consulting and Clinical Psychology, 50,* 345–352.

Currie, S. R. (2006). Sleep dysfunction. In M. Hersen (Ed.), *Clinician's handbook of adult behavioural assessment* (pp. 401–430). New York: Elsevier Inc.

Currie, S. R., Clark, S., Hodgins, D. C., & el-Guebaly, N. (2004). Randomized controlled trial of brief cognitive-behavioural interventions for insomnia in recovering alcoholics. *Addiction, 99,* 1121–1132.

Currie, S. R., Clark, S., Rimac, S., & Malhotra, S. D. (2003). Comprehensive assessment of insomnia in recovering alcoholics using daily sleep diaries and ambulatory monitoring. *Alcoholism: Clinical and Experimental Research, 27,* 1262–1270.

Currie, S. R., Malhotra, S. D., & Clark, S. (2004). Agreement among objective, subjective, and collateral reports of poor sleep in recovering alcoholics. *Behavioral Sleep Medicine, 2,* 148–161.

Currie, S. R., Wilson, K. G., & Curran, D. (2002). Clinical significance and predictors of treatment response to cognitive-behaviour therapy for insomnia secondary to chronic pain. *Journal of Behavioural Medicine, 25,* 135–153.

Currie, S. R., Wilson, K. G., Pontefract, A. J., & deLaplante, L. (2000). Cognitive-behavioural treatment of insomnia secondary to chronic pain. *Journal of Consulting and Clinical Psychology, 68,* 407–416.

Domino, G., Blair, G., & Bridges, A. (1984). Subjective assessment of sleep by sleep questionnaire. *Perceptual and Motor Skills, 59,* 163–170.

Edinger, J. D., & Fins, A. I. (1995). The distribution and clinical significance of sleep time misperceptions among insomniacs. *Sleep, 18,* 232–239.

Edinger, J. D., Wohlgemuth, W. K., Radtke, R. A., Marsh, G. R., & Quillian, R. E. (2001). Cognitive behavioural therapy for treatment of chronic primary insomnia: A randomized controlled trial. *Journal of the American Medical Association, 285,* 1856–1864.

Espie, C. A. (1991). *The psychological management of insomnia.* Chichester, England: Wiley.

Espie, C. A., Inglis, S. J., Tessier, S., & Harvey, L. (2001). The clinical effectiveness of cognitive behaviour therapy for chronic insomnia: Implementation and evaluation of a sleep clinic in general medical practice. *Behaviour Research and Therapy, 39,* 45–60.

Fichten, C. S., Creti, L., Amsel, R., Brender, W., Weinstein, N., & Libman, E. (1995). Poor sleepers who do not complain of insomnia: Myths and realities about psychological and lifestyle characteristics of older good and poor sleepers. *Journal of Behavioural Medicine, 18,* 189–223.

First, M. B., Spitzer, R. L., Gibbon, M., & Williams, J. B. W. (1995). *Structured Clinical Interview for DSM-IV Axis I disorders.* Washington, DC: American Psychiatric Association.

Ford, D. E., & Kamerow, D. B. (1989). Epidemiological study of sleep disturbances and psychiatric disorders. *Journal of the American Medical Association, 262,* 1479–1484.

Gehrman, P., Matt, G., Turingan, M., Dinh, Q., & Ancoli-Israel, S. (2002). Towards an understanding of self-reports of sleep. *Journal of Sleep Research, 11,* 229–236.

Harvey, A. (2001). Insomnia: Symptom or diagnosis? *Clinical Psychology Review, 21,* 1037–1059.

Harvey, A. (2002). A cognitive model of insomnia. *Behaviour Research and Therapy, 40,* 869–894.

Haythornthwaite, J. A., Hegel, M. T., & Kerns, R. D. (1991). Development of a sleep diary for chronic pain patients. *Journal of Pain and Symptom Management, 6,* 65–72.

Hoddes, E., Zarcone, V., Smythe, H., Phillips, R., & Dement, W. C. (1973). Quantification of sleepiness: A new approach. *Psychophysiology, 10,* 431–436.

Hunsley, J., & Mash, E. J. (2006). Introduction to the special section on developing guidelines for the evidence-based assessment (EBA) of adult disorders. *Journal of Consulting and Clinical Psychology, 17,* 251–255.

Johns, M. W. (1991). A new method for measuring daytime sleepiness: The Epworth Sleepiness Scale. *Sleep, 14,* 540–545.

Kaplan, H. I., & Sadock, B. J. (2002). *Synopsis of psychiatry* (9th ed.). Baltimore, MD: Lippincott Williams & Wilkins.

Kump, K., Whalen, C., & Tishler, P. V. (1994). Assessment of the validity and utility of a sleep-symptom questionnaire (p. 542). *Amercian Journal of Respiratory Critical Care, 150,* 735–741.

Lacks, P. (1987). *Behavioural treatment for persistent insomnia.* Toronto, ON: Pergamon Press.

Lacks, P. (1988). Daily sleep diary. In M. Hersen & A. S. Bellack (Eds.), *Dictionary of behavioural assessment techniques* (pp. 162–164). New York: Pergamon.

Lacks, P., & Morin, C. M. (1992). Recent advances in the assessment and treatment of insomnia. *Journal of Consulting and Clinical Psychology, 60,* 586–594.

Lichstein, K. L., Durrence, H. H., Riedel, B. W., Taylor, D. J., & Bush, A. J. (2004). *Epidemiology of sleep.* Mahwah, NJ: Laurence Erlbaum Associates.

Lichstein, K. L., Durrence, H. H., Taylor, D. J., Bush, A. J., & Riedel, B. W. (2003). Quantitative criteria for insomnia. *Behaviour Research and Therapy, 41,* 427–455.

Lichstein, K. L., McCrae, C. S., & Wilson, N. M. (2003). Secondary insomnia: Diagnostic issues, cognitive-behavioural treatment, and future directions. In M. L. Perlis & K. L. Lichstein (Eds.), *Treating sleep disorders: Principles and practice of behavioural sleep medicine* (pp. 286–304). Toronto: John Wiley & Sons Canada, Ltd.

Lineberger, M. D., Carney, C. E., Edinger, J. D., & Means, M. K. (2006). Defining insomnia: Quantitative criteria for insomnia severity and frequency. *Sleep: Journal of Sleep and Sleep Disorders Research, 29,* 479–485.

McCall, W. V., & Reynolds, D. (2000). Psychiatric disorders and insomnia. In M. H. Kryger, T. Roth, & W. C. Dement (Eds.), *Principles and Practice of Sleep Medicine* (3rd ed., pp. 640–646). Toronto: W. B. Saunders Company.

Middlekoop, H. A. M., Van Hilton, B. J., Kramer, C. G. S., & Kamphuisen, H. A. C. (1993). Actigraphically recorded motor activity and immobility across sleep cycles and stages in healthy male participants. *Journal of Sleep Research, 2,* 28–33.

Mimeault, V., & Morin, C. M. (1999). Self-help treatment for insomnia: Bibliotherapy with and without professional guidance. *Journal of Consulting and Clinical Psychology, 67,* 511–519.

Montplaisir, J., Nicolas, A., Godbout, R., & Walters, A. (2005). Restless legs syndrome and periodic limb movement disorders. In M. H. Kryger, T. Roth, & W. C. Dement (Eds.), *Principles and practice of sleep medicine* (4th ed., pp. 839–852). Toronto: W. B. Saunders Company.

Morawetz, D. (2003). Insomnia and depression: Which came first? *Sleep Research Online, 5*, 77–81.

Morin, C. M. (1993). *Insomnia: Psychological assessment and management.* New York: The Guilford Press.

Morin, C. M. (2000). The nature of insomnia and the need to refine our diagnostic criteria. *Psychosomatic Medicine, 62*, 483–485.

Morin, C. M., Bastien, C., & Savard, J. (2003). Current status of cognitive-behavior therapy for insomnia: Evidence for treatment effectiveness and feasibility. In M. L. Perlis & K. L. Lichstein (Eds.), *Treating sleep disorders: Principles and practice of behavioral sleep medicine* (1st ed., pp. 262–285). Toronto: John Wiley & Sons Canada Ltd.

Morin, C. M., Colecchi, C., Stone, J., Sood, R., & Brink, D. (1999). Behavioural and pharmacological therapies for late-life insomnia: A randomized controlled trial. *Journal of the American Medical Association, 281*, 991–999.

Morin, C. M., Hauri, P. J., Espie, C. A., Spielman, A. J., Buysse, D., & Bootzin, R. R. (1999). Nonpharmacologic treatment of chronic insomnia. *Sleep, 22*, 1134–1156.

Murtagh, D. R. R., & Greenwood, K. M. (1995). Identifying effective psychological treatments for insomnia: A meta-analysis. *Journal of Consulting and Clinical Psychology, 63*, 79–89.

Ohayon, M. (2002). Epidemiology of insomnia: What we know and what we still need to learn. *Sleep Medicine Reviews, 6*, 97–111.

Ollendick, T. H., Alvarez, H. K., & Greene, R. W. (2004). Behavioural assessment: History of underlying concepts and methods. In M. Hersen (Ed.), *Comprehensive handbook of psychological assessment: Behavioural assessment* (pp. 19–34). Hoboken, NJ: John Wiley & Sons, Inc.

Partinen, M., & Hublin, C. (2005). Epidemiology of Sleep Disorders. In M. H. Kryger, T. Roth, & W. C. Dement (Eds.), *Principles and practice of sleep medicine* (4th ed., pp. 626–647). Toronto: W. B. Saunders Company.

Pilowsky, I., Crettenden, I., & Townley, M. (1985). Sleep disturbance in pain clinic patients. *Pain, 23*, 27–33.

Rechtschaffen, A., & Kales, A. (1968). *A manual of standardized terminology, techniques, and scoring system for sleep stages of human subjects.* Los Angeles: BIS/BRI, UCLA.

Reite, M., Buysse, D., Reynolds, C., & Mendelson, W. (1995). The use of polysomnography in the evaluation of insomnia. *Sleep, 18*, 58–70.

Rosa, R. R., & Bonnet, M. H. (2000). Reported insomnia is independent of poor sleep as measured by electroencephalography. *Psychosomatic Medicine, 62*, 474–482.

Roth, T. (2004). Measuring treatment efficacy in insomnia. *Journal of Clinical Psychology, 65*(Suppl. 8), 8–12.

Sadeh, A., Hauri, P. J., Kripke, D. F., & Lavie, P. (1995). The role of actigraphy in the evaluation of sleep disorders. *Sleep, 18*, 288–302.

Sateia, M. J., Doghramji, K., Hauri, P. J., & Morin, C. M. (2000). Evaluation of chronic insomnia. *Sleep, 23*, 243–308.

Schramm, E., Hohagen, F., Grasshoff, U., Riemann, D., Hajak, G., Hans-Gunther, W., et al. (1993). Test–retest reliability and validity of the structured interview for sleep disorders according to DSM-III-R. *American Journal of Psychiatry, 150*, 867–872.

Simon, A., & Von Korff, M. (1997). Prevalence, burden, and treatment of insomnia in primary care. *American Journal of Psychiatry, 154*, 1417–1423.

Sivertsen, B., Omvik, S., Pallesen, S., Bjorvatn, B., Havik, O. E., Kvale, G., et al. (2006). Cognitive behavioral therapy vs. zopiclone for treatment of chronic primary insomnia in older adults: A randomized controlled trial. *Journal of the American Medical Association, 295*, 2851–2858.

Smith, L. J., Nowakowski, S., Soeffing, J. P., Orff, H. J., & Perlis, M. L. (2003). The measurement of sleep. In M. L. Perlis & K. L. Lichstein (Eds.), *Treating sleep disorders: Principles and practice of behavioural sleep medicine* (pp. 29–73). Toronto, ON: John Wiley & Sons.

Smith, L. J., Smith, L. J., Nowakowski, S., & Perlis, M. L. (2003). Primary insomnia: diagnostic issues, treatment, and future directions. In M. L. Perlis & K. L. Lichstein (Eds.), *Treating sleep disorders: Principles and practice of behavioural sleep medicine* (pp. 214–261). Toronto: John Wiley & Sons Canada, Ltd.

Smith, S., & Trinder, J. (2001). Detecting insomnia: Comparison of four self-report measures of sleep in a young adult population. *Journal of Sleep Research, 10*, 229–235.

Stone, A. A., Shiffman, S., Schwartz, J. E., & Hufford, M. R. (2002). Patient non-compliance with paper diaries. *British Medical Journal, 324*, 1193–1194.

Thorpy, M. J. (2005). Classification of sleep disorders. In M. H. Kryger, T. Roth, & W. C. Dement (Eds.), *Principles and practice of sleep medicine* (4th ed., pp. 615–625). Toronto: W. B. Saunders Company.

Tryon, W. (2006). Activity measurement. In M. Hersen (Ed.), *Clinician's handbook of adult behavioral assessment* (pp. 85–113). San Diego, CA.: Elsevier Academic Press.

Tsai, P. S., Wang, S. Y., Wang, M. Y., Su, C. T., Yang, T. T., Huang, C. J., et al. (2005). Psychometric evaluation of the Chinese version of the Pittsburgh Sleep Quality Index (CPSQI) in primary insomnia and control subjects. *Quality of Life Research: An International Journal of Quality of Life Aspects of Treatment, Care & Rehabilitation, 14,* 1943–1952.

Üstün, T. B., Privett, M., Lecrubier, Y., Weiller, E., Simon, A., Korten, A., et al. (1996). Form, frequency, and burden of sleep problems in general health care: A report from the WHO Collaborative Study on Psychological Problems in General Health Care. *European Psychiatry, 11*(Suppl. 1), 5S–10S.

Weissman, M. M., Greenwald, S., Nino-Murcia, G., & Dement, W. C. (1997). The morbidity of insomnia uncomplicated by psychiatric disorders. *General Hospital Psychiatry, 19,* 245–250.

Wong, M. M., Brower, K. J., Fitzgerald, H. E., & Zucker, R. A. (2004). Sleep problems in early childhood and early onset of alcohol and other drug use in adolescence. *Alcoholism: Clinical and Experimental Research, 28,* 578–587.

Zammit, G. K., Weiner, J., & Damato, N. (1999). Quality of life in people with insomnia. *Sleep, 22*(Suppl. 2), 379–385.

25

Child and Adolescent Pain

Erin C. Moon

C. Meghan McMurtry

Patrick J. McGrath

The International Association for the study of pain defines pain as "an unpleasant sensory and emotional experience associated with actual or potential tissue damage, or described in terms of such damage" (Merskey & Bogduk, 1994, p. 210). The definition goes on to assert that pain is always subjective and always a psychological state. This definition is very widely accepted and serves as the starting point for all pain assessment. There has been an explosion of research in the scientific study of pain and its measurement in children and youth. One of the most important findings has been that pain is much more complex than was thought 50 years ago. The beginning of the modern era of pain research can be marked by Melzack and Wall's (1965) seminal paper proposing the Gate Control Theory of pain. They posited that pain was modulated by "gates" in the spinal cord, by descending signals from the brain, and by peripheral stimulation. More recently, both peripheral and central sensitization have been described (Taddio & Katz, 2005). In effect, our bodies have a memory for pain so that one experience of pain will trigger more pain during later experiences (Taddio, Katz, Illersich, & Koren, 1997). Rather than "getting used to" pain, we (and children and adolescents) actually become more sensitive to it (Fradet, McGrath, Kay, Adams, & Luke, 1990).

We now have sophisticated measures for many clinical situations and reasonable treatments for some types of pain (e.g., acute). However, the fact remains that many children and adolescents continue to suffer from inadequately treated acute and chronic/recurrent pain (Cummings et al., 1996; Perquin et al., 2000). Chronic pain, when severe and persistent, is soul-destroying (Angell, 1982) and requires the most aggressive, immediate, and effective relief. This relief can be difficult to achieve in the clinic as the causes of chronic pain are often unknown, its trajectory is difficult to predict, our assessments are inadequate, and our treatments are of limited utility.

Pain measurement is the application of some metric to a specific aspect of pain. Assessment is much broader than measurement and includes the selection of what aspects of pain to measure and what measures to use (McGrath & Unruh, 1987). Most commonly, the focus is on intensity of pain; however, its measurement fails to capture the overall experience of pain. Recently, the Initiative on Methods, Measurement, and Pain Assessment in Clinical Trials (IMMPACT; McGrath et al., 2006) has suggested that in addition to pain intensity, several other domains should be considered when developing measurement strategies for clinical trials focusing on pain in children and adolescents. These domains include global judgment of satisfaction with treatment, symptoms and adverse events, physical recovery, emotional response, economic factors, role functioning, and sleep. One strategy to capture the relevant domains is to use a standard battery of questions (e.g., Varni, Seid, & Kurtin, 2001). An alternative assessment strategy is to select specific measures for each aspect of the pain experience that is to be measured. Regardless of the method, the first step in the effective management of pain in children and adolescents is an evidence-based assessment.

In this chapter, we will review the pediatric pain assessment literature and provide recommendations for assessment tools that have demonstrated utility and feasibility in clinical settings or hold promise as clinical assessment tools. Assessment tools in pediatric pain can be thought of as behavioral (observational), physiological, self-report (Walco, Conte, Labay, Engel, & Zeltzer, 2005), or some combination of the three. For a systematic review of observational measures of pain for children and adolescents, the reader is directed to a recent article by von Baeyer and Spagrud (2007). Researchers have used physiological methods (such as heart rate and vagal tone) for measuring pain in very young children (infants in particular) but these methods are rarely used in clinical care outside of neonatal intensive care units. Furthermore, the output from these physiologically based assessments (e.g., heart rate) may reflect other biological states (e.g., arousal) rather than pain specifically. For more information, the reader is directed to a chapter by Sweet and McGrath (1998) on physiological measures of pain in children. The present chapter will focus on the assessment of pain in children between the ages of 3 and 18 years without severe cognitive impairment. The assessment of pain in cognitively impaired children is beyond the scope of this chapter and the reader is referred to a recent volume by Oberlander and Symons (2006). In recent times, the knowledge base in neonatal pain has expanded dramatically (Anand, Stevens, & McGrath, 2007). As assessment of pain in infants is quite specialized and differs from that in children and adolescents, it and will not be covered in this chapter.

As pain is always a subjective experience, self-report is often considered the "gold standard" in pain assessment. However, this view is somewhat controversial because self-report tools have a number of limitations (e.g., Craig, Lilley, & Gilbert, 1996; von Baeyer, 2006). For example, these tools require fairly sophisticated cognitive and communication abilities and ratings on them are likely influenced by self-interests (e.g., von Baeyer, 2006; Craig, Lilley, & Gilbert, 1996). Consider, a child who knows he/she will receive medication intravenously and under-reports his/her pain to avoid the needle (Eland & Anderson, 1977). Ideally, a thorough pain assessment would utilize a combination of behavioral and self-report tools. Unfortunately, in general clinical practice this is often not feasible. Many self-report tools have the advantage of being quick and cost-effective to administer in clinical settings. As such, they have received the most research attention and many have undergone rigorous psychometric testing. Therefore,

we will focus our review on self-report tools. When relevant, we will also discuss parental reports of child functioning and parental proxy reports of child pain.

Our discussion of the pediatric pain assessment literature is tailored to mental health professionals such as clinical psychologists, social workers, and psychiatrists working in various settings with children who suffer from pain. Although our recommendations may also help to guide other health-care professionals in their assessments of pediatric pain, we will not discuss pediatric pain assessment from a medical standpoint. The role of mental health practitioners in the assessment of pediatric pain is multifaceted and varies from setting to setting. However, mental health practitioners working with children and adolescents in pain are united by a focus that extends beyond assessing simple pain perception. They also examine the effects of pain on the functioning of children, adolescents, and their families across a wide variety of domains, such as physical, emotional, and social role functioning. For this reason, mental health practitioners require assessment tools that span all of these domains.

THE NATURE OF PAIN

The World Health Organization's International Classification of Functioning, Disability and Health (WHO, 2001) incorporates functioning, disability, as well as contextual factors that affect health. This system provides a useful framework for pain assessment (Matthews, McGrath, & Pigeon, 1993; McGrath & Unruh, 1987). In the first part of this classification system, body functions and structures, as well as activities and participation in various areas of life are taken into account. At the second level of classification, environmental and personal factors related to health are considered. As defined by the WHO classification system, body structures are the anatomical parts of the body such as organs, limbs, and their components. This chapter will not address the impairments in body structures underlying various pain conditions. Body functions refer to the physiological functions of body systems, including psychological functions. The experience of pain is both physiological and psychological; therefore, pain perception fits at the body functions level of the WHO classification system. In the area of pediatric psychology, much of the pain assessment literature to date focuses on pain perception. Although a comprehensive assessment of pediatric pain includes measures of pain perception, it is vital to include measures of how pain impacts daily activities and role functioning to fully understand the experience of children and adolescents who suffer from pain. It is also important to consider the environmental and personal factors that influence children's pain experiences.

Measurement and assessment of pain in children and adolescents must be considered within a developmental context for several reasons. First, there are developmental factors in the occurrence of different pains. For example, recurrent abdominal pain peaks at about 9 years of age (Apley, 1975) and migraine increases sharply after puberty, especially in females (Unruh & Campbell, 1999). Second, development limits children's understanding of pain. An 18-month-old child is unlikely to understand why he/she should receive a needle for a vaccination whereas an 11-year-old child can understand the reasons. Third, development is also a limiting factor in the use of self-report measures. Many children below 5 or 6 years of age cannot consistently use self-report measures for pain or show response biases such as endorsing the extremes of a scale (Chambers & Johnston, 2002). Conversely, older children may inhibit behavioral responses to pain and thus make observational measures less useful as the child grows up. In this chapter, we will focus on measures that have demonstrated validity across a broad age range (from 3 through 18 years). However, we have kept developmental factors in mind while formulating our recommendations.

Pain can be categorized in terms of its cause(s). Pain in children and adolescents can arise from medical procedures such as needles or surgery and can also be caused by disease or trauma. Some diseases such as sickle cell disease or juvenile arthritis frequently cause pain, but the amount of pain often does not correspond to the severity of the underlying disease. The origin of pain may also be unknown—a large proportion of children who attend pediatric pain clinics suffer from pain of unknown origin. Unfortunately, when the cause of pain cannot be ascertained, it is often assumed to be the result of psychological factors. This is an unfortunate and pernicious strategy because it alienates patients who believe they are being blamed for their pain and that they are being told their pain "is all in their head." This "leap to the head," as Wall (1989) called it, is not scientifically justified because there is seldom any positive evidence of psychological causation. However, psychological factors are important in the experience of chronic pain even when pain is of a known physiological cause.

Pain may also be categorized in terms of its time course, such as acute, recurrent, or chronic. Acute pain can be divided into short sharp pain that may last a few seconds to a few minutes and longer-lasting acute pain that may last from hours to days. Postoperative pain and pain from injuries are the most common longer-lasting acute pain. Examples of short sharp pain include pain from everyday accidents such as stubbing a toe or skinning a knee. Clinical short sharp pain is typically from medical procedures, such as needles that are inserted intravenously, intramuscularly, or subcutaneously or the insertion or removal of a chest tube. Recurrent pain is episodic. There may be bouts of pain interspersed with either pain-free or low pain periods of time. The most common clinically significant recurrent pains in children and adolescents are headache, abdominal pain, and limb pain (Perquin et al., 2000). Children who have severe interference with their normal activities and long-lasting pain are often described as having chronic pain. An example would be an adolescent who is missing school regularly because of migraine headaches. The term chronic pain is usually defined as continuous or near continuous pain that has lasted for 3 months or more beyond the expected period of healing (Merskey & Bogduk, 1994).

ASSESSMENT FOR DIAGNOSIS

As mentioned, most clinical short sharp pain is iatrogenic and of known cause (e.g., from a needle or a surgical procedure such as a tonsillectomy). Although a variety of acute pain perception measures have been empirically validated for use with children and adolescents undergoing medical procedures, these measures are not usually applied in standard clinical care. However, this type of pain assessment may be clinically relevant with children who undergo repeated acutely painful medical procedures, such as children with cancer or diabetes who require numerous needle sticks for blood work or intravenous line starts. Pain from needles or other invasive procedures does occur and should be minimized through the use of topical anesthetics and/or psychological interventions. With respect to the diagnosis of recurrent and chronic pain, there are several parameters of pain that are useful

TABLE 25.1 Ratings of Instruments Used for Diagnosis

Instrument	Norms	Internal Consistency	Inter-Rater Reliability	Test–Retest Reliability	Content Validity	Construct Validity	Validity Generalization	Clinical Utility	Highly Recommended
Pieces of Hurt Tool	NA	NA	NA	NA	A	G	G	G	✓
The Oucher	NA	NA	NA	NA	G	G	A	G	
FPS-R	NA	NA	NA	NA	A	G	E	G	✓
Visual analogue scales	NA	NA	NA	NA	NA	A	G	A	✓
APPT	NA	NA	NA	A	G	G	E	A	✓

Note: FPS-R = Faces Pain Scale-Revised; APPT = the Adolescent Pediatric Pain Tool; A = Adequate; G = Good; E = Excellent; NA = Not Applicable.

Pain Intensity

to consider, including pain intensity, localization, quality, frequency, and duration. Table 25.1 provides summary information on measures designed to assess some of these constructs.

Sensory intensity is often one of the first dimensions of pain assessed by clinicians. It is vital for clinicians to obtain quantitative ratings of intensity in order to understand the extent of children's pain. Although pain intensity measures are discussed in this section, these measures are also valuable for treatment planning and monitoring treatment effectiveness. In our discussion and in the information summarized in Table 25.1 the reader will note that we have not provided ratings for the internal consistency, test–retest reliability or inter-rater reliability of these measures. These tools are all single-item measures of a subjective and ever-fluctuating state; therefore, conventional indices of reliability are not generally applicable.

In addition, the meaning of norms for measures of pain is an interesting issue. In general, a pain-free state is the norm. Norms for painful conditions have little meaning because pain problems vary considerably. There is little meaning to the intensity of an average migraine headache. What would be of interest, but is not currently available, is the typical intensity, duration, and frequency of pain that produces a given level of functional disability. These are judgments that clinicians and parents make all the time without good normative data. The judgments are likely accurate in most situations. For example, the judgment that it is not "normal" for a 14-year-old girl with menstrual pain to miss 2 days of school each month is almost certainly statistically true. But, how severe might the pain have to be to make school absence typical and thus normative (even if it is not helpful)?

We do not yet have data to answer these types of questions and, therefore, we have not provided ratings of the availability of norms for the pain intensity measures we discuss.

Pieces of Hurt Tool

The Pieces of Hurt Tool (sometimes called the Poker Chip Tool; Hester, 1979) is a concrete ordinal rating tool. This tool consists of four plastic poker chips that represent "pieces of hurt." When the tool is administered, the child is asked, "did/does it hurt?" If the child says "no," a score of zero is recorded. If the child says "yes," he/she is asked to indicate his/her pain intensity by selecting between one and four poker chips, with one chip representing "a little hurt" and four chips representing "the most hurt." The number of chips selected is the child's score.

Psychometric data indicates that the Pieces of Hurt Tool is a valid self-report measure of child pain intensity (Stinson, Kavanaugh, Yamada, Gill, & Stevens, 2006a). It has adequate content validity (Hester, 1979) and good construct validity. It has been shown to correlate strongly with other pain intensity measures, such as vocal and verbal responses to pain on an observational scale (Hester, 1979), the Wong-Baker FACES Pain Scale, (Gharaibeh & Abu-Saad, 2002), the Faces Pain Scale (Goodenough et al., 1997), the Oucher (Beyer & Aradine, 1987, 1988) and verbal rating scales (Gharaibeh & Abu-Saad, 2002; Goodenough et al., 1997; Suraseranivongse et al., 2005). Evidence of discriminant validity is provided by a study in which it was found to have low correlations with two measures of fear (Beyer & Aradine, 1988).

In terms of validity generalization, the Pieces of Hurt Tool has been studied with children between the ages of 3 and 18 years (Stinson et al., 2006a) and has been used with hospitalized children (Beyer

& Aradine, 1987, 1988) and children with postoperative pain (Aradine, Beyer, & Tompkins, 1988; Suraseranivongse et al., 2005), as well as children undergoing venipunctures (Gharaibeh & Abu-Saad, 2002) and immunizations (Goodenough et al., 1997; Hester, 1979). The Pieces of Hurt Tool has been translated and validated for use with children in Thailand (Suraseranivongse et al., 2005) and Jordan (Gharaibeh & Abu-Saad, 2002).

The advantages of the Pieces of Hurt Tool include the fact that it is scored on a concrete ordinal rating scale. This type of scale is appealing for use with children because concrete representations (poker chips) enhance children's ability to understand the concept of levels of hurt/pain (Stinson et al., 2006a). The disadvantages include the need to sterilize the chips after each use and its rating scale, which ranges from 0 to 4, differs from the 0 to 10 scale widely accepted among pediatric pain researchers. The Pieces of Hurt Tool has the best psychometric evidence for use with preschool-aged children who have acute pain from medical procedures (Stinson et al., 2006a). We recommend it for use with children between the ages of 3 and 7 suffering from acute pain, as it requires further testing in preschool-aged children and children with chronic pain (Stinson et al., 2006a).

The Oucher

The Oucher (Beyer, 1984) consists of two separate scales in a poster format: a 0-to-100 numerical scale for older children and a photographic faces scale for younger children. The photographic scale is scored from 0 to 5 whereas the numerical scale is scored from 0 to 100. The original Oucher photographic scale shows the face of a 4-year-old Caucasian boy in increasing levels of discomfort, from "no hurt" to "the biggest hurt you could ever have." African American and Hispanic versions of the Oucher are available (Villaruel & Denyes, 1991), and a modified Asian version of the Oucher (with a numerical scale that ranges from 0 to 10) has also been developed (Yeh, 2005).

Extensive psychometric research has been carried out on the Oucher (Stinson et al., 2006a). Similar to other measures of child pain intensity, it does not lend itself to traditional examinations of reliability. However, Belter, McIntosh, Finch, and Saylor (1988) assessed reliability indirectly by asking young children to rate the intensity of pain depicted in various cartoon scenes. These authors found low to moderate

levels of test–retest reliability for the Oucher. Luffy and Grove (2003) also obtained ratings of test–retest reliability on the African American version by asking children to rate the pain they experienced from two past medical procedures/treatments. These authors reported a test–retest reliability score of $r = .70$.

A number of studies indicate that the Oucher is a valid measure of pediatric pain intensity. In terms of content validity, the conceptual framework behind the Oucher was clearly defined and informed each step in its creation (Beyer, Denyes, & Villaruel, 1992). It has been shown that 3- to 7-year-old children show strong agreement with the order of the six original photographs (Beyer & Aradine, 1986). Content validity has also been established for the African American, Hispanic, and Asian versions (Villarruel & Denyes, 1991; Yeh, 2005). The construct validity of the original Oucher is supported by a study carried out by Beyer and Aradine (1988), in which correlations with the Pieces of Hurt Tool and a visual analogue scale were strong and positive in a group of hospitalized children. Evidence for discriminant validity is provided by data showing low correlations between scores on this measure and two measures of children's fears (Beyer & Aradine, 1988). Similar evidence of convergent and discriminant validity has been found for the African American, Hispanic, and Asian versions (Beyer & Knott, 1998; Yeh, 2005).

There is evidence to support the use of the Oucher with hospitalized children (Beyer & Aradine, 1987, 1988) and children suffering from postoperative pain (Beyer & Knott, 1998; Ramritu, 2000). It has been validated with Caucasian, African American, and Hispanic children between the ages of 3 and 12 years (Beyer & Knott, 1998). In terms of patient preference, the data are inconclusive. In a study by Ramritu (2000), the majority of older school-age children preferred the Oucher numerical scale to a word-graphic scale. On the other hand, Luffy and Grove (2003) found that in a sample of African American children between the ages of 3 and 18 years, most children preferred the Wong-Baker FACES Pain Scale to the African American version of the Oucher.

One of the main advantages of the Oucher is that it is culturally sensitive. On the other hand, all versions depict male children and there is some informal evidence that female children may have difficulty relating to the photographs of male children, making it more difficult for them to use the scale (Beyer et al., 1992). Two factors to keep in mind for clinical use are the need to clean the laminated poster in between assessment sessions and its cost (currently about $3 USD; Stinson et al., 2006a).

In concordance with the systematic review conducted by Stinson and her colleagues (2006a), we recommend the numerical scale of the Oucher for use with children between the ages of 6 and 12 years, as it requires further psychometric testing with very young children (i.e., age 3 to 4 years; Stinson et al., 2006a). We also suggest that the photographic scale of the Oucher may be used with children between 3 and 6 years old who are not able to use the numerical scale. To determine which version a child should use, it is recommended that clinicians ask the child to count from 1 to 100 by ones, state which of two numbers is larger, and complete a seriation task (such as sequencing six equilateral triangles of increasing size). If the child completes all three tasks successfully, he/she should use the numerical scale; if not, he/she should use the photographic scale (Beyer et al., 1992).

Faces Pain Scale-Revised

The early development of the ability to recognize facial expressions of emotion may make it easier for children to use scales with faces that are also more concrete than abstract formats such as visual analogue scales and numerical rating scales (Bieri, Reeve, Champion, Addicoat, & Ziegler, 1990). However, to use a faces scale, children are still required to match their internal feelings of pain to a given face on the scale (Hicks, von Baeyer, Spafford, van Korlaar, & Goodenough, 2001). The Faces Pain Scale-Revised (FPS-R; Hicks et al, 2001) is a single-item self-report measure of pain intensity. The scale shows a series of six faces ranging from a neutral face showing "no pain" to a face showing "very much pain." The child is asked to rate his/her pain by indicating which face shows how much pain (hurt) he/she has. The FPS-R is based on the Faces Pain Scale developed by Bieri and colleagues (Bieri et al., 1990). The original version of the scale contains seven faces and is scored from 0 to 6 whereas the FPS-R has six faces and is scored from 0 to 10. The FPS-R was designed to provide a metric common to that employed in other pain measures (i.e., 0 to 5; 0 to 10). Empirical evidence indicates that the FPS-R is a psychometrically sound scale (Stinson et al., 2006a). In fact, in a recent systematic review, the FPS-R was recommended as a self-report measure of acute pain intensity in clinical trials for children between 4 and 12 years (Stinson et al., 2006a).

In terms of content validity, the faces for the original version of the scale were based on children's drawings of increasing pain expressions (Bieri et al., 1990). The six faces for the FPS-R were produced through a magnitude production task in which adults were asked to match faces to a given pain intensity (Hicks et al., 2001). Results of this task supported linear progression of the faces with an adult population.

The FPS-R has generally shown strong convergent validity with other measures of pain intensity including visual analogue scales (Hicks et al., 2001; Newman et al., 2005), the Wong-Baker FACES Pain Scale (Newman et al., 2005), as well as the Colored Analogue Scale (Hicks et al., 2001; Miro & Huguet, 2004). This convergent validity has even been shown with younger children (4 to 6 years old) who are sometimes thought to provide inconsistent ratings (Hicks et al., 2001). Discriminant validity of the FPS-R has been supported by comparisons between it and measures of pain intensity versus pain affect (Miro & Huguet, 2004).

Although most conventional indices of reliability are inapplicable for the FPS-R, parents' ratings using the FPS-R have been found to relate significantly to their children's self-report scores (e.g., Wood et al., 2004). Test–retest reliability (stability) was examined by Miro and Huguet (2004) by asking school children to rate pain intensity in response to hypothetical events at time one and then 4 weeks later. Overall, the test–retest reliability coefficient was considered acceptable at .63 (Miro & Huguet, 2004).

Regarding validity generalization, the FPS-R has been used with children between 4 and 15 years old (Hicks et al., 2001; Newman et al., 2005). It has been used with a non-clinical sample of children undergoing ear piercing (Hicks et al., 2001), healthy school children (Miro & Huguet, 2004), hospitalized samples of children undergoing surgery or with other painful conditions (Hicks et al., 2001; Miro & Huguet, 2004), children in a large clinical trial comparing two vaccinations (Wood et al., 2004), children with HIV (Newman et al., 2005), children in a clinical trial testing needle-free delivery of lidocaine (Migdal, Chudzynska-Pomianowska, Vause, Henry, & Lazar, 2005), and children undergoing tonsillectomy (Lister et al., 2006).

Advantages of the FPS-R include its strong psychometrics, quickness and ease of administration, and its availability (it is available free for clinical and research use online at www.painsourcebook.ca). In addition to English and French versions, the FPS-R has been translated into 24 languages. However, to our knowledge, only three of the translated versions have been validated for use with their respective populations: French (Wood et al., 2004), Thai (Newman et al., 2005), and Catalan (Miro & Huguet, 2004). One disadvantage of the FPS-R is that although the original FPS has shown evidence of interpretability with values of 3 or more indicating clinically significant pain (Gauthier, Finley, & McGrath, 1998), such evidence is not available for the FPS-R (Stinson et al., 2006a). In addition, one must be cautious in administering the FPS-R and similar scales to young children (i.e., 4 to 6 years) because children of this age have been found to use the extreme ends of the scale (Arts et al., 1994). Finally, the FPS-R may not have high acceptability as children, parents, and nurses have indicated preference for more cartoon-like scales that have a smiling no pain face (Chambers, Hardial, Craig, Court, & Montgomery, 2005). However, in a comparison with a non-facial scale of pain intensity, the majority of schoolchildren and children in hospital preferred the FPS-R (Miro & Huguet, 2004). Overall, as concluded by Stinson et al. (2006a), there is sufficient support to recommend the FPS-R for clinical use in assessing pain intensity in children between 4 and 12 years of age.

The Wong-Baker FACES Pain Scale (Wong & Baker, 1988) is another widely used, psychometrically sound, single item self-report measure of pain intensity (for a review see Stinson et al., 2006a). It contains six cartoonlike faces which, in contrast to the FPS-R, range from a smiling "no hurt" face to a face with tears for the "hurts worst" face. Parents, children, and nurses have indicated a preference for the Wong-Baker FACES Pain Scale over other faces scales (Chambers et al., 2005). However, scales with a smiling no pain face have been shown to confound affect with pain intensity (Chambers & Craig, 1998; Chambers, Giesbrecht, Craig, Bennett, & Huntsman, 1999). Furthermore, research has demonstrated that children reporting their pain on faces scales with a smiling no pain face endorse higher pain ratings than on those with a neutral face anchor (Chambers et al., 1999). Although these differences in ratings are statistically significant, it is not clear whether these differences affect the clinical care of children (Chambers et al., 2005).

Visual Analogue Scales

Usually, visual analogue scales consist of a 10 cm horizontal line drawn on a piece of paper, with stops (anchors) placed at each end of the line (Wewers & Lowe, 1990). The anchors are labeled from, for example, "no pain" to "the most extreme pain" and the child is asked to point or make a mark on the line to represent his/her current level of pain intensity. The recordings are typically measured in millimeters, yielding scores that range from 0 to 100. Research suggests that the minimum clinically significant difference on 10 cm visual analogue scales for child pain intensity is 10 mm (Powell, Kelly, & Williams, 2001). There are many versions of the visual analogue scale available for use with children that differ in the terminology they use for the anchors, the presence or absence of divisions along the line, the units of measurement, the length of the scale, and whether the scale is presented horizontally or vertically (Stinson et al., 2006a).

Visual analogue scales for child pain intensity have undergone extensive psychometric testing (Stinson et al., 2006a), which is summarized in Table 25.1. As stated earlier, it is difficult to test the reliability of single-item pain intensity measures such as visual analogue scales. In one study that examined children's ratings of past medical procedures/treatments, Luffy and Grove (2003) found that only 45% of children rated their pain intensity within 10 mm above or below their original rating. However, more research on children's recalled pain intensity is needed before any conclusions about the test–retest reliability of visual analogue scales can be drawn. The convergent validity of visual analogue scales has been demonstrated by studies showing that these scales have moderate to strong correlations with other child pain intensity measures such as the Oucher, the Pieces of Hurt Tool (Beyer & Aradine, 1987, 1988) and the FPS-R (Migdal et al., 2005). In terms of discriminant validity, visual analogue scales have been found to have low correlations with two measures of fear (Beyer & Aradine, 1988).

Visual analogue scales can be considered valid pain intensity rating tools for children 8 years and older (Stinson et al., 2006a). They have been used successfully with hospitalized children (Beyer & Aradine, 1987, 1988), children undergoing venipunctures (Migdal et al., 2005), children with acute pain in the emergency department (Powell et al., 2001), and children with chronic pain conditions such as arthritis (Beales, Keen, & Lennox-Holt, 1983). Child preference data on visual analogue scales are equivocal. In their sample of children between the ages of 3 and 18 years, Luffy and

Grove (2003) found that the Wong-Baker FACES Pain Scale and the Oucher were preferred over a visual analogue scale. However, Berntson and Svensson (2001) found that children aged 10 to 17 years preferred a visual analogue scale instead of a verbal descriptor scale.

Visual analogue scales are quick and easy to use. They can be easily and affordably photocopied for use (as long as photocopying does not change the length of the line). Another advantage is that they allow for measurement of pain on an interval scale, which allows for greater sensitivity (Champion, Goodenough, von Baeyer, & Thomas, 1998). One of the main disadvantages of visual analogue scales is that clinicians must be careful to ensure that children (especially younger children) understand the instructions for their use. These scales require children to seriate their perceptions from small to large and this ability does not appear until children are about 7 years of age (Shields, Palermo, Powers, Grewe, & Smith, 2003). For this reason, we recommend the use of visual analogue scales with children over the age of 8. Many versions of visual analogue scales have been created in an effort to make these scales appropriate for younger children (e.g., the Colored Analogue Scale; McGrath et al., 1996; the Visual Analogue Toy scale; White & Stow, 1985). At present, there are not enough psychometric data to recommend the use of these modified visual analogue scales.

Pain Localization

The location of a child's pain is an important assessment parameter. In clinical practice, children are often asked to tell or point to where they feel pain. These informal methods have limitations. Children may not have enough anatomical knowledge to accurately express where they hurt and/or may be hesitant to point to their pain sites (Savedra, Tesler, Holzemer, Wilkie, & Ward, 1989). Another limitation of asking children to tell or point to where they hurt is that these methods do not preserve empirical documentation of children's responses. In light of these limitations, pediatric pain researchers have developed body outline tools to aid in the assessment of pain localization. However, measures of localization have not received nearly as much research attention as measures of intensity in the pediatric pain literature.

Eland Color Tool

The Eland Color Tool (Eland & Anderson, 1977) is a measure of child pain intensity and localization. To use this tool, the child is asked to choose four crayon colors to represent "no hurt," "a little hurt", "more hurt," and "worst hurt." The child then selects the color that represents his/her level of pain and is asked to color in a body outline wherever he/she hurts. In an unpublished study, 98% of hospitalized children between the ages of 4 and 10 years could place a mark on this tool that coincided with their pathology, surgical procedure, or another painful event that occurred during hospitalization (Eland & Anderson, 1977). A modified version of the Eland Color Tool has been used successfully in a sample of children with developmental delays (Benini et al., 2004). The advantage of the Eland Color Tool is that it allows clinicians to assess children's self-reported pain, localization, and intensity. In our clinical experience, this tool has proven to be very appealing to young children, who are often eager to use a favorite activity (coloring) to communicate about their pain. Because the Eland Color Tool has not undergone rigorous psychometric testing to date, it must be interpreted with caution.

Adolescent Pediatric Pain Tool

The Adolescent Pediatric Pain Tool (APPT; Savedra, Holzemer, Tesler, & Wilkie, 1993) is a self-report multidimensional pain measure that can be used to assess pain intensity, localization, and quality. It is divided into 3 separate components: a body outline, a word-graphic ratings scale, and a qualitative descriptive word list. The APPT is presented on a single, two-sided sheet of paper with the body outline on one side and the word-graphic rating scale and word list on the other. The body outline is made up of two line drawings showing the front and back of the body. The word-graphic rating scale is a 10 cm visual analogue scale with 5 pain intensity anchors ("no pain," "little pain," "medium pain," "large pain," and "worst pain possible"). The word list is composed of 56 words that describe the sensory, affective, and evaluative dimensions of pain. Both the body outline and word list are based on a widely used adult pain assessment measure, the McGill Pain Questionnaire (Melzack, 1983). Adolescents indicate the location of their current pain on the body outline, rate their current pain intensity on the word graphic rating scale, and highlight words that describe their current pain experience on the word list.

The APPT has undergone rigorous psychometric testing with both healthy and hospitalized children from a wide range of ethnic backgrounds between the ages of 8 and 17 years old. The development of the APPT is documented in a series of published studies (Savedra et al., 1989; Tesler et al., 1991; Wilkie et al., 1990) that provide good evidence for the content validity of each of its three components. Evidence for the convergent validity of the body outline component of the APPT is supplied by a study in which hospitalized children's markings on the body outline were found to match nurses' observations and/or medical records (Savedra et al., 1989). The word-graphic rating scale has also shown evidence of convergent validity through moderate to strong correlations with a visual analogue scale, a graded-graphic rating scale, a 0-to-10 numeric scale, and a color scale (Tesler et al., 1991). Scores on the word list component of the APPT have been shown to have weak to moderate but significant correlations with pain intensity and number of pain sites, which provides some limited support for its convergent validity (Wilkie et al., 1990). Overall, there is good evidence for the construct validity of the APPT.

The creators of the APPT carried out some innovative evaluations providing evidence for the test–retest reliability of their measure. Savedra and her colleagues (1993) found that the correlations between the number of body sites marked by hospitalized children over 5 postoperative days were moderate to strong. These researchers also found evidence for strong test–retest reliability of the word-graphic rating component of the APPT by administering it twice (separated by four other pediatric pain intensity measures) to a group of hospitalized children (Tesler et al., 1991). The test–retest reliability of the word list was examined with a small sample of hospitalized children recovering from surgery whose pain intensity ratings remained stable over 3 postoperative days (Wilkie et al., 1990). This sample of children responded in a reliable fashion to the word list.

Although the APPT has been tested with children between 8 and 17 years of age, younger children may not be able to understand some of the words in the word list and may have difficulty with left/right reversal of body outline drawings (Savedra et al., 1989, 1993; Wilkie et al., 1990). The majority of studies on the reliability and validity of the APPT have been carried out with children suffering from postoperative pain, but this tool has also been used successfully with African American children with sickle cell disease in inpatient and outpatient settings (Franck, Treadwell, Jacob, & Vichinsky, 2002).

Average administration time for the APPT is about 3 to 6 minutes (Savedra et al., 1993). The tool is easily reproducible, provided that the correct scaling of the word-graphic rating scale is preserved. Scoring the tool requires placing a clear plastic template over the completed body outline to measure the number of separate locations marked by the child, measuring the child's mark on the word-graphic rating scale with a ruler, and calculating total and percentage sensory, affective, and evaluative subscale scores for the word list. This multistep scoring procedure may limit the APPT's feasibility in some busy clinical settings. Although no child preference data is available for the complete APPT, child preference was taken into account during the development of the word-graphic rating scale (Tesler et al., 1991).

The main advantage of the APPT is that it measures three important dimensions of pain (location, intensity, and quality). The body outline component of the APPT is the only pediatric pain tool of its kind with evidence to support its reliability and validity. It provides a measure of pain location in children who may not have enough anatomical knowledge to indicate the location of their pain verbally or who may be hesitant to point to their pain sites (Savedra et al., 1989). The body outline also provides empirical documentation that can be used to track changes in children's pain location over time. Although further psychometric testing by researchers who were not involved in the creation of the APPT would help to further establish its reliability and validity, there is enough evidence to date to recommend this tool for clinical use.

Pain Quality

The quality of pain is important for diagnosis because it may give an indication of the type of pain or particular disease causing the pain. For example, burning pain is a part of the diagnosis of neuropathic pain, pounding headache is one part of the criteria for migraine, steady headache is a component of a tension-type headache diagnosis, and pain in the flank radiating to the groin is indicative of kidney stones. There are no particular

TABLE 25.2 Ratings of Instruments Used for Case Conceptualization and Treatment Planning

Instrument	Norms	Internal Consistency	Inter-Rater Reliability	Test–Retest Reliability	Content Validity	Construct Validity	Validity Generalization	Clinical Utility	Highly Recommended
FDI	G	E	NA	A	A	E	G	G	✓
PedsQL™ 4.0	E	A	NA	A	G	G	G	A	

Note: FDI = Functional Disability Inventory (Walker & Green, 1991); PedsQL™ 4.0 = The Pediatric Quality of Life Inventory™ Generic Core Scales (PedsQL™ 4.0; Varni et al., 2001); NA = Not Applicable; A = Adequate; G = Good; E = Excellent.

measures for children and adolescents that have been mapped to specific disorders. Currently, the APPT word list is the only tool assessing pain quality that has undergone extensive psychometric testing with children and we recommend it for purpose.

Pain Frequency and Duration

Pain frequency and duration are important dimensions of the pain experience to take into account when formulating diagnoses. Diagnoses for chronic and recurrent pain conditions depend on the time course of the symptoms. For example, recurrent abdominal pain is typically defined as 3 or more episodes of abdominal pain that occur over at least 3 months and cause significant impairment in functioning (Apley, 1975). On multidisciplinary hospital teams, mental health professionals typically use pain diaries to augment diagnostic information provided by children's physicians. Pain diaries are discussed in more detail in the Assessment for Case Conceptualization and Treatment Planning section.

Overall Evaluation

To make accurate diagnoses in children and adolescents suffering from pain, clinicians must, at the minimum, assess the perceptual dimensions of pain, including intensity, localization, quality, duration, and frequency. The Pieces of Hurt Tool, FPS-R, visual analogue scales, and the Oucher have all undergone rigorous psychometric testing and we recommend their use in clinical settings for the assessment of pain intensity in preschool and school-aged children. We also recommend visual analogue scales and the word-graphic rating scale of the APPT for the measurement of pain intensity in older children and adolescents. For pain localization, we recommend the APPT body outline tool with older children and adolescents. For younger children, the Eland Color Tool may be useful for measuring pain intensity and

localization. However, this measure has not undergone rigorous psychometric testing to date. For pain quality, we recommend the APPT word list for older children and adolescents. Unfortunately, no similar measure has been validated for use with younger children. We recommend pain diaries for the assessment of pain frequency and duration for the purposes of diagnosis, with parental proxy-report for younger children.

ASSESSMENT FOR CASE CONCEPTUALIZATION AND TREATMENT PLANNING

For the most part, mental health practitioners will not be involved in case conceptualization or treatment planning for children undergoing isolated acutely painful procedures or injuries. The exception may be a case in which a child develops severe anxiety or a specific phobia about certain painful procedures, such as needles. In this case, the assessment typically focuses on the anxiety associated with the painful procedure, rather than the pain itself. The majority of pediatric pain assessments carried out by mental health practitioners are with children suffering from recurrent or chronic pain. To obtain a full case conceptualization for a child or adolescent suffering from recurrent or chronic pain, clinicians must assess basic pain perception parameters, such as pain intensity and frequency, over an extended period of time. It is also important for clinicians to assess the impact of the child's pain on his/her day-to-day functioning to define targets for intervention. Finally, there are a number of psychological factors related to pain that clinicians should consider when conceptualizing cases and formulating treatment plans. These psychological factors include pain catastrophizing, fear of pain, as well as general anxiety and depression. Table 25.2 provides summary information on measures designed to assess some of these constructs.

TABLE 25.3 Pain Diary of a Fictional 10-Year-Old Child with Chronic Headaches

Name: Jamie Trisco

Date	Time	Rating (0 = No Pain to 5 = Severe Pain)	What Happened Before the Headache	What Did You Do
Monday	Breakfast	0		
	Lunch	0		
	Dinner	4	Late dinner	took 2 Advil
	Bedtime	0		
Tuesday	Breakfast	3	Woke up with headache	took 2 Advil
	Lunch	4		took 2 Advil
	Dinner	3		Slept for 1 hour
	Bedtime	1		
Wednesday	Breakfast	0		
	Lunch	5	Late lunch	took 2 Advil, slept for 1 hour
	Dinner	2		Slept for 1 hour
	Bedtime	1		

Note: This diary suggests the possibility that headaches are triggered by delays in eating and are made somewhat better by Advil and by sleep. A lengthier observation period might support these ideas and specific manipulations could confirm them.

Pain Frequency and Duration

Information about pain frequency and duration augments basic diagnostic information and allows mental health professionals to form full psychological case conceptualizations and plan treatments for children suffering from recurrent or chronic pain. By working with children and their families to document pain frequency and duration, clinicians gain insight into possible patterns in children's pain experiences. For example, a child with recurrent abdominal pain may report that she/he typically has severe pain twice per week, on Mondays and Wednesdays during a challenging class at school. This might indicate a link between the child's abdominal pain and academic stress and suggest that psychological strategies targeting the management of academic stress may help decrease this child's pain. Pain diaries are the best method for investigating potential patterns in children's pain experiences.

Pain diaries

Paper-and-pencil pain diaries (see Table 25.3 for an example) combine numerical ratings with a calendar to allow for the assessment of pain over time. Diaries are commonly used for continuing or episodic pain such as headache, abdominal pain, or neuropathic pain. Although diaries are commonly used in clinical

contexts, they have not been the focus of thorough psychometric testing. Research conducted to date suggests that children who are queried retrospectively about their pain tend to overreport pain in comparison with data from prospective pain diaries (Andrasik, Burke, Attanasio, & Rosenblum, 1985; van den Brink, Bandell-Hoekstra, & Abu-Saad, 2001). For this reason, pain diaries help clinicians obtain a more accurate picture of children's pain experiences over time.

Pain diaries are most typically time-based and require the child and/or parent to make a rating 3 or 4 times a day. More frequent reporting by the respondents will increase the precision of the diary but will also increase the burden on the respondents and likely decrease compliance. Pain intensity ratings are most often recorded in diaries on a 0-to-5 or 0-to-10 scale; however, there is evidence to suggest that different pain intensity anchors may not significantly change the ratings given by respondents (Richardson, McGrath, Cunningham, & Humphreys, 1983). Event-based diaries are an alternative to time-based diaries. In this style of diary, respondents are asked to record the beginning and end of pain episodes. Event-based diaries have the advantage of being able to determine the duration of pain episodes more accurately but also carry the risk of being unable to distinguish between the absence of pain and the absence of reporting.

Whether the parent, child, or both fill out the diary will depend on the developmental level of the child. There is evidence to suggest that parents and children report similar intensities of the child's pain (Andrasik et al., 1985; Richardson et al., 1983); however, parents' and children's pain frequency ratings may differ under some circumstances. For example, pain experienced at school is unlikely to be recorded by a parent unless it is of sufficient severity that the child has to leave school. Similarly, mild pain may not result in behavior that is evident to parents even when it is present.

We recommend that clinicians routinely use paper-and-pencil pain diaries to inform their case conceptualizations and treatment plans for children suffering from chronic or recurrent pain. Although electronic diaries (programs run on computers or personal digital assistants) are generally unavailable to most children, they have several advantages over paper-and-pencil diaries. Research has suggested that respondents are more likely to complete electronic diary recordings and to make these recordings at the time when pain occurs (rather than recalling the pain experience later and making the recording retrospectively; Palermo, Valenzuela, & Stork, 2004). The usability of an electronic chronic pain diary was recently demonstrated in a small sample of adolescents with juvenile arthritis (Stinson et al., 2006b). Further research with larger samples of children is needed before we can determine whether the advantages of these tools over paper-and-pencil diaries outweigh their cost.

Physical, Social, and Role Functioning

In accordance with the WHO International Classification of Functioning, Disability, and Health (2001), clinicians need to assess how pain impacts children's physical, social, and role functioning in completing a full case conceptualization and treatment plan. When assessing physical functioning, clinicians should always include a measure of sleep, as it is often disrupted in children with chronic or recurrent pain (e.g., Walters & Williamson, 1999). It is beyond the scope of this chapter to discuss pediatric sleep assessment in detail. We refer the reader to a book by Mindell and Owens (2003) for recommendations in this area. Appetite and weight are two other aspects of physical functioning that should be assessed. This does not usually require formal assessment measures. In children, role functioning is often synonymous with academic functioning

because school is the "job" of children. In children with chronic or recurrent pain, it is also important to assess the extent to which children are taking on a "sick role" in their family and demonstrating lower functioning in their other roles (e.g., social).

Illness Behavior Encouragement Scale

The Illness Behavior Encouragement Scale (IBES; Walker & Zeman, 1992) is a brief questionnaire designed to measure parents' encouragement of their children's sick-role behavior. Sick-role behavior (which is synonymous with "illness behavior") can be defined as behavior that suggests illness, such as complaining about physical symptoms like pain or refusing to complete daily tasks such as attending school due to pain (Brace, Smith, McCauley, & Sherry, 2000). Parents who attend to or reward their children's sick-role behavior may unintentionally reinforce it (Walker & Zeman, 1992).

The original version of the IBES assesses parental encouragement of child cold symptoms (e.g., congestion) and gastrointestinal symptoms (e.g., stomach aches). Since the original version was published, the IBES has been adapted to measure parental encouragement of other child pain symptoms (such as headaches; Bijttebier & Vertommen, 1999). Both the original and adapted versions of the IBES consist of parallel 12-item parent and child-report forms. The parent-report form asks parents to indicate the frequency with which they respond to their children's symptoms in particular ways. For example, "How often do you let your child stay home from school when he/she has *symptom*." Similarly, the child-report form asks children to indicate the frequency with which their parents respond to their (the children's) symptoms in particular ways. For example, "How often do your parents let you stay home from school when you have *symptom*." Both forms are scored on a 5-point Likert scale ranging from 0 ("never") to 4 ("always"). Total scores are obtained by summing the items, with higher scores indicating more parental encouragement of the symptom in question.

There is some evidence that the IBES possesses adequate psychometric properties. However, this tool has not undergone rigorous psychometric evaluation since its initial development and validation. In terms of content validity, the IBES was modeled on work by Whitehead and colleagues showing that illness behavior in adults was positively correlated with their recollections of receiving rewards at times of illness during their childhood (Whitehead, Winget, Fedoravicius, Wooley, & Blackwell, 1982). In the initial validation study, the test–retest reliability of the IBES-Child Form was reported to be adequate (Walker & Zeman, 1992). To our knowledge, the test–retest reliability of the IBES-Parent Form has not been reported. Internal consistency for both the parent and child-report forms of the IBES appears to be adequate (Walker & Zeman, 1992; Walker, Garber, & Greene, 1993).

In terms of construct validity, the IBES has been found to correlate positively with other indices of child illness behavior (such as number of school days missed due to symptoms; Walker & Zeman, 1992) and negatively with adolescents' physical recovery from oral surgery (Gidron, McGrath, & Goodday, 1995). IBES scores have also been found to correlate positively with number of days of school missed in adolescents with juvenile arthritis (Brace et al., 2000) and functional disability in children with recurrent pain who report symptoms of depression and anxiety (Peterson & Palermo, 2004).

The IBES has been used by samples of children and adolescents with many different types of chronic and recurrent pain, including recurrent abdominal pain (Walker et al., 1993), headache (Bijttebier & Vertommen, 1999), juvenile arthritis (Brace et al., 2000), Familial Mediterranean Fever (characterized by inflammatory pain; Gidron, Berkovitch, & Press, 2003), irritable bowel syndrome (Levy et al., 2004), and sickle cell disease (Peterson & Palermo, 2004). In these samples, the participants ranged in age from 3 to 20 years and the IBES-Child Form was used with children 8 years and older. The IBES has been translated into Dutch and studies conducted with the Dutch version provide some preliminary evidence for its validity (Bijttebier & Vertommen, 1999; Merlijn et al., 2003, 2006).

Advantages of the IBES include its brevity and straightforward scoring procedure. It is also an advantage that the IBES has parallel parent and child-report forms, which allows clinicians to compare parent and child reports. Disadvantages include gaps in the data about its psychometric properties (such as the test–retest reliability of the parent-report form) and attention to only *parental* encouragement of illness behavior (i.e., it does not take the influence of other family members or peers into account). In our clinical experience, the IBES has proven very useful for identifying ways in which parents may unintentionally encourage their children's sick-role behavior related to pain. Until further psychometric testing is completed, we suggest that this measure may be used with caution in clinical contexts.

Functional Disability Inventory

The Functional Disability Inventory (FDI) is a 15-item global measure of children's physical and psychosocial functioning that has both self and parent-report components (FDI; Walker & Greene, 1991). Respondents are asked to indicate the perceived difficulty the child has had performing various activities (e.g., walking to the bathroom) in the previous few days. The response scale has the following options, scored 0 to 4, and summed across items: "no trouble," "a little trouble," "some trouble," "a lot of trouble," and "impossible." Total scores range from 0 to 60 for both self and parent-report forms, with higher scores indicating greater disability. Healthy children have been found to score on average between 2 and 3.5 on the FDI (Walker & Greene, 1991).

Two major studies have been conducted to examine the psychometric properties of the FDI (Claar & Walker, 2006; Walker & Greene, 1991) and many other studies have employed the FDI as an assessment or treatment outcome measure. The internal consistency of the FDI has ranged from good to excellent, with Cronbach alphas ranging from .85 to .95 for both child and parent versions (Walker & Greene, 1991). Further studies have shown that the high internal consistency values hold for both boys and girls (Claar & Walker, 2006). The inter-rater reliability of clinical judges on the FDI has not been assessed. This is likely due the fact that the scale measures perceived difficulty in everyday functioning, which would be difficult for a clinician to judge. Test–retest reliability of the FDI has been supported through significant moderate to high correlations between the scores of patients with chronic conditions over a 3-month period (Claar & Walker, 2006; Walker & Greene, 1991). Correlations in this range are expected for a measure of day-to-day functional disability.

There are a number of studies supporting the validity of the FDI. In terms of content validity, the FDI was developed based on adult measures of functional disability and pilot tested for usability with children and adolescents (Walker & Greene, 1991). Cross-informant (parent–child) correlations on the

FDI have ranged from moderate to strong (Reid, McGrath, & Lang, 2005; Walker & Greene, 1991). Significant low to moderate cross-informant correlations have been found for both male and female children, as well as for younger and older children. Concurrent and convergent validity of the FDI have been established by its moderate to strong relationships with other measures of child health and well-being, such as sleep disturbance (Palermo & Kiska, 2005), depression (Kashikar-Zuck, Vaught, Goldschneider, Graham, & Miller, 2002), somatization (Walker, Smith, Garber, & Claar, 2005), school absence, anxiety, physical symptoms (Claar & Walker, 2006; Walker & Greene, 1991), and catastrophizing (Lynch, Kashikar-Zuck, Goldschneider, & Jones, 2006). The FDI has also shown low to moderate correlations with measures of pain (Claar & Walker, 2006; Peterson & Palermo, 2004). In addition, children with a familial history of chronic pain had significantly higher scores on the FDI than children without such a familial history (Lynch et al., 2006).

Discriminant validity of the FDI has been supported through negative correlations with measures that would not be expected to be closely related to functional disability (e.g., social, academic, and athletic competence; Claar, Walker, & Smith, 1999) and through its ability to distinguish between groups of children and adolescents who are expected to have different levels of perceived disability (Walker & Greene, 1991; Walker, Guite, Duke, Barnard, & Greene, 1998). There is also evidence that scores on the FDI have incremental validity over other clinical measures in predicting the severity of sleep/wake problems (Palermo & Kiska, 2005), number of days a child spent in bed due to illness and school absences (Walker & Greene, 1991). In addition, significant correlations between baseline scores on the FDI and subsequent measures of illness, behavior (e.g., school absence, bed days, pain, depressive symptoms) support the predictive validity of this instrument (Claar & Walker, 2006; Walker & Greene, 1991).

The FDI has good validity generalization. While the measure has been used with a number of different patient groups, there has been little to no variation in the ethnicity of the children. The FDI has been administered to children as young as 6 and adults up to age 23, with the majority of the studies conducted with children between 8 and 17 years. There is evidence that girls may report greater disability than boys (Walker & Greene, 1991; Claar & Walker,

2006). The FDI has been used to assess disability in many different populations including children with recurrent abdominal pain (Campo et al., 2004; Claar & Walker, 2006; Walker & Greene, 1991), chronic back pain (e.g. Lynch et al., 2006), burns (Barnum, Synder, Rapoff, Mani, & Thompson, 1998), complex regional pain syndrome, juvenile idiopathic musculoskeletal pain (Eccleston, Crombez, Scotford, Clinch, & Connell, 2004), fibromyalgia (e.g. Kashikar-Zuck et al., 2002; Reid et al., 2005), recurrent headache (Palermo & Kiska, 2005), and sickle cell disease (Peterson & Palermo, 2004). The FDI has also been used with adolescents following oral surgery (Gidron, McGrath, & Goodday, 1995), outpatients with minor health complaints, and healthy controls (Walker & Greene, 1991).

An advantage of the FDI is that it is easy and relatively fast to administer. Furthermore, the tool has been used with a number of different populations and shows good psychometric data. Use of the measure may allow both children and parents to express the level of disruption that the child's health problems are creating for the child's daily functioning. A disadvantage is that it has primarily been used with Caucasian children. Further work needs to establish the use of the measure with children and adolescents of different ethnic backgrounds. In addition, there have been inconsistent relationships between scores on the FDI and socioeconomic status (Claar & Walker, 2006; Peterson & Palermo, 2004; Walker & Greene, 1991). Despite these limitations, there is sufficient psychometric support to recommend the use of the FDI to measure children's physical and psychosocial functioning in clinical settings.

The Pediatric Quality of Life Inventory™ Generic Core Scales

The Pediatric Quality of Life Inventory™ (PedsQL™) is a 23-item modular instrument that measures health-related quality of life (HRQOL), which can be defined as: "an individual's subjective perception of his or her functioning and emotional state vis-à-vis the effects of disease and treatment" (Connelly & Rapoff, 2006, p. 698). The PedsQL 4.0 Generic Core Scales (PedsQL 4.0; Varni et al., 2001) were designed to measure child physical, mental, and social health dimensions, as well as role (school) functioning. The measure is made up of parallel child self-report and parent proxy-report formats. The parent proxy-reports measure parents' perceptions of their children's HRQOL. Child self-reports include ages 5–7 (young child), 8–12 (child), and 13–18 (adolescent). Parent proxy-reports include ages 2–4 (toddler), 5–7 (young child), 8–12 (child), and 13–18 (adolescent).

Completion of the PedsQL 4.0 takes, on average, less than 5 minutes (Varni, 2007). Respondents indicate the extent to which the child is having problems in each of the four areas of functioning using a Likert scale. A 5-point scale is used for the child self-report forms (ages 8–18) and the parent proxy-report forms. To increase ease of use for young children, a simplified 3-point scale is used for young children. The young child self-report form is also anchored to a faces scale ranging from happy to sad. Items are reverse-scored and converted into a 0-to-100 scale, with higher scores indicating better HRQOL. The measure yields a Physical Health Summary Scale, a Psychosocial Health Summary Scale, and a Total Scale.

A large volume of empirical evidence supports the psychometric properties of the PedsQL 4.0. In terms of norms, measures of central tendency and distribution are available for total and scale scores in large samples of children and adolescents with chronic and acute health conditions, as well as samples of healthy children (Connelly & Rapoff, 2006; Powers, Patton, Hommel, & Hershey, 2004; Varni, Burwinkle, Limbers, & Szer, 2007; Varni et al., 2001; Varni, Seid, Knight, Uzark, & Szer, 2002). Internal consistency alpha values obtained for the majority of the child-report and parent-report scales meet or exceed .70, whereas alpha values for the child-report and parent-report total scale scores are .85 or above (Connelly & Rapoff, 2006; Varni et al., 2001; Varni et al., 2007). Two-week test–retest reliability of the Total Scale score has been estimated at $r = .86$ (Connelly & Rapoff, 2006).

The PedsQL 4.0 was designed to measure the core health dimensions outlined by the World Health Organization (WHO, 1948). Items for the original instrument were created based on a literature search, interviews with samples of children with cancer and their families, and discussions with pediatric health-care professionals (Varni, Seid, & Rode, 1999). This most recent version is the result of a number of iterations that have occurred since the publication of the original instrument (Varni et al., 1999).

There is good evidence for the construct validity of the PedsQL 4.0. Scores on this measure have been found to be significantly lower in samples of children with chronic pain conditions and acute health conditions (including children with migraines, recurrent headaches, fibromyalgia, and cardiac disease) than in samples of healthy children (Connelly & Rapoff, 2006; Powers et al., 2004; Varni et al., 2001, 2007). A number of studies provide evidence of concurrent validity. In a large sample of children and their parents recruited from pediatric health-care settings, child and parent-report scores were negatively correlated with number of days of hospital care over the past month and number of days missed from school (Varni et al., 2001). In addition, parent-report scores in this sample were negatively correlated with number of days missed from work. In another study with children suffering from recurrent headaches, summary scores were correlated in the expected direction with headache severity data and scores from a validated measure of headache-related disability (Connelly & Rapoff, 2006).

Empirical evidence supports the use of the PedsQL 4.0 with a wide age range (2–18 years). It is the only generic pediatric quality of life measure to span such a wide age range that has undergone rigorous psychometric testing (Eiser & Morse, 2001). The PedsQL 4.0 is appropriate for use with both healthy children and children with a wide variety of acute and chronic illnesses (e.g., Varni et al., 2001). This measure has been tested with samples of children from different ethnic backgrounds and their parents in both English and Spanish and ratings provided in both languages have been found to be equivalent (Varni et al., 2001). Translations in a wide range of other languages are also available (Varni, 2007), including Norwegian, Dutch, German, and Chinese versions that have all been validated by independent groups of authors (Bastiaansen, Koot, Bongers, Varni, & Verhulst, 2004; Chan, Chow, & Lo, 2005; Felder-Puig et al., 2004; Reinfjell, Diseth, Veenstra, & Vikan, 2006).

Because the PedsQL 4.0 is a generic HRQOL measure, it gives researchers and clinicians the ability to conduct comparisons across acute and chronic health conditions, as well as benchmark against healthy population norms (Varni et al., 2002). However, the generic nature of this instrument may make it necessary to administer supplementary disease-specific assessments to address the full range of functioning in some children with pain (Eiser & Morse, 2001). PedsQL disease-specific modules are currently available for asthma, rheumatology, diabetes, cancer, and cardiac conditions.

One of the main advantages of the PedsQL 4.0 is that it includes complementary child and parent proxy-report forms. Although patient self-report is considered the standard for measuring perceived HRQOL, it is parents' perception of their children's HRQOL that influences health-care utilization (Varni & Setoguchi, 1992). Correlations between child and parent ratings are in the moderate range, suggesting that it is important to obtain both the child's and the parent's perspective (e.g., Powers et al., 2004; Varni et al., 2007). Another advantage of the PedsQL is that it provides a multidimensional quality of life assessment with a quick administration time and relatively simple scoring procedure. This makes it practical for use in clinical settings. The PedsQL also has a useful website (http://www.pedsql.org) that provides detailed information about administration and scoring, along with an extensive reference list. The main disadvantage of the PedsQL 4.0 is that large noncommercial organizations such as hospitals and health-care systems must pay a license fee to use it (conditions of use are detailed on the Web site). Although clinicians must take this practical consideration into account, we feel that there is enough evidence for the clinical utility of this measure to recommend its use as part of multidimensional pain assessments.

Psychological Factors Related to Pain

Pain catastrophizing can be defined as "an exaggerated negative orientation" toward pain (Sullivan, Bishop, & Pivik, 1995, p. 524). Pain catastrophizing has been found to predict somatic complaints, pain severity, and functional disability in children (Vervoot, Goubert, Eccleston, Bijttebier, & Crombez, 2006) and should be assessed as a part of the treatment planning process. Fear of pain is another psychological factor that has been shown to predict disability in adult chronic pain patients (McCracken, Zayfert, & Gross, 1992). Two commonly used measures of fear of pain in adults are The Fear of Pain Questionnaire-III (FPQ-II; McNeil & Rainwater, 1998) and the Pain Anxiety Symptoms Scale (PASS; McCracken et al., 1992). Unfortunately, no measures of fear of pain have been developed to date for use with children. For older children and adolescents, clinicians may use the FPQ-III or PASS, but they must interpret the results of these tests with caution, as they have only been validated with adults.

The Pain Catastrophizing Scale for Children (PCS-C; Crombez et al., 2003) was adapted from the Pain Catastrophizing Scale (Sullivan et al., 1995). The PCS-C is a 13 item self-report measure with each item depicting various feelings or thoughts one might have while in pain. The child responds to each statement by choosing an intensity rating: "not at all," "mildly," "moderately," "severely," or "extremely." The items represent three related dimensions: Rumination, Magnification, and Helplessness. Total scores on the PCS-C range from 0 to 52, with higher scores indicating higher levels of pain catastrophizing. The PCS-C has been used with both healthy children and children with chronic pain between the ages of 9 and 16 years (Crombez et al., 2003). The initial validation study (Crombez et al., 2003) for the PCS-C showed evidence of internal consistency, criterion validity, construct validity, and validity generalization. However, there has been no further psychometric testing of the measure to date. Some advantages of the PCS-C are its relative brevity, ease of administration, and initial psychometric data. The disadvantages are that it has been primarily used within a research context by a particular research center and has not been used with a large clinical sample. At this time, the PCS-C must be used with caution in a clinical context, as there is insufficient evidence of its full psychometric properties (e.g., clinical norms) and clinical usefulness (e.g., treatment sensitivity).

Two other psychological factors that clinicians should take into account during case conceptualization and treatment planning are depression and anxiety. Symptoms of both depression and anxiety have been found at increased rates in children with recurrent pain (Palermo, 2000). The reader is referred to the chapters on child and adolescent depression and anxiety disorders in this volume for information on assessment of these factors.

Overall Evaluation

There are a number of factors that clinicians must take into account in forming case conceptualizations and planning treatments for children with chronic or recurrent pain. Detailed information about pain frequency and duration should be collected with a pain diary. Pain diaries are invaluable assessment tools because they allow clinicians to identify possible patterns in pain symptoms and target their interventions accordingly. Assessment of the child's physical, social, and role functioning are also essential components of treatment planning. We recommend the use of the

FDI for the assessment of physical and psychosocial functioning in older children between the ages of 8 and 17. We also recommend the PedsQL 4.0 for the assessment of physical, emotional, social, and school functioning for children and adolescents from age 2 through 18. For the assessment of encouragement of sick-role behavior, we suggest that clinicians consider the parent and child-report forms of the IBES for children 8 years and older, and the parent-report form of the IBES for children under 8 years. Results of the IBES must be interpreted with caution because further evaluation of the psychometric properties of this measure is needed.

We recommend that clinicians assess for sleep problems in children with chronic or recurrent pain. Psychological factors such as pain catastrophizing, as well as general depression and anxiety, should also be assessed before treatment plans are formulated. For pain catastrophizing, we suggest that clinicians consider using the PCS-C. Although this measure has some preliminary evidence of validity, it must be interpreted with caution pending further psychometric evaluation. For recommendations on depression and anxiety assessment measures for children, readers are directed to the other chapters in this volume. Although there is no formal tool for measuring fear of pain in young children, fear of pain is an important dimension to assess and it is suggested that clinicians consider using the FPQ-III or the PASS with older children and adolescents as long as they interpret the results with caution.

ASSESSMENT FOR TREATMENT MONITORING AND TREATMENT OUTCOME EVALUATION

The measures chosen for assessment of treatment monitoring and treatment outcome will reflect the areas of functioning identified during case conceptualization as major problem areas (e.g., poor school attendance, fear of pain, depression, anxiety, sleep) for a given child or adolescent. Assessment for treatment outcome will also include pain perception parameters such as pain intensity, duration, and frequency. Pain diaries that track when each intervention was implemented and the resulting pain levels are especially useful for tracking progress. However, more research is needed to formally document the treatment sensitivity of various pain diary formats. Table 25.4 presents

ratings for instruments relevant for use in treatment monitoring and treatment outcome evaluation.

Each of the pain intensity measures we recommended for formulating diagnoses has some evidence of treatment sensitivity. Specifically, there is some data to suggest that the Pieces of Hurt Tool is responsive to changes in pain intensity following surgery (Beyer & Aradine, 1987). Similarly, there is evidence to suggest that the Oucher is responsive to changes in pain following surgery and analgesic administration (Aradine et al., 1988; Beyer & Aradine, 1987; Beyer & Knott, 1998; Ramritu, 2000). There is also good evidence for the treatment sensitivity of the FPS-R. Scores on this measure are sensitive not only to pre-post needle differences in pain but also to group differences between children receiving two different types of vaccines (Wood et al., 2004). Children's pain ratings on the FPS-R have also reflected significant differences between treatment with lidocaine versus placebo for needle pain (Taddio, Kaur-Soin, Schuh, Koren, & Scolnik, 2005) and two different types of tonsillectomy surgery (Lister et al., 2006). Although the evidence for the treatment sensitivity of visual analogue scales is not as strong as it is for the FPS-R, these measures have also been shown to be responsive to changes in child pain intensity following the administration of analgesic medications (Aradine, Beyer, & Tompkins, 1988) and topical anesthetics (Migdal et al., 2005).

In terms of pain localization, preliminary evidence for the treatment sensitivity of the Eland Color Tool was demonstrated in a small sample of kindergarten children undergoing injections (Eland, 1982). The treatment sensitivity of the APPT is supported by more rigorous psychometric evaluations. In a pilot study of the APPT with 55 children (Savedra, Tesler, Holzemer, Wilkie, & Ward, 1990), all three components of this tool (body outline for localization; word-graphic rating scale for intensity; and descriptive word list for sensory, affective and evaluative dimensions of pain) were sensitive to changes in postoperative pain over 5 days. Similar results were reported in a later study with a group of 67 children who had undergone surgery (Savedra et al., 1993). In this later study, mean number of pain locations did not decrease over 5 postoperative days, which was consistent with the types of surgeries and ongoing medical interventions that these children experienced.

Unfortunately, some children and adolescents with chronic pain may not experience significant

TABLE 25.4 Ratings of Instruments Used for Treatment Monitoring and Treatment Outcome Evaluation

Instrument	Norms	Internal Consistency	Inter-Rater Reliability	Test–Retest Reliability	Content Validity	Construct Validity	Validity Generalization	Clinical Utility	Treatment Sensitivity	Highly Recommended
Pieces of hurt tool	NA	NA	NA	NA	A	G	G	G	A	
The oucher	NA	NA	NA	NA	G	G	A	G	A	✓
FPS-R	NA	NA	NA	NA	A	G	E	G	G	✓
Visual analogue scales	NA	NA	NA	NA	NA	A	G	A	A	✓
APPT	NA	NA	NA	A	G	G	E	A	A	✓
FDI	G	E	NA	A	A	E	G	G	A	
PedsQL™ 4.0	E	A	NA	A	G	G	G	A	G	✓

Note: FPS-R = Faces Pain Scale-Revised; APPT = the Adolescent Pediatric Pain Tool; FDI = the Functional Disability Inventory; PedsQL™ 4.0 = The Pediatric Quality of Life Inventory™ Generic Core Scales; A = Adequate; G = Good; E = Excellent; NA = Not Applicable.

decreases in pain intensity over the course of treatment; however, they may show dramatic improvement in their overall coping and functioning. For this reason, it is important for clinicians to include measures of overall functioning and quality of life in their treatment monitoring plans. The treatment sensitivity of two such measures, the FDI and the PedsQL 4.0., has received some empirical support. (Eccleston, Malleson, Clinch, Connell, & Sourbut, 2003) found that following residential treatment, FDI scores for adolescents with chronic pain significantly declined immediately after treatment and 3 months posttreatment compared with baseline. In another study, Walker and Greene (1991) showed that the FDI scores of children who had received medical treatment for their abdominal pain of organic etiology declined after treatment. A number of studies support the treatment sensitivity of the PedsQL 4.0. In a study conducted with children visiting an orthopedic clinic for treatment of fractures, scores were significantly lower at the initial clinic visit than at a follow-up phone call 6 to 8 months later (Varni et al., 2002). In another study, children with recurrent headaches showed significant improvements on the Total Scale, Physical Health Summary, and Psychosocial Health Summary scores following a cognitive-behavioral intervention (Connelly & Rapoff, 2006). Significant improvements in Total Scale scores following cognitive-behavioral treatment were also reported in a study of children with recurrent abdominal pain (Youssef et al., 2004).

As mentioned in our discussion of measures for case conceptualization and treatment planning, the IBES and PCS-C require further psychometric testing before they can be recommended for use in clinical settings. Preliminary evidence of the treatment sensitivity of the IBES is provided by a study with adolescents recovering from oral surgery (Gidron et al., 1995). To our knowledge, the treatment sensitivity of the PCS-C has not been examined to date.

Overall Evaluation

The choice of measures for treatment monitoring and treatment outcome should flow logically from information gathered during diagnosis, case conceptualization, and treatment planning. It is important for clinicians to monitor basic pain perception parameters, as well as overall functioning and quality of life in children and adolescents suffering from pain. Out of the pain intensity measures discussed above, the

FPS-R has received the most empirical support for its treatment sensitivity. There is some less rigorous evidence for the treatment sensitivity of the Pieces of Hurt Tool, the Ocher, visual analogue scales, and the APPT. In terms of overall functioning and quality of life, there is adequate evidence for the sensitivity of the FDI and good evidence for the sensitivity of the PedsQL 4.0. More data is needed on the treatment sensitivity of the IBES and the PCS-C.

CONCLUSIONS AND FUTURE DIRECTIONS

Assessment of pain requires an understanding of pain intensity, localization, quality, frequency, and duration. However, these perceptual dimensions are only part of the puzzle when we seek to understand a child or adolescent's total experience of pain. For example, two young people with the same chronic pain condition and similar pain intensity, localization, frequency, and duration can have very different levels of functional ability. Psychological factors, such as the presence of symptoms of depression or anxiety, as well as a person's specific orientation to pain (e.g., pain catastrophizing, fear of pain) are important pieces to take into account. For children and adolescents, it is also important to consider parents' orientation and behavior towards their children's pain (such as unintentional encouragement of illness behavior). The WHO's International Classification of Functioning, Disability and Health (2001) provides an ideal framework for assessment when working with children or adolescents who suffer from chronic/recurrent pain because it goes beyond a disease-based model to focus on overall health, functional ability, and quality of life. As reflected in our recommendations, we feel that it is just as important to assess the impact of children's pain on their physical, social, and role functioning as it is to assess the basic perceptual parameters of their pain.

Reviews have revealed that there are several areas in which child and adolescent pain assessment tools need to be developed, including pain quality and fear of pain. However, in general, future research should focus on establishing the psychometrics and feasibility of existing assessment tools rather than adding to the list of tools already available. This is particularly true for measures of pain intensity, a construct for which there are numerous tools, all of which have gaps in their psychometric data. Some of the pain intensity measures we have discussed in our review have been applied primarily to assess the intensity of acute pain. Their application in the assessment of chronic pain deserves further study.

Although there has been valuable research on the measurement of various aspects of pain in children, there has been insufficient attention paid to the development and validation of measures suitable for everyday clinical use. There is also a dearth of research on clinical issues such as interpretability of assessment tools and levels of clinically significant pain (e.g., when a child feels he/she would need pharmacological intervention; for an exception see Gauthier et al., 1998).

The growth of evidence-based clinical practice in pediatric pain depends on the use of psychometrically sound assessment tools. Close collaboration between clinicians practicing in busy clinics and pain measurement scientists is needed to ensure that the measures and assessments that are developed are easy to use and yield information that clinicians find helpful in clinical decision-making for diagnosis, case formulation, and evaluation of treatments. The integration of appropriate measures into routine care will be invaluable for ensuring that each child is given the most effective treatment.

References

Anand, K. J. S., Stevens, B. J., & McGrath, P. J. (Eds.). (2007). *Pain in neonates and infants* (3rd ed.). Amsterdam: Elsevier.

Andrasik, F., Burke, E. J., Attanasio, V., & Rosenblum, E. L. (1985). Child, parent, and physician reports of a child's headache pain: Relationships prior to and following treatment. *Headache: The Journal of Head and Face Pain, 25*, 421–425.

Angell, M. (1982). The quality of mercy. *New England Journal of Medicine, 306*, 98–99.

Apley, J. (1975). *The child with abdominal pains* (2nd ed.). Oxford: Blackwell Scientific Publications.

Aradine, C., Beyer, J., & Tompkins, J. (1988). Children's pain perception before and after analgesia: A study of instrument construct validity and related issues. *Journal of Pediatric Nursing, 3*, 11–23.

Arts, S. E., Abu-Saad, H. H., Champion, G. D., Crawford, M. R., Fisher, R. J., Juniper, K. H., et al. (1994). Age-related response to lidocaine-prilocaine (EMLA) emulsion and effect of music distraction on the pain of intravenous cannulation. *Pediatrics, 93*, 797–801.

Bastiaansen, D., Koot, H. M., Bongers, I. L., Varni, J. W., & Verhulst, F. C. (2004). Measuring quality of life in children referred for psychiatric problems: Psychometric properties of the PedsQL™ 4.0 generic core scales. *Quality of Life Research, 13*, 489–495.

Barnum, D. D., Snyder, C. R., Rapoff, M. A., Mani, M. M., & Thompson, R. (1998). Hope and social support in the psychological adjustment of children who have survived burn injuries and their matched controls. *Child Health Care, 27*, 15–30.

Beales, J. G., Keen, J. H., & Lennox-Holt, P. J. (1983). The child's perception of the disease and the experience of pain in juvenile chronic arthritis. *Journal of Rheumatology, 10*, 61–65.

Belter, R. W., McIntosh, J. A., Finch, A. J., & Saylor, C. F. (1988). Preschoolers' ability to differentiate levels of pain: Relative efficacy of three self-report measures. *Journal of Clinical Child Psychology, 17*, 329–335.

Benini, F., Trapanatto, M., Gobber, D., Agosto, C., Carli, G., Drigo, P., et al. (2004). Evaluating pain induced by venipuncture in pediatric patients with developmental delay. *Clinical Journal of Pain, 20*, 156–163.

Berntson, L., & Svensson, E. (2001). Pain assessment in children with juvenile chronic arthritis: A matter of scaling and rater. *Acta Pediatrica, 90*, 1131–1136.

Beyer, J. E. (1984). *The oucher: A user's manual and technical report.* Evanston, IL: Judson Press.

Beyer, J. E., & Aradine, C. R. (1986). Content validity of an instrument to measure young children's perceptions of the intensity of their pain. *Journal of Pediatric Nursing, 1*, 386–395.

Beyer, J. E., & Aradine, C. R. (1987). Patterns of pediatric pain intensity: A methodological investigation of a self-report scale. *The Clinical Journal of Pain, 3*, 130–141.

Beyer, J. E., & Aradine, C. R. (1988). Convergent and discriminant validity of a self-report measure of pain intensity for children. *Children's Health Care, 16*, 274–282.

Beyer, J. E., Denyes, M., & Villaruel, A. (1992). The creation, validation and continuing development of the oucher: A measure of pain intensity in children. *Journal of Pediatric Nursing, 7*, 335–346.

Beyer, J. E., & Knott, C. B. (1998). Construct validity estimation for the African-American and Hispanic versions of the Oucher scale. *Journal of Pediatric Nursing, 13*, 20–31.

Bieri, D., Reeve, R., Champion, G., Addicoat, L., & Ziegler, J. (1990). The faces pain scale for the self-assessment of the severity of pain experienced by children: Development, initial validation, and preliminary investigation for ratio scale properties. *Pain, 41,* 13–50.

Bijttebier, P., & Vertommen, H. (1999). Antecedents, concomitants, and consequences of pediatric headache: Confirmatory construct validation of two parent-report scales. *Journal of Behavioral Medicine, 22,* 437–456.

Brace, M. J., Smith, M. S., McCauley, E., & Sherry, D. D. (2000). Family reinforcement of illness behavior: A comparison of adolescents with chronic fatigue syndrome, juvenile arthritis, and healthy controls. *Journal of Developmental and Behavioral Pediatrics, 21,* 332–339.

Campo, J. V., Perel, J., Lucas, A., Bridge, J., Ehmann, M., Kalas, C., et al. (2004). Citalopram treatment of pediatric recurrent abdominal pain and comorbid internalizing disorders: An exploratory study. *Journal of the American Academy of Child & Adolescent Psychiatry, 43,* 1234–1242.

Chambers, C. T., & Craig, K. D. (1998). An intrusive impact of anchors in children's faces pain scales. *Pain, 78,* 27–37.

Chambers, C. T., Giesbrecht, K., Craig, K. D., Bennett, S., & Huntsman, E. (1999). A comparison of faces scales for the measurement of pediatric pain: Children's and parents' ratings. *Pain, 83,* 25–35.

Chambers, C. T., Hardial, J., Craig, K. D., Court, C., & Montgomery, C. (2005). Faces scales for the measurement of postoperative pain intensity in children following minor surgery. *Clinical Journal of Pain, 21,* 277–285.

Chambers, C. T., & Johnston, C. (2002). Developmental differences in children's use of rating scales. *Journal of Pediatric Psychology, 27,* 27–36.

Chan, L. F., Chow, S. M., & Lo, S. K. (2005). Preliminary validation of the Chinese version of the Pediatric Quality of Life Inventory™. *International Journal of Rehabilitation Research, 28,* 219–227.

Champion, G. D., Goodenough, B., von Baeyer, C. L., & Thomas, W. (1998). Measurement of pain by self-report. In G. A. Finley & P. J. McGrath (Eds.), *measurement of pain in infants and children, progress in pain research and management* (Vol. 10, pp. 123–160). Seattle, WA: IASP Press.

Claar, R. L., & Walker, L. S. (2006). Functional assessment of pediatric pain patients: Psychometric properties of the Functional Disability Inventory. *Pain, 121,* 77–84.

Claar, R. L., Walker, L. S., & Smith, C. A. (1999). Functional disability in adolescents and young adults with symptoms of irritable bowel syndrome: The role of academic, social, and athletic competence. *Journal of Pediatric Psychology, 24,* 271–280.

Connelly, M., & Rapoff, M. A. (2006). Assessing health-related quality of life in children with recurrent headache: Reliability and validity of the PedsQL™ in a pediatric headache sample. *Journal of Pediatric Psychology, 31,* 698–702.

Craig, K. D., Lilley, C. M., & Gilbert, C. A. (1996). Social barriers to optimal pain management in infants and children. *Clinical Journal of Pain, 12,* 232–242.

Crombez, G., Bijttebier, P., Eccleston, C., Mascagni, T., Mertens, G., Goubert, L., et al. (2003). The child version of the pain catastrophizing scale (PCS-C): A preliminary validation. *Pain, 104,* 639–646.

Cummings, E. A., Reid, G. J., Finley, G. A., McGrath, P. J., & Ritchie, J. A. (1996). Prevalence and source of pain in pediatric inpatients. *Pain, 68,* 25–31.

Eccleston, C., Crombez, G., Scotford, A., Clinch, J., & Connell, H. (2004). Adolescent chronic pain: Patterns and predictors of emotional distress in adolescents with chronic pain and their parents. *Pain, 108,* 221–229.

Eccleston, C., Malleson, P. N., Clinch, J., Connell, H., & Sourbut, C. (2003). Chronic pain in adolescents: Evaluation of a programme of interdisciplinary cognitive behavioral therapy. *Archives of Disease in Childhood, 88,* 881–885.

Eiser, C., & Morse, R. (2001). A review of measures of quality of life for children with chronic illness. *Archives of Disease in Childhood, 84,* 205–211.

Eland, J. M. (1982). Pain. In L. Hart, J. Reese, & M. Fearing (Eds.), *Concepts common to acute illness* (pp. 164–196). St. Louis, MO: Mosby.

Eland, J. M., & Anderson, J. E. (1977). The experience of pain in children. In A. Jacox (Ed.), *Pain: A sourcebook for nurses and other health care professionals.* Boston, MA: Little, Brown & Co.

Felder-Puig, R., Frey, E., Proksch, K., Varni, J. W., Gadner, H., & Topf, R. (2004). Validation of the German version of the Pediatric Quality of Life Inventory™ (PedsQL™) in childhood cancer patients off treatment and children with epilepsy. *Quality of Life Research, 13,* 223–234.

Fradet, C., McGrath, P. J., Kay, J., Adams, S., & Luke, B. (1990). A prospective survey of reactions to blood tests by children and Adolescents. *Pain, 40,* 53–60

Franck, L. S., Treadwell, M., Jacob, E., & Vichinsky, E. (2002). Assessment of sickle cell pain in children and young adolescents using the Adolescent Pediatric Pain Tool. *Journal of Pain and Symptom Management, 23,* 114–120.

Gharaibeh, M., & Abu-Saad, H. (2002). Cultural validation of pediatric pain assessment tools: Jordanian perspective. *Journal of Transcultural Nursing, 13,* 12–18.

Gauthier, J. C., Finley, G. A., & McGrath, P. J. (1998). Children's self-report of postoperative pain intensity and treatment threshold: Determining the adequacy of medication. *Clinical Journal of Pain, 14,* 116–120.

Gidron, Y., Berkovitch, M., & Press, J. (2003). Psychosocial correlates of incidence of attacks in children with familial Mediterranean fever. *Journal of Behavioral Medicine, 26,* 95–104.

Gidron Y., McGrath P. J., & Goodday, R. (1995). The physical and psychosocial predictors of adolescents' recovery from oral surgery. *Journal of Behavioral Medicine, 18,* 385–99.

Goodenough, B., Addicoat, L., Champion, G. D., McInerney, M., Young, B., Juniper, K., et al. (1997). Pain in 4- to 6-year-old children receiving intramuscular injections: A comparison of the faces pain scale with other self-report and behavioral measures. *The Clinical Journal of Pain, 13,* 60–73.

Hester, N. O. (1979). The preoperational child's reaction to immunization. *Nursing Research, 28,* 250–255.

Hicks, C. L., von Baeyer, C. L., Spafford, P. A., van Korlaar, I., & Goodenough, B. (2001). The Faces Pain Scale-Revised: Toward a common metric in pediatric pain measurement. *Pain, 93,* 173–183.

Kashikar-Zuck, S., Vaught, M. H., Goldschneider, K. R., Graham, T. B., & Miller, J. C. (2002). Depression, coping, and functional disability in juvenile primary fibromyalgia syndrome. *Journal of Pain, 3,* 412–419.

Levy, R. L., Whitehead, W. E., Walker, L. S., Von Korff, M., Feld, A. D., Garner, M., et al. (2004). Increased somatic complaints and health-care utilization in children: Effects of parent IBD status and parent response to gastrointestinal symptoms. *American Journal of Gastroenterology, 99,* 2442–2451.

Lister, M. T., Cunningham, M. J., Benjamin, B., Williams, M., Tirrell, A., Schaumberg, D. A., et al. (2006). Microdebrider tonsillotomy vs electrosurgical tonsillectomy: A randomized, double-blind, paired control study of postoperative pain. *Archives of Otolaryngology—Head and Neck Surgery, 132,* 599–604.

Luffy, R., & Grove, S. K. (2003). Examining the validity, reliability, and preference of three pediatric pain tools in African-American children. *Pediatric Nursing, 29,* 54–59.

Lynch, A. M., Kashikar-Zuck, S., Goldschneider, K. R., & Jones, B. A. (2006). Psychosocial risks for disability in children with chronic back pain. *Journal of Pain, 7,* 244–251.

Mathews, J. R., McGrath, P. J., & Pigeon, H. (1993). Assessment and measurement of pain in children. In N. L. Schechter, C. B. Berde, & M. Yaster (Eds.), *Pain in infants, children, and adolescents* (pp. 97–111). Baltimore, MD: Williams & Wilkins.

McCracken, L. M., Zayfert, C., & Gross, R. T. (1992). The Pain Anxiety Symptoms Scale: Development and validation of a scale to measure fear of pain. *Pain, 50,* 67–73.

McGrath, P. A., Seifert, C. E., Speechley, K. N., Booth, J. C., Stitt, L., & Gibson, M. C. (1996). A new analogue scale for assessing children's pain: An initial validation study. *Pain, 64,* 435–443.

McGrath, P. J., Turk, D. C., Dworkin, R. H., Brown, M. T., Davidson, K., Eccleston, C., et al. (2006). *Core outcome domains and measures for pediatric acute and chronic/recurrent pain clinical trials: PedIMMPACT recommendations.* Unpublished manuscript.

McGrath, P. J., & Unruh, A. (Eds.). (1987). *Pain in children and adolescents.* Amsterdam: Elsevier.

McNeil, D. W., & Rainwater, A. J., (1998). Development of the Fear of Pain Questionnaire-III. *Journal of Behavioral Medicine, 21,* 389–410.

Melzack, R. (1983). The McGill Pain Questionnaire. In R. Melzack (Ed.), *Pain measurement and assessment* (pp. 41–47). New York: Raven Press.

Melzack R., & Wall, P. D. (1965). Pain mechanisms: A new theory. *Science, 150,* 971–979.

Merlijn, V. P. B. M., Hunfeld, J. A. M., van der Wouden, J. C., Hazebroek-Kampschreur, A. A. J. M., & Passchier, J. (2003). Psychosocial factors associated with chronic pain in adolescents. *Pain, 101,* 33–43.

Merlijn, V. P. B. M., Hunfeld, J. A. M., van der Wouden, J. C., Hazebroek-Kampschreur, A. A. J. M., Passchier, J., & Koes, B. W. (2006). Factors related to the quality of life in adolescents with chronic pain. *Clinical Journal of Pain, 22,* 306–315.

Merskey, H., & Bogduk, N. (1994). *Classification of chronic pain: Description of chronic pain syndromes and definitions of pain terms* (2nd ed.). Seattle, WA: IASP Press.

Migdal, M., Chudzynska-Pomianowska, E., Vause, E., Henry, E., & Lazar, J. (2005). Rapid, needle-free delivery of lidocaine for reducing the pain of venipuncture among pediatric subjects. *Pediatrics, 115,* 393–398.

Mindell, J. A., & Owens, J. A. (2003). *A clinical guide to pediatric sleep: diagnosis and management of sleep problems in children and adolescents.* Philadelphia, PA: Lippincott Williams & Wilkins.

Miro, J., & Huguet, A. (2004). Evaluation of reliability, validity, and preference for a pediatric pain intensity scale: The Catalan version of the Faces Pain Scale—revised. *Pain, 111,* 59–64.

Newman, C. J., Lolekha, R., Limkittikul, K., Luangxay, K., Chotpitayasunondh, T. & Chanthavanich, P. A. (2005). A comparison of pain scales in Thai children. *Archives of Disease in Childhood, 90,* 269–70.

Oberlander, T. F., & Symons, F. J. (Eds.). (2006). *Pain in children and adults with developmental disabilities.* Baltimore, MD: Paul H. Brooks Publishing.

Palermo, T. M. (2000). Impact of recurrent and chronic pain on child and family daily functioning: A critical review of the literature. *Journal of Developmental and Behavioral Pediatrics, 21,* 58–69.

Palermo, T. M., & Kiska, R. (2005). Subjective sleep disturbances in adolescents with chronic pain: Relationship to daily functioning and quality of life. *Journal of Pain, 6,* 201–207.

Palermo, T. M., Valenzuela, D., & Stork, P. P. (2004). A randomized trial of electronic versus paper pain diaries in children: Impact on compliance, accuracy, and acceptability. *Pain, 107,* 213–219.

Perquin, C. W., Hazebroek-Kampschreur, A. A. J. M., Hunfeld, J. A. M., Bohnena, A. M., van Suijlekom-Smitd, L. W. A., Passchier, J., et al. (2000). Pain in children and adolescents: A common experience. *Pain, 87,* 51–58.

Peterson C. C., & Palermo, T. M. (2004). Parental reinforcement of recurrent pain: The moderating impact of child depression and anxiety on functional disability. *Journal of Pediatric Psychology, 29,* 331–341.

Powell, C. V., Kelly, A.-M., & Williams, A. (2001). Determining the minimum clinically significant difference in visual analogue pain score for children. *Annals of Emergency Medicine, 37,* 28–31.

Powers, S. W., Patton, S. R., Hommel, K. A., & Hershey, A. D. (2004). Quality of life in paediatric migraine: Characterization of age-related effects using PedsQL ™ 4.0. *Cephalagia, 24,* 120–127.

Ramritu, P. L. (2000). Use of the Oucher numeric and Word Graphic Scale in children aged 9–14 years with post-operative pain. *Journal of Clinical Nursing, 9,* 763–773.

Reid, G. J., McGrath, P. J., & Lang, B. A. (2005). Parent–child interactions among children with juvenile fibromyalgia, arthritis, and healthy controls. *Pain, 113,* 201–210.

Reinfjell, T., Diseth, T. H., Veenstra, M., & Vikan, A. (2006). Measuring health-related quality of life in young adolescents: Reliability and validity in the Norwegian version of the Pediatric Quality of Life Inventory™ 4.0 (PedsQL™) generic core scales. *Health and Quality of Life Outcomes,* Article 4:61. Retrieved May 1, 2007, from http://www.hqlo.com/content/4/1/61

Richardson, G. M., McGrath, P., Cunningham, S. J., & Humphreys, P. (1983). Validity of the headache diary for children. *Headache: The Journal of Head and Face Pain, 23,* 184–187.

Savedra, M., Holzemer, W., Tesler, M., & Wilkie, D. (1993). Assessment of postoperative pain in children and Adolescents using the Adolescent Pediatric Pain Tool. *Nursing Research, 42,* 5–9.

Savedra, M. C., Tesler, M. D., Holzemer, W. L., Wilkie, D. J., & Ward, J. A. (1990). Testing a tool to assess postoperative pediatric and adolescent pain. In D. C. Tyler & E. J. Krane (Eds.), *Advances in pain research and therapy* (pp. 85–93). New York: Raven Press Ltd.

Savedra, M. C., Tesler, M. D., Holzemer, W. L., Wilkie, D. J.,& Ward, J. A. (1989). Pain location: Validity and reliability of body outline markings by hospitalized children and adolescents. *Research in Nursing and Health, 12,* 307–314.

Shields, B. J., Palermo, T. M., Powers, J. D., Grewe, S. D., & Smith, G. A. (2003). Predictors of a child's ability to use a visual analogue scale. *Child: Care, Health and Development, 29,* 281–290.

Stinson, J. N., Kavanagh, T., Yamada, J., Gill, N., & Stevens, B. (2006a). Systematic review of the psychometric properties, interpretability, and feasibility of self-report pain intensity measures for use in clinical trials in children and adolescents. *Pain, 125,* 143–157.

Stinson, J. N., Petroz, G. C., Tait, G., Feldman, B. M., Streiner, D., McGrath, P. J., et al. (2006b). e-Ouch: Usability testing of an electronic chronic pain diary for adolescents with arthritis. *Clinical Journal of Pain, 22,* 295–305.

Sullivan, M. J. L., Bishop, S. R., & Pivik, J. (1995). The Pain Catastrophizing Scale: Development and validation. *Psychological Assessment, 7,* 524–532.

Suraseranivongse, S., Montapaneewat, T., Monon, J., Chainhop, P., Petcharatana, S., & Kraiprasit, K. (1985). Cross-validation of a self-report scale for post-operative pain in school-aged children. *Journal of the Medical Association of Thailand, 88,* 412–417.

Sweet, S. D., & McGrath, P. J. (1998). Physiological measures of pain. In G. A. Finley & P. J. McGrath (Eds.), *Measurement of pain in infants and children: Progress in pain research and management* (Vol. 10, pp. 59–81). Seattle, WA: IASP Press.

Taddio, A., & Katz, J. (2005). The effects of early pain experience in neonates on pain responses in infancy and childhood. *Paediatric Drugs, 7,* 245–257.

Taddio, A., Katz, J., Illersich, A. L., & Koren, G. (1997). Effect of neonatal circumcision on pain response during subsequent routine vaccination. *The Lancet, 349,* 599–603.

Taddio, A., Kaur Soin, H., Schuh, S., Koren, G., & Scolnik, D. (2005). Liposomal lidocaine to improve procedural success rates and reduce procedural pain among children: A randomized controlled trial. *Canadian Medical Association Journal, 172,* 1691–1695.

Tesler, M. D., Savedra, M. C., Holzemer, W. L., Wilkie, D. J., Ward, J. A., & Paul, S. M. (1991). The word-graphic rating scale as a measure of children's and adolescents' pain intensity. *Research in Nursing and Health, 14,* 361–371.

Unruh, A. M., & Campbell, M. (1999). Gender variation in children's pain experiences. In P. J. McGrath & G. A. Finley (Vol. Eds.), *Chronic and recurrent pain in children and adolescents: progress in pain research and management* (Vol. 13, pp. 199–241). Seattle, WA: IASP Press.

van den Brink, M., Bandell-Hoekstra, E. N. G., & Abu-Saad, H. H. (2001). The occurrence of recall bias in pediatric headache: A comparison of questionnaire and diary data. *Headache: The Journal of Head and Face Pain, 41,* 11–20.

Varni, J. W. (2007). PedsQL™ Web site. Retrieved April 23, 2007 from http://www.pedsql.org

Varni, J. W., Burwinkle, T. M., Limbers, C. A., & Szer, I. S. (2007). The PedsQL™ as a patient-reported outcome in children and adolescents with fibromyalgia: An analysis of OMERACT domains. *Health and Quality of Life Outcomes,* Article 5:9. Retrieved April 05, 2007 from http://www.hqlo.com/content/5/1/9

Varni, J. W., Seid, M., & Rode, C. A. (1999). The PedsQL™: Measurement model for the Pediatric Quality of Life Inventory™. *Medical Care, 37,* 126–139.

Varni, J. W., Seid, M., Knight, T. S., Uzark, K., & Szer, I. S. (2002). The PedsQL™ 4.0 Generic Core Scales: Sensitivity, responsiveness, and impact on clinical decision-making. *Journal of Behavioural Medicine, 25,* 175–193.

Varni, J. W., Seid, M., & Kurtin, P. S. (2001). PedsQL™ 4.0: Reliability and validity of the Pediatric Quality of Life Inventory™ Version 4.0 Generic Core Scales in healthy and patient populations. *Medical Care, 39,* 800–812.

Varni, J. W., & Setoguchi, Y. (1992). Screening for behavioral and emotional problems in children and adolescents with congenital or acquired limb deficiencies. *American Journal of Diseases of Children, 146,* 103–107.

Vervoot, T., Goubert, L., Eccleston, C., Bijttebier, P., & Crombez, G. (2006). Catastrophic thinking about pain is independently associated with pain severity, disability, and somatic complaints in schoolchildren and children with chronic pain. *Journal of Pediatric Psychology, 31,* 674–683.

Villarruel, A., & Denyes, M. (1991). Pain assessment in children: Theoretical and empirical validity. *Advances in Nursing Science, 14,* 32–41.

von Baeyer, C. L. (2006). Children's self-reports of pain intensity: Scale selection, limitations and interpretation. *Pain Research and Management, 11,* 157–162.

von Baeyer, C. L., & Spagrud, L. J. (2007). Systematic review of observational (behavioral) measures of pain for children and adolescents aged 3 to 18 years. *Pain, 127,* 140–150.

Wall, P. D. (1989). Introduction. In P. D. Wall & R. Melzack (Eds.), *Textbook of pain* (2nd ed., pp. 1–18). Edinburgh: Churchill Livingstone.

Walco, G. A., Conte, P. M., Labay, L. E., Engel, R., & Zeltzer, L. K. (2005). Procedural distress in children with cancer: Self-report, behavioral observations, and physiological parameters. *Clinical Journal of Pain, 21,* 498–490.

Walker, L. S., Garber, J., & Greene, J. W. (1993). Psychosocial correlates of recurrent childhood pain: A comparison of pediatric patients with recurrent abdominal pain, organic illness, and psychiatric disorders. *Journal of Abnormal Psychology, 102,* 248–258.

Walker, L. S., & Zeman, J. L. (1992). Parental response to child illness behavior. *Journal of Pediatric Psychology, 17,* 49–71.

Walters, A. S., & Williamson, G. M. (1999). The role of activity restriction in the association between pain and depression: A study of pediatric patients with chronic pain. *Children's Health Care, 28,* 33–50.

Walker, L. S., & Greene, J. W. (1991). The Functional Disability Inventory: Measuring a neglected dimension of child health status. *Journal of Pediatric Psychology, 16,* 39–58.

Walker, L. S., Guite, J. W., Duke, M., Barnard, J. A., & Greene, J. W. (1998). Recurrent abdominal pain: A potential precursor of irritable bowel syndrome in adolescents and young adults. *Journal of Pediatrics, 132,* 1010–1015.

Walker, L. S., Smith, C. A., Garber, J., & Claar, R. L. (2005). Testing a model of pain appraisal and coping in children with chronic abdominal pain. *Health Psychology, 24,* 364–374.

Wewers, M. E., & Lowe, N. K. (1990). A critical review of visual analogue scales in the measurement of clinical phenomena. *Research in Nursing & Health, 13,* 227–236.

White, J. B., & Stow, P. J. (1985). Rational and experience with visual analogue toys. *Anesthesia, 40,* 601–603.

Whitehead, W. E., Winget, C., Fedoravicius, A. S., Wooley, S., & Blackwell, B. (1982). Learned illness behavior in patients with irritable bowel syndrome and peptic ulcer. *Digestive Diseases and Sciences, 27,* 202–208.

Wilkie, D. J., Holzemer, W. L., Tesler, M. D., Ward, J. A., Paul, S. M., & Savedra, M. C. (1990). Measuring pain quality: Validity and reliability of children's and adolescents' pain language. *Pain, 41,* 151–159.

Wong, D. L., & Baker, C. M. (1988). Pain in children: Comparison of assessment scales. *Pediatric Nursing, 14,* 9–17.

Wood, C., von Baeyer, C. L., Bourrillon, A., Dejos-Conant, V., Clyti, N., & Abitbol, V. (2004). Self-assessment of immediate post-vaccination pain after two different MMR vaccines administered as second dose in 3- to 6-year old children. *Vaccine, 23,* 127–131.

World Health Organization (1948). *Constitution of the World Health Organization basic document.* Geneva: Word Health Organization.

World Health Organization (2001). *International classification of functioning, disability and health: ICF.* Geneva: World Health Organization.

Yeh, C.-H. (2005). Development and validation of the Asian version of the Oucher: A pain intensity scale for children. *Journal of Pain. 6,* 526–534.

Youssef, N. N., Rosh, J. R., Loughran, M., Schuckalo, S. G., Cotter, A. N., Verga, B. G., et al. (2004). Treatment of functional abdominal pain in childhood with cognitive behavioral strategies. *Journal of Pediatric Gastroenterology, 39,* 192–196.

26

Chronic Pain in Adults

Dennis C. Turk
Akiko Okifuji
Michelle Skinner

In this chapter, we focus on the psychological (behavioral medicine) evaluation of chronic pain patients. We first discuss the nature of chronic pain and the rationale behind the need to have a comprehensive psychological evaluation. We then review medical and physical evaluations for pain. In the section on psychological evaluation, we provide a description of measures that may be used for initial psychological screening and emphasize the importance of identifying those patients who are likely to require a more comprehensive psychological evaluation. We provide an overview of the general areas that are covered in a psychological evaluation through patient and significant other interviews. We also review a number of standardized psychometric tests that can be useful to provide corroborative information obtained from the interview.

THE NATURE OF CHRONIC PAIN

Pain is an extremely prevalent symptom. Chronic pain alone is estimated to affect 15% to 20% of the adult population of the United States (Von Korff et al., 2001), upwards of 50 million people (U.S. Department of Health and Human Services, Food and Drug Administration, 1997). In addition to being highly prevalent, pain is exceedingly costly, to the individual with chronic pain, his or her significant others, and society. The expenses for chronic pain involve not only traditional healthcare but also indirect costs such as lost productive time at work, lost tax revenue, legal services, and disability compensation.

Although exact figures for the cost of a wide variety of available medical and alternative treatments are difficult to ascertain, estimates of the total costs of chronic pain (including treatment, lost work days, disability payments, legal fees) in the United States reaches $150 to $215 billion per year (National Research Council, 2001; U.S. Bureau of the Census, 1996). Despite the soaring cost of treating people with chronic pain, relief for many remains elusive and complete elimination of pain is rare. Although there have been substantial advances in our knowledge of neurophysiology, along with the development of potent analgesic medications and other innovative medical and surgical interventions, people with conditions such as low back pain, headaches, fibromyalgia syndrome (FMS), and osteoarthritis continue to suffer from pain that impairs their quality of life, causing significant physical disability and considerable emotional distress.

How we think about symptoms such as pain influences the way in which we go about evaluating patients. Physicians and the lay public alike assume that some underlying pathology is both a necessary and a sufficient cause of the symptoms experienced. Consequently, medical assessment usually begins with taking a thorough history and performing physical examination, followed by, when deemed appropriate, laboratory tests and diagnostic imaging procedures in an attempt to identify or confirm the presence of an underlying pathology that *causes* the symptom. In the absence of identifiable organic pathology, the physician may assume that the report of symptoms stems from psychological factors.

A psychological evaluation may be requested to detect the underlying psychological factors that underlie the patient's reports. Thus, there is a duality where the report of symptoms is attributed to either somatic or psychogenic mechanisms. The assumption that symptoms that cannot be explained by medical findings must originate from psychological distress is, albeit unfortunately common, overly simplistic, and inconsistent with current scientific, understanding (Turk & Flor, 1999).

Over the years, research has revealed puzzling observations that would challenge the presumed isomorphism between pain and organic pathology. For example, the exact pathophysiology underlying some of the most common and recurring acute (e.g., primary headache) and chronic (e.g., back pain, FMS) pain problems is largely unknown. Conversely, several studies using plain radiography, computed tomography scans, and magnetic-resonance imaging, reveal that more than 30% of *asymptomatic* individuals have structural abnormalities such as herniated discs resulting in impingement of neural structures and spinal stenosis that would explain the pain if it was present (Boden, Davis, Dina, Patronas, & Wiesel, 1990; Jensen, Brant-Zawadski, Obuchowski, Modic, Malkasian, et al., 1994). In the case of FMS, although a number of endocrine, immunological, and neurochemical perturbations have been investigated, there is currently no consensus regarding the causal mechanisms for the symptoms reported (Pillemer, Bradley, Crofford, Moldofsky, & Chrousos, 1997). Thus, we are confronted with a rather strange set of circumstances: people with no identified organic pathology report severe pain and others with significant pathology who are apparently pain free.

Still other observations challenge the simple one-to-one relationship between organic pathology and pain. For example, the same surgical procedure performed following a standard protocol on patients with the same objective physical pathology, may have very different outcomes (North, Campbell, James, Conover-Walker, Wang, et al., 1991). In one patient the pain is eliminated immediately following surgery, whereas another patient finds no benefit and may even report worsening of the pain. Finally, only a modest association exists between patients' levels of functional impairment and the extent of tissue pathology (Waddell, 1987). Obviously, factors other than organic pathology must be contributing to these observations.

Chronic pain that is associated with significant physical, functional, and psychosocial dysfunction poses a difficult problem for the patient, his or her family, and health care providers. A comprehensive evaluation can provide information useful in identifying psychosocial and behavioral factors that may be contributing to, but not necessarily causing, the patients' pain and disability, as well as clarifying the impact that chronic pain may have on physical, psychological, and social functioning. A psychological evaluation can also provide important information for the development and implementation of an optimal treatment plan. We must be careful, however, not to confuse a psychological evaluation and a psychiatric evaluation. Many patients, as well as clinicians, may consider that the psychological evaluation is only to focus on mental health. The assessment of mental health is certainly an important part of the psychological evaluation for pain patients; however, it must also evaluate overall psychological and behavioral functions of the patient, including behavioral repertories, cognitive patterns, interpersonal situations, and lifestyle habits. For example, a number of studies have implicated the role of the patient's idiosyncratic appraisals of his or her symptoms, expectations regarding the cause of the symptoms, and the meaning of the symptoms, in addition to organic factors, as essential in understanding the individual's report of pain and subsequent disability (Jensen, Turner, Romano, & Lawler, 1994; Jensen, Romano, Turner, Good, & Wald, 1999). Moreover, the patient's current mood, ways of coping with symptoms, and responses by significant others, including physicians, may modulate the experience of pain, particularly chronic or recurrent pain (Fordyce, 1976; Turk, Okifuji, & Scharff, 1995). Failure to address these factors can result in poor response to treatments that focus exclusively on somatic causes.

A comprehensive psychological evaluation of a pain patient should help us gain insight as to how the person handles somatic and psychological distress and the level of the patient's coping resources, and guide us in developing a comprehensive treatment plan. In other words, providing a satisfactory explanation and appropriate treatment to a patient with chronic pain requires more than just an accurate evaluation of the organic pathology that may be causing the pain. It must also address the specific psychosocial, behavioral, and cognitive factors such as current mood (anxiety, depression, anger), interpretation of the symptoms, expectations about the meaning of symptoms, and the responses to the patient's symptoms by significant others (e.g., family members, coworkers), each of which contributes to the subjective experience of pain.

GENERAL ASSESSMENT CONSIDERATIONS

Turk and Meichenbaum (1984) suggested that three central questions should guide assessment of people who report pain:

1. What is the extent of the patient's disease or injury (physical impairment)?
2. What is the magnitude of the illness? That is, to what extent is the patient suffering, disabled, and unable to enjoy usual activities?
3. Does the individual's behavior seem appropriate to the disease or injury or is there any evidence of amplification of symptoms for any of a variety of psychological or social reasons or purposes?

In this section, we examine some of the issues related to addressing the first question.

Medical and Physical Evaluations

Appropriate assessment and treatment of a patient whose primary symptom is pain begins with a comprehensive history and physical examination. Patients are usually asked to describe the characteristics (e.g., stabbing, burning), location, severity of their pain, treatment history, current and past medications, and review of systems. Where appropriate, physical examination includes a trigger point assessment to determine whether there is significant myofacial component to the pain. A physical therapist typically assesses the level of physical functioning, such as range of motion, strength, gait, posture, and reflex. The nature and level of activities of daily living are also evaluated. Through this examination, the clinician may note the presence or absence of signs indicative of neurological deficit.

A physician may order some laboratory testing to be conducted to rule out any specific structural damages or endocrine and neurological abnormalities. A diagnostic nerve block may be of value, as it evaluates the involvement of the particular nerves and, thus, may provide some guidance for treatment. For example, the block itself may be beneficial, when this is the case the initially diagnostic procedure can be repeated as a treatment. If the pain is not eliminated during the block, then the source of the pain is likely not in the peripheral nerves affected by the level of the injection. However, in reality, the results often appear equivocal; for example, the patient may report a slight decline in pain during the procedure for a very short period of time. Thus, the results of the diagnostic blocks are best interpreted in conjunction with other aspects of the evaluations.

Sophisticated laboratory and imaging techniques are readily available for use in detecting organic pathology. Imaging and electrophysiological studies may reveal pathology that may be addressed medically or surgically. However, for a large portion of chronic pain patients, such evaluations are conducted at a fairly early stage of treatment. It is common to see that these tests fail to reveal any specific pathology that would explain the presence of persistent pain or the extent of such pain. Furthermore, for significant numbers of patients, no physical pathology can be identified using plain radiographs, CAT (Computed Axial Tomography) scans, or electromyography to validate the report of pain severity, making the diagnostic value of these studies for chronic pain somewhat dubious.

Because of these issues, it is often not possible to make any precise pathological diagnosis or even to identify an adequate anatomical or physiological origin for the pain. Despite these limitations, however, the patient's history and physical examination remain the basis of medical diagnosis and may be the best defense against over-interpreting results from sophisticated imaging procedures. Physicians must therefore be cautious not to over-interpret either the presence or absence of objective findings. An extensive literature is available focusing on physical assessment, radiographic, and laboratory assessment procedures to determine the physical basis of pain and the extent of impairments in adults (see Turk & Melzack, 1992/2001).

Quantifying Pain Severity

In evaluating pain patients, it is critical to understand the extent of pain severity, which will serve as a baseline with which the treatment effects will be determined. Because there is no "pain thermometer" that can provide an objective quantification of the amount or severity of pain experienced by a patient, it can only be assessed indirectly based on a patient's overt communication, both verbal and nonverbal (i.e., pain behaviors). However, even a patient's communications make pain assessment difficult, as pain is a complex, subjective phenomenon comprised of a range of factors and is uniquely experienced by each individual. Wide variability in pain severity, quality, and impact may be noted in reports of patients attempting to describe what appear to be objectively identical phenomena. Patient's descriptions of pain are also colored by cultural and sociological influences. Later in the chapter, we discuss some commonly used self-report inventories for the assessment of pain.

PURPOSES OF PSYCHOLOGICAL ASSESSMENT

On the basis of the multidimensional perspective espoused in this chapter, health-care providers need to examine not only the physical source of the pain through examination and diagnostic tests but also the patient's mood, fears, expectancies, coping efforts, resources, responses of significant others, and the impact of pain on the patients' lives. In short, the health-care provider must evaluate the whole patient, not just a primary complaint. Regardless of whether an organic basis for the pain can be documented or whether psychosocial problems preceded or resulted from the pain, the evaluation process can be helpful in identifying how biomedical, psychosocial, and behavioral factors interact to influence the nature, severity, and persistence of pain and disability.

In the remainder of this chapter, we focus on the second and third of Turk and Meichenbaum's (1984) questions: specifically, the extent of the patient's disability and the behavioral influences on the patient's pain, distress, and suffering. Evaluating these variables begins with gathering information from the patient, through clinical interview and/or through standard assessment instruments.

Interviews

When conducting an interview with chronic pain patients the health-care professional should focus on both factual information and on patients' and significant others' specific thoughts (e.g., expectations, meaning of symptoms), and feelings and they should observe specific behaviors. Thus, the intent of the interview is not solely gathering of subjective information provided by the patient but also interpreting how the information is conveyed. The patient's attitude about the health-care system and reaction to certain questions may provide an insightful clue for the person's psychological repertories.

Pain patients' beliefs about the cause of symptoms, their trajectory, and beneficial treatments will have important influences on emotional adjustment and adherence to therapeutic interventions. A habitual pattern of maladaptive thoughts may contribute to a sense of hopelessness, dysphoria, and unwillingness to engage in activity, and in turn, deactivate the patient and severely limit his or her coping resources. The interviewer should also determine both the patient's and the significant others' expectancies and goals for treatment. An expectation that pain will be eliminated completely may be unrealistic and will have to be addressed to prevent discouragement when this outcome does not occur. Setting appropriate and realistic goals is an important process in pain rehabilitation as it requires the patient to attain better understanding of chronic pain and goes beyond the dualistic, traditional medical model.

To help the patient understand the psychosocial aspects of pain, attention should focus on the patient's reports of specific thoughts, behaviors, emotions, and physiological responses that precede, accompany, and follow pain episodes or exacerbation, as well as the environmental conditions and consequences associated with cognitive, emotional, and behavioral responses in these situations. During the interview, the clinician should attend to the temporal association of these cognitive, affective, and behavioral events, their specificity versus generality across situations, and the frequency of their occurrence, to establish salient features of the target situations, including the controlling variables. The interviewer seeks information that will assist in the development of potential alternate responses, appropriate goals for the patient, and possible reinforcers for these alternatives.

A psychological interview with pain patients is typically semistructured. As discussed subsequently in this chapter, a structured format of psychiatric interview can be incorporated as a tool to examine psychopathology. However, a psychological interview

TABLE 26.1 Screening Questions

If there is a combination of more than 6 "Yes" to the first 13 questions and "No" to the last 3 questions below or if general concerns in any one area, a referral for a detailed psychological assessment should be considered.

1. Has the patient's pain persisted for three months or longer despite appropriate interventions and in the absence of progressive disease? [Yes]
2. Does the patient repeatedly and excessively use the health care system, persist in seeking invasive investigations or treatments after being informed these are inappropriate, or use opioid or sedative-hypnotic medications or alcohol in a pattern of concern to the patient's physician (e.g., escalating use)? [Yes]
3. Does the patient come in requesting specific opioid medication (e.g., dilaudid, oxycontin)? [Yes]
4. Does the patient have unrealistic expectations of the health care providers or the treatment offered (i.e., "total elimination of pain and related symptoms") [Yes]
5. Does the patient have a history of substance abuse or is he or she currently abusing mind altering substances? [Yes]
6. Does the patient display large number of pain behaviors that appear exaggerated (e.g., grimacing, rigid or guarded posture)? [Yes]
7. Does the patient have litigation pending? [Yes]
8. Is the patient seeking or receiving disability compensation? [Yes]
9. Does the patient have any other family members who had or currently suffer from chronic pain conditions? [Yes]
10. Does the patient demonstrate excessive depression or anxiety? [Yes]. Straightforward questions such as, "Have you been feeling down?" or "What effect has your pain had on your mood?" can clarify whether this area is in need of more detailed evaluation.
11. Can the patient identify a significant or several stressful life events previous to symptom onset or exacerbation? [Yes]
12. If married or living with a partner, does the patient indicate a high degree of interpersonal conflict? [Yes]
13. Has the patient given up many activities (recreational, social, familial, in addition to occupational and work activities) due to pain? [Yes]
14. Does the patient have any plans for renewed or increased activities if pain is reduced? [No]
15. Was the patient employed prior to pain onset? [No] If yes, does he or she wish to return to that job or any job? [No]
16. Does the patient believe that he or she will never be able to resume normal life and normal functioning? [No]

with pain patients needs to go beyond it, as the main purpose of conducting such an interview is to assess the psychosocial factors (not just psychopathology) related to his/her pain and disability.

Table 26.1 contains a list of 16 salient points that can be used as prescreening questions with patients who report persistent or recurring pain. When a number of these questions are endorsed, referral for more thorough evaluation by pain specialists should be considered. Generally, a referral for evaluation may be indicated where disability greatly exceeds what would be expected based on physical findings alone, when patients make excessive demands on the health-care system, when the patient persists in seeking medical tests and treatments when these are not indicated, when patients display significant emotional distress (e.g., depression or anxiety), or when the patient displays evidence of addictive behaviors or continual nonadherence to the prescribed regimen. Table 26.2 contains a detailed outline of the areas that should be addressed in a more extensive psychological interview for pain patients.

Patients with chronic pain problems often consume a variety of medications. It is important to discuss a patient's medications during the interview, as many pain medications (particularly opioids) are associated with side effects that may mimic emotional distress. A clinician, for example, should be familiar with side effects that result in fatigue, sleep difficulties, and mood changes to avoid misdiagnosis of depression. A general understanding of commonly used medications for chronic pain is important, as some patients also may use opioid analgesics to manage mood. During the interview potential psychological dependence and aberrant drug seeking behaviors on pain-relieving medications should be evaluated. In some states, a physician is able to obtain a record of prescriptions of controlled substances. When in doubt, a psychologist may recommend that such a record be obtained and urine toxicology screening performed to rule out substance abuse problems (including diversion) and aberrant opioid taking behaviors.

Assessment Instruments

In addition to interviews, a number of assessment instruments designed to evaluate patients' attitudes, beliefs, and expectancies about themselves, their

TABLE 26.2 Areas Addressed in Psychological Interviews

Experience of Pain and Related Symptoms
- Location and description of pain (e.g., "sharp", "burning")
- Onset and progression
- Perception of cause (e.g., trauma, virus, stress)
- Exacerbating and relieving factors (e.g., exercise, relaxation, stress, massage)
- Pattern of symptoms (e.g., symptoms worse certain times of day or following activity or stress)
- Sleep habits (e.g., difficulty falling to sleep or maintaining sleep, sleep hygiene)
- Thoughts, feelings, and behaviors that precede, accompany, and follow fluctuations in symptoms
- What has the patient been told about the symptoms and condition? Does the patient believe that this information is accurate?

Treatments Received and Currently Receiving
- Medication (prescribed and over-the-counter). How helpful have these been?
- Pattern of medication use (*prn*, time-contingent), changes in quantity or schedule
- Physical modalities (e.g., physical therapy). How helpful have these been?
- Exercise (e.g., Do they participate in a regular exercise routine? Is there evidence of deactivation and avoidance of activity due to fear of pain or exacerbation of injury?). Has the pattern changed (increased, decreased)?
- Complementary and alternative (e.g., chiropractic manipulation, relaxation training). How helpful have these been?
- Which treatments have they found the most helpful?
- Compliance/adherence with recommendations of health care providers
- Attitudes towards previous health care providers

Compensation/Litigation
- Current disability status (e.g., receiving or seeking disability, amount, percent of former job income, expected duration of support)
- Current or planned litigation

Responses by Patient and Significant Others
- Typical daily routine
- Changes in activities and responsibilities (both positive and obligatory) due to symptoms
- Changes in significant other's activities and responsibilities due to patient's symptoms
- Patient's behavior when pain increases or flares up
- Significant others' responses to behavioral expressions of pain
- What does the patient do when pain is not bothering him or her (uptime activities)?
- Significant other's response when patient is active
- Impact of symptoms on interpersonal, family, marital, and sexual relations (e.g., changes in desire, frequency, or enjoyment)
- Activities that patient avoids because of symptoms
- Activities continued despite symptoms.
- Pattern of activity and pacing of activity (can use activity diaries that ask patients to record their pattern of daily activities [time spent sitting, standing, walking, and reclining] for several days or weeks)

Coping
- How does the patient try to cope with his or her symptoms? Does patient view himself or herself as having any role in symptom management? If so, what role?
- Current life stresses
- Pleasant activities

Educational and Vocational History
- Level of education completed, including any special training
- Work history
- How long at most recent job?
- How satisfied with most recent job and supervisor?
- What like least about most recent job?
- Would the patient like to return to most recent job? If not what type of work would the patient like?
- Current work status, including homemaking activities
- Vocational and avocational plans

Social History
- Relationships with family or origin
- History of pain or disability in family members

(continued)

TABLE 26.2 (continued)

- History of substance abuse in family members
- History of, or current, physical, emotional, and sexual abuse. Was the patient a witness to abuse of someone else?
- Marital history and current status?
- Quality of current marital and family relations

Alcohol and Substance Use

- Current and history of alcohol use (quantity, frequency)
- History and current use of illicit psychoactive drugs
- History and current use of prescribed psychoactive medications
- Consider the CAGE questions as a quick screen for alcohol dependence (Mayfield, McLeod, & Hall, 1987) Depending on response consider, other instruments for alcohol and substance abuse (Allen & Litten, 1998)

Psychological Dysfunction

- Current psychological symptoms/diagnosis (depression including suicidal ideation, anxiety disorders, somatization, posttraumatic stress disorder). Depending on responses, consider conducting structured interview such as the Structured Clinical Interview for DSM-IV-TR (SCID; American Psychiatric Association, 1997)
- Is the patient currently receiving treatment for psychological symptoms? If yes, what treatments (e.g., psychotherapy or psychiatric medications). How helpful are the treatments?
- History of psychiatric disorders and treatment including family counseling
- Family history of psychiatric disorders

Concerns and Expectations

- Patient concerns/fears (e.g., Does the patient believe he/she has serious physical problems that have not been identified? Or that symptoms will become progressively worse and patient will become more disabled and more dependent? Does the patient worry that he or she will be told the symptoms are all psychological?)
- Explanatory models of pain held by the patient
- Expectations regarding the future and regarding treatment (will get better, worse, never change)
- Attitude toward rehabilitation versus cure
- Treatment goals

---

symptoms, and the health care system have been developed and published. One survey (Piotrowski, 1998) of clinicians who treated pain indicated that the five most frequently used instruments in the assessment of pain, in order of frequency, were the Minnesota Multiphasic Personality Inventory (Hathaway & McKinley, 1967), Beck Depression Inventory (Beck, Ward, Mendelson, Mock, & Erbaugh, 1961), McGill Pain Questionnaire (Melzack, 1975), Symptom Checklist-90 (Derogatis, 1983), and Multidimensional Pain Inventory (Kerns, Turk, & Rudy, 1985). Of this group, only the McGill Pain Questionnaire and the Multidimensional Pain Inventory were specifically developed for use with individuals with chronic pain. In Table 26.3 we list the descriptions of these and some of the most commonly used instruments.

Standardized instruments have advantages over semistructured and unstructured interviews. They are easy to administer, require less time, assess a wide range of behaviors, obtain information about behaviors that may be private (sexual relations) or unobservable (thoughts, emotional arousal), and, most importantly, can be submitted to analyses that permit determination of their reliability and validity.

These instruments should not be viewed as alternatives to interviews; rather, they may suggest issues to be addressed in more depth during an interview or investigated with other measures. In Table 26.4, we have the detailed rating for reliability and validity of each instrument.

A word of caution should be offered in interpreting the results of self-report inventories. Studies of the psychometric properties of self-report inventories typically involve data collection from a large number of patients. As reliability estimates are influenced by sample size, it follows that the measurement error of questionnaire data from one person should be expected to be much greater than that found in reports based on group data. One way to address concerns about reliability with some measures is to collect data at multiple points over time rather than simply comparing pretreatment and posttreatment data.

Assessment of Pain

Although a ubiquitous phenomenon, pain is inherently subjective. The only way to know about someone's pain is by what they say or show by their

TABLE 26.3 Description of Commonly Used Assessment Instruments

	Domains Assessed	# Items	Description of Score
Pain Intensity Questionnaires			
McGill Pain Questionnaire (MPQ), Melzack (1975)	Pain	20	78 pain-related words grouped in 20 subclasses; Respondants rank words according to pain intensity; Calculates sensory, affective, evaluative, and miscellaneous scores, and a total score ("Pain Rating Index")
McGill Pain Questionnaire— Short-Form (MPQ-SF), Melzack (1983)	Pain	15	Adjectives selected from the MPQ Calculates sensory and affective Scores
Pain Condition-Specific Measures			
Neuropathic Pain Scale (NPS), Galer and Jensen (1997)	Pain	10	Assesses qualities of neuropathic pain: sharpness, heat/cold, dullness, intensity, unpleasantness, and surface vs. deep pain
Pain-Related Disability/Functionality Measures			
Pain Disability Index (PDI), Pollard (1984)	Measures disability due to pain (degree to which patients believe pain interferes with family/home responsibilities, recreation, social activities, occupation, sexual behavior, self-care, life support activity)	7	Derives a total score
Oswestry Disability Scale, Fairbank, Couper, Davies, and O'Brien (1980).	Measures disability	20	Derives a total score
Pain-Related Psychosocial Pain Measures			
Chronic Pain Coping Inventory (CPCI), Jensen, Turner, Romano, and Strom (1995)	Illness and well-focused coping strategies	64	Calculates eight subscales: Guarding, Resting, Asking for Assistance, Relaxation, Task Persistence, Exercising/ Stretching, Coping Self-Statements, Seeking Social Support
Vanderbilt Multidimensional Pain Coping Inventory (VCPMI), Smith, Wallston, Dwyer, and Dowdy (1997)	Revised VPMI: assesses ways of coping with pain	49	Calculates 11 subscales: Planful Problem-Solving, Positive Reappraisal, Distraction, Confrontative Coping, Distancing/Denial, Stoicism, Use of Religion, Self-Blame, Self-Isolation
Coping Strategies Questionnaire (CSQ), Rosenstiel and Keefe (1983)	Assesses specific coping strategies (six cognitive coping strategies; one behavioral coping strategy)		Calculates seven subscales: Diverting Attention, Reinterpreting Pain, Coping Self-Statements, Ignoring Pain, Praying or Hoping, Catastrophizing, and Increasing Activity

(*continued*)

TABLE 26.3 (continued)

	Domains Assessed	# Items	Description of Score
Fear-Avoidance Beliefs Questionnaire (FABQ), Waddell, Newton, Henderson, Somerville, and Main (1993)	Evaluates patients' beliefs about how physical activity and work may affect their back pain	16	Calculates two scales: Fear-avoidance beliefs related to work, and Fear-avoidance beliefs about physical activity in general
Pain Beliefs and Perceptions Inventory (PBAPI), Williams and Thorn (1989)	Measures pain beliefs	16	Calculates three dimensions: Self-Blame, Mystery (i.e., perception of pain as mysterious), and Stability (i.e., beliefs about the stability of pain over time)
Pain Stages of Change Questionnaire (PSOCQ), Kerns, Rosenberg, Jamison, Caudill, and Haythorntwaite (1997)	Measures conditions that are relevant for a patients' readiness for change	30	Derives four stages of self-management: Precontemplation, Contemplation, Action, and Maintenance
Survey of Pain Attitudes (SOPA), Jensen, Karoly, and Huger (1987)	Measures beliefs about pain	57	Derives seven dimensions: Control, Disability, Harm, Emotion, Medication, Solicitude, and Medical Cure
Pain Anxiety Symptoms Scale (PASS), McCracken, Zayfert, and Gross (1992)	Assesses fear of pain across cognitive, psychological, and behavioral domains	53	Calculates 4 subscales: Fear of Pain, Cognitive Anxiety, Somatic Anxiety, and Fear and Avoidance
Pain Beliefs Questionnaire (PBQ), Edwards, Pearce, Turner-Stokes, and Jones (1992)	Assesses beliefs about pain	12	Calculates 2 subscales: Organic Beliefs (8 items) and Psychological Beliefs (4 items)
Pain Catastrophizing Scale (PCS), Sullivan, Bishop, and Pivik (1995)	Examines components of catastrophizing	13	Calculates three components: Rumination, Magnification, and Helplessness

Multidimensional/Pain-Related Quality of Life Measures

	Domains Assessed	# Items	Description of Score
Brief Pain Inventory, Cleeland and Ryan (1994)	Measures pain and interference of pain with functional activities	10	Derives 2 scores: Pain and Interference
West Haven-Yale Multidimensional Pain Inventory (WHY/MPI), Kerns, Turk, and Rudy (1985)	Measures pain severity, interference, support, life control, affective distress, others' responses to pain behaviors, and frequency of performance on 18 common activities	52	Higher scores on each scale reflect higher levels of that dimension; scores can be used to classify patients as "dysfunctional," "interpersonally distressed," or "adaptive copers"

Health-Related QOL Measures

	Domains Assessed	# Items	Description of Score
Short Form-36 (SF-36), Ware and Sherbourne (1992)		36	Calculate mental health and physical health scores; higher scores = better health status
Sickness Impact Profile (SIP), Bergner, Bobbitt, Carter, and Gibson (1981)	Measures ambulation, mobility, body care, social interaction, communication, alertness, sleep and rest, eating, work, home management, recreation and pastime activities, and emotional behavior	136	Calculate overall dysfunction score, and summary scores of physical and psychosocial dysfunction; Range of scores = 0% to 100% dysfunction

TABLE 26.4 Ratings of Instruments Used for Case Conceptualization/Treatment Planning and Treatment Monitoring/Evaluation

Instrument	Treatment Planning	Treatment Monitoring	Norms	Internal Consistency	Test–Retest Reliability	Content Validity	Construct Validity	Validity Generalization	Treatment Sensitivity	Clinical Utility	Highly Recommended
MPQ	X		G	A–G	G	G	E	E	G	G	
MPQ-SF		X	G	A–G	A	G	E	E	G	G	✓
NPS	X	X	A	NA	NA	A	A	A–G	A–G	A–G	
PDI	X	X	G	G	A	G	G	E	A	A–G	
Oswestry	X	X	G	G–E	A–G	G	E	E	G	G	✓
CPCI	X		A	A–E	A–G	G	G	E	NA	A	✓
VCPMI	X		G	A–G	A–G	G	E	G	NA	G	✓
CSQ	X	X	A	A–G	A	G	G	E	A	A–G	
FABQ	X		G	A–E	A–G	G	G	G	NA	A	
PBAPI	X		A	A–G	A	G	A	A	NA	A	
PSOCQ	X		A	A–G	A	G	E	G	NA	G	
SOPA	X		A	A–G	A	A	E	G	NA	A	
PASS	X		A	G–E	A	A	E	E	NA	A	
PBQ	X		G	A	A	A	A	A	NA	A	
PCS	X		G	A–G	A–G	G	G	E	NA	A–G	
BPI	X	X	G	G–E	A–E	A	G	E	G	A–G	✓
WHYMPI	X	X	G	A–E	A	G	E	E	E	A–G	✓
SF-36	X	X	E	A–E	G	E	G	E	E	A–G	✓
SIP	X	X	E	A–E	A–G	E	G	E	G	A–G	✓

Note: MPQ = McGill Pain Questionnaire; MPQ-SF = McGill Pain Questionnaire-Short Form; NPS = Neuropathic Pain Scale; PDI = Pain Disability Index; Oswestry = Oswestry Disability Scale; CPCI = Chronic Pain Coping Inventory; VCPMI = Vanderbilt Multidimensional Pain Coping Inventory; CSQ = Coping Strategies Questionnaire; FABQ = Fear-Avoidance Beliefs Questionnaire; PBAPI = Pain Beliefs and Perceptions Inventory; PSOCQ = Pain Stages of Change Questionnaire; SOPA = Survey of Pain Attitudes; PASS = Pain Anxiety Symptoms Scale; PBQ = Pain Beliefs Questionnaire; PCS = Pain Catastrophizing Scale; BPI = Brief Pain Inventory; WHYMPI = West Haven-Yale Multidimensional Pain Inventory; SF-36 = Short Form-36; SIP = Sickness Impact Profile; A = Adequate; G = Good; E = Excellent; NA = Not Applicable. When scales consist of many subscales, a range of ratings is given.

behavior. Because there is no "objective" method for assessing pain, self-report provides the gold standard in assessments of pain and its characteristics. Pain assessment therefore requires that patients and participants in clinical trials describe their own experiences. Although individuals interpret measures of pain in different and somewhat idiosyncratic ways, these interpretations can be expected to remain relatively constant within people over time. As a result, they can also provide valid measures of change in pain due to treatment or time.

Pain Intensity

Self-report measures of pain often ask patients to quantify their pain by providing a single, general rating of pain: "Is your usual level of pain 'mild,' 'moderate,' or 'severe?'" or "Rate your typical pain on a scale from 0 to 10 where 0 equals no pain and 10 is the worst pain you can imagine." There are a number of simple methods that can be used to evaluate current pain intensity—numerical scale (NRS), verbal ratings scales (VRS), and visual analogue scales (VAS).

Each of the commonly used methods of rating pain intensity, NRS, VRS, and VAS, appear sufficiently reliable and valid, and no one method consistently demonstrates greater responsiveness in detecting improvements associated with pain treatment (Jensen & Karoly, 2001). However, there are important differences among NRS, VRS, and VAS measures of pain intensity with respect to missing data stemming from failure to complete the measure, patient preference, ease of data recording, and ability to administer the measure by telephone or with electronic diaries. NRS and VRS measures tend to be preferred over VAS measures by patients, and VAS measures usually demonstrate more missing data than do NRS measures. Greater difficulty completing VAS measures is associated with increased age and greater opioid intake, and cognitive impairment has been shown to be associated with inability to complete NRS ratings of pain intensity (Jensen & Karoly, 2001). Patients who are unable to complete NRS ratings may be able to complete VRS pain ratings (e.g., none, mild, moderate, severe). Other measures are available to assess pain in children and those who are unable to verbally communicate (e.g., stroke patients, mentally impaired; Hadjistavropoulos, von Baeyer, & Craig, 2001).

There has been some concern expressed that retrospective reports may not be valid, as they may reflect current pain severity that serves as an anchor for recall of pain severity over some interval (Gendreau, Hufford, & Stone, 2003; Stone & Shiffman, 2002). More valid information may be obtained by asking about current level of pain, pain over the past week, worst pain of the last week, and lowest level of severity over the last week. This has also led to the use of daily diaries that are believed to be more accurate as they are based on real-time rather than recall. For example, patients are asked to maintain regular diaries of pain intensity with ratings recorded several times each day (e.g., at meals and bedtime) for several days or weeks. One problem noted with the use of paper-and-pencil diaries is that patients may not follow the instruction to provide ratings at specified intervals. Rather, patients may complete diaries in advance ("fill forward") or shortly before seeing a clinician ("fill backward"; Stone, Shiffman, Schwartz, Broderick, & Hufford, 2003). These two reporting approaches undermine the putative validity of diaries. As an alternative to the paper-and-pencil diaries, a number of commentators have advocated for the use of electronic devices that can prompt patients for ratings and "time stamp" the actual ratings, thus facilitating real-time data capture. Although there are numerous advantages to the use of advanced technology to improve the validity of patient ratings, they are not without potential problems, including hardware problems, software problems, and user problems (Turk, Burwinkle, & Showlund, 2007). These methods are also costly and, although they may be appropriate for research studies, their usefulness in clinical settings may be limited.

Pain Quality

Pain is known to have different sensory and affective qualities in addition to its intensity, and measures of these components of pain may be used to describe an individual's pain experience more fully (Melzack & Torgerson, 1971; Price, Harkins, & Baker, 1987). It is possible that the efficacy of pain treatments varies for different pain qualities, and measures of pain quality may therefore identify treatments that are efficacious for certain types of pain but not for overall pain intensity. Assessment of specific pain qualities at baseline also makes it possible to determine whether certain patterns of pain quality moderate the effects of treatment. The Short-Form McGill Pain Questionnaire (Melzack, 1987) assesses 15 sensory and affective pain descriptors and its sensory and affective subscales have demonstrated responsivity to treatment in a number of clinical trials (e.g., Dworkin et al., 2003; Rowbotham, Harden, Stacey, Bernstein, & Magnus-Miller, 1998).

Assessment of Overt Expressions of Pain

Patients display a broad range of responses that communicate to others that they are experiencing pain, distress, and suffering. Some of these pain behaviors may be controllable by the person, whereas others are not. Although there is no one-to-one correspondence between these, pain behaviors and self-report of pain, they are at least modestly correlated. A number of different observational procedures have been developed to quantify pain behaviors. Several investigators using the Pain Behavior Checklist (Turk, Wack, & Kerns, 1985) have found a significant association between these self-reports and behavioral observations. Health care providers can use observational methods to systematically quantify various pain behaviors and note the factors that increase or decrease them. For example, observing the patient in the waiting room, while being interviewed, or during a structured series of physical tasks. Behavioral observation scales can be used by patients' significant others as well.

Uses of the health-care system and analgesic medication are other ways to assess pain behaviors. Patients can record the times when they take medication over a specified interval such as a week. Diaries not only provide information about the frequency and quantity of medication but may also permit identification of the antecedent and consequent events of medication use. Antecedent events might include stress, boredom, or activity. Examination of antecedents is useful in identifying patterns of medication use that may be associated with factors other than pain per se. Similarly, patterns of response to the use of analgesic may be identified. Does the patient receive attention and sympathy whenever he or she is observed by significant others taking medication? That is, do significant others provide positive reinforcement for the taking of analgesic medication and thereby unwittingly increase medication use?

Assessment of Emotional Distress

The results of numerous studies suggest that chronic pain is often associated with emotional distress, particularly depression, anxiety, anger, and irritability.

The presence of emotional distress in people with chronic pain presents a challenge when assessing symptoms such as fatigue, reduced activity level, decreased libido, appetite change, sleep disturbance, weight gain or loss, and memory and concentration deficits. These symptoms are often associated with pain and have also been considered "vegetative" symptoms of depressive disorders. Improvements or deterioration in such symptoms, therefore, can be a result of changes in either pain or emotional distress.

Both the BDI and BDI-II (Beck, Ward, et al., 1961; Beck, Steer, Ball, & Ranieri, 1996) and the Profile of Mood States (POMS, McNair, Lorr, & Droppleman, 1971) have well-established reliability and validity in the assessment of symptoms of depression and emotional distress, and they have been used in numerous clinical trials in psychiatry and an increasing number of studies of patients with chronic pain (Kerns, 2003). In research in psychiatry and chronic pain, the BDI provides a well-accepted criterion of the level of psychological distress in a sample and its response to treatment. The POMS (McNair et al., 1971) assesses six mood states—tension-anxiety, depression-dejection, anger-hostility, vigor-activity, fatigue-inertia, and confusion-bewilderment—and also provides a summary measure of total mood disturbance. Although the discriminant validity of the POMS scales in patients with chronic pain has not been adequately documented, it has scales for the three most important dimensions of emotional functioning in chronic pain patients (depression, anxiety, anger) and also assesses three other dimensions that are very relevant to chronic pain and its treatment, including a positive mood scale of vigor-activity. Moreover, the POMS has demonstrated beneficial effects of treatment in some (but not all) chronic pain trials (e.g., Dworkin et al., 2003; Rowbotham et al., 1998). For these reasons, administration of the BDI and the POMS are reasonable choices as brief measures of emotional distress.

As noted earlier, various symptoms of depression—such as decreased libido, appetite or weight changes, fatigue, and memory and concentration deficits—are also commonly believed to be consequences of chronic pain and the medications used for its treatment (Gallagher & Verma, 2004). It is unclear whether the presence of such symptoms in patients with chronic pain (and other medical disorders) should nevertheless be considered evidence of depressed mood, or whether the assessment of mood in these patients should emphasize symptoms that are less likely to be secondary to physical disorders (Wilson, Mikail, D'Eon, & Minns, 2001).

Assessment of Function

The poor reliability and questionable validity of physical examination measures has led to the development of self-report functional status measures that seek to quantify symptoms, function, and behavior directly, rather than inferring them. Self-report measures have been developed to assess peoples' reports of their abilities to engage in a range of functional activities such as the ability to walk up stairs, to sit for specific periods of time, the ability to lift specific weights, performance of activities of daily living, as well as the severity of the pain experienced upon the performance of these activities have been developed. There are a number of well-established, psychometrically supported generic (e.g., Short Form-36; Ware & Sherbourne, 1992), disease-specific (e.g., Western Ontario McMaster Osteoarthritis Index [WOMAC]—Bellamy, Buchanan, Goldsmith, Campbell, & Stitt, 1988; Fibromyalgia Impact Questionnaire—Burchardt, Clark, & Bennett, 1991; Roland-Morris Back Pain Disability Questionnaire—Roland & Morris, 1983), and pain-specific (e.g., Brief Pain Inventory Interference Scale—Cleeland & Ryan, 1994; Pain Disability Index—Pollard, 1984; MPI Interference Scale—Kerns et al., 1985) measures of functional status.

Disease-specific measures are designed to evaluate the impact of a specific condition (e.g., ability to wear clothing in patients with postherpetic neuralgia). Such specific effects of a disorder may not be assessed by a generic measure, and disease-specific measures may therefore be more likely to reveal clinically important improvement or deterioration in function that is a consequence of treatment. In addition, responses on disease-specific measures will generally not reflect the effects of co-morbid conditions on physical functioning, which may confound the interpretation of change occurring over the course of a trial when generic measures are used. Disease-specific measures may be more sensitive to the effects of treatment on function, but generic measures provide information about physical functioning and treatment benefits that can be compared across different conditions and studies (Dworkin, Nagasako, Hetzel, & Farrar, 2001; Fowler, Cleary, Magaziner, Patrick, & Benjamin, 1994; Guyatt, Feeney, & Patrick, 1993).

Each of these approaches has strengths. Decisions regarding whether to use a disease-specific or generic measure, or some combination, will depend on the purpose of the assessment. For individual patients in clinical practice it would be most appropriate to use measures developed on samples with comparable characteristics. Therefore, for example, the WOMAC might be the preferred measure of function to use with patients with osteoarthritis. If the clinician wishes to compare across a group of patients, then one of the broader-based pain-specific measures should be considered. If the assessment is being performed as part of a research study, some combination might be appropriate to compare chronic pain samples with a larger population of people with diverse medical diseases (e.g., SF-36).

Assessment of Coping and Psychosocial Adaptation to Pain

Historically, psychological measures designed to evaluate psychopathology have been used to identify specific individual differences associated with reports of pain, even though these measures were usually not developed for or standardized on samples of medical patients. However, it is possible that responses by medical patients may be distorted as a function of the disease or the medications that they take. For example, common measures of depression ask patients about their appetites, sleep patterns, and fatigue. Because disease status and medication can affect responses to such items, patients' scores may be elevated, thereby distorting the meaning of their responses. As a result, a number of measures have been developed for use specifically with pain patients. Instruments have been developed to assess psychological distress, the impact of pain on patients' lives, feeling of control, coping behaviors, and attitudes about disease, pain, and health care providers and the patient's plight (Turk & Melzack, 1992/2001, see Table 26.3).

CONCLUSIONS

Pain is a complex, idiosyncratic experience. Assessment and treatment of pain can be complicated by the web of influential factors that modulate the overall pain experience and associated disability. Furthermore, traditional biomedical approaches with diagnostic tests are often not helpful because structural damage and persistent pain complaints do not necessarily coincide. Pain research in the past three decades has repeatedly shown that pain is not just a physiological phenomenon, and that a range of "person variables," such as psychosocial, environmental, and behavioral factors, play a significant role in determining the occurrence, severity, and quality of pain. Given the multifactorial nature of pain, adequate assessment requires an interdisciplinary team approach. In this chapter, we discussed medical, physical, and psychological assessments as well as introduced a range of self-report inventories that can be used in conjunction with interviews and medical examinations. As we repeatedly stressed, an adequate pain assessment means the evaluation of the person with chronic pain. We must not just focus on the pathology or complaint, but must reach out to understand the person and his/her well-being. Although there is no shortcut in this, the delineation of relevant medical, physical, psychosocial, and behavioral factors to pain in a patient are critical in planning and executing a successful treatment plan.

ACKNOWLEDGMENT   Preparation of this manuscript was supported in part by grants from the National Institute of Arthritis and Musculoskeletal and Skin Diseases (AR/AI44724, AR47298) awarded to the first author.

References

Allen, J. P., & Litten, R. Z. (1998). Screening instruments and biochemical screening. In A. W. Graham, T. K. Schultz, & B. B. Wilford (Eds.), *Principles of addiction medicine* (pp. 263–272). Annapolis Junction, MD: American Society of Addiction Medicine.

American Psychiatric Association. (1997). *User's Guide for the structured clinical interview for DSM-IV Axis I Disorders SCID-1: Clinician version.* Washington, DC: Author.

Beck, A. T., Steer, R. A., Ball, R., & Ranieri, W. F. (1996). Comparison of Beck Depression Inventories -IA and -II in Psychiatric Outpatients. *Journal of Personality, 67,* 588–597.

Beck, A. T., Ward, C. H., Mendelson, M., Mock, J., & Erbaugh, J. (1961). An inventory for measuring depression. *Archives of General Psychiatry, 4,* 561–571.

Bellamy, N., Buchanan, W. W., Goldsmith, C. H., Campbell, J., & Stitt, L. W. (1988). Validation study of WOMAC: A health status instrument for measuring clinically important patient relevant outcomes to antirheumatic drug therapy in patients with osteoarthritis of the hip or knee. *Journal of Rheumatology, 15,* 1833–1840.

Bergner, M., Bobbitt, R., Carter, W., & Gilson, B. (1981). The Sickness Impact Profile: Development and final revision of a health status measure. *Medical Care, 19,* 787–805.

Boden, S., Davis, D., Dina, T., Patronas, N. J., & Wiesel, S. W. (1990). Abnormal magnetic-resonance scans of the lumbar spine in asymptomatic subjects. A prospective investigation. *Journal of Bone and Joint Surgery, 72,* 403–408.

Burckhardt, C. S., Clark, S. R., & Bennett, R. M. (1991). The Fibromyalgia Impact Questionnaire: Development and validation. *Journal of Rheumatology, 18,* 728–733.

Cleeland, C. S., & Ryan, K. M. (1994). Pain assessment: Global use of the Brief Pain Inventory. *Annals of Academic Medicine, 23,* 129–138.

Derogatis, L. (1983). *The SCL-90-R: II: Administration, scoring and procedure.* Baltimore, MD: Clinical Psychometric Research.

Dworkin, R. H., Corbin, A. E., Young, J. P., Sharma, U., LaMoreaux, L., Bockbrader, H., et al. (2003). Pregabalin for the treatment of postherpetic neuralgia: A randomized, placebo-controlled trial. *Neurology, 60,* 1274–1283.

Dworkin, R. H., Nagasako, E. M., Hetzel, R. D., & Farrar, J. T. (2001). Assessment of Pain and pain-related quality of life in clinical trials. In D. C. Turk & R. Melzack (Eds.), *Handbook of pain assessment* (2nd ed., pp. 659–692). New York: Guilford.

Edwards, L. C., Pearce, S. A., Turner-Stokes, L., & Jones, A. (1992). The Pain Beliefs Questionnaire: An investigation of beliefs in the causes and consequences of pain. *Pain, 51,* 267–272.

Fairbank, J. C., Couper, J., Davies, J. B., & O'Brien, J. P. (1980). The Oswestry Low Back Pain Disability Questionnaire. *Physiotherapy, 66,* 271–273.

Fordyce, W. E. (1976). *Behavioral methods for chronic pain and illness.* St. Louis: CV Mosby.

Fowler, F. J., Cleary, P. D., Magaziner, J., Patrick, D. L., & Benjamin, K. L. (1994). Methodological issues in measuring patient-reported outcomes: The agenda of the work group on outcomes assessment. *Medical Care, 32,* JS65–JS76.

Galer, B. S., & Jensen, M. P. (1997). Development and preliminary validation of a pain measure specific to neuropathic pain: The Neuropathic Pain Scale. *Neurology, 48,* 332–338.

Gallagher, R. M., & Verma, S. (2004). Mood and anxiety disorders in chronic pain. In R. H. Dworkin & W. S. Breitbart (Eds.), *Psychosocial aspects of pain: A handbook for health care providers* (pp. 589–606). Seattle, WA: IASP Press.

Gendreau, M., Hufford, M. R., & Stone, A. A. (2003). Measuring clinical pain in chronic widespread pain: Selected methodological issues. *Best Practice and Research Clinical Rheumatology, 17,* 575–592.

Guyatt, G. H., Feeney, D. H., & Patrick, D. L. (1993). Measuring health-related quality of life. *Annals Internal Medicine, 118,* 622–629.

Hadjistavropoulos, T., von Baeyer, C., & Craig, K. D. (2001). Pain assessment in persons with limited ability to communicate. In D. C. Turk & R. Melzack (Eds.), *Handbook of pain assessment* (2nd ed., pp. 134–152). New York: Guilford Press.

Hathaway, S. R., & McKinley, J. C. (1967). *The Minnesota Multiphasic Personality Inventory Manual.* New York: Psychological Corporation.

Jensen, M., Brant-Zawadski, M., Obuchowski, N., Modic, M. T., Malkasian, D., & Ross, J. S. (1994). Magnetic resonance imaging of the lumbar spine in people with back pain. *New England Journal of Medicine, 331,* 69–73.

Jensen, M. P., & Karoly, P. (2001). Self-report scales and procedures for assessing pain in adults. In D. C. Turk & R. Melzack (Eds.), *Handbook of pain assessment* (2nd ed., pp. 15–34). New York: Guilford Press.

Jensen, M. P., Karoly, P., & Huger, R. (1987). The development and preliminary validation of an instrument to assess patient's attitudes toward pain. *Journal of Psychosomatic Research, 31,* 393–400.

Jensen, M. P., Romano, J. M., Turner, J. A., Good, A. B., & Wald, L. H. (1999). Patient beliefs predict patient functioning: further support for a cognitive-behavioral model of chronic pain. *Pain, 81,* 95–104.

Jensen, M. P., Turner, J. A., Romano, J. M., & Lawler, B. K. (1994). Relationship of pain-specific beliefs to chronic pain adjustment. *Pain, 57,* 301–309.

Jensen, M. P., Turner, J. A., Romano, J. M., & Strom, S. E. (1995). The chronic pain coping inventory: Development and preliminary validation. *Pain, 60,* 203–216.

Kerns, R. D. (2003) Assessment of emotional functioning in pain treatment outcome research. Presented at the second meeting of the *Initiative on Methods, Measurement, and Pain Assessment in Clinical Trials* (IMMPACT-II). Retrieved April 2003 from www.immpact.org/meetings.html

Kerns, R. D., Rosenberg, R., Jamison, R. N., Caudill, M. A., & Haythorntwaite, J. (1997). Readiness to adopt a self-management approach to chronic pain: The Pain Stages of Change Questionniare (PSOCQ). *Pain, 72,* 227–234.

Kerns, R. D., Turk, D. C., & Rudy, T. E. (1985). The West Haven-Yale Multidimensional Pain Inventory (WHYMPI). *Pain, 23,* 345–356.

Mayfield, D., McLeod, G., & Hall, P. (1987). The CAGE questionnaire. *American Journal of Psychiatry, 131,* 1121–1123.

McCracken, L. M., Zayfert, C., & Gross, R. T. (1992). The pain anxiety symptoms scale: Development and validation of a scale to measure fear of pain. *Pain, 50,* 67–73.

McNair, D. M., Lorr, M., & Droppleman, L. F. (1971) *Profile of Mood States.* San Diego, CA: Educational and Industrial Testing Service.

Melzack, R. (1975). The McGill pain questionnaire: Major properties and scoring methods. *Pain, 1,* 277–299.

Melzack, R. (1987). The short-form McGill Pain Questionnaire. *Pain, 30,* 191–197.

Melzack, R., & Torgerson, W. S. (1971). On the language of pain. *Anesthesiology, 34,* 50–59.

National Research Center/National Academies of Science. (2001). *Musculoskeletal disorders and the workplace.* Washington, DC: National Academies Press.

North, R. B., Campbell, J. N., James, C. S., Conover-Walker, M. K., Wang, H., Piantadosi, S., et al. (1991). Failed back surgery syndrome: 5-year follow-up in 102 patients undergoing repeated operation. *Neurosurgery, 28,* 685–690.

Pillemer, S., Bradley, L. A., Crofford, L. J., Moldofsky, H., & Chrousos, G. P. (1997). The neuroscience and endocrinology of fibromyalgia. *Arthritis and Rheumatism, 40,* 1928–1938.

Piotrowski, C. (1998). Assessment of pain: A survey of practicing clinicians. *Perceptual and Motor Skills, 86,* 181–182.

Pollard, C. A. (1984). Preliminary validity study of the Pain Disability Index. *Perceptual and Motor Skills, 59,* 974.

Price, D. D., Harkins, S. W., & Baker, C. (1987). Sensory-affective relationships among different types of clinical and experimental pain. *Pain, 28,* 297–307.

Roland, M., & Morris, R. (1983). A study of the natural history of back pain, part I: Development of a reliable and sensitive measure of disability in low back pain. *Spine, 8,* 141–144.

Rosenstiel, A. K., & Keefe, F. J. (1983). The use of coping strategies in chronic low back pain patients: Relationship to patient characteristics and current adjustment. *Pain, 17,* 33–44.

Rowbotham, M. C., Harden, N., Stacey, B., Bernstein, P., & Magnus-Miller, L. (1998). Gabapentin Postherpetic Neuralgia Study Group: Gabapentin for the treatment postherpetic neuralgia: A randomized controlled trial. *Journal of the American Medical Association, 280,* 1837–1842.

Smith, C. A., Wallston, K. A., Dwyer, K. A., & Dowdy, S. W. (1997). Beyond good and bad coping: A multidimensional examination of coping with pain in persons with rheumatoid arthritis. *Annals of Behavioral Medicine, 19,* 11–21.

Stone, A. A., & Shiffman, S. (2002). Capturing momentary, self-report data: A proposal for reporting guidelines. *Annals of Behavioral Medicine, 24,* 236–243.

Stone, A. A., Shiffman, S., Schwartz, J. E., Broderick, J. E., & Hufford, M. R. (2003). Patient compliance with paper and electronic diaries. *Controlled Clinical Trials, 24,* 182–199.

Sullivan, M. J. L., Bishop, S., & Pivik, J. (1995). The Pain Catastrophizing Scale: Development and validation. *Psychological Assessment, 7,* 524–532.

Turk, D. C., Burwinkle, T., & Showlund, M. (2007). Assessing the impact of chronic pain in real-time. In A. Stone, S. Shiffman, A. Atienza, & L. Nebeling (Eds.), *The science of real-time data capture: Self-reports in health research* (pp. 204–228). New York: Oxford University Press.

Turk, D. C., & Flor, H. (1999). Chronic pain: A biobehavioral perspective. In R. J. Gatchel & D. C. Turk (Eds.), *Psychosocial factors in pain: Critical perspectives* (pp. 18–34). New York: Guilford Press.

Turk, D. C., & Meichenbaum, D. (1984). A cognitive-behavioral approach to pain management. In P. D. Wall & R. Melzack (Eds.), *Textbook of pain* (pp. 787–794). New York: Churchill-Livingstone.

Turk, D. C., & Melzack, R. (Eds.) (1992/2001). *Handbook of pain assessment* (1st/2nd ed.). New York: Guilford.

Turk, D. C., Okifuji, A., & Scharff, L. (1995). Chronic pain and depression: Role of perceived impact and perceived control in different age cohorts. *Pain, 61,* 93–101.

Turk, D. C., Wack, J. T., & Kerns, R. D. (1985). An empirical examination of the "pain behavior" construct. *Journal of Behavioral Medicine, 9,* 119–130.

United States Bureau of the Census. (1996). *Statistical abstract of the United States: 1996* (116th edition), Washington, DC: Author.

United States Department of Health and Human Services. Food and Drug Administration (Docket No. 97D-0188) (1997). International Conference on Harmonisation; Guidance on General Considerations for Clinical Trials. *Federal Register, 62,* 66, 113–66, 119. Retrieved from www.fda.gov/cder/guidance/ 1857fnl.pdf

Von Korff, M., Crane, P., Lane, M., Miglioretti, D. L., Simon G., Ormel, E., et al. (2001). United States Department of Health and Human Services. *Prescription Drugs: Abuse and Addiction.* NIH Publication Number 01-48881, Rockville, MD: U.S. Department of Health and Human Services, National Institutes of Health.

Waddell, G. (1987). A new clinical model for the treatment of low-back pain. *Spine, 12,* 632–644.

Waddell, G., Newton, M., Henderson, I., Somerville, D., & Main, C. J. (1993). A Fear-Avoidance Beliefs Questionnaire (FABQ) and the role of fear-avoidance beliefs in chronic low back pain and disability. *Pain, 52,* 157–168.

Ware, J. E., & Sherbourne, C. D. (1992). The MOS 36-item short-form health survey (SF-36). *Medical Care, 30,* 473–483.

Williams, D. A., & Thorn, B. E. (1989). An empirical assessment of pain beliefs. *Pain, 36,* 351–358.

Wilson, K. G., Mikail, S. F., D'Eon. J. L., & Minns, J. E. (2001). Alternative diagnostic criteria for major depressive disorder in patients with chronic pain. *Pain, 91,* 227–234.

Assessment Instrument Index

Author Index

Subject Index

3

KETTERING COLLEGE
MEDICAL ARTS LIBRARY

WM 141 G9457 2008

A guide to assessments that
work